Select Material from

PSYCHOLOGY

THE SCIENCE OF

2

AN APPRECIATIVE VIEW

Laura A. King
University of Missouri, Columbia

University of Connecticut

Learning Solutions

Boston   Burr Ridge, IL   Dubuque, IA   New York   San Francisco   St. Louis
Bangkok   Bogotá   Caracas   Lisbon   London   Madrid
Mexico City   Milan   New Delhi   Seoul   Singapore   Sydney   Taipei   Toronto

The McGraw·Hill Companies

Select Material from
The Science of Psychology
An Appreciative View, Second Edition

3 4 5 6 7 8 9 0 BRP BRP 13 12

ISBN-13: 978-0-07-754944-2
ISBN-10: 0-07-754944-9

Learning Solutions Manager: Nick DiNardo
Production Editor: Nina Meyer
Printer/Binder: BR Printing

for *Sam*

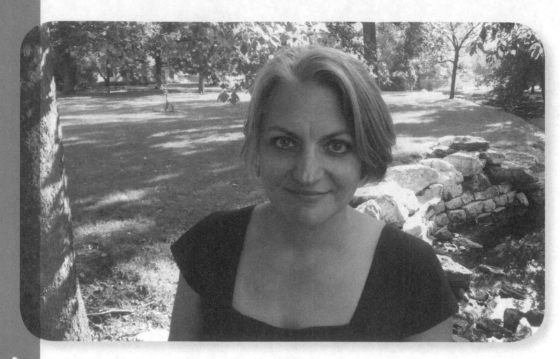

LAURA A. KING

Laura King did her undergraduate work at Kenyon College, where, an English major, she declared a second major, in psychology, during the second semester of her junior year. She completed her A.B. in English with high honors and distinction and in psychology with distinction in 1986. Laura then did graduate work at Michigan State University and the University of California, Davis, receiving her Ph.D. in personality psychology in 1991.

Laura began her career at Southern Methodist University in Dallas, moving to the University of Missouri in 2001, where she is now the Frederick A. Middlebush Professor of Psychological Sciences. In addition to seminars in the development of character, social psychology, and personality psychology, she has taught undergraduate lecture courses in introductory psychology, introduction to personality psychology, and social psychology. At SMU, she received six different teaching awards, including the "M" award for "sustained excellence" in 1999. At the University of Missouri, she received the Chancellor's Award for Outstanding Research and Creative Activity in 2004.

Her research, which has been funded by the National Institute of Mental Health, has focused on a variety of topics relevant to the question of what it is that makes for a good life. She has studied goals, life stories, happiness, well-being, and meaning in life. In general, her work reflects an enduring interest in studying what is good and healthy in people. In 2001, her research accomplishments were recognized by a Templeton Prize in positive psychology. Laura's research (often in collaboration with undergraduate and graduate students) has been published in *The American Psychologist*, the *Journal of Personality and Social Psychology*, *Psychological Science*, and other publications.

Currently editor-in-chief of the Personality and Individual Differences section of the *Journal of Research in Personality and Social Psychology*, Laura has also served as the editor-in-chief of the *Journal of Research in Personality* and associate editor for the *Journal of Personality and Social Psychology* and *Personality and Social Psychology Bulletin*, as well as on numerous grant panels. She has edited or co-edited special sections of the *Journal of Personality* and the *American Psychologist*. In "real life," Laura is an accomplished cook and enjoys listening to music (mostly jazz vocalists and singer-songwriters), gardening, and chasing Sam, her 6-year-old son.

BRIEF CONTENTS

CONTENTS

15
Psychological
Disorders   486

16
Therapies   520

17
Health
Psychology   552

PREFACE

Appreciating You!

When I set out to write the first edition of *The Science of Psychology: An Appreciative View*, I could not have imagined how well it would be received by instructors and students alike. Who knew that the focus on *why things go right* would strike such a strong chord in the classroom? Over the past three years I met dozens of faculty members across the country, and I continue to be awestruck by the hard work, dedication, and enthusiasm of introductory psychology instructors. So, I wanted to say thank you. You all continue to inspire me—to be a better teacher myself, to develop the best learning solutions for the introductory psychology course, and to make our field fun and relevant to today's students. I appreciate you!

The hallmarks of the first edition of *The Science of Psychology: An Appreciative View*—appreciating why things go right, appreciating psychology as an integrated whole, and appreciating what psychology has to say about human health and wellness—continue to be compelling today. The second edition extends these themes and enhances their pedagogical value by placing special emphasis on helping students "know what they know and learn what they don't know." Indeed, the new edition embodies a redoubled effort to show the relevance of studying psychology to students' health and well-being, and it features a wealth of systematically researched and developed test assessment items that mirror the topics and learning objectives of your course goals.

Appreciating That Today's Students Are Different

The Science of Psychology: An Appreciative View, Second Edition, recognizes that today's students are as different from the learners of the last generation as today's discipline of psychology is different from the field thirty years ago. Students now learn in multiple modalities; rather than sitting down and reading traditional printed chapters from beginning to end, their work preferences tend to be more visual and interactive. For many students, a traditional print textbook is no longer their sole tool when they have instant, 24/7 access to news and information from around the globe. They expect their course material to be an engaging and personal solution.

The Science of Psychology: An Appreciative View, Second Edition, draws on thousands of hours of research into faculty teaching and student behavior. To provide course material that actively engages students while saving instructors time, McGraw-Hill visited with faculty like you across the country and observed you preparing for class, delivering your lectures, and teaching in a variety of classroom settings—from the traditional face-to-face lecture hall, to fully online courses, to hybrids of the two—as well as watching students as they worked through assignments and studied for exams.

The result of this research and development is **Connect Psychology,** a response to the learning preferences of today's student. The groundbreaking adaptive diagnostic tool helps students "know what they know" while guiding them to experience and learn what they don't know through engaging interactivities, exercises, and readings. Instructors using Connect report their students' performance is increasing by a letter grade or more.

Designed for a variety of study habits and approaches to the course, *The Science of Psychology: An Appreciative View,* Second Edition, with its powerful diagnostic tool, provides a roadmap for success.

Appreciating Psychology's Role in Health and Wellness

The Science of Psychology: An Appreciative View, Second Edition, continues to emphasize the relevance of psychology to the health and well-being of students and the people in their lives. As in the first edition, substantial discussion and examples focus on the scientific understanding of human strengths and capacities, health, and wellness in order to cultivate students' appreciation for how extensively psychology applies to their lives.

A **new chapter on gender, sex, and sexuality (Chapter 11)** builds upon this attention to health and wellness. The chapter presents the latest thinking on such diverse topics as theories of gender development, the psychology of gender differences, sexual orientation, gay and lesbian functioning, and sexual health and wellness.

CHAPTER 11

CHAPTER OUTLINE
1 Defining Sex and Gender
2 Theories of Gender Development
3 The Psychology of Gender Differences
4 Sexual Orientation
5 Sexual Behaviors and Practices
6 Sexual Variations and Disorders
7 Sexuality and Health and Wellness

Gender, Sex, and Sexuality

Jazz Jennings: Declaring Herself Proudly

"Is it a boy or a girl?" That is so often our first, excited question when we hear that someone has given birth or even when we find out that she is pregnant. Although it may seem straightforward, the answer—and what it means for each newborn—can be quite complex. Consider the young girl known to the media as Jazz Jennings. Though born with a male body, Jazz has insisted throughout her young life that she is a girl (Goldberg & Adriano, 2008). At first her parents humored their son, allowing him to play with girls' toys and to dress like a girl at home. Eventually, after observing Jazz's sadness during a dance recital when he was not permitted to wear a tutu like the "other girls," Jazz's parents decided to allow her to be herself, to dress and to act like a girl everywhere she went. Jazz entered kindergarten with long hair and wearing earrings and a dress. Although ever mindful of the difficulties she might face along the way, Jazz's parents remain committed to supporting their child wherever her gender identity takes her.

Even for individuals whose biological sex seems a perfect fit, sexuality can be complex, and the impact of sex and gender can be just as profound. Issues of gender, sex, and sexuality are everywhere around us. Why do little boys gravitate toward toy trucks, and little girls toward dolls? Why are there so few male teachers, especially for preschool and kindergarten? Should women in the military be permitted to serve in combat? Should gay men and lesbian women be permitted to marry their same-sex partners? What kind of sex education is most effective? In this chapter we will explore the concepts, knowledge, and psychology behind these and other provocative questions related to gender, sex, and sexuality. ●

Appreciating Psychology's Role in Student Assessment: Raising the Bar for Test Development

Systematic research informs the development of every McGraw-Hill product— including test banks. As part of a broad-based research project, McGraw-Hill, in collaboration with Auburn University, tagged and mapped midterm and final exams from hundreds of instructors from schools across the country. Our objective: to see how well the learning objectives and test questions in its products match up with how instructors are assessing their students. The result for *The Science of Psychology: An Appreciative View,* Second Edition? A **comprehensive new test bank** with assessment items mirroring the highest frequency topics and learning objectives that reflect individual instructors' course goals and objectives. For professors, this means the test bank is tried and true and designed to meet the outcomes of your course.

WHAT ELSE IS NEW IN THE SECOND EDITION?

The Science of Psychology: An Appreciative View, Second Edition, builds on the hallmarks of the first edition and includes new coverage and features designed to help students master core content, making psychology real and relevant for them.

Appreciating Why Things Go Right

psychological inquiry

Schedules of Reinforcement and Different Patterns of Responding

This figure shows how the different schedules of reinforcement result in different rates of responding. The graph's X or horizontal axis represents time. The Y or vertical axis represents the cumulative responses. That means that as the line goes up, the total number of responses are building and building. In the figure, each hash mark indicates the delivery of reinforcement. That is, each of those little ticks indicates that a reward is being given.

Look closely at the pattern of responses over time for each schedule of reinforcement. On the fixed-ratio schedule, notice the dropoff in responding after each response; on the variable-ratio schedule, note the high, steady rate of responding. On the fixed-interval schedule, notice the immediate dropoff in responding after reinforcement and the increase in responding just before reinforcement (resulting in a scalloped curve); and on the variable-interval schedule, note the slow, steady rate of responding.

1. Which schedule of reinforcement represents the "most bang for the buck"? That is, which one is associated with the most responses for the least amount of reward?
2. Which schedule of reinforcement is most like pop quizzes?
3. Which is most like regular tests on a course syllabus?
4. Which schedule of reinforcement would be best if you have very little time for training?
5. Which schedule of reinforcement do you think is most common in your own life? Why?

The second edition of *The Science of Psychology: An Appreciative View* continues to place **function and dysfunction in balance.** Rather than focusing first on why things go wrong, the focus is first on why things go right.

One of the challenges instructors face in focusing on function first is going against the grain of human nature. Research in psychology itself tells us that the negative captures our attention more readily than the positive. There is no question that bad news makes headlines. A global recession, disturbing climate changes, a catastrophic oil spill, and the everyday demands of juggling work, family, and finances—these and other issues loom large for us all. We strive and struggle to find balance and to sculpt a happy life. The science of psychology has much to offer in terms of helping us understand the choices we make and the implications of these choices for ourselves and for others around the world.

The Science of Psychology: An Appreciative View, Second Edition, communicates the nature and breadth of psychology and its value as a science with an appreciative perspective. Its primary goal is to help students think like psychological scientists, which includes asking questions about their own life experiences. Throughout, students' curiosity is nurtured through timely, applied examples and a focus on what psychological science means for people going about daily life. A new feature, **Psychological Inquiry,** stimulates students' analytical thinking about psychology's practical applications. The selections reinforce student understanding of central aspects of research design, such as the difference between correlational and experimental studies and the concepts of independent and dependent variables. The two Psychological Inquiry selections in each chapter guide students' analysis of a figure, graph, or other illustration and include a set of critical thinking questions. For example, one of the Psychological Inquiry features in Chapter 6 on learning prompts students to analyze graphical schedules of reinforcement and different patterns of responding to them.

Appreciating Psychology as an Integrated Whole

INTERSECTION

Developmental Psychology and Clinical Psychology: Is "Girl Talk" Always a Good Thing?

Making friends, keeping friends, and being a friend are all tasks that face the developing human being. Friends are important to children's self-esteem, well-being, and school adjustment (Brengden & others, 2010; Erath & others, 2010; Rubin, Cheah, & Menzer, 2010). Having a friend means that there is someone to talk to when one has problems and someone to celebrate with when things go well. Thus, if a child has a lot of friends, we might think that he or she is doing pretty well. Are all friendships equally supportive, however? Research indicates that some friends might have a knack for making problems seem worse, not better.

Are some of your friends likely to co-ruminate over negative events? Why do you think co-rumination is worse for girls than boys?

Developmental psychologist Amanda Rose and her colleagues have studied how young friends' responses to their friends' problems influence the mental health of children and adolescents (Rose, 2002; Rose, Carlson, & Waller, 2007; Rose & Smith, 2009). Rose (2002) introduced the concept of co-rumination to describe the ways that some friends might make matters worse by giving their pals even more things to worry about

than they had originally realized. For example, if Janisa tells her friend Robin about doing poorly on a spelling test, does Robin encourage Janisa to study harder, or does she remind Janisa that not doing well now is a really bad sign because the words are only going to get harder in the future? Rumination is a way of thinking that involves worrying about a topic without finding a resolution. When we ruminate, we might dwell on all the possible horrible consequences of some negative life event or imagine everything that might go wrong in the future. Co-rumination is like that too, but it involves engaging in a conversation with someone and making a negative event that the person is going through seem even worse.

In a study of hundreds of grade-school and middle-school children, Rose (2002) found that girls were more likely than boys to engage in co-rumination, and this difference was particularly large among adolescents. Furthermore, longitudinal research has shown that co-rumination, even in the context of good friends, was associated with increased feelings of depression and anxiety, especially for girls (Rose, Carlson, & Waller, 2007). Rose and colleagues suggest that some friends might be a good sign of social functioning, but when those friends are people who hurt more than help, they can negatively influence girls' well-being.

As with the first edition, the continuing goal of *The Science of Psychology: An Appreciative View* is to present psychology as an integrated field in which the whole is greater than the sum of its parts but the parts are essential to the whole. Accordingly, this edition illuminates many areas where specialized subfields overlap and where research findings in one subfield support important studies and exciting discoveries in another. Students come to appreciate, for example, how neuroscientific findings inform social psychology and how discoveries in personality psychology relate to leadership in organizational settings. **Intersection** features showcase research at the crossroads of two areas and shed light on these intriguing connections. This second edition includes many new Intersections showing the influence of work in one field of psychology on another. For example, the Intersection in the chapter on human development, Chapter 9, links work in developmental psychology with clinical psychology to explore the topic "Is 'Girl Talk' Always a Good Thing?"

Appreciating Psychology as a Science

The second edition's attention to function before dysfunction, up-to-date coverage, and broad scope reflect the field of psychology *today.* These qualities underscore psychology's vital and ongoing role as a **science that ever advances knowledge** about ourselves and our interactions in the world. Psychology is a vigorous young science and one that changes quickly. The text narrative interweaves the most current research with classic findings to give students an appreciation of this vitality. In Chapter 13, for instance, the treatment of Milgram's classic study on obedience is complemented by analysis of Burger's recent attempts to re-create the study.

In conjunction with creating current and contemporary course materials, *The Science of Psychology: An Appreciative View*, Second Edition, includes citations that bring the most important recent and ongoing research into the text. These updated references give students and instructors the very latest that psychology has to offer on each topic.

Appreciating science also means appreciating disagreements in the field. Each chapter contains a **Critical Controversy** feature highlighting current psychological debates and posing thought-provoking questions that encourage students to examine the evidence on both sides. For example, Chapter 11's Critical Controversy investigates whether abstinence-only sex education can be effective.

Finally, appreciating science also means helping students master challenging scientific concepts. Two special inserts, **Touring the Brain and Nervous System** and **Touring the Senses,** feature detailed full-color transparency overlays of important figures. Conceived and developed with the input of an expert consultant, the overlays offer students hands-on practice in grasping key biological structures and processes that are essential to an appreciation of the role of science in psychology and success in the course. Finally, **Test Yourself questions** appear at the end of every major section to help students check what they know before moving on.

CRITICAL CONTROVERSY

Can Abstinence-Only Sex Education Ever Be Effective?

A recent study made the headlines when it reported that an abstinence-only intervention successfully delayed sexual intercourse in youth. Let's take a look at the study to get a sense of why it worked. John B. Jemmott III and his colleagues randomly assigned 662 African American sixth- and seventh-graders to different groups (Jemmott, Jemmott, & Fong, 2010). The groups included abstinence-only and safer-sex interventions. A group that received information about healthy behavior (but not about sexuality) served as a control. The dependent measure was whether participants had sexual intercourse in the two years following the interventions.

The abstinence-only intervention was built around the principles of social cognitive theory, focusing on building self-efficacy and a sense of personal control. The facilitators in the program emphasized that sexual activity is a serious step and that it might be best to delay it for some time in the future. They did not talk about sex moralistically and never mentioned that students should wait until marriage; nor did the instructors present sexual behavior negatively. Instead, the intervention included role-play exercises and other activities that helped students build skills to resist pressures to have sex. If the topics of birth control or condoms were broached by students, the facilitators provided medically accurate information and cleared up any misconceptions students might have.

Two years later, students in the abstinence-only program were less likely to report having had sex than those in the control group. Specifically, about one-third of the abstinence-only group reported they had had sexual intercourse, compared with nearly half of the control group. The safe-sex intervention students did not differ from the controls in terms of whether they reported having sex. Importantly, those in the abstinence-only group who did have sex were no less likely to use condoms than those in the safer-sex group.

Although these results might generally seem to support the effectiveness of abstinence-only education, particular aspects of the study might raise the eyebrows of abstinence-only advocates. First, some of the middle-schoolers in the study were as young as 10 years old, certainly younger than many abstinence-only advocates might envision. Second, the information provided about contraceptives and condoms does not conform with the typical expectations for abstinence-only education. Moreover, participants were not encouraged to wait until marriage to have sex, nor were they told that sexual behavior outside of marriage is generally harmful.

There are also features of the study that limit its validity and generalizability. Note that only students in the abstinence-only group were specifically encouraged to delay sexual activity and that the dependent measure was self-report. So, these students might not have been truthful about their sexual activity. Also, because the study included only youngsters, it is not clear whether the intervention would work for older teens.

Nevertheless, this research provides the first evidence that sex education aimed at abstinence can have an influence on the sexual behavior of young people. Importantly, though, the version of abstinence-only education used in the study may be one that surprises advocates of such interventions.

> **WHAT DO YOU THINK?**
> - What kind of sex education did you have in school? Was it adequate? Explain.
> - If, as a parent, you were asked to give consent for your child to participate in the study by Jemmott and others, how would the child's sex or age influence your decision?
> - How might an intervention like this one be used to reduce other risky behaviors in youth?

Appreciating Our Dynamic Field: Chapter-by-Chapter Changes

In this second edition, I have added important new material while streamlining where possible, and I have brought each chapter up-to-date to capture the latest trends and findings in the field. In addition, all of the chapter-opening vignettes—as well as many of the topics in the features, the Apply Your Knowledge exercises, and the examples— are new or updated.

The key content changes, chapter by chapter, include but are not limited to the following:

CHAPTER 1: WHAT IS PSYCHOLOGY?

- New material on genes, genetic characteristics, and natural selection
- New Critical Controversy selection, "Are Young Americans in the Middle of a Narcissism Epidemic?"
- New Intersection selection, "Social Psychology and Cross-Cultural Psychology: Is Success Always Sweeter Than Failure?"
- New Psychological Inquiry selection, "Explore Evolution from Giraffes to Human Beings"
- New Psychological Inquiry selection, "Questions That Psychology Specialists Ask"

CHAPTER 2: PSYCHOLOGY'S SCIENTIFIC METHOD

- New discussion of event-contingent responding
- Enhanced treatment of calculating the standard deviation
- New example applying research methods to the election of Barack Obama
- New section demonstrating the application of various research approaches to the same research question
- New health and wellness section on the health benefits of writing
- New Psychological Inquiry selection, "Miserable but Helpful?" on how mood relates to helping
- New Psychological Inquiry selection, "Experimentation in a Natural Setting"

CHAPTER 3: BIOLOGICAL FOUNDATIONS OF BEHAVIOR

- Expanded discussion of the neurotransmitter acetylcholine (ACh) and its effects
- New coverage of the neurotransmitter glutamate and its functions
- New discussion of transcranial magnetic stimulation (TMS)
- New information on left and right hemisphere function in the brain
- Updated coverage of the role of the hippocampus in memory and the reward areas of the brain
- Expanded coverage of the endocrine system and its interactions with the central nervous system
- New details on the role of genes in creating the amino acids that form the bases of body functioning
- Analysis of a new twin study comparing identical and fraternal twin pairs in Italy with respect to their self-esteem, life satisfaction, and optimism for the future
- New Psychological Inquiry selection, "The Brain in Different Species"
- New Psychological Inquiry selection, "The Jim Twins"

CHAPTER 4: SENSATION AND PERCEPTION

- New discussion of emotional stimuli, emotion-induced blindness, and inattentional blindness
- New description of phantom limb pain and its treatment
- New account of extrasensory perception
- Added coverage on the taste of *umami*
- New Psychological Inquiry selection, "Old Woman or Young Woman?"
- New section on subliminal perception, complemented by a new Psychological Inquiry selection, "Subliminal Perception: Working Up a Thirst"

CHAPTER 5: STATES OF CONSCIOUSNESS

- New discussion of the global brain workspace and its role in consciousness
- New material on sudden infant death syndrome (SIDS) and research linking it to sleep apnea
- Updated and expanded coverage of narcolepsy
- New section on sleep throughout the life span
- New material on the role of sleep in brain plasticity
- Treatment of incubation and its function in producing a solution to a problem
- New information on hypnotizability and the uses of hypnosis
- New Psychological Inquiry selection, "Taking a Ride on the Sleep Cycles"
- New Psychological Inquiry selection, "Drug Use by American Teenagers"

CHAPTER 6: LEARNING

- Revised treatment of avoidance learning
- New examination of learned helplessness and research on breaking its lock on individual functioning
- New description of classical conditioning effects on the immune and endocrine systems
- New material on preparedness and snake phobia in humans
- Added coverage of the classic Bobo doll study
- New material on the relationship between multicultural experience and insight learning
- New Psychological Inquiry selection, "From Acquisition to Extinction (to Spontaneous Recovery)"
- New Psychological Inquiry selection, "Schedules of Reinforcement and Different Patterns of Responding"

CHAPTER 7: MEMORY

- Expanded treatment of attention, covering divided attention, sustained attention, and multitasking
- New information on primacy and recency and their influence on individuals' feelings about various sensory stimuli
- Updated and expanded coverage of the tip-of-the-tongue phenomenon
- New Psychological Inquiry selection, "The Inner Workings of Working Memory"
- New Psychological Inquiry selection, "The Serial Position Effect: Lost in Midstream"

CHAPTER 8: THINKING, INTELLIGENCE, AND LANGUAGE

- Extensive new examination of system 1 and system 2 methods of reasoning and decision making
- New discussion of Spearman's *g*
- Updated account of intellectual disability
- New Critical Controversy, "Does Gender Influence Language?"
- Added coverage of the base rate fallacy and representativeness heuristic
- New material on the role of experience in enhancing cognitive skills
- New Psychological Inquiry selection, "Thinking Outside the Box"
- New Psychological Inquiry selection, "The Normal Curve"

CHAPTER 9: HUMAN DEVELOPMENT

- Detailed new presentation on research methods in developmental psychology
- Extensive new discussion of whether early or later life experiences play a larger role in human development
- Expanded treatment of Piaget's concepts of assimilation and accommodation
- Updated treatment of current research in moral development
- New, updated account of current research on socioemotional development and aging, including a look at Carstensen's socioemotional selectivity theory
- New Psychological Inquiry selection, "Thinking Critically About Object Permanence"
- New Psychological Inquiry selection, "Looking at Identity Exploration"

CHAPTER 10: MOTIVATION AND EMOTION

- All-new section on binge eating disorder
- All-new section on emotional expression in computer communications
- Updated coverage of the contemporary classification of emotion as a function of valence and arousal
- New section on resilience
- New health and wellness section on the pursuit of happiness
- New Psychological Inquiry selection, "Obeying the (Yerkes-Dodson) Law"
- New Psychological Inquiry selection, "The Full Circle of Emotions"

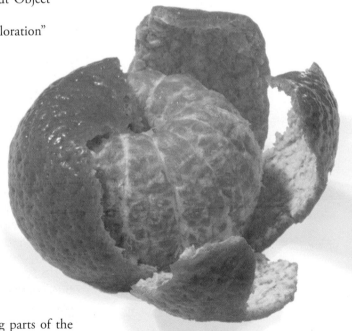

CHAPTER 11: GENDER, SEX, AND SEXUALITY

- New chapter, constructed of largely new content and including parts of the previous edition's chapters on biological foundations, development, motivation and emotion, social psychology, and health psychology
- New Psychological Inquiry selection, "Sex and Casual Sex"
- New Psychological Inquiry selection, "Sex in America"

CHAPTER 12: PERSONALITY

- Updated discussion of current research on the five-factor model of personality
- Expanded treatment of cross-cultural and animal studies on the big five personality traits
- All-new discussion of biological approaches to personality, including Eysenck's reticular activation system theory, Gray's reinforcement sensitivity theory, the neuroscience of personality, and behavior genetics
- New Intersection selection, "Personality and Organizational Psychology: Hey, What's Your Type?"
- New Psychological Inquiry selection, "Your Personality Traits: Who Are You?"
- New Psychological Inquiry selection, "A Can-Do Attitude Means You Can Quit Smoking"

CHAPTER 13: SOCIAL PSYCHOLOGY

- Expanded discussion of self-objectification
- New material on resisting persuasion and strategies for successful persuasion
- Added description of the classic cognitive dissonance study by Festinger and Carlsmith
- New material on Burger's recent attempt to replicate Milgram's classic study
- New treatment of sociocultural factors in altruism, focusing on recent research
- New discussion of media influences on prosocial behavior
- Streamlined analysis of close relationships
- New Intersection selection, "Social Psychology and Cognitive Neuroscience: Is the Brain Wired for Conformity?"
- New Psychological Inquiry selection, "Objectifying Sarah Palin"
- New Psychological Inquiry selection, "Obedience Now and Then"

CHAPTER 14: INDUSTRIAL AND ORGANIZATIONAL PSYCHOLOGY

- Streamlined presentation
- Updated discussion of the best places to work in the United States
- New details on transformational leadership, reflecting recent research
- Expanded, updated treatment of workplace aggression and violence
- Revised health and wellness section on job stress and how to manage it
- New Psychological Inquiry selection, "The Fastest-Growing Jobs in the United States"
- New Psychological Inquiry selection, "You Need a Vacation!"

CHAPTER 15: PSYCHOLOGICAL DISORDERS

- Focused treatment of personality disorders, highlighting antisocial personality disorder and borderline personality disorder
- Updated treatment of psychological factors in depression
- New information on sociocultural factors in suicide, including updated worldwide suicide rates
- New examples for dissociative amnesia, dissociative fugue, and dissociative identity disorder
- New Psychological Inquiry selection, "Depression Among Women and Men Across Cultures"
- New Psychological Inquiry selection, "The Association of Genes with Schizophrenia"

CHAPTER 16: THERAPIES

- New information on tetracyclic antidepressants (NaSSAs)
- Updated discussion on trends in the prescription of antidepressants
- New material on deep brain stimulation as a treatment for depression and other disorders

- New discussion on cybertherapy (e-therapy) and its advantages and disadvantages
- New coverage of the use of behavior therapies for obsessive-compulsive disorder
- New material on the therapeutic alliance and client factors in the success of psychotherapy
- New Psychological Inquiry selection, "Classical Conditioning: The Backbone of Aversive Conditioning"
- New Psychological Inquiry selection, "Does Therapy Work?"

CHAPTER 17: HEALTH PSYCHOLOGY

- New discussion on the fields of health promotion and public health
- New information on the hypothalamic-pituitary-adrenal axis (HPA axis) and its function in regulating stress
- New Psychological Inquiry selection, "Praying for Good Health"
- New Psychological Inquiry selection, "Physical Activity: A Matter of Life and Death"

Appreciating the Power of Customization: Create

Craft your teaching resources to match the way you teach! With McGraw-Hill Create, **www.mcgrawhillcreate.com,** you can easily rearrange chapters, combine material from other content sources, and quickly upload content you have written, such as your course syllabus or teaching notes. Find the content you need in Create by searching through thousands of leading McGraw-Hill textbooks. Arrange your book to fit your teaching style. Create even allows you to personalize your book's appearance by selecting the cover and adding your name, school, and course information. Order a Create book and you'll receive a complimentary print review copy in 3–5 business days or a complimentary electronic review copy (eComp) via e-mail in about an hour. Go to **www.mcgrawhillcreate.com** today and register. Experience how McGraw-Hill Create empowers you to teach *your* students *your* way.

Appreciating Instructor Support

What if . . .

- You could re-create the one-on-one experience of working through difficult concepts in office hours with every student without having to invest any office-hour time to do so?
- You could see at a glance how well each of your students (or sections) is performing in each segment of your course?
- You had all of the assignments and resources for your course pre-organized by learning objective and with point-and-click flexibility?

Over the course of developing *The Science of Psychology: An Appreciative View,* we asked these questions and many more. We did not stop at simply asking questions either. We visited with faculty across the country and also observed you doing what you do to prepare and deliver your courses. And we observed students as they worked through assignments and studied for exams. The result of these thousands of hours of research and development is a state-of-the-art learning environment tool that bolsters student performance at the same time as it makes instructors' lives easier and more efficient. To experience this environment for yourself, please visit **www.mcgraw-hillconnect.com.**

Online Learning Center for Instructors The password-protected instructor side of the Online Learning Center (**www.mhhe.com/king2e**) contains the Instructor's Manual, Test Bank files, PowerPoint slides, Classroom Performance System (CPS or "clicker") Questions, Image Gallery, and other valuable material to help you design and enhance your course. See more information about specific assets below. Ask your local McGraw-Hill representative for password information.

Instructor's Manual by Lorelei A. Carvajal, Triton Community College

The Instructor's Manual provides a wide variety of tools and resources for presenting the course, including learning objectives, ideas for lectures and discussions, and handouts. The Connections section serves as a roadmap outlining all the other ancillaries for that chapter and points out all the unique and interesting features available.

Test Bank by Ted A. Barker, Northwest Florida State College

By increasing the rigor of the test bank development process, McGraw-Hill has raised the bar for student assessment. Over 1,700 multiple-choice and 85 essay questions were prepared by a coordinated team of subject-matter experts. Each question and set of possible answers were methodically vetted by the team for accuracy, clarity, effectiveness, and accessibility, and each is annotated for level of difficulty, Bloom's taxonomy, APA learning outcomes, and corresponding coverage in the text. Organized by chapter, the questions are designed to test factual, applied, and conceptual understanding. The test bank is compatible with McGraw-Hill's computerized testing program, EZ Test, and most course management systems.

PowerPoint Presentations by Victor Broderick, Lincoln Land Community College

The PowerPoint Presentations cover the key points of each chapter and include figures and charts from the text. The presentations serve as an organizational and a navigational tool integrated with examples and activities from an expert teacher. The slides can be used as is or modified to meet the needs of the individual instructor.

Classroom Performance System (CPS) by Jason S. Spiegelman, Community College of Baltimore County

The Classroom Performance System's mix of factual and opinion questions allows instructors to know what concepts their students are variously mastering and those with which students are having difficulty. CPS, a "clicker" system, is a great way to give interactive quizzes, maximize student participation in class discussions, and take attendance.

Image Gallery

The Image Gallery features the complete set of figures and tables from the text. These images are available for download and can be easily embedded into instructors' PowerPoint slides.

Appreciating How Students Study

Today's students are different, and how they study is different as well. With this in mind, *The Science of Psychology: An Appreciative View* takes these changed realities into account in providing students with a roadmap for success.

Adaptive Diagnostic Tool This diagnostic tool is an unparalleled, intelligent learning system based on cognitive mapping that *diagnoses* your students' knowledge of a particular subject and then creates an individualized learning path geared toward student success in your course. It offers individualized assessment by delivering appropriate learning material in the form of questions at the right time, helping students attain mastery of the content. Whether the system is assigned by you or used independently by students as a study tool, the results can be recorded in an easy-to-use grade report that allows you to measure student progress at all times and coach your students to success.

As an added benefit, all content covered in this adaptive diagnostic is tied to learning objectives for your course so that you can use the results as evidence of subject mastery. This tool also provides a personal study plan that allows the student to estimate the time it will take and the number of questions required to learn the subject matter. Your students will learn faster, study more efficiently, and retain more knowledge when using *The Science of Psychology: An Appreciative View*.

***Online Learning Center for Students* by Alisha Janowsky, University of Central Florida** The Student Online Learning Center contains chapter-by-chapter quizzes, outlines, learning objectives, and key terms. The multiple choice, applied multiple choice, fill-in-the-blank, and true/false quizzes ask questions that build on conscientious reading of the text. To access the Online Learning Center, go to **www. mhhe.com/king2e.**

CourseSmart e-Textbook This text is available as an eTextbook at **www.CourseSmart. com.** At CourseSmart your students can take advantage of significant savings off the cost of a print textbook, reduce their impact on the environment, and gain access to powerful web tools for learning. CourseSmart eTextbooks can be viewed online or downloaded to a computer. The eTextbooks allow students to do full text searches, add highlighting and notes, and share notes with classmates. CourseSmart has the largest selection of eTextbooks available anywhere. Visit **www.CourseSmart.com** to learn more and to try a sample chapter.

Tegrity Tegrity Campus is a service that makes class time available all the time by automatically capturing every lecture in a searchable format for students to review when they study and complete assignments. With a simple one-click start and stop process, users capture all computer screens and corresponding audio. Students replay any part of any class with easy-to-use browser-based viewing on a PC or Mac.

Educators know that the more students can see, hear, and experience class resources, the better they learn. With Tegrity Campus, students quickly recall key moments by using Tegrity Campus's unique search feature. This search helps students efficiently find what they need, when they need it, across an entire semester of class recordings. Help turn all your students' study time into learning moments immediately supported by your lecture.

ACKNOWLEDGMENTS
APPRECIATING VALUABLE INSTRUCTOR AND STUDENT FEEDBACK

The quality of *The Science of Psychology: An Appreciative View,* Second Edition, is a testament to the skills and abilities of so many people, and I am tremendously grateful to the following individuals for their insightful contributions during the project's development and production.

SECOND EDITION CONTRIBUTORS

Manuscript Reviewers

Cheryl Anagnopoulos, *Black Hills State University*
David Andresen, *Metropolitan State College of Denver*
Lindette Baas, *Arizona Western College-Yuma*
Mita Banerjee, *Pitzer College*
Michael Barber, *Santa Fe College*
Ted A. Barker, *Northwest Florida State College*
Richard Bernstein, *Broward College-South*
Kenneth G. Brewer, *Northeast State Community College*
Deborah S. Briihl, *Valdosta State University*
Victor Broderick, *Lincoln Land Community College*
Ellen Broom, *Texas Christian University*
Susan D. Burleson, *Davidson County Community College*
Lorelei A. Carvajal, *Triton Community College*
David Cavalleri, *Santa Fe College*
Sharon E. Chacon-Mineau, *Northeast Wisconsin Technical College*
Wanda Clark, *South Plains College*
Verne Cox, *University of Texas-Arlington*
Trina Cyterski, *University of Georgia*
Sundi Donovan, *Liberty University*
Evelyn N. Doody, *College of Southern Nevada*
Kristin S. Edwards, *Ohio State University-Columbus*
Kathy Erickson, *Pima Community College*
Diane K. Feibel, *University of Cincinnati-Raymond Walters College*
Debra L. Frame, *University of Cincinnati-Raymond Walters College*
Betty Jane Fratzke, *Indiana Wesleyan University*
Laura Gaudet, *Chadron State College*
Katherine Gibbs, *University of California-Davis*
Gregg Gold, *Humboldt State University*
Nicholas Greco, *College of Lake County*
Gladys S. Green, *Manatee Community College*
Jerry Green, *Tarrant County College*

Laura Gruntmeir, *Redlands Community College*
Shawn M. Haake, *Iowa Central Community College*
Carrie E. Hall, *Miami University of Ohio*
Sheryl M. Hartman, *Miami Dade College*
Lesley Hathorn, *Metropolitan State College of Denver*
Kimberly Henderson, *Boise State University*
John Hensley, *Tulsa Community College*
Rebecca Henthorn, *Murray State College*
Jennifer K. Higa-King, *Honolulu Community College*
Wendy Johnson, *Borough of Manhattan Community College*
Linda Jones, *Blinn College*
Diana Joy, *Community College of Denver*
Hilary Kalagher, *Indiana University*
Patty M. Keller, *Saint Louis Community College-Kirkwood*
Shelia Kennison, *Oklahoma State University*
Yuthika Kim, *Oklahoma City Community College*
Kevin M. King, *University of Washington*
Cherie L. Kittrell, *State College of Florida*
Larry Kollman, *Northern Iowa Area Community College*
Jeff Lawley, *Louisiana State University-Shreveport*
Cathy Lawrenz, *Johnson County Community College*
Kristin Lazarova, *Northeast State Community College*
Juliet Lee, *Cape Fear Community College*
Kenneth J. Leising, *Texas Christian University*
Heather Lench, *Texas A&M University*
Eric Limegrover, *Miami University of Ohio*
Amy Lindsey, *Utica College*
Tammy Lochridge, *Itawamba Community College*
Ann Madden, *Florida State College-South Campus*
Betty Magjuka, *Gloucester County College*
Debra Matchinsky, *North Hennepin Community College*
Christopher Mayhorn, *North Carolina State University*
Dawn M. McBride, *Illinois State University*
Shawn Mikulay, *Elgin Community College*

Kristie Morris, *Rockland Community College*
Judith Ann Nichols, *Lincoln Land Community College*
Fabian Novello, *Clark State Community College*
Bernadette A. O'Leary, *California State University-Long Beach*
Debbie Palmer, *University of Wisconsin-Stevens Point*
Lisa L. Poole, *Northeast State Community College*
Helen J. Powell, *Baker College*
Marianna Rader, *Florida State College-Downtown*
Cynthia K. Shinabarger Reed, *Tarrant County College-NE*
Karen Clay Rhines, *Northampton Community College*
Michael C. Rhoads, *University of Northern Colorado*
Carol P. Russell, *Owens Community College*
Kristina L. Schaefer, *Moorpark College*
Chris Scribner, *Lindenwood University*
David Shepard, *South Texas College*
Barry Silber, *Hillsborough Community College*
Jason S. Spiegelman, *Community College of Baltimore County*

Krishna S. Stilianos, *Oakland Community College*
Michael W. Torello, *Capital University*
Alicia Uddin, *Tulsa Community College*
Glenn Valdez, *Grand Valley State University*
Thomas E. Van Canfort, *Fayetteville State University*
Jennifer Vaughn, *Metropolitan Community College*
Jacqueline J. von Spiegel, *Ohio State University-Columbus*
Jeff Wachsmuth, *Napa Valley College*
Andrew S. Walters, *Northern Arizona University*
Roger Ward, *University of Cincinnati-Raymond Walters College*
Shannon Welch, *University of Idaho*
Steve J. Withrow, *Guilford Tech Community College-Jamestown*

Design Reviewers

David Cavalleri, *Santa Fe College*
Gregg Gold, *Humboldt State University*
Gladys S. Green, *Manatee Community College*
Carrie E. Hall, *Miami University of Ohio*
Sheryl M. Hartman, *Miami Dade College*
Hilary Kalagher, *Indiana University*
Cheri L. Kittrell. *State College of Florida*
Heather Lench, *Texas A&M University*
Debbie Palmer, *University of Wisconsin-Stevens Point*
Marianna Rader, *Florida State College-Downtown*
Glenn Valdez, *Grand Valley State University*
Jeff Wachsmuth, *Napa Valley College*

Connect and LearnSmart Consultants

Lorelei A. Carvajal, *Triton Community College*
Jenel Cavazos, *University of Oklahoma*
Regina Hughes, *Collin College*
Cheri Kittrell, *Manatee Community College*

TestBank Reviewers

Jeff Henriques, *University of Wisconsin, Madison*
Jason Spiegelman, *Community College of Baltimore City*

Cover Survey Respondents

Lindette Baas, *Arizona Western College-Yuma*
Michael Barber, *Santa Fe College*
Ted A. Barker, *Northwest Florida State College*

Richard Bernstein, *Broward College-South*
Victor Broderick, *Lincoln Land Community College*
Lorelei A. Carvajal, *Triton College*
David Cavalleri, *Santa Fe College*
Sharon E. Chacon-Mineau, *Northeast Wisconsin Technical College*
Wanda Clark, *South Plains College*
Verne Cox, *University of Texas-Arlington*
Evelyn N. Doody, *College of Southern Nevada*
Kathy Erickson, *Pima Community College*
Diane K. Feibel, *University of Cincinnati-Raymond Walters College*
Laura Gaudet, *Chadron State College*
Nicholas Greco, *College of Lake County*
Shawn M. Haake, *Iowa Central Community College*
Carrie E. Hall, *Miami University of Ohio*
Lesley Hathorn, *Metropolitan State College of Denver*
Jennifer K. Higa-King, *Honolulu Community College*
Wendy Johnson, *Borough of Manhattan Community College*
Diana Joy, *Community College of Denver*
Hilary Kalagher, *Indiana University*
Larry Kollman, *Northern Iowa Area Community College*
Jeff Lawley, *Louisiana State University-Shreveport*
Cathy Lawrenz, *Johnson County Community College*
Kristin Lazarova, *Northeast State Community College*
Juliet Lee, *Cape Fear Community College*
Amy Lindsey, *Utica College*
Ann Madden, *Florida State College-South Campus*
Betty Magjuka, *Gloucester County College*
Christopher Mayhorn, *North Carolina State University*
Dawn M. McBride, *Illinois State University*
Bernadette A. O'Leary, *California State University-Long Beach*
Lisa L. Poole, *Northeast State Community College*
Marianna Rader, *Florida State College-Downtown*
Cynthia K. Shinabarger Reed, *Tarrant County College-NE*
Jason S. Spiegelman, *Community College of Baltimore County*
Krishna S. Stilianos, *Oakland Community College*
Alicia Uddin, *Tulsa Community College*
Jeff Wachsmuth, *Napa Valley College*

Expert Reviewers

Barbara Sayad, *California State University-Monterey Bay*
William Yarber, *Indiana University-Bloomington*

PsychInteractive Advisory Board

Melissa Acevedo, *Westchester Community College*
Jennifer Brooks, *Collin County Community College*
Jeffrey Green, *Virginia Commonwealth University*
Julie Bauer Morrison, *Glendale Community College*
Phil Pegg, *Western Kentucky University*
Tanya Renner, *Kapi'olani Community College; University of Hawaii*
Carla Strassle, *York College of Pennsylvania*
Jim Stringham, *University of Georgia*

Introductory Psychology Symposia Participants

Every year, McGraw-Hill conducts several Introductory Psychology Symposia that are attended by instructors from across the country. These events are an opportunity for editors from McGraw-Hill to gather information about the needs and challenges of instructors teaching the introductory psychology course. The symposia also offer a forum for the attendees to exchange ideas and experiences with colleagues whom they might not have otherwise met. The feedback we have received has been invaluable and has contributed to the development of *The Science of Psychology: An Appreciative View,* Second Edition.

Melissa Acevedo, *Westchester Community College*
Terry Scott Adcock, *Parkland College*
Carol Anderson, *Bellevue College*
Susan A. Anderson, *University of South Alabama*
Diane Davis Ashe, *Valencia Community College*
Thomas C. Bailey, *University of Maryland University College*
Steven Barnhart, *Middlesex County College*

David E. Baskind, *Delta College*
Shirley Bass-Wright, *St. Philip's College*
Scott C. Bates, *Utah State*
Jennifer Beck, *Austin Community College*
James L. Becker, *Pulaski Technical College*
Aileen M. Behan-Collins, *Chemeketa Community College*
Andrew Berns, *Milwaukee Area Tech Community College*
Joy L. Berrenberg, *University of Colorado-Denver*
Ginette Blackhart, *East Tennessee State University*
Stephen Blessing, *University of Tampa*
Susan Boatright, *University of Rhode Island*
Deborah S. Briihl, *Valdosta State University*
Tamara Brown, *University of Kentucky*
Brad Brubaker, *Indiana State University*
Carrie Canales, *West Los Angeles College*
Jessica Carpenter, *Elgin Community College*
Lorelei A. Carvajal, *Triton Community College*
Karen Christoff, *University of Mississippi*
Jack Chuang, *San Jacinto College-Central*
Douglas L. Chute, *Drexel University*
Diana Ciesko, *Valencia Community College-East*
Marsha G. Clarkson, *Georgia State University*
Doreen Collins-McHugh, *Seminole State College of Florida*
Laurie L. Couch, *Morehead State University*
Michaela DeCataldo, *Johnson & Wales University*
Bonnie Dennis, *Virginia Western Community College*
Anne Marie Donohue, *Montgomery County Community College*
Katherine Dowdell, *Des Moines Area Community College*
Laura Duvall, *Heartland Community College*
David Echevarria, *University of Southern Mississippi*
Penny Edwards, *Tri-County Technical College*
Andrea Ericksen, *San Juan College*
Michael Erickson, *University of California-Riverside*
Barbara Etzel, *Finger Lakes Community College*
Dan Fawaz, *Georgia Perimeter College*
Greg J. Feist, *San Jose State University*
Dave Filak, *Joliet Junior College*
Beth Finders, *Saint Charles Community College*
Tom Fischer, *Wayne State University*
Paul A. Fox, *Appalachian State University*
Debra L. Frame, *University of Cincinnati-Raymond Walters College*
Paula Frioli, *Truckee Meadows Community College*
Dale Fryxell, *Chaminade University*
Ellen Furlong, *Ohio State University*
Lynne Gabriel, *Lakeland Community College*
John Gambon, *Ozarks Technical and Community College*
Travis Gibbs, *Riverside Community College-Moreno Valley Campus*
Charles W. Ginn, *University of Cincinnati*
Robert L. Gordon, *Wright State University*
Sam Gosling, *University of Texas-Austin*
Bonnie Gray, *Scottsdale College*

Jeff Green, *Virginia Commonwealth University*
Jerry Green, *Tarrant County College*
Daine Grey, *Middlesex Community College*
Mark Griffin, *Georgia Perimeter College*
Paul Grocoff, *Scottsdale College*
Robert Guttentag, *University of North Carolina-Greensboro*
David T. Hall, *Baton Rouge Community College*
Ericka Hamilton, *Moraine Valley Community College*
Lora Harpster, *Salt Lake Community College*
Gregory Eugene Harris, *Polk Community College-Winter Haven, FL*
Lesley Hathorn, *Metropolitan State College of Denver*
Rose Hattoh, *Austin Community College*
Traci Haynes, *Columbus State Community College*
Brett Heintz, *Delgado Community College*
Carmon Weaver Hicks, *Ivy Tech Community College*
Natalie W. Hopson, *Salisbury University*
Rachel Hull, *Texas A&M University*
Mayte Insua-Auais, *Miami Dade College-North Campus*
Linda A. Jackson, *Michigan State University*
Nita Jackson, *Butler Community College*
Margaret Jenkins, *Seminole State College*
Sean P. Jennings, *Valencia Community College*
Joan Batelle Jenson, *Central Piedmont Community College*
Robin Joynes, *Kent State University*
Barbara Kennedy-Stein, *Brevard Community College-Palm Bay Campus*
Shelia Kennison, *Oklahoma State University*
Yuthika Kim, *Oklahoma City Community College*
Christina Knox, *College of the Sequoias*
Dana Kuehn, *Florida Community College-Deerwood Center*
Eric Landrum, *Boise State University*
Ladonna Lewis, *Glendale Community College*
Mary Lewis, *Oakland University*
Deborah Licht, *Pikes Peak Community College*
Maria Lopez, *Mt. San Jacinto College-San Jacinto Campus*
Sonya L. Lott-Harrison, *Community College of Philadelphia*
Jeff Love, *Penn State University*
Lea Ann Lucas, *Sinclair Community College*
Wade Lueck, *Mesa Community College*
Lynda Mae, *Arizona State University*
Mike Majors, *Delgado Community College*
Karen Marsh, *University of Minnesota-Duluth*
Diane Martichuski, *University of Colorado-Boulder*
Wanda C. McCarthy, *University of Cincinnati-Clermont College*
Sean Meegan, *University of Utah*
Kathleen Mentink, *Chippewa Valley Technical College*
Steven P. Mewaldt, *Marshall University*
Shawn Mikulay, *Elgin Community College*
Michelle D. Miller, *Northern Arizona University*

Joel Morgovsky, *Brookdale Community College*
Kathy Morrow, *Wayne County Community College*
Patricia Nation, *Bluegrass Community and Technical College*
Jeff Neubauer, *Pima Community College-Northwest Campus*
Glenda Nichols, *Tarrant County College-South Campus*
Jane Noll, *University of Southern Florida*
Eileen O'Brien, *University of Maryland-Baltimore County*
Donald Orso, *Anne Arundel Community College*
Jack A. Palmer, *University of Louisiana-Monroe*
Jeff Parsons, *Hunter College-CUNY*
David Perkins, *University of Louisiana-Lafayette*
Julie A. Penley, *El Paso Community College*
Frank Provenzano, *Greenville Technical College*
Reginald Rackley, *Southern University*
Cynthia K. S. Reed, *Tarrant County College*
Tanya Renner, *Kapi'olani Community College*
Vicki Ritts, *Saint Louis Community College-Meramec*
Alan Roberts, *Indiana University*
Caton F. Roberts, *University of Wisconsin-Madison*
Steven Ross, *Owens Community College*
Debra Rowe, *Oakland Community College*
Larry Rudiger, *University of Vermont*
Phyllis Rundhaug, *San Jacinto College*
Traci Sachteleben, *Southwestern Illinois College*
Sharleen Sakai, *Michigan State University*
Donna Love Seagle, *Chattanooga State Technical Community College*
James Shannon, *Citrus College*
Elizabeth Sheehan, *Georgia State University*
Maria Shpurik, *Florida International University*
Barry Silber, *Hillsborough Community College*
Peggy Skinner, *South Plains College*
Chris Smith, *Tyler Community College*
Lilliette Johnson Smith, *Southwest Tennessee Community College*
Wayne S. Stein, *Brevard Community College-Melbourne Campus*
Genevieve Stevens, *Houston Community College-Central*
Rick Stevens, *University of Louisiana-Monroe*
Richard Suplita, *University of Georgia*
Eva Szeli, *Arizona State University*
Shawn Talbot, *Kellogg Community College*
Helen Taylor, *Bellevue Community College*
Sheila E. Ten Eyck, *Pittsburgh Technical Institute*
Felicia Friendly Thomas, *California State Polytechnic University-Pomona*
Lisa Thomassen, *Indiana University-Bloomington*
Karen Tinker, *NorthWest Arkansas Community College*
Isabel Trombetti, *Community College of Rhode Island*

Margot Underwood, *Joliet Junior College*
Barbara Van Horn, *Indian River Community College*
Andrew Walters, *Northern Arizona University*
Martin Wolfger, *Ivy Tech Community College-Bloomington*
Andrew Woster, *South Dakota State University*
John W. Wright, *Washington State University*
Matt Yeazel, *Anne Arundel Community College*

FIRST EDITION CONTRIBUTORS

I would also like to thank the following instructors and students who provided thoughtful comments and insights on the first edition of *The Science of Psychology: An Appreciative View.*

Manuscript Reviewers

Debra Ahola, *Schenectady Community College*
Julie Wargo Aikens, *University of Connecticut*
Jim Backlund, *Kirkland Community College*
Michelle Bannoura, *Hudson Valley Community College*
Joyce Bateman-Jones, *Central Texas College*
Jeff Bergmann, *United States Military Academy*
Craig Bowden, *University of Wisconsin-Green Bay*
Josh Burke, *College of William and Mary*
Chrisanne Christensen, *Southern Arkansas University*
Diana Ciesko, *Valencia Community College*
Jane Cirillo, *Houston Community College-Central College*
Jennifer Clark, *University of Kentucky*
Patrick Courtney, *Central Ohio Tech College*
Don Daughtry, *South Texas College*
Neeru Deep, *Northwestern State University of Louisiana*
Delores Doench, *Southwestern Community College*
Heather Dore, *Florida Community College South Campus*
Kimberley Duff, *Cerritos College*
Curtis Dunkel, *Northwestern State University*
Sheri Dunlavy, *Ivy Tech Community College*
Tami J. Eggleston, *McKendree College*
Kenneth C. Elliott, *University of Maine-Augusta*
Scott Engel, *Sheridan College*
Tom Ersfeld, *Central Lakes College*
Gwen Fischer, *Hiram College*
Betty Jane Fratzke, *Indiana Wesleyan University*
Katrina Gantly, *Camosun College, Canada*

Noni Gaylord-Harden, *Loyola University*
Barbara Gfellner, *Brandon University, Canada*
Jessica Gilbert, *Northern Virginia Community College*
Jeffrey Green, *Virginia Commonwealth University*
Janelle Grellner, *University of Central Oklahoma*
Laura Gruntmeir, *Redlands Community College*
Elizabeth Yost Hammer, *Loyola University*
Carmon Hicks, *Ivy Tech Community College*
Cynthia Hoffman, *Indiana University*
Jean W. Hunt, *University of the Cumberlands*
Heather Jennings, *Mercer County Community College*
Brian Johnson, *University of Tennessee-Martin*
Arthur Kemp, *University of Central Missouri*
Sheryl Leytham, *Grand View College*
Angie MacKewn, *University of Tennessee*
Nancy Mann, *Southern Wesleyan University*
Amy J. Marin, *Phoenix College*
Randall Martinez, *Cypress College*
Jason McCartney, *Salisbury University*
David McCone, *United States Air Force Academy*
Will Mcintosh, *Georgia Southern University*
Ron Mulson, *Hudson Valley Community College*
Jeff Neubauer, *Pima Community College*
Geoffrey O'Shea, *State University of New York-Oneonta*
Barbara Oswald, *Midlands Technical College*
Laura Overstreet, *Tarrant County College*
Shana Pack, *Western Kentucky University*
Marc Patry, *St. Mary's University, Canada*
Jennifer Peluso, *Florida Atlantic University*
Stewart Perry, *California State University-Sacramento*
Deborah S. Podwika, *Kankakee Community College*
Charlotte Prokop, *State University of New York-Dutchess*
Amanda Rabidue, *University of Arizona*
Betsy Robinette, *Indiana Wesleyan University*
Traci Sachteleben, *Southwestern Illinois College*
Sherry Schnake, *St. Mary of the Woods College*
John Schulte, *Cape Fear Community College*
Janis Seeley, *Luzerne County Community College*
Stephanie Smith, *Indiana University*
Mary Anne Taylor, *Clemson University*
David Thompson, *Wake Technical Community College*
Angela Vaughn, *Wesley College*
Shelley Warm, *Palm Beach Community College-South*
Mary E. Wells, *Sinclair Community College*
Molly Wernli, *College of Saint Mary*
Melissa Weston, *El Centro College*
Colin William, *Ivy Tech Community College*

Introductory Psychology Symposia

Mark Alicke, *Ohio University*
Cheryl Almeida, *Johnson & Wales University*
Dan Bellack, *Trident Technical College*
Jeffrey Blum, *Los Angeles City College*
Tamara Brown, *University of Kentucky*
Nicole Judith Campbell, *University of Oklahoma*
Alexis Collier, *Ohio State University*
Layton Curl, *Metropolitan State College-Denver*
Barb DeFilippo, *Lane Community College*
Suzanne Delaney, *University of Arizona-Tucson*
Neeru Deep, *Northwestern State University of Louisiana*
Tom DiLorenzo, *University of Delaware*
Carol Donnelly, *Purdue University*
Joan Doolittle, *Anne Arundel Community College*
Dale Doty, *Monroe Community College*
Joelle Elicker, *University of Akron*
Jay Brophy Ellison, *University of Central Florida*
Don Forsyth, *Virginia Commonwealth University*
Regan A. R. Gurung, *University of Wisconsin-Green Bay*
Mike Hackett, *Westchester Community College*
Robin Hailstorks, *Prince George Community College*
Erin Hardin, *Texas Tech University*
Jeffrey B. Henriques, *University of Wisconsin-Madison*
Debra Hollister, *Valencia Community College*
Theresa Holt, *Middlesex City College*
Mark Hoyert, *Indiana University Northwest*
Charlie Huffman, *James Madison University*
Natalie Kerr, *James Madison University*
Shirin Khosropour, *Austin Community College*
Mark Laumakis, *San Diego State University*
Philip K. Lehman, *Virginia Tech*
Veronica Evans Lewis, *University of Louisiana-Monroe*
Mark Licht, *Florida State University*
Clem Magner, *Milwaukee Area Technical College*
Randall Martinez, *Cypress College*
Charlene Melrose, *Orange Coast College*
Glen Musgrove, *Broward Community College*

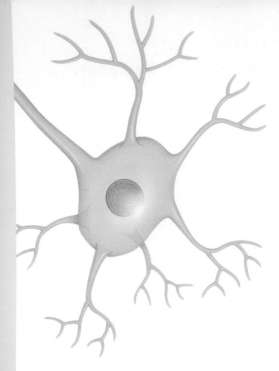

Jeff Neubauer, *Pima Community College*
John Nezlek, *College of William and Mary*
Glenda Nichols, *Tarrant County College-South*
Randall Osborne, *Texas State University-San Marcos*
John Pellew, *Greenville Tech College*
Jennifer Peluso, *Florida Atlantic University*
Deborah S. Podwika, *Kankakee Community College*
Susan Pollock, *Mesa Community College*
Bryan Porter, *Old Dominion University*
Alida Quick, *Wayne County Community College*
Christopher K. Randall, *Kennesaw State University*
Laura Reichel, *Front Range Community College*
Tanya Renner, *Kapi'olani Community College; University of Hawaii*
Tonja Ringgold, *Baltimore City Community College*
Edna Ross, *University of Louisville*
David A. Schroeder, *University of Arkansas*
Wayne Shebilske, *Wright State University*
Elisabeth Sherwin, *University of Arkansas-Little Rock*
Harvey Shulman, *Ohio State University*
Jennifer Siciliani, *University of Missouri-St. Louis*
Jamie Smith, *Ohio State University*
Vivian Smith, *Lakeland Community College*
Pam Stewart, *Northern Virginia Community College*
Nina Tarner, *Sacred Heart University*
Stephen Tracy, *Community College of Southern Nevada*
Lisa Valentino, *Seminole Community College*
Anre Venter, *University of Notre Dame*
Eduardo Vianna, *LaGuardia Community College*
Fred Whitford, *University of Montana*

Biological Art Consultants

Nicole Judith Campbell, *University of Oklahoma*
Neeru Deep, *Northwestern State University of Louisiana*
Carlos Grijalva, *University of California-Los Angeles*
Erin Hardin, *Texas Tech University*
Jeffrey B. Henriques, *University of Wisconsin-Madison*
Debra Hollister, *Valencia Community College*
Philip K. Lehman, *Virginia Tech*
Christopher K. Randall, *Kennesaw State University*
Genevieve Stevens, *Houston Community College-Central*
Ruth Wallace, *Butler Community College*

Design Consultants

Julie Wargo Aikens, *University of Connecticut*
Cheryl Almeida, *Johnson & Wales University*
Michelle Bannoura, *Hudson Valley Community College*
Joyce Bateman-Jones, *Central Texas College*
Craig Bowden, *University of Wisconsin-Green Bay*
Diana Ciesko, *Valencia Community College*
Jennifer Clarke, *University of Kentucky*
Patrick Courtney, *Central Ohio Tech College*
Neeru Deep, *Northwestern State University of Louisiana*
Delores Doench, *Southwestern Community College*
Joan Doolittle, *Anne Arundel Community College*
Sheri Dunlavy, *Ivy Tech Community College*
Tami J. Eggleston, *McKendree College*
Kenneth Elliot, *University of Maine-Augusta*
Scott Engel, *Sheridan College*
Jeffrey Green, *Virginia Commonwealth University*
Laura Gruntmeir, *Redlands Community College*
Regan Gurung, *University of Wisconsin-Green Bay*
Jeffrey B. Henriques, *University of Wisconsin-Madison*
Carmon Hicks, *Ivy Tech Community College*
Brian Johnson, *University of Tennessee-Martin*
Nicole T. Judice-Campbell, *University of Oklahoma*
David McCone, *United States Air Force Academy*
Nancy Mann, *Southern Wesleyan University*
Amy J. Marin, *Phoenix College*
Deborah S. Podwika, *Kankakee Community College*
Amanda Rabidue, *University of Arizona*
Betsye Robinette, *Indiana Wesleyan University*
Sherry Schnake, *St. Mary College of the Woods*
David A. Schroeder, *University of Arkansas*
John Schulte, *Cape Fear Community College*
Janis Wilson Seeley, *Luzerne County Community College*

Mary Anne Taylor, *Clemson University*
Donald Thompson, *Wake Technical Community College*
Eduardo Vianna, *LaGuardia Community College*
Shelley Warm, *Palm Beach Community College*
Molly Wernli, *College of St. Mary*
Melissa Weston, *El Centro College*

Expert Reviewers

Jamie Arndt, *University of Missouri-Columbia*
Bruce Bartholow, *University of Missouri, Columbia*
Scott Geller, *Virginia Tech*
Carlos Grijalva, *University of California-Los Angeles*
Christopher Robert, *University of Missouri-Columbia*
Amanda Rose, *University of Missouri-Columbia*
Timothy Trull, *University of Missouri-Columbia*
David Wolitzky, *New York University*

Class Testers

Diane Roche Benson, *Miller-Motte Technical College*
Wanda Clark, *South Plains College*
Patrick Courtney, *Central Ohio Tech College*
Tami J. Eggleston, *McKendree College*
Sheryl Leytham, *Grand View College*
Angie MacKewn, *University of Tennessee-Martin*
Elizabeth Pete, *Gibbs College of New Jersey*
Marianna Rader, *Florida Community College-Jacksonville, Downtown Campus*
Christine Selby, *University College of Bangor*
William E. Thomas, *Louisiana Technical College-Sabine Valley Campus*
Melissa Weston, *El Centro College*

PsychInteractive Advisory Board

Melissa Acevedo, *Westchester Community College*
Jennifer Brooks, *Collin County Community College*
Jeffrey Green, *Virginia Commonwealth University*
Julie Bauer Morrison, *Glendale Community College*
Phil Pegg, *Western Kentucky University*
Tanya Renner, *Kapi'olani Community College; University of Hawaii*
Carla Strassle, *York College of Pennsylvania*
Jim Stringham, *University of Georgia*

Student Focus Groups Participants

Joseph Aning, *City College of New York*
Melanie Bigenho, *San Francisco State University*
Allison Carroll, *San Francisco State University*

Diana Castro, *San Francisco State University*
Doris Corniell, *City University of New York-Brooklyn*
Tara Demoulin, *City College of San Francisco*
Jessica Frost, *San Francisco State University*
Marissa Holmes, *San Francisco State University*
Samula Jones, *City College of San Francisco*
Krupa Kothari, *San Francisco State University*
Ling Jung Li, *New York University*
Kyle Limin, *San Francisco State University*
Kristy Lin, *Cornell University*
Medeona Muca, *College of Staten Island*
Christina Ng, *State University of New York-Stony Brook*
Veronica Roman, *College of Staten Island*
Matt Russo, *State University of New York-Binghamton*
Brian Yu, *University of Michigan*

Student Reviewers

Melanie Bigenho, *San Francisco State University*
Andrea Brown, *State University of New York-New Paltz*
Allison Carroll, *San Francisco State University*
Tara DeMoulin, *City College of San Francisco*
Marissa Holmes, *San Francisco State University*
Samula Jones, *City College of San Francisco*

Krupa Kothari, *San Francisco State University*
David Zeng, *Baruch College*

Teleconference Attendees

Thomas Brandon, *University of South Florida-Tampa*
Julia Daniels, *Westchester Community College*
Don Daughtry, *South Texas College*
Robert Dunkle, *Ivy Tech Community College*
Jamie Goldenberg, *University of South Florida-Tampa*
Natalie Kerr, *James Madison University*
Chris LeGrow, *Marshall University*
Randall Martinez, *Cypress College*
Patrick McCarthy, *Middle Tennessee State University*
Steve Mewaldt, *Marshall University*
Julie Penley, *El Paso Community College*
Roger Pfeifer, *Valdosta State University*
Sandra Prince-Madison, *Delgado Community College*
Traci Sachteleben, *Southwestern Illinois College*

PERSONAL ACKNOWLEDGMENTS

I would like to extend my deepest appreciation to the many energetic and talented individuals at McGraw-Hill who have contributed so much to this work. Certainly, I owe a debt of gratitude to the amazing sales representatives whose hard work allowed the first edition of *The Science of Psychology* to be such a success. In addition, I thank Mike Sugarman, Mike Ryan, and Steve Debow for their encouragement throughout the process of this second edition. Thanks also to Sheryl Adams, Dawn Groundwater, and Beth Mejia for wonderful ideas and contributions along the way, as well as to James Headley and Julia Flohr for finding ways to "let me be me" in the service of the book.

Readers of this second edition will benefit from the conscientious efforts of development editor Sylvia Mallory, who continued this journey along with me, adding her personal energies and gifts to make the second edition a special and exciting new introduction to psychology. Thank you, Sylvia.

A special thanks to copyeditor Jennifer Gordon for her indefatigable sensibility and attention to detail. This second edition is better for her efforts. And I am grateful to production editor Cathrine Morris and to art manager Robin Mouat for their deep well of professionalism and skill. Thanks also to design manager Cassandra Chu, designer Linda Beaupré, lead photo researcher Alexandra Ambrose, and production supervisor Tandra Jorgensen for their hard work on this project.

I also want to acknowledge the energy and flair that Yasuko Okada brought to the marketing of *The Science of Psychology: An Appreciative View* (and also *Experience Psychology*). Yasuko was an amazing person who injected such vitality into her work. Her untimely death touched everyone who knew her, and I count myself fortunate to have been among those whose lives she influenced so positively. I will be ever grateful for the degree to which she devoted herself to my work, and her death will always be a reminder to live every day with excitement and zest, just as she did.

Thanks to the many introductory psychology instructors I have met over the last few years. Your enthusiasm for sharing psychology with students has inspired me throughout the process of creating this second edition. Thanks as well to the manuscript reviewers whom I have not met in person. Your critical and thoughtful appraisals of the book will benefit students in innumerable ways. I thank you for sharing your expertise with me.

I also have to thank my students at the University of Missouri, Columbia, especially my introductory psychology students, who manage (even at 8 A.M.) to keep me on my toes and thinking. They have been a fabulous testing ground for ideas. Thanks as well to Jason Trent, my graduate student, who has patiently managed to build a scholarly career while his advisor has juggled her writing and editing.

Finally, I thank my family for their love, support, patience, and encouragement. I must also acknowledge the many musicians who filled my office with inspiration while I worked on this second edition—especially Radiohead, Rufus Wainwright, and Sufjan Stevens.

HOW
The Science of Psychology: An Appreciative View,
Second Edition, HELPS YOU OVERCOME COURSE CHALLENGES!

COURSE CHALLENGE	HOW *The Science of Psychology: An Appreciative View* HELPS	WHERE CAN I FIND IT?
I want my students to read the material.	The adaptive diagnostic tool in Connect Psychology helps students "know what they know and learn what they don't know" through a personalized study plan that allows them quickly to identify their own areas of strength as well as concepts where they need additional practice.	Connect Psychology, **www.mcgraw-hillconnect.com**
Sometimes my students don't retain what they have read.	The adaptive diagnostic tool can help student performance jump by a letter grade or more by letting students know exactly where they stand—not just with their grade but with their learning, through every step of the course.	Connect Psychology, **www.mcgraw-hillconnect.com**
	Integrated self-tests that appear after every major section	Test Yourself questions in every chapter at the end of every major section
I want to foster students' critical thinking.	Psychological Inquiry selections help students think like psychological scientists, stimulating students' analytical reflection by calling on them to examine a photo, graph, or other illustration and to answer a set of critical thinking questions.	Psychological Inquiry appears in each chapter
	Critical Controversy selections highlight current psychological debates and pose thought-provoking questions that encourage students to examine the evidence on all sides.	Critical Controversy selections in each chapter; integrated critical thinking coverage, such as in Chapter 2, "Psychology's Scientific Method," and Chapter 8, "Thinking, Intelligence, and Language."

CHAPTER 1

What Is Psychology?

The Mystery That Is You

Do you have a hero? When you think about someone you truly admire, a government official, media personality, or star athlete might come to mind. In a December 2009 Gallup poll, the most admired American man was President Barack Obama. The previous president, George W. Bush, was a distant second, followed by Nelson Mandela (Page, 2009). For the most admired woman, Hillary Rodham Clinton edged out Sarah Palin, and Oprah Winfrey was third. These are all famous people who have made significant contributions in public life.

At the right moment, though, an "ordinary" person can become a hero. On January 15, 2009, US Airways Captain Chesley "Sully" Sullenberger was piloting a routine flight out of New York City. A few moments after takeoff, the plane hit a flock of geese, and the engines cut out. With 155 people on board, Captain Sullenberger faced a potential catastrophe. Realizing that the disabled plane would be unable to reach any nearby runways, he made a split-second decision to land in the Hudson River. He managed to glide the aircraft into the water with no engine power. Just six minutes after takeoff, all 155 on board began deplaning from the floating craft into waiting rescue boats. Sullenberger had calmly saved everyone on board, becoming a hero to the world (CBS News, 2009).

Even in less extraordinary circumstances, people make choices that might be called heroic. They are generous when they might be selfish. They are forgiving when they could hold a grudge. They work hard when they could slack off. You might not think of psychology as focusing on admirable aspects of everyday human behavior, but in fact the science of psychology is about *all* of human behavior. Indeed, ordinary human behavior is extraordinary when viewed in the right light and with a close lens.

Scientists, including psychologists, bring such powerful observations to their efforts. As scientists, moreover, psychologists are passionate about what they study—and what they study is you. As you are reading this book, thousands of dedicated scientists are studying things about you that you might have never considered, such as how your brain responds to a picture flashed on a screen and how your eyes adjust to a sunny day. There is not a single thing about you that is not fascinating to some psychologist somewhere. ●

PREVIEW

This introductory chapter begins by formally defining psychology and then gives context to that definition by reviewing the history and the intellectual underpinnings of the field. We next examine a number of contemporary approaches to the subject. We explore what psychologists do, including therapeutic practice and research, and consider the areas of specialization within psychology. Our introduction to this dynamic, practical field closes with a look at how understanding and applying psychological findings can positively influence human health and wellness.

1· DEFINING PSYCHOLOGY

● **psychology** The scientific study of behavior and mental processes.

● **science** The use of systematic methods to observe the natural world, including human behavior, and to draw conclusions.

When you think of the word *psychology,* what first comes to mind? Formally defined, **psychology** is the scientific study of behavior and mental processes. Let's consider the three key terms in this definition: *science, behavior,* and *mental processes.*

As a **science,** psychology uses systematic methods to observe human behavior and draw conclusions. The goals of psychological science are to describe, predict, and explain behavior. In addition, psychologists are often interested in controlling or changing behavior, and they use scientific methods to examine interventions that might help, for example, reduce violence or promote happiness.

Researchers might be interested in knowing whether individuals will help a stranger who has fallen down. The researchers could devise a study in which they observe people walking past a person who needs help. Through many observations, the researchers could come to *describe* helping behavior by counting how many times it occurs in particular circumstances. The researchers may also try to *predict* who will help, and when, by examining characteristics of the individuals studied. Are happy people more likely to help? Are women or men more likely to help? After psychologists have analyzed their data, they also will want to *explain* why helping behavior occurred when it did. Finally, these researchers might be interested in changing helping behavior, by devising strategies to increase helping.

● **behavior** Everything we do that can be directly observed.

● **mental processes** The thoughts, feelings, and motives that each of us experiences privately but that cannot be observed directly.

Behavior is everything we do that can be directly observed—two people kissing, a baby crying, a college student riding a motorcycle to campus. **Mental processes** are the thoughts, feelings, and motives that each of us experiences privately but that cannot be observed directly. Although we cannot directly see thoughts and feelings, they are nonetheless real. They include *thinking* about kissing someone, a baby's *feelings* when its mother leaves the room, and a student's *memory* of a motorcycle trip.

The Psychological Frame of Mind

What makes for a good job, a good marriage, or a good life? Although there are a variety of ways to come to answer the big questions of life, psychologists approach these questions as scientists. Psychology is a rigorous discipline that tests assumptions, bringing scientific data to bear on the questions of central interest to human beings (Stanovich, 2010). Psychologists conduct research and rely on that research to provide evidence for their conclusions. They examine the available evidence about some aspect of mind and behavior, evaluate how strongly the data (information) support their hunches, analyze disconfirming evidence, and carefully consider whether they have explored all of the possible factors and explanations (Sternberg, Roediger, & Halpern, 2007). At the core of this scientific approach are four attitudes: critical thinking, skepticism, objectivity, and curiosity.

Like all scientists, psychologists are critical thinkers. **Critical thinking** is the process of reflecting deeply and actively, asking questions, and evaluating the evidence. Thinking critically means asking ourselves *how* we know something. Critical thinkers question and test what some people say are facts. They examine research to see how soundly it supports an idea (McMillan, 2008). Critical thinking reduces the likelihood that conclusions will be based on unreliable personal beliefs, opinions, and emotions. *Thinking critically will be very important as you read this book.* Some of the things you read will fit with your current beliefs, and some will challenge you to reconsider your assumptions. Actively engaging in critical thinking is vital to making the most of psychology. As you read, think about how what you are learning relates to your life experiences and the assumptions you might have about people.

In addition, scientists are characterized by *skepticism* (Stanovich, 2010). Skeptical people challenge whether a supposed fact is really true. Being skeptical can mean questioning what "everybody knows." There was a time when "everybody knew" that women were morally inferior to men, that race could influence a person's IQ, and that the earth was flat. Psychologists, like all scientists, look at such assumptions in new and questioning ways and with a skeptical eye.

Psychology researchers often turn up the unexpected in human behavior. For example, it might seem obvious that couples who live together before marriage have a better chance of making the marriage last. After all, practice makes perfect, right? Yet researchers have found a higher rate of marital success for couples who did *not* live together before marriage (Rhoades, Stanley, & Markham, 2009; Wilson & Smallwood, 2008). You might use scientific skepticism the next time you encounter an infomercial about the latest diet craze that promises to help you lose weight "without diet or exercise." A skeptic knows that if something sounds too good to be true, it probably is.

Related to critical thinking and skepticism is the distinction between science and pseudoscience. *Pseudo* means "fake," and *pseudoscience* refers to information that is couched in scientific terminology but is not supported by sound scientific research. Astrology is an example of a pseudoscience. Although astrologers may present detailed information about an individual, supposedly based on when that person was born, no scientific evidence supports these assumptions and predictions. One way to tell that an explanation is pseudoscience rather than science is to look at how readily proponents of the explanation will accept evidence to the contrary.

Being open to the evidence means thinking *objectively*. Scientists are objective and believe that one of the best ways to be objective is to apply the empirical method to learn about the world (Beins, 2009; Stanovich, 2010). Using the **empirical method** means gaining knowledge through the observation of events, the collection of data, and logical reasoning. Being objective involves seeing things as they really are, *not as we would like them to be*. Objectivity means waiting to see what the evidence tells us rather than going with our hunches. Does the latest herbal supplement truly help relieve depression? An objective thinker knows that we must have sound evidence before answering that question.

A baby's interactions with its mother and the infant's crying are examples of behavior *because they are observable. The feelings underlying the baby's crying are an example of a* mental process *that is unobservable.*

● **critical thinking** The process of reflecting deeply and actively, asking questions, and evaluating the evidence.

● **empirical method** Gaining knowledge through the observation of events, the collection of data, and logical reasoning.

"According to this rubbish I'm going on a long journey."

© Roy Nixon. www.CartoonStock.com.

Last, scientists are curious. The scientist notices things in the world (a star in the sky, an insect, a happy person) and wants to know what it is and why it is that way. Science involves asking questions, even very big questions, such as where did the earth come from, and how does love between two people endure for 50 years? Thinking like a psychologist means opening your mind and imagination to wondering why things are the way they are. Once you begin to think like a psychologist, you might notice that the world looks like a different place. Easy answers and simple assumptions will not do.

As you can probably imagine, psychologists have many different opinions about many different things, and psychology, like any science, is filled with debate and controversy. Throughout this book, we will survey areas of hot debate in psychology in a feature called Critical Controversy. As the first example, check out this chapter's Critical Controversy concerning whether the generation of Americans born since the 1980s is experiencing an epidemic of self-love.

Debate and controversy are a natural part of thinking like a psychologist. Psychology has advanced as a field *because* psychologists do not always agree with one another about why the mind and behavior work as they do. Psychologists have reached a more accurate understanding of human behavior *because* psychology fosters controversies and *because* psychologists think deeply and reflectively and examine the evidence on all sides. A good place to try out your critical thinking skills is by revisiting the definition of psychology.

Psychology as the Science of All Human Behavior

As you consider the definition of psychology as the science of human behavior, you might be thinking, okay, where's the couch? Where's the mental illness? Psychology certainly does include the study of therapy and psychological disorders. *Clinical psychologists* in particular specialize in studying and treating psychological disorders. By definition, though, psychology is a much more *general* science (Ash & Sturm, 2007). Surely, psychological disorders are very interesting, and the media often portray psychologists as therapists. Yet the view of psychology as the science of what is wrong with people started long before television was invented. So how did we end up with the idea that psychology is only about mental illness?

When they think about psychology, many people think of Sigmund Freud (1856–1939). Freud believed that most of human behavior is caused by dark, unpleasant, unconscious impulses pressing for expression. For Freud, even the average person on the street is a mysterious well of unconscious desires. Certainly, Freud has had a lasting impact on psychology and on society; as recently as March 2006, on the occasion of his 150th birthday, Freud was featured on the cover of *Newsweek*. Consider, though, that Freud based his ideas about human nature on the patients whom he saw in his clinical practice—individuals who were struggling with psychological problems. His experiences with these clients, as well as his analysis of himself, colored his outlook on all of humanity. Freud (1996) once wrote, "I have found little that is 'good' about human beings on the whole. In my experience most of them are trash."

Freud's view of human nature has crept into general perceptions of what psychology is all about. Imagine, for example, that you are seated on a plane, having a pleasant conversation with the woman (a stranger) sitting next to you. At some point you ask your seatmate what she does for a living, and she informs you she is a psychologist. You might think to yourself, "Uh oh. What have I already told this person? What secrets does she know about me that I don't know about myself? Has she been analyzing me this whole time?" Would you be surprised to discover that this psychologist studies happiness? Or intelligence? Or the processes related to the experience of vision? The study of psychological disorders is a very important aspect of psychology, but it represents only one part of the science of psychology.

Psychology seeks to understand the truths of human life in *all* its dimensions, including people's best and worst experiences. Psychologists acknowledge that, as in the heroism of Sully Sullenberger, sometimes an individual's best moments emerge

CRITICAL CONTROVERSY

Are Young Americans in the Middle of a Narcissism Epidemic?

In reading status updates posted to Facebook and Twitter, it is easy to get the impression that many young adults think even the smallest details of their lives are fascinating. A lively controversy in psychology concerns whether young adults in the United States today are more likely to think of themselves as special and extraordinary compared to their counterparts in previous generations. Jean Twenge and her colleagues argue that Americans born since the 1980s are different in being unusually self-confident, self-assertive, and self-centered (Twenge, 2006; Twenge & Campbell, 2009; Twenge & Foster, 2008).

Examining evidence from nationally representative surveys of U.S. high school students over 30 years, Twenge and Keith Campbell (2008) found that students in 2006 gave themselves higher ratings as compared to students in 1975 in terms of their positive expectations as spouses, parents, and workers. Indeed, students in 1975 on average rated themselves as likely to be "good" in these roles, whereas students in 2006 rated themselves as likely to be "very good" (Twenge & Campbell, 2008). Imagine—an entire generation of swollen heads. What are the implications for educators trying to teach them and for employers trying to manage them (Twenge & S. M. Campbell, 2010)? Twenge refers to these individuals as Generation Me and suggests that there is an epidemic of *narcissism* (a condition of intense, unhealthy self-love) in this age group (2006). The popular media—including CBS News, National Public Radio, and several major newspapers—have jumped on the bandwagon to cover this "epidemic" (Associated Press, 2007).

Other psychologists sharply disagree with these conclusions. They argue that the positivity of Americans' self-views has remained stable over time (Donnellan, Trzesniewski, & Robins, 2009; Trzesniewski, Donnellan, & Robins, 2008). For example, Kali Trzesniewski and Brent

You're wonderful / I know

© Kate Taylor. www.CartoonStock.com.

Donnellan (2009) looked at Twenge and Campbell's data and noted that small differences in the order of the questions could produce the differences in the ratings students made. In most of their analyses, Twenge and Campbell focused on 1975, but 1975 might not have been a representative year, Trzesniewski and Donnellan assert, because the order of the questions was changed after that year. These changes may have rendered 1975 an unusually modest year (Trzesniewski & Donnellan, 2009). Looking at the data for 1975, 1976, and 1977 and comparing these to 2006, Trzesniewski and Donnellan found no evidence that students had developed increasingly positive self-views over time (2009). Thus, Trzesniewski and Donnellan caution against assuming that the young adults of today are especially likely to think of themselves as special or extraordinary (Trzesniewski & Donnellan, 2009, 2010).

This debate illustrates a number of important aspects of the science of psychology. First, solid scientific evidence is a vital part of psychology, and claims must be supported by that evidence. Further, scientists can look at the same data and reach strikingly different conclusions. The lesson here is that no matter how popular a research conclusion might be, it must be evaluated critically and objectively. In their search for answers to fascinating questions, psychologists rely on the empirical method for solid evidence.

WHAT DO YOU THINK?

- Where do you fall in this debate? What kind of research would be needed to change your mind about whether there is a narcissism epidemic among young Americans?

- What problems are inherent in drawing conclusions about the members of an entire generation?

---

amid the most difficult circumstances. Research on the human capacity for forgiveness demonstrates this point (Bono, McCullough, & Root, 2008; Lawler-Row & others, 2008; Legaree, Turner, & Lollis, 2007). Forgiveness is the act of letting go of our anger and resentment toward someone who has harmed us. Through forgiveness we cease seeking revenge or avoiding the person who did us harm, and we might even wish that person well.

A case in point: In October 2006, after Charles Carl Roberts IV took 10 young Amish girls hostage in a one-room schoolhouse in Pennsylvania, eventually murdering 5 of them and wounding 5 others before killing himself, the grief-stricken Amish community focused not on hatred and revenge but on forgiveness. As funds were being set up for the victims' families, the Amish insisted on establishing one for the murderer's family. As they prepared simple funerals for the dead girls, the community invited the killer's wife to attend. The science of psychology has much to offer to

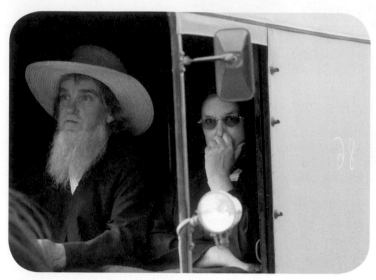

The murder in 2006 of five Amish schoolgirls evoked feelings in the community not of hatred and revenge but of forgiveness.

● **positive psychology** A branch of psychology that emphasizes human strengths.

test yourself

1. What makes psychology a science? What are the goals of psychological scientists?
2. What four attitudes are at the core of the scientific approach?
3. Which particular Freudian views of human nature have influenced general perceptions of what psychology is all about?

our understanding of not only the perpetrator's violence but also the victims' capacity for forgiveness.

The willingness of the Amish community to forgive this horrible crime is both remarkable and puzzling. Can we scientifically understand the human ability to forgive even what might seem to be unforgivable? As it happens, a number of psychologists have taken up the topic of forgiveness in research and clinical practice (Bono & McCullough, 2006; Cohen & others, 2006). Michael McCullough and his colleagues (2007) have shown that the capacity to forgive is an unfolding process that often takes time. For the Amish, their deep religious faith led them to embrace forgiveness, where many people might have been motivated to seek revenge and retribution. Researchers also have explored the relationship between religious commitment and forgiveness (McCullough, Bono, & Root, 2007). More recently, researchers have determined that forgiveness takes mental skills and abilities, not just emotional fortitude (Pronk & others, 2010).

Some argue that psychology has focused too much on the negative while neglecting qualities that reflect the best of humanity (Seligman & Csikszentmihalyi, 2000). From these criticisms positive psychology has emerged. **Positive psychology** is a branch of psychology that emphasizes human strengths. Research in positive psychology centers on topics such as hope, optimism, happiness, and gratitude (Snyder & Lopez, 2009). One goal of positive psychology is to bring a greater balance to the field by moving beyond focusing on how and why things go wrong in life to understanding how and why things go right. Positive psychology is not without its own critics, though. Indeed, some psychologists insist that human weaknesses are the most important topics to study (Lazarus, 2003).

To be a truly general science of human behavior, psychology must address *all* sides of human experience. Surely, controversy—such as that concerning positive psychology—is a part of any science. The healthy debate that characterizes the field of psychology can give rise to new psychological perspectives, and this is a sign of a lively discipline.

2· PSYCHOLOGY IN HISTORICAL PERSPECTIVE

Psychology seeks to answer questions that people have been asking for thousands of years—for example:

■ How do we learn?

■ What is memory?

■ Why does one person grow and flourish while another struggles?

It is a relatively new idea that such questions might be answered through scientific inquiry. From the time human language included the word *why* and became rich enough to enable people to talk about the past, people have created myths to explain why things are the way they are. Ancient myths attributed most important events to the pleasure or displeasure of the gods. When a volcano erupted, the gods were angry; if two people fell in love, they had been struck by Cupid's arrows. Gradually, myths gave way to *philosophy*—the rational investigation of the underlying principles of being and knowledge. People attempted to explain events in terms of natural rather than supernatural causes.

Western philosophy came of age in ancient Greece in the fourth and fifth centuries B.C.E. Socrates, Plato, Aristotle, and others debated the nature of thought and behavior, including the possible link between the mind and the body. Later philosophers, especially René Descartes, argued that the mind and body were completely separate, and they focused their attention on the mind. Psychology grew out of this tradition of thinking about the mind and body. The influence of philosophy on contemporary psychology persists today, as researchers who study emotion still talk about Descartes, and scientists who study happiness often refer to Aristotle (Biswas-Diener, Kashdan, & King, 2009).

In addition to philosophy, psychology also has roots in the natural sciences of biology and physiology (Johnson, 2008; Pinel, 2009). Read on to trace how the modern field of psychology developed.

Wundt's Structuralism and James's Functionalism

Wilhelm Wundt (1832–1920), a German philosopher-physician, put the pieces of the philosophy–natural science puzzle together to create the academic discipline of psychology. Some historians say that modern psychology was born in December 1879 at the University of Leipzig, when Wundt and his students, especially E. B. Titchener, performed an experiment to measure the time lag between the instant a person heard a sound and the moment he or she pressed a telegraph key to signal having heard it. What was so special about this experiment? Wundt's study was about the workings of the brain: He was trying to measure the time it took the human brain and nervous system to translate information into action. At the heart of this experiment was the idea that mental processes could be measured. This notion ushered in the new science of psychology.

Wundt and his collaborators concentrated on discovering the basic elements, or "structures," of mental processes. Their approach was thus called **structuralism** because of its focus on identifying the structures of the human mind, and their method of study was *introspection* (literally, "looking inside"). For this type of research, a person in Wundt's lab would be asked to think (introspect) about what was going on mentally as various events took place. For example, the individual might be subjected to a sharp, repetitive clicking sound and then might have to report whatever conscious feelings the clicking produced. What made this method scientific was the systematic, detailed self-reports required of the person in the controlled laboratory setting.

Although Wundt is most often regarded as the founding father of modern psychology, it was psychologist and philosopher William James (1842–1910), perhaps more than anyone else, who gave the field an American stamp. From James's perspective, the key question for psychology is not so much what the mind *is* (that is, its structures) as what it *is for* (its purposes or functions). James's view was eventually named *functionalism*.

In contrast to structuralism, which emphasized the components of the mind, **functionalism** probed the functions and purposes of the mind and behavior in the individual's adaptation to the environment. Whereas structuralists were looking inside the mind and searching for its structures, functionalists focused on human interactions with the outside world and the purpose of thoughts. If structuralism is about the "what" of the mind, functionalism is about the "why." Unlike Wundt, James did not believe in the existence of rigid structures in the mind. Instead, James saw the mind as flexible and fluid, characterized by constant change in response to a continuous flow of information from the world. James called this natural flow of thought a "stream of consciousness."

A core question in functionalism is, why is human thought *adaptive*—that is, why are people better off because they can think than they would be otherwise? When we talk about whether a characteristic is adaptive, we are focusing on how it makes an organism better able to survive. As we will see next, functionalism fit well with the theory of evolution through natural selection proposed by British naturalist Charles Darwin (1809–1882).

Darwin's Natural Selection

In 1859, Darwin published his ideas in *On the Origin of Species*. A centerpiece of his theory was the principle of **natural selection,** an evolutionary process in which organisms that are best adapted to their environment will survive and, importantly, produce offspring.

William Wundt (1832–1920) Wundt founded the first psychology laboratory (with his co-workers) in 1879 at the University of Leipzig.

● **structuralism** Wundt's approach to discovering the basic elements, or structures, of mental processes; so called because of its focus on identifying the structures of the human mind.

● **functionalism** James's approach to mental processes, emphasizing the functions and purposes of the mind and behavior in the individual's adaptation to the environment.

● **natural selection** Darwin's principle of an evolutionary process in which organisms that are best adapted to their environment will survive and produce offspring.

William James (1842–1910) James's approach became known as functionalism.

psychological *inquiry*

Explore Evolution from Giraffes to Human Beings

Evolution through natural selection and genetic mutation is a slow process that explains the various characteristics we see in creatures in the natural world. Darwin developed his theory of evolution through natural selection by observing phenomena in nature.

Let's take a look at a familiar creature of our natural world—the giraffe. Giraffes are the tallest mammals on earth, with some reaching a soaring height of 19 feet. Much of that height comes from the giraffe's very long neck. That neck poses a mystery that fascinates scientists: *Why* does the giraffe have such a long neck? Critically explore some possible reasons, below, and answer the questions with each.

1. An evolutionary explanation for the giraffe's neck would begin by assuming that, ages ago, some giraffes were genetically predisposed to have longer necks and others were genetically predisposed to have shorter necks. Take this evolutionary argument one step further: Why do we now see *only* giraffes with long necks?

2. You might reasonably guess that giraffes have long necks in order to reach leaves growing on tall trees—in other words, so that they can eat and survive. However, giraffes often prefer to eat from bushes and relatively low tree branches. Instead, male giraffes use their long necks in fights with other giraffes as they compete over mates. Those that win the fights are more likely to reproduce. Over the course of time, were the winners those with the longer necks or the shorter necks? Explain.

3. The process of evolution sheds light on why members of a particular species share common characteristics. If you were to apply evolutionary theory to human beings, what kinds of characteristics would you focus on, and why? Choose one human characteristic and apply the same kinds of questions you considered about the giraffe's long neck. Why are we humans the way we are?

Darwin noted that the members of any species are often locked in competition for scarce resources such as food and shelter. Natural selection is the process by which the environment determines who wins that competition. Darwin asserted that organisms with biological features that led to survival and reproduction would be better represented in subsequent generations. Over many generations, organisms with these characteristics would constitute a larger percentage of the population. Eventually, this process could change an entire species.

Importantly, a characteristic cannot be passed from one generation to the next unless it is recorded in the *genes,* those collections of molecules that are responsible for heredity. Genetic characteristics that are associated with survival and reproduction are passed down over generations. According to evolutionary theory, species change through random genetic mutation. That means that, essentially by accident, some members of a species are born with genetic characteristics that make them different from other members. If these changes are adaptive (if they help those members compete for food, survive, and reproduce), they become more common in the species. If environmental conditions were to change, however, other characteristics might become favored by natural selection, moving the process in a different direction.

Evolutionary theory implies that the way we are, at least in part, is the way that is best suited to survival in our environment (Cosmides, 2011). The Psychological Inquiry feature above lets you critically apply the principles of Darwin's theory of evolution.

Darwin's theory continues to influence psychologists today because it is strongly supported by observation. We can make such observations every day. Right now, for example, in your kitchen sink, various bacteria are locked in competition for scarce resources in the form of those tempting food particles from your last meal. When you use an antibacterial cleaner, you are playing a role in natural selection, because you are effectively killing off the bacteria that cannot survive the cleaning agents. However, you are also letting the bacteria that are genetically adapted to survive that cleanser to take over the sink. The same principle applies to taking an antibiotic medication at the first sign of a sore throat or an earache. By killing off the bacteria that may be causing the illness, you are creating an environment where their competitors (so-called antibiotic-resistant bacteria) may flourish. These observations powerfully demonstrate Darwinian selection in action.

If structuralism won the battle to be the birthplace of psychology, functionalism won the war. To this day, psychologists continue to talk about the adaptive nature of human characteristics, although they have branched out to study more aspects of human behavior than Wundt or James might ever have imagined. In a general way, since the days of those pioneers in the field, psychology has defined itself as the science of human behavior. The question of what exactly counts as human behavior, however, has fueled debate throughout the history of the field. For some psychologists, behavior has meant only observable actions; for others, it has included thoughts and feelings; for still others, unconscious processes have been the focal point. Traces of this debate can be seen today in the various contemporary approaches to the science of psychology that we will consider next.

test yourself

1. What is structuralism? How does functionalism contrast with structuralism?
2. What is meant when we say that a particular characteristic of an organism is adaptive?
3. In what ways is Darwin's work relevant to psychology?

3· CONTEMPORARY APPROACHES TO PSYCHOLOGY

In this section we survey seven different approaches that represent the intellectual backdrop of psychological science: biological, behavioral, psychodynamic, humanistic, cognitive, evolutionary, and sociocultural.

● **biological approach** An approach to psychology focusing on the body, especially the brain and nervous system.

● **neuroscience** The scientific study of the structure, function, development, genetics, and biochemistry of the nervous system, emphasizing that the brain and nervous system are central to understanding behavior, thought, and emotion.

The Biological Approach

Some psychologists examine behavior and mental processes through the **biological approach,** which is a focus on the body, especially the brain and nervous system. For example, researchers might investigate the way your heart races when you are afraid or how your hands sweat when you tell a lie. Although a number of physiological systems may be involved in thoughts and feelings, perhaps the largest contribution to physiological psychology has come through the emergence of neuroscience (Koch, 2011; Salzman & Fusi, 2010).

Neuroscience is the scientific study of the structure, function, development, genetics, and biochemistry of the nervous system. Neuroscience emphasizes that the brain and nervous system are central to understanding behavior, thought, and emotion. Neuroscientists believe that thoughts and emotions have a physical basis in the brain. Electrical impulses zoom throughout the brain's cells, releasing chemical substances that enable us to think, feel, and behave. Our remarkable human capabilities would not be possible without the brain and nervous system, which constitute the most complex, intricate, and elegant system imaginable. Although biological approaches might sometimes seem to reduce complex human experience into simple physical structures, developments in neuroscience have allowed psychologists to understand the brain as an amazingly complex organ, perhaps just as complex as the psychological processes linked to its functioning.

B. F. Skinner was a tinkerer who liked to make new gadgets. The younger of his two daughters, Deborah, was raised in Skinner's enclosed Air-Crib. Some critics accused Skinner of monstrous experimentation with his children; however, the early controlled environment has not had any noticeable harmful effects. Deborah, shown here as a child with her parents, is today a successful artist whose work strongly reflects her unique early childhood experience.

Sigmund Freud (1856–1939) Freud was the founding father of the psychodynamic approach.

● **behavioral approach** An approach to psychology emphasizing the scientific study of observable behavioral responses and their environmental determinants.

● **psychodynamic approach** An approach to psychology emphasizing unconscious thought, the conflict between biological drives (such as the drive for sex) and society's demands, and early childhood family experiences.

● **humanistic approach** An approach to psychology emphasizing a person's positive qualities, the capacity for positive growth, and the freedom to choose any destiny.

● **cognitive approach** An approach to psychology emphasizing the mental processes involved in knowing: how we direct our attention, perceive, remember, think, and solve problems.

The Behavioral Approach

The **behavioral approach** emphasizes the scientific study of observable behavioral responses and their environmental determinants. It focuses on an organism's visible interactions with the environment—that is, behaviors, not thoughts or feelings. The principles of the behavioral approach have been widely applied to help people change their behavior for the better (Miltenberger, 2008). The psychologists who adopt this approach are called *behaviorists*. Under the intellectual leadership of John B. Watson (1878–1958) and B. F. Skinner (1904–1990), behaviorism dominated psychological research during the first half of the twentieth century.

Skinner (1938) emphasized that psychology should be about what people do—their actions and behaviors—and should not concern itself with things that cannot be seen, such as thoughts, feelings, and goals. He believed that rewards and punishments determine our behavior. For example, a child might behave in a well-mannered fashion because her parents have previously rewarded this behavior. We do the things we do, behaviorists say, because of the environmental conditions we have experienced and continue to experience.

Contemporary behaviorists still emphasize the importance of observing behavior to understand an individual, and they use rigorous methods advocated by Watson and Skinner (Cheng & Holyoak, 2011). However, not every behaviorist today accepts the earlier behaviorists' rejection of thought processes, which are often called *cognition* (Shanks, 2010).

The Psychodynamic Approach

The **psychodynamic approach** emphasizes unconscious thought, the conflict between biological drives (such as the drive for sex) and society's demands, and early childhood family experiences. Practitioners of this approach believe that sexual and aggressive impulses buried deep within the unconscious mind influence the way people think, feel, and behave.

Sigmund Freud, the founding father of the psychodynamic approach, theorized that early relationships with parents shape an individual's personality. Freud's (1917) theory was the basis for the therapeutic technique that he called *psychoanalysis,* which involves an analyst's unlocking a person's unconscious conflicts by talking with the individual about his or her childhood memories, as well as the individual's dreams, thoughts, and feelings. Certainly, Freud's views have been controversial, but they remain a part of contemporary psychology. Today's psychodynamic theories tend to place less emphasis on sexual drives and more on cultural and social experiences as determinants of behavior.

The Humanistic Approach

The **humanistic approach** emphasizes a person's positive qualities, the capacity for positive growth, and the freedom to choose one's destiny. Humanistic psychologists stress that people have the ability to control their lives and are not simply controlled by the environment (Maslow, 1971; Rogers, 1961). They theorize that rather than being driven by unconscious impulses (as the psychodynamic approach dictates) or by external rewards (as the behavioral approach emphasizes), people can choose to live by higher human values such as *altruism*—unselfish concern for other people's well-being—and free will. Many aspects of this optimistic approach appear in research on motivation, emotion, and personality psychology (Ciani & others, 2010; Sheldon & Gunz, 2009).

The Cognitive Approach

According to cognitive psychologists, the human brain houses a "mind" whose mental processes allow us to remember, make decisions, plan, set goals, and be creative (Grigorenko & others, 2008; Sternberg, 2009). The **cognitive approach,** then, emphasizes the mental processes involved in knowing: how we direct our attention, perceive, remember, think, and solve problems. Many scientists who adopt this approach focus on *information processing,* the ways that the human mind interprets incoming information, weighs it, stores it, and applies it to decision making. Cognitive psychologists seek answers to questions such as how we solve math problems, why we remember some things for only a short time but others for a lifetime, and how we use our imagination to plan for the future.

Cognitive psychologists view the mind as an active and aware problem-solving system. This view contrasts with the behavioral view, which portrays behavior as controlled by external environmental forces. In the cognitive view, an individual's mental processes are in control of behavior through memories, perceptions, images, and thinking.

The Evolutionary Approach

Although arguably all of psychology emerges out of evolutionary theory, some psychologists emphasize an **evolutionary approach** that uses evolutionary ideas such as adaptation, reproduction, and natural selection as the basis for explaining specific human behaviors. David Buss (2008) argues that just as evolution molds our physical features, such as body shape, it also influences our decision making, level of aggressiveness, fears, and mating patterns. Thus, evolutionary psychologists argue, the way we adapt is traceable to problems early humans faced in adapting to their environment (Meston & Buss, 2009).

Evolutionary psychologists believe their approach provides an umbrella that unifies the diverse fields of psychology (Cosmides, 2011). Not all psychologists agree with this conclusion, however. For example, some critics stress that the evolutionary approach provides an inaccurate explanation of why men and women have different social roles and does not adequately account for cultural diversity and experiences (Wood & Eagly, 2010). Yet, even psychologists who disagree with applying the evolutionary approach to psychological characteristics still agree with the general principles of evolutionary theory.

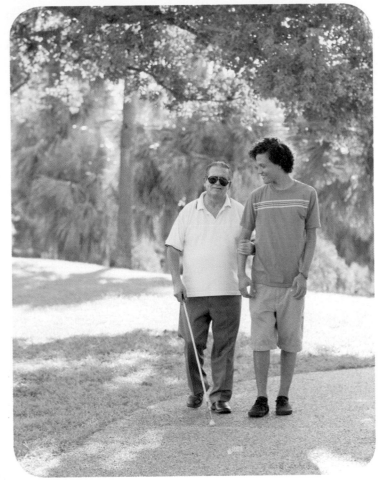

According to humanistic psychologists, warm, supportive behavior toward others helps us to realize our capacity for self-understanding.

● **evolutionary approach** An approach to psychology centered on evolutionary ideas such as adaptation, reproduction, and natural selection as the basis for explaining specific human behaviors.

● **sociocultural approach** An approach to psychology that examines the ways in which social and cultural environments influence behavior.

The Sociocultural Approach

The **sociocultural approach** examines the ways in which social and cultural environments influence behavior. Socioculturalists argue that understanding a person's behavior requires knowing about the cultural context in which the behavior occurs (Matthews & Gallo, 2011). Researchers who focus on sociocultural influences might compare people from different cultures to see whether they are similar or different in important ways (Kitayama, 2011).

The sociocultural view focuses not only on comparisons of behavior across countries but also on the behavior of individuals from different ethnic and cultural groups within a country (Grigorenko & Takanishi, 2010). Thus, in recent years, there has been increased interest in the United States on the behavior of African Americans, Latinos, and Asian Americans, especially with regard to the factors that have restricted or enhanced their ability to adapt and cope with living in a predominantly Euro-American society (Banks, 2010).

Summing Up the Seven Contemporary Approaches

These seven psychological approaches provide different views of the same behavior, and all of them may offer valuable insights that the other perspectives miss. Think about the simple experience of seeing a cute puppy. Looking at that puppy involves physical processes in the eyes, nervous system, and brain—the focus of the biological approach to psychology. The moment you spot that puppy, though, you might smile without thinking and reach down to pet the little guy. That reaction might be a response based on your past learning with your own dog (behavioral perspective), or on unconscious memories of a childhood dog (psychodynamic perspective), or on conscious memories that you especially like this dog breed (cognitive perspective), or even evolutionary processes that promoted cuteness to help offspring survive (evolutionary approach). You might find yourself striking up a conversation with the puppy's owner, based on your shared love of dogs (humanistic perspective). Further, sociocultural factors might play a role in your decision about whether to ask the owner if you could hold the puppy, whether you share those warm feelings about the puppy with others, and even whether (as in some cultures) you might view that puppy as food.

4· WHAT PSYCHOLOGISTS DO

People who think of themselves as psychologists work in a wide range of settings and engage in many different activities. Figure 1.1 shows the various settings in which psychologists practice their profession. In this section we look at what psychologists do, and then we zoom in on the areas of specialization.

Careers in Psychology

Individuals with undergraduate training in psychology might use their expertise in occupations ranging from human resources and business consulting to doing casework for individuals struggling with psychological disorders. Those with graduate training in psychology might work as therapists and counselors, researchers and teachers in universities, or as business consultants or marketing researchers.

Individuals who are primarily engaged in helping others are often called *practitioners* of psychology. They spend most of their time in clinical practice, seeing clients and offering them guidance as they work through problems. However, even psychologists who are primarily concerned with clinical practice pay attention to scientific research. For these individuals, rigorous research guides their therapeutic practice and their efforts to make improvements in the lives of their patients. Increasingly, psychologists who primarily provide therapy engage in *evidence-based practice*—that is, they use therapeutic tools whose effectiveness is supported by empirical research (Beidas & Kendall, 2010; Sandler, Wolchik, & Schoenfelder, 2011).

An important distinction that is often not well understood is the difference between a clinical psychologist and a psychiatrist. A clinical psychologist typically has a doctoral degree in psychology, which requires approximately four to five years of graduate work and one year of internship in a mental health facility. In contrast, a psychiatrist is a physician with a medical degree who subsequently specializes in abnormal behavior and psychotherapy. Another difference between a psychiatrist and a clinical psychologist is that a psychiatrist can prescribe drugs, whereas a clinical psychologist generally cannot. Despite these differences, clinical psychologists and psychiatrists are alike in sharing an interest in improving the lives of people with mental health problems.

Many psychologists who are employed at universities divide their time between teaching and doing research. Research in psychology creates the knowledge that is presented in this book and that you will be learning about in your introductory psychology course.

Human behavior is a vast, complex topic. Most psychologists specialize in a particular area of study, as we consider next.

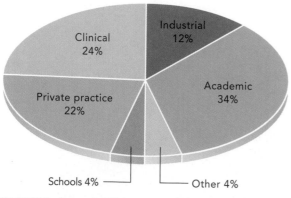

FIGURE 1.1 **Settings in Which Psychologists Work** More psychologists work in academic environments (34 percent), such as colleges and universities, than in any other setting. However, clinical (24 percent) and private practice (22 percent) settings—both of them contexts in which many psychologists in the mental health professions work—together make up almost half of the total settings.

Areas of Specialization

Psychology has many areas of specialization. Currently, there are 56 divisions in the American Psychological Association, each focusing on a specific subfield of psychology. Division 1, the Society of General Psychology, seeks to provide a coherent integration of the vast science of psychology. Division 2, the Society for the Teaching of Psychology, is dedicated to devising the best ways to help students learn about this fascinating science. The other main specializations in the field of psychology include the following:

Physiological Psychology and Behavioral Neuroscience   Researchers who study *physiological psychology* are interested in the physical processes that underlie mental operations such as vision and memory. Physiological psychologists may use animal models (that is, they may employ animals, such as rats, to study processes that are difficult or impossible to study in the same way in humans) to examine such topics as the development of the nervous system. The field of *behavioral neuroscience* also focuses on biological processes, especially the brain's role in behavior (Rilling & Sanfey, 2011). In Chapter 3 we will examine the many ways that physiological processes relate to psychological experience.

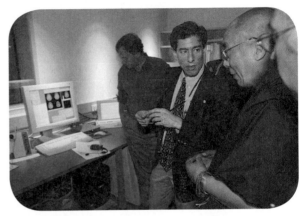

Sensation and Perception   Researchers who study *sensation and perception* focus on the physical systems and psychological processes that allow us to experience the world—to smell the Thanksgiving turkey in the oven (Yeshurun & Sobel, 2010) and to see the beauty of a sunset (Keen, 2011). These complex processes are the subject of Chapter 4.

Richard J. Davidson of the University of Wisconsin, Madison, shown with the Dalai Lama, is a leading researcher in behavioral neuroscience.

Learning   *Learning* is the intricate process by which behavior changes to adapt to changing circumstances (Cheng & Holyoak, 2011). Many researchers study the basic principles of learning using animals such as rats and pigeons (Ploog & Williams, 2010). Learning has been addressed from the behavioral and cognitive perspectives (Shanks, 2010). This topic is covered in Chapter 6.

Cognitive Psychology   *Cognitive psychology* (explored in Chapters 7 and 8) is the broad name given to the field of psychology that examines attention, consciousness, information processing, and memory. Cognitive psychologists are also interested in skills and abilities such as problem solving, decision making, expertise, and intelligence, topics covered in Chapter 8 (Margrett & others, 2010; Sternberg, 2011). Researchers in cognitive psychology and sensation perception are sometimes called *experimental psychologists.*

Developmental Psychology   *Developmental psychology* is concerned with how people become who they are, from conception to death. In particular, developmental psychologists concentrate on the biological and environmental factors that contribute to human development (Goldsmith, 2011). Developmentalists study child development (Grusec, 2011) but also adult development and aging (Staudinger & Gluck, 2011). Their inquiries range across the biological, cognitive, and social domains of life (Nelson, 2011). Chapter 9 reviews the key findings in this fascinating area.

Motivation and Emotion   Researchers from a variety of specializations are interested in *motivation and emotion,* two important aspects of experience. Research questions addressed by scientists who study motivation include how individuals persist to attain a difficult goal and how rewards affect the experience of motivation (Boekaerts, 2010).

Emotion researchers delve into such topics as the physiological and brain processes that underlie emotional experience, the role of emotional expression in health, and the possibility that emotions are universal (Izard, 2009). These fascinating questions are examined in Chapter 10.

Psychology of Women and Gender

The *psychology of women* studies psychological, social, and cultural influences on women's development and behavior. This field stresses the importance of integrating information about women with current psychological knowledge and beliefs and applying the information to society and its institutions (Martin & Ruble, 2010; Wood & Eagly, 2010). Psychologists are also interested in understanding the broad topic of *gender* and the ways in which our biological sex influences our ideas about ourselves as men and women. We consider these important topics in Chapter 11.

Personality Psychology

Personality psychology studies personality, consisting of the relatively enduring characteristics of individuals. Personality psychologists study such topics as traits, goals, motives, genetics, personality development, and well-being (McAdams & Olson, 2010). Researchers in personality psychology are interested in those aspects of your psychological makeup that make you uniquely you. The field of personality is explored fully in Chapter 12.

Social Psychology

Social psychology deals with people's interactions with one another, relationships, social perceptions, social cognition, and attitudes (Bohner & Dickel, 2011; Erber & Erber, 2011). Social psychologists are interested in the influence of groups on individuals' thinking and behavior and in the ways that the groups to which we belong influence our attitudes. The research questions that concern social psychologists include understanding and working to reduce racial prejudice, determining whether two heads really are better than one, and exploring how the presence of others influences performance. Social psychologists also study the important domain of close interpersonal relationships (Shaver & Mikulincer, 2011). Chapter 13 reviews the major research findings of social psychology.

● **psychopathology** The scientific study of psychological disorders and the development of diagnostic categories and treatments for those disorders.

The research of Carol S. Dweck of Stanford University spans developmental and social psychology. Her influential work looks at how our ideas of self play a role in motivation, self-regulation, and achievement.

Industrial and Organizational (I/O) Psychology

Industrial and organizational psychology (I/O psychology) centers on the workplace—both the workers and the organizations that employ them. I/O psychology is often divided into *industrial psychology* and *organizational psychology*. Among the main concerns of industrial psychology are personnel matters and human resource management (Aguinis & Kraiger, 2009). Thus, industrial psychology is increasingly referred to as *personnel psychology*. *Organizational psychology* examines the social influences in organizations (Aquino & Thau, 2009), as well as organizational leadership (Avolio, Walumbwa, & Weber, 2009; Gigerenzer, 2011). Chapter 14 probes the key concerns and findings of I/O psychology.

Clinical and Counseling Psychology

Clinical and counseling psychology is the most widely practiced specialization in psychology. Clinical and counseling psychologists diagnose and treat people with psychological problems (Hersen & Gross, 2008). Counseling psychologists sometimes work with people to help solve practical problems in life (Forrest, 2010). For example, counseling psychologists may work with students, advising them about personal problems and career planning. Clinical psychologists are interested in **psychopathology**—the scientific study of psychological disorders and the development of diagnostic categories and treatments for those disorders. Chapters 15 and 16 explore the intriguing world of psychological disorders and therapies.

Social psychologists explore the powerful influence of groups (such as, clockwise, Chinese Americans, members of motorcycle clubs, gay Americans, military families, and inner-city youths) on individuals' attitudes, thinking, and behavior.

Health Psychology   *Health psychology* is a multidimensional approach to human health that emphasizes psychological factors, lifestyle, and the nature of the healthcare delivery system (Miller, Chen, & Cole, 2009). Many health psychologists study the roles of stress and coping in people's lives (Carver & Connor-Smith, 2010; Holsboer & Ising, 2010). Health psychologists may work in physical or mental health areas. Some are members of multidisciplinary teams that conduct research or provide clinical services. Health psychology is examined in Chapter 17.

This list of specialties cannot convey the extraordinarily rich knowledge you will be gaining as a student in introductory psychology. To whet your appetite for what is to come, check out the Psychological Inquiry feature on p. 18 and try answering some of the questions that fascinate psychologists.

The specialties that we have discussed so far are the main areas of psychology that we cover in this book. However, they do not represent an exhaustive list of the interests of the field. Other specializations in psychology include the following.

Community Psychology   *Community psychology* concentrates on improving the quality of relationships among individuals, their community, and society at large. Community psychologists are practitioner scientists who provide accessible care for people with psychological problems. Community-based mental health centers are one means of delivering services such as outreach programs to people in need, especially those who traditionally have been underserved by mental health professionals (Trickett, 2009).

psychological *inquiry*

Questions That Psychology Specialists Ask

This table identifies, by chapter, the topics we will investigate in this book (column 1). For each topic, a question is posed that the chapter will answer (column 2). What do you think the research will show about each of these questions? In the space provided in the note pad, jot down your guesses. Be bold—there are no right answers (yet)!

Chapter and Topic	Question
2 Psychology's Scientific Method	How is self-esteem related to increased aggression?
3 Biological Foundations of Behavior	How does behavior change the brain?
4 Sensation and Perception	Is there evidence for the existence of ESP?
5 States of Consciousness	What do dreams mean?
6 Learning	How do pop quizzes influence studying?
7 Memory	Are you likely to remember what you've learned in intro psychology this year 50 years from now?
8 Thinking, Intelligence, and Language	Who talks more, men or women?
9 Human Development	What kind of parenting is associated with children who are responsible and kind?
10 Motivation and Emotion	Does pursuing happiness make people happier?
11 Gender, Sex, and Sexuality	Where does sexual orientation come from?
12 Personality	Are personality characteristics genetically determined?
13 Social Psychology	How can we best combat racial prejudice?
14 Industrial and Organizational Psychology	Are happy workers more productive?
15 Psychological Disorders	What role do genes play in psychological disorders?
16 Therapies	Does psychotherapy work?
17 Health Psychology	What is the role of religion and spirituality in influencing healthy choices?

Your Hunch

2.
3.
4.
5.
6.
7.
8.
9.
10.
11.
12.
13.
14.
15.
16.
17.

Community psychologists strive to create communities that are more supportive of their residents by pinpointing needs, providing services, and teaching people how to access resources that are already available (Moritsugu, Wong, & Duffy, 2010). Community psychologists are also concerned with prevention. That is, they try to prevent mental health problems by identifying high-risk groups and then intervening with appropriate services and resources in the community.

School and Educational Psychology   *School and educational psychology* centrally concerns children's learning and adjustment in school. School psychologists in elementary and secondary school systems test children, make recommendations about educational placement, and collaborate on educational planning teams. Educational psychologists work at colleges and universities, teach classes, and do research on teaching and learning (Banks, 2010).

Environmental Psychology   *Environmental psychology* is the study of the interactions between people and their physical environment. Environmental psychologists explore the effects of physical settings in most major areas of psychology, including perception, cognition, learning, development, abnormal behavior, and social relations (Gifford, 2009; Hartmann & Apaolaza-Ibanez, 2010). Topics that an environmental psychologist might study range from how different building and room arrangements influence behavior to what strategies might be used to reduce human behavior that harms the environment.

Forensic Psychology   *Forensic psychology* is the field of psychology that applies psychological concepts to the legal system (Campbell & Brown, 2010). Social and cognitive psychologists increasingly conduct research on topics related to psychology and law. Forensic psychologists are hired by legal teams to provide input about many aspects of trials, such as jury selection. Forensic psychologists with clinical training may also testify as experts in trials, such as when they are asked to evaluate whether a person is likely to be a danger to society.

Sport Psychology   *Sport psychology* applies psychology's principles to improving sport performance and enjoying sport participation (Rotella, 2010). Sport psychology is a relatively new field, but it is rapidly gaining acceptance. It is now common to hear about elite athletes working with a sport psychologist to improve their game.

Cross-Cultural Psychology   Cross-cultural psychology is the study of culture's role in understanding behavior, thought, and emotion (Greenfield, 2009; Kitayama, 2011). Cross-cultural psychologists compare the nature of psychological processes in different cultures with a special interest in whether psychological phenomena are universal or culture-specific.

Keep in mind that psychology is a collaborative science in which psychologists work together to examine a wide range of research questions. It is common for scholars from different specialties within psychology to join forces to study some aspect of human behavior. The Intersection feature reviews research that represents collaboration among scientists from different specialties to probe the same question. See how looking at psychology through the lens of culture can influence our conclusions by checking out this chapter's Intersection.

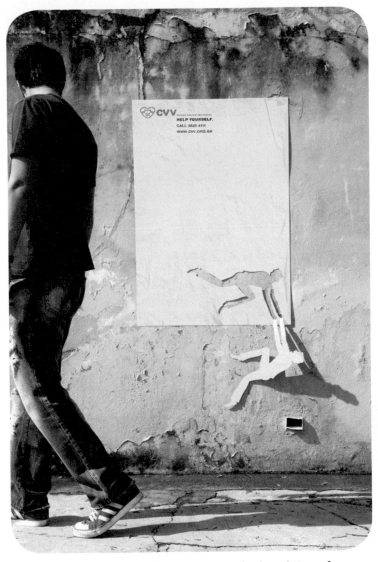

Community psychologists provide accessible care to local populations, often through efforts such as the suicide-prevention program advertised in this poster.

test yourself

1. What are some career options for a person with an undergraduate degree in psychology? What careers might someone with a graduate degree in psychology pursue?
2. What important distinctions are there between a clinical psychologist and a psychiatrist?
3. Name five areas of specialization in psychology and describe the primary concerns of each of them.

Social Psychology and Cross-Cultural Psychology:
Is Success Always Sweeter Than Failure?

At one time or another, all of us experience the high of success. At other times we endure the agony of failure. When we succeed, we often want to savor our moment of achievement, perhaps hanging up, for all to see, our hard-won diploma or the treasured essay on which we received an *A*. When we fail, we might hide the results in a drawer, literally or otherwise. Are these responses natural to all people, or does *culture*—the shared meanings that characterize a particular social group—matter when we are judging success and failure?

To get a feel for how researchers have addressed this question, imagine that you are in a psychological study in which you are asked to solve a number of puzzles. Some of the puzzles are easy, and you complete them with no problem. The other puzzles are difficult; try as you might, you cannot figure them out. After the study, you are left alone with the puzzles, and the researchers inform you that if you would like, you can keep working the puzzles while they prepare the rest of the study materials. Which puzzles will you be likely to choose?

If you are like most U.S. college students, you will gravitate toward the easy puzzles, choosing to work on what you know you are already good at. However, if you are like most Asian students, you will pick up the difficult puzzles and keep working on those that you have not yet solved (Heine, 2005; Heine &

Hamamura, 2007). These cultural differences are thought to emerge out of differing views of the self, goals, and learning. Compared to U.S. students, Asian students may be more likely to view failure as an opportunity to learn. What explains these differences?

Researchers interested in the influence of culture on psychological processes have distinguished individualistic cultures from collectivistic ones (Triandis, 2007). *Individualistic cultures* (such as the United States and western European nations) emphasize the uniqueness of each individual and his or her thoughts, feelings, and choices. Individualistic cultures view the person as having an independent sense of self, separate from his or her social group. In contrast, *collectivistic cultures* (such as those in East Asia) emphasize the social group and the roles the individual plays in that larger group. Collectivistic cultures view the person as embedded in the social network or as having an interdependent sense of self.

Participants from individualistic cultures tend to be more likely to emphasize their strengths and to show a tendency toward self-enhancing. Such individuals feel better about themselves when they are successful, and they enjoy focusing on success (Heine & others, 1999). On the

How does your cultural experience influence your perceptions of success and failure?

other hand, individuals from collectivistic cultures take a more self-critical view. They are more likely to switch away from tasks in which they have been successful and to pursue tasks in which they might instead improve themselves, a pattern that has been shown not only in Asian cultures (Falk & others, 2009; Heine & Hamamura, 2007) but also in Chile (Heine & Raineri, 2009) and among Mexican Americans (Tropp & Wright, 2003) and Native Americans (Fryberg & Markus, 2003).

These differences in responses to failure have prompted some observers to assert that feeling good about oneself is not a universal but rather a culturally specific need that applies only to individualists (Heine & Buchtel, 2009). By examining psychological processes across different cultures, psychologists can investigate whether the world around them is truly representative of human beings or is instead the product of culture.

5· THE SCIENCE OF PSYCHOLOGY AND HEALTH AND WELLNESS

We have reviewed a variety of ways that psychologists approach human behavior. Psychology has learned much about behavior that is relevant to you and your life. In this book, we seek to answer the question, what does psychology have to say about *you*, by tying research in psychology to your physical health and psychological wellness. At the close of each chapter, we will consider how the topics covered matter to your physical body and your mind. This link between the mind and the body has fascinated philosophers for centuries. Psychology occupies the very spot where the mind and body meet.

How the Mind Impacts the Body

When you think about psychology, your first thought might be about the mind and the complex feelings—love, gratitude, hate, anger, and others—that emanate from it. Psychology has come to recognize more and more the degree to which that mind is intricately connected to the body. As you will see when we examine neuroscience in Chapter 3, observations of the brain at work reveal that when mental processes change, so do physical processes (Hagner, 2007).

Health psychologists talk about health behavior as just a subset of behaviors that are relevant to physical health. These behaviors might include eating well, exercising, not smoking, performing testicular and breast self-exams, brushing your teeth, and getting enough sleep. But think about it: Is there ever really a time when your behavior is *not* relevant to your body, and therefore to your health? Is there ever a time when you are doing something—thinking, feeling, walking, running, singing—when your physical body is not present? As long as your body is there—with your heart, lungs, blood, and brain activated—your health is affected. In short, *everything* we do, see, think, and feel is potentially important to our health and well-being.

It might be instructive to think concretely about the ways the mind and body relate to each other, even as they are united in the physical reality of a person. Let's say you see a "Buns of Steel" infomercial on TV. You decide to embark on a quest for these legendary buns. Commitment, goal setting, and self-discipline will be among the many mental processes necessary to resculpt your rear. In this example, the mind works on the body by producing behaviors that change its shape and size.

How the Body Impacts the Mind

Similarly, the body can influence the mind in dramatic ways. Consider how fuzzy your thinking is after you stay out too late and how much easier it is to solve life's problems when you have had a good night's sleep. Also recall your outlook on the first day of true recovery from a nagging cold: Everything just seems better. Your mood and your work improve. Clearly, physical states such as illness and health influence the way we think.

The relationship between the body and mind is illustrated in a major question that psychologists regularly encounter: What is the impact of nature (genetic heritage) versus nurture (social experience) on a person's psychological characteristics? The influence of genetics on a variety

FRANK & ERNEST © Thaves/Distributed by Newspaper Enterprise Association, Inc.

of psychological characteristics, and the ways that genetic endowments can themselves be altered by social experience, will be addressed in many of the main topics in this book, from development (Chapter 9) to personality (Chapter 12) to psychological disorders (Chapter 15). You will see that your physical and mental selves are intertwined in ways you may have never considered (Diamond, Casey, & Munakata, 2011).

Throughout this book, we investigate the ways that all of the various approaches to psychology matter to your life. Psychology is crucially about you, essential to your understanding of your life, your goals, and the ways that you can use the insights of thousands of scientists to make your life healthier and happier. In taking introductory psychology, you have an amazing opportunity. You will learn a great deal about human beings, especially one particular human being: you. Whether the psychological research presented is about emotions and motivation or the structures of the nervous system, it is still essentially about the mystery that is you.

test yourself

1. What has psychology increasingly come to recognize about the relationship between the mind and the body?
2. What are some mental processes that might be involved in efforts to change your physical body, as through diet or exercise?
3. What is some real-life evidence of the body's impact on the mind? Give examples that are different from those in the text.

SUMMARY

1. DEFINING PSYCHOLOGY

Psychology is the scientific study of human behavior and mental processes. Psychologists approach human behavior as scientists who think critically and are curious, skeptical, and objective. Behavior includes everything organisms do that can be observed. Mental processes are thoughts, feelings, and motives.

As a truly general science, psychology addresses all sides of human experience—positive and negative, strengths and weaknesses. Psychology is characterized by controversy and debate, and new psychological perspectives sometimes arise when one scientist questions the views of another.

2. PSYCHOLOGY IN HISTORICAL PERSPECTIVE

Psychology emerged as a science from the fields of philosophy and physiology. Two founders of the science of psychology are Wilhelm Wundt and William James. Wundt's structuralism emphasized the conscious mind and its structures. James's functionalism focused on the functions of the mind in human adaptation to the environment. The functionalist emphasis on the mind's adaptive character fit well with the new understandings that came from Charles Darwin's theory of evolution.

3. CONTEMPORARY APPROACHES TO PSYCHOLOGY

Different approaches to psychology include biological, behavioral, psychodynamic, humanistic, cognitive, evolutionary, and sociocultural views. All of these consider important questions about human behavior from different but complementary perspectives.

The biological approach focuses on the body, especially the brain and nervous system. Technological advances in brain imaging have allowed researchers to examine the brain in all its complexity. The behavioral approach emphasizes the scientific study of observable behavioral responses and their environmental determinants. John B. Watson and B. F. Skinner were important early behaviorists. The psychodynamic approach emphasizes unconscious thought, the conflict between biological instincts and society's demands, and early family experiences. Sigmund Freud was the founding father of the psychodynamic approach. The humanistic approach emphasizes a person's capacity for positive growth, freedom to choose a destiny, and positive qualities. The cognitive approach emphasizes the mental processes involved in knowing. Cognitive psychologists study attention, think-ing, problem solving, remembering, and learning. The evolutionary approach stresses the importance of adaptation, reproduction, and "survival of the fittest." The sociocultural approach focuses on the social and cultural determinants of behavior and encourages us to attend to the ways that our behavior and mental processes are embedded in a social context.

4. WHAT PSYCHOLOGISTS DO

Psychologists work in a wide range of settings and engage in many different activities. Individuals with undergraduate training in psychology hold occupations ranging from human resources and business consulting to doing casework for individuals struggling with psychological disorders. Those with graduate training in psychology might work as therapists and counselors, researchers and teachers in universities, or as business consultants or marketing researchers.

A clinical psychologist typically has a doctoral degree in psychology, whereas a psychiatrist is a medical doctor who specializes in treating people with abnormal behavior. A psychiatrist treats patients with psychotherapy and can prescribe drugs; a clinical psychologist generally cannot prescribe medication.

Main areas of specialization in psychology include physiological psychology and behavioral neuroscience, developmental psychology, sensation and perception, cognitive psychology, learning, motivation and emotion, personality psychology, social psychology, industrial and organizational psychology, clinical and counseling psychology, and health psychology. Other specialties include community psychology, school and educational psychology, environmental psychology, the psychology of women, forensic psychology, sport psychology, and cross-cultural psychology.

5. THE SCIENCE OF PSYCHOLOGY AND HEALTH AND WELLNESS

Over time, the field of psychology has come to recognize that the mind and the body are intricately related. The mind can influence the body. The way we think has implications for our nervous system and brain. Our motives and goals can influence our bodies as we strive to be physically fit and eat well. In turn, the body can have an impact on the mind. We think differently when our bodies are rested versus tired, healthy versus unhealthy.

Plan to make the most of your experience in taking introductory psychology by applying your learning to your life. Psychology is, after all, the scientific study of you—your behavior, thoughts, goals, and well-being.

key *terms*

psychology, p. 4
science, p. 4
behavior, p. 4
mental processes, p. 4
critical thinking, p. 5

empirical method, p. 5
positive psychology, p. 8
structuralism, p. 9
functionalism, p. 9
natural selection, p. 9

biological approach, p. 11
neuroscience, p. 11
behavioral approach, p. 12
psychodynamic approach, p. 12
humanistic approach, p. 12

cognitive approach, p. 12
evolutionary approach, p. 13
sociocultural approach, p. 13
psychopathology, p. 16

apply your *knowledge*

1. Ask 10 friends and family members to tell you the first thing that comes to mind when they think of psychology or a psychologist. After hearing their answers, share with them the broad definition of psychology given in this chapter. How do they react?

2. Visit the website of a major book retailer (such as Amazon) and enter "psychology" as a search term. Read the descriptions of five to seven of the most popular psychology books listed. How well do the themes covered represent your perceptions of what psychology is? How well do they represent the approaches to psychology discussed in the text? Are any perspectives over- or underrepresented? If so, why do you think that is?

3. In the directory for your school (or for another institution), look up the psychology faculty. Select several faculty members and see what the areas of specialization are for each person (be careful, they may not be the same as the classes they teach). How do you think their areas of academic training might affect the way they teach their classes?

4. Human beings evolved long ago in a very different environment than we occupy today. The survivors were those who were most able to endure extremely difficult circumstances, struggling to find food, avoid predators, and create social groups. What do you think were the most adaptive traits for these early humans? Are those traits still adaptive? To what specific environments are humans adapting today?

5. Adopt Wilhelm Wundt's approach to understanding the human mind and behavior. Invite three friends to listen to a piece of music, and then ask them to reflect on the experience. Examine what they each say about various aspects of the music. What does this exercise tell you about the subjectivity of introspection? In what ways do you think the method is worthwhile, and in what ways is it limited?

CHAPTER

2:23 PM

Psychology's Scientific Method

The Thrill of Third

As officials handed out the Olympic medals for the 1,500-meter speed skating event at the 2010 Vancouver Winter Games, Jung-Su Lee of South Korea accepted the gold and Apolo Ohno of the United States took the silver. No one, though, was smiling more broadly than J. R. Celski as he accepted the bronze. For Celski, a 19-year-old American who was recovering from an injury and had not been expected to medal at all, the thrill of third place was written all over his face. Perhaps surprisingly, the sheer joy he felt in coming in third is common.

Psychologist Tom Gilovich and his colleagues noticed this interesting phenomenon as they watched the 1992 Summer Olympic Games in Barcelona: Silver medalists generally looked noticeably less happy than the bronze medalists whom they had just beaten (Medvec, Madey, & Gilovich, 1995). The researchers surmised that these varying reactions came from the different ways in which the athletes thought about "what might have been." Silver medalists, Gilovich and his colleagues proposed, might be tortured by the thought "I almost won the gold." In contrast, bronze medalists might take solace in thinking, "I almost missed the medals altogether."

In a series of studies to investigate their theory, the researchers asked individuals who had not watched the 1992 Olympics to look at videos of the games and to rate how happy the athletes looked at two different moments—just as the events ended and as they stood on the medal podium. In support of the researchers' hunches, the silver medalists were rated as appearing less happy than the bronze medalists both right after the event and on the podium. Moreover, in post-event interviews, the silver medalists were more likely to say how things might have gone *better*, while the bronze medalists were more likely to consider how things could have been *much worse*. Second place is objectively better than third, but in many ways coming in second can be a mixed blessing. Achieving third, on the other hand, is apparently "all good."

This example demonstrates how psychologists can take an observation from everyday life, develop a theory that might explain that observation, and then test their ideas systematically using the scientific method. ●

PREVIEW

Being a psychologist means being a scientist who studies psychology. In this chapter, we review the scientific method. You will read about the ways that psychologists have applied this general method to a variety of important topics and about the steps that are involved in recognizing research questions, developing methods to test them, and using statistical techniques to understand the results. Later in the chapter we consider some of the ethical issues that are involved in scientific inquiry. Psychology shares a great deal with other sciences, but as you will see, topics that psychologists study sometimes require special methodological and ethical consideration. To close the chapter, we examine the role of psychological research in health and wellness.

1· PSYCHOLOGY'S SCIENTIFIC METHOD

Science is defined not by *what* it investigates but by *how* it investigates. Whether you want to study photosynthesis, butterflies, Saturn's moons, or happiness, the *way* you study your question of interest determines whether your approach is scientific. The scientific method is how psychologists gain knowledge about mind and behavior.

It is the use of the scientific method that makes psychology a science (Langston, 2011; McBurney & White, 2010). Indeed, most of the studies psychologists publish in research journals follow the scientific method, which comprises these five steps (Figure 2.1):

1. Observing some phenomenon
2. Formulating hypotheses and predictions
3. Testing through empirical research
4. Drawing conclusions
5. Evaluating the theory

Step 1. Observing Some Phenomenon

The first step in conducting a scientific inquiry involves observing some phenomenon in the world. The curious, critically thinking psychologist sees something in the world and wants to know why or how it is the way it is. The phenomena that scientists study are called variables, a word related to the verb *to vary*. A **variable** is anything that can change. For example, one variable that interests psychologists is happiness. Some people seem to be generally happier than others. What might account for these differences?

As scientists consider answers to such questions, they often develop theories. A **theory** is a broad idea or set of closely related ideas that attempts to explain observations. Theories tell us about the relationships between variables on a conceptual level. Theories seek to explain why certain things have happened, and they can be used to make predictions about future observations. For instance, some psychologists theorize that the most important human need is the need to belong to a social group (Baumeister & Leary, 2000).

Science is defined not by what it studies but by how it investigates. Photosynthesis, butterflies, and happiness all can be studied in a scientific manner.

1

Observing Some Phenomenon

We feel good when we give someone a gift. However, do we genuinely feel better giving something away than we might feel if we could keep it? Elizabeth Dunn, Lara Aknin, and Michael Norton (2008) decided to test this question.

2

Formulating Hypotheses and Predictions

These researchers hypothesized that spending money on other people would lead to greater happiness than spending money on oneself.

3

Testing Through Empirical Research

In an experiment designed to examine this prediction, the researchers randomly assigned undergraduate participants to receive money ($5 or $20) that the students had to spend on either themselves or someone else by 5 P.M. that day. Those who spent the money on *someone else* reported greater happiness that night.

4

Drawing Conclusions

The experiment supported the hypothesis that spending money on others can be a strong predictor of happiness. Money might not buy happiness, the researchers concluded, but spending money in a particular way, that is, on other people, may enhance happiness.

5

Evaluating the Theory

The experimental results were published in the prestigious journal *Science*. Now that the findings are public, other researchers might investigate related topics and questions inspired by this work, and their experiments might shed further light on the original conclusions.

FIGURE 2.1   Steps in the Scientific Method: Is It Better to Give Than to Receive? This figure shows how the steps in the scientific method were applied in a research experiment examining how spending money on ourselves or others can influence happiness (Dunn, Aknin, & Norton, 2008).

Step 2. Formulating Hypotheses and Predictions

The second step in the scientific method is stating a hypothesis. A **hypothesis** is an educated guess that derives logically from a theory. It is a prediction that can be tested. A theory can generate many hypotheses. If more and more hypotheses related to a theory turn out to be true, the theory gains in credibility. So, a researcher who believes that social belonging is the most important aspect of human functioning might predict that people who belong to social groups will be happier than those who do not. Another hypothesis from the theory that belongingness is important to human functioning might be that individuals who have been socially excluded should feel less happy than those who have been socially included.

Step 3. Testing Through Empirical Research

The next step in the scientific method is to test the hypothesis by conducting *empirical research,* that is, by collecting and analyzing data. At this point, it is time to design a study that will test predictions that are based on the theory. To do so, a researcher first needs a concrete way to measure the variables of interest.

An **operational definition** provides an objective description of how a variable is going to be measured and observed in a particular study. Operational definitions eliminate the fuzziness that might creep into thinking about a problem. Imagine, for instance, that everyone in your psychology class is asked to observe a group of children and to keep track of kind behaviors. Do you think that all your classmates will define "kind behaviors" in the same way? Establishing an operational definition ensures that everyone agrees on what a variable means.

To measure personal happiness, for example, prominent psychologist Ed Diener and his students (1985) devised a self-report questionnaire that measures how satisfied a person is with his or her life, called the Satisfaction with Life Scale. (You will get a chance to complete the questionnaire later in this chapter.) Scores on this questionnaire

● **variable** Anything that can change.

● **theory** A broad idea or set of closely related ideas that attempts to explain observations and to make predictions about future observations.

● **hypothesis** An educated guess that derives logically from a theory; a prediction that can be tested.

● **operational definition** A definition that provides an objective description of how a variable is going to be measured and observed in a particular study.

Researchers have identified Duchenne smiling (notice the wrinkles) as a sign of genuine happiness.

are then used as measures of happiness. Research using this scale and others like it has shown that certain specific factors—marriage, religious faith, purpose in life, and good health—are strongly related to being happy (Diener, 1999; Pavot & Diener, 2008).

Importantly, there is not just one operational definition for any variable. While Diener and colleagues used a questionnaire, consider that in the study of silver and bronze medalists described at the beginning of this chapter, researchers used ratings of facial expressions as an operational definition of happiness. In yet another study, one that examined happiness as a predictor of important life outcomes, Lee Anne Harker and Dacher Keltner (2001) looked at the yearbook pictures of college women who had graduated three decades earlier and coded the photographs for the appearance of *Duchenne smiling*. This type of smiling is genuine smiling—the kind that creates little wrinkles around the outer corner of the eyes. Duchenne smiling has been shown to be a sign of true happiness. (If you want to see whether someone in a photograph is smiling genuinely, cover the bottom of the person's face. Can you still tell that he or she is smiling? A genuine smile is evident in the eyes, not just the mouth.) So, while Diener and colleagues operationally defined happiness as a score on a questionnaire, Harker and Keltner operationally defined happiness as Duchenne smiling. Harker and Keltner found that happiness, as displayed in these yearbook pictures, predicted positive life outcomes, such as successful marriages and satisfying lives, some 30 years later.

Devising satisfactory operational definitions for the variables in a study is a crucial step in designing psychological research. To study anything, we have to have a way to see it or measure it. Clearly, in order to establish an operational definition for any variable, we first must agree on what we are trying to measure. If we think of happiness as something that people know about themselves, then a questionnaire score might be a good operational definition of the variable. If we think that people might not be aware of how happy they are (or are not), then a facial expression might be a better operational definition. In other words, our definition of a variable must be set out clearly before we operationally define it. You might try your hand at operationally defining the following variables: generosity, love, maturity, exhaustion, and physical attractiveness. What are some things that *you* find interesting? How might you operationally define these variables?

Because operational definitions allow for the measurement of variables, researchers have a lot of numbers to deal with once they have conducted a study. A key aspect of the process of testing hypotheses is *data analysis*. *Data* refers to all the information (all those numbers) researchers collect in a study—say, the questionnaire scores or the behaviors observed. Data analysis means "crunching" those numbers mathematically to see if they support predictions. We will cover some of the basics of data analysis later in this chapter.

The following example demonstrates the first three steps in the scientific method. One theory of well-being is *self-determination theory* (Deci & Ryan, 2000; Ryan & Deci, 2009). According to this theory, people are likely to feel fulfilled when their lives meet three important needs: relatedness (warm relations with others), autonomy (independence), and competence (mastering new skills). One hypothesis that follows logically from this theory is that people who value money, material possessions, prestige, and physical appearance (that is, *extrinsic rewards*) over the needs of relatedness, autonomy, and competence (which are *intrinsic rewards*) should be less fulfilled, less happy, and less well adjusted. In a series of studies entitled "The Dark Side of the American Dream," researchers Timothy Kasser and Richard Ryan asked participants to complete self-report measures of values and of psychological and physical functioning (Kasser & Ryan, 1993, 1996; Kasser & others, 2004). Thus, the operational definitions of values and psychological functioning were questionnaire scores. The researchers found that individuals who value material rewards over more intrinsic rewards do indeed tend to suffer as predicted.

Step 4. Drawing Conclusions

Based on the results of the data analyses, scientists then draw conclusions from their research. It is important to keep in mind that usually a theory is revised only after a number of studies produce similar results. Before we change a theory, we want to be sure that the research can be replicated, or repeated, by other scientists using different methods. If a research finding is shown again and again—that is, if it is *replicated*—across different researchers and different specific methods, it is considered reliable. It is a result on which we can depend.

Step 5. Evaluating the Theory

The final step in the scientific method is one that never really ends. Researchers submit their work for publication, and it undergoes rigorous review. Afterward, the published studies are there for all to see, read, and evaluate continually. Scholars go back and consider the theory that started it all. Do the studies really support the theory?

One special type of study involves a meta-analysis. **Meta-analysis** is a statistical procedure that summarizes a large body of evidence from the research literature on a particular topic. For a meta-analysis, a researcher tries to find all of the studies that have been done on a topic of interest. The researcher then compares all the studies and their findings. A meta-analysis allows researchers to conclude whether a result is consistent in the literature and to estimate the magnitude of the relationship between variables (McDonald & others, 2010). An example of a meta-analysis is a study conducted by Sonja Lyubomirsky and her colleagues examining the relationship between happiness and work success (Lyubomirsky, King, & Diener, 2005). They found that across 43 different studies, happy people were less likely to be "burned out" and to think about quitting their jobs and more likely to receive positive evaluations from their supervisors.

The research community maintains an active conversation about what scientists know, and this dialogue constantly questions conclusions. From published studies, a scholar may come up with a new idea that will eventually change the thinking on some topic. Steps 3, 4, and 5 in the scientific method are part of an ongoing process. That is, researchers go back and do more research, revise their theories, hone their methods, and draw and evaluate their new conclusions.

● **meta-analysis** A method that allows researchers to combine the results of several different studies on a similar topic in order to establish the strength of an effect.

test yourself

1. What are the five steps in the scientific method?
2. What is an operational definition, and what is its value in a study?
3. What is a meta-analysis? Why do researchers use this procedure?

2· TYPES OF PSYCHOLOGICAL RESEARCH

Psychologists commonly use three types of research. *Descriptive research* involves finding out about the basic dimensions of some variable (for example, what the average level of happiness is for men in the United States). *Correlational research* is interested in discovering relationships between variables (for instance, whether being married predicts greater happiness for men). *Experimental research* concerns establishing causal relationships between variables (for example, whether women perceive men as more attractive if the men are smiling). In this section, we examine each of these types of research.

Descriptive Research

Just as its name suggests, **descriptive research** is about describing some phenomenon—determining its basic dimensions and defining what this thing is, how often it occurs, and so on. By itself, descriptive research cannot prove what causes some phenomenon, but it can reveal important information about people's behaviors and attitudes (Stake, 2010). Descriptive research methods include observation, surveys and interviews, and case studies.

● **descriptive research** Research that determines the basic dimensions of a phenomenon, defining what it is, how often it occurs, and so on.

OBSERVATION

Imagine that you are going to conduct a study on how children who are playing together resolve conflicts that arise. The data that are of interest to you concern conflict resolution. As a first step, you might go to a playground and simply observe what the children do—how often you see conflict resolution occur and how it unfolds. You would likely keep careful notes of what you observe.

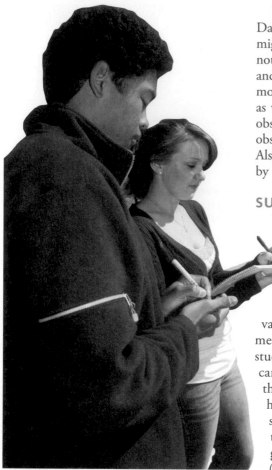

This type of scientific observation requires an important set of skills (R. A. Smith & Davis, 2010). Unless you are a trained observer and practice your skills regularly, you might not know what to look for, you might not remember what you saw, you might not realize that what you are looking for is changing from one moment to the next, and you might not document and communicate your observations effectively. Furthermore, you might not realize the value of having one or more others do the observations as well, so that you develop a sense of the accuracy of your observations. In short, for observations to be effective, they must be systematic. You must know whom you are observing, when and where you will observe, and how you will make the observations. Also, you need to know in advance in what form you will document them: in writing, by sound recording, or by video.

SURVEYS AND INTERVIEWS

Sometimes the best and quickest way to get information about people is to ask them for it. One technique is to interview them directly. A related method that is especially useful when information from many people is needed is the *survey,* or questionnaire. A survey presents a standard set of questions, or *items,* to obtain people's self-reported attitudes or beliefs about a particular topic.

Although surveys can be a straightforward way to measure psychological variables, constructing them requires care (Stangor, 2011). For example, surveys can measure only what people think about themselves. Thus, if we are interested in studying a variable that we think is unconscious, such as a psychodynamic drive, we cannot use a survey. Furthermore, people do not always know the truth about themselves. If you were answering a survey that asked, "Are you a generous person?" how might your answer compare to that of a friend who is asked to make that same rating about you? One particular problem with surveys and interviews is the tendency of participants to answer questions in a way that will make them look good rather than in a way that communicates what they truly think or feel (McMillan & Wergin, 2010).

Another challenge in survey construction is that when a questionnaire is used to define variables operationally, it is crucial that the items clearly probe the specific topic of interest and not some other characteristic. The language used in a survey therefore must be clear and understandable if the responses are to reflect the participants' actual feelings.

Surveys and interviews can examine a wide range of topics, from religious beliefs to sexual habits to attitudes about gun control (Rosnow & Rosenthal, 2008). Some survey and interview questions are unstructured and open-ended, such as "How fulfilling would you say your marriage is?" Such questions allow for unique responses from each person surveyed. Other survey and interview questions are more structured and ask about quite specific things. For example, a structured question might ask, "How many times have you talked with your partner about a personal problem in the past month: 0, 1–2, 3–5, 6–10, 11–30, every day?"

CASE STUDIES

● **case study or case history** An in-depth look at a single individual.

A **case study,** or **case history,** is an in-depth look at a single individual. Case studies are performed mainly by clinical psychologists when, for either practical or ethical reasons, the unique aspects of an individual's life cannot be duplicated and tested in other individuals. A case study provides information about one person's goals, hopes, fantasies, fears, traumatic experiences, family relationships, health, and anything else that helps the psychologist understand the person's mind and behavior. Case studies can also involve in-depth explorations of particular families or social groups.

An example of a case study is the analysis of India's spiritual leader Mahatma Gandhi (1869–1948) by psychodynamic theorist Erik Erikson (1969). Erikson studied Gandhi's life in great depth to discover how his positive spiritual identity developed, especially during his youth. In piecing together Gandhi's identity development, Erikson described the contributions of culture, history, family, and various other factors that might affect the way other people form an identity.

Case histories provide dramatic, detailed portrayals of people's lives, but we must be cautious about applying what we learn from one person's life to other people. The subject of a case study is unique, with a genetic makeup and personal history that no one else shares. Case studies can be very valuable at the first step of the scientific method, in that they often provide vivid observations that can then be tested in a variety of ways in psychological research. However, and importantly, an in-depth study of a single case may not be generalizable to the general population.

THE VALUE OF DESCRIPTIVE RESEARCH

Descriptive research allows researchers to get a sense of a subject of interest, but it cannot answer questions about how and why things are the way they are. Nevertheless, descriptive research does explore intriguing topics, such as the experience of happiness in different cultures. Before reading about and considering the value of that research, complete the measure below. Specifically, using the 7-point scale, indicate your agreement with each item that follows the scale.

Mahatma Gandhi was India's spiritual leader in the mid-twentieth century. Erik Erikson conducted an extensive case study of Gandhi's life to determine what contributed to his identity development.

7	6	5	4	3	2	1
Strongly Agree	Agree	Slightly Agree	Neither Agree nor Disagree	Slightly Disagree	Disagree	Strongly Disagree

1. In most ways my life is close to my ideal.

2. The conditions of my life are excellent.

3. I am satisfied with my life.

4. So far I have gotten the important things I want in life.

5. If I could live my life over, I would change almost nothing.

You have just completed the Satisfaction with Life Scale (or SWLS; Diener & others, 1985), one operational definition of happiness. To find out your score, add up your ratings and divide by 5. This average rating could be considered your level of general happiness. A broad range of studies in many different countries have used this scale and others like it to measure happiness levels. Based on such research, Ed and Carol Diener (1996) concluded that most people are pretty happy because they score above the midpoint, 3.5, on the scale you just completed. However, research on happiness in various cultures has generally centered on relatively industrialized countries. What about non-industrialized societies?

One study examined levels of happiness in groups of people who have not generally been included in psychological studies (Biswas-Diener, Vitterso, & Diener, 2005). The research examined three groups: the Inughuits (Inuits) of Greenland, the Maasai of southern Kenya, and American Old Order Amish. All three groups completed measures essentially the same as the one you just did.

The Inuit tribe studied (the Inughuits) live at 79 degrees latitude (very far north), in the harshest climate inhabited by a traditional human society. Rocks, glaciers, and the sea dominate the landscape. Farming is impossible. The Inughuits have some modern conveniences, but they generally adhere to a traditional hunting culture. It is not uncommon to find an Inughuit hunter carving a seal or caribou on the kitchen floor while children watch TV in the next room. Most of us might feel a little blue in the winter months when gloomy weather seems to stretch on, day after day. For the Inughuits, however, the sun never rises at all throughout the winter months, and in the summer, it never sets. How happy could an individual be in such a difficult setting? Pretty happy, it turns out, as the Inughuits averaged a 5.0 on the Satisfaction with Life Scale.

The Maasai are an indigenous (native) African nomadic group who live in villages of about 20 people, with little exposure to the West. Maasai are fierce warriors, and their culture has many traditional ceremonies built around a boy's passage from childhood to manhood. Boys are circumcised between the ages of 15 and 22, and they are forbidden from moving or making a sound during the procedure. Girls also experience circumcision as they enter puberty, in a controversial rite that involves the removal of the clitoris and that makes childbirth extremely difficult. The Maasai practice child marriage and polygamy. Maasai women have very little power and are generally expected to do most of the work. How happy could an individual be in this context? Maasai men and women who completed the measure orally in their native tongue, Maa, averaged a 5.4 on the life satisfaction scale (Biswas-Diener, Vitterso, & Diener, 2005).

Finally, the Old Order Amish of the midwestern and northeastern United States belong to a strict religious sect that explicitly rejects modern aspects of life. The Amish separate themselves from mainstream society and travel by horse and buggy. The women wear bonnets, and the men sport beards, dark clothes, and dark brimmed hats. The Amish farm without modern machinery and dedicate their lives to simplicity—without radios, TVs, CDs, DVDs, iPods, cell phones, washing machines, and cars. Still, the Amish are relatively happy, averaging 4.4 on the 7-point happiness scale (Biswas-Diener, Vitterso, & Diener, 2005).

Like a host of other studies in industrialized nations, these results indicate that most individuals are pretty happy. Such descriptive findings provide researchers of well-being a valuable foundation for further examining the processes that lead to these feelings of happiness in different cultural settings. If a researcher wanted to extend these findings to investigate predictors of happiness in different cultures, he or she would then turn to a correlational design.

Correlational Research

● **correlational research** Research that examines the relationships between variables, whose purpose is to examine whether and how two variables change together.

We have seen that descriptive research tells us about the basic dimensions of a variable. In contrast, **correlational research** tells us about the relationship between two variables. The purpose of correlational research is to examine whether and how two variables *change together*. That is, correlational research looks at a co-relationship. For instance, if one of the variables increases, what happens to the other one? When two variables change together, we can predict one from the other, and we say that the variables are correlated.

Correlational research is so named because of the statistical technique *correlation* that is typically used to analyze these types of data. The key feature of a correlational study is that the factors of interest are measured or observed to see how they are related (Kiess & Green, 2010; Levin & Fox, 2011). If we wanted to know whether shy people are happy, we might give the same people two questionnaires—one that measures shyness and another that measures happiness. For each person we would have two scores, and we would then see whether shyness and happiness relate to each other in a systematic way.

The degree of relationship between two variables is expressed as a numerical value called a *correlational coefficient,* which is most commonly represented by the letter *r*. The correlation coefficient is a statistic that tells us two things about the relationship between two variables—its strength and its direction. The value of a correlation always falls between −1.00 and +1.00. The number or magnitude of the correlation tells us about the *strength* of the relationship. The closer the number is to ±1.00, the stronger the relationship. The sign (+ or −) tells us about the *direction* of the relationship between the variables. A positive sign means that as one variable increases, the other also increases. A negative sign means that as one variable increases, the other decreases. A zero correlation means that there is no systematic relationship between the variables.

Examples of scatter plots (a type of graph that plots scores on the two variables) showing positive and negative correlations appear in Figure 2.2. Note that every dot in this figure represents both scores for one person.

CORRELATION IS NOT CAUSATION

Look at the terms in bold type in the following newspaper headlines:

Researchers **Link** Coffee Consumption to Cancer of Pancreas

Brain Size Is **Associated** with Gender

Psychologists Discover **Relationship** Between Religious Faith and Good Health

Positive Correlations

The longer the lecture, the more you yawn.

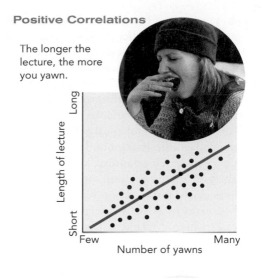

Negative Correlations

The longer the lecture, the lower your attentiveness.

FIGURE 2.2 Scatter Plots Showing Positive and Negative Correlations A positive correlation is a relationship in which two factors vary in the same direction, as shown in the two scatter plots on the left. A negative correlation is a relationship in which two factors vary in opposite directions, as shown in the two scatter plots on the right.

The more you study, the higher your test grade.

The more you party, the lower your test grade.

● **third variable problem** The circumstance where a variable that has not been measured accounts for the relationship between two other variables. Third variables are also known as confounds.

Reading these headlines, one might conclude that coffee causes pancreatic cancer, gender causes differences in brain size, and religious faith causes good health. The boldface words are synonymous only with correlation, however, not with causality.

Correlation does not equal causation. Remember, correlation means only that two variables change together. Being able to predict one event based on the occurrence of another event does not necessarily tell us anything about the cause of either event (Aron, Aron, & Coups, 2011; Heiman, 2011). At times some other variable that has not been measured accounts for the relationship between two others. Researchers refer to this circumstance as the **third variable problem.**

To understand the third variable problem, consider the following example. A researcher measures two variables: the number of ice cream cones sold in a town and the number of violent crimes that occur in that town throughout the year. The researcher finds that ice cream cone sales and violent crimes are positively correlated, to the magnitude of +.50. This high positive correlation would indicate that as ice cream sales increase, so does violent crime. Would it be reasonable for the local paper to run the headline "Ice Cream Consumption Leads to Violence"? Should concerned citizens gather outside the local Frosty Freeze to stop the madness? Probably not. Perhaps you have already thought of the third variable that might explain this correlation—heat. Indeed, when it is hot outside, people are more likely both to purchase ice cream and to act aggressively (Anderson & Bushman, 2002). Such a third variable is also called a *confound.*

THE VALUE OF CORRELATIONAL RESEARCH

Given the potential problems with third variables, why do researchers bother to conduct correlational studies? There are several very good reasons. Although correlational studies

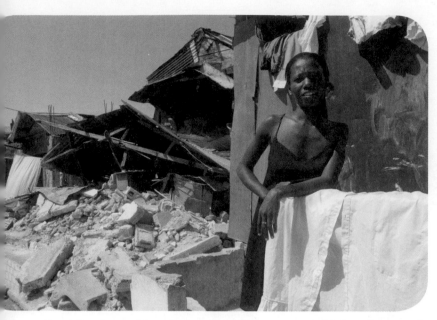

Correlational research is useful for studying the impact on people's lives of events such as the Haitian earthquake of early 2010.

cannot show a causal relationship between variables, they do allow us to use one variable to predict a person's score on another. This is the reasoning behind tests such as the SAT and ACT, which provide a measure of academic ability that will predict performance in college. In addition, some important questions can be investigated only through correlational studies. Such questions may involve variables that can only be measured or observed, such as biological sex, personality traits, genetic factors, and ethnic background. Another reason why researchers conduct correlational studies is that sometimes the variables of interest are real-world events that influence people's lives, such as Hurricane Katrina in 2005 and the earthquake in Haiti in 2010. Correlational research is also valuable in cases where it would not be ethical to do research in any other way. For example, it would be unethical for an experimenter to direct expectant mothers to smoke varying numbers of cigarettes in order to see how cigarette smoke affects birth weight and fetal activity.

Although we have predominantly focused on relationships between just two variables, researchers often measure many variables in their studies. This way, they can examine whether a relationship between two variables is explained by a third variable (or a fourth or fifth variable). An interesting question that researchers have probed in this fashion is, do happy people live longer? In one study, 2,000 Mexican Americans aged 65 and older were interviewed twice over the course of two years (Ostir & others, 2000). In the first assessment, participants completed measures of happiness but also reported about potential third variables such as diet, physical health, smoking, marital status, and distress. Two years later, the researchers contacted the participants again to see who was still alive. Even with these many potential third variables taken into account, happiness predicted who was still living two years later.

Correlational studies are useful, too, when researchers are interested in studying everyday experience. For example, correlational researchers have begun to use daily journal keeping, known as the *experience sampling method (ESM),* to study people in their natural settings. ESM studies involve having people report on their experiences in a diary a few times a day or to complete measures of their mood and behavior whenever they are beeped by an electronic organizer. A similar method, *event-contingent responding,* asks participants to complete a report each time they engage in a particular behavior, such as drinking alcohol or having sex (Cooper, 2010). Such methods allow researchers to get close to real life as it happens.

Although the correlation coefficient is often used to express the relationship between two variables, it is important to keep in mind that what makes a study correlational is not the statistic researchers use to analyze the data. Rather, a study is correlational when it relies on measuring variables to see how they are related. To get a sense of this distinction and learn about some clever ways in which psychologists have operationalized variables, check out the Psychological Inquiry on p. 35.

LONGITUDINAL DESIGNS

● **longitudinal design** A special kind of systematic observation, used by correlational researchers, that involves obtaining measures of the variables of interest in multiple waves over time.

One way that correlational researchers can deal with the issue of causation is to employ a special kind of systematic observation called a **longitudinal design.** Longitudinal research involves obtaining measures of the variables of interest in multiple waves over time. This type of research can suggest potential causal relationships because if one variable is thought to cause changes in another, it should at least come before that variable in time.

One intriguing longitudinal study is the Nun Study, conducted by David Snowdon and his colleagues (Grossi & others, 2007; Mortimer, Snowdon, & Markesbery, 2009; Snowdon, 2003). The study began in 1986 and has followed a sample of 678 School

psychological *inquiry*

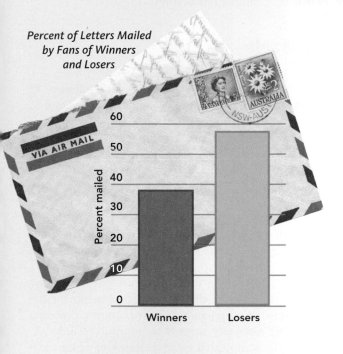

Percent of Letters Mailed by Fans of Winners and Losers

Miserable but Helpful?

Many studies have shown that happy individuals are more helpful than people in a negative mood. Social psychologist R. F. Soames Job (1987) was interested in examining how mood relates to helping. In a clever study, he used naturally occurring mood and an unusual measure of helpfulness.

The study took place outside a major rugby match pitting Canterbury-Bankstown against St. George, in Sydney, Australia. Rugby is enormously popular in Sydney, and more than 40,000 people attended the match. While the game was going on, the researchers placed 100 stamped letters on the windshields of cars parked around the sporting grounds. The letters were addressed to the same person, and a handwritten note on each letter said, "Found near your car." Cars belonging to supporters of each team were identified by different colored streamers, team stickers, and posters. Fifty letters were placed on the cars of supporters of each team. The researchers then waited to see which type of fan was most likely to put the letter in the mailbox—a fan of the winning team or of the losing team. The figure shows the results. Try your hand at the questions below.

1. What were the variables of interest in this study?
2. How did the study operationally define these variables?
3. Why is this a correlational study?
4. Job concluded that these data support the notion that negative mood relates to helping. Is this conclusion justified, in your opinion? Why or why not?
5. Identify at least one third variable that might explain the results of this study.

Sisters of Notre Dame (SSND) ever since. The nuns ranged in age from 75 to 103 when the study began. These women complete a variety of psychological and physical measures annually. This sample is unique in many respects. However, certain characteristics render the participants an excellent group for correlational research. For one thing, many potential extraneous third variables are relatively identical for all the women in the group. Specifically, their biological sex, living conditions, diet, activity levels, marital status, and religious participation are essentially held constant, so there is little chance that differences would arise in these variables that might explain the study's results.

Researchers examined the relationship between happiness and longevity using this rich dataset. All of the nuns had been asked to write a spiritual autobiography when they entered the convent (for some, as many as 80 years before). Deborah Danner and her colleagues (2001) were given access to these documents and used them as indicators of happiness earlier in life by counting the number of positive emotions expressed in the autobiographies (note that here we have yet another operational definition of happiness). Higher levels of positive emotion expressed in autobiographies written at an average age of 22 were associated with a 2.5-fold difference in risk of mortality when the nuns were in their 80s and 90s. That is, women who included positive emotion in their autobiographies when they were in their early 20s were two-and-a-half times more likely to survive some 60 years later.

Longitudinal designs provide ways by which correlational researchers may attempt to demonstrate causal relations among variables (Gibbons, Hedeker, & DuToit, 2010). Still, it is important to be aware that even in longitudinal studies, causal relationships are not completely clear. For example, the nuns who wrote happier autobiographies may have had happier childhood experiences that might be influencing their longevity, or a particular genetic factor might explain both their happiness and their survival. As you read about correlational research studies throughout this book, do so critically, and with

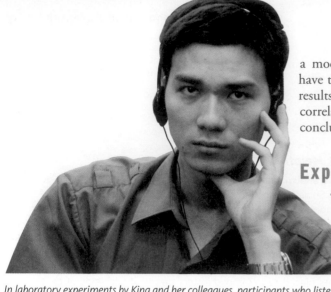

In laboratory experiments by King and her colleagues, participants who listened to happy music rated their lives as more meaningful than those who listened to neutral music.

a modicum of skepticism; consider that even the brightest scientist may not have thought of all of the potential third variables that could have explained the results. It is easy to assume causality when two events or characteristics are merely correlated. Remember those innocent ice cream cones, and critically evaluate conclusions that may be drawn from simple observation.

Experimental Research

To determine whether a causal relationship exists between variables, researchers must use experimental methods (Christensen, Johnson, & Turner, 2011). An **experiment** is a carefully regulated procedure in which the researcher manipulates one or more variables that are believed to influence some other variable. Imagine, for example, that a researcher notices that people who listen to classical music seem to be of above average intelligence. A correlational study on this question would not tell us if listening to classical music *causes* increases in intelligence. In order to demonstrate causation, the researcher would manipulate whether or not people listen to classical music. He or she might create two groups: one that listens to classical music and one that listens to pop music. To test for differences in intelligence, the researcher would then measure intelligence.

If that manipulation led to differences between the two groups on intelligence, we could say that the manipulated variable *caused* those differences: The experiment has demonstrated cause and effect. This notion that experiments can demonstrate causation is based on the idea that if participants are *randomly assigned* to groups, the only systematic difference between them must be the manipulated variable. **Random assignment** means that researchers assign participants to groups by chance. This technique reduces the likelihood that the experiment's results will be due to any preexisting differences between groups (Graziano & Raulin, 2010).

To get a sense of what experimental studies, as compared to correlational studies, can reveal, consider the following example. Psychologists have long assumed that experiencing one's life as meaningful is an important aspect of psychological well-being (Frankl, 1963/1984; Steger & Frazier, 2005). Because surveys that measure meaning in life and well-being correlate positively (that is, the more meaningful your life, the happier you are), the assumption has been that experiencing meaning in life causes greater happiness. Because the studies involved in exploring this relationship have been correlational, however, the cause is unclear. Meaning in life may lead people to be happier, but the reverse might also be true: Happiness might make people feel that their lives are more meaningful.

To address this issue, Laura King and her colleagues conducted a series of laboratory experiments (King & Hicks, 2010; King & others, 2006). In one study, the researchers put some participants in a positive mood by having them listen to happy music. Other participants listened to neutral music. Participants who listened to happy music rated their lives as more meaningful than did individuals who listened to neutral music. Note that participants were randomly assigned to one of two conditions, happy music or neutral music, and then rated their meaning in life using a questionnaire. In this case happiness was operationally defined by the type of music participants heard, and meaning in life was operationally defined by ratings on a questionnaire. Because participants were randomly assigned to conditions, we can assume that the only systematic difference between the two groups was the type of music they heard. As a result, we can say that the happy music caused people to rate their lives as more meaningful.

INDEPENDENT AND DEPENDENT VARIABLES

Experiments have two types of variables: independent and dependent. An **independent variable** is a manipulated experimental factor. The independent variable is the variable that the experimenter changes to see what its effects are; it is a potential

● **experiment** A carefully regulated procedure in which the researcher manipulates one or more variables that are believed to influence some other variable.

● **random assignment** Researchers' assignment of participants to groups by chance, to reduce the likelihood that an experiment's results will be due to preexisting differences between groups.

● **independent variable** A manipulated experimental factor; the variable that the experimenter changes to see what its effects are.

cause. Any experiment may include several independent variables, or factors that are manipulated, to determine their effect on some outcome. In the study of positive mood and meaning in life, the independent variable is mood (positive versus neutral), operationally defined by the type of music participants heard.

Sometimes the independent variable is the individual's social context. Social psychologists often manipulate the social context with the help of a confederate. A **confederate** is a person who is given a role to play in a study so that the social context can be manipulated. For example, if a researcher is interested in reactions to being treated rudely, he or she might assign a confederate to treat participants rudely (or not).

A **dependent variable** in an experiment is the variable that may change as a result of manipulations of the independent variable. It represents the outcome (effect) in an experiment. As researchers manipulate the independent variable, they measure the dependent variable to test for any effect of the manipulated variable. In the study by King and others of music type and meaning in life, meaning in life was the dependent variable.

Independent and dependent variables are two of the most important concepts in psychological research. Remember that the independent variable is the *cause,* and the dependent variable is the *effect*.

EXPERIMENTAL AND CONTROL GROUPS

Experiments can involve one or more experimental groups and one or more control groups. In an experiment, the researcher manipulates the independent variable to create these groups. An **experimental group** consists of the participants in an experiment who receive, say, the drug or other treatment under study—that is, those who are exposed to the change that the independent variable represents. A **control group** in an experiment is as much like the experimental group as possible and is treated in every way like the experimental group except for that change. The control group provides a comparison against which the researcher can test the effects of the independent variable. In the study of meaning in life above, participants who listened to happy music were the experimental group, and those who heard neutral music were the control group.

To see how experimental and correlational research can be applied to the same research question, check out the Intersection.

SOME CAUTIONS ABOUT EXPERIMENTAL RESEARCH

Validity refers to the soundness of the conclusions that a researcher draws from an experiment. Two broad types of validity matter to experimental designs. The first is **external validity,** which refers to the degree to which an experimental design actually reflects the real-world issues it is supposed to address. That is, external validity is concerned with the question, do the experimental methods and the results *generalize*—do they apply—to the real world?

Imagine, for example, that a researcher is interested in the influence of stress (the independent variable) on creative problem solving (the dependent variable). The researcher randomly assigns individuals to be blasted with loud noises at random times during the session (the high-stress or experimental group) or to complete the task in relative quiet (the control group). As the task, the researcher gives all participants a chance to be creative by asking them to list every use they can think of for a cardboard box. Counting up the number of uses that people list, the researcher discovers that those in the high-stress group generated fewer uses of the box. This finding might seem to indicate that stress reduces creativity. In considering the external validity of this study, however, we might appropriately ask some questions: How similar are the blasts of loud, random noises to the stresses people experience every day? Is listing uses for a cardboard box really an indicator of creativity? We are asking, in other words, if these operational definitions do a good job of reflecting the real-world processes they are supposed to represent.

● **confederate** A person who is given a role to play in a study so that the social context can be manipulated.

● **dependent variable** The outcome; the factor that can change in an experiment in response to changes in the independent variable.

● **experimental group** The participants in an experiment who receive the drug or other treatment under study—that is, those who are exposed to the change that the independent variable represents.

● **control group** The participants in an experiment who are as much like the experimental group as possible and who are treated in every way like the experimental group except for a manipulated factor, the independent variable.

● **external validity** The degree to which an experimental design actually reflects the real-world issues it is supposed to address.

Social Psychology and Developmental Psychology: Is High Self-Esteem Such a Good Thing?

Low self-esteem is frequently implicated in society's ills, from juvenile delinquency to violent acts of aggression. It often seems as if we could make the world a better place if we could help everyone achieve higher self-esteem. Yet in the late 1990s, psychologist Roy Baumeister presented a provocative idea: He suggested that *high* self-esteem, not low self-esteem, is associated with aggressive acts (Baumeister, 1999; Baumeister, Bushman, & Campbell, 2000; Baumeister & Butz, 2005; Baumeister & others, 2007; Bushman & Baumeister, 2002). In a variety of experimental studies, he showed that individuals who scored very high on a measure of self-esteem were more likely than their counterparts with low self-esteem to behave aggressively toward others when their self-esteem was threatened. For example, individuals with high self-esteem might have been more likely to blast someone with loud noise in the lab after being told that they did not perform well on an intelligence test. These findings conflicted with a long-held belief in psy-

chology that self-esteem was a central component of psychological health.

Following the publication of Baumeister's work, research conducted by developmental psychologists (who study the ways human beings mature from earliest childhood to old age) challenged the notion that high self-esteem was bad. These researchers used longitudinal data collected from a large sample of individuals in Dunedin, New Zealand, to show that contrary to Baumeister's conclusions, low (not high) self-esteem was associated with a variety of negative outcomes, including aggression, delinquency, poor health, and limited economic prospects through the middle adulthood years (Donnellan & others, 2005; Trzesniewski & others, 2006).

How can we resolve this apparent conflict between experimental evidence and longitudinal correlational evidence? One possibility is that individuals with high self-esteem might act aggressively in the artificial setting of a laboratory when given the chance to do so, but would not engage in actual aggressive behavior in real life. Another possibility is that Baumeister was talking about a particular kind of high self-esteem: inflated and unstable high self-esteem (W. K. Campbell & others, 2004; Konrath, Bushman, & Campbell, 2006). Individuals with unrealistically high self-esteem appear to be prone to react aggressively in response to a threat. Such individuals might be best described not as psychologically healthy but rather as narcissistic. For most people, though, it is more likely that low self-esteem rather than high self-esteem is linked to higher levels of aggression.

Do you know anyone who is aggressive? Do you think the person has high or low self-esteem?

● **internal validity** The degree to which changes in the dependent variable are due to the manipulation of the independent variable.

The second type of validity is **internal validity,** which refers to the degree to which changes in the dependent variable are genuinely due to the manipulation of the independent variable. In the case of internal validity, we want to know whether the experimental methods are free from biases and logical errors that may render the results suspect. Although experimental research is a powerful tool, it requires safeguards (Leary, 2008). Expectations and biases can, and sometimes do, tarnish results (Ray, 2009; Rosnow & Rosenthal, 2008), as we next consider.

● **experimenter bias** Occurs when the experimenter's expectations influence the outcome of the research.

● **demand characteristics** Any aspects of a study that communicate to the participants how the experimenter wants them to behave.

Experimenter Bias Experimenters may subtly (and often unknowingly) influence their research participants. **Experimenter bias** occurs when the experimenter's expectations influence the outcome of the research. No one designs an experiment without wanting meaningful results. Consequently, experimenters can sometimes subtly communicate to participants what they want the participants to do. **Demand characteristics** are any aspects of a study that communicate to participants how the experimenter wants them to behave. The influence of experimenter expectations can be very difficult to avoid.

In a classic study, Robert Rosenthal (1966) turned college students into experimenters. He randomly assigned the participants rats from the same litter. Half of the students were told that their rats were "maze bright," whereas the other half were told that their rats were "maze dull." The students then conducted experiments to test their rats' ability to navigate mazes. The results were stunning. The so-called maze-bright rats were more successful than the maze-dull rats at running the mazes. The only explanation for the results is that the college students' expectations, conveyed in their behaviors, affected the rats' performance.

Often the participants in psychological studies are not rats but people. Imagine that you are an experimenter, and you know that a participant is going to be exposed to disgusting pictures in a study. Is it possible that you might treat the person differently than you would if you were about to show him photos of cute kittens? The reason experimenter bias is important is that it introduces systematic differences between the experimental group and the control groups; this means that we cannot know if those who looked at disgusting pictures were more, say, upset because of the pictures or because of different treatment by the experimenter.

Like third variables in correlational research, these systematic biases are called *confounds*. In experimental research, confounds are factors that "ride along" with the experimental manipulation, systematically and undesirably influencing the dependent variable. Experimenter bias, demand characteristics, and confounds may all lead to biased results.

Research Participant Bias and the Placebo Effect

Like experimenters, research participants may have expectations about what they are supposed to do and how they should behave, and these expectations may affect the results of experiments (Christensen, 2007). **Research participant bias** occurs when the behavior of research participants during the experiment is influenced by how they think they are supposed to behave or by what their expectations are about what is happening to them.

One example of the power of participant expectations is the placebo effect. The **placebo effect** occurs when participants' expectations, rather than the experimental treatment, produce a particular outcome. Participants in a drug study might be assigned to an experimental group that receives a pill containing an actual painkiller or to a control group that receives a placebo pill. A **placebo** is a harmless substance that has no physiological effect. This placebo is given to participants in a control group so that they are treated identically to the experimental group except for the active agent—in this case, the painkiller. Giving individuals in the control group a placebo pill allows researchers to determine whether changes in the experimental group are due to the active drug agent and not simply to participants' expectations.

"We close at six!"

© Mike Williams. www.CartoonStock.com.

● **research participant bias** Occurs when the behavior of research participants during the experiment is influenced by how they think they are supposed to behave or their expectations about what is happening to them.

● **placebo effect** Occurs when participants' expectations, rather than the experimental treatment, produce an outcome.

● **placebo** In a drug study, a harmless substance that has no physiological effect, given to participants in a control group so that they are treated identically to the experimental group except for the active agent.

Advertisements for prescription drugs usually describe not only the side effects on people taking the actual drug but also the effects experienced by individuals receiving a placebo.

Observation
Psychologists are using observational methods to examine President Obama's inaugural address, focusing on the words he used and the themes he stressed to make predictions about his presidency. Other observational data might include facial expressions of the crowd during the inaugural ceremony and the content of various post-election blogs.

Survey and Interview
Researchers can use surveys and telephone interviews to track popular approval of the president and to gauge public support for his various initiatives and programs. Survey research can also probe how different demographic groups (for example, African Americans and Euro-Americans) might differ in their expectations about the president.

Case Study
President Obama has published two autobiographical books, *The Audacity of Hope* and *Dreams from My Father*. These works provide valuable data for psychologists who are interested in using case studies to understand his life story and his path to presidential office.

Correlational Research
Correlational research can track the ways that attitudes toward African Americans may have changed with Obama's candidacy and election. In addition, examining the aspirations of children of various ethnicities before and after the election allows psychologists to study the influence of this new role model on American children.

Experimental Research
Psychologists interested in attitudes and behaviors toward different ethnic groups can use images of President Obama in experimental research to examine how visual reminders of the president influence such attitudes and behaviors.

FIGURE 2.3 **Psychology's Research Methods Applied to Studying President Barack Obama** Psychologists can apply very different methods to study the same phenomenon. The historic election of Barack Obama, the first African American president, opened up a host of new research questions for psychologists.

●**double-blind experiment** An experimental design in which neither the experimenter nor the participants are aware of which participants are in the experimental group and which are in the control group until the results are calculated.

Another way to ensure that neither the experimenter's nor the participants' expectations affect the outcome is to design a **double-blind experiment.** In this design, neither the experimenter administering the treatment nor the participants are aware of which participants are in the experimental group and which are in the control group until the results are calculated. This setup ensures that the experimenter cannot, for example, make subtle gestures signaling who is receiving a drug and who is not. A double-blind study allows researchers to distinguish the specific effects of the independent variable from the possible effects of the experimenter's and the participants' expectations about it.

Applications of the Three Types of Research

All three types of research—descriptive, correlational, and experimental—can be used to address the same topic (Figure 2.3). For instance, various researchers have used different research methods to explore the role of intensely positive experiences in human functioning, as follows.

Abraham Maslow believed that people who were the healthiest and the happiest were capable of having intense moments of awe; he used the descriptive case study approach (1971) to examine the role of such "peak experiences" in the lives of such individuals, who seemed to enjoy the best of life. In contrast, Dan McAdams (2001) used correlational research to probe individuals' descriptions of their most powerful positive experiences. He found that individuals who were motivated toward warm interpersonal experiences tended to mention such experiences as the best memories of their lives. Finally, experimental researchers have also investigated this topic by randomly assigning individuals to write about their most intensely positive experiences for a few minutes each day for two or three days. Those who wrote about emotional and happy topics experienced enhanced positive mood as well as fewer physical illnesses two months later, as compared to individuals in control groups who wrote about topics that were not emotional (Burton & King, 2004, 2008). So, researchers coming from many different methodological perspectives can address the same topic, leading to different but valuable contributions to knowledge.

test yourself

1. Define descriptive, correlational, and experimental research.
2. Explain why correlation is not the same as causation.
3. What is the difference between an experimental group and a control group?

3· RESEARCH SAMPLES AND SETTINGS

Regardless of whether a study is correlational or experimental, among the important decisions to be made about collecting data are whom to choose as the participants and where to conduct the research. Will the participants be people or animals? Will they be children, adults, or both? Where will the research take place—in a lab or in a natural setting?

The Research Sample

When psychologists conduct a study, they usually want to be able to draw conclusions that will apply to a larger group of people than the participants they actually study. The entire group about which the investigator wants to draw conclusions is the **population.** The subset of the population chosen by the investigator for study is a **sample.** The researcher might be interested only in a particular group, such as all children who are gifted and talented, all young women who embark on science and math careers, or all gay men. The key is that the sample studied must be representative of the population to which the investigator wants to generalize his or her results. That is, the researcher might study only 100 gifted adolescents, but he or she wants to apply these results to all gifted and talented adolescents. A representative sample for the United States would reflect the U.S. population's age, socioeconomic status, ethnic origins, marital status, geographic location, religion, and so forth.

● **population** The entire group about which the investigator wants to draw conclusions.

● **sample** The subset of the population chosen by the investigator for study.

The research sample might include a particular group, such as all gay men or all women runners.

● **random sample** A sample that gives every member of the population an equal chance of being selected.

To mirror the population as closely as possible, the researcher uses a **random sample,** a sample that gives every member of the population an equal chance of being selected. Random sampling improves the chances that the sample is representative of the population. In actual practice, however, random sampling typically only *approximates* this ideal—for example, by randomly sampling people who have telephones or people who live in a particular town or state. Note that a random sample is *not* the same thing as random assignment. Random assignment is about making sure experimental and control groups are equivalent, and a random sample is about selecting participants from a population so that the sample is representative of that population.

In selecting a sample, researchers must strive to minimize bias, including gender bias. Because psychology is the scientific study of human behavior, it should pertain to *all* humans, and so the participants in psychological studies ought to be representative of humanity as a whole. Early research in the field often included just the male experience—not only because the researchers themselves were often male, but also because the participants too were typically male (Etaugh & Bridges, 2010). For a long time, the human experience studied by psychologists was primarily the male experience.

There is also a growing realization that psychological research needs to include more people from diverse ethnic groups (Swanson, Edwards, & Spencer, 2010; Tamis-LeMonda & McFadden, 2010). Because a great deal of psychological research involves college student participants, individuals from groups that have not had as many educational opportunities have not been strongly represented in that research. Given the fact that individuals from diverse ethnic groups have been excluded from psychological research for so long, we might reasonably conclude that people's real lives are more varied than past research data have indicated.

These issues are important because scientists want to be able to predict human behavior broadly speaking, not just the behavior of non-Latino White, male college students. Imagine if policymakers planned their initiatives for a wide range of Americans based on research derived from only a small group of individuals from a particular background. What might the results be?

The Research Setting

All three types of research we examined in the preceding section can take place in different physical settings. The setting of the research does not determine the type of research it is. Common settings include the research laboratory and natural settings.

Natural settings and laboratories are common locales for psychological studies. (Left) Jane Goodall, who specializes in animal behavior, has carried out extensive research on chimpanzees in natural settings. Her work has contributed a great deal to our understanding of these intelligent primates. (Right) Barbara L. Fredrickson, a psychologist at the University of North Carolina, Chapel Hill, whose work investigates topics such as positive emotions and human flourishing, conducts a laboratory study.

Because psychological researchers often want to control as many aspects of the situation as possible, they conduct much of their research in a laboratory—a controlled setting with many of the complex factors of the real world, including potential confounds, removed (Kantowitz, Roediger, & Elmes, 2009). Although laboratory research provides a great deal of control, doing research in the laboratory has drawbacks. First, it is almost impossible to conduct research in the lab without the participants knowing they are being studied. Second, the laboratory setting is not the real world and therefore can cause the participants to behave unnaturally. A third drawback of laboratory research is that individuals who are willing to go to a university laboratory may not be representative of groups from diverse cultural backgrounds. Those who are unfamiliar with university settings and with the idea of "helping science" may be intimidated by the setting. Fourth, some aspects of the mind and behavior are difficult if not impossible to examine in the laboratory.

Research can also take place in a natural setting. **Naturalistic observation** is viewing behavior in a real-world setting (Leedy & Ormrod, 2010). Psychologists conduct naturalistic observations at sporting events, child-care centers, work settings, shopping malls, and other places that people frequent. If you wanted to study the level of civility on your campus for a research project, most likely you would include naturalistic observation of how people treat one another in such gathering places as the cafeteria and the library reading room. In another example of a natural setting, researchers who use survey methods are increasingly relying on web-based assessments that allow participants to complete the measures using the Internet.

● **naturalistic observation** The observation of behavior in a real-world setting.

The type of research a psychologist conducts, the operational definitions of the variables of interest, and the choice of sample and setting are decisions that ideally are guided by the research question itself. However, sometimes these decisions represent a compromise between the psychologist's key objective (for example, to study a representative sample of Americans) and the available resources (for instance, a sample of 100 college students). For a closer look at the process of conducting an experiment in a real-world setting, check out the Psychological Inquiry on p. 44.

test yourself
1. With respect to a research study, what is meant by a population? What is a sample?
2. What is the difference between a random sample and random assignment?
3. What are two common physical settings for research?

4· ANALYZING AND INTERPRETING DATA

Once psychologists collect data, whether they do so in a lab or a natural setting, it is time to analyze and interpret them. For this task they use *statistics,* mathematical methods for reporting data (Howell, 2010). There are two basic categories of statistics: descriptive statistics, which are used to describe and summarize data, and inferential statistics, which are used to draw conclusions about those data.

Psychology students are sometimes surprised to learn that a statistics course is often a requirement for the major. In this section, as we look at how psychologists analyze and interpret research data, you will get a flavor of the ways in which math plays an important role in the science of psychology.

Descriptive Statistics

Most psychological studies generate considerable numerical data. Simply listing all of the scores (or other measures) generated by a study—for each individual in the study—is not very meaningful. **Descriptive statistics** are the mathematical procedures researchers have developed to describe and summarize sets of data in a meaningful way. Descriptive statistics reveal the "big picture"—the overall characteristics of the data and the variation among them.

● **descriptive statistics** Mathematical procedures that are used to describe and summarize sets of data in a meaningful way.

MEASURES OF CENTRAL TENDENCY

A *measure of central tendency* is a single number that indicates the overall characteristics of a set of data. The three measures of central tendency are the mean, the median, and the mode.

psychological *inquiry*

Experimentation in a Natural Setting

A team of social psychologists was interested in examining how mood influences helping behavior in the real world. They hypothesized that, especially among the less experienced members of a sales staff, mood would guide behavior, so that happy salespersons would be most helpful to customers and unhappy salespersons less so. Researchers Joseph Forgas, Elizabeth Dunn, and Stacey Granland (2008) conducted an experiment in a Target department store, as follows.

First, the experimenters trained two confederates. The first confederate was in charge of manipulating the employees' mood. There were three mood conditions:

- In the *positive mood condition,* the confederate said, "I just wanted to let someone know that I am so impressed with the service at this store! The store looks great and the staff is so nice. I was able to get what I wanted and will be coming back to this store again."

- In the *negative mood condition,* the confederate said, "I just wanted to let someone know that I am so disappointed with the service at this store. The store looks terrible and the staff is rude. I couldn't get anything I wanted and won't be coming back here again."

- In the *neutral mood condition,* the confederate simply observed, "Interesting, I have been coming here quite regularly and this store seems always the same, nothing much changes."

Employees were chosen randomly by the confederate and were randomly assigned to the conditions.

Then, after the first confederate left the employees, the second confederate, who was blind to the mood procedure (meaning unaware of the mood condition for each participant), approached the employees individually and asked, "Excuse me, could you tell me where I could find the book *The White Bear*?" This confederate surreptitiously recorded (1) the number of helpful responses, (2) the number of actual attempts to help, and (3) the time spent helping. These three values were averaged to create an overall helpfulness score. (If the staff salesperson saw the confederate jotting things down, the confederate pretended to be checking a shopping list.) The figure shows the results for the less experienced sales staff.

Answer these questions to see how much you remember about experimental design.

1. Despite the natural setting, this was an experiment. Why?
2. What was the independent variable and what was its operational definition?
3. What was the dependent variable and what was its operational definition?
4. Why is it important that the second confederate was "blind" to the mood condition?
5. Why were the employees assigned to mood condition randomly?
6. The store management was aware of the study, but the employees were not. Do you think the experiment was ethical? Why or why not?

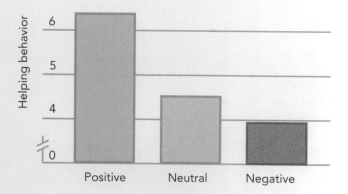

Target Employee Helping as a Function of Mood Condition

Adapted from Forgas, Dunn, & Granland, 2008.

Most quantitative techniques in psychological science begin with the mean. The **mean** is what people often call the average. The mean is calculated by adding all the scores in a set of scores and then dividing by the number of scores. As a good indicator of the central tendency for a group of scores, the mean is the measure that is used most often. When your instructor provides students with their exam grades, he or she might mention the test mean, because this average gives the class a general idea of how the group performed.

● **mean** A measure of central tendency that is the average for a sample.

The mean is not so helpful, however, when a group of scores contains a few extreme scores, especially if the number of cases in the group is small. Consider the annual earnings for the two groups of five people shown in the table below.

Group 1		Group 2	
	$19,000		$19,000
	19,000		19,000
	23,000		23,000
	24,000		24,000
	25,000		45,000,000
Mean	$22,000	Mean	$9,017,000
Median	$23,000	Median	$23,000
Mode	$19,000	Mode	$19,000

Group 1 lists the earnings of five ordinary people. Group 2 is composed of the earnings of four ordinary people plus the approximate earnings of movie director Steven Spielberg. Now look at the means that have been calculated for the two groups. The vast difference between them is due to the one extreme score. In such a situation, one of the other two measures of central tendency, the median or the mode, would give a more accurate picture of the data overall.

The **median** is the score that falls exactly in the middle of the distribution of scores after they have been arranged (or ranked) from highest to lowest. When you have an odd number of scores (say, five or seven), the median is the score with the same number of scores above it as below it. In the table above, each group has a median income of $23,000. Notice that, unlike the mean, the median is unaffected by extreme scores. The medians are the same for both groups ($23,000), but their means are extremely different ($22,000 versus $9,017,000). Of course, if there is an even number of scores, there is no "middle" score. This problem is dealt with by averaging the scores that share the middle location.

● **median** A measure of central tendency that is the middle score in a sample.

● **mode** A measure of central tendency that is the most common score in a sample.

The **mode** is the score that occurs most often in a dataset. In our earnings example, the mode is $19,000, which occurs twice in each group. All of the other annual incomes occur only once. The mode is the least used measure of central tendency. Yet the mode can be particularly useful, for example, in cases in which information is desired about preference or popularity. Consider a teacher who wants to know the most popular or least popular child in her classroom. She might create a questionnaire and ask students which of their classmates they like the most or the least. The most frequently nominated child would be the mode in these instances.

MEASURES OF DISPERSION

In addition to revealing the central characteristics of a sample, descriptive statistics can also give us *measures of dispersion,* which describe how much the scores in a sample differ from one another. That is, these measures give us a sense of the spread of scores, or how much variability exists in the data. Let's look at some common ways that researchers measure dispersion.

To begin, suppose that four students rate their positive mood on a scale from 1 (not at all positive) to 7 (extremely positive), as follows:

Positive Mood

Sarah	7
Sun Mee	6
Josh	2
Rodney	5

● **range** A measure of dispersion that is the difference between the highest and lowest scores.

(You might note that the mean for these data is 20/4, or 5.) One common measure of dispersion is the **range,** which is the distance between the highest and the lowest scores. In the example above, the range in positive mood is 5 (that is, the highest score, 7, minus the lowest score, 2). Generally speaking, the range is a rather simplistic estimate of the variability within a group of scores. Because the range takes into account only the lowest and highest scores, it can produce a misleading picture of how different from one another scores in the dataset actually are. Note that for positive mood, most people in the example have fairly similar high scores, but using the range alone gives the impression that scores are very widely dispersed.

● **standard deviation** A measure of dispersion that tells us how much scores in a sample differ from the mean of the sample.

A more informative measure of dispersion, and the one most commonly used in psychological research, is the standard deviation. The **standard deviation** measures how much scores vary, on average, around the mean of the sample. There is a little hitch, however. One of the mathematical properties of the mean is that if you add up each person's difference from the mean, the sum will always be 0. So, we cannot calculate the average difference (or deviation) from the mean and get a meaningful answer.

To get around this problem, we take each person's difference from the mean and multiply it by itself. This removes the negative numbers, and the sum of these differences will no longer equal 0. We add these squared deviations together and then divide by the number of cases (minus 1). Finally, we take the square root of that number. Essentially, then, the standard deviation is the square root of the average squared deviation from the mean. The smaller the standard deviation, the less variability in the dataset. A small standard deviation indicates that, on average, scores are close to the mean.

The following table presents the information needed to calculate the standard deviation for the positive mood ratings given above.

	A	**B**	**C**
Participant	Rating	Difference from the mean (5)	*Squared* difference from the mean (5)
Sarah	7	2	4
Sun Mee	6	1	1
Josh	2	−3	9
Rodney	5	0	0
MEAN = $\frac{(7 + 6 + 2 + 5)}{4}$ = 5.0		Sum of this column = 0	Sum of these differences = 4 + 1 + 9 + 0 = 14

Column A presents the ratings by each participant. Column B shows the differences of these scores from the mean (5). Notice that if we add up Column B, the answer is 0. Column C shows the squared deviations from the mean for each participant. Adding up those squared differences, we get 14. Next, we divide 14 by the number of participants minus 1, in this case 14 divided by 3 = 4.67, and then we take the square root of that number, which is 2.16. This is the standard deviation of our sample, which, compared to the range of 5, tells us that the group is actually fairly closely arranged around the mean.

The mean and standard deviation together yield a lot of information about a sample. Indeed, given the raw scores, the means, and the standard deviations of two variables, we can calculate the correlation coefficient in no time. The correlation coefficient is not a descriptive statistic but rather an inferential statistic, our next topic.

Inferential Statistics

Imagine that, inspired by the research of Lee Anne Harker and Dacher Keltner on college yearbooks (see p. 28), you conduct a study on the relationship between expressions of positive emotion and interpersonal success. In your project, you video-record job candidates being interviewed, code the videos for Duchenne smiling by the candidates, and document which of the job seekers were called back for a second interview. Let's say you calculate that the mean number of smiles for candidates who were not called back was 3.5, and the mean number of smiles for candidates who were called back was 6.5. So, those who were called back generated, on average, 3 more smiles than those who were not called back. Does that difference matter? It seems pretty big, but is it big enough? Could we have obtained the same difference simply by chance?

To draw conclusions about differences we observe in studies, we want to know that the difference is likely to be one that can be replicated or found consistently in a variety of studies. Inferential statistics are the tools that help us to state whether a difference is unlikely to be the result of chance. More specifically, **inferential statistics** are the mathematical methods used to indicate whether data sufficiently support a research hypothesis (Kiess & Green, 2010).

The logic behind inferential statistics is relatively simple. Inferential statistics yield a statement of probability about the differences observed between two or more groups; this probability statement gives the odds that the observed differences were due simply to chance. In psychological research the standard is that if the odds are 5 out of 100 (or .05) or less that the differences are due to chance, the results are considered *statistically significant*. In statistical language, this is referred to as the .05 level of statistical significance, or the .05 confidence level. Put another way, statistical significance means that the differences observed between two groups are large enough that it is highly unlikely that those differences are merely due to chance. The .05 level of statistical significance is considered the minimum level of probability that scientists will accept for concluding that the differences observed are real, thereby supporting a hypothesis.

Recall that although we study a sample, we typically wish to generalize our findings to a population. Inferential statistics are the bridge between a sample and a population, because they tell us the likelihood that the results we found with a sample reflect differences in the larger population. It makes sense that the larger our sample is, the more likely it is to represent that population. Thus, significance tests are based in part on the number of cases in a sample. The higher the number of cases, the easier it is to get statistical significance. As a result, with a very large sample, even very small differences may be significant.

However, statistical significance is not the same thing as real-world significance. Even if a difference is found to be statistically significant, its real-world value remains to be evaluated by critically thinking scientists.

● **inferential statistics** Mathematical methods that are used to indicate whether results for a sample are likely to generalize to a population.

test yourself

1. What is meant by a measure of central tendency? Name three measures of central tendency.
2. What do measures of dispersion describe?
3. What does standard deviation measure?

Being part of a research study can potentially lead to unintended consequences for the participants. After taking part in a study of young dating couples (Rubin & Mitchell, 1976), some participants identified problems in their relationship and ended it.

5· CONDUCTING ETHICAL RESEARCH

Ethics is a crucial consideration for all science. This fact came to the fore in the aftermath of World War II, for example, when it became apparent that Nazi doctors had used concentration camp prisoners as unwilling participants in experiments. These atrocities spurred scientists to develop a code of appropriate behavior—a set of principles about the treatment that participants in research have a right to expect. In general, ethical principles of research focus on balancing the rights of the participants with the rights of scientists to ask important research questions (Smith & Davis, 2010).

The issue of ethics in psychological research may affect you personally if at some point you participate in a study. In that event, you need to know your rights as a participant and the researchers' responsibilities in ensuring that these rights are safeguarded. Experiences in research can have unforeseen effects on people's lives.

One investigation of young dating couples asked them to complete a questionnaire that coincidentally stimulated some of the participants to think about potentially troublesome issues in the relationship (Rubin & Mitchell, 1976). One year later, when the researchers followed up with the original sample, 9 of 10 participants said they had discussed their answers with their dating partners. In most instances, the discussions helped to strengthen the relationships. In some cases, however, the participants used the questionnaire as a springboard to discuss problems or concerns previously hidden. One participant said, "The study definitely played a role in ending my relationship with Larry." In this case, the couple had different views about how long they expected to be together. She was thinking of a short-term dating relationship, whereas he was thinking in terms of a lifetime. Their answers to the questions brought the disparity in their views to the surface and led to the end of their relationship. Researchers have a responsibility to anticipate the personal problems their study might cause and, at least, to inform the participants of the possible fallout.

Ethics comes into play in every psychological study. Even smart, conscientious students sometimes think that members of their church, athletes in the Special Olympics, or residents of the local nursing home present great samples for psychological research. Without proper permission, though, the most well-meaning, kind, and considerate researchers still violate the rights of the participants.

Ethics Guidelines

A number of guidelines have been developed to ensure that research is conducted ethically. At the base of all of these guidelines is the notion that a person participating in psychological research should be no worse off coming out of the study than he or she was on the way in.

Today colleges and universities have a review board (typically called the *institutional review board,* or *IRB*) that evaluates the ethical nature of research conducted at their institutions. Proposed research plans must pass the scrutiny of a research ethics committee before the research can be initiated. In addition, the American Psychological Association (APA) has developed ethics guidelines for its members. The code of ethics instructs psychologists to protect their participants from mental and physical harm. The participants' best interests need to be kept foremost in the researcher's mind (Gravetter, 2009; Ray, 2009). The APA's guidelines address four important issues:

- *Informed consent:* All participants must know what their participation will involve and what risks might develop. For example, participants in a study on dating should be told beforehand that a questionnaire might stimulate thoughts about issues in their relationships that they have not considered. Participants also should be informed that in some instances a discussion of the issues might improve their relationships but that in others it might worsen the relationships and even end them. Even after informed consent is given, participants must retain the right to withdraw from the study at any time and for any reason.

- *Confidentiality:* Researchers are responsible for keeping all of the data they gather on individuals completely confidential and, when possible, completely anonymous. Confidential data are not the same as anonymous. When data are confidential, it is possible to link a participant's identity to his or her data.

- *Debriefing:* After the study has been completed, the researchers should inform the participants of its purpose and the methods they used. In most cases, the experimenters also can inform participants in a general manner beforehand about the purpose of the research without leading the participants to behave in a way that they think that the experimenters are expecting. When preliminary information about the study is likely to affect the results, participants can at least be debriefed after the study's completion.

- *Deception:* This is an ethical issue that psychologists debate extensively. In some circumstances, telling the participants beforehand what the research study is about substantially alters the participants' behavior and invalidates the researcher's data. For example, suppose a psychologist wants to know whether bystanders will report a theft. A mock theft is staged, and the psychologist observes which bystanders report it. Had the psychologist informed the participants beforehand that the study intended to discover the percentage of bystanders who will report a theft, the whole study would have been ruined. Thus, the researcher deceives participants about the purpose of the study, perhaps leading them to believe that it has some other purpose. In all cases of deception, however, the psychologist must ensure that the deception will not harm the participants and that the participants will be told the true nature of the study (will be debriefed) as soon as possible after the study is completed.

The federal government also takes a role in ensuring that research involving human participants is conducted ethically. The Office for Human Research Protection is devoted to ensuring the well-being of participants in research studies. Over the years, the office has dealt with many challenging and controversial issues—among them, informed consent rules for research on mental disorders, regulations governing research on pregnant women and fetuses, and ethical issues regarding AIDS vaccine research.

For generations, psychologists have used animals in some research. Animal studies have provided a better understanding of and solutions for many human problems (Pinel, 2009). Neal Miller (1985), who has made important discoveries about the effects of biofeedback on health, listed the following areas in which animal research has benefited humans:

- Psychotherapy techniques and behavioral medicine
- Rehabilitation of neuromuscular disorders
- Alleviation of the effects of stress and pain
- Drugs to treat anxiety and severe mental illness
- Methods for avoiding drug addiction and relapse
- Treatments to help premature infants gain weight so they can leave the hospital sooner
- Methods used to alleviate memory deficits in old age

About 5 percent of APA members use animals in their research. Rats and mice account for 90 percent of all psychological research with animals. It is true that researchers sometimes use procedures with animals that would be unethical with humans, but they are guided by a set of standards for housing, feeding, and maintaining the psychological and physical well-being of their animal subjects. Researchers are required to weigh potential benefits of the research against possible harm to the animal and to avoid inflicting unnecessary pain. In short, researchers must follow stringent ethical guidelines, whether animals or humans are the subjects in their studies.

The Place of Values in Psychological Research

Questions are asked not only about the ethics of psychology but also about its values and its standards for judging what is worthwhile and desirable. Some psychologists argue that psychology should be value-free and morally neutral. From their perspective, the psychologist's role as a scientist is to present facts as objectively as possible. Others believe that because psychologists are human, they cannot possibly be value-free. Indeed, some people go so far as to argue that psychologists should take stands on certain issues. For example, psychological research shows that children reared by gay male and lesbian parents are no more likely to be gay than other children and tend to show levels of psychological health that are equal to or higher than those of children reared by heterosexual parents (Patterson & Hastings, 2007). To the extent that some have argued against the rights of gays and lesbians to adopt children or to retain custody of their biological children, psychologists may have a role to play in the debate about these issues.

To explore questions about the ethics of research further, read the Critical Controversy feature about reality TV.

test yourself

1. What two things do the ethical principles used in research seek to balance?
2. With respect to the participants in a study, what do the various ethical guidelines covering research all fundamentally seek to protect?
3. What four key issues do the APA's ethics guidelines address?

CRITICAL CONTROVERSY

Would Reality TV Pass the Institutional Review Board?

*S*urvivor, American Idol, Big Brother—these are just a few of the many popular reality shows that fill the U.S. television airwaves. While critics debate the quality of these shows, reality TV watchers may think that they are learning a lot about human nature by tuning in to see who will get voted off, who will willingly eat ground-up rats, or who will be ridiculed by the *American Idol* judges.

For you as a student of psychology, an appropriate question might be, would these reality TV shows ever gain the approval of the IRB of an institution of higher learning? This issue was of interest to Barbara Spellman, a founding member of the American Psychological Society Committee on Human Subject Protection, who examined reality TV programming with an eye toward the ethical issues these shows present. If we were to consider reality TV from the perspective of the APA ethical guidelines we have considered in this chap-

Would Survivor *gain the approval of your school's institutional review board?*

ter, at least five issues that Spellman (2005) identified would come to the fore.

First, how do reality shows achieve informed consent? The principle of informed consent means that all participants must know what their participation will involve and what risks might develop. Yet the very thing that makes reality shows exciting is the element of the unknown—the potential for surprise. Clearly the producers of *Survivor* are not going to inform contestants upfront that for their particular episode they will be asked to eat live bugs, because the element of shock and the dramatic moment of the decision would diminish greatly if it occurred off camera while the person perused the consent form. On the other hand, we might note that it is highly unlikely that anyone who participates on such a show has not watched a few episodes, and therefore most participants will have a pretty good idea that they must expect the unexpected.

A second, related problem with at least some reality shows is the use of deception. Fooling a group of women into believing that a semi-employed construction worker is actually a millionaire is probably not likely to satisfy APA ethical considerations.

A third issue that might arise is that of risk. Many reality shows pose a great deal of psychological and/or physical risk. Some reality shows include children (for example, *Wife Swap*), and it is very unlikely that an IRB would consider posing any kind of risk to children justified.

A fourth major stumbling block for reality TV is the potential for huge cash awards to compel people to behave in ways they would not otherwise do. Is it "really" lying if you are doing it in order to win a million dollars? If a person does something to "play the game" that he or she would never do outside of the game, haven't we shown that money has compelled the individual to act in ways he or she might later regret or be judged for?

Remember that ethical considerations involve balancing the rights of participants with the scientist's right to know. Thus, a fifth question pertinent to a study of reality TV is, what is the value of what we can learn from these "experiments"? This brings up the issue of how "natural" reality shows are. Are people truly themselves when the cameras are rolling?

WHAT DO YOU THINK?

- Do reality TV shows represent natural human behavior? Explain.
- What kind of reality show would you design if you were interested in exploring important psychological processes? What ethical safeguards would you build into the design to protect participants?

6· THINKING CRITICALLY ABOUT PSYCHOLOGICAL RESEARCH

Not all psychological information that is presented for public consumption comes from professionals with excellent credentials and reputations at colleges or universities or in applied mental health settings (Stanovich, 2010). Because journalists, television reporters, and other media personnel are not usually trained in psychological research, they often have trouble sorting through the widely varying material they find and making sound decisions about the best information to present to the public. In addition, the media often focus on sensationalistic and dramatic psychological findings to capture public attention. Media reports may go beyond what actual research articles and clinical findings really say. For example, recall from Chapter 1 the research controversy over the alleged epidemic of narcissism in members of Generation Me. The popular media latched on to this work, although subsequent research has called its conclusions into question.

Even when the media present the results of excellent research, they sometimes have trouble accurately informing people about the findings and their implications for people's lives. This entire book is dedicated to carefully introducing, defining, and elaborating on key concepts and issues, research, and clinical findings. The media, however, do not have the luxury of so much time and space to detail and specify the limitations and qualifications of research. In the end, *you* have to take responsibility for evaluating media reports on psychological research. To put it another way, you have to consume psychological information critically and wisely. Five guidelines follow.

Avoid Overgeneralizing Based on Little Information

Media reports of psychological information often leave out details about the nature of the sample used in a given study. Without information about sample characteristics—such as the number of participants, their sex, or their ethnic representation—it is wise to take research results with a grain of salt. For example, research that demonstrated the classic "fight or flight" response to stress has had great impact on how we understand the body's response to threatening situations. Yet the original work on this topic included only male participants (Taylor, 2011). The implications of the lack of women in these studies will be explored in Chapter 3.

Distinguish Between Group Results and Individual Needs

Just as we cannot generalize from a small group to all people, we also cannot apply conclusions from a group to an individual. When you learn about psychological research through the media, you might be disposed to apply the results to your life. It is important to keep in mind that statistics about a group do not necessarily represent each individual in the group equally well. Imagine, for example, taking a test in a class and being told that the class average was 75 percent, but you got 98 percent. It is unlikely that you would want the instructor to apply the group average to your score.

Sometimes consumers of psychological research can get the wrong idea about whether their own experience is "normal" if it does not match group statistics. New parents face this issue all the time. They read about developmental milestones that supposedly characterize an entire age group of children; one such milestone might be that most 2-year-olds are conversing with their parents. However, this group information does not necessarily characterize *all* children who are developing normally. Albert Einstein did not start talking until he was the ripe old age of 3.

Look for Answers Beyond a Single Study

The media might identify an interesting piece of research and claim that its conclusions are phenomenal and have far-reaching implications. Although such pivotal studies do occur, they are rare. It is safer to assume that no single study will provide conclusive answers to an important question, especially answers that apply to all people. In fact, in most psychological domains that prompt many investigations, conflicting results are common. Answers to questions in research usually emerge after many scientists have conducted similar investigations that yield similar conclusions. Remember that you should not take one research study as the absolute, final answer to a problem, no matter how compelling the findings.

Avoid Attributing Causes Where None Have Been Found

Drawing causal conclusions from correlational studies is one of the most common mistakes the media make. For example, the results of the Nun Study described earlier suggest that happy people live longer. However, we cannot state that happiness *caused* them to live longer. When a true experiment has not been conducted—that is, when participants have not been randomly assigned to treatments or experiences—two variables might have only a non-causal relationship to each other. Remember from the discussion of correlation earlier in the chapter that causal interpretations cannot be made when two or more factors are simply correlated. We cannot say that one causes the other. When you hear about correlational studies, be skeptical of words indicating causation until you know more about the particular research.

Consider the Source of Psychological Information

Studies conducted by psychologists are not automatically accepted by the rest of the research community. The researchers usually must submit their findings to an academic journal for review by their colleagues, who make a decision about whether to publish the paper, depending on its scientific merit. Although the quality of research and findings is not uniform among all psychology journals, in most cases journals submit the findings to far greater scrutiny than do the popular media (Stanovich, 2010).

Within the media, though, you can usually draw a distinction. The reports of psychological research in respected newspapers such as the *New York Times* and the *Washington Post,* as well as in credible magazines such as *Time* and the *Atlantic Monthly,* are far more trustworthy than reports in tabloids such as the *National Enquirer* and *Star.* Yet whatever the source—serious publication, tabloid, or even academic journal—you are responsible for reading the details behind the reported findings and for analyzing the study's credibility.

7· THE SCIENTIFIC METHOD AND HEALTH AND WELLNESS

Throughout this book we examine a host of ways that psychological research has implications for health and wellness. In this chapter's concluding section, we focus on a research topic in which the scientific method has played a particularly important role

test yourself

1. For what reasons are media reports on psychological studies often problematic?
2. Why is it wise to look beyond the conclusions of just one research study?
3. How does the submission of research findings to a respectable academic journal aid both researchers and the public?

in the conclusions drawn—the power of expressive writing to enhance health and wellness.

James Pennebaker has conducted a number of studies that converge on the same conclusion: that writing about one's deepest thoughts and feelings concerning one's most traumatic life event leads to a number of health and well-being benefits (Pennebaker & Chung, 2007). This research began with a correlational study comparing two groups of individuals—those who had lost a spouse to suicide and those who had lost a spouse to an accident (Pennebaker & O'Heeron, 1984). The results of the study showed that survivors of a suicide were more likely to have become sick in the months after the death, compared to accident survivors. Importantly, the difference was explained by the fact that individuals whose spouses had committed suicide were much less likely to talk about their loss, compared to the other participants.

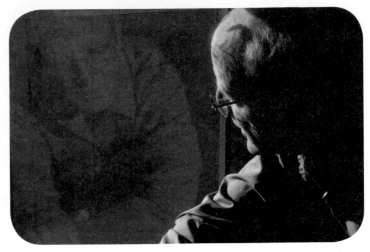

The research of James Pennebaker of the University of Texas, Austin, probes the connections among traumatic life experience, expressive writing, physical and mental health, and work performance.

These correlational findings led Pennebaker to wonder whether it might be possible to manipulate expressing one's thoughts and feelings about a traumatic event *experimentally* and thereby to receive the benefits of socially sharing the trauma. So, in subsequent studies, participants have been randomly assigned to write about one of two topics— either the individual's most traumatic life event or a relatively uninteresting topic (for example, his or her plans for the day). Assignment of the specific topic is meant to control for the act of writing itself so that the control group is as much like the experimental group as possible (Baddeley & Pennebaker, 2009; Pennebaker & Graybeal, 2001).

The participants write about the same topic for three or four consecutive days for about 20 minutes each day. Weeks or months after writing, participants in the trauma writing group have better physical health than those in the control group. Since the first traumatic writing study, a host of researchers have replicated these effects, showing that writing about trauma is associated with superior immune function, better response to a vaccine, higher psychological well-being, better adjustment to coming to college, and more quickly finding employment after being laid off from work (Lepore & Smyth, 2002; Pennebaker, 1997a, 1997b, 2004). Thus, we might conclude that documenting one's deepest thoughts and feelings about traumatic life events is necessary to attain the "healing power" of writing.

Note, however, that the participants in the trauma group were not just writing about a trauma. They were also documenting an important personal experience. Thinking about these results in terms of the internal validity of the conclusions, we might ask if focusing on a trauma is the key ingredient in producing health benefits. Might there be other, less negative aspects of life that are equally meaningful and that might promote good health when they are the subject of personal writing? Indeed, subsequent research shows that health benefits can emerge from writing about a variety of topics, including how one has grown from a negative experience (King & Miner, 2000; Low, Stanton, & Danoff-Burg, 2006), one's life dreams (King, 2001), and one's most intensely positive experiences (Burton & King, 2004, 2009). In a recent study, participants who wrote about either a traumatic life event or an extremely positive event for just two minutes a day over two days reported fewer illnesses a month later (Burton & King, 2008).

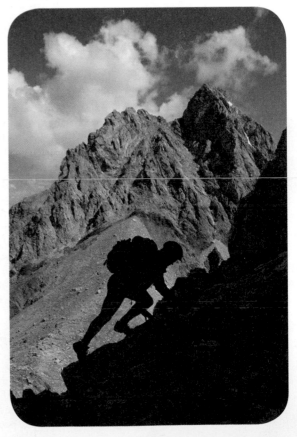

The body of evidence for the effects of expressive writing on health is substantial and has been subjected to two meta-analyses, the procedure described earlier in this chapter. These meta-analyses indicate that individuals who write over days that are spaced apart tend to benefit most from writing, and that feeling distressed while writing is not necessary to enjoy these benefits (Frattaroli, 2006; Smyth, 1998).

If you would like to explore the healing power of writing in your own life, use the simple guidelines below:

- Find a quiet place to write.
- Pick just one topic to explore through writing.
- Dedicate yourself to a few minutes of writing each day, perhaps writing once a week for a few weeks.
- While writing, do not worry about punctuation, grammar, or spelling—just let yourself go and write about all of the thoughts, emotions, and feelings associated with the experience you are documenting.
- If you feel that writing about something negative is not for you, try writing about your most positive life experiences, the people you care about, or all the things for which you feel grateful.

The long and growing literature on the effects of expressive writing on health demonstrates how research methods influence the conclusions that scientists reach and how the process of scientific research builds from one study to the next. This literature also demonstrates how psychological research is relevant to the daily life of everyone with a story to write—and how an individual can benefit from writing that story.

test yourself

1. Briefly describe Pennebaker's initial correlational study comparing two groups of individuals who had lost a spouse.
2. What did Pennebaker's subsequent experimental research show?
3. What does the accumulated body of evidence indicate about the effects of expressive writing on health?

SUMMARY

1. PSYCHOLOGY'S SCIENTIFIC METHOD

Psychologists use the scientific method to address research questions. This method involves starting with a theory and then making observations, formulating hypotheses, testing these through empirical research, drawing conclusions, and evaluating the theory. The science of psychology is an ongoing conversation among scholars.

2. TYPES OF PSYCHOLOGICAL RESEARCH

Three types of research commonly used in psychology are descriptive research (finding out about the basic dimensions of some variable), correlational research (finding out if and how two variables change together), and experimental research (determining the causal relationship between variables). Descriptive research includes observation, surveys, interviews, and case studies. Correlational research often includes surveys and interviews as well as observation. Experimental research often occurs in a lab but can also be done in a natural setting.

In an experiment, the independent variable is manipulated to see if it produces changes in the dependent variable. An experiment involves comparing two groups: the experimental group (the one that receives the treatment or manipulation of the independent variable) and the control group (the comparison group or baseline that is equal to the experimental group in every way except for the independent variable). Experimental research relies on random assignment to ensure that the groups are roughly equivalent before the manipulation of the independent variable.

3. RESEARCH SAMPLES AND SETTINGS

Two important decisions that must be made for psychological research are whom to study and where to study them. A sample is the group that participates in a study; a population is the group to which the researcher wishes to generalize the results. A random sample is the best way of ensuring that the sample reflects the population.

Research settings include both the laboratory and real-world, naturalistic contexts. The laboratory allows a great deal of control, but naturalistic settings may give a truer sense of natural behavior.

4. ANALYZING AND INTERPRETING DATA

Descriptive statistics are used to describe and summarize samples of data in a meaningful way. Two types of descriptive statistics are measures of central tendency and measures of variability. Measures of central tendency are the mean (or mathematical average), the median (the middle score), and the mode (the most common score). Measures of variability include the range (the difference between the highest and lowest scores) and the standard deviation (the square root of the average squared deviation from the mean).

Inferential statistics are used to draw conclusions about data. Inferential statistics aim to uncover statistical significance, which means that the differences observed between groups (or the correlation between variables) are unlikely to be the result of chance.

5. CONDUCTING ETHICAL RESEARCH

For all kinds of research, ethical treatment of participants is crucial. Participants should leave a psychological study no worse off than they were when they entered. Some guiding principles for ethical research in psychology include informed consent, confidentiality, debriefing (participants should be fully informed about the purpose of a study once it is over), and explaining fully the use of deception in a study.

6. THINKING CRITICALLY ABOUT PSYCHOLOGICAL RESEARCH

In your everyday life and in introductory psychology, you will be exposed to psychological research findings. In approaching psychological research in the media, you should adopt the attitude of a scientist and critically evaluate the research presented. This means being careful to avoid overgeneralizing based on little information, realizing that group results may not apply to every individual, looking for answers beyond a single study, and avoiding attributing causation when none has been found. Finally, it is important to consider the source when you encounter research in the popular media.

7. THE SCIENTIFIC METHOD AND HEALTH AND WELLNESS

A great deal of psychological research has relevance to health and wellness. An example is research by James Pennebaker on the effects of expressive writing on health and well-being. This research has shown that individuals who are randomly assigned to write about a traumatic life event for a few minutes a day over three or four days show a host of health and well-being benefits compared to those in a control condition. Subsequent research has shown that these health benefits can be obtained by writing about very positive life experiences and even just writing for a couple of minutes.

This research demonstrates how a research question can begin as a correlational study and then move to the laboratory to demonstrate causation. When many studies have been done on a topic, a meta-analysis can provide a sense of the overall importance of the results. This example also shows how psychological research can have important implications for everyday life.

key *terms*

variable, p. 26
theory, p. 26
hypothesis, p. 27
operational definition, p. 27
meta-analysis, p. 29
descriptive research, p. 29
case study or case history, p. 30
correlational research, p. 32
third variable problem, p. 33

longitudinal design, p. 34
experiment, p. 36
random assignment, p. 36
independent variable, p. 36
confederate, p. 37
dependent variable, p. 37
experimental group, p. 37
control group, p. 37
external validity, p. 37

internal validity, p. 38
experimenter bias, p. 38
demand characteristics, p. 38
research participant bias, p. 39
placebo effect, p. 39
placebo, p. 39
double-blind experiment, p. 40
population, p. 41
sample, p. 41

random sample, p. 42
naturalistic observation, p. 43
descriptive statistics, p. 43
mean, p. 45
median, p. 45
mode, p. 45
range, p. 46
standard deviation, p. 46
inferential statistics, p. 47

apply your *knowledge*

1. It's time to get out those old photos from the prom, wedding, or family reunion and see just how happy people were (or weren't). Look at some pictures from your own life and see who was genuinely smiling and who was faking it. Just cover the mouths with your finger—you can see who is happy from their eyes.

2. Is an old diary of yours hanging around somewhere? Pull it out and take a look at what you wrote. Count up your positive emotion words or negative emotion words. Are there themes in your diary from years ago that are still relevant to your life today? Does looking at your own diary change the way you might think about the results of the Nun Study? Explain.

3. What are some positive and negative correlations that you have observed in your own experience? What are some third variables that might explain these relationships? Do you think these relationships may be causal? How would you design an experiment to test that possibility?

4. In the next few days, look through several newspapers and magazines for reports about psychological research. Also notice what you see and hear on television about psychology. Apply the guidelines for being a wise consumer of information about psychology to these media reports.

5. The study of the Olympic athletes that was described at the beginning of this chapter was a correlational study. Design an experiment that would test the prediction that those who finish second are likely to be less happy than those who finish third.

6. Pick a topic of interest to you and define the variables. Then list as many ways to operationalize the variables as you can. Come up with at least one behavioral measure of the variable. Would your topic be best studied using a correlational or an experimental method? How would you conduct the study?

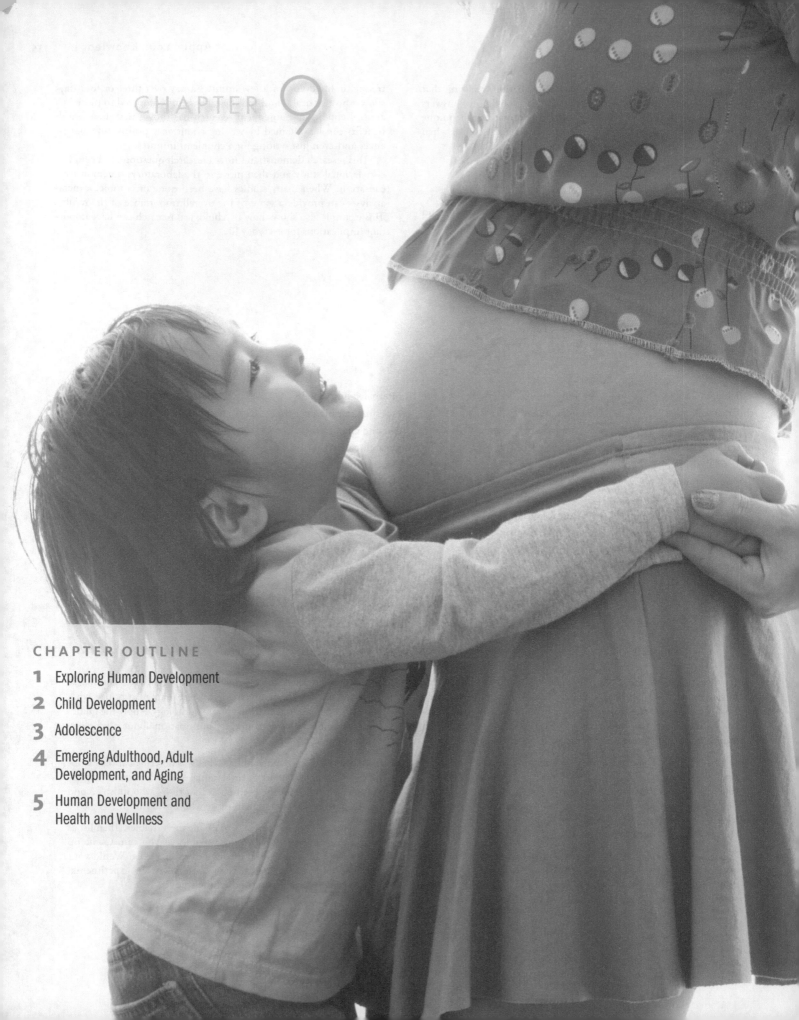

CHAPTER 9

Human Development

Welcome to the World

On any given day, about 384,000 babies are born worldwide. That translates to 16,000 babies every hour. In fact, in the time it takes you to read these few words, about 16 people have entered the world and begun their life's journey. For their parents it is a life-changing moment: a Monday or a Thursday that is not just a square on the calendar but a day they will never forget. Children are being born everywhere—in homes and hospitals, at birthing centers, and even in parking lots, as was the case for Wyatt Dean Overman, who was born in his parents' car outside a Cambridge, Minnesota, convenience store on January 12, 2010. Newborn babies are cute and fascinating, a few pounds of complete mystery. Whom does she resemble? What will her personality be like? What will she be when she grows up?

Reflect on your birthday—not the date but the actual day you were born. You cannot remember it, but you were much smaller, virtually helpless, and full of possibilities. Those possibilities have been unfolding throughout your life. Today, you are quite a bit taller and heavier (not to mention toilet trained). Some of these developments—physical growth, for instance—have "just happened." Some, such as reading and writing, you have learned through instruction and practice. Other things—such as studying psychology—have happened because you have wanted them to. Just as learning to walk was a developmental milestone, accomplishing the goals you set for yourself as an adult may also qualify as developmental changes. ●

PREVIEW

Developmental psychologists are interested in tracking and understanding the changes that occur throughout a person's life—all the steps toward being the person you are now and the person you are becoming. We begin this chapter by examining the meaning of development and exploring some key questions and issues in the field. We then study the processes of physical, cognitive, and socioemotional development throughout the life span: prenatally (before birth), during childhood, and later, in adolescence and adulthood. We round off our tour of the human life span with a look at development and wellness. Throughout, we consider how the active developer—whether an infant, a toddler, a teenager, or an adult—can influence the path and meaning of development.

1· EXPLORING HUMAN DEVELOPMENT

● **development** The pattern of continuity and change in human capabilities that occurs throughout life, involving both growth and decline.

Development refers to the pattern of continuity and change in human capabilities that occurs throughout the course of life. Most development involves growth, although it also is concerned with decline (for example, physical abilities may decline with age). Developmental psychology is interested in how people change, physically and psychologically as they age. These changes occur on three different levels:

■ *Physical processes* involve changes in an individual's biological nature. Genes inherited from parents; the hormonal changes of puberty and menopause; and changes throughout life in the brain, height and weight, and motor skills—all of these reflect the developmental role of biological processes. Such biological growth processes are called *maturation*.

■ *Cognitive processes* involve changes in an individual's thought, intelligence, and language. Observing a colorful mobile as it swings above a crib, constructing a sentence about the future, imagining oneself as a movie star, memorizing a new telephone number—these activities reflect the role of cognitive processes in development.

■ *Socioemotional processes* involve changes in an individual's relationships with other people, in emotions, and in personality. An infant's smile in response to her mother's touch, a girl's development of assertiveness, an adolescent's joy at the senior prom, a young man's aggressiveness in sport, and an older couple's affection for each other all reflect the role of socioemotional processes.

Human development is complex because it is the product of several processes. A child's growth in height and weight, a phone user's tapping out a friend's number from memory, and a young couple's joy on the occasion of their prom reflect physical, cognitive, and socioemotional processes, respectively.

These physical, cognitive, and socioemotional processes are intricately interwoven (Diamond, 2009; Diamond, Casey, & Munakata, 2011). Think of Hannah, an infant whose parents place a teddy bear in her crib. As an infant she might simply look at the teddy bear when her parents jiggle it in front of her. Over time, she not only can see the teddy bear but also can reach for it. She might even remember that the teddy bear exists and might cry for it when it is not with her. As a toddler, when she carries it around, she is demonstrating her physical abilities to do so, as well as her capacity to use the teddy bear as a source of comfort. As an adolescent, Hannah might no longer sleep with her teddy, but she might give it a place of honor on a shelf.

As you read this chapter, remember that you are studying the development of an integrated human being, like Hannah, in whom body, mind, and emotion are interdependent. Researchers in developmental psychology are interested in the ways that these three processes—physical, cognitive, and socioemotional—change over the human life span. Their work centrally probes how a person's *age* relates to different aspects of his or her physical, cognitive, and socioemotional characteristics. Because age is a variable that cannot be experimentally manipulated, studies on the relationship between age and other characteristics are by definition correlational in nature. This aspect of developmental research carries important implications for research design, as we now consider.

Research Methods in Developmental Psychology

Human development is about the changes that occur with age. To know what age-related differences mean, however, we must consider the kind of research presented.

In *cross-sectional studies,* a number of people of different ages are assessed at one point in time, and differences are noted. By examining how the ages of these individuals relate to the characteristics measured, researchers can find out whether younger individuals differ from older ones. Age differences, however, are not the same as developmental change.

One problem in cross-sectional studies is cohort effects. *Cohort effects* are differences between individuals that stem not necessarily from their ages but from the historical and social time period in which they were born and developed (Schaie, 2009, 2010, 2011). For instance, individuals who were born in the 1940s might be less likely to have attended college than those born in the 1990s. Differences observed between these groups might be due not to their age but rather to these differing experiences. Consider your own cohort. How might experiences that are unique to your age group lead you and your peers to be different from other generations?

In contrast to a cross-sectional study, a *longitudinal study,* as described in Chapter 2, assesses the same participants multiple times over a lengthy period. A longitudinal study can find out not only whether age groups differ but also whether the same individuals change with respect to a particular characteristic as they age.

To get a sense of the difference between a cross-sectional and a longitudinal design, consider a large-scale cross-sectional U.S. study of approximately 28,000 individuals aged 18 to 88 indicating that happiness increased with age (Y. Yang, 2008). About 33 percent of the participants were very happy at 88 years of age, compared to only about 24 percent of those in their late teens and early 20s. From this work we *might* conclude that people become happier as they age, but this conclusion is limited by the cross-sectional nature of the design used. We simply do not know if the happy 88-year-olds were less happy when they were in their 20s. Indeed, it may be the case that these individuals were very happy even in their 20s. Perhaps the explanation is that relatively more happy people survive into their senior years. Clearly, strong statements about developmental changes in psychological characteristics require longitudinal designs. Using these and other methods, human development researchers have grappled with three big questions that are relevant to all of psychology, as we consider next.

How Do Nature and Nurture Influence Development?

● **nature** An individual's biological inheritance, especially his or her genes.

● **nurture** An individual's environmental and social experiences.

Developmental psychologists seek to understand how nature and nurture influence development. **Nature** refers to a person's biological inheritance, especially his or her genes; **nurture** refers to the individual's environmental and social experiences. In Chapter 3 we considered the concept of a *genotype* (the individual's genetic heritage—his or her actual genetic material). We also examined the idea of a *phenotype* (the person's observable characteristics). The phenotype shows the contributions of both nature (genetic heritage) and nurture (environment). The genotype may be expressed in various ways, depending on both the environment and characteristics of the genotype itself. Recall, for example, that a recessive gene, though part of the genotype, will not show up in the phenotype at all if it is paired with a dominant gene.

In a long debate over the influence of nature (heredity) versus nurture (environment), some commentators have gone so far as to suggest that parenting—an environmental factor—is not especially important for children's development. To read about this debate, see the Critical Controversy.

One illustration of the role of environmental influences in genetic expression is a genetic condition called *phenylketonuria* (PKU). Caused by two recessive genes, PKU results in an inability to metabolize the amino acid phenylalanine (a major component of the artificial sweetener aspartame, which substitutes for sugar in soft drinks and many other products you might consume). Decades ago, it was thought that the genotype for PKU led to a specific phenotype—namely, irreversible brain damage, developmental disabilities, and seizures. However, scientists now know that as long as individuals with the genotype for PKU stick to a diet that is very low in phenylalanine, these phenotypic characteristics can be avoided (Grosse, 2010). Thus, environmental precautions can change the phenotype associated with this genotype.

PKU demonstrates that a person's observable and measurable characteristics (phenotype) might not reflect his or her genetic heritage (genotype) very precisely because of the particular experiences the person has had. Instead, for each genotype, a *range* of phenotypes may be expressed, depending on environmental factors. In concrete terms, an individual can inherit the genetic potential to grow very tall, but good nutrition, an environmental factor, is important for achieving that potential. The person whom we see before us emerges through an interplay of genetic and environmental experiences. In short, development is the product of nature, nurture, and the complex interaction of the two (Diamond, Casey, & Munakata, 2011).

One of the factors that must be taken into account in the development process is the developer himself or herself, as we consider next.

What Is the Developer's Role in Development?

Nature and nurture have at least one thing in common. Because we cannot pick our genes or our parents, each of us would seem to be stuck with the genes and environment we got at birth. However, importantly, the developing human being also has a role to play in development (Brandstadter, 2006). Although you might think of nature and nurture as the raw ingredients of yourself as a person, the fact is that you take those ingredients and make them into the person you are.

Indeed, some psychologists believe that we can develop beyond what our genetic inheritance and our environment give us. They argue that a key aspect of development involves seeking optimal experiences in life (Armor, Massey, & Sackett, 2008). They cite examples of individuals who go beyond what life has given them to achieve extraordinary things. These individuals build and shape their own lives, authoring a unique developmental path and sometimes transforming negative characteristics into real strengths.

In our efforts to experience our lives in optimal ways, we develop *life themes* that involve activities, social relationships, and life goals (Csikszentmihalyi & Rathunde, 1998; Rathunde & Csikszentmihalyi, 2006). Some individuals are more successful at

CRITICAL CONTROVERSY

Genes or Superparents: Which Matters More to Kids?

Compared to past generations, today's parents are more likely to be preoccupied with their children's lives and behaviors. Whereas decades ago parents might have worried about getting their children into the right college, today some parents obsess over enrolling their little ones in the right preschool and kindergarten. Is this obsession necessary to ensure healthy development? Some experts would give that question a definite no.

Judith Harris (1998), author of the book *The Nurture Assumption,* argues that what parents do makes no difference in children's behavior. Spank them. Hug them. Read to them. Ignore them. It will not influence how they turn out, because genes and peers are far more important than parents in children's development, Harris maintains. Similarly, developmental researcher Sandra Scarr (1992, 2000) suggests that "superparenting" is unnecessary. She asserts that the genotype is so strong that it makes most environmental experiences unimportant. Scarr suggests that the only parenting that has a negative effect on a child is parenting that is far outside the normal range—for example, chronic physical abuse. Apart from such extremes, Scarr asserts, genes are the primary determinant of developmental outcomes. So, can parents take a breather? Not necessarily.

Claims such as those of Harris and Scarr have met with a firestorm of criticism. Diana Baumrind (1993) countered that "good enough" parenting *is not* good enough, and she cited evidence that

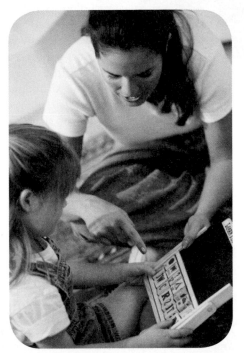

highly demanding and highly responsive parents are more likely to have high-achieving and socially well-adjusted children. A longitudinal study by W. Andrew Collins and his colleagues (2000) supported Baumrind's claims; it showed that even with genetic influences taken into account, parenting practices made a difference in children's lives. Baumrind also expressed concern that Scarr's opinion might lead parents to give up the important responsibility of childrearing or to conclude that their efforts on behalf of their children are not worthwhile. So, in the view of those in the Baumrind and Collins camp, although a person's genetic heritage certainly has a role to play in development, we cannot cuddle our genes, be scolded by them, laugh with them, or look to them for advice. For those important aspects of experience we need parents—super or otherwise (Sandler, Wolchik, & Schoenfelder, 2011).

Despite the strong criticism of her views, Harris (2009) recently published a revised and updated edition of her earlier book, restating her claim that parents matter far less than most people think.

WHAT DO YOU THINK?

- If you have children or decide to have them in the future, how might the information in this Critical Controversy affect your approach to parenting?
- Why might today's parents be more likely than parents in the past to try to be superparents?

constructing optimal life experiences than others. Among the public figures who have succeeded are Martin Luther King, Jr., Mother Teresa, Nelson Mandela, Bill and Melinda Gates, and Oprah Winfrey. These individuals looked for and found meaningful life themes as they developed. Their lives were not restricted to simple biological survival or to simply settling for their particular life situations. Many of them, in fact, faced hardships early in life and yet managed to contribute to the world in meaningful ways.

A developmental question that naturally flows from this discussion is, are early or later life experiences more important to a person's development over the life span? Let's dig into that issue.

Are Early or Later Life Experiences More Important in Development?

A key question in developmental psychology centers on the extent to which childhood experiences (nurture) determine aspects of later life. If early experiences provide the foundation for later development, does that mean that childhood experiences are

Microsoft founder Bill Gates and his wife, Melinda, have quested after—and carved out—meaningful life experiences as they have progressed through their development.

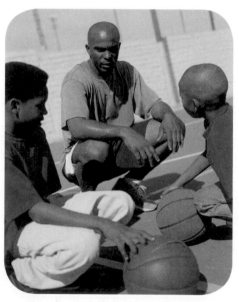

Having a supportive relationship with a parent or a competent adult outside the home can contribute to childhood resilience.

● **resilience** A person's ability to recover from or adapt to difficult times.

test yourself

1. What three broad processes of change do developmental psychologists study?
2. Why are longitudinal studies commonly used to investigate developmental questions? What are the limitations of cross-sectional studies with respect to studying such questions?
3. In what ways can the developing individual play a role in his or her own development?

likely to influence (and limit or damage) us for the rest of our lives? Developmental psychologists debate whether early experiences or later experiences are more important (Kagan, 2010; Staudinger & Gluck, 2011; R. A. Thompson, 2010). Some believe that unless infants receive warm, nurturing caregiving in their first year or so of life, they will not develop to their full potential (Phillips & Lowenstein, 2011; Sroufe, Coffino, & Carlson, 2010). Other psychologists emphasize the power of later experience, arguing that important development occurs later on in life as well (Scheibe & Carstensen, 2010). Life-span developmentalists, who study both children and adults, in fact stress that researchers have given too little attention to adult development and aging. They argue that although early experiences contribute powerfully to development, they are not necessarily more influential than later experiences (Park & Huang, 2010; Schaie, 2010, 2011). These experts say that both early and later experiences make significant contributions to development and thus no one is doomed to be a prisoner of his or her childhood.

In approaching the question of which life-span experiences—early or later—are more important, we must look at the wide variation that can occur in individual responses to any particular life event. Consider, for example, the relationship between parental divorce and the emotional adjustment of children. According to leading researcher E. Mavis Hetherington, adjustment difficulties characterize approximately 25 percent of children and adolescents of divorced parents, compared with only 10 percent of children and adolescents of non-divorced parents (Hetherington, 2006; Hetherington & Stanley-Hagen, 2002). Note that this finding means that approximately 75 percent of children of divorced parents do *not* have adjustment problems. Among the factors that predict better adjustment for children in divorced families are harmony between the divorced partners, warm and attentive parenting, and the child's own personality characteristics (Amato, 2006; Hetherington, 2006; Ziol-Guest, 2009).

A key concept in understanding the role of negative early experiences in later development is resilience. **Resilience** refers to a person's ability to recover from or adapt to difficult times. Resilience means that even in the face of adversity, a person shows signs of positive functioning (Ong, Bergeman, & Boker, 2009; Vetter & others, 2010). Resilience can refer to factors that compensate for difficulties, buffering the individual from the effects of these, or to the fact that moderate difficulties may themselves help to promote development (Blum & Blum, 2009). Despite undergoing hardship time and time again, resilient children grow up to be capable adults. Researchers have found that resilient children have one or more advantages—such as strong intellectual functioning or a close, supportive relationship with a parent or other adult—that help them to overcome their disadvantages (Masten, 2007, 2009; Masten, Obradovic, & Burt, 2006). Although often studied as an aspect of childhood and adolescence (Montgomery, 2010), resilience can also characterize development in adulthood and old age (McFadden & Basting, 2010; Ryff & Singer, 2009).

2· CHILD DEVELOPMENT

In this section we focus on the three fundamental developmental processes—physical, cognitive, and socioemotional—of childhood. To understand childhood in all its dimensions, we must begin before it even starts, with *prenatal* ("before birth") development. Childhood continues through the elementary school years. To begin exploring child development, we first trace the ways that we grow and change physically before the life span starts, during prenatal development.

Prenatal Development

Prenatal development is a time of astonishing change, beginning with conception. *Conception* occurs when a single sperm cell from the male merges with the female's ovum (egg) to produce a *zygote,* a single cell with 23 chromosomes from the mother and 23 from the father.

THE COURSE OF PRENATAL DEVELOPMENT

Development from zygote to fetus is divided into three periods:

- *Germinal period—weeks 1 and 2:* The germinal period begins with conception. After 1 week and many cell divisions, the zygote is made up of 100 to 150 cells. By the end of 2 weeks, the mass of cells has attached to the uterine wall.

- *Embryonic period—weeks 3 through 8:* The rate of cell differentiation intensifies, support systems for the cells develop, and the beginnings of organs appear (Figure 9.1a). In the third week, the neural tube, which eventually becomes the spinal cord, starts to take shape. Within the first 28 days after conception, the neural tube is formed and closes, encased inside the embryo. By the end of the embryonic period, the heart begins to beat, the arms and legs become more differentiated, the face starts to form, and the intestinal tract appears (Figure 9.1b).

- *Fetal period—months 2 through 9:* At 2 months, the fetus is the size of a kidney bean and has started to move around. At 4 months, the fetus is 5 inches long and weighs about 5 ounces (Figure 9.1c). At 6 months, the fetus has grown to a pound and a half. The last three months of pregnancy are the time when organ functioning increases and the fetus puts on considerable weight and size, adding baby fat.

Although it floats in a well-protected womb, the fetus is not immune to the larger environment surrounding the mother. Sometimes, as we will now see, normal development is disrupted by environmental insults.

THREATS TO THE FETUS

A *teratogen* is any agent that causes a birth defect. Teratogens include chemical substances ingested by the mother (such as nicotine if the mother smokes and alcohol if

(a)   (b)   (c)

FIGURE 9.1   From Embryo to Fetus (*a*) At about 4 weeks, an embryo is about 0.2 inch (less than 1 centimeter) long. The head, eyes, and ears begin to show; the head and neck are half the length of the body; the shoulders will be located where the whitish arm buds are attached. (*b*) At 8 weeks, the developing individual is about 1.6 inches (4 centimeters) long and has reached the end of its embryonic phase. It has become a fetus. Everything that will be found in the fully developed human being has now begun to form. The fetal stage is a period of growth and perfection of detail. The heart has been beating for a month, and the muscles have just begun their first exercises. (*c*) At 4½ months, the fetus is just over 7 inches (about 18 centimeters) long. When the thumb comes close to the mouth, the head may turn, and the lips and tongue begin their sucking motions—a reflex for survival.

The photograph shows Tiffany Field massaging a newborn infant. Field's research has demonstrated the power of massage in improving the developmental outcome of at-risk infants. Under her direction, the Touch Research Institute in Miami, Florida, investigates the role of touch in a number of domains of health and well-being.

she drinks) and certain illnesses (such as rubella, or German measles). Substances that are ingested by the mother can lead to serious birth defects. For example, *fetal alcohol spectrum disorders* (FASD) are a cluster of abnormalities and problems that appear in the offspring of mothers who drink alcohol heavily during pregnancy. These abnormalities include a small head, defects in the limbs and heart, and below-average intelligence (Klingenberg & others, 2010). Heavy drinking is linked to FASD, but even moderate drinking can lead to serious problems (Sayal & others, 2007). The best advice for a woman who is pregnant or thinking of becoming pregnant is to avoid alcohol.

The effects of chemical teratogens depend on the timing of exposure. The body part or organ system that is developing when the fetus encounters the teratogen is most vulnerable (Rojas & others, 2010; Torchinsky & Toder, 2010). Genetic characteristics may buffer or worsen the effects of a teratogen. Perhaps most importantly, the environment the child encounters *after birth* can influence the ultimate effects of prenatal insults.

Sexually transmitted infections (STIs) also threaten the fetus. Some STIs, such as gonorrhea, can be transferred to the baby during delivery. Others, including syphilis and the human immunodeficiency virus (HIV), the virus that causes AIDS, can also infect the fetus while it is in the womb. Besides transmission of infections to the fetus and newborns, STI exposure enhances the risk of stillbirth, as well as a number of other problems, such as eye infections and blindness (in the case of gonorrhea). Many STIs also increase the risk of preterm birth.

A *preterm infant,* one who is born prior to 37 weeks after conception, may also be at risk for developmental difficulties. Whether a preterm infant will have developmental problems is a complex issue, however. Very small preterm infants are more likely than their larger counterparts to have developmental problems (Minde & Zelkowitz, 2008). Preterm infants who grow up in poverty are more likely to have problems than are those who live in better socioeconomic conditions (Madan & others, 2006). Postnatal experience plays a crucial role in determining the ultimate effects of preterm birth. For example, research has shown that massage can improve developmental outcomes for premature infants (Field, Diego, & Hernandez-Reif, 2010).

Physical Development in Childhood

Human infants are the world's most helpless newborns. One reason for their helplessness is that they are born not quite finished. Our enormous brain sets humans apart from other animals. Getting that big brain out of the relatively small birth canal is a challenge that nature has met by sending human babies out of the womb before the brain has fully developed. The first months and years of life allow the developing human (and his or her environment) to put the finishing touches on that important organ.

REFLEXES

Newborns come into the world equipped with several genetically wired reflexes that are crucial for survival. Babies are born with the ability to suck and swallow. If they are dropped in water, they will naturally hold their breath, contract their throats to keep water out, and move their arms and legs to stay afloat at least briefly. Some reflexes persist throughout life—coughing, blinking, and yawning, for example. Others, such as automatically grasping something that touches the fingers, disappear in the months following birth as higher brain functions mature and infants develop voluntary control over many behaviors. Figure 9.2 shows some examples of reflexes.

MOTOR AND PERCEPTUAL SKILLS

Relative to the rest of the body, a newborn's head is gigantic, and it flops around uncontrollably. Within 12 months, the infant becomes capable of sitting upright, standing, stooping, climbing, and often walking. During the second year, growth decelerates, but

Rooting	Gripping	Toe curling	Moro or startle	Galant
What provokes the response? Stroking of the infant's cheek	*What provokes the response?* Something that is placed in the infant's hand	*What provokes the response?* Stroking of the inner or outer sole of the infant's foot	*What provokes the response?* Sudden noise or movement	*What provokes the response?* Stroking of the infant's lower back, next to the spinal cord
What the infant does Head turns in the direction of the touch, and the infant opens his or her mouth for feeding.	*What the infant does* The infant grasps the item and can hold on very well—almost enough to support his or her own weight.	*What the infant does* If the inner sole is stroked, the infant curls his or her toes. If the outer sole is stroked, the toes spread out.	*What the infant does* The infant throws his or her head back and arms and legs out (and then cries).	*What the infant does* The infant curves toward the side that was stroked—and looks like a fencer when doing so.

FIGURE 9.2   Some Infant Reflexes Infants are born with a number of reflexes to get them through life, and they are incredibly cute when they perform them. These reflexes disappear as infants mature.

rapid gains occur in such activities as running and climbing. Researchers used to think that motor milestones—such as sitting up, crawling, and walking—unfolded as part of a genetic plan. However, psychologists now recognize that motor development is not the consequence of nature or nurture alone (Adolph, Berger, & Leo, 2010; Karasik & others, 2010).

For example, environmental experiences play a role in reaching and grasping (Needham, 2009). In one study, 3-month-old infants participated in play sessions wearing "sticky mittens"—mittens with palms that stick to the edges of toys and allow the infants to pick up the toys (Needham, Barrett, & Peterman, 2002) (Figure 9.3). Infants who participated in sessions with the mittens grasped and manipulated objects earlier in their development than a control group of infants who did not have the "mitten" experience. The experienced infants looked at the objects longer, swatted at them, and were more likely to put the objects in their mouths.

Infants are active developers, and their motor and perceptual skills develop together and mutually promote each other. Because a baby can see a new toy, she wants to reach out for it, and her motivation to do so may foster the development of her motor abilities. Babies are continually coordinating their movements with information they perceive through their senses to learn how to maintain their balance, reach for objects in space, and move across various surfaces and terrains (Adolph & others, 2009). Action in turn informs perception. For example, holding and touching an object while watching it helps infants to learn about its texture, size, and hardness. Moving from place to place in the environment teaches babies how objects and people look from different perspectives and whether surfaces will support their weight (Gibson, 2001).

Psychologists face a daunting challenge in studying infant perception. Infants cannot talk, so how can scientists learn whether they can see or hear certain things? Psychologists who study infants have no choice but to become extraordinarily clever methodologists, relying on what infants can do to understand what they know (S. P. Johnson, 2010a, 2010b; Slater & others,

FIGURE 9.3   Infants' Use of "Sticky Mittens" to Explore Objects Amy Needham and her colleagues (2002) found that "sticky mittens" enhance young infants' object exploration skills.

FIGURE 9.4   Dendritic Spreading

Note the increase in connections among neurons over the course of the first two years of life. Reprinted by permission of the publisher from *The Postnatal Development of the Human Cerebral Cortex,* Volumes I–VIII, by Jesse LeRoy Conel, Cambridge, MA.: Harvard University Press, Copyright © 1939, 1941, 1947, 1951, 1955, 1959, 1963, 1967 by the President and Fellows of Harvard College. Copyright © renewed 1967, 1969, 1975, 1979, 1983, 1987, 1991.

| At birth | 1 month | 3 months | 15 months | 24 months |

● **preferential looking** A research technique that involves giving an infant a choice of what object to look at.

2011). One thing infants can do is look. The **preferential looking** technique involves giving an infant a choice of what object to look at. If an infant shows a reliable preference for one stimulus (say, a picture of a face) over another (a scrambled picture of a face) when these are repeatedly presented in differing locations, we can infer that the infant can tell the two images apart.

Using this technique, researchers have found that as early as *7 days old,* infants are already engaged in organized perception of faces and are able to put together sights and sounds. If presented with two faces with mouths moving, infants will watch the face whose mouth matches the sounds they are hearing (Pascalls & Kelly, 2008). At 3 months, infants prefer real faces to scrambled faces, and their mother's face to a stranger's (Slater, Field, & Reif-Hernandez, 2007). These techniques have provided a great deal of information about infants' remarkable abilities, but they are also limited. Research using brain imaging suggests that infants may know more than even these clever strategies reveal.

THE BRAIN

As an infant plays, crawls, shakes a rattle, smiles, and frowns, his or her brain is changing dramatically. At birth and in early infancy, the brain's 100 billion neurons have only minimal connections. The infant brain literally is ready and waiting for the experiences that will create these connections (C. A. Nelson, 2011). During the first two years of life, the dendrites of the neurons branch out, and the neurons become far more interconnected (Figure 9.4). Myelination, the process of encasing axons with fat cells (the myelin sheath described in Chapter 3), begins prenatally and continues after birth well into adolescence and young adulthood (Tamnes & others, 2010).

During childhood, *synaptic connections* increase dramatically (C. A. Nelson, 2011). Recall from Chapter 3 that a *synapse* is a gap between neurons that is bridged by chemical neurotransmitters. Nearly twice as many synapses are available as will ever be used (Huttenlocher & Dabholkar, 1997). The connections that are made become stronger and will survive; the unused ones will be replaced by other neural pathways or disappear. In the language of neuroscience, these unused connections will be "pruned." Figure 9.5 illustrates the steep growth and later pruning of synapses during infancy in specific areas of the brain.

Brain-imaging studies demonstrate that children's brains also undergo amazing anatomical changes (Gogtay & Thompson, 2010; Paus, 2009). Repeated brain scans of the same children for up to 4 years of age show that the amount of brain material in some areas can nearly double within as little as a year, followed by a drastic loss of tissue as unneeded cells are purged and the brain continues to reorganize itself. From 3 to 6 years of age, the most rapid growth takes place in the frontal lobe areas, which are involved in planning and organizing new actions and in maintaining attention to tasks (Gogtay & Thompson, 2010; P. M. Thompson & others, 2000). These brain changes are not simply the result of nature; new experiences in the world also promote brain

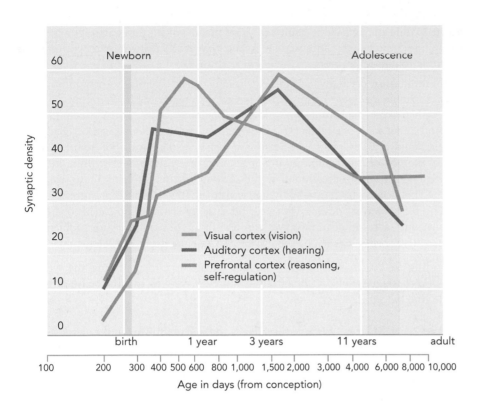

FIGURE 9.5 Synaptic Density in the Human Brain from Infancy to Adulthood The graph shows the dramatic increase and then pruning in synaptic density in three regions of the brain: visual cortex, auditory cortex, and prefrontal cortex. Synaptic density is believed to be an important indication of the extent of connectivity between neurons.

development (C. A. Nelson, 2011). Thus, as in other areas of development, nature and nurture operate together in the development of the child's brain (Diamond, Casey, & Munakata, 2011).

A key activity that children perform with their brains is to think. The quality of a child's thinking develops in childhood, as we consider next.

Cognitive Development in Childhood

Cognitive development refers to how thought, intelligence, and language processes change as people mature. *Cognition* refers to the way individuals think and also to their cognitive skills and abilities. Jean Piaget (1896–1980), the famous Swiss developmental psychologist, presented a theory of cognitive development that has had a lasting impact on our understanding of how children think. His theory traced cognitive development through childhood into adulthood.

PIAGET'S THEORY OF COGNITIVE DEVELOPMENT

Piaget believed that children *actively construct* their cognitive world as they go through a series of stages. In Piaget's view, children use schemas to make sense of their experience.

Recall from Chapter 7 that a *schema* is a mental concept or framework that organizes information and provides a structure for interpreting it. Schemas are expressed as various behaviors and skills that the child can exercise in relation to objects or situations. For example, sucking is a simple early schema. More complex schemas that occur later in childhood include blowing, crawling, and hiding. In adulthood, schemas may represent more complex expectations and beliefs about the world.

Piaget (1952) described two processes responsible for how people use and adapt their schemas:

■ **Assimilation** occurs when individuals incorporate new information into existing knowledge. That is, people *assimilate* the environment into a schema. Assimilation means that, faced with a new experience, the person applies old ways of doing things. For infants, this might mean applying the schema of *sucking* to whatever new thing they encounter. For an adolescent, it might mean using the skills

● **assimilation** An individual's incorporation of new information into existing knowledge.

Jean Piaget (1896–1980) Piaget, the famous Swiss developmental psychologist, changed the way we think about the development of children's minds.

● **accommodation** An individual's adjustment of his or her schemas to new information.

learned while playing video games to drive a car. For an adult it might mean solving a conflict with a spouse using ways that worked in the past with friends or previous romantic partners.

■ **Accommodation** occurs when individuals adjust their schemas to new information. That is, people *accommodate* their schemas to the environment. Accommodation means that rather than using one's old ways of doing things, a new experience promotes new ways of dealing with experience. Existing schemas can be changed and new schemas can be developed in response to new experiences. For example, after several months of experience, the infant who has been sticking everything in her mouth might begin to accommodate the sucking schema by being more selective with it. The adolescent who has typically gone with the flow of social pressure might develop a new way of dealing with peer pressure by standing up for his or her beliefs. For an adult, accommodation may mean rethinking old strategies for problem solving when a new challenge, such as the loss of a job or the onset of illness, presents itself.

According to Piaget, we go through four stages in understanding the world (Figure 9.6). Each stage involves a qualitatively different way of making sense of the world than the one before it.

● **sensorimotor stage** Piaget's first stage of cognitive development, lasting from birth to about 2 years of age, during which infants construct an understanding of the world by coordinating sensory experiences with motor (physical) actions.

Sensorimotor Stage   Piaget's first stage, the **sensorimotor stage,** lasts from birth to about 2 years of age. In this stage, infants construct an understanding of the world by coordinating sensory experiences (such as seeing and hearing) with motor (physical) actions—hence the term *sensorimotor*. As newborns they have little more than reflexive patterns with which to work. By the end of this stage, 2-year-olds show complex sensorimotor patterns and are beginning to use symbols or words in their thinking.

Object permanence is Piaget's term for the crucial accomplishment of understanding that objects and events continue to exist even when they cannot directly be seen, heard, or touched. Piaget believed that "out of sight" literally was "out of mind" for very young infants. Object permanence is an enormous developmental milestone. In the absence of

Sensorimotor Stage	**Preoperational Stage**	**Concrete Operational Stage**	**Formal Operational Stage**
The infant constructs an understanding of the world by coordinating sensory experiences with physical actions. An infant progresses from reflexive, instinctual action at birth to the beginning of symbolic thought toward the end of the stage.	The child begins to represent the world with words and images. These words and images reflect increased symbolic thinking and go beyond the connection of sensory information and physical action.	The child can now reason logically about concrete events and classify objects into different sets.	The adolescent reasons in more abstract, idealistic, and logical ways.
Birth to 2 Years of Age	**2 to 7 Years of Age**	**7 to 11 Years of Age**	**11 Years of Age Through Adulthood**

FIGURE 9.6   Piaget's Four Stages of Cognitive Development Jean Piaget described how human beings, through development, become ever more sophisticated thinkers about the world.

FIGURE 9.7 **Object Permanence** Piaget regarded object permanence as one of infancy's landmark cognitive accomplishments. According to Piaget, for this 5-month-old boy, out of sight is literally out of mind. The infant looks at the toy dog (*left*), but when his view of the toy is blocked (*right*), he does not search for it. Piaget assumed that if the child does not search for the toy, the child does not know the object still exists. We will investigate this assumption a little later in this chapter.

object permanence, the world and its objects change from one moment to the next. Once the infant knows that objects still exist even if he or she cannot see them, the infant can think about future events, such as, "When will I see Mommy again?" The most common way to study object permanence was to show an infant an interesting toy and then cover the toy with a blanket. Piaget reasoned that if infants understood that the toy still existed, they would try to uncover it (Figure 9.7).

Preoperational Stage Piaget's second stage of cognitive development, the **preoperational stage,** lasts from approximately 2 to 7 years of age. Preoperational thought is more symbolic than sensorimotor thought. In preschool years, children begin to represent their world with words, images, and drawings. Thus, their thoughts begin to exceed simple connections of sensorimotor information and physical action.

The type of symbolic thinking that children are able to accomplish during this stage is limited. They still cannot perform what Piaget called *operations,* by which he meant mental representations that are reversible. Preoperational children have difficulty understanding that reversing an action may restore the original conditions from which the action began.

A well-known test of whether a child can think "operationally" is to present a child with two identical beakers, A and B, filled with liquid to the same height (Figure 9.8).

● **preoperational stage** Piaget's second stage of cognitive development, lasting from about 2 to 7 years of age, during which thought is more symbolic than sensorimotor thought.

FIGURE 9.8 **Piaget's Conservation Task** The beaker test determines whether a child can think operationally   that is, can mentally reverse action and understand conservation of the substance. (*a*) Two identical beakers are presented to the child, each containing the same amount of liquid. As the child watches, the experimenter pours the liquid from B into C, which is taller and thinner than A and B. (*b*) The experimenter then asks the child whether beakers A and C have the same amount of liquid. The preoperational child says no. When asked to point to the beaker that has more liquid, the child points to the tall, thin one.

Next to them is a third beaker, C. Beaker C is tall and thin, whereas beakers A and B are short and wide. The liquid is poured from B into C, and the child is asked whether the amounts in A and C are the same. The 4-year-old child invariably says that the amount of liquid in the tall, thin beaker (C) is greater than that in the short, wide beaker (A). The 8-year-old child consistently says the amounts are the same. The 4-year-old child, a preoperational thinker, cannot mentally reverse the pouring action; that is, she cannot imagine the liquid going back from container C to container B. Piaget said that such a child has not grasped the concept of *conservation,* a belief in the permanence of certain attributes of objects despite superficial changes.

To sharpen your sense of how operational thinking differs from preoperational thought, consider the following example. Babysitting for two thirsty 4-year-olds, you might give them each the same amount of apple juice poured into two different cups, one tall and thin and the other short and wide. Try as you might to explain to them that the amounts are the same, they will fight over the tall, thin cup because *it looks like more*. However, in the same situation, older children—who are more sophisticated, operational thinkers— would not bat an eye, because they understand that the amounts are equal.

Children's thought in the preoperational stage is egocentric—not in the sense that they are self-centered or arrogant but because preoperational children cannot put themselves in someone else's shoes or take another person's mental state into account. Preoperational thinking is also intuitive, meaning that preoperational children make judgments based on gut feelings rather than logic. In reaching a basic level of operational understanding, children progress to the third of Piaget's cognitive stages.

● **concrete operational stage** Piaget's third stage of cognitive development, lasting from about 7 to 11 years of age, during which the individual uses operations and replaces intuitive reasoning with logical reasoning in concrete situations.

Concrete Operational Stage
Piaget's **concrete operational stage** (7 to 11 years of age) involves using operations and replacing intuitive reasoning with logical reasoning in concrete situations. Children in the concrete operational stage can successfully complete the beaker task described above. They are able to imagine the operation of reversing the pouring of the liquid back into the wide beaker. Many of the concrete operations identified by Piaget are related to the properties of objects. For instance, when playing with Play-doh, the child in the concrete operational stage realizes that *the amount* of Play-doh is not changed by changing its shape.

One important skill at this stage of reasoning is the ability to classify or divide things into different sets or subsets and to consider their interrelations. Children in the concrete operational stage might enjoy playing games that involve sorting objects into types and identifying objects that do not fit with a group. Concrete operational thought involves logical reasoning in concrete but not hypothetical contexts. According to Piaget, this kind of abstract, logical reasoning occurs in the fourth, and final, cognitive stage.

● **formal operational stage** Piaget's fourth stage of cognitive development, which begins at 11 to 15 years of age and continues through the adult years; it features thinking about things that are not concrete, making predictions, and using logic to come up with hypotheses about the future.

Formal Operational Stage
Individuals enter the **formal operational stage** of cognitive development at 11 to 15 years of age. This stage continues through the adult years. Formal operational thought is more abstract and logical than concrete operational thought. Most important, formal operational thinking includes thinking about things that are not concrete, making predictions, and using logic to come up with hypotheses about the future.

Unlike elementary schoolchildren, adolescents can conceive of hypothetical, purely abstract possibilities. This type of thinking is called *idealistic* because it involves comparing how things are to how they might be. Adolescents also think more logically. They begin to think more as a scientist thinks, devising plans to solve problems and systematically testing solutions. Piaget called this type of problem solving *hypothetical-deductive reasoning*. The phrase denotes adolescents' ability to develop hypotheses, or best hunches, about ways to solve a problem such as an algebraic equation. It also denotes their ability to systematically deduce, or come to a conclusion about, the best path for solving the problem. In contrast, before adolescence, children are more likely to solve problems by trial and error. Many of the topics we covered in Chapter 8 on thinking and problem solving fall into Piaget's formal operational stage.

In summary, over the course of Piaget's four developmental stages, a person progresses from sensorimotor cognition to abstract, idealistic, and logical thought. Piaget based his

psychological *inquiry*

Thinking Critically About Object Permanence

Let's revisit the classic object permanence task developed by Piaget. To begin with, we can consider how the methodological aspects of this task might have led Piaget to underestimate infants' abilities. Remember that from Piaget's perspective, "proving" object permanence meant that the child must search for the hidden toy, reach out, and retrieve it.

Let's assume that the child has attained the developmental milestone of object permanence. That is, the child believes that the toy exists even if he or she cannot see it. What skills must the child possess in order to enact the behaviors that Piaget thought would indicate object permanence? Answer the following questions to sharpen your understanding of this landmark developmental achievement.

1. Look at the two photos. Assuming that the child does understand that the toy still exists behind the board, what behavior must the child exhibit to indicate that understanding?
2. What motor and perceptual skills are required for the child to enact those behaviors?
3. What motivational states (or goals) are required for the child to enact them?
4. If the child does not reach out for the toy even though he or she knows it still exists, what might the failure to do so mean?
5. Why do you think it took over 50 years for psychologists to question the appropriateness of Piaget's methods? What other methods, beyond Piaget's classic object permanence task, might a researcher use to demonstrate object permanence?

stages on careful observation of children's behavior, but there is always room to evaluate theory and research. Let's consider the current thinking about Piaget's theories of cognitive development.

EVALUATING PIAGET'S THEORY

Piaget opened up a new way of looking at how the human mind develops (P. H. Miller, 2011). We owe him for a long list of masterful concepts that have enduring power and fascination. These include the concepts of schemas, assimilation, accommodation, cognitive stages, object permanence, egocentrism, and conservation. We also owe Piaget for the currently accepted vision of children as active, constructive thinkers who play a role in their own development.

Nevertheless, just as other psychological theories have been criticized and amended, so have Piaget's. As methods have improved for assessing infants and children, researchers have found that many cognitive abilities emerge earlier in children than Piaget envisioned (Bauer, Larkina, & Deocampo, 2011; de Hevia & Spelke, 2010; Meltzoff, 2011; Quinn, 2011). Piaget's object permanence task, for example, has been criticized for not giving infants a chance to show their stuff. To get a sense of the limitations of Piaget's task, check out the Psychological Inquiry above.

Renée Baillargeon (1997; Baillargeon & others, 2009, 2011) has documented that infants as young as 3 months of age know that objects continue to exist even when hidden, and that these very young infants have expectations about objects in the world. In one study (Luo & Baillargeon, 2005), researchers showed 3-month-old infants a puppet show featuring Minnie Mouse. In the center of the stage was a flat cardboard cut-out of a castle. Minnie entered stage right and proceeded toward the castle, disappearing behind it. When Minnie went behind the castle walls from one side, the infants looked for her to come out on the other side. Their behavior suggested that even though Minnie was out of sight, she was not out of mind. Not only did these 3-month-olds realize that Minnie still existed, but they also *had expectations* about where she was heading.

Just as Piaget may have *under*estimated infants, he may have *over*estimated adolescents and adults. Formal operational thought does not emerge as consistently and universally in early adolescence as Piaget envisioned (Kuhn, 2008, 2009), and many adolescents and even adults do not reason as logically as Piaget proposed.

Piaget did not think that culture and education play important roles in children's cognitive development. For Piaget, the child's active interaction with the physical world was all that was needed to go through these stages. The Russian psychologist Lev Vygotsky (1962) took a different approach, recognizing that cognitive development is very much an interpersonal process that happens in a cultural context (Gauvain & Parke, 2010). Vygotsky thought of children as apprentice thinkers who develop as they interact in dialogue with more knowledgeable others, such as parents and teachers (Daniels, 2011; Holzman, 2009). Vygotsky theorized that these expert thinkers spur cognitive development by interacting with a child in a way that is just above the level of sophistication the child has mastered. In effect, these interactions provide *scaffolding* that allows the child's cognitive abilities to be built higher and higher. Teachers and parents, then, provide a framework for thinking that is always just at a level the child can strive to attain.

Furthermore, in Vygotsky's view, the goal of cognitive development is to learn the skills that will allow the individual to be competent in his or her particular culture. Expert thinkers are not simply guiding a child into a level of cognitive sophistication but also, along the way, sharing with the child important aspects of culture, such as language and customs. For Vygotsky, a child is not simply learning to think about the world—he or she is learning to think about *his or her own world*.

Socioemotional Development in Childhood

Emotionally speaking, an infant does not enter the world as a blank slate. When we observe the newborns behind the window of a hospital nursery, one thing is clear: Humans differ from one another in terms of their emotional demeanor from the very beginning of life. Some are easygoing, and some are prone to distress. Furthermore, in the earliest days of life, infants encounter a social network that will play an important role as they develop their sense of self and the world. To begin our exploration of the socioemotional aspects of development, we focus first on these early raw ingredients of emotional and social characteristics that are present very early in life—infant temperament and attachment.

TEMPERAMENT

● **temperament** An individual's behavioral style and characteristic way of responding.

Temperament refers to an individual's behavioral style and characteristic way of responding. There are a number of ways to think about infant temperament. For example, psychiatrists Alexander Chess and Stella Thomas (1977, 1996) identified three basic types of temperament in children:

- *The easy child* generally is in a positive mood, quickly establishes regular routines in infancy, and easily adapts to new experiences.
- *The difficult child* tends to react negatively and to cry frequently, engages in irregular daily routines, and is slow to accept new experiences.
- *The slow-to-warm-up child* has a low activity level, is somewhat negative, is inflexible, and displays a low intensity of mood.

Other researchers have suggested that we should think about infants as being high or low on different dimensions, such as *effortful control* or *self-regulation* (controlling arousal and not being easily agitated), *inhibition* (being shy and showing distress in an unfamiliar situation), and *negative affectivity* (tending to be frustrated or sad) (Kagan, 2010; Rothbart & Gartstein, 2008; Sheese & others, 2009). These emotional characteristics that a child brings into the world are thought to serve as a foundation for later personality (Evans & Rothbart, 2009). Similarly, the child's earliest social bonds might set the stage for later social relationships.

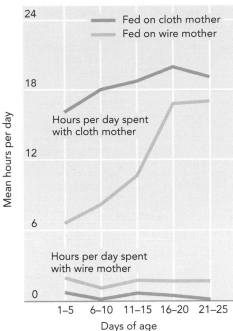

FIGURE 9.9   **Contact Time with Wire and Cloth Surrogate Mothers**
Regardless of whether the infant monkeys were fed by a wire or a cloth mother, they overwhelmingly preferred to spend contact time with the cloth mother.

ATTACHMENT IN INFANCY

Just as infants require nutrition and shelter, they need warm social interaction to survive and develop. A classic study by Harry Harlow (1958) demonstrates the essential importance of warm contact. Harlow separated infant monkeys from their mothers at birth and placed them in cages in which they had access to two artificial "mothers." One of the mothers was a physically cold wire mother; the other was a warm, fuzzy cloth mother (the "contact comfort" mother). Each mother could be outfitted with a feeding mechanism. Half of the infant monkeys were fed by the wire mother; the other half, by the cloth mother. The infant monkeys nestled close to the cloth mother and spent little time on the wire one, even if it was the wire mother that gave them milk (Figure 9.9). When afraid, the infant monkeys ran to the comfy mom.

Harlow's classic work is important because it clearly demonstrates that what the researchers described as contact comfort, not feeding, is crucial to an infant's attachment to its caregiver. This work set the stage for our modern understanding of the vital role of warm physical contact between caregivers and infants. Even if an otherwise healthy child's physical needs for food and shelter are met, the child is unlikely to thrive in the absence of warmth.

Infant attachment is the close emotional bond between an infant and its caregiver. British psychiatrist John Bowlby (1969, 1989) theorized that the infant and the mother instinctively form an attachment. For Bowlby, the newborn comes into the world equipped to stimulate the caregiver to respond; it cries, clings, smiles, and coos. Bowlby thought that this early relationship with our primary caregiver was internalized so that it served as our schema for our sense of self and the social world. Many developmental psychologists concur that such attachment during the first year provides an important foundation for later development (Fearon & others, 2010; Sroufe, Coffino, & Carlson, 2010).

Mary Ainsworth devised a way to study differences in children's attachment, called the *strange situation* (Ainsworth, 1979; Ainsworth & others, 1978). In this procedure, caregivers leave infants alone with a stranger and then return. Children's responses to this situation are used to classify their attachment style. The term **secure attachment** means that infants use the caregiver, usually the mother, as a secure base from which to explore the environment. In the strange situation, the secure infant is upset when the mother leaves, but calms down and appears happy to see her when she returns. The

● **infant attachment** The close emotional bond between an infant and its caregiver.

● **secure attachment** The ways that infants use their caregiver, usually their mother, as a secure base from which to explore the environment.

In the Hausa culture, siblings and grandmothers provide a significant amount of care for infants.

Trust versus mistrust

Developmental period: Infancy (Birth to 1½ years)

Characteristics: A sense of trust requires a feeling of physical comfort and minimal amount of fear about the future. Infants' basic needs are met by responsive, sensitive caregivers.

Autonomy versus shame and doubt

Developmental period: Toddlerhood (1½ to 3 years)

Characteristics: After gaining trust in their caregivers, infants start to discover that they have a will of their own. They assert their sense of autonomy, or independence. They realize their will. If infants are restrained too much or punished too harshly, they are likely to develop a sense of shame and doubt.

Initiative versus guilt

Developmental period: Early childhood (preschool years, ages 3–5)

Characteristics: As preschool children encounter a widening social world, they are challenged more and need to develop more purposeful behavior to cope with these challenges. Children are now asked to assume more responsibility. Uncomfortable guilt feelings may arise, though, if children are irresponsible and are made to feel too anxious.

Industry versus inferiority

Developmental period: Middle and late childhood (elementary school years, 6 years–puberty)

Characteristics: At no other time are children more enthusiastic than at the end of early childhood's period of expansive imagination. As children move into the elementary school years, they direct their energy toward mastering knowledge and intellectual skills. The danger at this stage involves feeling incompetent and unproductive.

FIGURE 9.10 Erikson's Eight Stages of Human Development Erikson changed the way psychologists think about development by tracing the process of growth over the entire life span.

Erik Erikson (1902–1994) Erikson generated one of the most important developmental theories of the twentieth century.

securely attached infant moves freely away from the mother but also keeps tabs on her by periodically glancing at her. An insecurely attached infant, in contrast, avoids the mother or is ambivalent toward her. In the strange situation, such an infant might not even notice the mother has gone, or conversely might respond with intense distress, only to rage at the mother when she returns.

One criticism of attachment theory is that it does not adequately account for cultural variations (van IJzendoorn & Sagi-Schwartz, 2008). For example, in some cultures infants show strong attachments to many people, not just to their primary caregiver. In the African Hausa culture, both grandmothers and siblings provide a significant amount of care to infants (Harkness & Super, 1995). Another critique of attachment theory is that it may not account for temperamental differences among infants that might color the attachment relationship. In addition, caregivers and infants likely share genetic characteristics, and it might be that the attachment relationship is really a product of these shared genes (Gervai, 2009). Despite such criticisms, there is ample evidence that secure attachment is important to development (Sroufe, Coffino, & Carlson, 2010; Thompson & Newton, 2009).

Given these raw ingredients of temperament and attachment, how does a human being develop in the socioemotional domain? This question was addressed by Erik Erikson, who devised a theory of what he called *psychosocial* development. Like Piaget's theory of cognitive development, Erikson's theory has guided thinking about how human beings develop in their social and emotional capacities.

ERIKSON'S THEORY OF SOCIOEMOTIONAL DEVELOPMENT

Erik Erikson (1902–1994) proposed eight psychosocial stages of development from infancy through old age. In Erikson's (1968) view, the first four stages take place in childhood; the last four, in adolescence and adulthood (Figure 9.10). One reason why Erikson's theory is so important is that he fully expected socioemotional development to occur throughout the life span. For Erikson, movement toward greater competence and maturity was a lifelong process, marked by important developmental milestones in young and middle adulthood and into old age. Each of Erikson's stages represents the developmental task that the individual must master at a particular place in the life span.

Identity versus identity confusion	Intimacy versus isolation	Generativity versus stagnation	Integrity versus despair
Developmental period: Adolescence (10–20 years)	**Developmental period:** Eary adulthood (20s, 30s)	**Developmental period:** Middle adulthood (40s, 50s)	**Developmental period:** Late adulthood (60s–)
Characteristics: Individuals are faced with finding out who they are, what they are all about, and where they are going in life. An important dimension is the exploration of alternative solutions to roles. Career exploration is important.	**Characteristics:** Individuals face the developmental task of forming intimate relationships with others. Erikson described intimacy as finding oneself yet losing oneself in another person.	**Characteristics:** A chief concern is to assist the younger generation in developing and leading useful lives.	**Characteristics:** Individuals look back and evaluate what they have done with their lives. The retrospective glances can be either positive (integrity) or negative (despair).

According to Erikson, these developmental tasks are represented by two possible outcomes, such as trust versus mistrust (Erikson's first stage). If an infant's physical and emotional needs are well taken care of, he or she will experience an enduring sense of trust in others. If, on the other hand, these needs are frustrated, the individual might carry concerns about trust throughout his or her life, with bits of this unfinished business being reflected in the rest of the stages. For Erikson, each stage is a turning point with two opposing possible outcomes: one, greater personal competence; and the other, greater weakness and vulnerability. Using Erikson's stages as a guide, let's consider the various ways that human beings develop in terms of their capacities for interpersonal relationships and emotional well-being in infancy and childhood.

Socioemotional Development in Childhood: From Trust to Industry   We examine Erikson's adolescence and adult stages later in this chapter. His four childhood stages are:

1. *Trust versus mistrust* (the first 18 months of life): Trust is built when a baby's basic needs—such as comfort, food, and warmth—are met. If infants' needs are not met by responsive, sensitive caregivers, the result is mistrust. Trust in infancy sets the stage for a lifelong expectation that the world will be a good and pleasant place to live.

2. *Autonomy versus shame and doubt* (18 months through 3 years): Children can develop either a positive sense of independence and autonomy or negative feelings of shame and doubt. In seeking autonomy, they are likely to develop a strong sense of independence. A toddler who is experiencing toilet training is learning the beginnings of self-control. The toddler's growing independence is evident in the child's insistence that no matter how difficult the task, "I can do it myself!" Similarly common is the toddler's assertion of autonomy with a simple two-letter word: "No!"

3. *Initiative versus guilt* (3 to 5 years): During these years, children's social worlds are widening. When asked to assume more responsibility for themselves, children can develop initiative. When allowed to be irresponsible or made to feel anxious, they can develop too much guilt. The preschooler is more likely to engage in imaginative play propelled by his or her own fantasies. The child may make friends of his or her own choosing for the first time.

4. *Industry versus inferiority* (age 6 to puberty): Children can achieve industry by mastering knowledge and intellectual skills. When they do not, they can feel inferior. At the end of early childhood, children are ready to turn their energy to learning academic skills. If they do not, they can develop a sense of being incompetent and unproductive. During the beginnings of elementary school, children learn the value of what Erikson called *industry,* gaining competence in academic skills and acquiring the ability to engage in self-discipline and hard work.

From Erikson's perspective, then, children should grow toward greater levels of autonomy and self-confidence as they progress from infancy to school age and beyond. At each stage, Erikson said, either parents can facilitate the child's growth or they can thwart it by being overly protective or neglectful.

EVALUATING ERIKSON'S THEORY

Like Piaget's theory, Erikson's conclusions have had their critics (Kroger, 2007). Erikson mainly practiced case study research, which some reject as the sole research foundation for his approach. Critics also argue that Erikson's attempt to capture each developmental stage with a single concept leaves out other important developmental tasks. For example, as we will see, Erikson said that the main task for young adults is to resolve a conflict between intimacy and isolation, yet another important developmental task at this life stage revolves around careers and work. Such criticisms do not tarnish Erikson's monumental contributions, however. Like Piaget, he is a giant in developmental psychology.

PARENTING AND CHILDHOOD SOCIOEMOTIONAL DEVELOPMENT

Various researchers have tried to identify styles of parenting associated with positive developmental outcomes. Diana Baumrind (1991, 1993) described four basic styles of interaction between parents and their children:

● **authoritarian parenting** A restrictive, punitive style in which the parent exhorts the child to follow the parent's directions and to value hard work and effort.

■ **Authoritarian parenting** is a strict punitive style. The authoritarian parent firmly limits and controls the child with little verbal exchange. In a difference of opinion about how to do something, for example, the authoritarian parent might say, "You do it my way or else." Children of authoritarian parents sometimes lack social skills, show poor initiative, and compare themselves with others. Importantly, culture influences the effects of authoritarian parenting. In one study (Rudy & Grusec, 2006), collectivist mothers (in this case Iranian, Indian, Egyptian, and Pakistani) described themselves as more authoritarian but did not express negative attitudes about their children, and the children did not show these more negative outcomes. For Latino families, some psychologists have suggested that authoritarian parenting may express culturally valued childrearing goals such as family, respect, and education and that this parenting style must be understood in the context of these cultural ideals (Halgunseth, Ispa, & Rudy, 2006).

● **authoritative parenting** A parenting style that encourages the child to be independent but that still places limits and controls on behavior.

■ **Authoritative parenting** encourages the child to be independent but still places limits and controls on behavior. This parenting style is more collaborative. Extensive verbal give-and-take is allowed, and parents are warm and nurturing toward the child. An authoritative father might put his arm around the child in a comforting way and say, "You know you should not have done that; let's talk about how you can handle the situation better next time." Children whose parents are authoritative tend to be socially competent, self-reliant, and socially responsible.

● **neglectful parenting** A parenting style characterized by a lack of parental involvement in the child's life.

■ **Neglectful parenting** is distinguished by a lack of parental involvement in the child's life. Children of neglectful parents might develop a sense that other aspects of their parents' lives are more important than they are. Children whose parents are neglectful tend to be less competent socially, to handle independence poorly, and (especially) to show poor self-control.

Developmental Psychology and Clinical Psychology: Is "Girl Talk" Always a Good Thing?

Making friends, keeping friends, and being a friend are all tasks that face the developing human being. Friends are important to children's self-esteem, well-being, and school adjustment (Brengden & others, 2010; Erath & others, 2010; Rubin, Cheah, & Menzer, 2010). Having a friend means that there is someone to talk to when one has problems and someone to celebrate with when things go well. Thus, if a child has a lot of friends, we might think that he or she is doing pretty well. Are all friendships equally supportive, however? Research indicates that some friends might have a knack for making problems seem worse, not better.

Are some of your friends likely to co-ruminate over negative events? Why do you think co-rumination is worse for girls than boys?

Developmental psychologist Amanda Rose and her colleagues have studied how young friends' responses to their friends' problems influence the mental health of children and adolescents (Rose, 2002; Rose, Carlson, & Waller, 2007; Rose & Smith, 2009). Rose (2002) introduced the concept of *co-rumination* to describe the ways that some friends might make matters worse by giving their pals even more things to worry about

than they had originally realized. For example, if Janisa tells her friend Robin about doing poorly on a spelling test, does Robin encourage Janisa to study harder, or does she remind Janisa that not doing well now is a really bad sign because the words are only going to get harder in the future? Rumination is a way of thinking that involves worrying about a topic without finding a resolution. When we ruminate, we might dwell on all the possible horrible consequences of some negative life event or imagine everything that might go wrong in the future. Co-rumination is like that too, but it involves engaging in a conversation with someone and making a negative event that the person is going through seem even worse.

In a study of hundreds of grade-school and middle-school children, Rose (2002) found that girls were more likely than boys to engage in co-rumination, and this difference was particularly large among adolescents. Furthermore, longitudinal research has shown that co-rumination, even in the context of good friends, was associated with increased feelings of depression and anxiety, especially for girls (Rose, Carlson, & Waller, 2007). Rose and colleagues suggest that some friends represent a trade-off, especially for girls. Having close friends might be a good sign of social functioning, but when those friends are people who hurt more than help, they can negatively influence girls' well-being.

■ **Permissive parenting** involves placing few limits on the child's behavior. A permissive parent lets the child do what he or she wants. Some parents deliberately rear their children this way because they believe that the combination of warm involvement and few limits will produce a creative, confident child. However, children with very permissive parents typically rate poorly in social competence. They often fail to learn respect for others, expect to get their own way, and have difficulty controlling their behavior. Recall that socioemotional development involves becoming increasingly adept at controlling and regulating one's emotions and behaviors (Vazsonyi & Huang, 2010). Children may require structure from their caregivers in order to acquire these skills.

● **permissive parenting** A parenting style characterized by the placement of few limits on the child's behavior.

Parents are crucial to child development. However, as the Intersection explores, peers play a large role in socioemotional development as well.

MORAL DEVELOPMENT

Another aspect of development that psychologists study is how an individual becomes not only physically able, cognitively skilled, and emotionally well but also a person of character— someone who behaves morally. This aspect of development features yet another classic theory in developmental psychology, that of Lawrence Kohlberg (1927–1987). Moral development involves changes with age in thoughts, feelings, and behaviors regarding the

Lawrence Kohlberg (1927–1987)
Kohlberg created a provocative theory of moral development. In his view, "Moral development consists of a sequence of qualitative changes in the way an individual thinks."

principles and values that guide what people should do. Much research on moral reasoning and thinking has revolved around Kohlberg's theory of moral development and reactions to it.

Kohlberg's Theory Kohlberg (1958) began his study of moral thinking by creating a series of stories and asking children, adolescents, and adults questions about the stories. One of the stories goes something like this. A man, Heinz, whose wife is dying of cancer, knows about a drug that might save her life. He approaches the pharmacist who has the drug, but the pharmacist refuses to give it to him without being paid a very high price. Heinz is unable to scrape together the money and eventually decides to steal the drug.

After reading the story, each person interviewed was asked a series of questions about the moral dilemma. Should Heinz have stolen the drug? Kohlberg was less interested in the answer to this question than he was to the next one: Why? Based on the reasons people gave for their answers, Kohlberg (1986) evaluated their level of moral development. Kohlberg's stages of moral development consisted of three levels, as follows, with two stages at each level (Figure 9.11).

1. The *preconventional level* is based primarily on punishments and rewards from the external world. Moral reasoning is guided by not wanting Heinz to go to jail or concern for the druggists' profits.

2. At the *conventional level,* the individual abides by standards such as those learned from parents or society's laws. At this level the person might reason that Heinz should act in accord with expectations or his role as a good husband or reason that Heinz should follow the law no matter what.

3. At the *postconventional level,* the individual recognizes alternative moral courses, explores the options, and then develops an increasingly personal moral code. At this level, the person might reason that Heinz's wife's life is more important than a law.

Kohlberg believed that moral development advances because of the maturation of thought, the availability of opportunities for role taking, and the chance to discuss moral issues with a person who reasons at a stage just above one's own. Kohlberg studied with Piaget, and Kohlberg's approach to moral reasoning emphasized the individual's capacity to reason in a sophisticated way, as did Piaget's theory of cognitive development. As we will see, subsequent theories of moral development have focused on its social and emotional components. For Kohlberg, a sense of justice was at the heart of moral reasoning, which he believed laid the foundation for moral behavior.

LEVEL 1 **Preconventional Level** **No Internalization**	**LEVEL 2** **Conventional Level** **Intermediate Internalization**	**LEVEL 3** **Postconventional Level** **Full Internalization**
Stage 1 Heteronomous Morality *Individuals pursue their own interests but let others do the same. What is right involves equal exchange.*	**Stage 3** Mutual Interpersonal Expectations, Relationships, and Interpersonal Conformity *Individuals value trust, caring, and loyalty to others as a basis for moral judgments.*	**Stage 5** Social Contract or Utility and Individual Rights *Individuals reason that values, rights, and principles undergird or transcend the law.*
Stage 2 Individualism, Purpose, and Exchange *Children obey because adults tell them to obey. People base their moral decisions on fear of punishment.*	**Stage 4** Social System Morality *Moral judgments are based on understanding and the social order, law, justice, and duty.*	**Stage 6** Universal Ethical Principles *The person has developed moral judgments that are based on universal human rights. When faced with a dilemma between law and conscience, a personal, individualized conscience is followed.*

FIGURE 9.11 **Kohlberg's Three Levels and Six Stages of Moral Development** Kohlberg proposed that human moral development could be characterized by a sequence of age-related changes.

Evaluating Kohlberg's Theory   Kohlberg's ideas have stimulated considerable research about how people think about moral issues (Narvacz & Lapsley, 2009; Walker & Frimer, 2011). At the same time, his theory has numerous critics. One criticism is that moral *reasoning* does not necessarily mean moral *behavior*. When people are asked about their moral reasoning, what they say might fit into Kohlberg's advanced stages, but their actual behavior might involve cheating, lying, and stealing. The cheaters, liars, and thieves might know what is right but still do what is wrong.

Another criticism is that Kohlberg's view does not adequately reflect concern for other people and social bonds (Carlo, 2006). Kohlberg's theory is called a *justice perspective* because it focuses on the rights of the individual as the key to sound moral reasoning. In contrast, the *care perspective,* which lies at the heart of Carol Gilligan's (1982) approach to moral development, views people in terms of their connectedness with others and emphasizes interpersonal communication, relationships, and concern for others. From Gilligan's perspective, this weakness in Kohlberg's approach explains why, using his measures, women generally score lower than men on moral development. Similarly, culture can influence whether a person approaches a moral dilemma from the perspective of justice or care (Gibbs, 2010). In Western cultures, where people generally tend toward an individualistic sense of self and are therefore inclined to take a justice perspective, individuals might score higher in Kohlberg's scheme than their counterparts in collectivistic Asian cultures, where people have a sense of the self as part of a larger group.

Current Research on Moral Development   Researchers interested in moral development have increasingly studied **prosocial behavior,** behavior that is intended to benefit other people (N. Eisenberg, 2010; N. Eisenberg & others, 2009). For example, researchers are probing how, when, and why children engage in everyday acts of kindness toward others (Carlo, 2006). Studies have found that supportive parenting and parental monitoring relate to increased helping and comforting of others (Dodge, Coie, & Lynam, 2006). Furthermore, research suggests that the capacities to empathize with others and engage in prosocial behavior are linked with the ability to engage in self-control more generally (N. Eisenberg, 2010).

Other recent work has focused on when a child first shows signs of possessing a conscience (Kochanska & others, 2008; R. A. Thompson, 2009b). Having a conscience means hearing that voice in our head that tells us that something is morally good or bad. Deborah Laible and Ross Thompson (2000, 2002, 2007) have examined the conversations between mothers and toddlers at times when the child did something well or got into trouble. They have found that by 3 years of age, children begin to show signs of early conscience development. This development is fostered by parent–child interactions that are clear, elaborate, and rich with emotional content and that include shared positive emotion. Childhood characteristics are important because longitudinal research shows that kind, moral children are more likely to be kind, moral adults (N. Eisenberg, 2010; Eisenberg, Fabes, & Spinrad, 2006).

How can parents successfully rear a child to be considerate of others and to understand the difference between right and wrong? Researchers have found that the following parenting strategies are most often helpful in rearing a moral child (Eisenberg & Murphy, 1995; Eisenberg & Valiente, 2002; N. Eisenberg & others, 2009):

- Being warm and supportive rather than overly punishing and rigid
- When disciplining, using reasoning the child can understand
- Providing opportunities for the child to learn about others' perspectives and feelings
- Involving children in family decision making and in thinking about moral decisions
- Modeling moral behaviors and thinking, and providing children with opportunities to engage in such behaviors and thought

Note that the last strategy includes modeling moral behaviors. That is, it calls for parents to demonstrate moral behavior to the child. However, significantly, parents are themselves still developing, even as they model this behavior for the child. Human development, then, occurs in the context of generations relating to each other, teaching each other lessons, and working in tandem.

Carol Gilligan (b. 1936) Gilligan argues that Kohlberg's approach does not give adequate attention to relationships. In Gilligan's view, "Many girls seem to fear, most of all, being alone—without friends, family, and relationships."

● **prosocial behavior** Behavior that is intended to benefit other people.

test yourself

1. What are teratogens? Give several examples of them.
2. According to Piaget, what two processes are responsible for how people use and adapt their schemas, and what is involved in each process?
3. What are Erikson's four childhood stages of development, and with what is each centrally concerned?

3· ADOLESCENCE

Adolescence is the developmental period of transition from childhood to adulthood, beginning around 10 to 12 years of age and ending at 18 to 21 years of age. Adolescents are not all the same (Diamond & Savin-Williams, 2009). Variations in ethnicity, culture, history, gender, socioeconomic status, and lifestyle characterize their life trajectories (Galambos, Berenbaum, & McHale, 2009). Any image of adolescents should take into account the particular adolescent or group of adolescents one is considering. In this section we examine the changes that occur in adolescence in the domains of physical, cognitive, and socioemotional development.

Physical Development in Adolescence

Dramatic physical changes characterize adolescence, especially early adolescence. Among the major physical changes of adolescence are those involving puberty and the brain.

PUBERTAL CHANGE

● **puberty** A period of rapid skeletal and sexual maturation that occurs mainly in early adolescence.

● **androgens** The main class of male sex hormones.

● **estrogens** The main class of female sex hormones.

The signature physical change in adolescence is **puberty,** a period of rapid skeletal and sexual maturation that occurs mainly in early adolescence. We will look at these developments more specifically in Chapter 11.

Hormonal changes lie at the core of pubertal development. The concentrations of certain hormones increase dramatically during puberty (Susman & Dorn, 2009). *Testosterone*—an **androgen,** which is the main class of male sex hormones—is associated in boys with the development of genitals, an increase in height, and voice change. *Estradiol*—an **estrogen,** the main class of female sex hormones—is associated in girls with breast, uterine, and skeletal development. Developmental psychologists believe that hormonal changes account for at least some of the emotional ups and downs of adolescence, but hormones are not alone responsible for adolescent behavior (Graber, 2007).

Remember that physical and socioemotional development are intertwined. Nowhere is this link more apparent than in the timing of puberty. Boys who mature earlier than their peers tend to show more positive socioemotional outcomes, such as being popular with their peers and having higher self-esteem (Graber, Brooks-Gunn, & Warren, 2006). Longitudinal studies have shown that boys who matured early in adolescence were more successful and less likely to drink alcohol, smoke cigarettes, or engage in delinquent behaviors than late-maturing boys (Taga, Markey, & Friedman, 2006; van der Geest, Blokland, & Bijleveld, 2009). In contrast, girls who are early bloomers tend to be less outgoing and less popular, and they are more likely to smoke, use drugs, become sexually active, and engage less in academic pursuits (Engels, 2009; Susman & Dorn, 2009).

THE BRAIN

Brain-imaging studies have revealed important changes in the brain during adolescence (Paus, 2009; Steinberg, 2009). These changes focus on the earlier development of the amygdala, which involves emotion, and the later development of the prefrontal cortex, which is concerned with reasoning and decision making (Figure 9.12). These changes in the brain may help to explain why adolescents often display very strong emotions but cannot yet control these passions. It is as if the adolescent brain does not have the brakes to slow down emotions. Because of the relatively slow development of the prefrontal cortex, which continues to mature into early adulthood, adolescents may lack the cognitive skills to control their

Prefrontal cortex
Involved in higher-order cognitive functioning, such as decision making

Amygdala
Involved in processing information about emotion

FIGURE 9.12 Developmental Changes in the Adolescent's Brain The amygdala, which is responsible for processing information about emotion, matures earlier than the prefrontal cortex, which is responsible for making decisions and other higher-order cognitive functions.

pleasure seeking effectively. This developmental disjunction may account for increased risk taking and other problems in adolescence (Steinberg, 2009).

Biological changes in the brain are linked with experiences (Lerner, Boyd, & Du, 2008). For instance, one study of adolescents found that resisting peer pressure was correlated with prefrontal cortex thickening and more brain connections (Paus & others, 2008). This correlational study cannot tell us if the brain changes promoted peer-pressure resistance or if this resistance promoted changes in the brain, but it does highlight the nature–nurture question that permeates the study of development.

Cognitive Development in Adolescence

As they advance into Piaget's formal operational thinking, adolescents undergo other significant cognitive changes (Byrnes, 2008; Kuhn, 2009, 2011). One characteristic of adolescent thinking, especially in early adolescence, is egocentrism. Although children are also considered egocentric, *adolescent egocentrism* has a different focus; it involves the individual's belief that others are as preoccupied with him or her as the adolescent himself or herself is and that the individual is both unique and invincible (that is, incapable of being harmed) (Elkind, 1978). Egocentric adolescents perceive others as observing them more than actually is the case—think of the eighth-grade boy who senses that everyone has noticed the small pimple on his face. However, recent research is calling into question whether adolescents believe they are invincible. In one study, 12- to 18-year-olds who were asked about their chance of dying in the next year and before age 20 greatly overestimated their chance of dying (Fischhoff & others, 2010).

Socioeomotional Development in Adolescence: The Emergence of Identity

Erikson's approach to the formation of identity during adolescence is one of his most important contributions. His ideas changed the way we think about adolescence (Kroger, Martinussen, & Marcia, 2010). Recall from Figure 9.10 that Erikson (1968) viewed the key challenge of adolescence (his fifth stage) as **identity versus identity confusion.** In seeking an *identity,* adolescents face the challenges of finding out who they are, what they are all about, and where they are going in life. Adolescents are confronted with many new roles and adult statuses—from jobs and careers to friendships and romantic relationships. If they do not adequately explore their identity during this stage, they end up confused about who they are. Therefore, Erikson argues, parents should allow adolescents to explore many different roles and many paths within a particular role. Adolescents who spend this time in their lives exploring alternatives can reach some resolution of the identity crisis and emerge with a new sense of self. Those who do not successfully resolve the crisis suffer what Erikson calls *identity confusion,* which is expressed in one of two ways: the individual either withdraws, becoming isolated from peers and family, or loses himself or herself in the crowd.

Copyright by Mark Parisi, www.offthemark.com.

● **identity versus identity confusion** Erikson's fifth psychological stage, in which adolescents face the challenges of finding out who they are, what they are all about, and where they are going in life.

© Hilary B. Price.

psychological *inquiry*

Has the person made a commitment?

		Yes	No
Has the person explored meaningful alternatives regarding some identity question?	**Yes**	Identity Achievement	Identity Moratorium
	No	Identity Foreclosure	Identity Diffusion

Looking at Identity Exploration

This figure summarizes Marcia's conceptualization of identity development. Notice that the different quadrants of the square represent the crossings of the two factors of commitment and exploration and that every possible combination of the two is represented. Answer the following questions.

1. Imagine a young woman who has grown up in a family of doctors. Everyone in her family expects her to follow this same course. What outcomes might be expected if she simply "goes with the flow" of her family's wishes?

2. Imagine a young woman who comes from a family in which no one ever attended college. What sorts of experiences might influence her journey to identity? How might her background influence her identity exploration?

3. Find yourself in this figure. That is, in which quadrant is your own identity located? Do you feel that you fully explored your potential identities? Why or why not?

4. Which path to identity do you think is most challenging? Why?

5. Which path to identity do you believe is most common in young people today? Why?

6. Finding one's path in life is a common theme in popular books, TV, and film. Can you identify a book or movie that depicts the combination of exploration and resolution? Why do you think this theme is so popular?

MARCIA'S THEORY OF IDENTITY STATUS

Building on Erikson's ideas, James Marcia (1980, 2002) proposed the concept of *identity status* to describe a person's position in the development of an identity. In Marcia's view, two dimensions of identity, exploration and commitment, are important. *Exploration* refers to a person's investigating various options for a career and for personal values. *Commitment* involves making a decision about which identity path to follow and making a personal investment in attaining that identity. Various combinations of exploration and commitment give rise to one of four identity statuses.

Notably, Marcia's approach focuses on identity as an active construction, an outcome of a process of thinking about and trying on different identities (Klimstra & others, 2009). To master Marcia's approach, check out the Psychological Inquiry above.

ETHNIC IDENTITY

Developing an identity in adolescence can be especially challenging for individuals from ethnic minority groups (Gonzales-Backen & Umana-Taylor, 2010; Juang & Syed, 2010). As they mature cognitively, many adolescents become acutely aware of the evaluation of their ethnic group by the majority culture. In addition, an increasing number of minority adolescents face the challenge of *biculturalism*—identifying in some ways with their ethnic minority group and in other ways with the majority culture (Phinney & others, 2006).

Research has shown that for ethnic minority youth, feeling both a positive attachment to their minority group and an attachment to the larger culture is related to more positive academic and emotional outcomes (Iturbide, Raffaelli, & Carlo, 2009; Yip, Kiang, & Fuligni, 2008). Although it might seem that being a member of an ethnic minority would make life more stressful, studies have indicated that having a strong

Michelle Chin, age 16, reflecting on her identity, commented, "Parents do not understand that teenagers need to find out who they are, which means a lot of experimenting, a lot of mood swings, a lot of emotions and awkwardness. Like any teenager, I am facing an identity crisis. I am still trying to figure out whether I am a Chinese American or an American with Asian eyes."

ethnic identity can buffer adolescents from the effects of discrimination (Iturbide, Raffaelli, & Carlo, 2009; Sellers & others, 2006). For both minority and majority adolescents, developing a positive identity is an important life theme (Kroger, Martinussen, & Marcia, 2010; Swanson, 2010). In addition to ethnic identity, adolescence can be a time when other aspects of one's identity come to the fore, such as sexual orientation and gender role (see Chapter 11).

The managerial role of parenting involves effective monitoring of the adolescent's friends, social activities, and academic efforts.

PARENTAL AND PEER ROLES IN IDENTITY FORMATION

Parents and peers can help the adolescent answer the central questions of identity, "Who am I, and who do I hope to become?" (Brown & Dietz, 2009; Rodriquez & Walden, 2010). To help adolescents reach their full potential, a key parental role is to be an effective manager—one who locates information, makes contacts, helps to structure offsprings' choices, and provides guidance. By assuming this managerial role, parents help adolescents to avoid pitfalls and to work their way through the decisions they face (Gauvain & Parke, 2010).

Although adolescence is a time of establishing independence, a crucial aspect of the managerial role of parenting is effective monitoring (Collins & Steinberg, 2006). Monitoring includes supervising the adolescent's choice of social settings, activities, and friends, as well as his or her academic efforts. A research review concluded that when African American parents monitored their sons' academic achievement—by ensuring that they completed homework; by restricting the time spent on activities like video games and TV; and by participating in a consistent, positive dialogue with teachers—their sons' academic achievement benefited (Mandara, 2006).

How competent the adolescent will become often depends on access to legitimate opportunities for growth, such as a quality education, community and societal support for achievement and involvement, and good jobs. Especially important in adolescent development is long-term, deeply caring support from adults (Lerner & others, 2009). Successfully parenting an adolescent means allowing one's son or daughter to explore his or her own identity and assume increasing levels of autonomy, while also remaining an involved parent (Smetana & others, 2009).

During adolescence, individuals spend more time with peers than they did in childhood. These peer influences can be positive or negative (Asher & McDonald, 2009). A significant aspect of positive peer relations is having one or more close friends. Adolescents can learn to be skilled and sensitive partners in intimate relationships by forging close friendships with selected peers. However, some peers and friends can negatively impact adolescents' development. Researchers have found that hanging out with delinquent peers in adolescence can be a strong predictor of substance abuse, delinquent behavior, and depression (Dishion & Piehler, 2009; Farrington, 2009).

test yourself

1. What characteristics of the adolescent brain help to explain why adolescents often display strong emotions that they cannot control?

2. According to Erikson, what challenges do adolescents face in trying to establish an identity, and what happens if they do not successfully resolve this crisis?

3. In what ways do parents and peers help an adolescent develop an identity?

4· EMERGING ADULTHOOD, ADULT DEVELOPMENT, AND AGING

Development continues throughout adulthood. Developmental psychologists identify three approximate periods in adult development: early adulthood (20s and 30s), middle adulthood (40s and 50s), and late adulthood (60s until death). Each phase features distinctive physical, cognitive, and socioemotional changes.

Erikson believed that once the issues of identity are resolved, the young adult turns to the important domain of intimate relationships. However, more recently, scholars have noted that during the life stage after adolescence, many young people are putting off the commitments to marriage, family, and career that are traditionally associated with adult life. Jeffrey Arnett (2004, 2007, 2010) introduced the concept of *emerging adulthood* to describe this transitional period, which is in part an extended adolescence and in part a "trying on" of adult roles. If you are a traditional-age college student, you are at this point in the life span. We begin our survey of post-adolescent development by briefly examining this transitional life stage.

● **emerging adulthood** The transitional period from adolescence to adulthood, spanning approximately 18 to 25 years of age.

Emerging Adulthood

Emerging adulthood is the transitional period from adolescence to adulthood (Arnett, 2004, 2006, 2007). The age range for emerging adulthood is approximately 18 to 25 years of age. Experimentation and exploration characterize the emerging adult. At this point in their development, many individuals are still exploring which career path they want to follow, what they want their identity to be, and what kinds of close relationships they will have.

Jeffrey Arnett (2006, 2010) identified five main features of emerging adulthood:

- *Identity exploration, especially in love and work:* Emerging adulthood is the time of significant changes in identity for many individuals.
- *Instability:* Residential changes peak during emerging adulthood, a time during which there also is often instability in love, work, and education.
- *Self-focus:* Emerging adults "are self-focused in the sense that they have little in the way of social obligations, [and] little in the way of duties and commitments to others, which leaves them with a great deal of autonomy in running their own lives" (Arnett, 2006, p. 10).
- *A feeling of being "in between":* Many emerging adults consider themselves neither adolescents nor full-fledged adults.
- *Access to various life possibilities and an opportunity to transform one's life:* Arnett (2006) describes two ways in which emerging adulthood is the age of possibilities: (1) Many emerging adults are optimistic about their future, and (2) for emerging adults who have experienced difficult times while growing up, emerging adulthood presents an opportunity to guide their lives in a positive direction.

Other research suggests that emerging adulthood is a time of increasing well-being (Schulenberg & Zarrett, 2006). One possible reason for this improvement is that emerging adults have more choices and more control over those choices in their daily lives. Emerging adulthood provides an opportunity for individuals who engaged in problem behavior during adolescence to get their lives together.

Physical Development in Adulthood

Like other developmental periods, our bodies change during adulthood. Most of the changes that occur following adolescence involve declines in physical and perceptual abilities, as we now consider.

PHYSICAL CHANGES IN EARLY ADULTHOOD

Most adults reach their peak physical development during their 20s and are the healthiest then. Early adulthood, however, is also the time when many physical skills begin to decline. The decline in strength and speed often is noticeable in the 30s. Another realm in which physical changes occur with age is in the ability to perceive the world. Hearing loss is very common with age. In fact, starting at about age 18, hearing begins a gradual decline, though it is so slow that most people do not notice it until the age of 50 or so.

PHYSICAL CHANGES IN MIDDLE AND LATE ADULTHOOD

By the 40s or 50s, the skin has begun to wrinkle and sag because of the loss of fat and collagen in underlying tissues. Small, localized areas of pigmentation in the skin produce age spots, especially in areas exposed to sunlight such as the hands and face (McCullough & Kelly, 2006). Hair becomes thinner and grayer due to a lower replacement rate and a decline in melanin production. Individuals lose height in middle age, and many gain weight (Page & others, 2009). The decrease in height is due to bone loss in the vertebrae. On average, body fat accounts for about 10 percent of body weight in adolescence; it makes up 20 percent or more in middle age. Once individuals hit their 40s, age-related vision changes usually become apparent, especially difficulty in seeing things up close. The sense of taste can also be affected by age, as taste buds (described in Chapter 4) are less likely to be replaced.

For women, entering middle age means that menopause will soon occur. Usually in the late 40s or early 50s, a woman's menstrual periods cease completely. With menopause comes a dramatic decline in the ovaries' production of estrogen. Estrogen decline produces uncomfortable symptoms in some menopausal women, such as *hot flashes* (sudden, brief flushing of the skin and a feeling of elevated body temperature), nausea, fatigue, and rapid heartbeat. Some menopausal women report depression and irritability (K. A. Matthews & others, 2007), but menopause does not produce serious psychological or physical problems for most women (Bauld & Brown, 2009; Weismiller, 2009).

For both men and women, a variety of bodily systems are likely to show the effects of wear and tear as the body becomes less and less able to repair damage and regenerate itself (Effros, 2009; Zou & others, 2009). Physical strength declines and motor speed slows, bones may become more brittle (especially for women), and nearly every bodily system may change with age. Significantly, however, even as age is associated with some inevitable decline, important aspects of successful aging are within the person's control (Martin-Joy & Vaillant, 2010). For instance, a healthy diet and regular exercise can help to prevent or slow these effects. Regular physical activity can have wide-reaching benefits not only for physical health but for cognitive functioning as well (Rolland, van Kan, & Vellas, 2010; Weis & others, 2010).

On the island of Okinawa (part of Japan), individuals live longer than anywhere else in the world, and Okinawa has the world's highest prevalence of *centenarians*—individuals who live to 100 years or beyond. Examination of Okinawans' lives provides insights into their longevity. Specific factors are diet (they eat nutritious foods such as grains, fish, and vegetables); lifestyle (they are easygoing and experience low stress); community (Okinawans look out for one another and do not isolate or ignore older adults); activity (they lead active lifestyles, and many older adults continue to work); and spirituality (they find a sense of purpose in spiritual matters) (Willcox & others, 2008). Just as physical changes are interwoven with socioemotional processes in childhood and adolescence, so they are as human beings enter the later stages of life.

". . . All the lab work confirms it—I'm sorry Mr. Franklin . . . You're old."

© Harry Bliss. Reprinted by permission of TMS/MCT Reprints

BIOLOGICAL THEORIES OF AGING

Of the many proposed biological theories of aging, three especially merit attention. The first is the *cellular-clock theory,* Leonard Hayflick's (1977) view that cells can divide a maximum of about 100 times and that, as we age, our cells become less capable of dividing. Hayflick found that cells extracted from adults in their 50s to 70s had divided fewer than 100 times. The total number of cell divisions was roughly related to the individual's age. Based on the way cells divide, Hayflick places the human life span's upper limit at about 120 years.

Recently, scientists have been examining why cells lose their ability to divide (Davoli, Denchi, & de Lange, 2010; Sahin & Daphino, 2010). The answer may lie at the tips of chromosomes. Each time a cell divides, the *telomeres* protecting the ends of chromosomes shorten. After about 100 replications, the telomeres are dramatically reduced, and the cell no longer can reproduce (Shay & Wright, 2007). There is considerable interest in discovering ways to maintain high levels of the telomere-extending enzyme—telomerase—through genetic manipulation of chemical telomerase activators (Effros, 2009).

The *free-radical theory* of aging states that people age because unstable oxygen molecules known as *free radicals* are produced inside their cells. These molecules damage DNA and other cellular structures (Hepple, 2009; van Remmen & Jones, 2009). The damage done by free radicals may lead to a range of disorders, including cancer and arthritis.

Hormonal stress theory argues that aging in the body's hormonal system can lower resistance to stress and increase the likelihood of disease. As individuals age, the hormones stimulated by stress stay in the bloodstream longer than when they were younger (Brown-Borg, 2008). These prolonged, elevated levels of stress hormones are linked to increased risks for many diseases, including cardiovascular disease, cancer, and diabetes (Wolkowitz

FIGURE 9.13 **The Brains of the Mankato Nuns** At 90 years old, Nun Study participant Sister Rosella Kreuzer, SSND (School Sisters of Notre Dame), remains an active contributing member of her community of sisters. Sister Rosella articulated the Nun Study's mission as "That You May Have Life to the Full." (*Inset*) A neuroscientist holds a brain donated by one of the Mankato Nun Study participants.

FIGURE 9.14 **The Decrease in Brain Lateralization in Older Adults** Younger adults primarily used the right prefrontal region of the brain (*top left photo*) during a memory recall task, while older adults used both the left and the right prefrontal regions (*bottom two photos*).

& others, 2010). Recently, the hormonal stress theory of aging has focused on the role of chronic stress in reducing immune system functioning (Bauer, Jeckel, & Luz, 2009).

AGING AND THE BRAIN

Just as the aging body has a greater capacity for renewal than previously thought, so does the aging brain (Imayoshi & others, 2009; Prakash & others, 2010). For decades, scientists believed that no new brain cells are generated past early childhood. However, researchers have recently discovered that adults can grow new brain cells throughout life (Eisch & others, 2008; Gould & others, 1999), although the evidence is limited to the hippocampus and the olfactory bulb (Arenkiel, 2010; L. Zou & others, 2010). Researchers currently are studying factors that might inhibit and promote neurogenesis, including various drugs, stress, and exercise (Gil-Mohapel & others, 2010; Marlatt, Lucassen, & van Pragg, 2010). They also are examining how grafting neural stem cells to various brain regions, such as the hippocampus, might increase neurogenesis (Farin & others, 2009; Szulwach & others, 2010).

Research from the Nun Study (described in Chapter 2) provides evidence for the role of experience in maintaining the brain. Recall that this study involves nearly 700 nuns in a convent in Mankato, Minnesota (Snowdon, 2003, 2007) (Figure 9.13). Although in Chapter 2 we surveyed the aspects of the study related to happiness, this research has also investigated brain functioning. By examining the nuns' donated brains as well as those of others, neuroscientists have documented the aging brain's remarkable ability to grow and change. Even the oldest Mankato nuns lead intellectually challenging lives, and neuroscientists believe that stimulating mental activities increase dendritic branching. Keeping the brain actively engaged in challenging activities can help to slow the effects of age, as we saw in Chapters 7 and 8.

Even in late adulthood, the brain has remarkable repair capability (Grady, 2008). Stanley Rapaport (1994) compared the brains of younger and older adults when they were engaged in the same tasks. The older adults' brains literally rewired themselves to compensate for losses. If one neuron was not up to the job, neighboring neurons helped to pick up the slack. Rapaport concluded that as brains age, they can shift responsibilities for a given task from one region to another.

Changes in lateralization may provide one type of adaptation in aging adults (Angel & others, 2009; Zhu, Zacks, & Slade, 2010). *Lateralization* is the specialization of function in one hemisphere of the brain or the other. Using neuroimaging techniques, researchers have found that brain activity in the prefrontal cortex is lateralized less in older adults than in younger adults when they are engaging in mental tasks (Cabeza, 2002; Cabeza, Nyberg, & Park, 2005). For example, Figure 9.14 shows that when younger adults are given the task of recognizing words they have previously seen, they process the information primarily in the right hemisphere, whereas older adults are more likely to use both hemispheres (Madden & others, 1999). The decrease in lateralization in older adults might play a compensatory role in the aging brain. That is, using both hemispheres may help to maintain the mental abilities of older adults.

Cognitive Development in Adulthood

Recall that for Piaget, each stage of cognitive development entails a way of thinking that is *qualitatively different* from the stage before. From Piaget's perspective, meaningful cognitive development ceases after the individual reaches the formal operational stage. Subsequent research has examined not qualitative differences in thinking over time, but the ebb and flow of cognitive abilities as a function of age. What kind of cognitive changes occur in adults?

COGNITION IN EARLY ADULTHOOD

Just as physical abilities peak in early adulthood, intellectual skills are often considered to be at their peak during this time in life (Kitchener, King, & DeLuca, 2006). Some experts on cognitive development argue that the typical idealism of Piaget's formal operational stage is replaced in young adulthood by more realistic, pragmatic thinking (Labouvie-Vief, 1986). Gisela Labouvie-Vief (2006) proposed that the increasing complexity of cultures in the past century has generated a greater need for reflective, more complex thinking that takes into account the changing nature of knowledge and the kinds of challenges contemporary thinkers face. She emphasizes that key aspects of cognitive development for young adults include deciding on a particular worldview, recognizing that the worldview is subjective, and understanding that diverse worldviews should be acknowledged. In her perspective, considerable individual variation characterizes the thinking of young adults, with the highest level of thinking attained only by some.

COGNITION IN MIDDLE ADULTHOOD

What happens to cognitive skills in middle adulthood? Although some cross-sectional studies indicate that middle adulthood is a time of cognitive decline, longitudinal evidence presents a somewhat rosier picture. K. Warner Schaie is conducting an extensive longitudinal study of intellectual abilities in adulthood. Five hundred individuals initially were tested in 1956 and have been tested repeatedly over the years (Schaie, 1994, 2007, 2010, 2011). New waves of participants are added periodically. Schaie has measured a host of different cognitive abilities. As shown in Figure 9.15, the highest level of functioning for four of the six intellectual abilities occurred in middle adulthood (Schaie, 2006, 2010, 2011). Only two of the six abilities—numerical ability and perceptual speed—declined in middle age. Perceptual speed showed the earliest decline, beginning in early adulthood. Schaie found middle adulthood to be a time of peak performance for some aspects of both *crystallized intelligence* (vocabulary) and *fluid intelligence* (spatial orientation and inductive reasoning). Based on the longitudinal data he has collected so far, Schaie (2006, 2007, 2010, 2011) concluded that middle adulthood, not early adulthood, is the period when many people reach their peak for a range of intellectual skills.

COGNITION IN LATE ADULTHOOD

Many contemporary psychologists conclude that as in middle adulthood, some dimensions of intelligence decline in late adulthood, whereas others are maintained or may even increase (Blair, 2011; Staudinger & Gluck, 2011). One of the most consistent findings is that when the speed of processing information is involved, older adults do

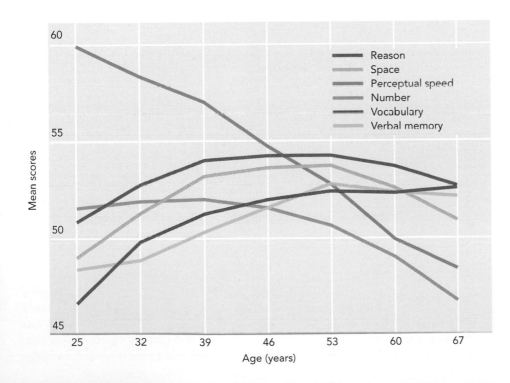

FIGURE 9.15 **Longitudinal Changes in Six Intellectual Abilities from Age 25 to Age 67** Some abilities show sharp declines with age. Others—such as vocabulary, reasoning, and perceptual speed—remain stable and high throughout late life.

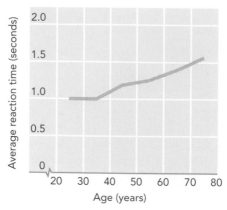

FIGURE 9.16 **The Relationship Between Age and Reaction Time** In one study, the average reaction time slowed in the 40s, and this decline accelerated in the 60s and 70s (Salthouse, 1994). The task used to assess reaction time required individuals to match numbers with symbols on a computer screen.

● **wisdom** Expert knowledge about the practical aspects of life.

Copyright by Mark Parisi, www.offthemark.com.

more poorly than their younger counterparts (Figure 9.16). This decline in speed of processing is apparent in middle-aged adults and becomes more pronounced in older adults (Deary, Johnson, & Starr, 2010; Salthouse, 2009).

Older adults also tend to do more poorly than younger adults in most aspects of memory (Bialystok & Craik, 2011). In the area of memory involving knowledge of the world (for instance, the capital of Peru or the chemical formula for water), older adults usually take longer than younger adults to remember the information, but they often are able to remember it (Hoyer & Roodin, 2009). Further, in the important area of memory in which individuals manipulate and assemble information to solve problems and make decisions, decline occurs in older adults.

Some aspects of cognition might improve with age. One such area is **wisdom,** expert knowledge about the practical aspects of life (Staudinger & Gluck, 2011). Wisdom may increase with age because of the buildup of life experiences, but individual variations characterize people throughout their lives (Grossman & others, 2010). Thus, not every older person has wisdom, and some young people are wise beyond their years.

Do we all face the prospect of gradually becoming less competent intellectually? Not necessarily. Even for those aspects of cognitive aging that decline, older adults can improve their cognitive skills with training (Schaie, 2006, 2011; Willis & Schaie, 2005). Researchers have demonstrated that training older adults to use specific strategies can enhance their memory, and there is increasing evidence that physical fitness training sharpens the thinking skills of older adults (Etnier, 2009; Hillman, Erickson, & Kramer, 2008; La Rue, 2010; Park & Reuter-Lorenz, 2009). However, many experts conclude that older adults are less able to adapt than younger adults and thus are limited in how much they can improve their cognitive skills (Finch, 2009; Salthouse, 2009).

Socioemotional Development in Adulthood

In the physical and the cognitive domains, the developmental story is generally one of rapid growth during childhood, with continuing gains in adolescence, followed by steady decline with age. Does a similar pattern hold for socioemotional development? We now consider the changes that characterize adult socioemotional development, first returning to Erikson's stage theory of life-span development and then looking at what current research has to say.

SOCIOEMOTIONAL DEVELOPMENT IN EARLY ADULTHOOD

According to Erikson (1968), during early adulthood, people face a developmental dilemma involving *intimacy versus isolation* (see Figure 9.10). At this stage, individuals either form intimate relationships with others or become socially isolated. Erikson describes intimacy as both finding oneself and losing oneself in another person. If the young adult develops healthy friendships and an intimate relationship with a partner, intimacy will likely be achieved. One key way that a young adult achieves intimacy is through a long-term relationship with a romantic partner, often in the form of marriage.

Just as the notion of emerging adulthood would indicate, men and women have been waiting longer to marry in the last few decades. For example, in 2007, the median age for a first marriage in the United States climbed to just over 27.5 years for men and 25.6 years for women, compared to 20.8 for women and 23.2 for men in the 1970s (U.S. Bureau of the Census, 2008). This trend may be good news, because a woman's age at her first marriage is related to the ultimate survival of the marriage. As many as 59 percent of marriages in which the wife is less than 18 years old end in divorce within 15 years, compared to just 36 percent of marriages in which the woman is age 20 or older (Center for Family and Demographic Research, 2002).

What makes a marriage successful? John Gottman has been studying married couples' lives since the early 1970s (Gottman, 1994, 2006; Gottman, Gottman, & Declaire, 2006; Gottman & Silver, 1999). He interviewed couples, filmed them interacting with each other, and even took measures of their heart rate and blood pressure during their interactions. He also checked back with the couples every year to see how their marriages were faring. Gottman and his colleagues continue to follow married couples, as well as same-sex partners, to try to understand what makes relationships thrive. A significant issue, according to Gottman, is getting past the notion that love is a magical thing. From his perspective, love is a decision and a responsibility, and individuals have control over extramarital temptations (Gottman, Gottman, & Declaire, 2006).

Gottman (2006) has found these four principles at work in successful marriages:

- *Nurturing fondness and admiration:* Partners sing each other's praises. When couples put a positive spin on their talk with and about each other, the marriage tends to work.
- *Turning toward each other as friends:* Partners see each other as friends and turn toward each other for support in times of stress and difficulty.
- *Giving up some power:* Bad marriages often involve one partner who is a powermonger. Abuse of power is more common in husbands, but some wives have the problem as well.
- *Solving conflicts together:* Couples work to solve problems, regulate their emotion during times of conflict, and compromise to accommodate each other.

SOCIOEMOTIONAL DEVELOPMENT IN MIDDLE ADULTHOOD

According to Erikson, following the resolution of intimacy versus isolation dilemma, the adult turns to concerns about *generativity versus stagnation* (see Figure 9.10). *Generativity* means making a contribution to the next generation. The feeling that one has made a lasting and memorable contribution to the world is related to higher levels of psychological well-being (McAdams & others, 1997). One way in which individuals make a lasting contribution to the world is by having children and being positively involved in their development.

Research shows that engaged parenting may have benefits not only for children but also for parents. John Snarey (1993) followed fathers and their children for four decades. He found that children, especially girls, were better off if their fathers were actively engaged in their lives—especially with regard to athletic pursuits. In addition, and perhaps more importantly for fathers, those who were constructively engaged in childrearing were themselves better off in terms of marital satisfaction, life satisfaction, and even career success.

SOCIOEMOTIONAL DEVELOPMENT AND AGING

From Erikson's perspective, the person who has entered the later years of life is engaged in looking back—evaluating his or her life and seeking meaning. Erikson called this stage of life *integrity versus despair* (see Figure 9.10). Through this process of life review and reminiscence, the older adult comes to a sense of meaning or despair, Erikson theorized. The individual is also occupied with coming to terms with his or her own death, according to Erikson. If the individual had a strong sense of integrity, experiencing life as a meaningful and coherent whole, he or she faces the later years with a strong sense of meaning and low fear of death. In the absence of integrity, the older adult is filled with despair and fear.

RESEARCH ON ADULT SOCIOEMOTIONAL DEVELOPMENT

Current research on socioemotional development and aging reveals that Erikson was correct in his view that meaning is a central concern for older adults. However, he may have overlooked that this meaning derives not necessarily just from the past but also from the present. To understand the ways in which older adults maximize a sense of meaning in life, let's conclude our look at socioemotional development in adulthood by considering recent research findings about how adults' lives change socially and emotionally over time.

In terms of social relationships, older adults may become more selective about their social networks (Carstensen, 2006, 2008). This observation was first made decades

"We only live once. Hop in."

ago, and it was interpreted as indicating that older adults, in preparation for death, were disengaging from social life (Cumming & Henry, 1961). Old age, according to the view of those earlier times, was characterized not as a stage of enjoying life, hobbies, and one's children and grandchildren but as a lonely period of disengagement from society and waiting to leave the earth. This older view stands in contrast to the perspectives that have emerged from various recent studies demonstrating that older adults are happier than their younger counterparts (Cornwell, Schumm, & Laumann, 2008; Mroczek, 2001; Mroczek & Kolarz, 1998; Ram & others, 2008) and that satisfaction with life increases with age, peaking at age 65 (Mroczek & Spiro, 2005).

Laura Carstensen developed *socioemotional selectivity theory* to address the narrowing of social contacts and the increase in positive emotion that occur with age (Carstensen, 2006; Charles & Carstensen, 2010). The theory states that because they recognize their limited time on earth, older adults tend to be selective in their social interactions, striving to maximize positive and meaningful experiences. Although younger adults may gain a sense of meaning in life from long-term goals and hopes for the future, older adults gain a sense of meaning by focusing on satisfying relationships and activities in the *present*. Unlike younger adults, who may be preoccupied with the future and stressing out over how they will accomplish their life goals, older adults may embrace the present moment with increasing vitality (Lachman & others, 2008). Socioemotional selectivity theory further posits that it is not old age itself that spurs people to focus on maximizing the positive meaning experienced in the present but, rather, limited time. Young adults who are asked to imagine having limited time (for instance, because they are about to go on a long trip) show the same pattern of maximizing time they spend with a narrow set of important friends and family members (Charles & Carstensen, 2010; Kurtz, 2008).

Research has found that with age, engagement in one's *present life* can be a vital source of meaning. The more active and involved older people are, the more satisfied they are and the more likely they are to stay healthy (Hendricks & Hatch, 2006). Researchers have found that older people who go to church, attend meetings, take trips, and exercise are happier than those who sit at home (George, 2006). In other words, the capacity to regulate emotions, maximizing positive experiences, appears to be a central feature of aging. Researchers have found that across diverse samples—Norwegians, Catholic nuns, African Americans, Chinese Americans, and Euro-Americans—older adults report better control of their emotions than younger adults (Carstensen & Charles, 2003).

Just as physical changes can influence socioemotional experience, socioemotional factors can influence physical health. One longitudinal study demonstrated that over time, women who avoided their problems (rather than confronting them) and who experienced low levels of positive emotion were more likely to show physical changes associated with diabetes (Tsenkova & others, 2008). Further, in one study, adults who had expressed positive attitudes about aging some 20 years previously, lived, on average, 7.5 years longer than those with more negative attitudes about aging (Levy, Slade, & Kasl, 2002). An important factor in the relationship between attitudes and longevity was a person's belief that life was full, hopeful, and worthwhile.

test yourself

1. What are the five main features of emerging adulthood?
2. What is brain lateralization, and how might a decrease in lateralization in older adults play a role in the aging brain?
3. What do longitudinal studies indicate about intellectual abilities in middle adulthood?

5· HUMAN DEVELOPMENT AND HEALTH AND WELLNESS

It may be that adult development is especially important *because* it occurs in the context of some declines. Unlike childhood growth, adult growth is more likely to be a conscious process and therefore a truer mark of an individual's accomplishment (King & Hicks,

2007; Levenson & Crumpler, 1996). In this concluding section we will consider the active developer as he or she meets the challenges of adulthood. We will seek to answer the question, how do adults "grow themselves"?

Coping and Adult Development

One way that adults develop is through coping with life's difficulties. Psychologist Carolyn Aldwin and her colleagues have suggested that stress and coping play a role in development (Aldwin, 2007; Aldwin, Levenson, & Kelly, 2009; Aldwin, Spiro, & Park, 2006; Aldwin, Yancura, & Boeninger, 2007; Boeninger & others, 2009). To understand how, consider that Piaget's ideas of assimilation and accommodation in childhood cognitive development may be applied to adult development as well (Block, 1982).

In assimilation, existing cognitive structures are used to make sense out of the current environment. Assimilation allows the person to enjoy a feeling of meaning because experiences fit into his or her preexisting schemas (King & Hicks, 2007). However, life does not always conform to our expectations. When our experience conflicts with our existing schemas, it is necessary to modify current ways of thinking. Accommodation is the process whereby existing schemas are modified or new structures are developed. Accommodation helps us to change so that we can make sense of life's previously incomprehensible events. When we encounter a negative life circumstance such as an illness or a loss, we have the opportunity to change—to develop and to mature (M. C. Davis & others, 2007). Indeed, research suggests that individuals who are faced with difficulties in life are more likely to come to a rich, complex view of themselves and the world (King & Hicks, 2007).

One of the negative events that people begin to experience in middle adulthood is death, especially the death of parents and older relatives. Also faced with less time in their own life, many individuals at this stage of life think more than before about what life is all about and what they want the rest of their life to be like. Austrian psychiatrist Victor Frankl confronted this issue personally and then shared his insights with the world. His mother, father, brother, and wife died in the concentration camps and gas chambers in Auschwitz, Poland. Frankl survived the camps and went on to write *Man's Search for Meaning* (1963/1984), in which he emphasized each person's uniqueness and the finite nature of life. Given the limited time we have to live, Frankl proposed that people actively ask themselves questions such as why they exist, what they want from life, and what their lives really mean.

Life Themes and Life-Span Development

Frankl's ideas fit with the concept of a life theme. As we saw earlier in this chapter, a life theme involves a person's efforts to cultivate meaningful optimal experiences (Csikszentmihalyi & Rathunde, 1998; Massimini & Delle Fave, 2000; Rathunde & Csikszentmihalyi, 2006). Consider someone who has spent much of his or her adult life pursuing wealth and career success and who turns to more selfless pursuits in middle age. To contribute to the well-being of the next generation, the individual devotes more energy and resources to helping others—for example, by volunteering or working with young people. This reorientation can ease the individual into a positive and meaningful old age. Remaining actively engaged in life is an essential part of successful adulthood (Hillman, Erickson, & Kramer, 2008).

These motivations are demonstrated by numerous individuals who are using their successes for the betterment of the world. Among the celebrities who are exploring life themes, consider Bono, the lead singer of the rock group U2. Enriched by tremendous music sales and concert proceeds, the Grammy Award

Volunteering our time and talents and working with younger people can contribute to our well-being and life satisfaction as we age.

winner has spent the last few years lobbying political leaders on behalf of African nations beset with debt. More recently, he has been an advocate for DATA, a nonprofit organization dedicated to eradicating AIDS and poverty in Africa.

As children, our psychological development occurs in tandem with physical development. As we become strong and skilled enough to walk, the horizons of our world open up to new discoveries. In adulthood, we receive our developmental cues from ourselves—where do we go, once we have managed the many tasks that human beings face in childhood and adolescence? This chapter began by reminding you of the day of your birth, a day when you were the center of attention and a mystery waiting to unfold. From a developmental psychology perspective, today could be as important as that day. On the day you were born, you were full of possibilities—and you still are.

SUMMARY

1. EXPLORING HUMAN DEVELOPMENT

Development is the pattern of change in human capabilities that begins at birth and continues throughout the life span. Research on human development can be cross-sectional, which demonstrates age differences, or longitudinal, which demonstrates age-related change. To make strong conclusions about development, longitudinal data are necessary.

Both nature (biological inheritance) and nurture (environmental experience) extensively influence development. However, people are not at the mercy of either their genes or their environment when they actively construct optimal experiences. Resilience refers to the capacity of individuals to thrive during difficulties at every stage of development.

2. CHILD DEVELOPMENT

Prenatal development progresses through the germinal, embryonic, and fetal periods. Particular drugs, such as alcohol and nicotine, as well as certain illnesses, can adversely affect the fetus. These environmental threats are called teratogens. Preterm birth is another potential problem, especially if the infant is very small or grows up in an adverse environment.

The infant's physical development is dramatic in the first year, and a number of motor milestones are reached in infancy. Extensive changes in the brain, including denser connections between synapses, take place in infancy and childhood.

With regard to cognitive development, in Piaget's view, children use schemas to actively construct their world, either assimilating new information into existing schemas or adjusting schemas to accommodate that information. Piaget identified four stages of cognitive development: the sensorimotor stage, the preoperational stage, the concrete operational stage, and the formal operational stage.

Socioemotional development in childhood includes consideration of Erikson's psychosocial stages as well as moral development. Erikson presented a major, eight-stage psychosocial view of life-span development; its first four stages occur in childhood. In each stage, the individual seeks to resolve a particular socioemotional conflict. Kohlberg proposed a cognitive theory of moral development with three levels (preconventional, conventional, and postconventional).

3. ADOLESCENCE

Puberty is a period of rapid skeletal and sexual maturation that occurs mainly in early adolescence. Its onset occurs about two years earlier in girls than in boys. Hormonal changes trigger pubertal development.

According to Piaget, cognitive development in adolescence is characterized by the appearance of formal operational thought, the final stage in his theory. This stage involves abstract, idealistic, and logical thought.

One of the most important aspects of socioemotional development in adolescence is identity. Erikson's fifth stage of psychosocial development is identity versus identity confusion. Marcia proposed four statuses of identity based on crisis and commitment. A special concern is the development of ethnic identity. Despite great differences among adolescents, the majority of them develop competently.

4. EMERGING ADULTHOOD, ADULT DEVELOPMENT, AND AGING

Psychologists refer to the period between adolescence and adulthood as emerging adulthood. This period is characterized by the exploration of identity through work and relationships, instability, and self-focus.

Most adults reach their peak physical performance during their 20s and are healthiest then. Physical skills begin to decline during the 30s. The cellular-clock, free-radical, and hormonal stress theories are three important biological explanations for aging. Even in late adulthood, the brain has remarkable repair capacity and plasticity.

Piaget argued that no new cognitive changes occur in adulthood. However, some psychologists have proposed that the idealistic thinking of adolescents is replaced by the more realistic, pragmatic thinking of young adults. Longitudinal research on intelligence shows that many cognitive skills peak in middle age. Overall, older adults do not do as well on memory and other cognitive tasks and are slower to process information than younger adults. However, older adults may have greater wisdom than younger adults.

Erikson's three stages of socioemotional development in adulthood are intimacy versus isolation (early adulthood), generativity versus stagnation (middle adulthood), and integrity versus despair (late adulthood). A special concern, beginning when individuals are in their 50s, is the challenge of understanding life's meaning. Researchers have found that remaining active increases the likelihood that older adults will be happy and healthy. They also have found that older adults often reduce their general social affiliations and instead are motivated to spend more time with close friends and family members. Older adults also experience more positive emotion, are happier, and are more satisfied with their lives than younger adults.

Until recently, the positive dimensions of aging were largely ignored. Developmentalists now recognize that many adults can sustain or even improve their functioning as they age. Researchers today widely view adult development as a self-motivated process limited only by the individual's imagination.

5. HUMAN DEVELOPMENT AND HEALTH AND WELLNESS

Though often associated with childhood, psychological development can continue throughout life. Psychologists have suggested that coping with life's difficulties is one way in which adults may develop. For adults, taking an active approach to developing oneself may be an im-

portant motivator in development. Piaget's concepts of assimilation and accommodation have been applied to the process of developing through difficult times. An individual may experience meaning in life by applying his or her current understanding of the world (assimilation). In contrast, the individual may find that some experiences require a revision of that understanding (accommodation). In adulthood, people have the opportunity to pursue new goals that represent important life themes, such as leaving a legacy for the future.

key *terms*

development, p. 278
nature, p. 280
nurture, p. 280
resilience, p. 282
preferential looking, p. 286
assimilation, p. 287
accommodation, p. 288

sensorimotor stage, p. 288
preoperational stage, p. 289
concrete operational stage, p. 290
formal operational stage, p. 290
temperament, p. 292
infant attachment, p. 293
secure attachment, p. 293

authoritarian
    parenting, p. 296
authoritative
    parenting, p. 296
neglectful parenting, p. 296
permissive parenting, p. 297
prosocial behavior, p. 299

puberty, p. 300
androgens, p. 300
estrogens, p. 300
identity versus identity
    confusion, p. 301
emerging adulthood, p. 304
wisdom, p. 308

apply your *knowledge*

1. Consider the style of parenting with which you were raised. It might help to think of specific situations or moments when your parents put limits on your behavior (or did not). If you have one or more siblings, ask for their opinion, too. Do you agree with one another about your parents' style? Now give these definitions to your parents, and ask which, if any, describes them. Sometimes there are as many different views of a family as there are members of that family.

2. A major part of any child's life is playing—and when kids are playing, they are often playing with toys. Using the information on perceptual and cognitive development reviewed in this chapter, design a toy that you think is a perfect fit for a child of 2 months, 2 years, and 10 years old. With respect to the child's development, what features of the toy are especially good for the child of each age group?

3. Go online and Google "parenting discussion boards." Click on one or two of the many sites that come up, and see what parents are talking about. What issues seem to concern them most? Do

these parents appear to have a sense of the issues addressed by developmental psychologists? Does the advice that parents share with one another seem to be based on the science of psychology?

4. Set aside 15 minutes to write a brief essay as follows. Think about your life in the future, when you are 70 or 80 years old. Imagine that everything has gone as well as it possibly could, and you have achieved your life dreams. What is your life like at this stage? What things about you are the same as they are for you now as a student of psychology? What things have changed? What is your best possible older adult self? How have aspects of your life today contributed to this happily-older-after?

5. You might have heard the statement that "40 is the new 30" or "50 is the new 40." What trend do these statements reflect? What might explain this trend? What might it mean for our understanding of adult development?

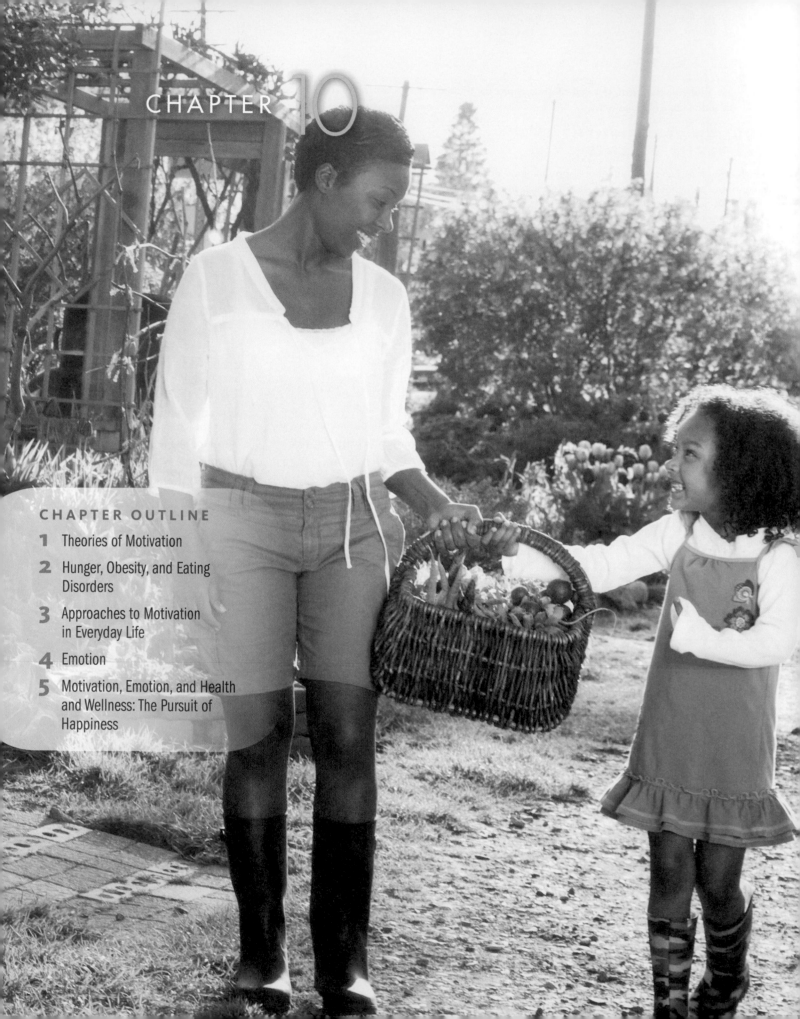

Motivation and Emotion

Climbing Unseen Mountains

In 1995, Erik Weihenmayer and his team were ascending Mount McKinley, the highest peak in North America. His wife and family arranged to fly over them in a plane. All the climbers in the team were dressed in red gear, and as they waved their ski poles madly at the plane overhead, Weihenmayer asked a friend, "Do you think they know which one is me?" His friend assured him that they probably did, because he was the only one waving in the wrong direction.

Erik Weihenmayer—an exceptional athlete, skier, and marathon runner—has been completely blind since age 13. He is also one of an elite group that has made it to the top of all the Seven Summits, including Mount Everest, which he climbed in 2001. Considering the obstacles Weihenmayer faces, we might ask why he did it. More pointedly, why did he *even imagine* doing it? For Weihenmayer, part of the motivation has been to inspire others to look beyond physical disabilities and to imagine the possibilities in every human circumstance. Although he has shattered stereotypes about what a blind person can accomplish, his tremendous efforts have also allowed him to stand on the peak of Everest as "just another climber."

When we ask "why," we are asking about motivation. The terms *motivation* and *emotion* come from the Latin word *movere*, which means "to move." Motivation and emotion are the "go" of human life, providing the steam that propels us to overcome obstacles and to accomplish the great and little things we do every day. Our emotions often define for us what we really want: We feel joy or sorrow depending on how events influence our most cherished life dreams. ●

PREVIEW

This chapter examines the ways psychologists study motivation and emotion. We first review some general approaches to motivation and consider one important physiological source of motivation: hunger. We then examine motivation as it applies to everyday life. Next, we explore the rich topic of emotion. We close by considering the ways that motivation and emotion intertwine in the pursuit of happiness.

1· THEORIES OF MOTIVATION

● **motivation** The force that moves people to behave, think, and feel the way they do.

Motivation is the force that moves people to behave, think, and feel the way they do. Motivated behavior is energized, directed, and sustained. Psychologists have proposed a variety of theories about why organisms are motivated to do what they do. In this section we explore some of the main theoretical approaches to motivation.

The Evolutionary Approach

In the early history of psychology, the evolutionary approach emphasized the role of instincts in motivation. *Ethology*—the study of animal behavior—also has described motivation from an evolutionary perspective.

● **instinct** An innate (unlearned) biological pattern of behavior that is assumed to be universal throughout a species.

An **instinct** is an innate (unlearned) biological pattern of behavior that is assumed to be universal throughout a species. Generally, an instinct is set in motion by a *sign stimulus*—something in the environment that turns on a fixed pattern of behavior. Instincts may explain a great deal of nonhuman animal behavior. In addition, some human behavior is instinctive. Recall, for example, the discussion of infant reflexes in Chapter 9. Babies do not have to learn to suck; they instinctively do it when something is placed in their mouth. So, for infants, an object touching the lips is a sign stimulus. After infancy, though, it is hard to think of specific behaviors that all human beings engage in when presented with a particular stimulus.

According to evolutionary psychologists, the motivations for sex, aggression, achievement, and other behaviors are rooted in our evolutionary past, and we can understand similarities among members of the human species through these shared evolutionary roots. Because evolutionary approaches emphasize the passing on of one's genes, these theories focus on domains of life that are especially relevant to reproduction. For example, evolutionary theorists note that in terms of romantic partners, across many cultures, men prefer younger women to older women, and women prefer men who have resources (Cosmides, 2011; Geary, 2010).

In general, however, most human behavior is far too complex to be explained on the basis of instinct. Indeed, it would hardly seem adaptive for humans to have a fixed action pattern that is invariably set in motion by a particular signal in the environment. To understand human behavior, psychologists have developed a variety of other approaches, as we now consider.

Drive Reduction Theory

● **drive** An aroused state that occurs because of a physiological need.

Another way to think about motivation is through the constructs of drive and need. A **drive** is an aroused state that occurs because of a physiological need. You can think of a drive as a psychological itch that requires scratching. A **need** is a deprivation that energizes the drive to eliminate or reduce the deprivation. Generally, psychologists think of needs as underlying our drives. You may have a need for water; the drive that accompanies that need is your feeling of being thirsty. Usually but not always, needs

● **need** A deprivation that energizes the drive to eliminate or reduce the deprivation.

and drives are closely associated. For example, when your body needs food, your hunger drive will probably be aroused. An hour after you have eaten a hamburger, your body might still need essential nutrients (thus you need food), but your hunger drive might have subsided.

This example should reinforce the concept that drive pertains to a psychological state, whereas need involves a physiological one. Drives do not always follow from needs. For example, if you are deprived of oxygen because of a gas leak, you have a need for oxygen. You may feel lightheaded but may never realize that your condition is the result of a gas leak that is creating a need for air. That is, you might never experience the drive for oxygen that might lead you to open a window. Moreover, drives sometimes seem to come out of nowhere. Imagine having eaten a fine meal and feeling full to the point of not wanting another single bite—until the waiter wheels over the dessert cart. Suddenly you feel ready to tackle the Double Chocolate Oblivion, despite your lack of hunger.

Drive reduction theory explains that as a drive becomes stronger, we are motivated to reduce it. The goal of drive reduction is **homeostasis,** the body's tendency to maintain an equilibrium, or a steady state. Hundreds of biological states in the body must be maintained within a certain range; these include temperature, blood sugar level, potassium and sodium levels, and oxygenation. When you dive into an icy swimming pool, your body uses energy to maintain its normal temperature. When you walk out of an air-conditioned room into the heat of a summer day, your body releases excess heat by sweating. These physiological changes occur automatically to keep your body in an optimal state of functioning.

Most psychologists conclude that drive reduction theory does not provide a comprehensive framework for understanding motivation because people often behave in ways that increase rather than reduce a drive. For example, when dieting, you might choose to skip meals, but this tactic can increase your hunger drive rather than reduce it. Similarly, many other things that you might opt to do involve increasing (not decreasing) tensions—for example, taking a challenging course in school, raising a family, and working at a difficult job.

Optimum Arousal Theory

When psychologists talk about arousal, they are generally referring to a person's feelings of being alert and engaged. When we are very excited, our arousal levels are high. When we are bored, they are low. You have probably noticed that motivation influences arousal levels. Sometimes you can want something (for example, to do well on a test) so much that you can become overly motivated and anxious. On the other hand, you might be so unmotivated for a task (such as doing dishes) that you can hardly force yourself to complete it. Sometimes, to do well, you need to have an arousal level that is "just right" (Keeley, Zayac, & Correia, 2008).

Early in the twentieth century, two psychologists described how arousal can influence performance. According to their formulation, now known as the **Yerkes-Dodson law,** performance is best under conditions of moderate arousal rather than either low or high arousal. At the low end of arousal, you may be too lethargic to perform tasks well; at the high end, you may not be able to concentrate. To master the Yerkes-Dodson law, check out the Psychological Inquiry on p. 318.

The relationship between arousal and performance is one reason that individuals in many professions are trained to overlearn important procedures. **Overlearning** means learning to perform a task so well that it becomes automatic. Recall Captain Chesley "Sully" Sullenberger, the pilot who landed the U.S. Airways plane safely in the Hudson River. For individuals who must perform at their best in a crisis, success depends on knowing what to do so well that it requires little or no thought. With this extra learning, when these individuals are under conditions of high arousal, they can rely on automatic pilot to do what needs to be done.

● **homeostasis** The body's tendency to maintain an equilibrium, or steady state.

● **Yerkes-Dodson law** The psychological principle stating that performance is best under conditions of moderate arousal rather than either low or high arousal.

● **overlearning** Learning to perform a task so well that it becomes automatic.

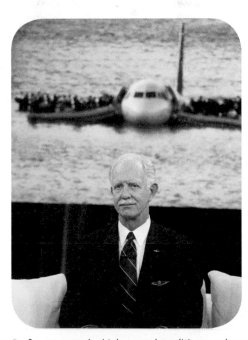

Performance under high-arousal conditions, such as those pilot Chesley Sullenberger faced when he had to land his damaged plane in the Hudson River, requires being trained to the point of overlearning.

test yourself

1. What is motivation?
2. What are three theoretical approaches to motivation?
3. What is overlearning, and how can it help an individual who must perform at his or her best?

psychological *inquiry*

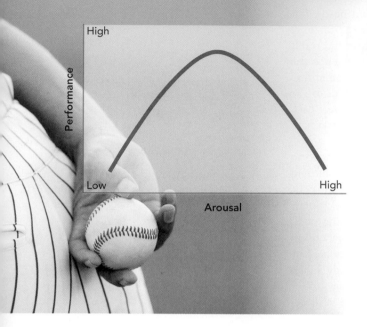

Performance

High

Low

High

Arousal

Obeying the (Yerkes-Dodson) Law

The graph displays the relationship between arousal (shown on the X, or horizontal, axis) and performance (shown on the Y, or vertical, axis). Note that the curve is in the form of an inverted *U*. Using the figure as a reference, answer the questions below.

1. What was your arousal level the last time you took an exam? If you were very nervous, your arousal level would be considered high. If you were excited and engaged but not too worried, it would be in the medium range. If you were feeling sluggish, your arousal level would be low.

2. How did you actually do on that test? Plot your performance on the graph. Does it fit with the Yerkes-Dodson prediction?

3. Now think about performance in sports or the arts. Imagine your favorite athlete, musician, or actor. How might that person feel when he or she is on the spot, trying to sink a winning free-throw, strike out the last batter, or impress an audience? How might arousal influence performance in those cases?

4. In many professions, individuals are forced to perform under conditions of very high arousal. These include EMTs, lifeguards, and emergency room medical professionals. (Name some others.) How might such individuals train themselves to perform even under conditions of extreme arousal?

2· HUNGER, OBESITY, AND EATING DISORDERS

Part of the power of motivation in life is tied to physiological needs. We experience strong motivational forces, for example, when we are hungry or thirsty. Furthermore, the physiological state of being hungry has often been used as a path toward understanding a variety of human motivations. We might even use words about hunger in non-physiological contexts, such as when we say that someone is "craving" attention or "starving" for affection. In this section we examine the basic motivational processes underlying hunger and eating, including the related topic of eating disorders.

The Biology of Hunger

You know you are hungry when your stomach growls and you feel those familiar hunger pangs. What role do such signals play in hunger?

GASTRIC SIGNALS

In 1912, Walter Cannon and A. L. Washburn conducted an experiment that revealed a close association between stomach contractions and hunger (Figure 10.1). In one step of the procedure, a partially inflated balloon was passed through a tube inserted in Washburn's mouth and pushed down into his stomach. A machine that measures air pressure was connected to the balloon to monitor Washburn's stomach contractions. Every time Washburn reported hunger pangs, his stomach was also contracting. Sure enough, a growling stomach needs food. The stomach tells the brain not only how full it is but also how much nutrient is present, which is why rich food stops hunger faster than the same amount of water. The hormone cholecystokinin (CCK) helps start the digestion of food, travels to the brain through the bloodstream, and signals us to stop eating (Nefti & others, 2009). Hunger involves a lot more than an empty stomach, however.

BLOOD CHEMISTRY

Three key chemical substances play a role in hunger, eating, and *satiety* (the state of feeling full): glucose, insulin, and leptin.

Glucose (blood sugar) is an important factor in hunger, probably because the brain critically depends on sugar for energy. One set of sugar receptors, located in the brain itself, triggers hunger when sugar levels fall too low. Another set of sugar receptors is in the liver, which stores excess sugar and releases it into the blood when needed. The sugar receptors in the liver signal the brain when its sugar supply falls, and this signal also can make you hungry.

The hormone *insulin* also plays a role in glucose control (Dominquez Coello & others, 2010; Oliver & others, 2009). When we eat complex carbohydrates such as bread and pasta, insulin levels go up and fall off gradually. When we consume simple sugars such as candy, insulin levels rise and then fall sharply—the all-too-familiar "sugar low" (Rodin, 1984). Blood glucose levels are affected by complex carbohydrates and simple sugars in similar ways, so we are more likely to eat within the next several hours after eating simple sugars than after eating complex carbohydrates.

Released by fat cells, the chemical substance *leptin* (from the Greek word *leptos,* meaning "thin") decreases food intake and increases energy expenditure or metabolism (Bluher & Mantzoros, 2009; Kaiyala & others, 2010). Leptin's functions were discovered in a strain of genetically obese mice, called *ob mice* (Pelleymounter & others, 1995). Because of a genetic mutation, the fat cells of ob mice cannot produce leptin. The ob mouse has a low metabolism, overeats, and gets extremely fat. Leptin appears to act as an anti-obesity hormone (Friedman, 2009; Kovalszky & others, 2010). If ob mice are given daily injections of leptin, their metabolic rate increases, and they become more active, eat less, and lose weight. Figure 10.2 shows an untreated ob mouse and an ob mouse that has received injections of leptin.

In humans, leptin concentrations have been linked with weight, body fat, and weight loss in response to dieting (Lee & Fried, 2009). Scientists continue to explore the possibility that disorders in the production and uptake of leptin may explain human obesity (Adam, 2010).

FIGURE 10.1   Cannon and Washburn's Classic Experiment on Hunger In this experiment, the researchers demonstrated that stomach contractions, which were detected by the stomach balloon, accompany a person's hunger feelings, which were indicated by pressing the key. Line A in the chart records increases and decreases in the volume of the balloon in the participant's stomach. Line B records the passage of time. Line C records the participant's manual signals of feelings of hunger. Line D records a reading from the belt around the participant's waist to detect movements of the abdominal wall and ensure that such movements are not the cause of changes in stomach volume.

BRAIN PROCESSES

Chapter 3 described the central role of the hypothalamus in regulating important body functions, including hunger. More specifically, activity in two areas of the hypothalamus contributes to our understanding of hunger. The *lateral hypothalamus* is involved in stimulating eating. When this area is electrically stimulated in a well-fed animal, the animal begins to eat. If this part of the hypothalamus is destroyed, even a starving animal will show no interest in food. The *ventromedial hypothalamus* is involved in reducing hunger and restricting eating. When this area of an animal's brain is stimulated, the animal stops eating. When the area is destroyed, the animal eats profusely and quickly becomes obese.

Although the lateral and ventromedial hypothalamuses both influence hunger, there is much more to the brain's role in determining hunger than these on/off centers in the hypothalamus. Neurotransmitters (the chemical messengers that convey information from neuron to neuron) and neural circuits (clusters of neurons that often involve different parts of the brain) also function in hunger (Fulton, 2010; Minor,

FIGURE 10.2   Leptin and Obesity The ob mouse on the left is untreated; the one on the right has been given injections of leptin.

Chang, & de Cabo, 2009). Leptin influences eating by inhibiting the production of a neurotransmitter in the hypothalamus that induces eating. The neurotransmitter serotonin is partly responsible for the satiating effect of CCK, and serotonin antagonists have been used to treat obesity in humans (Garfield & Heisler, 2009; Rodgers, Holch, & Tallett, 2010; Zhang & others, 2010).

Obesity

Given that the brain and body are so elegantly wired to regulate eating behavior, why do so many people in the United States overeat and suffer the effects of this behavior? According to the Centers for Disease Control and Prevention (CDC), 60 percent of Americans are overweight, and one-third are considered obese (dangerously overweight) (CDC, 2009a). Being obese or overweight raises one's risk for a variety of health problems, such as cardiovascular disease, diabetes, and depression (Shelton & Miller, 2010; Vega, Barlow, & Grundy, 2010). Currently, the number of people considered overweight around the world is 20 percent higher than the number suffering from hunger.

The reason so many people overeat to the point of becoming obese is a motivational puzzle, because it involves eating when one is not in need of nutrition. As is the case with much behavior, in eating, biological, cognitive, and sociocultural factors interact in diverse ways in different individuals, making it difficult to point to a specific cause (Adler & Stewart, 2009).

THE BIOLOGY OF OBESITY

Obesity clearly has a genetic component. After the discovery of an ob gene in mice, researchers found a similar gene in humans. Some individuals do inherit a tendency to be overweight (Keller & Attie, 2010). Only 10 percent of children who do not have obese parents become obese themselves, whereas 40 percent of children who have one obese parent become obese, and 70 percent of children who have two obese parents become obese. Identical human twins have similar weights, even when they are reared apart (Maes, Neal, & Eaves, 1997).

● **set point** The weight maintained when the individual makes no effort to gain or lose weight.

Another factor in weight is **set point,** the weight maintained when the individual makes no effort to gain or lose weight. Set point is determined in part by the amount of stored fat in the body (Levin, 2010). Fat is stored in *adipose cells,* or fat cells. When these cells are filled, you do not get hungry. When people gain weight—because of genetic predisposition, childhood eating patterns, or adult overeating—their fat cell number increases, and they might not be able to get rid of extra ones. A normal-weight individual has 10 to 20 billion fat cells. An obese individual can have up to 100 billion fat cells (Fried, 2008). Consequently, an obese individual has to eat more to feel satisfied.

PSYCHOLOGICAL FACTORS IN HUNGER AND OBESITY

Psychologists used to think that obesity stemmed from factors such as unhappiness and external food cues. These ideas make some sense; drowning one's sorrows in chocolate or eating some cookies just because they are there seems common enough to explain overeating. However, a number of factors are more important than emotional state and external stimuli (Rodin, 1984).

Time and place affect our eating. Learned associations of food with a particular place and time are characteristic of many organisms (Fiese, Foley, & Spagnola, 2006). If it is noon, we are likely to feel hungry even if we ate a big breakfast. We also associate eating with certain places. Many people link watching television with eating and feel uncomfortable if they are not eating something while watching TV.

From an evolutionary framework, we might note that human taste preferences developed at a time when reliable food sources were scarce. Our earliest ancestors probably developed a preference for sweets and fatty foods because ripe fruit, a concentrated source of sugar (and calories), was accessible and because high-fat foods carried much-needed calories. Today many people still have a taste for such foods, but unlike our ancestors' ripe fruit (containing sugar *plus* vitamins and minerals), the soft drinks and candy bars we snack on fill us with nutrient-free calories. Furthermore, in modern life we rarely require the calorie counts that our ancestors needed to survive.

Dieting is a continuing U.S. obsession. In Chapter 17, we will consider ways that individuals can successfully lose weight. However, some people who focus on losing weight do so not for reasons of good health but because they have eating disorders, our next topic.

Disordered Eating

Many Americans feel that life would improve greatly if they could just lose those last 5 pounds. However, for some people, concerns about weight and body image become a serious, debilitating disorder (Miller & Golden, 2010; Treasure, Claudino, & Zucker, 2010). For such individuals, the very act of eating, an activity essential for survival, becomes an arena where a variety of complex biological, psychological, and cultural issues are played out, often with tragic consequences.

A number of famous people have coped with eating disorders, including Princess Diana, Paula Abdul, Mary-Kate Olsen, and Kelly Clarkson. Eating disorders are characterized by extreme disturbances in eating behavior—from eating very, very little to eating a great deal. In this section we examine three eating disorders— anorexia nervosa, bulimia nervosa, and binge eating disorder.

ANOREXIA NERVOSA

Anorexia nervosa is an eating disorder that involves the relentless pursuit of thinness through starvation. Anorexia nervosa is much more common in girls and women than boys and men and affects between 0.5 and 3.7 percent of young women (NIMH, 2009). The American Psychiatric Association (2005) lists these main characteristics of anorexia nervosa:

● **anorexia nervosa** Eating disorder that involves the relentless pursuit of thinness through starvation.

- Weight less than 85 percent of what is considered normal for age and height and refusing to maintain weight at a healthy level.

- An intense fear of gaining weight that does not decrease with weight loss.

- A distorted body image (Costa, Vasconcelos, & Peres, 2010). Even when individuals with anorexia nervosa are extremely thin, they never think they are thin enough. They weigh themselves frequently, take their body measurements often, and gaze critically at themselves in mirrors.

- Amenorrhea (lack of menstruation) in girls who have reached puberty.

Over time, anorexia nervosa can lead to physical changes, such as the growth of fine hair all over the body, thinning of bones and hair, severe constipation, and low blood pressure (NIMH, 2009). Dangerous and even life-threatening complications of anorexia nervosa include damage to the heart and thyroid. Anorexia nervosa is said to have the highest mortality rate (about 5.6 percent of individuals with anorexia nervosa die within 10 years of diagnosis) of any psychological disorder (Hoek, 2006; NIMH, 2009).

Anorexia nervosa typically begins in the teenage years, often following an episode of dieting and some type of life stress (Lo Sauro & others, 2008; Sigel, 2008). Most individuals with anorexia nervosa are non-Latino White female adolescents or young adults from well-educated middle- and upper-income families. They are often high-achieving perfectionists (Forbush, Heatherton, & Keel, 2007). In addition to perfectionism, obsessive thinking about weight and compulsive exercise are related to anorexia nervosa (Finzi-Dottan & Zubery, 2009).

● **bulimia nervosa** Eating disorder in which an individual (typically female) consistently follows a binge-and-purge eating pattern.

Uruguayan model Eliana Ramos posed for the camera in her native country. Tragically, the super-thin Eliana died at age 18 in February 2007, two years after this picture was taken, reportedly from health problems associated with anorexia nervosa.

BULIMIA NERVOSA

Bulimia nervosa is an eating disorder in which an individual (typically female) consistently follows a binge-and-purge eating pattern. The individual goes on an eating binge and then purges by self-induced vomiting or the use of laxatives. Most people with bulimia nervosa are preoccupied with food, have a strong fear of becoming overweight, and are depressed or anxious (Speranza & others, 2003). Because bulimia nervosa occurs within a normal weight range, the disorder is often difficult to detect (Mizes & Miller, 2000). A person with bulimia nervosa usually keeps the disorder a secret and experiences a great deal of disgust and shame.

Bulimia nervosa can lead to complications such as a chronic sore throat, kidney problems, dehydration, and gastrointestinal disorders (NIMH, 2009). The disorder is also related to dental problems, as persistent exposure to the stomach acids in vomit can wear away tooth enamel.

Bulimia nervosa typically begins in late adolescence or early adulthood (Levine, 2002). The disorder affects between 1 and 4 percent of young women (NIMH, 2008). Like those with anorexia nervosa, many young women who develop bulimia nervosa are highly perfectionistic (Forbush, Heatherton, & Keel, 2007). At the same time, they tend to have low levels of self-efficacy (Bardone-Cone & others, 2006). In other words, these are young women with very high standards but very low confidence that they can achieve their goals. Impulsivity, negative emotion, and childhood obsessive-compulsive disorder (see Chapter 15) are also related to bulimia (Tchanturia & others, 2004; Vervaet, van Heeringen, & Audenaert, 2004). Bulimia nervosa is associated, too, with a high incidence of sexual and physical abuse in childhood (Lo Sauro & others, 2008).

ANOREXIA NERVOSA AND BULIMIA NERVOSA: CAUSES AND TREATMENTS

What is the etiology (cause) of anorexia nervosa and bulimia nervosa? For many years researchers thought that sociocultural factors, such as media images of very thin women and family pressures, were the central determinant of these disorders (le Grange & others, 2010). Certainly the U.S. popular media bombard their audiences with images of extremely thin women. Media images that glorify extreme thinness can influence women's body image, and emphasis on the thin ideal is related to anorexia nervosa and bulimia nervosa (Harrison & Hefner, 2006; Stice & others, 2007; Treasure, Claudino, & Zucker, 2010).

However, as powerful as these media messages might be, countless females are exposed to media images of unrealistically thin women, but relatively few develop eating disorders. Many young women embark on diets, but comparatively few of them develop eating disorders. Thus, since the 1980s, researchers have moved beyond a sole focus on sociocultural factors and have increasingly probed the potential biological underpinnings of these disorders. This research has examined the interplay of social and biological factors in eating disorders.

Genes play a substantial role in both anorexia nervosa and bulimia nervosa (Calati & others, 2010; Sokol & others, 2009). In fact, genes influence many psychological characteristics (for example, perfectionism, impulsivity, obsessive-compulsive tendencies, and thinness drive) and behaviors (restrained eating, binge eating, self-induced vomiting) that are associated with anorexia nervosa and bulimia nervosa (Bulik & others, 2000; Mikolajczyk, Grzywacz, & Samochowiec, 2010; Schur, Heckbert, & Goldberg, 2010). These genes are also factors in the regulation of serotonin, and problems in regulating serotonin are related to both anorexia nervosa and bulimia nervosa (Capasso, Putrella, & Milano, 2009).

Keep in mind that even as biological factors play a role in the emergence of eating disorders, eating disorders themselves affect the body, including the brain. Most psychologists believe that while social factors and experiences may play a role in triggering dieting, the physical effects of dieting, bingeing, and purging may change the neural networks that then sustain the disordered pattern, in a kind of vicious cycle (Kaye, 2008; le Grange & others, 2010; Treasure, Claudino, & Zucker, 2010).

Although anorexia and bulimia nervosa are serious disorders, recovery is possible (Treasure, Claudino, & Zucker, 2010; van Son & others, 2010). Anorexia nervosa may require hospitalization. The first target of intervention is promoting weight gain, in extreme cases through the use of a feeding tube. A common obstacle in the treatment of anorexia nervosa is that individuals with the disorder deny that anything is wrong. They maintain their belief that thinness and restrictive dieting are correct and not a sign of mental illness (Wilson, Grilo, & Vitousek, 2007). Still, drug therapies and psychotherapy have been shown to be effective in treating anorexia nervosa, as well as bulimia nervosa (Thompson-Brenner, Boisseau, & Satir, 2010).

BINGE EATING DISORDER

Binge eating disorder (BED) is characterized by recurrent episodes of consuming large amounts of food during which the person feels a lack of control over eating (NIMH, 2009; Striegel-Moore & Franko, 2008). Unlike an individual with bulimia nervosa, someone with BED does not try to purge. Most individuals with BED are overweight or obese.

Individuals with BED often eat quickly, eat a great deal when they are not hungry, and eat until they are uncomfortably full. They frequently eat alone because of embarrassment or guilt, and they experience disgust and shame after overeating. BED is the most common of all eating disorders—affecting men, women, and ethnic groups within the United States more similarly than anorexia nervosa or bulimia nervosa (Azarbad & others, 2010; Striegel-Moore & Franko, 2008). An estimated 2 to 5 percent of Americans will suffer from BED in their lifetime (NIMH, 2009).

BED is thought to characterize approximately 8 percent of individuals who are obese. Unlike obese individuals who do not suffer from BED, binge eaters are more likely to place great value on their physical appearance, weight, and body shape (Grilo, Masheb, & White, 2010). The complications of BED are those of obesity more generally, including diabetes, hypertension, and cardiovascular disease.

BINGE EATING DISORDER: CAUSES AND TREATMENTS

Researchers are examining the role of biological and psychological factors in BED. Genes play a role (Akkermann & others, 2010), as does dopamine, the neurotransmitter related to reward pathways in the brain (C. Davis & others, 2010). The fact that binge eating often occurs after stressful events suggests that binge eaters use food as a way to regulate their emotions (Wilson, Grilo, & Vitousek, 2007). The areas of the brain and endocrine system that respond to stress are overactive in individuals with BED (Lo Sauro & others, 2008), and this overactivity leads to high levels of circulating cortisol, the hormone most associated with stress. Individuals with BED may be more likely to perceive events as stressful and then seek to manage that stress by binge eating.

Just as treatment for anorexia nervosa focuses on weight gain first, some believe that treatment for BED should focus on weight loss first (De Angelis, 2002). Others argue that individuals with BED must be treated for disordered eating per se, and insist that if the underlying psychological issues are not addressed, weight loss will not be successful or permanent (de Zwaan & others, 2005; Hay & others, 2009).

Food is unquestionably necessary for survival. Individuals struggling with disordered eating must change their relationship with this vital resource in order to survive and, eventually, thrive. Clearly, though, human thriving involves more than food. We next turn to the broader implications of motivation in everyday life.

3· APPROACHES TO MOTIVATION IN EVERYDAY LIFE

Think about the wide range of human actions and achievements reported in the news, such as a man's donation of his kidney to a best friend and the appointment of a woman who grew up in poverty as the CEO of a major corporation. Such

● **binge eating disorder (BED)** Eating disorder characterized by recurrent episodes of consuming large amounts of food during which the person feels a lack of control over eating.

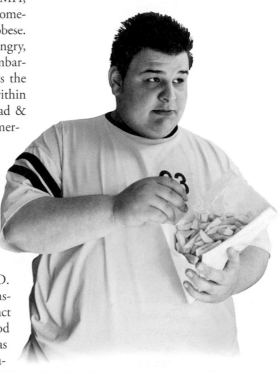

Unlike individuals with anorexia nervosa or bulimia nervosa, most people with binge eating disorder (BED) are overweight or obese.

test yourself

1. In Cannon and Washburn's classic study on hunger, what bodily associations were revealed?
2. What is leptin, and how does it function in the body?
3. What are some key ways that bulimia nervosa and binge eating disorder differ?

individuals' behaviors are not easily explained by motivational approaches that focus on physiological needs. Psychologists have begun to appreciate the role of the goals that people set for themselves in motivation (Mayer, 2011). In this section, we explore the ways that psychologists have come to understand the processes that underlie everyday human behavior.

Maslow's Hierarchy of Human Needs

● **hierarchy of needs** Maslow's theory that human needs must be satisfied in the following sequence: physiological needs, safety, love and belongingness, esteem, and self-actualization.

Humanistic theorist Abraham Maslow (1954, 1971) proposed a **hierarchy of needs** that must be satisfied in the following sequence: physiological needs, safety, love and belongingness, esteem, and self-actualization (Figure 10.3). The strongest needs are at the base of the hierarchy (physiological), and the weakest are at the top (self-actualization).

According to this hierarchy, people are motivated to satisfy their need for food first and to fulfill their need for safety before their need for love. If we think of our needs as calls for action, hunger and safety needs shout loudly, while the need for self-actualization beckons with a whisper. Maslow asserted that each lower need in the hierarchy comes from a deficiency—such as being hungry, afraid, or lonely—and that we can only see the higher-level needs in a person who is relatively satisfied in these most basic needs. Such an individual can then turn his or her attention to the fulfillment of a higher calling.

● **self-actualization** The motivation to develop one's full potential as a human being—the highest and most elusive of Maslow's proposed needs.

Self-actualization, the highest and most elusive of Maslow's needs, is the motivation to develop one's full potential as a human being. According to Maslow, self-actualization is possible only after the other needs in the hierarchy are met. Maslow cautions that most people stop moving up the hierarchy after they have developed a high level of esteem and thus do not become self-actualized. We will return to Maslow's notion of self-actualization in Chapter 12.

The idea that human motives are hierarchically arranged is appealing; however, Maslow's ordering of the needs is debatable (Kenrick & others, 2010). Some people might seek greatness in a career to achieve self-esteem, while putting on hold their needs for love and belongingness. Certainly history is full of examples of individuals who, in the most difficult circumstances, were still able to engage in acts of kindness that seem to come from higher-level needs. Often, the poorest individuals are most likely to give generously to others.

● **self-determination theory** Deci and Ryan's theory asserting that all humans have three basic, innate organismic needs: competence, relatedness, and autonomy.

Perhaps Maslow's greatest contribution to our understanding of motivation is that he asked the key question about motivation for modern people: How can we explain what humans do, once their bellies are full? That is, how do we explain the "why" of human behavior when survival is not the most pressing need? This is the kind of questioning that inspired *self-determination theory* (Deci & Ryan, 2002; Ryan & Deci, 2009).

FIGURE 10.3 Maslow's Hierarchy of Needs Abraham Maslow developed the hierarchy of human needs to show that we have to satisfy basic physiological needs before we can satisfy other, higher needs.

Self-Determination Theory

Building from Maslow's humanistic perspective, Edward Deci and Richard Ryan have explored the role of motivation in optimal human functioning from a perspective that emphasizes particular kinds of needs as factors in psychological and physical well-being (Deci & Ryan, 2000; Ryan & Deci, 2009). Their **self-determination theory** asserts that there are three basic organismic needs: competence, relatedness, and autonomy. The word *organismic* here means that these psychological needs are innate and exist in every person. They are basic to human growth and functioning, just as water, soil, and sunshine are necessary for plant growth. This metaphor is especially apt, because once we plant a seed, all it requires to thrive and grow is a supportive environment. Similarly, self-determination theory holds that we all have the capacity for growth and fulfillment in us, ready to emerge if given the right context.

Importantly, from the perspective of self-determination theory, these organismic needs do not arise from deficits. Self-determination theory is not a drive reduction theory. Like Maslow, Deci and Ryan (2000) argue that these needs concern personal growth, not the filling of deficiencies. Let's examine each of these needs in depth.

The first organismic need described by self-determination theory, *competence,* is met when we feel that we are able to bring about desired outcomes (Reis & others, 2000). Competence motivation involves *self-efficacy* (the belief that you have the competence to accomplish a given goal or task) and *mastery* (the sense that you can gain skills and overcome obstacles). Competence is also related to expectancies for success. One domain in which competence needs may be met is in the realm of achievement. Some individuals are highly motivated to succeed and spend considerable effort striving to excel.

The second organismic need described by self-determination theory is *relatedness,* the need to engage in warm relations with other people. Some psychologists have proposed that the need to belong is the strongest human motivator (Baumeister & Leary, 2000). The need for relatedness is reflected in the importance of parents' nurturing children's development, the intimate moments of sharing private thoughts in friendship, the uncomfortable feelings we have when we are lonely, and the powerful attraction we have for someone else when we are in love.

The critical role of social bonds is also demonstrated in research examining the effects of being socially excluded (Hess & Pickett, 2010; K. D. Williams, 2007). When people are left out, they tend to engage in a variety of self-defeating behaviors, such as overeating and drinking to excess (Twenge, 2008). Research has shown that even when the exclusion is unintentional (for instance, when someone is ignored, though not purposely), it can lead to distress and the feeling that one's life is meaningless (K. D. Williams, 2007).

The third need proposed by self-determination theory is *autonomy*—the sense that we are in control of our own life. Autonomy means being independent and self-reliant, and it is a key aspect of feeling that one's behavior is self-motivated and emerging from genuine interest. Of course, many of the behaviors we engage in may feel like things we are forced to do, but a sense of autonomy is strongly related to well-being (Sheldon & others, 2005). Kennon Sheldon and colleagues (2005) have found that age relates to the experience of autonomy. For example, older Americans feel more autonomous than younger Americans when paying taxes, voting, and tipping.

Research on the role of motivation in well-being supports the idea that progress on goals that serve the three organismic needs is strongly related to well-being (Sheldon & Elliot, 1998). Further, valuing more extrinsic qualities—such as money, prestige, and physical appearance—over these organismic concerns is associated with lowered well-being, lowered self-actualization, and physical illness (Kasser & Ryan, 1996; Kasser & others, 2004).

Like any theory, self-determination theory has its controversies. One important issue is the extent to which the three needs are indeed universal. Cultures vary in how strongly they promote the needs for competence, relatedness, and autonomy. Many Western cultures—among them, the United States, Canada, and western European countries— are termed *individualistic* because they emphasize individual achievement, independence, and self-reliance. In contrast, many Eastern cultures—such as China, Japan, and Korea—are called *collectivistic* because they stress affiliation, cooperation, and interdependence (Triandis, 2000). However, cross-cultural evidence suggests that the needs emphasized by self-determination theory are likely to be valued in both Western and Eastern cultures (Sheldon & others, 2001).

Self-determination theory maintains that one of the most important aspects of healthy motivation is the sense that we do the things we do because we have freely chosen to do them. When we can choose our behaviors and feel ownership over those choices, we are likely to experience heightened fulfillment (Blumenfeld, Kempler, & Krajcik, 2006). When our behaviors follow from the needs for competence, autonomy, and relatedness, we experience intrinsic motivation. When our behavior serves needs for other values—such as prestige, money, or approval—our behavior is extrinsically motivated (Ryan & Deci, 2000, 2009). We examine this important distinction between intrinsic and extrinsic motivation next.

"Mr. Frimley, sir, can I have a word about the motivational artwork . . ."

© Clive Goddard. www.CartoonStock.com.

● **intrinsic motivation** Motivation based on internal factors such as organismic needs (competence, relatedness, and autonomy), as well as curiosity, challenge, and fun.

● **extrinsic motivation** Motivation that involves external incentives such as rewards and punishments.

● **self-regulation** The process by which an organism effortfully controls behavior in order to pursue important objectives.

Copyright by Mark Parisi, www.offthemark.com.

Intrinsic Versus Extrinsic Motivation

One way psychologists understand the "why" of our goals is by distinguishing between intrinsic and extrinsic motivation. **Intrinsic motivation** is based on internal factors such as organismic needs (competence, relatedness, and autonomy), as well as curiosity, challenge, and fun. When we are intrinsically motivated, we engage in a behavior because we enjoy it. **Extrinsic motivation** involves external incentives such as rewards and punishments. When we are extrinsically motivated, we engage in a behavior for some external payoff or to avoid an external punishment. Some students study hard because they are internally motivated to put forth considerable effort and achieve high quality in their work (intrinsic motivation). Other students study hard because they want to make good grades or avoid parental disapproval (extrinsic motivation).

Which type of motivation is related to superior performance—intrinsic or extrinsic? Do extrinsic rewards interfere with intrinsic motivation? We delve into these questions in the Critical Controversy.

Many very successful individuals are both intrinsically motivated (they have high personal standards of achievement and emphasize personal effort) and extrinsically motivated (they are strongly competitive) (Schunk, 2011). For the most part, however, psychologists believe that intrinsic motivation is the key to achievement (Blumenfeld, Kempler, & Krajcik, 2006), although elite athletes, such as members of Olympic teams, may be motivated by both intrinsic and extrinsic rewards (Ciani & Sheldon, 2010). Indeed, many of us might think of the ideal occupation as one in which we get paid (an extrinsic reward) for doing the very thing we love to do (intrinsic motivation).

Self-Regulation: The Successful Pursuit of Goals

Today many psychologists approach motivation in the way that you yourself might—by asking about goals and values and seeking to understand how these motivational forces shape behavior. Psychologists have referred to goals by various names, including *personal projects, best possible selves, life tasks,* and *personal strivings* (King, 2008). All of these terms reflect the goals a person is trying to accomplish in everyday life. Self-generated goals can range from trivial matters (such as letting a bad haircut grow out) to life tasks (such as becoming a good parent).

Goal approaches to motivation include the concept of self-regulation. **Self-regulation** is the process by which an organism effortfully controls behavior in order to pursue important objectives (Carver & Scheier, 2009a). A key aspect of self-regulation is getting feedback about how we are doing in our goal pursuits. Our daily mood has been proposed as a way that we may receive this feedback—that is, we feel good or bad depending on how we are doing in the areas of life we value. Note that the role of mood in self-regulation means that we cannot be happy all the time. In order to effectively pursue our goals, we have to be open to the bad news that might occasionally come our way (King, 2008).

Putting our personal goals into action is a potentially complex process that involves setting goals, planning for their implementation, and monitoring our progress. Individuals' success improves when they set goals that are specific and moderately challenging (Bandura, 1997; Schunk, 2011). A fuzzy, nonspecific goal is "I want to be successful." A concrete, specific goal is "I want to have a 3.5 average at the end of the semester."

You can set both long-term and short-term goals. When you set long-term goals, such as "I want to be a clinical psychologist," make sure that you also create short-term goals as steps along the way, such as "I want to get an *A* on my next psychology test." Make commitments in manageable chunks. Planning how to reach a goal and monitoring progress toward the goal are critical aspects of achievement (Wigfield & others, 2006). Researchers have found that high-achieving individuals monitor their own

CRITICAL CONTROVERSY

Does Extrinsic Motivation Undermine Intrinsic Motivation?

Many psychologists believe that intrinsic motivation leads to more positive outcomes than extrinsic motivation (Blumenfeld, Kempler, & Krajcik, 2006; Patell, Cooper, & Robinson, 2008; Ryan & Deci, 2009). They argue that intrinsic motivation is more likely to produce competent behavior and mastery. Extrinsic motivation, in fact, is thought to reduce intrinsic motivation (Lepper, Greene, & Nisbett, 1973). A wide variety of social (extrinsic) events—such as deadlines, surveillance, and coercive rewards—can reduce the enjoyment (intrinsic motivation) associated with work, play, and study (Blumenfeld, Kempler, & Krajcik, 2006).

A decade ago, two reviews of studies on intrinsic and extrinsic motivation reached opposite conclusions (Cameron, Banko, & Pierce, 2001; Deci, Koestner, & Ryan, 1999). Edward Deci and his colleagues (1999) analyzed 128 studies and concluded that the main negative effect of external rewards was to restrict self-determination and interfere with intrinsic motivation. However, an analysis of 145 studies by Judy Cameron and her colleagues yielded mixed results (Cameron, Banko, & Pierce, 2001). Cameron's group found that extrinsic rewards sometimes produced the expected negative effects on intrinsic motivation but at other times had a positive effect or no effect at all. The truth, Cameron and her colleagues suggested, is that extrinsic motivation has no overall effect on intrinsic motivation.

Think back to Chapter 6, where we examined the role of rewards in operant conditioning. Rewarding a behavior should increase the likelihood that it will happen again, right? In fact, research on extrinsic rewards seems to indicate just the opposite: Rewarding a behavior will *reduce* the performance of that behavior, as well as the enjoyment associated with it. How can we make sense of this apparent contradiction? According to Cameron and her colleagues, a prime issue is *which behavior*, exactly, is rewarded (Cameron & Pierce, 2002; Cameron & others, 2005). When extrinsic rewards are given for the quality and creativity of a behavior, they actually enhance that behavior (Eisenberger & Aselage, 2009). Furthermore, when extrinsic rewards are provided for mastering skills, intrinsic motivation itself increases (Cameron & others, 2005).

In daily life, people often do things that are not intrinsically motivating, such as, perhaps, mowing the lawn and studying mathematics. Without external rewards, they may simply lose interest in performing those tasks. In such cases, extrinsic motivation may help foster intrinsic motivation. For example, a creative mathematics teacher might use rewards such as extra credit, math games, and verbal praise as a way to instill a lifelong love of mathematics. Similarly, if an employee is producing shoddy work, seems bored, or has a negative attitude, offering an external incentive may improve motivation. There are times, though, when external rewards can diminish intrinsic motivation. The problem with using a reward as an incentive is that individuals may perceive that the reward rather than their own motivation caused their achievement behavior.

A richer understanding of intrinsic and extrinsic motivation might allow for more accurate predictions of when extrinsic motivation will reduce, increase, or not affect intrinsic motivation. It might then be possible for employers and teachers to help employees and students develop the deep intrinsic motivation that most experts agree is indispensable to well-being.

WHAT DO YOU THINK?
- What are some instances in your own life in which your intrinsic motivation was *reduced* by external rewards? What are some instances in which your intrinsic motivation was *increased* by external rewards?
- What other factors might determine whether extrinsic motivation influences intrinsic motivation?

---

learning and systematically evaluate their progress toward their goals more than low-achieving individuals (Schunk, 2011; Schunk, Pintrich, & Meece, 2008).

Even as we keep our nose to the grindstone in pursuing short-term goals, it is also important to have a sense of the big picture. Dedication to a long-term dream or personal mission can enhance the experience of purpose in life. *Purpose* is an intention to accomplish a goal that is meaningful to oneself and to contribute something to the world (Damon, 2008). Although short-term goals can provide a sense of accomplishment, attaching these goals to a future dream can allow individuals to experience a sense of meaning and to maintain their efforts in the face of short-term failure (Houser-Marko & Sheldon, 2008).

It can be difficult to recruit all of your willpower to pursue a goal you have consciously chosen. To learn more about the ways motivation and cognition relate to sticking with a goal, see the Intersection.

test yourself

1. What is Maslow's theory of a hierarchy of needs? Explain.
2. What is self-actualization, according to Maslow, and on what does it depend?
3. How do intrinsic motivation and extrinsic motivation differ?

Motivation and Cognition: How Do We Resist Temptation?

It is bound to happen. On Friday you commit to studying all weekend, and then a friend invites you to a party on Saturday night. You commit to losing those last 10 pounds, and without fail the Girl Scouts show up peddling their delicious cookies. Motivation is about committing to the pursuit of valued goals, but often it seems the world conspires against you, dangling temptation at every turn (Mischel & Ayduk, 2004). How do you stick with the program when daily life so often tries to derail you from steadfastly pursuing your goals?

One of the most important underlying problems in resisting temptation is *delay of gratification*—putting off a pleasurable experience in the interest of some larger but later reward. Successful delay of gratification is evident in the student who does not go out with friends but instead stays in and studies for an upcoming test, thinking, "There will be time to party after this test is over." Delay of gratification is challenging. Think about it—future payoffs are simply much less certain than current rewards.

Walter Mischel and his colleagues examined how children managed to delay gratification (Mischel, Cantor, & Feldman, 1996; Mischel & Moore, 1980). They placed children in a difficult situation—alone in a room with a very tempting cookie in their reach. The children were told that if they wanted to at any time, they could ring a bell and eat the cookie. Otherwise, they could wait until the experimenter returned, and then they would get two cookies. The children were then left alone to face this self-control dilemma. The researchers were interested in measuring how long the children could wait before giving in to temptation and eating the cookie.

There were a variety of responses to this unusual situation. Some children sat dead still, focused on the tempting cookie. Some smelled the cookie. Others turned away, sang songs, picked their noses, or did anything but pay attention to the cookie. How did the children who were able to resist temptation do it? Mischel and colleagues found that the kids who were able to distract themselves from the cookie by focusing on "cool thoughts" (that is, non-cookie-related things) were better able to delay gratification. In contrast, children who remained focused on the cookie and all its delightful qualities—what Mischel called "hot thoughts"—ate the cookie sooner (Metcalfe & Mischel, 1999).

What do these findings mean for self-control in your life? Imagine that you are in a long-term romantic relationship that you wish to continue, and you meet someone new to whom you are physically attracted. Should you cultivate a friendship with that person? Maybe not, if you want to avoid temptation and preserve your current relationship. Think about all the current and potential "cookies" in your life—those things that have the power to distract you from achieving your long-term plans. Mischel's research with children demonstrates that avoiding these hot issues might be a good way to see a long-term plan through to its completion.

What are some of the "cookies" in your life? How do you avoid being sidetracked by temptation?

4· EMOTION

Motivation and emotion are closely linked. We can feel happy or sad depending on how events influence the likelihood of our getting the things we want in life. Sometimes our emotions take us by surprise and give us a reality check about what we really want. We might think, for example, that we have lost interest in our romantic partner until that person initiates a breakup. Suddenly, we realize how much the partner really means to us and to our happiness.

Anyone who has watched an awards show on television surely knows the link between motivation and emotion. Strolling in on the red carpet, the celebrities stress how honored they are to be nominated; but behind the Hollywood smiles is the longing to win. When the announcement is made, "And the Oscar goes to . . . ," the cameras zoom in to catch a glimpse of real emotion: the winner's face lighting up with joy and, of course, the moment of disappointment for the others.

Emotions are certainly complex. The body, the mind, and the face play key roles in emotion, although psychologists debate which of these components is most significant in emotion and how they mix to produce emotional experiences (Davidson, Scherer, & Goldsmith, 2002; Werner & Gross, 2010). For our purposes, **emotion** is feeling, or affect, that can involve physiological arousal (such as a fast heartbeat), conscious experience (thinking about being in love with someone), and behavioral expression (a smile or grimace).

● **emotion** Feeling, or affect, that can involve physiological arousal (such as a fast heartbeat), conscious experience (thinking about being in love with someone), and behavioral expression (a smile or grimace).

Biological Factors in Emotion

A friend whom you have been counseling about a life problem calls you to say, "We need to talk." As the time of your friend's visit approaches, you get nervous. What could be going on? You feel burdened—you have a lot of work to do, and you do not have time for a talk session. You also worry that she is angry or disappointed about something you have done. When she arrives with a gift-wrapped package and a big smile, your nerves give way to relief. She announces, "I wanted to give you this present to say thanks for all your help over the last few weeks." Your heart warms, and you feel a strong sense of your enduring bond with her. As you moved through the emotions of worry, relief, and joy, your body changed. Indeed, the body is a crucial part of our emotional experience.

AROUSAL

Recall from Chapter 3 that the *autonomic nervous system* (ANS) takes messages to and from the body's internal organs, monitoring such processes as breathing, heart rate, and digestion. The ANS is divided into the sympathetic and the parasympathetic nervous systems (Figure 10.4). The *sympathetic nervous system* (SNS) is involved in the body's arousal; it is responsible for a rapid reaction to a stressor, sometimes referred to as the "fight or flight" response. The SNS immediately causes an increase in blood pressure, a faster heart rate, more rapid breathing for greater oxygen intake, and more efficient blood flow to the brain and major muscle groups. All of these changes prepare us for action. At the same time, the body stops digesting food, because it is not necessary for immediate action (which could explain why just before an exam, students usually are not hungry).

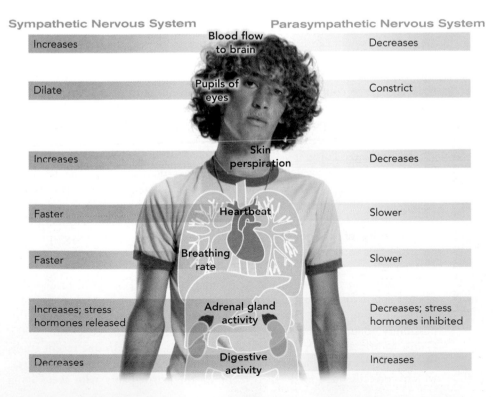

Sympathetic Nervous System		Parasympathetic Nervous System
Increases	Blood flow to brain	Decreases
Dilate	Pupils of eyes	Constrict
Increases	Skin perspiration	Decreases
Faster	Heartbeat	Slower
Faster	Breathing rate	Slower
Increases; stress hormones released	Adrenal gland activity	Decreases; stress hormones inhibited
Decreases	Digestive activity	Increases

FIGURE 10.4 **The Autonomic Nervous System and Its Role in Arousing and Calming the Body** The two parts of the autonomic nervous system work in different ways. The sympathetic nervous system arouses the body in reaction to a stressor, evoking the "fight or flight" response. In contrast, the parasympathetic nervous system calms the body, promoting relaxation and healing.

The *parasympathetic nervous system* (PNS) calms the body. Whereas the sympathetic nervous system prepares the individual for fighting or running away, the parasympathetic nervous system promotes relaxation and healing. When the PNS is activated, heart rate and blood pressure drop, stomach activity and food digestion increase, and breathing slows down.

The sympathetic and parasympathetic nervous systems evolved to improve the human species' likelihood for survival, but it does not take a life-threatening situation to activate them. Emotions such as anger and fear are associated with elevated SNS activity as exemplified in heightened blood pressure and heart rate. States of happiness and contentment also activate the SNS to a lesser extent.

MEASURING AROUSAL

Because arousal includes a physiological response, researchers have been intrigued by how to measure it accurately. One aspect of emotional arousal is *skin conductance level* (SCL) response, a rise in the skin's electrical conductivity when sweat gland activity increases. A sweaty palm conducts electricity better than a dry palm, and this difference provides the basis for SCL, which produces an index of arousal that has been used in many studies of emotion.

● **polygraph** A machine, commonly called a lie detector, that monitors changes in the body, used to try to determine whether someone is lying.

Another measure of arousal is the **polygraph** or lie detector, a machine examiners use to try to determine whether someone is lying. The polygraph monitors changes in the body—heart rate, breathing, and SCL—thought to be influenced by emotional states. In a typical polygraph test, the examiner asks the individual a number of neutral questions and several key, less neutral questions. If the individual's heart rate, breathing, and SCL responses increase substantially when the key questions are asked, the individual is assumed to be lying. Lying also has been linked with certain emotional facial expressions (Porter & ten Brinke, 2008; Warren, Schertler, & Bull, 2009).

How accurate is the lie detector? Although it measures the degree of arousal to a series of questions, no one has found a unique physiological response to telling lies (Lykken, 1987, 2001; Seymour & others, 2000). Heart rate and breathing can increase for reasons other than lying, and this effect can make it difficult to interpret the physiological indicators of arousal.

Accurately identifying truth or deception is linked with the skill of the examiner and the skill of the individual being examined. Body movements and the presence of certain drugs in the person's system can interfere with the polygraph's accuracy. Sometimes the mere presence of the polygraph and the individual's belief that it is accurate in detecting deception trigger a confession of guilt. Police may use the polygraph in this way to get a suspect to confess. However, in too many instances it has been misused and misrepresented. Experts argue that the polygraph errs just under 50 percent of the time, especially as it cannot distinguish between such feelings as anxiety and guilt (Iacono & Lykken, 1997).

The Employee Polygraph Protection Act of 1988 restricts polygraph testing outside government agencies, and most courts do not accept the results of polygraph testing. However, some psychologists defend the polygraph's use, saying that polygraph results are as sound as other admissible forms of evidence, such as hair fiber analysis (Grubin & Madsen, 2006; Honts, 1998). The majority of psychologists, though, argue against the polygraph's use because of its inability to tell who is lying and who is not (Iacono & Lykken, 1997; Lykken, 1998; Saxe, 1998; Steinbrook, 1992).

Recently, functional magnetic brain imaging (fMRI) has been proposed as a better option for detecting deception than the polygraph (Langleben & Dattilio, 2008; Simpson, 2008). However, researchers are just beginning to study this possibility (Baumgartner & others, 2009; Fullam, McKie, & Dolan, 2009; Ganis, Morris, & Kosslyn, 2009; Kozel & others, 2009). In one recent study, the best results were obtained for changes in a region of the prefrontal cortex, which correctly identified 71 percent of the participants who were lying

Examiners use a polygraph to tell whether someone is lying. A polygraph monitors changes in the body believed to be influenced by emotional states. Controversy has swirled about the polygraph's use because it is unreliable.

(Monteleone & others, 2008). As the authors of this study concluded, their findings were better than chance but well below perfection.

THEORIES OF EMOTION

Imagine that you and your date are enjoying a picnic in the country. Suddenly, a bull runs across the field toward you. Why are you afraid? Two well-known theories of emotion that involve physiological processes provide answers to this question.

Common sense tells you that you are trembling and running away from the bull because you are afraid, but William James (1950) and Carl Lange (pronounced "Long-uh") (1922) said emotion works in the opposite way. According to the **James-Lange theory,** emotion results from physiological states triggered by stimuli in the environment: Emotion occurs *after* physiological reactions. Moreover, each emotion—from anger to rapture—has a distinct set of physiological changes, evident in changes in heart rate, breathing patterns, sweating, and other responses. Essentially, the James-Lange theory proposes that after the initial perception, the experience of the emotion results from the perception of one's own physiological changes.

● **James-Lange theory** The theory that emotion results from physiological states triggered by stimuli in the environment.

Let's see how the James-Lange theory would explain fear in the situation with the bull. You see the bull scratching its hoof on the ground, and you begin to run away. Your aroused body then sends sensory messages to your brain, at which point emotion is perceived. According to this theory, you do not run away because you are afraid; rather, you are afraid because you are running away. In other words, you perceive a stimulus in the environment, your body responds, and you interpret the body's reaction as emotion.

Walter Cannon (1927) objected to the assumption in the James-Lange theory that each emotional experience has its own particular set of physiological changes. He argued that different emotions could not be associated with specific physiological changes because autonomic nervous system responses are too diffuse and slow to account for rapid and differentiated emotional responses.

To understand Cannon's view, imagine the bull and the picnic once again. Seeing the bull scratching its hoof causes the thalamus of your brain to do two things simultaneously: First, it stimulates your autonomic nervous system to produce the physiological changes involved in emotion (increased heart rate, rapid breathing); second, it sends messages to your cerebral cortex, where the experience of emotion is perceived. Philip Bard (1934) supported this analysis, and so the theory became known as the **Cannon-Bard theory**—the proposition that emotion and physiological reactions occur simultaneously. In the Cannon-Bard theory, the body plays a less important role than in the James-Lange theory. Figure 10.5 shows how the James-Lange and Cannon-Bard theories differ.

● **Cannon-Bard theory** The proposition that emotion and physiological reactions occur simultaneously.

The question of whether emotions involve discrete autonomic nervous system responses continues to be debated (Keltner & Ekman, 2000). Recent studies have documented some emotion-specific autonomic nervous system responses (Christie & Friedman, 2004). For example, fear, anger, and sadness are associated with increased heart rate, but disgust is not (Bryant, 2006; Hamer & others, 2007). Also, anger is linked with increased blood flow to the hands, an effect that is not triggered by fear.

NEURAL CIRCUITS AND NEUROTRANSMITTERS

Contemporary researchers are keenly interested in charting the neural circuitry of emotions and in discovering the role of neurotransmitters (Kindt, Soeter, & Vervliet, 2009; Pessoa, 2009). The focus of much of their work has been on the amygdala, the almond-shaped structure in the limbic system that we considered in Chapter 3. The amygdala houses circuits that are activated when we experience negative emotions.

Research by Joseph LeDoux and his colleagues has investigated the neural circuitry of one particular emotion: fear (Cowansage, LeDoux, & Monfils, 2010; Cunha, Monfils, & LeDoux, 2010; Debiec & others, 2010; LeDoux, 1996, 2002, 2009; Sotres-Bayon & others, 2009). The amygdala plays a central role in fear. When the amygdala determines that danger is present, it shifts into high gear, marshaling the brain's resources in an effort to protect the organism from harm. This fear system

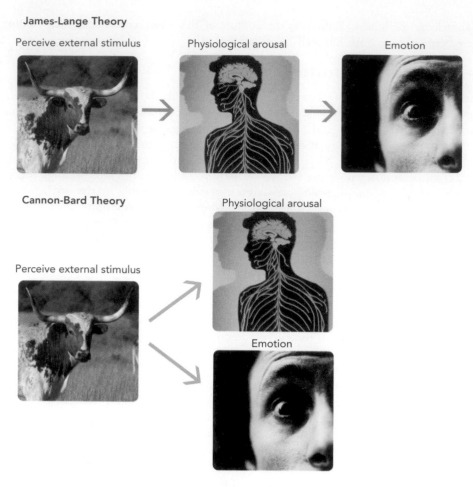

FIGURE 10.5 **James-Lange and Cannon-Bard Theories** From the James-Lange perspective, the experience of fear is an outcome of physiological arousal. In the Cannon-Bard view, fear occurs at the same time as the physiological response.

James-Lange Theory

Perceive external stimulus → Physiological arousal → Emotion

Cannon-Bard Theory

Perceive external stimulus → Physiological arousal / Emotion

FIGURE 10.6 **Direct and Indirect Brain Pathways in the Emotion of Fear** Information about fear can follow two pathways in the brain when an individual sees a snake. The direct pathway (*broken arrow*) conveys information rapidly from the thalamus to the amygdala. The indirect pathway (*solid arrows*) transmits information more slowly from the thalamus to the sensory cortex (here, the visual cortex) and then to the amygdala.

Visual thalamus

Visual cortex

Amygdala

evolved to detect and respond to predators and other types of natural dangers that threaten survival or territory.

The brain circuitry that involves the emotion of fear can follow two pathways: a direct pathway from the thalamus to the amygdala or an indirect pathway from the thalamus through the sensory cortex to the amygdala (Figure 10.6). The direct pathway does not convey detailed information about the stimulus, but it has the advantage of speed—and speed clearly is an important characteristic of information for an organism facing a threat to its survival. The indirect pathway carries nerve impulses from the sensory organs (eyes and ears, for example) to the thalamus (recall that the thalamus is a relay station for incoming sensory stimuli); from the thalamus, the nerve impulses travel to the sensory cortex, which then sends appropriate signals to the amygdala.

Recall from Chapter 7 that the amygdala is linked with emotional memories. LeDoux and his colleagues say that the amygdala hardly ever forgets (Duvarci, Nader, & LeDoux, 2008; LeDoux, 2000, 2001, 2009). This quality is useful, because once we learn that something is dangerous, we do not have to relearn it. However, we pay a penalty for this ability. Many people carry fears and anxieties around with them that they would like to get rid of but cannot seem to shake. We will look at such fears when we explore phobias in Chapter 15.

Part of the reason fears are so difficult to change is that the amygdala is well connected to the cerebral cortex, in which thinking and decision making primarily occur (Rauch, Shin, & Phelps, 2006). The amygdala is in a much better position to influence the cerebral cortex than the other way around, because it sends more connections to the cerebral cortex than it gets back. This may explain why it is so hard to control our emotions, and why, once fear is learned, it is so hard to erase.

The amygdala is not only involved in negative emotions but also appears to participate in positive emotions (Hurleman & others, 2010; Ritchey, Labar, & Cabeza, 2010; Winecoff & others, 2010). Research reviews concluded that various regions of the limbic system, including the amygdalae, are involved in the experience of positive emotions (Burgdorf & Panksepp, 2006; Koepp & others, 2009). The neurotransmitter dopamine is especially active in the limbic system during positive emotions.

Researchers are also finding that the cerebral hemispheres may be involved in understanding emotion. Richard Davidson and his colleagues have shown that the cerebral hemispheres work differently in positive and negative emotions (Davidson, 2000, 2010a; Davidson, Shackman, & Pizzagalli, 2002; Light & others, 2009; Reuter-Lorenz & Davidson, 1981; Urry & others, 2004). Recall that research we reviewed in Chapter 3 suggests that people who show relatively more left than right prefrontal activation tend to be happier. Researchers are also intrigued by the roles that neurotransmitters play in the neural pathways of emotions. Endorphins and dopamine are involved in positive emotions such as happiness (Koepp & others, 2009), and norepinephrine functions in regulating arousal (Berridge & Kringelbach, 2008; Greeson & others, 2009).

Cognitive Factors in Emotion

Does emotion depend on the tides of the mind? Are we happy only when we think we are happy? Cognitive theories of emotion center on the premise that emotion always has a cognitive component (Frijda, 2007; Johnson-Laird, Mancini, & Gangemi, 2006). Thinking is said to be responsible for feelings of love and hate, joy and sadness. While cognitive theorists do recognize the role of the brain and body in emotion, they give cognitive processes the main credit for these responses.

THE TWO-FACTOR THEORY OF EMOTION

In the **two-factor theory of emotion** developed by Stanley Schachter and Jerome Singer (1962), emotion is determined by two factors: physiological arousal and cognitive labeling (Figure 10.7). Schachter and Singer argued that we look to the external world for an explanation of why we are aroused. We interpret external cues and label the emotion. For example, if you feel good after someone has made a pleasant comment to you, you might label the emotion "happy." If you feel bad after you have done something wrong, you may label the feeling "guilty."

To test their theory of emotion, Schachter and Singer (1962) injected volunteer participants with epinephrine, a drug that produces high arousal. After participants received the drug, they observed someone else behave in either a euphoric way (shooting papers at a wastebasket) or an angry way (stomping out of the room). As predicted, the euphoric and angry behavior influenced the participants' cognitive interpretation of their own arousal. When they were with a happy person, they rated themselves as happy; when they were with an angry person, they said they were angry. This effect occurred, however, only when the participants were not told about the true effects of the injection. When they were told that the drug would increase their heart rate and make them jittery, they said the reason for their own arousal was the drug, not the other person's behavior.

In general, research supports the belief that misinterpreted arousal intensifies emotional experiences (Leventhal & Tomarken, 1986). An intriguing study by Donald Dutton and Arthur Aron (1974) substantiates this conclusion. In the study, an attractive woman approached men while they were walking across the Capilano River Bridge in British Columbia. Only men without a female companion were approached. The woman asked the men to make up a brief story for a project she was doing on creativity. The Capilano River Bridge sways dangerously more than 200 feet above rapids and

● **two-factor theory of emotion** Schachter and Singer's theory that emotion is determined by two factors: physiological arousal and cognitive labeling.

FIGURE 10.7 **Schachter and Singer's Two-Factor Theory of Emotion**
The two-factor theory includes not only arousal but also cognitive labeling: You feel afraid of the bull because you label your physiological response "fear."

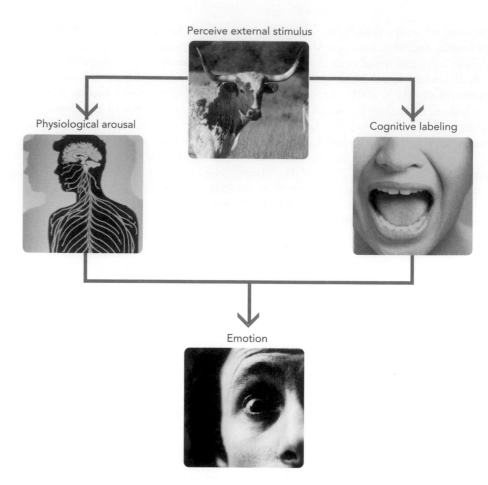

Perceive external stimulus

Physiological arousal

Cognitive labeling

Emotion

FIGURE 10.8 **Capilano River Bridge Experiment: Misinterpreted Arousal Intensifies Emotional Experiences** (*Top*) The precarious Capilano River Bridge in British Columbia. (*Bottom*) The experiment in progress. An attractive woman approached the men while they were crossing the bridge; she asked them to make up a story to help her with a creativity project. She also made the same request on a lower, much safer bridge. The men on the Capilano River Bridge told more sexually oriented stories, probably because they were aroused by the fear or excitement of being up so high on a swaying bridge and interpreted their arousal as sexual attraction for the female interviewer.

rocks (Figure 10.8). The female interviewer made the same request of other men crossing a much safer, lower bridge. The men on the Capilano River Bridge told more sexually oriented stories and rated the female interviewer as more attractive than did men on the lower, less frightening bridge.

Imagine that you are late for class on an important exam day. You sprint across campus as fast as you can, arriving just in time for the test. As you look over the questions, your heart is racing, your breathing is fast, and you feel sweaty. Are you nervous about the test or just recovering from your run to the classroom? The two-factor theory suggests that you just might mistake your bodily sensations as indications that you are scared of the test.

THE PRIMACY DEBATE: COGNITION OR EMOTION?

Which comes first, thinking or feeling? Fans of the vintage episodes of TV's *Star Trek* may recognize this theme from the frequent arguments between Mr. Spock, the logical Vulcan, and Dr. McCoy, the emotional doctor on the *Enterprise*. In the 1980s and 1990s, two eminent psychologists, Richard Lazarus (1922–2002) and Robert Zajonc (1923–2008), debated the question of which is central—cognition or emotion.

Recall from Chapter 8 that Lazarus said that we cognitively appraise ourselves and our social circumstances and that these appraisals determine how we feel about events and experiences. For Lazarus (1991), then, thinking is primary—he believed cognitive activity to be a precondition for emotion. Our appraisals—which are guided by values, goals, commitments, beliefs, and expectations—determine our emotions (Urry, 2010; Wilkowski & Robinson, 2010). People may feel happy because they have a deep religious commitment, angry because they did not get the raise they anticipated, or fearful because they expect to fail an exam. Zajonc (1984) disagreed with Lazarus. Emotions are primary, he said, and our thoughts are a result of them. Zajonc famously argued that "preferences need no inferences," meaning that the way we feel about something on a "gut level" requires no thought.

Which of the two psychologists is right? *Both* are likely correct. Lazarus talked mainly about a cluster of related events that occur over a period of time, whereas Zajonc described single events or a simple preference for one stimulus over another. Lazarus was concerned with love over the course of months and years, a sense of value to the community, and plans for retirement; Zajonc spoke about a car accident, an encounter with a snake, and a preference for ice cream rather than spinach.

Some of our emotional reactions are virtually instantaneous and probably do not involve cognitive appraisal, such as shrieking upon detecting a snake (Young & Claypool, 2010). Other emotional circumstances, especially long-term feelings such as a depressed mood or anger toward a friend, are more likely to involve cognitive appraisal (Smith & Kirby, 2009). Indeed, the direct and indirect brain pathways described earlier support the idea that some of our emotional reactions do not involve deliberate thinking, whereas others do (LeDoux, 2001, 2009).

Behavioral Factors in Emotion

Vintage Star Trek *episodes explored the question, what comes first—thinking or feeling?*

Remember that our definition of emotion includes not only physiological and cognitive components but also a behavioral component. The behavioral component can be verbal or nonverbal. Verbally, a person might show love for someone by professing it in words or might display anger by saying nasty things. Nonverbally, a person might smile, frown, show a fearful expression, look down, or slouch.

The most interest in the behavioral dimension of emotion has focused on the nonverbal behavior of facial expressions (Hasegawa & Unuma, 2010; Sacco & Hugenberg, 2009; Todd & others, 2010). Emotion researchers have been intrigued by people's ability to detect emotion from a person's facial expression (Sato & others, 2010; Stein & others, 2010; Yoon, Joormann, & Gotlib, 2009). In a typical research study, participants, when shown photographs like those in Figure 10.9, are usually able to identify six emotions: happiness, anger, sadness, surprise, disgust, and fear (Ekman & O'Sullivan, 1991).

FIGURE 10.9   Recognizing Emotions in Facial Expressions Look at the six photographs and determine the emotion reflected in each of the six faces: (*top*) happiness, anger, sadness; (*bottom*) surprise, disgust, fear.

● **facial feedback hypothesis** The idea that facial expressions can influence emotions as well as reflect them.

Might our facial expressions not only reflect our emotions but also influence them? According to the **facial feedback hypothesis,** facial expressions can influence emotions as well as reflect them (Davis, Senghas, & Ochsner, 2009). In this view, facial muscles send signals to the brain that help us to recognize the emotion we are experiencing (Keillor & others, 2002). For example, we feel happier when we smile and sadder when we frown.

Support for the facial feedback hypothesis comes from an experiment by Paul Ekman and his colleagues (1983). In this study, professional actors moved their facial muscles in very precise ways, such as raising their eyebrows and pulling them together, raising their upper eyelids, and stretching their lips horizontally back to their ears (you might want to try this yourself). They were asked to hold their expression for 10 seconds, during which time the researchers measured their heart rate and body temperature. When the actors moved facial muscles in the ways described, they showed a rise in heart rate and a steady body temperature—physiological reactions that characterize fear. When they made an angry facial expression (with a penetrating stare, brows drawn together and downward, and lips pressed together or opened and pushed forward), their heart rate and body temperature both increased. The facial feedback hypothesis provides support for the James-Lange theory of emotion discussed earlier—namely, that emotional experiences can be generated by changes in and awareness of our own bodily states.

Sociocultural Factors in Emotion

Are the facial expressions that are associated with different emotions largely innate, or do they vary across cultures? Are there gender variations in emotion? Answering these questions requires a look at research findings on sociocultural influences in emotions.

CULTURE AND THE EXPRESSION OF EMOTION

In *The Expression of the Emotions in Man and Animals,* Charles Darwin stated that the facial expressions of human beings are innate, not learned; are the same in all cultures around the world; and have evolved from the emotions of animals (1965). Today psychologists still believe that emotions, especially facial expressions of emotion, have strong biological ties (Gelder & others, 2006). For example, children who are blind from birth and have never observed the smile or frown on another person's face smile or frown in the same way that children with normal vision do. If emotions and facial expressions that go with them are unlearned, then they should be the same the world over. Is that in fact the case?

Extensive research has examined the universality of facial expressions and the ability of people from different cultures accurately to label the emotion that lies behind facial expressions (Sauter & others, 2010). Paul Ekman's careful observations reveal that the many faces of emotion do not differ significantly from one culture to another (Ekman, 1980, 1996, 2003). For example, Ekman and his colleague photographed people expressing emotions such as happiness, fear, surprise, disgust, and grief. When they showed the photographs to people from the United States, Chile, Japan, Brazil, and Borneo (an Indonesian island in the western Pacific), the participants recognized the emotions the faces were meant to show, across the various cultures (Ekman & Friesen, 1969).

Another study focused on the way the Fore tribe, an isolated Stone Age culture in New Guinea, matched descriptions of emotions with facial expressions (Ekman & Friesen, 1971). Before Ekman's visit, most of the Fore had never seen a Caucasian face. Ekman's team showed them photographs of faces expressing emotions such as fear, happiness, anger, and surprise. Then they read stories about people in emotional situations and asked the tribespeople to pick out the face that matched the story. The Fore were able to match the descriptions of emotions with the facial expressions in the photographs. Figure 10.10 shows the similarity of facial expressions

FIGURE 10.10 **Emotional Expressions in the United States and New Guinea** (*Top*) Two women from the United States. (*Bottom*) Two men from the Fore tribe in New Guinea. Notice the similarity in their expressions of disgust and happiness. Psychologists believe that the facial expression of emotion is virtually the same in all cultures.

of emotions by persons in New Guinea and the United States. More recently, one study found that East Asians and Westerners differed in their capacity to tell the difference between facial expressions of fear and surprise as well as expressions of anger and disgust (Jack & others, 2009). These differences were explained by the tendency of East Asians to focus more on the eyes (than the mouth) when judging faces.

Although facial expressions of basic emotions may be universal, display rules for emotion vary (Fischer, 2006; Matsumoto & others, 2008). **Display rules** are sociocultural standards that determine when, where, and how emotions should be expressed. For example, although happiness is a universally expressed emotion, when, where, and how people display it may vary from one culture to another (Sauter & others, 2010). The same is true for other emotions, such as fear, sadness, and anger. Members of the Utku culture in Alaska, for example, discourage anger by cultivating acceptance and by dissociating themselves from any display of anger. If an unexpected snowstorm hampers a trip, the Utku do not express frustration but accept the storm and build an igloo. The importance of display rules is especially evident when we evaluate the emotional expression of another. Does that grieving husband on a morning talk show seem appropriately distraught over his wife's murder? Or might he be a suspect?

Like facial expressions, some other nonverbal signals appear to be universal indicators of certain emotions. For example, regardless of where they live, when people are depressed, their emotional state shows not only in their sad facial expressions but also in their slow body movements, downturned heads, and slumped posture. Many nonverbal signals of emotion, though, vary from one culture to another (Mesquita, 2002). For example, male-to-male kissing is commonplace in Yemen but uncommon in the United States. The "thumbs up" sign, which in most cultures means either that everything is okay or that one wants to hitch a ride, is an insult in Greece, similar to a raised third finger in the United States—a cultural difference to keep in mind if you find yourself backpacking through Greece.

In the Middle Eastern country of Yemen, male-to-male kissing is commonplace, but in the United States it is less common.

● **display rules** Sociocultural standards that determine when, where, and how emotions should be expressed.

EMOTIONAL EXPRESSION IN COMPUTER COMMUNICATIONS

Recently psychologists have become interested in examining the expression of emotion in computer-mediated communications, including e-mails, blogs, and instant messages. You have probably used emoticons in your own communications. First introduced by computer scientist Scott Fahlman in 1982 (Fahlman, 2003), emoticons are used to express a variety of feelings, from joy **:D** to sadness **:-(** to silliness **;P** to great shock and dismay **: - O.**

Emoticons allow us to compensate for the loss of information from other expressive channels, such as vocal tone and facial expression (Derks, Bos, & von Grumbkow, 2008; Lo, 2008). People use emoticons as they do other displays of emotion, such as laughter, often at the end of the statement they are trying to clarify (Provine, Spencer, & Mandell, 2007).

Just as culture influences emotional expressions, it has also influenced emoticons. For instance, East Asian emoticons are less likely to be presented sideways, so that a Japanese student might convey her level of exhaustion with **(-.-)Zzzzzz** rather than **l-)Zzzzzz**. Even with emoticons, display rules can be important. A Japanese student expressing a thumbs up **d(^_^)b** might encounter an American who thinks he is saying he has big ears.

Emoticons reveal a potentially unique aspect of computer-mediated communication. Consider that back when people often communicated by writing letters (an art that would seem to share the limitations of e-mail and texting), emoticons were not used. Looking at the letters of great writers, we do not find smileys and frownies explaining their feelings. Thus, computer-mediated communication such as instant messaging might be considered a mixture of spoken conversation and the written word (Tagliamonte & Denis, 2008). As texting and IMing have become more common, it is no wonder that humans have devised a way to inject emotional meanings into their online discourse. Emoticons certainly demonstrate how crucial emotions are to our communications.

"... close with 'Yours truly, Phil'—and could you sprinkle a few appropriate emoticons around?"

© Chris Wildt. www.CartoonStock.com.

GENDER INFLUENCES

Unless you have been isolated on a mountaintop, you probably know the stereotype about gender and emotion: She is emotional; he is not. This stereotype is a powerful and pervasive image in U.S. culture (Shields, 1991).

Does science support this stereotype? Researchers have found that men and women are often more alike in the way they experience emotion than the stereotype would lead us to believe. Women and men often use the same facial expressions, adopt the same language, and describe their emotional experiences similarly when they keep diaries about their experiences. For many emotional experiences, researchers do not find gender differences—both sexes are equally likely to experience love, jealousy, anxiety in new social situations, anger when they are insulted, grief when close relationships end, and embarrassment when they make mistakes in public (Tavris & Wade, 1984).

When we go beyond stereotypes and consider some specific emotional experiences, contexts in which emotion is displayed, and certain beliefs about emotion, gender does matter in understanding emotion (Brannon, 1999; Brody, 1999; Shields, 1991). Research has shown that women are more accurate at recognizing the emotional content of faces, especially when the task is made challenging by showing the faces for a very short time (Hall & Matsumoto, 2004). Women also report themselves as experiencing emotions for a longer period than men (Birditt & Fingerman, 2003) and use more emoticons than men in their computer communications (Wolf, 2000).

It is important to keep in mind that both women and men are certainly aware of the gender-specific expectations for emotional behavior (Blakemore, Berenbaum, & Liben, 2009). Indeed, men who embrace a stereotypically masculine gender identity are more likely to report themselves as less emotional (Jakupcak & others, 2003). Gender differences in emotion are much more tied to social context than to biological sex (Brody, 1999).

Classifying Emotions

There are more than 200 words for emotions in the English language, indicating the complexity and variety of emotions. Not surprisingly, psychologists have created ways to classify emotions—to summarize these many emotions along various dimensions (Izard, 2009), including their valence and arousal.

VALENCE

● **negative affect** Unpleasant emotions such as anger, guilt, and sadness.

● **positive affect** Pleasant emotions such as joy, happiness, and interest.

The *valence* of an emotion refers to whether it feels pleasant or unpleasant. You probably are not surprised to know that happiness, joy, pleasure, and contentment are positively valenced emotions. In contrast, sadness, anger, worry, and feeling upset are negatively valenced emotions. Research has shown that emotions tend to go together based on their valence, so that if someone is sad, he or she is also likely to be angry or worried, and if a person is happy, he is or she is also likely to be feeling confident, joyful, and content (D. Watson, 2001).

We can classify many emotional states on the basis of valence. Indeed, according to some experts in emotion (D. Watson, 2001), there are two broad dimensions of emotional experience: negative affect and positive affect. **Negative affect** refers to emotions such as anger, guilt, and sadness. **Positive affect** refers to emotions such as joy, happiness, and interest. Although it seems essential to consider the valence of emotions as a way to classify them, valence does not fully capture all that we need to know about emotional states. The joy a person experiences at the birth of a child and the mild high at finding a $5 bill are both positive states, but they clearly differ. One way in which they differ is in their level of arousal.

AROUSAL LEVEL

The *arousal level* of an emotion is the degree to which the emotion is reflected in an individual's being active, engaged, or excited versus more passive, relatively disengaged, or

psychological *inquiry*

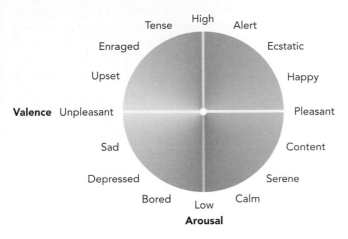

The Full Circle of Emotions

The figure shows a commonly used representation of human emotions, the circumplex model. Note that the circle is created by two independent dimensions: valence and arousal. Emotions that are similar are closer together, and those that differ are farther apart. Using the figure as a reference, answer the following questions.

1. Locate the emotions "upset" and "sad" on the circumplex. According to the circumplex, these two feelings differ primarily in terms of their arousal. Which is higher in arousal? Do you agree with this placement of these emotions? Explain.

2. According to the model, which emotion is the exact opposite of "serene"?

3. Where would you place the following feelings on the circle: worried, proud, angry, embarrassed?

calm. Positive and negative emotions can be high or low in arousal. Ecstasy and excitement are examples of high-arousal positive emotions, whereas contentment and tranquility are low-arousal positive emotions. Examples of high-arousal negative emotions are rage, fury, and panic, while irritation and boredom represent low-arousal negative emotions.

Valence and arousal level are independent dimensions that together describe a vast number of emotional states. Using these dimensions, psychologists have created a wheel of mood states that they call a *circumplex model of mood* (Posner, Russell, & Peterson, 2005). A circumplex is a graph that creates a circle from two independent dimensions. Using the dimensions of valence and arousal level, we can arrange emotional states in an organized fashion. To view the circumplex model and grasp its usefulness, see the Psychological Inquiry above.

The Adaptive Functions of Emotions

In considering the functions of emotions, it is fairly easy to come up with a good reason for us to have emotions such as fear and anger. Negative emotions carry direct and immediate adaptive benefits in situations that threaten survival. Negative emotions indicate clearly that something is wrong and that we must take action. Positive emotions do not signal a problem. So, what is the adaptive function of positive emotions?

Confronting this question, Barbara Fredrickson proposed the **broaden-and-build model** of positive emotion (Fredrickson, 1998, 2001, 2006, 2009). She argues that the function of positive emotions lies in their effects on our attention and our ability to build resources. The broaden-and-build model begins with the influence of positive emotions on cognitive processing.

Positive moods, such as contentment and humor, have been shown to broaden our attentional focus; they allow us to see the forest for the trees. As a result, when in a good mood, we may be more disposed to think outside the box—to see unusual possibilities that escaped us before. In addition, a good mood, Fredrickson says, gives us a chance to build resources—to make friends, to exercise to promote our health, to branch out in new ways. These activities allow us to build up strengths that we can use when we encounter life's difficulties (Kok, Catalino, & Fredrickson, 2008; Papousek & others, 2010). For example, joy broadens people by creating the urge to play, push the limits, and be creative. Interest broadens people by creating the motivation to explore, absorb new information and experiences, and expand the self (Csikszentmihalyi, 1990; Ryan & Deci, 2000). Positive emotions facilitate "approach" behavior, meaning that when we are feeling

● **broaden-and-build model** Fredrickson's model of positive emotion, stating that the function of positive emotions lies in their effects on an individual's attention and ability to build resources.

According to Fredrickson's broaden-and-build model, a good mood paves the way for building resources such as close friends and health-promoting activities.

good, we are more likely to go after the rewards we want and to face our problems head on (Otake & others, 2006; D. Watson, 2001).

RESILIENCE

Recall from Chapter 9 that resilience has been associated with the capacity to thrive during difficult times (Masten, 2006, 2009). Resilience refers to the ability to bounce back from negative experiences, to be flexible and adaptable when things are not going well. Resilient individuals might be thought of as tall trees that have the ability to bend but do not break in response to strong winds. In contrast, people who lack resilience might be characterized as more brittle—more likely to snap or break in the face of adversity (Block & Kremen, 1996).

Positive emotions might play an important role in the ability of resilient individuals to cope successfully with life's challenges. Resilient individuals are zestful, optimistic, and energetic in their approach to life (Block & Kremen, 1996). They cultivate positive emotion through the use of humor (Segerstrom, 2006). Michelle Tugade, Barbara Frederickson, and Lisa Feldman Barrett (2004) found that the superior coping of resilient individuals came from their ability to use positive emotions to bounce back from negative emotional experiences. Using measures of cardiovascular activity, the researchers found that resilient individuals were better able to regulate their responses to stressful situations (for instance, being told they were about to give an important speech) by strategically experiencing positive emotion.

Resilient individuals seem to show a kind of emotional wisdom; they capitalize on the power of positive emotions to reverse the stress of negative feelings. This skill has been demonstrated in response to a specific stressful event: the terrorist attacks of September 11, 2001. In one study, resilient individuals were found to be less likely to fall prey to depression after 9/11, and this capacity to flourish in the face of the crisis was a result of their attention to positive emotions (Fredrickson & others, 2003).

5· MOTIVATION, EMOTION, AND HEALTH AND WELLNESS: THE PURSUIT OF HAPPINESS

Motivation is about what people want, and a quick scan of the bestseller list or the self-help section of any bookstore would seem to indicate that one thing people want very much is to be happy—or happier. Can people get happier? Let's consider the evidence.

Biological Factors in Happiness

As we have seen, the brain is certainly at work in the experience of positive emotions. Genes also play a role. For instance, research on the heritability of well-being has tended to show that a substantial proportion of well-being differences among people can be explained by genetics. The heritability estimates for happiness range from 50 to 80 percent (Lykken, 1999). Remember from Chapter 8 that heritability is a statistic that describes characteristics of a group, that heritability estimates can vary across groups and over time, and that even highly heritable characteristics can be influenced by experience. Thus, a person is not necessarily doomed to an unhappy life, even if the person knows that he or she has particularly miserable parents.

Recall the concept of *set point* in our discussion of weight. As it happens, there may also be a happiness set point—a person's basic level of happiness when the individual is not intentionally trying to increase his or her happiness (Sheldon & Lyubomirsky, 2007). Like weight, the happiness level may fluctuate around this set point. In investigating how to increase happiness, we must consider the role of this powerful starting spot, which is likely the result of genetic factors and personal disposition.

test yourself

1. What are the key differences between the James-Lange theory and the Cannon-Bard theory of emotion?
2. What is the facial feedback hypothesis, and how has it been supported experimentally?
3. What is meant by the *valence* of an emotion and by the terms *positive affect* and *negative affect*?

Well, you could try being happy for a while and if it doesn't work you can go back to being miserable.

Machlis. Artizans.com.

Other factors also complicate the pursuit of happiness. As we shall see, these include getting caught up on the hedonic treadmill and making happiness itself the direct goal.

Obstacles in the Pursuit of Happiness

The first key challenge individuals encounter in trying to increase their happiness is the hedonic (meaning "related to pleasure") treadmill (Brickman & Campbell, 1971; Fredrick & Loewenstein, 1999). The term *hedonic treadmill* captures the idea that any aspect of life that enhances one's positive feelings is likely to do so for only a short time, because individuals generally adapt rapidly to any life change that would presumably influence their happiness. Winning the lottery, moving into a dream home, or falling in love may lead to temporary gains in the experience of joy, but eventually people go back to their baseline (Schkade & Kahneman, 1998). Whether it is the switch from CDs to iTunes or from dial-up to wireless, what a person first experiences as a life-changing improvement eventually fades to a routine (but still necessary) aspect of life, all too soon to be taken for granted. How can individuals increase their happiness if such pleasure enhancers quickly lose their power? Clearly, happiness is not about shopping at the right stores, because new possessions will likely lead to only a momentary burst of pleasure, eventually giving way to the set point.

A second obstacle in the goal of enhancing happiness is that pursuing happiness for its own sake is rarely a good way to get happy or happier. When happiness is the goal, the pursuit is likely to backfire (Schooler, Ariely, & Loewenstein, 2003). Indeed, those who explicitly link the pursuit of their everyday goals to happiness fare quite poorly (McIntosh, Harlow, & Martin, 1995).

In light of this difficult path, how can we enhance our happiness without having any new capacity for joy become ho-hum? How might we achieve happiness without pursuing it in and of itself?

Happiness Activities and Goal Striving

Sonja Lyubomirsky and her colleagues have proposed a promising approach to enhancing happiness (Lyubomirsky, 2008; Sheldon & Lyubomirsky, 2007; Sin & Lyubomirsky, 2009). Lyubomirsky suggests beginning with intentional activities. For example, she notes that physical activity, kindness, and positive self-reflection all enhance positive affect (Sheldon & Lyubomirsky, 2007). Engaging in altruistic behavior—habitually helping others, especially through a wide range of acts of service—is another powerful way to enhance happiness, according to Lyubomirsky (2008).

One technique for engaging in positive self-reflection is to keep a gratitude journal. Studies by Robert Emmons and Michael McCullough (2004) have demonstrated the ways that being grateful can lead to enhanced happiness and psychological well-being. In one study, they asked individuals to keep a diary in which the participants counted their blessings every day. Those who counted their blessings were better off on various measures of well-being. Although some individuals seem to be naturally more grateful than others, experimental evidence indicates that even people who are not naturally grateful can benefit from taking a moment to count their blessings (Emmons & McCullough, 2003; McCullough, Emmons, & Tsang, 2002).

Another potentially useful approach to enhancing happiness is to commit to the pursuit of personally meaningful goals. Stop for a minute and write down the things you are typically trying to accomplish in your everyday behavior. You might identify a goal such as "to get better grades" or "to be a good friend (or partner or parent)." Such everyday goals and the pursuit of them have been shown to relate strongly to subjective well-being (Brunstein, 1993; Sheldon, 2002). Goal pursuit provides the glue that meaningfully relates a chain of life events, endowing life with beginnings, middles, and ends (King, 2008).

The scientific literature on goal investment offers a variety of ideas about the types of goals that are likely to enhance happiness. To optimize the happiness payoffs of goal pursuit, one ought to set goals that are important and personally valuable and that reflect the intrinsic needs of relatedness, competence, and autonomy (Sheldon, 2002). These goals also should be moderately challenging and should share an instrumental relationship with each other—so that the pursuit of one goal facilitates the accomplishment of another (Emmons & King, 1988).

With regard to the hedonic treadmill, goal pursuit has a tremendous advantage over many other ways of trying to enhance happiness. Goals change and are changed by life experience. As a result, goal pursuit may be less susceptible to the dreaded hedonic treadmill over time. Goals accentuate the positive but do not necessarily eliminate the negative. When we fail to reach our goals, we may experience momentary increases in unhappiness (Pomerantz, Saxon, & Oishi, 2000), which can be a very good thing. Because goals can make us happy and unhappy, they keep life emotionally interesting, and their influence on happiness does not wear off over time.

Overall, goal pursuit may lead to a happier life. Goals keep the positive possible and interesting. The conclusion to be drawn from the evidence, assuming that you want to enhance your happiness, is to strive mightily for the goals that you value. You may fail now and then, but missing the mark will only make your successes all the sweeter.

test yourself

1. Explain the term *hedonic treadmill* and give some real-world examples of it.
2. According to Lyubomirsky, how can individuals cultivate positive emotion?
3. How does committing oneself to personally meaningful goals relate to well-being?

SUMMARY

1. THEORIES OF MOTIVATION

Motivated behavior is energized, directed, and sustained. Early evolutionary theorists considered motivation to be based on instinct—the innate biological pattern of behavior.

A drive is an aroused state that occurs because of a physiological need or deprivation. Drive reduction theory was proposed as an explanation of motivation, with the goal of drive reduction being homeostasis: the body's tendency to maintain equilibrium.

Optimum arousal theory focuses on the Yerkes-Dodson law, which states that performance is best under conditions of moderate rather than low or high arousal. Moderate arousal often serves us best, but there are times when low or high arousal is linked with better performance.

2. HUNGER, OBESITY, AND EATING DISORDERS

Stomach signals are one factor in hunger. Glucose (blood sugar) and insulin both play an important role in hunger. Glucose is needed for the brain to function, and low levels of glucose increase hunger. Insulin can cause a rise in hunger.

Leptin, a protein secreted by fat cells, decreases food intake and increases energy expenditure. The hypothalamus plays an important role in regulating hunger. The lateral hypothalamus is involved in stimulating eating; the ventromedial hypothalamus, in restricting eating.

Obesity is a serious problem in the United States. Heredity, basal metabolism, set point, and fat cells are biological factors involved in obesity. Time and place affect eating. Our early ancestors ate fruits to satisfy nutritional needs, but today we fill up on the empty calories in sweets.

Three eating disorders are anorexia nervosa, bulimia nervosa, and binge eating disorder. Anorexia nervosa is characterized by extreme underweight and starvation. Anorexia nervosa is related to perfectionism and obsessive-compulsive tendencies. Bulimia nervosa involves a pattern of binge eating followed by purging through self-induced vomiting or laxatives. Binge eating disorder involves binge eating without purging.

Anorexia nervosa and bulimia nervosa are much more common in women than men, but there is no gender difference in binge eating disorder. Although sociocultural factors were once thought to be primary in explaining eating disorders, more recent evidence points to the role of biological factors.

3. APPROACHES TO MOTIVATION IN EVERYDAY LIFE

According to Maslow's hierarchy of needs, our main needs are satisfied in this sequence: physiological needs, safety, love and belongingness, esteem, and self-actualization. Maslow gave the most attention to self-actualization: the motivation to develop to one's full potential.

Self-determination theory states that intrinsic motivation occurs when individuals are engaged in the pursuit of organismic needs that are innate and universal. These needs include competence, relatedness, and autonomy. Intrinsic motivation is based on internal factors. Extrinsic motivation is based on external factors, such as rewards and punishments.

Self-regulation involves setting goals, monitoring progress, and making adjustments in behavior to attain desired outcomes. Research suggests that setting intermediate goals on the path toward a long-term goal is a good strategy.

4. EMOTION

Emotion is feeling, or affect, that has three components: physiological arousal, conscious experience, and behavioral expression. The biology of emotion focuses on physiological arousal involving the autonomic nervous system and its two subsystems. Skin conductance level and the polygraph have been used to measure emotional arousal.

The James-Lange theory states that emotion results from physiological states triggered by environmental stimuli: Emotion follows physiological reactions. The Cannon-Bard theory states that emotion and physiological reactions occur simultaneously. Contemporary biological views of emotion increasingly highlight neural circuitry and neurotransmitters. LeDoux has charted the neural circuitry of fear, which focuses on the amygdala and consists of two pathways, one direct and the other indirect. It is likely that positive and negative emotions use different neural circuitry and neurotransmitters.

Schachter and Singer's two-factor theory states that emotion is the result of both physiological arousal and cognitive labeling. Lazarus believed that cognition always directs emotion, but Zajonc argued that emotion directs cognition. Both probably were right.

Research on the behavioral component of emotion focuses on facial expressions. The facial feedback hypothesis states that facial expressions can influence emotions, as well as reflect them.

Most psychologists believe that facial expressions of basic emotions are the same across cultures. However, display rules—nonverbal signals of body movement, posture, and gesture—vary across cultures. Differences in emoticons across cultures reinforce the idea that display rules depend on culture.

Emotions can be classified based on valence (pleasant or unpleasant) and arousal (high or low). Using the dimensions of valence and arousal, emotions can be arranged in a circle, or circumplex model.

Positive emotions likely play an important role in well-being by broadening our focus and allowing us to build resources. Resilience is an individual's capacity to thrive even during difficult times. Research has shown that one way resilient individuals thrive is by experiencing positive emotions.

5. MOTIVATION, EMOTION, AND HEALTH AND WELLNESS: THE PURSUIT OF HAPPINESS

Happiness is highly heritable, and there is reason to consider each person as having a happiness set point. Still, many people would like to increase their level of happiness. One obstacle to changing happiness is the hedonic treadmill: the idea that we quickly adapt to changes that might enhance happiness. Another obstacle is that pursuing happiness for its own sake often backfires.

Ways to enhance happiness include engaging in physical activity, helping others, and engaging in positive self-reflection and experiencing meaning (such as by keeping a gratitude journal). Another way to enhance happiness is to pursue personally valued goals passionately.

key *terms*

motivation, p. 316

instinct, p. 316

drive, p. 316

need, p. 316

homeostasis, p. 317

Yerkes-Dodson law, p. 317

overlearning, p. 317

set point, p. 320

anorexia nervosa, p. 321

bulimia nervosa, p. 322

binge eating disorder (BED), p. 323

hierarchy of needs, p. 324

self-actualization, p. 324

self-determination theory, p. 324

intrinsic motivation, p. 326

extrinsic motivation, p. 326

self-regulation, p. 326

emotion, p. 329

polygraph, p. 330

James-Lange theory, p. 331

Cannon-Bard theory, p. 331

two-factor theory of emotion, p. 333

facial feedback hypothesis, p. 336

display rules, p. 337

negative affect, p. 338

positive affect, p. 338

broaden-and-build model, p. 339

apply your *knowledge*

1. Ask your friends and your parents to define the word *motivation*. Compare your friends' and parents' definitions with the way psychologists define and approach motivation. What are the similarities? What are the differences? How do the definitions of your friends differ from those of your parents? Why do you think all of these variations exist?

2. To explore your own goals and sense of purpose, try the following activity. First list the top 5 or 10 goals that you are trying to accomplish in your everyday behavior. Then write your responses to the following questions that Damon used in his interviews (Damon, 2008, p. 135):

   - Do you have any long-term goals?
   - What does it mean to have a good life?
   - What does it mean to be a good person?
   - If you were looking back on your life now, how would you like to be remembered?

   Finally, consider: Are your everyday goals leading to the fulfillment of your long-term dream? How are you working in your everyday behavior to achieve your grander purposes?

3. Some psychologists believe that the ability to identify and regulate one's emotions is a kind of intelligence. Emotionally intelligent people are also thought to be better at reading the emotional expressions of others. Do a web search for "emotional intelligence tests" and take some online quizzes, or try the one at http://www.testcafe.com/ei/. Do you think you are emotionally intelligent? Does your performance on the test seem to reflect your actual experience? What is your opinion of the test you tried? Is there information on the site showing its validity and reliability?

4. This chapter reviewed the use of autonomic nervous system activity in the detection of deception. Psychologists have devised various ways to detect lying. Go online and search for information on detecting deception and lies. Is there a good way to tell if someone is being truthful? Explain.

CHAPTER 11

Gender, Sex, and Sexuality

Jazz Jennings: Declaring Herself Proudly

"Is it a boy or a girl?" That is so often our first, excited question when we hear that someone has given birth or even when we find out that she is pregnant. Although it may seem straightforward, the answer—and what it means for each newborn—can be quite complex.

Consider the young girl known to the media as Jazz Jennings. Though born with a male body, Jazz has insisted throughout her young life that she is a girl (Goldberg & Adriano, 2008). At first her parents humored their son, allowing him to play with girls' toys and to dress like a girl at home. Eventually, after observing Jazz's sadness during a dance recital when he was not permitted to wear a tutu like the "other girls," Jazz's parents decided to allow her to be herself, to dress and to act like a girl everywhere she went. Jazz entered kindergarten with long hair and wearing earrings and a dress. Although ever mindful of the difficulties she might face along the way, Jazz's parents remain committed to supporting their child wherever her gender identity takes her.

Even for individuals whose biological sex seems a perfect fit, sexuality can be complex, and the impact of sex and gender can be just as profound. Issues of gender, sex, and sexuality are everywhere around us. Why do little boys gravitate toward toy trucks, and little girls toward dolls? Why are there so few male teachers, especially for preschool and kindergarten? Should women in the military be permitted to serve in combat? Should gay men and lesbian women be permitted to marry their same-sex partners? What kind of sex education is most effective? In this chapter we will explore the concepts, knowledge, and psychology behind these and other provocative questions related to gender, sex, and sexuality. ●

PREVIEW

We begin the chapter by defining some key terms and concepts related to gender, sex, and sexuality. We then consider the major theoretical approaches to gender development, followed by a review of the psychology of gender differences. Next, we delve into the science behind sexual orientation and examine sexual practices and behaviors. A look at several sexual variations and disorders follows, and we close by taking stock of the important place of sexuality in physical health and psychological wellness.

1· DEFINING SEX AND GENDER

Let's begin by defining the two terms we will use throughout this chapter. You have no doubt heard and used the words *sex* and *gender* frequently in your life. Their technical definitions are key to understanding how scientists study these concepts.

Sex and Its Biological Components

● **sex** The properties of a person that determine his or her classification as male or female.

Sex refers to the properties of a person that determine his or her classification as male or female. One structure of our physical bodies that scientists use to classify us as male or female is chromosomes. We have seen that chromosomes are the packages of DNA that carry our genes. In Chapter 3 we saw that human beings have 23 pairs of chromosomes, with one of each pair being provided by each of our parents. Twenty-two of these pairs are generally the same in males and females, but the 23rd pair differs across the sexes. Scientists call this differing pair of genes the **sex chromosomes** because the pair determines a person's genetic sex (male or female). In females, both sex chromosomes are similar and are called X chromosomes. Males have one X and one Y chromosome—the latter so named because it looks like an upside-down Y (Figure 11.1).

● **sex chromosomes** In humans, the pair of genes that differs between the sexes and determines a person's sex as male or female.

Another set of physical structures used to classify us as male or female is our gonads, a part of the endocrine system. **Gonads** are glands that produce sex hormones and generate ova (eggs) in females and sperm in males; collectively called *gametes,* the ova and sperm are the cells that will eventually be used in reproduction. In females the gonads are the *ovaries* (located on either side of the abdomen), and in males they are the *testes* (located in the *scrotum,* the pouch of skin that hangs below the penis).

● **gonads** Glands that produce sex hormones and generate ova (eggs) in females and sperm in males; collectively called gametes, the ova and sperm are the cells that will eventually be used in reproduction.

Sex may also be classified by the hormones that these gonads produce. Recall that hormones are chemicals produced by the endocrine system's glands. There are no hormones that are unique to one sex, but the levels of hormones vary by sex. The levels of estrogen and progesterone are higher in women than in men, and the levels of androgens (the most

FIGURE 11.1 The Genetic Difference Between Males and Females
The chromosome structures of a male (*left*) and female (*right*). The 23rd pair is shown at bottom right. Notice that the male's Y chromosome is smaller than his X chromosome. To obtain pictures of chromosomes, a cell is removed from a person's body, usually from inside the mouth, and the chromosomes are photographed under magnification.

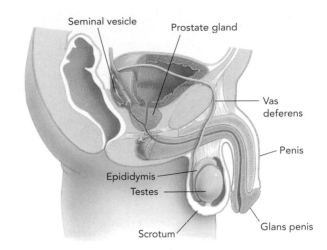

FIGURE 11.2 **Female and Male Internal Sex Organs and External Genitalia** These figures show the female (*left*) and male (*right*) internal sex organs and external genitalia.

common being testosterone) are higher in men than in women. In women, androgens are produced by the adrenal glands, and in men some of the androgens that are produced by the testes are converted into estrogens. These hormones play a role in the development of our internal reproductive structures, our external genitalia, and the secondary sex characteristics (see below) that are also used in classifying us as male or female.

Figure 11.2 shows the internal sex organs of females and males. In women, these organs allow the ovum to travel from the ovaries to the uterus, and they also play roles in sexual functioning, the menstrual cycle, and pregnancy. In men, the internal sex organs include the structures involved in the production and storage of sperm, as well as those that play a role in sexual arousal and orgasm.

The external genitalia of males and females are found between their legs, as Figure 11.2 also illustrates. The external genitalia of females, collectively called the *vulva,* include the *mons pubis* (a fleshy area just above the vagina), the *labia* (the lips surrounding the vaginal opening), and the *clitoris* (a small sensory organ at the top where the labia meet). For males, the external genitalia include the *penis* and *scrotum.*

Recall from Chapter 9 that puberty is a period of rapid skeletal and sexual maturation that occurs mainly in early adolescence (Figure 11.3). At puberty, individuals develop **secondary sex characteristics,** traits that differ between the two sexes but are not part of the reproductive system. Breasts in females and facial hair in males are secondary sex characteristics.

To reemphasize, these many physical attributes may play a role in classifying a person as male or female. However, as we will see, physical characteristics may or may not match a person's psychological experience of himself or herself as male or female—that is, the person's gender.

Gender

Gender refers to the social and psychological aspects of being female or male. Gender goes beyond biological sex to include a person's understanding of the meaning to his or her own life of being male or female. Although checking off "male" or "female" on a questionnaire may seem like a simple choice, gender is a complex variable influenced by biological factors, as well as socialization and experience.

Gender identity is an individual's sense of belonging to the male or female sex. Gender identity is multifaceted. Specifically, people differ in the extent to which they experience gender identity as central to their sense of self; in their comfort level with their own gender category; and in the degree to which they feel socially encouraged to conform to a particular gender identity (Berenbaum, 2006; Martin & Ruble, 2010).

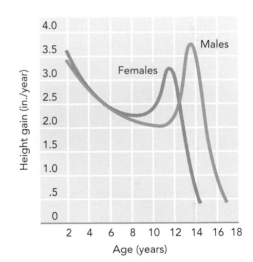

FIGURE 11.3 **Pubertal Growth Spurt** On average, the pubertal growth spurt begins and peaks about two years earlier for girls (starts at 9, peaks at 11½) than for boys (starts at 11½, peaks at 13½). From J. M. Tanner et al., in *Archives of Diseases in Childhood, 41,* 1966. Reproduced with permission from the BMJ Publishing Group.

● **secondary sex characteristics** Traits that differ between the two sexes but are not part of the reproductive system; they include breasts in females and facial hair in males.

● **gender** The social and psychological aspects of being female or male; gender goes beyond biological sex to include a person's understanding of the meaning to his or her own life of being male or female.

● **gender identity** An individual's multifaceted sense of belonging to the male or female sex.

In describing a person's gender identity, we might talk about attributes such as masculinity and femininity. Technically speaking, these words mean, respectively, "being like a man" and "being like a woman." Psychologists have studied these gender-related characteristics using the terms *instrumentality* (for more masculine traits) and *expressiveness* (for more feminine traits) to represent broad dimensions that may or may not be strongly associated with a particular sex. Instrumental attributes include being assertive, brave, independent, and dominant. Expressive traits include being nurturing, warm, gentle, and sensitive to others.

Instrumentality and expressiveness are not systematically related to each other, so every possible combination of these characteristics is possible. We might call someone who is highly instrumental but not very expressive "masculine," and someone else who is highly expressive but not very instrumental "feminine." Individuals who are *high* on both dimensions are considered **androgynous,** meaning that they have attributes that we typically associate with both genders (Bem, 1993). Individuals who are *low* on both dimensions are referred to as undifferentiated. Importantly, although there are differences between men and women regarding these traits, with men scoring as more instrumental and women as more expressive (Fink & others, 2007; Lippa, 2008), they are not as strong as you might expect. Indeed, the degree of instrumentality or expressiveness a person feels can depend on the social context and the activity in which he or she is engaged (Leszczynski, 2009). A father playing with his toddler may feel quite expressive; a WNBA guard who is running up the basketball court on a fast break may feel quite instrumental.

● **androgynous** Having attributes that we typically associate with both genders.

Research has shown that individuals who are not strongly gender-typed according to these scales tend to have better psychological adjustment and resilience than those rated as extremely masculine or feminine (Lam & McBride-Chang, 2007). In fact, a balance between instrumentality and expressiveness relates to a variety of positive outcomes (Bruch, 2002; Danoff-Burg, Mosher, & Grant, 2006; Helgeson, 1994; Mosher & Danoff-Burg, 2008).

It is tempting to think of *sex* as the term for biologically based differences between males and females, and *gender* as the word for differences that are a product of environment or socialization. Many psychologists do in fact distinguish sex and gender in this way (Caplan & Caplan, 2005; Halpern & others, 2007). In this chapter we generally reserve the word *sex* to refer to biological characteristics, and we use *gender* for psychosocial attributes that are related to sex but that may or may not reflect biological differences.

Sex and gender are linked in ways that might surprise you. Let's take a close look at the processes that lead from sex to gender.

From Genes to Sex to Gender

In the first few weeks after conception, male and female embryos look alike. Moreover, the raw materials of male and female genitals and gonads are essentially the same. The penis and clitoris take shape from the same embryonic structures. Similarly, the same embryonic structures develop into the testes (in males) and ovaries (in females), and the same is true for the scrotum and the labia. What causes the differentiation of the sexes is a particular gene on the Y chromosome, the *SRY gene,* which is activated early in the first trimester (the first three months of the pregnancy). The SRY gene causes the development of embryonic testes. These testes begin to manufacture androgens (including

Some successful entertainers, among them Adam Lambert and Lady Gaga, challenge common notions of gender.

Gender and Neuroscience: Are There His and Hers Brains?

Do men's and women's brains differ systematically? Research using the brain-imaging techniques we examined in Chapter 3 shows that male and female brains do differ from each other in significant ways.

Female brains are smaller than male brains by between 8 and 10 percent (Cahill, 2006), and this difference is not explained by the fact that women are generally smaller than men (Goldstein & others, 2001). Perhaps because of its smaller size, the female brain may use its real estate more judiciously. Compared to the male brain, a woman's brain has higher cortical volume (meaning that more of the brain is devoted to the cortex, the brain's outermost part). The female brain also has more *gray matter* (brain tissue made up of neurons that send signals), but the male brain has more *white matter* (brain tissue composed of myelinated axons that send signals rapidly to and from the gray matter). In terms of brain structures, in women, the prefrontal cortex and the hippocampus are larger, while in men the amygdalae are larger (Goldstein & others, 2001; Hamann, 2005).

Why do you think male and female brains differ?

Male and female brains differ not only in structure but in function as well (McCarthy & others, 2009). The hippocampus in women is less reactive to stress (Andreano & Cahill, 2006; Cahill, 2006) and may not be affected as strongly by chronic stress compared to the male hippocampus. Men's right amygdala is more active than the left in response to happy faces. In women the opposite pattern holds (Killgore & Yurgelun-Todd, 2001).

The hippocampus and amygdala are involved in learning, memory, and emotion. So, do sex differences in these areas translate into differences in learning, memory, and emotion? Research has begun to suggest that they might (Andreano & Cahill, 2006). For example, one study examined the release of noradrenaline (also called *norepinephrine,* a chemical that is emitted into the synapses of the brain as part of the "fight or flight" response described in Chapter 3) in reaction to emotionally arousing pictures and investigated the memory for those pictures in men and women (Segal & Cahill, 2009). Although there was no sex difference in memory performance, the brain processes that had occurred differed between the sexes. For women, noradrenaline release was more likely to occur in response to emotional pictures. Furthermore, in women, this release was related to better long-term memory. Men's memory was similarly accurate but was not a function of noradrenaline release.

These results suggest that when performing the same task, men and women may tap into different regions of the brain to produce identical-looking results. Sex *differences* in the brain may explain the *lack of differences* in behavior, as the brains of each sex compensate for their various differences to produce the same behavior (De Vries, 2004).

Research on the neuroscience of sex differences tells us that even when the sexes look alike behaviorally, different brain processes may be responsible for these behaviors, depending on the person's sex. A key lesson from this intriguing research is that sex matters to neuroscience—in sometimes unexpected ways. We cannot study one sex and make generalizations about the other, even when we are studying the brain (Cahill, 2006).

testosterone) that spread throughout the developing embryo, influencing the growing body and brain. Through this process, the XY embryo essentially turns itself into a male. Low levels of androgen in a female embryo allow for the development of the female body and brain.

Although often called the sex chromosomes, the 46th pair broadly influences human development, affecting not only sexual characteristics but other bodily systems as well (Goldstein & Reynolds, 1999; Hagerman, 2009). Given their extensive effects, might these chromosomal differences between the sexes lead to differences in the development of the brain? To explore this intriguing question, check out the Intersection.

Disorders of Sexual Development

Genes and prenatal hormones play crucial roles in the development of the genitals, and these physical structures are generally used to identify a child's sex prenatally through

● **disorders of sexual development (DSD)** Congenital conditions in which the development of chromosomal, gonadal, or anatomical sex is atypical; formerly called intersex conditions or hermaphroditism.

an ultrasound or at birth (Berenbaum, 2006; Blakemore, Berenbaum, & Liben, 2009). Although typically the sex of a baby is straightforward, some individuals are born with external genitalia that are not clearly male or female. Prenatal hormonal exposure, chromosomal abnormalities, and environmental factors (such as exposure to radiation, chemicals, or some medications while in the womb) can affect the developing genitals. The result may be sexually ambiguous—that is, not clearly male or female—external organs such as a very small penis, an enlarged clitoris, or genitals that appear to include both a penis and vaginal labia. Formerly called *intersex conditions* (or *hermaphroditism*), these conditions now fall under the category of **disorders of sexual development (DSD)** (Hughes & others, 2006), which refers to *congenital* (that is, present at birth) conditions in which the development of chromosomal, gonadal, or anatomical sex is atypical (P. A. Lee & others, 2006). Professionals debate about how best to handle such cases.

Imagine being the parent of a child born with genitals that are not clearly male or female. How would you feel, and what would you do? Experts long believed that immediate surgery and sex assignment were crucial for both parents and children (Money, Hampson, & Hampson, 1955, 1957). Decades ago, professionals assumed that a child could not develop normally with ambiguous genitals and that gender identity was entirely determined by socialization rather than being influenced by biological factors (Berenbaum, 2006; Meyer-Bahlburg, 1998). Interestingly, these assumptions were originally supported by a case in which a child was born with *unambiguously* male genitalia.

John Money, a well-known sex researcher, believed strongly that socialization was the main determinant of gender. In the 1960s, a case presented itself that gave Money the opportunity to test this theory. In 1965 twin boys were born, and a few months after birth, one twin's penis was destroyed during circumcision. Money persuaded the boy's parents to allow him to surgically transform the injured male genitals into female genitals and to agree to treat the child as a girl. The former boy was reared as a girl and, according to Money, essentially became a girl (Money & Tucker, 1975). The "John/Joan" case became famous as an example of nurture's triumph over nature. For many years, this case was used as evidence for the amazing flexibility of gender.

Milton Diamond, a biologist and strong critic of Money's theory, decided to follow up on Money's most famous case (Diamond & Sigmundson, 1997). Diamond found that over time, "Joan" became less and less interested in being a girl and eventually refused to continue the process of feminization that Money had devised. We now know that "Joan" was really David Reimer, whose biography, *As Nature Made Him,* written by John Colapinto (2000), revealed the difficulties of his life as a boy, then a girl, then a boy, and finally a man. David struggled with traumatic gender-related life experiences and depression, eventually committing suicide in 2004.

David's story seems to indicate that biological factors powerfully guide the way from sex to gender identity. Yet this one case may not represent the full picture. Remember from Chapter 2 that it is difficult to make generalizations based on a single case study. However tragic, this case does not close the door on the possibility that socialization can significantly shape gender development. Indeed, there have been other cases in which genetic males have lost their penis to trauma, animal attacks, or vehicular accidents at a very young age. In such cases, doctors and parents must consider their options: to reassign the individual's sex to female and rear the child as a girl, or to rear him as a boy with eventual surgery to re-create the penis. However, regarding the latter option, male sexual anatomy is extremely complex, and such surgery is difficult. Perhaps for this reason, some parents have decided to reassign the child's sex, and a number of cases have had positive outcomes (Bradley & others, 1998; Lippa, 2005; Zucker, 1999).

What about evidence beyond vivid cases? One clear conclusion from that evidence is that the sex in which an individual is reared is the single strongest predictor of eventual gender identity (Berenbaum, 2006; Meyer-Bahlburg, 2005; Zucker, 1999). In

Colapinto's biography documents the dramatic John/Joan case—one of the most infamous in modern medicine—in which David Reimer, who had suffered a botched circumcision as an infant, was raised as a girl until he was a teenager.

other words, socialization is powerfully (but not perfectly) related to eventual gender identity. For example, one study showed that among genetic males born without a penis (due to a birth defect) and reared as females, fully 78 percent lived their adult lives as women. Of those who were reared as male, 100 percent were living as male (Meyer-Bahlburg, 2005).

After reviewing the evidence, Sheri Berenbaum (2006), an expert on sexual development, concluded that despite their distress, parents and healthcare providers might need to live with a child's unusual physical condition until the child is able to have some say in the decision. The idea that a child cannot experience healthy development with ambiguous genitals is simply an assumption that has not been systematically tested. Policies about treatment ought to be based on reproductive potential, the possibility of future sexual functioning, and a minimization of medical procedures. Further, Berenbaum stressed that all involved in the decision must realize that the child might initiate a gender change later in life. Most important, experts agree that these decisions should be made based on the child's well-being, not parental distress (Consortium on the Management of Disorders of Sexual Development, 2006).

When Genetic Sex and Gender Conflict: Transgender Experience

This chapter began with the story of Jazz Jennings, the child who was born with a boy's body but is convinced that she is a girl. Among other people who feel as if they were born into the wrong sex is Chastity Bono, the daughter of pop singers Sonny and Cher; Chastity recently came out as transgendered and changed her name to Chaz. **Transgender** refers to experiencing one's psychological gender as different from one's physical sex. Transgender individuals can be biological males who identify as female, or biological females who identify as male.

How do psychologists understand transgender individuals? The American Psychiatric Association classifies individuals who feel trapped in the wrong biological sex as suffering from gender identity disorder (previously referred to as "transsexualism") (APA, 2000). **Gender identity disorder (GID)** refers to strong, persistent cross-sex identification and a continuing discomfort with, or sense of inappropriateness of, one's assigned sex. To meet the criteria for GID, the person cannot have experienced a disorder of sexual development, and the distress must be such that it interferes with daily life. Quite rare, GID occurs in an estimated 1 in 11,000–30,000 genetic males and 1 in 30,400–100,000 genetic females (APA, 2000).

The defining feature of GID is *gender dysphoria,* distress over one's born sex (Cohen-Kettenis & Pfafflin, 2010; Gijs & Brewaeys, 2007). The only empirically evaluated treatment for GID is *sex reassignment surgery,* which involves the removal of secondary sex characteristics, hormone treatments, and the surgical reconstruction of the genitals. The surgical challenges that female-to-male transgender individuals face are more complex than those for male-to-female transgender people. Studies of individuals who have undergone these procedures generally find that they express little or no regret and are satisfied with the surgery (Cohen-Kettenis & Pfafflin, 2010; Gijs & Brewaeys, 2007).

A controversial diagnosis, GID is no longer viewed as a disorder in France or Great Britain. Nonetheless, should individuals who experience themselves as one gender psychologically and another physically be considered mentally ill? Should their treatment be seen as primarily a way to alleviate suffering? Increasingly, transgender individuals have urged that society consider them as not suffering from a disorder but rather as individuals who require help in dealing with a distressing error in nature (Cohen-Kettenis & Pfafflin, 2010).

● **transgender** Experiencing one's psychological gender as different from one's physical sex, as in the cases of biological males who identify as female, and biological females who identify as male.

● **gender identity disorder (GID)** Strong, persistent cross-sex identification and a continuing discomfort with, or sense of inappropriateness of, one's assigned sex.

Chaz Bono, who has recently completed the transition from female to male, is an activist for the lesbian, gay, bisexual, and transgender communities.

test yourself

1. Explain the difference between sex and gender.
2. Discuss the causes of the differentiation of the sexes.
3. What is gender identity disorder (GID)? What is the only treatment for GID that has been evaluated by research?

Many transgender individuals do not desire sex reassignment surgery (Cohen-Kettenis & Pfafflin, 2010). Some opt for hormone treatment only. Others prefer to think of their gender identity in an alternative, broader way: They embrace their identity as a quality that challenges the notion of sexual identity as one of two opposing categories. For such individuals, being transgender means living according to the belief that a person can experience life as a man who happens to have a vagina or as a woman who has a penis (Lev, 2007)—as an individual who occupies a different but valid gender territory (Meyer-Bahlburg, 2010; Pfafflin, 2010).

For most people, genetic sex and psychological gender are experienced as a pretty good fit. Nevertheless, we might wonder how a person who is XX or XY comes to think of him- or herself as female or male. Various theories of gender development have addressed this question.

2· THEORIES OF GENDER DEVELOPMENT

In this section we examine the major theoretical approaches to gender development. Theorists debate the relative contributions of nature and nurture to gender identity. In general, psychologists acknowledge that gender identity is complex and that to understand it we need to consider both biological and psychosocial processes (Berenbaum, 2006; Blakemore, Berenbaum, & Liben, 2009).

Biological Approaches

We have seen that a number of biological factors—including genes, gonads, and hormones—identify a person as male or female. Biological approaches to gender draw links between these aspects of the person's biological sex and his or her eventual psychological feelings of gender. Individuals who study biological factors in gender development focus on variables such as genes, prenatal hormones, and brain structures and functions, as these differ between males and females and potentially account for the experiences of ourselves in those sexes.

Biologically based research has looked at differences between the sexes in infancy, searching for clues to gender-related characteristics in the earliest days of life. One study examined 1-day-old male and female infants. The infants were shown two stimuli: a human face and a mobile made out of a picture of that face (Connellan & others, 2000). The researchers found that the baby girls spent more time looking at the human face, while the baby boys were more interested in the mobile (Connellan & others, 2000). Similarly, research on infants from 3 to 8 months of age found that males spent more time looking at typical boy toys, including trucks and machines, and females spent more time looking at typical girl toys, such as dolls (Alexander, Wilcox, & Woods, 2009). Nonhuman primates exhibit similar differences (Alexander & Hines, 2002; Hassett, Siebert, & Wallen, 2008). In humans, such differences are thought to be biologically, not socially, based because very young children have not yet had social experiences that might influence gender development.

Evolutionary Psychology

The evolutionary psychology approach to gender views the biological differences between the sexes through the lens of natural selection and adaptation. From this perspective, the factors that produce gender are the product of millions of years of natural selection.

Recall from Chapter 1 that, according to Charles Darwin's theory of evolution, a species' characteristics reflect natural selection, the process by which the environment

Research on infants from 3 to 8 months of age found that males spent more time looking at boy toys, such as trucks and machines, than other toys.

determines the adaptiveness of particular genetic characteristics. Organisms with the fittest genes are most likely to survive and reproduce. This slow process is responsible for creating the typical characteristics of any species. Applying these ideas to gender, evolutionary psychologists assert that the differences we see between contemporary men and women can be explained by the *selection pressures,* or environmental challenges, that confronted our distant human ancestors (Buss, 2011; Cosmides, 2011; Geary, 2010; Meston & Buss, 2009).

SEXUAL SELECTION

Differences between male and female members of the same species abound in nature. For instance, the beautiful peacock with the colorful tail and the cardinal with brilliant red feathers are both males, while the female members of those species are duller in appearance. What accounts for these sex differences within species? Darwin (1871) proposed that many sex differences that occur within species have evolved through sexual selection. **Sexual selection** means that the male and female members of a species differ from each other because of differences in competition and choice. *Competition* occurs among members of the same sex as they vie for the opportunity to mate with members of the opposite sex. Members of that opposite sex in turn exercise *choice,* selecting the lucky one (or ones) with whom they will mate. In peacocks, the males use their amazing plumage to compete with one another for females, and the female selects the prettiest male with whom to reproduce.

Who competes and who chooses? Generally, the sex that invests the most in producing offspring is the one that chooses, and the other sex is the one that competes (Andersson & Simmons, 2006; Bateman, 1948; Clutton-Brock, 2007, 2010). Applying these ideas to humans, evolutionary psychologists believe that sex differences observed in women and men are evidence that sexual selection has occurred in our species. Women are the sex that gives birth, and as such they ought to do the choosing. Men, on the other hand, show characteristics that are thought to be well suited for competing. For example, men are physically larger and stronger than women. Evolutionary psychologists explain human males' physical size as an adaptation that helps men to compete against one another for female mates.

Sexual selection is more complicated in human beings than in other species. Specifically, because human infants are so helpless, it makes sense from a survival standpoint for men to invest in their offspring—so sometimes men get to be the choosers, and women are the competitors vying for those men who are likely to invest in their children (Andersson & Simmons, 2006; Halpern & others, 2007). This aspect of sexual selection is of particular interest in humans because of the different challenges men and women face in reproducing.

REPRODUCTIVE CHALLENGES FOR MEN AND WOMEN

Men and women share the same evolutionary goal—to reproduce—but accomplishing that objective presents different challenges to each sex. Women are the sex that experiences pregnancy and childbirth. They can reproduce only about once per year and have a limited time of fertility. Thus, women must be choosy in selecting sexual partners, putting a premium on high *quality.* Evolutionary psychologists stress that women should be picky and should seek sexual partners who have adequate resources to invest in a family.

In contrast, according to evolutionary theorists, because men are generally fertile from puberty through the rest of life, they can focus on *quantity,* reproducing as often as possible with a broad range of partners. A sticking point for this strategy, though, is that as noted above, babies are so helpless that it is adaptive for men to invest in their offspring.

Further, men have an additional problem. Because the moment when the egg is fertilized by the sperm is a mystery for the parties involved, a man cannot be certain

This male peacock uses his beautiful plumage to attract female mates.

● **sexual selection** According to Darwin's theory of evolution, the differentiation between the male and female members of a species because of the differences between the two in competition and choice.

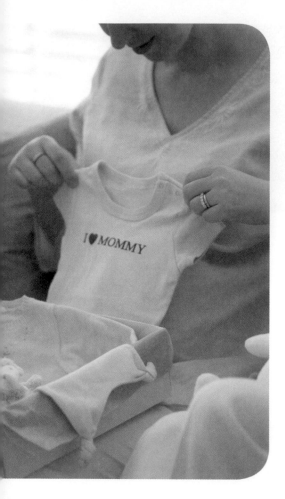

whether the child in whom he is investing his resources is genetically *his* child. Evolutionarily speaking, for a man, the worst-case scenario is to invest his resources to ensure the survival of someone else's offspring.

How might men avoid this dreaded outcome? Evolutionary psychologists point out that across cultures, men are likely to prefer women who are younger than they are (Buss, 2011). This preference for younger women may be a way for a man to minimize the chances that his betrothed is already pregnant with someone else's offspring. Evolutionary psychologists suggest that, compared to women, men should be less selective about sexual behavior and more interested in physical appearance (which is thought to represent health and fertility), seeking partners who are young and beautiful (Buss, 2011; Geary, 2010).

The sex differences that have been discovered shortly after birth, as well as cross-cultural similarities in mate preferences, would seem strongly to support biological and evolutionary theories of gender development. However, let's stop and think beyond these theories and also look at the potential role of the *social* environment in the emergence of gender. Family and friends begin to buy pink and blue baby clothes before a child is even born. That child is introduced to a social network with strong expectations about gender-appropriate behavior. If a little boy shows a preference for playing with a truck or a ball, we might smile and conclude, "He's *all boy*." If the same child expresses interest in trying on a dress or playing with a doll, we might respond quite differently. Might not these different social responses influence the child's developing sense of self?

Furthermore, consider that the male preference for younger sexual partners may reflect social expectations or the power differences that exist between men and women in many cultures. These considerations reflect concerns that are represented in two additional views of gender development: social cognitive approaches and social role theory.

Social Cognitive Approaches

Social cognitive theories of gender development focus on how children learn about gender and how they come to occupy a particular gender identity. These approaches emphasize both the way that children internalize information about gender (Bem, 1983, 1993) and the way the environment reinforces gender-related behavior (Bussey & Bandura, 2004).

Social cognitive approaches examine how experience influences the formation of the person's sense of gender. From this perspective, gender behavior is learned through reward and punishment, observational learning, and modeling (Bandura & Bussey, 2004; Bussey & Bandura, 2004), processes we examined in Chapter 6. According to Albert Bandura, modeling is an especially potent mechanism for transmitting values (Bandura, 1986; Bussey & Bandura 2004). Children gain information about gender from models of each sex. Who goes to work every day? Who does the housekeeping? When children see their parents and other adults engaging in gender-related behavior (and as they observe whether and how these behaviors are reinforced), they learn about how men and women behave.

In subtle ways, children may be rewarded for engaging in gender-conforming behavior and punished for engaging in behavior that does not fit with expectations for their sex, what is called *gender-nonconforming behavior*. Examples of gender-conforming behavior include playing with dolls (for girls) and playing with trucks (for boys). Examples of gender-nonconforming behavior are a girl's playing with a train set and a boy's playing dress-up or house. The child's social environment responds to behaviors in various ways, coloring his or her perception of their appropriateness. A girl might learn that pretending to be a professional football player is not a way to please her parents. A boy might pick up on his mother's subtle frown when he announces that he wants to try on her high-heeled shoes.

Peers also play an important role in gender development. Especially after age 6, peer groups often segregate into boy groups and girl groups (Maccoby, 2002) (Figure 11.4). Peers are stricter than most parents in rewarding gender-conforming behavior and punishing gender-nonconforming behavior. For example, children can be punitive toward boys who engage in behaviors that are not typically boyish (Herek, 1991; Bailey & Zucker, 1995; Lippa, 2008).

Through these varied experiences, children develop a *gender schema*—a mental framework for understanding what is considered appropriate behavior for females and males in their culture (Martin & Ruble, 2010). Children learn that gender is an important organizing principle in social life, and they come to recognize that boys and girls, and men and women, are different in ways that matter. This gender schema then serves as a cognitive framework by which children interpret further experiences related to gender.

While acknowledging biological differences between males and females, social cognitive psychologists believe that social and cultural factors have a much stronger influence on eventual gender identity (Bandura & Bussey, 2004). From this perspective, differences in men's and women's career and life choices can be explained by differences in the availability of role models and beliefs about self-efficacy and personal control. Social cognitive practitioners would say, for example, that men and women differ in their career choices primarily because they have different beliefs about their ability to achieve their career goals—and about the extent to which success is in their control.

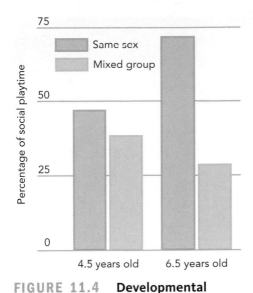

FIGURE 11.4 **Developmental Changes in Percentage of Time Spent in Same-Sex and Mixed-Group Settings** Observations of children show that they are more likely to play in same-sex than mixed-sex groups. This tendency increases between 4 and 6 years of age.

Social Role Theory

Alice Eagly has proposed that to understand gender, we must recognize the larger social and cultural institutions surrounding the psychological phenomenon of gender identity (Eagly, 1987, 2010a, 2010b; Eagly & Fischer, 2009; Eagly & Sczesny, 2009; Eagly & Wood, 2010; Wood & Eagly, 2010). Eagly's approach, *social role theory,* starts off by acknowledging the very same physical differences between the sexes that were noted by evolutionary psychologists: Women are more innately and directly involved in reproduction than men, and men are larger and stronger than women. Eagly proposed that these differences resulted in a division of labor between the sexes, with women being more involved in the home and with childrearing, and men being more likely to work outside the home.

From Eagly's perspective, this division of labor can lead to the belief that the things that men and women *do* are the things that men and women *should do.* The activities and occupations we see men and women performing give rise to expectations and beliefs about what it means to be male or female, what a male or female person *ought* to do, and what we believe that person *can* do. In this way, the division of labor spawns the social construct of **gender roles,** expectations for how females and males should think, act, and feel (Leaper & Friedman, 2007). Social role theory argues that each culture creates its own sense of what is a man and what is a woman (Eagly, 2010a, 2010b; Eagly & Wood, 2010).

Gender roles are related to **gender stereotypes**—overly general beliefs and expectations about what women and men are like. Gender stereotypes might suggest that women are warm, caring, and emotional and that men are strong, dominant, and rational. These stereotypes might influence how we interpret behavior. For example, if a woman is assertive, we might view her as bossy or manly, and if a man is gentle, we might evaluate him as wimpy.

Social role theory asserts that each of us internalizes these roles and stereotypes and comes to evaluate our own behavior and life choices according to their gender typicality (Deaux & LaFrance, 1998; Eagly & Wood, 2010). For example, gender roles and gender stereotypes might influence our life goals (Diekman & Eagly,

● **gender roles** Expectations for how females and males should think, act, and feel.

● **gender stereotypes** Overly general beliefs and expectations about what women and men are like.

Traditional gender roles and gender stereotypes often (but not always, as the photo shows) shape individuals' life goals and career choices.

2008; Evans & Diekman, 2009). If a particular occupation (say, an engineer, a nurse, or a kindergarten teacher) conflicts with our perceived gender role, we may view it as less desirable and less likely to bring us success. Notably, when men and women make choices that are guided by gender roles and gender stereotypes, they tend to become more and more different from each other in their behaviors, attitudes, and aspirations, with each sex engaging in more stereotypical pursuits (Eagly, Wood, & Johannesen-Schmidt, 2004). In turn, these sex-based differences, driven by gender roles and stereotypes, maintain the social structure (Eagly, 1987; Eagly & Wood, 2010).

Social role theory also takes into account the institutional structures and patterns of opportunity that perpetuate gender differences (Eagly, 1987; Eagly & Wood, 2010; Wood & Eagly, 2010). Differences between men and women in access to education and in the treatment they receive from teachers, for instance, helps to explain differences in career choices.

One prediction from social role theory is that as social structures change, gender differences should decrease—and this prediction has been borne out (Eagly & Diekman, 2003). For example, in cultures in which women have greater access to economic opportunities, education, and careers, women are much less likely to prefer men with resources as suggested by the evolutionary perspective (Eagly & Wood, 2010; Kasser & Sharma, 1999). Importantly, social role theory asserts that thinking about men and women simply in terms of their sex misses big differences among people within each group. Indeed, in Eagly's view, lumping people together according to their sex (assuming that biological sex means the same thing as gender) is essentially engaging in gender stereotyping.

Evaluating the Theoretical Approaches to Gender

In summary, scholars think about gender and its origins in a number of persuasive ways, including biological, evolutionary, social cognitive, and social role perspectives. These theories are not mutually exclusive, and a comprehensive understanding of gender might well take all of them into account.

Biology alone would not seem to offer a sufficient explanation for gender. Indeed, wide variations occur within each sex, for there are certainly girls and women who are assertive and dominant, as well as boys and men who are submissive and subordinate. Yet biological differences between the sexes are perhaps more significant than the social cognitive approach acknowledges: Just ask the parents whose daughter insists on playing with dolls instead of trucks or who witness their son turning a stuffed bunny into a weapon.

Similarities in patterns of gender differences across different cultures support evolutionary psychology approaches. However, the application of sexual selection to human behavior has been strongly criticized. Some suggest that gender differences between men and women can be better explained by social factors, among them group cooperation, than by natural selection (Roughgarden, Oishi, & Akcay, 2006).

Certainly, having role models is a vital factor in the attitudes that men and women form about their choices of life goals, as the social cognitive view suggests. Further, there is no question that social roles are also important. Indeed, it is shocking to think that although we live in a world where in some nations a woman can serve as national leader, in other countries a girl is not permitted even to go to school and a woman cannot leave home without an escort.

Biological, evolutionary, social cognitive, and social role theorists approach gender development from different levels of analysis, and each approach poses different research questions to answer (Figure 11.5). Throughout the rest of this chapter, we will regularly refer to these broad perspectives to see how each one applies with regard to the specific topics and issues addressed. Each of these theories, for example, has something to say about whether and how the sexes should differ from each other on various attributes, our next topic.

test yourself

1. What are four major theoretical approaches to gender development? What is the main idea behind each?

2. Explain sexual selection, a key concept of the evolutionary psychology approach.

3. What are gender roles and gender stereotypes? What does social role theory say about them?

Theoretical Approach	Summary	Research Questions
Biological	Focuses on the various biological processes that underlie differences between men and women. Researchers from this perspective examine variables such as genes, hormones, and brain structures and functions to identify the biological underpinnings of gender.	• How does prenatal hormone exposure relate to later sex-typed behavior? • How do genetic factors influence the development of gender identity?
Evolutionary	Focuses on the ways that differences between men and women can be understood as serving adaptive functions for our distant ancestors. Sexual selection is used to explain gender differences in behavior, and sex differences in reproductive challenges are thought to underlie differences in sexual behavior.	• How do men and women differ in terms of engaging in casual sex? • Do sex differences in nonhuman primates show the same patterns as those found in humans?
Social Cognitive	Focuses on how processes such as learning (including modeling and rewards and punishers) and the development of cognitive schemas associated with sex lead to conceptions of male and female.	• When do children learn that a person's sex makes a difference in how he or she is treated by others? • How do peer groups react to children who behave in gender-atypical ways?
Social Role	Focuses on the ways that the division of labor between the sexes leads to expectations about what is appropriate behavior for members of each sex. The division of labor leads to the construction of gender roles and stereotypes that influence the opportunities and aspirations of men and women.	• Do women seek out different opportunities in cultures that have more egalitarian attitudes toward the sexes? • Do gender differences we see in one culture translate to another?

FIGURE 11.5   Summary of Major Theoretical Approaches to Gender and Gender Development Note how each approach focuses on a different aspect of human life, ranging from genetic and hormonal influences to relationships, psychological processes, and social structures.

3· THE PSYCHOLOGY OF GENDER DIFFERENCES

To think about gender differences, let's start with a game we will call "Who are more _____?" For each adjective below, answer as quickly as you can with either "Men" or "Women."

Who are more...   Assertive   Rational
                   Emotional   Aggressive
                   Strong   Sexually adventurous
                   Creative   Reserved
                   Verbal   Active

Now for each of those descriptors, think of someone you know who is of the opposite sex to your answer and who is very high on the quality described. What does this game tell you about gender stereotypes? Might it suggest that even though you may have ready stereotypes for gender differences, in fact men and women vary widely with respect to a number of qualities?

In this section we will review the research on gender differences in three main areas: cognitive ability, aggression, and sexuality. As we do, keep in mind that because gender cannot be manipulated, research comparing men and women is by definition correlational, so that causal claims are not justified.

Cognitive Differences

A gender difference that is a source of interest for many researchers, as well as for the public at large, is the underrepresentation of women in math and science careers. For example, in 1980, the percentage of PhDs in the physical sciences and engineering that were awarded to women in the United States was 12 percent and 4 percent, respectively. By 2001 these percentages had increased to 26 percent for the physical sciences and 17 percent for engineering (Halpern & others, 2007)—still a very large gap.

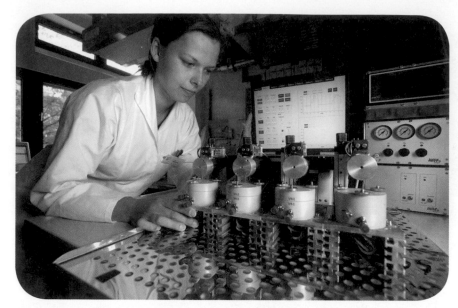

Research findings indicate that aptitude for science is similarly predicted by genes for both males and females. This female scientist is working on medical applications of stem cell technology.

This discrepancy has been a focal point at many conferences. At just such a gathering in January 2005, Larry Summers, then president of Harvard University, sparked a major controversy. Summers commented that he believed that a key determinant of such underrepresentation of women was gender differences in innate ability in math and science—specifically, women's lack of natural cognitive ability relevant to careers in math and science. Summers's words met a firestorm of criticism. Many observers were shocked and dismayed that he would suggest such a thing, and others felt that he had been victimized by the forces of political correctness.

What do the data tell us about cognitive differences between men and women? First, the data point to no gender differences in general intellectual ability. Further, research shows that in terms of academic performance, girls tend to get better grades in school than boys, regardless of the topic (Halpern & others, 2007). Nevertheless, clearly, more boys eventually pursue careers in math and science than do girls. Why?

Many studies have examined gender differences in performance on different cognitive tasks and found that when differences emerge, they tend to be in two directions. First, girls are more likely to outperform boys on tasks of verbal ability; and second, boys are more likely to outperform girls on tasks requiring a certain type of cognitive skill—visuospatial ability (Halpern & others, 2007). For example, research has probed the verbal performance of fourth-graders in 33 different countries (Mullis & others, 2003; Ogle & others, 2003). In every country, the average performance of girls on verbal tasks was higher than the average performance of boys. In turn, research has revealed that, at least by preschool age, boys show greater accuracy in performing tasks requiring mental rotation of objects in space (S. C. Levine & others, 1999; Loring-Meier & Halpern, 1999). As children age, these differences are most likely to show up on tasks requiring the person to imagine objects moving in space—for instance, to state when two objects will crash (Liu & Huang, 1999).

What might explain these differences? Biological theorists might look to genetic or hormonal differences, although aptitude for science is similarly predicted by genes for both males and females (Haworth, Dale, & Plomin, 2009). From an evolutionary perspective, the differences are thought to be tied to females' important roles in socializing offspring and negotiating the interpersonal landscape and to ancestral males' need to traverse the landscape for food and to find their way home again (Geary, 2010). From a social cognitive and social role perspective, theorists might say that these differences reflect parents' expectations for their children. The female advantage in verbal skills and the male advantage in visuospatial tasks might emerge out of parents' greater expectations for their daughters to be socially engaged and for their sons to be good at stereotypically male activities such as playing video games.

The observed gender differences in verbal and visuospatial skills are relatively consistent—but they are also rather small. Janet Shibley Hyde (2005) conducted a review of major meta-analytic studies of gender differences in a wide range of characteristics. (Recall that meta-analysis is a statistical technique that allows researchers to pull together findings from a range of studies that all addressed the same questions, so that they can get a much better sense of whether differences from one study represent real differences in the world and estimate the size of those differences.) With regard to cognitive variables, Hyde found that where differences did emerge, they were quite small, with girls scoring higher on some measures of verbal ability and boys scoring higher on spatial tasks. Overall, however, Hyde found strong support for what she came to call the **gender similarities hypothesis**—the idea that men and women (and boys and girls) are much more similar than they are different (Hyde, 2005, 2006, 2007a).

● **gender similarities hypothesis** Hyde's proposition that men and women (and boys and girls) are much more similar than they are different.

Hyde's conclusion suggests that the very large gender difference in the pursuit of careers in math and science is unlikely to result from these small cognitive differences between males and females. In trying to explain the shortage of women in math and science, we might therefore think about the *multiple* factors that lead an individual to pursue a particular career. That choice is likely to be a product of many interrelated factors, including what the person feels he or she is especially good at and likes to do, the role models encountered, the social support from family and friends, and the likelihood that a particular career path will ultimately lead to the life the person envisions for himself or herself in the future (Halpern & others, 2007).

Gender Differences in Aggression

Aggression is defined as behaviors that are intended to harm another person (Crick & Grotpeter, 1995). Are men or women more aggressive? The answer depends on the particular *type* of aggression we are talking about.

● **aggression** Behaviors that are intended to harm another person.

Overt aggression refers to physically or verbally harming another person directly. Males tend to be higher on overt aggression than females. As children, boys are more likely than girls to get in fights in which they are physically aggressive toward one another (Bukowski, Brendgen, & Vitaro, 2007). As adolescents, males are more likely to join gangs and to commit violent acts (Dodge, Coie, & Lynam, 2006). Children and adolescents who are diagnosed with **conduct disorder**—a pattern of offensive behavior that violates the basic rights of others—are three times more likely to be boys than girls (Kjelsberg, 2005). As adults, men are more likely than women to be chronically hostile and to commit violent crimes (White & Frabutt, 2006).

● **overt aggression** Physically or verbally harming another person directly.

● **conduct disorder** A pattern of offensive behavior that violates the basic rights of others.

Women's smaller physical size may be one reason they are less likely to engage in overt aggression. In probing aggressive tendencies in girls and women, researchers have focused instead on **relational aggression,** behavior that is meant to harm the social standing of another person through activities such as gossiping and spreading rumors (Crick & Grotpeter, 1995). Relational aggression differs from overt aggression in that it requires that the aggressor have a considerable level of social and cognitive skill. To be relationally aggressive, an individual must have a strong understanding of the social environment and must be able to plant rumors that are most likely to damage the intended party. Relational aggression is more subtle than overt aggression, and the relationally aggressive individual may not seem to be aggressive to others, as the aggressive acts typically are committed secretly. Research has shown that girls are more relationally aggressive than boys (Archer, 2004; Card & others, 2008) and that this difference increases with age (Smith, Rose, & Schwartz-Mette, 2010).

● **relational aggression** Behavior that is meant to harm the social standing of another person.

Generally, both overt aggression and relational aggression are related to reduced peer acceptance (Crick & Rose, 2000). Relational aggression in girls is associated in particular with less acceptance by other girls; in contrast, relationally aggressive adolescent girls are more likely to enjoy acceptance by boys. This pattern suggests that girls who relationally aggress toward other girls may do so to improve their standing with boys (Smith, Rose, & Schwartz-Mette, 2010).

Although relational aggression may not lead to the physical injury that is often the result of overt aggression, it can be extremely painful nevertheless. In 2010, Phoebe Prince, a 15-year-old who had recently moved from Ireland to the United States with her family, became the target of unrelenting rumors and harassment from a group of popular girls at her high school after she had a brief relationship with a popular senior boy. Prince became so distraught that she hanged herself after school one day. Even after her suicide, the girls who had harassed her posted rumors about her on the Facebook page that was set up as a memorial (Cullen, 2010).

The various theoretical approaches we reviewed earlier would explain these gender differences in aggression in different ways. With regard to the overt aggression of boys

Phoebe Prince's family buried her in her native Ireland because "they wanted an ocean between her and the people who hounded her to the grave" (Cullen, 2010).

and men, biological researchers might focus on the role of a hormone such as testosterone, which circulates at higher levels in men than women (van Bokhoven & others, 2006). The evolutionary psychology perspective would view the overt aggression of males as an outgrowth of ancestral male competition for females with whom to mate. Evolutionary psychologists would see the propensity for relational aggression as coming from females' need to compete for male partners with resources. From a social cognitive perspective, gender differences in styles of aggression would reflect differences in boys' and girls' socialization, with girls being taught early on that overt aggression is inappropriate (Archer, 2004). Similarly, social role theory would see these differences as emerging out of gender roles, and responses to these forms of aggression would reflect stereotypes of male and female.

Gender Differences in Sexuality

● **sexuality** The ways people experience and express themselves as sexual beings.

Broadly speaking, **sexuality** refers to the ways people experience and express themselves as sexual beings. Sexuality involves activity that is associated with sexual pleasure. The evolutionary perspective on gender strongly predicts gender differences in sexual behavior—specifically, that women should be more selective, and men less selective, when it comes to engaging in sex. In 1989, Russell D. Clark III and Elaine Hatfield conducted a study examining this prediction.

The researchers sent five men and five women experimenters (who were judged to range from slightly unattractive to moderately attractive) to the Florida State University campus. They were told to approach members of the opposite sex whom they found to be quite attractive. For each person they approached, the experimenters were instructed to say "I have been noticing you around campus. I find you very attractive" and then to ask one of three questions: (1) "Would you like to go out with me?" (2) "Would you like to go to my apartment with me?" or (3) "Would you like to go to bed with me?" (These data were collected in 1978 and 1982, before AIDS became a known and widespread problem.)

The Psychological Inquiry on p. 361 illustrates the results of the study. As you can see, men and women did not differ in terms of their answers to the "going out" question—about half of each sex said yes to this query. However, dramatic sex differences emerged for the other two questions. Nearly 70 percent of men said yes to the "apartment" question, while very few women answered in the affirmative. Finally, with regard to the "bed" question, 75 percent of the men said yes, but *none* of the women did. In fact, more men said yes to the go-to-bed question than to the go-on-a-date question. Men who said no to the request to go to bed with the female experimenters were more likely to explain themselves with a statement such as "I have a girlfriend" or "I'm married." In contrast, women who were asked if they would like to go to bed with a male experimenter were more likely to give responses such as "You've got to be kidding" and "What is wrong with you? Leave me alone" (Clark & Hatfield, 1989, p. 52).

More recently, a study conducted with college students in Germany, Italy, and the United States replicated these gender differences in students who were asked to imagine being in the study (Schutzwohl & others, 2009). Other relevant research shows that women tend to have fewer lifetime sex partners compared to men, and these differences are true regardless of whether the person is homosexual or heterosexual (Peplau & Fingerhut, 2007; Savin-Williams & Diamond, 2004). So, the data suggest that women do appear to be more selective than men when it comes to casual sex.

Men and women differ sexually in other ways as well. Men report more frequent feelings of sexual arousal, are more prone to lust, have more frequent sexual fantasies, and rate the strength of their own sex drive higher than do women (Baumeister, Catanese, & Vohs, 2001). Men also are more likely than women to masturbate, to have more permissive attitudes about casual premarital sex, and to have a more difficult time adhering to their vows of sexual fidelity when married (Oliver & Hyde, 1993; Peplau, 2003).

Compared to men, women tend to show more changes in their sexual patterns and sexual desires over their lifetime (Baumeister, 2000; Baumeister & Stillman, 2006;

psychological *inquiry*

Percent responding yes

Male
Female

80
60
40
20
0

Would you go on a date with me?
Would you go to my apartment with me?
Would you go to bed with me?

Sex and Casual Sex

The figure shows the results of the Clark and Hatfield study (1989). Recall that the experimenters approached men and women on a college campus and asked one of three questions. Review the details of the study and answer the following questions.

1. This study was an experiment. What are the independent and dependent variables?

2. Why do you think that men were more likely to say yes to the "bed" question than they were to the "date" question?

3. Recall that in this study, the experimenters were judged to range from slightly unattractive to moderately attractive and were told to approach people whom they found to be quite attractive. How might these circumstances have influenced the results?

4. Perhaps the most striking aspect of this experiment's results is the big gender difference on the "bed" question. Most men said yes, and not a single woman did. What is another question that might have produced such a stunning gender difference?

5. Imagine that you strongly favor the social role theory of gender development. How would you explain these results from that perspective?

Diamond, 2008a). Women are more likely than men, for instance, to have had sexual experiences with same- and opposite-sex partners, even if they identify themselves strongly as heterosexual or lesbian. In one study of 9,000 twins and their siblings, participants were asked about their *potential* for same-sex sexual behavior (Santtila & others, 2008). The researchers asked the participants whether they would be able to engage in sexual activity with an attractive same-sex person whom they liked, if no one would find out about it. Nearly twice as many women (65 percent) as men (33 percent) said they would, even though more than 90 percent of these individuals had had no same-sex sexual contacts in the previous year.

In contrast, male sexuality may be more limited to particular targets of attraction. One study compared the sexual arousal of heterosexual women, lesbian women, heterosexual men, and homosexual men while they watched erotic films of various sexual acts featuring male and female actors or bonobo apes. The films included scenes of sexual activity between same- and opposite-sex human partners and between opposite-sex bonobos, and scenes of men and women masturbating alone or engaging in aerobic exercise while naked. Sexual arousal was measured physiologically by monitoring the sex organs of men and women for indicators of arousal. Both heterosexual women and lesbian women were aroused by all of the films showing sexual activity (including those featuring the bonobos). However, gay men were aroused only by the films that included men, and heterosexual men were aroused only by the films that included women (Chivers, Seto, & Blanchard, 2007).

How extensive are these gender differences in sexuality? A recent meta-analysis revealed that overall, men reported having *slightly more* sexual experience and more permissive attitudes than women for most aspects of sexuality (Petersen & Hyde, 2010).

For the following factors, stronger gender differences in sexuality were found: Men engaged in more masturbation, viewed more pornography, engaged in more casual sex, and had more permissive attitudes about casual sex than did women.

How would the various theoretical approaches interpret gender differences in sexuality? From the biological perspective, differences in sexuality can be explained by genetic and hormonal differences between men and women. The evolutionary psychology approach would see these differences as supporting the role of sexual selection in human evolution. Social cognitive theories would focus on the ways that boys and girls learn about what is considered appropriate sexual behavior for each gender. Finally, social role theory would assert that these gender differences reflect the differing gender roles, stereotypes, and opportunities that cultures construct for men and women. In some cultures, for example, women cover their heads and faces when they are out in public. Their husbands are the only men who ever see them uncovered. Clearly, biological explanations are not needed to explain why these women would be very unlikely to engage in sexual activity outside of marriage.

Evaluating the Evidence for Gender Differences

It is safe to say that in talking about gender differences, people can be prone to extremes. For instance, a bestselling book suggested that men and women are so different that they must have come from different planets, with men hailing from warlike, competitive Mars and women from the love planet, Venus (Gray, 2004). Clearly, our survey of gender differences does not support such a radical view. Gender differences appear to be strongest in the areas of aggression and sexuality and seem to be consistent but relatively weaker in the cognitive domain. On the whole, we can state with certainty that men and women are indeed both from planet Earth.

One way in which men and women clearly differ is that men generally are sexually attracted to women, whereas women typically are sexually attracted to men. Of course, these patterns of attraction are not always the case, as human beings differ from one another in their sexual orientation, our next topic.

4· SEXUAL ORIENTATION

An individual's **sexual orientation** is the direction of his or her erotic interests. Sexual orientation does not mean simply sexual behavior. A man who has sex with other men while in prison may not think of himself as homosexual, and once released from prison he may never engage in such behavior again. A woman might always find herself sexually attracted to other women but never act on those feelings. When we talk about sexual orientation, we mean a *whole range* of human experiences that interest psychologists, including not only behaviors but also desires, feelings, fantasies, and a person's sense of identity.

Defining Sexual Orientation

An individual who self-identifies as **heterosexual** is generally sexually attracted to members of the opposite sex. An individual who self-identifies as **homosexual** is generally sexually attracted to members of the same sex. Today, sexual orientation is commonly viewed as a continuum from exclusive male–female relations to exclusive same-sex relations (B. M. King, 2005). Some individuals self-identify as **bisexual,** meaning that they are sexually attracted to people of both sexes.

Despite the widespread use of labels such as "homosexual," "gay," "lesbian," and "bisexual," some researchers argue that they are misleading. Instead, erotic attractions may be fluid, and references to such a construct as a fixed sexual orientation ignores the potential flexibility of human sexual attraction and behavior (Diamond, 2008a, 2009). In some cultures, engaging in same-sex sexual activity is not viewed as an

test yourself

1. What is the gender similarities hypothesis? How might even small gender differences lead to larger differences later in life?
2. How do overt aggression and relational aggression differ? Which sex is more likely to engage in each?
3. Identify at least four ways in which males and females differ in their patterns of sexual behavior, thoughts, and/or feelings.

● **sexual orientation** The direction of an individual's erotic interests.

● **heterosexual** Referring to a sexual orientation in which the individual is generally sexually attracted to members of the opposite sex.

● **homosexual** Referring to a sexual orientation in which the individual is generally sexually attracted to members of the same sex.

● **bisexual** Referring to a sexual orientation in which the individual is sexually attracted to people of both sexes.

indication of the person's identity (Nanda, 2008), but in Western societies, there is a strong belief that sexual orientation is a stable personal attribute. Stability of sexual orientation might also depend on the orientation. Longitudinal studies have shown very high stability for heterosexuality over time (Kinnish, Strassberg, & Turner, 2005). Non-heterosexual individuals may be more likely to shift their erotic interests, especially in adolescence (Diamond & Savin-Williams, 2011; Savin-Williams & Ream, 2007).

Related to this issue is the very definition of bisexuality. People sometimes think that bisexuality is simply a steppingstone to homosexuality, while others view it as a sexual orientation itself or as an indicator of sexual fluidity. (Comedian Woody Allen once quipped that at least bisexuality doubles your chances of finding a date on a Saturday night.) In a decade-long longitudinal study of non-heterosexual women, Lisa Diamond (2008b) found evidence for the existence of a stable bisexual identity. Among women who identified themselves as lesbian or bisexual in 1995, change was more likely to occur in the direction of lesbian women moving toward bisexuality rather than bisexual women changing to a lesbian or heterosexual orientation. Demonstrating the difference between sexual behavior and sexual orientation, Diamond's study found that although bisexual orientation was unlikely to change, sexual behavior did. Women who self-identified as bisexual were more likely, over time, to engage in exclusively homosexual or heterosexual behavior, because many of them had settled into a long-term relationship with one partner by the end of the study (Diamond, 2008b).

Occurrence of the Different Sexual Orientations

Homosexual behavior is relatively common in nature, having been observed in 1,500 different species, including rats, nonhuman primates, giraffes, ostriches, guppies, cats, bison, dolphins, and fruit flies (Sommer & Vasey, 2006). Furthermore, long-term same-sex partnerships occur in nonhuman species. In 2004, the *New York Times* reported the story of Roy and Silo, two male penguins who appeared to share a long-term monogamous sexual relationship at the Central Park Zoo, even raising their adopted daughter Tango (they have since broken up) (D. Smith, 2004). In humans, homosexuality is present in all cultures, regardless of whether a culture is tolerant or not. Obviously, the majority of people, regardless of culture, are heterosexual.

It is difficult to know precisely how many gays, lesbians, and bisexuals there are in the world, partly because fears of discrimination may prevent individuals from answering honestly on surveys. Estimates of the frequency of homosexuality range from 2 percent to10 percent of the population and are typically higher for men than women (Zietsch & others, 2008). With respect to the United States, a Centers for Disease Control national survey reported that the percentage of Americans who identify themselves as heterosexual was 90 percent for men and women. Approximately 4.1 percent reported themselves as homosexual or bisexual—essentially, 5 million Americans between the ages of 18 and 44 (Mosher, Chandra, & Jones, 2005).

Origins of Sexual Orientation: A Scientific Puzzle

What is the source of sexual orientation? Scientists have speculated extensively about this question (Kelly, 2006; Rahman, 2005). Charles Darwin (1862) himself commented that "we do not even in the least know the final cause of sexuality. The whole subject is hidden in darkness."

Since Darwin's time, scientists have learned something about factors that *do not* predict sexual orientation. First, being reared by a gay parent *does not* increase the chances of being gay (Golombok & Tasker, 1996; Patterson & Farr, 2010; Patterson & Wainright, 2010). In fact, the vast majority of gay individuals have heterosexual parents. Nor does a particular parenting style relate to the emergence of homosexuality (Bell, Weinberg, & Hammersmith, 1981). Further, same-sex sexual experience or experimentation in childhood does not predict eventual adult homosexuality (Bailey, 2003; Bogaert, 2000).

So, what factors might account for sexual orientation? Before we probe this intriguing question, let's pause to consider some key issues in the science behind sexual orientation.

Roy and Silo, same-sex partners who raised their adopted daughter Tango, are chinstrap penguins like these.

THINKING CRITICALLY ABOUT SEXUAL ORIENTATION

There is controversy over the origin of sexual orientation. Scientists approach this puzzle dispassionately and must remain open to the different potential answers the empirical data suggest. Before exploring the current evidence for various explanations of sexual orientation, it may be helpful to review five important issues for critical thinkers.

- *Unlikelihood of a single cause:* Whatever the psychological characteristic of interest, it is unlikely that a single cause can be identified, and sexual orientation is no exception. As we consider the accumulated data on this topic, keep in mind that it is very probable that *many factors work together* to foster sexual orientation and that factors that have not even been considered yet will likely emerge in the future.

- *Within-group variation:* There is a great deal of variation within any group of people who share the same sexual orientation. All heterosexual men are sexually attracted to women, but that attraction may be the only thing that any two heterosexual men have in common. Similarly, all gay men share a sexual attraction to men, but any two gay men may have little else in common.

- *Research challenges:* Comparing individuals from different sexual orientations presents research design challenges. One such challenge bears on the matter of representativeness, for in some studies the heterosexual and homosexual participants are recruited in very different ways. Gay and lesbian participants are sometimes recruited only from gay pride events, for example, and so they may not be representative of all homosexual and bisexual individuals. Similarly, small sample size can be an issue because of the difficulty involved in recruiting gay participants. Indeed, in a study reported in 2000, just 6 gay men were compared to 256 "non-gay" men (Lippa, 2000). Recall that studies using larger samples are more likely to yield results that generalize to the general population.

- *The meaning of cross-sex similarities:* In presenting research on the origins of sexual orientation, the popular media often emphasize similarities between gay men and heterosexual women and between lesbian women and heterosexual men. Keep in mind that, regardless of their sexual orientation, gay men are men, and lesbian women are women.

- *Explaining sexual orientation does not mean explaining only homosexuality:* Finally, and perhaps most importantly, keep in mind as you read this section that any good theory of sexual orientation should explain how *any of us* (gay or straight) becomes sexually oriented toward individuals *of a particular* sex. As scientists, we want to explain the sexual orientations of men and women who are attracted to men or women or both.

With these cautions in mind, let's look at the evidence concerning sexual orientation.

GENETIC INFLUENCES

Researchers have examined genes as a factor in sexual orientation by using twins to estimate the heritability of sexual orientation. Recall from Chapter 8 that heritability is a statistic that tells us the extent to which we can explain observed differences in a given characteristic based on differences in genes. Recently, a study of nearly 4,000 twins in Sweden demonstrated that the heritability of same-sex sexual behavior was about 35 percent in men and 19 percent in women (Langstrom & others, 2010). These heritability estimates suggest that although genes play a role in sexual orientation, genes are not as strong an influence as they are for other characteristics, such as intelligence.

Of course, genes do not impact psychological characteristics as directly as they do a physical characteristic like hair color or eye color. We therefore need to consider other factors that might provide the bridge between genes and the psychological experience of sexual orientation.

BRAIN DIFFERENCES

One way in which genes might influence sexual orientation is through their effect on brain development. Two particular types of brain differences have garnered the most attention among researchers: the thickness of the corpus callosum (the bundle of fibers that connects the two hemispheres) and the symmetry between the brain's two hemispheres. Evidence from brain-imaging studies suggests that gay men may have thicker corpus callosa than heterosexual men (Witelson & others, 2008). In terms of hemispheric symmetry, a recent brain-imaging study found that heterosexual women and gay men show a similar pattern in which the two hemispheres are alike, while heterosexual men and lesbian women display a similar pattern of having a larger right hemisphere relative to left (Savic & Lindström, 2008).

Where do these brain differences come from? Differences in the corpus callosum are thought to have a genetic basis because the corpus callosum's size is strongly heritable (Witelson & others, 2008). Differences in hemispheric symmetry are believed to emerge from prenatal hormone exposure (Savic & Lindström, 2008), another biological factor studied in the origins of sexual orientation, as we consider just below. A word of caution, however: In trying to interpret these brain characteristics, we must keep in mind that habitual patterns of *behavior* can also influence brain structure and function—and we must consider that these cross-sex similarities may therefore be explained by behavioral similarities between heterosexual women and gay men, as well as between heterosexual men and lesbian women.

PRENATAL HORMONES

In another approach to understanding sexual orientation, studies have examined the role of prenatal hormones. Recall that the development of male sexual characteristics is triggered by high levels of prenatal androgens. Researchers have examined whether this prenatal hormone exposure might be responsible for creating a brain that is sexually attracted to women. Because prenatal androgen levels can vary for female embryos, we can examine whether females who were exposed to prenatal androgens are more likely to be bisexual or lesbian than heterosexual. Researchers have tested this possibility in a variety of ways (Meyer-Bahlburg & others, 2008).

One strategy for examining the link between prenatal hormones and sexual orientation is to identify physical features that are associated with prenatal testosterone. These features potentially provide a window into prenatal hormonal exposure (McFadden, 2008; Rahman, 2005; Rahman, Clarke, & Morera, 2009). The idea is that once we identify the effects of prenatal testosterone on various physical features of the body, we can look at those features and see whether they differ in adults who are either gay or straight (McFadden, 2008).

The best known of these features is the ratio between the second and fourth digits on the hand (the pointer and the ring finger), called the *2D:4D ratio*. Men tend to have a ring finger that is longer than their pointer, while for women the two fingers are nearly the same length (Manning, 2002; Medland & Loehlin, 2008). Thus, women tend to have larger 2D:4D ratios than men. This ratio is influenced by prenatal testosterone (Lutchmaya & others, 2004; McFadden & others, 2005). If prenatal testosterone exposure is related to developing a brain that is attracted to females, we might expect lesbian women to show a pattern more similar to heterosexual men—that is, a smaller 2D:4D ratio. Some studies have supported such a pattern for lesbian women (Kraemer & others, 2006; McFadden & Shubel, 2002; Rahman & Wilson, 2003) or specifically for lesbian women who identify themselves as "butch," or masculine (W. M. Brown & others, 2002; James, 2005).

SOCIAL FACTORS

A great deal of current research on the origins of sexual orientation focuses on genetic, hormonal, and neurobiological mechanisms. What about social experience? We have seen that there is no evidence that specific parenting styles "cause" sexual orientation. Given the many different ways in which parents interact with their children and the fact that the vast majority of people are heterosexual, it seems unlikely that the emergence of heterosexuality is explained by particular parenting strategies. Furthermore, the fact that most homosexual and bisexual individuals have heterosexual parents contradicts the influence of observational learning or modeling in the development of sexual orientation.

Some scientists have attempted to explain sexual orientation as a function of early childhood experience. A particular focus has been gender-nonconforming behaviors, activities that run counter to gender stereotypes (Bem, 1996; Rieger, Linsenmeier, & Bailey, 2009; Rieger & others, 2008). Research shows that homosexual adults are more likely than heterosexual adults to remember themselves as having engaged in gender-nonconforming behaviors (Bailey & Zucker, 1995; Lippa, 2008). Moreover, some evidence suggests that in videos of their childhood activities, gay and lesbian adults pursued more gender-atypical activities as children (Rieger & others, 2008).

For boys, gender-nonconforming behavior may be related to eventual sexual development, but the picture is not clear-cut. For example, one study compared 66 extremely gender-nonconforming boys to 56 gender-conforming boys (Green, 1987). Among the nonconforming boys, 75 percent were either bisexual or homosexual at a follow-up during adolescence or young adulthood. Among the gender-conforming boys, 96 percent were heterosexual at follow-up.

Although this study is sometimes used as evidence of the role of gender-nonconforming behavior in the development of sexual orientation (Bem, 1996), take a good look at those percentages. It may be true that gender-nonconforming boys were more likely to be homosexual or bisexual—but note that the percentage of boys in the gender-*conforming* group who eventually emerged as gay or bisexual falls within the typical percentages found in the general population. Thus, boys who are quite gender typical in their behavior can certainly turn out to be gay (or bisexual or straight).

Studies of childhood behavior and sexual orientation are correlational. As we saw in Chapter 2, one challenge of correlational research is the potential for a third variable to explain the relationship between the variables of interest. In thinking about an individual's gender-nonconforming behavior in childhood and his or her eventual sexual orientation, you might note that factors such as genes and prenatal hormone exposure might explain both of these variables (Cohen-Bendahan, van de Beek, & Berenbaum, 2005).

Consider, too, that gender-nonconforming boys may experience a very different social response than gender-nonconforming girls. In fact, many women report having been a tomboy as a child (Peplau & others, 1999). Girls who engage in boyish activities are frequently viewed as more popular by their peers, and the vast majority of tomboys turn out to be heterosexual (Peplau & others, 1999). Social responses to gender-nonconforming boys may be more negative and may play a role in eventual gender identity and sexual orientation. Parents and peers may label a gender-nonconforming boy as "homosexual," and that labeling may influence the boy's sense of self and his emerging identity (Hegarty, 2009).

AN UNSOLVED PUZZLE

Clearly, scientists have devised a number of clever ways to identify factors associated with sexual orientation. However, as we have seen, many questions remain. Although we may not still be in the "darkness" described by Darwin, it is fair to say at least that the room remains not very well lit.

Similar to many other psychological characteristics, an individual's sexual orientation most likely depends on a combination of genetic, hormonal, cognitive, and environmental factors (Langstrom & others, 2010). Most experts on sexual orientation believe that no one factor alone causes sexual orientation and that the relative weight of each factor can vary within people of the same orientation. Just as individuals can have the same sexual orientation but be different in many other respects, the underlying processes that lead to sexual orientation may differ from one person to the next. We know that whether heterosexual, homosexual, or bisexual, a person cannot be talked out of his or her sexual orientation. Indeed, Qazi Rahman, a researcher who studies the neurobiology of sexual orientation, asserted that "there is no argument anymore—if you are gay, you are born gay" (quoted in Nicholson, 2008). This work tells us that whether one is homosexual, heterosexual, or bisexual, sexual orientation is not a choice but an integral part of the functioning human being and his or her sense of self (Katz, 1995; Worthington & others, 2008).

Gay and Lesbian Functioning

We may not know definitively why individuals are gay or lesbian, but research has uncovered some interesting things about gay men and women. Here we briefly review selected findings as they relate to individual adjustment and well-being, gay and lesbian relationships, and gay and lesbian families.

INDIVIDUAL ADJUSTMENT AND WELL-BEING

Research shows that gay and lesbian individuals are similar to their heterosexual counterparts in many ways. Researchers typically find no differences among lesbians, gays, bisexuals, and heterosexuals in a wide range of attitudes and behaviors, as well as in psychological adjustment (Hyde & DeLamater, 2011). Gay men and lesbian women are likely to differ from heterosexuals in terms of the gender typicality of their hobbies, activities, and occupations (Lippa, 2000). Note, however, that if gay men and women live in households that are headed by two men or two women, they will inevitably engage in gender-atypical behavior (for instance, women doing the yard work or men cooking and cleaning) simply because someone has to take care of those tasks.

Lesbian women and gay men are similar to heterosexual women and heterosexual men in many respects.

One factor in the well-being of gays and lesbians is coping with prejudice and discrimination (Balsam & Mohr, 2007). Among gay and lesbian participants polled in a 2006 survey, 83 percent reported themselves as "out," including having revealed their sexual orientation to their acquaintances, family, and friends. More than half, however, reported themselves as concerned that coming out could increase their risk of being the victim of a hate crime. A third of the individuals sampled reported that they might choose not to come out primarily because of concern over rejection by family and friends or the loss of a job (Harris Interactive, 2006).

The good news for homosexual individuals is that attitudes toward gays and lesbians have become increasingly more positive in U.S. society (Kaiser Family Foundation, 2001). This increased acceptance likely stems in part from gay men's and lesbian women's greater openness with others about their lives. Individuals who know someone who is gay or lesbian are less likely to report prejudicial attitudes toward gays and lesbians (Smith, Axelton, & Saucier, 2009). In 2006, a U.S. survey found that 70 percent of the heterosexuals polled knew someone who was gay, lesbian, or bisexual—a large increase from 1984, when only 24 percent of those surveyed knew a gay or bisexual person (Harris Interactive, 2006). Younger Americans are particularly likely to support gay rights. A survey of members of Generation Next (those born between 1981 and 1988) found that 58 percent believed that homosexuality ought to be accepted, and nearly half felt that same-sex marriage should be legal (Pew Research Center, 2007).

For gays, lesbians, and bisexuals, being open about their sexual orientation not only is related to progress in changing cultural attitudes but also is a strong predictor of psychological and physical health (Savin-Williams, 2006). For gay men and lesbian women, living in accord with their sexual orientation is a matter of living authentically, and being "out" to the people around them is part of being true to themselves (King, Burton, & Geise, 2009). The more comfortable gay, lesbian, and bisexual individuals feel about coming out, the better will be scientists' chances to study them and to understand their lives.

GAY AND LESBIAN RELATIONSHIPS

Research consistently shows that gay men and lesbian women report themselves as more satisfied in their relationships compared to heterosexual couples. For example, in an 11-year longitudinal study by Lawrence Kurdek (2004), gay and lesbian couples and heterosexual married couples rated their relationships on a host of characteristics, including psychological adjustment, conflict, satisfaction, intimacy, and social support. Kurdek found that gay and lesbian couples scored higher than heterosexual marriage partners on 76 percent of the variables measured. Nevertheless, these same individuals were more likely to end their relationships than heterosexual married couples, especially heterosexual couples with children (Kurdek, 2004).

Why might gay and lesbian couples be more likely to break up than heterosexual couples? One possibility is that heterosexual couples may be more likely to stay in unsatisfying relationships out of concern for their children's welfare, and heterosexual couples are more likely than gay couples to have children.

Another possible reason for this difference is that married heterosexual couples face a legal barrier—divorce—that makes dissolving their relationships difficult. In 2000, the state of Vermont legally recognized same-sex civil unions, allowing for a test of this possibility. Kimberly Balsam and her colleagues (2008) studied three samples of couples: gay and lesbian couples who had been united in a civil union; gay and lesbian couples who had not had a civil union; and heterosexual married couples. Three years later, gay and lesbian couples who had not been joined in a civil union were more likely to have broken up—or to be on the brink of breaking up—than either gay couples who were in a civil union or heterosexual married couples. These results suggest that the legal tie of marriage is associated with relationship stability. In this study, as in Kurdek's earlier work, the gay and lesbian couples (regardless of whether they were in a civil union) reported higher relationship quality, better compatibility, and less conflict than their heterosexual counterparts.

What might explain the higher satisfaction with their relationships that gay and lesbian individuals report? One possibility is that heterosexual individuals may feel more pressure to get married and stay married, regardless of their personal choices, and they may be supported to stay in unsatisfying relationships (Green, Bettinger, & Zacks, 1996). Another factor is that having children is generally associated with lower levels of marital satisfaction, and, as mentioned above, heterosexual couples are more likely than homosexual couples to have children (Kurdek, 2004).

John Gottman and his colleagues (2003) conducted a longitudinal study of couple functioning that included video-recorded interactions over 12 years. The participants comprised gay and lesbian couples, as well as heterosexual couples. Gottman's team found that compared to heterosexual couples, gay and lesbian partners were better able to manage conflicts. They were more likely to use humor and affection in dealing with conflicts, took a more positive attitude toward negative feedback from their partners, and let conflicts go once they were resolved (Gottman & others, 2003).

It may also be the case that individuals in same-sex couples have more in common with each other because they are of the same sex (Balsam & others, 2008). In their romantic relationships, gay and lesbian couples do not have to negotiate the sorts of gender differences we reviewed earlier in this chapter.

GAY AND LESBIAN FAMILIES

Although gay and lesbian couples may be less likely than heterosexual couples to have children, increasingly gay families do include kids. Available evidence suggests that gay and lesbian households exist in 99 percent of counties throughout the United States, and approximately one in four of these households includes children (O'Barr, 2006). Children reared by gay men and lesbian women tend to be as well adjusted as those from heterosexual households, are no more likely to be homosexual themselves, and are no less likely to be accepted by their peers (Chan, Raboy, & Patterson, 1998; Golombok & others, 2003; Patterson & Farr, 2010; Patterson & Wainright, 2010). A study comparing adolescents who had two mothers with adolescents who had opposite-sex parents revealed no differences in self-reported or peer-reported functioning. For both sets of adolescents, what mattered were their close, warm relationships with their parents (Wainwright & Patterson, 2008).

In the United States, gay marriage and gay parenting have generated strong controversy, especially in political election years. In addressing the central issues in the debate, psychologists rely on scientific evidence. Based on the research we reviewed above, the

American Psychological Association issued a press release supporting gay marriage and opposing discrimination against gay men and lesbian women in matters such as parenting, adoption, and child custody (American Psychological Association, 2004).

5· SEXUAL BEHAVIORS AND PRACTICES

Talking about sexual behaviors, practices, and attitudes can sometimes be uncomfortable or embarrassing. It can also be interesting, enlightening, and exhilarating. In this section, we take up these hot topics and explore the ways that research has addressed them.

Sexual Behaviors

What constitutes sexual behavior—what we commonly refer to as "sex"? When President Bill Clinton was asked whether he had engaged in sex with White House intern Monica Lewinsky, he was widely ridiculed for replying that "it depends" on what sex is. Yet Clinton may have been representing a more general confusion. What counts as sex? Most people might answer that question with "vaginal intercourse," but what about other sexual behaviors, such as anal sex and oral sex? If someone has engaged in these practices, is he or she still a "virgin"? If your significant other reported to you that he or she had recently engaged in oral sex with another person, would you consider that sexual infidelity? What if he or she spent an hour sexting an attractive friend? These are the kinds of questions that come up in trying to define sexual behavior (Medley-Rath, 2007).

One possibility is to define sex as activities that are involved in reproduction and fertilization. By this interpretation, many gay men and women are virgins, as are adolescents who engage exclusively in, say, oral sex. Further, from this point of view, too, masturbation would not be a sexual behavior.

Another approach is to define sexual behavior by the arousal and sexual response that occur when the behavior is performed. Though broader, this definition still might leave out individuals who themselves might say that they are engaged in sexual behavior. For instance, if a person is unable to experience sexual arousal but performs oral sex on a partner, has that person engaged in sexual behavior? Alternatively, we might broaden the definition a great deal and define sexual behaviors to include behaviors that are specific to each individual and that are pleasurable in a particular way—one that is unusually intimate and personal.

Confusion over what counts as sex can lead to potentially risky behavior. For example, as Figure 11.6 shows, oral sex has become relatively common during the teen years (National Center for Health Statistics, 2002). For many adolescents, oral sex appears to be a recreational activity, and because many individuals under age 20 do not view the practice as sex, they believe that it is a safe alternative to intercourse (Brady & Halpern-Felsher, 2007; Brewster, Harker, & Tillman, 2008). As we will consider later in this chapter, however, oral sex exposes individuals to the risk of contracting sexually transmitted infections.

Sexual Practices

When people in the United States engage in sexual behavior, what do they do, and how often? The earliest research on this topic was conducted by Alfred Kinsey and his colleagues in 1948. Kinsey is widely recognized as the father of sexology, a pioneer who brought scientific attention to sexual behavior. Kinsey was interested in studying sex objectively without concern about guilt or shame. He collected data wherever he could find it, interviewing anyone willing to discuss the intimate details of his or her sex life.

The Kinsey Reports, published in two volumes, presented his findings for men (Kinsey, Pomeroy, & Martin, 1948) and women (Kinsey, Martin, & Pomeroy, 1953). Among the findings that shocked his readers were Kinsey's estimates of the frequency of bisexuality in men (nearly 12 percent) and women (7 percent)

test yourself

1. Name various factors that might influence sexual orientation.
2. What is gender-nonconforming behavior? What is the evidence for the role of gender-nonconforming behavior in the development of sexual orientation?
3. What are some factors associated with gay and lesbian well-being?

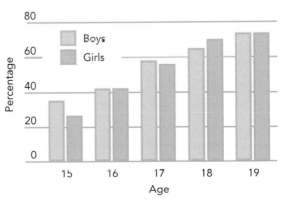

FIGURE 11.6   Percentage of U.S. 15- to 19-Year-Old Boys and Girls Who Report Engaging in Oral Sex Is it really sex? This figure shows the percentage of young people under the age of 20 who report having engaged in oral sex. SOURCE: National Center for Health Statistics (2002).

psychological *inquiry*

Noncohabiting

Men

7% 23% 19% 26% 25%

Cohabiting (married)

7% 1% 13% 36% 43%

Women

5% 15% 32% 24% 23%

7% 3% 12% 32% 47%

● Never
● A few times a year
● A few times a month
● 2–3 times a week
● 4 or more times a week

Sex in America

These pie charts show the responses of non-cohabiting and cohabiting (married) men and women to the question "How often have you had sex in the past year?" (Michael & others, 1994). Notice that for this type of graph, the area of the pie that is taken up by a response is proportional to the percentage of people giving that response. After studying the charts, answer these questions:

1. Overall, who reported having the most and the least sex?

2. The graphs separate those who were married from those who were not. For which gender did being married matter most in terms of frequency of sex?

3. When the respondents reported on having had sex, what behaviors do you think they included? Do you think these behaviors were the same for men and women? Explain.

4. Do you think that self-report is a good way to find out about sexual behavior? What other methods might researchers use to measure this variable?

and his estimate that at least 50 percent of married men had been sexually unfaithful. Although acknowledged for initiating the scientific study of sexual behavior, Kinsey's work was limited by the lack of representative samples.

Not until 1994 were more accurate data obtained from a well-designed, comprehensive study of U.S. sexual patterns. Robert Michael and his colleagues (1994) interviewed nearly 3,500 randomly selected people from 18 to 50 years of age. Although 17 percent of the men and 3 percent of the women said they had had sex with at least 21 partners, the overall impression from the survey was that for most Americans, marriage and monogamy rule sexual behavior. Married couples reported having sex most often and were the most likely to have orgasms when they did. The Psychological Inquiry above shows the frequency of sex for married and non-cohabiting individuals in the year before the survey was taken. Nearly 75 percent of the married men and 85 percent of the married women indicated that they had never been unfaithful. More recent surveys have shown similar results. For instance, in 2004 ABC polled a nationally representative sample and found that individuals in committed relationships had more sex than singles, and the vast majority reported themselves as sexually faithful (ABC News, 2004).

What exactly are people doing when they say they are having sex, and how often are they doing it? In 2002, the Centers for Disease Control conducted a study of sexual behaviors in the United States (Mosher, Chandra, & Jones, 2005). The findings were that among people aged 15 to 44, 10 percent of men and 8 percent of women had never had sex, including vaginal intercourse, oral sex, and anal sex. Among adults aged 25 to 44 years, 97 percent had had vaginal intercourse, and 90 percent had had oral sex. Among men, 40 percent had had anal sex, and among women 35 percent had done so.

A recent study comprising a representative sample of nearly 3,000 Swedes examined the frequency of different sexual behaviors in the previous month (Brody & Costa, 2009). The behaviors studied were vaginal intercourse, masturbation, oral sex, and anal sex. The results showed that on average, men reported having vaginal intercourse 5 times and masturbating 4.5 times in the previous month. On average, women reported having vaginal intercourse about 5 times but masturbated less than 2 times during the previous month. For both men and women, oral sex occurred approximately 2 times and anal sex less than once (Brody & Costa, 2009).

What do gay men and lesbian women do when they "have sex"? Research is limited and generally posed in terms of risk for sexually transmitted infection. Among gay men, mutual masturbation, oral sex, and anal sex are common, although as many as a third of gay men report never having engaged in anal sex (Reisner & others, 2009). Among lesbian women, practices include genital-to-genital contact (body rubbing), mutual fondling and masturbation, penetration with the hands or other objects, and oral sex (Marrazzo, Coffey, & Bingham, 2005; Mercer & others, 2007).

The Human Sexual Response Pattern

Regardless of the specific behavior, similar physical processes are involved in sexual responses. To examine the physiological processes involved in sexual activity, William Masters and Virginia Johnson (1966) carefully observed and measured the physiological responses of 382 female and 312 male volunteers as they masturbated or had vaginal intercourse. Masters and Johnson identified a **human sexual response pattern** consisting of four phases—excitement, plateau, orgasm, and resolution.

The *excitement phase* begins the process of erotic responsiveness; it lasts from several minutes to several hours, depending on the nature of the sex play involved. Engorgement of blood vessels and increased blood flow in genital areas, along with muscle tension, characterize the excitement phase. The most obvious signs of response in this phase are lubrication of the vagina and partial erection of the penis.

The second phase of the human sexual response, the *plateau phase,* is a continuation and heightening of the arousal begun in the excitement phase. The increases in breathing, pulse rate, and blood pressure that occurred during the excitement phase become more intense, penile erection and vaginal lubrication are more complete, and orgasm is closer.

The third phase of the human sexual response cycle is *orgasm.* How long does orgasm last? Some individuals sense that time is standing still when it takes place, but in fact orgasm lasts for only about 3 to 15 seconds. Orgasm involves an explosive discharge of neuromuscular tension and an intensely pleasurable feeling. With orgasm comes the release of the neurotransmitter oxytocin, which, as we saw in Chapter 3, plays a role in social bonding.

Following orgasm, the individual enters the *resolution phase,* in which blood vessels return to their normal state. A sex difference in this phase is that females may be stimulated to orgasm again without delay, whereas males enter a *refractory period* during which they cannot have another orgasm.

Working around the same time as Masters and Johnson was sex therapist Helen Singer Kaplan (1974). Kaplan studied sexual response through the lens of her clinical practice, during which she talked with individuals about their sexual experiences. Kaplan's view of the sexual response differed from Masters and Johnson's in that she added a key initial stage: desire. Kaplan discovered that for many of her clients, sexual desire was sometimes lacking. Kaplan's work highlighted the very important role of motivation in sexual activity. Clearly, she argued, without the desire to have sex, the stages described by Masters and Johnson may never get started. We will return to the human sexual response and the issue of desire later in this chapter when we survey sexual disorders.

Cognition and Other Factors in Sexual Behavior

Sexual behavior is influenced by a variety of factors, ranging from sensation and perception to the ways we think about sexuality (Crooks & Baur, 2011). Finding someone sexually attractive may involve seeing the person, getting to know him or her, and feeling emotionally attached. From experience, we know that our thoughts play an important role in our sexuality (Kelly, 2006). We might be sexually attracted to someone but understand that we must inhibit our sexual urges until the relationship has time to develop. We have the cognitive capacity to respect our partners and not take sexual advantage of them. We also have the cognitive resources to generate sexual images—to become sexually aroused just by thinking about something erotic.

● **human sexual response pattern** Masters and Johnson's model of human sexual response, consisting of four phases—excitement, plateau, orgasm, and resolution.

Recall from Chapter 7 that scripts are mental schemas for events. Sexuality is influenced by *sexual scripts,* patterns of expectancies for how people should behave sexually (Stulhofer, Busko, & Landripet, 2010). We carry these scripts with us in our memories (McCabe, Tanner, & Heiman, 2010). Typically, women and men have different sexual scripts, which contain their beliefs and expectations about sex and what it means (R. Jones, 2006; McCabe, Tanner, & Heiman, 2010). For men, sex may center more on what's going on in the genitals, with orgasm being a crucial aspect; for women, sex may be more an expression of intimacy, with orgasm an optional feature (van Lankveld, 2008).

Cognitive interpretation of sexual activity also involves our perceptions of the individual with whom we are having sex, and his or her perceptions of us (Miller, Perlman, & Brehm, 2009). Is this sexual encounter a symbol of a more enduring relationship or simply a hook-up? Amid the wash of hormones in sexual activity is the cognitive ability to control, reason about, and try to make sense of the activity.

THE INFLUENCE OF CULTURE

The influence of culture on sexuality was demonstrated dramatically in a classic analysis by John Messenger (1971) of the people living on the small island of Inis Beag off the coast of Ireland. They knew nothing about tongue kissing or hand stimulation of the penis, and they detested nudity. For both females and males, premarital sex was out of the question. Men avoided most sexual experiences because they believed that sexual intercourse reduced their energy level and was bad for their health. Under these repressive conditions, sexual intercourse occurred only at night, taking place as quickly as possible. As you might suspect, female orgasm was rare in this culture (Messenger, 1971).

In contrast, around the same time that Messenger was studying the people of Inis Beag, Donald Marshall (1971) conducted research on the Mangaian culture in the South Pacific. In Mangaia, young boys were taught about masturbation and were encouraged to engage in it as much as they liked. At age 13, the boys underwent a ritual initiating them into sexual manhood. First, their elders instructed them about sexual strategies, including how to aid their female partner in having orgasms. Two weeks later, the boy had intercourse with an experienced woman who helped him hold back from ejaculation until she experienced orgasm with him. By the end of adolescence, Mangaians had sex pretty much every day. Mangaian women reported a high frequency of orgasm.

Few cultures are as isolated and homogeneous as those of Inis Beag and Mangaia. In the United States, sexual behaviors and attitudes reflect the country's diverse multicultural population, and Americans fall somewhere in the middle of a continuum going from repressive to liberal. We are more conservative in our sexual habits than once thought but somewhat more open-minded regarding sexual orientation than a century ago.

Culture influences not only attitudes about sexual behavior but also ideas about sexual orientation. In many traditional cultures, there are accepted roles for individuals who are homosexual, lesbian, or transgender (Nanda, 2008).

SEX EDUCATION

One way that societies teach youth about sex and sexuality is through formal education. Although many topics associated with sex and sexuality are likely to spur controversy, most people concerned with sex education share two simple and relatively uncontroversial goals: to encourage the very young to delay sexual activity and to reduce teen pregnancy and sexually transmitted infections. Despite this consensus, there are many different opinions on *how* to achieve these goals.

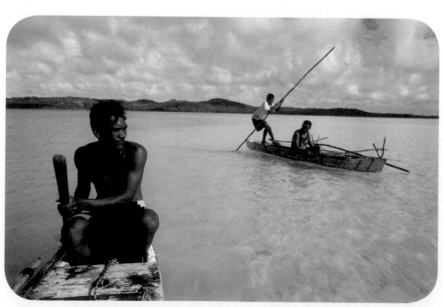

Donald Marshall's work focused on the sexual practices of the people of the South Pacific island of Mangaia.

One form of sex education is the *abstinence-only* approach, which has become increasingly common in the United States over the past two decades. According to federal guidelines (Family and Youth Services Bureau, 2004), abstinence-only educational programs must emphasize that any sexual behavior outside of marriage is harmful to individuals of any age. In addition, instructors can present contraceptives and condoms only in terms of their failure rates. Abstinence-only sex education promotes the notion that abstinence is the only effective way to avoid pregnancy and sexually transmitted infections (Family and Youth Services Bureau, 2004).

An alternative approach is *comprehensive* sex education; this involves providing students with comprehensive knowledge about sexual behavior, birth control, and the use of condoms in protecting against sexually transmitted infections, while encouraging them to delay sexual activity and practice abstinence.

Which approach to sex education most effectively delays sexual activity and prevents teen pregnancy? Research strongly indicates that comprehensive sex education outstrips abstinence-only programs in achieving these goals. Two recent research reviews found that abstinence-only programs do not delay the initiation of sexual intercourse and do not reduce HIV-risk behaviors (Kirby, 2008; Kirby, Laris, & Rolleir, 2007; Underhill, Montgomery, & Operario, 2007). Further, a recent study revealed that adolescents who experienced comprehensive sex education were less likely to report adolescent pregnancies than those who received abstinence-only sex education or no sex education (Kohler, Manhart, & Lafferty, 2008).

A number of leading experts on adolescent sexuality now conclude that sex education programs that emphasize contraceptive knowledge do not increase the incidence of sexual intercourse and are more likely to reduce the risk of adolescent pregnancy and sexually transmitted infections than abstinence-only programs (Constantine, 2008; M. E. Eisenberg & others, 2008; Hampton, 2008; Hyde & DeLamater, 2011). An additional key concern with abstinence-only education is that it often includes negative and even misleading information about the effectiveness of condoms, leading adolescents to be less likely to use them when they do have sex.

In many communities in the United States, educational practices have not caught up with the research findings. Indeed, inadequate knowledge about contraception, coupled with inconsistent use of effective contraceptive methods, has given Americans a dubious distinction: The United States has one of the highest rates of adolescent pregnancy and childbearing in the developed world, with as many as one-third of young women under the age of 20 becoming pregnant (Guttmacher Institute, 2010). Births to adolescent girls had fallen over the years, reaching a record low in 2004, but they took an upturn in 2006 (Guttmacher Institute, 2010), coinciding with the national trend toward abstinence-only sex education.

U.S. adolescent pregnancy rates are nearly twice those of Canada and Great Britain and at least four times the rates in France, Sweden, Germany, and Japan (Figure 11.7). Although U.S. adolescents are no more sexually active than their counterparts in countries such as France and Sweden, their adolescent pregnancy rate is much higher—perhaps because, compared to these other nations, the United States has less comprehensive sex education and less availability and use of condoms. Clearly, education and prevention are crucial to progress in reducing pregnancy among adolescents.

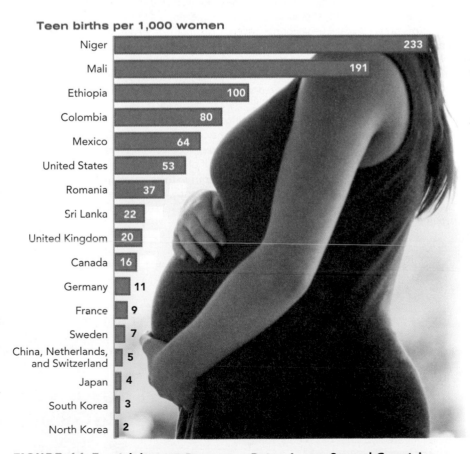

Teen births per 1,000 women

Country	
Niger	233
Mali	191
Ethiopia	100
Colombia	80
Mexico	64
United States	53
Romania	37
Sri Lanka	22
United Kingdom	20
Canada	16
Germany	11
France	9
Sweden	7
China, Netherlands, and Switzerland	5
Japan	4
South Korea	3
North Korea	2

FIGURE 11.7   Adolescent Pregnancy Rates Across Several Countries
Comprehensive sex education is one reason for the difference in teen pregnancy rates among countries. What other factors might be at work?

CRITICAL CONTROVERSY

Can Abstinence-Only Sex Education Be Effective?

A recent study made the headlines when it reported that an abstinence-only intervention successfully delayed sexual intercourse in youth. Let's take a look at the study to get a sense of why it worked.

John B. Jemmott III and his colleagues randomly assigned 662 African American sixth- and seventh-graders to different groups (Jemmott, Jemmott, & Fong, 2010). The groups included abstinence-only and safer-sex interventions. A third group that received information about healthy behavior (but not about sexuality) served as a control. The dependent measure was whether participants reported having sexual intercourse in the two years following the interventions.

The abstinence-only intervention was built around the principles of social cognitive theory, focusing on building self-efficacy and a sense of personal control. The facilitators in the program emphasized that sexual activity is a serious step and that it might be best to delay it for some time in the future. They did not talk about sex moralistically and never mentioned that students should wait until marriage; nor did the instructors present sexual behavior negatively. Instead, the intervention included role-play exercises and other activities that helped students build skills to resist pressures to have sex. If the topics of birth control or condoms were broached by students, the facilitators provided medically accurate information and cleared up any misconceptions students might have.

Two years later, students in the abstinence-only group were less likely to report having had sex than those in the control group. Specifically, about one-third of the abstinence-only group reported they had had sexual intercourse, compared with nearly half of the control group. The safer-sex intervention students did not differ from the controls in terms of whether they reported having sex. Importantly, those in the abstinence-only group who did have sex were no less likely to use condoms than those in the safer-sex group.

Although these results might generally seem to support the effectiveness of abstinence-only education, particular aspects of the study might raise the eyebrows of abstinence-only advocates. First, some of the middle-schoolers in the study were as young as 10 years old, certainly younger than many abstinence-only advocates might envision. Second, the information provided about contraceptives and condoms does not conform with the typical expectations for abstinence-only education. Moreover, participants were not encouraged to wait until marriage to have sex, nor were they told that sexual behavior outside of marriage is generally harmful.

There are also features of the study that limit its validity and generalizability. Note that only students in the abstinence-only group were specifically encouraged to delay sexual activity and that the dependent measure was self-report. So, these students might not have been truthful about their sexual activity. Also, because the study included only youngsters, it is not clear whether the intervention would work for older teens.

Nevertheless, this research provides the first evidence that sex education aimed at abstinence can have an influence on the sexual behavior of young people. Importantly, though, the version of abstinence-only education used in the study may be one that surprises advocates of such interventions.

WHAT DO YOU THINK?
- What kind of sex education did you have in school? Was it adequate? Explain.
- If, as a parent, you were asked to give consent for your child to participate in the study by Jemmott and others, how would the child's sex or age influence your decision?
- How might an intervention like this one be used to reduce other risky behaviors in youth?

test yourself

1. What are some different ways that people define sexual behavior, or "sex"?
2. What do studies indicate about the frequency of sex among married partners and among people in committed relationships versus single people?
3. What are two kinds of sex education, and how effective is each?

A recent study of a specific kind of abstinence-only sex education challenged ideas about whether abstinence-only programs can at least delay sex among younger adolescents. To read more about this study, check out the Critical Controversy.

6· SEXUAL VARIATIONS AND DISORDERS

If we think of sexual behavior as any behavior that involves sexual pleasure, then we can say that there are many different kinds of sexual behavior. When it comes to sexual pleasure, in fact, variation is the norm. In this section we consider some variant sexual behaviors and draw a contrast between behavior that is pleasurable but not harmful versus behavior that is potentially distressing and therefore abnormal. We also consider some common disorders of sexual response and desire.

Fetishes

People are sexually aroused by different activities. A man might be sexually stimulated by wearing women's clothing. A woman might be turned on by wearing a necktie. A **fetish** is an object or activity that arouses sexual interest and desire. Fetishes include erotic materials (such as pornographic images and films), clothing, and other physical objects (Gijs, 2008). A person with a *transvestic fetish* (who may be heterosexual or homosexual) gets sexual pleasure from wearing clothing of the opposite sex. Other fetishes include activities such as dressing up like an animal or a baby. In yet another fetish, *sadomasochism,* one person (the sadistic partner) gains sexual pleasure from dominating another person (the masochist), who in turn enjoys being dominated.

These behaviors may be unusual, but they are not generally considered abnormal. Indeed, unusual sexual practices are typically considered harmless variations as long as these three principles are not violated: The individuals are consenting adults; they do not experience personal distress; and they are not putting themselves in danger of physical harm or death as a result of their activities (Gijs, 2008). When a variation in sexual behavior violates one or more of these principles, however, it may qualify as a paraphilia, which is a psychological disorder and may be illegal.

● **fetish** An object or activity that arouses sexual interest and desire.

Paraphilias

The American Psychiatric Association (APA) defines **paraphilias** as sexual disorders that feature recurrent sexually arousing fantasies, urges, or behaviors involving (1) nonhuman objects, (2) the suffering or humiliation of oneself or one's partner, or (3) children or other nonconsenting persons (APA, 2000). While some paraphilias may be relatively harmless, a paraphilia is considered to require treatment if the person experiencing it feels distress or impairment in social or occupational life domains. Men are far more likely than women to suffer from paraphilias (Gijs, 2008).

Certain paraphilias, such as exhibitionism (exposing one's genitals to another person to gain sexual pleasure) and voyeurism (watching another person to experience sexual pleasure), are considered problematic even when the paraphilic individual does not suffer from personal distress, because they involve the violation of someone who is not consenting. Sexual sadism without the consent of one's partner is similarly violating. Pedophilia, which we examine below, involves sexual behavior with children; it is certainly a psychological disorder, even in the absence of personal distress, because children are not old enough to legally consent to such behavior. Figure 11.8 lists the various paraphilias that the American Psychiatric Association recognizes.

What is the etiology of paraphilias? (*Etiology* means "the causes or significant preceding conditions.") There is no one answer to this question. Each paraphilia may have its own origin. Some experts have suggested that principles of classical conditioning can explain the emergence of some paraphilias (Gijs, 2008). Recall that in classical conditioning, a conditioned stimulus (CS) is paired with another stimulus, the unconditioned stimulus (UCS), which provokes an unconditioned response (UCR). After frequent pairings, the CS comes to evoke the response even in the absence of the UCS. Using this framework, we might say that a man with a shoe fetish might have been around shoes when he masturbated as a boy and that these experiences led to the fetish. For other paraphilias, however, it is likely that more than associative learning is involved.

● **paraphilias** Sexual disorders that feature recurrent sexually arousing fantasies, urges, or behaviors involving nonhuman objects; the suffering or humiliation of oneself or one's partner; or children or other nonconsenting persons.

Pedophilia

Pedophilia is a paraphilia in which an adult or an older adolescent sexually fantasizes about or engages in sexual behavior with individuals who have not reached puberty.

● **pedophilia** A paraphilia in which an adult or an older adolescent sexually fantasizes about or engages in sexual behavior with individuals who have not reached puberty.

FIGURE 11.8 Types of Paraphilias
Sexual variations are considered harmless if they (1) do not cause a person distress or physical harm and (2) do not violate another person. For some of the paraphilias in the figure, the issue is one of consent; for others, the variations may qualify as a disorder only if they cause the person distress or interfere with daily living. Notice that fetishism is included as a paraphilia if a fetish causes personal distress or interferes with daily life. Can you identify which of these principles apply to each of the other paraphilias?

Paraphilia	Focus
Exhibitionism	Exposing one's genitals to a stranger
Fetishism	Using nonliving objects for sexual pleasure
Frotteurism	Touching and rubbing against a person who has not given consent—for instance, in a crowded subway train
Pedophilia	Sexual activity with a prepubescent child
Sexual masochism	The act of being humiliated, beaten, bound, or otherwise made to suffer
Sexual sadism	Acts in which the individual derives sexual excitement from the psychological or physical suffering of the victim
Transvestic fetishism	Cross-dressing by a male in women's clothing
Voyeurism	Observing unsuspecting individuals—usually strangers who are naked, in the process of disrobing, or engaged in sexual activity

Pedophilia is more common in men than women, but it is not an exclusively male disorder (Seto, 2009).

The causes of this disorder are not well understood. Although it was once thought that most individuals who sexually abuse children were themselves sexually abused as children, this explanation has not held up to the evidence (U.S. General Accounting Office, 1996). Adults who sexually abuse children are more likely than other sex offenders to report themselves as having experienced sexual abuse in childhood (Jesperson, Lalumiere, & Seto, 2009), but the vast majority of individuals who have been sexually molested as children do not themselves go on to molest others.

Pedophilia is associated with low self-esteem, poor social skills, low IQ (Hall & Hall, 2007), and a history of head injuries (causing unconsciousness) in childhood (Seto, 2009). The disorder is related to a pattern of cognitive distortions, including minimizing the harm of pedophilic activities, believing that sexual impulses are uncontrollable, and thinking that sexual relationships with children are consensual (Hall & Hall, 2007). Brain-imaging studies suggest that individuals who are sexually attracted to children show a pervasive pattern of brain dysfunction, related to connections between brain regions (Cantor & others, 2008).

Given the potential damage that pedophilic behavior can inflict on its victims, identifying strategies for treatment and prevention is paramount. Therapies have targeted the learned associations between children and sexual arousal or have focused on training offenders in skills needed to recognize and avoid risky situations, such as being around children. Unfortunately, these treatments have not been effective (Marques & others, 2005; Seto, 2009).

In recent years castration (either surgically, through removal of the testes, or chemically, through drugs that reduce testosterone) has been used to treat sex offenders who victimize children. Hundreds of surgical castrations of sex offenders have been performed throughout Europe, and nine U.S. states have laws that *require* chemical or surgical castration for sex offenders who commit crimes against children as a condition of parole (Seto, 2009). It is difficult to evaluate the effectiveness of castration, however, because individuals are not randomly assigned to the treatment, and those who undergo the procedure may be particularly motivated to change their behavior (Seto, 2009). Furthermore, some critics have suggested that castration is used primarily to punish, not to treat, and as such is unethical (Spaulding, 1998; R. G. Wright, 2008).

Acknowledging the difficulties in treating pedophilia, Michael Seto (2009), an expert on the disorder, concluded that efforts should focus on prevention—both preventing pedophilia itself and implementing interventions aimed at child-victims. With respect to actually preventing pedophilia, Seto argues that, given the evidence for a neuro-developmental basis to the problem, enhanced prenatal care and early parenting interventions might be helpful in reducing pedophilia's occurrence, in addition to having other positive benefits. With respect to preventing abuse and protecting children, Seto advocates educating children to distinguish appropriate and inappropriate touch and empowering them to share their feelings with a trusted adult if someone is making them uncomfortable.

Disorders of Sexual Desire and Sexual Response

Paraphilias are unusual. More common disorders of sexuality involve problems either in sexual desire or in the physical sexual response described by Masters and Johnson.

With regard to sexual desire disorders, studies suggest that up to a quarter of men and nearly half of women report sometimes being troubled with a general lack of interest in sex (Laumann & others, 2005; van Lankveld, 2008). Lack of sexual desire in both men and women can stem from low levels of androgen, stress, anxiety and depression, physical illnesses, and various drugs used to treat psychological and physical conditions (Hackett, 2008; van Lankveld, 2008). Treatments for lack of sexual desire include drug therapies, psychological therapies, and relationship counseling.

In terms of disorders related to sexual response, two common disorders in men are *erectile dysfunction,* the failure of the penis to become erect, and *premature ejaculation,* the experience of orgasm before the person wishes it. As we have seen, the male genitalia are complex, and the male sexual response involves a number of physiological reactions, from erection to ejaculation. It is not surprising that, at times, this elegant machinery does not function optimally.

Erectile dysfunction was once believed to be primarily psychological, but experts now agree that most cases involve a combination of psychological and physical factors (Heidelbaugh, 2010; Lewis, Yuan, & Wang, 2008). Erectile dysfunction may be a symptom of an underlying physical illness, such as diabetes, and is more likely to occur with age. Treatment typically involves medications, such as Viagra, that allow the individual to experience erection (Althof & others, 2010; Claes, 2010). Premature ejaculation is the most common sexual complaint among men under the age of 40 (Rowland & McMahon, 2008). Psychological, physical, and relationship factors can play a role in premature ejaculation. The problem may be treated with drugs or therapy and may also involve working together with one's sexual partner to develop greater mastery over the sexual response.

Women can also suffer from disorders of sexual response, including problems in sexual arousal as well as in the experience of orgasm. For some women, dysfunction in arousal is explained by problems in the autonomic nervous system that disrupt the engorgement of the labia and lubrication of the vagina; for other women, the subjective feeling of arousal is absent even when these physical changes occur (Meston, Seal, & Hamilton, 2008). Disorders of sexual orgasm in women involve delayed or absent orgasm during sexual activity (Meston, Seal, & Hamilton, 2008). Both of these types of disorders can be related to the experience of childhood sexual abuse, as well as to strict religious beliefs and negative sexual attitudes (van Lankveld, 2008). These disorders of sexual response may be treated with androgens or through psychotherapy. Addressing underlying physical causes can also sometimes bring relief.

The occasional occurrence of erectile dysfunction or premature ejaculation in males, and of problems with arousal and orgasm in females, is common and normal. It is when these problems cause distress for the individual or difficulties in important relationships that they are considered disorders in need of treatment.

test yourself

1. What three principles must not be violated for a variation in sexual behavior to be considered harmless?
2. Why is it difficult to determine the effectiveness of surgical or chemical castration as a treatment for pedophilia?
3. Give examples of sexual response disorders experienced by men, as well as examples of such disorders experienced by women.

Variations, Disorders, and the Meaning of Normality

A theme throughout this discussion has been whether variations in sexual behavior are problems that require professional help or whether they represent harmless differences that simply reflect human diversity. The difficulties people have in talking about sexuality only perpetuate anxiety, shame, and concern about sex. People are not ashamed to admit that they like certain foods and dislike others. Imagine if we treated sexual tastes in a similarly open way.

If you feel concern about your own sexual behaviors or experiences, seeking the advice of a counselor or therapist is a great way to get clarity about the issues. Sexuality can be powerful and confusing, but it is also an amazing expression of the capacity of humans to bond with others.

7· SEXUALITY AND HEALTH AND WELLNESS

Many of us would agree that healthy sexual activity is an important component of the good life. Yet, for a variety of reasons, we often do not talk about this aspect of our behavior. In this concluding section, we consider two aspects of the intersection of sexuality with health and wellness—first, its implications for physical health; and second, its role in psychological well-being.

Sexual Behavior and Physical Health

● **sexually transmitted infection (STI)** An infection that is contracted primarily through sexual activity—vaginal intercourse as well as oral and anal sex.

● **acquired immune deficiency syndrome (AIDS)** A sexually transmitted infection, caused by the human immunodeficiency virus (HIV), that destroys the body's immune system.

A key consideration in any discussion of sexual health is sexually transmitted infections. A **sexually transmitted infection (STI)** is an infection that is contracted primarily through sexual activity—vaginal intercourse as well as oral and anal sex. STIs affect about one of every six adults in the United States (National Center for Health Statistics, 2005).

TYPES AND CAUSES OF SEXUALLY TRANSMITTED INFECTIONS

Some STIs are bacterial in origin, as are gonorrhea and syphilis. Others are caused by viruses, as in the case of genital herpes and HIV. STIs are a top health concern because they can have implications for a person's future fertility, risk of cancer, and life expectancy.

No single STI has had a greater impact on sexual behavior in the past decades than HIV. **Acquired immune deficiency syndrome (AIDS)** is caused by the *human immunodeficiency virus (HIV)*, a sexually transmitted infection that destroys the body's immune system. Without treatment, most people who contract HIV are vulnerable to germs that a normal immune system can destroy. Through 2007, more than 1 million Americans had been diagnosed with AIDS, and more than 560,000 Americans had died of complications from the infection (National Center for Health Statistics, 2010).

Recent improvements in drug therapies have given rise to the view that HIV is a chronic rather than terminal condition. Responses to treatment vary among individuals, and keeping up with the "cocktail" of drugs necessary to continuously fight HIV can be challenging. The treatment known as highly active antiretroviral therapy (HAART) can

Along with a number of other factors, sexual activity plays a role in romantic partners' well-being.

involve taking between 6 and 22 pills each day, although in 2006 the FDA approved the first one-pill-per-day treatment for HIV (Laurence, 2006).

Because of increased education and the development of more effective drug therapies, deaths due to AIDS have begun to decline in the United States (National Center for Health Statistics, 2010). There are no solid estimates for the life expectancy of someone who is HIV positive, because the existing treatments have been around for only about a decade. Even in this era of improved treatments, however, HIV remains an incurable infection that can lead to early death. Importantly, it has been estimated that as many as one-half of individuals who are HIV positive are not in treatment and that one-quarter of individuals who are HIV positive do not know that they are (National Center for Health Statistics, 2010).

PRACTICING SAFE SEX

Anyone who is sexually active is at risk of contracting HIV and other STIs. The only 100 percent safe behavior is abstinence from sex, which most individuals do not view as an option. Sensual activities such as kissing, French kissing, cuddling, massage, and mutual masturbation (that does not involve the exchange of bodily fluids) involve no risk of an STI. Sexual activities that involve penetration, including vaginal and anal intercourse as well as oral sex, are riskier behaviors that can be made less risky with the use of proper protection.

Generally, condoms are a key tool in efforts to protect oneself from sexually transmitted infections. In your own sexual experience, it may be difficult to gauge the accuracy of a partner's estimates of risk and his or her status with respect to having an STI. The wisest course of action is always to protect yourself by using a latex condom. When correctly used, latex condoms help to prevent the transmission of many STIs.

Condoms are most effective in preventing gonorrhea, syphilis, chlamydia, and HIV. Research suggests that consistent condom use also significantly reduces the risk that males will transmit to their female partners the human papilloma virus (HPV), which can cause cervical cancer (Winer & others, 2006). Although condoms are less effective against the spread of herpes than against other STIs, the consistent use of condoms significantly reduces the risk of herpes infection for both men and women (Wald, Langenberg, & Krantz, 2005). In short, anyone who thinks that condom use is inconvenient or will ruin the mood might well consider this question: Which is more inconvenient—using a condom or contracting gonorrhea or AIDS?

Research has shown that programs to promote safe sex are especially effective if they include the eroticization of condom use—that is, making condoms a part of the sensual experience of foreplay (Scott-Sheldon & Johnson, 2006). Analyses of HIV prevention programs (including over 350 intervention groups and 100 control groups) by Delores Albarracin and her colleagues have produced important recommendations for the best ways to influence behavior (Albarracin, Durantini, & Earl, 2006; Albarracin & others, 2005; Durantini & others, 2006). The studies have found that fear tactics are relatively less effective and that programs emphasizing active skill building (for example, role playing the use of condoms), self-efficacy, and positive attitudes about condom use are effective with most groups. Making safe sex sexy is a great way to practice safe sex.

Sexual Behavior and Psychological Well-Being

Researchers have been particularly interested in people's motives for having sex. Lynne Cooper and her colleagues (Cooper, Shapiro, & Powers, 1998) examined the sex motives of a sample of adolescents and young adults whom they followed longitudinally over several years. The researchers examined the reasons these individuals gave for having sex. The participants' reported motives included the following: to connect intimately with someone, to enhance their own self-esteem, to gain a partner's and peers' approval, and to avoid feeling distressed or lonely. The researchers also found that engaging in sex as a form of intimacy with another person was related to having fewer sex partners overall and to practicing less risky sex (Cooper, Shapiro, & Powers, 1998). Conversely, individuals who had sex to cope with negative feelings were less likely to have stable long-term relationships and tended to engage in more unsafe sex. Subsequent research has shown that having sex in

test yourself

1. What is a sexually transmitted infection (STI)?

2. What contraceptive device is key in efforts to protect individuals from contracting STIs? Against what does it offer the most protection?

3. What motives for having sex are associated with increased well-being? With decreased well-being?

order to be close to another person is related to enhanced well-being, but engaging in sex to avoid bad feelings is linked with decreases in well-being (Impett, Peplau, & Gable, 2005).

Research has solidly supported the role of sexual activity in well-being. In the Swedish study described earlier, frequency of vaginal intercourse was strongly related to life satisfaction for men and women (Brody & Costa, 2009). Furthermore, although the frequency of sexual behavior may decline with age, sexuality remains a significant part of human identity and relationships throughout life (DeLamater & Moorman, 2007; Lindau & Gavrilova, 2010). Importantly, partnered sexual activity is a strong predictor of satisfaction in relationships even when those activities do not include vaginal intercourse (DeLamater & Moorman, 2007; Kennedy, Haque, & Zarankow, 1997). Throughout the life span, then, sexual activities remain a source of pleasure and an avenue for the experience of intimacy with another.

SUMMARY

1. DEFINING SEX AND GENDER

Sex refers to biological aspects of the person that are used to classify him or her as male or female. Biological features that serve in this capacity include genes, gonads, hormones, genitals, and secondary sexual characteristics. *Gender* refers to the person's psychological sense of himself or herself as male or female. Gender is sometimes described in terms of a person's level of instrumentality or expressiveness.

Disorders of sexual development are conditions in which a person's genetic, genital, or gonadal sex is atypical. In these cases, the sex in which the child was raised is the most consistent predictor of eventual gender identity.

Individuals who feel trapped in the wrong biological sex are referred to as *transgender*. Transgender individuals are sometimes considered to be suffering from gender identity disorder, which involves intense distress over one's birth sex. The only evaluated treatment for gender identity disorder is sex reassignment surgery. There is controversy about whether transgender should be considered a psychological disorder. Many transgender individuals feel that they do not have a disorder but rather occupy a different gender territory that goes beyond male versus female.

2. THEORIES OF GENDER DEVELOPMENT

Perspectives on gender development include biological, evolutionary psychology, social cognitive, and social role theories. Biological approaches focus on the ways that genes, hormones, and brain structures relate to gender differences. Evolutionary psychology theory views gender through the lens of Darwinian natural selection and states that human beings have evolved through a process of sexual selection in which males compete for mates and females choose their male partners. Social cognitive approaches to gender emphasize how learning, modeling, and cognitive schemas influence the development of gender. Social role theory states that a division of labor between the sexes that is based on male–female physical differences can lead to the social construction of gender roles and gender stereotypes. Social role theory predicts that as social structures change, gender differences should decline.

3. THE PSYCHOLOGY OF GENDER DIFFERENCES

Research indicates that girls are better at verbal tasks and boys are better at visuospatial tasks, though these differences are relatively small. In terms of aggression, males tend to be more overtly aggressive than females, but females may be more relationally aggressive than males.

Sexuality refers to the ways people experience and express themselves as sexual beings. Men are more likely to engage in casual sex and to have more lifetime sex partners compared to women. Men also report more frequent sexual arousal, are more prone to lust and sexual fantasies, and are more likely than women to masturbate. They have more permissive attitudes about casual premarital sex as well, and have a more difficult time being sexually faithful when married. Women are more likely than men to show fluidity in their sexual attractions.

4. SEXUAL ORIENTATION

Sexual orientation refers to the direction of a person's erotic interest and includes heterosexuality, homosexuality, and bisexuality. Sexual orientation is generally measured using questionnaires. The vast majority of people are heterosexual; the number of homosexual or bisexual individuals is between 2 and 10 percent of the population.

Possible explanations for sexual orientation include genetic factors, brain differences, and prenatal hormone exposure. Genes explain a relatively small amount of the variation we see in sexual orientation. Some research indicates that gay men have thicker corpus callosa than heterosexual men. Other research suggests that lesbian women may be more similar to heterosexual men in terms of brain hemisphere asymmetry. Prenatal testosterone exposure shows some links to eventual lesbian and bisexual orientation in women. Social factors do not seem to play a large role in sexual orientation.

Gay men and lesbian women are similar to their heterosexual counterparts in many ways, but they do show higher levels of relationship satisfaction and are more likely to break up than heterosexual married couples. Gay men and lesbian women in civil unions are less likely to break up than those without such unions. Children with gay parents tend to be as well adjusted as children with heterosexual parents.

5. SEXUAL BEHAVIORS AND PRACTICES

Although it is difficult to study sexual behaviors and practices, research suggests that married couples have sex more often than unmarried couples and singles. Vaginal intercourse is the most common sexual practice for men and women. Both men and women report engaging in oral sex and anal sex. Regardless of the particular sexual activity, the human sexual response pattern is characterized by four stages—excitement, plateau, orgasm, and resolution.

Sexual desire is also a key element in sexual behavior. Sensation, perception, and cognition are all important components of sexual activity. Culture plays a role in sexuality as well.

Some people worry that providing adolescents with comprehensive sex education will lead to premature sexual activity. However, research strongly suggests that education is crucial to preventing unwanted pregnancy.

6. SEXUAL VARIATIONS AND DISORDERS

With regard to sexual tastes and activities, variation is the norm. A fetish is an object that a person finds sexually arousing. Paraphilias are disorders in which a person experiences strong sexual interest in certain objects or activities. Paraphilias may require treatment if they violate the rights of others or put the individual at risk of physical harm.

Pedophilia is a particularly harmful paraphilia involving sexual attraction to children. Pedophilia is very difficult to treat.

More common than paraphilias are disorders of sexual desire and sexual response. Two common disorders of sexual response in men are erectile dysfunction and premature ejaculation. In women, common sexual response disorders include problems in arousal and in experiencing orgasm.

7. SEXUALITY AND HEALTH AND WELLNESS

Sexually transmitted infections (STIs) are infections that can be spread through sexual contact, including vaginal, anal, and oral sex. When used properly and consistently, latex condoms offer excellent protection against many STIs, including AIDS.

The relationship between sexual behavior and psychological wellness depends on the reasons people have sex. Those who engage in sexual activity based on intimacy motives have fewer overall sex partners and are more likely to practice safe sex. Those who engage in sex to win a partner's approval or to cope with negative feelings tend to show decreases in well-being and to engage in more sexual risk taking. Sexuality is an important aspect of psychological well-being throughout the life span.

key *terms*

sex, p. 346
sex chromosomes, p. 346
gonads, p. 346
secondary sex
 characteristics, p. 347
gender, p. 347
gender identity, p. 347
androgynous, p. 348
disorders of sexual development
 (DSD), p. 350

transgender, p. 351
gender identity disorder
 (GID), p. 351
sexual selection, p. 353
gender roles, p. 355
gender stereotypes, p. 355
gender similarities
 hypothesis, p. 359
aggression, p. 359
overt aggression, p. 359

conduct disorder, p. 359
relational aggression, p. 359
sexuality, p. 360
sexual orientation, p. 362
heterosexual, p. 362
homosexual, p. 362
bisexual, p. 362
human sexual response
 pattern, p. 371

fetish, p. 375
paraphilias, p. 375
pedophilia, p. 375
sexually transmitted
 infection (STI), p. 378
acquired immune deficiency
 syndrome (AIDS), p. 378

apply your *knowledge*

1. Ask your parents about your gender-related behavior as a child and about their views on how their parenting influenced your gender development. Do their recollections ring true with your memories? What factors do you think played a role in your gender development?

2. Set aside a day and keep a gender-awareness diary. Try to notice every time you have an experience in which your gender matters to your life. From the moment you get up in the morning until you go to bed at night, if you are man, ask yourself, "Would I be doing this if I were a woman?" If you are a woman, ask yourself, "Would I be doing this if I were a man?" When you see a woman performing an activity, ask yourself, "Would this seem appropriate to me if a man were doing it?" Write down your thoughts and feelings about these activities, and reflect on the role of gender in your daily life.

3. The evolutionary psychology approach to gender suggests that men are more likely to seek women who are younger than they are and that women are more likely to seek older men with resources. Sit down with the personal ads from a local paper and examine the ads placed by men and women. Does the ads' content support predictions about what men and women look for?

4. States differ in terms of their laws regarding gay and lesbian marriage, adoption rights, and employment protections. Research your own state's legal policies toward the rights of gay men and women. Summarize those rights. Does your state also have laws about the protection of transgender rights?

5. Conduct web searches for "transgender experience" and "gender identity disorder." How do the sites you find differ in terms of their discussion of a person who feels trapped in the wrong sex?

CHAPTER 12

Personality

Revealing Who We *Really* Are

When you meet someone for the first time, do you ever wonder whether the person is putting on a front, maybe trying to show himself or herself in the best possible light? Increasingly, such first meetings are occurring on online social networking sites such as Facebook and MySpace. More than 700 million people worldwide have profiles on social networking sites (ComScore, 2008). How accurately do these online profiles reflect their owners?

Recently, a team of personality psychologists, led by Mitja Back, sought to address this very question, and the results might surprise you. The researchers asked 236 U.S. and 103 German college students to complete a measure of their personality characteristics. Back and colleagues then compared these reports to the information on each student's online profile (Back & others, 2010). The results? The online profiles were well matched to the students' actual characteristics. In other words, rather than presenting an idealized version of themselves, the participants had used their online profile to express their *real personality*. Indeed, Back and colleagues suggest that this is the very reason for the popularity of social networking sites: They give us a chance to share who we genuinely are.

We leave evidence of "the real us" in many of the settings we occupy in life—not just on websites but also in offices, classrooms, bedrooms, and dorm rooms (Gosling, 2008a). "Who we really are" is the topic that occupies personality psychology, our focus in this chapter. Personality psychologists are interested in identifying the characteristics that make each of us different from everyone else and in understanding how these characteristics relate to behavior. Personality psychology explores the psychological attributes that underlie who we really are—the unified and enduring core characteristics that account for our existence as one and the same person throughout the life span. ●

PREVIEW

In this chapter, we first survey theories of personality from a variety of perspectives. We begin with classic theories from psychodynamic and humanistic thinkers and then examine more contemporary approaches, including the trait, life story, social cognitive, and biological perspectives. We then look at personality assessment, the domain in which personality psychologists have grappled with the question of how to measure who we really are. Finally, we consider the role of personality characteristics in health and wellness.

1· PSYCHODYNAMIC PERSPECTIVES

● **personality** A pattern of enduring, distinctive thoughts, emotions, and behaviors that characterize the way an individual adapts to the world.

● **psychodynamic perspectives** Theoretical views emphasizing that personality is primarily unconscious (beyond awareness).

Personality is a pattern of enduring, distinctive thoughts, emotions, and behaviors that characterize the way an individual adapts to the world. Psychologists have approached these enduring characteristics in a variety of ways, focusing on different aspects of the person.

Psychodynamic perspectives on personality emphasize that personality is primarily unconscious (that is, beyond awareness). According to this viewpoint, those enduring patterns that make up personality are largely unavailable to our conscious awareness, and they powerfully shape our behaviors in ways that we cannot consciously comprehend. Psychodynamic theorists use the word *unconscious* differently from how other psychologists might use the term. From the psychodynamic perspective, aspects of our personality are unconscious because they *must* be; this lack of awareness is motivated. These mysterious, unconscious forces are simply too frightening to be part of our conscious awareness.

Psychodynamic theorists believe that behavior is only a surface characteristic and that to truly understand someone's personality, we have to explore the symbolic meanings of that behavior and the deep inner workings of the mind (C. Levin, 2010; Westen, Gabbard, & Soto, 2008). Psychodynamic theorists also stress the role of early childhood experience in adult personality. From this perspective, the adult is a reflection of those childhood experiences that shape our earliest conceptions of ourselves and others. These characteristics were sketched by the architect of psychoanalytic theory, Sigmund Freud.

Freud's Psychoanalytic Theory

Sigmund Freud, one of the most influential thinkers of the twentieth century, was born in Freiberg, Moravia (today part of the Czech Republic), in 1856 and died in London at the age of 83. Freud spent most of his life in Vienna, but he left the city near the end of his career to escape the Holocaust.

Freud has had such a phenomenal impact that just about everyone has an opinion about him, even those who have never studied his work. If you ask others what they think of Freud, you will likely get a variety of interesting answers. Some might comment that Freud was a cocaine addict. Freud did use cocaine early in his career, but he stopped using the drug when he discovered its harmful effects. Others might claim that Freud hated women. As we will see, Freud's theory of development did include the notion that women are morally inferior to men. In truth, however, Freud was never satisfied with his approach to the psychology of women. He welcomed women interested in pursuing careers in psychoanalysis, and many of his earliest and most influential followers were women. Finally, people might declare that Freud thought everything was about sex. That claim, it turns out, is quite true, except by *sex* Freud did not mean sexual activity in the usual sense. Instead, Freud defined sex as organ pleasure. *Anything* that is pleasurable is sex, according to Freud.

For Freud, the sexual drive was the most important motivator of all human activity. As we will see, Freud thought that the human sex drive was the main determinant of personality development, and he felt that psychological disorders, dreams, and all human

Sigmund Freud (1856–1939) Freud's theories have strongly influenced how people in Western cultures view themselves and their world.

behavior represent the conflict between this unconscious sexual drive and the demands of civilized human society.

Freud developed *psychoanalysis,* his approach to personality, through his work with patients suffering from hysteria. *Hysteria* refers to physical symptoms that have no physical cause. For instance, a person might be unable to see, even with perfectly healthy eyes, or unable to walk, despite having no physical injury.

In Freud's day (the Victorian era, a time marked by strict rules regarding sex), many young women suffered from physical problems that could not be explained by actual physical illness. In his practice, Freud spent long hours listening to these women talk about their symptoms. Freud came to understand that the hysterical symptoms stemmed from unconscious psychological conflicts. These conflicts centered on experiences in which the person's drive for pleasure was thwarted by the social pressures of Victorian society. Furthermore, the particular symptoms were symbolically related to these underlying conflicts. One of Freud's patients, Fraulein Elisabeth Von R., suffered from excruciating leg pains that prevented her from standing or walking. The fact that Fraulein Elisabeth could not walk was no accident. Through analysis, Freud discovered that Fraulein Elisabeth had had a number of experiences in which she wanted nothing more than to take a walk but had been prevented from doing so by her duty to her ill father.

Importantly, Freud believed that hysterical symptoms were *overdetermined*—that is, they had *many* causes in the unconscious. Eventually, Freud came to use hysterical symptoms as his metaphor for understanding dreams, slips of the tongue, and all human behavior. Everything we do, he said, has a multitude of unconscious causes.

Drawing from his work in analyzing patients (as well as himself), Freud developed his model of the human personality. He described personality as like an iceberg, existing mostly below the level of awareness, just as the massive part of an iceberg lies beneath the surface of the water. Figure 12.1 illustrates this analogy and depicts how extensive the unconscious part of our mind is, in Freud's view.

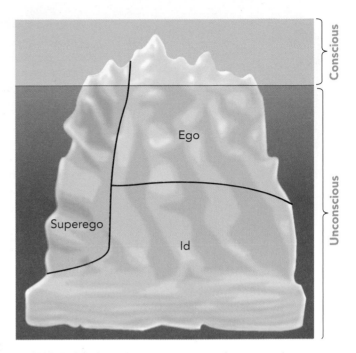

FIGURE 12.1 **The Conscious and Unconscious Mind: The Iceberg Analogy** The iceberg analogy illustrates how much of the mind is unconscious in Freud's theory. The conscious mind is the part of the iceberg above water; the unconscious mind, the part below water. Notice that the id is totally unconscious, whereas the ego and the superego can operate at either the conscious or the unconscious level.

STRUCTURES OF PERSONALITY

The three parts of the iceberg in Figure 12.1 reflect the three structures of personality described by Freud. Freud (1917) called these structures the id, the ego, and the superego. You can get a better feel for these Latin labels by considering their English translations: The id is literally the "it," the ego is the "I," and the superego is the "above-I."

The **id** consists of unconscious drives and is the individual's reservoir of sexual energy. This "it" is a pool of amoral and often vile urges pressing for expression. In Freud's view, the id has no contact with reality. The id works according to the *pleasure principle,* the Freudian concept that the id always seeks pleasure.

The world would be dangerous and scary, however, if personalities were all id. As young children mature, they learn that they cannot slug other children in the face, that they have to use the toilet instead of diapers, and that they must negotiate with others to get the things they want. As children experience the constraints of reality, a new element of personality is formed—the **ego,** the Freudian structure of personality that deals with the demands of reality. Indeed, according to Freud, the ego abides by the *reality principle.* That is, it tries to bring the individual pleasure within the norms of society. The ego helps us to test reality, to see how far we can go without getting into trouble and hurting ourselves. Whereas the id is completely unconscious, the ego is partly conscious. It houses our higher mental functions—reasoning, problem solving, and decision making, for example.

The id and ego do not consider whether something is right or wrong. Rather, the **superego** is the harsh internal judge of our behavior. The superego is reflected in what we often call conscience and evaluates the morality of our behavior. Like the id, the

● **id** The part of the person that Freud called the "it," consisting of unconscious drives; the individual's reservoir of sexual energy.

● **ego** The Freudian structure of personality that deals with the demands of reality.

● **superego** The Freudian structure of personality that serves as the harsh internal judge of our behavior; what we often call conscience.

Anna Freud (1895–1982) The youngest of Freud's six children, Anna Freud not only did influential work on defense mechanisms but also pioneered in the theory and practice of child psychoanalysis.

● **defense mechanisms** Tactics the ego uses to reduce anxiety by unconsciously distorting reality.

superego does not consider reality; it considers only whether the id's impulses can be satisfied in acceptable moral terms.

The ego acts as a mediator between the conflicting demands of the id and the superego, as well as the real world. Your ego might say, for example, "I will have sex only in a committed relationship and always practice safe sex." Your id, however, screams, "Sex! Now!" and your superego commands, "Sex? Don't even think about it."

DEFENSE MECHANISMS

The conflicts that erupt among the demands of the id, the superego, and reality create a great deal of anxiety for the ego. The ego has strategies for dealing with this anxiety, called defense mechanisms. **Defense mechanisms** are tactics the ego uses to reduce anxiety by unconsciously distorting reality. For example, imagine that Jason's id is pressing to express an unconscious desire to have sex with his mother. Clearly, acting on this impulse would not please the superego or society at large. If he became aware of this impulse, Jason might recoil in horror. Instead, Jason's ego might use the defense mechanism of *displacement,* and he might develop a relationship with a girlfriend who looks and acts like his mother. Displacement means directing unacceptable impulses at a less threatening target. Through displacement, the ego allows Jason to express his id impulse in a way that will not land him in trouble. Of course, Jason's friends might chuckle at the resemblance between his mother and his girlfriend, but you can bet that Jason will never notice.

Figure 12.2 describes several defense mechanisms, many of which were introduced and developed by Freud's daughter Anna, who followed in her father's career footsteps. All these mechanisms work to reduce anxiety.

Defense Mechanism	How It Works	Example
Repression	The master defense mechanism; the ego pushes unacceptable impulses out of awareness, back into the unconscious mind.	A young girl was sexually abused by her uncle. As an adult, she can't remember anything about the traumatic experience.
Rationalization	The ego replaces a less acceptable motive with a more acceptable one.	A college student does not get into the fraternity of his choice. He tells himself that the fraternity is very exclusive and that a lot of students could not get in.
Displacement	The ego shifts feelings toward an unacceptable object to another, more acceptable object.	A woman can't take her anger out on her boss, so she goes home and takes it out on her husband.
Sublimation	The ego replaces an unacceptable impulse with a socially acceptable one.	A man with strong sexual urges becomes an artist who paints nudes.
Projection	The ego attributes personal shortcomings, problems, and faults to others.	A man who has a strong desire to have an extramarital affair accuses his wife of flirting with other men.
Reaction Formation	The ego transforms an unacceptable motive into its opposite.	A woman who fears her sexual urges becomes a religious zealot.
Denial	The ego refuses to acknowledge anxiety-producing realities.	A man won't acknowledge that he has cancer even though a team of doctors has diagnosed his cancer.
Regression	The ego seeks the security of an earlier developmental period in the face of stress.	A woman returns home to mother every time she and her husband have a big argument.

FIGURE 12.2 **Defense Mechanisms** Defense mechanisms reduce anxiety in various ways, in all instances by distorting reality.

Repression is the most powerful and pervasive defense mechanism. Repression pushes unacceptable id impulses back into the unconscious mind. Repression is the foundation for *all* of the psychological defense mechanisms, whose goal is to *repress* threatening impulses, that is, to push them out of awareness. Freud said, for example, that our early childhood experiences, many of which he believed were sexually laden, are too threatening for us to deal with consciously, so we reduce the anxiety of childhood conflict through repression.

Two final points about defense mechanisms are important. First, defense mechanisms are unconscious; we are not aware that we are calling on them. Second, when used in moderation or on a temporary basis, defense mechanisms are not necessarily unhealthy (Cramer, 2008a). For example, the defense mechanism of *denial* can help people cope upon first getting the news that their death is impending, and the defense mechanism of *sublimation* involves transforming unconscious impulses into activities that benefit society. Note that the defense mechanism of sublimation means that even the very best things that human beings accomplish—a beautiful work of art, an amazing act of kindness—are still explained by unconscious sexual drives and defenses.

PSYCHOSEXUAL STAGES OF PERSONALITY DEVELOPMENT

Freud believed that human beings go through universal stages of personality development and that at each developmental stage we experience sexual pleasure in one part of the body more than in others. Each stage is named for the location of sexual pleasure at that stage. *Erogenous zones* are parts of the body that have especially strong pleasure-giving qualities at particular stages of development. Freud thought that our adult personality is determined by the way we resolve conflicts between these early sources of pleasure—the mouth, the anus, and then the genitals—and the demands of reality.

- *Oral stage (first 18 months):* The infant's pleasure centers on the mouth. Chewing, sucking, and biting are the chief sources of pleasure that reduce tension in the infant.
- *Anal stage (18 to 36 months):* During a time when most children are experiencing toilet training, the child's greatest pleasure involves the anus and urethra and their functions. Freud recognized that there is pleasure in "going" and "holding it" as well as in the experience of control over one's parents in deciding when to do either.
- *Phallic stage (3 to 6 years):* The name of Freud's third stage comes from the Latin word *phallus,* which means "penis." Pleasure focuses on the genitals as the child discovers that self-stimulation is enjoyable.

  In Freud's view, the phallic stage has a special importance in personality development because it triggers the Oedipus complex. This name comes from the Greek tragedy in which Oedipus unknowingly kills his father and marries his mother. The **Oedipus complex** is the boy's intense desire to replace his father and enjoy the affections of his mother. Eventually, the boy recognizes that his father might punish him for these incestuous wishes, specifically by cutting off the boy's penis. *Castration anxiety* refers to the boy's intense fear of being mutilated by his father. To reduce this conflict, the boy identifies with his father, adopting the male gender role. The intense castration anxiety is repressed into the unconscious and serves as the foundation for the development of the superego.

  Freud recognized that there were differences between boys and girls in the phallic stage. Because a girl does not have a penis, she cannot experience castration anxiety, Freud reasoned. Instead, she compares herself to boys and realizes that she is missing something—a penis. Without experiencing the powerful force of castration anxiety, a girl cannot develop a superego in the same sense that boys do. Given this inability, Freud concluded, women were morally inferior to men, and this inferiority explained their place as second-class citizens in Victorian society. Freud believed that girls experience "castration completed," resulting in penis envy—the intense desire to obtain a penis by eventually marrying and bearing a son.

● **Oedipus complex** According to Freud, a boy's intense desire to replace his father and enjoy the affections of his mother.

While noting that his views ran counter to the early feminist thinkers of his time, Freud stood firm that the sexes are not equal in every way. He considered women to be somewhat childlike in their development and thought it was good that fathers, and eventually husbands, should guide them through life. He asserted that the only hope for women's moral development was education.

■ *Latency period (6 years to puberty):* This phase is not a developmental stage but rather a kind of psychic time-out. After the drama of the phallic stage, the child sets aside all interest in sexuality. Although we now consider these years extremely important to development, Freud felt that this was a time in which no psychosexual development occurred.

■ *Genital stage (adolescence and adulthood):* The genital stage is the time of sexual reawakening, a point when the source of sexual pleasure shifts to someone outside the family. Freud believed that in adulthood the individual becomes capable of the two hallmarks of maturity: love and work. However, Freud felt that human beings are inevitably subject to intense conflict, reasoning that everyone, no matter how healthy or well adjusted, still has an id pressing for expression. Adulthood, even in the best of circumstances, still involves reliving the unconscious conflicts of childhood.

Freud argued that the individual may become stuck in any of these developmental stages if he or she is underindulged or overindulged at a given stage. For example, a parent might wean a child too early (or not early enough) or be too strict (or too lax) in toilet training. *Fixation* occurs when a particular psychosexual stage colors an individual's adult personality. For instance, an *anal retentive* person (someone who is obsessively neat and organized) is fixated at the anal stage. The construct of fixation thus explains how, according to Freud's view, childhood experiences can have an enormous impact on adult personality. Figure 12.3 illustrates possible links between adult personality characteristics and fixation at the oral, anal, and phallic stages.

Psychodynamic Critics and Revisionists

Because Freud was among the first theorists to explore personality, some of his ideas have needed updating and revision over time, while others have been tossed out altogether. In particular, Freud's critics have said that his ideas about sexuality, early experience, social factors, and the unconscious mind were misguided (Adler, 1927; Erikson, 1968; Fromm, 1947; Horney, 1945; Jung, 1917; Kohut, 1977; Rapaport, 1967; Sullivan, 1953). They stress the following points:

■ Sexuality is not the pervasive force behind personality that Freud believed it to be. Furthermore, the Oedipus complex is not as universal as Freud maintained.

Stage	Adult Extensions (Fixations)	Sublimations	Reaction Formations
Oral	Smoking, eating, kissing, oral hygiene, drinking, chewing gum	Seeking knowledge, humor, wit, sarcasm, being a food or wine expert	Speech purist, food faddist, prohibitionist, dislike of milk
Anal	Notable interest in one's bowel movements, love of bathroom humor, extreme messiness; or, alternatively, extreme cleanliness, stubbornness, and a strong desire for simplicity and structure	Interest in painting or sculpture, being overly giving, great interest in statistics	Extreme disgust with feces, fear of dirt, prudishness, irritability
Phallic	Heavy reliance on masturbation, flirtatiousness, expressions of virility	Interest in poetry, love of love, interest in acting, striving for success	Puritanical attitude toward sex, excessive modesty

FIGURE 12.3 Defense Mechanisms and Freudian Stages If a person is fixated at a psychosexual stage, the fixation can color his or her personality in many ways, including the defense mechanisms the person might use to cope with anxiety.

Freud's concepts were heavily influenced by the setting in which he lived and worked—turn-of-the-century Vienna, a society that, compared with contemporary society, was sexually repressed and male-dominated.

- The first five years of life are not as powerful in shaping adult personality as Freud thought. Later experiences deserve more attention.

- The ego and conscious thought processes play a more dominant role in our personality than Freud believed; he claimed that we are forever captive to the instinctual, unconscious clutches of the id. In addition, the ego has a separate line of development from the id, so achievement, thinking, and reasoning are not always tied to sexual impulses.

- Sociocultural factors are much more important than Freud believed. In stressing the id's dominance, Freud placed more emphasis on the biological basis of personality. More contemporary psychodynamic scholars have especially emphasized the interpersonal setting of the family and the role of early social relationships in personality development (Hirsch, 2010; Leon, 2010).

A number of dissenters and revisionists to Freud's theory have been influential in the development of psychodynamic theories. Erik Erikson, whose psychosocial stages we examined in Chapter 9, is among these. Here we consider three other thinkers—Karen Horney, Carl Jung, and Alfred Adler—who made notable revisions to Freud's approach.

HORNEY'S SOCIOCULTURAL APPROACH

Karen Horney (1885–1952) rejected the classical psychoanalytic concept that anatomy is destiny and cautioned that some of Freud's most popular ideas were only hypotheses. She insisted that these hypotheses be supported with observable data before being accepted as fact. She also argued that sociocultural influences on personality development should be considered.

Consider Freud's concept of penis envy, which attributed some of the behavior of his female patients to their repressed desire to have a penis. Horney pointed out that women might envy the penis not because of these unconscious issues but because of the status that society bestows on those who have one. Further, she suggested that both sexes envy the attributes of the other, with men coveting women's reproductive capacities (Horney, 1967).

Horney also believed that the need for security, not for sex, is the prime motive in human existence. Horney reasoned that an individual whose needs for security are met should be able to develop his or her capacities to the fullest extent. She viewed psychological health as allowing the person to express talents and abilities freely and spontaneously.

JUNG'S ANALYTICAL THEORY

Freud's contemporary Carl Jung (1875–1961) had a different complaint about psychoanalytic theory. Jung shared Freud's interest in the unconscious, but he believed that Freud underplayed the unconscious mind's role in personality. In fact, Jung believed that the roots of personality go back to the dawn of humanity. The **collective unconscious** is Jung's term for the impersonal, deepest layer of the unconscious mind, shared by all human beings because of their common ancestral past. In Jung's theory, the experiences of a common past have made a deep, permanent impression on the human mind.

Jung posited that the collective unconscious contains **archetypes,** emotionally laden ideas and images that have rich and symbolic meaning for all people. Jung concluded that these archetypes emerge in art, literature, religion, and dreams (Faber & Mayer, 2009; Kradin, 2009; Merchant, 2006). He used archetypes to help people understand themselves (Urban, 2008). Archetypes are essentially predispositions to respond to the environment in particular ways.

Jung used the terms *anima* and *animus* to identify two common archetypes. He believed each of us has a passive feminine side—the anima—and an assertive masculine side—the animus. The *persona* is another archetype; Jung thought that the persona

Karen Horney (1885–1952) Horney developed the first feminist criticism of Freud's theory. Horney's view emphasizes women's positive qualities and self-evaluation.

● **collective unconscious** Jung's term for the impersonal, deepest layer of the unconscious mind, shared by all human beings because of their common ancestral past.

● **archetypes** Jung's term for emotionally laden ideas and images in the collective unconscious that have rich and symbolic meaning for all people.

Carl Jung (1875–1961) Jung, a Swiss psychoanalytic theorist, developed the concepts of the collective unconscious and archetypes.

represents the public mask that we all wear during social interactions. Jung believed that the persona is an essential archetype because it allows us always to keep some secret part of ourselves (who we really are) hidden from others.

ADLER'S INDIVIDUAL PSYCHOLOGY

● **individual psychology** Adler's view that people are motivated by purposes and goals and that perfection, not pleasure, is thus the key motivator in human life.

Alfred Adler (1870–1937) was one of Freud's earliest followers, although his relationship with Freud was quite brief and his approach to personality was drastically different. In Adler's **individual psychology,** people are motivated by purposes and goals—thus, perfection, not pleasure, is the key motivator in human life. Adler argued that people have the ability to take their genetic inheritance and their environmental experiences and act upon them creatively to become the person they want to be.

Adler thought that everyone strives for superiority by seeking to adapt, improve, and master the environment. Striving for superiority is our response to the uncomfortable feelings of inferiority that we experience as infants and young children when we interact with bigger, more powerful people. *Compensation* is Adler's term for the individual's attempt to overcome imagined or real inferiorities or weaknesses by developing one's own abilities. Adler believed that compensation is normal, and he said that we often make up for a weakness in one ability by excelling in a different one. For example, a person of small stature and limited physical abilities (like Adler himself) might compensate by excelling in academics.

Adler believed that birth order could influence how successfully a person could strive for superiority. He viewed firstborn children to be in a particularly vulnerable state given that they begin life as the center of attention but then are knocked off their pedestal by their siblings. Adler in fact believed that the firstborn are more likely to suffer from psychological disorders and to engage in criminal behavior. Youngest children, however, also are potentially in trouble because they are most likely to be spoiled. The healthiest birth order? According to Adler, all of us (including Adler) who are middle-born are in a particularly advantageous situation because we have our older siblings as built-in inspiration for superiority striving. Importantly, though, Adler did not believe that anyone was doomed by birth order. Rather, sensitive parents could help children at any place in the family to negotiate their needs for superiority.

Evaluating the Psychodynamic Perspectives

Although psychodynamic theories have diverged from Freud's original psychoanalytic version, they share some core principles:

- Personality is determined both by current experiences and, as the original psychoanalytic theory proposed, by early life experiences.

- Personality can be better understood by examining it developmentally—as a series of stages that unfold with the individual's physical, cognitive, and socioemotional development.

- We mentally transform our experiences, giving them meaning that shapes our personality.

  - The mind is not all consciousness; unconscious motives lie behind some of our puzzling behavior.

    - The individual's inner world often conflicts with the outer demands of reality, creating anxiety that is not easy to resolve.

      - Personality and adjustment—not just the experimental laboratory topics of sensation, perception, and learning—are rightful and important topics of psychological inquiry.

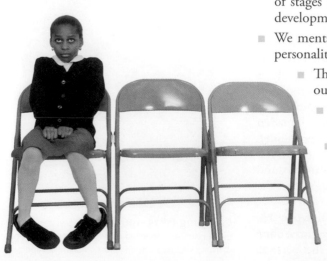

Psychodynamic perspectives have come under fire for a variety of reasons. Some critics say that psychodynamic theorists overemphasize the influence of early family experiences on personality and do not acknowledge that people retain the capacity for change and adaptation throughout life. Moreover, some psychologists believe that Freud and Jung put too much faith in the unconscious mind's ability to control behavior. Others object that Freud placed too much importance on sexuality in explaining personality; we humans are not born into the world with only a bundle of sexual and aggressive instincts, this camp insists.

Some have argued, too, that psychoanalysis is not a theory that researchers can test through empirical studies. However, numerous empirical studies on concepts such as defense mechanisms and the unconscious have proved this criticism to be unfounded (Cramer, 2008a, 2009; Hibbard & others, 2010; Strick, Dijksterhuis, & van Baaren, 2010). At the same time, another version of this argument may be accurate. Although it is certainly possible to test hypotheses derived from psychoanalytic theory through research, the question remains whether psychoanalytically oriented individuals who believe strongly in Freud's ideas would be open to research results that call for serious changes in the theory.

In light of these criticisms, it may be hard to appreciate why Freud continues to have an impact on psychology. It is useful to keep in mind that Freud made a number of important contributions, including being the first to propose that childhood is crucial to later functioning, that development might be understood in terms of stages, and that unconscious processes might play a significant role in human life.

2· HUMANISTIC PERSPECTIVES

Humanistic perspectives stress a person's capacity for personal growth and positive human qualities. Humanistic psychologists believe that we all have the ability to control our lives and to achieve what we desire (Cain, 2001; M. Cooper & others, 2010; M. B. Smith, 2001).

Humanistic perspectives contrast with both psychodynamic perspectives and behaviorism, discussed in Chapter 6. Humanistic theorists sought to move beyond Freudian psychoanalysis and behaviorism to a theory that might capture the rich and potentially positive aspects of human nature.

Maslow's Approach

A leading architect of the humanistic movement was Abraham Maslow (1908–1970), whose hierarchy of needs we considered in Chapter 10. Maslow referred to humanistic psychology as *third force* psychology because it stressed neither Freudian drives nor the stimulus–response principles of behaviorism. Maslow believed that we can learn the most about human personality by focusing on the very best examples of human beings—self-actualizers.

Recall that at the top of Maslow's (1954, 1971) hierarchy was the need for self-actualization. Self-actualization is the motivation to develop one's full potential as a human being. Maslow described self-actualizers as spontaneous, creative, and possessing a childlike capacity for awe. According to Maslow, a person at this optimal level of existence would be tolerant of others, have a gentle sense of humor, and be likely to pursue the greater good. Self-actualizers also maintain a capacity for "peak experiences," or breathtaking moments of spiritual insight. As examples of self-actualized individuals, Maslow included Pablo Casals (cellist), Albert Einstein (physicist), Ralph Waldo Emerson (writer), William James (psychologist), Thomas Jefferson (politician), Eleanor Roosevelt (humanitarian, diplomat), and Albert Schweitzer (humanitarian).

Created four decades ago, Maslow's list of self-actualized individuals is clearly biased. Maslow focused on highly successful individuals who he thought represented the best of the human species. Because Maslow concentrated on people who were successful in a particular historical context, his self-actualizers were limited to those who had opportunities for success in that setting. Maslow thus named considerably more men than women, and most of the individuals were from Western cultures and of European

test yourself

1. What three structures of personality did Freud describe, and how did he define each?
2. What are Freud's psychosexual stages of personality development?
3. What criticisms have been leveled at psychodynamic theories of personality?

● **humanistic perspectives** Theoretical views stressing a person's capacity for personal growth and positive human qualities.

Carl Rogers (1902–1987) Rogers was a pioneer in the development of the humanistic perspective.

● **unconditional positive regard** Rogers's construct referring to the individual's need to be accepted, valued, and treated positively regardless of his or her behavior.

● **conditions of worth** The standards that the individual must live up to in order to receive positive regard from others.

ancestry. Today, we might add to Maslow's list individuals such as the Dalai Lama, Tibetan spiritual and political leader; Wangari Maathai, a Kenyan woman acclaimed for her work on behalf of democracy and the environment; and Muhammad Yunus, a Bangladeshi banker and crusader against poverty. All are recipients of the Nobel Peace Prize in recent years.

Rogers's Approach

The other key figure in the development of humanistic psychology, Carl Rogers (1902–1987), began his career as a psychotherapist struggling to understand the unhappiness of the individuals he encountered in therapy. Rogers's groundbreaking work established the foundations for more contemporary studies of personal growth and self-determination.

Like Freud, Rogers began his inquiry into human nature with troubled people. In the knotted, anxious verbal stream of his clients, Rogers (1961) noted the things that seemed to be keeping them from reaching their full potential. Based on his clinical observations, Rogers devised his own approach to personality. He believed that we are all born with the raw ingredients of a fulfilling life. We simply need the right conditions to thrive. Just as a sunflower seed, once planted in rich soil and given water and sunshine, will grow into a strong and healthy flower, all humans will flourish in the appropriate environment.

This analogy is particularly apt and reveals the differences between Rogers's view of human nature and Freud's. A sunflower seed does not have to be shaped away from its dark natural tendencies by social constraints, nor does it have to reach a difficult compromise between its vile true impulses and reality. Instead, given the appropriate environment, it will grow into a beautiful flower. Rogers believed that, similarly, each person is born with natural capacities for growth and fulfillment. We are also endowed with an innate sense—a gut feeling—that allows us to evaluate whether an experience is good or bad for us. Finally, we are all born with a need for positive regard from others. We need to be loved, liked, or accepted by people around us. As children interacting with our parents, we learn early on to value the feeling that they value us, and we gain a sense of self-worth.

EXPLAINING UNHAPPINESS

If we have innate tendencies toward growth and fulfillment, why are so many people so unhappy? The problem arises when our need for positive regard from others is not met *unconditionally*. **Unconditional positive regard** is Rogers's term for being accepted, valued, and treated positively regardless of one's behavior. Unfortunately, others often value us only when we behave in particular ways that meet what Rogers called **conditions of worth.** These conditions are the standards we must live up to in order to receive positive regard from others. For instance, parents might give their son positive regard only when he achieves in school, succeeds on the soccer field, or chooses a profession that they themselves value. According to Rogers, as we grow up, people who are central to our lives condition us to move away from our genuine feelings, to earn their love by pursuing those goals that they value, even if those goals do not reflect our deepest wishes.

Rogers's theory includes the idea that we develop a *self-concept,* our conscious representation of who we are and who we wish to become, during childhood. Optimally, this self-concept reflects our genuine, innate desires, but it also can be influenced by conditions of worth. Conditions of worth can become part of who we think we ought to be. As a result, we can become alienated from our genuine feelings and strive to actualize a self that is not who we were meant to be. A person who dedicates himself or herself to such goals might be very successful by outward appearances but might feel utterly unfilled. Such an individual might be able to check off all the important boxes in life's to-do lists and complete all that he or she is "supposed to do," but never feel truly happy.

PROMOTING OPTIMAL FUNCTIONING

To remedy this situation, Rogers believed that the person must reconnect with his or her true feelings and desires. He proposed that to achieve this reconnection, the individual must experience a relationship that includes three essential qualities: unconditional positive regard (as defined above), empathy, and genuineness. We consider each in turn.

First, Rogers said that regardless of what they do, people need unconditional positive regard. Although an individual might lack unconditional positive regard in childhood, he or she can experience this unconditional acceptance from others later, in friendships and/or romantic relationships or during sessions with a therapist. Even when a person's behavior is inappropriate, obnoxious, or unacceptable, he or she still needs the respect, comfort, and love of others (Assor, Roth, & Deci, 2004).

Second, Rogers said that individuals can become more fulfilled by interacting with people who are empathic toward them. Empathy involves being a sensitive listener and understanding another's true feelings.

Genuineness is a third requirement in the individual's path to become fully functioning. Being genuine means being open with one's feelings and dropping all pretenses and facades. The importance that Rogers placed on the therapist's acting genuinely in the therapeutic relationship demonstrates his strong belief in the positive character of human nature. For Rogers, we can help others simply by being present for them as the authentic individuals we really are.

Thus, according to Rogers, unconditional positive regard, empathy, and genuineness are three essential ingredients of healthy human relations. Anyone—a manager, teacher, counselor, member of the clergy—who is interested in promoting optimal human functioning can apply these principles.

Evaluating the Humanistic Perspectives

The humanistic perspectives emphasize that the way we perceive ourselves and the world around us is an essential element of personality. Humanistic psychologists also stress that we need to consider the whole person and the positive bent of human nature (Schneider, 2009). Their emphasis on conscious experience has given us the view that personality contains a well of potential that can be developed to its fullest (C. E. Hill, 2000).

Some critics believe that humanistic psychologists are too optimistic about human nature and that they overestimate people's freedom and rationality. Others say that the humanists may promote excessive self-love and narcissism by encouraging people to think so positively about themselves. Still others argue that humanistic approaches do not hold individuals accountable for their behaviors, if all negative human behavior is seen as emerging out of negative situations.

Self-determination theory, which we considered in Chapter 10, demonstrates the way that psychologists have studied humanistic ideas that might appear too abstract and difficult to test. Their work bears witness to the enduring impact of humanistic perspectives on contemporary personality psychology.

3· TRAIT PERSPECTIVES

If you are setting up a friend on a blind date, you are likely to describe the person in terms of his or her *traits,* or lasting personality characteristics. Trait perspectives on personality have been the dominant approach for the past three decades.

Trait Theories

According to **trait theories,** personality consists of broad, enduring dispositions (traits) that tend to lead to characteristic responses. In other words, we can describe people in terms of the ways they behave, such as whether they are outgoing, friendly, private, or hostile. People who have a strong tendency to behave in certain ways are referred to as

test yourself

1. What do the humanistic perspectives on personality emphasize?
2. What name did Maslow give to the motivation to develop one's full human potential?
3. According to Rogers, what three qualities do individuals need in order to connect with their feelings and desires? How did Rogers define each?

● **trait theories** Theoretical views stressing that personality consists of broad, enduring dispositions (traits) that tend to lead to characteristic responses.

"Gerry's downloading a personality."

© Rob Murray. www.CartoonStock.com

"high" on the traits; those with a weak tendency to behave in these ways are "low" on the traits. Although trait theorists differ about which traits make up personality, they agree that traits are the fundamental building blocks of personality (De Pauw & Mervielde, 2010; McCrae & Sutin, 2009). The trait approach was founded by Gordon Allport (1897–1967).

Allport, sometimes referred to as the father of American personality psychology, was particularly bothered by the negative view of humanity that psychoanalysis portrayed. He rejected the notion that the unconscious was central to an understanding of personality. He further believed that to understand healthy people, we must focus on their lives in the present, not on their childhood experiences. Allport, who took a pragmatic approach to understanding the person, asserted that if you want to know something about someone, you should "just ask him" (or her).

Allport believed that personality psychology should focus on understanding healthy, well-adjusted individuals. He described such persons as showing a positive but objective sense of self and others, interest in issues beyond their own experience, a sense of humor, common sense, and a unifying philosophy of life—typically but not always provided by religious faith (Allport, 1961). Allport dedicated himself to the idea that psychology should have relevance to social issues facing modern society, and his scholarship has influenced not only personality psychology but also the psychology of religion and prejudice.

In defining personality, Allport (1961) stressed each person's uniqueness and capacity to adapt to the environment. For Allport, the unit we should use to understand personality is the trait. He defined traits as mental structures that make different situations the same for the person. For Allport, traits are structures that are inside a person that cause behavior to be similar even in different situations. For instance, if Carly is sociable, she is likely to behave in an outgoing, happy fashion whether she is at a party or in a group study session. Allport's definition implies that behavior should be consistent across different situations.

We get a sense of the down-to-earth quality of Allport's approach to personality by looking at his study of traits. In the late 1930s, Allport and his colleague H. S. Odbert (1936) sat down with two big unabridged dictionaries and pulled out all the words that could be used to describe a person—a method called the *lexical approach.*

This approach reflects the idea that if a trait is important to people in real life, it ought to be represented in the natural language people use to talk about one another. Furthermore, the more important a trait is, the more likely it is that it should be represented by a single word. Allport and Odbert started with 18,000 words and gradually pared down that list to 4,500.

As you can appreciate, 4,500 traits make for a very long questionnaire. Imagine that you are asked to rate a person, Ignacio, on some traits. You use a scale from 1 to 5, with 1 meaning "not at all" and 5 meaning "very much." If you give Ignacio a 5 on "outgoing," what do you think you might give him on "shy"? Clearly, we may not need 4,500 traits to summarize the way we describe personality. Still, how might we whittle down these descriptors further without losing something important?

With advances in statistical methods and the advent of computers, the lexical approach became considerably less unwieldy, as researchers began to analyze the words to look for underlying structures that might account for their overlap. Specifically, a statistical procedure called *factor analysis* allowed researchers to identify which traits go together in terms of how they are rated. Factor analysis essentially tells us what items on a scale people are responding to as if they mean the same thing. For example, if Ignacio got a 5 on "outgoing," he probably would get a 5 on "talkative" and a 1 or 2 on "shy."

One important characteristic of factor analysis is that it relies on the scientist to interpret the meaning of the factors, and the researcher must make some decisions about how many factors are enough to explain the data (Goldberg & Digman, 1994). In 1963, W. T. Norman reanalyzed the Allport and Odbert traits and concluded that only five factors were needed to summarize these traits. Norman's research set the stage for the dominant approach in personality psychology today: the five factor model (Digman, 1990).

The Five-Factor Model of Personality

Pick a friend and jot down 10 of that person's most notable personality traits. Did you perhaps list "reserved" or "a good leader"? "Responsible" or "unreliable"? "Sweet," "kind," or "friendly"? Maybe even "creative"? Researchers in personality psychology have found that there are essentially five broad personality dimensions that are represented in the natural language; these dimensions also summarize the various ways psychologists have studied traits (Costa & McCrae, 2006; Digman, 2002; Hogan, 2006; Rammstedt, Goldberg, & Borg, 2010).

The **big five factors of personality**—the broad traits that are thought to describe the main dimensions of personality—are neuroticism (which refers to the tendency to worry and experience negative emotions and is sometimes identified by its opposite, emotional stability), extraversion, openness to experience, agreeableness, and conscientiousness. Although personality psychologists typically refer to the traits as N, E, O, A, and C on the basis of the order in which they emerge in a factor analysis, if you create an anagram from these first letters of the trait names, you get the word *OCEAN*.

Figure 12.4 more fully defines the big five traits. Before reading further, to find out where you stand on these traits, see the Psychological Inquiry on p. 396.

Each of the big five traits has been the topic of extensive research (McCrae & Sutin, 2007; Ozer & Benet-Martinez, 2006). The following sampling of research findings on each trait sheds light on the interesting work that the five-factor model has inspired:

● **big five factors of personality** The five broad traits that are thought to describe the main dimensions of personality: neuroticism (emotional instability), extraversion, openness to experience, agreeableness, and conscientiousness.

- *Neuroticism* is related to feeling negative emotion more often than positive emotion in one's daily life and to experiencing more lingering negative states (Widiger, 2009). Neuroticism has been shown as well to relate to more health complaints (Carver & Connor-Smith, 2010). In a longitudinal study, individuals were tracked for nearly seven years. Neuroticism was associated with dying during the study (Fry & Debats, 2009). In general, neurotic individuals appear to suffer in silence: Acquaintances and observers have difficulty detecting how neurotic another person is (Vazire, 2010).

- Individuals high in *extraversion* are more likely than others to engage in social activities (Emmons & Diener, 1986) and to experience gratitude (McCullough, Emmons, & Tsang, 2002) and a strong sense of meaning in life (King & others, 2006). In addition, extraverts are more forgiving (L. Thompson & others, 2005). People rate extraverts as smiling and standing energetically and as dressing stylishly (Naumann & others, 2009), and observers know an extravert when they see one (Vazire, 2010). One study found that extraverted salespeople sold more cars, especially if they were also good at picking up interpersonal cues (Blickle, Wendel, & Ferris, 2010).

- *Openness to experience* is related to liberal values, open-mindedness, tolerance (McCrae & Sutin, 2009), and creativity (Silvia & others, 2009). Openness is also associated with superior cognitive functioning and IQ across the life span (Sharp & others, 2010). Individuals who rate themselves as open to experience are more likely to dress distinctively (Naumann & others, 2009), to pursue entrepreneurial goals (for instance, starting their own business), and to experience success in those pursuits (Zhao, Seibert, & Lumpkin, 2010). Individuals high on openness to experience are also more likely to interact with others on Internet websites and to use social media (Correa, Hinsley, & de Zuniga, 2010).

Openness	**C**onscientiousness	**E**xtraversion	**A**greeableness	**N**euroticism (emotional instability)
• Imaginative or practical	• Organized or disorganized	• Sociable or retiring	• Softhearted or ruthless	• Calm or anxious
• Interested in variety or routine	• Careful or careless	• Fun-loving or somber	• Trusting or suspicious	• Secure or insecure
• Independent or conforming	• Disciplined or impulsive	• Energetic or reserved	• Helpful or uncooperative	• Self-satisfied or self-pitying

FIGURE 12.4   The Big Five Factors of Personality Each of the broad traits encompasses more narrow traits and characteristics. Use the acronym *OCEAN* to remember the big five personality factors: openness, conscientiousness, extraversion, agreeableness, and neuroticism.

psychological *inquiry*

Your Personality Traits: Who Are You?

Use the following scale to rate yourself on the trait items listed below. That is, next to each trait, write the number that best corresponds to how you rate yourself with respect to that trait.

Disagree strongly	Disagree moderately	Disagree a little	Neither agree nor disagree	Agree a little	Agree moderately	Agree strongly
1	**2**	**3**	**4**	**5**	**6**	**7**

I see myself as:

1. ____ Extraverted, enthusiastic.

2. ____ Critical, quarrelsome.

3. ____ Dependable, self-disciplined.

4. ____ Anxious, easily upset.

5. ____ Open to new experiences, complex.

6. ____ Reserved, quiet.

7. ____ Sympathetic, warm.

8. ____ Disorganized, careless.

9. ____ Calm, emotionally stable.

10. ____ Conventional, uncreative.

You have just completed the Ten-Item Personality Inventory, or TIPI (Gosling, Rentfrow, & Swann, 2003), a brief measure of the big five personality traits. All of the even-numbered items are *reverse-scored*, meaning your ratings should be reversed for these. (Reverse items are included in scales to fully identify a characteristic and to make sure that respondents are actually reading the items carefully.) So, if you gave item number 2 a rating of 7, it should be a 1; a rating of 6 should be a 2, and so on. The first step in calculating your scores is to reverse your scores on these even-numbered items. Then average together your ratings for the following items for each trait, using the steps in the table below.

Trait	Items	Sum of Your Ratings	Your Score (divide the sum by 2)	Low Score	Medium Score	High Score
Emotional Stability (the opposite of neuroticism)	4, 9	____	____	3.41	4.83	6.25
Extraversion	1, 6	____	____	2.99	4.44	5.89
Openness to Experience	5, 10	____	____	4.13	5.38	6.45
Agreeableness	2, 7	____	____	4.12	5.23	6.34
Conscientiousness	3, 8	____	____	4.08	5.40	6.72

The last three columns provide information about what those scores mean. The "medium scores" reflect the mean score found in a sample of 1,813 participants. The "low scores" are that mean minus one standard deviation. The "high scores" are the mean plus one standard deviation. Now answer the following questions.

1. Do your scores reflect your sense of who you really are? Explain.

2. Why do you think the researchers included one reverse-scored item for each scale?

3. The guides for low, medium, and high scores were provided by data from a sample of college students at the University of Texas. Do you think these norms might differ at your institution? Why or why not?

4. Although this is a very short assessment, research supports the idea that it does measure these traits because scores on this short scale are highly correlated with scores on longer scales measuring the same traits (Ehrhart & others, 2009). What does it mean to say that the scores are highly correlated?

- *Agreeableness* is related to generosity and altruism (Caprara & others, 2010), to reports of religious faith (Saroglou, 2010), and to more satisfying romantic relationships (Donnellan, Larsen-Rife, & Conger, 2005). There are also links between agreeableness and viewing other people positively (Wood, Harms, & Vazire, 2010). In online dating profiles, agreeable individuals are less likely than people who score low on this trait to lie about themselves (Hall & others, 2010).

- *Conscientiousness* is a key factor in a variety of life domains. Researchers have found that conscientiousness is positively related to high school and college students' grade point averages (Noftle & Robins, 2007). Conscientiousness is also linked to better-quality friendships (Jensen-Campbell & Malcolm, 2007), to higher levels of religious faith (Saroglou, 2010), and to a forgiving attitude (Balliet, 2010). Conscientiousness is associated with dressing neatly, especially in the case of men (Naumann & others, 2009), and, like openness, is related to entrepreneurial success (Zhao, Seibert, & Lumpkin, 2010). Low levels of conscientiousness are associated with criminal behavior (Wiebe, 2004) and substance abuse (Walton & Roberts, 2004).

Keep in mind that because the five factors are theoretically independent of one another, a person can be any combination of them. Do you know a neurotic extravert or an agreeable introvert, for example?

CROSS-CULTURAL STUDIES ON THE BIG FIVE

Some research on the big five factors addresses the extent to which the factors appear in personality profiles in different cultures (Lingjaerde, Foreland, & Engvik, 2001; Miacic & Goldberg, 2007; Pukrop, Sass, & Steinmeyer, 2000). The question is, do the big five show up in the assessment of personality in cultures around the world? Some research suggests that they do: A version of the five factors appears in people in countries as diverse as Canada, Finland, Poland, China, and Japan (Paunonen & others, 1992; X. Zhou & others, 2009). Among the big five, the factors most likely to emerge across cultures and languages are extraversion, agreeableness, and conscientiousness, with neuroticism and openness to experience being more likely to emerge only in English-speaking samples (De Raad & others, 2010).

ANIMAL STUDIES ON THE BIG FIVE

Researchers have found evidence for at least some of the big five personality traits in animals, including domestic dogs (Gosling, 2008; Gosling, Kwan, & John, 2003) and hyenas (Gosling & John, 1999). In addition, studies have turned up evidence for general personality traits (such as overall outgoingness) in orangutans, geese, lizards, fish, cockatiels, and squid (Fox & Millam, 2010; McGhee & Travis, 2010; Sinn, Gosling, & Moltschaniwskyj, 2008; Weinstein, Capitanio, & Gosling, 2008; Wilson & Godin, 2010), though some researchers have found that squid "personality" may be more a function of environmental factors than stable individual differences (Sinn & others, 2010).

Evaluating the Trait Perspectives

Despite strong evidence for the big five, some personality researchers say that these traits might not end up being the ultimate list of broad traits; they argue that more specific traits are better predictors of behavior (Fung & Ng, 2006; Moskowitz, 2010; Simms, 2007). One alternative, the HEXACO model, incorporates a sixth dimension, honesty/humility, to capture the moral dimensions of personality (Ashton & Kibeom, 2008). Other researchers argue that five factors is too many and that we can best understand personality as one big dimension, with extraversion, agreeableness, openness to experience, and conscientiousness at one end, and with neuroticism at the other end (Erdle & others, 2010). In this single-dimension view, high-scoring individuals might be described as being outgoing, nice, creative, reliable, and emotionally stable—in other words, having a "really good" personality.

More generally, studying people in terms of their personality traits has practical value. Identifying a person's traits allows us to know that individual better. Psychologists have

Sam Gosling, a professor at the University of Texas, is a personality psychologist who has conducted research on animal personality as well as the ways that we express our traits through websites, dorm room decoration, and other contexts.

● **personological and life story perspectives** Theoretical views stressing that the way to understand the person is to focus on his or her life history and life story.

learned a great deal about the connections between personality and health, ways of thinking, career success, and relations with others using traits (Fry & Debats, 2009; Leary & Hoyle, 2009a; Levenson & Aldwin, 2006; Roberts & others, 2007).

The trait approach has been faulted, however, for missing the importance of situational factors in personality and behavior (Leary & Hoyle, 2009b). For example, a person might rate herself as introverted among new people but very outgoing with family and friends. Further, some have criticized the trait perspective for painting an individual's personality with very broad strokes. They say that although traits can tell us much about someone whom we have never met, they reveal little about the nuances of an individual's personality.

4· PERSONOLOGICAL AND LIFE STORY PERSPECTIVES

If two people have the same levels of the big five traits, do they essentially have the same personality? Researchers who approach personality from the personological and life story perspectives do not think so (McAdams & Olson, 2010). One of the goals of personality psychology is to understand how each of us is unique and in some ways like no other human being on earth. **Personological and life story perspectives** stress that the way to understand the uniqueness of each person is to focus on his or her life history and life story.

Murray's Personological Approach

Henry Murray (1893–1988) was a young biochemistry graduate student when he became interested in the psychology of personality after meeting Carl Jung and reading his work. Murray went on to become the director of the Psychological Clinic at Harvard at the same time that Gordon Allport was on the faculty there. Murray and Allport saw personality very differently. Whereas Allport was most comfortable focusing on conscious experience and traits, Murray embraced the psychodynamic notion of unconscious motivation.

Murray coined the word *personology* to refer to the study of the whole person. He believed that to understand a person, we have to know that person's history, including the physical, psychological, and sociological aspects of the person's life. Murray applied his insights into personality during World War II, when he was called upon by the Office of Strategic Services (or OSS, a precursor to the CIA) to develop a psychological profile of Adolf Hitler. That document, produced in 1943, accurately predicted that Hitler would commit suicide rather than be taken alive by the Allies. Murray's analysis of Hitler was the first "offender profile," and it has served as a model for modern criminal profiling.

The aspect of Murray's research that has had the most impact on contemporary personality psychology is his approach to motivation. Murray believed that our motives are largely unknown to us. This circumstance complicates the study of motivation: Researchers cannot simply ask people to say what it is they want. To address the issue, Murray, along with Christiana Morgan, developed the Thematic Apperception Test (TAT), to which we return later in this chapter (Morgan & Murray, 1935). For the TAT, a person looks at an ambiguous picture and writes or tells a story about what is going on in the scene. A variety of scoring procedures have been devised for analyzing the unconscious motives that are revealed in imaginative stories (C. P. Smith, 1992). These scoring procedures involve *content analysis,* a procedure in which a psychologist takes the person's story and codes it for different images, words, and so forth. Although Murray posited 22 different unconscious needs, three have been the focus of most current research:

■ *Need for achievement:* an enduring concern for attaining excellence and overcoming obstacles

■ *Need for affiliation:* an enduring concern for establishing and maintaining interpersonal connections

■ *Need for power:* an enduring concern for having impact on the social world

Henry Murray's psychological profile of Adolf Hitler, developed in 1943 during World War II, serves as a model for criminal profiling today.

David Winter (2005) analyzed the motives revealed in inaugural addresses of U.S. presidents. He found that certain needs revealed in these speeches corresponded to later events during the person's presidency. For instance, presidents who scored high on need for achievement (such as Jimmy Carter) were less successful during their terms. Note that the need for achievement is about striving for personal excellence and may have little to do with playing politics, negotiating interpersonal relationships, or delegating responsibility. Presidents who scored high on need for power tended to be judged as more successful (John F. Kennedy, Ronald Reagan), and presidents whose addresses included a great deal of imagery about making positive interpersonal connections or avoiding rejection (suggesting a high need for affiliation) tended to experience scandal during their presidencies (Richard M. Nixon).

Research by David Winter (2005) has analyzed presidential motives in inaugural addresses such as those delivered by Richard M. Nixon (left) and John F. Kennedy (right). Winter found that certain needs revealed in these speeches corresponded to later events during these individuals' terms in office.

The Life Story Approach to Identity

Following in the Murray tradition, Dan McAdams (2001, 2006; McAdams & Olson, 2010) developed the *life story approach* to identity. His work centers on the idea that each of us has a unique life story, full of ups and downs. Our life story represents our memories of what makes us who we are. This life story is a constantly changing narrative that provides us with a sense of coherence. For McAdams, our life story is our very identity.

McAdams (1989) also introduced the concept of intimacy motivation. The *intimacy motive* is an enduring concern for warm interpersonal encounters for their own sake. Intimacy motivation is revealed in the warm, positive interpersonal imagery in the stories people tell. Intimacy motive has been shown to relate to positive outcomes. For instance, college men who were high on intimacy motivation showed heightened levels of happiness and lowered work strain some 30 years later (McAdams & Bryant, 1987). A study of the coming-out stories of gay men and lesbians demonstrated that intimacy-related imagery (for example, experiencing falling in love or warm acceptance from others) was associated with well-being and personality development (King & Smith, 2005).

Other personality psychologists have relied on narrative accounts of experiences as a means of understanding how individuals create meaning in life events (King & others, 2000). In one study, parents of children with Down syndrome wrote down the story of how they found out about their child's diagnosis. Parents whose stories ended happily scored higher on measures of happiness, life meaning, and personal growth than others. Parents who told stories about struggling to make sense of the experience tended to mature psychologically over time (King & others, 2000). By using narratives, personal documents (such as diaries), and even letters and speeches, personality psychologists search for the deeper meaning that cannot be revealed through tests that ask people directly about whether specific items capture their personality traits.

Finally, some personality psychologists take very seriously Murray's commitment to understanding the whole person, by focusing on just one case. *Psychobiography* is a means of inquiry in which the personality psychologist attempts to apply a personality theory to a single person's life (Runyon, 2007; W. T. Schultz, 2005). Erik Erikson's study of Gandhi's life, described in Chapter 2, is an example of a psychobiography. Psychobiographies have been written about a diverse array of figures, including Sigmund Freud, Gordon Allport, George W. Bush, Osama bin Laden, and Elvis Presley (W. T. Schultz, 2005).

● **social cognitive perspectives** Theoretical views emphasizing conscious awareness, beliefs, expectations, and goals.

Albert Bandura (b. 1925) Bandura's practical, problem-solving social cognitive approach has made a lasting mark on personality theory and therapy.

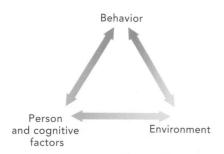

FIGURE 12.5   Bandura's Social Cognitive Theory Bandura's social cognitive theory emphasizes reciprocal influences of behavior, environment, and person/cognitive factors.

Evaluating the Personological and Life Story Perspectives

Studying individuals through narratives and personal interviews provides an extraordinarily rich opportunity for the researcher. Imagine having the choice of reading someone's diary versus seeing that person's scores on a questionnaire measuring traits. Not many would pass up the chance to read the diary.

However, life story studies are difficult and time-consuming. Personologist Robert W. White (1992) referred to the study of narratives as exploring personality "the long way." Collecting interviews and narratives is often just the first step. Turning these personal stories into scientific data means transforming them into numbers, and that process involves extensive coding and content analysis. Further, for narrative studies to be worthwhile, they must tell us something we could not have found out in a much easier way (King, 2003). Moreover, psychobiographical inquiries are prone to the biases of the scholars who conduct them and may not serve the scientific goal of generalizability.

5· SOCIAL COGNITIVE PERSPECTIVES

Social cognitive perspectives on personality emphasize conscious awareness, beliefs, expectations, and goals. While incorporating principles from behaviorism (see Chapter 6), social cognitive psychologists explore the person's ability to reason; to think about the past, present, and future; and to reflect on the self. They emphasize the person's individual interpretation of situations and thus focus on the uniqueness of each person by examining how behavior is tailored to the diversity of situations in which people find themselves. Social cognitive theorists are not interested in broad traits such as the big five. Rather, they investigate how more specific factors, such as beliefs, relate to behavior and performance. In this section we consider the two major social cognitive approaches, developed respectively by Albert Bandura and Walter Mischel.

Bandura's Social Cognitive Theory

B. F. Skinner, whose work we examined in Chapter 6, believed that there is no such thing as "personality"; rather, he emphasized behavior and felt that internal mental states were irrelevant to psychology. Albert Bandura found Skinner's approach to be far too simplistic for understanding human functioning (1986, 2001, 2009, 2010a, 2010b). Bandura took the basic tenets of behaviorism and added a recognition of the role of mental processes in determining behavior. Whereas Skinner saw behavior as caused by the situation, Bandura pointed out that the person can cause situations, and sometimes the very definition of the situation itself depends on the person's beliefs about it. For example, is that upcoming exam an opportunity to show your stuff or a threat to your ability to achieve your goals? The test is the same either way, but a person's unique take on the test can influence a host of behaviors (studying hard, worrying, and so on).

Bandura's social cognitive theory states that behavior, environment, and person/cognitive factors are *all* important in understanding personality. Bandura coined the term *reciprocal determinism* to describe the way behavior, environment, and person/cognitive factors interact to create personality (Figure 12.5). The environment can determine a person's behavior, and the person can act to change the environment. Similarly, person/cognitive factors can both influence behavior and be influenced by behavior. From Bandura's perspective, then, behavior is a product of a variety of forces, some of which come from the situation and some of which the person brings to the situation. We now review the important processes and variables Bandura used to understand personality.

OBSERVATIONAL LEARNING

Recall from Chapter 6 Bandura's belief that observational learning is a key aspect of how we learn. By observing others behave and noticing the consequences of their actions, we might come to adopt the behavior ourselves. For example, a boy might observe that his mother's hostile exchanges with people are an effective way to get what she wants. Later, when the boy is with his peers, he might adopt the same strategy. Social cognitive theorists believe that we acquire a wide range of behaviors, thoughts, and feelings by watching others' behavior and that our observations strongly shape our personality (Bandura, 2010a).

PERSONAL CONTROL

Social cognitive theorists emphasize that we can regulate and control our own behavior despite our changing environment (Bandura, 2008, 2009; Mischel, 2004). For example, a young executive who observes her boss behave in an overbearing and sarcastic manner toward his subordinates may find the behavior distasteful and go out of her way to encourage and support her own staff. Psychologists commonly describe a sense of behavioral control as coming from inside the person (an *internal locus of control*) or outside the person (an *external locus of control*). When we feel that we ourselves are controlling our choices and behaviors, the locus of control is internal, but when other influences are controlling them, the locus of control is external.

Consider the question of whether you will perform well on your next test. With an internal locus of control, you believe that you are in command of your choices and behaviors, and your answer will depend on what you can realistically do (for example, study hard or attend a special review session). With an external locus of control, however, you might say that you cannot predict how things will go because so many outside factors influence performance, such as whether the test is difficult, how the curve is set in the course, and whether the instructor is fair. Feeling a strong sense of personal control is vital to many aspects of performance, well-being, and physical health (Bandura, 2009; Morrison, Ponitz, & McClelland, 2010). Self-efficacy is an important aspect of the experience of control, as we next consider.

SELF-EFFICACY

Self-efficacy is the belief that one can master a situation and produce positive change. Bandura and others have shown that self-efficacy is related to a number of positive developments in people's lives, including solving problems and becoming more sociable (Bandura, 2001, 2009, 2010b; Schunk, 2011). Self-efficacy influences whether people even try to develop healthy habits, as well as how much effort they expend in coping with stress, how long they persist in the face of obstacles, and how much stress and pain they experience (Brister & others, 2006; Sarkar, Fisher, & Schillinger, 2006). Self-efficacy is also related to whether people initiate psychotherapy to deal with their problems and whether it succeeds (Longo, Lent, & Brown, 1992). In addition, researchers have found that self-efficacy is linked with successful job interviewing and job performance (Tay, Ang, & Van Dyne, 2006). We will return to the topics of personal control and self-efficacy at the end of this chapter.

● **self-efficacy** The belief that one can master a situation and produce positive change.

Mischel's Contributions

Like Bandura, Walter Mischel is a social cognitive psychologist who has explored how personality influences behavior. Mischel has left his mark on the field of personality in two notable ways. First, his critique of the idea of consistency in behavior ignited a flurry of controversy. Second, he has proposed the CAPS model, a new way of thinking about personality.

MISCHEL'S CRITIQUE OF CONSISTENCY

Whether we are talking about unconscious sexual conflicts, traits, or motives, all of the approaches we have considered so far maintain that these various personality characteristics are an enduring influence on behavior. This shared assumption was attacked in 1968 with the publication of Walter Mischel's *Personality and Assessment,* a book that nearly ended the psychological study of personality.

To understand Mischel's argument, recall Gordon Allport's definition of a trait as a characteristic that ought to make different situations equivalent for a given person. This quality of traits suggests that a person should behave consistently in different situations—in other words, the individual should exhibit *cross-situational consistency*. For example, an outgoing person should act highly sociably whether she is at a party or in the library. However, Mischel looked at the research compiled on trait prediction of behavior and found it to be lacking. He concluded that there was no evidence for cross-situational consistency in behavior—and thus no evidence for the existence of personality as it had been previously conceptualized.

Rather than understanding personality as consisting of broad, internal traits that make for consistent behavior across situations, Mischel said that personality often changes according to a given situation. Mischel asserted that behavior is discriminative—that is, a person looks at each situation and responds accordingly. Mischel's view is called *situationism*, the idea that personality and behavior often vary considerably from one context to another.

Personality psychologists responded to Mischel's situationist attack in a variety of ways (Donnellan, Lucas, & Fleeson, 2009; Funder, 2009; Hogan, 2009). Researchers showed that it is not a matter of *whether* personality predicts behavior but *when and how* it does so, often in combination with situational factors (Sherman, Nave, & Funder, 2010). The research findings were that

- The narrower and more limited a trait is, the more likely it will predict behavior.
- Some people are consistent on some traits, and other people are consistent on other traits.
- Personality traits exert a stronger influence on an individual's behavior when situational influences are less powerful. A very powerful situation is one that contains many clear cues about how a person is supposed to behave. For example, even a highly talkative person typically sits quietly during a class lecture. In weaker situations, however, such as during leisure time, the person may spend most of the time talking.

Moreover, individuals select the situations they are in. Consequently, even if situations determine behavior, traits play a role by influencing which situations people choose—such as going to a party or staying home to study (Sherman, Nave, & Funder, 2010).

Let's pause and reflect on what it means to be consistent. You might believe that being consistent is part of being a genuine, honest person and that tailoring behavior to different situations means being fake. On the other hand, consider that a person who never changes his or her behavior to fit a situation might be unpleasant to have around. For example, think about someone who cannot put aside his competitive drive even when playing checkers with a 4-year-old. Clearly, adaptive behavior might involve sometimes being consistent and sometimes tailoring behavior to the situation.

Over time, Mischel (2004, 2009) has developed an approach to personality that he feels is better suited to capturing the nuances of the relationship between the individual and situations in producing behavior. Imagine trying to study personality without using traits or broad motives. What would you focus on? Mischel's answer to this dilemma is his CAPS theory.

CAPS THEORY

Recall Mischel's (2004) work on delay of gratification from Chapter 10. In that work, children were left in a room with a tempting cookie. Mischel measured the amount of time the kids were able to delay eating the cookie, and he and his colleagues continued to study those children for many years. They found that the amount of time the children were able to delay gratification predicted their academic performance in high school and even college (Mischel, 2004). These results indicate remarkable stability in personality over time.

Mischel's revised approach to personality is concerned with just such stability (or coherence) in the pattern of behavior *over time,* not with consistency across differing situations. That is, Mischel and his colleagues have studied how behaviors in very different situations have a coherent pattern, such as a child's waiting to eat the cookie versus that same individual's (as a grown college student) deciding to stay home and study instead of going out to party.

In keeping with the social cognitive emphasis on the person's cognitive abilities and mental states, Mischel conceptualizes personality as a set of interconnected **cognitive affective processing systems (CAPS)** (Mischel, 2004, 2009; Mischel & Shoda, 1999; Orom & Cervone, 2009). According to this approach, our thoughts and emotions about ourselves and the world affect our behavior and become linked in ways that matter to behavior. Personal control and self-efficacy are psychological connections that a person has made among situations, beliefs, and behaviors. Take the example of Raoul, who is excited by the challenge of a new assignment from his boss. Raoul may think about all the possible strategies to complete the project and get down to work immediately. Yet this go-getter may respond differently to other challenges, depending on who gives the assignment, what it is, or whether he feels he can do a good job.

CAPS is concerned with how personality works, not with what it is (Shoda & Mischel, 2006). From the CAPS perspective, it makes no sense to ask a person "How extraverted are you?" because the answer is always, "It depends." A person may be outgoing in one situation (on the first day of class) and not so in another (right before an exam), and that unique pattern of flexibility is what personality is all about.

Not surprisingly, CAPS theory focuses on how people behave in different situations and how they uniquely interpret situational features. From this perspective, knowing that Crystal is an extravert tells us little about how she will behave in a group discussion in her psychology class. We need to know about Crystal's beliefs and goals in the discussion. For example, does she want to impress the instructor? Is she a psychology major? We also need to know about her personal understanding of the situation itself: Is this an opportunity to shine, or is she thinking about her test for the next class? Research using the CAPS approach generally involves observing individuals behaving in a variety of contexts in order to identify the patterns of associations that exist among beliefs, emotions, and behavior for each person across different situations (Romero-Canyas & others, 2010).

● **cognitive affective processing systems (CAPS)** Mischel's theoretical model for describing that our thoughts and emotions about ourselves and the world affect our behavior and become linked in ways that matter to behavior.

Evaluating the Social Cognitive Perspectives

Social cognitive theory focuses on the interactions of individuals with their environments. The social cognitive approach has fostered a scientific climate for understanding personality that highlights the observation of behavior. Social cognitive theory emphasizes the influence of cognitive processes in explaining personality and suggests that people have the ability to control their environment.

Critics of the social cognitive perspective on personality take issue with one or more aspects of the theory. For example, they charge that

- The social cognitive approach is too concerned with change and situational influences on personality. It does not pay adequate tribute to the enduring qualities of personality.
- Social cognitive theory ignores the role biology plays in personality.
- In its attempt to incorporate both the situation and the person into its view of personality, social cognitive psychology tends to lead to very specific predictions for each person in any given situation, making generalizations impossible.

test yourself

1. In what ways did Bandura react to and modify Skinner's approach to understanding human functioning?
2. What is self-efficacy, and to what kinds of positive life developments has research linked it?
3. With what is Mischel's cognitive affective processing systems (CAPS) approach centrally concerned?

6· BIOLOGICAL PERSPECTIVES

The notion that physiological processes influence personality has been around since ancient times. Around 400 B.C.E., Hippocrates, the father of medicine, described human beings as having one of four basic personalities based on levels of particular bodily fluids (called *humours*). For Hippocrates, a "sanguine" personality was a happy, optimistic individual who happened to have an abundance of blood. A "choleric" person was quick-tempered with too much yellow bile. A "phlegmatic" personality referred to a placid, sluggish individual with too much phlegm (mucus), and a "melancholic" pessimist had too much black bile.

Even though Hippocrates' ideas about bodily fluids have fallen by the wayside, personality psychologists have long acknowledged that personality involves both the brain and biological processes. Psychologists' beliefs about these interacting processes in personality, though, were based on assumptions rather than on direct study. For instance, Freud's psychosexual stages bear witness to his strong belief in the connection between the mind (personality) and the body; Allport defined traits as "*neuro*psychic" structures, and personality as a "psycho*physical*" system; and Murray once declared, "No brain, no personality." More recently, advances in method and theory have led to fascinating research on the role of biological processes in personality.

Personality and the Brain

The brain is clearly important in personality as in other psychological phenomena. Recall the case of Phineas Gage, described in Chapter 3. One of the key effects of Gage's horrific accident was that it changed his personality. He went from being gentle, kind, and reliable to being angry, hostile, and untrustworthy.

A great deal of research is currently addressing the ways in which brain activity is associated with various personality traits. For example, research has shown that an extraverted person's left prefrontal cortex is more responsive to positive stimuli and that the same area in neurotic individuals is more responsive to negative stimuli (Canli, 2008a, 2008b; Haas & others, 2007; Schmidtke & Heller, 2004). The amygdalae in extraverts are more responsive to seeing happy faces than are those in introverts (Canli & others, 2002). Two theoretical approaches to the biology of personality, by Hans Eysenck and Jeffrey Gray, have garnered the most interest.

EYSENCK'S RETICULAR ACTIVATION SYSTEM THEORY

British psychologist Hans Eysenck (1967) was among the first to describe the role of a particular brain system in personality. He developed an approach to extraversion/introversion based on the *reticular activation system* (RAS).

Recall from Chapters 3 and 5 that the reticular formation is located in the brain stem and plays a role in wakefulness or arousal. The RAS is the name given to the reticular formation and its connections. Eysenck posited that all of us share an optimal arousal level, a level at which we feel comfortably engaged with the world. However, Eysenck proposed, the RAS of extraverts and introverts differs with respect to the baseline level of arousal. You know that an extravert tends to be outgoing, sociable, and dominant and that an introvert is quieter and more reserved and passive. According to Eysenck, these outward differences in behavior reflect different arousal regulation strategies (Figure 12.6). Extraverts wake up in the morning under-aroused, *below* the optimal level, whereas introverts start out *above* the optimal level.

If *you* were feeling under-engaged with life, what might you do? You might listen to loud music or hang out with friends—in other words, behave like an extravert. If, on the other hand, you were feeling over-aroused or too stimulated, what would you do?

FIGURE 12.6 **Eysenck's Reticular Activation System Theory** Eysenck viewed introversion and extraversion as characteristic behavioral patterns that aim to regulate arousal around the individual's baseline level.

You might spend time alone, keep distractions to a minimum, maybe sit quietly and read a book—in other words, you might act like an introvert.

Thus, from Eysenck's perspective, we can understand the traits of extraversion/introversion as characteristic patterns of behavior that aim to regulate arousal around our baseline. Research has not shown that extraverts and introverts differ in terms of baseline arousal but, rather, that introverts may be more sensitive to arousing stimuli.

GRAY'S REINFORCEMENT SENSITIVITY THEORY

Building from Eysenck's work, Jeffrey Gray proposed a neuropsychology of personality, called *reinforcement sensitivity theory,* that has been the subject of much research (Gray, 1987; Gray & McNaughton, 2000). On the basis of animal learning principles, Gray posited that two neurological systems—the *behavioral activation system* (BAS) and the *behavioral inhibition system* (BIS)—could be viewed as underlying personality, as Figure 12.7 shows.

According to Gray, these systems explain differences in an organism's attention to rewards and punishers in the environment. An organism sensitive to rewards is more likely to learn associations between behaviors and rewards and therefore to show a characteristic pattern of seeking out rewarding opportunities. In contrast, an organism with a heightened sensitivity to punishers in the environment is more likely to learn associations between behaviors and negative consequences. Such an organism shows a characteristic pattern of avoiding such consequences.

In Gray's theory, the BAS is sensitive to rewards in the environment, predisposes one to feelings of positive emotion, and underlies the trait of extraversion. In contrast, the BIS is sensitive to punishments and is involved in avoidance learning; it predisposes the individual to feelings of fear and underlies the trait of neuroticism (Berkman, Lieberman, & Gable, 2009; Corr, 2008; Gray & McNaughton, 2000). Psychologists often measure the BAS and BIS in humans by using questionnaires that assess a person's attention to rewarding or punishing outcomes (Schmeichel, Harmon-Jones, & Harmon-Jones, 2010).

Gray's conceptual model of reinforcement sensitivity proposed interacting brain systems as primarily responsible for the behavioral manifestations of the BAS and BIS. Research has provided some evidence for the biological underpinnings of these systems. The amygdala, the prefrontal cortex, and the anterior cingulated cortex appear to serve together as a system for affective style (Davidson, 2005; McNaughton & Corr, 2008) and are particularly implicated in the BAS or extraversion (Pickering & Smillie, 2008).

THE ROLE OF NEUROTRANSMITTERS

Neurotransmitters have also been implicated in personality in ways that fit Gray's model. Recall from Chapter 6 the function of the neurotransmitter dopamine in the experience of reward. Dopamine is a "feel good" neurotransmitter vital to learning that certain behaviors are rewarding and to sending the message to "do it again!" Research has shown that dopamine is also a factor in BAS or extraversion (Munafo & others, 2008). Studies have suggested that early encounters with warm caregivers and positive life experiences can promote the growth of dopamine-producing cells and receptors. These early experiences can make the brain especially sensitive to rewards, setting the neurochemical stage for extraversion (Depue & Collins, 1999).

Perhaps even stronger than the link between dopamine and extraversion is the relationship between the neurotransmitter serotonin and neuroticism (Brummett & others, 2008; Middeldorp & others, 2007). Neuroticism is especially related to a certain serotonin transporter gene and to the binding of serotonin in the thalamus (Gonda & others, 2009; Harro & others, 2009; Vinberg & others, 2010). Individuals who have less circulating serotonin are prone to negative mood; giving them drugs that inhibit the reuptake of serotonin tends to decrease negative mood and enhance feelings of sociability (Ksir, Hart, & Ray, 2008). Serotonin is also implicated in aggressive behavior (Neumann, Veenema, & Beiderbeck, 2010), as we will see in Chapter 13, as well as in the experience of depression (Popova & others, 2010), as we will consider in Chapter 15.

Behavioral Approach System

Sensitive to
Environmental reward

Behavior
Seek positive consequences/rewards

Character of emotion
Positive

Personality trait
Extraversion

Behavioral Inhibition System

Sensitive to
Environmental punishment

Behavior
Avoid negative consequences/punishments

Character of emotion
Negative

Personality trait
Neuroticism

FIGURE 12.7   Gray's Reinforcement Sensitivity Theory Gray theorized that two neurological systems, the BAS and the BIS, explain differences in an organism's attention to environmental rewards and punishments and in this way shape personality.

● **behavioral genetics** The study of the inherited underpinnings of behavioral characteristics.

Keep in mind that finding associations between brain activity or neurotransmitters and personality does not tell us about the potential causal pathways between these variables. Behavior can influence brain processes, and patterns of behavior can therefore determine brain activity. One thing that behavior cannot influence, at least not yet, is genes, another important biological factor in personality.

Personality and Behavioral Genetics

Behavioral genetics is the study of the inherited underpinnings of behavioral characteristics. A great deal of research in behavioral genetics has involved twin studies, and the hub of this work is, appropriately, the University of Minnesota, Twin Cities.

Twin study findings demonstrate that genetic factors explain a substantial amount of the observed differences in each of the big five traits. Remember that to conduct these studies, researchers compare identical twins, who share 100 percent of their genes, with fraternal twins, who share just 50 percent. All of the participants complete questionnaires measuring their traits. Then the researchers see if the identical twins are more similar to each other than the fraternal twins. Heritability estimates for the five factors are about 50 percent (Bouchard & Loehlin, 2001; Jang, Livesley, & Vernon, 1996; South & Krueger, 2008; Veselka & others, 2009).

Even aspects of personality that are not traits reveal some genetic influence. For example, research has shown that autobiographical memories about one's childhood and early family experiences (the kind of data that the personologist might find interesting) are influenced by genetics. Robert Krueger and his colleagues examined retrospective reports on the quality of family environments in a sample of twins who were reared apart (Krueger, Markon, & Bouchard, 2003). Participants rated their adoptive families on a variety of characteristics such as parental warmth, feelings of being wanted, and the strictness of their parents. These twins, though obviously sharing genetics, were reared by different families, so they were describing different experiences. Yet their recollections of their early family experiences were similar, and the heritability estimate for family cohesion ranged from 40 to 60 percent.

As we saw in Chapter 8's discussion of intelligence and Chapter 10's examination of happiness, the heritability statistic describes a group, not an individual, and heritability does not mean that traits are set in stone. Understanding the role of genetic factors in personality is enormously complex. Research on non-twin samples often suggests much lower heritability, for reasons that are not well understood (South & Krueger, 2008). Furthermore, because genes and environment are often intertwined, it is very difficult to tease apart whether, and how, genes or experience explains enduring patterns of behavior. For instance, a little girl who is genetically predisposed to disruptive behavior may often find herself in a time-out or involved in arguments with parents or teachers. When that child emerges as an adult with a "fighting spirit" or lots of "spunk," are those adult traits the product of genes, experiences, or both? Finally, most traits are probably influenced by multiple genes (P. T. Costa & others, 2010), making the task of identifying specific molecular links very challenging.

Evaluating the Biological Perspectives

Research that explores the biological aspects of personality is clearly important, and it is likely to remain a key avenue of research. This work ties the field of personality to animal learning models, advances in brain imaging, and evolutionary theory (Revelle, 2008). However, a few cautions are necessary in thinking about biological variables and their place in personality.

As we considered above, biology can be the effect, not the cause, of personality. To be sure that you grasp this idea, first recall that personality is the individual's characteristic pattern of behavior, thoughts, and feelings. Then recall from previous chapters that behavior, thoughts, and feelings are physical events in the body and brain. If traits predispose individuals to particular, consistent behaviors, thoughts, and emotional

CRITICAL CONTROVERSY

Can Personality Change?

As you talk on the phone with a friend, she tells you for what seems like the hundredth time about her boyfriend troubles. He never calls when he says he will. He always seems to have forgotten his wallet when they go out. Now she thinks he might be cheating on her *again*. As you count silently to 10, you are tempted to blurt it out: "Dump him already! He's never going to change!"

Of course, your friend might be banking on the notion that he *will* change. Can people genuinely change? The answer to this question has implications for a variety of important life domains. For example, can criminals be rehabilitated? Can addicts truly recover from addictions? Will all those self-help books ever help you to stop worrying and enjoy life? Will that lousy boyfriend turn out to be suitable husband material after all?

Whether personality can change has been a topic of controversy throughout the history of the field of personality. William James once wrote that "it is well for the world that in most of us, by the age of 30, the character has set like plaster, and will never soften again." Trait psychologists Paul Costa and Robert McCrae concluded from their own work that James was on target: They suggested that most traits are indeed "essentially fixed" by age 30, with little meaningful change occurring throughout the rest of adulthood (Costa & McCrae, 1992, 2006; McCrae & Costa, 2006). However, other research has provided evidence that meaningful personality change continues over time (Noftle & Fleeson, 2010; Roberts & Mroczek, 2008; Roberts, Wood, & Caspi, 2008).

Strong evidence that personality traits do change is provided by longitudinal studies that follow the same individuals over a long period. Brent Roberts and his colleagues analyzed 92 different longitudinal studies that included thousands of participants ranging from 12 years old to over 80 years old and that measured aspects of the big five across the life course (Edmonds & others, 2007; Roberts, Walton, & Viechtbauer, 2006; Roberts, Wood, & Caspi, 2008; Roberts & others, 2009). They found strong, consistent evidence for trait changes throughout life, even into adulthood. Social dominance (a facet of extraversion), conscientiousness, and emotional stability (the opposite of neuroticism) were found to increase especially between the ages of

20 and 40. Social vitality, another facet of extraversion, and openness to experience increased most during adolescence but then declined in old age. Agreeableness showed a steady rise over the life course. Over time, people were not just getting older—they were getting more responsible, kinder, and less worried.

Research has also shown that especially between age 17 and 24, individuals are likely to become more responsible and less distressed (Blonigen & others, 2008; Klimstra & others, 2009). In general, changes in personality traits across adulthood occur in a positive direction (Roberts & Mroczek, 2008). Over time, individuals become more confident and responsible, as well as warmer and calmer. Such positive changes equate with becoming more socially mature.

What can we conclude about stability and change in personality development during the adult years? The evidence does not support the view that personality traits become completely fixed at a certain age in adulthood (Caspi & Roberts, 2001; Noftle & Fleeson, 2010; Roberts, Wood, & Caspi, 2008). Keep in mind that, by definition, traits are considered to be stable. They might be the least likely aspect of personality to change, as compared, for example, to beliefs or goals. To find change in even these relatively stable dimensions is extraordinary and speaks to the important possibility that people can grow and change, especially in positive ways, over the life span. Researchers have discovered that other aspects of personality—such as resilience, wisdom, complexity, and insight—also increase through life experience (Helson & Soto, 2005; Helson, Soto, & Cate, 2006).

What do these findings mean for your friend and her loser boyfriend? Maybe he will shape up, but she might have to wait a very long time.

WHAT DO YOU THINK?

- In your opinion, can personality change throughout a person's life? Explain.
- Reflect on what you were like five years ago. Which aspects of your personality have changed? Which have stayed the same?
- If you have a friend who wants to be more outgoing, what would your advice be?

responses, traits may play a role in forging particular habitually used pathways in the brain. Recall, too, from Chapter 7 that memory may be thought of as patterns of activation among neurons. The autobiographical memories that interest personologists, then, might be viewed as well-worn patterns of activation. To the extent that personality represents a person's characteristic pattern of thought or the accumulation of memories over the life span, personality may not only be influenced by the brain—it may also play a role in the brain's very structure and functions.

One issue that biological approaches bring to the fore is the question of whether personality is plastic—that is, whether it can change throughout a person's life. If personality is "caused" by biological processes, does that mean it is fixed? To explore this issue, see the Critical Controversy.

test yourself

1. According to Eysenck, what part of the brain influences whether a person is an introvert or an extravert?
2. How does Gray's reward sensitivity theory of personality explain extraversion and neuroticism?
3. What is behavioral genetics, and what kind of study is commonly used in research in this area?

7· PERSONALITY ASSESSMENT

One of the great contributions of personality psychology is its development of rigorous methods for measuring mental processes. Psychologists use a number of scientifically developed methods to evaluate personality. They assess personality for different reasons—from clinical evaluation to career counseling and job selection (J. N. Butcher, 2010; Heine & Buchtel, 2009).

Self-Report Tests

● **self-report test** Also called an objective test or an inventory, a method of measuring personality characteristics that directly asks people whether specific items describe their personality traits.

The most commonly used method of measuring personality characteristics is self-report. A **self-report test,** which is also called an *objective test* or *inventory,* directly asks people whether specific items describe their personality traits. Self-report personality tests include items such as

- I am easily embarrassed.
- I love to go to parties.
- I like to watch cartoons on TV.

Respondents choose from a limited number of answers (yes or no, true or false, agree or disagree).

One problem with self-report tests is a factor called *social desirability.* To grasp the idea of social desirability, imagine answering the item "I am lazy at times." This statement is probably true for everyone, but would you feel comfortable admitting it? When motivated by social desirability, individuals say what they think the researcher wants to hear or what they think will make them look better. One way to measure the influence of social desirability is to give individuals a questionnaire that is designed to tap into this tendency. Such a scale typically contains many universally true but threatening items ("I like to gossip at times," "I have never said anything intentionally to hurt someone's feelings"). If scores on a trait measure correlate with this measure of social desirability, we know that the test takers were probably not being straightforward with respect to the trait measure. That is, if a person answers one questionnaire in a socially desirable fashion, he or she is probably answering all the questionnaires that way.

● **empirically keyed test** A type of self-report test that presents many questionnaire items to two groups that are known to be different in some central way.

Another way to get around social desirability issues is to design scales so that it is virtually impossible for the respondent to know what the researcher is trying to measure. One means of accomplishing this goal is to use an **empirically keyed test,** a type of self-report test that is created by first identifying two groups that are known to be different. The researcher would give these two groups a large number of questionnaire items and then see which items show the biggest differences between the groups. Those items would become part of the scale to measure the group difference. For instance, a researcher might want to develop a test that distinguishes between individuals with a history of substance abuse and those with no such history. The researcher might generate a long list of true/false items that ask about a variety of topics but do not mention substance abuse. These questions would be presented to the members of the two groups, and on the basis of the responses, the researcher can then select the items that best discriminate between the members of the differing groups (Segal & Coolidge, 2004).

Note that an empirically keyed test avoids the issue of social desirability because the items that distinguish between the two groups are not related in any obvious way to the actual purpose of the test. For instance, those without a substance abuse history might typically respond "true" to the item "I enjoy taking long walks," while those with a history of substance abuse might respond "false"; but this item does not mention substance use, and there is no clear reason why it should distinguish between these groups.

"I like the way I look, but I hate my personality."

Indeed, an important consideration with respect to empirically keyed tests is that researchers often do *not* know why a given test item distinguishes between two groups. Imagine, for example, that an empirically keyed test of achievement motivation includes an item such as "I prefer to watch sports on TV instead of romantic movies." A researcher might find that this item does a good job of distinguishing between higher-paid versus lower-paid managers in a work setting. However, does an item such as this example measure achievement motivation or, instead, simply the respondents' gender?

MMPI

The **Minnesota Multiphasic Personality Inventory (MMPI)** is the most widely used and researched empirically keyed self-report personality test. The MMPI was initially constructed in the 1940s to assess "abnormal" personality tendencies. The most recent version of the inventory, the MMPI-2, is still widely used around the world to assess personality and predict outcomes (J. N. Butcher, 2010; Handel & others, 2010). The scale features 567 items and provides information on a variety of personality characteristics. The MMPI also includes items meant to assess whether the respondent is lying or trying to make a good impression (social desirability). Not only is the MMPI used by clinical psychologists to assess mental health (S. R. Smith & others, 2010), but it is also a tool in hiring decisions (Caillouet & others, 2010) and in forensic settings, assessing criminal risk (Bow, Flens, & Gould, 2010; Sellbom & others, 2010).

ASSESSMENT OF THE BIG FIVE FACTORS

Paul Costa and Robert McCrae (1992) constructed the Neuroticism Extraversion Openness Personality Inventory—Revised (or NEO-PI-R, for short), a self-report test geared to assessing the five-factor model: openness, conscientiousness, extraversion, agreeableness, and neuroticism (emotional instability). The test also evaluates six subdimensions that make up the five main factors. Other measures of the big five traits have relied on the lexical approach and offer the advantage of being available without a fee.

Unlike empirically keyed tests, measures of the big five generally contain straightforward items; for instance, the trait "talkative" might show up on an extraversion scale. These items have what psychologists call face validity. A test item has **face validity** if it seems on the surface to be testing the characteristic in question. Measures of the big five typically involve items that are obvious in terms of what they measure, but not all self-report assessments have this quality.

The MMPI and the NEO-PIR are well-established measures of personality characteristics. Yet, you may be more familiar with another assessment tool that is popular in business settings, called the Myers-Briggs Type Indicator. To learn about the way personality psychologists regard this questionnaire, see the Intersection.

It is likely that you could give a reasonably good assessment of your own levels of traits such as neuroticism and extraversion. What about the more mysterious aspects of yourself and others? If you are like most people, you think of psychological assessments as tools to find out things you do not already know about yourself. For that objective, psychologists might turn to projective tests.

Projective Tests

A **projective test** presents individuals with an ambiguous stimulus and asks them to describe it or tell a story about it—in other words, to *project* their own meaning onto the stimulus. Projective tests are based on the assumption that the ambiguity of the stimulus allows individuals to interpret it based on their feelings, desires, needs, and attitudes. The test is especially designed to elicit the individual's unconscious feelings and conflicts, providing an assessment that goes deeper than the surface of personality (Bram, 2010; Hibbard & others, 2010; Husain, 2009).

● **Minnesota Multiphasic Personality Inventory (MMPI)** The most widely used and researched empirically keyed self-report personality test.

● **face validity** The extent to which a test item appears to be a good fit to the characteristic it measures.

● **projective test** A personality assessment test that presents individuals with an ambiguous stimulus and asks them to describe it or tell a story about it—to project their own meaning onto the stimulus.

© Dan Reynolds. www.CartoonStock.com.

Personality and Organizational Psychology: Hey, What's Your Type?

Personality assessment has become increasingly useful in business settings. Personality psychologists and industrial and organizational psychologists (specialists we discuss in Chapter 14) have investigated the ways that personality characteristics relate to success in the workplace. One of the most popular assessment tools for personnel decisions is the Myers Briggs Type Indicator (MBTI) developed in the 1940s by the mother–daughter team of Katherine Briggs and Isabel Briggs Myers (Briggs & Myers, 1998), neither of whom was trained in psychology or assessment (Saunders, 1991).

Based on a book by Carl Jung, the Myers Briggs questionnaire provides people with feedback on their personality "type" based on four dimensions:

- *Extraversion* (basing one's actions on outward conditions) versus *introversion* (being more introspective)
- *Sensing* (relying on what can be sensed about reality) versus *intuiting* (relying on gut feelings and unconscious processes)
- *Thinking* (relying on logic) versus *feeling* (relying on emotion)
- *Judgment* (using thinking and feeling) versus *perception* (using sensing and intuiting)

These MBTI dimensions are used to create categories that are labeled with letters; for example, an extraverted person who relies on sensation, thinking, and judgment would be called an ESTJ.

The MBTI has become so popular that people in some organizations introduce themselves as an INTJ or an INSP in the same way that people might exchange their astrological signs. Unfortunately, as in the case of astrology, strong evidence for the actual value of the MBTI types for personnel selection and job performance is very weak at best (Hunsley, Lee, & Wood, 2004; Pittenger, 2005). In fact, the MBTI is neither reliable (people get different scores with repeated testing) nor valid (it does not predict what it should). For example, there is no evidence that particular MBTI types are better suited to particular occupations (Bjork & Druckman, 1991; Boyle, 1995; Gardner & Martinko, 1996).

Given this lack of empirical support, why does MBTI remain popular? Some practitioners have found it to be quite useful in their own work (McCaulley, 2000), whether or not they are aware of the lack of scientific evidence for the types. The MBTI has been well marketed, and those who pay for the scale and its training may be motivated to find evidence in their own lives to support the notion that it works.

It can be fun to learn about our personalities and to be given these letter labels. When we read that an INTJ is someone who is "introspective and likely to sometimes argue a point just for the sake of argument," we might think, "They really figured me out." However, this description could be true of virtually anyone, as is the case for most astrological profiles. The tendency to see ourselves in such vague descriptions is called the *Barnum effect,* after P. T. Barnum, the famous showman. The wily Barnum—simply by dispensing vague, general descriptions that would likely be true of anyone—convinced people that he could read minds.

The popularity of the Myers Briggs letter typology attests to the power of marketing, the persistence of confirmation bias (the tendency to use information that supports our ideas rather than refutes them), and the Barnum effect. Most troubling to personality psychologists is that although other psychological measures may not be as exciting and mysterious as those four letters, they are more likely to provide reliable and valid information about job performance (Hunsley, Lee, & Wood, 2004).

If you were a manager, what personality characteristics would you look for in job candidates?

Projective tests attempt to get inside the mind to discover how the test taker really feels and thinks; that is, they aim to go beyond the way the individual overtly presents himself or herself. Projective tests are theoretically aligned with the psychodynamic perspectives on personality, which give more weight to the unconscious than do other perspectives. Projective techniques also require content analysis. The examiner must code the responses for the underlying motivations revealed in the story.

Perhaps the most famous projective test is the **Rorschach inkblot test,** developed in 1921 by the Swiss psychiatrist Hermann Rorschach. The test consists of 10 cards, half in

● **Rorschach inkblot test** A famous projective test that uses an individual's perception of inkblots to determine his or her personality.

black and white and half in color, which the individual views one at a time (Figure 12.8). The person taking the Rorschach test is asked to describe what he or she sees in each of the inkblots. For example, the individual may say, "I see two fairies having a tea party" or "This is the rabbit's face from the movie *Donnie Darko*." These responses are scored based on indications of various underlying psychological characteristics (Exner, 2003; Leichtman, 2009).

The Rorschach's usefulness in research is controversial. From a scientific perspective, researchers are skeptical about the Rorschach (Feshbach & Weiner, 1996; Garb & others, 2001; Hunsley & Bailey, 2001; Weiner, 2004). The test's reliability and validity have both been criticized. If the Rorschach were reliable, two different scorers would agree on the personality characteristics of the individual being tested. If the Rorschach were valid, it would predict behavior outside of the testing situation; that is, it would predict, for example, whether an individual will attempt suicide, become severely depressed, cope successfully with stress, or get along well with others. Conclusions based on research evidence suggest that the Rorschach does not meet these criteria of reliability and validity (Lilienfeld, Wood, & Garb, 2000). Thus, many psychologists have serious reservations about the Rorschach's use in diagnosis and clinical practice.

Although still administered in clinical (Bram, 2010) and applied (Del Giudice, 2010) circles, the Rorschach is not commonly used in personality research. However, the projective method itself remains a tool for studying personality, especially in the form of the Thematic Apperception Test (TAT).

The **Thematic Apperception Test (TAT),** developed by Henry Murray and Christiana Morgan in the 1930s, is designed to elicit stories that reveal something about an individual's personality. The TAT consists of a series of pictures like the one in Figure 12.9, each on an individual card or slide. The TAT test taker is asked to tell a story about each of the pictures, including events leading up to the situation described, the characters' thoughts and feelings, and the way the situation turns out. The tester assumes that the person projects his or her own unconscious feelings and thoughts into the story (Hibbard & others, 2010).

In addition to being administered as a projective test in clinical practice, the TAT is used in research on people's need for achievement, affiliation, power, intimacy, and a variety of other needs (Brunstein & Maier, 2005; Schultheiss & Brunstein, 2005; C. P. Smith, 1992); unconscious defense mechanisms (Cramer, 2008a, 2008b; Cramer & Jones, 2007); and cognitive styles (Woike, 2008; Woike & Matic, 2004; Woike, Mcleod, & Goggin, 2003). In contrast to the Rorschach, TAT measures have shown high inter-rater reliability and validity (Woike, 2001).

Other Assessment Methods

Self-report questionnaires and projective techniques are just two of the multitude of assessment methods developed and used by personality psychologists. Personality psychologists might also measure behavior directly, by observing a person either live or in a video. In addition, cognitive assessments have become more common in personality psychology, as researchers probe such topics as the relation between personality and processes of attention and memory. Many personality psychologists incorporate friend or peer ratings of individuals' traits or other characteristics. Personality psychologists also use a host of psychophysiological measures, such as heart rate and skin conductance. Increasingly, personality psychologists are incorporating brain imaging as well.

Whether personality assessments are being used by clinical psychologists, psychological researchers, or other practitioners, the choice of assessment instrument depends greatly on the researcher's theoretical perspective. Figure 12.10 summarizes which methods are associated with each of the theoretical perspectives. The figure also summarizes each approach, including its major assumptions, and gives a sample research question addressed by each. Personality psychology is a diverse field, unified by a shared interest in understanding the person you really are.

FIGURE 12.8   Type of Stimulus Used in the Rorschach Inkblot Test What do you see in this figure? Do you see two green seahorses? Or a pair of blue spiders? A psychologist who relies on the Rorschach test would examine your responses to find out who you are.

● **Thematic Apperception Test (TAT)** A projective test that is designed to elicit stories that reveal something about an individual's personality.

FIGURE 12.9   Picture from the Thematic Apperception Test (TAT) What are these two women thinking and feeling? How did they come to this situation, and what will happen next? A psychologist who uses the TAT would analyze your story to find out your unconscious motives. Reprinted by permission of the publishers from *Thematic Apperception Test* by Henry A. Murray, Card 12F, Cambridge, MA: Harvard University Press. Copyright © 1943 by the President and the Fellows of Harvard College. Copyright © 1971 by Henry A. Murray.

Approach	Summary	Assumptions	Typical Methods	Sample Research Question
Psychodynamic	Personality is characterized by unconscious processes. Childhood experiences are of great importance to adult personality.	The most important aspects of personality are unconscious.	Case studies, projective techniques.	How do unconscious conflicts lead to dysfunctional behavior?
Humanistic	Personality evolves out of the person's innate, organismic motives to grow and actualize the self. These healthy tendencies can be undermined by social pressure.	Human nature is basically good. By getting in touch with who we are and what we really want, we can lead happier, healthier lives.	Questionnaires, interviews, observation.	Can situations be changed to support individuals' organismic values and enhance their well-being?
Trait	Personality is characterized by five general traits that are represented in the natural language that people use to describe themselves and others.	Traits are relatively stable over time. Traits predict behavior.	Questionnaires, observer reports.	Are the five factors universal across cultures?
Personological and Life Story	To understand personality, we must understand the whole person. We all have unique life experiences, and the stories we tell about those experiences make up our identities.	The life story provides a unique opportunity to examine the personality processes associated with behavior, development, and well-being.	Written narratives, TAT stories, autobiographical memories, interviews, and psychobiography.	How do narrative accounts of life experiences relate to happiness?
Social Cognitive	Personality is the pattern of coherence that characterizes a person's interactions with the situations he or she encounters in life. The individual's beliefs and expectations, rather than global traits, are the central variables of interest.	Behavior is best understood as changing across situations. To understand personality, we must understand what each situation means for a given person.	Multiple observations over different situations; video-recorded behaviors rated by coders; questionnaires.	When and why do individuals respond to challenging tasks with fear versus excitement?
Biological	Personality characteristics reflect underlying biological processes such as those carried out by the brain, neurotransmitters, and genes. Differences in behaviors, thoughts, and feelings depend on these processes.	Biological differences among individuals can explain differences in their personalities.	Brain imaging, twin studies, molecular genetic studies.	Do genes explain individual differences in extraversion?

FIGURE 12.10 **Approaches to Personality Psychology** This figure summarizes the broad approaches to personality described in this chapter. Many researchers in personality do not stick with just one approach but apply the various theories and methods that are most relevant to their research questions.

test yourself

1. What is an empirically keyed test?
2. What is a common problem with self-report tests?
3. What technique does the Thematic Apperception Test (TAT) involve?

8· PERSONALITY AND HEALTH AND WELLNESS

Personality comprises a set of enduring characteristics that influence behavior. As such, personality affects many behaviors that impact physical health and psychological wellness, as we consider in this concluding section.

Personality and Physical Health

We first survey personality characteristics that are linked, respectively, to health and to illness.

CONSCIENTIOUSNESS

Conscientiousness is not the sexiest personality trait, but it might well be the most important of the big five when it comes to longevity and healthy living (Roberts & Mroczek, 2008; Roberts & others, 2009). In a longitudinal study of more than 1,200 individuals across seven decades, conscientiousness predicted a lower mortality risk from childhood through late adulthood (Martin, Friedman, & Schwartz, 2007). A variety of studies show that conscientious people tend to do all the things that they are told are good for their health, such as getting regular exercise, avoiding drinking and smoking, wearing seatbelts, and checking smoke detectors (D. B. O'Connor & others, 2009; Rush, Becker, & Curry, 2009). This capacity to follow a sensible plan may be just what it takes to do the mundane tasks required to live a long, healthy life. Indeed, research has shown that conscientious individuals are less likely to die than their counterparts who are less conscientious (Fry & Debats, 2009; Iwassa & others, 2008, 2009; Kern & Friedman, 2008; R. S. Wilson & others, 2004).

PERSONAL CONTROL

Another personality characteristic associated with taking the right steps toward a long, healthy life is personal control (Baumeister & Alquist, 2009; Forgas, Baumeister, & Tice, 2009). Feeling in control can reduce stress during difficult times and can lead to the development of problem-solving strategies to deal with hardship (Taylor, 2011; S. C. Thompson, 2001). An individual with a good sense of personal control might reason, "If I stop smoking now, I will not develop lung cancer" or "If I exercise regularly, I won't develop cardiovascular disease."

A sense of personal control has been linked to a lower risk for common chronic diseases such as cancer and cardiovascular disease (Sturmer, Hasselbach, & Amelang, 2006). Further, like conscientiousness, a sense of personal control might help people avoid a risky lifestyle that involves health-compromising behaviors. Consider a study of East German migrants to West Germany who found themselves unemployed (Mittag & Schwarzer, 1993). Individuals in the study often turned to heavy drinking for solace—unless, that is, they had a sense of personal control (as measured by such survey items as "When I'm in trouble, I can rely on my ability to deal with the problem effectively"). Overall, across a wide range of studies, a sense of personal control has been related to emotional well-being, successful coping with a stressful event, healthy behavior change, and good health (Little, Snyder, & Wehmeyer, 2006; Stanton, Revenson, & Tennen, 2007; Taylor, 2011; Taylor & Stanton, 2007).

SELF-EFFICACY

Research has shown that self-efficacy is related to success in a wide variety of positive life changes, including achieving weight loss (Annesi, 2007), exercising regularly (Lippke & Plotnikoff, 2006), quitting smoking (Gwaltney & others, 2009), ending substance abuse (Warren, Stein, & Grella, 2007), and practicing safe sex (Abbey & others, 2007). Recent evidence suggests that self-efficacy is also strongly linked to cardiovascular functioning following heart failure and that individuals high in self-efficacy are not only less likely to suffer a second hospitalization due to heart failure but also likely to live longer (Sarkar, Ali, & Whooley, 2009).

If there is a problem to be fixed, self-efficacy—having a can-do attitude—is related to finding a solution. In one study, smokers were randomly assigned to one of three conditions. In the *self-efficacy condition,* individuals were told they had been chosen for the study because they had great potential to quit smoking (Warnecke & others, 2001). Then they participated in a 14-week program on smoking cessation. In the *treatment-alone condition,* individuals participated in the 14-week smoking cessation program but were told that they had been randomly selected for it. In the *no-treatment control condition,* individuals did not participate in the smoking cessation program. At the end of the 14 weeks, individuals in the self-efficacy condition were more likely to have quit smoking than their counterparts in the other two conditions. The Psychological Inquiry on p. 414 shows the results.

OPTIMISM

A factor that is often linked to positive functioning and adjustment is optimism (Carver & Connor-Smith, 2010; Peterson & Seligman, 2003; Seligman & Pawelski, 2003;

psychological *inquiry*

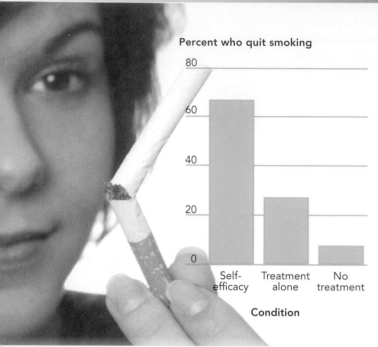

Percent who quit smoking

[Bar graph with Y-axis labeled 0, 20, 40, 60, 80. X-axis labeled "Self-efficacy", "Treatment alone", "No treatment". The bars show approximately 65% for Self-efficacy, 28% for Treatment alone, and 7% for No treatment.]

Condition

A Can-Do Attitude Means You Can Quit Smoking

The figure shows the results of the study on self-efficacy and smoking cessation (discussed in the text) in which smokers were randomly assigned to one of three conditions—self-efficacy, treatment alone, and no treatment (Warnecke & others, 2001). Notice that the Y or vertical axis shows the dependent variable, the percentage of participants who quit smoking. The X or horizontal axis shows the independent variable, the groups to which participants were assigned. Try your hand at the following questions.

1. Why were participants randomly assigned to groups?

2. If the researchers concluded that the self-efficacy manipulation caused these differences, would their conclusion be justified? Explain.

3. How might the results of this study be generalized to groups who wish to change other behaviors?

4. How would you design a correlational study that would examine the relationship between self-efficacy and smoking cessation?

Smith & MacKenzie, 2006). Martin Seligman's (1990) theory and research view optimism as a matter of how a person explains the causes of bad events. Optimists explain the causes of bad events as external, unstable, and specific, whereas pessimists explain them as internal, stable, and global. Studies have associated explaining life events optimistically with a variety of positive outcomes (Reivich & Gillham, 2002).

Other researchers define optimism as the expectancy that good things, and not bad things, are more likely to occur in the future (Carver & Connor-Smith, 2010; Carver & Scheier, 2009; Solberg Nes, Evans, & Segerstrom, 2009; Solberg Nes & Segerstrom, 2006). This view focuses on how people pursue their goals and values. Even when faced with misfortune, optimists believe that they can attain their goals and live according to their values.

Numerous studies reveal that optimists generally function more effectively and are physically and mentally healthier than pessimists (Segerstrom, 2006). In one study, people who had been classified as optimistic at age 25 were healthier at ages 45 to 60 than those who had been classified as pessimistic (Peterson, Seligman, & Vaillant, 1988). In other studies, optimism has been linked to more effective immune system functioning and better health (Segerstrom, 2003, 2005; Solberg Nes & Segerstrom, 2006).

Whereas optimism, sense of personal control, and self-efficacy can promote effective coping with stress, other personality characteristics have been shown to exacerbate stress with special significance for cardiovascular illness. In particular, people who are impatient or quick to anger or who display frequent hostility have an increased risk for cardiovascular disease (Chida & Steptoe, 2009), as we now consider.

THE TYPE A/TYPE B BEHAVIOR PATTERN

In the late 1950s, a secretary for two California cardiologists, Meyer Friedman and Ray Rosenman, observed that the chairs in their waiting rooms were tattered and worn, but only on the front edges. The cardiologists themselves had noticed the impatience of their cardiac patients, who often arrived exactly on time and were in a great hurry to leave. Intrigued by this consistency, they conducted a study of 3,000 healthy men between the ages of 35 and 59 over eight years to find out whether people with certain behavioral

Martin Seligman (b. 1942) Seligman went from pessimist to optimist and believes that others can, too. Seligman (1990) provided the details in his book *Learned Optimism*.

characteristics might be prone to heart problems (Friedman & Rosenman, 1974). During the eight years, one group of men had twice as many heart attacks or other forms of heart disease as the other men. Autopsies of the men who died revealed that the coronary arteries of this group were more obstructed than those of the other group.

Friedman and Rosenman described the common personality characteristics of the men who developed coronary disease as the **Type A behavior pattern.** They theorized that a cluster of characteristics—being excessively competitive, hard-driven, impatient, and hostile—is related to the incidence of heart disease. Rosenman and Friedman labeled the behavior of the healthier group, who were commonly relaxed and easygoing, the **Type B behavior pattern.**

Further research on the link between Type A behavior and coronary disease indicates that the association is not as strong as Friedman and Rosenman believed (Suls & Swain, 1998; R. B. Williams, 2001, 2002). However, researchers have found that certain components of Type A behavior are more precisely linked with coronary risk (Spielberger, 2004), especially hostility (Chida & Steptoe, 2009). People who are hostile outwardly or who turn anger inward are more likely to develop heart disease than their less angry counterparts (Eng & others, 2003; K. A. Matthews & others, 2004). Such people have been called "hot reactors" because of their intense physiological reactions to stress—racing heart, quickened breathing, and increased muscle tension. Research on hostility demonstrates that just as personality can relate to better health outcomes, some personality characteristics can be associated with health risks.

Personality and Psychological Well-Being

Among the most consistent findings in personality research is the strong association between personality traits and psychological well-being. Specifically, neuroticism is strongly related to lower levels of well-being, whereas extraversion is related to higher levels (Steel, Schmidt, & Schultz, 2008; Wilt & Revelle, 2009). The links between these two traits and well-being have even been found in orangutans (Weiss, King, & Perkins, 2006). What explains these connections?

As defined by psychologists, **subjective well-being** is a person's assessment of his or her level of positive affect and negative affect, and an evaluation of his or her life in general (Diener, 2000). This definition provides a clue as to why the traits of neuroticism and extraversion are so strongly related to psychological state. Neuroticism is the tendency to worry, to feel distressed, and to experience negative emotion. Neurotic individuals experience more negative mood than others, and their moods are more changeable. David Watson, a personality and clinical psychologist who specializes in the study of mood, has suggested that negative emotion is at the very core of the trait of neuroticism (Miller, Vachon, & Lynam, 2009; Watson & Clark, 1997).

Interestingly, however, research has shown that neurotics can be happy—especially if they are also extraverted (Hotard & others, 1989). Indeed, Watson suggests that positive emotion is that core of the trait of extraversion (Watson & Naragon, 2009). Research has shown that extraverts are happier than introverts even when they are alone (Lucas, 2008). In fact, research has supported the conclusion that extraverts are happier regardless of what they are doing or with whom they are doing it (Lucas, 2007; McNiel, Lowman, & Fleeson, 2010).

If you are not very conscientious, or you are a pessimist with an external locus of control, or you are hostile, or neurotic, or an introvert—or a hostile, neurotic introvert—you may be feeling your mood deflating. If personality is stable, what good is it to find out that your personality—who you really are—might put you at risk for illness and make you miserable?

A positive way to think about these issues is to focus on the difference between traits and states (Marine & others, 2006). Recall that traits are enduring characteristics—the way you generally are. In contrast, states (such as positive or negative moods) are briefer experiences. Having a trait, such as neuroticism, that predisposes you to feelings of worry (a state) does not mean that your overall well-being must suffer. Instead, recognizing that you tend to be neurotic may be an important step in noting when your negative moods

● **Type A behavior pattern** A cluster of characteristics—such as being excessively competitive, hard-driven, impatient, and hostile—related to the incidence of heart disease.

● **Type B behavior pattern** A cluster of characteristics—such as being relaxed and easygoing—related to good health.

● **subjective well-being** A person's assessment of his or her own level of positive affect relative to negative affect, and the individual's evaluation of his or her life in general.

test yourself

1. What are four personality characteristics that are associated with positive functioning and positive life changes?
2. How have various researchers defined optimism?
3. What is the Type A behavior pattern, and what specific aspect of it is most often linked to coronary disease?

are potentially being fed by this trait and are not necessarily the result of objective events. Finding out that you have a personality style associated with higher levels of stress or lower levels of happiness does not mean that you are doomed. Rather, you can use this information to cultivate good habits and to make the most of your unique qualities.

Remember, too, that personality characteristics influence health through their relationships to behaviors and the experience of stress. Even a person very low in conscientiousness can engage in healthy behaviors. Consider that characteristics such as locus of control and self-efficacy are about your beliefs about the world, and these aspects of personality are changeable. Recall that in the Psychological Inquiry on page 414, self-efficacy was manipulated by simply telling people they had high potential to change. Believing in *your own* potential may be the first step to enhancing your health and wellness.

SUMMARY

1. PSYCHODYNAMIC PERSPECTIVES

Freud developed psychoanalysis through his work with patients suffering from hysterical symptoms (physical symptoms with no physical cause). Freud viewed these symptoms as representing conflicts between sexual drive and duty. Freud believed that most personality—which, in his theory, includes components he called the id, ego, and superego—is unconscious. The ego uses various defense mechanisms, Freud said, to reduce anxiety.

A number of theorists criticized and revised Freud's approach. Horney said that the need for security, not sex or aggression, is our most important need. Jung developed the concept of the collective unconscious, a storehouse of archetypes. Adler's individual psychology stresses that people are striving toward perfection.

Weaknesses of the psychodynamic perspectives include overreliance on reports from the past and overemphasis of the unconscious mind. Strengths of psychodynamic approaches include recognizing the importance of childhood, conceptualizing development through stages, and calling attention to the role of unconscious processes in behavior.

2. HUMANISTIC PERSPECTIVES

Humanistic perspectives stress a person's capacity for personal growth and positive human qualities. Maslow developed the concept of a hierarchy of needs, with self-actualization being the highest human need. In Rogers's approach, each of us is born with a tendency toward growth, a sense of what is good and bad for us, and a need for unconditional positive regard. Because we are often denied unconditional positive regard, we may become alienated from our innate growth tendencies. In order to reconnect with these innate tendencies, Rogers felt, a person required a relationship that included unconditional positive regard, empathy, and genuineness.

The humanistic perspectives promote the positive capacities of human beings. The weaknesses of the approach are a tendency to be too optimistic and an inclination to downplay personal responsibility.

3. TRAIT PERSPECTIVES

Trait theories emphasize that personality consists of traits—broad, enduring dispositions that lead to characteristic responses. Allport stated that traits should produce consistent behavior in different situations, and he used the lexical approach to personality traits, which involves using all the words in the natural language that could describe a person as a basis for understanding the traits of personality.

The current dominant perspective in personality psychology is the five-factor model. The big five traits include openness to experience, conscientiousness, extraversion, agreeableness, and neuroticism. Extraversion is related to enhanced well-being, and neuroticism is linked to lowered well-being.

Studying people in terms of their traits has value. However, trait approaches are criticized for focusing on broad dimensions and not attending to each person's uniqueness.

4. PERSONOLOGICAL AND LIFE STORY PERSPECTIVES

Murray described personology as the study of the whole person. Contemporary followers of Murray study personality through narrative accounts and interviews. McAdams introduced the life story approach to identity, which views identity as a constantly changing story with a beginning, a middle, and an end. Psychobiography is a form of personological investigation that applies personality theory to one person's life.

Life story approaches to personality reveal the richness of each person's unique life story. However, this work can be very difficult to carry out.

5. SOCIAL COGNITIVE PERSPECTIVES

Social cognitive theory states that behavior, environment, and person/cognitive factors are important in understanding personality. In Bandura's view, these factors reciprocally interact.

Two important concepts in social cognitive theory are self-efficacy and personal control. Self-efficacy is the belief that one can master a situation and produce positive outcomes. Personal control refers to individuals' beliefs about whether the outcomes of their actions depend on their own acts (internal) or on events outside of their control (external).

Mischel's controversial book *Personality and Assessment* stressed that people do not behave consistently across different situations but rather tailor their behavior to suit particular situations. Personality psychologists countered that personality does predict behavior for some people some of the time. Very specific personality characteristics predict behavior better than very general ones, and personality characteristics are more likely to predict behavior in weak versus strong situations.

Mischel developed a revised approach to personality centered on cognitive affective processing systems (CAPS). According to CAPS, personality is best understood as a person's habitual emotional and cognitive reactions to specific situations.

A particular strength of social cognitive theory is its focus on cognitive processes. However, social cognitive approaches have not given adequate attention to enduring individual differences, to biological factors, and to personality as a whole.

6. BIOLOGICAL PERSPECTIVES

Eysenck suggested that the brain's reticular activation system (RAS) plays a role in introversion/extraversion. He thought of these traits as the outward manifestations of arousal regulation. Gray developed a reward sensitivity theory of personality, suggesting that extraversion and neuroticism can be understood as two neurological systems that respond to rewards (the behavioral approach system, or BAS) and punishments (the behavioral inhibition system, or BIS) in the environment.

Research has found that dopamine is associated with behavioral approach (extraversion) and serotonin with behavioral avoidance (neuroticism). Behavioral genetic studies have shown that the heritability of personality traits is approximately 50 percent. Studies of biological processes in personality are valuable but can overestimate the causal role of biological factors.

7. PERSONALITY ASSESSMENT

Self-report tests assess personality by asking participants about their preferences and behaviors. One problem in self-report research is the tendency for individuals to respond in socially desirable ways. Empirically keyed tests avoid social desirability problems by using items that distinguish between groups even if we do not know why the items do so.

The most popular test for assessing the big five traits is the NEO-PI-R, which uses self-report items to measure each of the traits. The Minnesota Multiphasic Personality Inventory (MMPI) is the most widely used empirically keyed personality test.

Projective tests, designed to assess unconscious aspects of personality, present individuals with an ambiguous stimulus, such as an inkblot or a picture, and ask them to tell a story about it. Projective tests are based on the assumption that individuals will project their personalities onto these stimuli. The Thematic Apperception Test (TAT) is a projective test that has been used in personality research. Other assessment methods include behavioral observation, reports from peers, and psychophysiological and neuropsychological measures.

8. PERSONALITY AND HEALTH AND WELLNESS

Conscientiousness and personal control relate to health and longevity through their association with healthy lifestyle choices. Self-efficacy is also related to the ability to make positive changes in lifestyle. Optimism is another personality characteristic that is related to better health.

The Type A behavior pattern is a set of characteristics that may put an individual at risk for the development of heart disease. Type A behavior includes hostility, time urgency, and competitiveness. Type B behavior, in contrast, refers to a more easygoing style. The crucial aspect of Type A appears to be hostility.

Personality traits that are related to health and wellness can also be thought of as states. Thus, even if you are low on these wellness traits, you can still benefit by seeking out states that foster positive attributes.

key *terms*

personality, p. 384

psychodynamic perspectives, p. 384

id, p. 385

ego, p. 385

superego, p. 385

defense mechanisms, p. 386

Oedipus complex, p. 387

collective unconscious, p. 389

archetypes, p. 389

individual psychology, p. 390

humanistic perspectives, p. 391

unconditional positive regard, p. 392

conditions of worth, p. 392

trait theories, p. 393

big five factors of personality, p. 395

personological and life story perspectives, p. 398

social cognitive perspectives, p. 400

self-efficacy, p. 401

cognitive affective processing systems (CAPS), p. 403

behavioral genetics, p. 406

self-report test, p. 408

empirically keyed test, p. 408

Minnesota Multiphasic Personality Inventory (MMPI), p. 409

face validity, p. 409

projective test, p. 409

Rorschach inkblot test, p. 410

Thematic Apperception Test (TAT), p. 411

Type A behavior pattern, p. 415

Type B behavior pattern, p. 415

subjective well-being, p. 415

apply your *knowledge*

1. Consider a facet of your personality that you might want to change. From the perspective of Freud's psychoanalytic theory and Rogers's humanistic theory, could you change this aspect of your personality? If so, how?

2. How important has your childhood been in the development of your adult personality? Choose an experience or series of experiences in childhood and describe how they are represented in your current personality.

3. If you are a fan of reality television, try your hand at identifying the personality characteristics of the individuals involved. Are any of the folks from *Jersey Shore* or *Real Housewives* particularly neurotic or conscientious? If you prefer fictional shows, consider your favorite characters: What are the traits these individuals express?

4. Look at your own social networking profile. Do you think you are expressing the "real you"? If so, how?

CHAPTER 13

Social Psychology

Are 180,000 Heads Better Than One?

Whether it is solving a problem, making a decision, or having influence on the world, a group of people acting together can sometimes accomplish much more than a single individual acting alone. The value of many different perspectives is illustrated in the experience of Tiffany Philippou, a 21-year-old recent college graduate from the U.K. Philippou entered a website competition in hopes of landing a summer internship at the Saatchi and Saatchi ad agency. She started with a Facebook page, called Secret London, where people could share their tips for travel to London—their favorite hotels and restaurants, along with less common travel advice. In just two weeks, Philippou had 180,000 Facebook friends who were sharing enormous amounts of information about the city. Using a technique called *crowdsourcing*, in which the web is used as a forum for brainstorming from all sides, Philippou put all those heads together and amassed a wealth of creative and interesting ideas, certainly more than any one person could have compiled. In no time, her site became more than just an entry in a competition—it became Philippou's very own startup company (Butcher, 2010).

Philippou's experience reveals that brainstorming by a (very) large group can accomplish far more than one person thinking alone. A noteworthy aspect of crowdsourcing is that it may bypass many of the issues that arise when human beings interact in person. Whether face-to-face or online, the ways that people come together—to solve problems, interact, and form bonds with one another—is the essence of social psychology. ●

PREVIEW

We begin our survey of social psychology by examining humans' social cognitive nature and by subsequently exploring social behavior, zeroing in on its extreme forms: altruism and aggression. We next look at the two-way street of social influence—how we influence others and how they influence us. After that, we consider how the groups to which we belong shape our interactions with other groups. Then we probe the world of close relationships, including attraction and love. Finally, we consider the vital role of social connections in physical health and psychological wellness.

1· SOCIAL COGNITION

● **social psychology** The study of how people think about, influence, and relate to other people.

Social psychology is the study of how people think about, influence, and relate to other people. As you will see, social psychologists take many of the topics we have covered so far—including perception, cognition, and emotion—and examine them in a social context. Social psychologists are especially interested in the ways that social situations influence behavior.

Social cognition is the area of social psychology that explores how people select, interpret, remember, and use social information (Spaulding, 2010). Essentially, it is the way in which individuals think in social situations (Maddux, 2010; Strack & Forster, 2009).

Person Perception

Person perception refers to the processes by which we use social stimuli to form impressions of others (Smith & Collins, 2009). One important social cue is the face (Olivola & Todorov, 2010; Rule & others, 2010). The power of the face is demonstrated in research by Alexander Todorov and his colleagues (2005), who examined the ways that perceptions of faces can influence political elections. These researchers asked people to rate the competence of individuals from photographs of their faces. The faces were of candidates in the 2000, 2002, and 2004 U.S. House and Senate elections. Respondents' ratings accurately predicted the outcome for about *70 percent* of the elections. Those faces gave away information about the candidates that was meaningful to the perceivers, including how competent the perceivers felt each office-seeker would be (Mattes & others, 2010). Other aspects of faces can also have important implications for social perception, as we now consider.

PHYSICAL ATTRACTIVENESS AND OTHER PERCEPTUAL CUES

Physical attractiveness has been recognized as a powerful social cue (Berneburg & others, 2010). Judith Langlois and her colleagues found that even infants as young as 3 to 6 months of age showed a preference for looking at attractive faces versus unattractive faces, as rated by adults (Hoss & Langlois, 2003; Ramsey & others, 2004). Attractive individuals are generally assumed to have a variety of other positive characteristics, including being better adjusted, socially skilled, friendly, likable, extraverted, and likely to achieve superior job performance (Langlois & others, 2000). These positive expectations for physically attractive individuals have been referred to as the "beautiful is good" stereotype.

● **stereotype** A generalization about a group's characteristics that does not consider any variations from one individual to another.

A **stereotype** is a generalization about a group's characteristics that does not consider any variations from one individual to another. Stereotypes are a natural extension of the limits on human cognitive processing and our reliance on concepts in cognitive processing (Cook, Cusack, & Dickens, 2010; Wegener, Clark, & Petty, 2006).

We simplify the task of understanding people by classifying them as members of groups or categories with which we are familiar. It takes more mental effort to consider a person's individual characteristics than it does to label him or her as a member of a particular group or category. Thus, when we categorize an individual, the categorization is often based on stereotypes.

Is there any truth to the "beautiful is good" stereotype? Research has shown that attractive people may indeed possess a number of positive characteristics (Langlois & others, 2000). Does that mean that attractiveness is naturally related to, for example, better social skills? Not necessarily.

One way that stereotypes can influence individuals is through a phenomenon called *self-fulfilling prophecy*. In a self-fulfilling prophecy, expectations cause individuals to act in ways that serve to make the expectations come true. Robert Rosenthal and Lenore Jacobsen conducted the classic self-fulfilling prophecy study in 1968. The researchers told grade-school teachers that five students were likely to be "late bloomers"—that these students had high levels of ability that would likely shine forth over time. In reality, however, the students had been randomly selected by the researchers. Nonetheless, a year later, the researchers found that teachers' expectations for the "late bloomers" were reflected in student performance—the academic performance of these five was beyond that of other students. Self-fulfilling prophecy effects show the potential power of stereotypes and other sources of expectations on human behavior.

How might self-fulfilling prophecy effects apply when people interact with physically attractive versus unattractive individuals? Consider that attractive people may receive differential treatment from others throughout their lives. This special treatment increases the likelihood that the attractive individuals might well develop enhanced social skills and be more self-confident than others.

Another relevant question is, what makes a face attractive? *People* magazine's "50 Most Beautiful People" issue might lead you to conclude that attractiveness is about being exceptional in some physical way: Consider Julia Roberts's radiant smile or George Clooney's dreamy eyes. For some time, researchers relied on ratings to tell them who was or was not attractive. They assumed that beauty was something about which social perceivers would agree, along the lines of the editors of *People* magazine.

Researchers have examined what specifically makes a face attractive. Using computer technology that allowed them to average together digitized photographs of a large group of individuals of varying attractiveness, Langlois and her colleagues (1994) created composite faces. A large sample of college students then rated the individual faces and the composites. The results showed that individual faces were less attractive than faces that were created by averaging 8, 16, or 32 other faces. These researchers concluded that attractive faces are actually "just average." Although "averageness" is not the only predictor of attractiveness, Langlois and her colleagues suggest that being average is an essential component (along with variables such as symmetry and youthfulness) of facial attractiveness.

FIRST IMPRESSIONS

When we first meet someone, typically the new acquaintance quickly makes an impression. That first impression can have lasting effects (Ambady & Skowronski, 2009). Recall the primacy effect from Chapter 7—people's tendency to attend to and remember what they learned first (N. H. Anderson, 1965). The power of first impressions is likely due to just such an effect. How quickly do we make these initial impressions of others? In one study, judgments made after just a 100-millisecond exposure time to unfamiliar faces was sufficient for individuals to form an impression (Willis & Todorov, 2006).

Of course, once you become acquainted with someone, you have a lot more information to use to form an opinion of the person. The process by which we come to understand the causes of others' behavior and form an impression of them as individuals is called *attribution*.

What makes a face attractive? Research has found that "averageness" is an essential component.

"Thank God we're cute. You only get one chance to make a good first impression."

Attribution

Trying to understand why people do the things they do is a puzzle that fascinates all of us. We can observe people's behavior and listen to what they say, but to determine the underlying cause of their behavior we often have to make inferences from these observations. Making inferences means taking the information we have and coming up with a good guess about who someone is and what they are likely to do in the future (Gaunt & Trope, 2007; Krueger, 2007).

● **attribution theory** The view that people are motivated to discover the underlying causes of behavior as part of their effort to make sense of the behavior.

Attribution theory views people as motivated to discover the underlying causes of behavior as part of their effort to make sense of the behavior (Heider, 1958; Kelley, 1973; Weiner, 2006). Attributions vary along three dimensions (Jones, 1998):

- *Internal/external causes:* Internal attributions include all causes inside and specific to the person, such as his or her traits and abilities. External attributions include all causes outside the person, such as social pressure, aspects of the social situation, money, the weather, and luck. Did Beth get an *A* on the test because she is smart or because the test was easy?

- *Stable/unstable causes:* Is the cause relatively enduring and permanent, or is it temporary? Did Aaron blow up at his girlfriend because he is a hostile guy or because he was in a bad mood that day?

- *Controllable/uncontrollable causes:* We perceive that people have power over some causes (for instance, by preparing delicious food for a picnic) but not others (rain on picnic day). So, if Henry's picnic is spoiled by a rainstorm, we would not hold that against him.

● **fundamental attribution error** Observers' overestimation of the importance of internal traits and underestimation of the importance of external situations when they seek explanations of an actor's behavior.

● **false consensus effect** Observers' overestimation of the degree to which everybody else thinks or acts the way they do.

ATTRIBUTIONAL ERRORS AND BIASES

In attribution theory, the person who produces the behavior to be explained is called the *actor.* The person who offers a causal explanation of the actor's behavior is called the *observer.* Actors often explain their own behavior in terms of external causes. In contrast, observers frequently explain the actor's behavior in terms of internal causes. Susannah might explain that she honked her car horn at someone who was slow to move when the light turned green because she was in a hurry to get to the hospital to see her ill father, but the other driver might think she was rude.

In committing the **fundamental attribution error,** observers overestimate the importance of internal traits and underestimate the importance of external situations when they seek explanations of an actor's behavior (Jones & Harris, 1967; Kressel & Uleman, 2010; Ramsey & de C. Hamilton, 2010) (Figure 13.1). For example, seeing news coverage of the prisoner abuse that occurred in the Abu Ghraib prison in Iraq, an observer might have concluded, "Those guards were cruel people." In fact, situational factors, such as orders from their superiors, may have influenced their behavior (Haney & Zimbardo, 2009).

Observer Tends to give internal, trait explanations of actor's behavior

"She's late with her report because she can't concentrate on her own responsibilities."

Actor Tends to give external, situational explanations of own behavior

"I'm late with my report because other people keep asking me to help them with their projects."

FIGURE 13.1 The Fundamental Attribution Error In this situation, the supervisor is the observer, and the employee is the actor.

HEURISTICS IN SOCIAL INFORMATION PROCESSING

Heuristics, as described in Chapter 8, are cognitive shortcuts that allow us to make decisions rapidly. Just as heuristics are useful in general information processing, they can play a role in social information processing (Chaiken & Ledgerwood, 2007; Reimer & Rieskamp, 2007). Indeed, heuristics are helpful tools for navigating the complex social landscape, although they can lead to mistakes (Weaver & others, 2007). Stereotypes can be considered a type of heuristic in that they allow us to make quick judgments using very little information.

A common heuristic is the false consensus effect. Ask yourself: "How many students at your school support the death penalty?" Your answer is likely to depend on whether *you* support the death penalty. The **false consensus effect** is the overestimation of the degree to which everybody else thinks or acts the way we do. False consensus effects can be important in social interactions. Imagine, for example, that someone in a group to which you belong makes a racially insensitive remark. According to the false consensus effect, that person is likely to interpret silence on the part of others in the group as agreement.

Note that the fundamental attribution error and the false consensus effect are both related to the special significance of our own thoughts and circumstances. Both of these effects reflect the vast amount of information we have about ourselves relative to the more limited information we have about other people, and they suggest the special place of the self in social information processing.

The Self as a Social Object

Each of us carries around mental representations of ourselves. We can think of the self as our schema, as described in Chapter 7, for who we are, what we are like (and not like), and how we feel about these perceptions. The self is different from other social objects because we know so much more about ourselves than we do about others. While we are more likely to think that behavior is very important to understanding who other people really are, we are more likely to think that our private thoughts and feelings are most indicative of our true self (Johnson, Robinson, & Mitchell, 2004).

The self is special not only because we have direct access to these private experiences but also because we value ourselves. One of the most important self-related variables is *self-esteem,* the degree to which we have positive or negative feelings about ourselves (Harter, 2006). In general, research has shown that it is good to feel good about oneself (Bosson & Swann, 2009).

Individuals with high self-esteem often possess a variety of **positive illusions**—rosy views of themselves that are not necessarily rooted in reality. Constantine Sedikides and his colleagues have shown that many of us think of ourselves as above average on a number of valued characteristics, including how trustworthy and attractive we are (Gregg & Sedikides, 2010; Hepper & Sedikides, 2010; Sedikides, 2007, 2009; Sedikides, Gaertner, & Vevea, 2005; Sedikides & Gregg, 2008; Sedikides & Skowronski, 2009). Of course, the very definition of *average* indicates that not all of us can be "above average."

Shelley Taylor and her colleagues have demonstrated that having positive illusions about the self is often related to heightened well-being (Taylor, 2011; Taylor & Sherman, 2008; Taylor & others, 2003a, 2003b, 2007). Individuals who tend to have positive illusions about themselves are psychologically healthier and more likely to be judged positively by others. Self-esteem also affects our attributions about our own behavior. Individuals with high self-esteem, for instance, tend to give themselves breaks when it comes to judging their own behavior.

Self-serving bias refers to the tendency to take credit for our successes and to deny responsibility for our failures. Think about taking a psychology exam. If you do well, you are likely to take credit for that success ("I'm smart" or "I knew that stuff"); you tend to make internal attributions. If you do poorly, however, you are more likely to blame situational factors ("The test was too hard"); you tend to make external attributions.

SELF-OBJECTIFICATION

Barbara Fredrickson and Tomi-Ann Roberts (1997) examined how another aspect of the self might relate to important outcomes. **Self-objectification** refers to the tendency to see oneself primarily as an object in others' eyes. According to these researchers, women have been socialized to think of themselves and their physical bodies as objects in the social world.

● **positive illusions** Positive views of the self that are not necessarily rooted in reality.

● **self-serving bias** The tendency to take credit for our successes and to deny responsibility for our failures.

● **self-objectification** The tendency to see oneself primarily as an object in the eyes of others.

psychological *inquiry*

Competence

| Appearance | Personal characteristics |

Adapted from Heflick & Goldenberg, 2009.

Objectifying Sarah Palin

The graph shows the results of a study in which participants first evaluated Sarah Palin (or, alternatively, Angelina Jolie) in terms of her appearance or her personal characteristics and then rated her competence. The Y axis shows the competence ratings; the X axis shows the dimension on which she was first evaluated. Answer the questions below.

1. What were the independent and dependent variables in this study?

2. Participants were randomly assigned to evaluate Sarah Palin (or Angelina Jolie) in terms of either her appearance or her personal qualities. Why was random assignment important?

3. If this study had been conducted *after* it was widely known that the Republican Party had paid for a $150,000 makeover for Palin, how do you think that might have influenced the results?

4. Objectification theory focuses primarily on appearance concerns for women. Can you think of a quality that would produce similar results for men?

In a series of studies, Fredrickson and her colleagues asked men and women first to try on certain clothing—either a sweater or a swimsuit—and then to complete a math test. The researchers found that after trying on a swimsuit, women performed much more poorly on the math test. They surmised that trying on the swimsuit had heightened women's experience of self-objectification and body shame and reduced their mental resources for completing the math test (Fredrickson & others, 1998).

Subsequent studies have demonstrated that making woman aware of their status as sexual objects can induce body image concerns, shame, and restricted eating (Moradi & Huang, 2008). Chronic feelings of objectification are associated with lower self-esteem and higher levels of depression (Miner-Rubino, Twenge, & Fredrickson, 2002). Thus, research suggests that the social importance given to women's physical appearance has significant consequences for women. How might focusing on physical appearance influence *others'* perceptions of women?

Consider that in the 2008 U.S. presidential election, the media and others commented regularly on the physical appearance of Governor Sarah Palin, John McCain's vice presidential running mate. The fact that Palin had once been a beauty queen was also a common topic of discussion. Could such commentary influence perceptions of Palin's qualifications to be vice president? To address this question, in a study conducted just weeks before the election, Nathan Heflick and Jamie Goldenberg (2009) asked participants to look at pictures of either Sarah Palin or Angelina Jolie and to evaluate these women based on either their appearance or their personal characteristics. Then the participants rated the competence of the woman whose picture they had viewed. The results showed that regardless of which woman they were rating—Palin or Jolie—the participants rated her as less competent when they had first focused on evaluating her appearance. The Psychological Inquiry above explores these results.

STEREOTYPE THREAT

Stereotypes not only influence our views of others but also sometimes influence the feelings and performance of individuals in stereotyped groups (Rydell & Boucher, 2010;

Seacat & Mickelson, 2009). **Stereotype threat** is an individual's fast-acting, self-fulfilling fear of being judged based on a negative stereotype about his or her group. A person who experiences stereotype threat is well aware of stereotypical expectations for him or her as a member of the group. In stereotype-relevant situations, the individual experiences anxiety about living "down" to expectations and consequently underperforms (Armenta, 2010; Schmader & others, 2009). Claude Steele and Eliot Aronson (1995, 2004) have shown that when a test is presented to African American and Euro-American students who have first simply checked a box indicating their ethnicity, the African Americans perform more poorly. In situations where ethnicity was not made salient, no differences in performance emerged.

Research has also demonstrated that stereotype threat affects performance on math tests by women compared to men, even when both groups have equally strong math training (Spencer, Steele, & Quinn, 1999). White men, too, can fall prey to stereotype threat; in a study of golf ability, Euro-American men performed more poorly than African American men when they were told the test measured "natural athletic ability" (Stone, 2002). Asian women did better on a math test if asked first for their ethnicity, but they scored more poorly if asked first about their gender (Shih & others, 2007).

Researchers have begun to identify factors that may help prevent the consequences of stereotype threat. For example, in one study, African American schoolchildren who were asked their race prior to a math test performed more poorly unless the test was presented to them as a challenge, not as a threat (Alter & others, 2010). Some research suggests that self-esteem may help buffer the effects of stereotype threat in women, especially if women are reminded of another aspect of the self (for instance, "college student") that is positively associated with math performance (Rydell & Boucher, 2010).

SOCIAL COMPARISON

Have you ever felt a sense of accomplishment about getting a *B* on a test, only to feel deflated when you found out that your friend in the class got an *A*? We gain self-knowledge from our own behavior, of course, but we also acquire it from others through **social comparison,** the process by which we evaluate our thoughts, feelings, behaviors, and abilities in relation to other people. Social comparison helps us to evaluate ourselves, tells us what our distinctive characteristics are, and aids us in building an identity.

More than 50 years ago, Leon Festinger (1954) proposed a theory of social comparison. According to this theory, when no objective means are available to evaluate our opinions and abilities, we compare ourselves with others. Furthermore, to get an accurate appraisal of ourselves, we are most likely to compare ourselves with others who are similar to us. Social comparison theory has been extended and modified over the years and continues to provide an important rationale for how we come to know ourselves (Dijkstra, Gibbons, & Buunk, 2010; Mussweiler, 2009).

Festinger concentrated on comparisons with those who are similar to us; other researchers have focused on downward social comparisons, that is, comparisons with those whom we consider inferior to us. Individuals under threat (from negative feedback or low self-esteem, for example) try to feel better by comparing themselves with others who are less fortunate (Wayment & O'Mara, 2008). It can be comforting to think, "Well, at least I'm not as bad off as that guy."

Attitudes

Attitudes are our feelings, opinions, and beliefs about people, objects, and ideas. We have attitudes about all sorts of things. Social psychologists are interested in how attitudes relate to behavior and in whether and how attitudes can change (Bohner & Dickel, 2011; Jost, Federico, & Napier, 2009).

CAN ATTITUDES PREDICT BEHAVIOR?

People sometimes say one thing but do another. You might report positive attitudes about recycling on a survey but still pitch an aluminum soda can in the trash. Studies

● **stereotype threat** An individual's fast-acting, self-fulfilling fear of being judged based on a negative stereotype about his or her group.

● **social comparison** The process by which individuals evaluate their thoughts, feelings, behaviors, and abilities in relation to other people.

● **attitudes** Our feelings, opinions, and beliefs about people, objects, and ideas.

over the past half-century indicate some of the conditions under which attitudes guide actions (McGuire, 2004; Schomerus, Matschinger, & Angermeyer, 2009):

■ *When the person's attitudes are strong* (Ajzen, 2001): For example, senators whose attitudes toward the president are "highly favorable" are more likely to vote for the president's policies than are senators who have only "moderately favorable" attitudes toward the chief executive.

■ *When the person shows a strong awareness of his or her attitudes and when the person rehearses and practices them* (Fazio & Olsen, 2007; Fazio & others, 1982): For example, a person who has been asked to give a speech about the benefits of recycling is more likely to recycle than is an individual with the same attitude about recycling who has not put the idea into words or defined it in public.

■ *When the person has a vested interest* (Sivacek & Crano, 1982): People are more likely to act on attitudes when the issue at stake is something that will affect them personally. For example, a classic study examined whether students would show up for a rally protesting a change that would raise the legal drinking age from 18 to 21 (Sivacek & Crano, 1982). Although students in general were against the change, only those in the critical age group (from 18 to 20) turned out to protest.

CAN BEHAVIOR PREDICT ATTITUDES?

Just as attitudes guide behavior, ample evidence also exists that changes in behavior sometimes precede changes in attitudes. Social psychologists offer two main explanations for why behavior influences attitudes: cognitive dissonance theory and self-perception theory.

● **cognitive dissonance** An individual's psychological discomfort (dissonance) caused by two inconsistent thoughts.

Cognitive Dissonance Theory **Cognitive dissonance,** a concept developed by Festinger (1957), is an individual's psychological discomfort (*dissonance*) caused by two inconsistent thoughts. According to the theory, we feel uneasy when we notice an inconsistency between what we believe and what we do. Cognitive dissonance is at the root of that uncomfortable feeling of being a hypocrite (McConnell & Brown, 2010).

In their classic study of cognitive dissonance, Festinger and J. Merrill Carlsmith (1959) asked college students to engage in a series of very boring tasks, such as sorting spools into trays and turning wooden pegs. These participants were later asked to persuade another student (who was in fact a confederate) to participate in the study by telling him that the task was actually interesting and enjoyable. Half of the participants were randomly assigned to be paid $1 for telling this white lie, and the other half received $20. Afterward, all of the participants rated how interesting and enjoyable the task really was.

Curiously, those who were paid only $1 to tell the lie rated the task as significantly more enjoyable than those who were paid $20. Festinger and Carlsmith reasoned that those paid $20 to tell the lie could attribute their behavior to the high value of the money they received. On the other hand, those who were paid $1 experienced cognitive dissonance. The inconsistency between what they *did* (tell a lie) and what they *were paid for it* (just $1) moved these individuals to change their attitudes about the task ("I wouldn't lie for just $1. If I said I liked the task, I must have really liked it.").

We can reduce cognitive dissonance in one of two ways: change our behavior to fit our attitudes or change our attitudes to fit our behavior. In the classic study above, participants changed their attitudes about the task to match their behavior. Thus, when our attitudes and behavior are at odds, our behavior can influence our attitudes. After you have pitched that soda can, for example, you might feel guilty and relieve that guilt by deciding, "Recycling is not really that important."

Effort justification, one type of dissonance reduction, means rationalizing the amount of effort we put into something. Psychologists have used the concept of effort justification to explain an individual's strong feelings of loyalty toward a group after enduring experiences such as the initiation rites to get into Greek organizations, boot camp in the Marines, and the rigors of medical school en route to becoming a physician. From a cognitive dissonance perspective, individuals in these situations are likely to think, "If it's this tough to get into, it must be worth it." Thus, working hard to get into an organization or a profession can change our attitudes about it.

Self-Perception Theory   **Self-perception theory** is Daryl Bem's (1967) take on how behavior influences attitudes. According to self-perception theory, individuals make inferences about their attitudes by perceiving their behavior. That is, behaviors can cause attitudes, because when we are questioned about our attitudes, we think back on our behaviors for information. When asked about your attitude toward exercise, for example, you might think, "Well, I run every morning, so I must like it." From Bem's perspective, your behavior has led you to recognize something about yourself that you had not noticed before. Bem believes that we are especially likely to look to our own behavior to determine our attitudes when our attitudes are not completely clear.

Figure 13.2 compares cognitive dissonance theory and self-perception theory. Both theories have merit in explaining the connection between attitudes and behavior, and these opposing views bring to light the complexity that may exist in this connection. Both theories suggest that attitudes can be changed by behavior. Another route to attitude change is persuasion.

Working hard to get into a group inspires loyalty through cognitive dissonance.

● **self-perception theory** Bem's theory on how behaviors influence attitudes, stating that individuals make inferences about their attitudes by perceiving their behavior.

PERSUASION

Persuasion involves trying to change someone's attitude—and often his or her behavior as well (Perrin & others, 2010). There are two central questions with respect to persuasion: What makes an individual decide to give up an original attitude and adopt a new one, and what makes a person decide to act on an attitude that he or she has not acted

FIGURE 13.2   Two Theories of the Connections Between Attitudes and Behavior Although we often think of attitudes as causing behavior, behavior can change attitudes, through either dissonance reduction or self-perception.

Festinger Cognitive Dissonance Theory

We are motivated toward consistency between attitudes and behavior and away from inconsistency.

Example: "I hate my job. I need to develop a better attitude toward it or else quit."

Bem Self-Perception Theory

We make inferences about our attitudes by perceiving and examining our behavior and the context in which it occurs, which might involve inducements to behave in certain ways.

Example: "I am spending all of my time thinking about how much I hate my job. I really must not like it."

on before? Teachers, lawyers, and sales representatives study techniques that will help them sway their audiences (children, juries, and buyers). Presidential candidates have arsenals of speechwriters and image consultants to help ensure that their words are persuasive. Perhaps the most skilled persuaders of all are advertisers, who draw on a full array of techniques to sell everything from cornflakes to carpets to cars. Let's review the various elements of persuasion, which were originally identified by Carl Hovland and his colleagues (Hovland, Janis, & Kelley, 1953; Janis & Hovland, 1959):

- *The communicator (source):* Suppose you are running for president of the student body. You tell your fellow students that you are going to make life at your college better. Will they believe you? Most likely, that will depend on your characteristics as a communicator. Whether the students believe you will depend in large part on your credibility—how much other students trust what you say. Trustworthiness, expertise, power, attractiveness, likability, and similarity are all credibility characteristics that help a communicator change people's attitudes or convince them to act.

- *The medium:* Another persuasion factor is the medium or technology used to get the message across. Consider the difference between watching a presidential debate on television and reading about it in the newspaper. Because it presents live images, television is generally a more powerful medium than print sources for changing attitudes.

- *The target (audience):* Age and attitude strength are two characteristics of the audience that determine whether a message will be effective. Younger people are more likely to change their attitudes than older ones. As well, it is easier to change weak attitudes than strong ones.

- *The message:* What kind of message is persuasive? Some messages involve strong logical arguments, and others focus on exciting emotions such as fear and anger in the audience. Which is more likely to work and when? The elaboration likelihood model addresses this question.

● **elaboration likelihood model** Theory identifying two ways to persuade: a central route and a peripheral route.

The **elaboration likelihood model** identifies two ways to persuade: a central route and a peripheral route (DeMarree & Petty, 2007; Petty & Brinol, 2008; Petty & Cacioppo, 1986). The central route to persuasion works by engaging someone thoughtfully with a sound, logical argument. The peripheral route involves non-message factors such as the source's credibility and attractiveness or emotional appeals. The peripheral route is effective when people are not paying close attention or do not have the time or energy to think about what the communicator is saying (Brewer, Barnes, & Sauer, 2010). As you might guess, television advertisers often use the peripheral route to persuasion on the assumption that during the commercials you are probably not paying full attention to the screen. However, the central route is more persuasive when people have the ability and the motivation to pay attention to the facts (Sparks & Areni, 2008).

Successful Persuasion Sooner or later, nearly everyone will be in a position of selling someone something. Social psychologists have studied a variety of ways in which social psychological principles influence whether a salesperson makes that sale (Cialdini, 1993).

One strategy for making a sale is called the *foot-in-the-door* technique (Freedman & Fraser, 1966). The foot-in-the-door strategy involves making a smaller request ("Would you be interested in a three-month trial subscription to a magazine?") at the beginning, saving the biggest demand ("How about a full year?") for last. The foot-in-the-door strategy relies on the notion that in agreeing to the smaller offer, the customer has created a relationship with the seller, expressing some level of trust.

Robert Cialdini and his colleagues introduced a different strategy, called the *door-in-the-face* technique (Cialdini & others,

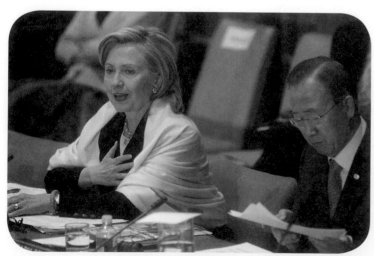

Hillary Clinton called on her powers of persuasion when she ran for president in 2008, and she relies on persuasion today in her role as secretary of state.

1975). The door-in-the-face strategy involves making the biggest pitch at the beginning ("Would you be interested in a full-year subscription?"), which the customer probably will reject, and then making a smaller, "concessionary" demand ("Okay, then, how about a three-month trial?"). The door-in-the-face technique relies on the fact that the customer feels a sense of reciprocity and obligation: Because you let him off the hook with that big request, maybe he should be nice and take that smaller offer.

Cognitive dissonance can also be a powerful tool in sales. Sometimes the harder we work to buy something, the more we want it. After all, did you *buy* that strange lamp on eBay—or did you *win* it?

Resisting Persuasion   Advertisers and salespeople work their hardest to persuade us to buy their products. How do we resist their appeals? According to William McGuire, one way to resist persuasion is through *inoculation* (McGuire, 2003; McGuire & Papageorgis, 1961). McGuire proposed that just as administering a vaccine inoculates individuals from a virus by introducing a weakened or dead version of that virus to the immune system, giving people a weak version of a persuasive message and allowing them time to argue against it can help individuals avoid persuasion.

Research has shown that such "inoculation" helps college students resist plagiarism (Compton & Pfau, 2008) as well as credit card marketing appeals (Compton & Pfau, 2004). When individuals are warned that they are going to be hit with persuasive appeals and are given arguments to help them resist these pitches, they are able to do so. Consider yourself inoculated: Credit card companies often prey on college students.

2· SOCIAL BEHAVIOR

Of course, we do not just think socially; we also behave in social ways. Two particular types of behavior that have interested psychologists represent the extremes of human social activity: altruism and aggression.

Altruism

In 2009, Rick Hohl, a Florida man, heard about a sheriff's deputy in dire need of a kidney transplant. Hohl made an on-the-spot decision to be tested, and he eventually donated his kidney to Johnnie Briggs, a complete stranger (Farris, 2009). Asked why he did it, Hohl replied, in tears, "I'm a Christian." He added, "And I just want to make a difference."

Such a selfless act of kindness is a part of our social experience, as are the huge relief efforts that have followed disasters such as the massive earthquakes in Haiti and Chile in 2010. In everyday life, we witness and perform "random acts of kindness"—maybe adding a quarter to someone's expired parking meter or giving up our seat on a bus to someone in need. We may volunteer for the Special Olympics or serve as a literacy tutor. What all of these acts have in common is **altruism,** an unselfish interest in helping another person (N. Eisenberg & others, 2009).

In examining potentially altruistic behavior (or *prosocial behavior*), psychologists have questioned just how genuinely selfless it is. Some psychologists even argue that true altruism has never been demonstrated (Cialdini, 1991; Maner & others, 2002). True altruism means giving to another person with the ultimate goal of benefiting that person. In contrast to altruism is **egoism,** which involves giving to another person to gain self-esteem; to present oneself as powerful, competent, or caring; or to avoid censure, both from oneself and from society, for failing to live up to expectations. Egoism may also entail helping another person because we want to increase the chances that the person will return the favor someday—that is, we may be kind to another person to ensure *reciprocity.*

The principle of reciprocity encourages us to do unto others as we would have them do unto us. Reciprocity lies at the heart of the Golden Rule. Reciprocity involves an

test yourself

1. What do psychologists mean by a stereotype, and how do they define a stereotype threat?
2. What is involved in making a fundamental attribution error? Give an example of such an error.
3. Identify and briefly explain the four elements of persuasion.

● **altruism** Unselfish interest in helping another person.

● **egoism** Giving to another person to ensure reciprocity; to gain self-esteem; to present oneself as powerful, competent, or caring; or to avoid censure from oneself and others for failing to live up to society's expectations.

expression of trust for another person, as well as feelings of obligation and guilt. The principle of reciprocity means that we behave kindly, as kidney donor Rick Hohl did, under the assumption that someone will show us the same kindness someday.

EVOLUTIONARY VIEWS OF ALTRUISM

Altruism has presented a puzzle for evolutionary psychologists (Leigh, 2010; Phillips, Ferguson, & Rijsdijk, 2010). How can a behavior that rewards others, and not oneself, be adaptive? Interestingly, kindness is not exclusive to humans. Ethologists studying nonhuman primates have shown that altruistic acts of kindness also occur in other species (de Waal, Leimgruber, & Greenberg, 2008). Perhaps kindness is not a mystery but an important adaptation.

Evolutionary theorists note that helping is especially likely to occur among family members, because helping a relative also means promoting the survival of the family's genes (Leigh, 2010). Evolutionary theorists believe that reciprocity in relationships with nonfamily members is essentially the mistaken application of a heuristic that made sense in human evolutionary history—to engage in selfless acts of kindness to one's own family (Nowak, Page, & Sigmund, 2000).

Dale Miller (1999, 2001) suggested that altruism may be an expression of true human nature. From Miller's perspective, although human beings are socialized to believe that the human species is naturally selfish, a great deal of research indicates that humans are not necessarily self-centered and do not engage in selfish acts as a natural response (Holmes, Miller, & Lerner, 2002).

PSYCHOLOGICAL FACTORS IN ALTRUISM

A number of psychological factors have been examined as playing a role in prosocial behavior. Here we examine mood and empathy.

Mood and Helping A distinct psychological component of altruistic behavior is mood. The research literature strongly concludes that happy people are more likely to help others than are unhappy people (Snyder & Lopez, 2007). Does it then follow that when they are in a bad mood, people are less likely to help? Not necessarily, because adults (especially) generally understand that doing good for another person can be a mood booster. Thus, when in a bad mood, they might be likely to help if they think that doing so will improve their mood. Even seeing another person act kindly can be a mood booster. The feelings we have when we see someone else do a good deed—referred to as *feelings of elevation*—also increase the chances that we will, in turn, do something kind ourselves (Schnall, Roper, & Fessler, 2010). Furthermore, sometimes those who have experienced distressing traumatic events find helping others to be an effective and meaningful way of coping (Staub & Vollhardt, 2008).

● **empathy** A feeling of oneness with the emotional state of another person.

Empathy and Helping Another significant element of altruism is empathy (Saarni & others, 2006). **Empathy** is a person's feeling of oneness with the emotional state of another. Daniel Batson (2002, 2006; Batson & others, 2007) has spent the better part of his career searching for proof that truly altruistic behavior does exist. The key to such altruism, he believes, is the extent to which we are able to put ourselves in another person's shoes. When we are feeling empathy for someone else's plight, we are moved to action—not to make ourselves feel better but out of genuine concern for the other person. Empathy can produce altruistic behavior even toward members of rival groups and even when we believe no one will ever hear about our kind act (Fultz & others, 1986).

SOCIOCULTURAL FACTORS IN ALTRUISM

Sociocultural research has examined the characteristics of cultures that are associated with the emergence of altruism and with the belief that everyone deserves fair treatment. A recent study comparing 15 different cultures examined two particular factors: market economies and investment in established religion (Henrich & others, 2010).

A market economy is a decentralized system featuring the free exchange of products and services between producers and consumers. Market economies, such as the U.S. economy, require individuals to extend the principle of reciprocity to strangers, because the normal flow of business requires a certain degree of trust. For example, when you order a book online, you assume a great deal on the part of the strangers who are selling you that book. You give them your credit card information, confident that they will not use it to purchase things and will not share it with someone else. Even though you have no personal knowledge of these sellers, you assume that they will not take advantage of you.

Another important factor in prosocial behavior across cultures is established religions. World religions tend to share an emphasis on the Golden Rule and on treating others fairly. A series of studies conducted with participants in places as varied as Papua New Guinea, Samburu in Kenya, and the U.S. state of Missouri demonstrated that prosocial behaviors were more common in communities characterized by market economies and by investment in established religion (Henrich & others, 2010).

In addition to these two broad cultural factors, social psychologists have examined other sociocultural variables as predictors of altruism and helping, including gender, the influence of bystanders, and the media.

Altruism and Gender   Given the role of empathy in helping, we might think that women should be more likely to help than men. After all, stereotypes tell us that women are by nature more empathic than men. However, as in most domains, it is useful to think about gender in context (Best, 2010; N. Eisenberg & others, 2009). Researchers have found that women are more likely than men to help when the context involves nurturing, such as volunteering time to help a child with a personal problem. Men, on the other hand, are more likely to help in situations in which a perceived danger is present (for instance, picking up a hitchhiker) and in which they feel competent to help (as in assisting someone with a flat tire) (Eagly & Crowley, 1986).

The Bystander Effect   Nearly 50 years ago, a young woman named Kitty Genovese was brutally murdered in New York City. She was attacked at about 3 A.M. in a courtyard surrounded by apartment buildings. It took the slayer approximately 30 minutes to kill Genovese. Thirty-eight neighbors watched the gory scene from their windows and heard Genovese's screams. No one helped or called the police.

Inspired by the Genovese case, social psychologists John Darley and Bibb Latané (1968) conducted a number of studies on the **bystander effect,** the tendency of an individual who observes an emergency to help less when other people are present than when the observer is alone. Most bystander studies show that when alone, a person will help 75 percent of the time, but when another bystander is present, the figure drops to 50 percent. Apparently the difference is due to diffusion of responsibility among witnesses and the tendency to look to the behavior of others for cues about what to do. We may think that someone else will call the police or that, because no one else is helping, possibly the person does not need help.

The bystander effect is still in evidence today. In October 2009, in Richmond, California, a 15-year-old high school girl was raped and beaten by as many as 10 people outside a homecoming dance (CBS News, 2009a). During the assault, more than 20 people watched—and no one called for help.

Media Influences   Psychologists have long considered media influences to be a factor in aggressive behavior. Researchers are also investigating whether media can elicit prosocial behavior as well. Studies suggest that the answer is yes. For example, listening to music with prosocial lyrics can promote kindness (Greitemeyer, 2009), and watching television shows with positive content has been associated with prosocial behavior (Hearold, 1986).

Recently, a series of studies examined the effects of playing prosocial video games on behavior. In those studies, participants who had played a video game such as *Lemmings,* in which the player tries to save the hapless creatures from a variety of disasters, were

● **bystander effect** The tendency of an individual who observes an emergency to help less when other people are present than when the observer is alone.

more likely than those who had played either a neutral or a violent game to help an experimenter pick up a cup of spilled pencils (Greitemeyer & Osswald, 2010). Moreover, in another study, participants who played a prosocial video game were more likely to intervene when a confederate posing as the experimenter's ex-boyfriend came in and began to harass her (Greitemeyer & Osswald, 2010). Thus, exposure to prosocial media may be an important way to spread kindness.

This discussion of altruism highlights the capacity of human beings to help one another, whether through a simple gesture like picking up pencils or a selfless act such as donating an organ. This ability to engage in kindness sits alongside other capacities, such as the capacity to cause others harm. Some evolutionary scientists have suggested that altruism, especially when it is directed at the members of one's own group, may coexist with hostile feelings and actions toward other groups (Arrow, 2007; Choi & Bowles, 2007). For example, a soldier may perform selfless, heroic acts of altruism for his or her country, but for a person on the other side of the combat, that behavior is harmful. Thus, altruism within a group may be linked to aggression.

Aggression

● **aggression** Social behavior whose objective is to harm someone, either physically or verbally.

Aggression refers to social behavior whose objective is to harm someone, either physically or verbally. Aggression is an all-too-common occurrence in contemporary society. Murders in the United States take place at the rate of about 20,000 per year (U.S. Department of Justice, 2007).

BIOLOGICAL INFLUENCES IN AGGRESSION

There is nothing new about human aggression. The primate ancestors of human beings and the earliest humans are thought to have committed aggressive acts against others of their own kind. Researchers who approach aggression from a biological viewpoint examine the influence of evolutionary tendencies, genetics, and neurobiological factors.

In the animal world, aggression often is ritualistic and typically involves threat displays such as a cat's arching its back, baring its teeth, and hissing.

Evolutionary Views Ethologists say that certain stimuli release innate aggressive responses (Lorenz, 1965; Tinbergen, 1969). For example, a male robin will attack another male bird when it sees the red patch on the other bird's breast. When the patch is removed, no attack takes place. However, in the animal kingdom, most hostile encounters do not escalate to killing or even severe harm. Much of the fighting is ritualistic and involves threat displays, for example, a cat arching its back, baring its teeth, and hissing or a chimpanzee staring, stomping the ground, and screaming.

Evolutionary theorists believe that human beings are not much different from other animals. A basic theme of their theory is the survival of the fittest (Barber, 2009; Cosmides, 2011). Thus, they conclude that early in human evolution the survivors were probably aggressive individuals.

Genetic Basis Genes are important in explaining the biological basis of aggression (Brooker & others, 2010). The selective breeding of animals provides evidence for genetic influences in aggression. After a number of breedings among only aggressive animals and among only docile animals, vicious and timid strains of animals emerge. The vicious strains attack nearly anything in sight; the timid strains rarely fight, even when attacked.

The genetic basis for aggression is more difficult to demonstrate in humans than animals and may depend on the type of aggression studied (L. A. Baker & others, 2008; Brendgen & others, 2008). Specifically, twin studies have shown that physical aggression that is proactive in nature may be more influenced by genes, but more reactive aggression and social aggression (for instance, starting rumors about someone) may be more susceptible to environmental effects. Also, genetic influences may be stronger for males than for females (L. A. Baker & others, 2008).

Neurobiological Factors In 1966, Charles Whitman climbed to the top of the campus tower at the University of Texas at Austin, killed 15 people below with a high-powered rifle, and then took his own life. An autopsy revealed a tumor in the limbic system of Whitman's brain, an area (including the amygdalae and hippocampus) associated with emotion. Indeed, although humans do not appear to have a specific aggression center in the brain, aggressive behavior often results when areas such as the limbic system are stimulated by electric currents (Herbert, 1988; Wood & Liossi, 2006).

The frontal lobes of the brain—the areas most involved in executive functions such as planning and self-control—have also been implicated in aggression. Research by Adriane Raine and his colleagues has examined the brains of individuals who have committed the ultimate act of violence: murder (Raine, 2008; Yang, Glen, & Raine, 2008). The results indicate that murderers may differ from others in deficits in the functioning of these areas of the brain.

Neurotransmitters—particularly, lower levels of serotonin—have been linked to aggressive behavior (Neumann, Veenema, & Beiderbeck, 2010; Rosell & others, 2010). In one study, young men whose serotonin levels were low relative to those of other men their age were far more likely to have committed a violent crime (Moffitt & others, 1998). Similarly, aggressive children have lower levels of serotonin than do children who display low rates of aggression (Blader, 2006; Nevels & others, 2010).

Hormones are another biological factor that may play a role in aggression, as noted in Chapter 11. The hormone that is typically implicated in aggressive behavior is testosterone. Research on rats and other animals has shown that testosterone relates to aggression (Cunningham & McGinnis, 2007). However, results with humans have been less consistent (van Bokhoven & others, 2006).

A fascinating study examined how testosterone is influenced by experience and how experience and testosterone together might help explain aggression (Klinesmith, Kasser, & McAndrew, 2006). In this study, college men interacted with either a gun or a child's toy. Testosterone was measured before and after this phase of the study. Men who interacted with the gun showed higher increases in testosterone, compared to the control group. Furthermore, later in the study, the men who had interacted with the gun were more aggressive (they put more hot sauce in a cup of water they thought someone else was going to drink). The role of testosterone in this increase in aggression suggests that testosterone changes may shed light on why some people respond more aggressively to violent cues than do others (Klinesmith, Kasser, & McAndrew, 2006).

At this point it is worth noting that many of the studies of aggression that have been conducted in social psychology laboratories rely on a variety of behaviors that may be considered aggressive even if they do not involve, for example, actually punching someone in the face. In studies on aggression, participants might have an opportunity to "aggress" against another, for instance, by subjecting the individual to a blast of loud noise, dispensing a mild electrical shock, or even, as in the study described above, administering a large dose of Tabasco to swallow. Whether these operational definitions of aggression are applicable to real-life violence is a matter of much debate (Savage & Yancey, 2008).

Social psychologists sometimes ask the participants in a study to assign the amount of hot sauce a person must drink as a measure of aggression. Do you think that is a good operational definition of aggression?

PSYCHOLOGICAL INFLUENCES IN AGGRESSION

Numerous psychological factors appear to be involved in aggression. They include individuals' responses to circumstances, as well as cognitive and learning factors.

Frustrating and Aversive Circumstances   Many years ago, John Dollard and his colleagues (1939) proposed that *frustration,* the blocking of an individual's attempts to reach a goal, triggers aggression. The *frustration-aggression hypothesis* states that frustration always leads to aggression. Soon, however, psychologists found that aggression is not the only possible response to frustration. Some individuals who experience frustration become passive, for example (N. E. Miller, 1941).

Psychologists later recognized that, besides frustration, a broad range of aversive experiences can cause aggression. They include physical pain, personal insults, crowding, and unpleasant events. Aversive circumstances also include factors in the physical environment,

Aversive circumstances that might stimulate aggression include factors in the physical environment such as noise, crowding, and heat waves.

such as the weather. Murder, rape, and assault increase when temperatures are the highest, as well as in the hottest years and the hottest cities (Anderson & Bushman, 2002).

Cognitive Determinants   Aspects of the environment may prime us to behave aggressively (Englander, 2006). Recall from Chapter 7 that priming can involve making something salient to a person, even subliminally or without the person's awareness. Leonard Berkowitz (1993; Berkowitz & LePage, 1996) has shown how the mere presence of a weapon (such as a gun) may prime hostile thoughts and produce aggression (Anderson, Benjamin, & Bartholow, 1998). Indeed, in accordance with Berkowitz's ideas, a well-known study in 1993 found that individuals who lived in a household with a gun were 2.7 times more likely to be murdered than those dwelling in a household without a gun (Kellerman & others, 1993).

A variety of other cognitive factors determine whether an individual responds aggressively to aversive situations (Baumeister, 1999; Berkowitz, 1990; DeWall & others, 2009). For instance, if a person perceives that another's actions are unfair or intentionally hurtful, aggression is more likely to occur. Indeed, in the workplace, individuals who perceive that they have been treated unfairly are more likely to aggress, verbally and physically, against supervisors (Dupre & Barling, 2006).

Observational Learning   Social cognitive theorists believe that individuals learn aggression through reinforcement and observational learning (Englander, 2006). Watching others engage in aggressive actions can evoke aggression, as you might recall from the classic Bobo doll study described in Chapter 6 (Bandura, 1986). One of the most frequent opportunities people have to observe aggression in our culture is to watch violence on television, which we consider further in the discussion below on media violence.

SOCIOCULTURAL INFLUENCES IN AGGRESSION

Aggression involves not only biological and cognitive factors but also factors in the wider social world. Among the sociocultural factors in aggression are variations in economic inequity, the "culture of honor," and the extent to which people watch violence in the media.

Cultural Variations and the Culture of Honor   Aggression and violence are more common in some cultures than others (Kitayama, 2011; Kitayama & Cohen, 2007; Sorrentino & others, 2005). The U.S. homicide rate does not compare well with rates for other countries. For example, the U.S. homicide rate in 2004 was 5.5 per 100,000 (U.S. Bureau of Justice Statistics, 2006), five times the rate in Germany (BKA, 2006) and more than twice that of Canada (Canadian Statistics, 2005).

Crime rates tend to be higher in countries and communities with a considerable gap between the rich and poor (Messner, Raffalovich, & Shrock, 2002; Popp, 2006). The Gini index is a measure of income disparities between the richest and poorest citizens of a nation. The lower the number on the Gini index, the smaller the income disparity. In the United States the Gini index for 2005 was 45, compared to 30 for Germany and 31 for Canada (CIA, 2005).

Dov Cohen has examined the ways in which some cultural norms about masculine pride and family honor may foster aggressive behavior (Cohen, 2001; Vandello & Cohen, 2008; Vandello & others, 2009). In cultures of honor, a man's reputation is thought to be an essential aspect of his economic survival. Such cultures see insults to a man's honor as diminishing his reputation and view violence as a way to compensate for that loss. In these cultures, family pride might lead to so-called honor killings in which, for example, a female rape victim is slain by her male family members so that they, in turn, are not "contaminated" by the rape. In April 2009, a Jordanian man confessed to stabbing his pregnant sister with a meat cleaver because she had left her husband, and he believed she was seeing other men. He felt that he had to kill her to protect his family honor (Gavlak, 2009).

Cohen has examined how, in the United States, southerners are more likely than northerners to be aggressive when honor is at stake. In one study, Cohen and his colleagues (1996) had White men who were from either the North or the South take part in an experiment that required them to walk down a hallway. A confederate passed all the men, bumping against them and quietly calling them a derogatory name. The southerners were more likely than the northerners to think their masculine reputation was threatened, to become physiologically aroused by the insult, and to engage in actual aggressive or dominant acts. In contrast, the northerners were less likely to perceive a random insult as "fightin' words."

Media Violence   Images of violence pervade the U.S. popular media: newscasts, television shows, sports broadcasts, movies, video games, and song lyrics. Evildoers kill and get killed; police and detectives violently uphold or even break society's laws; sports announcers glorify players regardless of whether their behavior is sportsmanlike or contributes to their team's success.

One reason that violence seems so alluring on TV and in the movies is that it usually is portrayed unrealistically. Viewers rarely see its lasting effects, and it is easy to get the message that aggression and violence are the norm—in fact, are the preferred mode of behavior—in the United States.

Although some critics reject the conclusion that TV violence causes aggression (Savage & Yancey, 2008), many scholars insist that TV violence can prompt aggressive or antisocial behavior in children (Anderson & Huesmann, 2007; Comstock & Scharrer, 2006; Dubow, Huesmann, & Greenwood, 2007). Of course, television violence is not the only cause of aggression in children or adults. There is no *one* cause of any social behavior. Aggression, like all other social behaviors, has multiple determinants. The link between TV violence and aggression in children is influenced by children's aggressive tendencies, by their attitudes toward violence, and by the monitoring of children's exposure to it. Perhaps the strongest predictor of aggression is witnessing aggression in one's own family (Ferguson & others, 2008).

Another type of media violence that has interested social psychologists is violent pornography. Violent pornography comprises films, videos, websites, and magazines portraying the degradation of women in a sexual context. An often asked question is, do such media foster violence toward women? Based on several meta-analyses and on research of their own, Neil Malamuth and his colleagues concluded that pornography consumption does have a small effect on male sexual aggression and is related to more accepting attitudes about violence toward women (Hald, Malamuth, & Yuen, 2010; Malamuth, Addison, & Koss, 2000). Yet Malamuth and his colleagues caution that pornography is only one of a number of factors that may lead to sexual violence against

CRITICAL CONTROVERSY

Do Violent Video Games Lead to Violence?

On April 20, 1999, two teenagers, Eric Harris and Dylan Klebold, carried out a shooting rampage on their classmates and teachers at Columbine High School near Littleton, Colorado. Before killing themselves, they shot and killed 12 students and a teacher and wounded 24 others. In the wake of the slayings, the media reported that Harris and Klebold were fans of violent video games, including *Doom* and *Wolfenstein*. Some people began to wonder if the boys had been so obsessively occupied with these violent games that they could no longer distinguish between fantasy and reality. Indeed, the parents of some of the victims filed lawsuits against video game manufacturers, though with no success. Is it possible that video games promote violence?

Video games are an extremely potent medium. It has been suggested that violent video games engage children and adolescents so intensely that they experience an altered state of consciousness in which "rational thought is suspended and highly arousing aggressive scripts are increasingly likely to be learned" (Roberts, Henriksen, & Foehr, 2009, p. 328). Unlike other media, such as TV shows, video games allow the individual to play an active role in perpetrating violence.

Psychologists have examined the role of violent video games in empathy, attitudes about violence, and aggression. A recent meta-analysis concluded that children and adolescents who play violent video games extensively are more aggressive, less sensitive to real-life violence, more likely to engage in delinquent acts, and more likely to get lower grades in school than their counterparts who spend less time playing the games or do not play them at all (Anderson & others, 2010).

Social psychologist Craig Anderson has been a vocal spokesperson against media violence, especially violent video games (Anderson, 2003; Anderson & Huesmann, 2007; Bushman & Anderson, 2007; Gentile & Anderson, 2006). Critics of the work of Anderson and his colleagues have pointed out that the acts of aggression (for instance, blasting someone with loud noise) studied in the laboratory are not generalizable to real-world criminal violence (Ritter & Elsea, 2005; Savage, 2008; Savage & Yancey, 2008). Furthermore, they stress that many studies have not measured important third variables, such as family violence, in predicting both video game use and aggression (Ferguson & others, 2008; Ferguson & Kilburn, 2010).

The controversy over violent video games and aggression highlights the links among social psychology, public policy, and current events. Every technological innovation opens a new set of questions to be addressed by social psychologists.

WHAT DO YOU THINK?

- Do you or people you know play violent video games? If so, what impact, if any, do you think this activity has on your or their thoughts and feelings?
- Would you allow your child to play violent video games? Why or why not?
- What do you think policymakers should do with regard to the controversy over the effects of playing video games?

---

women (Hald, Malamuth, & Yuen, 2010; Vega & Malamuth, 2007). The most problematic materials are those that depict women enjoying being the victims of male sexual violence (Hald, Malamuth, & Yuen, 2010). Such violent pornography reinforces the *rape myth*—the false belief that women desire coercive sex.

Violent video games are another form of media that might influence aggressive behavior. To read about this topic, see the Critical Controversy.

test yourself

1. What is the difference between altruism and egoism?
2. Explain the bystander effect, and give an example.
3. What have researchers found about the influence of prosocially oriented video games? What have they learned about the effects of violent video games?

REDUCING AGGRESSION

Social cognitive theorists believe that people who act aggressively often are rewarded for their aggression and that individuals learn to be aggressive by watching others behave aggressively. Research has supported this view (Bandura, 1997). Thus, the strategies for reducing aggression that seem most promising are those designed to decrease rewards for aggression and to lessen exposure to it. Parents in particular have been targeted to help children to reduce aggression (Leaper & Friedman, 2007). Recommended parenting strategies include encouraging young children to develop empathy toward others and more closely monitoring adolescents' activities (Denham, Bassett, & Wyatt, 2007; N. Eisenberg & others, 2009).

3· SOCIAL INFLUENCE

Another topic of interest to social psychologists is how our behavior is influenced by other individuals and groups (Judd & Park, 2007; Monin, 2007; Perrin & others, 2010). This section explores key aspects of social influence: conformity, obedience, and group influence.

Conformity and Obedience

Research on conformity and obedience started in earnest after World War II. Psychologists sought answers to the disturbing question of how ordinary people could be influenced to commit the sort of atrocities inflicted on Jews, Gypsies, and other minorities during the Holocaust. Researchers wanted to know to what extent people would change their behavior to conform to the behavior of others.

CONFORMITY

Conformity is a change in a person's behavior to coincide more closely with a group standard. Conformity takes many forms and affects many aspects of people's lives, in negative and positive ways. Conformity is at work, for example, when a person comes to college and starts to drink alcohol heavily at parties, even though he or she might have never been a drinker before. Conformity is also at work when we obey the rules and regulations that allow society to run smoothly. Consider how chaotic it would be if people did not conform to social norms such as stopping at a red light, driving on the correct side of the road, and not punching others in the face. Conformity can also be a powerful way to increase group cohesion. Even something as simple as marching in step together or singing a song along with a group can lead to enhanced cooperation among group members (Wiltermuth & Heath, 2009).

Asch's Experiment   Put yourself in this situation: You are taken into a room where you see five other people seated along a table. A person in a white lab coat enters the room and announces that you are about to participate in an experiment on perceptual accuracy. The group is shown two cards—the first having only a single vertical line on it and the second having three vertical lines of varying length. You are told that the task is to determine which of the three lines on the second card is the same length as the line on the first card. You look at the cards and think, "What a snap. It's so obvious which is the same."

What you do not know is that the other people in the room are confederates who are working with the experimenter. On the first several trials, everyone agrees about which line matches the standard. Then on the fourth trial, each of the others picks the same incorrect line. As the last person to make a choice, you have the dilemma of responding as your eyes tell you or conforming to what the others before you said. How do you think you would answer?

● **conformity** A change in a person's behavior to coincide more closely with a group standard.

Homogeneous Originality **by CIAgent**

www.funnytimes.com

Standard line

A   B   C
Comparison lines

Solomon Asch conducted this classic experiment on conformity in 1951 (Figure 13.3). Asch instructed the confederates to give incorrect responses on 12 of 18 trials. To his surprise, Asch (1951) found that the volunteer participants conformed to the incorrect answers 35 percent of the time. Subsequent research has supported the notion that the pressure to conform is strong (Pines & Maslach, 2002). Why do people go along with a group even when they have clear-cut information disputing the others, such as the lines in the Asch experiment? Social psychologists have addressed this question as well.

Going Along to Be Right and Going Along to Be Liked
In general, two main factors have been identified as contributing to conformity: informational social influence and normative social influence.

Informational social influence refers to the influence other people have on us because we want to be right. The social group can provide us with information that we did not know or may help us see things in ways that had not occurred to us. As a result, we may conform because we have come to agree with the group. The tendency to conform based on informational social influence depends especially on two factors: how confident we are in our own independent judgment and how well informed we perceive the group to be. For example, in a discussion with three of your acquaintances who are IT geeks, you might just go along with their opinions about which new computer you should buy, especially if you do not know much about computers.

In contrast, **normative social influence** is the influence others have on us because we want them to like us. Whether the group is an inner-city gang or members of a profession such as medicine or law, if a particular group is important to us, we

FIGURE 13.3   Asch's Conformity Experiment The figures at the top show the stimulus materials for the Asch conformity experiment on group influence. The photograph captures the puzzlement of one student after five confederates of the experimenter chose the incorrect line.

● **informational social influence** The influence other people have on us because we want to be right.

● **normative social influence** The influence others have on us because we want them to like us.

● **obedience** Behavior that complies with the explicit demands of the individual in authority.

might adopt a clothing style that people in the group wear or use the same slang words, and we might assume the attitudes that characterize the group's members (Hewlin, 2009).

Conformity is a powerful social force, and on many occasions we undoubtedly feel more comfortable when we are able to go along with the crowd. You can feel the pressure of conformity for yourself if, the next time you get on an elevator with other people, you do not turn around to face the door. Why does it feel so wrong to face the back of the elevator? Recent research in social psychology and neuroscience has provided an interesting answer, as we shall see in the Intersection.

OBEDIENCE

Obedience is behavior that complies with the explicit demands of the individual in authority. We are obedient when an authority figure demands that we do something, and we do it. Note that in conformity, people change their thinking or behavior so that it will be more like that of others, while in obedience, there is an explicit demand to comply (Blass, 2007).

Obedient behavior sometimes can be distressingly cruel. One of the most infamous examples of the destructive nature of obedience is the Nazi crimes against Jews and others during World War II. More recent examples include the obedience of radical Muslims instructed to participate in suicide attacks against Israelis and Westerners (McCauley & Segal, 2009), as well as that of U.S. military personnel at Abu Ghraib prison in Iraq, who justified their horrendous abuse of detainees by asserting that they were "just following orders" (A. G. Miller, 2004). Millions of people throughout history have obeyed commands to commit terrible acts.

Social Psychology and Cognitive Neuroscience: Is the Brain Wired for Conformity?

Conformity involves changing our behavior to match that of a group. Just as the brain is involved in all human behavior, it is involved in conformity. Recent research has provided intriguing insights into the ways the brain responds to moments when we do not fit in with a group. The research results suggest that our brain may actually "feel better" when we fit in.

In a recent study using fMRI, the brain-imaging technique described in Chapter 3, Vasily Klucharev and his colleagues examined what happens in the brain when people find out that their opinions conflict with those of others (Klucharev & others, 2009). Women were asked to rate a variety of female faces for attractiveness, and their brains were scanned while they received feedback about whether their ratings agreed with those of the other group members. When participants were told that their ratings differed from the group's ratings, they showed enhanced activation in the brain area typically associated with monitoring for errors. In other words, the brain responded to judgments that differed from the group judgments as if they were *mistakes*. Furthermore, when the women's ratings were different from the group's ratings, women experienced less activation in the nucleus accumbens and the ventral tegmental area, the brain's reward centers. The greater the degree to which women's brains responded to being different as an error and as

Why would humans be wired for conformity? Could the brain learn to enjoy being different?

not rewarding, the more they tended to conform when given a chance to re-rate the faces at the end of the study. Klucharev and colleagues suggest that their findings demonstrate that humans *learn* that conformity is rewarding.

In a second study, the researchers found that these effects were specific to social conformity. In that study, the women were given feedback about a *computer's* ratings of the faces. Results showed that the brain did not mind being different from a computer nearly as much as being different from a group of other humans.

A classic series of experiments by Stanley Milgram (1965, 1974) provides insight into such obedience. Imagine that, as part of an experiment in psychology, you are asked to deliver a series of painful electric shocks to another person. You are told that the purpose of the study is to determine the effects of punishment on memory. Your role is to be the "teacher" and to punish the mistakes made by the "learner." Each time the learner makes a mistake, you are to increase the intensity of the shock.

You are introduced to the learner, a nice 50-year-old man who mumbles something about having a heart condition. He is strapped to a chair in the next room; he communicates with you through an intercom. The apparatus in front of you has 30 switches, ranging from 15 volts (slight) to 450 volts (marked as beyond dangerous, "XXX").

As the trials proceed, the learner quickly runs into trouble and is unable to give the correct answers. Should you shock him? As you increase the intensity of the shock, the learner says that he is in pain. At 150 volts, he demands to have the experiment stopped. At 180 volts, he cries out that he cannot stand it anymore. At 300 volts, he yells about his heart condition and pleads to be released. If you hesitate in shocking the learner, however, the experimenter tells you that you have no choice; the experiment must continue. Eventually the learner stops responding altogether, and the experimenter tells you that not responding is the same as a wrong answer. At this point, the learner appears to be injured or even dead. Would you keep going?

Prior to doing the study, Milgram asked 40 psychiatrists how they thought individuals would respond to this situation. The psychiatrists predicted that most teachers

"I don't care if you do think I'm 'dissing' you . . . I want you in the story corner NOW!"

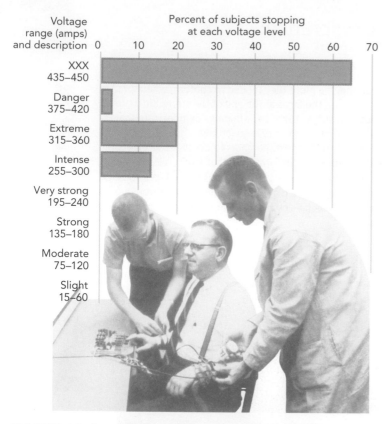

FIGURE 13.4 **Milgram Obedience Study** A 50-year-old man, the "learner," is strapped into a chair. The experimenter makes it look as if a shock generator is being connected to his body through several electrodes. The chart shows the percentage of "teachers" who stopped shocking the learner at each voltage level. Adapted from Stanley Milgram, "Behavioral Study of Obedience" in *Journal of Abnormal and Social Psychology*, 67: 371–378, 1963.

would go no farther than 150 volts, that fewer than 1 in 25 would go as far as 300 volts, and that only 1 in 1,000 would deliver the full 450 volts. The psychiatrists were way off. As shown in Figure 13.4, the majority of the teachers obeyed the experimenter: Almost two-thirds delivered the full 450 volts.

By the way, the 50-year-old man was a confederate in the experiment. In Milgram's study, the learner was not being shocked at all. Of course, the teachers were unaware that the learner was only pretending to be shocked.

At very strong voltage levels, the learner quit responding. When the teacher asked the experimenter what to do, the experimenter simply replied, "You must go on. The experiment requires that you continue." Imagine that with those simple statements the experimenter was able to calmly command people to (as far as they knew) shock a man to unconsciousness and possibly death. Such is the power of obedience to authority.

In variations of the experiment, Milgram discovered that more people would disobey in certain circumstances. Specifically, disobedience was more common when participants could see others disobey, when the authority figure was not perceived to be legitimate and was not close by, and when the victim was made to seem more human.

The ethics of Milgram's studies has been a subject of controversy since he began them. The teachers in the experiment clearly felt anguish; some were very disturbed about "harming" another individual. All of the participants had been deceived by Milgram as part of the study. Even though they found out that they had not actually shocked or harmed anyone, was the anguish imposed on them ethical? Milgram's studies certainly revealed a great deal about human nature, and none of the volunteers expressed regret that they had taken part.

Under today's ethical guidelines, it is unlikely that these experiments would have been approved. Nonetheless, we are still learning from Milgram's data. A recent meta-analysis of his experiments suggested that the critical decision was at the 150-volt level, when the learner first requested that the experiment be halted. At that point, 80 percent of those who were going to stop did so (Packer, 2008). Apparently, individuals who were going to disobey were those who responded not to the later anguished cries of pain but to the learner's first request to be set free.

You might wonder whether Milgram's results would still apply in contemporary society. To examine this question, in 2006 social psychologist Jerry Burger (2009) re-created Milgram's study at Santa Clara University in California. Burger's study was very similar to Milgram's, except that in Burger's experiment the participants were never allowed to go higher than 150 volts. At 150 volts, the confederate asked to end the study, and immediately after participants decided whether to continue, the experiment was ended. Surprisingly, Burger's participants were only slightly less likely to obey than Milgram's had been. The Psychological Inquiry on p. 441 probes the results of Burger's study.

EXERTING PERSONAL CONTROL

"If a man does not keep pace with his companions, perhaps it is because he hears a different drummer. Let him step to the music which he hears, however measured or far away." American essayist and philosopher Henry David Thoreau's words suggest that some of us resist social influence, just as Thoreau himself did. It is safe to say that as we go through life, we are both conformists and nonconformists. Sometimes we stand up and stand out, and sometimes we go with the flow.

Our relationship to the social world is reciprocal. Individuals may try to control us, but we can exert personal control over our actions and influence others in turn (Bandura,

psychological *inquiry*

Percent (Y axis): 0, 20, 40, 60, 80

2006 sample   Milgram's sample

☐ Stopped at 150 volts or earlier
■ Continued after 150 volts

Adapted from Burger, 2009.

Obedience Now and Then

The figure shows, side by side, the results of Burger's (2009) study of obedience and the results of one of Milgram's studies. The vertical or Y axis shows the percent of participants who stopped or continued shocking the learner after that individual first expressed a desire to end the study. Try out the following questions.

1. Comparing the two studies, are you surprised at the similarities? Why or why not?

2. Burger did not allow participants who had learned about Milgram's study to take part in his study. Do you think that decision was justified? Explain. How might the results have differed if these individuals had been permitted to participate?

3. If you had been a "teacher" in Burger's study—that is, involved in administering the shocks—what do you think you would have done?

2009; Doerr & Baumeister, 2010; Knowles, Nolan, & Riner, 2007). Although it may not be easy to resist authority, living with the knowledge that you compromised your own moral integrity may be more difficult in the long run.

Group Influence

On February 2, 2005, Chico State University student Matthew Carrington died following a fraternity hazing in the basement of the Chi Tau house. He and another pledge were verbally taunted and forced to do pushups in raw sewage. They were also compelled to drink gallons and gallons of water. Eventually, Carrington suffered a seizure and died of water intoxication. Among those who were convicted in his death were four fraternity brothers who had never been in trouble before. Indeed, the group's ringleader was Gabriel Maestretti, a deeply religious former altar boy, high school homecoming king, and volunteer coach. Why and how do individuals who would never perform destructive acts, if alone, perpetrate them when in a group? This is the central question that has driven research in the social psychology of group influence.

DEINDIVIDUATION

One process that sheds light on the behavior of individuals in groups is **deindividuation,** which occurs when being part of a group reduces personal identity and erodes the sense of personal responsibility (Levine, Cassidy, & Jentzsch, 2010; Zimbardo, 2007). An example of the effects of deindividuation is the wild street celebrations that erupt after a team's victory in the World Series or Super Bowl.

One explanation for the effects of deindividuation is that groups give us anonymity. When we are part of a group, we may act in an uninhibited way because we believe that no one will be able to identify us. The Ku Klux Klan demonstrates a variety of ways that human beings can deindividuate: acting in groups, often under cover of darkness, and wearing white hoods to conceal identity.

SOCIAL CONTAGION

Have you ever noticed that a movie you watched in a crowded theater seemed funnier than it did when you watched the DVD alone at home? People laugh more when others

● **deindividuation** The reduction in personal identity and erosion of the sense of personal responsibility when one is part of a group.

These Ku Klux Klan members illustrate a variety of ways that human beings can deindividuate: turning out in a group, acting under cover of darkness, and concealing identity through special clothing.

The research of Norman Triplett (1898) of Indiana University, viewed by some to be the first North American sport psychologist, found that cyclists performed better when they raced in groups than when they rode by themselves, against the clock.

● **social contagion** Imitative behavior involving the spread of actions, emotions, and ideas.

● **social facilitation** Improvement in an individual's performance because of the presence of others.

● **social loafing** Each person's tendency to exert less effort in a group because of reduced accountability for individual effort.

are laughing. Babies cry when other babies are crying. The effects of others on our behavior can take the form of **social contagion,** imitative behavior involving the spread of actions, emotions, and ideas (Cohen & Prinstein, 2006; Gino, Ayal, & Ariely, 2009). Social contagion effects can be observed in such varied phenomena as social fads, the popularity of dog breeds (Herzog, 2006), the spread of unhealthy behaviors such as smoking and drinking among adolescents (Rodgers, 2007), and symptoms of eating disorders among young women (Crandall, 2004; Forman-Hoffman & Cunningham, 2008).

One way to observe social contagion is to sit in a quiet but crowded library and start coughing. You will soon notice others doing the same thing. Similarly, imagine that you are walking down the sidewalk and come upon a group of people who are all looking up. How likely is it that you can avoid the temptation of looking up to see what is so interesting to them?

GROUP PERFORMANCE

Are two or three heads better than one? Some studies reveal that we do better in groups; others show that we are more productive when we work alone (Mojzisch & Schulz-Hardt, 2010). We can make sense out of these contradictory findings by looking closely at the circumstances in which performance is being analyzed (Nijstad, 2009).

Social Facilitation If you have ever given a presentation in a class, you might have noticed that you did a much better job standing in front of your classmates than during any of your practice runs. **Social facilitation** occurs when an individual's performance improves because of the presence of others (Mendes, 2007). Robert Zajonc (1965) argued that the presence of other individuals arouses us. The arousal produces energy and facilitates our performance in groups. If our arousal is too high, however, we are unable to learn new or difficult tasks efficiently. Social facilitation, then, improves our performance on well-learned tasks. For new or difficult tasks, we might be best advised to work things out on our own before trying them in a group.

Social Loafing Another factor in group performance is the degree to which one's behavior is monitored. **Social loafing** refers to each person's tendency to exert less effort in a group because of reduced accountability for individual effort. The effect of social loafing is lowered group performance (Latané, 1981). The larger the group, the more likely it is that an individual can loaf without detection.

Social loafing commonly occurs when a group of students is assigned a class project, and it is one reason that some students intensely dislike group assignments. These same individuals will not be surprised to learn that under certain conditions, working with others can increase individual effort (D. S. Levine, 2000). For example, a person who views the group's task as important (say, a student who strongly wants an *A* on the project) and who does not expect other group members to contribute adequately is likely to work harder than usual—and perhaps to do most of the work himself or herself.

Researchers have identified ways to decrease social loafing. They include making individuals' contributions more identifiable and unique, simplifying the evaluation of these contributions, and making the group's task more attractive (Karau & Williams, 1993).

GROUP DECISION MAKING

Many of the decisions we make take place in groups—juries, teams, families, clubs, school boards, and the U.S. Senate, for example (Gastil, 2009; Kerr, 2010; Mojzisch & Schulz-Hardt, 2010). What happens when people put their minds to the task of making a group decision? How do they decide whether a criminal is guilty, whether a country should attack another, whether a family should stay home or go on vacation, or whether sex education should be part of a school curriculum? Three aspects of group decision making bear special mention: risky shift and group polarization; groupthink; and major-ity and minority influence.

Risky Shift and Group Polarization   Imagine that you have a friend, Lisa, who works as an accountant. All her life Lisa has longed to be a writer. In fact, she believes that she has the next great American novel in her head and that she just needs time and energy to devote to writing it. Would you advise Lisa to quit her job and go for it? What if you knew beforehand that her chances of success were 50–50? How about 60–40? How much risk would you advise Lisa to take?

In one investigation, participants were presented with fictitious dilemmas like this one and were asked how much risk the characters in the scenarios should take (Stoner, 1961). When the individuals discussed the dilemmas as a group, they were more willing to endorse riskier decisions than when they were queried alone. The so-called **risky shift** is the tendency for a group decision to be riskier than the average decision made by the individual group members (Goethals & Demorest, 1995).

However, people do not always make riskier decisions in a group than when alone. Instead, a group discussion can move individuals more strongly in the direction of the position they initially held (Moscovici, 1985). The **group polarization effect** is the solidification and further strengthening of an individual's position as a consequence of a group discussion or interaction. For example, let's say that while in a class where the students and instructor are discussing the effects of obedience on human behavior, you start out with a somewhat negative view of obedience. After hearing the full class dis-cussion and adding your two cents, you find that your attitude toward obedience is quite a bit more negative than at first. What might explain your more extreme views at the end of the discussion? Such polarization may occur because, during the discus-sion, you heard new, more persuasive arguments that strengthened your original posi-tion. Group polarization might also be a product of social comparison. In the example of your classroom discussion, you might have discovered that your opinion was not as extreme as others' opinions, and you might have been influenced to take a stand at least as strong as the most extreme advocate's position.

Groupthink: Getting Along but Being Very Wrong   **Groupthink** refers to the impaired group decision making that occurs when making the right decision is less important than maintaining group harmony. Instead of engaging in an open discussion of all the available information, in groupthink, members of a group place the highest value on conformity and unanimity. Members are encouraged to "get with the program," and dissent meets with very strong disapproval.

Groupthink can result in disastrous decisions. Irving Janis (1972) introduced the concept of groupthink to explain a number of enormous decision-making errors throughout history. Such errors include the lack of U.S. preparation for the Japanese bombing of Pearl Harbor during World War II, the escalation of the Vietnam War in the 1960s, the Watergate cover-up in 1974, and the *Challenger* space shuttle disaster in 1986. After the 9/11 terrorist attacks, the possibility that groupthink interfered with the proper implementation of intelligence reared its head. Whistleblower Colleen Rowley, an FBI special agent, revealed that the FBI power hierarchy had been unresponsive to information that might have helped prevent the attacks. More recently, many criticized former President George W. Bush and his cabinet for not listening to dissenting voices in the days leading up to the Iraq War.

Symptoms of groupthink include overestimating the power and morality of one's group, close-mindedness and lack of willingness to hear all sides of an argument, and pressure for uniformity. Groupthink can occur whenever groups value conformity over accuracy (Degnin, 2009). However, groupthink can be prevented if groups avoid isola-tion, allow the airing of all sides of an argument, have an impartial leader, include

● **risky shift** The tendency for a group decision to be riskier than the average decision made by the individual group members.

● **group polarization effect** The solidification and further strengthening of an individual's posi-tion as a consequence of a group discussion or interaction.

● **groupthink** The impaired group decision making that occurs when making the right deci-sion is less important than maintaining group harmony.

outside experts in the debate, and encourage members who are strongly identified with the group to speak out in dissent (Packer, 2009).

Majority and Minority Influence   Most groups make decisions by voting, and, even in the absence of groupthink, the majority usually wins. The majority exerts influence on group decision making through both informational influence (they have greater opportunity to share their views) and normative influence (they set group norms). Those who do not go along may be ignored or even given the boot.

Prospects might seem dim for minority opinion holders, but they *can* make a difference. Because it is outnumbered, the minority cannot win through normative pressure. Instead, it must do its work through informational pressure. If the minority presents its views consistently and confidently, then the majority is more likely to listen to the minority's perspectives. A powerful way that minority opinion holders can have influence is by winning over former majority members to their points of view.

4· INTERGROUP RELATIONS

Conflicts between groups, especially ethnic and cultural groups, are rampant around the world (Stevens & Gielen, 2007). The Islamic terrorist organization al Qaeda attacks the United States and other countries that its members perceive to be too secular and materialistic. The wronged nations retaliate. Israelis and Palestinians fight over territory in the Middle East, each claiming religious and historical rights to the disputed land. In countries across Africa, tribal chiefs try to craft a new social order favorable to their own rule. A variety of concepts introduced by social psychologists can help us understand the intensity of such cultural and ethnic conflicts and can provide insight into how to reduce their number and magnitude (Sanchez-Burks, 2007).

Group Identity: Us Versus Them

Think about the groups of which you are a member—religious and social organizations, your ethnic group, your nationality. When someone asks you to identify yourself, how often do you respond by mentioning these group memberships? And how much does it matter whether the people you associate with are members of the same groups as you?

SOCIAL IDENTITY

Social identity refers to the way we define ourselves in terms of our group membership. In contrast to personal identity, which can be highly individualized, social identity assumes some commonalities with others (Dovidio, Gaertner, & Saguy, 2009; Wenzel, 2009). A person's social identity might include identifying with a religious group, a country, a social organization, a political party, and many other groups (Carney & others, 2007; Haslam & Reicher, 2006; Vaes, Heflick, & Goldenberg, 2010). These diverse forms of social identity reflect the numerous ways people connect to groups and social categories (Abrams & Hogg, 2004; Hogg & Abrams, 2007; Postmes & Jetten, 2006). Social psychologist Kay Deaux (2001) identified five distinct types of social identity: ethnicity and religion, political affiliation, vocations and avocations, personal relationships, and stigmatized groups (Figure 13.5).

For many people, ethnic identity and religious identity are central to their social identity (Charmaraman & Grossman, 2010; King & Roeser, 2009). Ethnic identity can be a source of pride for individuals (Umana-Taylor & Guimond, 2010). In the United States, special events celebrate the rich cultural contributions of

test yourself

1. Compare and contrast informational social influence and normative social influence.
2. What is the difference between conformity and obedience?
3. What do the concepts of risky shift and group polarization have to say about decision making in a group context?

● **social identity** The way we define ourselves in terms of our group membership.

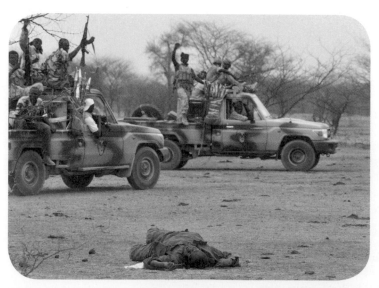

Ethnic conflict in the African country of Chad has increased in recent years. In this photograph from May 2009, a rebel soldier lies dead while Chad soldiers carry out cleanup operations in the area of Am Dam.

Ethnicity & Religion	Relationships	Vocations & Avocations	Political Affiliation	Stigmatized Identities
Jewish Asian American Southern Baptist West Indian	Parent Mother Son Widow	Artist Athlete Psychologist Military veteran	Environmentalist Feminist Republican	Overweight person Person with AIDS Homeless person Alcoholic

FIGURE 13.5   Types of Identity When we identify ourselves, we draw on a host of different characteristics associated with the various social groups to which we belong.

many different groups to the society. Such experiences may provide individuals with an important resource in coping with biases they may encounter in life (Crocker, Major, & Steele, 1998). Feeling connected to one's ethnic group may buffer individuals from the stressful effects of injustice (Sellers & others, 2006).

Social psychologist Henry Tajfel (1978), a Holocaust survivor, wanted to explain the extreme violence and prejudice that his religious group (Jews) experienced. Tajfel's **social identity theory** states that our social identities are a crucial part of our self-image and a valuable source of positive feelings about ourselves. To feel good about ourselves, we need to feel good about the groups to which we belong. For this reason, individuals invariably think of the group to which they belong as an *in-group,* a group that has special value in comparison with other groups, called *out-groups.* To improve our self-image, we continually compare our in-groups with out-groups (Parks, 2007). In the process, we often focus more on the differences between the two groups than on their similarities.

Research by Tajfel (1978) and many others who have used his theory shows how easy it is to lead people to think in terms of "us" and "them." In one experiment, Tajfel had participants look at a screen featuring a huge number of dots and estimate how many dots were displayed. He then assigned the participants to groups based on an arbitrary situation—whether they overestimated or underestimated the number of dots. Once assigned to one of the two groups, the participants were asked to award money to other participants. Taifel found that individuals awarded money to members of their in-group, not to participants in the out-group, even though the group assignment had been essentially arbitrary. If we favor the members of a group that was formed on such trivial bases, it is no wonder that we show intense in-group favoritism when differences are not so trivial.

ETHNOCENTRISM

The tendency to favor one's own ethnic group over other groups is called **ethnocentrism.** Ethnocentrism does not simply mean taking pride in one's group; it also involves asserting the group's superiority over other groups (Gormley & Lopez, 2010; Hall, Matz, & Wood, 2010). As such, ethnocentrism encourages in-group/out-group, we/they thinking (Brewer, 2007; Smith, Bond, & Kagitcibasi, 2006). Consequently, ethnocentrism implies that ethnic out-groups are not simply different; they are worse than one's group. Hence ethnocentrism may underlie prejudice.

Prejudice

Prejudice is an unjustified negative attitude toward an individual based on the individual's membership in a particular group. The group can be made up of people of a specific ethnicity, sex, age, religion—essentially, people who are different in some way from a prejudiced person (Brandt & Reyna, 2010; Graziano & Habashi, 2010; Jefferson & Bramlett, 2010; T. D. Nelson, 2009). Prejudice as a worldwide phenomenon can be

● **social identity theory** Tajfel's theory that our social identities are a crucial part of our self-image and a valuable source of positive feelings about ourselves.

● **ethnocentrism** The tendency to favor one's own ethnic group over other groups.

● **prejudice** An unjustified negative attitude toward an individual based on the individual's membership in a particular group.

Ethnic identity evokes ethnic pride. Here, Italian American soccer fans in Boston's North End rejoice at the Italian soccer team's World Cup win; Chinese American children touch the "lion" in the streets of New York City's Chinatown on the day of Chinese New Year, in hopes of receiving good luck and prosperity; and children and adults dance during a Kwanzaa celebration at Philadelphia's Canaan Baptist Church to strengthen their ties to their African heritage.

seen in many eruptions of hatred in human history. In the Balkan Peninsula of eastern Europe, the Serbs' prejudice against Bosnians prompted the Serb policy of "ethnic cleansing." The prejudice of the Hutus against the Tutsis in Rwanda led them to go on a murderous rampage, attacking the Tutsis with machetes.

A powerful example of destructive prejudice within U.S. society is racial prejudice against African Americans. When Africans were brought to colonial America as slaves, they were considered property and treated inhumanely. In the first half of the twentieth century, most African Americans still lived in the South and remained largely segregated from White society by law; restaurants, movie theaters, and buses had separate areas for Whites and African Americans.

Despite progress in racial equality over the years, a much higher percentage of African Americans than Whites still live in impoverished neighborhoods and lack access to good schools, jobs, and healthcare, even decades after the abolition of legal segregation. Recent national events also make it clear that there is still work to be done. Following Hurricane Katrina, news reports referred to White victims as "finding" food but described African Americans who were doing the same things as "looting" (Kinney, 2005). In a revealing study, Marianne Bertrand and Sendhil Mullainathan (2004) sent out 5,000 résumés in response to 1,200 job ads placed in newspapers in Chicago and Boston. They constructed résumés so that applicants were identical in qualifications but differed in how stereotypically White or Black their names sounded. "White" names included Meredith, Emily, Brad, and Greg. "Black" names included Tamika, Lakisha, Darnell, and Kareem. The researchers found that even with identical qualifications, the applicants with "White-sounding" names were 50 percent more likely to be called for an interview.

Because racial prejudice is socially unacceptable, few people today would readily admit to racist or prejudicial views. In a CNN poll (2006), 88 percent of individuals answered no to the question "Are you racist?" It is not clear whether such results reflect a genuine change of heart or simply the recognition of this shifting social standard. Today, prejudiced individuals are more likely than before to appear unprejudiced on the surface while nevertheless holding racist views at a deeper level (Sears, 2008; Sears & Henry, 2007). Indeed, individuals may not be consciously aware of their own racial (or gender or age) biases.

To confront this problem, social psychologists examine prejudicial attitudes on two levels—explicit or overt racism and implicit or covert racism. *Explicit racism* is a person's conscious and openly shared attitude, which might be measured using a questionnaire. *Implicit racism* refers to attitudes that exist on a deeper, hidden level. Implicit attitudes must be measured with a method that does not require awareness (Trawaiter & Shapiro,

2010). For example, implicit racism is sometimes measured using the Implicit Associations Test (IAT), a computerized survey that assesses the ease with which a person can associate a Black or White person with good things (for example, flowers) or bad things (for example, misery) (Greenwald & others, 2009; Nosek & Banaji, 2007; Sriram & Greenwald, 2009). This test is based on the idea that preexisting biases may make it easier to associate some social stimuli with positive rather than negative items.

In one study, a sample of White college students completed measures of explicit and implicit attitudes toward Black people using an implicit measure similar to the IAT (Dovidio, Kawakami, & Gaertner, 2002). The students then interacted with a Black student partner. Explicit prejudice predicted what people said to a person of a different race—that is, White students who said they were not prejudiced were unlikely to say overtly racist things. Explicit prejudice also predicted how friendly White individuals felt they had behaved toward their Black partner. However, implicit prejudice related to nonverbal aspects of the interaction, such as how close the White students sat to their partners, as well as their facial expressions.

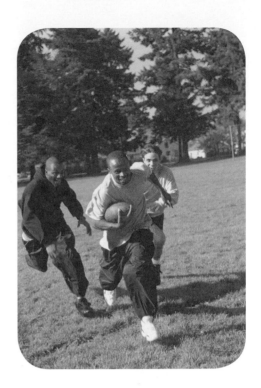

Why do people develop prejudice? Social psychologists have explored a number of possible reasons. Competition between groups, especially when resources are scarce, can contribute to prejudice. For example, immigrants often compete with established low-income members of a society for jobs—a situation that can lead to persistent conflict between the two groups. Cultural learning is also clearly involved. Children can adopt the prejudicial attitudes of their families and friends before they even meet a person from an out-group. In addition, when people feel bad about themselves, they might bolster their self-esteem by demeaning out-group members.

A final factor that might underlie prejudice comes from the limits on our information-processing abilities. As already noted, human beings are limited in their capacity for effortful thought, but they face a complex social environment. To simplify the challenge of understanding others' behavior, people use categories or stereotypes. Stereotypes can be a powerful force in developing and maintaining prejudicial attitudes.

STEREOTYPING AND PREJUDICE

Recall that stereotypes are generalizations about a group that deny variations within the group. Researchers have found that we are less likely to detect variations among individuals who belong to "other" groups than among individuals who belong to "our" group. So, we might see the people in our in-group as varied, unique individuals while viewing the members of out-groups as "all the same" (Amodio & Mendoza, 2010). Thinking that "they all look alike" can be a particular concern in the context of eyewitness identification (Brigham, 1986). At the root of prejudice is a particular kind of stereotype: a negative generalization about a group that is applied to all members of that group (Stangor, 2009).

DISCRIMINATION

Discrimination is an unjustified negative or harmful action toward a member of a group simply because the person belongs to that group. Discrimination occurs when negative emotional reactions combine with prejudicial beliefs and are translated into behavior (Bretherton, 2007; Major & Sawyer, 2009). Many forms of discrimination are illegal in the U.S. workplace. Since the Civil Rights Act of 1964 (revised in 1991), it has been unlawful to deny someone employment on the basis of gender or ethnicity (Parker, 2006). We will revisit workplace discrimination—and, in particular, look at sexual harassment, a form of discrimination based on gender—in Chapter 14.

● **discrimination** An unjustified negative or harmful action toward a member of a group simply because the person belongs to that group.

Ways to Improve Intergroup Relations

Martin Luther King, Jr., said, "I have a dream that my four little children will one day live in a nation where they will not be judged by the color of their skin but by the content of their character." How might we attain the world that King envisioned?

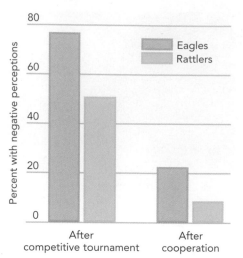

FIGURE 13.6 Attitudes Toward the Out-Group Following Competitive and Cooperative Activities In Sherif's research, hostility peaked after an athletic tournament, as reflected in the high percentage of Eagles and Rattlers who perceived the other group unfavorably following this event. However, after the groups worked together to reach a goal, their unfavorable attitudes toward each other dropped considerably.

One way might be for people to come to know one another better so that they can get along. However, in daily life many people interact with individuals from other ethnic groups, and this contact does not necessarily lead to tolerance or warm relations. Indeed, researchers have consistently found that contact by itself—attending the same school or working in the same company—does not necessarily improve relations among people of different ethnic backgrounds. So, rather than focusing on contact per se, researchers have examined how *various features* of a contact situation may be optimal for reducing prejudice and promoting intergroup harmony.

Gordon Allport (1954), whose contributions to personality psychology we examined in Chapter 12, theorized that particular aspects of the contact between groups could help to reduce prejudice. According to Allport, intergroup contact is likely to reduce prejudice when group members

- Think that they are of equal status
- Feel that an authority figure sanctions their positive relationships
- Believe that friendship might emerge from the interaction
- Engage in cooperative tasks in which everyone has something to contribute

Research has demonstrated support for many of Allport's ideas (Pettigrew & Tropp, 2006). In particular, studies have examined the role of *task-oriented cooperation*—working together on a shared goal—in reducing tensions between groups. Two examples of the power of task-oriented cooperation are Sherif's Robbers Cave Study and Aronson's jigsaw classroom.

It may be hard to imagine in our post-*Survivor* era, but even before Jeff Probst started handing out color-coded "buffs" on the TV show *Survivor,* Muzafer Sherif and his colleagues (1961) had the idea of exploring group processes by assigning 11-year-old boys to two competitive groups (the "Rattlers" and the "Eagles") in a summer camp called Robbers Cave. Sherif, disguised as a janitor so that he could unobtrusively observe the Rattlers and the Eagles, arranged for the two groups to compete in baseball, touch football, and tug-of-war. If you have watched reality television, you have some idea how this experiment went. In short order, relations between the groups got downright ugly. Members of each group expressed negative opinions of members of the other group, and the Rattlers and Eagles became battling factions.

What would bring these clashing groups together? Sherif created tasks that required the joint efforts of both groups, such as working together to repair the camp's only water supply and pooling their money to rent a movie. When the groups were required to work cooperatively to solve problems, the Rattlers and Eagles developed more positive relationships. Figure 13.6 shows how competitive and cooperative activities changed perceptions of the out-group.

Sherif's idea was later tested in the real world in Austin, Texas, when ethnic tensions increased and violence erupted among African Americans, Mexican Americans, and Whites in desegregated schools. Social psychologist Eliot Aronson was asked to help address the problem. Aronson (1986) devised the *jigsaw classroom,* where all of the students have to pull together to get the "big picture." Let's say a class consists of 30 students, some White, some African American, and some Latino. The academic goal for all students is to learn about the life of the Indian leader Mahatma Gandhi. The class might be broken up into five study groups of six students each, with the groups being as equal as possible in ethnic composition and academic achievement level. Learning about Gandhi's life becomes a class project divided into six parts, with one part given to each member of the six-person group. The components might be various books about Gandhi or information about different aspects of his life. The parts are like the pieces of a jigsaw puzzle: They have to be put together to form the complete puzzle.

U.S. classrooms have widely used the jigsaw approach (Deutsch, 2006; Deutsch, Coleman, & Marcus, 2006). This model has been associated with increased self-esteem, better academic performance, friendships among classmates, and improved interethnic perceptions (Slavin, 2006).

test yourself

1. What does social identity theory say about groups?
2. What is prejudice? Give two real-world examples, either historical or contemporary.
3. According to Allport, what particular aspects of the contact between groups could help to reduce prejudice?

5· CLOSE RELATIONSHIPS

Along with good health and happiness, close relationships figure prominently in most people's notions of a good life. Every day we see or hear commercials lauding the ability of this or that Internet dating service to link us up with the love of our life. U.S. consumers spent more than $490 million on Internet personals and dating services in 2005 (Online Publishers Association, 2005). Because close romantic relationships are so crucially important for most of us, it is no wonder that social psychologists should be interested in studying this fascinating aspect of human existence. Indeed, a vast literature has accumulated in social psychology, examining attraction, love, and intimacy.

© Ralph Hagen. www.CartoonStock.com.

Attraction

At the beginning of this chapter, we discussed one key factor in interpersonal attraction, namely, physical attractiveness. Research on interpersonal attraction has illuminated a variety of other factors that play a role in the dynamic of attraction.

PROXIMITY, ACQUAINTANCE, AND SIMILARITY

Even in the age of Internet dating, it is very unlikely that you are going to become attracted to someone without meeting the person. *Proximity,* or physical closeness, is a strong predictor of attraction. You are more prone to become attracted to an individual you pass in the hall every day than to someone you see rarely. One potential mechanism for the role of proximity in attraction is the mere exposure effect (Zajonc, 1968, 2001). The **mere exposure effect** is the phenomenon that the more we encounter someone or something (a person, a word, an image), the more probable it is that we will start liking the person or thing even if we do not realize we have seen it before.

● **mere exposure effect** The phenomenon that the more we encounter someone or something, the more probable it is that we will start liking the person or thing even if we do not realize we have seen it before.

We not only tend to be attracted to people whom we have seen before, but also are more likely to like someone if we are led to believe we will be meeting that person. Let's say you are sitting in a room and an experimenter tells you there are two strangers next door, one of whom you will be meeting and the other not. Research shows that you will probably begin to like the first person, in anticipation of your interaction (Insko & Wilson, 1977). In addition, if we find out that someone whom we do not know yet already likes us, it is a sure sign that we will find ourselves attracted to that person—in other words, we like those who like us. (For one thing, we know that they have excellent taste.)

In addition to proximity and the promise of acquaintanceship, similarity plays an important role in attraction (Qian, 2009). We have all heard that opposites attract, but what is true of magnets is not true of human beings, at least not typically. We like to associate with people who are similar to us (Berscheid, 2000). Our friends and lovers are much more like us than unlike us. We have similar attitudes, behavior patterns, taste in clothes, intelligence, personality, other friends, values, lifestyle, physical attractiveness, and so on.

The concept of *consensual validation* explains why people are attracted to others who are similar to them. Our own attitudes and behavior are supported when someone else's attitudes and behavior are similar to ours—their attitudes and behavior validate ours. Another reason that similarity matters is that we tend to shy away from the unknown. Similarity implies that we will enjoy doing things with another person who has similar tastes and attitudes.

Love

Some relationships never progress much beyond the attraction stage. Others deepen to friendship and perhaps even to love. Social psychologists have long puzzled over exactly

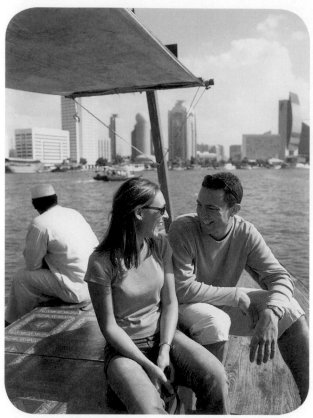

As love matures, passionate love tends to give way to affectionate love.

● **romantic love** Also called passionate love; love with strong components of sexuality and infatuation, often dominant in the early part of a love relationship.

● **affectionate love** Also called companionate love; love that occurs when individuals desire to have another person near and have a deep, caring affection for the person.

● **social exchange theory** The view of social relationships as involving an exchange of goods, the objective of which is to minimize costs and maximize benefits.

● **investment model** A model of long-term relationships that examines the ways that commitment, investment, and the availability of attractive alternative partners predict satisfaction and stability in relationships.

what love is (Berscheid, 2006, 2010). One way to think about love is to consider the types of love that characterize different human relationships—for instance, friendships versus romantic relationships (Hendrick & Hendrick, 2009). Here we consider two types of love: romantic love and affectionate love.

Poets, playwrights, and musicians through the ages have celebrated the fiery passion of romantic love—and lamented the searing pain when it fails. Think about songs and books that hit the top of the charts. Chances are, they are about romantic love. **Romantic love,** also called *passionate love,* is love with strong components of sexuality and infatuation, and it often predominates in the early part of a love relationship (Hendrick & Hendrick, 2006). Ellen Berscheid (1988) says that it is romantic love we mean when we say that we are "in love" with someone. It is romantic love that she believes we need to understand if we are to learn what love is all about. Berscheid judges sexual desire to be the most important ingredient of romantic love.

Love is more than just passion, however. **Affectionate love,** also called *companionate love,* is the type of love that occurs when individuals desire to have the other person near and have a deep, caring affection for the person. There is a growing belief that the early stages of love have more romantic ingredients and that as love matures, passion tends to give way to affection (Berscheid & Regan, 2005).

Models of Close Relationships

What makes long-term romantic relationships last? Two theoretical approaches to this sometimes bewildering question include social exchange theory and the investment model.

SOCIAL EXCHANGE THEORY

The social exchange approach to close relationships focuses on the costs and benefits of one's romantic partner. **Social exchange theory** is based on the notion of social relationships as involving an exchange of goods, the objective of which is to minimize costs and maximize benefits. This theory looks at human relations as an exchange of rewards between actors. From the social exchange perspective, the most important predictor of a relationship's success is *equity*—a feeling on the part of the individuals in the relationship that each is doing his or her "fair share." Essentially, social exchange theory asserts that the partners keep a mental balance sheet, tallying the plusses and minuses associated with each other—what they put in ("I paid for our last date") and what they get out ("He brought me flowers").

As relationships progress, equity may no longer apply. In fact, research shows that over time, this kind of accounting not only is less likely to explain what happens in a relationship but also becomes distasteful to the partners. Happily married couples are less likely to keep track of "what I get versus what I give," and they avoid thinking about the costs and benefits of their relationships (Buunk & Van Yperen, 1991; Clark & Chrisman, 1994). Surely we can all think of long-term relationships in which one partner remains committed even when the benefits are hard for the outsider to see—as in the case where the person's romantic partner is gravely ill for a long time.

THE INVESTMENT MODEL

Another way to think about long-term romantic relationships is to focus on the underlying factors that characterize stable, happy relationships compared to others. The **investment model** examines the ways that commitment, investment, and the availability of attractive alternative partners predict satisfaction and stability in relationships (Rusbult & Agnew, 2010; Rusbult & others, 2004).

From the investment model perspective, long-term relationships are likely to continue when both partners are committed to the relationship and both have invested a great deal; in addition, relationships are more enduring when there are few tempting alternatives for the partners. For example, college students who are committed to their romantic partners are less likely to cheat on them sexually during spring break (Drigotas, Safstrom, & Gentilia, 1999). Commitment to a relationship also predicts a willingness to sacrifice for a romantic partner. In one study, individuals were given a chance to climb up and down a short staircase, over and over, to spare their partner from having to do so. Those who were more committed to their partner worked harder to climb up and down repeatedly, in order to spare their loved one the burden (Van Lange & others, 1997). When two partners are deeply invested in a relationship, they can also bring the best out in each other, mutually helping themselves grow into their best possible selves (Rusbult, Finkel, & Kumashiro, 2009).

test yourself

1. Explain the concept of consensual validation.
2. What is the difference between romantic love and affectionate love, and what is another name for each?
3. What does social exchange theory say about happy romantic relationships?

6· SOCIAL PSYCHOLOGY AND HEALTH AND WELLNESS

The principles of social psychology have provided a strong foundation for ongoing research in the areas of health and wellness (Kok & de Vries, 2006; Taylor, 2011). In this concluding section, we glimpse some of the significant connections that researchers have uncovered among social contacts, physical health, and psychological wellness.

A long list of studies has shown that social ties are an important, if not the *most* important, variable in predicting health. For example, in a landmark study, social isolation had six times the effect on mortality rates that cigarette smoking had (House, Landis, & Umberson, 1988). In another study involving 1,234 heart attack patients, those living alone were nearly twice as likely to have a second heart attack (Case & others, 1992). Further, in a study of leukemia patients, of those who said that they had little support prior to undergoing a bone marrow transplant, only 20 percent were alive two years later, compared to 54 percent who reported that they felt strong support (Colón & others, 1991). Research shows, too, that widows die at a rate that is 3 to 13 times higher than that of married women for every known cause of death (Wortman & Boerner, 2007). Loneliness is linked with impaired physical health (Cacioppo & others, 2006; Hawkley, Preacher, & Cacioppo, 2010; Hawkley, Thisted, & Cacioppo, 2009; Munoz-Laboy, Hirsch, & Quispe-Lazaro, 2009). Chronic loneliness can lead to an early death (Cornwell & Waite, 2009; Cuijpers, 2001). Without a doubt, being connected to others is crucial to human survival.

Having many different social ties may be especially important during difficult times (Hawkley & Cacioppo, 2009; Taylor, 2011). Individuals who participate in more diverse social networks—for example, having a close relationship with a partner; interacting with family members, friends, neighbors, and fellow workers; and belonging to social and religious groups—live longer than those with a narrower range of social relationships (Vogt & others, 1992). One study investigated the effects of diverse social ties on the susceptibility to getting a common cold (S. Cohen & others, 1998). Individuals reported the extent of their participation in 12 types of social ties. Then they were given nasal drops containing a cold virus and monitored for the appearance of a cold. Individuals with more diverse social ties were less likely to get a cold than their counterparts with less diverse social networks.

Each of us has times in our life when we feel lonely, particularly when we are going through major life transitions. For example, when individuals leave the familiar world of their hometown and family to begin college, they can feel especially lonely. Indeed, experiencing loneliness at the beginning of one's college career is quite common and normal (Cutrona, 1982).

If you are lonely, there are strategies you can use to become better connected with others. You might consider joining activities, such as volunteering your time for a cause in which you believe. When interacting with others, you will improve your chances of

test yourself

1. What are some physical illnesses in which social isolation plays a significant role, according to researchers?
2. What kinds of social networks are especially important in times of trouble?
3. If a friend were struggling with loneliness, what strategy would you recommend for coping with it?

developing enduring relationships if you are considerate, honest, trustworthy, and cooperative. If you cannot get rid of your loneliness on your own, you might want to contact the counseling services at your college.

Having completed this chapter's survey of social psychology, you may be surprised to learn that we have barely scratched the surface of this broad and deep field: The branch of psychology that focuses on the ways human beings relate to one another is a rich, intriguing area of study. In the next few days, think about the stories that are making the headlines and that you are talking about with your friends. Reflecting back on this chapter, you might notice that social psychology would have something to say about most of these topics.

SUMMARY

1. SOCIAL COGNITION

The face conveys information to social perceivers, including attractiveness. Self-fulfilling prophecy means that our expectations of others can have a powerful impact on their behavior.

Attributions are our thoughts about why people behave as they do and about who or what is responsible for the outcome of events. Attribution theory views people as motivated to discover the causes of behavior as part of their effort to make sense of it. The dimensions used to make sense of the causes of human behavior include internal/external, stable/unstable, and controllable/uncontrollable.

The fundamental attribution error is observers' tendency to overestimate traits and to underestimate situations when they explain an actor's behavior. Self-serving bias means attributing our successes to internal causes and blaming our failures on external causes. Heuristics are used as shortcuts in social information processing. One such heuristic is a stereotype—a generalization about a group's characteristics that does not consider any variations among individuals in the group.

The self is our mental representation of our own characteristics. Self-esteem is important and is related to holding unrealistically positive views of ourselves. Stereotype threat is an individual's fast-acting, self-fulfilling fear of being judged based on a negative stereotype about his or her group. In order to understand ourselves better, we might engage in social comparison, evaluating ourselves by comparison with others.

Attitudes are our feelings—about people, objects, and ideas. We are better able to predict behavior on the basis of attitudes when an individual's attitudes are strong, when the person is aware of his or her attitudes and expresses them often, and when the attitudes are specifically relevant to the behavior. Sometimes changes in behavior precede changes in attitude.

According to cognitive dissonance theory, our strong need for cognitive consistency causes us to change our behavior to fit our attitudes or to change our attitudes to fit our behavior. Self-perception theory stresses the importance of making inferences about attitudes by observing our own behavior, especially when our attitudes are not clear.

2. SOCIAL BEHAVIOR

Altruism is an unselfish interest in helping someone else. Reciprocity often is involved in altruism. Individuals who are in a good mood are more helpful. Empathy is also linked to helping. The bystander effect means that individuals who observe an emergency help less when someone else is present than when they are alone.

Women are more likely to help in situations that are not dangerous and involve caregiving. Men are more likely to help in situations that involve danger or in which they feel competent.

One view of the biological basis of aggression is that early in human evolution, the most aggressive individuals were likely to be the survivors. Neurobiological factors involved in aggressive behavior include the neurotransmitter serotonin and the hormone testosterone. Psychological factors in aggression include frustrating and aversive circumstances. Sociocultural factors include cross-cultural variations, the culture of honor, and violence in the media. Males are consistently more physically aggressive than females.

3. SOCIAL INFLUENCE

Conformity involves a change in behavior to coincide with a group standard. Factors that influence conformity include informational social influence (going along to be right) and normative social influence (going along to be liked).

Obedience is behavior that complies with the explicit demands of an authority. Milgram's classic experiment demonstrated the power of obedience.

People often change their behaviors when they are in a group. Deindividuation refers to the lack of inhibition and diffusion of responsibility that can occur in groups. Social contagion refers to imitative behaviors involving the spread of behavior, emotions, and ideas. Our performance in groups can be improved through social facilitation and lowered because of social loafing.

Risky shift refers to the tendency for a group decision to be riskier than the average decision made by the individual group members. The group polarization effect is the solidification and further strengthening of a position as a consequence of group discussion. Groupthink involves impaired decision making and avoidance of realistic appraisal to maintain harmony in the group.

4. INTERGROUP RELATIONS

Social identity is our definition of ourselves in terms of our group memberships. Social identity theory states that when individuals are assigned to a group, they invariably think of it as the in-group. Identifying with the group allows the person to have a positive self-image. Ethnocentrism is the tendency to favor one's own ethnic group over others.

Prejudice is an unjustified negative attitude toward an individual based on membership in a group. The underlying reasons for prejudice include competition between groups over scarce resources, a person's motivation to enhance his or her self-esteem, cognitive processes that tend to categorize and stereotype others, and cultural learning. Prejudice is also based on stereotypes. The cognitive process of stereotyping can lead to discrimination, an unjustified negative or harmful action toward a member of a group simply because he or she belongs to that group. Discrimination results when negative emotional reactions combine with prejudicial beliefs and are translated into behavior.

An effective strategy for enhancing the effects of intergroup contact is to set up task-oriented cooperation among individuals from different groups.

5. CLOSE RELATIONSHIPS

We tend to be attracted to people whom we see often, whom we are likely to meet, and who are similar to us. Romantic love (passionate love) includes feelings of infatuation and sexual attraction. Affectionate love (companionate love) is more akin to friendship and includes deep, caring feelings for another.

Social exchange theory states that a relationship is likely to be successful if individuals feel that they get out of the relationship what they put in. The investment model focuses on commitment, investment,

and the availability of attractive alternatives in predicting relationship success.

6. SOCIAL PSYCHOLOGY AND HEALTH AND WELLNESS

Social isolation is a strong risk factor for a range of physical illnesses and even death. Loneliness relates to a number of negative health outcomes, including impaired physical health and early death. Individuals who participate in more diverse social networks live longer than those with a narrower range of social relationships. Loneliness often emerges when people make life transitions, so it is not surprising that loneliness is common among college freshmen. Strategies that can help to reduce loneliness include participating in activities with others and taking the initiative to meet new people.

key *terms*

social psychology, p. 420

stereotype, p. 420

attribution theory, p. 422

fundamental attribution error, p. 422

false consensus effect, p. 422

positive illusions, p. 423

self-serving bias, p. 423

self-objectification, p. 423

stereotype threat, p. 425

social comparison, p. 425

attitudes, p. 425

cognitive dissonance, p. 426

self-perception theory, p. 427

elaboration likelihood model, p. 428

altruism, p. 429

egoism, p. 429

empathy, p. 430

bystander effect, p. 431

aggression, p. 432

conformity, p. 437

informational social influence, p. 438

normative social influence, p. 438

obedience, p. 438

deindividuation, p. 441

social contagion, p. 442

social facilitation, p. 442

social loafing, p. 442

risky shift, p. 443

group polarization effect, p. 443

groupthink, p. 443

social identity, p. 444

social identity theory, p. 445

ethnocentrism, p. 445

prejudice, p. 445

discrimination, p. 447

mere exposure effect, p. 449

romantic love, p. 450

affectionate love, p. 450

social exchange theory, p. 450

investment model, p. 450

apply your *knowledge*

1. Check out this website to see how the averaging of faces works: http://www.faceresearch.org/demos/average. Pick some faces you consider unattractive. What happens when you average them together? If you have a digital photograph of yourself and some friends, see what happens when you average those faces. Do you agree that average faces are more attractive than any single face?

2. Many people are surprised by the results of the IAT when they take this implicit measure. Try it out at https://implicit.harvard .edu/implicit. Do you think your results are valid? Explain.

3. We are often unaware of how many attributions we make about the behavior of others. To demonstrate this point to yourself, spend some time in a crowded area observing the interactions of others (or instead watch some scenes in television shows or movies). Take careful notes about the social behaviors that occur and

then document your impression of why the individuals behaved as they did. What cues did you use in making your attributions about their behavior? Did your knowledge of the fundamental attribution error influence your attributions? Why or why not?

4. Take a day and engage in altruistic behavior. Act as kindly toward others as you can, without telling anyone what you are up to. Keep track of your thoughts and feelings as you experience this day of kindness. How does it influence your feelings about altruism?

5. Interview the happiest couple you know. Ask the partners individually about the things that they think help make their relationship work. Then examine your notes. How do the characteristics of your "ideal" couple's relationship compare with the findings of research on close relationships?

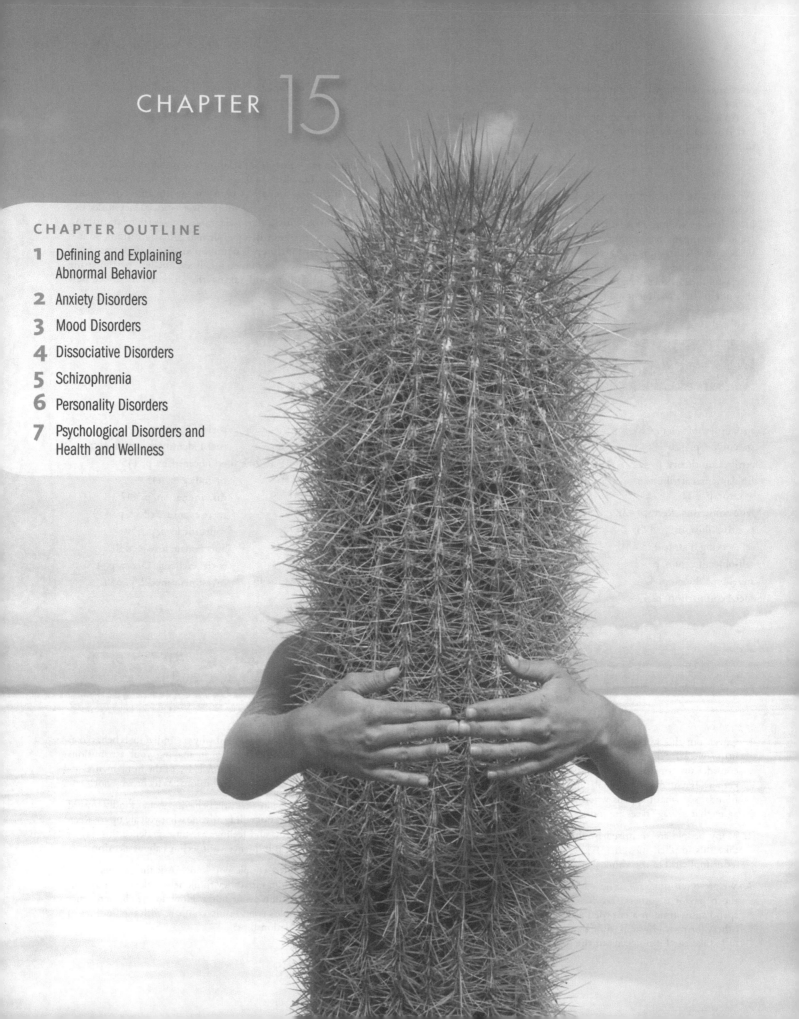

CHAPTER 15

Psychological Disorders

The Courage to Wake Up Every Morning

Bill Garrett was a freshman at Johns Hopkins University, where he had won a full four-year scholarship, when he began to hear strange voices inside his head. Those voices told him profoundly disturbing things: that he was stupid and fat, that soap and shampoo were toxic, that his father had poisoned the family dog, and that his grandmother was putting human body parts in his food. Bill withdrew into this terrifying inner world, convinced that there were conspiracies out to get him. Eventually, he was diagnosed with schizophrenia, a disorder characterized by disturbed thought. Failing in all of his classes, this previously excellent student (and track and lacrosse star) was forced to leave school and return home to struggle with his disorder.

Bill's mother realized what her son had been experiencing only when she found herself at a support group for families of individuals with schizophrenia. At one point, surrounded by 10 people all speaking to her at once, she was overwhelmed by the confusing cacophony. Afterward she told her son, "You have to be the most courageous person. You wake up every morning" (M. Park, 2009). Bill had told her that sleep was his only escape from the constant terror of those voices.

At home, Bill was faced with evidence of his previous successes. Looking at his trophies and awards, he said, "Mom, I was on top of the world. Now I'm in the gutter." His mother, however, has offered Bill a different perspective. She has encouraged him to think of his disorder not as a sign of failure but as an opportunity to use the gifts he still possesses—symbolized by those past accomplishments—to fight for the rights of individuals who, like him, find their lives turned upside-down by psychological disorders. ●

PREVIEW

In this chapter we survey psychological orders, such as the schizophrenia with which Bill Garrett is struggling. We explore the meaning of the word *abnormal* as it relates to psychology. We examine various theoretical approaches to understanding abnormal behavior and survey the main psychological disorders. In the concluding section, we consider the influence of the stigma associated with psychological disorders on the health and wellness of those who must deal with them.

1· DEFINING AND EXPLAINING ABNORMAL BEHAVIOR

What makes behavior "abnormal"? The American Psychiatric Association (2001, 2006) defines abnormal behavior in medical terms—as a mental illness that affects or is manifested in a person's brain and can affect the way the individual thinks, behaves, and interacts with others.

Three criteria help distinguish normal from abnormal behavior. **Abnormal behavior** is behavior that is *deviant, maladaptive,* or *personally distressful* over a relatively long period of time. Let's take a look at what each of the three characteristics of abnormal behavior entails:

● **abnormal behavior** Behavior that is deviant, maladaptive, or personally distressful over a relatively long period of time.

- Abnormal behavior is *deviant.* Abnormal behavior is certainly atypical or statistically unusual. People such as Alicia Keys, Peyton Manning, and Steven Spielberg are atypical—but we do not categorize them as abnormal. When atypical behavior deviates from what is acceptable in a culture, it often is considered abnormal. A woman who washes her hands three or four times an hour and takes seven showers a day is abnormal because her behavior deviates from what we consider acceptable.

- Abnormal behavior is *maladaptive.* Maladaptive behavior interferes with a person's ability to function effectively in the world. A man who believes that he can endanger other people through his breathing may go to great lengths to avoid people so that he will not harm anyone. He might isolate himself from others, for what he believes is their own good. His belief separates him from society and prevents his everyday functioning; thus, his behavior is maladaptive. Behavior that presents a danger to the person or those around him or her would also be considered maladaptive (and abnormal).

- Abnormal behavior involves *personal distress* over a long period of time. The person engaging in the behavior finds it troubling. A woman who secretly makes herself

Accomplished people—such as recording artist-actor Alicia Keys, NFL superstar Peyton Manning, and award-winning film director Steven Spielberg—are atypical but not abnormal. However, when atypical behavior deviates form cultural norms, it often is considered abnormal.

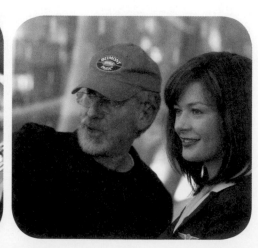

vomit after every meal may never be seen by others as deviant (because they do not know about it), but this pattern of behavior may cause her to feel intense shame, guilt, and despair. Personal distress may exist in the context of great success. Imagine a highly successful business executive who feels profound sadness because of family difficulties.

Note that the *context* of a behavior may help to determine whether the behavior is abnormal. Consider the woman who washes her hands three or four times an hour and takes repeated showers. If she works in a sterile lab with live viruses or radioactive material, her behavior might be quite adaptive rather than abnormal.

Only one of the three criteria described above needs to be present for behavior to be labeled "abnormal," but typically two or all three may be present. When abnormal behavior persists, it may lead to the diagnosis of a psychological disorder.

Theoretical Approaches to Psychological Disorders

What causes people to develop a psychological disorder, that is, to behave in deviant, maladaptive, and personally distressful ways? Theorists have suggested various approaches to this question.

THE BIOLOGICAL APPROACH

The biological approach attributes psychological disorders to organic, internal causes. This approach primarily focuses on the brain, genetic factors, and neurotransmitter functioning as the sources of abnormality.

The biological approach is evident in the **medical model,** which describes psychological disorders as medical diseases with a biological origin. From the perspective of the medical model, abnormalities are called *mental illnesses,* the afflicted individuals are *patients,* and they are treated by *doctors.*

● **medical model** The view that psychological disorders are medical diseases with a biological origin.

THE PSYCHOLOGICAL APPROACH

The psychological approach emphasizes the contributions of experiences, thoughts, emotions, and personality characteristics in explaining psychological disorders. Psychologists might focus, for example, on the influence of childhood experiences or of personality traits in the development and course of psychological disorders. Behavioral psychologists probe the rewards and punishers in the environment that determine abnormal behavior, whereas social cognitive psychologists focus on observational learning, cognitions, and beliefs as factors that foster or maintain abnormal behavior.

THE SOCIOCULTURAL APPROACH

The sociocultural approach emphasizes the social contexts in which a person lives, including the individual's gender, ethnicity, socioeconomic status, family relationships, and culture. For instance, individuals from low-income, minority neighborhoods have the highest rates of psychological disorders (Schwartz & Corcoran, 2010). Socioeconomic status plays a much stronger role in disorders than does ethnicity: The living conditions of poverty create stressful circumstances that can contribute to the development of a psychological disorder (E. Davis & others, 2010; Kohrt & others, 2009; South & Krueger, 2010).

The sociocultural perspective stresses the ways that cultures influence the understanding and treatment of psychological disorders. The frequency and intensity of psychological disorders vary and depend on social, economic, technological, and religious aspects of cultures (Alegria, 2011; Shiraev & Levy, 2010). Some disorders are culture-related, as indicated in Figure 15.1.

THE BIOPSYCHOSOCIAL MODEL

Abnormal behavior can be influenced by biological factors (such as genes), psychological factors (such as childhood experiences), and sociocultural factors (such as gender).

Disorder	Culture	Description/Characteristics
Amok	Malaysia, Philippines, Africa	This disorder involves sudden, uncontrolled outbursts of anger in which the person may injure or kill someone. Amok is often found in males who are emotionally withdrawn before the onset of the disorder. After the attack on someone, the individual feels exhausted and depressed and does not remember the rage and attack.
Anorexia Nervosa	Western cultures, especially the United States	This eating disorder involves a relentless pursuit of thinness through starvation and can eventually lead to death.
Windigo	Algonquin Indian hunters	This disorder involves a fear of being bewitched. The hunter becomes anxious and agitated, worrying he will be turned into a cannibal with a craving for human flesh.

FIGURE 15.1 Some Culture-Related Disorders Although many psychological disorders are universal, some are associated with specific cultures, as this figure illustrates.

These factors can operate alone, but they often act in combination with one another (Scheid & Brown, 2010).

To appreciate how these factors work together, let's back up for a moment. Consider that not everyone with a genetic predisposition to schizophrenia develops the disorder. Similarly, not everyone who experiences childhood neglect develops depression. Moreover, even women who live in cultures that strongly discriminate against them do not always develop psychological disorders. Thus, to understand the development of psychological disorders, we must consider a variety of *interacting* factors from each of the domains of experience.

Sometimes this approach is called *biopsychosocial.* From the biopsychosocial perspective, none of the factors considered is necessarily viewed as more important than another; rather, biological, psychological, and social factors are *all* significant ingredients in producing both normal and abnormal behavior. Furthermore, these ingredients may combine in unique ways, so that one depressed person might differ from another in terms of the key factors associated with the development of the disorder.

Classifying Abnormal Behavior

To understand, prevent, and treat abnormal behavior, psychiatrists and psychologists have devised systems classifying those behaviors into specific psychological disorders. Classifying psychological disorders provides a common basis for communicating. If one psychologist says that her client is experiencing depression, another psychologist understands that a particular pattern of abnormal behavior has led to this diagnosis. A classification system can also help clinicians make predictions about how likely it is that a particular disorder will occur, which individuals are most susceptible to it, how the disorder progresses, and what the prognosis (or outcome) for treatment is (Cuthbert & Insel, 2010; First, 2011; Nenadic, Sauer, & Gaser, 2010).

Further, a classification system may benefit the person suffering from psychological symptoms. The fact that an individual's disorder has a name can be a comfort and a signal that the person may reasonably expect relief. On the other hand, officially labeling a problem can also have serious negative implications for the person because of the potential for creating *stigma,* a mark of shame that may cause others to avoid or to act negatively toward an individual. Indeed, being diagnosed with a psychological disorder can profoundly influence a person's life, not only because of the effects of the disorder itself, but because of what the diagnosis means with respect to the person, his or her family, and the individual's larger social world. We return to the important issue of stigma at the end of this chapter.

THE *DSM-IV* CLASSIFICATION SYSTEM

In 1952, the American Psychiatric Association (APA) published the first major classification of psychological disorders in the United States, the *Diagnostic and Statistical Manual of Mental Disorders.* Its current version, the ***DSM-IV*** (APA, 1994), was introduced in 1994 and revised in 2000, producing the *DSM-IV-TR* (text revision) (APA, 2000). *DSM-V* is due in 2013. Throughout the development of the *DSM,* the number of diagnosable disorders has increased dramatically. The first *DSM* listed 112 disorders; the *DSM-IV-TR* includes 374.

The *DSM-IV* classifies individuals on the basis of five dimensions, or *axes,* that take into account the individual's history and highest level of functioning in the previous year. The system's creators meant to ensure that the individual is not merely assigned to a psychological disorder category but instead is characterized in terms of a number of factors. The five axes of *DSM-IV* are

Axis I: All diagnostic categories except personality disorders and mental retardation

Axis II: Personality disorders and mental retardation

● **DSM-IV** The *Diagnostic and Statistical Manual of Mental Disorders;* the major classification of psychological disorders in the United States.

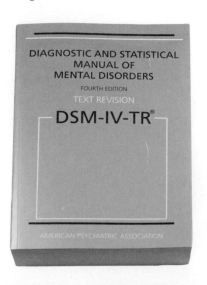

Axis III: General medical conditions

Axis IV: Psychosocial and environmental problems

Axis V: Current level of functioning

Axes I and II are concerned with the classification of psychological disorders. Figure 15.2 describes the major categories of these disorders. Axes III through V may not

Major Categories of Psychological Disorders	Description
Axis I Disorders	
Disorders usually first diagnosed in infancy, childhood, or adolescence and communication disorders	Include disorders that appear before adolescence, such as attention deficit hyperactivity disorder, autism, and learning disorders (stuttering, for example).
Anxiety disorders	Characterized by motor tension, hyperactivity, and apprehensive expectations/thoughts. Include generalized anxiety disorder, panic disorder, phobic disorder, obsessive-compulsive disorder, and post-traumatic stress disorder.
Somatoform disorders	Occur when psychological symptoms take a physical form even though no physical causes can be found. Include hypochondriasis and conversion disorder.
Factitious disorders	Characterized by the individual's deliberate fabrication of a medical or mental disorder, but not for external gain (such as a disability claim).
Dissociative disorders	Involve a sudden loss of memory or change of identity. Include the disorders of dissociative amnesia, dissociative fugue, and dissociative identity disorder.
Delirium, dementia, amnesia, and other cognitive disorders	Consist of mental disorders involving problems in consciousness and cognition, such as substance-induced delirium or dementia related to Alzheimer disease.
Mood disorders	Disorders in which there is a primary disturbance in mood; include depressive disorders and bipolar disorder (which involves wide mood swings from deep depression to extreme euphoria and agitation).
Schizophrenia and other psychotic disorders	Disorders characterized by distorted thoughts and perceptions, odd communication, inappropriate emotion, and other unusual behaviors.
Substance-related disorders	Include alcohol-related disorders, cocaine-related disorders, hallucinogen-related disorders, and other drug-related disorders.
Sexual and gender identity disorders	Consist of three main types of disorders: gender-identity disorders (person is not comfortable with identity as a female or male), paraphilias (person has a preference for unusual sexual acts to stimulate sexual arousal), and sexual dysfunctions (impairments in sexual functioning).
Eating disorders	Include anorexia nervosa, bulimia nervosa, and binge eating disorder.
Sleep disorders	Consist of primary sleep disorders, such as insomnia and narcolepsy (see Chapter 5), and sleep disorders due to a general medical condition.
Impulse control disorders not elsewhere classified	Include kleptomania, pyromania, and compulsive gambling.
Adjustment disorders	Characterized by distressing emotional or behavioral symptoms in response to an identifiable stressor.
Axis II Disorders	
Intellectual disability	Low intellectual functioning and an inability to adapt to everyday life (see Chapter 8).
Personality disorders	Develop when personality traits become inflexible and maladaptive. Include antisocial personality disorder and borderline personality disorder.
Other conditions that may be a focus of clinical attention	Include relational problems (with a partner, sibling, and so on), problems related to abuse or neglect (physical abuse of a child, for example), or additional conditions (such as bereavement, academic problems, religious or spiritual problems).

FIGURE 15.2   Main Categories of Psychological Disorders in the *DSM-IV* The *DSM-IV* provides a way for mental health professionals and researchers to communicate with one another about these well-defined psychological disorders.

● **attention deficit hyperactivity disorder (ADHD)** One of the most common psychological disorders of childhood, in which individuals show one or more of the following: inattention, hyperactivity, and impulsivity.

be needed to diagnose a psychological disorder, but they are included so that the person's overall life situation is considered. Axis III information helps to clarify if symptoms may be rooted in physical illness. Axis IV focuses on whether the person is experiencing disruptions in various life domains, including important social relationships, his or her job, or living conditions. On Axis V, the clinician evaluates the highest level of adaptive functioning the person has attained in the preceding year in social, occupational, or school activities.

CRITIQUES OF THE *DSM-IV*

A number of criticisms of the *DSM-IV* have been made (Hyman, 2010; Katschnig, 2010; Langstrom, 2010; Ronningstam, 2010). The most controversial aspect of the *DSM-IV* is that the manual classifies individuals based on their symptoms, using medical terminology in the psychiatric tradition of thinking about mental disorders in terms of disease (Oltmanns & Emery, 2010). This emphasis implies that the abnormalities have an internal cause that is relatively independent of environmental factors (Kring & others, 2007). So, even though researchers have begun to shed light on the complex interaction of genetic, neurobiological, cognitive, and environmental factors in psychological disorders, the *DSM-IV* continues to reflect the medical model (APA, 2006).

Another criticism is that the *DSM-IV* focuses strictly on pathology and problems. Critics argue that emphasizing *strengths* as well as weaknesses might help to destigmatize labels such as "schizophrenic." Indeed, professionals avoid such labels, using what is called *people-first language.* Bill Garrett, whom you met in the chapter-opening vignette, is a *person with schizophrenia,* not "a schizophrenic." Identifying a person's strengths can be an important step toward maximizing his or her ability to contribute to society (Roten, 2007).

Of course, labels such as those described by the *DSM-IV* are based on the idea that psychological disorders are real and often medically treatable. Some individuals have questioned this very assumption. To read about this controversy, see the Critical Controversy.

Before we begin our survey of the various psychological disorders, take a moment to consider this caution. It is very common for individuals who are learning about psychological disorders to recognize the symptoms and behaviors of disorders in themselves or in people around them. Keep in mind that only trained professionals can diagnose a psychological disorder.

test yourself

1. What three main criteria distinguish abnormal behavior from normal behavior?
2. Why is it important to have formal systems for classifying abnormal behaviors into specific psychological disorders?
3. What is the *DSM-IV*, and what did its authors strive to ensure with respect to individuals with psychological disorders?

2· ANXIETY DISORDERS

Think about how you felt before a make-or-break exam or a big presentation—or perhaps as you noticed police lights flashing behind your speeding car. Did you feel jittery and nervous and experience tightness in your stomach? These are the feelings of normal anxiety. Anxiety is an unpleasant feeling of fear and dread.

Individuals with high levels of anxiety worry a lot, but their anxiety does not necessarily impair their ability to function. In contrast, **anxiety disorders** involve fears that are uncontrollable, disproportionate to the actual danger the person might be in, and disruptive of ordinary life (Cisler & others, 2010). They feature motor tension (jumpiness, trembling), hyperactivity (dizziness, a racing heart), and apprehensive expectations and thoughts. In this section we survey five types of anxiety disorders:

● **anxiety disorders** Psychological disorders involving fears that are uncontrollable, disproportionate to the actual danger the person might be in, and disruptive of ordinary life.

- Generalized anxiety disorder
- Panic disorder
- Phobic disorder
- Obsessive-compulsive disorder
- Post-traumatic stress disorder

CRITICAL CONTROVERSY

Are Psychological Disorders a Myth?

In a 2005 broadcast of NBC's *Today Show,* Matt Lauer interviewed Tom Cruise, who was embroiled in a heated media debate with Brooke Shields. Shields had published a book about her experience with post-partum (following childbirth) depression and her positive experience with prescription antidepressants to treat her disorder. Cruise vehemently criticized the very idea of depression and scorned the use of prescription drugs to treat psychological disorders, dubbing psychiatry "a pseudo science."

In response, the National Alliance for the Mentally Ill (NAMI), the American Psychiatric Association, and the National Mental Health Association (NMHA) issued a joint statement declaring, "While we respect the right of individuals to express their own points of view, they are not entitled to their own facts. Mental illnesses are real medical conditions that affect millions of Americans" (NAMI/APA/NMHA, 2005).

Cruise's argument was very similar to one made 50 years ago by psychiatrist Thomas Szasz (1961) in his book *The Myth of Mental Illness.* Szasz argued that psychological disorders are not illnesses and are better labeled "problems of living." Szasz said that it makes no sense to refer to a person's problems of living as "mental illness" and to treat him or her through a medical model. If a man's bizarre beliefs do nothing more than offend or frighten other people, what right do we have to label him "mentally ill" and to administer drugs to him? Szasz's arguments carry weight to this day (Cresswell, 2008; Eghigian, 2010).

The controversy over attention deficit hyperactivity disorder provides a thought-provoking example. In **attention deficit hyperactivity disorder (ADHD),** individuals show one or more of the following symptoms: inattention, hyperactivity, and impulsivity. ADHD is one of the most common psychological disorders of childhood, and the growth in diagnosis of this disorder in recent years is staggering (Rosenberg, Westling, & McLeskey, 2011). Whereas in 1988 just 500,000 cases were diagnosed, currently *4 million* children are diagnosed with ADHD each year (Bloom & Cohen, 2007). The sheer number of ADHD diagnoses has prompted some observers to wonder whether psychiatrists, parents, and teachers are actually labeling normal childhood behavior as psychopathology (Carey, 2002). After all, the impulsivity, hyperactivity, and inattention that characterize ADHD are typical of most children, especially boys.

Non-Latino White boys are much more likely to be diagnosed with ADHD than any other group (National Center for Health Statistics, 2006). The potential overdiagnosing of ADHD is of some significance, because animal research has shown that in the absence of ADHD, exposure to stimulants such as Ritalin (a common drug treatment for ADHD) can predispose individuals to later addiction problems (Leo, 2005).

In response to the debate, the National Institute of Mental Health sponsored a conference to review the scientific evidence. The result was a "consensus statement" signed by 75 psychiatrists and psychologists, declaring that ADHD is a real psychological disorder with a biological basis in the brain, associated with a number of problems, including dropping out of school, teen pregnancy, and antisocial behavior (Barkley & 74 others, 2002). Denying that ADHD is a real disorder, the statement asserted, amounts to believing that the earth is flat.

In turn, critics of the consensus statement argued that the biological basis of ADHD is not unique to ADHD but is a pattern shared with other childhood disorders (Timimi, 2004). Furthermore, the critics argued, the use of prescription drugs removes responsibility from parents and teachers and leads society to ignore possible environmental factors in ADHD (Timimi, 2004). Finally, critics pointed out that some of those signing the consensus statement were researchers funded by the pharmaceutical companies that produce the drugs used to treat ADHD.

ADHD is not the only controversial diagnosis, nor is ADHD alone in its link to pharmaceutical companies. Drug companies commonly fund research that focuses on a disease model of psychological disorders.

Does this controversy have a resolution? Clearly, psychological disorders are "real" in the sense that they lead to objectively negative outcomes in people's lives. The controversy over ADHD is a reminder of the important role of research in clarifying and defining diagnostic categories. Nobody wants to label inappropriately, to misdiagnose, or to mistreat people who are already suffering.

WHAT DO YOU THINK?

- When do you think it is appropriate to label someone as having a psychological disorder?
- When do you think medical treatments for psychological disorders are appropriate?
- If a teacher suggested that your child be tested for ADHD, what would you do? Why?

Diagnoses of attention deficit hyperactivity disorder have increased sharply in recent years.

Sleep disturbance is a common problem for people with generalized anxiety disorder.

● **generalized anxiety disorder** Psychological disorder marked by persistent anxiety for at least six months and in which the individual is unable to specify the reasons for the anxiety.

Generalized Anxiety Disorder

When you are worrying about getting a speeding ticket, you know why you are anxious; there is a specific cause. **Generalized anxiety disorder** is different from such everyday feelings of anxiety in that sufferers of this disorder experience persistent anxiety for at least six months and are unable to specify the reasons for the anxiety (Fisher, Granger, & Newman, 2010). People with generalized anxiety disorder are nervous most of the time. They may worry about their work, relationships, or health. That worry can also take a physical toll, so that individuals with generalized anxiety disorder may suffer from fatigue, muscle tension, stomach problems, and difficulty sleeping.

What is the etiology of generalized anxiety disorder? (*Etiology* means the causes or significant preceding conditions.) Among the biological factors involved in generalized anxiety disorder are genetic predisposition, deficiency in the neurotransmitter GABA, sympathetic nervous system activity, and respiratory system abnormalities (Fisher, Granger, & Newman, 2010; Garner & others, 2009; Katzman, 2009).

The psychological and sociocultural factors include having harsh (or even impossible) self-standards, overly strict and critical parents, automatic negative thoughts when feeling stressed, and a history of uncontrollable traumas or stressors (such as an abusive parent).

Panic Disorder

Much like everyone else, you might have a specific experience that sends you into a panic. For example, you work all night on a paper, only to have your computer crash before you printed it out or saved your last changes, or you are just about to dash across a street when you see a large truck coming right at you. Your heart races, your hands shake, and you might break into a sweat. In these situations, you know why you are experiencing feelings of panic.

In a **panic disorder,** however, a person experiences recurrent, sudden onsets of intense apprehension or terror, often without warning and with no specific cause. Panic attacks can produce severe palpitations, extreme shortness of breath, chest pains, trembling, sweating, dizziness, and a feeling of helplessness (Dammen & others, 2006). People with panic disorder fear that they will die, go crazy, or do something they cannot control. They may feel that they are having a heart attack.

Charles Darwin, the scientist who proposed the theory of evolution, suffered from intense panic disorder (Barloon & Noyes, 1997). Actor Kim Basinger and former NFL running back Earl Campbell also have dealt with this disorder.

What is the etiology of panic disorder? In terms of biological factors, individuals may have a genetic predisposition to the disorder (Battaglia & others, 2009; Maron, Hettema, & Shlik, 2010). One biological view is that individuals who experience panic disorder may have an autonomic nervous system that is predisposed to be overly active (Durand & Barlow, 2010; Hazlett-Stevens & Craske, 2009). Another biologically based possibility is that panic disorder may stem from problems involving either or both of two neurotransmitters: norepinephrine and GABA (P. L. Johnson & others, 2010).

Many experts interpret Edvard Munch's painting The Scream *as an expression of the terror brought on by a panic attack.*

With respect to psychological factors, one theory about panic disorder is that individuals misinterpret harmless indicators of physiological arousal (for example, a slightly raised heartbeat) as an emergency (such as a heart attack). However, this model of panic disorder remains controversial (Hazlett-Stevens & Craske, 2009).

In terms of sociocultural factors in the United States, American women are twice as likely as American men to have panic attacks (Altemus, 2006). Possible reasons for this difference include biological differences in hormones and neurotransmitters (Altemus, 2006; Fodor & Epstein, 2002). Research also suggests that women may cope with anxiety-provoking situations differently than men, and these differences may explain the gender difference in panic disorder (Schmidt & Koselka, 2000).

● **panic disorder** Anxiety disorder in which the individual experiences recurrent, sudden onsets of intense apprehension or terror, often without warning and with no specific cause.

Phobic Disorder

Many people are afraid of spiders and snakes; indeed, thinking about letting a tarantula crawl over one's face is likely to give anyone the willies. It is not uncommon to be afraid of particular objects or specific environments such as extreme heights. For most of us, these fears do not interfere with daily life. Some of us, however, have an irrational, overwhelming, persistent fear of a particular object or situation—an anxiety disorder called a **phobic disorder** or **phobia.** Whereas individuals with generalized anxiety disorder cannot pinpoint the cause of their nervous feelings, individuals with phobias can (Ollendick & others, 2010; Schienle & others, 2009).

A fear becomes a phobia when a situation is so dreaded that an individual goes to almost any length to avoid it. As with any anxiety disorder, phobias are fears that are uncontrollable, disproportionate, and disruptive. A snake phobia that keeps a city-dweller from leaving his apartment is clearly disproportionate to the actual chances of encountering a snake. John Madden—former NFL coach, football commentator, and video game consultant—has a famous fear of flying that led him to take a bus to the games that he broadcast.

Another phobic disorder, *social phobia,* is an intense fear of being humiliated or embarrassed in social situations (Carter & Wu, 2010; Rapee, Gaston, & Abbott, 2009). Individuals with this phobia are afraid that they will say or do the wrong thing. Singers Carly Simon and Barbra Streisand have dealt with social phobia.

Phobias usually begin in childhood and come in many forms (National Institute of Mental Health, 2008). Figure 15.3 labels and describes a number of phobias.

What is the etiology of phobic disorder? Genes appear to play a role in social phobia (Reich, 2009). Researchers have proposed that there is a neural circuit for social phobia

● **phobic disorder or phobia** Anxiety disorder characterized by an irrational, overwhelming, persistent fear of a particular object or situation.

Acrophobia	Fear of high places	Arachnophobia	Fear of spiders	Mysophobia	Fear of dirt
Aerophobia	Fear of flying	Astrapophobia	Fear of lightning	Nyctophobia	Fear of darkness
Ailurophobia	Fear of cats	Cynophobia	Fear of dogs	Ophidiophobia	Fear of nonpoisonous snakes
Algophobia	Fear of pain	Gamophobia	Fear of marriage		
Amaxophobia	Fear of vehicles, driving	Hydrophobia	Fear of water	Thanatophobia	Fear of death
		Melissophobia	Fear of bees	Xenophobia	Fear of strangers

FIGURE 15.3   **Phobias** This figure features some examples of phobic disorder—an anxiety disorder characterized by irrational and overwhelming fear of a particular object or experience.

● **obsessive-compulsive disorder (OCD)** Anxiety disorder in which the individual has anxiety-provoking thoughts that will not go away and/or urges to perform repetitive, ritualistic behaviors to prevent or produce some future situation.

that includes the thalamus, amygdala, and cerebral cortex (Damsa, Kosel, & Moussally, 2009). Also, a number of neurotransmitters may be involved in social phobia, especially serotonin (Christensen & others, 2010).

With regard to psychological factors, some theorists consider phobias learned fears (Clark & others, 2006). According to learning researchers, perhaps the individual with the fear of falling off a building experienced a fall from a high place earlier in life and therefore associates heights with pain (a classical conditioning explanation). Alternatively, he or she may have heard about or watched others who demonstrated terror of high places (an observational learning explanation), as when a little girl develops a fear of heights after sitting next to her terrified mother and observing her clutch the handrails, white-knuckled, as the roller coaster creeps steeply uphill.

"Since you have a complete record of my life, could you tell me if I remembered to turn the stove off?"

© Mike Baldwin. www.CartoonStock.com.

Obsessive-Compulsive Disorder

Just before leaving on a long road trip, you find yourself checking to be sure you locked the front door. As you pull away in your car, you are stricken with the thought that you forgot to turn off the coffeemaker. Going to bed the night before an early flight, you check your alarm clock a few times to be sure it will wake you for your 8 A.M. plane. This kind of checking behavior is a normal part of worrying.

In contrast, the anxiety disorder known as **obsessive-compulsive disorder (OCD)** features anxiety-provoking thoughts that will not go away and/or urges to perform repetitive, ritualistic behaviors to prevent or produce some future situation. *Obsessions* are recurrent thoughts, and *compulsions* are recurrent behaviors. Individuals with OCD dwell on normal doubts and repeat their routines sometimes hundreds of times a day (Abramowitz, 2009). Game show host Howie Mandel has coped with OCD, and David Beckham and Leonardo DiCaprio have each described mild cases of the disorder.

The most common compulsions are excessive checking, cleansing, and counting. An individual with OCD might believe that she has to touch the doorway with her left hand whenever she enters a room and count her steps as she walks across the room. If she does not complete this ritual, she may be overcome with a sense of fear that something terrible will happen. Indeed, most individuals do not enjoy their ritualistic behavior but feel extraordinarily anxious when they do not carry it out (Victor & Bernstein, 2009).

What is the etiology of obsessive-compulsive disorder? In terms of biological factors, there seems to be a genetic component (Gelernter & Stein, 2009; Sampaio & others, 2010). Also, brain-imaging studies have suggested neurological links for OCD (Nakao & others, 2009). One interpretation of these data is that the frontal cortex or basal ganglia are so active in OCD that numerous impulses reach the thalamus, generating obsessive thoughts or compulsive actions (Figure 15.4) (Rotge & others, 2009).

Studies using fMRI have examined the brain activity of individuals with OCD before and after treatment. Following effective treatment, a number of areas in the frontal cortex show decreased activation (Freyer & others, 2010; Nakao & others, 2005). Interestingly, the amygdala, which is associated with the experience of anxiety, may be smaller in individuals with OCD compared to those who do not have the disorder (Atmaca & others, 2008). Low levels of the neurotransmitters serotonin and dopamine likely are

FIGURE 15.4 **PET Scans of Individuals with Obsessive-Compulsive Disorder** (*Top*) Brain images of normal individuals. (*Bottom*) Brain images of individuals with obsessive-compulsive disorder (OCD). The brain images of the individuals with OCD show more activity in the frontal cortex, basal ganglia, and thalamus than the scans of normal individuals.

involved in the brain pathways linked with OCD (Koo & others, 2010; Olver & others, 2009).

In terms of psychological factors, OCD sometimes occurs during a period of life stress such as that surrounding the birth of a child or a change in occupational or marital status (Uguz & others, 2007). According to the cognitive perspective, what differentiates individuals with OCD from those who do not have it is the inability to turn off negative, intrusive thoughts by ignoring or effectively dismissing them (Belloch & others, 2010; Foa & Franklin, 2011; Storch & others, 2010).

Post-Traumatic Stress Disorder

If you have ever been in even a minor car accident, you may have had a nightmare or two about it. You might have even found yourself reliving the experience for some time. This normal recovery process takes on a particularly devastating character in post-traumatic stress disorder. **Post-traumatic stress disorder (PTSD)** is an anxiety disorder that develops through exposure to a traumatic event that has overwhelmed the person's abilities to cope (O'Donnell & others, 2010). The symptoms of PTSD vary but include

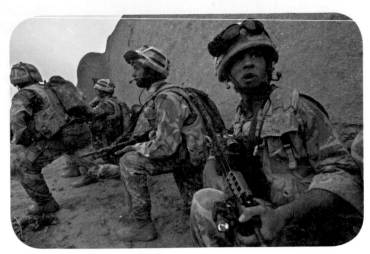

Prior to deployment, troops receive stress-management training aimed at helping to prevent PTSD and other disorders that might be triggered by the high-stress conditions of war.

● **post-traumatic stress disorder (PTSD)** Anxiety disorder that develops through exposure to a traumatic event that has overwhelmed the person's abilities to cope.

- Flashbacks in which the individual relives the event. A flashback can make the person lose touch with reality and reenact the event for seconds, hours, or, very rarely, days. A person having a flashback—which can come in the form of images, sounds, smells, and/or feelings—usually believes that the traumatic event is happening all over again.

- Avoidance of emotional experiences and of talking about emotions with others.

- Reduced ability to feel emotions, often reported as feeling numb, resulting in an inability to experience happiness, sexual desire, or enjoyable interpersonal relationships.

- Excessive arousal, resulting in an exaggerated startle response or an inability to sleep.

- Difficulties with memory and concentration.

- Feelings of apprehension, including nervous tremors.

- Impulsive outbursts of behavior, such as aggressiveness, or sudden changes in lifestyle.

PTSD symptoms can follow a trauma immediately or after months or even years (de Roon-Cassini & others, 2010; McFarlane, 2010). Most individuals who are exposed to a traumatic event experience some of the symptoms in the days and weeks following exposure (National Center for Post-Traumatic Stress Disorder, 2006). However, not every individual exposed to the same event develops PTSD (Gil & Caspi, 2006).

Researchers have examined PTSD associated with a variety of different experiences. These experiences include combat and war-related traumas (Kennedy & others, 2010; Ling & others, 2009); sexual abuse and assault (Mouilso, Calhoun, & Gidycz, 2010); natural disasters such as hurricanes and earthquakes (Irmansyah & others, 2010); and unnatural disasters such as plane crashes and terrorist attacks (Dedert & others, 2009; B. J. Hall & others, 2010).

Clearly, one cause of PTSD is the traumatic event itself. However, because not everyone who experiences the same traumatic life event develops PTSD, other factors (aside from the event) may influence a person's vulnerability to the disorder (Markowitz & others, 2009). These factors include a history of previous traumatic events and conditions, such as abuse and psychological disorders (Walter & others, 2010), as well as genetic predispositions (Voisey & others, 2009).

test yourself

1. What are the main characteristics of anxiety disorders?
2. Define phobic disorder (phobia) and give at least three examples of common phobias.
3. With what kinds of experiences is post-traumatic stress disorder (PTSD) associated?

This painting by Vincent Van Gogh, Portrait of Dr. Gachet, *reflects the extreme melancholy that characterizes the depressive disorders.*

● **mood disorders** Psychological disorders—the main types of which are depressive disorders and bipolar disorder—in which there is a primary disturbance of mood: prolonged emotion that colors the individual's entire emotional state.

● **depressive disorders** Mood disorders in which the individual suffers from depression—an unrelenting lack of pleasure in life.

● **major depressive disorder (MDD)** Psychological disorder involving a significant depressive episode and depressed characteristics, such as lethargy and hopelessness, for at least two weeks.

● **dysthymic disorder (DD)** Mood disorder that is generally more chronic and has fewer symptoms than MDD; the individual is in a depressed mood for most days for at least two years as an adult or at least one year as a child or an adolescent.

3· MOOD DISORDERS

Mood disorders are psychological disorders in which there is a primary disturbance of *mood:* prolonged emotion that colors the individual's entire emotional state. This mood disturbance can include cognitive, behavioral, and somatic (physical) symptoms, as well as interpersonal difficulties. In this section we examine the two main types of mood disorders: depressive disorders and bipolar disorder. In addition, we consider a tragic correlate of these disorders—suicide.

Depressive Disorders

Everyone feels blue sometimes. A romantic breakup, the death of a loved one, or a personal failure can cast a dark cloud over life. Sometimes, however, a person might feel unhappy and not know why. **Depressive disorders** are mood disorders in which the individual suffers from *depression:* an unrelenting lack of pleasure in life. The severity of depressive disorders varies. Some individuals experience what is classified as *major depressive disorder,* whereas others are given the diagnosis of *dysthymic disorder,* a more chronic depression with fewer symptoms than major depression (Ingram, 2009; Rafanelli & others, 2010).

Depressive disorders are common, and a number of successful individuals have been diagnosed with depression. They include musicians Sheryl Crow, Eric Clapton, and Peter Gabriel; actors Drew Barrymore and Jim Carrey; and artist Pablo Picasso, photographer Diane Arbus, astronaut Buzz Aldrin (the second man to walk on the moon), and famed architect Frank Lloyd Wright.

Major depressive disorder (MDD) involves a significant depressive episode and depressed characteristics, such as lethargy and hopelessness, for at least two weeks. MDD impairs daily functioning, and it has been called the leading cause of disability in the United States (National Institute of Mental Health, 2008). Nine symptoms (at least five of which must be present during a two-week period) define a major depressive episode:

■ Depressed mood most of the day

■ Reduced interest or pleasure in all or most activities

■ Significant weight loss or gain or significant decrease or increase in appetite

■ Trouble sleeping or sleeping too much

■ Psychological and physical agitation, or, in contrast, lethargy

■ Fatigue or loss of energy

■ Feeling worthless or guilty in an excessive or inappropriate manner

■ Problems in thinking, concentrating, or making decisions

■ Recurrent thoughts of death and suicide

■ No history of manic episodes (periods of euphoric mood)

Dysthymic disorder (DD) is a mood disorder that is generally more chronic and has fewer symptoms than MDD. The individual is in a depressed mood for most days for at least two years as an adult or at least one year as a child or an adolescent. To be classified as having dysthymic disorder, the individual must not have experienced a major depressive episode, and the two-year period of depression must not have been broken by a normal mood lasting more than two months. Two or more of these six symptoms must be present:

■ Poor appetite or overeating

■ Sleep problems

■ Low energy or fatigue

- Low self-esteem
- Poor concentration or difficulty making decisions
- Feelings of hopelessness

A variety of biological, psychological, and sociocultural factors have been implicated in the development of these depressive disorders.

BIOLOGICAL FACTORS

Genetic influences play a role in depression (Shyn & Hamilton, 2010; Y. Yuan & others, 2010). In addition, specific brain structures and neurotransmitters are involved in depressive disorders. For example, depressed individuals show lower levels of brain activity in a section of the prefrontal cortex that is involved in initiating behavior (Friedel & others, 2009; M. Roy & others, 2010).

Research has revealed that activity in the brain region that is associated with the perception of rewards in the environment (the ventromedial prefrontal cortex) may differ for depressed and non-depressed individuals (Tye & Janak, 2007). This discovery suggests that a depressed person's brain may not recognize opportunities for pleasurable experiences.

Depression likely involves problems in the body's regulation of a number of neurotransmitters. Recall from Chapter 3 that neurotransmitters are chemicals that carry impulses from neuron to neuron. In order for the brain to function smoothly, these neurotransmitters must ebb and flow, often in harmony with one another. Individuals with major depressive disorder appear to have difficulty regulating the neurotransmitter serotonin or too few receptors for serotonin and norepinephrine (Bobo & Shelton, 2010; Tourian, Jiang, & Ninan, 2010).

PSYCHOLOGICAL FACTORS

Psychological explanations of depression have drawn on behavioral learning theories and cognitive theories. One behavioral view of depression focuses on learned helplessness (see Chapter 6), an individual's acquisition of feelings of powerlessness when exposed to aversive circumstances, such as prolonged stress, over which the individual has no control. When people cannot control their stress, they eventually feel helpless and stop trying to change their situations. This helplessness spirals into a feeling of hopelessness (Becker-Weidman & others, 2009).

Cognitive explanations of depression have focused on the kinds of thoughts and beliefs that can contribute to this sense of hopelessness (Fiske, Wetherell, & Gatz, 2009; Wellen, 2010). Psychiatrist Aaron Beck (1967) proposed that negative thoughts reflect self-defeating beliefs that shape the experiences of individuals who are depressed. These habitual negative thoughts magnify and expand these individuals' negative experiences (de Graaf & others, 2010; Joorman, Teachman, & Gotlib, 2009). For example, a person who is depressed might overgeneralize about a minor occurrence—say, turning in a work assignment late—and think that he or she is worthless, or the individual might view a minor setback such as getting a *D* on a paper as the end of the world. The accumulation of cognitive distortions can lead to depression (de Graaf, Hollon, & Huibers, 2010; Gibbons & others, 2010).

The course of depression can be influenced by not only what people think but also *how* they think (Brinker & Dozois, 2009; Mathew & others, 2010). Depressed individuals may ruminate on negative experiences and negative feelings, playing them over and over again in their mind (Aldao, Nolen-Hoeksema, & Schweizer, 2010; Nolen-Hoeksema, 2011). This tendency to ruminate is associated with the development of depression as well as other psychological problems, such as binge eating and substance abuse (Aldao, Nolen-Hoeksema, & Schweizer, 2010). Combining the findings with research on the brain, we might say that individuals with depression have a brain that is wired for attention to negative information and that their habitual patterns of thought produce well-worn neurological pathways for unhappiness (De Raedt & Koster, 2010).

Another cognitive view of depression focuses on the *attributions* people make—their attempts to explain what caused something to happen (Hartley & Maclean, 2009; Wong, Kim, & Tran, 2010). Depression is thought to be related to a pessimistic attributional style. In this style, individuals regularly explain negative events as having internal causes ("It is my fault I failed the exam"), stable causes ("I'm going to fail again and again"), and global causes ("Failing this exam shows that I won't do well in any of my courses"). Pessimistic attributional style means blaming oneself for negative events and expecting the negative events to recur in the future (Abramson, Seligman, & Teasdale, 1978).

- **bipolar disorder** Mood disorder characterized by extreme mood swings that include one or more episodes of mania, an overexcited, unrealistically optimistic state.

This pessimistic attributional style can be contrasted with an optimistic attributional style. Optimists make external attributions for bad things that happen ("I did badly on the test because it's hard to know what a professor wants on the first exam"). They also recognize that these causes can change ("I'll do better on the next one") and that they are specific ("It was only one test"). Optimistic attributional style has been related to lowered depression and decreased suicide risk in a variety of samples (Giltay, Zitman, & Kromhout, 2006; Hirsch & others, 2009).

SOCIOCULTURAL FACTORS

Individuals with a low socioeconomic status (SES), especially people living in poverty, are more likely to develop depression than their higher-SES counterparts (Bryant-Davis & others, 2010). A longitudinal study of adults revealed that depression increased as standard of living and employment circumstances worsened (Lorant & others, 2007). Studies have found very high rates of depression in Native American groups, among whom poverty, hopelessness, and alcoholism are widespread (LaFromboise, Albright, & Harris, 2010; Teesson & Vogl, 2006).

In terms of gender, women are nearly twice as likely as men to be diagnosed with depression (J. Yuan & others, 2009). This gender difference occurs in many countries (Inaba & others, 2005; Nolen-Hoeksema, 2011). Incidence of depression is high as well among single women who are the heads of households and among young married women who work at unsatisfying, dead-end jobs (Whiffen & Demidenko, 2006). Minority women also are a high-risk group for depression (Diefenbach & others, 2009). The Psychological Inquiry on p. 501 provides a closer look at gender differences in depression.

So far, we have concentrated on depression in adults. However, there also is concern about the development of depression in children, as the Intersection on p. 502 explores.

The incidence of depression is high among people living in poverty, as well as single women who are the heads of households.

Bipolar Disorder

Just as we all have our down times, there are times when things seem to be going phenomenally well. For individuals with bipolar disorder, the ups and downs of life take on an extreme and often harmful tone. **Bipolar disorder** is a mood disorder that is characterized by extreme mood swings that include one or more episodes of *mania*, an overexcited, unrealistically optimistic state. A manic episode is like the flipside of a depressive episode

psychological *inquiry*

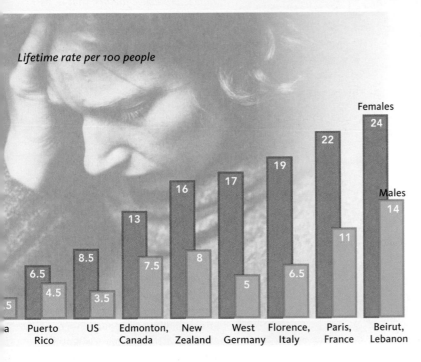

Lifetime rate per 100 people

Depression Among Women and Men Across Cultures

The graph shows the rates of depression for women and men in nine different cultures (Weissman & Olfson, 1995). The rates represent the number of diagnosed cases per 100 people.

1. Which cultures have the highest and lowest levels of depression overall? What might account for these differences?

2. Which places have the biggest gender difference in depression? What might account for these differences?

3. In order to be diagnosed with depression, a person has to seek treatment for the disorder. How might gender influence a person's willingness to seek treatment?

4. How does your answer to question 3 influence the conclusions you would draw from the data illustrated in the graph?

(Last, 2009). The person feels euphoric and on top of the world. An individual who experiences mania has tremendous energy and might sleep very little. A manic state also features an impulsivity that can get the individual in trouble. For example, the sufferer might spend his or her life savings on a foolish business venture.

The severity of manic episodes is used to distinguish between two types of bipolar disorder. *Bipolar I disorder* refers to individuals who have extreme manic episodes during which they may experience hallucinations, that is, seeing or hearing things that are not there. We will discuss this symptom in more detail later when we examine schizophrenia. *Bipolar II disorder* refers to the milder version. In bipolar II disorder, the individual may not experience full-blown mania but rather a less extreme level of euphoria.

Most individuals with bipolar disorder experience multiple cycles of depression interspersed with mania. These people can have manic and depressive episodes four or more times a year, but they usually are separated by six months to a year. Unlike depressive disorders, which are more likely to occur in women, bipolar disorder is equally common in women and men. Bipolar disorder does not prevent a person from being successful. Academy Award–winning actor Patty Duke, famed dancer and choreographer Alvin Ailey, and actor Carrie Fisher (Princess Leia in *Star Wars*) have been diagnosed with bipolar disorder.

What factors play a role in the development of bipolar disorder? Genetic influences are stronger predictors of bipolar disorder than of depressive disorder (Craddock & Forty, 2006). An individual with an identical twin who has bipolar disorder has a more than 60 percent probability of also having the disorder, and a fraternal twin more than 10 percent (Figure 15.5). Researchers are zeroing in on the specific genetic location of bipolar disorder (Barnett & Smoller, 2009; X. Zhou & others, 2009a).

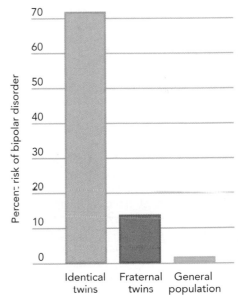

FIGURE 15.5 **Risk of Bipolar Disorder in Identical and Fraternal Twins If One Twin Has the Disorder, and in the General Population** Notice how much stronger the similarity of bipolar disorder is in identical twins, compared with fraternal twins and the general population. These statistics suggest a strong genetic role in the disorder.

Clinical Psychology and Developmental Psychology: Will New Discoveries Bring Depressed Children a Happier Future?

Imagine once again living the life of a typical 3-year-old. Your daily routine would likely revolve around eating, playing, napping, and perhaps watching cartoons. For most children in these early years, life would seem to be a time of simple happiness. For some children, however, childhood is clouded by depression. The prevalence of major depressive disorder among children ranges from 1.5 to 2.5 percent in school-age children and 15 to 20 percent in adolescents (Graber & Sontag, 2009).

Childhood depression is a significant problem (Domènech-Llaberia & others, 2009; Korczak & Goldstein, 2009). Because childhood is a time of building skills and abilities that are essential in later life, childhood depression may interfere with the normal course of development. Children who develop depression are at a higher risk of a variety of problems, including substance abuse, academic problems, increased physical illness, susceptibility to future depression, and a 30-fold increase in suicide risk (Cullen, Klimes-Dougan, & Kumra, 2009; Horowitz & Garber, 2006). How can we as a society come to better understand, treat, and prevent this debilitating childhood disorder?

Developmental psychopathology represents the merging of developmental and clinical psychology to understand, treat, and prevent childhood psychological disorders (Fontaine & others, 2009; Masten, 2009; Masten & Wright, 2009; Montgomery, 2010). Rather than applying knowledge about adult psychological disorders to children, developmental psychopathologists focus on the special developmental circumstances of children in seeking to understand what leads to negative outcomes.

Using longitudinal studies to track the relationships that exist in the unfolding of abnormal and normal behavior patterns (Ge & others, 2009; Zimmer-Gembeck & others, 2009), developmental psychopathology seeks to identify *risk factors* that might predispose a child to depression (Bureau,

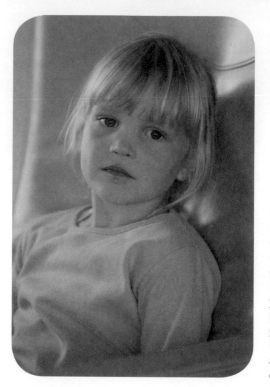

Easterbrooks, & Lyons-Ruth, 2009), as well as *protective factors*, that is, aspects of a child's psychological or social experience that may provide a shield against the development of depression (Wingo & others, 2010). The identification of risk factors might suggest avenues for both prevention and treatment. For example, researchers have identified parental psychopathology as a risk factor for childhood depression: Specifically, parents who suffer from depression, an anxiety disorder, or substance abuse are more likely to have children who experience depression (Burstein & others, 2010; Shaw & others, 2009). A research review revealed that interventions aimed at youth who were at risk for depression promoted wellness in the targeted groups (Horowitz & Garber, 2006). Interventions might include training at-risk children to engage in more effective attributions for negative events or to manage their emotions in a healthier way. Protective factors might include a supportive adult who provides the child with love, encouragement, and a role model or a strong extended family that supports the child's attempts to cope with difficulties. Genetic characteristics might be both risk factors and protective factors for children (Benjet, Thompson, & Gotlib, 2010).

Childhood is a time of extraordinary development and learning. Developmental psychopathologists are taking the problems of persistently sad and disengaged children seriously and striving to understand the sources of their suffering in order to give them a more promising future (Brumariu & Kerns, 2010; Hankin, Stone, & Wright, 2010).

In what ways might you be a protective factor in the life of a child you know?

Other biological processes are also a factor. Like depression, bipolar disorder is associated with differences in brain activity. Figure 15.6 shows the metabolic activity in the cerebral cortex of an individual cycling through depressive and manic phases. Notice the decrease in metabolic activity in the brain during depression and the increase in metabolic activity during mania (Baxter & others, 1995). In addition to high levels of norepinephrine and low levels of serotonin, studies show that high levels of the neurotransmitter glutamate occur in bipolar disorder (Singh & others, 2010; Sourial-Bassillious & others, 2009). These differences between depression and bipolar disorder have led to differences in treatment, as we will see in Chapter 16.

Suicide

Life with a psychological disorder can be so difficult that some individuals choose to end it. Suicide is not a diagnosable disorder but is, rather, a tragic consequence of psychological disorders, most commonly depression and anxiety (Black & others, 2010; Nrugham, Holen, & Sund, 2010; Oyama & others, 2010). Individuals suffering from depression are also likely to attempt suicide more than once (da Silva Cais & others, 2009). Although it is not uncommon for individuals to contemplate suicide at some point in life and thinking about suicide is not necessarily abnormal, attempting or completing the act of suicide *is* abnormal.

According to the National Institute of Mental Health (NIMH), in 2004, 32,439 people in the United States committed suicide, and suicide was the 11th-highest cause of death (NIMH, 2008). Research indicates that for every completed suicide, 8 to 25 attempted suicides occur (NIMH, 2008). Suicide is the third-leading cause (after automobile accidents and homicides) of death today among U.S. adolescents 13 through 19 years of age (National Center for Health Statistics, 2005a). Even more shocking, suicide is the third-leading cause of death among children in the United States aged 10 to 14 (Centers for Disease Control and Prevention, 2007).

Given these grim statistics, psychologists work with individuals to reduce the frequency and intensity of suicidal impulses (Pirucello, 2010). You can do your part. Figure 15.7 provides good advice on what to do and what not to do if you encounter someone who is threatening suicide.

What might prompt an individual to end his or her own life? Biological, psychological, and sociocultural circumstances can be contributing factors.

FIGURE 15.6   Brain Metabolism in Mania and Depression
PET scans of an individual with bipolar disorder, who is described as a rapid cycler because of how quickly severe mood changes occurred. (*Top and bottom*) The person's brain in a depressed state. (*Middle*) A manic state. The PET scans reveal how the brain's energy consumption falls in depression and rises in mania. The red areas in the middle row reflect rapid consumption of glucose.

BIOLOGICAL FACTORS

Genetic factors appear to play a role in suicide, which tends to run in families (Brezo & others, 2009; Wasserman, Wasserman, & Sokolowski, 2010). One famous family that has been plagued by suicide is the Hemingways. Five members of that family, spread across generations, committed suicide, including the writer Ernest Hemingway and his granddaughter Margaux, a model and actor. Similarly, in 2009, Nicholas Hughes—a successful marine biologist and the son of Sylvia Plath, a poet who had killed herself—tragically hanged himself. (In considering these examples, you might note that Margaux Hemingway and Nicholas Hughes had experienced the suicide of a family member—and might therefore have been more likely than most people to view ending their life as a way to cope with life's difficulties.)

A number of studies have linked suicide with low levels of the neurotransmitter serotonin (Pompili & others, 2010). Individuals who attempt suicide and who have low serotonin levels are 10 times more likely to attempt suicide again than are attempters who have high serotonin levels (Courtet & others, 2004). Poor physical health, especially when it is long-standing and chronic, is another risk factor for suicide. Ernest Hemingway had been in failing health for a number of years when he committed suicide.

PSYCHOLOGICAL FACTORS

Psychological factors that can contribute to suicide include mental disorders and traumas such as sexual abuse. Struggling with the stress of a psychological disorder can leave a person feeling hopeless, and the disorder itself may tax the person's ability

What to Do

1. Ask direct, straightforward questions in a calm manner. For example, "Are you thinking about hurting yourself?"

2. Be a good listener and be supportive. Emphasize that unbearable pain can be survived.

3. Take the suicide threat very seriously. Ask questions about the person's feelings, relationships, and thoughts about the type of method to be used. If a gun, pills, rope, or other means is mentioned and a specific plan has been developed, the situation is dangerous. Stay with the person until help arrives.

4. Encourage the person to get professional help and assist him or her in getting help. If the person is willing, take the person to a mental health facility or hospital.

What Not to Do

1. Don't ignore the warning signs.

2. Don't refuse to talk about suicide if the person wants to talk about it.

3. Don't react with horror, disapproval, or repulsion.

4. Don't offer false reassurances ("Everything will be all right") or make judgments ("You should be thankful for . . .").

5. Don't abandon the person after the crisis seems to have passed or after professional counseling has begun.

FIGURE 15.7 When Someone Is Threatening Suicide Do not ignore the warning signs if you think someone you know is considering suicide. Talk to a counselor if you are reluctant to say anything to the person yourself.

Suicide tends to run in families. Five suicides occurred in different generations of the Hemingway family, including author Ernest (left) and his granddaughter Margaux (right).

to cope with life difficulties. Indeed, approximately 90 percent of individuals who commit suicide are estimated to have a diagnosable psychological disorder (NIMH, 2008).

An immediate and highly stressful circumstance—such as the loss of a loved one or a job, flunking out of school, or an unwanted pregnancy—can lead people to threaten and/or to commit suicide (Videtic & others, 2009). In addition, substance abuse is linked with suicide more today than in the past (Britton & Conner, 2010).

In a fascinating set of studies, Thomas Joiner and his colleagues have focused on distinguishing between the suicide notes of suicide attempters and completers (Conner & others, 2007; Joiner, 2005; Joiner, Hollar, & Van Orden, 2006; Van Orden & others, 2008). They found that suicide attempters were more likely than suicide completers to feel a sense of belonging with others. Furthermore, completers were more likely to feel that their lives posed a burden on others (Selby & others, 2010; Van Orden & others, 2010).

SOCIOCULTURAL FACTORS

Chronic economic hardship can be a factor in suicide (Ferretti & Coluccia, 2009; Rojas & Stenberg, 2010). Cultural and ethnic contexts also are related to suicide attempts. In the United States, adolescents' suicide attempts vary across ethnic groups. As Figure 15.8 illustrates, more than 20 percent of American Indian/Alaska Native (AI/AN) female adolescents reported that they had attempted suicide in the previous year, and suicide accounts for almost 20 percent of AI/AN deaths in 15- to 19-year-olds (Goldston & others, 2008). As the figure also shows, African American and non-Latino White males reported the lowest incidence of suicide attempts. A major risk factor in the high rate of suicide attempts by AI/AN adolescents is their elevated rate of alcohol abuse.

Suicide rates vary worldwide; the lowest rates occur in countries with cultural and religious norms against ending one's own life. Among the nations with the highest suicide rates are several eastern European nations—including Belarus, Bulgaria, and Russia—along with Japan and South Korea. Among the nations with the lowest rates are Haiti, Antigua and Barbuda, Egypt, and Iran (World Health Organization, 2009). Of the 104 nations ranked by the WHO, the United States ranks 40th.

There are gender differences in suicide as well (Sarma & Kola, 2010). Women are three times more likely to attempt suicide than men. Men, however, are four times more likely to complete suicide than women (Kochanek & others, 2004). Men are also more likely than women to use a firearm in a suicide attempt (Maris, 1998). The highest suicide rate is among non-Latino White men aged

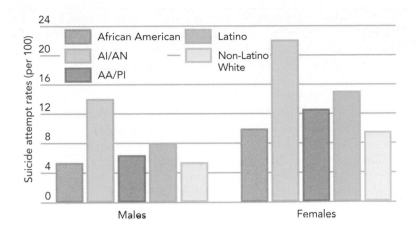

85 and older (NIMH, 2008). Although women are more likely than men to be diagnosed with depression, men are more likely to commit suicide. The explanation for these patterns may be that men are less likely to seek treatment when they are suffering from depression.

test yourself

1. How do major depressive disorder (MDD) and dysthymic disorder (DD) differ?
2. What are the essential characteristics of bipolar disorder?
3. Give at least two biological, two psychological, and two sociocultural factors in suicide.

4· DISSOCIATIVE DISORDERS

Have you ever been on a long car ride and completely lost track of time, so that you could not even remember a stretch of miles along the road? Have you been so caught up in a daydream that you were unaware of the passage of time? These are examples of normal dissociation. *Dissociation* refers to psychological states in which the person feels disconnected from immediate experience.

At the extreme of dissociation are individuals who feel a sense of disconnection *persistently*. **Dissociative disorders** are psychological disorders that involve a sudden loss of memory or change in identity. Under extreme stress or shock, the individual's conscious awareness becomes *dissociated* (separated or split) from previous memories and thoughts (Espirito-Santo & Pio-Abreu, 2009). Individuals who develop dissociative disorders may have problems putting together different aspects of consciousness, so that experiences at different levels of awareness might be felt as if they are happening to someone else (Dell & O'Neil, 2009).

Psychologists believe that dissociation is an individual's way of dealing with extreme stress (Spiegel, 2006). Through dissociation the individual mentally protects his or her conscious self from the traumatic event. Dissociative disorders often occur in individuals who also show signs of PTSD (Zucker & others, 2006). Both psychological disorders are thought to be rooted, in part, in extremely traumatic life events (Foote & others, 2006). The notion that dissociative disorders are related to problems in pulling together emotional memories is supported by findings showing lower volume in the hippocampus and amygdala in individuals with dissociative disorders (Vermetten & others, 2006). The hippocampus is especially involved in consolidating memory and organizing life experience into a coherent whole (Spiegel, 2006).

Dissociative disorders are perhaps the most controversial of all diagnostic categories, with some psychologists believing that they are often mistakenly diagnosed (Freeland & others, 1993) while others believe that they are underdiagnosed (Sar, Akyuz, & Dogan, 2007; Spiegel, 2006). Three kinds of dissociative disorders are dissociative amnesia, dissociative fugue, and dissociative identity disorder.

● **dissociative disorders** Psychological disorders that involve a sudden loss of memory or change in identity due to the dissociation (separation) of the individual's conscious awareness from previous memories and thoughts.

Dissociative Amnesia and Dissociative Fugue

Recall from Chapter 7 that *amnesia* is the inability to recall important events (Dewar & others, 2010a). Amnesia can result from a blow to the head that produces trauma

● **dissociative amnesia** Dissociative disorder characterized by extreme memory loss that is caused by extensive psychological stress.

in the brain. **Dissociative amnesia** is a type of amnesia characterized by extreme memory loss that stems from extensive psychological stress. A person experiencing dissociative amnesia still remembers things like how to hail a cab or use a phone. Only aspects of their own identity and autobiographical experiences are forgotten.

One case of dissociative amnesia involved a 28-year-old married woman who had given birth to her sixth child four months before (Tharoor & others, 2007). After she delivered the child, her family noticed that she did not acknowledge her newborn as her own baby and that she had neither a recollection of having given birth nor a sense of her own identity. She took care of the baby as advised by her family members but maintained a belief that, although she had been pregnant, she had not given birth. Under the influence of sodium pentathol (a narcotic sometimes referred to as "truth serum" because it renders people talkative and likely to share information), the young mother eventually described how she had not wanted to continue her sixth pregnancy, but her spouse, who lived in another country, had refused to consent to an abortion. She described herself as physically drained and stressed by the pregnancy. Eventually, through hypnosis and memory exercises, the woman recovered autobiographical memory for her identity as well as for the experience of having given birth.

● **dissociative fugue** Dissociative disorder in which the individual not only develops amnesia but also unexpectedly travels away from home and sometimes assumes a new identity.

Dissociative fugue (*fugue* means "flight") is a dissociative disorder in which the individual not only develops amnesia but also unexpectedly travels away from home and sometimes assumes a new identity. What makes dissociative fugue different from dissociative amnesia is this tendency to run away.

A recent case of dissociative fugue involved the disappearance of a middle school teacher in New York City. Twenty-three-year-old Hannah Upp disappeared while out for a run on August 28, 2008 (Marx & Didziulis, 2009). She had no wallet, no identification, no cell phone, and no money. Her family, friends, and roommates posted flyers around the city and messages on the Internet. As days went by, they became increasingly concerned that something terrible had happened. Finally, Hannah was found floating face down in the New York harbor on September 16, sunburned and dehydrated but alive. She remembered nothing of her experiences. To her, it felt like she had gone out for a run and 10 minutes later was being pulled from the harbor. To this day, she does not know what event might have led to her dissociative fugue, nor does she remember how she survived during her two-week disappearance. At one point during her fugue, Hannah was approached by someone who asked if she was the Hannah everyone was looking for, and she answered no.

● **dissociative identity disorder (DID)** Formerly called multiple personality disorder, a dissociative disorder in which the individual has two or more distinct personalities or identities, each with its own memories, behaviors, and relationships.

Dissociative Identity Disorder

Dissociative identity disorder (DID), formerly called *multiple personality disorder,* is the most dramatic, least common, and most controversial dissociative disorder. Individuals with this disorder have two or more distinct personalities or identities. Each identity has its own memories, behaviors, and relationships. One identity dominates at one time, another takes over at another time. Individuals sometimes report that a wall of amnesia separates their different identities (Dale & others, 2009); however, research suggests that memory does transfer across these identities, even if the person believes it does not (Kong, Allen, & Glisky, 2008). The shift between identities usually occurs under distress (Sar & others, 2007) but sometimes can also be controlled by the person (Kong, Allen, & Glisky, 2008).

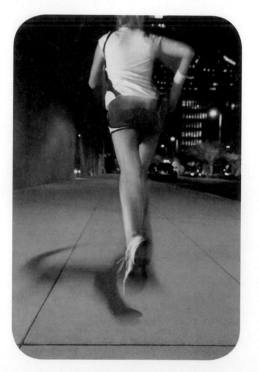

One of the most famous real-life cases of dissociative identity disorder involves the "three faces of Eve" (Thigpen & Cleckley, 1957) (Figure 15.9). Eve White was the original dominant personality. She had no knowledge of her second personality, Eve Black, although Eve Black had been alternating with Eve White for a number of years. Eve White was bland, quiet, and serious. By contrast, Eve Black was carefree, mischievous, and uninhibited. Eve Black would emerge at the most inappropriate times, leaving Eve White with hangovers, bills, and a reputation in local bars that she could not explain. During treatment, a third personality, Jane, emerged. More mature than the other two, Jane seems to have developed as a result of therapy.

More recently, former Heisman Trophy winner and legendary NFL running back Herschel Walker (2008) revealed his experience with dissociative disorder in his book *Breaking Free: My Life with Dissociative Identity Disorder.*

Research on dissociative identity disorder suggests that a high rate of extraordinarily severe sexual or physical abuse during early childhood is related to the condition (Sar, Akyuz, & Dogan, 2007). Some psychologists believe that a child can cope with intense trauma by dissociating from the experience and developing other alternate selves as protectors. Sexual abuse has occurred in as many as 70 percent or more of dissociative identity disorder cases (Foote & others, 2006); however, the majority of individuals who have been sexually abused do not develop dissociative identity disorder. The vast majority of individuals with dissociative identity disorder are women. A genetic predisposition might also exist, as the disorder tends to run in families (Dell & Eisenhower, 1990).

Until the 1980s, only about 300 cases of dissociative identity disorder had ever been reported (Suinn, 1984). In the past 30 years, hundreds more cases have been diagnosed. Social cognitive approaches to dissociative identity disorder point out that cases have tended to increase whenever the popular media present a case, such as the film *The Three Faces of Eve,* the miniseries *Sybil,* or the Showtime drama *The United States of Tara.* From this perspective, individuals develop multiple identities through a process of social contagion (as described in Chapter 13). After exposure to these examples, people may be more likely to view multiple identities as a real condition.

Some experts believe, in fact, that dissociative identity disorder is a *social construction*—that it represents a category some people adopt to make sense out of their experiences (Spanos, 1996). Rather than being a single person with many conflicting feelings, wishes, and potentially awful experiences, the individual compartmentalizes different aspects of the self into independent identities. In some cases, therapists have been accused of creating alternate personalities. Encountering an individual who appears to have a fragmented sense of self, the therapist may begin to treat each fragment as its own "personality" (Spiegel, 2006).

FIGURE 15.9   The Three Faces of Eve Chris Sizemore, the subject of *The Three Faces of Eve,* is shown here with a work she painted, titled *Three Faces in One.*

test yourself

1. What are the main characteristics of dissociative disorders? What does the word *dissociative* mean in reference to them?
2. Identify the characteristics of dissociative fugue. How is it different from dissociative amnesia?
3. What explanations have experts given for the development of dissociative identity disorder (DID) in individuals?

5· SCHIZOPHRENIA

Have you had the experience of watching a movie and suddenly noticing that the film bears an uncanny resemblance to your life? Have you ever listened to a radio talk show and realized that the host was saying exactly what you were just thinking? Do these moments mean something special about you, or are they coincidences? For people with schizophrenia, such experiences may take on special and personal meaning.

Schizophrenia is a severe psychological disorder that is characterized by highly disordered thought processes. These disordered thoughts are referred to as *psychotic* because they are far removed from reality. Individuals with schizophrenia may see things that are not there, hear voices inside their heads, and live in a strange world of twisted logic. They may say odd things, show inappropriate emotion, and move their bodies in peculiar ways. Often, they are socially withdrawn and isolated.

As much as schizophrenia might sound disturbing to those who have not experienced it, the ordeal of those living with it seems unimaginable. Often the experience of schizophrenia is one of extraordinary terror (NIMH, 2008). Typically diagnosed in early adulthood, the disorder can be debilitating. About one-half of the patients in psychiatric hospitals are afflicted with schizophrenia. Moreover, the suicide risk for individuals with schizophrenia is eight times that for the general population (Pompili & others, 2007).

● **schizophrenia** Severe psychological disorder characterized by highly disordered thought processes, referred to as psychotic because they are so far removed from reality.

For many people with the disorder, controlling it means using powerful medications to combat symptoms. The most common cause of relapse is that individuals stop taking their medication. They might do so because they feel better, because they do not realize that their thoughts are disordered, or because the side effects of the medications are so unpleasant. Recall Bill Garrett's story from the beginning of this chapter. Some medications made him drowsy and lethargic; others made him volatile. On one medication he rapidly gained 75 pounds (M. Park, 2009).

Symptoms of Schizophrenia

Psychologists generally classify the symptoms of schizophrenia as positive symptoms, negative symptoms, and cognitive deficits (NIMH, 2008).

POSITIVE SYMPTOMS

The *positive symptoms* of schizophrenia are marked by a distortion or an excess of normal function. They are "positive" because they reflect something added above and beyond normal behavior. Positive symptoms of schizophrenia include hallucinations, delusions, thought disorders, and disorders of movement.

Hallucinations are sensory experiences in the absence of real stimuli. Hallucinations are usually auditory—the person might complain of hearing voices—or visual, and much less commonly they take the form of smells or tastes (Bhatia & others, 2009). Visual hallucinations involve seeing things that are not there. For example, consider the case of Moe Armstrong. At the age of 21, while serving in Vietnam as a Marine medical corpsman, Armstrong experienced a psychotic break. Dead Vietcong soldiers appeared to talk to him and beg him for help and did not seem to realize that they were dead. Armstrong, now a successful businessman and a sought-after public speaker who holds two master's degrees, relies on medication to keep such experiences at bay (Bonfatti, 2005).

Delusions are false, unusual, and sometimes magical beliefs that are not part of an individual's culture. A delusional person might think that he is Jesus Christ or Muhammad; another might imagine that her thoughts are being broadcast over the radio. It is crucial to distinguish delusions from cultural ideas such as the religious belief that a person can have divine visions or communicate personally with a deity. Generally, psychology and psychiatry do not treat these ideas as delusional.

For individuals with schizophrenia, delusional beliefs that might seem completely illogical to the outsider are experienced as all too real. At one point in his life, Bill Garrett was convinced that a blister on his hand was a sign of gangrene. So strong was his belief that he tried to cut off his hand with a knife, before being stopped by his family (M. Park, 2009).

Thought disorder refers to the unusual, sometimes bizarre thought processes that are characteristic positive symptoms of schizophrenia. The thoughts of persons with schizophrenia can be disorganized and confused. Often individuals with schizophrenia do not make sense when they talk or write. For example, someone with schizophrenia might say, "Well, Rocky, babe, happening, but where, when, up, top, side, over, you know, out of the way, that's it. Sign off." Such speech has no meaning for the listener. These incoherent, loose word associations are called "word salad." The individual might also make up new words (*neologisms*) (Kerns & others, 1999). In addition, a person with schizophrenia can show **referential thinking,** which means ascribing personal meaning to completely random events. For instance, the individual might believe that a traffic light has turned red *because* he or she is in a hurry.

A final type of positive symptom is *disorders of movement*. A person with schizophrenia may show unusual mannerisms, body movements, and facial expressions. The individual may repeat certain motions over and over or, in extreme cases, may become catatonic. **Catatonia** is a state of immobility and unresponsiveness that lasts for long periods of time (Figure 15.10).

● **hallucinations** Sensory experiences in the absence of real stimuli.

● **delusions** False, unusual, and sometimes magical beliefs that are not part of an individual's culture.

● **referential thinking** Ascribing personal meaning to completely random events.

● **catatonia** State of immobility and unresponsiveness lasting for long periods of time.

FIGURE 15.10 **Disorders of Movement in Schizophrenia** Unusual motor behaviors are positive symptoms of schizophrenia. Individuals may cease to move altogether (a state called catatonia), sometimes holding bizarre postures.

NEGATIVE SYMPTOMS

Whereas schizophrenia's positive symptoms are characterized by a distortion or an excess of normal functions, schizophrenia's *negative symptoms* reflect social withdrawal, behavioral deficits, and the loss or decrease of normal functions. One negative symptom is **flat affect,** which means the display of little or no emotion (Alvino & others, 2007). Individuals with schizophrenia also may be lacking in the ability to read the emotions of others (Chambon, Baudouin, & Franck, 2006). They may experience a lack of positive emotional experience in daily life and show a deficient ability to plan, initiate, and engage in goal-directed behavior.

● **flat affect** The display of little or no emotion— a common negative symptom of schizophrenia.

COGNITIVE SYMPTOMS

Cognitive symptoms of schizophrenia include difficulty sustaining attention, problems holding information in memory, and inability to interpret information and make decisions (Kerns, 2007; Sitnikova, Goff, & Kuperberg, 2009). These cognitive symptoms may be quite subtle and are often detected only through neuropsychological tests.

Causes of Schizophrenia

A great deal of research has investigated schizophrenia's causes. Here we consider the biological, psychological, and sociocultural factors involved in the disorder.

BIOLOGICAL FACTORS

Research provides strong support for biological explanations of schizophrenia. Particularly compelling is the evidence for a genetic predisposition, but structural brain abnormalities and problems with neurotransmitter regulation also are linked to this severe psychological disorder (Horn & others, 2010; Kegeles & others, 2010).

Heredity   Research supports the notion schizophrenia is at least partially caused by genetic factors (Paul-Samojedny & others, 2010). As genetic similarity to a person with schizophrenia increases, so does a person's risk of developing schizophrenia (Cardno & Gottesman, 2000). Such data strongly suggest that genetic factors play a role in schizophrenia. Researchers are seeking to pinpoint the chromosomal location of genes involved in susceptibility to schizophrenia (Duan, Sanders, & Gejman, 2010; Holliday & others, 2009). The Psychological Inquiry on p. 510 shows the results of research examining the role of genetics in schizophrenia.

Structural Brain Abnormalities   Studies have found structural brain abnormalities in people with schizophrenia. Imaging techniques such as MRI scans clearly show enlarged ventricles in their brain (Acer & others, 2010; Killgore & others, 2009). Ventricles are fluid-filled spaces, and enlargement of the ventricles indicates deterioration in other brain tissue.

Individuals with schizophrenia also have a small prefrontal cortex and lower activity in this area of the brain than individuals who do not have schizophrenia (Smieskova & others, 2010). The prefrontal cortex is the region where thinking, planning, and decision making take place. Recall from Chapter 9 that the prefrontal cortex continues to develop throughout adolescence and into young adulthood. It may be that the emergence of symptoms of schizophrenia in young adulthood occurs because this is the time when the prefrontal cortex becomes fully functioning.

Still, differences between the brains of healthy individuals and those with schizophrenia are surprisingly small (NIMH, 2008). Microscopic studies of brain tissue after death reveal small changes in the distribution or characteristics of brain cells in persons with schizophrenia. It appears that many of these changes occurred prenatally because they are not accompanied by glial cells, which are always present when a brain injury occurs after birth (Vuillermot & others, 2010). It may be that problems in prenatal development such as prenatal infections (A. S. Brown, 2006) predispose a brain to

psychological *inquiry*

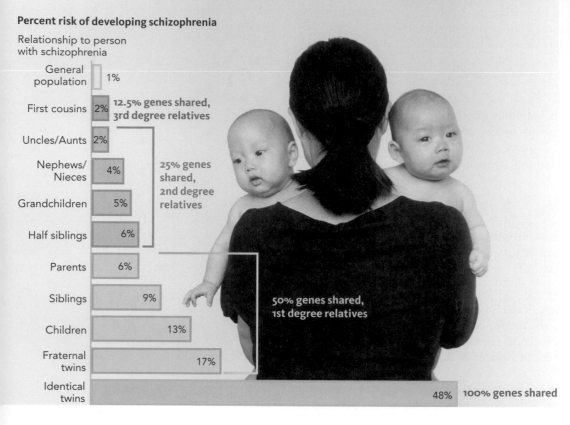

Percent risk of developing schizophrenia

Relationship to person with schizophrenia

Relationship	Risk
General population	1%
First cousins	2%
Uncles/Aunts	2%
Nephews/Nieces	4%
Grandchildren	5%
Half siblings	6%
Parents	6%
Siblings	9%
Children	13%
Fraternal twins	17%
Identical twins	48%

12.5% genes shared, 3rd degree relatives

25% genes shared, 2nd degree relatives

50% genes shared, 1st degree relatives

100% genes shared

The Association of Genes with Schizophrenia

This figure shows that as genetic relatedness to an individual with schizophrenia increases, so does the lifetime risk of developing schizophrenia. Using the graph, answer these questions:

1. Which familial relations have the lowest and highest level of genetic overlap (shared genes)?

2. What is the difference in genetic overlap between identical twins and non-twin siblings?

3. What is the difference in risk of schizophrenia between identical twins and non-twin siblings of individuals with schizophrenia?

4. What do you think accounts for the differences in your answers to questions 2 and 3?

developing schizophrenic symptoms during puberty and young adulthood (Fatemi & Folsom, 2009).

Problems in Neurotransmitter Regulation An early biological explanation for schizophrenia linked excess dopamine production to schizophrenia. The link between dopamine and psychotic symptoms was first noticed when the drug L-dopa (which increases dopamine levels) was given to individuals as a treatment for Parkinson disease. In addition to relieving their Parkinson symptoms, L-dopa caused some individuals to experience disturbed thoughts (Janowsky, Addario, & Risch, 1987). Furthermore, drugs that reduce psychotic symptoms often block dopamine (van Os & Kapur, 2009). Whether it is differences in amount of dopamine, its production, or its uptake, there is good evidence that overactivation of pathways in the brain associated with dopamine plays a role in schizophrenia (D. P. Eisenberg & others, 2010; Howes & others, 2009).

As noted in the chapters about states of consciousness (Chapter 5) and learning (Chapter 6), dopamine is a "feel good" neurotransmitter that helps us recognize rewarding stimuli in the environment. As described in the chapter on personality (Chapter 12), dopamine is related to being outgoing and sociable. How can a neurotransmitter that is associated with good things play a crucial role in the most devastating psychological disorder?

One way to think about this puzzle is to view dopamine as a neurochemical messenger that in effect shouts out, "Hey! This is important!" whenever we encounter opportunities for reward. Imagine what it might be like to be bombarded with such messages about even the smallest details of life (Kapur, 2003; Rosier & others, 2010). The person's own thoughts might take on such dramatic proportions that they sound like someone else's voice talking inside the individual's head. Fleeting ideas, such as

"It's raining today *because* I didn't bring my umbrella to work," suddenly seem not silly but true. Shitij Kapur (2003) has suggested that hallucinations, delusions, and referential thinking may be expressions of the individual's attempts to make sense of such extraordinary feelings.

A problem with the dopamine explanation of schizophrenia is that antipsychotic drugs reduce dopamine levels very quickly, but delusional beliefs take much longer to disappear. Even after dopamine levels are balanced, a person might still cling to the bizarre belief that members of a powerful conspiracy are watching his or her every move. If dopamine causes these symptoms, why do the symptoms persist even after the dopamine is under control? According to Kapur, delusions serve as explanatory schemes that have helped the person make sense of the random and chaotic experiences caused by out-of-control dopamine. Bizarre beliefs might disappear only after experience demonstrates that such schemes no longer carry their explanatory power (Kapur, 2003). That is, with time, experience, and therapy, the person might come to realize that there is, in fact, no conspiracy.

PSYCHOLOGICAL FACTORS

Psychologists used to explain schizophrenia as rooted in an individual's difficult childhood experiences with parents. Such explanations have mostly fallen by the wayside, but contemporary theorists do recognize that stress may contribute to the development of this disorder. The **diathesis-stress model** argues that a combination of biogenetic disposition and stress causes schizophrenia (Meehl, 1962). (The term *diathesis* means "physical vulnerability or predisposition to a particular disorder.") For instance, genetic characteristics might produce schizophrenia only when (and if) the individual experiences extreme stress.

● **diathesis-stress model** View of schizophrenia emphasizing that a combination of biogenetic disposition and stress causes the disorder.

SOCIOCULTURAL FACTORS

Sociocultural background is not considered a *cause* of schizophrenia, but sociocultural factors do appear to affect the *course* of the disorder. That is, sociocultural factors influence how schizophrenia progresses. Across cultures, individuals with schizophrenia in developing, nonindustrialized nations tend to have better outcomes than those in developed, industrialized nations (Jablensky, 2000). This difference may be due to the fact that in developing nations, family and friends are more accepting and supportive of individuals with schizophrenia.

In addition, in Western samples, marriage, warm supportive friends (Jablensky & others, 1992; Wiersma & others, 1998), and employment are related to better outcomes for individuals diagnosed with schizophrenia (Rosen & Garety, 2005). At the very least, this research suggests that some individuals with schizophrenia enjoy marriage, productive work, and friendships (Drake, Levine, & Laska, 2007; Fleischhaker & others, 2005; Marshall & Rathbone, 2006).

test yourself

1. What is schizophrenia?
2. What are some positive and negative symptoms of schizophrenia?
3. Give three biological explanations for schizophrenia.

6· PERSONALITY DISORDERS

Are there aspects of your personality that you would like to change? Maybe you worry too much or fall in love too easily. Imagine that your very personality—who you really are—is the core of your life difficulties. That is what happens with **personality disorders,** which are chronic, maladaptive cognitive-behavioral patterns that are thoroughly integrated into an individual's personality. Personality disorders are relatively common. In a study of a representative U.S. sample, researchers found that 15 percent had a personality disorder (Grant & others, 2004).

The *DSM-IV* lists 10 different personality disorders. Below we survey the two that have been the object of greatest study: antisocial personality disorder and borderline personality disorder. These disorders are associated with dire consequences, including criminal activity and violence (in the case of antisocial personality disorder) and self-harm and suicide (borderline personality disorder).

● **personality disorders** Chronic, maladaptive cognitive-behavioral patterns that are thoroughly integrated into an individual's personality.

Antisocial Personality Disorder

● **antisocial personality disorder (ASPD)** A psychological disorder characterized by guilt-lessness, law-breaking, exploitation of others, irresponsibility, and deceit.

Antisocial personality disorder (ASPD) is a psychological disorder characterized by guiltlessness, law-breaking, exploitation of others, irresponsibility, and deceit. Although they may be superficially charming, individuals with ASPD do not play by the rules, and they often lead a life of crime and violence. ASPD is far more common in men than in women and is related to criminal behavior, vandalism, substance abuse, and alcoholism (Cale & Lilienfeld, 2002).

The *DSM-IV* criteria for antisocial personality disorder include

- Failure to conform to social norms or obey the law
- Deceitfulness, lying, using aliases, or conning others for personal profit or pleasure
- Impulsivity or failure to plan ahead
- Irritability and aggressiveness, getting into physical fights or perpetrating assaults
- Reckless disregard for the safety of self or others
- Consistent irresponsibility, inconsistent work behavior, not paying bills
- Lack of remorse, showing indifference to the pain of others, or rationalizing, having hurt or mistreated another

Generally, ASPD is not diagnosed unless a person has shown persistent antisocial behavior before the age of 15.

Although ASPD is associated with criminal behavior, not all individuals with ASPD engage in crime, and not all criminals suffer from ASPD. Some individuals with ASPD can have successful careers. There are antisocial physicians, clergy members, lawyers, and just about any other occupation. Still, such individuals tend to be exploitative of others and to lack empathy. They break the rules, even if they are never caught.

What is the etiology of ASPD? Biological factors include genetic, brain, and autonomic nervous system differences. We consider these in turn.

ASPD is genetically heritable (L. F. Garcia & others, 2010). Certain genetic characteristics associated with ASPD may interact with testosterone (the hormone that is most associated with aggressive behavior) to promote antisocial behavior (Sjoberg & others, 2008). Although the experience of childhood abuse may be implicated in ASPD, there is evidence that genetic differences may distinguish abused children who go on to commit violent acts themselves from those who do not (Caspi & others, 2002; Lynam & others, 2007).

In terms of the brain, research has linked ASPD to low levels of activation in the prefrontal cortex and has related these brain differences to poor decision making and problems in learning (Yang & Raine, 2009). With regard to the autonomic nervous system, researchers have found that individuals with ASPD are less stressed than others by aversive circumstances, including punishment (Fung & others, 2005), and that they have the ability to keep their cool while engaging in deception (Verschuere & others, 2005). These findings suggest that people with ASPD might be able to fool a polygraph. The underaroused autonomic nervous system may be a key difference between adolescents who become antisocial adults and those whose behavior improves during adulthood (Raine, Venables, & Williams, 1990).

Psychopaths are one subgroup of individuals with ASPD (Weber & others, 2008). Psychopaths are remorseless predators who engage in violence to get what they want. Examples of psychopaths include serial killers John Wayne Gacy (who murdered 33 boys and young men) and Ted Bundy (who confessed to murdering at least 30 young women).

Psychopaths tend to show less prefrontal activation than normal individuals and to have structural abnormalities in the amygdala, as well as the hippocampus, the brain structure most closely associated with memory (Weber & others, 2008). Importantly, these brain differences are most pronounced in "unsuccessful psychopaths"—individuals who have been arrested for their behaviors (Y. Yang & others, 2005). In contrast, "successful psychopaths"—individuals who have engaged in antisocial behavior but have not

John Wayne Gacy (top) and Ted Bundy (bottom) exemplify the subgroup of people with ASPD who are also psychopathic.

gotten caught—are more similar to healthy controls in terms of brain structure and function (Gao & Raine, 2010).

However, in their behavior, successful psychopaths show a lack of empathy and a willingness to act immorally; they victimize other people to enrich their own lives. Successful psychopaths may even get away with murder (Y. Yang & others, 2005). Psychopaths show deficiencies in learning about fear, have difficulty processing information related to the distress of others, such as sad or fearful faces (Dolan & Fullam, 2006), and show deficits in theory of mind (Shamay-Tsoory & others, 2010).

A key challenge in treating individuals with ASPD, including psychopaths, is their ability to con even sophisticated mental health professionals. Many never seek therapy, and others end up in prison, where treatment is rarely an option.

Borderline Personality Disorder

According to the *DSM-IV,* **borderline personality disorder (BPD)** is a pervasive pattern of instability in interpersonal relationships, self-image, and emotions, and of marked impulsivity beginning by early adulthood and present in various contexts. Individuals with BPD are insecure, impulsive, and emotional (Aggen & others, 2009). BPD is related to self-harming behaviors such as cutting, which is injuring oneself with a sharp object but without suicidal intent (Chapman, 2009) and also to suicide (Soloff & others, 1994).

The *DSM-IV* specifies that BPD is indicated by the presence of five or more of the following symptoms:

● **borderline personality disorder (BPD)** A psychological disorder characterized by a pervasive pattern of instability in interpersonal relationships, self-image, and emotions, and of marked impulsivity beginning by early adulthood and present in a variety of contexts.

- Frantic efforts to avoid being abandoned
- Unstable and intense interpersonal relationships characterized by extreme shifts between idealization and devaluation
- Markedly and persistently unstable self-image or sense of self
- Impulsivity in at least two areas that are potentially self-damaging (for example, spending, sex, substance abuse, reckless driving, and binge eating)
- Recurrent suicidal behavior, gestures, or threats or self-mutilating behavior
- Unstable and extreme emotional responses
- Chronic feelings of emptiness
- Inappropriate, intense anger or difficulty controlling anger
- Temporary stress-related *paranoia* (a pattern of disturbed thought featuring delusions of grandeur or persecution) or severe dissociative symptoms

BPD is far more common in women than men. Women make up 75 percent of those with the disorder (Korzekwa & others, 2008). Individuals with BPD are prone to wild mood swings and are very sensitive to how others treat them. They often feel as if they are riding a nonstop emotional rollercoaster (Selby & others, 2009), and their loved ones may have to work hard to avoid upsetting them. Individuals with BPD tend to see the world in black-and-white terms, a thinking style called *splitting.* For example, they typically view other people as either hated enemies with no positive qualities or as beloved, idealized friends who can do no wrong. To cope with their unstable emotional lives, individuals with BPD may engage in a variety of maladaptive behaviors, among them drinking alcohol and using illicit substances (Waugaman, 2005).

The potential causes of BPD are likely complex and include biological factors as well as childhood experiences (Barnow & others, 2010; Steele & Siever, 2010). The role of genes in BPD has been demonstrated in a variety of studies and across cultures, and researchers estimate the heritability of BPD to be about 40 percent (Distel & others, 2008).

Impulsivity of the type that can lead to self-harm can be a symptom of borderline personality disorder.

Many individuals with BPD report experiences of childhood sexual abuse, as well as physical abuse and neglect (Al-Alem & Omar, 2008; Lobbestael & Arntz, 2010). It is not clear, however, whether abuse is a primary cause of the disorder (Trull & Widiger, 2003). Childhood abuse experiences may combine with genetic factors in promoting BPD, and this possibility suggests a diathesis-stress explanation for the disorder.

Cognitive factors associated with BPD include a tendency to hold a set of irrational beliefs. These include thinking that one is powerless and innately unacceptable and that other people are dangerous and hostile (Arntz, 2005). Individuals with BPD also display *hypervigilance:* the tendency to be constantly on the alert, looking for threatening information in the environment (Sieswerda & others, 2007).

As recently as within the past 20 years, experts thought that BPD was unlikely to be treatable, but newer evidence suggests that many individuals with BPD show improvement over time. As many as 50 percent of individuals with BPD improve within two years, and once improved they are not likely to relapse (Gunderson, 2008). One key aspect of improvement appears to be reductions in social stress, such as leaving an abusive romantic partner or establishing a sense of trust in a therapist (Gunderson & others, 2003).

7· PSYCHOLOGICAL DISORDERS AND HEALTH AND WELLNESS

Putting a label on a person with a psychological disorder can make the disorder seem like something that happens only to other people (Baumann, 2007). The truth is that psychological disorders are not just about *other* people; they are about people, period. Over 26 percent of Americans aged 18 and older suffer from a diagnosable psychological disorder in a given year—an estimated 57.7 million U.S. adults (Kessler & others, 2005; NIMH, 2008). Chances are that you or someone you know will experience a psychological disorder. Figure 15.11 shows how common many psychological disorders are in the United States.

Psychological disorders clearly present a challenge to living a healthy, fulfilling life. For the many individuals who are diagnosed with one or more such disorders, a significant obstacle in the pursuit of that life is the fear of stigma, stereotypes, prejudice, and discrimination. To appreciate the power of the labels that are attached to individuals with psychological disorders, consider a classic and controversial study by David Rosenhan (1973). He recruited eight adults (including a stay-at-home mother, a psychology graduate student, a pediatrician, and some psychiatrists), none with a psychological disorder, to see a psychiatrist at various hospitals. These "pseudo patients" were instructed to act in a normal way except to complain about hearing voices that said things like "empty" and "thud." All eight expressed an interest in leaving the hospital and behaved cooperatively. Nevertheless, all eight were labeled with schizophrenia and kept in the hospital from 3 to 52 days. None of the mental health professionals they encountered ever questioned the diagnosis that had been given to these individuals, and all were discharged with the label "schizophrenia in remission." The label "schizophrenia" had stuck to the pseudo-patients and caused the professionals around them to interpret their quite normal behavior as abnormal. Clearly, then, once a person has been labeled with a psychological disorder, that label colors how others perceive everything else he or she does.

Labels of psychological disorder carry with them a wide array of implications for the individual. Is he or she still able

	Number of Americans in a given year (millions)	Percent of Americans
Anxiety Disorders		
General anxiety disorder	6.8	3.1%
Panic disorder	6.0	2.7%
Phobic disorder	19.2	8.7%
PTSD	7.7	3.5%
Mood Disorders		
Major depressive disorder	14.8	6.7%
Dysthymic disorder	3.3	1.5%
Bipolar disorder	5.7	2.6%
Schizophrenia	2.4	1.1%

FIGURE 15.11 **The 12-Month Prevalence of the Most Common Psychological Disorders** If you add up the numbers in this figure, you will see that the totals are higher than the numbers given in the text. The explanation is that people are frequently diagnosed with more than one psychological disorder. An individual who has both a depressive and an anxiety disorder would be counted in both of those categories.

to be a good friend? A good parent? A competent worker? A significant concern for individuals with psychological disorders is the negative attitudes that others might have about people struggling with mental illness (Phelan & Basow, 2007). Stigma can be a significant barrier for individuals coping with a psychological disorder, as well as for their families and loved ones (Corrigan, 2007; Hinshaw, 2007). Fear of stigma can prevent individuals from seeking treatment and from talking about their problems with family and friends. To test your own attitudes about people with psychological disorders, complete the exercise in Figure 15.12.

Consequences of Stigma

The stigma attached to psychological disorders can provoke prejudice and discrimination toward individuals who are struggling with these problems, thus adding a complication to an already difficult situation. Having a disorder and experiencing the stigma associated with it can also negatively affect the physical health of such individuals.

PREJUDICE AND DISCRIMINATION

Labels of psychological disorders can be damaging because they may lead to negative stereotypes, which, as reviewed in Chapter 13, play a role in prejudice. For example, the label "schizophrenic" often has negative connotations such as "frightening" and "dangerous."

Vivid cases of extremely harmful behavior by individuals with psychological disorders can perpetuate the stereotype that people with such disorders are violent. For example, Cho Seung-Hui, a 23-year-old college student, murdered 32 students and faculty at Virginia Tech University in April 2007 before killing himself. The widely reported fact that Cho had struggled with psychological disorders throughout his life may have reinforced the notion that individuals with disorders are dangerous. In fact, however, people with psychological disorders (especially those in treatment) are no more likely to commit violent acts than the general population. Cho was no more representative of people with psychological disorders than he was representative of students at Virginia Tech.

Individuals who are diagnosed with psychological disorders are often aware of the negative stigma attached to these conditions (Brohan & others, 2010; Moses, 2010). They themselves may have previously held such negative attitudes. People with psychological disorders need help, but seeking that assistance may involve accepting a stigmatized identity (Thornicroft & others, 2009; Yen & others, 2009). They must face the prospect of sacrificing their status as mentally healthy for a new status as disordered. Even mental health professionals can fall prey to prejudicial attitudes toward those who are coping with psychological disorders (Nordt, Rossler, & Lauber, 2006).

Among the most feared aspects of stigma is discrimination. As we saw in Chapter 13, discrimination means acting prejudicially toward a person who is a member of a stigmatized group. In the workplace, discrimination against a person with a psychological disorder is against the law. As described in Chapter 14, the Americans with Disabilities Act (ADA) of 1990 made it illegal to refuse employment or a promotion to someone with a psychological disorder when the person's condition does not prevent performance

Rate the following items using a scale of 1–5, with 1 indicating that you completely *disagree* with the statement and 5 indicating that you completely *agree* with the statement.

*1=completely disagree 2=slightly agree
3=moderately agree 4=strongly agree
5=completely agree*

____ 1. I would rather not live next door to a person with a psychological disorder.

____ 2. A person with a psychological disorder is unfit to raise children.

____ 3. I would be afraid to be around a person with a psychological disorder.

____ 4. I would not want to live in the same neighborhood as a group home for persons with psychological disorders.

____ 5. A person with a psychological disorder cannot hold a job.

____ 6. A person with a psychological disorder is dangerous or potentially violent.

Total _____

Add up your score and divide by 6. If your score is 3 or higher, you may want to rethink your attitudes about individuals with psychological disorders.

It may be revealing to ask yourself how you would respond to these statements if the words "person with a psychological disorder" were replaced with "woman," "African American," or "gay man or lesbian." Sometimes even individuals who would not think of themselves as being prejudiced against other groups find themselves biased against the mentally ill.

FIGURE 15.12   Test Your Attitudes About People with Psychological Disorders Take the survey to discover and evaluate your own attitudes.

Although Sheila Hollingsworth struggles with schizophrenia, her story is one of success, not failure. She has refused to allow her disorder to rob her of a good life.

of the job's essentials functions (Cleveland, Barnes-Farrell, & Ratz, 1997). A person's appearance or behavior may be unusual or irritating, but as long as that individual is able to complete the duties required of a position, he or she cannot be denied employment or promotion.

PHYSICAL HEALTH

Individuals with psychological disorders are more likely to be physically ill and two times more likely to die than their psychologically healthy counterparts (Gittelman, 2008; Kumar, 2004). They are also more likely to be obese, to smoke, to drink excessively, and to lead sedentary lives (Beard, Weisberg, & Keller, 2010; J. Y. Kim & others, 2007; Lindwall & others, 2007; Mykletun & others, 2007).

You might be thinking that these physical health issues are the least of their worries. If someone struggling with schizophrenia wants to smoke, why not? This type of thinking reveals the subtle way that prejudice toward those with psychological disorders can affect their lives. It sells short the capacity of psychological and psychiatric treatments to help those with psychological disorders, and, more important, it demonstrates a lack of appreciation of the fact that individuals with serious mental disorders can lead healthy, meaningful lives.

Research has shown that health-promotion programs can work well even for individuals with a severe psychological disorder (Addington & others, 1998; Chafetz & others, 2008). When we disregard the potential of physical health interventions for people with psychological disorders to make positive life changes, we reveal our own biases.

Overcoming Stigma

How can we effectively combat the stigma of psychological disorders? One obstacle to changing people's attitudes toward individuals with psychological disorders is that mental illness is often invisible. That is, sometimes a person can have a disorder without those of us around him or her ever knowing. Indeed, we may be unaware of *many* courageous lives around us that are being lived within the challenging context of psychological disorders, because worries about being stigmatized keep the affected individuals from "coming out." Thus, stigma leads to a catch-22: Positive examples of individuals coping with psychological disorders are often missing from our experience because those who are doing well shun public disclosure of their disorders (Jensen & Wadkins, 2007).

A critical step toward eliminating stigma is to resist thinking of people with disorders as limited individuals whose disorder colors everything they do. Instead, it is vital to recognize their strengths—both in confronting their disorder and in carrying on despite their problems—and their achievements. By creating a positive environment for people with disorders, we encourage more of them to become confidently visible, and we empower them to be positive role models for others.

Sheila Hollingsworth—a 51-year-old divorced mother of two—is such a role model. She has a master's degree and works at the Baltic Street Mental Health Board. She is so beloved at work that everyone calls her "Sheila Love." She sings in her church choir, takes calligraphy classes, and is determined to lose 30 pounds (Bonfatti, 2005). Notably, Sheila has schizophrenia. However, she has not allowed the stigma of this disorder to rob her of a good life. She works as a peer counselor and helps others by leading groups and modeling effective treatment. It can be enormously positive for individuals coping with severe psychological disorders to have a role model, like Sheila, who is making it, one day at a time. Each of us can benefit from exposure to success stories such as Sheila's.

After reading this chapter, you know that many admired individuals have dealt with psychological disorders. Their diagnoses do not detract from their accomplishments. Quite the contrary, their accomplishments are all the more remarkable in the context of the challenging, courageous lives in which they have occurred.

test yourself

1. What did the classic study by Rosenhan reveal about the power of labels that are applied to individuals?
2. What social and physical effects can result from the stigma with which some people view psychological disorders?
3. What are some critical considerations in efforts to eliminate stigmas toward individuals with psychological disorders?

1. DEFINING AND EXPLAINING ABNORMAL BEHAVIOR

Abnormal behavior is deviant, maladaptive, or personally distressful. Theoretical perspectives on the causes of psychological disorders include biological, psychological, sociocultural, and biopsychosocial approaches.

Biological approaches to disorders describe psychological disorders as diseases with origins in structural, biochemical, and genetic factors. Psychological approaches include the behavioral, social cognitive, and trait perspectives. Sociocultural approaches place emphasis on the larger social context in which a person lives, including marriage, socioeconomic status, ethnicity, gender, and culture. Biopsychosocial approaches view the interactions among biological, psychological, and social factors as significant forces in producing both normal and abnormal behavior.

The classification of disorders provides a shorthand for communication, allows clinicians to make predictions about disorders, and helps them to decide on appropriate treatment. The *Diagnostic and Statistical Manual of Mental Disorders (DSM)* is the classification system clinicians use to diagnose psychological disorders. Some psychologists contend that the *DSM-IV* perpetuates the medical model of psychological disorders, labels everyday problems as psychological disorders, and fails to address strengths.

2. ANXIETY DISORDERS

Generalized anxiety disorder is anxiety that persists for at least 6 months with no specific reason for the anxiety. Panic disorder involves attacks marked by the sudden onset of intense terror. Biological, psychological, and sociocultural factors may contribute to the development of panic disorder.

Phobic disorders involve an irrational, overwhelming fear of a particular object, such as snakes, or a situation, such as flying. Obsessive-compulsive disorder is an anxiety disorder in which the individual has anxiety-provoking thoughts that will not go away (obsession) and/or urges to perform repetitive, ritualistic behaviors to prevent or produce some future situation (compulsion). Post-traumatic stress disorder (PTSD) is an anxiety disorder that develops through exposure to traumatic events, sexual abuse and assault, and natural and unnatural disasters. Symptoms include flashbacks, emotional avoidance, emotional numbing, and excessive arousal. A variety of experiential, psychological, and genetic factors have been shown to relate to these disorders.

3. MOOD DISORDERS

Two types of mood disorders are depressive disorders and bipolar disorder. The depressive disorders include major depressive disorder and dysthymic disorder. In major depressive disorder, the individual experiences a serious depressive episode and depressed characteristics such as lethargy and hopelessness. Dysthymic disorder is generally more chronic and has fewer symptoms than major depressive disorder.

Biological explanations of depressive disorders focus on heredity, neurophysiological abnormalities, and neurotransmitter deregulation. Psychological explanations include behavioral and cognitive perspectives. Sociocultural explanations emphasize socioeconomic and ethnic factors, as well as gender.

Bipolar disorder is characterized by extreme mood swings that include one or more episodes of mania (an overexcited, unrealistic, optimistic state). Individuals with bipolar I disorder have more extreme manic episodes, while those with bipolar II disorder have less extreme episodes. Most individuals with bipolar disorder go through multiple cycles of depression interspersed with mania. Genetic influences are stronger predictors of bipolar disorder than depressive disorder, and biological processes are also a factor in bipolar disorder.

Severe depression and other psychological disorders can cause individuals to want to end their lives. Theorists have proposed biological, psychological, and sociocultural explanations of suicide.

4. DISSOCIATIVE DISORDERS

Dissociative amnesia involves memory loss caused by extensive psychological stress. Dissociative fugue also involves memory loss, but individuals with this disorder unexpectedly travel away from home or work, sometimes assume a new identity, and do not remember the old identity. In dissociative identity disorder, formerly called multiple personality disorder, two or more distinct personalities are present in the same individual; this disorder is rare.

5. SCHIZOPHRENIA

Schizophrenia is a severe psychological disorder characterized by highly disordered thought processes. Positive symptoms of schizophrenia are behaviors and experiences that are present in individuals with schizophrenia but absent in healthy people; they include hallucinations and delusions. Negative symptoms of schizophrenia are behaviors and experiences that are part of healthy human life that are absent for those with this disorder; they include flat affect and an inability to plan or engage in goal-directed behavior.

Biological factors (heredity, structural brain abnormalities, and problems in neurotransmitter regulation, especially dopamine), psychological factors (diathesis-stress model), and sociocultural factors may be involved in schizophrenia. Psychological and sociocultural factors are not viewed as stand-alone causes of schizophrenia, but they are related to the course of the disorder.

6. PERSONALITY DISORDERS

Personality disorders are chronic, maladaptive cognitive-behavioral patterns that are thoroughly integrated into an individual's personality. Two common types are antisocial personality disorder (ASPD) and borderline personality disorder (BPD).

Antisocial personality disorder is characterized by guiltlessness, law-breaking, exploitation of others, irresponsibility, and deceit. Individuals with this disorder often lead a life of crime and violence. Psychopaths—remorseless predators who engage in violence to get what they want—are a subgroup of individuals with ASPD.

Borderline personality disorder is a pervasive pattern of instability in interpersonal relationships, self-image, and emotions, and of marked impulsivity beginning by early adulthood and present in a variety of contexts. This disorder is related to self-harming behaviors such as cutting and suicide.

Biological factors for ASPD include genetic, brain, and autonomic nervous system differences. The potential causes of BPD are complex and include biological and cognitive factors as well as childhood experiences.

7. PSYCHOLOGICAL DISORDERS AND HEALTH AND WELLNESS

Stigma can create a significant barrier for people coping with a psychological disorder, as well as for their loved ones. Fear of being labeled can prevent individuals with a disorder from getting treatment

SUMMARY

and from talking about their problems with family and friends. In addition, the stigma attached to psychological disorders can lead to prejudice and discrimination toward individuals who are struggling with these problems. Having a disorder and experiencing the stigma associated with it can also negatively affect the physical health of such individuals.

We can help to combat stigma by acknowledging the strengths and the achievements of individuals coping with psychological disorders. By creating a positive environment for people with disorders, we encourage more of them to be open about their struggles and to thrive, with the result that they can become positive role models for others.

key *terms*

abnormal behavior, p. 488

medical model, p. 489

DSM-IV, p. 490

attention deficit hyperactivity disorder (ADHD), p. 492

anxiety disorders, p. 492

generalized anxiety disorder, p. 494

panic disorder, p. 495

phobic disorder or phobia, p. 495

obsessive-compulsive disorder (OCD), p. 496

post-traumatic stress disorder (PTSD), p. 497

mood disorders, p. 498

depressive disorders, p. 498

major depressive disorder (MDD), p. 498

dysthymic disorder (DD), p. 498

bipolar disorder, p. 500

dissociative disorders, p. 505

dissociative amnesia, p. 506

dissociative fugue, p. 506

dissociative identity disorder (DID), p. 506

schizophrenia, p. 507

hallucinations, p. 508

delusions, p. 508

referential thinking, p. 508

catatonia, p. 508

flat affect, p. 509

diathesis-stress model, p. 511

personality disorders, p. 511

antisocial personality disorder (ASPD), p. 512

borderline personality disorder (BPD), p. 513

apply your *knowledge*

1. Spend 15 to 20 minutes observing an area with a large number of people, such as a mall, a cafeteria, or a stadium during a game. Identify and make a list of behaviors you would classify as abnormal. How does your list of behaviors compare with the definition of *abnormal* provided above? What would change in the list if you were in a different setting, such as a church, a bar, or a library? What does this exercise tell you about the meaning of *abnormal*?

2. If you have never met anyone with schizophrenia, check out a blog that is kept by Moe Armstrong at http://www.moearmstrong .com/Site/Welcome.html and view one of his speeches on YouTube at http://www.youtube.com/watch?v=p-_j1ZNKzsg.

3. Although we might think of people who contend with psychological disorders as troubled and downtrodden, they (like all people)

have the capacity to be astonishingly creative. Check out the website maintained by the National Art Exhibitions of the Mentally Ill (NAEMI) to experience some amazing creations of artists who suffer from mental illness. Go to http://www.naemi.org and click on "Artists." How does your exploration of this artwork influence your feelings about mental illness?

4. Go online and search for message boards where individuals with different psychological disorders share with each other. How do the discussion boards reflect what you have learned about these disorders?

CHAPTER 16

Therapies

Rebuilding Houses and Lives

On Monday, August 29, 2005, a category 5 hurricane named Katrina made violent landfall in the city of New Orleans and elsewhere along the Gulf Coast. Katrina would be the costliest—and one of the deadliest—hurricanes in U.S. history. Media coverage of the devastation in New Orleans was nonstop. Even now, years later, the rebuilding of the city is an ongoing process—and one that was recently made more complicated by the massive British Petroleum oil spill in the Gulf of Mexico in the spring of 2010.

The physical reconstruction of their city has been only one part of the recovery for the people of New Orleans. In addition, these uprooted survivors have been rebuilding their sense of hope and their very lives, with the help of teams of psychologists. Clinical psychologists from all over the United States have flocked to New Orleans many times since that day in the summer of 2005, lending an ear, teaching new skills, and dispensing therapies of all kinds to help the stricken residents manage their profound sense of loss and develop new goals toward which to strive. Just as Habitat for Humanity, a nonprofit organization dedicated to constructing decent and affordable housing, has helped the victims repair the storm's physical damage and rebuild their homes, psychologists have helped them repair the psychological damage of trauma and rebuild their lives (Borchardt, 2008).

For countless Katrina survivors, asking for help to rebuild their city was natural, but asking for psychological help was a different—and often difficult—matter. Indeed, for many of us, whatever the cause, seeking aid when we are troubled seems a mark of weakness. To the contrary, however, seeking help is a sign that we are strong enough and courageous enough to admit that we cannot go it alone. ●

PREVIEW

The science of psychology has led to the development of various treatment approaches to help relieve psychological suffering. These different forms of therapy are the focus of this chapter. We review biological, psychological, and sociocultural approaches to the use of therapy to improve the lives of individuals with psychological disorders. We then examine the effectiveness of therapy and explore the factors contributing to its success. Finally, we consider the broad array of benefits that therapy offers for physical health and psychological wellness.

1· BIOLOGICAL THERAPIES

● **biological therapies** Also called biomedical therapies, treatments that reduce or eliminate the symptoms of psychological disorders by altering aspects of body functioning.

Biological therapies, also called *biomedical therapies,* are treatments that reduce or eliminate the symptoms of psychological disorders by altering aspects of body functioning. Drug therapy is the most common form of biomedical therapy. Electroconvulsive therapy and psychosurgery are much less commonly used biomedical therapies.

As medical doctors, psychiatrists can prescribe drugs as part of therapy. Family doctors can also prescribe drugs for psychological disorders. In contrast, psychologists, who are not trained as medical doctors, cannot administer drugs therapeutically in most states.

Drug Therapy

Although people have long used medicine and herbs to alleviate symptoms of emotional distress, it was not until the twentieth century that drug treatments revolutionized mental healthcare. Psychotherapeutic drugs are used mainly in three diagnostic categories: anxiety disorders, mood disorders, and schizophrenia. In this section we explore the effectiveness of drugs for these various disorders—respectively, antianxiety drugs, antidepressant drugs, and antipsychotic drugs. As you read about these various treatments, you will note that the reasons why a particular drug works for a particular problem are not always understood. Rather, these drugs are used because they work—and research continues to explore the reasons for their effectiveness.

ANTIANXIETY DRUGS

● **antianxiety drugs** Commonly known as tranquilizers, drugs that reduce anxiety by making the individual calmer and less excitable.

Antianxiety drugs are commonly known as *tranquilizers.* These drugs reduce anxiety by making the individual calmer and less excitable. Benzodiazepines are the antianxiety drugs that generally offer the greatest relief for anxiety symptoms, though these drugs are potentially addictive, through the processes described in Chapter 5. They work by binding to the receptor sites of neurotransmitters that become overactive during anxiety (Bastien, 2010; Poisnel & others, 2009). The most frequently prescribed benzodiazepines include Xanax, Valium, and Librium. A nonbenzodiazepine—buspirone, or BuSpar—is commonly used to treat generalized anxiety disorder (Mokhber & others, 2010; Pollack, 2009). Benzodiazepines are relatively fast-acting medications, taking effect within hours. In contrast, buspirone must be taken daily for two to three weeks before the patient feels benefits.

Benzodiazepines, like all drugs, have some side effects, including drowsiness, loss of coordination, fatigue, and mental slowing (Fields, 2010). These effects can be hazardous when a person is driving or operating machinery, especially when the individual first starts taking benzodiazepines. Benzodiazepines also have been linked to abnormalities in babies born to mothers who took them during pregnancy (Istaphanous & Loepke, 2009). The combination of benzodiazepines with other medications can cause problems (Vakily & others, 2009). When combined with alcohol, anesthetics, antihistamines, sedatives, muscle relaxants, and some prescription pain medications, benzodiazepines can lead to depression.

People have used medicinal herbs to treat emotional distress since ancient times.

Why are antianxiety drugs so widely used? Many individuals experience stress, anxiety, or both. Family physicians or psychiatrists prescribe these drugs to improve people's ability to cope with their problems effectively. Antianxiety medications are best used only temporarily for symptomatic relief. Too often, they are overused and can become addictive (Lader, Tylee, & Donoghue, 2009; Reeves & Burke, 2010).

ANTIDEPRESSANT DRUGS

Antidepressant drugs regulate mood. The four main classes of antidepressant drugs are tricyclics, such as Elavil; tetracyclics such as Avanza; monoamine oxidase (MAO) inhibitors, such as Nardil; and selective serotonin reuptake inhibitors, such as Prozac. These antidepressants are all thought to help alleviate depressed mood through their effects on neurotransmitters in the brain. In different ways, they all allow the person's brain to increase or maintain its level of important neurotransmitters, especially serotonin and norepinephrine. Let's take a close look at each of these types of antidepressants.

Tricyclics, so-called because of their three-ringed molecular structure, are believed to work by increasing the level of certain neurotransmitters, especially norepinephrine and serotonin (Lopez-Munoz & Alamo, 2009; Racagni & Popoli, 2010). You might recall the role of low serotonin levels in negative mood (Chapter 12) and aggression (Chapter 13). The tricyclics reduce the symptoms of depression in approximately 60 to 70 percent of cases; these drugs usually take two to four weeks to improve mood. Adverse side effects may include restlessness, faintness, trembling, sleepiness, and memory difficulties.

Related to the tricyclics are *tetracyclic* antidepressants (named for their four-ringed structure). Tetracyclics are also called *noradrenergic and specific serotonergic antidepressants,* or NaSSAs. These drugs have effects on both norepinephrine and serotonin, enhancing brain levels of these neurotransmitters. According to a recent analysis, the tetracylic Remeron (mertazapine) was more effective in reducing depression than any other antidepressant drug (Cipriani & others, 2010).

MAO inhibitors are thought to work because they block the enzyme monoamine oxidase. This enzyme breaks down the neurotransmitters serotonin and norepinephrine in the brain (Hazell, 2009; Pitychoutis & others, 2010). Scientists believe that the blocking action of MAO inhibitors allows these neurotransmitters to stick around in the brain's synapses and help regulate mood. MAO inhibitors are not as widely used as the tricyclics because they are more potentially harmful to the body. However, some individuals who do not respond to the tricyclics do respond to MAO inhibitors. MAO inhibitors may be especially risky because of their potential interactions with certain fermented foods (such as cheese) and drugs, leading to high blood pressure and risk of stroke (Nishida & others, 2009).

Psychiatrists and general practitioners increasingly are prescribing a type of antidepressant drug called *selective serotonin reuptake inhibitors* (SSRIs). SSRIs target serotonin, and work mainly by interfering only with the reabsorption of serotonin in the brain (Cipriani & others, 2010; Z. Zhou & others, 2009). Figure 16.1 shows how this process works.

Three widely prescribed SSRIs are Prozac (fluoxetine), Paxil (paroxetine), and Zoloft (sertraline). The increased prescription of these drugs reflects their effectiveness in reducing the symptoms of depression with fewer side effects than other antidepressants (Amsterdam & Shults, 2010; Gentile, 2010; Ksir, Hart, & Ray, 2008). Nonetheless, they can have negative effects, including insomnia, anxiety, headache, and diarrhea (Keeton, Kolos, & Walkup, 2009). They also can impair sexual functioning and produce severe withdrawal symptoms if the individual abruptly stops taking them (Frohlich & Meston, 2005).

The number of Americans who had ever been prescribed an antidepressant doubled between 1996 and 2005, with 10 percent of Americans taking an antidepressant at some point in their life (Olfson & Marcus, 2009). Beyond their usefulness in treating mood disorders, antidepressant

● **antidepressant drugs** Drugs that regulate mood.

FIGURE 16.1   How the Antidepressant Prozac Works Secreted by a transmitting neuron, serotonin moves across the synaptic gap and binds to receptors in a receiving neuron. Excess serotonin in the synaptic gap is normally reabsorbed by the transmitting neuron. The antidepressant Prozac blocks this reuptake of serotonin by the transmitting neuron, however, leaving excess serotonin in the synaptic gap. The excess serotonin is transmitted to the receiving neuron and circulated through the brain. The result is a reduction of the serotonin deficit found in individuals with depression.

drugs are often effective for a number of anxiety disorders, including generalized anxiety disorder, panic disorder, obsessive-compulsive disorder, social phobia, and post-traumatic stress disorder, as well as some eating and sleep disorders (Ahmed & Thorpy, 2010; Davidson, 2009; Hollingsworth, Burgess, & Whiteford, 2010). Increasingly, antidepressants are prescribed for other common problems, among them sleeplessness and chronic pain. In fact, in 2005, less than half of the individuals in the United States who had taken prescribed antidepressants were doing so for depression (Olfson & Marcus, 2009).

Lithium is widely used to treat bipolar disorder. Lithium is the lightest of the solid elements in the periodic table of elements. If you have ever used a lithium battery (or are a fan of Nirvana or Evanescence), you know that lithium has uses beyond treating psychological disorders. The amount of lithium that circulates in the bloodstream must be carefully monitored because the effective dosage is precariously close to toxic levels (Paton & others, 2010). Kidney and thyroid gland complications as well as weight gain can arise as a consequence of lithium therapy (Bauer & others, 2007). Lithium is thought to stabilize moods by influencing norepinephrine and serotonin, but the exact mechanism of its effect is largely unknown (Perlis & others, 2009; Serretti, Drago, & DeRonchi, 2009). The effectiveness of lithium of course depends on the person's staying on the medication. Some may be troubled by the association between lithium and weight gain, and others may go off the drug when they are feeling well.

The use of antidepressant drugs to treat depression in children is controversial. To read more about this issue, see the Critical Controversy.

ANTIPSYCHOTIC DRUGS

Antipsychotic drugs are powerful drugs that diminish agitated behavior, reduce tension, decrease hallucinations, improve social behavior, and produce better sleep patterns in individuals who have a severe psychological disorder, especially schizophrenia (Uchida & Mamo, 2009; Yamin & Vaddadi, 2010). Before antipsychotic drugs were developed in the 1950s, few, if any, interventions brought relief from the torment of psychotic symptoms.

Neuroleptics are the most extensively used class of antipsychotic drugs (Garver, 2006). Numerous well-controlled investigations reveal that, when used in sufficient doses, neuroleptics reduce a variety of schizophrenic symptoms (Nasrallah & others, 2009). The most widely accepted explanation for the effectiveness of neuroleptics is their ability to block dopamine's action in the brain (Agatonovic-Kustrin, Davies, & Turner, 2009).

Neuroleptics do not cure schizophrenia. They treat only the symptoms of the disorder, not its causes. If an individual with schizophrenia stops taking the drug, the symptoms return. Neuroleptic drugs have substantially reduced the length of hospital stays for individuals with schizophrenia. However, when these individuals are able to return to the community (because the drug therapy reduces their symptoms), many have difficulty coping with the demands of society. In the absence of symptoms, many struggle to justify to themselves that they should continue to take the very medications that have reduced their symptoms—especially because neuroleptic drugs can have severe side effects (J. W. Y. Lee, 2010; Tural & Onder, 2010). Drugs that treat disturbed thought by reducing dopamine (which plays a role in positive, rewarding experiences) can also induce a lack of pleasure (Kapur, 2003).

Another potential side effect of neuroleptic drugs is *tardive dyskinesia,* a neurological disorder characterized by involuntary random movements of the facial muscles, tongue, and mouth, as well as twitching of the neck, arms, and legs (Go & others, 2009). Up to 20 percent of individuals with schizophrenia who take neuroleptics develop this disorder. As you may recall from Chapter 15, movement disorders are a positive symptom of schizophrenia, and tardive dyskinesia can also occur in individuals suffering from psychiatric disorders who have not taken neuroleptic drugs (Chouinard, 2006).

Newer drugs called *atypical antipsychotic medications,* introduced in the 1990s, carry a much lower risk of these side effects (Remington, 2007). The precise mechanism by which these drugs work is unknown, but they appear to influence dopamine as well as

● **lithium** The lightest of the solid elements in the periodic table of elements, widely used to treat bipolar disorder.

● **antipsychotic drugs** Powerful drugs that diminish agitated behavior, reduce tension, decrease hallucinations, improve social behavior, and produce better sleep patterns in individuals with a severe psychological disorder, especially schizophrenia.

"Lab Rat Rehab"

CRITICAL CONTROVERSY

Do Antidepressants Increase Suicide Risk in Children?

In 2000, Caitlin McIntosh, a 12-year-old straight-*A* student, artist, and musician, hanged herself with her shoelaces in the girls' room of her middle school. Caitlin had been struggling with depression and had been prescribed antidepressants shortly before her suicide. Tragic cases such as Caitlin's have stirred deep concerns among parents and mental health professionals. Could the very drugs prescribed to alleviate depression be causing children to become suicidal?

In 2004, the FDA held hearings to address the concerns of parents and health professionals about the potential risk of suicide as an unexpected, tragic side effect of antidepressant treatment. Many of the stories that parents told indicated no apparent previous risk of suicide and starkly illustrated the impulsiveness of the suicides. Some of the children had made plans for family activities for the very day after their suicides. Some had left sad evidence of the apparent randomness of their acts—a half-drunk glass of soda, an unfinished letter on the computer. Such real-life case studies can be emotionally engaging and persuasive, but are they generalizable to the population as a whole? What about the scientific evidence?

During the hearings, the FDA reviewed clinical trials of antidepressant use with children, including 23 clinical trials involving 4,300 children who were randomly assigned to receive either an antidepressant or a placebo (Hammad, 2004). None of the children in the studies committed or attempted suicide. In studies that included participants' self-report ratings of their suicidal thoughts and behaviors, no differences were found between the antidepressant and placebo groups. Another variable examined was "adverse event reports"—spontaneous statements of thoughts about suicide reported by the participants or their parents. The research did show an increase in adverse event reports in the participants in the treatment group. While the placebo participants showed 2 percent of such spontaneous reports of suicidal thoughts, those taking antidepressants showed a 4 percent rate. This last finding, along with the dramatic personal cases presented by families, was the basis of the FDA's subsequent action.

In October 2004, the FDA required prescription antidepressants to carry the severest "black box" warning, describing the potential of antidepressants to be associated with suicidal thoughts and behaviors in children and adolescents (FDA, 2004). The black box warning had a chilling effect: Following the black box warning edict (and even before the box started appearing on the drug containers), prescriptions for antidepressants for children declined dramatically. Between March 2004 and June 2005, the number of prescriptions fell 20 percent compared to the same time frame the year before (Rosack, 2007). This drop in prescriptions might indicate that health professionals were being more careful about prescribing antidepressants to youth. It might also indicate that professionals were hesitant to prescribe these drugs even when they might be of real help to children with depression.

Sorting out the possible connection between antidepressants and suicide in adolescents is complex for a variety of reasons (Brent &

others, 2009; Healy, 2009; Weissman, 2009). As many as 17 percent of adolescents think about suicide in any given year, and most teen suicides do not involve antidepressants (CDC, 2004). As noted in Chapter 15, some 90 percent of individuals who attempt suicide are thought to suffer from a psychological disorder, with depression being the most typical factor. Would an adolescent with depression be just as likely to commit suicide with or without taking antidepressants? Studies examining the effects of antidepressants generally exclude from participation individuals who are suicidal at the outset. As a result, positive effects of these drugs on reducing suicidal thoughts and behaviors are difficult to detect. Indeed, in a large-scale population study, the number of prescriptions for Prozac was negatively related to suicide rates over time (Milane & others, 2006).

Since the FDA called for the black box warning, a number of studies have found no link between antidepressants and suicide in either adults or children (Dudley, Goldney, & Hadzi-Pavlovic, 2010; Hammond, Laughren, & Racoosin, 2006; Markowitz & Cuellar, 2007). One study revealed that Prozac and cognitive-behavior therapy were both effective in reducing depression in children and adolescents, with a drop in suicidal thoughts from 29 percent to 10 percent in the treatment groups (March & others, 2004).

Importantly, drug therapy may not be the first-choice treatment for children with depression (Jerrell, 2010). Many children and adolescents have uncomplicated depression that responds well to psychotherapy alone (Emslie, Croarkin, & Mayes, 2010; Kennard & others, 2008). Indeed, in Great Britain, guidelines allow the prescription of Prozac only in conjunction with ongoing psychotherapy (Boseley, 2006). In the United Kingdom and France, Paxil and Zoloft are not approved for pediatric use.

This controversy highlights many of the issues addressed throughout this book. How do we weigh dramatic case study evidence against less vivid scientific data that do not bear out those cases? Are special considerations required when professionals suggest the use of drug therapy in children? How can we best balance the potential benefits of drug treatment against the risks of that treatment? Throughout the debate looms the profound tragedy of suicide, and certainly professionals have been moved to change their thinking and practices with regard to treating depression in youth.

WHAT DO YOU THINK?

- Have antidepressants helped anyone you know? If so, were you aware of negative side effects? Positive side effects? What was the nature of these effects?

- What do you think of the common practice of treating depression with medication first?

- Do you think occasional bouts of depression might play a normal role in psychological development? Why or why not?

serotonin (Leucht, Kissling, & Davis, 2009; C. Lin & others, 2009). The two most widely used drugs in this group, Clozaril (clozapine) and Risperdal (risperidone), show promise for reducing schizophrenia's symptoms without the side effects of neuroleptics (Kinon & others, 2010; Smith, Weston, & Lieberman, 2009).

Strategies to increase the effectiveness of the antipsychotic drugs involve administering small dosages over time, rather than a large initial dose, and combining drug therapy with psychotherapy. Along with drug treatment, individuals with schizophrenia may need training in vocational, family, and social skills.

Figure 16.2 summarizes the drugs used to treat various psychological disorders, the disorders they target, their effectiveness, and their side effects. Notice that for some types of anxiety disorders, such as agoraphobia, MAO inhibitors (antidepressant drugs) might be used rather than antianxiety drugs.

Electroconvulsive Therapy

● **electroconvulsive therapy (ECT)** Also called shock therapy, a treatment, commonly used for depression, that sets off a seizure in the brain.

The goal of **electroconvulsive therapy (ECT),** commonly called *shock therapy,* is to set off a seizure in the brain, much like what happens spontaneously in some forms of epilepsy (W. A. Brown, 2007). The notion that causing someone to have a seizure might help cure a psychological disorder may seem strange, but this idea has been around for quite some time. Hippocrates, the ancient Greek father of medicine, first noticed that malaria-induced convulsions would sometimes cure individuals who were thought to be insane (Endler, 1988). Following Hippocrates, many other medical doctors noted that

Psychological Disorder	Drug	Effectiveness	Side Effects
Everyday Anxiety and Anxiety Disorders			
Everyday anxiety	Antianxiety drugs; antidepressant drugs	Substantial improvement short term	Antianxiety drugs: less powerful the longer people take them; may be addictive Antidepressant drugs: see below under depressive disorders
Generalized anxiety disorder	Antianxiety drugs	Not very effective	Less powerful the longer people take them; may be addictive
Panic disorder	Antianxiety drugs	About half show improvement	Less powerful the longer people take them; may be addictive
Agoraphobia	Tricyclic drugs and MAO inhibitors	Majority show improvement	Tricyclics: restlessness, fainting, and trembling MAO inhibitors: toxicity
Specific phobias	Antianxiety drugs	Not very effective	Less powerful the longer people take them; may be addictive
Mood Disorders			
Depressive disorders	Tricyclic drugs, MAO inhibitors, SSRI drugs, and tetracyclic drugs	Majority show moderate improvement	Tricyclics: cardiac problems, mania, confusion, memory loss, fatigue MAO inhibitors: toxicity SSRI drugs: nausea, nervousness, insomnia, and in a few cases, suicidal thoughts Tetracyclics: drowsiness, increased appetite, weight gain
Bipolar disorder	Lithium	Large majority show substantial improvement	Toxicity
Schizophrenic Disorders			
Schizophrenia	Neuroleptics; atypical antipsychotic medications	Majority show partial improvement	Neuroleptics: irregular heartbeat, low blood pressure, uncontrolled fidgeting, tardive dyskinesia, and immobility of face Atypical antipsychotic medications: less extensive side effects than with neuroleptics, but can have a toxic effect on white blood cells

FIGURE 16.2   Drug Therapy for Psychological Disorders This figure summarizes the types of drugs used to treat various psychological disorders.

head traumas, seizures, and convulsions brought on by fever would sometimes lead to the apparent cure of psychological problems.

In the early twentieth century, doctors induced seizures by insulin overdose and other means and used this procedure primarily to treat schizophrenia. In 1937, Ugo Cerletti, an Italian neurologist specializing in epilepsy, developed the procedure by which seizures could be induced using electrical shock. With colleagues, he developed a fast, efficient means of causing seizures in humans, and ECT gained wide use in mental institutions (Faedda & others, 2010). Unfortunately, in earlier years, ECT was used indiscriminately, sometimes even to punish patients, as illustrated in the classic film *One Flew Over the Cuckoo's Nest*. Among the individuals who underwent ECT were Ernest Hemingway and Sylvia Plath, both of whom struggled with depression and ultimately committed suicide.

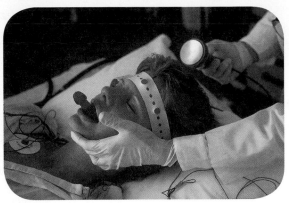

Electroconvulsive therapy (ECT), commonly called shock therapy, causes a seizure in the brain. ECT is still given to as many as 100,000 people a year, mainly to treat major depressive disorder.

Today, doctors use ECT primarily to treat severe depression (Birkenhager & others, 2010; Damm & others, 2010). As many as 100,000 individuals a year undergo ECT, primarily as treatment for major depressive disorder (Mayo Foundation, 2006). ECT has also been used in cases of severe chronic post-traumatic stress disorder (Margoob, Zaffar Ali, & Andrade, 2010). Fortunately, the contemporary use of ECT bears little resemblance to its earlier uses. Treatment involves passing a small electrical current of a second or less through two electrodes placed on the individual's head. The current excites neural tissue, stimulating a seizure that lasts for approximately a minute.

Today, ECT is given mainly to individuals who have not responded to drug therapy or psychotherapy, and its administration involves little discomfort. The patient receives anesthesia and muscle relaxants before the current is applied; this medication allows the individual to sleep through the procedure, minimizes convulsions, and reduces the risk of physical injury. Although in the past, electrical current was passed through the person's entire brain, increasingly ECT is applied only to the right side. The individual awakens shortly afterward with no conscious memory of the treatment.

How effective is ECT? One analysis of the use of ECT compared its effectiveness in treating depression with that of cognitive therapy and antidepressant drugs (Seligman, 1994). ECT was as effective as cognitive therapy or drug therapy, with about four of five individuals showing marked improvement in all three therapies. However, as with the other therapies, the relapse rate for ECT is moderate to high. What sets ECT apart from other treatments is the rapid relief it can produce in a person's mood (Merkl, Heuser, & Bajbouj, 2009; Popeo, 2009). ECT may be especially effective as a treatment for acute depression in individuals who are at great risk of suicide (Kellner & others, 2006).

ECT is controversial. Its potential side effects remain a source of debate and contradictory findings (Crowley & others, 2008; Nordenskjold, Knorring, & Engstrom, 2010). These possible effects include memory loss and other cognitive impairments and are generally more severe than drug side effects (Caverzasi & others, 2008); such problems are less likely to occur, however, when only one side of the brain is stimulated (Sienaert & others, 2010). Some individuals treated with ECT have reported prolonged and profound memory loss (Koitabashi, Oyaizu, & Ouchi, 2009). Despite these potential problems, some psychiatrists argue that for certain individuals, this invasive treatment can have life-enhancing—and even life-saving—benefits (O'Connor & others, 2009; Sherman, 2009).

More recently, rather than using electricity to set off a seizure, practitioners have begun to apply electrical stimulation in very precise locations in the brain (Sachdev & Chen, 2009). In **deep brain stimulation,** doctors surgically implant electrodes in the brain that emit signals to alter the brain's electrical circuitry (Connor, 2010). Deep brain stimulation involving the transmission of high-frequency electrical impulses to targeted areas of the brain is now being used to treat individuals with treatment-resistant depression and obsessive-compulsive disorder (Haq & others, 2010; Moreines, McClintock, & Holtzheimer, 2010). For instance, deep brain stimulation of the nucleus accumbens (part of the brain's reward pathways) has been effective in treating severe depression (Bewernick & others, 2010).

● **deep brain stimulation** A procedure for treatment-resistant depression that involves the implantation of electrodes in the brain that emit signals to alter the brain's electrical circuitry.

● **psychosurgery** A biological therapy, with irreversible effects, that involves removal or destruction of brain tissue to improve the individual's adjustment.

Psychosurgery

Psychosurgery is a biological intervention that involves the removal or destruction of brain tissue to improve the individual's adjustment. The effects of psychosurgery cannot be reversed.

In the 1930s, Portuguese physician Antonio Egas Moniz developed a surgical procedure to treat psychological disorders. In this operation, an instrument is inserted into the brain and rotated, severing fibers that connect the frontal lobe, which is important in higher thought processes, and the thalamus, which plays a key role in emotion. Moniz theorized that by severing the connections between these structures, the surgeon could alleviate the symptoms of severe mental disorders. In 1949, Moniz received the Nobel Prize for developing this procedure. Although some patients may have benefited from these lobotomies, many were left in a vegetable-like state because of the massive assaults on their brains. Moniz himself felt that the procedure should be used with extreme caution and only as a last resort.

After hearing about Moniz's procedure, American physician and neurologist Walter Freeman became the champion of *prefrontal lobotomies* (a term he coined). With his colleague James Watts, he performed the first lobotomy in the United States in 1936 (El-Hai, 2005). Freeman eventually developed his own technique, which he performed using a device similar to an ice pick, in surgeries that lasted mere minutes. Freeman was a dynamic and charismatic showman who argued strongly for the usefulness of the technique. In the 1950s and 60s, he traveled the country in a van he called the "lobotomobile," demonstrating the surgery in state-run mental institutions. In his career, Freeman performed over 3,000 lobotomies (El-Hai, 2005). Indeed, prefrontal lobotomies were conducted on tens of thousands of patients from the 1930s through the 1960s. These numbers speak not only to Freeman's persuasive charm but also to the desperation many physicians felt in treating institutionalized patients with severe psychological disorders (Lerner, 2005).

Subsequent research called the lobotomy procedure into question, with critics pointing to the considerable damage that resulted (Landis & Erlick, 1950; Mettler, 1952). Many individuals who received lobotomies suffered permanent and profound brain damage (Whitaker, 2002). Ethical concerns arose because, in many instances, giving consent for the lobotomy was a requirement for release from a mental hospital. Like ECT, lobotomies were being used as a form of punishment and control.

By the 1950s, drug therapies had emerged as alternatives to the invasive procedure of lobotomy (Juckel & others, 2009). By the late 1970s new regulations classified the procedure as experimental and established safeguards for patients. Fortunately, crude lobotomies are no longer performed, and Freeman's techniques are certainly not typical of contemporary psychosurgery. Indeed, psychosurgery today is quite precise (Heller & others, 2006; Kopell, Machado, & Rezai, 2006) and involves making just a small lesion in the amygdala or another part of the limbic system (Fountas & Smith, 2007).

Today, only several hundred patients who have severely debilitating conditions undergo psychosurgery each year. Psychosurgery may be performed for OCD, major depression, or bipolar disorders rather than for schizophrenia (Elias & Cosgrove, 2008; Shelton & others, 2010). Just as Moniz originally suggested, the procedure is now used only as a last resort—and with the utmost caution (Ruck, 2003). Psychiatrists and psychologists recognize that science should tamper with the brain only in extreme cases (Pressman, 1998).

test yourself

1. How do antianxiety drugs work, and why do so many people take them?
2. What are SSRIs, and through what process do they have their effect?
3. Describe the procedure used in electroconvulsive therapy (ECT).

2· PSYCHOTHERAPY

● **psychotherapy** A nonmedical process that helps individuals with psychological disorders recognize and overcome their problems.

Although their ability to prescribe drugs is limited, psychologists and other mental health professionals may provide **psychotherapy,** a nonmedical process that helps individuals with psychological disorders recognize and overcome their problems. Psychotherapy may be given alone or in conjunction with biological therapy administered by psychiatrists and other medical doctors (Davidson, 2009). Indeed, in many instances, a combination of psychotherapy and medication is a desirable course of treatment (Nolen-Hoeksema, 2011). Unfortunately, even as prescriptions for medications have increased dramatically over the years, the number of people receiving psychotherapy has dropped. According to a recent study, among individuals receiving antidepressant medication, the number in therapy fell from 32 percent in 1996 to less than 20 percent in 2005 (Olfson & Marcus, 2009).

Psychotherapists employ a number of strategies to alleviate symptoms of psychological disorders: talking, interpreting, listening, rewarding, and modeling, for example (Prochaska & Norcross, 2010). Although most psychotherapy is conducted face-to-face, many contemporary therapists communicate with clients through e-mail or text messaging (Berger, Hohl, & Caspar, 2009; Wangberg, Gammon, & Spitznogle, 2007).

Another recent development is *cybertherapy,* or *e-therapy,* in which an online source provides help to people seeking therapy for psychological disorders (Klein & others, 2010; Marks & Cavanaugh, 2009; Postel, de Haan, & de Jong, 2010; Reger & Gahm, 2009). E-therapy websites are controversial among mental health professionals (Abbott, Klein, & Ciechomski, 2008). For one thing, many of these sites do not include the most basic information about the therapists' qualifications (Recupero & Rainey, 2006). In addition, because cybertherapy occurs at a distance, such sites typically exclude individuals who are having thoughts of suicide. Further, confidentiality, a crucial aspect of the therapeutic relationship, cannot always be guaranteed on a website. On the plus side, though, individuals who might be unwilling or unable to seek out face-to-face therapy may be more disposed to get help online (Postel, de Jong, & de Haan, 2005; Van Voorhees & others, 2009).

Psychotherapy is practiced by a variety of mental health professionals, including clinical psychologists, psychiatrists, counselors, and social workers. Figure 16.3 lists the

Professional Type	Degree	Education Beyond Bachelor's Degree	Nature of Training
Clinical psychologist	PhD or PsyD	5–7 years	Requires both clinical and research training. Includes a 1-year internship in a psychiatric hospital or mental health facility. Some universities have developed PsyD programs, which have a stronger clinical than research emphasis. The PsyD training program takes as long as the clinical psychology PhD program and also requires the equivalent of a 1-year internship.
Psychiatrist	MD	7–9 years	Four years of medical school, plus an internship and residency in psychiatry, is required. A psychiatry residency involves supervision in therapies, including psychotherapy and biomedical therapy.
Counseling psychologist	MA, PhD, PsyD, or EdD	3–7 years	Similar to clinical psychologist but with emphasis on counseling and therapy. Some counseling psychologists specialize in vocational counseling. Some counselors complete master's degree training, others PhD or EdD training, in graduate schools of psychology or education.
School psychologist	MA, PhD, PsyD, or EdD	3–7 years	Training in graduate programs of education or psychology. Emphasis on psychological assessment and counseling practices involving students' school-related problems. Training is at the master's or doctoral level.
Social worker	MS W/DSW or PhD	2–5 years	Graduate work in a school of social work that includes specialized clinical training in mental health facilities.
Psychiatric nurse	RN, MA, or PhD	0–5 years	Graduate work in a school of nursing with special emphasis on care of mentally disturbed individuals in hospital settings and mental health facilities.
Occupational therapist	BS, MA, or PhD	0–5 years	Emphasis on occupational training with focus on physically or psychologically handicapped individuals. Stresses getting individuals back into the mainstream of work.
Pastoral counselor	None to PhD or DD (Doctor of Divinity)	0–5 years	Requires ministerial background and training in psychology. An internship in a mental health facility as a chaplain is recommended.
Counselor	MA or MEd	2 years	Graduate work in a department of psychology or department of education with specialized training in counseling techniques.

FIGURE 16.3   Main Types of Mental Health Professionals A wide range of professionals with varying levels of training have taken on the challenge of helping people with psychological disorders.

main types of mental health professionals, their degrees, the years of education required, and the nature of their training. Licensing and certification are two ways in which society retains control over psychotherapy practitioners. Laws at the state level are used to license or certify such professionals. These laws vary in toughness from one state to another, but invariably they specify the training the mental health professional must have and provide for some assessment of an applicant's skill through formal examination.

Regardless of their particular occupation, psychotherapists use a variety of techniques to help alleviate suffering. This section focuses on four main approaches to psychotherapy: psychodynamic, humanistic, behavioral, and cognitive.

Psychodynamic Therapies

● **psychodynamic therapies** Treatments that stress the importance of the unconscious mind, extensive interpretation by the therapist, and the role of early childhood experiences in the development of an individual's problems.

The **psychodynamic therapies** stress the importance of the unconscious mind, extensive interpretation by the therapist, and the role of early childhood experiences in the development of an individual's problems. The goal of psychodynamic therapies is to help individuals recognize the maladaptive ways in which they have been coping with problems and the sources of their unconscious conflicts. Many psychodynamic approaches grew out of Freud's psychoanalytic theory of personality. Today some therapists with a psychodynamic perspective practice Freudian techniques, but others do not (Busch, Milrod, & Sandberg, 2009; Cardoso Zoppe & others, 2009).

PSYCHOANALYSIS

● **psychoanalysis** Freud's therapeutic technique for analyzing an individual's unconscious thoughts.

Psychoanalysis is Freud's therapeutic technique for analyzing an individual's unconscious thoughts. Freud believed that a person's current problems could be traced to childhood experiences, many of which involved unconscious sexual conflicts. Only through extensive questioning, probing, and analyzing was Freud able to put together the pieces of the client's personality and help the individual become aware of how these early experiences were affecting present behavior. The psychoanalyst's goal is to bring unconscious conflicts into conscious awareness, thus giving the client insight into his or her core problems and freeing the individual from unconscious influences (Dougherty, 2010).

To reach the shadowy world of the unconscious, psychoanalytic therapists use the therapeutic techniques of free association, interpretation, dream analysis, analysis of transference, and analysis of resistance. We survey each in turn.

● **free association** A psychoanalytic technique that involves encouraging individuals to say aloud whatever comes to mind, no matter how trivial or embarrassing.

Free association involves encouraging individuals to say aloud whatever comes to mind, no matter how trivial or embarrassing. When Freud detected a person resisting the spontaneous flow of thoughts, he probed further. He believed that the crux of the person's problem lurked below this point of resistance. Encouraging people to talk freely, Freud thought, would allow their deepest thoughts and feelings to emerge. *Catharsis* is the release of emotional tension a person experiences when reliving an emotionally charged and conflicting experience.

● **interpretation** A psychoanalyst's search for symbolic, hidden meanings in what the client says and does during therapy.

Interpretation plays an important role in psychoanalysis. The analyst does not take the patient's statements and behavior at face value. To understand what is causing the

MOTHER GOOSE & GRIMM © 2010 Grimmy, Inc. King Features Syndicate.

person's conflicts, the therapist constantly searches for symbolic, hidden meanings in what the individual says and does (Kligman, 2010). From time to time, the therapist suggests possible meanings of the person's statements and behavior.

Dream analysis is a psychoanalytic technique for interpreting a person's dreams. Psychoanalysts believe that dreams contain information about unconscious thoughts, wishes, and conflicts (Freud, 1911). From this perspective, dreams give us an outlet to express our unconscious wishes, a mental theater in which our deepest and most secret desires can be played out (Ferro, 2009; Ogden, 2010). According to Freud, every dream, even our worst nightmare, contains a hidden, disguised wish. The sheer horror we feel during a nightmare might itself disguise that unconscious wish.

Freud distinguished between the dream's manifest and latent content. *Manifest content* is the psychoanalytic term for the conscious, remembered aspects of a dream. For instance, if you wake up in the morning remembering a dream about being back in sixth grade with your teacher scolding you for not turning in your homework, that is the manifest content of the dream. *Latent content* is the unconscious, hidden aspects that are symbolized by the manifest content. In order to understand the meaning of your dream, a psychoanalyst might ask you to free-associate to each of the elements of the manifest content: What comes to your mind when you think of being in sixth grade? When you think of your teacher? According to Freud, the latent meaning of a dream is locked inside the unconscious mind of the dreamer. The goal of analysis is to unlock that secret meaning by probing into the deeper layers of the person's mind through free association about the manifest dream elements.

The psychoanalyst interprets the dream by analyzing the manifest content for disguised unconscious wishes and needs, especially those that are sexual and aggressive. Dream symbols can mean different things to different dreamers. Although countless books and websites today claim to provide guidance as to the meaning of dream symbols, Freud (1911) believed that the true meaning of any dream symbol depends on the individual dreamer.

Freud viewed transference as an inevitable—and essential—aspect of the analyst–patient relationship. **Transference** is the psychoanalytic term for the person's relating to the analyst in ways that reproduce or relive important relationships in the individual's life. A person might interact with an analyst as if the analyst were a parent or lover, for example. According to Freud, transference is a necessary part of the psychoanalytic relationship, as it models the way that individuals relate to important people in their lives (Meissner, 2009; Rycroft, 2010).

Resistance is the psychoanalytic term for the client's unconscious defense strategies that prevent the analyst from understanding the person's problems. Resistance occurs because it is painful for the client to bring conflicts into conscious awareness. By resisting analysis, the individual does not have to face the threatening truths that underlie his or her problems (Hoffman, 2006). Showing up late or missing sessions, arguing with the psychoanalyst, and faking free associations are examples of resistance.

CONTEMPORARY PSYCHODYNAMIC THERAPIES

Psychodynamic therapy has changed extensively since its beginnings almost a century ago. Nonetheless, many contemporary psychodynamic therapists still probe unconscious thoughts about early childhood experiences to gain insight into their clients' current problems (Cortina, 2010; Gotthold, 2009; Messer & Abbass, 2010; Rustin, 2009). However, contemporary psychoanalysts accord more power to the conscious mind and to a person's current relationships, and they generally place less emphasis on sex (Holmes, 2010; Knoblauch, 2009). In addition, clients today rarely lie on a couch, as they did in Freud's time, or see their therapist several times a week, as was the norm in early psychodynamic therapy. Instead, they sit in a comfortable chair facing the therapist, and weekly appointments are typical.

Some contemporary psychodynamic therapists (Busch, 2007) focus on the self in social contexts, as was suggested by Heinz Kohut (1977). In Kohut's view, early social relationships with attachment figures such as one's parents are critical. As we develop,

● **dream analysis** A psychoanalytic technique for interpreting a person's dreams.

● **transference** A client's relating to the psychoanalyst in ways that reproduce or relive important relationships in the individual's life.

● **resistance** A client's unconscious defense strategies that interfere with the psychoanalyst's understanding of the individual's problems.

● **humanistic therapies** Treatments, unique in their emphasis on people's self-healing capacities, that encourage clients to understand themselves and to grow personally.

● **client-centered therapy** Also called Rogerian therapy or nondirective therapy, a form of humanistic therapy, developed by Rogers, in which the therapist provides a warm, supportive atmosphere to improve the client's self-concept and to encourage the client to gain insight into problems.

● **reflective speech** A technique in which the therapist mirrors the client's own feelings back to the client.

"I see. So what you're saying is that you woke up this morning and your woman had done left you."

we internalize those relationships, and they serve as the basis for our sense of self. Kohut (1977) believed that the therapist's job is to replace unhealthy childhood relationships with the healthy relationship provided by the therapist. In Kohut's view, the therapist needs to interact with the client in empathic and understanding ways. Empathy and understanding are also cornerstones for humanistic therapies, our next topic.

Humanistic Therapies

The underlying philosophy of humanistic therapies is captured by the metaphor of how an acorn, if provided with appropriate conditions, will grow in positive ways, pushing naturally toward its actualization as an oak (Schneider, 2002). In **humanistic therapies,** people are encouraged toward self-understanding and personal growth. The humanistic therapies are unique in their emphasis on the person's self-healing capacities. In contrast to psychodynamic therapies, humanistic therapies emphasize conscious rather than unconscious thoughts, the present rather than the past, and self-fulfillment rather than illness.

Client-centered therapy (also called *Rogerian therapy* or *nondirective therapy*) is a form of humanistic therapy, developed by Carl Rogers, in which the therapist provides a warm, supportive atmosphere to improve the client's self-concept and to encourage the client to gain insight into problems (Rogers, 1961, 1980). Compared with psychodynamic therapies, which emphasize analysis and interpretation by the therapist, client-centered therapy places far more emphasis on the client's self-reflection (C. E. Hill, 2000). In client-centered therapy, the goal of therapy is to help the client identify and understand his or her own genuine feelings (Hazler, 2007).

One way to achieve this goal is through active listening and **reflective speech,** a technique in which the therapist mirrors the client's own feelings back to the client. For example, as a woman is describing her grief over the traumatic loss of her husband in a drunk-driving accident, the therapist, noting her voice and facial expression, might suggest, "You sound angry" to help her identify her feelings. According to Rogers, the therapist must enter into an authentic relationship with the client, not as a physician diagnosing a disease but as one human being connecting with another. Indeed, in talking about those he was trying to help, Rogers referred to the "client," and eventually to the "person," rather than to the "patient."

Rogers believed that each of us is born with the potential to be fully functioning, but that we live in a world in which we are valued only if we live up to conditions of worth. That is, others value us only if we meet certain standards, and we come to apply those standards to ourselves. When we do, we become alienated from our own genuine feelings and desires.

As noted in Chapter 12, Rogers believed that humans require three essential elements to grow: unconditional positive regard, empathy, and genuineness. These three elements are reflected in his approach to therapy. To free a person from conditions of worth, the therapist engages in unconditional positive regard, which involves creating a warm and caring environment and never disapproving of the client as a person. Rogers believed this unconditional positive regard provides a context for personal growth and self-acceptance, just as soil, water, and sunshine provide a context for the acorn to become an oak.

In addition to unconditional positive regard, Rogers emphasized the importance of empathy and genuineness. Through empathy the therapist strives to put himself or herself in the client's shoes—to feel the emotions the client is feeling. Genuineness involves letting the client know the therapist's feelings and not hiding behind a façade. For genuineness to coexist with unconditional positive regard, that regard must be a sincere expression of the therapist's true feelings. The therapist may distinguish between the person's behavior and the person himself or herself. Although the client is always acknowledged as a valuable human being, his or her behavior can be evaluated negatively: "You are a good person but your actions are not." Rogers's positive view of humanity extended to his view of therapists. He believed that by being genuine with the client, the therapist could help the client improve.

Behavior Therapies

Psychodynamic and humanistic approaches are called *insight therapies* because they encourage self-awareness as the key to psychological health. We now turn to therapies that take a different approach: the behavior therapies. Behavior therapists do not search for unconscious conflicts, as psychodynamic therapists do, or encourage individuals to develop accurate perceptions of their feelings and selves, as humanistic therapists do. Insight and self-awareness are not the keys to helping individuals develop more adaptive behavior patterns, the behavior therapists say. Rather, changing behavior is the key. Indeed, behavior therapies offer action-oriented strategies to help people change behavior, not underlying thoughts or emotions (Spiegler & Guevremont, 2010).

Behavior therapies use principles of learning to reduce or eliminate maladaptive behavior. Behavior therapies are based on the behavioral and social cognitive theories of learning. Behavior therapists assume that overt symptoms are the central problem and that even if clients discover why they are depressed, that does not mean the depression will cease. To alleviate depression, then, behavior therapists focus on eliminating the problematic symptoms or behaviors rather than on helping individuals gain an understanding of why they are depressed (Yamanishi & others, 2009).

Although initially based almost exclusively on the learning principles of classical and operant conditioning, behavior therapies have become more diverse in recent years. As social cognitive theory grew in popularity, behavior therapists increasingly included observational learning, cognitive factors, and self-instruction—encouraging people to change what they say to themselves—in their practice (Vassilopoulos & Watkins, 2009).

CLASSICAL CONDITIONING TECHNIQUES

Classical conditioning has been used in treating phobias. Recall that phobias are irrational fears that interfere with an individual's life, such as fear of heights, dogs, flying, or public speaking. Specifically for this purpose, therapists use **systematic desensitization,** a method of behavior therapy that treats anxiety by teaching the client to associate deep relaxation with increasingly intense anxiety-producing situations (Wolpe, 1963). A therapist might first ask the client which aspects of the feared situation are the most and least frightening. The therapist then arranges these circumstances in order from most to least frightening. The next step is to teach the individual to relax. The client learns to recognize the presence of muscular contractions or tension in various parts of the body and then to contract and relax different muscles. Once the individual is relaxed, the therapist asks him or her to imagine the least feared stimulus in the hierarchy. Subsequently, the therapist moves up the list of items, from least to most feared, while the client remains relaxed. Eventually, the client can imagine the most fearsome circumstance without fear.

In systematic desensitization, if you are afraid of, say, spiders, the therapist might initially have you watch someone handle a spider and then ask you to engage in increasingly more feared behaviors. You might first go into the same room with a spider, next approach the spider, and then touch the spider. Eventually, you might play with the spider. Figure 16.4 shows an example of a desensitization hierarchy. Desensitization involves exposing someone to a feared situation in a real or an imagined way (Figueroa-Moseley & others, 2007).

A more intense form of exposure is *flooding*—exposing an individual to feared stimuli to an excessive degree while not allowing the person to avoid the stimuli (Berry, Rosenfield, & Smits, 2009; Wolitzky & Telch, 2009). In flooding, the patient is essentially forced to confront the frightening situation and survive. Desensitization and flooding are based on the process of extinction in classical conditioning. During extinction, the conditioned stimulus is presented without the unconditioned stimulus, leading to a decreased conditioned response.

Recall from Chapter 6 that aversive conditioning consists of repeated pairings of an undesirable behavior with aversive stimuli to decrease the behavior's positive associations. Through aversive conditioning, people can learn to avoid such behaviors as smoking, overeating, and drinking alcohol. Electric shocks, nausea-inducing substances, and verbal

● **behavior therapies** Treatments, based on the behavioral and social cognitive theories of learning, that use principles of learning to reduce or eliminate maladaptive behavior.

● **systematic desensitization** A method of behavior therapy that treats anxiety by teaching the client to associate deep relaxation with increasingly intense anxiety-producing situations.

1 A month before an examination
2 Two weeks before an examination
3 A week before an examination
4 Five days before an examination
5 Four days before an examination
6 Three days before an examination
7 Two days before an examination
8 One day before an examination
9 The night before an examination
10 On the way to the university on the day of an examination
11 Before the unopened doors of the examination room
12 Awaiting distribution of examination papers
13 The examination paper lies facedown before her
14 In the process of answering an examination paper

FIGURE 16.4   A Desensitization Hierarchy Involving Test Anxiety In this hierarchy, the individual begins with her least feared circumstance (a month before the exam) and moves through each of the circumstances until reaching her most feared circumstance (being in the process of answering the exam questions). At each step of the way, the person replaces fear with deep relaxation and successful visualization.

psychological *inquiry*

Before Aversive Conditioning

UCS $\longrightarrow$ UCR

Nausea-inducing drug $\longrightarrow$ Nausea

During Aversive Conditioning

Neutral stimulus + UCS $\longrightarrow$ UCR

Alcohol + Nausea-inducing $\longrightarrow$ Nausea
drug

After Aversive Conditioning

CS $\longrightarrow$ CR

Alcohol $\longrightarrow$ Nausea

Classical Conditioning: The Backbone of Aversive Conditioning

This figure demonstrates how classical conditioning principles underlie the process of aversive conditioning. It specifically shows how classical conditioning can provide a conditional aversion to alcohol. In studying the figure, recall the abbreviations UCS (unconditioned stimulus), UCR (unconditioned response), CS (conditioned stimulus), and CR (conditioned response). Try your hand at the questions below.

1. In the example illustrated in the figure, what is the conditioned stimulus?

2. What is the likely effect of alcohol *prior to* aversion therapy? Is this effect learned (that is, a conditioned response) or not (an unconditioned response)?

3. What role, if any, does the person's motivation play in the process of conditioning?

4. Looking over the steps in aversive conditioning, how do you think classical conditioning might be applied to prevent psychological problems?

insults are some of the noxious stimuli used in aversive conditioning (Sommer & others, 2006). The Psychological Inquiry above illustrates conditioning principles in practice.

OPERANT CONDITIONING TECHNIQUES

The idea behind using operant conditioning as a therapy approach is that just as maladaptive behavior patterns are learned, they can be unlearned. Therapy involves conducting a careful analysis of the person's environment to determine which factors need modification. Especially important is changing the consequences of the person's behavior to ensure that healthy, adaptive replacement behaviors are followed by positive reinforcement.

Applied behavior analysis, described in Chapter 6, involves establishing positive reinforcement connections between behaviors and rewards so that individuals engage in appropriate behavior and extinguish inappropriate behavior. Consider, for example, a woman with obsessive-compulsive disorder (OCD) who engages in a compulsive ritual such as touching the door frame three times every time she enters a room. If she does not complete her ritual, she is overcome with anxiety that something dreadful will happen. Note that whenever she completes the ritual, nothing dreadful does happen and her anxiety is relieved. Her compulsion is a behavior that is reinforced by the relief of anxiety and the fact that nothing dreadful happens. Such a ritual, then, could be viewed as avoidance learning. An operant conditioning–based therapy would involve stopping the behavior to extinguish this avoidance. Specifically, allowing the woman to experience the lack of catastrophic consequences in the absence of the touching the door frame, as well as training her to relax, might help to eliminate the compulsive rituals. Indeed, behavior therapy has been shown to be effective in treating OCD (Bonchek, 2009; Rosa-Alcazar & others, 2008).

It may strike you as unusual that behavioral approaches do not emphasize gaining insight and self-awareness. However, for the very reason that they do not stress these goals, such treatments may be particularly useful in individuals whose cognitive abilities are limited, such as adults with developmental disabilities or children. Applied behavior analysis can be used, for instance, with individuals with autism who engage in self-injurious behaviors such as head banging (Vismara & Rogers, 2010).

Cognitive Therapies

Cognitive therapies emphasize that cognitions, or thoughts, are the main source of psychological problems; these therapies attempt to change the individual's feelings and behaviors by changing cognitions. *Cognitive restructuring,* a general concept for changing a pattern of thought that is presumed to be causing maladaptive behavior or emotion, is central to cognitive therapies.

Cognitive therapies differ from psychoanalytic therapies by focusing on overt symptoms rather than on deep-seated unconscious thoughts, by providing more structure to the individual's thoughts, and by being less concerned about the origin of the problem. Compared with humanistic therapies, cognitive therapies provide a more structured framework and more analysis, and they are based on specific cognitive techniques. Cognitive therapists guide individuals in identifying their irrational and self-defeating thoughts. Then they use various techniques to get clients to challenge these thoughts and to consider different, more positive ways of thinking.

Cognitive therapies all involve these basic assumptions: Human beings have control over their feelings, and how individuals feel about something depends on how they think about it. In the next section we examine three main types of cognitive therapy: Albert Ellis's rational-emotive behavior therapy, Aaron Beck's cognitive therapy, and cognitive-behavior therapy.

ELLIS'S RATIONAL-EMOTIVE BEHAVIOR THERAPY

Rational-emotive behavior therapy (REBT) was developed by Albert Ellis (1913–2007), who believed that individuals develop a psychological disorder because of irrational and self-defeating beliefs. Ellis said our emotional reactions to life events are a product of our irrational beliefs and expectations along with the central false belief that we cannot control our feelings (1962, 1996, 2000, 2002, 2005). Ellis was a very confrontational therapist who aggressively attacked these irrational beliefs.

Ellis (2000, 2002) believed that many individuals construct three basic demands, which he called "musterbating": (1) I absolutely *must* perform well and win the approval of other people; (2) other people *must* treat me kindly and fairly; and (3) my life conditions *must* not be frustrating. Once people convert their important desires into demands, they often create dysfunctional, exaggerated beliefs, such as "Because I'm not performing well, as I absolutely must, I'm an inadequate person."

The goal of REBT is to get the individual to eliminate self-defeating beliefs by rationally examining them (Sava & others, 2009). A client is shown how to dispute his or her dysfunctional beliefs—especially the absolute "musts"—and how to convert them to realistic and logical thoughts. Homework assignments provide opportunities to engage in the new self-talk and to experience the positive results of not viewing life in such a catastrophic way. For Ellis, a successful outcome means getting the client to live in reality, where life is sometimes tough and bad things happen.

BECK'S COGNITIVE THERAPY

Aaron Beck developed a somewhat different form of cognitive therapy to treat psychological problems, especially depression (Beck, 1976, 1993). He began with the basic assumption that a psychological problem such as depression results when people think illogically about themselves, their world, and the future (Beck, 2005, 2006). Similar to Ellis's method, Beck's approach derives from the idea that the goal of therapy is to help people to recognize and discard self-defeating cognitions.

● **cognitive therapies** Treatments that point to cognitions (thoughts) as the main source of psychological problems and that attempt to change the individual's feelings and behaviors by changing cognitions.

● **rational-emotive behavior therapy (REBT)** A therapy based on Ellis's assertion that individuals develop a psychological disorder because of irrational and self-defeating beliefs and whose goal is to get clients to eliminate these beliefs by rationally examining them.

Albert Ellis (1913–2007) Ellis's rational-emotive behavior therapy aims to eliminate individuals' rigid, irrational beliefs through a process of rational self-examination.

Aaron Beck (b. 1921) Beck's method stresses that the goal of therapy should be to help people to recognize and eliminate illogical and self-defeating thinking.

In the initial phases of Beck's therapy, individuals learn to make connections between their patterns of thinking and their emotional responses. From Beck's perspective, emotions are a product of cognitions. By changing cognitions, people can change how they feel. Unfortunately, thoughts that lead to emotions can happen so rapidly that a person is not even aware of them. Thus, the first goal of therapy is to bring these automatic thoughts into awareness so that they can be changed. The therapist helps clients to identify their own automatic thoughts and to keep records of their thought content and emotional reactions.

With the therapist's assistance, clients learn to recognize logical errors in their thinking and to challenge the accuracy of these automatic thoughts. Logical errors in thinking can lead individuals to the following erroneous beliefs (Carson, Butcher, & Mineka, 1996):

- Perceiving the world as harmful while ignoring evidence to the contrary—for example, when a young woman still feels worthless after a friend has just told her how much other people genuinely like her.

- Overgeneralizing on the basis of limited examples—such as a man's seeing himself as worthless because one individual stopped dating him.

- Magnifying the importance of undesirable events—such as seeing the loss of a dating partner as the end of the world.

- Engaging in absolutist thinking—such as exaggerating the importance of someone's mildly critical comment and perceiving it as proof of total inadequacy.

Figure 16.5 describes some of the most widely used cognitive therapy techniques.

The following case study gives you a glimpse of what happens in Beck's cognitive therapy. In this dialogue, the therapist guides a depressed 26-year-old graduate student toward understanding the connection between how she interprets her experiences and how she feels. The goal is to help her see the inaccuracy of her interpretations:

> Student: I agree with the description of me, but I guess I don't agree that the way I think makes me depressed.
> Therapist: How do you understand it?
> Student: I get depressed when things go wrong. Like when I fail a test.
> Therapist: How can failing a test make you depressed?
> Student: Well, if I fail I'll never get into law school.
> Therapist: So failing the test means a lot to you. But if failing a test could drive people into clinical depression, wouldn't you expect everyone who failed the test to have depression? Did everyone who failed the test get depressed enough to require treatment?
> Student: No, but it depends on how important the test was to the person.
> Therapist: Right, and who decides the importance?
> Student: I do.
> Therapist: And so, what we have to examine is your way of viewing the test or the way that you think about the test and how it affects your chances of getting into law school. Do you agree?
> Student: Right . . .
> Therapist: Now what did failing mean?
> Student: (*Tearful*) That I couldn't get into law school.
> Therapist: And what does that mean to you?
> Student: That I'm just not smart enough.
> Therapist: Anything else?
> Student: That I can never be happy.
> Therapist: And how do these thoughts make you feel?
> Student: Very unhappy.
> Therapist: So it is the meaning of failing a test that makes you very unhappy. In fact, believing that you can never be happy is a powerful factor in producing unhappiness. So, you get yourself into a trap—by definition, failure to get into law school equals, "I can never be happy." (Beck & others, 1979, pp. 145–146).

Cognitive Therapy Technique	Description	Example
Challenge idiosyncratic meanings	Explore personal meaning attached to the client's words and ask the client to consider alternatives.	When a client says he will be "devastated" by his spouse leaving, ask just how he would be devastated and ways he could avoid being devastated.
Question the evidence	Systematically examine the evidence for the client's beliefs or assertions.	When a client says she can't live without her spouse, explore how she lived without the spouse before she was married.
Reattribution	Help the client distribute responsibility for events appropriately.	When a client says that his son's failure in school must be his fault, explore other possibilities, such as the quality of the school.
Examine options and alternatives	Help the client generate alternative actions to maladaptive ones.	If a client considers leaving school, explore whether tutoring or going part-time to school are good alternatives.
Decatastrophize	Help the client evaluate whether he is overestimating the nature of a situation.	If a client states that failure in a course means he or she must give up the dream of medical school, question whether this is a necessary conclusion.
Fantasize consequences	Explore fantasies of a feared situation: if unrealistic, the client may recognize this; if realistic, work on effective coping strategies.	Help a client who fantasizes "falling apart" when asking the boss for a raise to role-play the situation and develop effective skills for making the request.
Examine advantages and disadvantages	Examine advantages and disadvantages of an issue, to instill a broader perspective.	If a client says he "was just born depressed and will always be that way," explore the advantages and disadvantages of holding that perspective versus other perspectives.
Turn adversity to advantage	Explore ways that difficult situations can be transformed to opportunities.	If a client has just been laid off, explore whether this is an opportunity for her to return to school.
Guided association	Help the client see connections between different thoughts or ideas.	Draw the connections between a client's anger at his wife for going on a business trip and his fear of being alone.
Scaling	Ask the client to rate her emotions or thoughts on scales to help gain perspective.	If a client says she was overwhelmed by an emotion, ask her to rate it on a scale from 0 (not at all present) to 100 (I fell down in a faint).
Thought stopping	Provide the client with ways of stopping a cascade of negative thoughts.	Teach an anxious client to picture a stop sign or hear a bell when anxious thoughts begin to snowball.
Distraction	Help the client find benign or positive distractions to take attention away from negative thoughts or emotions temporarily.	Have a client count to 200 by 13s when he feels himself becoming anxious.
Labeling of distortions	Provide labels for specific types of distorted thinking to help the client gain more distance and perspective.	Have a client keep a record of the number of times a day she engages in all-or-nothing thinking—seeing things as all bad or all good.

FIGURE 16.5 Cognitive Therapy Techniques Cognitive therapists develop strategies to help change the way people think.

The cognitive therapies of Beck and Ellis share some differences as well as similarities. Rational-emotive behavior therapy is very directive and confrontational; in contrast, Beck's cognitive therapy involves more of an open-ended dialogue between the therapist and the individual. The aim of this dialogue in Beck's approach is to get individuals to reflect on personal issues and discover their own misconceptions. Beck also encourages clients to gather information about themselves and to try out unbiased experiments that reveal the inaccuracies of their beliefs. So whereas Ellis's approach was to bring a sledgehammer down on irrational beliefs, Beck's involves a more subtle process of coaxing a client to recognize that these beliefs promote thoughts that influence feelings. Despite the differences in their approaches, a recent study showed that both Ellis's rational-emotive behavior therapy and Beck's cognitive therapy were more effective in treating depression than drug therapy (Sava & others, 2009).

● **cognitive-behavior therapy** A therapy that combines cognitive therapy and behavior therapy with the goal of developing self-efficacy.

COGNITIVE-BEHAVIOR THERAPY

Cognitive-behavior therapy is a combination of cognitive therapy, with its emphasis on reducing self-defeating thoughts, and behavior therapy, with its emphasis on changing behavior. An important aspect of cognitive-behavior therapy is *self-efficacy,* Albert Bandura's concept that one can master a situation and produce positive outcomes (1997, 2001, 2009, 2010b). Bandura believes in fact that self-efficacy is the key to successful therapy. At each step of the therapy process, clients need to bolster their confidence by telling themselves messages such as "I'm going to master my problem," "I can do it," "I'm improving," and "I'm getting better." As they gain confidence and engage in adaptive behavior, the successes become intrinsically motivating. Before long, individuals persist (with considerable effort) in their attempts to solve personal problems because of the positive outcomes that were set in motion by self-efficacy.

Self-instructional methods are cognitive-behavior techniques aimed at teaching individuals to modify their own behavior (Spiegler & Guevremont, 2010). Using self-instructional techniques, cognitive-behavior therapists prompt clients to change what they say to themselves. The therapist gives the client examples of constructive statements, known as *reinforcing self-statements,* which the client can repeat in order to take positive steps to cope with stress or meet a goal. The therapist also encourages the client to practice the statements through role playing and strengthens his or her newly acquired skills through reinforcement.

COGNITIVE THERAPY FOR PSYCHOLOGICAL DISORDERS

Cognitive therapy has successfully treated some anxiety disorders, mood disorders, schizophrenia, and personality disorders (Peters & others, 2010; Sava & others, 2009). In many instances, cognitive therapy used together with drug therapy is an effective treatment for psychological disorders (Starcevic, 2006).

Cognitive therapy is often used to treat panic disorder, one of the anxiety disorders (Schmidt & Keough, 2003; van Apeldoorn & others, 2010). The central concept in the cognitive model of panic is that individuals catastrophically misinterpret relatively harmless physical or psychological events. In cognitive therapy, the therapist encourages individuals to test the catastrophic misinterpretations by inducing an actual panic attack. The individuals then can test the notion that they will die or go crazy, which they find out is not the case.

Cognitive therapy also shows considerable promise in the treatment of post-traumatic stress disorder, especially when therapists encourage clients to relive traumatic experiences so that they can come to grips with the threatening cognitions precipitated by those experiences (Cockram, Drummond, & Lee, 2010; Vickerman & Margolin, 2009). In addition, cognitive therapy has been successful in treating generalized anxiety disorder, certain phobias, and obsessive-compulsive disorder (Foa & Franklin, 2011; Jaurrieta & others, 2009; Roy-Byrne & others, 2010).

In one study, cognitive-behavior therapy was given to children (as well as their parents) who were highly anxious about going to school (Dadds & others, 1999). As shown in Figure 16.6, the therapy (provided over a 10-week period) was considerably more effective in reducing anxiety than no therapy at all, and the positive effects of the therapy were still present two years later.

One of the earliest applications of cognitive therapy was in the treatment of depression. A number of studies have shown that cognitive therapy can be just as successful as, or in some cases superior to, drug therapy in the treatment of depressive disorders (Sado & others, 2009; Sava & others, 2009). Some studies also have demonstrated that individuals treated with cognitive therapy are less likely to relapse into depression than individuals treated with drug therapy (Jarrett & others, 2001).

Practitioners have made considerable strides in recent years in applying cognitive therapy to the treatment of schizophrenia.

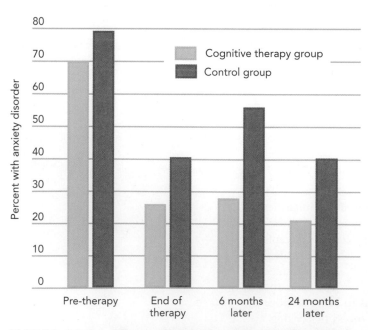

FIGURE 16.6 **Effects of Cognitive-Behavior Therapy on Children's Anxiety About School** Children and their parents participated in a 10-week cognitive-behavior therapy program. Compared with a control group, the children in the cognitive therapy program were less likely to have an anxiety disorder through 24 months after the therapy.

	Cause of Problem	Therapy Emphasis	Nature of Therapy and Techniques
Psychodynamic Therapies	Client's problems are symptoms of deep-seated, unresolved unconscious conflicts.	Discover underlying unconscious conflicts and work with client to develop insight.	Psychoanalysis, including free association, dream analysis, resistance, and transference: therapist interprets heavily, operant conditioning.
Humanistic Therapies	Client is not functioning at an optimal level of development.	Develop awareness of inherent potential for growth.	Person-centered therapy, including unconditional positive regard, genuineness, accurate empathy, and active listening; self-appreciation emphasized.
Behavior Therapies	Client has learned maladaptive behavior patterns.	Learn adaptive behavior patterns through changes in the environment or cognitive processes.	Observation of behavior and its controlling conditions; specific advice given about what should be done; therapies based on classical conditioning, operant conditioning.
Cognitive Therapies	Client has developed inappropriate thoughts.	Change feelings and behaviors by changing cognitions.	Conversation with client designed to get him or her to change irrational and self-deflating beliefs

FIGURE 16.7   Therapy Comparisons Different therapies address the same problems in very different ways. Many therapists take an eclectic approach, using the techniques that seem right for a given client and his or her problems.

Although not a substitute for drug therapy in the treatment of this disorder, cognitive therapy has been effective in reducing some schizophrenia symptoms such as belief in delusions and acting out impulsively (Christopher Frueh & others, 2009). Cognitive therapy also has proved effective in treating personality disorders (McMain & Pos, 2007). The focus is on using cognitive therapy to change individuals' core beliefs and to reduce their automatic negative thoughts.

So far, we have studied the biological therapies and psychotherapies. The four psychotherapies—psychodynamic, humanistic, behavior, and cognitive—are compared in Figure 16.7.

The cognitive approach to therapy assumes that how we think is an important part of how we feel, and that if we can change how we think about things—reinterpret events in more positive ways—we can feel better. A goal for cognitive-behavior therapy is to help us to alter our routine, automatic thinking habits (Jaurrieta & others, 2008). Remember that thinking is not only a mental event but also a physical event in the brain. How does changing our thoughts change the brain? To read about research addressing this fascinating question, see the Intersection.

Therapy Integrations

Having read about the major approaches to psychotherapy, you may be surprised to learn that as many as 50 percent of therapists do not identify themselves as adhering to one particular method. Rather, they refer to themselves as "integrative" or "eclectic." **Integrative therapy** is a combination of techniques from different therapies based on the therapist's judgment of which particular methods will provide the greatest benefit for the client (Prochaska & Norcross, 2010). Integrative therapy is characterized by openness to various ways of applying diverse therapies. For example, a therapist might use a behavioral approach to treat an individual with panic disorder and a cognitive therapy approach to treat a client with major depressive disorder.

Because clients present a wide range of problems, it makes sense for therapists to use the best tools for each individual rather than to take a "one size fits all" approach. Sometimes a given psychological disorder is so difficult to treat that it requires the therapist to bring all of his or her tools to bear (de Groot, Verheul, & Trijsburg, 2008; Kozaric-Kovacic, 2008). For example, borderline personality disorder, as described in Chapter 15, involves emotional instability, impulsivity, and self-injurious behaviors. This disorder responds to a form of therapy called *dialectical behavior therapy,* or DBT (Dimeff, Koerner, & Linehan, 2007; Harley & others, 2008; Neacsiu & others, 2010; Paris, 2010). Like psychodynamic approaches, DBT assumes that early childhood experiences are important to the development of borderline personality disorder. DBT includes a variety of techniques, including homework assignments, cognitive interventions, intensive individual therapy, and group

● **integrative therapy** A combination of techniques from different therapies based on the therapist's judgment of which particular methods will provide the greatest benefit for the client.

Clinical Psychology and Neuroscience: How Does Therapy Change the Brain?

When we change our habitual patterns of thinking, we are also making physical changes in the brain. We might be activating brain areas we have not used, and we might be establishing new physical connections in the brain. Remarkably, advances in brain-imaging technology such as functional magnetic resonance imaging (or fMRI, discussed in Chapter 3) have allowed researchers to examine what actually happens in the brain when, through therapy, we change the way we think (Costafreda & others, 2009; Dichter, Felder, & Smoski, 2010).

A striking example is provided by research showing that therapeutic interventions can "wake up" dormant parts of the brain. As noted in Chapter 15, schizophrenia is associated with low levels of activity in the prefrontal cortex, the brain area thought to be associated with high-order functions such as problem solving, judgment, and planning. In one study, a treatment called *cognitive-remediation therapy* (CRT) was administered to a group of individuals who were profoundly disabled by schizophrenia for 10 years or more (Wykes & others, 2002).

CRT is a psychological intervention that involves giving individuals practice in problem solving and information processing. The client essentially completes a variety of paper-and-pencil tasks that require skills such as cognitive flexibility, planning, and the use of working memory. Individuals with schizophrenia (who were on medication) and a control group of healthy individuals were scanned while engaging in a problem-solving task before and after those with schizophrenia completed CRT. Before CRT, the individuals with schizophrenia showed lower activation in the prefrontal cortex when solving such problems, compared with the healthy individuals. After CRT, however, participants with schizophrenia not only showed increases in activation, but they also were no longer different from the healthy participants. This result suggests that CRT had helped to normalize their brain function. This study is remarkable because it shows that a psychological intervention that focuses on engaging particular brain areas can lead to changes in the brain, even for patterns that were previously thought to be stable characteristics of a disorder.

The growing literature applying sophisticated scanning techniques to therapeutic interventions sheds light on how researchers can use knowledge about the brain to track psychological processes and to pinpoint brain changes associated with improved functioning (Pine, 2009; Reinhardt & others, 2010). Because the brain is a physical organ, we might assume that it is most sensitive to biological interventions. However, research is showing that psychological interventions also can powerfully affect the brain. In a sense, the dramatic findings are revealing how, with the help of therapy, the brain is capable of changing itself.

How does learning about these brain effects influence your view of treating disorders with therapy versus medication?

---

sessions with others with the disorder. Group sessions focus on mindfulness training as well as emotional and interpersonal skills training.

Integrative therapy also is at work when individuals are treated with both psychotherapy and drug therapy. For example, combined cognitive therapy and drug therapy has been effective in treating anxiety and depressive disorders (Koszycki & others, 2010), eating disorders (Wilson, Grilo, & Vitousek, 2007), and schizophrenia (Rector & Beck, 2001). This integrative therapy might be conducted by a mental health team that includes a psychiatrist and a clinical psychologist. At their best, integrative therapies are effective, systematic uses of a variety of therapy approaches (Prochaska & Norcross, 2010). However, some have voiced concern that increased use of integrative therapies will result in an unsystematic, haphazard use of techniques that are no better than a narrow, dogmatic, therapeutic approach (Lazarus, Beutler, & Norcross, 1992).

Therapy integrations are conceptually compatible with the biopsychosocial model of abnormal behavior described in Chapter 15. That is, many therapists believe that abnormal behavior involves biological, psychological, and social factors. Many single-therapy approaches concentrate on one aspect of the person more than others; for example, drug therapies focus on biological factors, and cognitive therapies probe psychological factors. Therapy integrations take a broader look at individuals' problems, and such breadth is also implied in sociocultural approaches to therapy, our next topic.

test yourself

1. Describe what psychotherapy is, and identify four psychotherapeutic approaches.
2. What is psychoanalysis? Who developed it?
3. What specific behavior therapy technique is used to treat phobias? How does it work?

3· SOCIOCULTURAL APPROACHES AND ISSUES IN TREATMENT

In the treatment of psychological disorders, biological therapies change the person's body, behavior therapies modify the person's behavior, and cognitive therapies alter the person's thinking. This section focuses on sociocultural approaches to the treatment of psychological disorders. These methods view the individual as part of a system of relationships that are influenced by various social and cultural factors (Nolen-Hoeksema, 2011).

We first review some common sociocultural approaches, including group therapy, family and couples therapy, self-help support groups, and community mental health. We then examine various cultural perspectives on therapy.

Group Therapy

There is good reason to believe that individuals who share a psychological problem may benefit from observing others cope with a similar problem and that helping others cope can in turn improve individuals' feelings of competence and efficacy. The sociocultural approach known as **group therapy** brings together individuals who share a psychological disorder in sessions that are typically led by a mental health professional.

Advocates of group therapy stress that individual therapy is limited because it puts the client outside the normal context of relationships. It is these very relationships, they argue, that may hold the key to successful therapy. Many psychological problems develop in the context of interpersonal relationships—within one's family, marriage, or peer group, for example. By taking into account the context of these important groups, therapy may be more successful.

Group therapy takes many diverse forms. These include psychodynamic, humanistic, behavior, and cognitive therapy, in addition to approaches that do not reflect the major psychotherapeutic perspectives (Hornsey & others, 2009; van Ingen & Novicki, 2009). Six features make group therapy an attractive treatment format (Yalom & Leszcz, 2006):

- *Information:* Individuals receive information about their problems from either the group leader or other group members.
- *Universality:* Many individuals develop the sense that no one else has frightening and unacceptable impulses. In the group, individuals observe that others feel anguish and suffering as well.
- *Altruism:* Group members support one another with advice and sympathy and learn that they have something to offer others.
- *Experiencing a positive family group:* A therapy group often resembles a family (in family therapy, the group is a family), with the leaders representing parents and the other members of the group representing siblings. In this new family, old wounds may be healed and new, more positive family ties made.
- *Development of social skills:* Corrective feedback from peers may correct flaws in the individual's interpersonal skills. An individual may come to see that he or she is self-centered if five other group members comment on the person's self-centeredness; in individual therapy, the individual might not believe the therapist.
- *Interpersonal learning:* The group can serve as a training ground for practicing new behaviors and relationships. A hostile person may learn that he or she can get along better with others by behaving less aggressively, for example.

Family and Couples Therapy

Our relationships with family members and significant others are certainly an important part of human life. Sometimes these vital relationships can benefit from a helpful outsider. **Family therapy** is group therapy among family members. **Couples therapy** is group therapy with married or unmarried couples whose major problem lies within

● **group therapy** A sociocultural approach to the treatment of psychological disorders that brings together individuals who share a particular psychological disorder in sessions that are typically led by a mental health professional.

● **family therapy** Group therapy with family members.

● **couples therapy** Group therapy with married or unmarried couples whose major problem lies within their relationship.

In family therapy, the assumption is that particular patterns of interaction among the family members cause the observed abnormal symptoms.

their relationship. These approaches stress that although one person may have some abnormal symptoms, those symptoms are a function of the family or couple relationships (Gehar, 2010; Hazell, 2009; Keitner, Ryan, & Solomon, 2009). Psychodynamic, humanistic, and behavior therapies may be used in family and couples therapy.

Four of the most widely used family therapy techniques are

- *Validation:* The therapist expresses an understanding and acceptance of each family member's feelings and beliefs and thus validates the person. When the therapist talks with each family member, he or she finds something positive to say.

- *Reframing:* The therapist helps families reframe problems as family problems, not as an individual's problems. A delinquent adolescent boy's problems are reframed in terms of how each family member contributed to the situation. The mother's or father's lack of attention to the boy and marital conflict may be involved, for example.

- *Structural change:* The family therapist tries to restructure the coalitions in a family. In a mother–son coalition, the therapist might suggest that the father take a stronger disciplinarian role to relieve the mother of some of the burden. Restructuring might be as simple as suggesting that the parents explore satisfying ways of being together. The therapist may recommend, for example, that the parents go out once a week for a quiet dinner together.

- *Detriangulation:* In some families, one member is the scapegoat for two other members who are in conflict but pretend not to be. For example, parents of a girl with anorexia nervosa or a son who is acting out aggressively at school might insist that their marriage is fine but find themselves in subtle conflict over how to handle the child. The therapist tries to disentangle, or detriangulate, this situation by shifting attention away from the child to the conflict between the parents.

Couples therapy proceeds in much the same way as family therapy. Conflict in marriages and in relationships between unmarried individuals frequently involves poor communication. In some instances, communication has broken down entirely. The therapist tries to improve the communication between the partners (Kauffman & Silberman, 2009; Ro & Wampler, 2009). In some cases, the therapist will focus on the roles partners play: One may be strong, the other weak; one may be responsible, the other spoiled, for example. Couples therapy addresses diverse problems such as alcohol abuse, jealousy, sexual issues, delayed childbearing, infidelity, gender roles, two-career families, divorce, remarriage, and the special concerns of stepfamilies (Hernandez, Siegel, & Almeida, 2009).

Self-Help Support Groups

© David Sipress

Self-help support groups are voluntary organizations of individuals who get together on a regular basis to discuss topics of common interest. The groups are not conducted by a professional therapist but by a paraprofessional or a member of the common interest group. *Paraprofessionals* are individuals who have been taught by a professional to provide some mental health services but who do not have *formal* mental health training. Some paraprofessionals may themselves have had a disorder; for example, a chemical dependency counselor may also be a recovering addict. The group leader and members provide support to help individuals with their problems.

Self-help support groups play a key and valuable role in our nation's mental health. A survey in 2002 revealed that for mental health support alone, nearly 7,500 such groups existed in the United States, with more than 1 million members (Goldstrom & others, 2006). In addition to reaching so many people in need of help, these groups are important because they use community resources and are relatively inexpensive. They also serve people who are less likely to receive help otherwise, such as those with less education and fewer financial resources.

Self-help support groups provide members with a sympathetic audience for confession, sharing, and emotional release. The social support, role modeling, and sharing of concrete strategies for solving problems that unfold in self-help groups add to their effectiveness. A woman who has been raped might not believe a therapist who tells her that, with time, she will put the pieces of her shattered life back together. The same message from another rape survivor—someone who has had to work through the same feelings of rage, fear, and violation—might be more believable.

Alcoholics Anonymous (AA), founded in 1935 by a reformed alcoholic and a physician, is one of the best-known self-help groups. Mental health professionals often recommend AA for their clients struggling with alcoholism (Kaskutas & others, 2009; Kelly & others, 2010; Slaymaker & Sheehan, 2008). A research review revealed that some studies show a positive effect for AA but others do not (Kaskutas, 2009).

Another self-help organization is Compeer, which matches community volunteers in supportive friendship relationships with children and adults receiving mental health treatment (McCorkle & others, 2008). In some cases, both partners in a Compeer relationship may have psychological disorders. There are myriad other self-help groups, such as lesbian and gay support groups, cocaine abuse support groups, Weight Watchers and TOPS (Take Off Pounds Sensibly), child abuse support groups, and many medical (heart disease, cancer) support groups.

For individuals who tend to cope by seeking information and affiliation with similar peers, self-help support groups can reduce stress and promote adjustment. However, as with any group therapy, there is a possibility that negative emotions will spread through the group, especially if the members face circumstances that deteriorate over time, as terminal cancer patients do. Group leaders who are sensitive to the spread of negative emotions can minimize such effects.

A multitude of online support groups has also emerged (Andersson & others, 2006; Davison, Pennebaker, & Dickerson, 2000). Many individuals feel more comfortable sharing their intimate life experiences with a group of people they cannot actually see. Although it may seem as if an online support group exists for just about every problem imaginable, that is not necessarily the case. Research has shown that an online support group is more likely to emerge for problems that are potentially stigmatizing (such as depression and AIDS) and for problems that are more likely to be suffered by women than men (such as breast cancer) (Davison, Pennebaker, & Dickerson, 2000; Thaxton, Emshoff, & Guessous, 2005; Ussher & others, 2006).

Despite their benefits, online support groups can be problematic. In the absence of guidance from a trained professional, group members may lack the expertise and

"We're organizing a tantrum support group."

© Randy Glasbergen

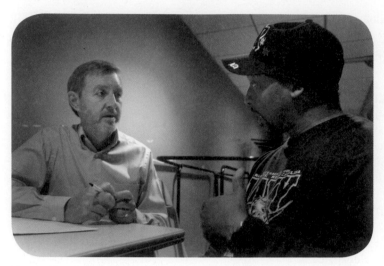

Community mental health counselors can serve as a lifeline to many local citizens.

knowledge to provide optimal advice. The emergence of pro-anorexia (or "pro-ana") websites, which *promote* anorexia, exemplifies the potentially negative side of the online "support" phenomenon (Harshbarger & others, 2009). Technological advances certainly have influenced therapy in some positive ways. However, they also present their own challenges—and even dangers.

Community Mental Health

The community mental health movement was born in the 1960s as society's attitude toward people with psychological disorders began to change. The deplorable conditions of some psychiatric facilities at the time were one catalyst for the movement. Advocates of community mental health maintained that individuals with psychological disorders ought to remain within society and with their families rather than being locked away in institutions; the troubled individuals should receive treatment in community mental health centers. This movement also reflected economic concerns, as it was thought that institutionalizing people was certainly more expensive than treating them in the community.

With the passage of the Community Mental Health Act of 1963, large numbers of individuals with psychological disorders were transferred from mental institutions to community-based facilities, a process called *deinstitutionalization*. Although at least partially motivated by a desire to treat individuals with psychological disorders more effectively and humanely, deinstitutionalization has been implicated in rising rates of homelessness. The success of community mental health services depends on the resources and commitment of the communities in which they occur.

Community mental health involves training teachers, ministers, family physicians, nurses, and others who directly interact with community members to offer lay counseling and workshops. Clients receive help in areas ranging from coping with stress to reducing their drug use to developing assertiveness (Moritsugu, Wong, & Duffy, 2010). Advocates and providers of community mental health believe that the best way to treat a psychological disorder is to prevent it from happening in the first place (Shinn & Thaden, 2010).

An explicit goal of community mental health is to help people who are disenfranchised from society, such as those living in poverty, to lead happier, more productive lives (L. Jackson & others, 2009). A key concept involved in this effort is empowerment—assisting individuals to develop the skills they need to control their own lives. Importantly, all of these programs may rely on financial support from local, state, and federal governments.

Cultural Perspectives

The psychotherapies discussed earlier in this chapter—psychodynamic, humanistic, behavior, and cognitive—focus mainly on the individual. This focus is compatible with the needs of many people in Western cultures such as the United States, where the emphasis is on the individual rather than the group (family, community, or ethnic group). However, these psychotherapies may not be as effective with people who live in cultures that place more importance on the group—called *collectivistic cultures*. Some psychologists argue that family therapy is likely to be more effective with people in cultures that place a high value on the family, such as Latino and Asian cultures (Guo, 2005).

ETHNICITY

Many ethnic minority individuals prefer discussing problems with parents, friends, and relatives rather than mental health professionals (Sue, Sue, & Sue, 2010). Might therapy progress best, then, when the therapist and the client are from the same ethnic background? Researchers have found that when there is an ethnic match between the therapist and the client and when ethnic-specific services are provided, clients are less likely to drop out of therapy early and in many cases have better treatment outcomes (Jackson & Greene, 2000). Ethnic-specific services include culturally appropriate greetings and arrangements (for example, serving tea rather than coffee to Chinese American clients), providing flexible hours for treatment, and employing a bicultural/bilingual staff (Nystul, 1999).

Nonetheless, therapy can still be effective when the therapist and client are from different ethnic backgrounds if the therapist has excellent clinical skills and is culturally sensitive (Akhtar, 2006). Culturally skilled psychotherapists have good knowledge of their clients' cultural groups, understand sociopolitical influences, and have competence in working with culturally diverse groups (Austad, 2009). Would you be comfortable sharing with a therapist who is different from you in terms of ethnic background? Gender? Religion?

GENDER

One byproduct of changing gender roles for women and men is reevaluation of the goal of psychotherapy (Gilbert & Kearney, 2006; Nolen-Hoeksema, 2011). Traditionally, therapy has focused on enhancing self-reliance and independence. However, this goal may reflect gender role expectations (as discussed in Chapter 11) for men more than for women. Thus, some psychologists argue that the therapeutic goal should reflect the client's life circumstances, as well as establish a balance between independence and relatedness to others (Notman & Nadelson, 2002).

Feminist therapists believe that traditional psychotherapy continues to carry considerable gender bias and has not adequately addressed the specific concerns of women. Thus, several alternative therapies have arisen that aim to help the client break free from traditional gender roles and stereotypes. In terms of improving the client's life, the goals of feminist therapists are no different from those of other therapists. However, feminist therapists maintain that the client's improvement depends in part on understanding how the nature of women's roles in U.S. society can contribute to the development of a psychological disorder. In other words, feminist therapists believe that women must become alert to the possibility of bias and discrimination in their own life in order to achieve their mental health goals (Herlihy & McCollum, 2007).

4- THE EFFECTIVENESS OF PSYCHOTHERAPY

Do individuals who go through therapy get better? Are some approaches more effective than others? How would we know if a therapy worked? During the past several decades, a large volume of research has addressed these questions (Kazdin, 2007).

Research on the Effectiveness of Psychotherapy

A large body of research points to the conclusion that psychotherapy works (Beck, 2005; Butler & others, 2006; Clemens, 2010; Lambert, 2001; Luborsky & others, 2002). Researchers have carried out literally hundreds of studies examining the effects of psychotherapy. The strategy used to analyze these diverse studies is meta-analysis, in which, as we have seen, the researcher statistically combines the results of many different studies (Rosenthal & DiMatteo, 2001). A number of persuasive meta-analyses have concluded that psychotherapy does work, and works well, for many psychological disorders (Lipsey & Wilson, 1993; Wampold, 2001). In a review of studies, more than 70 percent of individuals who saw a therapist improved, whereas less than 40 percent who received a placebo

test yourself

1. Why might group therapy be more successful than individual therapy?
2. What are four common family therapy techniques? Briefly describe each.
3. What social and economic forces drove the community mental health movement?

psychological *inquiry*

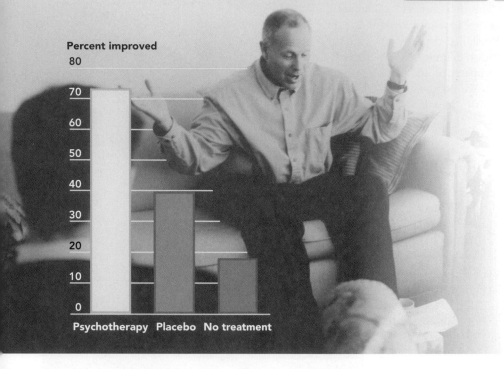

Percent improved

(Bar graph showing: Psychotherapy ~70, Placebo ~38, No treatment ~16)

Psychotherapy   Placebo   No treatment

Does Therapy Work?

This figure provides a summary of numerous studies and reviews of research in which clients were randomly assigned to a no-treatment control group, a placebo control group, or a psychotherapy treatment (Lambert, 2001). Note that the group to which individuals were assigned is indicated on the X or horizontal axis and the percent of individuals who improved is shown on the Y or vertical axis. Use the graph to answer the following questions.

1. Which group improved most and which improved least?

2. Why might those in the "no treatment" group have improved?

3. What does the difference between the psychotherapy group and the placebo group indicate?

4. Do these results allow us to infer causal relationships between therapy and improvement? Explain.

---

and less than 20 percent who received no treatment improved (Lambert, 2001). The Psychological Inquiry above summarizes these results.

People who are contemplating seeing a psychotherapist do not just want to know *whether* psychotherapy in general is effective but also, especially, *which form* of psychotherapy is most effective. There is no easy answer to that question. In fact, there is a term in psychotherapy describing this problem—the *Dodo bird hypothesis*—that comes from the Dodo bird in *Alice's Adventures in Wonderland*. Dodo was asked to judge the winner of a race. He proclaimed, "Everybody has won and all must have prizes." Many studies of psychotherapy lend support to the Dodo bird hypothesis—all "win" and all must have "prizes." That is, although research strongly supports the notion that therapy works, no one therapy has been shown to be significantly better than the others (Hubble & Miller, 2004; Lambert, 2001; Luborsky & others, 2002; Wampold, 2001). These results suggest that individuals considering psychotherapy should find out all they can about the various treatments and think about which might best suit their personality and problem.

Prospective clients also want to know how long it will take them to get better. In one study, people in therapy showed substantial improvement over the first six months, with diminishing returns after that (Howard & others, 1996). In another study, individuals rated their symptoms, interpersonal relations, and quality of life on a weekly basis before each treatment session (Anderson & Lambert, 2001). Figure 16.8 shows that one-third of the individuals had improved outcomes by the 10th session, 50 percent by the 20th session, and 70 percent by the 45th session. In sum, psychotherapy benefits most individuals at least through the first six months of treatment and possibly longer.

FIGURE 16.8 Number of Therapy Sessions and Improvement In one study, a large number of people undergoing therapy rated their well-being (based on symptoms, interpersonal relations, and quality of life) before each treatment session (Anderson & Lambert, 2001). The percentage of people who showed improved outcomes after each additional session of treatment indicated that about one-third of the individuals recovered by the 10th session, 50 percent by the 20th session, and 70 percent by the 45th session.

Common Themes in Effective Psychotherapy

In this brief section, we look at some common threads in successful psychotherapy. After carefully studying the nature of psychotherapy for more than 25 years, Jerome Frank concluded that effective psychotherapies have the common elements of expectations, mastery, and emotional arousal (Frank, 1982; Frank & Frank, 1993). By inspiring expectations of help, the therapist motivates the client to continue going to therapy (Jennings & Skovholt, 1999). These expectations are powerful morale builders and symptom relievers in themselves (Arnkoff, Glass, & Shapiro, 2002). The therapist also increases the client's sense of mastery and competence (Brammer & MacDonald, 1999). For example, the client begins to feel that he or she can cope effectively with the world. Therapy also arouses the individual's emotions, an essential motivator for behavior change, according to Frank.

In addition, two specific underlying factors that have been shown to play a key role in successful therapy are the therapeutic alliance and client factors, as we now consider.

THE THERAPEUTIC ALLIANCE

The **therapeutic alliance** is the relationship between the therapist and client. This alliance is an important element of successful psychotherapy (Prochaska & Norcross, 2010; Strupp, 1995). Effective psychotherapy depends on the client's having confidence and trust in the therapist (Knapp, 2007).

In one study, the most common ingredient in the success of different psychotherapies was the therapist's supportiveness of the client (Wallerstein, 1989). The client and therapist engage in a healing ritual that requires the active participation of both parties (Figure 16.9). As part of this ritual, the client becomes more hopeful and less alienated. It also is important for therapists to monitor the quality of the relationships with each client. Clients of therapists who did not assess the quality of the alliance were two times more likely to drop out of therapy (Hubble & Miller, 2004). Among those who completed therapy, clients of therapists who failed to assess their alliance were three to four times more likely to have a negative outcome (Hubble & Miller, 2004).

THE CLIENT AS AN ESSENTIAL FACTOR

Meta-analytic studies of therapeutic outcomes have shown that one major factor in predicting effectiveness is the client. Indeed, the quality of the client's participation is the most important determinant of whether therapy is successful (Bohart & Tallman, 2010; McKay, Imel, & Wampold, 2006; Wampold, 2001). Even though individuals often seek therapy due to difficulties and problems in their life, it is their strengths, abilities, skills, and motivation that account for therapeutic success (Hubble & Miller, 2004; Wampold & Brown, 2005). A review of the extensive evidence on therapeutic efficacy concluded: "the data make abundantly clear that therapy does not make clients work, but rather clients make therapy work" (Hubble & Miller, 2004, p. 347). Therapy can be viewed as a mechanism for bringing clients' own strengths to the forefront of their life.

5- THERAPIES AND HEALTH AND WELLNESS

Therapy is generally aimed at relieving psychological symptoms. A therapy is considered effective if it frees a person from the negative effects of psychological disorders. Does therapy have larger implications related to a person's psychological wellness and even physical health? Researchers have examined this interesting question in a variety of ways.

For example, people who learn that they have cancer are undoubtedly under stress. Might psychotherapeutic help aimed at reducing this stress improve patients' ability to cope with the disease? New research is indicating that therapy is having such a positive effect. One study revealed that group-based cognitive therapy that focused on improving prostate cancer patients' stress management skills was effective in improving their quality of life (Penedo & others, 2006). Another study found that individual cognitive-behavior

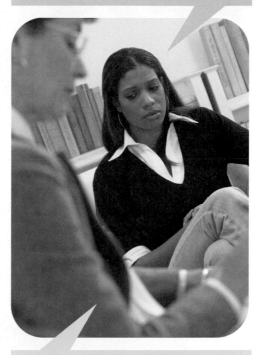

- Participates actively
- Draws on personal strengths, abilities, skills, and motivation
- Develops confidence and trust in therapist
- Becomes more hopeful and less alienated

- Participates actively
- Provides genuine support
- Monitors quality of relationship with client

FIGURE 16.9   Factors in a Successful Therapeutic Alliance This figure emphasizes the qualities and behaviors of therapists and clients that are essential to a successful therapeutic alliance and effective psychotherapy.

● **therapeutic alliance** The relationship between the therapist and client—an important element of successful psychotherapy.

test yourself

1. What are three general questions that people commonly ask about psychotherapy?
2. Describe the factors in a successful therapeutic alliance.
3. According to meta-analyses, what is a major factor in predicting the outcome of psychotherapy?

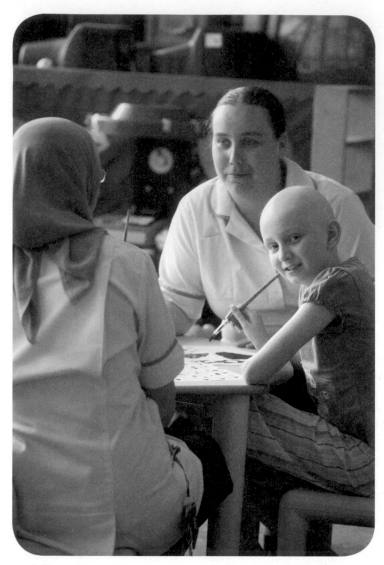

Psychotherapy can improve cancer patients' ability to cope with the disease.

therapy reduced symptom severity in cancer patients undergoing chemotherapy (Sikorskii & others, 2006).

As well, psychotherapy directed at relieving psychological disorders such as depression can have important benefits for physical health. Depression is associated with coronary heart disease, for example (Linke & others, 2009). Psychotherapy that reduces depression is likely, then, to reduce the risk of heart disease (K. W. Davidson & others, 2006). A research review also showed evidence of positive effects of psychotherapy on health behavior and physical illness, including habits and ailments such as smoking, chronic pain, chronic fatigue syndrome, and asthma (Eells, 2000).

Psychotherapy might also be a way to *prevent* psychological and physical problems. One study demonstrated the benefits of incorporating therapy into physical healthcare (Smit & others, 2006). Individuals waiting to see their primary healthcare provider received either physical health treatment as usual or that same treatment plus brief psychotherapy (a simple version of minimal contact cognitive-behavior therapy). The brief psychotherapy included a self-help manual, instructions in mood management, and six short telephone conversations with a prevention worker. The overall rate of depression was lowered significantly in the psychotherapy group, and this difference was cost effective. That is, the use of brief psychotherapy as a part of regular physical checkups was both psychologically and economically advantageous.

Finally, although typically targeted at relieving distressing symptoms, might psychotherapy enhance psychological well-being? This question is important because the absence of psychological symptoms (the goal of most psychotherapy) is not the same thing as the presence of psychological wellness. Just as an individual who is without serious physical illness is not necessarily at the height of physical health, a person who is relatively free of psychological symptoms still might not show the qualities we associate with psychological thriving. Studies have found that a lack of psychological wellness may predispose individuals to relapse or make them vulnerable to problems (Ryff & Singer, 1998; Ryff, Singer, & Love, 2004; Thunedborg, Black, & Bech, 1995). Research has demonstrated that individuals who show not only a decrease in symptoms but also an increase in well-being are less prone to relapse (Fava, 2006; Ruini & Fava, 2004).

Recently, therapists have developed a new type of treatment, aimed at enhancing well-being. **Well-being therapy (WBT)** is a short-term, problem-focused, directive therapy that encourages clients to accentuate the positive (Fava, 2006; Ruini & Fava, 2009). The first step in WBT is recognizing the positive in one's life when it happens. The initial WBT homework assignment asks clients to monitor their own happiness levels and keep track of moments of well-being. Clients are encouraged to note even small pleasures in their lives—a beautiful spring day, a relaxing chat with a friend, the great taste of morning coffee. Clients then identify thoughts and feelings that are related to the premature ending of these moments. WBT is about learning to notice and savor positive experiences and coming up with ways to promote and celebrate life's good moments. WBT is effective in enhancing well-being, and it may also allow individuals to enjoy sustained recovery from mental disorders (Fava, Ruini, & Belaise, 2007; Ruini & Fava, 2009; Ruini & others, 2006).

Life is complicated and filled with potential pitfalls. We all need help from time to time, and therapy is one way to get that help. Through therapy we can improve ourselves—physically and psychologically—to become the best person we can be. Like all human relationships, a therapeutic relationship is complex and challenging but potentially rewarding, making positive change possible for an individual through a meaningful association with another (Joseph & Linley, 2004).

● **well-being therapy (WBT)** A short-term, problem-focused, directive therapy that encourages clients to accentuate the positive.

test yourself

1. Discuss specific research findings about whether psychotherapy can improve a person's ability to cope with the effects of a disease such as cancer.
2. For what health-related behavior and chronic ailments is psychotherapy helpful, according to a research review?
3. What is well-being therapy, and what steps does it involve on the client's part?

1. BIOLOGICAL THERAPIES

Biological approaches to therapy include drugs, electroconvulsive therapy (ECT), and psychosurgery. Psychotherapeutic drugs that treat psychological disorders fall into three main categories: antianxiety drugs, antidepressant drugs, and antipsychotic drugs.

Benzodiazepines are the most commonly used antianxiety drugs. Antidepressant drugs regulate mood; the three main classes are tricyclics, MAO inhibitors, and SSRI drugs. Lithium is used to treat bipolar disorder. Antipsychotic drugs are administered to treat severe psychological disorders, especially schizophrenia.

Practitioners use electroconvulsive therapy to alleviate severe depression when other interventions have failed. Psychosurgery is an irreversible procedure in which brain tissue is destroyed. Though rarely used today, psychosurgery is more precise than in the days of prefrontal lobotomies.

2. PSYCHOTHERAPY

Psychotherapy is the process that mental health professionals use to help individuals recognize, define, and overcome their disorders and improve their adjustment. In Freudian psychoanalysis, psychological disorders stem from unresolved unconscious conflicts, believed to originate in early family experiences. A therapist's interpretation of free association, dreams, transference, and resistance provides paths for understanding the client's unconscious conflicts. Although psychodynamic therapy has changed, many contemporary psychodynamic therapists still probe the unconscious mind for early family experiences that might provide clues to clients' current problems.

In humanistic therapies, the analyst encourages clients to understand themselves and to grow personally. Client-centered therapy, developed by Rogers, is a type of humanistic therapy that includes active listening, reflective speech, unconditional positive regard, empathy, and genuineness.

Behavior therapies use principles of learning to reduce or eliminate maladaptive behavior. They are based on the behavioral and social cognitive theories of personality. Behavior therapies seek to eliminate the symptoms or behaviors rather than to help individuals to gain insight into their problems.

The two main behavior therapy techniques based on classical conditioning are systematic desensitization and aversive conditioning. In systematic desensitization, anxiety is treated by getting the individual to associate deep relaxation with increasingly intense anxiety-producing situations. In aversive conditioning, pairings of the undesirable behavior with aversive stimuli are repeated to decrease the behavior's pleasant associations.

In operant conditioning approaches to behavior therapy, a careful analysis of the person's environment is conducted to determine which factors need modification. Applied behavior analysis is the application of operant conditioning to change human behavior. Its main goal is to replace maladaptive behaviors with adaptive ones.

Cognitive therapies emphasize that the individual's cognitions (thoughts) are the main source of abnormal behavior. Cognitive therapies attempt to change the person's feelings and behaviors by changing cognitions. Three main forms of cognitive therapy are Ellis's rational-emotive behavior therapy (REBT), Beck's cognitive therapy, and cognitive-behavior therapy.

Ellis's approach is based on the idea that individuals develop psychological disorders because of their beliefs, especially irrational beliefs. In Beck's cognitive therapy, which has been especially effective in treating depression, the therapist assists the client in learning about logical errors in thinking and then guides the client in challenging these thinking errors. Cognitive-behavior therapy combines cognitive therapy and behavior therapy techniques. Self-efficacy and self-instructional methods are used in this approach.

As many as 50 percent of practicing therapists refer to themselves as "integrative" or "eclectic." Integrative therapy uses a combination of techniques from different therapies based on the therapist's judgment of which particular techniques will provide the greatest benefit for the client.

3. SOCIOCULTURAL APPROACHES AND ISSUES IN TREATMENT

Group therapies emphasize that relationships can hold the key to successful therapy. Family therapy is group therapy with family members. Four widely used family therapy techniques are validation, reframing, structural change, and detriangulation. Couples therapy is group therapy with married or unmarried couples whose major problem is within their relationship.

Self-help support groups are voluntary organizations of individuals who get together on a regular basis to discuss topics of common interest. They are conducted without a professional therapist.

The community mental health movement was born out of the belief that individuals suffering from psychological disorders should not be locked away from their families and communities. The deinstitutionalization that resulted from the movement caused the homeless population to rise, however. Empowerment is often a goal of community mental health.

Psychotherapies' traditional focus on the individual may be successful in individualistic Western cultures. However, individual-centered psychotherapies may not work as well in collectivistic cultures. Therapy is often more effective when there is an ethnic match between the therapist and the client, although culturally sensitive therapy can be provided by a therapist with a different background than the client's.

Psychotherapies' emphasis on independence and self-reliance may be problematic for the many women who place a strong emphasis on connectedness in relationships. To address that problem, feminist therapies have emerged.

4. THE EFFECTIVENESS OF PSYCHOTHERAPY

Using meta-analysis, researchers have found that psychotherapies are successful in treating psychological disorders. The Dodo bird hypothesis states that therapy works but that no therapy is conclusively more effective than any other. People considering psychotherapy should find out all they can about the various types of treatments and think about which might best suit their personality and problem.

The therapeutic alliance and client factors are two important variables that influence therapeutic success. The key to successful therapy may lie not in a particular therapist or technique but in the client. Although an individual may be in distress when beginning treatment, his or her internal resources and strengths are brought forth by therapy, as a result of which the individual might expect a healthier, more satisfying life.

5. THERAPIES AND HEALTH AND WELLNESS

Psychotherapy has been shown to help individuals cope with serious physical diseases. Psychotherapy can also aid individuals by alleviating physical symptoms directly or by reducing psychological problems, such as depression, that are related to physical illness. Research has shown moreover that brief psychotherapy may be a cost-effective way to *prevent* serious psychological disorders.

Psychotherapy aims not only at reducing the presence of psychological illness but also at enhancing psychological wellness and personal growth. Individuals who gain in wellness are less likely to fall prey to recurrent psychological distress. Interventions such as well-being therapy have been designed to promote wellness itself.

key *terms*

biological therapies, p. 522

antianxiety drugs, p. 522

antidepressant drugs, p. 523

lithium, p. 524

antipsychotic drugs, p. 524

electroconvulsive therapy (ECT), p. 526

deep brain stimulation, p. 527

psychosurgery, p. 528

psychotherapy, p. 528

psychodynamic therapies, p. 530

psychoanalysis, p. 530

free association, p. 530

interpretation, p. 530

dream analysis, p. 531

transference, p. 531

resistance, p. 531

humanistic therapies, p. 532

client-centered therapy, p. 532

reflective speech, p. 532

behavior therapies, p. 533

systematic desensitization, p. 533

cognitive therapies, p. 535

rational-emotive behavior therapy (REBT), p. 535

cognitive-behavior therapy, p. 538

integrative therapy, p. 539

group therapy, p. 541

family therapy, p. 541

couples therapy, p. 541

therapeutic alliance, p. 547

well-being therapy (WBT), p. 548

apply your *knowledge*

1. To experience Rogerian therapy firsthand, watch a video of Carl Rogers describing his approach and participating in a session with a client at http://www.viddler.com/explore/digizen/videos/14/.

2. The Beck Institute maintains a website chronicling the latest developments in cognitive therapy and including a variety of videos of Beck himself. Check out the site at http://www.beckinstituteblog.org/.

3. Behavioral and cognitive approaches may be helpful in modifying a behavior that would not be considered abnormal but that an individual might still want to change (for example, procrastinating, eating unhealthy food, or watching too much TV). Think about a behavior that you would like to do more or less frequently; then imagine that you are a behavior therapist or a cognitive therapist, and describe the kinds of recommendations you might make during a therapy session.

4. For which kinds of problems would you be most likely to choose one of the sociocultural approaches to therapy? Which method would you choose? Do some research and see whether you can find a local group or therapist who would be helpful to someone with these kinds of problems. Where would you turn if an appropriate resource were not available in your area?

CHAPTER 17

Health Psychology

Does It Take a Village to Lose Weight?

Troubled by the growing problem of childhood obesity, Mayor Margaret Finlay of Duarte, California, issued a challenge in February 2010 for city residents to start losing weight (Sand, 2010). Increasingly, U.S. community leaders are recognizing that the obesity epidemic requires immediate action. Their counterparts around the world share these concerns, as the problem of obesity has reached global proportions.

Some localities have formed community weight-loss clubs through churches and other organizations. In Ghent, Belgium, the city council declared their community officially vegetarian (at least one day a week) in order to reduce obesity as well as the city's environmental footprint (Mason, 2009). Advocates for change are charging that by making life too easy and far too accommodating to cars and drivers, urban designers have created an *obesogenic* (obesity-promoting) environment—a context where it is quite challenging for people to engage in healthy activities (Henderson, 2008). Countries such as the Netherlands and Denmark have adopted urban planning strategies that promote walking and biking and discourage car use. As a result, in the Netherlands, 60 percent of all journeys taken by people over age 60 are by bicycle (Henderson, 2008).

Embracing a healthy lifestyle is a choice that is made not only by individuals but sometimes by whole communities. Clearly, our physical health is influenced by our contexts, behaviors, motivations, thoughts, and feelings—in other words, by factors at the very heart of the science of psychology. ●

PREVIEW

In this chapter, we focus on health psychology: the field devoted to promoting healthy practices and understanding the psychological processes that underlie health and illness. We begin by defining the field. Then we examine the various ways that psychologists explain the process of making healthy life changes and the resources on which individuals can draw to effect positive change. Next we survey what psychologists know about stress and coping, and we consider psychological perspectives on making wise choices in three vital areas: physical activity, diet, and the decision to smoke or not to smoke. We end with a look at psychology's role in shaping a good life.

1· HEALTH PSYCHOLOGY AND BEHAVIORAL MEDICINE

● **health psychology** A subfield of psychology that emphasizes psychology's role in establishing and maintaining health and preventing and treating illness.

● **behavioral medicine** An interdisciplinary field that focuses on developing and integrating behavioral and biomedical knowledge to promote health and reduce illness; overlaps with health psychology.

Health psychology emphasizes psychology's role in establishing and maintaining health and preventing and treating illness. This subfield of psychology reflects the belief that lifestyle choices, behaviors, and psychological characteristics can play important roles in health (Suls, Davidson, & Kaplan, 2010; Taylor, 2011). A related discipline, **behavioral medicine,** is an interdisciplinary field that focuses on developing and integrating behavioral and biomedical knowledge to promote health and reduce illness. The concerns of health psychology and behavioral medicine overlap: Health psychology primarily focuses on behavioral, social, and cognitive influences (Brannon & Feist, 2010; Norris & others, 2009), whereas behavioral medicine centers on behavioral, social, and biomedical factors (Mann & others, 2009).

Health psychology and behavioral medicine both inform two related fields: health promotion and public health. *Health promotion* involves helping people change their lifestyle to optimize health and assisting them in achieving balance in physical, emotional, social, spiritual, and intellectual health and wellness. *Public health* is concerned with studying health and disease in large populations to guide policymakers. Public health experts identify public health concerns, set priorities, and design interventions for health promotion. An important goal of public health is to ensure that all populations have access to cost-effective healthcare and health promotion services. If you have seen a "Click It or Ticket" sign on the highway or one of thetruth.com's antismoking ads on TV, you have a good feel for what health promotion and public health are all about.

The "Click It or Ticket" program, publicizing seatbelt use, reflects the efforts of individuals working in the related fields of health promotion and health psychology.

The Biopsychosocial Model

The interests of health psychologists and behavioral medicine researchers are broad (Baker & others, 2009; Gurung, 2010). The biopsychosocial model we examined in Chapter 15 in the context of psychological disorders applies to health psychology as well, because health psychology integrates biological, psychological, and social factors in health (Mihashi & others, 2009).

For example, stress is a focal point of study across the broad field of psychology. Study of the brain and behavior (Chapter 3 of this book), for instance, acknowledges the impact of stress on the autonomic nervous system. Furthermore, an individual's state of consciousness (Chapter 5), as well as the particular ways in which that person thinks about events (Chapter 8), can influence the experience of stress. Stressful events also affect our emotions (Chapter 10), which are themselves psychological and physical events. Aspects of our personalities, too, may be associated with stress (Chapter 12) and can influence our health. Finally, social contexts, relationships (Chapter 13), and work experiences (Chapter 14) can shape both an individual's experience of stress and his or her ability to cope with it.

The Relationship Between Mind and Body

From the biopsychosocial perspective, the many diverse aspects of the person are strongly intertwined. Our bodies and minds are deeply connected, a link introduced in Chapter 1. After suffering a heart attack, one health psychologist ruefully noted that none of his colleagues in the field had thought to ask him whether heart disease was part of his family history, ignoring the obvious question that a medical doctor would ask first. Although the mind is responsible for much of what happens in the body, it is not the only factor. Even as we consider the many ways that psychological processes contribute to health and disease, we must understand that sometimes illness happens for other reasons—affecting even those who have led healthy lives.

Although it might be more exciting to think about ways the mind may influence health, it is important to appreciate that the body may influence the mind as well. That is, how we feel physically may have implications for how we think. Health psychology and behavioral medicine are concerned not only with how psychological states influence health, but also with how health and illness may influence the person's psychological experience, including cognitive abilities, stress, and coping (Holsboer & Ising, 2010; Mellon & others, 2009). For instance, one of the first symptoms experienced by someone with AIDS may be cognitive changes that are not immediately recognized as part of the disease. A person who is feeling psychologically run-down may not realize that the level of fatigue is in fact the beginning stage of an illness. In turn, being physically healthy can be a source of psychological wellness.

test yourself

1. What factors does the field of health psychology emphasize as keys to good health?
2. With what is the field of health promotion concerned?
3. Name three societal issues you might be concerned with if you worked in the field of public health.

2· MAKING POSITIVE LIFE CHANGES

One of health psychology's missions is to help individuals identify and implement ways they can effectively change their behaviors for the better (Norris & others, 2009; Taylor, 2011). **Health behaviors**—practices that have an impact on physical well-being—include adopting a healthy approach to stress, exercising, eating right, brushing one's teeth, performing breast and testicular exams, not smoking, drinking in moderation (or not at all), and practicing safe sex. Before exploring what health psychologists have learned about the best ways to make healthy behavioral changes, we focus on the process of change itself.

● **health behaviors** Practices that have an impact on physical well-being, such as adopting a healthy approach to stress, exercising, eating right, brushing one's teeth, performing breast and testicular exams, not smoking, drinking in moderation (or not at all), and practicing safe sex.

Theoretical Models of Change

In many instances, changing behaviors begins by changing attitudes. Psychologists have sought to understand specifically how changing attitudes can lead to behavioral changes.

A number of theoretical models have addressed the factors that probably play a role in healthy behavior changes. For example, the **theory of reasoned action** suggests that effective change requires individuals to have specific intentions about their behaviors, as well as positive attitudes about a new behavior, and to perceive that their social group looks favorably on the new behavior as well (Ajzen & Albarracin, 2007; Ajzen & Fishbein, 1980, 2005; Fishbein & Ajzen, 2010). If you smoke and want to quit smoking, you will be more successful if you devise an explicit intention of quitting, feel good about it, and believe that your friends support you. Icek Ajzen (pronounced "I-zen") modified the theory of reasoned action to include the fact that not all of our behaviors are under our control. The **theory of planned behavior** includes the basic ideas of the theory of reasoned action but adds the person's perceptions of control over the outcome (Ajzen, 2002). As we will see later, perceiving that one has control can have important implications for a number of life domains.

The theory of reasoned action and its extension, the theory of planned behavior, have accurately predicted whether individuals successfully engage in healthy behaviors (Ajzen & Manstead, 2007), including cancer screening (Ross & others, 2007), HIV prevention (Kalichman, 2007), prevention of smoking and marijuana use in youth (Guo & others, 2007; Lac & others, 2009), and exercise (B. H. Park & others, 2009). Other theories

● **theory of reasoned action** Theoretical model stating that effective change requires individuals to have specific intentions about their behaviors, as well as positive attitudes about a new behavior, and to perceive that their social group looks favorably on the new behavior as well.

● **theory of planned behavior** Theoretical model that includes the basic ideas of the theory of reasoned action but adds the person's perceptions of control over the outcome.

have stressed the importance of awareness of the health threats posed by potentially harmful behaviors such as smoking and unprotected sex (Floyd, Prentice-Dunn, & Rogers, 2000; Fry & Prentice-Dunn, 2006). Social cognitive theories emphasize the crucial role of beliefs about one's ability to make healthy changes, as well as of the individual's knowledge and skills (Bandura, 2008, 2009, 2010b). All theoretical models of health-related behavioral changes make predictions about the type of intervention that should be most successful in producing durable change.

The Stages of Change Model

● **stages of change model** Theoretical model describing a five-step process by which individuals give up bad habits and adopt healthier lifestyles.

The **stages of change model** describes the process by which individuals give up bad habits and adopt healthier lifestyles. The model breaks down behavioral changes into five steps, recognizing that real change does not occur overnight with one monumental decision (Prochaska, DiClemente, & Norcross, 1992; Prochaska, Norcross, & DiClemente, 1994) (Figure 17.1). Rather, change occurs in progressive stages, each characterized by particular issues and challenges. Those stages are

- Precontemplation
- Contemplation
- Preparation/Determination
- Action/Willpower
- Maintenance

PRECONTEMPLATION

The *precontemplation stage* occurs when individuals are not yet genuinely thinking about changing. They may not even be aware that they have a problem behavior. Individuals who drink to excess but are not aware that their drinking is affecting their work may be in this precontemplation phase. At this stage, raising one's consciousness about the problem is crucial.

FIGURE 17.1 Stages of Change Model Applied to Losing Weight The stages of change model has been applied to many different health behaviors, including losing weight.

Stage	Description	Example
Precontemplation 1	Individuals are not yet ready to think about changing and may not be aware that they have a problem that needs to be changed.	Overweight individuals are not aware that they have a weight problem.
Contemplation 2	Individuals acknowledge that they have a problem but may not yet be ready to change.	Overweight individuals know they have a weight problem but aren't yet sure they want to commit to losing weight.
Preparation/ Determination 3	Individuals are preparing to take action.	Overweight individuals explore options they can pursue in losing weight.
Action/Willpower 4	Individuals commit to making a behavioral change and enact a plan.	Overweight individuals begin a diet and start an exercise program.
Maintenance 5	Individuals are successful in continuing their behavior change over time.	Overweight individuals are able to stick with their diet and exercise regimens for 6 months.

A woman who smokes may find her consciousness raised by the experience of becoming pregnant. A man who is stopped for drunk driving may be forced to take a good look at his drinking. Similarly, overweight individuals may not recognize their problem until they see photos of themselves taken at a family reunion—or until they learn that an order of a McDonald's Big Mac, large fries, and large chocolate shake amounts to over 2,000 calories, the recommended adult caloric intake for an entire day.

Consciousness-raising sometimes comes from the media. If you have seen Morgan Spurlock's documentary film *Super Size Me,* you know how harmful fast food can be to your health. Spurlock ate every meal at McDonald's for a month. By the end of filming he felt ill, had gained weight (he jumped from 185 to 210 pounds), and could not wait for the experience to end. His doctors were appalled by his increasingly fatty liver, and his (vegan) girlfriend noted the decline in his sexual energy.

It is common for people in the precontemplation phase to deny that their current pattern of behavior is a problem. The individual might defend such behaviors, claiming that "I don't drink/smoke/eat that much." Those who are overweight may discover that they do eat "that much" when they start keeping track of calories.

CONTEMPLATION

In the *contemplation stage,* people acknowledge the problem but may not be ready to commit to change. As the name of the stage suggests, at this point individuals are actively thinking about change. They might engage in a reevaluation of themselves and the place of this behavior in their life. They understandably may have mixed feelings about giving up a bad habit. For example, how will they deal with missing their friends on a smoke break? Or going out drinking? Or packing a healthy lunch instead of heading to the drive-thru? They may weigh the short-term gains of the harmful behavior against the long-term benefits of changing. As we considered in Chapter 6, future rewards can be difficult to pursue when immediate pleasures beckon. Sure, it would be nice to be thinner, but losing weight is going to take time, and that hot fudge sundae is right there, looking very delicious. Nevertheless, in the contemplation phase, individuals may begin to separate themselves, mentally, from the typical overeater or smoker and start to define themselves as someone who is ready to change.

PREPARATION/DETERMINATION

At the *preparation/determination stage,* people are getting ready to take action. At this point, self-belief and especially beliefs about one's ability to "see it through" are very important. A key consideration in this stage is whether individuals truly feel they are ready to change. In a study of New Year's resolutions, readiness to change predicted success at achieving those resolutions (Norcross, Mrykalo, & Blagys, 2002).

During this stage, individuals start thinking concretely about how they might take on their new challenge. For example, they explore options of the best ways to quit smoking or drinking or to start an exercise program. Some smokers might consider trying a nicotine patch or participating in a support group for people trying to quit. Individuals who are seeking to lose weight might think about joining a gym to get regular exercise or setting the alarm clock for a 6 A.M. run.

ACTION/WILLPOWER

At the *action/willpower stage,* individuals commit to making a real behavioral change and enact an effective plan. An important challenge at this stage is to find ways to support the new, healthy behavior pattern. One approach is to find reinforcements or rewards for the new behavior. Individuals who have quit smoking might focus on how much better food tastes after they have given up cigarettes. Successful dieters might treat themselves to a shopping run to buy new, smaller-size clothes. Acknowledging, enjoying, and celebrating accomplishments can motivate consistent behavior.

"Every year it's the same thing. I resolve to lose a ton, and you say you're going to control your anger."

© Ralph Hagen. www.CartoonStock.com.

Another source of support for new behaviors is the individual's social network (Taylor, 2011). Friends, family, and even members of a support group can help through their encouraging words and supportive behaviors. Members of a family might all quit smoking at the same time or join the individual in physical activities or healthier eating.

Finally, people may focus on alternative behaviors that replace the unhealthy ones. Perhaps, instead of bar hopping, they join a group dedicated to activities not associated with drinking alcohol, such as a dance club or community theater group. In other words, effective change also means avoiding tempting situations.

MAINTENANCE

In the *maintenance stage,* individuals successfully avoid temptation and consistently pursue healthy behaviors. They may become skilled at anticipating tempting situations and avoid them or actively prepare for them. If smokers seeking to kick the habit know that they always enjoy a cigarette after a big meal out with friends, they might mentally prepare themselves for that temptation before going out. Successful dieters might post a consciousness-raising photograph on the refrigerator.

At some point, people in maintenance may find that actively fighting the urge to indulge in unhealthy behaviors is no longer necessary. *Transcendence* means that they are no longer consciously engaged in maintaining their healthy lifestyle; rather, the lifestyle has become a part of who they are. They are now nonsmokers, healthy eaters, or committed runners.

RELAPSE

● **relapse** A return to former unhealthy patterns.

One challenge during the maintenance stage is to avoid **relapse,** a return to the former unhealthy patterns. Contrary to popular belief, relapse is a common aspect of change. That is, for most people, real change takes many attempts. Relapse can be discouraging and can lead a person to feel like a failure. However, the *majority* of people who eventually do change do not succeed on the first try. Rather, they try and fail and try again, cycling through the five stages several times before achieving a stable healthy lifestyle. Consequently, individuals who are experts in health behavior change consider relapse to be normal (Prochaska & Norcross, 2010; Prochaska, Norcross, & DiClemente, 1994).

If you have ever tried to adopt a healthier lifestyle by dieting, starting an exercise program, or quitting smoking, you might know how bad you feel when you experience relapse. One slip, however, does not mean you will never reach your goal. Rather, when a slipup occurs, you have an opportunity to learn, to think about what led to the relapse, and to devise a strategy for preventing it in the future. Successful dieters, for example, do not let one lapse ruin the week. Individuals who successfully keep weight off are those who do not get too down on themselves when they relapse (Phelan & others, 2003).

EVALUATION OF THE STAGES OF CHANGE MODEL

The stages of change model has been applied successfully to a broad range of behaviors. These include cigarette smoking (C. L. Kohler & others, 2008; Schumann & others, 2006), exercise (Lippke & Plotnikoff, 2006), safe-sex practices (Arden & Armitage, 2008; Naar-King & others, 2006), marijuana use in teenagers (Walker & others, 2006), substance abuse more broadly (DiClemente, 2006; Migneault, Adams, & Read, 2005), and weight loss (MacQueen, Brynes, & Frost, 2002).

Although the stages of change model has proved to be relevant to a variety of behaviors, the model still has its critics (Brug & others, 2004; Joseph, Breslin, & Skinner, 1999). Some have questioned whether the stages are mutually exclusive and whether individuals move from one stage to another sequentially as has been proposed (Littrell & Girvin, 2002). For example, some individuals might feel themselves to be in both action/willpower and maintenance at the same time or may move from contemplation back to precontemplation. Critics of the model

BILL PROUD

"No, honestly, it's just diet and exercise."

also point out that it refers more to attitudes that change than to behaviors (West, 2005). Recall from Chapter 13 that the relationship between attitudes and behavior can be quite complex. Furthermore, all of the stages might be understood as promoting readiness to change rather than change itself (West, 2005).

Nevertheless, recent evidence suggests that the stages of change model does a good job of capturing the ways that individuals make positive life changes (Lippke & others, 2009; Schuz & others, 2009). Experts have argued that the stages of change model can be a tool for therapists who are trying to help clients institute healthy behavior patterns. Sometimes, sharing the model with individuals who are trying to change provides them with a useful language to use in understanding the change process, to reduce uncertainty, and to develop realistic expectations for the difficult journey ahead (Hodgins, 2005; Schuz & others, 2009).

3· RESOURCES FOR EFFECTIVE LIFE CHANGE

Making positive changes to promote health can be very challenging. Fortunately, we all have various psychological, social, and cultural resources and tools at our disposal to help us in the journey to a healthier lifestyle. In this section we consider some of the tools that can help us achieve effective change and, ultimately, a healthier life.

Motivation

Recall from Chapter 10 that motivation refers to the "why" of behavior. Motivational tools for self-change involve changing for the right reasons. Change is most effective when you are doing it for you—because you want to. An analysis of intervention programs aimed at reducing childhood and adolescent obesity found that a strong predictor of program success (that is, weight loss in the children and adolescents) was whether the participants had been required to join the program or had done so voluntarily (Stice, Shaw, & Marti, 2006). Those who had joined voluntarily were more likely to lose weight than their counterparts who had been required to join.

Self-determination theory, presented in Chapter 10, distinguishes between intrinsic motivation (doing something because you want to) and extrinsic motivation (doing something for external rewards). Research has shown that creating a context in which people feel more in control, more autonomous, and more competent is associated with enhanced outcomes for a broad array of health behaviors, including controlling diabetes through diet (Julien, Senecal, & Guay, 2009), quitting smoking (Gwaltney & others, 2009), and getting regular physical exercise (Hurkmans & others, 2010; Russell & Bray, 2010). Indeed, individuals are more likely to succeed in their New Year's resolutions if they approach them with a sense of both self-efficacy and autonomy—the latter meaning that they have chosen on their own to make a life change (Koestner & others, 2006).

Planning and goal setting are also crucial to making effective change. Researchers have found that individuals who are able to come up with specific strategies, or **implementation intentions,** for dealing with the challenges of making a life change are more successful than others at negotiating the road to change (Armitage, 2006; Gallo & others, 2009; Tam, Bagozzi, & Spanjol, 2010). Setting short-term, achievable goals also allows individuals to experience the emotional payoff of small successes along the way to self-change (R. F. Kushner, 2007). The dieter

test yourself

1. How does the theory of planned behavior expand upon, or extend, the theory of reasoned action?
2. Name and briefly describe the five stages of the stages of change model.
3. What positive advice would you give to someone who experiences relapse when dieting or trying to quit smoking?

● **implementation intentions** Specific strategies for dealing with the challenges of making a life change.

Children and adolescents who voluntarily join a weight-loss program are more likely to shed pounds than those who are required to join.

Health Psychology and Motivation: Why Do We Do the Things We Shouldn't Do?

Motivation can be a powerful force for positive life change. What about behaviors that are not so positive, however, such as drinking too much, smoking, and having unsafe sex? Are these behaviors motivated as well? Health psychologists recognize that probing the motives that guide even unhealthy behavior is important for understanding, changing, and preventing these behaviors.

Some health psychologists have been especially interested in analyzing why individuals consume alcohol. Lynne Cooper and her colleagues have identified three motivations for drinking (Cooper, 1994; Cooper & others, 1992):

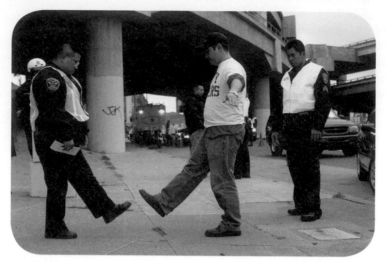

- *Social motives* include drinking alcohol because it is what your friends do or because you want to be sociable.
- *Coping motives* center on drinking alcohol to help you relax, to deal with stress, or to forget your worries.
- *Enhancement motives* include drinking because it is fun, because you like how it feels, or because it is exciting.

Research has shown that young adults most commonly drink for social reasons, with enhancement motives coming in a distant second (Kuntsche & others, 2006). Like enhancement motives, coping motives are not as common in young adults. Although all three motives for drinking are related to higher levels of drinking frequency (with enhancement motives being especially linked to drinking for men—Cooper & others, 1992), the motives that drive drinking can have implications for whether the behavior is harmful or harmless. Drinking to cope with life's negative events is typically associated with negative outcomes, such as social and work problems or potential substance abuse.

Research has related drinking motives to difficulties an individual might experience in reducing alcohol consumption. Individuals who drink because of coping or enhancement motives—that is, for internal reasons—are more likely to experience preoccupation with drinking when they try to limit their alcohol consumption (Stewart & Chambers, 2000).

Researchers conclude that motivation is a factor even in behaviors that might seem obviously self-defeating, such as smoking and unsafe sex (Cooper, 2010; Cooper & others, 2006, 2008; Gynther & others, 1999). Although this Intersection has focused primarily on young adults, examining the motives that drive unhealthy behavior patterns can be useful for anyone, at any age or life stage.

Viewing maladaptive behavior from a motivational perspective helps us not only to understand the "why" behind those behaviors but also to think about how we might meet our needs for social interaction, coping, and enhancement without alcohol (or cigarettes or unsafe sex). If you recognize that you drink—and occasionally drink too much—because of a desire for positive social interactions, you might think about ways to enjoy your social network without putting your health at risk.

What motives might underlie unhealthy behaviors in your own life?

who can take her skinny jeans out of the closet and zip them up is likely to feel a sense of accomplishment. The novice exerciser who catches a glimpse of his new biceps in the mirror gets a mood boost. These feelings of satisfaction can help to motivate continued effort toward achieving important health goals (Finch & others, 2005).

Enjoying the payoffs of our efforts to change also means that we must monitor our goal progress (Stadler, Oettingen, & Gollwitzer, 2010). As those who have watched *The Biggest Loser* will attest, stepping on a scale can be a scary prospect for someone who is trying to lose weight. However, it is important to get feedback on progress in the pursuit of any goal. If an individual finds out that she is falling short, she can try to identify areas that need work. If on the other hand she discovers that she is doing well, it is a potent motivator for future progress.

As we have seen, motivation is instrumental to engaging in healthier behaviors. For further insight into its influence on health, see the Intersection.

Social Relationships

One way that social connections make a difference in our lives is through social support. **Social support** is information and feedback from others indicating that one is loved and cared for, esteemed and valued, and included in a network of communication and mutual obligation. Social support has three types of benefits: tangible assistance, information, and emotional support (Taylor, 2011):

- *Tangible assistance:* Family and friends can provide goods and services in stressful circumstances. For example, gifts of food are often given after a death in the family occurs, so that bereaved family members will not have to cook at a time when their energy and motivation are low.

- *Information:* Individuals who provide support can also recommend specific actions and plans to help the person under stress cope more successfully. Friends may notice that a co-worker is overloaded with work and suggest ways for him or her to manage time or to delegate tasks more effectively.

- *Emotional support:* In stressful situations, individuals often suffer emotionally and may develop depression, anxiety, and loss of self-esteem. Friends and family can reassure the person under stress that he or she is valuable and loved. Knowing that others care allows a person to manage stress with greater assurance.

One way that people gain support during difficult times is through *social sharing*—turning to others who act as a sounding board or a willing ear. Individuals who are striving to make healthy life changes might join a group of others who are also struggling with the same issue. Such social sharing can also occur in online support groups.

Getting support from others is important, but *giving* support can have benefits, too. A study of 423 older adult couples who were followed for five years revealed how helping others benefits physical health (S. L. Brown & others, 2003). At the beginning of the study, the couples were asked about the extent to which they had given or received emotional or practical help in the past year. Five years later, those who said they had helped others were half as likely to have died. One possible reason for this finding is that helping others may reduce the output of stress hormones, an effect that improves cardiovascular health and strengthens the immune system (Cacioppo, Berntson, & Aue, 2010; Decety & Cacioppo, 2011; Hawkley & others, 2010; Norman & others, 2010).

Experiencing the emotional payoff of small successes is important in achieving long-term goals. Being able to zip up skinny jeans, for example, gives a dieter a sense of accomplishment.

● **social support** Information and feedback from others indicating that one is loved and cared for, esteemed and valued, and included in a network of communication and mutual obligation.

Both getting and giving support can benefit individuals.

psychological *inquiry*

Healthy lifestyle
Not smoking, drinking moderately or not at all, walking regularly, wearing seatbelts, etc.

Social support
Membership in a faith community, availability of help in times of need, buffer against loneliness

Religious faith

Sense of life meaning
Maintaining one's perspective, keeping a big-picture view on life's problems

Buffer against the effects of stress
Hope and motivation for positive life change, slower disease progression, protection against job burnout

Better health

Longer life

Praying for Good Health

This figure presents a model of the relationship between religious faith and health and longevity. Notice that the placement of the boxes and arrows suggests that religious faith has its influence on health through four intervening variables. Answer the questions below:

1. Of the four factors included in this model, which do you think is most important? Why?
2. Give another variable that ought to be added to this model. Where would it be placed?
3. According to this model, religious faith "comes first," and the other four variables are consequences of religious involvement. Do you think this schema is accurate, or would you change the placement of any of the variables? Explain.
4. How might this model be applied to individuals who are not religious at all?

Religious Faith

Religious faith is strongly related to the maintenance of a healthy lifestyle and to good health (Sapp, 2010; Waddell & Jacobs-Lawson, 2010). Many religions frown on excess and promote moderation. Indeed, weekly religious attendance relates to a host of healthy behaviors, including not smoking, taking vitamins, walking regularly, wearing seatbelts, exercising strenuously, sleeping soundly, and drinking moderately or not at all (T. D. Hill & others, 2006). A number of studies have definitively linked religious participation to a longer and healthier life (Campbell, Yoon, & Johnstone, 2010; Hummer & others, 2004; Krause, 2006; McCullough & Willoughby, 2009; McCullough & others, 2000). For example, a recent study revealed that religious affiliation, frequent attendance at religious services, and religious strength and comfort were linked to reduced risk of premature death from any cause (Schnall & others, 2010). The Psychological Inquiry above breaks down the various factors that might play a role in the association between religious faith and health.

Religious participation may also benefit health through its relation to social support (George, 2009; Taylor, 2011). Belonging to a faith community may give people access to a warm group of others who are available during times of need. This community is "there" to provide transportation to the doctor, to check in with the individual during hard times, and simply to stand next to the individual during a worship service, as a fellow member of the community. The social connections promoted by religious activity can forestall anxiety and depression and can help to prevent isolation and loneliness (Rosmarin, Krumrei, & Andersson, 2009; Ross & others, 2009a).

Religious faith, and spirituality more generally, may also be important factors in good health because they provide a sense of life meaning and a buffer against the effects of stressful events (Emmons, 2005; C. Park, 2009). Religious thoughts can play a role in maintaining hope and stimulating motivation for positive life changes. For example, studies have shown that some individuals with AIDS who lived much longer than expected had used religion as a coping strategy—specific benefits came from participating in religious activities such as praying and attending church services (Ironson &

others, 2001)—and that an increase in spirituality after testing positive for HIV is associated with slower disease progression over four years (Ironson, Stuetzle, & Fletcher, 2006). Faith may also help individuals to avoid burnout at work (Murray-Swank & others, 2006) and to negotiate life's difficulties without feeling overwhelmed (Mascaro & Rosen, 2006). Belief in the enduring meaningfulness of one's life can help one keep perspective and see life's hassles in the context of the big picture (C. Park, 2009).

In summary, making positive life changes can be complex and challenging. Fortunately, though, we have powerful resources and tools to help us attain a healthier life.

test yourself

1. Name three tools or resources on which we can draw in trying to make positive life changes.
2. Discuss the importance of motivation in efforts at self-change.
3. Identify and describe three types of benefits provided by social support.

4· TOWARD A HEALTHIER MIND (AND BODY): CONTROLLING STRESS

Complete the following sentence: "I wish I could stop_____." If you could change one thing about your behavior, what would you choose? Would the change perhaps have to do with feeling stressed out much of the time? Maybe you wish you could quit worrying so much or stop facing every daily challenge with tension. Let's look at the problems that can arise when you feel chronically stressed and the ways you can better manage your stress.

Stress and Its Stages

As described in Chapter 3, *stress* is an individual's response to environmental *stressors,* the circumstances and events that threaten the person and tax his or her coping abilities. We often think of negative life events as stressful, but positive occasions—such as graduating from college, getting married, and starting a new job—can also produce stress if these events present significant changes. Hans Selye (1974, 1983), the founder of stress research, focused on the physical response to stressors, especially the wear and tear on the body due to the demands placed on it. After observing patients with different problems—the death of someone close, loss of income, arrest for embezzlement—Selye concluded that any number of environmental events or stimuli would produce the same stress symptoms: loss of appetite, muscular weakness, and decreased interest in the world.

General adaptation syndrome (GAS) is Selye's term for the common effects on the body when stressful demands are placed on it (Figure 17.2). The GAS consists of three stages: alarm, resistance, and exhaustion. Selye's model is especially useful in helping us understand the link between stress and health.

The body's first reaction to a stressor, in the *alarm stage,* is a temporary state of shock during which resistance to illness and stress falls below normal limits. In trying to cope with the initial effects of stress, the body quickly releases hormones that, in a short time, adversely affect the functioning of the immune system, our body's network of natural defenses. During this time the individual is prone to infections from illness and injury.

In the *resistance stage* of Selye's general adaptation syndrome, a number of glands throughout the body manufacture different hormones that protect the individual in many ways. Endocrine and sympathetic nervous system activity are not as high as in the alarm stage, although they still are elevated. During the resistance stage, the body's immune system can fight off infection with remarkable efficiency. Similarly, hormones that reduce the inflammation normally associated with injury circulate at high levels.

If the body's all-out effort to combat stress fails and the stress persists, the individual moves into the *exhaustion stage.* At this point, the wear and tear on the body takes its toll—the person might collapse in a state of exhaustion, and vulnerability to disease increases. Serious, possibly irreversible damage to the body, such as a heart attack, or even death may occur.

● **general adaptation syndrome (GAS)** Selye's term for the common effects of stressful demands on the body, consisting of three stages: alarm, resistance, and exhaustion.

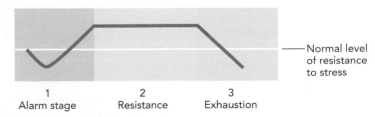

FIGURE 17.2   Selye's General Adaptation Syndrome The general adaptation syndrome (GAS) describes an individual's response to stress in terms of three stages: (1) alarm, in which the body mobilizes its resources; (2) resistance, in which the body strives mightily to endure the stressor; and (3) exhaustion, in which resistance becomes depleted.

● **hypothalamic-pituitary-adrenal axis (HPA axis)** The complex set of interactions among the hypothalamus, the pituitary gland, and the adrenal glands that regulates various body processes and controls reactions to stressful events.

● **psychoneuroimmunology** A new field of scientific inquiry that explores connections among psychological factors (such as attitudes and emotions), the nervous system, and the immune system.

The body system that plays the greatest role in Selye's GAS is called the **hypothalamic-pituitary-adrenal axis (HPA axis).** The HPA axis is a complex set of interactions among the hypothalamus (part of the brain's limbic system), the pituitary gland (the master gland of the endocrine system), and the adrenal glands (endocrine system glands that are located on top of each kidney). The HPA axis regulates various body processes, including digestion, immune system responses, emotion, and energy expenditure. The axis also controls reactions to stressful events, and these responses will be our focus here.

When the brain detects a threat in the environment, it signals the hypothalamus to release corticotropin-releasing hormone (CRH). In turn, CRH stimulates the pituitary gland to produce another hormone that causes the adrenal glands to release cortisol. Cortisol is itself the "stress hormone" that directs cells to make sugar, fat, and protein available so the body can take quick action. Cortisol also suppresses the immune system.

In Chapter 3 we distinguished between acute stress and chronic stress. Acute stress can sometimes be adaptive, and in acute stress cortisol plays an important role in helping us to take the necessary action to avoid dire consequences. Typically, once the body has dealt with a given stressor, our cortisol level returns to normal. However, under chronic stress, the HPA axis can remain activated over the long haul.

The activity of the HPA axis varies from one person to the next. These differences may be explained by genes as well as by particular stressful experiences (Hatzinger & others, 2010). Research with rats has shown that prenatal stress can influence the development of the HPA axis (Kjaer & others, 2010; Murray & others, 2010). When the HPA is chronically active, various systems in the body suffer, as we now consider.

Stress and the Immune System

Chronic stress can have serious implications for the body, in particular for the immune system. Interest in links between the immune system and stress spawned a new field of scientific inquiry, **psychoneuroimmunology,** which explores connections among psychological factors (such as attitudes and emotions), the nervous system, and the immune system (Kiecolt-Glaser, 2009, 2010; Leonard & Myint, 2009).

The immune system and the central nervous system are similar in their modes of receiving, recognizing, and integrating signals from the external environment (Sternberg & Gold, 1996). The central nervous system and the immune system both possess "sensory" elements, which receive information from the environment and other parts of the body, and "motor" elements, which carry out an appropriate response. Both systems also rely on chemical mediators for communication. CRH, the hormone discussed above, is shared by the central nervous system and the immune system, uniting the stress and immune responses.

A variety of research supports the idea that stress can profoundly influence the immune system (Bob & others, 2009; Grippo & Johnson, 2009; Ho & others, 2010). Acute stressors (sudden, stressful, one-time life events or stimuli) can produce immunological changes. For example, in relatively healthy HIV-infected individuals, as well as in individuals with cancer, acute stressors are associated with poorer immune system functioning (Pant & Ramaswamy, 2009). In addition to acute stressors, chronic stressors (long-lasting agents of stress) are associated with an increasing downturn in immune system responsiveness. This effect has been documented in a number of circumstances, including worries about living next to a damaged nuclear reactor, failures in close relationships (divorce, separation, and marital distress), and burdensome caregiving for a family member with progressive illness (Glaser & Kiecolt-Glaser, 2005; Gouin, Hantsoo, & Kiecolt-Glaser, 2009; Graham, Christian, & Kiecolt-Glaser, 2006).

Psychoneuroimmunology is a relatively young field. As it continues to develop, researchers hope to determine the precise links among psychological factors, the brain, and the immune system (Bauer, Jeckel, & Luz, 2009; Campbell & Edwards, 2009;

Kiecolt-Glaser & others, 2010). Preliminary hypotheses about the interaction that causes vulnerability to disease include the following:

- Stressful experiences lower the efficiency of immune systems, making individuals more susceptible to disease.
- Stress directly promotes disease-producing processes.
- Stressful experiences may cause the activation of dormant viruses that diminish the individual's ability to cope with disease.

These hypotheses may lead to clues for more successful treatments for some of the most challenging diseases to conquer—cancer and AIDS among them (Armaiz-Pena & others, 2009; Bormann & others, 2008).

Sheldon Cohen and his colleagues have conducted a number of studies on the effects of stress, emotion, and social support on immunity and susceptibility to infectious disease (Cohen, Doyle, & Skoner, 1999; Cohen & Janicki-Deverts, 2009; Cohen & Lemay, 2007; Cohen & others, 2009; Doyle & others, 2010; Janicki-Deverts, Cohen, & Doyle, 2010). Cohen and his colleagues (1998) found that adults who faced interpersonal or work-related stress for at least one month were more likely than their less-stressed counterparts to catch a cold after exposure to viruses. In the study, 276 adults were exposed to viruses and then quarantined for five days. The longer people had experienced major stress, the more likely they were to catch a cold. Individuals who reported high stress for the preceding two years tripled their risk of catching a cold (Figure 17.3). Those who experienced work-related stress for a month or longer were nearly five times more likely to develop colds than individuals without chronic stress. Those who experienced interpersonal stress for a month or more were twice as likely to catch a cold. Cohen concluded that stress-triggered changes in the immune system and hormones might create greater vulnerability to infection. The findings suggest that when we know we are under stress, we need to take better care of ourselves than usual, although often we do just the opposite (Cohen & Janicki-Deverts, 2009; Cohen & others, 2009; Doyle & others, 2010).

FIGURE 17.3 **Stress and the Risk of Developing a Cold** In a study by Cohen and others (1998), the longer individuals had a life stressor, the more likely they were to develop a cold. The four-point scale is based on the odds (0 = lower; 4 = higher) of getting a cold.

Stress and Cardiovascular Disease

There is also reason to believe that stress can increase an individual's risk for cardiovascular disease (Kibler, 2009; Williams & Davidson, 2009). Chronic emotional stress is associated with high blood pressure, heart disease, and early death (Schulz, 2007). Apparently, the surge in adrenaline caused by severe emotional stress causes the blood to clot more rapidly, and blood clotting is a major factor in heart attacks (Strike & others, 2006). Emotional stress also can contribute to cardiovascular disease in other ways. Individuals who have had major life changes (such as the loss of a spouse or another close relative and the loss of a job) have a higher incidence of cardiovascular disease and early death (Nakao, 2010; Taylor, 2011). A longitudinal study of involuntary job loss among workers 50 years and older over a 10-year period revealed that displaced workers have a twofold increase in the risk of developing a stroke (Gallo & others, 2006). Recall the Type A behavior pattern described in Chapter 12. Individuals who are Type A tend to be very reactive to stressful circumstances and to become hostile when frustrated.

The body's internal reactions to stress are not the only risk. People in a chronically stressed condition are more likely to take up smoking, start overeating, and avoid exercising. All of these stress-related behaviors are linked with the development of cardiovascular disease (Kodama & others, 2009; Patel & others, 2009).

Stress and Cancer

Given the association of stress with poor health behaviors such as smoking, it is not surprising that stress has also been related to cancer risk (Hamer, Chida, & Molloy, 2009). Stress sets in motion biological changes involving the autonomic, endocrine, and

FIGURE 17.4   NK Cells and Cancer
Two natural killer (NK) cells (*yellow*) are shown attacking a leukemia cell (*red*). Notice the blisters that the leukemia cell has developed to defend itself. Nonetheless, the NK cells are surrounding the leukemia cell and are about to destroy it.

immune systems. If the immune system is not compromised, it appears to help provide resistance to cancer and slow its progress. Researchers have found, however, that the physiological effects of stress inhibit a number of cellular immune responses (Anderson, Golden-Kreutz, & DiLillo, 2001). Cancer patients show diminished natural killer (NK)-cell activity in the blood (Bagnara & others, 2009) (Figure 17.4). Low NK-cell activity is linked with the development of further malignancies, and the length of survival for the cancer patient is related to NK-cell activity (Cho & Campana, 2009).

Thus, stress is clearly a factor not only in immune system functioning and cardiovascular health but also in the risk for cancer. In light of these links, understanding the psychological processes by which individuals can effectively handle stressful circumstances is a crucial topic in health psychology (Faul & others, 2009).

Coping with Stress

What stresses you out? Stressors can be anything from losing irreplaceable notes from a class, to being yelled at by a friend, to failing a test, to being in a car wreck.

Although everyone's body may have a similar response to stressors, not everyone perceives the same events as stressful. Indeed, whether or not an experience stresses us out depends on how we think about that experience. As reviewed in Chapter 8, *cognitive appraisal* refers to an individual's interpretation of an experience either as harmful and threatening or as challenging, and the person's determination of whether he or she has the resources to cope effectively with the event. Coping means managing taxing circumstances, expending effort to solve life's problems, and seeking to master or reduce stress.

● **problem-focused coping** The coping strategy of squarely facing one's troubles and trying to solve them.

TYPES OF COPING

Research has identified two types of coping. **Problem-focused coping** is the cognitive strategy of squarely facing one's troubles and trying to solve them. For example, if you are having trouble with a class, you might go to the campus study skills center and sign up for a program to learn how to study more effectively. In taking this step, you have faced your problem and attempted to do something about it. Problem-focused coping might involve coming up with goals and implementation intentions, the problem-solving steps we examined earlier in this chapter. A recent meta-analysis revealed that problem-focused coping was linked to a lower level of psychopathology in such areas as anxiety, depression, eating disorders, and substance use disorders (Aldao, Nolen-Hoeksema, & Schweizer, 2010).

Emotion-focused coping involves responding to the stress that you are feeling—trying to manage your emotional reaction—rather than confronting the problem itself. In emotion-focused coping, you might avoid the source of your stress, rationalize what has happened to you, deny the problem is occurring, laugh it off, or call on your religious faith for support. If you use emotion-focused coping, you might avoid going to a class that is a problem for you. You might say the class does not matter, deny that you are having difficulty with it, joke about it with your friends, or pray that you will do better.

Although problem-focused coping is generally associated with better outcomes, in some circumstances emotion-focused coping can help a person deal with life's problems. Denial is one of the main protective psychological mechanisms for navigating the flood of feelings that occurs when the reality of death or dying becomes too great. For example, one study found that following the death of a loved one, bereaved individuals who directed their attention away from their negative feelings had fewer health problems and were rated as better adjusted by their friends, compared to bereaved individuals who did not use this coping strategy (Coifman & others, 2007). Denial can be used to avoid the destructive impact of shock by postponing the time when a person has to deal with stress. In other circumstances, however, emotion-focused coping can be problematic. Denying that your ex does not love you anymore keeps you from getting on with life. Yet emotion-focused coping may be useful in situations in which there is no solution to a problem, such as long-term grieving over the loss of a loved one. In such cases, the emotion itself might be the stressor.

Many individuals successfully use both problem-focused and emotion-focused coping when adjusting to a stressful circumstance. For example, in one study individuals said they used both problem-focused and emotion-focused coping strategies in 98 percent of the stressful encounters they face (Folkman & Lazarus, 1980). Over the long term, though, problem-focused coping rather than emotion-focused coping usually works best (Nagase & others, 2009).

Strategies for Successful Coping

Successful coping can improve even the most stressful situations. Several specific factors are associated with effective coping, including a sense of personal control, a healthy immune system, personal resources, and positive emotions.

When one is experiencing stressful life events, multiple coping strategies often work better than a single strategy, as is true with any problem-solving challenge (Folkman & Moskowitz, 2004). People who have experienced a stressful life event or a cluster of difficulties (such as a parent's death, a divorce, and a significant loss of income) might actively embrace problem solving and consistently take advantage of opportunities for positive experiences, even in the context of the bad times they are going through. Positive emotion can give them a sense of the big picture, help them devise a variety of possible solutions, and allow them to make creative connections.

Optimism can play a strong role in effective coping. Recall from Chapter 12 that optimism is the expectancy that good things are likely to occur in the future (Carver & Scheier, 2009; Solberg Nes, Evans, & Segerstrom, 2009). Having an optimistic view of what lies ahead tends to help people engage constructively with potentially threatening information (Aspinwall, 1998; Aspinwall & Brunhart, 1996; Aspinwall, Leaf, & Leachman, 2009; Aspinwall & Tedeschi, 2010a, 2010b). Lisa Aspinwall views optimism as a resource that allows individuals to address their problems. Optimists are more likely than others to seek out genetic testing in order to learn about their risk for disease (Aspinwall, Leaf, & Leachman, 2009). Furthermore, optimists face life's challenges from a place of strength, so, for instance, when an optimist finds out that tanning, a favorite pastime, is related to an elevated risk of skin cancer, the information is important but not overwhelming. In contrast, pessimists are already living in a bleak world and prefer not to hear more bad news.

Another personal quality that appears to promote thriving during difficult times is hardiness. **Hardiness** is characterized by a sense of commitment rather than alienation,

● **emotion-focused coping** The coping strategy that involves responding to the stress that one is feeling—trying to manage one's emotional reaction—rather than focusing on the problem itself.

● **hardiness** A personal quality characterized by a sense of commitment rather than alienation, and of control rather than powerlessness; a hardy person sees problems as challenges rather than threats.

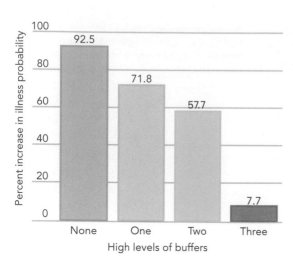

FIGURE 17.5 **Illness in High-Stress Business Executives** In one study of high-stress business executives (all of whom were selected for this analysis because they were above the stress mean for the entire year of the study), a low level of all three buffers (hardiness, exercise, and social support) involved a high probability of at least one serious illness in that year. High levels of one, two, and all three buffers decreased the likelihood of at least one serious illness occurring in the year of the study.

● **stress management program** A regimen that teaches individuals how to appraise stressful events, how to develop skills for coping with stress, and how to put these skills into use in everyday life.

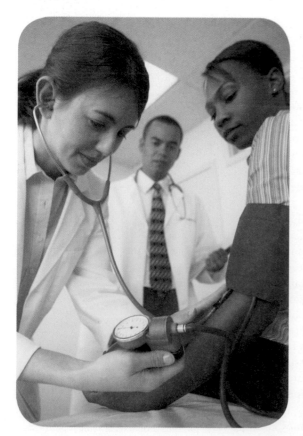

and of control rather than powerlessness; a hardy individual sees problems as challenges rather than threats (Maddi & others, 2006). Hardiness is exemplified by the basketball player whose team is down by two points with seconds remaining on the clock when he shouts, "Coach! Give me the ball!"

The links among hardiness, stress, and illness were the focus of the Chicago Stress Project, which studied male business managers 32 to 65 years of age over a five-year period (Kobasa, Maddi, & Kahn, 1982; Maddi, 1998). During the five years, most of the managers experienced stressful events such as divorce, job transfers, the death of a close friend, inferior performance evaluations at work, and reporting to an unpleasant boss. In one aspect of the study, managers who developed an illness, ranging from the flu to a heart attack, were compared with those who did not (Kobasa, Maddi, & Kahn, 1982). Those who did not were more likely to have hardy personalities. Another aspect of the study investigated whether hardiness, along with exercise and social support, provided a buffer against stress and reduced illness in executives' lives (Kobasa & others, 1986). When all three factors were present in an executive's life, the level of illness dropped dramatically (Figure 17.5).

Other researchers also have found support for the role of hardiness in illness and health (Heckman & Clay, 2005). The results of this research on hardiness suggest the power of multiple factors, rather than any single factor, in cushioning individuals against stress and maintaining their health (Maddi, 1998, 2008; Maddi & others, 2006).

Stress Management Programs

Nearly every day we are reminded that stress is bad for our health. "Avoid stress" may be a good prescription, but life is full of potentially stressful experiences. Sometimes just checking e-mail or answering a cell phone can be an invitation for stress. Sometimes, too, trying to manage stress on our own can be overwhelming. Thus, it makes sense to explore options for breaking the stress habit.

Because many people have difficulty in regulating stress, psychologists have developed various techniques that people can learn to apply themselves (Marshall, Walizer, & Vernalis, 2009; Willert, Thulstrup, & Hertz, 2009). **Stress management programs** teach individuals how to appraise stressful events, develop coping skills, and put these skills into use in everyday life. Effective stress management programs are generally based on the principles of cognitive-behavior therapy (Mercer, 2009), as described in Chapter 16. Some stress management programs are broad in scope, teaching a range of techniques to handle stress; others teach a specific technique, such as relaxation or assertiveness training (Fahey, Insel, & Roth, 2011).

Stress management programs are often taught through workshops, which are becoming more common in the workplace (Taylor, 2011). Aware of the costs in lost productivity due to stress-related disorders, many organizations have become increasingly motivated to help their workers identify and cope with the stressful circumstances in their lives. Colleges and universities similarly run stress management programs for students. If you are finding the experience of college extremely stressful and having difficulty coping with the pressures, you might consider enrolling in a stress management program at your school or in your community.

Do stress management programs work? In one study, researchers randomly assigned men and women with hypertension (blood pressure greater than 140/90) to one of three groups (Linden, Lenz, & Con, 2001). One group received 10 hours of individual stress management training; a second group was placed in a wait-list control group and eventually received stress management training; and a third group (a control group) received no such training. The two groups that received the stress management training showed significantly reduced blood pressure. The control group experienced no reduction in blood pressure. Also, the reduced blood pressure in the first two groups was linked to a reported decrease in psychological stress and improved ability to cope with anger.

Coping effectively with stress is essential for physical and mental health (Lim, Bogossian, & Ahern, 2010; Nagase & others, 2009). Still, there is a lot more we can do to promote our health. Healthful living—establishing healthy habits and evaluating and changing behaviors that interfere with good health—helps us avoid the damaging effects of stress (Frosch & others, 2009; Kodama & others, 2009). Just as the biopsychosocial perspective predicts, healthy changes in one area of life can have benefits that overflow to others. In the next section, we take a close look at habits and behaviors that directly influence our physical (and psychological) health and wellness.

5· TOWARD A HEALTHIER BODY (AND MIND): BEHAVING AS IF YOUR LIFE DEPENDS UPON IT

There's no escaping it: Getting stress under control is crucial for a healthy mind and body. Where health and wellness are concerned, it is also important to make wise behavioral choices when it comes to physical activity, diet and nutrition, and smoking.

Becoming Physically Active

Imagine that there was a time when, to change a TV channel, people had to get up and walk a few feet to turn a knob. Consider the time when people physically had to go to the library and hunt through card catalogs and shelves to find information rather than going online and Googling. As our daily tasks have become increasingly easy, we have become less active, and inactivity is a serious health problem (Carnethon & others, 2010; Puterman & others, 2010).

Any activity that expends physical energy can be part of a healthy lifestyle. It can be as simple as taking the stairs instead of an elevator, walking or biking to class instead of driving, going ice skating instead of to a movie, or getting up and dancing instead of sitting at the bar. One study of older adults revealed that the more they expended energy in daily activities, the longer they were likely to live (Manini & others, 2006).

In addition to being related to life expectancy, physical activity corresponds with a host of other positive outcomes, including a lower probability of developing cardiovascular disease (Lewis & others, 2010; Sui & others, 2009), diabetes (Colagiuri, 2010), weight loss in overweight individuals (Ades, Savage, & Harvey-Berino, 2010), improved cognitive functioning (Erickson & Kramer, 2009; Klusmann & others, 2010), positive coping with stress (Collins & others, 2009), and increased self-esteem (Hallal & others, 2006). Physical exercise has also been shown to reduce levels of anxiety (Rethorst, Wipfli, & Landers, 2009) and depression (Ryan, 2008).

Even a real pig can benefit from exercise; Figure 17.6 shows a hog getting a workout. In this study, a group of hogs was trained to run approximately 100 miles a week (Bloor & White, 1983). After training, the researchers narrowed the arteries that supplied blood to the hogs' hearts. Compared to a control group of untrained hogs, the jogging hogs developed extensive alternative pathways that provided a blood supply to their hearts. These results suggest that being physically active is like investing energy in a wellness bank account: Activity enhances physical well-being and gives us the ability to face life's potential stressors energetically.

Exercise is one special type of physical activity. **Exercise** formally refers to structured activities whose goal is to improve health. Although exercise designed to strengthen

test yourself

1. What is Selye's term for the pattern of common effects on the body when demands are placed on it?
2. How does the HPA axis function in regulating stress? How is the body affected when the HPA axis is chronically active?
3. What personality characteristic applies to an individual who faces difficulties with a sense of commitment and control, and who perceives problems as challenges rather than threats?

● **exercise** Structured activities whose goal is to improve health.

FIGURE 17.6   The Jogging Hog Experiment Jogging hogs reveal the dramatic effects of exercise on health. In one investigation, a group of hogs was trained to run approximately 100 miles per week (Bloor & White, 1983). Then the researchers narrowed the arteries that supplied blood to the heart. The hearts of the jogging hogs developed extensive alternate pathways for blood supply, and 42 percent of the threatened heart tissue was salvaged, compared with only 17 percent in a control group of non-jogging hogs.

psychological *inquiry*

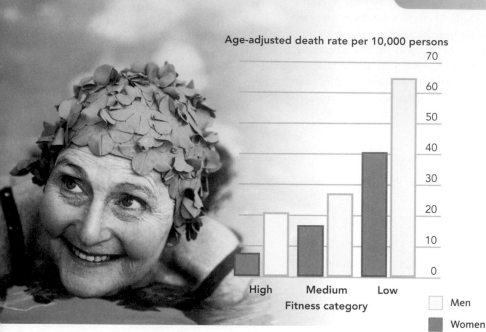

Age-adjusted death rate per 10,000 persons

(Fitness category: High, Medium, Low — Men and Women)

Physical Activity: A Matter of Life and Death

This graph shows the results of an 8-year-long longitudinal study of over 10,000 men and women (Blair & others, 1989). The X or horizontal axis shows the fitness level of participants, and the Y or vertical axis shows the death rates within those groups. Note that results are separated for men and women. Using the figure, answer the questions below.

1. Which groups had the highest and lowest death rates?

2. Comparing the results for men and women separately, what role does gender play in mortality? What might explain this difference?

3. Because this is a correlational study, the results cannot be assumed to show that a low fitness level causes mortality. What third variables might explain the relationship between activity level and mortality?

● **aerobic exercise** Sustained activity—jogging, swimming, or cycling, for example—that stimulates heart and lung functioning.

muscles and bones or to improve flexibility is important to fitness, many health experts stress the benefits of **aerobic exercise,** which is sustained activity—jogging, swimming, or cycling, for example—that stimulates heart and lung functioning.

In one study, exercise literally meant the difference between life and death for middle-aged and older adults (Blair & others, 1989). More than 10,000 men and women were divided into categories of low fitness, medium fitness, and high fitness. Then they were studied over eight years. Sedentary participants (low fitness) were more than twice as likely to die during the study's eight-year time span than those who were moderately fit, and more than three times as likely to die as those who were highly fit. The positive effects of physical fitness occurred for both men and women. The Psychological Inquiry above examines the study's results. Furthermore, a recent study revealed that adults aged 60 and over who were in the lowest fifth in terms of physical fitness as determined by a treadmill test were four times more likely to die over a 12-year period than their counterparts who were in the top fifth of physical fitness (Sui & others, 2007). This study also showed that older adults who were overweight but physically fit had a lower mortality risk over the 12 years than their normal-weight counterparts who were low in fitness. In addition, a recent study of more than 11,000 women found that low cardiorespiratory fitness was a significant factor for all causes of early mortality (Farrell & others, 2010).

One reason that exercise plays a role in how long people live may involve telomeres. Recall from Chapter 9 that telomeres protect the tips of chromosomes and become significantly shorter as individuals age; that shortening is theorized to be a main reason for aging (Davoli, Denchi, & de Lange, 2010; Sahin & DePinho, 2010). A recent study revealed that vigorous physical activity protected individuals who were experiencing high stress by reducing telomere shortening (Puterman & others, 2010).

Health experts recommend that adults engage in at least 30 minutes of moderate physical activity on most, preferably all, days of the week and that children exercise for 60 minutes. Most advise that you should try to raise your heart rate to at least 60 percent of your maximum rate. However, only about one-fifth of adults are active at these recommended levels of physical activity. Figure 17.7 lists examples

Moderate	Vigorous
Walking briskly (3–4 mph)	Walking briskly uphill or with a load
Swimming, moderate effort	Swimming, fast treading crawl
Cycling for pleasure or transportation (≤10 mph)	Cycling, fast or racing (>10 mph)
Racket sports, table tennis	Racket sports, singles tennis, racketball
Conditioning exercise, general calisthenics	Conditioning exercise, stair ergometer, ski machine
Golf, pulling cart or carrying clubs	Golf, practice at driving range
Canoeing, leisurely (2.0–3.9 mph)	Canoeing, rapidly (≥4 mph)
Home care, general cleaning	Moving furniture
Mowing lawn, power mower	Mowing lawn, hand mower
Home repair, painting	Fix-up projects

FIGURE 17.7 **Moderate and Vigorous Physical Activities** At minimum, adults should strive for 30 minutes of moderate activity each day. That activity can become even more beneficial if we "pump it up" to vigorous.

of the physical activities that qualify as moderate (and, for comparison, vigorous) activities.

Research suggests that both moderate and intense activities may produce important physical and psychological gains (Aihara & others, 2010; Paschalis & others, 2010). Some people enjoy intense exercise; others prefer moderate exercise. The enjoyment derived from exercise, added to its aerobic benefits, makes exercise one of life's most important activities.

One hint for becoming more physically active is not to limit yourself to only a few options. There are many activities that require physical exertion. Choose one that you genuinely like. Important factors in sticking to an exercise plan include self-efficacy, making active choices, and experiencing positive reinforcement and social support (Cress & others, 2005). Finding a buddy who is interested in working out with you might be a powerful motivator.

One often-welcome payoff for increasing physical activity is weight loss. Researchers have found that the most effective component of weight-loss programs is regular exercise (Duncan, 2010; Nagashima & others, 2010). Another way to combat weight problems is through changes in diet, our next topic.

Eating Right

The biggest health risk facing modern North Americans is being overweight or obese (Flegal & others, 2010). "Overweight" and "obese" are labels for ranges of weight that are greater than what experts consider healthy for an individual's height (Ogden & Carroll, 2010). In recent years, the percentage of individuals who are overweight or obese has been increasing at an alarming rate. As Figure 17.8 indicates, the prevalence of being overweight or obese in the United States changed little from 1960 to 1980 (Ogden & Carroll, 2010). However, the percentage of overweight and obese adults in the United States increased from less than 50 percent in 1960 to almost 70 percent in 2008. At

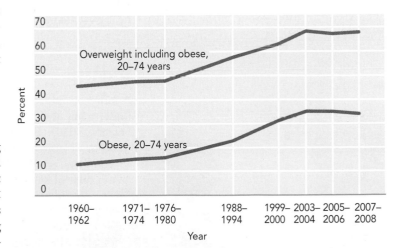

FIGURE 17.8 **Changes in the Percentage of U.S. Adults 20 to 74 Years of Age Classified as Overweight or Obese, 1960–2008** Obesity and overweight continue to be major public health concerns in the United States.

FIGURE 17.9 Comparison of Strategies in Successful and Unsuccessful Dieters Losing weight—and keeping it off—can be challenging, but reaching these goals is not impossible. Success in dieting depends on engaging in physical activity, planning meals, and monitoring progress.

this rate, it has been estimated that by 2030, the percentage of overweight or obese Americans could reach as high as *86 percent* (Beydoun & Wang, 2009).

Exercising regularly is one great way to lose weight (Fahey, Insel, & Roth, 2011). Making healthy dietary choices is another (Ross & others, 2009b). Eating right means eating sensible, nutritious foods that maximize health and wellness. Despite the growing variety of choices Americans can make in the grocery store, many of us are unhealthy eaters. We take in too much sugar and not enough foods high in vitamins, minerals, and fiber, such as fruits, vegetables, and grains. We eat too much fast food and too few well-balanced meals—choices that increase our fat and cholesterol intake, both of which are implicated in long-term health problems (Schiff, 2011).

Healthy eating does not mean trying out every fad diet that comes along but rather incorporating tasty, healthy foods into meals and snacks. Healthy eating is not something that people should do just to lose weight—it is about committing to lifelong healthy food habits. Several health goals can be accomplished through a sound nutritional plan. Not only does a well-balanced diet provide more energy, but it also can lower blood pressure and lessen the risk for cancer and tooth decay (Levitan, Wolk, & Mittleman, 2009; Wardlaw & Smith, 2011).

Losing weight and opting for healthier foods can be difficult, especially when one is just starting out. Many weight-loss fads promise weight loss with no effort, no hunger, and no real change in one's food consumption. These promises are unrealistic. Making genuine, enduring changes in eating behavior is hard work. This reality does not mean adopting a pessimistic attitude. Rather, positive expectations and self-efficacy are important because the task at hand is a challenging one.

The National Weight Control Registry is an ongoing study of people who have lost at least 40 pounds and kept it off for at least two years. Research on these successful dieters gives us important tips on how people who keep the weight off achieve this goal (Raynor & others, 2005).

Successful dieters also show consistency in what they eat, sticking to the same regimen even on the weekends and during the holiday season (Gorin & others, 2004). A study of approximately 2,000 U.S. adults found that exercising 30 minutes a day, planning meals, and weighing themselves daily were the main strategies of successful dieters (Kruger, Blanck, & Gillespie, 2006) (Figure 17.9).

The truth is that keeping weight off is an ongoing process. Moreover, the longer a dieter keeps the weight off, the less likely he or she is to gain it back (McGuire & others, 1999). The goal is difficult, but accomplishing it is a testament to the power of belief in oneself.

We have considered how exercise and nutrition can help individuals live healthily. In the Critical Controversy, we explore a question related to fitness, nutrition, and health—whether a person can be fat *and* fit.

Quitting Smoking

Another health-related goal is giving up smoking. Evidence from a number of studies underscores the dangers of smoking and being around smokers (American Cancer Society, 2010). For example, smoking is linked to 30 percent of cancer deaths, 21 percent of heart disease deaths, and 82 percent of chronic pulmonary disease deaths. Secondhand smoke is implicated in as many as 9,000 lung cancer deaths a year. Children of smokers are at special risk for respiratory and middle-ear diseases (Butz & others, 2010; Goodwin & Cowles, 2008).

Fewer people smoke today than in the past, and almost half of the living adults who ever smoked have quit. In 2008, 20.6 percent of all adults in the United States smoked, with men being more likely to smoke (23.1 percent) than women (18.3 percent) (National Center for Health Statistics, 2009). Although these numbers represent a substantial decline from 40 years ago, when 50 percent of men smoked, many individuals still smoke.

CRITICAL CONTROVERSY

Can You Be Fat and Fit?

What does a healthy body look like? During your spinning class, you notice that your instructor is overweight. Is she really healthy? Later, while watching your favorite baseball team, you check out the dugout. How many of the players are truly thin? Even Babe Ruth, perhaps the greatest baseball player of all time, was a rotund guy, known for his hearty appetite. One day at Coney Island, Ruth ate four steaks and eight hot dogs and drank eight sodas. The workout favored by "the Bambino" was generally limited to running the bases after hitting one of his many home runs.

Body weight is certainly an important factor in physical health. On the basis of longitudinal studies on large numbers of people, researchers have estimated that individuals who are obese at age 40 will live six to seven years less than their thin counterparts, and individuals who are overweight at 40 lose three years of life on average (Peeters & others, 2003).

How do we know if someone is overweight or obese? One of the most commonly used measures is the *body mass index* (BMI), which quantifies the relationship between a person's weight and his or her height (National Heart, Lung, and Blood Institute, 2009).

Figure 17.10 features a chart for determining BMI. Generally, body mass index gauges a person's weight in relation to his or her height. Measures of BMI may overestimate body fat in athletic individuals because muscle weighs more than fat. According to the Centers for Disease Control and Prevention (2009b), a healthy BMI for an adult ranges between 18.5 and 24. Overweight refers to a BMI that is greater than or equal to 25, and obese is greater than or equal to 30. (Babe Ruth's BMI? A solidly overweight 28.)

Another important factor in physical health and the risk for serious illness is fitness. *Cardiorespiratory fitness* (CRF) refers to the ability of the body's circulatory and respiratory systems to supply fuel during sustained physical activity. CRF, usually measured with a treadmill test, is increased by engaging in aerobic exercise regularly (Kodama & others, 2009).

One study that compared BMI and CRF challenged the notion that BMI is an important risk factor for disease (Lee, Blair, & Jackson, 1999). The researchers measured leanness, obesity, and CRF in nearly 22,000 men 30 to 83 years of age. The men were followed over eight years. During that time, 428 died. The researchers were interested in the contributions of weight and cardiorespiratory fitness to risk for death. Controlling for age, smoking, alcohol consumption, and parental history of heart disease, unfit lean men had double the risk of mortality of fit lean men, from all causes. Unfit lean men also had a higher risk of dying than *fit obese* men. Regardless of body size, unfit men were more likely to die than fit men.

Although the idea that one can be fat and still fit has popular appeal, the scientific community has been skeptical about its validity. A wide range of studies have examined whether being fit can compensate for being fat. Although research has supported the importance of CRF (Gerson & Braun, 2006), studies have not found support for the idea that fitness can compensate for being overweight (Duncan, 2010; Hu & others, 2004). Being fit does not protect a person from the health risks of being fat, and being thin does not protect the person from the risks associated with being unfit (Church & others, 2005; Sullivan & others, 2005).

The conclusion is that fitness and fatness are two independent predictors of health risk, and both have an impact on longevity. Can a

	Weight (pounds)													
	120	130	140	150	160	170	180	190	200	210	220	230	240	250
4'6"	29	31	34	36	39	41	43	46	48	51	53	56	58	60
4'8"	27	29	31	34	36	38	40	43	45	47	49	52	54	56
4'10"	25	27	29	31	34	36	38	40	42	44	46	48	50	52
5'0"	23	25	27	29	31	33	35	37	39	41	43	45	47	49
5'2"	22	24	26	27	29	31	33	35	37	38	40	42	44	46
5'4"	21	22	24	26	28	29	31	33	34	36	38	40	41	43
5'6"	19	21	23	24	26	27	29	31	32	34	36	37	39	40
5'8"	18	20	21	23	24	26	27	29	30	32	34	35	37	38
5'10"	17	19	20	22	23	24	26	27	29	30	32	33	35	36
6'0"	16	18	19	20	22	23	24	26	27	28	30	31	33	34
6'2"	15	17	18	19	21	22	23	24	26	27	28	30	31	32
6'4"	15	16	17	18	20	21	22	23	24	26	27	28	29	30
6'6"	14	15	16	17	19	20	21	22	23	24	25	27	28	29
6'8"	13	14	15	17	18	19	20	21	22	23	24	25	26	28

(Height on vertical axis)

■ Underweight ■ Healthy weight ■ Overweight ■ Obese

FIGURE 17.10 **Determining Your Body Mass Index** Body mass index is a measure of weight in relation to height. Anyone with a BMI of 25 or more is considered overweight, and people who have a body mass index of 30 or more (a BMI of 30 is roughly 30 pounds over a healthy weight) are considered obese. BMI has some limitations: It can overestimate body fat in people who are very muscular, and it can underestimate body fat in people who have lost muscle mass, such as the elderly.

person be both fat and fit? Yes, but fat and fit people are not as healthy as lean and fit people. Similarly, fat and fit people may be healthier than lean sedentary individuals. Essentially, research has shown that there are two avenues to pursue for optimal health: being physically active *and* maintaining a reasonable weight.

This controversy has highlighted the common tendency to equate a healthy body with a thin one. However, lean individuals who are inactive, smoke, drink to excess, or otherwise fail to take care of their bodies are not healthier than individuals who carry a few extra pounds but engage in vigorous exercise and otherwise take good care of themselves. A healthy body is more than a number on a scale or a slim silhouette in the mirror. As with most things in life, it is what's on the inside that counts.

WHAT DO YOU THINK?

- Find your BMI using Figure 17.10. What does it tell you about your health?
- If you had to work on one health goal, which would be easier—becoming fitter or losing weight? Why?

FIGURE 17.11 Fatal Lung Cancer and Years Since Quitting Smoking One study compared more than 43,000 former male smokers with almost 60,000 males who had never smoked (Enstrom, 1999). For comparison purposes, a zero level was assigned as the risk for fatal lung cancer for men who had never smoked. Over time, the relative risk for smokers who had quit declined, but even after 15 years it was still above that of nonsmokers.

"I told you smoking was bad for you."

© Adey Bryant. www.CartoonStock.com.

Quitting smoking has enormous health benefits. Figure 17.11 shows that when individuals quit smoking, their risk of fatal lung cancer declines over time. It is difficult to imagine that there is a person living today who is not aware that smoking causes cancer, and there is little doubt that most smokers would like to quit. However, their addiction to nicotine makes quitting a challenge. Nicotine, the active drug in cigarettes, is a stimulant that increases the smoker's energy and alertness, a pleasurable and reinforcing experience. In addition, nicotine stimulates neurotransmitters that have a calming or pain-reducing effect (Johnstone & others, 2006; Plaza-Zabala & others, 2010).

Research confirms that giving up smoking can be difficult, especially in the early days of quitting (Pilnick & Coleman, 2010). There are various ways to quit smoking (Fant & others, 2009; McRobbie & others 2010; Tong & others, 2010). Common methods include:

- *Going cold turkey:* Some individuals succeed by simply stopping smoking without making any major changes in their lifestyle. They decide they are going to quit, and they do. Lighter smokers usually have more success with this approach than heavier smokers.

- *Using a substitute source of nicotine:* Nicotine gum, the nicotine patch, the nicotine inhaler, and nicotine spray work on the principle of supplying small amounts of nicotine to diminish the intensity of withdrawal (Frishman & others, 2006). *Nicotine gum,* available without a prescription, delivers nicotine orally when an individual gets the urge to smoke. The *nicotine patch* is a nonprescription adhesive pad that releases a steady dose of nicotine to the individual. The dose is gradually reduced over an 8- to 12-week period. *Nicotine spray* delivers a half-milligram squirt of nicotine to each nostril. The usual dosage is one to two administrations per hour and then as needed to reduce cravings. The spray is typically used for three to six months. Success rates for nicotine substitutes are encouraging. All of these nicotine replacement therapies have been shown to enhance the chances of quitting and remaining smoke-free.

- *Seeking therapeutic help:* Some smokers get professional help to kick the habit. Therapies for quitting include prescribing medication such as antidepressants and teaching behaviorally based therapeutic techniques. Bupropion SR, an antidepressant sold as Zyban, helps smokers control their cravings while they ease off nicotine. Zyban works at the neurotransmitter level in the brain by inhibiting the uptake of dopamine, serotonin, and norepinephrine. Smokers using Zyban to quit have had a 21 percent average success rate after 12 months of taking the antidepressant (Paluck & others, 2006), which is similar to results for individuals using nicotine replacement. More recently, varenicline (trade name Chantix) has been approved to help smokers quit. This drug partially blocks nicotine receptors, reducing cravings and also decreasing the pleasurable sensations of smoking.

Varenicline, especially when combined with counseling/psychotherapy, is more effective for smoking cessation than buproprion SR (Garrison & Dugan, 2009;

Nides, 2008). For example, a recent study that combined varenicline with cognitive-behavior therapy resulted in a 58 percent smoking cessation rate after12 weeks (Ramon & Bruguera, 2009). One concern about the use of varenicline is an increase in suicide attempts by users of the drug. A recent study indicated this concern may pertain only to individuals with a history of suicide attempts before taking the drug and/or those experiencing a highly stressful event while taking the drug (Kasliwal, Wilton, & Shakir, 2009).

No one method is foolproof for quitting smoking (Fant & others, 2009). Often a combination of these approaches is the best strategy. Furthermore, quitting for good typically requires more than one try, as the stages of change model would suggest.

6· PSYCHOLOGY AND YOUR GOOD LIFE

In this chapter, we have examined how the mental and physical aspects of your existence intertwine and influence each other in dynamic ways. The field of health psychology serves to illustrate how all of the various areas of psychology converge to reveal that interplay.

As a human being, you are both a physical entity and a system of mental processes that are themselves reflected in that most complex of physical organs, the human brain. At every moment, both body and mind are present and affecting each other. Caring for your brain and mind—the resources that make it possible for you to read this book, study for tests, listen to lectures, fall in love, share with friends, help others, and make a difference in the world—is worthy of being a life mission.

Many pages ago, we defined psychology as the scientific study of behavior and mental processes, broadly meaning the things we do, think, and feel. Reflect for a moment on the psychological dimensions of vision, which we explored in Chapter 4. When we studied the human visual system, we examined the processes by which those amazing sense organs, our eyes, detect color, light, dark, shape, and depth. We probed the ways that the brain takes that information and turns it into perception—how a pattern of colors, shapes, and light comes to be perceived as a flower, a fall day, a sunset. Visual systems, we discovered, are generally the same from one person to the next. Thus, you can memorize the different parts of the human eye and know that your understanding is true for just about all the human eyes you will encounter in life.

However, even something as deceptively simple as perceiving a sunset through the sense of vision becomes amazingly complex when we put it in the context of a human life. Is that sunset the first you see while on your honeymoon, or right after a painful romantic breakup, or on the eve of the first day of your life as a new parent? Placing even the most ordinary moment in the context of a human life renders it remarkably complex and undeniably fascinating.

This fascination is one of the primary motivations for the science of psychology itself. From time immemorial, individuals have pondered the mysteries of human behavior, thought, and emotion. Why do we do the things we do? How do we think and feel? In this book, we have explored the broad range of topics that have interested psychologists throughout the history of this young science.

Coming to the close of this introduction to psychology allows you to look back but also ahead. It allows you to take stock of what psychology has come to mean to you now, as well as to consider what it might mean to you in the future. Whether or not you continue coursework in psychology, this book has highlighted opportunities for your future exploration about yourself and your world. In each of the real-life examples of human experience we have considered in the text—moments of heroism, weakness, joy, pain, and more—psychology has had a lesson to share with respect to the person that is *you*. Making the most of what you have learned about psychology means making the most of yourself and your life.

An everyday experience such as taking in and perceiving a sunset (or a painting of a sunset) becomes complex when we put it in the context of our life.

© Joseph Farris. www.CartoonStock.com.

SUMMARY

1. HEALTH PSYCHOLOGY AND BEHAVIORAL MEDICINE

Health psychology is a multidimensional field that emphasizes biological, psychological, and social factors in human health. Closely aligned with health psychology is behavioral medicine, which combines medical and behavioral knowledge to reduce illness and promote health. Related fields are health promotion, which is concerned with identifying ways to foster healthy behaviors, and public health, which focuses on understanding disease at the population level and directing public policy.

Health psychology and behavioral medicine demonstrate the biopsychosocial model by examining the interaction of biological, psychological, and social variables as they relate to health and illness. Stress is an example of a biological, psychological, and social construct.

Health psychology and behavioral medicine bring the relationship of the mind and body to the forefront. These approaches examine the reciprocal relationships between the mind and body: how the body is influenced by psychological states and how mental life is influenced by physical health.

2. MAKING POSITIVE LIFE CHANGES

The theory of reasoned action suggests that we can make changes by devising specific intentions for behavioral change. We are more likely to follow through on our intentions if we feel good about the change and if we feel that others around us also support the change. The theory of planned behavior incorporates these factors as well as our perceptions of control over the behavior.

The stages of change model posits that personal change occurs in a series of five steps: precontemplation, contemplation, preparation/determination, action/willpower, and maintenance. Each stage has its own challenges. Relapse is a natural part of the journey toward change.

3. RESOURCES FOR EFFECTIVE LIFE CHANGE

Motivation is an important part of sustaining behavioral change. Change is more effective when the person does it for intrinsic reasons (because he or she really wants to) rather than extrinsic reasons (to gain rewards). Implementation intentions are the specific ways individuals plan to institute changes successfully.

Social relationships are strongly related to health and survival. Social support refers to the aid provided by others to a person in need. Support can take the form of tangible assistance, information, or emotional support. Social support has been found to have strong relations to functioning and coping with stress.

Religious faith is associated with enhanced health. One reason for this association is that religions often frown on excess and promote healthy behavior. Religious participation also allows individuals to benefit from a social group. Finally, religion provides a meaning system on which to rely in times of difficulty.

4. TOWARD A HEALTHIER MIND (AND BODY): CONTROLLING STRESS

Stress is the response of individuals when life circumstances threaten them and tax their ability to cope. Selye characterized the stress response with his concept of a general adaptation syndrome (GAS), which has three stages: alarm, resistance, and exhaustion.

The hypothalamic-pituitary-adrenal axis (HPA axis) comprises the interactions among the hypothalamus, pituitary gland, and adrenal glands. This axis plays an important role in human responses to stress. Chronic stress takes a toll on the body's natural disease-fighting abilities. Stress is also related to cardiovascular disease and cancer.

Kicking the stress habit means remembering that stress is a product of how we think about life events. Coping may be divided into the categories of problem-focused coping and emotion-focused coping. Overall, problem-focused coping is more adaptive than emotion-focused coping. Hardiness is associated with thriving during stressful times.

5. TOWARD A HEALTHIER BODY (AND MIND): BEHAVING AS IF YOUR LIFE DEPENDS UPON IT

Exercise has many positive psychological and physical benefits. Tips for increasing one's activity level include starting small by making changes in one's routine to incorporate physical activity (such as walking instead of driving to school); trying a variety of activities to find something one likes; finding an exercise partner; and swapping exercise for sedentary activities such as TV viewing. Keeping track of progress helps the individual to monitor his or her goal progress.

Overweight and obesity pose the greatest health risks to Americans today. They can be largely avoided by eating right, which means selecting nutritious foods and maintaining healthy eating habits for a lifetime, not just while on a diet. A combination of healthy eating and exercise is the best way to achieve weight loss.

Despite widespread knowledge that smoking causes cancer, some people still smoke. Methods of quitting include going cold turkey, using a substitute source of nicotine, and seeking therapy. While difficult at first, quitting smoking can be achieved, though quitting for good usually takes more than one try. Usually a combination of methods is the best strategy for quitting.

6. PSYCHOLOGY AND YOUR GOOD LIFE

More than any other science, psychology is about you—understanding how you work. This book has aimed to show the relevance of psychology to your health and wellness and to help you appreciate the many, and deep, connections between this comparatively new science and your everyday life.

key *terms*

apply your *knowledge*

1. Take one day and become a stress detective. Every time a friend mentions how stressed out he or she is feeling, ask your friend to describe the source of the stress. What is the stressful event? How is the person appraising the event? How might he or she appraise the situation in ways that would help decrease stress?

2. Interview someone you know who has successfully lost weight, quit smoking, or started an exercise program. Ask the person about his or her experience of each of the stages of change. Does the theory fit your friend's experience? Why or why not?

3. Select one bad habit you would like to break for one week—for example, smoking, eating sugary foods, or putting off getting aerobic exercise. Keep a journal of your progress each day in avoiding the bad habit. How easy or difficult did you find this little test in healthy life change?

4. Search the web on the topic of stress management or coping with stress. Visit three or four sites and critically evaluate the suggestions made on the sites. How are they similar to the suggestions given in the text? How much information is available to evaluate the claims on the sites? Based on your critical evaluation, is the advice something you would follow or not? Explain.

5. One method that has helped to decrease unhealthy behaviors, such as smoking, is to make them more expensive. Some local governments have suggested imposing taxes on unhealthy foods, such as sugary soft drinks. Would such a tax be useful? Would you be in favor of such a tax, or opposed? Why?

6. Turn to the Table of Contents of this book. Consider which chapters or topics you found most interesting as you explored psychology. Go to your school's library and locate the journals that are devoted to that area (you can ask a librarian for help). Browse a recent issue of one of the journals. What kinds of topics are scientists studying? If a particular study described in this book sounded interesting, you can probably obtain it online. Do a Google "scholar" search on the authors and take a look at the original article. What did the authors conclude? What did you learn?

GLOSSARY

A

abnormal behavior Behavior that is deviant, maladaptive, or personally distressful over a relatively long period of time.

absolute threshold The minimum amount of stimulus energy that a person can detect.

accommodation An individual's adjustment of his or her schemas to new information.

acquired immune deficiency syndrome (AIDS) A sexually transmitted infection, caused by the human immunodeficiency virus (HIV), that destroys the body's immune system.

acquisition The initial learning of the connection between the unconditioned stimulus and the conditioned stimulus when these two stimuli are paired.

action potential The brief wave of positive electrical charge that sweeps down the axon.

activation-synthesis theory Theory that dreaming occurs when the cerebral cortex synthesizes neural signals generated from activity in the lower part of the brain and that dreams result from the brain's attempts to find logic in random brain activity that occurs during sleep.

addiction Either a physical or a psychological dependence, or both, on a drug.

adrenal glands Glands at the top of each kidney that are responsible for regulating moods, energy level, and the ability to cope with stress.

aerobic exercise Sustained activity—jogging, swimming, or cycling, for example—that stimulates heart and lung functioning.

affectionate love Also called companionate love; love that occurs when individuals desire to have another person near and have a deep, caring affection for the person.

affective commitment A kind of job commitment deriving from the employee's emotional attachment to the workplace.

afferent nerves Also called sensory nerves; nerves that carry information about the external environment *to* the brain and spinal cord via sensory receptors.

aggression Behaviors that are intended to harm another person.

alcoholism A disorder that involves long-term, repeated, uncontrolled, compulsive, and excessive use of alcoholic beverages and that impairs the drinker's health and social relationships.

algorithms Strategies—including formulas, instructions, and the testing of all possible solutions—that guarantee a solution to a problem.

all-or-nothing principle The principle that once the electrical impulse reaches a certain level of intensity (its threshold), it fires and moves all the way down the axon without losing any intensity.

altruism Unselfish interest in helping another person.

amnesia The loss of memory.

amygdala An almond-shaped structure within the base of the temporal lobe that is involved in the discrimination of objects that are necessary for the organism's survival, such as appropriate food, mates, and social rivals.

androgens The main class of male sex hormones.

androgynous Having attributes that we typically associate with both genders.

anorexia nervosa Eating disorder that involves the relentless pursuit of thinness through starvation.

anterograde amnesia A memory disorder that affects the retention of new information and events.

antianxiety drugs Commonly known as tranquilizers, drugs that reduce anxiety by making individuals calmer and less excitable.

antidepressant drugs Drugs that regulate mood.

antipsychotic drugs Powerful drugs that diminish agitated behavior, reduce tension, decrease hallucinations, improve social behavior, and produce better sleep patterns in individuals with a severe psychological disorder, especially schizophrenia.

antisocial personality disorder (ASPD) A psychological disorder characterized by guiltlessness, law-breaking, exploitation of others, irresponsibility, and deceit.

anxiety disorders Psychological disorders involving fears that are uncontrollable, disproportionate to the actual danger the person might be in, and disruptive of ordinary life.

apparent movement The perception that a stationary object is moving.

applied behavior analysis Also called behavior modification, the use of operant conditioning principles to change human behavior.

archetypes Jung's term for emotionally laden ideas and images in the collective unconscious that have rich and symbolic meaning for all people.

artificial intelligence (AI) A scientific field that focuses on creating machines capable of performing activities that require intelligence when they are done by people.

assimilation An individual's incorporation of new information into existing knowledge.

association cortex Sometimes called association areas, the region of the cerebral cortex that is the site of the highest intellectual functions, such as thinking and problem solving.

associative learning Learning that occurs when we make a connection, or an association, between two events.

Atkinson-Shiffrin theory Theory stating that memory storage involves three separate systems: sensory memory, short-term memory, and long-term memory.

attention The process of focusing awareness on a narrowed aspect of the environment.

attention deficit hyperactivity disorder (ADHD) One of the most common psychological disorders of childhood, in which individuals show one or more of the following: inattention, hyperactivity, and impulsivity.

attitudes Our feelings, opinions, and beliefs about people, objects, and ideas.

attribution theory The view that people are motivated to discover the underlying causes of behavior as part of their effort to make sense of the behavior.

auditory nerve The nerve structure that receives information about sound from the hair cells of the inner ear and carries these neural impulses to the brain's auditory areas.

authoritarian parenting A restrictive, punitive style in which the parent exhorts the child to follow the parent's directions and to value hard work and effort.

authoritative parenting A parenting style that encourages the child to be independent but that still places limits and controls on behavior.

autobiographical memory A special form of episodic memory, consisting of a person's recollections of his or her life experiences.

automatic processes States of consciousness that require little attention and do not interfere with other ongoing activities.

autonomic nervous system The body system that takes messages to and from the body's internal organs, monitoring such processes as breathing, heart rate, and digestion.

availability heuristic A prediction about the probability of an event based on the ease of recalling or imagining similar events.

aversive conditioning A form of treatment that consists of repeated pairings of a stimulus with a very unpleasant stimulus.

avoidance learning An organism's learning that it can altogether avoid a negative stimulus by making a particular response.

axon The part of the neuron that carries information away from the cell body toward other cells.

B

barbiturates Depressant drugs, such as Nembutal and Seconal, that decrease central nervous system activity.

basal ganglia Large neuron clusters located above the thalamus and under the cerebral cortex that work with the cerebellum and the cerebral cortex to control and coordinate voluntary movements.

base rate fallacy The tendency to ignore information about general principles in favor of very specific but vivid information.

behavior Everything we do that can be directly observed.

behavioral approach An approach to psychology emphasizing the scientific study of observable behavioral responses and their environmental determinants.

behavioral genetics The study of the inherited underpinnings of behavioral characteristics.

behavioral medicine An interdisciplinary field that focuses on developing and integrating behavioral and biomedical knowledge to promote health and reduce illness; overlaps with health psychology.

behaviorism A theory of learning that focuses solely on observable behaviors, discounting the importance of such mental activity as thinking, wishing, and hoping.

behavior therapies Treatments, based on the behavioral and social cognitive theories of learning, that use principles of learning to reduce or eliminate maladaptive behavior.

big five factors of personality The five broad traits that are thought to describe the main dimensions of personality: neuroticism (emotional instability), extraversion, openness to experience, agreeableness, and conscientiousness.

binding In the sense of vision, the bringing together and integration of what is processed by different neural pathways or cells.

binge eating disorder (BED) Eating disorder characterized by recurrent episodes of consuming large amounts of food during which the person feels a lack of control over eating.

binocular cues Depth cues that depend on the combination of the images in the left and right eyes and on the way the two eyes work together.

biological approach An approach to psychology focusing on the body, especially the brain and nervous system.

biological rhythms Periodic physiological fluctuations in the body, such as the rise and fall of hormones and accelerated and decelerated cycles of brain activity, that can influence our behavior.

biological therapies Also called biomedical therapies, treatments that reduce or eliminate the symptoms of psychological disorders by altering aspects of body functioning.

bipolar disorder Mood disorder characterized by extreme mood swings that include one or more episodes of mania, an overexcited, unrealistically optimistic state.

bisexual Referring to a sexual orientation in which the individual is sexually attracted to people of both sexes.

borderline personality disorder (BPD) A psychological disorder characterized by a pervasive pattern of instability in interpersonal relationships, self-image, and emotions, and of marked impulsivity beginning by early adulthood and present in a variety of contexts.

bottom-up processing The operation in sensation and perception in which sensory receptors register information about the external environment and send it up to the brain for interpretation.

brain stem The stemlike brain area that includes much of the hindbrain (it does not include the cerebellum) and the midbrain; it connects with the spinal cord at its lower end and then extends upward to encase the reticular formation in the midbrain.

broaden-and-build model Fredrickson's model of positive emotion, stating that the function of positive emotions lies in their effects on an individual's attention and ability to build resources.

bulimia nervosa Eating disorder in which an individual (typically female) consistently follows a binge-and-purge eating pattern.

burnout A distressed psychological state in which a person experiences emotional exhaustion and little motivation for work.

bystander effect The tendency of an individual who observes an emergency to help less when other people are present than when the observer is alone.

C

Cannon-Bard theory The proposition that emotion and physiological reactions occur simultaneously.

case study or case history An in-depth look at a single individual.

catatonia State of immobility and unresponsiveness lasting for long periods of time.

cell body The part of the neuron that contains the nucleus, which directs the manufacture of substances that the neuron needs for growth and maintenance.

central nervous system (CNS) The brain and spinal cord.

cerebral cortex Part of the forebrain, the outer layer of the brain, responsible for the most complex mental functions, such as thinking and planning.

chromosomes In the human cell, threadlike structures that come in 23 pairs, one member of each pair originating from each parent, and that contain the remarkable substance DNA.

circadian rhythms Daily behavioral or physiological cycles. Daily circadian rhythms involve the sleep/wake cycle, body temperature, blood pressure, and blood sugar level.

classical conditioning Learning process in which a neutral stimulus becomes associated with a meaningful stimulus and acquires the capacity to elicit a similar response.

client-centered therapy Also called Rogerian therapy or nondirective therapy, a form of humanistic therapy, developed by Rogers, in which the therapist provides a warm, supportive atmosphere to improve the client's self-concept and to encourage the client to gain insight into problems.

cognition The way in which information is processed and manipulated in remembering, thinking, and knowing.

cognitive affective processing systems (CAPS) Mischel's theoretical model for describing that our thoughts and emotions about ourselves and the world affect our behavior and become linked in ways that matter to behavior.

cognitive appraisal Individuals' interpretation of the events in their lives as harmful, threatening, or challenging and their determination of whether they have the resources to cope effectively with the events.

cognitive approach An approach to psychology emphasizing the mental processes involved in knowing: how we direct our attention, perceive, remember, think, and solve problems.

cognitive-behavior therapy A therapy that combines cognitive therapy and behavior therapy with the goal of developing self-efficacy.

cognitive dissonance An individual's psychological discomfort (dissonance) caused by two inconsistent thoughts.

cognitive reappraisal Regulating one's feelings about an experience by reinterpreting that experience or thinking about it in a different way or from a different angle.

cognitive theory of dreaming Theory proposing that we can understand dreaming by applying the same cognitive concepts we use in studying the waking mind; rests on the idea that dreams are essentially subconscious cognitive processing involving information and memory.

cognitive therapies Treatments that point to cognitions (thoughts) as the main source of psychological problems and that attempt to change the individual's feelings and behaviors by changing cognitions.

collective unconscious Jung's term for the impersonal, deepest layer of the unconscious mind, shared by all human beings because of their common ancestral past.

concept A mental category that is used to group objects, events, and characteristics.

concrete operational stage Piaget's third stage of cognitive development, lasting from about 7 to 11 years of age, during which the individual uses operations and replaces intuitive reasoning with logical reasoning in concrete situations.

conditioned response (CR) The learned response to the conditioned stimulus that occurs after conditioned stimulus–unconditioned stimulus pairing.

conditioned stimulus (CS) A previously neutral stimulus that eventually elicits a conditioned response after being paired with the unconditioned stimulus.

conditions of worth The standards that the individual must live up to in order to receive positive regard from others.

conduct disorder A pattern of offensive behavior that violates the basic rights of others.

cones The receptor cells in the retina that allow for color perception.

confederate A person who is given a role to play in a study so that the social context can be manipulated.

confirmation bias The tendency to search for and use information that supports our ideas rather than refutes them.

conformity A change in a person's behavior to coincide more closely with a group standard.

connectionism Also called parallel distributed processing (PDP), the theory that memory is stored throughout the brain in connections among neurons, several of which may work together to process a single memory.

consciousness An individual's awareness of external events and internal sensations under a condition of arousal, including awareness of the self and thoughts about one's experiences.

continuance commitment A kind of job commitment deriving from the employee's perception that leaving the organization would be too costly, both economically and socially.

control group The participants in an experiment who are as much like the experimental group as possible and who are treated in every way like the experimental group except for a manipulated factor, the independent variable.

controlled processes The most alert states of human consciousness, during which individuals actively focus their efforts toward a goal.

convergence A binocular cue to depth and distance in which the muscle movements in our two eyes provide information about how deep and/or far away something is.

convergent thinking Thinking that produces the single best solution to a problem.

coping Managing taxing circumstances, expending effort to solve life's problems, and seeking to master or reduce stress.

corpus callosum The large bundle of axons that connects the brain's two hemispheres, responsible for relaying information between the two sides.

correlational research Research that examines the relationships between variables, whose purpose is to examine whether and how two variables change together.

counterconditioning A classical conditioning procedure for changing the relationship between a conditioned stimulus and its conditioned response.

couples therapy Group therapy with married or unmarried couples whose major problem lies within their relationship.

creativity The ability to think about something in novel and unusual ways and to devise unconventional solutions to problems.

critical thinking The process of reflecting deeply and actively, asking questions, and evaluating the evidence.

culture-fair tests Intelligence tests that are intended to be culturally unbiased.

D

decay theory Theory stating that when we learn something new, a neurochemical memory trace forms, but over time this trace disintegrates; suggests that the passage of time always increases forgetting.

decision making The mental activity of evaluating alternatives and choosing among them.

deductive reasoning Reasoning from a general case that is known to be true to a specific instance.

deep brain stimulation A procedure for treatment-resistant depression that involves the implantation of electrodes in the brain that emit signals to alter the brain's electrical circuitry.

defense mechanisms Tactics the ego uses to reduce anxiety by unconsciously distorting reality.

deindividuation The reduction in personal identity and erosion of the sense of personal responsibility when one is part of a group.

delusions False, unusual, and sometimes magical beliefs that are not part of an individual's culture.

demand characteristics Any aspects of a study that communicate to the participants how the experimenter wants them to behave.

dendrites Treelike fibers projecting from a neuron, which receive information and orient it toward the neuron's cell body.

deoxyribonucleic acid (DNA) A complex molecule in the cell's chromosomes that carries genetic information.

dependent variable The outcome; the factor that can change in an experiment in response to changes in the independent variable.

depressants Psychoactive drugs that slow down mental and physical activity.

depressive disorders Mood disorders in which the individual suffers from depression—an unrelenting lack of pleasure in life.

depth perception The ability to perceive objects three-dimensionally.

descriptive research Research that determines the basic dimensions of a phenomenon, defining what it is, how often it occurs, and so on.

descriptive statistics Mathematical procedures that are used to describe and summarize sets of data in a meaningful way.

development The pattern of continuity and change in human capabilities that occurs throughout life, involving both growth and decline.

diathesis-stress model View of schizophrenia emphasizing that a combination of biogenetic disposition and stress causes the disorder.

difference threshold The degree of difference that must exist between two stimuli before the difference is detected.

discrimination An unjustified negative or harmful action toward a member of a group simply because the person belongs to that group.

discrimination (in classical conditioning) The process of learning to respond to certain stimuli and not others.

discrimination (in operant conditioning) Responding appropriately to stimuli that signal that a behavior will or will not be reinforced.

disorders of sexual development (DSD) Congenital conditions in which the development of chromosomal, gonadal, or anatomical sex is atypical; formerly called *intersex conditions* (or *hermaphroditism*).

display rules Sociocultural standards that determine when, where, and how emotions should be expressed.

dissociative amnesia Dissociative disorder characterized by extreme memory loss that is caused by extensive psychological stress.

dissociative disorders Psychological disorders that involve a sudden loss of memory or change in identity due to the dissociation (separation) of the individual's conscious awareness from previous memories and thoughts.

dissociative fugue Dissociative disorder in which the individual not only develops amnesia but also unexpectedly travels away from home and sometimes assumes a new identity.

dissociative identity disorder (DID) Formerly called multiple personality disorder, a dissociative disorder in which the individual has two or more distinct personalities or identities, each with its own memories, behaviors, and relationships.

divergent thinking Thinking that produces many solutions to the same problem.

divided attention Concentrating on more than one activity at the same time.

divided consciousness view of hypnosis Hilgard's view that hypnosis involves a splitting of consciousness into two separate components, one of which follows the hypnotist's commands and the other of which acts as a "hidden observer."

dominant-recessive genes principle The principle that, if one gene of a pair is dominant and one is recessive, the dominant gene overrides the recessive gene. A recessive gene exerts its influence only if both genes of a pair are recessive.

double-blind experiment An experimental design in which neither the experimenter nor the participants are aware of which participants are in the experimental group and which are in the control group until the results are calculated.

downsizing A dramatic cutting of the workforce that is an increasingly popular business strategy to enhance profitability.

dream analysis A psychoanalytic technique for interpreting a person's dreams.

drive An aroused state that occurs because of a physiological need.

DSM-IV The *Diagnostic and Statistical Manual of Mental Disorders;* the major classification of psychological disorders in the United States.

dysthymic disorder (DD) Mood disorder that is generally more chronic and has fewer symptoms than MDD; the individual is in a depressed mood for most days for at least two years as an adult or at least one year as a child or an adolescent.

E

efferent nerves Also called motor nerves; nerves that carry information *out of* the brain and spinal cord to other areas of the body.

ego The Freudian structure of personality that deals with the demands of reality.

egoism Giving to another person to ensure reciprocity; to gain self-esteem; to present oneself as powerful, competent, or caring; or to avoid censure from self and others for failing to live up to society's expectations.

elaboration The formation of a number of different connections around a stimulus at a given level of memory encoding.

elaboration likelihood model Theory identifying two ways to persuade: a central route and a peripheral route.

electroconvulsive therapy (ECT) Also called shock therapy, a treatment, commonly used for depression, that sets off a seizure in the brain.

emerging adulthood The transitional period from adolescence to adulthood, spanning approximately 18 to 25 years of age.

emotion Feeling, or affect, that can involve physiological arousal (such as a fast heartbeat), conscious experience (thinking about being in love with someone), and behavioral expression (a smile or grimace).

emotion-focused coping The coping strategy that involves responding to the stress that one is feeling—trying to manage one's emotional reaction—rather than focusing on the problem itself.

empathy A feeling of oneness with the emotional state of another person.

empirically keyed test A type of self-report test that presents many questionnaire items to two groups that are known to be different in some central way.

empirical method Gaining knowledge through the observation of events, the collection of data, and logical reasoning.

encoding The first step in memory; the process by which information gets into memory storage.

endocrine system The body system consisting of a set of glands that regulate the activities of certain organs by releasing their chemical products into the bloodstream.

episodic memory The retention of information about the where, when, and what of life's happenings—that is, how individuals remember life's episodes.

ergonomics Also called human factors, a field that combines engineering and psychology and that focuses on understanding and enhancing the safety and efficiency of the human–machine interaction.

estrogens The main class of female sex hormones.

ethnocentrism The tendency to favor one's own ethnic group over other groups.

evolutionary approach An approach to psychology centered on evolutionary ideas such as adaptation, reproduction, and natural selection as the basis for explaining specific human behaviors.

exercise Structured activities whose goal is to improve health.

experiment A carefully regulated procedure in which the researcher manipulates one or more variables that are believed to influence some other variable.

experimental group The participants in an experiment who receive the drug or other treatment under study—that is, those who are exposed to the change that the independent variable represents.

experimenter bias Occurs when the experimenter's expectations influence the outcome of the research.

explicit memory Also called declarative memory, the conscious recollection of information, such as specific facts or events and, at least in humans, information that can be verbally communicated.

external validity The degree to which an experimental design actually reflects the real-world issues it is supposed to address.

extinction (in classical conditioning) The weakening of the conditioned response when the unconditioned stimulus is absent.

extinction (in operant conditioning) Decreases in the frequency of a behavior when the behavior is no longer reinforced.

extrinsic motivation Motivation that involves external incentives such as rewards and punishments.

F

face validity The extent to which a test item appears to be a good fit to the characteristic it measures.

facial feedback hypothesis The idea that facial expressions can influence emotions as well as reflect them.

false consensus effect Observers' overestimation of the degree to which everybody else thinks or acts the way they do.

family therapy Group therapy with family members.

feature detectors Neurons in the brain's visual system that respond to particular features of a stimulus.

fetish An object or activity that arouses sexual interest and desire.

figure-ground relationship The principle by which we organize the perceptual field into stimuli that stand out (figure) and those that are left over (ground).

fixation Using a prior strategy and failing to look at a problem from a fresh new perspective.

flashbulb memory The memory of emotionally significant events that people often recall with more accuracy and vivid imagery than everyday events.

flat affect The display of little or no emotion—a common negative symptom of schizophrenia.

flow The optimal experience of a match between one's skills and the challenge of a task.

forebrain The brain's largest division and its most forward part.

formal operational stage Piaget's fourth stage of cognitive development, which begins at 11 to 15 years of age and continues through the adult years; it features thinking about things that are not concrete, making predictions, and using logic to come up with hypotheses about the future.

free association A psychoanalytic technique that involves encouraging individuals to say aloud whatever comes to mind, no matter how trivial or embarrassing.

frequency theory Theory on how the inner ear registers the frequency of sound, stating that the perception of a sound's frequency depends on how often the auditory nerve fires.

frontal lobes The portion of the cerebral cortex behind the forehead, involved in personality, intelligence, and the control of voluntary muscles.

functional fixedness Failing to solve a problem as a result of fixation on a thing's usual functions.

functionalism James's approach to mental processes, emphasizing the functions and purposes of the mind and behavior in the individual's adaptation to the environment.

fundamental attribution error Observers' overestimation of the importance of internal traits and underestimation of the importance of external situations when they seek explanations of an actor's behavior.

G

gender The social and psychological aspects of being female or male; gender goes beyond biological sex to include a person's understanding of the meaning to his or her own life of being male or female.

gender identity An individual's multifaceted sense of belonging to the male or female sex.

gender identity disorder (GID) Strong, persistent cross-sex identification and a continuing discomfort with, or sense of inappropriateness of, one's assigned sex.

gender roles Expectations for how females and males should think, act, and feel.

gender similarities hypothesis Hyde's proposition that men and women (and boys and girls) are much more similar than they are different.

gender stereotypes Overly general beliefs and expectations about what women and men are like.

general adaptation syndrome (GAS) Selye's term for the common effects of stressful demands on the body, consisting of three stages: alarm, resistance, and exhaustion.

generalization (in classical conditioning) The tendency of a new stimulus that is similar to the original conditioned stimulus to elicit a response that is similar to the conditioned response.

generalization (in operant conditioning) Performing a reinforced behavior in a different situation.

generalized anxiety disorder Psychological disorder marked by persistent anxiety for at least six months and in which the individual is unable to specify the reasons for the anxiety.

genes The units of hereditary information, consisting of short segments of chromosomes composed of DNA.

genotype An individual's genetic heritage; his or her actual genetic material.

gestalt psychology A school of thought interested in how people naturally organize their perceptions according to certain patterns.

gifted Possessing high intelligence (an IQ of 130 or higher) and/or superior talent in a particular area.

glands Organs or tissues in the body that create chemicals that control many of our bodily functions.

glial cells Also called glia; the second of two types of cells in the nervous system; glial cells provide support, nutritional benefits, and other functions and keep neurons running smoothly.

gonads Glands that produce sex hormones and generate ova (eggs) in females and sperm in males; collectively called gametes, the ova and sperm are the cells that will eventually be used in reproduction.

group polarization effect The solidification and further strengthening of an individual's position as a consequence of a group discussion or interaction.

group therapy A sociocultural approach to the treatment of psychological disorders that brings together individuals who share a particular psychological disorder in sessions that are typically led by a mental health professional.

groupthink The impaired group decision making that occurs when making the right decision is less important than maintaining group harmony.

H

habituation Decreased responsiveness to a stimulus after repeated presentations.

hallucinations Sensory experiences that occur in the absence of real stimuli.

hallucinogens Also called psychedelics, psychoactive drugs that modify a person's perceptual experiences and produce visual images that are not real.

halo effect A bias, common in performance ratings, that occurs when a rater gives a person the same rating on all of the items being evaluated, even though the individual varies across the dimensions being assessed.

hardiness A personal quality characterized by a sense of commitment rather than alienation, and of control rather than powerlessness; a hardy person sees problems as challenges rather than threats.

Hawthorne effect The tendency of individuals to perform better simply because of being singled out and made to feel important.

health behaviors Practices that have an impact on physical well-being, such as adopting a healthy approach to stress, exercising, eating right, brushing one's teeth, performing breast and testicular exams, not smoking, drinking in moderation (or not at all), and practicing safe sex.

health psychology A subfield of psychology that emphasizes psychology's role in establishing and maintaining health and preventing and treating illness.

heritability The proportion of observable differences in a group that can be explained by differences in the genes of the group's members.

heterosexual Referring to a sexual orientation in which the individual is generally sexually attracted to members of the opposite sex.

heuristics Shortcut strategies or guidelines that suggest a solution to a problem but do not guarantee an answer.

hierarchy of needs Maslow's theory that human needs must be satisfied in the following sequence: physiological needs, safety, love and belongingness, esteem, and self-actualization.

hindbrain Located at the skull's rear, the lowest portion of the brain, consisting of the medulla, cerebellum, and pons.

hindsight bias The tendency to report falsely, after the fact, that we accurately predicted an outcome.

hippocampus The structure in the limbic system that has a special role in the storage of memories.

homeostasis The body's tendency to maintain an equilibrium, or steady state.

homosexual Referring to a sexual orientation in which the individual is generally sexually attracted to members of the same sex.

hormones Chemical messengers that are produced by the endocrine glands and carried by the bloodstream to all parts of the body.

humanistic approach An approach to psychology emphasizing a person's positive qualities, the capacity for positive growth, and the freedom to choose any destiny.

humanistic perspectives Theoretical views stressing a person's capacity for personal growth and positive human qualities.

humanistic therapies Treatments, unique in their emphasis on people's self-healing capacities, that encourage clients to understand themselves and to grow personally.

human relations approach A management approach emphasizing the psychological characteristics of workers and managers, stressing the importance of factors such as morale, attitudes, values, and humane treatment of workers.

human sexual response pattern Masters and Johnson's model of human sexual response, consisting of four phases—excitement, plateau, orgasm, and resolution.

hypnosis An altered state of consciousness or a psychological state of altered attention and expectation in which the individual is unusually receptive to suggestions.

hypothalamic-pituitary-adrenal axis (HPA axis) The complex set of interactions among the hypothalamus, the pituitary gland, and the adrenal glands that regulates various body processes and controls reactions to stressful events.

hypothalamus A small forebrain structure, located just below the thalamus, that monitors three pleasurable activities—eating, drinking, and sex—as well as emotion, stress, and reward.

hypothesis An educated guess that derives logically from a theory; a prediction that can be tested.

I

id The part of the person that Freud called the "it," consisting of unconscious drives; the individual's reservoir of sexual energy.

identity versus identity confusion Erikson's fifth psychological stage, in which adolescents face the challenges of finding out who they are, what they are all about, and where they are going in life.

implementation intentions Specific strategies for dealing with the challenges of making a life change.

implicit memory Also called nondeclarative memory, memory in which behavior is affected by prior experience without a conscious recollection of that experience.

independent variable A manipulated experimental factor; the variable that the experimenter changes to see what its effects are.

individual psychology Adler's view that people are motivated by purposes and goals and that perfection, not pleasure, is thus the key motivator in human life.

inductive reasoning Reasoning from specific observations to make generalizations.

infant attachment The close emotional bond between an infant and its caregiver.

inferential statistics Mathematical methods that are used to indicate whether results for a sample are likely to generalize to a population.

infinite generativity The ability of language to produce an endless number of meaningful sentences.

informational social influence The influence other people have on us because we want to be right.

inner ear The part of the ear that includes the oval window, cochlea, and basilar membrane and whose function is to convert sound waves into neural impulses and send them to the brain.

insight learning A form of problem solving in which the organism develops a sudden insight into or understanding of a problem's solution.

instinct An innate (unlearned) biological pattern of behavior that is assumed to be universal throughout a species.

instinctive drift The tendency of animals to revert to instinctive behavior that interferes with learning.

integrative therapy A combination of techniques from different therapies based on the therapist's judgment of which particular methods will provide the greatest benefit for the client.

integrity test A type of job-screening examination that is designed to assess whether a candidate will be honest on the job.

intellectual disability A condition of limited mental ability in which an individual has a low IQ, usually below 70 on a traditional intelligence test, and has difficulty adapting to everyday life.

intelligence All-purpose ability to do well on cognitive tasks, to solve problems, and to learn from experience.

intelligence quotient (IQ) An individual's mental age divided by chronological age multiplied by 100.

interference theory The theory that people forget not because memories are lost from storage but because other information gets in the way of what they want to remember.

internal validity The degree to which changes in the dependent variable are due to the manipulation of the independent variable.

interpretation A psychoanalyst's search for symbolic, hidden meanings in what the client says and does during therapy.

intrinsic motivation Motivation based on internal factors such as organismic needs (competence, relatedness, and autonomy), as well as curiosity, challenge, and fun.

investment model A model of long-term relationships that examines the ways that commitment, investment, and the availability of attractive alternative partners predict satisfaction and stability in relationships.

J

James-Lange theory The theory that emotion results from physiological states triggered by stimuli in the environment.

job analysis The process of generating a description of what a job involves, including the knowledge and skills that are necessary to carry out the job's functions.

job crafting The physical and cognitive changes individuals can make within the constraints of a task to make the work "their own."

job satisfaction The extent to which a person is content in his or her job.

job stress The experience of stress on the job and in the workplace setting.

K

kinesthetic senses Senses that provide information about movement, posture, and orientation.

KSAOs (KSAs) Common elements in a person-oriented job analysis; an abbreviation for knowledge, skills, abilities, and other characteristics.

L

language A form of communication—whether spoken, written, or signed—that is based on a system of symbols.

latent content According to Freud, a dream's hidden content; its unconscious and true meaning.

latent learning Also called implicit learning, unreinforced learning that is not immediately reflected in behavior.

law of effect Thorndike's law stating that behaviors followed by positive outcomes are strengthened and that behaviors followed by negative outcomes are weakened.

learned helplessness An organism's learning through experience with unavoidable negative stimuli that it has no control over negative outcomes.

learning A systematic, relatively permanent change in behavior that occurs through experience.

leisure The pleasant times before or after work when individuals are free to pursue activities and interests of their own choosing, such as hobbies, sports, and reading.

levels of processing A continuum of memory processing from shallow to intermediate to deep, with deeper processing producing better memory.

limbic system A loosely connected network of structures under the cerebral cortex, important in both memory and emotion. Its two principal structures are the amygdala and the hippocampus.

lithium The lightest of the solid elements in the periodic table of elements, widely used to treat bipolar disorder.

longitudinal design A special kind of systematic observation, used by correlational researchers, that involves obtaining measures of the variables of interest in multiple waves over time.

long-term memory A relatively permanent type of memory that stores huge amounts of information for a long time.

M

major depressive disorder (MDD) Psychological disorder involving a significant depressive episode and depressed characteristics, such as lethargy and hopelessness, for at least two weeks.

manifest content According to Freud, the surface content of a dream, containing dream symbols that disguise the dream's true meaning.

mean A measure of central tendency that is the average for a sample.

median A measure of central tendency that is the middle score in a sample.

medical model The view that psychological disorders are medical diseases with a biological origin.

memory The retention of information or experience over time as the result of three key processes: encoding, storage, and retrieval.

mental age (MA) An individual's level of mental development relative to that of others.

mental processes The thoughts, feelings, and motives that each of us experiences privately but that cannot be observed directly.

mentoring A relationship between an experienced employee—a mentor—and a novice, in which the more experienced employee serves as an advisor, a sounding board, and a source of support for the newer employee.

mere exposure effect The phenomenon that the more we encounter someone or something, the more probable it is that we will start liking the person or thing even if we do not realize we have seen it before.

meta-analysis A method that allows researchers to combine the results of several different studies on a similar topic in order to establish the strength of an effect.

midbrain Located between the hindbrain and forebrain, an area in which many nerve-fiber systems ascend and descend to connect the higher and lower portions of the brain; in particular, the midbrain relays information between the brain and the eyes and ears.

middle ear The part of the ear that channels sound through the eardrum, hammer, anvil, and stirrup to the inner ear.

mindfulness The state of being alert and mentally present for one's everyday activities.

Minnesota Multiphasic Personality Inventory (MMPI) The most widely used and researched empirically keyed self-report personality test.

mode A measure of central tendency that is the most common score in a sample.

monocular cues Powerful depth cues available from the image in one eye, either the right or the left.

mood disorders Psychological disorders—the main types of which are depressive disorders and bipolar disorder—in which there is a primary disturbance of mood: prolonged emotion that colors the individual's entire emotional state.

morphology A language's rules for word formation.

motivated forgetting Forgetting that occurs when something is so painful or anxiety-laden that remembering it is intolerable.

motivation The force that moves people to behave, think, and feel the way they do.

motor cortex A region in the cerebral cortex that processes information about voluntary movement, located just behind the frontal lobes.

myelin sheath A layer of fat cells that encases and insulates most axons.

N

naturalistic observation The observation of behavior in a real-world setting.

natural selection Darwin's principle of an evolutionary process in which organisms that are best adapted to their environment will survive and produce offspring.

nature An individual's biological inheritance, especially his or her genes.

need A deprivation that energizes the drive to eliminate or reduce the deprivation.

negative affect Unpleasant emotions such as anger, guilt, and sadness.

negative punishment The removal of a positive stimulus following a given behavior in order to decrease the frequency of that behavior.

negative reinforcement An increase in the frequency of a behavior in response to the subsequent removal of something that is unpleasant.

neglectful parenting A parenting style characterized by a lack of parental involvement in the child's life.

neocortex The outermost part of the cerebral cortex, making up 80 percent of the cortex in the human brain.

nervous system The body's electrochemical communication circuitry.

neural networks Networks of nerve cells that integrate sensory input and motor output.

neurons One of two types of cells in the nervous system; neurons are the nerve cells that handle the information-processing function.

neuroscience The scientific study of the structure, function, development, genetics, and biochemistry of the nervous system, emphasizing that the brain and nervous system are central to understanding behavior, thought, and emotion.

neurotransmitters Chemical substances that are stored in very tiny sacs within the terminal buttons and involved in transmitting information across a synaptic gap to the next neuron.

noise Irrelevant and competing stimuli—not only sounds but also any distracting stimuli for our senses.

normal distribution A symmetrical, bell-shaped curve, with a majority of the scores falling in the middle of the possible range and few scores appearing toward the extremes of the range.

normative commitment A kind of job commitment deriving from the employee's sense of obligation to the organization for the investment it has made in the individual's personal and professional development.

normative social influence The influence others have on us because we want them to like us.

nurture An individual's environmental and social experiences.

O

obedience Behavior that complies with the explicit demands of the individual in authority.

observational learning Learning that occurs when a person observes and imitates another's behavior.

obsessive-compulsive disorder (OCD) Anxiety disorder in which the individual has anxiety-provoking thoughts that will not go away and/or urges to perform repetitive, ritualistic behaviors to prevent or produce some future situation.

occipital lobes Structures located at the back of the head that respond to visual stimuli.

Oedipus complex According to Freud, a boy's intense desire to replace his father and enjoy the affections of his mother.

olfactory epithelium The lining of the roof of the nasal cavity, containing a sheet of receptor cells for smell.

open-mindedness The state of being receptive to other ways of looking at things.

operant conditioning Also called instrumental conditioning, a form of associative learning in which the consequences of a behavior change the probability of the behavior's occurrence.

operational definition A definition that provides an objective description of how a variable is going to be measured and observed in a particular study.

opiates Opium and its derivatives; narcotic drugs that depress activity in the central nervous system and eliminate pain.

opponent-process theory Theory stating that cells in the visual system respond to complementary pairs of red-green and blue-yellow colors; a given cell might be excited by red and inhibited by green, whereas another cell might be excited by yellow and inhibited by blue.

optic nerve The structure at the back of the eye, made up of axons of the ganglion cells, that carries visual information to the brain for further processing.

organizational citizenship behavior (OCB) Discretionary actions on the part of an employee that promote organizational effectiveness but are not included in the person's formal responsibilities.

organizational culture An organization's shared values, beliefs, norms, and customs.

organizational identity Employees' feelings of oneness with the organization and its goals.

orientation A program by which an organization introduces newly hired employees to the organization's goals, familiarizes them with its rules and regulations, and lets them know how to get things done.

outer ear The outermost part of the ear, consisting of the pinna and the external auditory canal.

ovaries Sex-related endocrine glands in the uterus that produce hormones related to women's sexual development and reproduction.

overlearning Learning to perform a task so well that it becomes automatic.

overt aggression Physically or verbally harming another person directly.

P

pain The sensation that warns us of damage to our bodies.

pancreas A dual-purpose gland under the stomach that performs both digestive and endocrine functions.

panic disorder Anxiety disorder in which the individual experiences recurrent, sudden onsets of intense apprehension or terror, often without warning and with no specific cause.

papillae Rounded bumps above the tongue's surface that contain the taste buds, the receptors for taste.

parallel processing The simultaneous distribution of information across different neural pathways.

paraphilias Sexual disorders that feature recurrent sexually arousing fantasies, urges, or behaviors involving nonhuman objects; the suffering or humiliation of oneself or one's partner; or children or other nonconsenting persons.

parasympathetic nervous system The part of the autonomic nervous system that calms the body.

parietal lobes Structures at the top and toward the rear of the head that are involved in registering spatial location, attention, and motor control.

pedophilia A paraphilia in which an adult or an older adolescent sexually fantasizes about or engages in sexual behavior with individuals who have not reached puberty.

perception The process of organizing and interpreting sensory information so that it has meaning.

perceptual constancy The recognition that objects are constant and unchanging even though sensory input about them is changing.

perceptual set A predisposition or readiness to perceive something in a particular way.

performance appraisal The evaluation of a person's success at meeting his or her organization's goals.

peripheral nervous system (PNS) The network of nerves that connects the brain and spinal cord to other parts of the body.

permissive parenting A parenting style characterized by the placement of few limits on the child's behavior.

personality A pattern of enduring, distinctive thoughts, emotions, and behaviors that characterize the way an individual adapts to the world.

personality disorders Chronic, maladaptive cognitive-behavioral patterns that are thoroughly integrated into an individual's personality.

personological and life story perspectives Theoretical views stressing that the way to understand the person is to focus on his or her life history and life story.

phenotype An individual's observable characteristics.

phobic disorder or phobia Anxiety disorder characterized by an irrational, overwhelming, persistent fear of a particular object or situation.

phonology A language's sound system.

physical dependence The physiological need for a drug that causes unpleasant withdrawal symptoms such as physical pain and a craving for the drug when it is discontinued.

pituitary gland A pea-sized gland just beneath the hypothalamus that controls growth and regulates other glands.

placebo In a drug study, a harmless substance that has no physiological effect, given to participants in a control group so that they are treated identically to the experimental group except for the active agent.

placebo effect Occurs when participants' expectations, rather than the experimental treatment, produce an outcome.

place theory Theory on how the inner ear registers the frequency of sound, stating that each frequency produces vibrations at a particular spot on the basilar membrane.

plasticity The brain's special capacity for change.

polygraph A machine, commonly called a lie detector, that monitors changes in the body, used to try to determine whether someone is lying.

population The entire group about which the investigator wants to draw conclusions.

positive affect Pleasant emotions such as joy, happiness, and interest.

positive illusions Positive views of the self that are not necessarily rooted in reality.

positive psychology A branch of psychology that emphasizes human strengths.

positive punishment The presentation of an unpleasant stimulus following a given behavior in order to decrease the frequency of that behavior.

positive reinforcement An increase in the frequency of a behavior in response to the subsequent presentation of something that is good.

post-traumatic stress disorder (PTSD) Anxiety disorder that develops through exposure to a traumatic event that has overwhelmed the person's abilities to cope.

pragmatics The useful character of language and the ability of language to communicate even more meaning than is said.

preferential looking A research technique that involves giving an infant a choice of what object to look at.

prejudice An unjustified negative attitude toward an individual based on the individual's membership in a particular group.

preoperational stage Piaget's second stage of cognitive development, lasting from about 2 to 7 years of age, during which thought is more symbolic than sensorimotor thought.

preparedness The species-specific biological predisposition to learn in certain ways but not others.

primary reinforcer A reinforcer that is innately satisfying; one that does not take any learning on the organism's part to make it pleasurable.

priming The activation of information that people already have in storage to help them remember new information better and faster.

proactive interference Situation in which material that was learned earlier disrupts the recall of material that was learned later.

problem-focused coping The coping strategy of squarely facing one's troubles and trying to solve them.

problem solving The mental process of finding an appropriate way to attain a goal when the goal is not readily available.

procedural memory Memory for skills.

projective test A personality assessment test that presents individuals with an ambiguous stimulus and asks them to describe it or tell a story about it—to project their own meaning onto the stimulus.

prosocial behavior Behavior that is intended to benefit other people.

prospective memory Remembering information about doing something in the future; includes memory for intentions.

prototype model A model emphasizing that when people evaluate whether a given item reflects a certain concept, they compare the item with the most typical item(s) in that category and look for a "family resemblance" with that item's properties.

psychoactive drugs Drugs that act on the nervous system to alter consciousness, modify perception, and change mood.

psychoanalysis Freud's therapeutic technique for analyzing an individual's unconscious thoughts.

psychodynamic approach An approach to psychology emphasizing unconscious thought, the conflict between biological drives (such as the drive for sex) and society's demands, and early childhood family experiences.

psychodynamic perspectives Theoretical views emphasizing that personality is primarily unconscious (beyond awareness).

psychodynamic therapies Treatments that stress the importance of the unconscious mind, extensive interpretation by the therapist, and the role of early childhood experiences in the development of an individual's problems.

psychological dependence The strong desire to repeat the use of a drug for emotional reasons, such as a feeling of well-being and reduction of stress.

psychology The scientific study of behavior and mental processes.

psychoneuroimmunology A new field of scientific inquiry that explores connections among psychological factors (such as attitudes and emotions), the nervous system, and the immune system.

psychopathology The scientific study of psychological disorders and the development of diagnostic categories and treatments for those disorders.

psychosurgery A biological therapy, with irreversible effects, that involves removal or destruction of brain tissue to improve the individual's adjustment.

psychotherapy A nonmedical process that helps individuals with psychological disorders recognize and overcome their problems.

puberty A period of rapid skeletal and sexual maturation that occurs mainly in early adolescence.

punishment A consequence that decreases the likelihood that a behavior will occur.

R

random assignment Researchers' assignment of participants to groups by chance, to reduce the likelihood that an experiment's results will be due to preexisting differences between groups.

random sample A sample that gives every member of the population an equal chance of being selected.

range A measure of dispersion that is the difference between the highest and lowest scores.

rational-emotive behavior therapy (REBT) A therapy based on Ellis's assertion that individuals develop a psychological disorder because of irrational and self-defeating beliefs and whose goal is to get clients to eliminate these beliefs by rationally examining them.

reasoning The mental activity of transforming information to reach conclusions.

referential thinking Ascribing personal meaning to completely random events.

reflective speech A technique in which the therapist mirrors the client's own feelings back to the client.

reinforcement The process by which a rewarding stimulus or event (a reinforcer) following a particular behavior increases the probability that the behavior will happen again.

relapse A return to former unhealthy patterns.

relational aggression Behavior that is meant to harm the social standing of another person.

reliability The extent to which a test yields a consistent, reproducible measure of performance.

REM sleep An active stage of sleep during which dreaming occurs.

renewal The recovery of the conditioned response when the organism is placed in a novel context.

representativeness heuristic The tendency to make judgments about group membership based on physical appearances or the match between a person and one's stereotype of a group rather than on available base rate information.

research participant bias Occurs when the behavior of research participants during the experiment is influenced by how they think they are supposed to behave or their expectations about what is happening to them.

resilience A person's ability to recover from or adapt to difficult times.

resistance A client's unconscious defense strategies that interfere with the psychoanalyst's understanding of the individual's problems.

resting potential In an inactive neuron, the voltage between the inside and outside of the axon wall.

reticular formation A system in the midbrain comprising a diffuse collection of neurons involved in stereotyped patterns of behavior such as walking, sleeping, and turning to attend to a sudden noise.

retina The multilayered light-sensitive surface in the eye that records electromagnetic energy and converts it to neural impulses for processing in the brain.

retrieval The memory process that occurs when information that was retained in memory comes out of storage.

retroactive interference Situation in which material that was learned later disrupts the retrieval of information that was learned earlier.

retrograde amnesia Memory loss for a segment of the past but not for new events.

retrospective memory Remembering information from the past.

risky shift The tendency for a group decision to be riskier than the average decision made by the individual group members.

rods The receptor cells in the retina that are sensitive to light but not very useful for color vision.

role conflict The kind of stress that arises when a person tries to meet the demands of more than one important life role, such as worker and mother.

romantic love Also called passionate love; love with strong components of sexuality and infatuation, often dominant in the early part of a love relationship.

Rorschach inkblot test A famous projective test that uses an individual's perception of inkblots to determine his or her personality.

S

sample The subset of the population chosen by the investigator for study.

schedules of reinforcement Specific patterns that determine when a behavior will be reinforced.

schema A preexisting mental concept or framework that helps people to organize and interpret information. Schemas from prior encounters with the environment influence the way we encode, make inferences about, and retrieve information.

schizophrenia Severe psychological disorder characterized by highly disordered thought processes, referred to as psychotic because they are so far removed from reality.

science The use of systematic methods to observe the natural world, including human behavior, and to draw conclusions.

scientific management The managerial philosophy that emphasizes the worker as a well-oiled machine and the determination of the most efficient methods for performing any work-related task.

script A schema for an event, often containing information about physical features, people, and typical occurrences.

secondary reinforcer A reinforcer that acquires its positive value through an organism's experience; a secondary reinforcer is a learned or conditioned reinforcer.

secondary sex characteristics Traits that differ between the two sexes but are not part of the reproductive system; they include breasts in females and facial hair in males.

secure attachment The ways that infants use their caregiver, usually their mother, as a secure base from which to explore the environment.

selective attention The process of focusing on a specific aspect of experience while ignoring others.

self-actualization The motivation to develop one's full potential as a human being—the highest and most elusive of Maslow's proposed needs.

self-determination theory Deci and Ryan's theory asserting that all humans have three basic, innate organismic needs: competence, relatedness, and autonomy.

self-efficacy The belief that one can master a situation and produce positive change.

self-objectification The tendency to see oneself primarily as an object in the eyes of others.

self-perception theory Bem's theory on how behaviors influence attitudes, stating that individuals make inferences about their attitudes by perceiving their behavior.

self-regulation The process by which an organism effortfully controls behavior in order to pursue important objectives.

self-report test Also called an objective test or an inventory, a method of measuring personality characteristics that directly asks people whether specific items describe their personality traits.

self-serving bias The tendency to take credit for our successes and to deny responsibility for our failures.

semantic memory A person's knowledge about the world, including his or her areas of expertise; general knowledge, such as of things learned in school; and everyday knowledge.

semantics The meaning of words and sentences in a particular language.

semicircular canals Three fluid-filled circular tubes in the inner ear containing the sensory receptors that detect head motion caused when we tilt or move our head and/or body.

sensation The process of receiving stimulus energies from the external environment and transforming those energies into neural energy.

sensorimotor stage Piaget's first stage of cognitive development, lasting from birth to about 2 years of age, during which infants construct an understanding of the world by coordinating sensory experiences with motor (physical) actions.

sensory adaptation A change in the responsiveness of the sensory system based on the average level of surrounding stimulation.

sensory memory Memory system that involves holding information from the world in its original sensory form for only an instant, not much longer than the brief time it is exposed to the visual, auditory, and other senses.

sensory receptors Specialized cells that detect stimulus information and transmit it to sensory (afferent) nerves and the brain.

serial position effect The tendency to recall the items at the beginning and end of a list more readily than those in the middle.

set point The weight maintained when the individual makes no effort to gain or lose weight.

sex The properties of a person that determine his or her classification as male or female.

sex chromosomes In humans, the pair of genes that differs between the sexes and determines a person's sex as male or female.

sexual harassment Unwelcome behavior or conduct of a sexual nature that offends, humiliates, or intimidates another person.

sexuality The ways people experience and express themselves as sexual beings.

sexually transmitted infection (STI) An infection that is contracted primarily through sexual activity—vaginal intercourse as well as oral and anal sex.

sexual orientation The direction of an individual's erotic interests.

sexual selection According to Darwin's theory of evolution, the differentiation between the male and female members of a species because of the differences between the two in competition and choice.

shaping Rewarding approximations of a desired behavior.

short-term memory Limited-capacity memory system in which information is usually retained for only as long as 30 seconds unless we use strategies to retain it longer.

signal detection theory A theory of perception that focuses on decision making about stimuli in the presence of uncertainty.

sleep A natural state of rest for the body and mind that involves the reversible loss of consciousness.

social cognitive behavior view of hypnosis Theory that hypnosis is a normal state in which the hypnotized person behaves the way he or she believes that a hypnotized person should behave.

social cognitive perspectives Theoretical views emphasizing conscious awareness, beliefs, expectations, and goals.

social comparison The process by which individuals evaluate their thoughts, feelings, behaviors, and abilities in relation to those of other people.

social contagion Imitative behavior involving the spread of actions, emotions, and ideas.

social exchange theory The view of social relationships as involving an exchange of goods, the objective of which is to minimize costs and maximize benefits.

social facilitation Improvement in an individual's performance because of the presence of others.

social identity The way we define ourselves in terms of our group membership.

social identity theory Tajfel's theory that our social identities are a crucial part of our self-image and a valuable source of positive feelings about ourselves.

social loafing Each person's tendency to exert less effort in a group because of reduced accountability for individual effort.

social psychology The study of how people think about, influence, and relate to other people.

social support Information and feedback from others indicating that one is loved and cared for, esteemed and valued, and included in a network of communication and mutual obligation.

sociocultural approach An approach to psychology that examines the ways in which social and cultural environments influence behavior.

somatic nervous system The body system consisting of the sensory nerves, whose function is to convey information from the skin and muscles to the CNS about conditions such as pain and temperature, and the motor nerves, whose function is to tell muscles what to do.

somatosensory cortex A region in the cerebral cortex that processes information about body sensations, located at the front of the parietal lobes.

spontaneous recovery The process in classical conditioning by which a conditioned response can recur after a time delay, without further conditioning.

stages of change model Theoretical model describing a five-step process by which individuals give up bad habits and adopt healthier lifestyles.

standard deviation A measure of dispersion that tells us how much scores in a sample differ from the mean of the sample.

standardization The development of uniform procedures for administering and scoring a test, and the creation of norms (performance standards) for the test.

stem cells Unique primitive cells that have the capacity to develop into most types of human cells.

stereotype A generalization about a group's characteristics that does not consider any variations from one individual to another.

stereotype threat An individual's fast-acting, self-fulfilling fear of being judged based on a negative stereotype about his or her group.

stimulants Psychoactive drugs that increase the central nervous system's activity. The most widely used stimulants are caffeine, nicotine, amphetamines, and cocaine.

storage The retention of information over time and how this information is represented in memory.

stream of consciousness Term used by William James to describe the mind as a continuous flow of changing sensations, images, thoughts, and feelings.

strengths-based management A management style emphasizing that maximizing an employee's existing strengths is much easier than trying to build such attributes from the ground up.

stress The responses of individuals to environmental stressors.

stress management program A regimen that teaches individuals how to appraise stressful events, how to develop skills for coping with stress, and how to put these skills into use in everyday life.

stressors Circumstances and events that threaten individuals and tax their coping abilities and that cause physiological changes to ready the body to handle the assault of stress.

structuralism Wundt's approach to discovering the basic elements, or structures, of mental processes; so called because of its focus on identifying the structures of the human mind.

structured interview A kind of interview in which candidates are asked specific questions that methodically seek to obtain truly useful information for the interviewer.

subgoals Intermediate goals or intermediate problems that put us in a better position for reaching the final goal or solution.

subjective well-being A person's assessment of his or her own level of positive affect relative to negative affect, and the individual's evaluation of his or her life in general.

subliminal perception The detection of information below the level of conscious awareness.

superego The Freudian structure of personality that serves as the harsh internal judge of our behavior; what we often call conscience.

suprachiasmatic nucleus (SCN) A small brain structure that uses input from the retina to synchronize its own rhythm with the daily cycle of light and dark; the mechanism by which the body monitors the change from day to night.

sustained attention Also called vigilance, the ability to maintain attention to a selected stimulus for a prolonged period of time.

sympathetic nervous system The part of the autonomic nervous system that arouses the body.

synapses Tiny spaces between neurons; the gaps between neurons are referred to as synaptic gaps.

syntax A language's rules for combining words to form acceptable phrases and sentences.

systematic desensitization A method of behavior therapy that treats anxiety by teaching the client to associate deep relaxation with increasingly intense anxiety-producing situations.

T

temperament An individual's behavioral style and characteristic way of responding.

temporal lobes Structures in the cerebral cortex that are located just above the ears and are involved in hearing, language processing, and memory.

testes Sex-related endocrine glands in the scrotum that produce hormones related to men's sexual development and reproduction.

thalamus The forebrain structure that sits at the top of the brain stem in the brain's central core and serves as an important relay station.

Thematic Apperception Test (TAT) A projective test that is designed to elicit stories that reveal something about an individual's personality.

theory A broad idea or set of closely related ideas that attempts to explain observations and to make predictions about future observations.

theory of planned behavior Theoretical model that includes the basic ideas of the theory of reasoned action but adds the person's perceptions of control over the outcome.

theory of reasoned action Theoretical model stating that effective change requires individuals to have specific intentions about their behaviors, as well as positive attitudes about a new

behavior, and to perceive that their social group looks positively on the new behavior as well.

Theory X managers Managers who assume that work is innately unpleasant and that people have a strong desire to avoid it; such managers believe that employees need direction, dislike responsibility, and must be kept in line.

Theory Y managers Managers who assume that engaging in effortful behavior is natural to human beings; they recognize that people seek out responsibility and that motivation can come from allowing employees to suggest creative and meaningful solutions.

therapeutic alliance The relationship between the therapist and client—an important element of successful psychotherapy.

thermoreceptors Sensory nerve endings under the skin that respond to changes in temperature at or near the skin and provide input to keep the body's temperature at 98.6 degrees Fahrenheit.

thinking The mental process of manipulating information mentally by forming concepts, solving problems, making decisions, and reflecting critically or creatively.

third variable problem The circumstance where a variable that has not been measured accounts for the relationship between two other variables. Third variables are also known as confounds.

360-degree feedback A method of performance appraisal whereby an employee's performance is rated by a variety of individuals, including himself or herself, a peer, a supervisor, a subordinate, and perhaps a customer or client.

tip-of-the-tongue (TOT) phenomenon A type of effortful retrieval that occurs when we are confident that we know something but cannot quite pull it out of memory.

tolerance The need to take increasing amounts of a drug to get the same effect.

top-down processing The operation in sensation and perception, launched by cognitive processing at the brain's higher levels, that allows the organism to sense what is happening and to apply that framework to information from the world.

training Teaching a new employee the essential requirements to do the job well.

trait theories Theoretical views stressing that personality consists of broad, enduring dispositions (traits) that tend to lead to characteristic responses.

tranquilizers Depressant drugs, such as Valium and Xanax, that reduce anxiety and induce relaxation.

transactional leader An individual in a leadership capacity who emphasizes the exchange relationship between the worker and the leader and who applies the principle that a good job should be rewarded.

transference A client's relating to the psycho-analyst in ways that reproduce or relive important relationships in the individual's life.

transformational leader An individual in a leadership capacity who is concerned not with enforcing the rules but with changing them.

transgender Experiencing one's psychological gender as different from one's physical sex, as in the cases of biological males who identify as female, and biological females who identify as male.

triarchic theory of intelligence Sternberg's theory that intelligence comes in three forms: analytical, creative, and practical.

trichromatic theory Theory stating that color perception is produced by three types of cone receptors in the retina that are particularly sensitive to different, but overlapping, ranges of wavelengths.

two-factor theory of emotion Schachter and Singer's theory that emotion is determined by two factors: physiological arousal and cognitive labeling.

Type A behavior pattern A cluster of characteristics—such as being excessively competitive, hard-driven, impatient, and hostile—related to the incidence of heart disease.

Type B behavior pattern A cluster of characteristics—such as being relaxed and easygoing—related to good health.

U

unconditional positive regard Rogers's construct referring to the individual's need to be accepted, valued, and treated positively regardless of his or her behavior.

unconditioned response (UCR) An unlearned reaction that is automatically elicited by the unconditioned stimulus.

unconditioned stimulus (UCS) A stimulus that produces a response without prior learning.

unconscious thought According to Freud, a reservoir of unacceptable wishes, feelings, and thoughts that are beyond conscious awareness; Freud's interpretation viewed the unconscious as a storehouse for vile thoughts.

V

validity The extent to which a test measures what it is intended to measure.

variable Anything that can change.

vestibular sense Sense that provides information about balance and movement.

volley principle Modification of frequency theory stating that a cluster of nerve cells can fire neural impulses in rapid succession, producing a volley of impulses.

W

waigawa system A management system dedicated to the idea that when the corporation faces a difficult problem, all rank-related concerns are temporarily set aside so that anyone from any level of the organization can propose a solution.

Weber's law The principle that two stimuli must differ by a constant minimum percentage (rather than a constant amount) to be perceived as different.

well-being therapy (WBT) A short-term, problem-focused, directive therapy that encourages clients to accentuate the positive.

wisdom Expert knowledge about the practical aspects of life.

working memory A three-part system that allows us to hold information temporarily as we perform cognitive tasks; a kind of mental workbench on which the brain manipulates and assembles information to help us understand, make decisions, and solve problems.

Y

Yerkes-Dodson law The psychological principle stating that performance is best under conditions of moderate arousal rather than either low or high arousal.

REFERENCES

A

Abbott, B. B., Schoen, L. S, & Badia, P. (1984). Predictable and unpredictable shock: Behavioral measures of aversion and physiological measures of stress. *Psychological Bulletin, 96,* 45–71.

Abbott, J. M., Klein, B., & Ciechomski, L. (2008). Best practices in online therapy. *Journal of Technology in Human Services, 26,* 360–375.

ABC News. (2004, October 21). Poll: American sex survey. http://abcnews.go.com/Primetime/PollVault/story?id=156921&page=1

Abraham, A., & Windmann, S. (2007). Creative cognition: The diverse operations and the prospect of applying a cognitive neuroscience perspective. *Methods, 42,* 38–48.

Abramowitz, J. S. (2009). *Getting over OCD.* New York: Guilford.

Abrams, D., & Hogg, M. A. (2004). Metatheory: Lessons from social identity research. In A. W. Kruglanski & E. T. Higgins (Eds.), *Theory construction in social-personality psychology.* Mahwah, NJ: Erlbaum.

Abrams, L., & Rodriguez, E. L. (2005). Syntactic class influences phonological priming of tip-of-the-tongue resolution. *Psychonomic Bulletin & Review, 12* (6), 1018–1023.

Abramson, L. Y., Seligman, M. E. P., & Teasdale, J. (1978). Learned helplessness in humans: Critique and reformulation. *Journal of Abnormal Psychology, 87,* 49–74.

Acer, N., & others. (2010). Comparison of two volumetric techniques for estimating volume of intracerebral ventricles using magnetic resonance imaging: A stereological study. *Anatomical Science International.* (in press)

Achim, A. M., & Lepage, M. (2005). Neural correlates of memory for items and for associations: An event-related functional magnetic resonance imaging study. *Journal of Cognitive Neuroscience, 17,* 652–667.

Adam, C. L. (2010). Leptin: Primary central site of action? *Endocrinology, 151,* 1975–1979.

Addington, J., el-Guebaly, N., Campbell, W., Hodgkins, D. C., & Addington, D. (1998). Smoking cessation treatment for patients with schizophrenia. *American Journal of Psychiatry, 155,* 974–976.

Ader, R. (1974). Letter to the editor: Behaviorally conditioned immunosuppression. *Psychosomatic Medicine, 36,* 183–184.

Ader, R. (2000). On the development of psycho-neuroimmunology. *European Journal of Pharmacology, 405,* 167–176.

Ader, R., & Cohen, N. (1975). Behaviorally conditioned immunosuppression. *Psychosomatic Medicine, 37,* 333–340.

Ader, R., & Cohen, N. (2000). Conditioning and immunity. In R. Ader, D. L. Felton, & N. Cohen (Eds.), *Psychoneuroimmunology* (3rd ed.). San Diego: Academic.

Ades, P. A., Savage, P. D., & Harvey-Berino, J. (2010). The treatment of obesity in cardiac rehabilitation. *Journal of Cardiopulmonary Rehabilitation and Prevention.* (in press)

Adlard, P. A., Parncutt, J. M., Finkeelstein, D. I., & Bush, A. L. (2010). Cognitive loss in zinc transporter-3 knock-out mice: A phenocopy for the synaptic and memory deficits of Alzheimer's disease. *Journal of Neuroscience, 30,* 1631–1636.

Adler, A. (1927). *The theory and practice of individual psychology.* Fort Worth, TX: Harcourt Brace.

Adler, N. E., & Stewart, J. (2009). Reducing obesity: Motivating action while not blaming the victim. *Milbank Quarterly, 87,* 49–70.

Adolph, K. E., Berger, S. E., & Leo, A. (2010). Developmental continuity? Crawling, cruising, and walking. *Developmental Science.* (in press)

Adolph, K. E., Eppler, M. A., & Joh, A. S. (2010). Infants' perception of affordances of slopes under low and high friction conditions. *Journal of Experimental Psychology: Human Perception and Performance.* (in press)

Adolphs, R. (2009). The social brain: Neural basis of social knowledge. *Annual Review of Psychology* (vol. 60). Palo Alto, CA: Annual Reviews.

Agatonovic-Kustrin, S., Davies, P., & Turner, J. V. (2009). Structure-activity relationships for serotonin transporter and dopamine receptor selectivity. *Medicinal Chemistry, 5,* 271–278.

Aggen, S. H., Neale, M. C., Roysamb, E., Reichborn-Kjennerud, T., & Kendler, K. S. (2009). A psychometric evaluation of the DSM-IV borderline personality disorder criteria: Age and sex moderation of criterion functioning. *Psychological Medicine, 39,* 1967–1978.

Aguinis, H. (2009). *Performance management* (2nd ed.). Upper Saddle River, NJ: Prentice-Hall.

Aguinis, H. (2010). Organizational responsibility: Doing good and doing well. In S. Zedeck (Ed.), *APA handbook of industrial and organizational psychology.* Washington, DC: APA. (in press)

Aguinis, H., & Kraiger, K. (2009). Benefits of training and development for individuals and teams, organizations, and society. *Annual Review of Psychology* (vol. 60). Palo Alto, CA: Annual Reviews.

Ahmadi, J., Kampman, K. M., Oslin, D. M., Pettinati, H. M., Dackis, C., & Sparkman, T. (2009). Predictors of treatment outcome in outpatient cocaine and alcohol dependency treatment. *American Journal of Addiction, 18,* 81–86.

Ahmed, I., & Thorpy, M. (2010). Clinical features, diagnosis, and treatment of narcolepsy. *Clinics in Chest Medicine, 31,* 371–381.

Ahmed, N. U., Smith, G. L., Flores, A. M., Pamies, R. J., Mason, H. R., Woods, K. F., & Stain, S. C. (2005). Racial/ethnic disparity and predictors of leisure-time activity among U.S. men. *Ethnicity and Disease, 15,* 40–52.

Ahola, K., Honkonen, T., Kivimaki, M., Virtanen, M., Isometsa, E., Aromaa, A., & Lonnqvist, J. (2006). Contribution of burnout to the association between job strain and depression: The Health 2000 Study. *Journal of Occupational and Environmental Medicine, 48,* 1023–1030.

Aihara, Y., Minai, J., Aoyama, A., & Shiman-ouchi, S. (2010). Depressive symptoms and past lifestyle among Japanese elderly people. *Community Mental Health Journal.* (in press)

Ainsworth, M. D. S. (1979). Infant–mother attachment. *American Psychologist, 34,* 932–937.

Ainsworth, M. S., Blehar, M. C., Waters, E., & Wall, S. (1978). *Patterns of attachment: A psychological study of the strange situation.* Oxford, U.K.: Erlbaum.

Ajzen, I. (2001). Nature and operation of attitudes. *Annual Review of Psychology* (vol. 52). Palo Alto, CA: Annual Reviews.

Ajzen, I. (2002). Perceived behavioral control, self-efficacy, locus of control, and the theory of planned behavior. *Journal of Applied Social Psychology, 32,* 665–683.

Ajzen, I., & Albarracin, D. (2007). Predicting and changing behavior: A reasoned action approach. In I. Ajzen, D. Albarracin, & R. Hornik (Eds.), *Prediction and change in health behavior.* Mahwah, NJ: Erlbaum.

Ajzen, I., & Fishbein, M. (1980). *Understanding attitudes and predicting social behavior.* Englewood Cliffs, NJ: Prentice-Hall.

Ajzen, I., & Fishbein, M. (2005). The influence of attitudes on behavior. In D. Albarracin, B. T. Johnson, & M. P. Zanna (Eds.), *The handbook of attitudes* (pp. 173–221). Mahwah, NJ: Erlbaum.

Ajzen, I., & Manstead, A. S. R. (2007). Changing health-related behaviours: An approach based on the theory of planned behaviour. In M. Hewstone, H. Schut, J. de Wit, K. van den Bos, & M. S. Stroebe (Eds.), *The scope of social psychology: Theory and applications* (pp. 43–63). New York: Psychology Press.

Akhtar, S. (2006). Technical challenges faced by the immigrant psychoanalyst. *Psychoanalytic Quarterly, 75,* 21–43.

Akkermann, K., Nordquist, N., Oreland, L., & Harro, J. (2010). Serotonin transporter gene promoter polymorphism affects the severity of binge eating in general population. *Progress in Neuro-Psychopharmacology and Biological Psychiatry, 34,* 111–114.

Al-Alem, L., & Omar, H. A. (2008). Borderline personality: An overview of history, diagnosis, and treatment in adolescents. *International Journal of Adolescent Medicine, 20,* 395–404.

Albarracin, D., Durantini, M. R., & Earl, A. (2006). Empirical and theoretical conclusions of an analysis of outcomes of HIV-prevention interventions. *Current Directions in Psychological Science, 15,* 73–78.

Albarracin, D., Gillette, J. C., Earl, A. N., Glasman, L. R., Durantini, M. R., & Ho, M. (2005). A test of major assumptions about behavior change: A comprehensive look at the effects of passive and active HIV-prevention interventions since the beginning of the epidemic. *Psychological Bulletin, 131,* 856–897.

Alberto, P. A., & Troutman, A. C. (2009). *Applied behavior analysis for teachers* (8th ed.). Upper Saddle River, NJ: Prentice-Hall.

Aldao, A., Nolen-Hoeksema, S., & Schweizer, S. (2010). Emotion-regulation strategies across psychopathology: A meta-analytic review. *Clinical Psychology Review, 30,* 217–237.

Aldwin, C. M., Levenson, M. R., & Kelly, L. L. (2009). Lifespan developmental perspectives on stress-related growth. In C. L. Park, S. Lechner, A. Stanton, & M. Antoni (Eds.), *Positive life changes in the context of medical illness.* Washington, DC: APA Press.

Aldwin, C. M., Spiro, A., & Park, C. L. (2006). Health, behavior, and optimal aging. In J. E. Birren & K. W. Schaie (Eds.), *Handbook of the psychology of aging* (6th ed.). San Diego: Academic.

Aldwin, C. M., Yancura, L. A., & Boeninger, D. K. (2007). In C. M. Aldwin, C. L. Park, & A. Spiro (Eds.), *Handbook of health and aging.* New York: Guilford.

Alegria, M. (2011). Epidemiology of mental disorders in Latino and Asian populations. *Annual Review of Clinical Psychology* (vol. 7). Palo Alto, CA: Annual Reviews.

Alexander, G. M., & Hines, M. (2002). Sex differences in response to children's toys in nonhuman primates (*Cercopithecus aethiops sabaeus*). *Evolution and Human Behavior, 23,* 467–479.

Alexander, G. M., Wilcox, T., & Woods, R. (2009). Sex differences in infants' visual interest in toys. *Archives of Sexual Behavior, 38,* 427–433.

Allan, K. (2010). Vantage theory and linguistic relativity. *Language Sciences, 32,* 158–169.

Allen, J. J. B., Harmon-Jones, E., & Cavender, J. H. (2001). Manipulation of frontal EEG asymmetry through biofeedback alters self-reported emotional responses and facial EMG. *Psychophysiology, 38,* 685–693.

Allport, G. W. (1954). *The nature of prejudice.* Cambridge, MA: Perseus.

Allport, G. W. (1961). *Pattern and growth in personality.* New York: Holt, Rinehart & Winston.

Allport, G. W., & Odbert, H. (1936). *Trait-names: A psycho-lexical study. No. 211.* Princeton, NJ: Psychological Review Monographs.

Altemus, M. (2006). Sex differences in depression and anxiety disorders: Potential biological determinants. *Hormones and Behavior, 50,* 534–538.

Altenor, A., Volpicelli, J. R., & Seligman, M. E. P. (1979). Debilitated shock escape is produced by both short- and long-duration inescapable shock: Learned helplessness vs. learned inactivity. *Bulletin of the Psychonomic Society, 14,* 337–339.

Alter, A. L., Aronson, J., Darley, J. M., Rodriguez, C., & Ruble, D. N. (2010). Rising to the threat: Reducing stereotype threat by reframing the threat as a challenge. *Journal of Experimental Social Psychology, 46,* 166–171.

Althof, S. E., & others. (2010). Impact of tadalafil once daily in men with erectile dysfunction— including a report of the partner's evaluation. *Urology.* (in press)

Alvino, C., Kohlber, C., Barrett, F., Gur, R. E., Gur, R. C., & Verma, R. (2007). Computerized measurement of facial expression of emotions in schizophrenia. *Journal of Neuroscience Methods, 163,* 350–361.

Alyahri, A., & Goodman, R. (2008). Harsh corporal punishment of Yemeni children: Occurrence, type, and associations. *Child Abuse and Neglect, 32,* 766–773.

Amato, P. R. (2006). Marital discord, divorce, and children's well-being: Results from a 20-year longitudinal study of two generations. In A. Clarke-Stewart & J. Dunn (Eds.), *Families count.* New York: Cambridge University Press.

Ambady, N., Krabbenhoft, M. A., & Hogan, D. (2006). The 30-sec sale: Using thin-slice judgments to evaluate sales effectiveness. *Journal of Consumer Psychology, 16,* 4–13.

Ambady, N., & Skowronski, J. J. (Eds.). (2009). *First impressions.* New York: Guilford.

Ambrosi, G., Armentero, M. T., Levandis, G., Bramanti, P., Nappi, G., & Blandini, F. (2010). Effects of early and delayed treatment with an mGluR5 antagonist on motor impairment, nigrostriatal damage and neuroinflammation in a rodent model of Parkinson disease. *Brain Research Bulletin.* (in press)

American Association of University Women (AAUW). (2006). *Drawing the line: Sexual harassment on campus (2006).* Washington, DC: Author.

American Association on Intellectual and Developmental Disabilities. (2010). Diagnostic Adaptive Behavior Scale. http://www.aamr.org/content_106.cfm?navID=23 (accessed April 2, 2010)

American Cancer Society. (2010). *Guide to quitting smoking.* Washington, DC: Author.

American Psychiatric Association (APA). (1994). *Diagnostic and statistical manual of mental disorders* (4th ed.). Washington, DC: Author.

American Psychiatric Association (APA). (2000). *Diagnostic and statistical manual of mental disorders* (4th ed., text revision). Washington, DC: Author.

American Psychiatric Association (APA). (2001). *Mental illness.* Washington, DC: Author.

American Psychiatric Association (APA). (2005). *Let's talk about eating disorders.* Arlington, VA: Author.

American Psychiatric Association (APA). (2006). *American Psychiatric Association practice guidelines for the treatment of psychiatric disorders.* Washington, DC: Author.

American Psychological Association. (2004, July 28). *APA supports legalization of same-sex civil marriages and opposes discrimination against lesbian and gay parents: Denying same-sex couples legal access to civil marriage is discriminatory and can adversely affect the psychological, physical, social, and economic well-being of gay and lesbian individuals.* Washington, DC: Author.

American Sleep Apnea Association (ASAA). (2006). *Get the facts about sleep apnea.* Washington, DC: Author.

Amiot, C. E., Terry, D. J., Jimmieson, N. L., & Callan, V. J. (2006). A longitudinal investigation of coping processes during a merger: Implications for job satisfaction and organizational identification. *Journal of Management, 32,* 552–574.

Amodio, D. M., & Mendoza, S. A. (2010). Implicit outgroup bias: Cognitive, affective, and motivational underpinnings. In B. Gawronski & B. K. Payne (Eds.), *Handbook of implicit social cognition.* New York: Guilford.

Amsterdam, J. D., & Shults, J. (2010). Efficacy and safety of long-term fluoxetine versus lithium monotherapy of bipolar II disorder: A randomized, double-blind, placebo-substitution study. *American Journal of Psychiatry.* (in press)

Amunts, K., Schlaug, G., Jancke, L., Steinmetz, H., Schleicher, A., Dabringhaus, A., & Zilles, K. (1997). Motor cortex and hand motor skills: Structural compliance in the human brain. *Human Brain Mapping, 5* (3), 206–215.

Anastasi, A., & Urbina, S. (1996). *Psychological testing* (7th ed.). Upper Saddle River, NJ: Prentice-Hall.

Ancelet, C., Pedersen, N. P., Fuller, P. M., & Lu, J. (2010). Brainstem circuitry regulation phasic activation and trigeminal motoneurons during REM sleep. *PLoS One, 5,* e8788.

Andel, R., Crowe, M., Pedersen, N. L., Mortimer, J., Crimmins, E., Johansson, B., & Gatz, M. (2005). Complexity of work and risk of Alzheimer's disease: A population-based study of Swedish twins. *Journals of Gerontology: Series B: Psychological Sciences and Social Sciences, 60B,* 251–258.

Anderman, E. M., & Anderman, L. H. (2010). *Classroom motivation.* Upper Saddle River, NJ: Merrill.

Anderson, B. A., Golden-Kreutz, D. M., & DiLillo, V. (2001). Cancer. In A. Baum, T. A.

Revenson, & J. E. Singer (Eds.), *Handbook of health psychology*. Mahwah, NJ: Erlbaum.

Anderson, C. A. (2003). Video games and aggressive behavior. In D. Ravitch and J. P. Viteritti (Eds.), *Kid stuff: Marketing sex and violence to America's children* (pp. 143–167). Baltimore: Johns Hopkins University Press.

Anderson, C. A., & Arciniegas, D. B. (2010). Cognitive sequelae of hypoxic-ischemic brain injury: A review. *NeuroRehabilitation, 26,* 47–63.

Anderson, C. A., Benjamin, A. J., Jr., & Bartholow, B. D. (1998). Does the gun pull the trigger? Automatic priming effects of weapon pictures and weapon names. *Psychological Science, 9,* 308–314.

Anderson, C. A., & Bushman, B. J. (2002). Human aggression. *Annual Review of Psychology* (vol. 53). Palo Alto, CA: Annual Reviews.

Anderson, C. A., & Huesmann, L. R. (2007). Human aggression. In M. A. Hogg & J. Cooper (Eds.), *The Sage handbook of social psychology* (concise 2nd ed.). Thousand Oaks, CA: Sage.

Anderson, C. A., & Kilduff, G. J. (2009). Why do dominant personalities attain influence in face-to-face groups? The competence-signaling effects of trait dominance. *Journal of Personality and Social Psychology, 96,* 491–503.

Anderson, C. A., Shibuya, A., Ihori, N., Swing, E. L., Bushman, B. J., Sakamoto, A., Rothstein, H. R., & Saleem, M. (2010). Violent video game effects on aggression, empathy, and prosocial behavior in Eastern and Western countries: A meta-analytic review. *Psychological Bulletin, 136,* 151–173.

Anderson, E. M., & Lambert, M. J. (2001). A survival analysis of clinically significant change in outpatient psychotherapy. *Journal of Clinical Psychology, 57,* 875–888.

Anderson, N. H. (1965). Primacy effects in personality impression formation using a generalized order effect paradigm. *Journal of Personality and Social Psychology, 2,* 1–9.

Andersson, M., & Simmons, L. W. (2006). Sexual selection and mate choice. *Trends in Ecology and Evolution, 21,* 296–302.

Andreano, J. M., & Cahill, L. (2006). Glucocorticoid release and memory consolidation in men and women. *Psychological Science, 17,* 466–470.

Ang, S., & van Dyne, L. (Eds.). (2009). *Handbook on cultural intelligence.* New York: M. E. Sharpe.

Angel, L., Fay, S., Bourazzaouli, B., Granjon, L., & Isingrini, M. (2009). Neural correlates of cued recall in younger and older adults: An event-related potential study. *NeuroReport, 20,* 75–79.

Angel, L., & others. (2010). The amount of retrieval support modulates age effects on episodic memory: Evidence from event-related potentials. *Brain Research.* (in press)

Annesi, J. J. (2007). Relations of changes in exercise self-efficacy, physical self-concept, and body satisfaction with weight changes in obese white and African American women initiating a physical activity program. *Ethnicity and Disease, 17,* 19–22.

Aquino, K., & Thau, S. (2009). Workplace victimization: Aggression from the target's perspective. *Annual Review of Psychology* (vol. 60), Palo Alto, CA: Annual Reviews.

Archer, J. (2004). Sex differences in aggression in real-world settings: A meta-analytic review. *Review of General Psychology, 8,* 291–322.

Arden, M., & Armitage, C. J. (2008). Predicting and explaining transtheoretical model stage transitions in relation to condom-carrying behaviour. *British Journal of Health Psychology, 13,* 719–735.

Ardiel, E. L., & Rankin, C. H. (2010). An elegant mind: Learning and memory in *Caenorhabditis elegans. Learning and Memory, 17,* 191–201.

Arendt, J. (2009). Managing jet lag: Some of the problems and possible new solutions. *Sleep Medicine Reviews, 13,* 247–248.

Arenkiel, B. R. (2010). Adult neurogenesis supports short-term olfactory memory. *Journal of Neurophysiology.* (in press)

Armaiz-Pena, G. N., Lutgendorf, S. K., Cole, S. W., & Sood, A. K. (2009). Neuroendocrine modulation of cancer progression. *Brain, Behavior, and Immunity, 23,* 10–15.

Armenta, B. E. (2010). Stereotype boost and stereotype threat effects: The moderating role of ethnic identification. *Cultural Diversity and Ethnic Minority Psychology.* (in press)

Armitage, C. J. (2006). Evidence that implementation intentions promote transitions between the stages of change. *Journal of Consulting and Clinical Psychology, 74,* 141–151.

Armor, D. A., Massey, C., & Sackett, A. M. (2008). Prescribed optimism. *Psychological Science, 19,* 329–331.

Arnell, K. M., Killman, K. V., & Fijavz, D. (2007). Blinded by emotion: Target misses follow attention capture by arousing distractors in RSVP. *Emotion, 7,* 465–477.

Arnett, J. J. (2004). *Emerging adulthood.* New York: Oxford University Press.

Arnett, J. J. (2006). Emerging adulthood: Understanding the new way of coming of age. In J. J. Arnett & J. L. Tanner (Eds.), *Emerging adults in America.* Washington, DC: American Psychological Association.

Arnett, J. J. (2007). Socialization in emerging adulthood. In J. E. Grusec & P. D. Hastings (Eds.), *Handbook of socialization.* New York: Oxford University Press.

Arnett, J. J. (2010). Oh, grow up! Generational grumbling and the new life stage of emerging adulthood. *Perspectives on Psychological Science.* (in press)

Arnkoff, D. B., Glass, C. R., & Shapiro, S. J. (2002). Expectations and preferences. In J. C. Norcross (Ed.), *Psychotherapy relationships that work.* New York: Oxford University Press.

Arntz, A. (2005). Cognition and emotion in borderline personality disorder. *Journal of Behavior Therapy and Experimental Psychiatry, 36,* 167–172.

Aron, A., Aron, E. N., & Coups, E. (2011). *Statistics for the behavioral and social sciences* (5th ed.). Upper Saddle River, NJ: Prentice-Hall.

Aronson, E. (1986, August). *Teaching students things they think they already know all about: The case of prejudice and desegregation.* Paper presented at the meeting of the American Psychological Association, Washington, DC.

Arrow, H. (2007). The sharp end of altruism. *Science, 318,* 581–582.

Artazcoz, L., Cortes, I., Escriba-Aguir, V., Cascant, L., & Villegas, R. (2009). Understanding the relationship of long working hours with health status and health-related behaviors. *Journal of Epidemiology and Community Health, 63,* 521–527.

Arthur, W. J., Bennett, W. J., Edens, P., & Bell, S. T. (2003). Effectiveness of training in organizations: A meta-analysis of design and evaluation features. *Journal of Applied Psychology, 88,* 234–245.

Arvey, R. D., Harpaz, I., & Liao, H. (2004). Work centrality and post-award work behavior of lottery winners. *Journal of Psychology: Interdisciplinary and Applied, 138,* 404–420.

Arvey, R. D., Rotundo, M., Johnson, W., Zhang, Z., & McGue, M. (2006). The determinants of leadership role occupancy: Genetic and personality factors. *Leadership Quarterly, 17* (1), 1–20.

Arvey, R. D., Zhang, Z., Avolio, B. J., & Krueger, R. F. (2007). Developmental and genetic determinants of leadership role occupancy among women. *Journal of Applied Psychology, 92* (3), 693–706.

Asch, S. E. (1951). Effects of group pressure on the modification and distortion of judgments. In H. S. Guetzkow (Ed.), *Groups, leadership, and men.* Pittsburgh: Carnegie University Press.

Ash, M., & Sturm, T. (Eds.). (2007). *Psychology's territories.* Mahwah, NJ: Erlbaum.

Ashcraft, M. H., & Radvansky, G. (2009). *Cognition* (5th ed.). Upper Saddle River, NJ: Prentice-Hall.

Ashcroft, W., Argiro, S., & Keohane, J. (2010). *Success strategies for teaching kids with autism.* Waco, TX: Prufrock Press.

Asher, S. R., & McDonald, K. L. (2009). Friendship in childhood and adolescence. In B. McGraw, P. L. Peterson, & E. Baker (Eds.), *International encyclopedia of education* (3rd ed.). Amsterdam: Elsevier.

Ashton, M. C., & Kibeom, L. (2008). The HEXACO model of personality structure and the importance of the H factor. *Social and Personality Psychology Compass, 2,* 1952–1962.

Aspinwall, L. G. (1998). Rethinking the role of positive affect in self-regulation. *Motivation and Emotion, 22,* 1–32.

Aspinwall, L. G., & Brunhart, S. M. (1996). Distinguishing optimism from denial: Optimistic beliefs predict attention to health threats. *Personality and Social Psychology Bulletin, 22,* 993–1003.

Aspinwall, L. G., Leaf, S. L., & Leachman, S. A. (2009). Meaning and agency in the context of genetic testing for familial cancer. To appear in P. T. P. Wong (Ed.), *The human quest for meaning* (2nd ed.). Hillsdale, NJ: Erlbaum.

Aspinwall, L. G., & Tedeschi, R. G. (2010a). The value of positive psychology for health psychology: Progress and pitfalls in examining the relation of positive phenomena to health. *Annals of Behavioral Medicine, 39,* 4–15.

Aspinwall, L. G., & Tedeschi, R. G. (2010b). Of babies and bathwater: A reply to Coyne and Tennen's views on positive psychology and health. *Annals of Behavioral Medicine, 39,* 27–34.

Associated Press. (2007). College students think they're so special. www.msnbc.msn.com/id/17349066/ (accessed October 5, 2007)

Assor, A., Roth, G., & Deci, E. L. (2004). The emotional costs of parents' conditional regard: A self-determination theory analysis. *Journal of Personality, 72,* 47–88.

Atkinson, R. C., & Shiffrin, R. M. (1968). Human memory: A proposed system and its control processes. In K. W. Spence & J. T. Spence (Eds.), *The psychology of learning and motivation* (vol. 2). San Diego: Academic.

Atmaca, M., Yildirim, H., Ozdemir, H. N., Ozler, S., Kara, B., Ozler, Z., Kanmaz, E., Mermi, O., & Tezcan, E. (2008). Hippocampus and amygdalar volumes in patients with refractory obsessive-compulsive disorder. *Progress in Neuro-Psychopharmacology & Biological Psychiatry, 32,* 1283–1286.

Aton, S. J., Seibt, J., Dumoulin, M., Steinmetz, N., Coleman, T., Naidoo, N., & Frank, M. G. (2009). Mechanisms of sleep-dependent consolidation of cortical plasticity. *Neuron, 61,* 454–466.

Austad, C. S. (2009). *Counseling and psychotherapy today.* New York: McGraw-Hill.

Austin, J. T., & Crespin, T. R. (2006). Problems of criteria in industrial and organizational psychology. In W. Bennett, C. E. Lance, & D. J. Woehr (Eds.), *Performance measurement.* Mahwah, NJ: Erlbaum.

Avey, J. B., Luthans, F., Smith, R. M., & Palmer, N. F. (2010). Impact of positive psychological capital on employee well-being over time. *Journal of Occupational Health Psychology, 15,* 17–28.

Avolio, B. J., Rotundo, M., & Walumbwa, F. O. (2009). Early life experiences as determinants of leadership role occupancy: The importance of parental influence and rule breaking behavior. *Leadership Quarterly, 20,* 329–342.

Avolio, B. J., Walumbwa, F. O., & Weber, T. J. (2009). Leadership: Current theories, research, and future directions. *Annual Review of Psychology* (vol. 60). Palo Alto, CA: Annual Reviews.

Azarbad, L., Corsica, J., Hall, B., & Hood, M. (2010). Psychosocial correlates of binge eating in Hispanic, African American, and Caucasian women presenting for bariatric surgery. *Eating Behaviors, 11,* 79–84.

Azboy, O., & Kaygisiz, Z. (2009). Effects of sleep deprivation on cardiorespiratory functions of the runners and volleyball players during rest and exercise. *Acta Physiologica Hungarica, 96,* 29–36.

Azevedo, F. A., & others. (2009). Equal numbers of neuronal and nonneuronal cells make the human brain an isometrically scaled-up primate brain. *Journal of Comparative Neurology, 513,* 532–541.

B

Baars, B. J. (2010). Spontaneous repetitive thoughts can be adaptive: Postscript on "mind wandering." *Psychological Bulletin, 136,* 208–210.

Babiloni, C., Vecchio, F., Cappa, S., Pasqualetti, P., Rossi, S., Miniussi, C., & Rossini, P. M. (2006). Functional frontoparietal connectivity during encoding and retrieval processes follows HERA model: A high resolution study. *Brain Research Bulletin, 68,* 203–212.

Babson, K. A., Trainor, C. D., Feldner, M. T., & Blumenthal, H. (2010). A test of the effects of acute sleep deprivation on general and specific self-reported anxiety and depressive symptoms: An experimental extension. *Journal of Behavior Therapy and Experimental Psychiatry.* (in press)

Back, M. D., Stopfer, J. M., Vazire, S., Gaddis, S., Schmukle, S. C., Egloff, B., & Gosling, S. D. (2010). Facebook profiles reflect actual personality, not self idealization. *Psychological Science, 21,* 372–374.

Baddeley, A. D. (2001). *Is working memory still working?* Paper presented at the meeting of the American Psychological Association, San Francisco.

Baddeley, A. D. (2006). Working memory: An overview. In S. Pickering (Ed.), *Working memory and education.* San Diego: Academic.

Baddeley, A. D. (2008). What's new in working memory? *Psychological Review, 13,* 2–5.

Baddeley, A. D. (2009). Baddeley, A. *Current Biology, 19,* R1019–R1020.

Baddeley, A. D. (2010). Working memory. *Current Biology, 20,* R136–R140.

Baddeley, A. D., Allen, R., & Vargh-Khadem, F. (2010). Is the hippocampus necessary for visual and verbal binding in working memory? *Neuropsychologia, 48,* 1089–1095.

Baddeley, J. L., & Pennebaker, J. W. (2009). Expressive writing. In W. T. O'Donohue & J. E. Fisher (Eds.), *General principles and empirically supported techniques of cognitive behavior therapy* (pp. 295–299). Hoboken, NJ: Wiley.

Baddeley, J. L., & Singer, J. A. (2008). Telling losses: Personality correlates and functions of bereavement narratives. *Journal of Research in Personality, 42,* 421–438.

Bagetta, V., Ghiglieri, V., Sgobio, C., Calabresi, P., & Picconi, B. (2010). Synaptic dysfunction in Parkinson's disease. *Biochemical Society Transactions, 38,* 493–497.

Bagnara, D., & others. (2009). Adoptive immunotherapy mediated by ex vivo expanded natural killer T cells against CD1d-expressing lymphoid neoplasms. *Haematologica, 94* (7), 967–974.

Bahrick, H. P. (1984). Semantic memory content in permastore: Fifty years of memory for Spanish learned in school. *Journal of Experimental Psychology: General, 113,* 1–29.

Bahrick, H. P. (2000). Long-term maintenance of knowledge. In E. Tulving & F. I. M. Craik (Eds.), *The Oxford handbook of memory* (pp. 347–362). New York: Oxford University Press.

Bahrick, H. P. (2005). The long-term neglect of long-term memory: Reasons and remedies. In A. F. Healey (Ed.), *Experimental cognitive psychology and its applications.* (pp. 89–100). Washington, DC: American Psychological Association.

Bahrick, H. P., Bahrick, P. O., & Wittlinger, R. P. (1974). Long-term memory: Those unforgettable high-school days. *Psychology Today, 8,* 50–56.

Bahrick, H. P., Hall, L. K., & Da Costa, L. A. (2008). Fifty years of memory of college grades: Accuracy and distortions. *Emotion, 8,* 13–22.

Bailey, J. M. (2003). Biological perspectives on sexual orientation. In L. D. Garnets & D. C. Kimmel (Eds.), *Psychological perspectives on lesbian, gay, and bisexual experiences* (2nd ed., pp. 50–85). New York: Columbia University Press.

Bailey, J. M., & Zucker, K. J. (1995). Childhood sex-typed behavior and sexual orientation: A conceptual and quantitative review. *Developmental Psychology, 31,* 43–55.

Baillargeon, R., Li, J., Gertner, Y., & Wu, D. (2011). How do infants reason about physical events? In U. Goswami (Ed.), *Wiley-Blackwell handbook of childhood cognitive development* (2nd ed.). New York: Wiley Blackwell.

Baillargeon, R., Wu, D., Yan, S., Li, J., & Luo, Y. (2009). Young infants' expectations about self-propelled objects. In B. Hood & L. Santos (Eds.), *The origins of object knowledge.* New York: Oxford University Press.

Baker, C. K., Norris, F. H., Jones, E. C., & Murphy, A. D. (2009). Childhood trauma and adult physical health in Mexico. *Journal of Behavioral Medicine, 32,* 255–269.

Baker, L. A., Raine, A., Liu, J., & Jacobson, K. C. (2008). Differential genetic and environmental influences on reactive and proactive aggression in children. *Journal of Abnormal Child Psychology, 36,* 1265–1278.

Baldwin, T. T., & Padgett, M. Y. (1993). Management development: A review and commentary. In C. L. Cooper & I. T. Robertson (Eds.), *International review of industrial and organizational psychology* (pp. 35–38). Chichester, U.K.: Wiley.

Balliet, D. (2010). Conscientiousness and forgivingness: A meta-analysis. *Personality and Individual Differences, 48,* 259–263.

Balsam, K. F., Beauchaine, T. P., Rothblum, E. D., & Solomon, S. E. (2008). Three-year follow-up of same-sex couple who had civil unions in Vermont, same-sex couples not in civil unions, and heterosexual married couples. *Developmental Psychology, 44,* 102–116.

Balsam, K. F., & Mohr, J. J. (2007). Adaptation to sexual orientation stigma: A comparison of bisexual and lesbian/gay adults. *Journal of Counseling Psychology, 54,* 306–319.

Bamford, C., & Lagattuta, K. H. (2010). A new look at children's understanding of mind and emotion: The case of prayer. *Developmental Psychology, 46*, 78–92.

Bandura, A. (1986). *Social foundations of thought and action.* Englewood Cliffs, NJ: Prentice-Hall.

Bandura, A. (1997). *Self-efficacy.* New York: Freeman.

Bandura, A. (2001). Social cognitive theory. *Annual Review of Psychology* (vol. 52). Palo Alto, CA: Annual Reviews.

Bandura, A. (2007a). Self-efficacy in health functioning. In S. Ayers & others (Eds.), *Cambridge handbook of psychology, health, and medicine.* New York: Cambridge University Press.

Bandura, A. (2007b). Social cognitive theory. In W. Donsbach (Ed.), *International handbook of communication.* Thousand Oaks, CA: Sage.

Bandura, A. (2008). Reconstrual of "free will" from the agentic perspective of social cognitive theory. In J. Baer, J. C. Kaufman, & R. F. Baumeister (Eds.), *Are we free? Psychology and free will.* Oxford, U.K.: Oxford University Press.

Bandura, A. (2009). Social and policy impact of social cognitive theory. In M. Mark, S. Donaldson, & B. Campbell (Eds.), *Social psychology and program/policy evaluation.* New York: Guilford.

Bandura, A. (2010a). Vicarious learning. In D. Matsumoto (Ed.), *Cambridge dictionary of psychology.* New York: Cambridge University Press. (in press)

Bandura, A. (2010b). Self-efficacy. In D. Matsumoto (Ed.), *Cambridge dictionary of psychology.* New York: Cambridge University Press. (in press)

Bandura, A., & Bussey, K. (2004). On broadening the cognitive, motivational, and sociostructural scope of theorizing about gender development and functioning: Comment on Martin, Ruble, and Szkrybalo (2002). *Psychological Bulletin, 130*, 690–701.

Bandura, A., Ross, D., & Ross, S. A. (1961). Transmission of aggression through imitation of aggressive models. *Journal of Abnormal and Social Psychology, 63*, 575–582.

Banks, J. A. (Ed.). (2010). *Routledge international handbook of multicultural education.* New York: Routledge.

Banthia, R., Malcarne, V. L., Ko, C. M., Varni, J. W., & Sadler, G. R. (2009). Fatigued breast cancer survivors: The role of sleep quality, depressed mood, stage, and age. *Psychology & Health, 24*, 965–980.

Banyard, V. L., & Williams, L. M. (2007). Women's voices on recovery: A multi-method study of the complexity of recovery from child sexual abuse. *Child Abuse and Neglect, 31*, 275–290.

Barber, N. (2009). Evolutionary social science: A new approach to violent crime. *Aggression and Violent Behavior, 13*, 237–250.

Barclay, L. J., & Aquino, K. (2010). Workplace aggression and violence. In S. Zedeck (Ed.), *APA handbook of industrial and organizational psychology.* Washington, DC: APA. (in press)

Bard, P. (1934). Emotion. In C. Murchison (Ed.), *Handbook of general psychology.* Worcester, MA: Clark University Press.

Bardone-Cone, A. M., Abramson, L. Y., Vohs, K. D., Heatherton, T. F., & Joiner, T. E., Jr. (2006). Predicting bulimic symptoms: An interactive model of self-efficacy, perfectionism, and perceived weight status. *Behaviour Research and Therapy, 44*, 27–42.

Bargh, J. A. (2005). Bypassing the will: Towards demystifying the nonconscious control of social behavior. In R. Hassin, J. Uleman, & J. Bargh (Eds.), *The new unconscious.* New York: Oxford University Press.

Bargh, J. A. (2006). Agenda 2006: What have we been priming all these years? On the development, mechanism, and ecology of nonconscious social behavior. *European Journal of Social Psychology, 36*, 147–168.

Bargh, J. A., Chen, M., & Burrows, L. (1996). The automaticity of social behavior: Direct effects of trait concept and stereotype activation on action. *Journal of Personality and Social Psychology, 71*, 230–244.

Bargh, J. A., Gollwitzer, P. M., Lee-Chai, A., Barndollar, K., & Trotschel, R. (2001). The automated will: Nonconscious activation and pursuit of behavioral goals. *Journal of Personality and Social Psychology, 81*, 1014–1027.

Bargh, J. A., & Morsella, E. (2009). Unconscious behavioral guidance systems. In C. Agnew & others (Eds.), *Then a miracle occurs: Focusing on behavior and social psychological theory and research.* New York: Oxford University Press.

Barker, A. T., Jalinous, R., & Freeston, I. L. (1985). Non-invasive magnetic stimulation of human motor cortex. *Lancet, 1*, 1106–1107.

Barkley, R., & 74 others. (2002). International consensus statement on ADHD. *Clinical Child and Family Psychology, 5*, 89–111.

Barkus, E. & others. (2010). Distress and metacognition in psychosis prone individuals: Comparing high schizotypy to the at-risk mental state. *Journal of Nervous and Mental Disease, 198*, 99–104.

Barling, J., Christie, A., & Hoption, C. (2010). Leadership. In S. Zedeck (Ed.), *APA handbook of industrial and organizational psychology.* Washington, DC: APA. (in press)

Barling, J., Dupré, K., & Kelloway, E. K. (2009). Predicting workplace violence and aggression, *Annual Review of Psychology* (vol. 60). Palo Alto, CA: Annual Reviews.

Barling, J., Weber, T., & Kelloway E. K. (1996). Effects of transformational leadership training on attitudinal and financial outcomes: A field experiment. *Journal of Applied Psychology, 81*, 827–832.

Barloon, T., & Noyes, R., Jr. (1997). Charles Darwin and panic disorder. *Journal of the American Medical Association, 277*, 138–141.

Barlow, A., Qualter, P., & Stylianou, M. (2010). Relationships between Machiavellianism, emotional intelligence, and theory of mind in children. *Personality and Individual Differences, 48*, 78–82.

Barnett, J. H., & Smoller, J. W. (2009). The genetics of bipolar disorder. *Neuroscience, 164* (1), 331–343.

Barnow, S., & others. (2010). Borderline personality disorder and psychosis: A review. *Current Psychiatry Reports, 12*, 186–195.

Baron, N. (1992). *Growing up with language.* Reading, MA: Addison-Wesley.

Baron-Cohen, S. (2002). The extreme male brain theory of autism. *Trends in Cognitive Science, 6*, 248–254.

Baron-Cohen, S. (2003). *The essential difference: Men, women, and the extreme male brain.* New York: Basic.

Baron-Cohen, S. (2006). The hyper-systemizing, assortative mating theory of autism. *Progress in Neuro-Psychopharmacology & Biological Psychiatry, 30*, 865–872.

Baron-Cohen, S. (2008). Autism, hypersystemizing, and the truth. *Quarterly Journal of Experimental Psychology, 61*, 64–75.

Baron-Cohen, S., Knickmeyer, R. C., & Belmonte, M. K. (2006). Sex differences in the brain: Implications for explaining autism. *Science, 311*, 952.

Barrett, G. V., & Kernan, M. G. (1987). Performance appraisal and terminations: A review of court decisions since Brito v. Zia with implications for personnel practices. *Personnel Psychology, 40*, 489–503.

Barrouillet, P., & Camos, V. (2009). Interference: Unique source of forgetting in working memory. *Trends in Cognitive Science, 13*, 145–146.

Bartel, C. A., Blader, S., & Wrzesniewski, A. (Eds.). (2007). *Identity and the modern organization.* Mahwah, NJ: Erlbaum.

Bartolo, A., Benuzzi, F., Nocetti, L., Baraldi, P., & Nichelli, P. (2006). Humor comprehension and appreciation: An fMRI study. *Journal of Cognitive Neuroscience, 18*, 1789–1798.

Bartoshuk, L. (2008). Chemical senses: Taste and smell. *Annual Review of Psychology* (vol. 59). Palo Alto, CA: Annual Reviews.

Baskerville, T. A., Allard, J., Wayman, C., & Douglas, A. J. (2009). Dopamine-oxytocin interactions in penile erection. *European Journal of Neuroscience, 30*, 2151–2164.

Bass, B. M. (1985). *Leadership and performance beyond expectations.* New York: Free Press.

Bastien, C. H., St-Jean, G., Turcotte, I., Morin, C. M., Lavallee, M., & Carrier, J. (2009). Sleep spindles in chronic psychophysiological insomnia. *Journal of Psychosomatic Research, 66*, 59–65.

Bastien, D. L. (2010). Pharmacological treatment of combat-induced PTSD: A literature review. *British Journal of Nursing, 19*, 318–321.

Bateman, A. J. (1948). Intra-sexual selection in *Drosophila. Heredity, 2*, 349–358.

Bateman, T. S., & Snell, S. A. (2011). *Management* (9th ed.). New York: McGraw-Hill.

Batson, C. D. (2002). Addressing the altruism question experimentally. In S. G. Post, L. G. Underwood, J. P. Schloss, & W. B. Hurlbut (Eds.), *Altruism and altruistic love.* New York: Oxford University Press.

Batson, C. D. (2006). "Not all self-interest after all": Economics of empathy-induced altruism. In D. DeCremer, M. Zeelenberg, & J. K. Murnigham (Eds.), *Social psychology and economics* (pp. 281–299). Mahwah, NJ: Erlbaum.

Batson, C. D., Duncan, B. D., Ackerman, P., Buckley, T., Birch, K., Cialdini, R. B., Schaller, M., Houlihan, D., Arps, K., Fultz, J., & Beaman, A. L. (2007). Issue 17: Does true altruism exist? In J. A. Nier (Ed.), *Taking sides: Clashing views in social psychology* (2nd ed., pp. 348–371). New York: McGraw-Hill.

Battaglia, M., Pesenti-Gritti, P., Medland, S. E., Ogilari, A., Tambs, K., & Spatola, C. A. (2009). A genetically informed study of the association between childhood separation anxiety, sensitivity to CO(2), panic disorder, and the effect of childhood parental loss. *Archives of General Psychiatry, 66,* 64–71.

Bauer, J. J., McAdams, D. P., & Sakaeda, A. R. (2005). The crystallization of desire and the crystallization of discontent in narratives of life-changing decisions. *Journal of Personality, 73,* 1181–1213.

Bauer, M., & others. (2007). Using ultrasonography to determine thyroid size and prevalence of goiter in lithium-treated patients with affective disorders. *Journal of Affective Disorders, 104* (1–3), 45–51.

Bauer, M. E., Jeckel, C. M., & Luz, C. (2009). The role of stress factors during aging of the immune system. *Annals of the New York Academy of Sciences, 1153,* 139–152.

Bauer, P. J., Larkina, M., & Deocampo, J. (2011). Early memory development. In U. Goswami (Ed.), *Wiley-Blackwell handbook of childhood cognitive development* (2nd ed.). New York: Wiley Blackwell.

Bauld, R., & Brown, R. F. (2009). Stress, psychological stress, psychosocial factors, menopause symptoms, and physical health in women. *Maturitas, 62,* 160–165.

Baumann, A. E. (2007). Stigmatization, social distance and exclusion because of mental illness: The individual with mental illness as a "stranger." *International Review of Psychiatry, 19,* 131–135.

Baumeister, R. F. (1999). *Evil: Inside human violence and cruelty.* New York: Freeman.

Baumeister, R. F. (2000). Gender differences in erotic plasticity: The female sex drive as socially flexible and responsive. *Psychological Bulletin, 126* (3), 347–374.

Baumeister, R. F., & Alquist, J. L. (2009). Self-regulation as limited resource: Strength model of control and depletion. In J. P. Forgas, R. F. Baumeister, & D. M. Tice (Eds.), *Psychology of self-regulation.* New York: Psychology Press.

Baumeister, R. F., Bushman, B. J., & Campbell, W. K. (2000). Self-esteem, narcissism, and aggression: Does violence result from low self-esteem or from threatened egotism? *Current Directions in Psychological Science, 9,* 26–29.

Baumeister, R. F., & Butz, D. A. (2005). Roots of hate, violence, and evil. In R. J. Sternberg (Ed.), *The psychology of hate* (pp. 87–102). Washington, DC: American Psychological Association.

Baumeister, R. F., Campbell, J. D., Krueger, J. I., Vohs, K. D., DuBois, D. L., & Tevendale, H. D. (2007). Issue 5: Applying social psychology: Are self-esteem programs misguided? In J. A. Nier (Ed.), *Taking sides: Clashing views in social psychology* (2nd ed., pp. 92–115). New York: McGraw-Hill.

Baumeister, R. F., Catanese, K. R., & Vohs, K. D. (2001). Is there a gender difference in strength of sex drive? *Personality and Social Psychology Review, 5,* 242–273.

Baumeister, R. F., & Leary, M. R. (2000). The need to belong: Desire for interpersonal attachments as a fundamental human motivation. In E. T. Higgins & A. W. Kruglanski (Eds.), *Motivational science: Social and personality perspectives* (pp. 24–49). New York: Psychology Press.

Baumeister, R. F., & Stillman, T. (2006). Erotic plasticity: Nature, culture, gender, and sexuality. In R. D. McAnulty & M. M. Burnette (Eds.), *Sex and sexuality: Sexuality today: Trends and controversies* (vol. 1, pp. 343– 359, 377). Westport, CT: Praeger/Greenwood.

Baumgartner, T., Fischbacher, U., Feierabend, A., Lutz, K., & Fehr, E. (2009). The neural circuitry of a broken promise. *Neuron, 64,* 756–770.

Baumrind, D. (1991). Parenting styles and adolescent development. In J. Brooks-Gunn, R. Lerner, & A. C. Petersen (Eds.), *The encyclopedia of adolescence* (vol. 2). New York: Garland.

Baumrind, D. (1993). The average expectable environment is not good enough: A response to Scarr. *Child Development, 64,* 1299–1307.

Baumrind, D., Larzelere, R. E., & Cowan, P. A. (2002). Ordinary physical punishment: Is it harmful? Comment on Gershoff (2002). *Psychological Bulletin, 128,* 590–595.

Baxter, L. R., Jr., Phelps, M. E., Mazziotta, J. C., Schwartz, J. M., Gerner, R. H., Selin, C. E., & Sumida, R. M. (1995). Cerebral metabolic rates for glucose in mood disorders: Studies with positron emission tomography and fluorodeoxyglucose F 18. *Archives of General Psychiatry, 42,* 441–447.

Baylor, D. (2001). *Seeing, hearing, and smelling the world* [Commentary]. http://www.hhmi.org/senses (accessed October 2001)

BBC News. (2005, July 5). Japanese breaks *pi* record. http://news.bbc. co.uk/2/hi/asia-pacific/4644103.stm (accessed October 10, 2006)

Beard, C., Weisberg, R. B., & Keller, M. B. (2010). Health-related quality of life across the anxiety disorders: Findings from a sample of primary care patients. *Journal of Anxiety Disorders.* (in press)

Beck, A. (1967). *Depression.* New York: Harper & Row.

Beck, A. T. (1976). *Cognitive therapies and the emotional disorders.* New York: International Universities Press.

Beck, A. T. (1993). Cognitive therapy: Past, present, and future. *Journal of Consulting and Clinical Psychology, 61,* 194–198.

Beck, A. T. (2005). The current state of cognitive therapy: A 40-year retrospective. *Archives of General Psychiatry, 62,* 953–959.

Beck, A. T. (2006). How an anomalous finding led to a new system of psychotherapy. *Nature Medicine, 12,* 1139–1141.

Beck, A. T., Rush, A. J., Shaw, B. F., & Emery, G. (1979). *Cognitive therapy of depression.* New York: Guilford.

Beckers, T., Miller, R. R., De Houwer, J., & Urushihara, K. (2006). Reasoning rats: Forward blocking in Pavlovian animal conditioning is sensitive to constraints of causal inference. *Journal of Experimental Psychology: General, 135,* 92–102.

Becker-Weidman, E. G., Reinecke, M. A., Jacobs, R. H., Martinovich, Z., Silva, S. G., & March, J. S. (2009). Predictors of hopelessness among clinically depressed youth. *Behavioral and Cognitive Psychotherapy, 37* (3), 267–291.

Beeler, C. K. (2010). Leader traits, skills and behaviors. In M. D. Mumford (Ed.), *Leadership 101* (pp. 87–116). New York: Springer.

Beeli, G., Esslen, M., & Jancke, L. (2005). Synaesthesia: When coloured sounds taste sweet. *Nature, 434,* 38.

Beeson, M., Davison, I., Vostanis, P., & Windwo, S. (2006). Parenting programs for behavioral problems: Where do tertiary units fit in a comprehensive service? *Clinical Child Psychology and Psychiatry, 11,* 335–348.

Beidas, R. S., & Kendall, P. C. (2010). Training therapists in evidence-based practice: A critical review of studies from a systems-contextual perspective. *Clinical Psychology: Science and Practice, 17,* 1–30.

Bekinschtein, T. A., Dehaene, S., Rohaut, B., Tadel, F., Cohen, L., & Naccache, L. (2009). Neural signature of the conscious processing of auditory regularities. *Proceedings of the National Academy of Sciences USA, 106,* 1672–1677.

Bell, A. P., Weinberg, M. S., & Hammersmith, S. K. (1981). *Sexual preference: Its development in men and women.* Bloomington: Indiana University Press.

Belloch, A., Cabedo, E., Carrio, C., & Larsson, C. (2010). Cognitive therapy for autogenous and reactive obsessions: Clinical and cognitive outcomes at post-treatment and 1-year follow-up. *Journal of Anxiety Disorders.* (in press)

Bem, D. (1967). Self-perception: An alternative explanation of cognitive dissonance phenomena. *Psychological Review, 74,* 183–200.

Bem, D. J. (1996). The exotic becomes erotic: A developmental theory of sexual orientation. *Psychological Review, 103,* 320–335.

Bem, S. L. (1983). Gender schema theory and its implications for child development: Raising gender-aschematic children in a gender-schematic society. *Signs, 8,* 598–616.

Bem, S. L. (1993). *The lenses of gender: Transforming the debate on sexual inequality.* New Haven, CT: Yale University Press.

Bender, H. L., Allen, J. P., McElhaney, K. B., Antonishak, J., Moore, C. M., Kello, H. O.,

& Davis, S. M. (2007). Use of harsh physical discipline and developmental outcomes in adolescence. *Development and Psychopathology, 19,* 227–242.

Benedetti, F., and others. (2003). Conscious expectation and unconscious conditioning in analgesic; motor and hormonal placebo/nocebo responses. *Journal of Neuroscience, 23,* 4315–4323.

Beneventi, H., Tonnessen, F. E., Ersland, L., & Hugdahl, K. (2010). Executive working memory processes in dyslexia: Behavioral and fMRI evidence. *Scandinavian Journal of Psychology.* (in press)

Benjamin, A. S., Diaz, M., & Wee, S. (2009). Signal detection with criterion noise: Applications to recognition memory. *Psychological Review, 116,* 84–115.

Benjet, C., Thompson, R. J., & Gotlib, I. H. (2010). 5-HTTLPR moderates the effect of relational peer victimization on depressive symptoms in adolescent girls. *Journal of Child Psychology and Psychiatry, 51,* 173–179.

Benoit, R. G., Werkle-Bergner, M., Mecklinger, A., & Kray, J. (2009). Adapting to changing memory retrieval demands: Evidence from event-related potentials. *Brain and Cognition, 70,* 123–135.

Benoit-Bird, K. J., & Au, W. W. (2009). Phonation behavior of cooperatively foraging spinner dolphins. *Journal of the Acoustical Society of America, 125,* 539–546.

Berdahl, J. L., & Raver, J. L. (2010). Sexual harassment. In S. Zedeck (Ed.), *APA handbook of industrial and organizational psychology.* Washington, DC: APA. (in press)

Berenbaum, S. A. (2006). Psychological outcome in children with disorders of sex development: Implications for treatment and understanding typical development. *Annual Review of Sex Research, 17,* 1–38.

Berg, J. M., Wrzesniewski, A., & Dutton, J. E. (2010). Perceiving and responding to challenges in job crafting at different ranks: When proactivity requires adaptivity. *Journal of Organizational Behavior, 31,* 158–186.

Berger, T., Hohl, E., & Caspar, F. (2009). Internet-based treatment for social phobia. *Journal of Clinical Psychology, 65* (10), 1021–1035.

Bergman, M. E., Langhout, R. D., Palmieri, P. A., Cortina, L. M., & Fitzgerald, L. F. (2002). The (un)reasonableness of reporting: Antecedents and consequences of reporting sexual harassment. *Journal of Applied Psychology, 87,* 230–242.

Berkman, E. T., Lieberman, M. D., & Gable, S. L. (2009). BIS, BAS, and response conflict: Testing predictions of the revised reinforcement sensitivity theory. *Personality and Individual Differences, 46,* 586–591.

Berko Gleason, J. (2009). The development of language: An overview. In J. Berko Gleason & N. Ratner (Eds.), *The development of language* (7th ed.). Boston: Allyn & Bacon.

Berkowitz, L. (1990). On the formation and regulation of anger and aggression: A cognitive neoassociationistic analysis. *American Psychologist, 45,* 494–503.

Berkowitz, L. (1993). *Aggression.* New York: McGraw-Hill.

Berkowitz, L., & LePage, A. (1996). Weapons as aggression-eliciting stimuli. In S. Fein & S. Spencer (Eds.), *Readings in social psychology: The art and science of research* (pp. 67–73). Boston: Houghton Mifflin.

Bernadin, H. J. (2010). *Human resource management* (5th ed.). New York: McGraw-Hill.

Berneburg, M., Dietz, K., Niederle, C., & Goz, G. (2010). Changes in esthetic standards since 1940. *American Journal of Orthodontics and Dentofacial Orthopedics, 137,* e1–e9.

Bernstein, I. L., & Koh, M. T. (2007). Molecular signaling during taste aversion learning. *Chemical Senses, 32* (1), 99–103.

Berntsen, D., & Rubin, D. C. (2002). Emotionally charged autobiographical memories across the life span: The recall of happy, sad, traumatic, and involuntary memories. *Psychology and Aging, 17,* 636–652.

Berntsen, D., & Rubin, D. C. (2006). Flashbulb memories and posttraumatic stress reactions across the life span: Age-related effects of the German occupation of Denmark during World War II. *Psychology of Aging, 21,* 127–139.

Berridge, K. C., & Kringelbach, M. L. (2008). Affective neuroscience of pleasure: Reward in humans and animals. *Psychopharmacology, 199,* 457–480.

Berry, A. C., Rosenfield, D., & Smits, J. A. (2009). Extinction retention predicts improvement in social anxiety symptoms following exposure therapy. *Depression and Anxiety, 26,* 22–27.

Berscheid, E. (1988). Some comments on love's anatomy. Or, whatever happened to an old-fashioned lust? In R. J. Sternberg & M. L. Barnes (Eds.), *Anatomy of love.* New Haven, CT: Yale University Press.

Berscheid, E. (2000). Attraction. In A. Kazdin (Ed.), *Encyclopedia of psychology.* Washington, DC, & New York: American Psychological Association and Oxford University Press.

Berscheid, E. (2006). Searching for the meaning of "love." In R. J. Sternberg & K. Weis (Eds.), *The new psychology of love* (pp. 171–183). New Haven, CT: Yale University Press.

Berscheid, E. (2010). Love in the fourth dimension. *Annual Review of Psychology* (vol. 61). Palo Alto, CA: Annual Reviews.

Berscheid, E., & Regan, P. C. (2005). *The psychology of interpersonal relationships.* New York: Prentice-Hall.

Bertrand, M., & Mullainathan, S. (2004). Are Emily and Greg more employable than Lakisha and Jamal? A field experiment on labor market discrimination. *American Economic Review, 94,* 991–1013.

Best, D. L. (2010). Gender. In M. H. Bornstein (Ed.), *Handbook of cultural developmental science.* New York: Psychology Press.

Bethus, I., Tse, D., & Morris, R. G. (2010). Dopamine and memory: Modulation of the persistence of memory for novel hippocampal NMDA receptor-dependent paired associates. *Journal of Neuroscience, 30,* 1610–1618.

Bewernick, B. H., Hurlemann, R., Matusch, A., Kayser, S., Grubert, C., Hadrysiewicz, B.,

Axmacher, N., Lemke, M., Cooper-Mahkorn, D., Cohen, M. X., Brockmann, H., Lenartz, D., Sturm, V., & Schlaepfer, T. E. (2010). Nucleus accumbens deep brain stimulation decreases ratings of depression and anxiety in treatment-resistant depression. *Biological Psychiatry, 67,* 110–116.

Beydoun, M. A., & Wang, Y. (2009). Gender-ethnic disparity in BMI and waist circumference distribution shifts in U.S. adults. *Obesity, 17,* 169–176.

Bhatia, T., Garg, K., Pogue-Geile, M., Nimaonkar, V. L., & Deshpande, S. N. (2009). Executive functions and cognitive deficits in schizophrenia: Comparisons between probands, parents, and controls in India. *Journal of Postgraduate Medicine, 55,* 3–7.

Bialystok, E., & Craik, F. I. M. (2011). Structure and process in life-span cognitive development. In R. M. Lerner & W. F. Overton (Eds.), *Handbook of life-span development* (vol. 1). New York: Wiley.

Birditt, K. S., & Fingerman, K. L. (2003). Age and gender differences in adults' descriptions of emotional reactions to interpersonal problems. *Journals of Gerontology: Series B: Psychological Sciences and Social Sciences, 58B,* 237–245.

Birkenhager, T. K., & others. (2010). Influence of age on the efficacy of electroconvulsive therapy in major depression: A retrospective study. *Journal of Affective Disorders.* (in press)

Bisiacchi, P. S., Tarantino, V., & Ciccola, A. (2008). Aging and prospective memory: The role of working memory and monitoring processes. *Aging: Clinical and Experimental Research, 20,* 569–577.

Bisley, J., & Goldberg, M. E. (2010). Attention, intention, and priority in the parietal lobe. *Annual Review of Neuroscience* (vol. 33). Palo Alto, CA: Annual Reviews.

Biswas-Diener, R., Kashdan, T., & King, L. A. (2009). Two traditions of happiness research, not two distinct types of happiness. *Journal of Positive Psychology, 4,* 208–211.

Biswas-Diener, R., Vitterso, J., & Diener, E. (2005). Most people are pretty happy, but there is cultural variation: The Inughuit, the Amish, and the Maasai. *Journal of Happiness Studies, 6,* 205–226.

Bjork, R. S., & Druckman, D. (1991). *In the mind's eye: Enhancing human performance.* Washington, DC: National Academy Books.

Black, D. W., Gunter, T., Loveless, P., Allen, J., & Sieleni, B. (2010). Antisocial personality disorder in incarcerated offenders: Psychiatric comorbidity and quality of life. *Annals of Clinical Psychiatry, 22,* 113–120.

Blackman, M. (2008). The effective interview. In S. Cartwright & C. L. Cooper (Eds.), *The Oxford handbook of personnel psychology* (pp. 194–214). New York: Oxford University Press.

Blackwell, L. S., & Dweck, C. S. (2008). *The motivational impact of a computer-based program that teaches how the brain changes with learning.* Unpublished manuscript, Department of Psychology, Stanford University.

Blackwell, L. S., Trzesniewski, K. H., & Dweck, C. S. (2007). Implicit theories of intelligence predict achievement across an adolescent transition: A longitudinal study and an intervention. *Child Development, 78,* 246–263.

Blader, J. C. (2006). Pharmacotherapy and postdischarge outcomes of child inpatients admitted for aggressive behavior. *Journal of Clinical Psychopharmacology, 26,* 419–425.

Blades, H. B. (2006). Killer coworker: The case of Michael McDermott, the Christmas killer. *Forensic Examiner, 156,* 49–52.

Blagrove, M., & Akehurst, L. (2000). Personality and dream recall frequency: Further negative findings. *Dreaming, 10,* 139–148.

Blair, C. (2011). Fluid cognitive abilities and general intelligence: A life-span neuroscience perspective. In R. M. Lerner & W. F. Overton (Eds.), *Handbook of life-span development* (vol. 1). New York: Wiley.

Blair, S. N., Kohl, H. W., Paffenbarger, R. S., Clark, D. G., Cooper, K. H., & Gibbons, L. W. (1989). Physical fitness and all-cause mortality: A prospective study of healthy men and women. *Journal of the American Medical Association, 262,* 2395–2401.

Blakemore, J. E. O., Berenbaum, S. E., & Liben, L. S. (2009). *Gender development.* New York: Psychology Press.

Blanco, M., & others. (2009). *Investigating critical incidents, driver restart period, sleep quantity, and crash countermeasures in commercial operations using naturalistic data collection: A final report* (Contract No. DTFH61-01-00049, Task Order #23). Washington, DC: Federal Motor Carrier Safety Administration.

Blass, T. (2007). Unsupported allegations about a link between Milgram and the CIA: Tortured reasoning in *A Question of Torture. Journal of the History of the Behavioral Sciences, 43,* 199–203.

Blickle, G., Wendel, S., & Ferris, G. R. (2010). Political skill as moderator of personality—Job performance relationships in socioanalytic theory: Test of the getting ahead motive in automobile sales. *Journal of Vocational Behavior, 76,* 326–335.

Block, J. (1982). Assimilation, accommodation, and the dynamics of personality development. *Child Development, 53,* 281–295.

Block, J., & Kremen, A. M. (1996). IQ and ego-resiliency: Conceptual and empirical connections and separateness. *Journal of Personality and Social Psychology, 70,* 349–361.

Blonigen, D. M., Carlson, M. D., Hicks, B. M., Krueger, R. F., & Iacono, W. G. (2008). Stability and change in personality traits from late adolescence to early adulthood: A longitudinal twin study. *Journal of Personality, 76,* 229–266.

Bloom, B. (1985). *Developing talent in young people.* New York: Ballantine.

Bloom, B., & Cohen, R. A. (2007). Summary health statistics for U.S. children: National Health Interview Survey, 2006. National Center for Health Statistics. *Vital Health Statistics, 10* (234).

Bloom, F., Nelson, C. A., & Lazerson, A. (2001). *Brain, mind, and behavior* (3rd ed.). New York: Worth.

Bloom, P. (2004). Myths of word learning. In D. G. Hall & S. R. Waxman (Eds.), *Weaving a lexicon* (pp. 205–224). Cambridge, MA: MIT Press.

Bloor, C., & White, F. (1983). Unpublished manuscript. LaJolla, CA: University of California, San Diego.

Bluher, S., & Mantzoros, C. S. (2009). Leptin in humans: Lessons from translational research. *American Journal of Clinical Nutrition, 89,* 991S–997S.

Blum, L. M., & Blum, R. W. (2009). Resilience in adolescence. In R. A. Crosby (Ed.), *Adolescent health: Understanding and preventing risk behaviors* (pp. 51–76). San Francisco: Jossey-Bass.

Blumenfeld, P. C., Kempler, T. M., & Krajcik, J. S. (2006). Motivation and cognitive engagement in learning environments. In R. K. Sawyer (Ed.), *The Cambridge handbook of learning sciences.* New York: Cambridge University Press.

Boatright-Horowitz, S. L., Langley, M., & Gunnip, M. (2009). Depth-of-processing effects as college students use academic advising web sites. *CyberPsychology & Behavior, 12,* 331–335.

Bob, P., & others. (2009). Depression, traumatic stress, and interleukin-6. *Journal of Affective Disorders, 120,* 231–234.

Bobo, W. V., & Shelton, R. C. (2010). Efficacy, safety, and tolerability of Symbyax for acute-phase management of treatment-resistant depression. *Expert Review of Neurotherapeutics, 10,* 651–670.

Bocanegra, B. R., & Zeelenberg, R. (2009). Dissociating emotion-induced blindness and hypervision. *Emotion, 9,* 865–873.

Bocker, S., Briesemeister, S., & Klau, G. W. (2009). On optimal comparability editing with applications to molecular diagnostics. *BMC Bioinformatics, 10, Suppl. 1,* S61.

Boeddeker, N., & Memmi, J. M. (2010). Visual gaze control during peering flight manoeuvres in honeybees. *Proceedings. Biological Sciences.* (in press)

Boekaerts, M. (2010). Goal-directed behavior in the classroom. In K. Wentzel & A. Wigfield (Eds.), *Handbook of motivation at school.* New York: Routledge.

Boeninger, D. K., Shiraishi, R. W., Aldwin, C. M., & Spiro, A. (2009). Why do older men report lower stress ratings? Findings from the Normative Aging Study. *International Journal of Aging and Human Development, 2,* 149–170.

Boeve, B. F. (2010). REM sleep disorder: Updated review of the core features, the REM sleep disorder-neurodegenerative disease association, evolving concepts, controversies, and future directions. *Annals of the New York Academy of Sciences, 1184,* 15–54.

Bogaert, A. F. (2000). Birth order and sexual orientation in a national probability sample. *Journal of Sex Research, 37,* 361–368.

Bohannon, J. N., & Bonvillian, J. D. (2009). Theoretical approaches to language acquisition. In J. Berko Gleason & N. Ratner (Eds.), *The development of language* (7th ed.). Boston: Allyn & Bacon.

Bohart, A. C., & Tallman, K. (2010). Clients: The neglected common factor in psychotherapy. In B. L. Duncan, S. D. Miller, B. E. Wampold, & M. A. Hubble (Eds.), *The heart and soul of change: Delivering what works in therapy* (2nd ed., pp. 83–111). Washington, DC: American Psychological Association.

Bohner, G., & Dickel, N. (2011). Attitudes and attitude change. *Annual Review of Psychology* (vol. 62). Palo Alto, CA: Annual Reviews.

Bonchek, A. (2009). What's broken with cognitive behavior therapy treatment of obsessive-compulsive disorder and how to fix it. *American Journal of Psychotherapy, 63,* 69–86.

Bonfatti, J. F. (2005). Hope holds the key: Finding inspiration. *Schizophrenia Digest* (Summer), 31–34. www.schizophreniadigest.com

Bongers, K. C. A., & Dijksterhuis, A. (2009). Consciousness as a trouble shooting device? The role of consciousness in goal pursuit. In E. Morsella, J. A. Bargh, & P. Gollwitzer (Eds.), *The Oxford handbook of human action.* New York: Oxford University Press.

Bono, G., & McCullough, M. E. (2006). Positive responses to benefit and harm. Bringing forgiveness and gratitude into cognitive psychotherapy. *Journal of Cognitive Psychotherapy, 20,* 147–158.

Bono, G., McCullough, M. E., & Root, L. M. (2008). Forgiveness, feeling connected to others, and well-being: Two longitudinal studies. *Personality and Social Psychology Bulletin, 34,* 182–195.

Boonen, K., & others. (2010). Identification and relative quantification of neuropeptides from the endocrine tissues. *Methods in Molecular Biology, 615,* 191–206.

Borchardt, J. (2008, May 16). MU volunteers reach trauma victims worldwide. *Columbia Missourian.* http://www.Columbiamissourian.com/stories/2008/06/16/mu-volunteers-reach-trauma-victims-worldwide.htm (accessed April 15, 2009)

Bormann, J. E., Aschbacher, K., Wetherell, J. L., Roesch, S., & Redwine, L. (2008). Effects of faith/assurance on cortisol levels are enhanced by a spiritual mantram intervention in adults with HIV: A randomized trial. *Journal of Psychosomatic Research, 66,* 161–171.

Borst, A., Haag, J., & Reiff, D. F. (2010). Fly motion vision. *Annual Review of Neuroscience* (vol. 33). Palo Alto, CA: Annual Reviews.

Boseley, S. (2006, June 12). Tough curbs on Prozac prescribed for children. *The Guardian.*

Bosson, J. K., & Swann, W. B. (2009). Self-esteem. In M. R. Leary & R. H. Hoyle (Eds.), *Handbook of individual differences in social behavior* (pp. 527–546). New York: Guilford.

Bouchard, T. J. (2004). Genetic influences on human psychological traits. *Current Directions in Psychological Science, 13,* 148–151.

Bouchard, T. J., Jr., & Loehlin, J. C. (2001). Genes, evolution, and personality. *Behavior Genetics, 31,* 243–273.

Bouchard, T. J., Jr., & McGue, M. (2003). Genetic and environmental influences on human psychological differences. *Journal of Neurobiology, 54,* 4–45.

Bouchard, T. J., Lykken, D. T., Tellegen, A., & McGue, M. (1996). Genes, drives, environment, and experience. In D. Lubinski & C. Benbow (Eds.), *Psychometrics and social issues concerning intellectual talent.* Baltimore: Johns Hopkins University Press.

Bow, J. N., Flens, J. R., & Gould, J. W. (2010). MMPI-2 and MCMI-III in forensic evaluations: A survey of psychologists. *Journal of Forensic Psychology Practice, 10,* 37–52.

Bower, J. E., Moskowitz, J. T., & Epel, E. (2009). Is benefit finding good for your health? Pathways linking positive life changes after stress and physical health outcomes. *Current Directions in Psychological Science, 18,* 337–341.

Bowlby, J. (1969). *Attachment and loss* (vol. 1). London: Hogarth Press.

Bowlby, J. (1989). *Secure and insecure attachment.* New York: Basic.

Bowling, N. A. (2010). Effects of job satisfaction and conscientiousness on extra-role behaviors. *Journal of Business and Psychology, 25,* 119–130.

Boyd, J. H. (2008). Have we found the holy grail? Theory of mind as a unifying concept. *Journal of Religion and Health, 47,* 366–385.

Boyle, G. J. (1995). Myers-Briggs Type Indicator (MBTI): Some psychometric limitations. *Australian Psychologist, 30,* 71–74.

Bradley, S. J., Oliver, G. D., Chernick, A. B., & Zucker, K. J. (1998). Experiments of nurture: Ablatio penis at 2 months, sex reassignment at 7 months, and a psychosexual follow-up in young adulthood. *Pediatrics, 102,* e9.

Brady, S. S., & Halpern-Felsher, B. L. (2007). Adolescents' reported consequences of having oral sex versus vaginal sex. *Pediatrics, 119,* 229–236.

Bram, A. D. (2010). The relevance of the Rorschach and patient-examiner relationship in treatment planning and outcome assessment. *Journal of Personality Assessment, 92,* 91–115.

Brammer, L. M., & MacDonald, G. (1999). *The helping relationship* (7th ed.). Boston: Allyn & Bacon.

Brandstadter, J. (2006). Action perspectives in human development. In W. Damon & R. Lerner (Eds.), *Handbook of child psychology* (6th ed.). New York: Wiley.

Brandt, M. J., & Reyna, C. (2010). The role of prejudice and the need for closure in religious fundamentalism. *Personality and Social Psychology Bulletin.* (in press)

Brannick, M. T., & Levine, E. L. (2002). *Job analysis: Methods, research, and applications.* Thousand Oaks, CA: Sage.

Brannon, L. (1999). *Gender: Psychological perspectives* (2nd ed.). Boston: Allyn & Bacon.

Brannon, L., & Feist, P. (2010). *Health psychology* (7th ed.). Boston: Cengage.

Bransford, J., & others. (2006). Learning theories and education: Toward a decade of synergy. In P. A. Alexander & P. H. Winne (Eds.), *Handbook of educational psychology* (2nd ed.). Mahwah, NJ: Erlbaum.

Brasher, E. E., & Chen, P. Y. (1999). Evaluation of success criteria in job search: A process

perspective. *Journal of Occupational and Organizational Psychology, 72,* 57–70.

Breland, K., & Breland, M. (1961). The misbehavior of organisms. *American Psychologist, 16,* 681–684.

Brendgen, M., Boivin, M., Vitaro, F., Bukowski, W. M., Dionne, G., Tremblay, R. E., & Perusse, D. (2008). Linkages between children's and their friends' social and physical aggression: Evidence for a gene-environment interaction? *Child Development, 79,* 13–29.

Brendgen, M., Lamarche, V., Wanner, B., & Vitaro, F. (2010). Links between friendship relations and early adolescents' trajectories of depressed mood. *Developmental Psychology, 46,* 491–501.

Brent, D. A., & others. (2009). Predictors of spontaneous and systematically assessed suicidal adverse events in the treatment of SSRI-resistant depression in adolescents (TORDIA) study. *American Journal of Psychiatry, 166,* 418–426.

Brett, J. G., & Atwater, L. E. (2001). 360-degree feedback: Accuracy, reactions, and perceptions of usefulness. *Journal of Applied Psychology, 86,* 930–942.

Brettell, C. B., & Sargent, C. F. (2009). *Gender in cross-cultural perspective.* Upper Saddle River, NJ: Prentice-Hall.

Brewer, G. A., Knight, J. B., Marsh, R. L., & Unsworth, N. (2010). Individual differences in event-based prospective memory: Evidence for multiple processes supporting cue detection. *Memory and Cognition, 38,* 304–311.

Brewer, M. B. (2007). The social psychology of intergroup relations: Social categorization, ingroup bias, and outgroup prejudice. In A. W. Kruglanski & E. Tory Higgins (Eds.), *Social psychology: Handbook of basic principles* (2nd ed.). New York: Guilford.

Brewer, N., Barnes, J., & Sauer, J. (2010). The effects of peripheral message cues on clinicians' judgments about clients' psychological status. *British Journal of Clinical Psychology.* (in press)

Brewster, K. L., & Harker Tillman, K. (2008). Who's doing it? Patterns and predictors of youths' oral sexual experiences. *Journal of Adolescent Health, 42,* 73–80.

Brezo, J., & others. (2009). Differences and similarities in the serotonergic diathesis for suicide attempts and mood disorders: A 22-year longitudinal gene-environment study. *Molecular Psychiatry.* doi: 10.1038/mp.2009.19.

Brickman, P., & Campbell, D. T. (1971). Hedonic relativism and planning the good society. In M. H. Appley (Ed.), *Adaptation-level theory* (pp. 287–302). New York: Academic.

Bridge, D. J., Chiao, J. Y., & Paller, K. A. (2010). Emotional context at learning systematically biases memory for facial information. *Memory and Cognition, 38,* 125–133.

Bridgman, T. (2007). Review of the three faces of leadership: Manager, artist, priest. *Personnel Review, 36,* 494–496.

Briggs, K. C., & Myers, I. B. (1998). *Myers-Briggs Types Indicator.* Palo Alto, CA: Consulting Psychologists Press.

Brigham, J. C. (1986). Race and eyewitness identifications. In S. Worschel & W. G. Austin (Eds.), *Psychology of intergroup relations.* Chicago: Nelson-Hall.

Brigham, J. C., Bennett, L. B., Meissner, C. A., & Mitchell, T. L. (2007). The influence of race on eyewitness memory. In R. C. L. Lindsay, D. F. Ross, J. D. Read, & M. P. Toglia (Eds.), *The handbook of eyewitness memory: Vol II.* Mahwah, NJ: Erlbaum.

Brink, S. (2001, May 7). Your brain on alcohol. *U.S. News & World Report, 130* (18), 50–57.

Brinker, J. K., & Dozois, D. J. (2009). Ruminative thought style and depressed mood. *Journal of Clinical Psychology, 65,* 1–19.

Brister, H., Turner, J. A., Aaron, L. A., & Manci, L. (2006). Self-efficacy is associated with pain, functioning, and coping in patients with chronic temporomandibular disorder pain. *Journal of Orofacial Pain, 20,* 115–124.

Britton, P. C., & Conner, K. R. (2010). Suicide attempts within 12 months of treatment for substance use disorders. *Suicide and Life-Threatening Behavior, 40,* 14–21.

Brizendine, L. (2006). *The female brain.* New York: Random House.

Broberg, D. J., & Bernstein, I. L. (1987). Candy as a scapegoat in the prevention of food aversions in children receiving chemotherapy. *Cancer, 60,* 2344–2347.

Brody, L. R. (1999). *Gender, emotion and the family.* Cambridge, MA: Harvard University Press.

Brody, N. (2007). Does education influence intelligence? In P. C. Kyllonen, R. D. Roberts, & L. Stankov (Eds.), *Extending intelligence.* Mahwah, NJ: Erlbaum.

Brody, S., & Costa, R. M. (2009). Satisfaction (sexual, life, relationship, and mental health) is associated directly with penile-vaginal intercourse, but inversely with other sexual behavior frequencies. *Journal of Sexual Medicine, 6,* 1947–1954.

Brohan, E., Eglie, R., Sartorius, N., & Thornicroft, G., for the GAMIAN-Europe Study Group. (2010). Self-stigma, empowerment, and perceived discrimination among people with schizophrenia in 14 European countries: The GAMIAN-Europe study. *Schizophrenia Research.* (in press)

Bronfenbrenner, U., & Morris, P. A. (2006). The bioecological model of human development. In W. Damon & R. Lerner (Eds.), *Handbook of child psychology* (6th ed.). New York: Wiley.

Brooker, R. J., Widmaier, E. P., Graham, L. E., & Stiling, P. D. (2010). *Biology* (2nd ed.). New York: McGraw-Hill.

Brooks, J. G., & Brooks, M. G. (2001). *In search of understanding: The case for the constructivist classroom.* Upper Saddle River, NJ: Prentice-Hall.

Brown, A. S. (2006). Prenatal infection as a risk factor for schizophrenia. *Schizophrenia Bulletin, 32,* 200–202.

Brown, B. B., & Dietz, E. L. (2009). Informal peer groups in middle childhood and adolescence. In K. H. Rubin, W. M. Bukowski, &

B. Laursen (Eds.), *Handbook of peer interactions, relationships, and groups*. New York: Guilford.

Brown, D. (2007). Evidence-based hypnotherapy for asthma: A critical review. *International Journal of Clinical and Experimental Hypnosis, 55*, 220–249.

Brown, G. D. A., & Lewandowsky, S. (2010). Forgetting in memory models: Arguments against trace theory and consolidation failure. In S. D. Sala (Ed.), *Forgetting*. New York: Psychology Press.

Brown, K. G., & Sitzmann, T. (2010). Training and employee development for improved performance In S. Zedeck (Ed.), *APA handbook of industrial and organizational psychology*. Washington, DC: APA. (in press)

Brown, P. L., & Jenkins, H. M. (2009). On the law of effect. In D. Shanks (Ed.), *Psychology of learning*. Thousand Oaks, CA: Sage.

Brown, R. (1973). *A first language: The early stages*. Cambridge, MA: Harvard University Press.

Brown, S. L., Nesse, R. N., Vinokur, A. D., & Smith, D. M. (2003). Providing social support may be more beneficial than receiving it: Results from a prospective study of mortality. *Psychological Science, 14*, 320–327.

Brown, W. A. (2007). Treatment response in melancholia. *Acta Psychiatrica Scandinavica, 433*, 125–129.

Brown, W. M., Finn, C. J., Cooke, B. M., & Breedlove, S. M. (2002). Differences in finger length ratios between self-defined "butch" and "femme" lesbians, *Archives of Sexual Behavior, 31*, 123–127.

Brown-Borg, H. M. (2008). Hormonal regulation of longevity in mammals. *Aging Research Reviews, 6*, 28–45.

Bruch, M. A. (2002). The relevance of mitigated and unmitigated agency and communion for depression vulnerabilities and dysphoria. *Journal of Counseling Psychology, 49*, 449–459.

Brug, J., Conner, M., Harré, N., Kremers, S., McKellar, S., & Whitelaw, S. (2004). The transtheoretical model and stages of change: A critique. Observations by five commentators on the paper by Adams, J. and White, M. (2004) Why don't stage-based activity promotion interventions work? *Health Education Research, 20*, 244–258.

Brumariu, L. E., & Kerns, K. A. (2010). Parent-child attachment and internalizing symptoms in adolescence: A review of empirical findings and future directions. *Development and Psychopathology, 22*, 177–203.

Brummett, B. H., Boyle, S. H., Kuhn, C. M., Siegler, I. C., & Williams, R. B. (2008). Associations among central nervous system serotonergic function and neuroticism are moderated by gender. *Biological Psychology, 78*, 200–203.

Brunborg, G. S., & others. (2010). The relationship between aversive conditioning and risk-avoidance in gambling. *Journal of Gambling Studies*. (in press)

Bruning, R. H., Schraw, G. J., Norby, M. M., & Ronning, R. R. (2004). *Cognitive psychology and instruction* (4th ed.). Upper Saddle River, NJ: Prentice-Hall.

Brunstein, J. (1993). Personal goals and subjective well-being: A longitudinal study. *Journal of Personality and Social Psychology, 65*, 1061–1070.

Brunstein, J., & Maier, G. W. (2005). Implicit and self-attributed motives to achieve: Two separate but interacting needs. *Journal of Personality and Social Psychology, 89*, 205–222.

Bryant, J. B. (2009). Language in social contexts: Communication competence in the preschool years. In J. Berko Gleason & N. Ratner (Eds.), *The development of language* (7th ed.). Boston: Allyn & Bacon.

Bryant, R. A. (2006). Longitudinal psychophysiological studies of heart rate: Mediating effects and implications for treatment. *Annals of the New York Academy of Science, 1071*, 19–26.

Bryant-Davis, T., Ullman, S. E., Tsong, Y., Tillman, S., & Smith, K. (2010). Struggling to survive: Sexual assault, poverty, and mental health outcomes of African American women. *American Journal of Orthopsychiatry, 80*, 61–70.

Bucherelli, C., Baldi, E., Mariottini, C., Passani, M. B., & Blandina, P. (2006). Aversive memory reactivation engages in the amygdala only some neurotransmitters involved in consolidation. *Learning and Memory, 13*, 426–430.

Budson, A. E. (2009). Understanding memory dysfunction. *Neurologist, 15*, 71–79.

Bukowski, W. M., Brendgen, M., & Vitaro, F. (2007). Peers and socialization: Effects on externalizing and internalizing problems. In J. E. Grusec & P. D. Hastings (Eds.), *Handbook of socialization: Theory and research* (pp. 355–381). New York: Guilford.

Bulik, C. M., & others. (2000). Twin studies of eating disorders: A review. *International Journal of Eating Disorders, 27*, 1–20.

Bureau, J.-F., Easterbrooks, M. A., & Lyons-Ruth, K. (2009). Maternal depressive symptoms in infancy: Unique contribution to children's depressive symptoms in childhood and adolescence? *Development and Psychopathology, 21*, 519–537.

Burgdorf, J., & Panksepp, J. (2006). The neurobiology of positive emotions. *Neuroscience and Biobehavioral Reviews, 30*, 173–187.

Burger, J. (2009). Replicating Milgram: Would people still obey today? *American Psychologist, 64*, 1–11.

Burger, J. M., & Caldwell, D. F. (2000). Personality, social activities, job-search behavior and interview success: Distinguishing between PANAS trait positive affect and NEO extraversion. *Motivation and Emotion, 24*, 51–62.

Burstein, M., Ginsburg, G. S., Petras, H., & Ialongo, N. (2010). Parent psychopathology and youth internalizing symptoms in an urban community sample: A latent growth model analysis. *Child Psychiatry and Human Development, 41*, 61–87.

Burton, C. M., & King, L. A. (2004). The health benefits of writing about peak experiences. *Journal of Research in Personality, 38*, 150–163.

Burton, C. M., & King, L. A. (2008). The effects of (very) brief writing on health: The 2-minute miracle. *British Journal of Health Psychology, 13*, 9–14.

Burton, C. M., & King, L. A. (2009). The benefits of writing about positive experiences: Applying the broaden and build model. *Psychology and Health, 24*, 867–879.

Busch, F. (2007). "I noticed": The emergence of self-observation in relationship to pathological attractor sites. *International Journal of Psychoanalysis, 88*, 423–441.

Busch, F. N., Milrod, B. L., & Sandberg, L. S. (2009). A study demonstrating efficacy of a psychoanalytic psychotherapy for panic disorder: Implications for psychoanalytic research, theory, and practice. *Journal of the American Psychoanalytic Association, 57*, 131–148.

Bushman, B. J., & Anderson, C. A. (2007). Measuring the strength of the effect of violent media on aggression. *American Psychologist, 62*, 253–254.

Bushman, B. J., & Baumeister, R. F. (2002). Does self-love or self-hate lead to violence? *Journal of Research in Personality, 36*, 543–545.

Buss, D. M. (2011). *Evolutionary psychology* (4th ed.). Boston: Allyn & Bacon.

Bussey, K., & Bandura, A. (2004). Social cognitive theory of gender development and functioning. In A. H. Eagly, A. Beall, & R. Sternberg (Eds.), *The psychology of gender* (2nd ed., pp. 92–119). New York: Guilford.

Butcher, J. N. (2010). Personality assessment from the nineteenth century to the early twenty-first century: Past achievements and contemporary challenges. *Annual Review of Psychology* (vol. 61). Palo Alto, CA: Annual Reviews.

Butcher, M. (2010, February 10). Startup to launch after secret London facebook group amasses 180,000 members. *Techcrunch.com.* http://eu.techcrunch.com/2010/02/07/startup-to-launch-after-secret-london-facebook-group-amasses-180000/ (accessed February 15, 2010)

Butler, A. C., Chapman, J. E., Forman, E. M., & Beck, A. T. (2006). The empirical status of cognitive-behavioral therapy: A review of meta-analyses. *Clinical Psychology Review, 26*, 17–31.

Butz, A. M., & others. (2010). Household smoking behavior: Effects on indoor air quality and health of urban children with asthma. *Maternal and Child Health Journal.* (in press)

Buunk, B. P., & Van Yperen, N. W. (1991). Referential comparisons, relational comparisons, and exchange orientation: Their relation to marital satisfaction. *Personality and Social Psychology Bulletin, 17*, 709–717.

Byard, R. W., & Krous, H. F. (2004). Research and sudden infant death syndrome: Definitions, diagnostic difficulties and discrepancies. *Journal of Paediatrics and Child Health, 40*, 419–421.

Byrnes, J. P. (2008). Piaget's cognitive developmental theory. In M. M. Haith & J. B. Benson (Eds.), *Encyclopedia of infant and early childhood development*. Oxford, U.K.: Elsevier.

C

Cabanac, M., Cabanac, A. J., & Parent, A. (2009). The emergence of consciousness in phylogeny. *Behavioral Brain Research, 198,* 267–272.

Cabeza, R. (2002). Hemispheric asymmetry reduction in older adults: The HAROLD model. *Psychology and Aging, 17,* 85–100.

Cabeza, R., Nyberg, L., & Park, D. (Eds.). (2005). *Cognitive neuroscience of aging.* New York: Oxford University Press.

Cacioppo, J. T., Bernsten, G. G., & Aue, T. (2010). Social psychophysiology. In I. Wiener & E. Craighead (Eds.), *Corsini encyclopedia of psychology* (4th ed.). New York: Wiley.

Cacioppo, J. T., Hughes, M. E., Waite, L. J., Hawkley, L. C., & Thisted, R. A. (2006). Loneliness as a specific risk factor for depressive symptoms: Cross-sectional and longitudinal analyses. *Psychology and Aging, 21,* 140–151.

Cahill, L. (2006). Why sex matters for neuroscience. *Nature Reviews Neuroscience, 7,* 477–484.

Cai, D. J., & others (2009). REM, not incubation, improves creativity by priming associative networks. *PNAS, 106,* 10130–10134.

Caillouet, B. A., Boccaccini, M. T., Varela, J. G., Davis, R. D., & Rostow, C. D. (2010). Predictive validity of the MMPI-2 PSY-5 scales and facets for law enforcement officer employment outcomes. *Criminal Justice and Behavior, 37,* 217–238.

Cain, D. J. (2001). Defining characteristics, history, and evolution of humanistic psychotherapies. In D. J. Cain & J. Seeman (Eds.), *Humanistic psychotherapies.* Washington, DC: American Psychological Association.

Calati, R., De Ronchi, D., Bellini, M., & Serretti, A. (2010). The 5-HTTLPR polymorphism and eating disorders: A meta-analysis. *International Journal of Eating Disorders.* (in press)

Cale, E. M., & Lilienfeld, S. O. (2002). Sex differences in psychopathy and antisocial personality disorder: A review and integration. *Clinical Psychology Review, 22,* 1179–1207.

Calkins, S. D., & Bell, M. A. (Eds.). (2010). *Child development at the intersection of emotion and cognition.* Washington, DC: American Psychological Association.

Cameron, J., Banko, K. M., & Pierce, W. D. (2001). Pervasive negative effects of rewards on intrinsic motivation: The myth continues. *Behavior Analyst, 24,* 1–44.

Cameron, J., & Pierce, W. D. (2002). *Rewards and intrinsic motivation: Resolving the controversy.* Westport, CT: Bergin & Garvey.

Cameron, J., Pierce, W. D., Banko, K. M., & Gear, A. (2005). Achievement-based rewards and intrinsic motivation: A test of cognitive mediators. *Journal of Educational Psychology, 97,* 641–655.

Cameron, K. S. (2003). Organizational virtuousness and performance. In K. S. Cameron, J. E. Dutton, & R. E. Quinn (Eds.), *Positive organizational scholarship: Foundations of a new discipline* (pp. 48–65). San Francisco: Berrett-Koehler.

Cameron, K. S. (2005). Organizational downsizing. In N. Nicholson, P. G. Audia, & M. M. Pilluta (Eds.), *The Blackwell encyclopedia of management.* Malden, MA: Blackwell.

Cameron, K. S. (2007). Positive organizational change. In S. Clegg & B. James (Eds.), *International encyclopedia of organizational studies.* Thousand Oaks, CA: Sage.

Campbell, C. M., & Edwards, R. R. (2009). Mind-body interactions in pain: The neurophysiology of anxious and catastrophic pain-related thoughts. *Translational Research, 153,* 97–101.

Campbell, F. A. (2006). The malleability of the cognitive development of children of low income African-American families. In P. C. Kyllonen, R. D. Roberts, & L. Stankov (Eds.), *Extending intelligence.* Mahwah, NJ: Erlbaum.

Campbell, J. D., Yoon, D. P., & Johnstone, B. (2010). Determining relationships between physical health and spiritual experience, religious practice, and congregational support in a heterogeneous sample. *Journal of Religion and Health, 49,* 3–17.

Campbell, J. M., & Brown, E. A. (2010). *Cambridge handbook of forensic psychology.* Cambridge, U.K.: Cambridge University Press.

Campbell, L., Campbell, B., & Dickinson, D. (2004). *Teaching and learning through multiple intelligences.* Boston: Allyn & Bacon.

Campbell, W. K., Bonacci, A. M., Shelton, J., Exline, J. J., & Bushman, B. J. (2004). Psychological entitlement: Interpersonal consequences and validation of a self-report measure. *Journal of Personality Assessment, 83,* 29–45.

Canadian Statistics. (2005). Crime in Canada. http://www.statcan.ca/Daily/English/050721/ d050721a.htm|title=Crime in Canada (accessed June 13, 2007)

Canals, S., Beyerlein, M., Merkle, H., & Logothetis, N. K. (2009). Functional MRI evidence for LTP-induced neural network reorganization. *Current Biology, 19,* 398–403.

Canino, G., & others. (2004). The DSM-IV rates of child and adolescent disorders in Puerto Rico. *Archives of General Psychiatry, 61,* 85–93.

Canli, T. (2008a). Toward a neurogenetic theory of neuroticism. In D. W. Pfaff & B. L. Kieffer (Eds.), *Molecular and biophysical mechanisms of arousal, alertness, and attention* (pp. 153–174). Malden, MA: Blackwell.

Canli, T. (2008b). Toward a "molecular psychology" of personality. In O. P. John, R. W. Robins, & L. A. Pervin (Eds.), *Handbook of personality theory and research* (3rd ed., pp. 311–327). New York: Guilford.

Canli, T., Sivers, H., Whitfield, S. L., Gotlib, I. H., & Gabrieli, J. D. E. (2002). Amygdala response to happy faces as a function of extraversion. *Science, 296,* 2191.

Cannon, W. B. (1927). The James-Lange theory of emotions: A critical examination and an alternative theory. *American Journal of Psychology, 39,* 106–124.

Cannon, W. B., & Washburn, A. L. (1912). An explanation of hunger. *American Journal of Physiology, 29,* 441–454.

Cantor, J. M., Kabani, N., Christensen, B. K., Zipursky, R. B., Barbaree, H. E., Dickey, R., Klassen, P. E., Mikulis, D. J., Kuban, M. E., Blak, T., Richards, B. A., Hanratty, M. K., & Blanchard, R. (2008). Cerebral white matter deficiencies in pedophilic men. *Journal of Psychiatric Research, 42,* 167–183.

Cantor, N., & Sanderson, C. A. (1999). Life task participation and well-being: The importance of taking part in daily life. In D. Kahneman, E. Diener, & N. Schwarz (Eds.), *Well-being: The foundations of hedonic psychology* (pp. 230–243). New York: Russell Sage Foundation.

Capasso, A., Putrella, C., & Milano, W. (2009). Recent clinical aspects of eating disorders. *Reviews on Recent Clinical Trials, 4,* 63–69.

Caplan, J. B., & Caplan, P. J. (2005). The perseverative search for sex differences in mathematics ability. In A. M. Gallagher & J. C. Kaufman (Eds.), *Gender differences in mathematics* (pp. 25–47). Cambridge, U.K.: Cambridge University Press.

Caprara, G. V., Alessandri, G., Di Giunta, L., Panerai, L., & Eisenberg, N. (2010). The contribution of agreeableness and self-efficacy beliefs to prosociality. *European Journal of Personality, 24,* 36–55.

Caprara, G. V., Fagnani, C., Alessandri, G., Steca, P., Gigantesco, A., Sforza, L., Cavalli, L., & Stazi, M. A., (2009). Human optimal functioning: The genetics of positive orientation towards self, life, and the future. *Behavior Genetics, 39,* 277–284.

Card, N. A., Stucky, B. D., Sawalani, G. M., & Little, T. D. (2008). Direct and indirect aggression during childhood and adolescence: A meta-analytic review of gender differences, intercorrelations, and relations to maladjustment. *Child Development, 79,* 1185–1229.

Cardno, A. G., & Gottesman, I. I. (2000). Twin studies of schizophrenia: From bow-and-arrow concordances to Star Wars Mx and functional genomics. *American Journal of Medical Genetics, 97,* 12–17.

Cardoso Zoppe, E. H., Schoueri, P., Castro, M., & Neto, F. L. (2009). Teaching psychodynamics to psychiatric residents through psychiatric outpatient interviews. *Academic Psychiatry, 33,* 51–55.

Carey, B. (2009, August 9). After injury, fighting to regain a sense of self. *New York Times.* http://www.nytimes.com/2009/08/09/health/ research/09brain.html

Carey, W. B. (2002). Is ADHD a valid disorder? In P. Jensen & J. Cooper (Eds.), *Attention deficit hyperactivity disorder: State of the science, best practices.* Kingston, NJ: Civic Research Institute.

Carlo, G. (2006). Care-based and altruistically-based morality. In M. Killen & J. Smetana (Eds.), *Handbook of moral development.* Mahwah, NJ: Erlbaum.

Carlsson, M. A., & Swedberg, M. D. (2010). A behavioural operant discrimination model for assessment and pharmacological manipulation of visual function in rats. *Brain Research, 1321,* 78–87.

Carmona, J. E., Holland, A. K., & Harrison, D. W. (2009). Extending the functional cerebral theory of emotion to the vestibular modality: A systematic and integrative approach. *Psychological Bulletin, 135*, 286–302.

Carnethon, M. R., & others. (2010). Joint associations of physical activity and aerobic fitness on the development of incident hypertension: Coronary artery risk development in young adults. *Hypertension*. (in press)

Carney, D. R., Nosek, B. A., Greenwald, A. G., & Banaji, M. R. (2007). Implicit Association Test (IAT). In R. Baumeister & K. Vohs (Eds.), *Encyclopedia of social psychology*. Thousand Oaks, CA: Sage.

Carota, F., Posada, A., Harquel, S., Delpuech, C., Bertrand, O., & Sirigu, A. (2010). Neural dynamics of intention to speak. *Cerebral Cortex*. (in press)

Carpenter, S. K., & DeLosh, E. L. (2006). Impoverished cue support enhances subsequent retention: Support for the elaborative retrieval explanation of the testing effect. *Memory and Cognition, 34*, 268–276.

Carskadon, M. A. (2006, March). *Too little, too late: Sleep bioregulatory processes across adolescence.* Paper presented at the meeting of the Society for Research on Adolescence, San Francisco.

Carskadon, M. A., Mindell, J., & Drake, C. (2006, September). *Contemporary sleep patterns in the USA: Results of the 2006 National Sleep Foundation Poll.* Paper presented at the European Sleep Research Society, Innsbruck, Austria.

Carson, C. M. (2005). A historical view of Douglas McGregor's Theory Y. *Management Decision, 43*, 450–460.

Carson, R. C., Butcher, J. N., & Mineka, S. (1996). *Abnormal psychology and life* (10th ed.). New York: HarperCollins.

Carstensen, L. L. (2006). The influence of a sense of time on human development. *Science, 312*, 1913–1915.

Carstensen, L. L. (2008, May). *Long life in the twenty-first century.* Paper presented at the meeting of the Association of Psychological Science, Chicago.

Carstensen, L. L., & Charles, S. T. (2003). Human aging: Why is even good news taken as bad? In L. A. Aspinall & U. M. Staudinger (Eds.), *A psychology of human strengths*. Washington, DC: American Psychological Association.

Carter, S. A., & Wu, K. D. (2010). Symptoms of specific and generalized social phobia: An examination of discriminant validity and structural relations with mood and anxiety symptoms. *Behavior Therapy, 41*, 254–265.

Cartwright, S., & Cooper, C. L. (Eds.). (2008). *The Oxford handbook of personnel psychology.* New York: Oxford University Press.

Carver, C. S., & Connor-Smith, J. (2010). Personality and coping. *Annual Review of Psychology* (vol. 61). Palo Alto, CA: Annual Reviews.

Carver, C. S., & Scheier, M. F. (2009). Optimism. In M. R. Levy & R. H. Hoyle (Eds.), *Handbook of individual differences in social behavior* (pp. 330–342). New York: Guilford.

Carver, C. S., & Scheier, M. F. (2009a). Action, affect, multitasking, and layers of control. In J. P. Forgas, R. F. Baumeister, & D. M. Tice (Eds.), *Psychology of self-regulation: Cognitive, affective, and motivational processes* (pp. 109–126). New York: Psychology Press.

Cascio, W. (2010). *Managing human resources* (8th ed.). New York: McGraw-Hill.

Cascio, W. F., & Aguinis, H. (2011). *Applied psychology in human resource management* (7th ed.). Upper Saddle River, NJ: Prentice-Hall.

Case, R. B., Moss, A. J., Case, N., McDermott, M., & Eberly, S. (1992). Living alone after myocardial infarction. Impact on prognosis. *Journal of the American Medical Association, 267*, 515–519.

Caspi, A., McClay, J., Moffitt, T. E., Mill, J., Martin, J., Craig, I. W., Taylor, A., & Poulton, R. (2002). Role of genotype in the cycle of violence in maltreated children. *Science, 297*, 851–854.

Caspi, A., & Roberts, B. W. (2001). Personality development across the life course: The argument for change and continuity. *Psychological Inquiry, 12*, 49–66.

Cassimatis, N. L., Murugesan, A., & Bignoli, P. G. (2009). Reasoning as simulation. *Cognitive Processing, 10*, 343–353.

Cathers-Schiffman, T. A., & Thompson, M. S. (2007). Assessment of English- and Spanish-speaking students with the WISC-III and Leiter-R. *Journal of Psychoeducational Assessment, 25*, 41–52.

Cattaneo, L., & Rizzolatti, G. (2009). The mirror neuron system. *Archives of Neurology, 66*, 557–560.

Cauller, L. (2001, May). Review of *Santrock, Psychology* (7th ed.). New York: McGraw-Hill.

Cavallaro, F. I., & others. (2010). Hypnotizability-related EEG alpha and theta activities during visual and somesthetic imageries. *Neuroscience Letters, 470*, 13–18.

Caverzasi, E., & others. (2008). Complications in major depressive disorder therapy: A review of magnetic resonance spectroscopy studies. *Functional Neurology, 23*, 129–132.

Cavina-Pratesi, C., Kentridge, R. W., Heywood, C. A., & Milner, A. D. (2010). Separate channels for processing form, texture, and color: Evidence from fMRI adaptation and visual object agnosia. *Cerebral Cortex*. (in press)

CBS News. (2006, March 15). Ambien may prompt sleep eating. http://www.cbsnews.com/stories/2006/03/15/earlyshow/health/health_news/main1404632.shtml (accessed December 15, 2006)

CBS News. (2009). Sullenberger recalls moment engines died. http://www.cbsnews.com/stories/2009/01/30/60minutes/main4764852.shtml (accessed February 3, 2010)

CBS News. (2009a, December 2). Richmond High gang rape: Six plead not guilty to raping teen while others watched. http://www.cbsnews.com/8301-504083_162-5697504083.html (accessed December 15, 2009)

Centers for Disease Control and Prevention (CDC), National Center for Injury Prevention and Control. (2004). *Web-based injury statistics query and reporting system* (WISQARS). http://www.cdc.gov/ncipc/wisqars/default.Htm (accessed June 21, 2004)

Centers for Disease Control and Prevention (CDC). (2005). National Youth Risk Behavior Survey: 1991–2005. U.S. Department of Health and Human Services, Centers for Disease Control and Prevention.

Centers for Disease Control and Prevention (CDC). (2007, September 7). Suicide trends among youths and young adults aged 10–24 Years—United States, 1990–2004. *Morbidity and Mortality Weekly Report, 56*, 905–908.

Centers for Disease Control and Prevention (CDC). (2009a). *Obesity: Halting the epidemic by making health easier.* Atlanta: Author.

Centers for Disease Control and Prevention (CDC). (2009b). *Defining obesity and overweight.* Atlanta: Author.

Centers for Disease Control and Prevention (CDC). (2009c). *HIV/AIDS.* Atlanta: Author.

Centers for Disease Control and Prevention (CDC). (2009, November 13). Cigarette smoking among adults and trends in smoking cessation—United States, 2008. *Morbidity and Mortality Weekly Report, 58*, 1227–1232.

Cetinel, S., & others. (2010). Oxytocin treatment alleviates stress-activated colitis by a receptor-dependent mechanism. *Regulatory Peptides, 160*, 146–152.

Chabris, C., & Simons, D. (2010). *The invisible gorilla, and other ways our intuitions deceive us.* New York: Crown.

Chafetz, L., White, M., Collins-Bride, G., Cooper, B. A., & Nickens, J. (2008). Clinical trial of wellness training: Health promotion for severely mentally ill adults. *Journal of Nervous and Mental Disease, 196*, 475–483.

Chaiken, S., & Ledgerwood, A. (2007). Heuristic processing. In R. Baumeister & K. D. Vohs (Eds.), *Encyclopedia of social psychology*. Thousand Oaks, CA: Sage.

Chakraborty, S., Kaushik, D. K., Gupta, M., & Basu, A. (2010). Inflammasome signaling at the heart of central nervous system pathology. *Journal of Neuroscience Research*. (in press)

Chambon, V., Baudouin, J., & Franck, N. (2006). The role of configural information in facial emotion recognition in schizophrenia. *Neuropsychologia, 44*, 2437–2444.

Chan, R. W., Raboy, B., & Patterson, C. J. (1998). Psychosocial adjustment among children conceived via donor insemination by lesbian and heterosexual mothers. *Child Development, 69*, 326–332.

Chance, P. (2009). *Learning and behavior* (6th ed.). Belmont, CA: Cengage.

Chapman, A. L. (2009). Borderline personality disorder. In D. McKay, J. S. Abramowitz, & S. Taylor (Eds.), *Cognitive-behavioral therapy for refractory cases: Turning failure into success* (pp. 347–367). Washington, DC: American Psychological Association.

Chapman, D. S., & Webster, J. (2003). The use of technologies in the recruiting, screening, and selection processes for job candidates. *International Journal of Selection and Assessment, 11*, 113–120.

Charbonneau, D., Barling, J., & Kelloway, E. K. (2001). Transformational leadership behaviors, upward trust, and satisfaction in self-managed work teams. *Organizational Development Journal, 17,* 13–28.

Charles, S. T., & Carstensen, L. L. (2010). Social and emotional aging. *Annual Review of Psychology* (vol. 61). Palo Alto, CA: Annual Reviews.

Charmaraman, L., & Grossman, J. M. (2010). Importance of race and ethnicity: An exploration of Asian, Black, Latino, and multiracial ethnic identity. *Cultural Diversity and Ethnic Minority Psychology, 16,* 144–151.

Chassin, L., Hussong, A., & Beltran, I. (2009). Adolescent substance use. In R. M. Lerner & L. Steinberg (Eds.), *Handbook of adolescent psychology* (3rd ed.). New York: Wiley.

Chater, N., Reali, F., & Christiansen, M. H. (2009). Restrictions on biological adaptation in language evolution. *Proceedings of the National Academy of Sciences, 106,* 1015–1020.

Cheng, P. W., & Holyoak, K. J. (2011). Learning and inference with causal models. *Annual Review of Psychology* (vol. 62). Palo Alto, CA: Annual Reviews.

Chess, S., & Thomas, A. (1977). Temperamental individuality from childhood to adolescence. *Journal of Child Psychiatry, 16,* 218–226.

Chess, S., & Thomas, A. (1996). *Temperament: Theory and practice.* Philadelphia: Brunner/Mazel.

Cheung, O. S., & Gauthier, I. (2010). Selective interference on the holistic processing of faces in working memory. *Journal of Experimental Psychology: Human Perception and Performance.* (in press)

Chiang, M., Barysheva, M., Shattuck, D. W., Lee, A. D., Madsen, S. K., Avedissian, C., Klunder, A. D., Toga, A. W., McMahon, K. L., de Zubicaray, G. I., Wright, M. J., Srivastava, A., Balov, N., & Thompson, P. M. (2009). Genetics of brain fiber architecture and intellectual performance. *Journal of Neuroscience, 29,* 2212–2224.

Chiang, M. C., & others. (2009). Genetics of brain fiber architecture and intellectual performance. *Journal of Neuroscience, 29,* 2214–2224.

Chica, A. B., & others. (2010). Exogenous attention can capture perceptual consciousness. ERP and behavioral evidence. *NeuroImage.* (in press)

Chida, Y., & Steptoe, A. (2009). The association of anger and hostility with future coronary heart disease: A meta-analytic review of prospective evidence. *Journal of the American College of Cardiology, 53,* 936–946.

Chiesa, A., & Serretti, A. (2010). A systematic review of neurobiological and clinical features of mindfulness meditations. *Psychological Medicine.* (in press)

Chiesa, M., & Hobbs, S. (2008). Making sense of social research: How useful is the Hawthorne effect? *European Journal of Social Psychology, 38,* 67–74.

Chivers, M. L., Seto, M. C., & Blanchard, R. (2007). Gender and sexual orientation differences in sexual response to sexual activities versus gender of actors in sexual films. *Journal of Personality and Social Psychology, 93,* 1108–1121.

Cho, D., & Campana, D. (2009). Expansion and activation of natural killer cells for cancer immunotherapy. *Korean Journal of Laboratory Medicine, 29,* 89–96.

Choi, J. K., & Bowles, S. (2007). The co-evolution of parochial altruism and war. *Science, 318,* 636–640.

Chomsky, N. (1975). *Reflections on language.* New York: Pantheon.

Chouinard, G. (2006). Interrelations between psychiatric symptoms and drug-induced movement disorder. *Journal of Psychiatry and Neuroscience, 31,* 177–180.

Christensen, H., & others. (2010). Protocol for a randomized trial investigating the effectiveness of an online e-health application compared to attention placebo or sertraline in the treatment of generalized anxiety disorder. *Trials.* (in press)

Christensen, L. B. (2007). *Experimental methodology* (10th ed.). Boston: Allyn & Bacon.

Christensen, L. B., Johnson, R. B., & Turner, L. (2011). *Research design, methods, and analysis* (11th ed.). Upper Saddle River, NJ: Prentice-Hall.

Christie, I. C., & Friedman, B. H. (2004). Autonomic specificity of discrete emotion and dimensions of affective space: A multivariate approach. *International Journal of Psychophysiology, 51,* 143–153.

Christopher Frueh, B., Grubaugh, A. L., Cusack, K. J., Kimble, M. O., Elhai, J. D., & Knapp, R. G. (2009). Exposure-based cognitive-behavioral treatment of PTSD in adults with schizophrenia or schizoaffective disorder: A pilot study. *Journal of Anxiety Disorders, 23,* 665–675.

Chun, M. M., Turk-Browne, N., & Golomb, J. (2011). Toward a taxonomy of attention. *Annual Review of Psychology* (vol. 62). Palo Alto, CA: Annual Reviews.

Church, T. S., LaMonte, M. J., Barlow, C. E., & Blair, S. N. (2005). Cardiorespiratory fitness and body mass index as predictors of cardiovascular disease mortality among men with diabetes. *Archives of Internal Medicine, 165,* 2114–2120.

CIA. (2005). *CIA world fact book.* https://www.cia.gov/library/publications/the-world-factbook/index.html

Cialdini, R. B. (1991). Altruism or egoism? That is (still) the question. *Psychological Inquiry, 2,* 124–126.

Cialdini, R. B. (1993). *Influence. Science and practice.* New York: HarperCollins.

Cialdini, R. B., Vincent, J. E., Lewis, S. K., Catalan, J., Wheeler, D., & Darby, B. L. (1975). Reciprocal concessions procedure for inducing compliance: The door-in-the-face technique. *Journal of Personality and Social Psychology, 31,* 206–215.

Ciani, K. D., Middleton, M. J., Summers, J. J., & Sheldon, K. M. (2010). Buffering against performance classroom goal structures: The importance of autonomy support and classroom community. *Contemporary Educational Psychology, 35,* 88–99.

Ciani, K. D., & Sheldon, K. M. (2010). Evaluating the mastery-avoidance goal construct: A study of elite college baseball players. *Psychology of Sport and Exercise, 11,* 127–132.

Cicchetti, D., Rogosch, F. A., Gunnar, M. R., & Toth, S. L. (2010). The differential impacts of early physical and sexual abuse and internalizing problems on daytime cortisol rhythm in school-aged children. *Child Development, 81,* 252–269.

Cipriani, A., La Ferla, T., Furukawa, T. A., Signoretti, A., Nakagawa, A., Churchill, R., McGuire, H., & Barbui, C. (2010). Sertraline versus other antidepressive agents for depression. *Cochrane Database of Systematic Reviews,* 4: CD006117. doi: 10.1002/14651858.CD006117.pub4

Cisler, J. M., Olatunji, B. O., Feldner, M. T., & Forsyth, J. P. (2010). Emotion regulation and the anxiety disorders: An integrative review. *Journal of Psychopathology and Behavioral Assessment, 32,* 68–82.

Claes, H. I. (2010). Understanding the effects of sildenafil on erection maintenance and erection hardness. *Journal of Sexual Medicine.* (in press)

Clark, B. (2008). *Growing up gifted* (7th ed.). Upper Saddle River, NJ: Prentice-Hall.

Clark, D. M., Ehlers, A., Hackmann, A., McManus, F., Fennell, M., Grey, N., Waddington, L., & Wild, J. (2006). Cognitive therapy versus exposure and applied relaxation in social phobia: A randomized controlled trial. *Journal of Consulting and Clinical Psychology, 74,* 568–578.

Clark, M. J., & others (2010). U87MG decoded: The genomic sequence of a cytogenetically aberrant human cancer cell line. *PLoS Genetics, 6,* e1000832.

Clark, M. S., & Chrisman, K. (1994). Resource allocation in intimate relationships: Trying to make sense of a confusing literature. In M. J. Lerner & G. Mikula (Eds.), *Entitlement and the affectional bond: Justice in close relationships* (pp. 65–88). New York: Plenum.

Clark, R. D., & Hatfield, E. (1989). Gender differences in receptivity to sexual offers. *Journal of Psychology and Human Sexuality, 2,* 39–55.

Clark, R. E., & Squire, L. R. (2010). An animal model of recognition memory and medial temporal lobe amnesia: History and current issues. *Neuropsychologia.* (in press)

Cleeremans, A., & Sarrazin, J. C. (2007). Time, action, and consciousness. *Human Movement Science, 26,* 180–202.

Clemens, N. A. (2010). Evidence base for psychotherapy: Two perspectives. *Journal of Psychiatric Practice, 16,* 183–186.

Cleveland, J. N., Barnes-Farrell, J. L., & Ratz, J. M. (1997). Accommodation in the workplace. *Human Resource Management Review, 7,* 77–107.

Clifton, D. O., & Harter, J. K. (2003). Strengths investment. In K. S. Cameron, J. E. Dutton, & R. E. Quinn (Eds.), *Positive organizational scholarship* (pp. 111–121). San Francisco: Berrett & Koehler.

Clifton, D. O., & Nelson, P. (1992). *Soar with your strengths.* New York: Delacourt.

Clore, G. L., Gasper, K., & Garvin, E. (2001). Affect as information. In J. P. Forgas (Ed.), *Handbook of affect and social cognition* (pp. 121–144). Mahwah, NJ: Erlbaum.

Clore, G. L., & Palmer, J. (2009). Affective guidance of intelligent agents: How emotion controls cognition. *Cognitive Systems Research, 10,* 21–30.

Cloud, J. (2008, August 27). Failing our geniuses. *Time,* 40–47.

Clutton-Brock, T. H. (2007). Sexual selection in males and females. *Science, 318,* 1882–1885.

Clutton-Brock, T. H. (2010) We do not need a sexual selection 2.0—nor a theory of genial selection. *Animal Behaviour.* (in press)

CNN Poll. (2006, December 12). Most Americans see lingering racism—in others. http://www.cnn.com/2006/US/12/12/racism.poll/index.html (accessed June 13, 2007)

Coch, D., Fischer, K. W., & Dawson, G. (Eds.). (2007). *Human behavior, learning, and the developing brain.* New York: Guilford.

Cockram, D. M., Drummond, P. D., & Lee, C. W. (2010). Role and treatment of early maladaptive schemas in Vietnam veterans with PTSD. *Clinical Psychology and Psychotherapy, 17,* 165–182.

Cohen, D. (2001). Cultural variation: Considerations and implications. *Psychological Bulletin, 127,* 451–471.

Cohen, D., Nisbett, R. E., Bowdle, B. F., & Schwarz, N. (1996). Insult, aggression, and the southern culture of honor: An "experimental ethnography." *Journal of Personality and Social Psychology, 70,* 945–960.

Cohen, F., & others. (2007). Immune system declines with unemployment and recovers after stress termination. *Psychosomatic Medicine, 69,* 225–234.

Cohen, G. L., & Prinstein, M. J. (2006). Peer contagion of aggression and health risk behavior among adolescent males: An experimental investigation of effects on public conduct and private attitudes. *Child Development, 77,* 967–983.

Cohen, P. J. (2009). Medical marijuana: The conflict between scientific evidence and political ideology. Part one of two. *Journal of Pain & Palliative Care Pharmacotherapy, 23,* 4–25.

Cohen, S., Alper, C. M., Doyle, W. J., Treanor, J. J., & Turner, R. B. (2006). Positive emotional style predicts resistance to illness after experimental exposure to rhinovirus or influenza a virus. *Psychosomatic Medicine, 68,* 809–815.

Cohen, S., Doyle, W. J., & Skoner, D. P. (1999). Psychological stress, cytokine production, and severity of upper respiratory illness. *Psychosomatic Medicine, 61,* 175–180.

Cohen, S., Doyle, W. J., Alper, C. M., Janicki-Deverts, D., & Turner, R. B. (2009). Sleep habits and susceptibility to the common cold. *Archives of Internal Medicine, 169,* 62–67.

Cohen, S., Frank, E., Doyle, W., Skoner, D. P., Rabin, B. S., & Gwaltney, J. M. (1998). Types of stressors that increase susceptibility to the common cold in healthy adults. *Health Psychology, 17,* 214–223.

Cohen, S., & Janicki-Deverts, D. (2009). Can we improve our physical health by altering our social networks? *Perspectives on Psychological Science, 4* (4), 375–378.

Cohen, S., & Lemay, E. (2007). Why would social networks be linked to affect and health practices? *Health Psychology, 27,* 410–417.

Cohen-Bendahan, C. C. C., van de Beek, C., & Berenbaum, S. (2005). Prenatal sex hormone effects on child and adult sex-typed behavior: Methods and findings. *Neuroscience & Biobehavioral Reviews, 29,* 353–384.

Cohen-Charash, Y., & Spector, P. E. (2001). The role of justice in organizations: A meta-analysis. *Organizational Behavior and Human Decision Processes, 86,* 278–321.

Cohen-Kettenis, P. T., & Pfafflin, F. (2010). The DSM diagnostic criteria for gender identity disorder in adolescents and adults. *Archives of Sexual Behavior, 39* (2), 499–513.

Coifman, K. G., Bonanno, G. A., Ray, R. D., & Gross, J. J. (2007). Does repressing coping promote resilience? Affective-autonomic response discrepancy during bereavement. *Journal of Personality and Social Psychology, 92,* 745–758.

Colagiuri, S. (2010). Disabesity: Therapeutic options. *Diabetes and Obesity Medicine, 12,* 463–473.

Colangelo, J. J. (2009). The recovered memory controversy: A representative case study. *Journal of Child Sexual Abuse, 18,* 103–121.

Colapinto, J. (2000). *As nature made him.* New York: Harper Academic.

Colella, A. J., & Bruyère, S. M. (2010). Disability and employment: New directions for industrial and organizational psychology. In S. Zedeck (Ed.), *APA handbook of industrial and organizational psychology.* Washington, DC: APA. (in press)

Collins, A., Hill, L. E., Chandramohan, Y., Witcomb, D., Droste, S. K., & Reul, J. M. (2009). Exercise improves cognitive responses to stress through enhancement of epigenetic mechanisms and gene expression in the dentate gyrus. *PLoS One, 4,* e4330.

Collins, W. A., Maccoby, E. E., Steinberg, L., Hetherington, E. M., & Bornstein, M. H. (2000). Contemporary research on parenting: The case for nature and nurture. *American Psychologist, 55,* 218–232.

Collins, W. A., & Steinberg, L. (2006). Adolescent development in interpersonal context. In W. Damon & R. Lerner (Eds.), *Handbook of child psychology* (6th ed.). New York: Wiley.

Colón, E. A., Callies, A. L., Popkin, M. K., & McGlave, P. B. (1991). Depressed mood and other variables related to bone marrow transplantation survival in acute leukemia. *Psychosomatics, 32,* 420–425.

Colquitt, J. A., LePine, J. A., & Wesson, M. J. (2011). *Organizational behavior* (2nd ed.). New York: McGraw-Hill.

Commonwealth of Massachusetts vs. Porter 31285–330. (1993, Massachusetts).

Compton, J. A., & Pfau, M. (2004). Use of inoculation to foster resistance to credit card marketing targeting college students. *Journal of Applied Communication Research, 32,* 343–364.

Compton, J. A., & Pfau, M. (2008). Inoculating against pro-plagiarism justifications: Rational and affective strategies. *Journal of Applied Communication Research, 36,* 98–119.

Compton, R. J., Wirtz, D., Pajoumand, G., Claus, E., & Heller, W. (2004). Association between positive affect and attentional shifting. *Cognitive Therapy and Research, 28,* 733–744.

ComScore. (2008). *Social networking explodes worldwide as sites increase their focus on cultural relevance.* http://www.comscore.com/press/release/.asp?/press=2396 (accessed April 15, 2010)

Connellan, J., Baron-Cohen, S., Wheelwright, S., Batki, A., & Ahluwalia, J. (2000). Sex differences in human neonatal social perception. *Infant Behavior & Development, 23,* 113–118.

Connor, D. F. (2010). Electroconvulsive therapy, transcranial magnetic stimulation, and deep brain stimulation. In M. K. Dulcan (Ed.), *Dulcan's textbook of child and adolescent psychiatry* (pp. 795–804). Arlington, VA: American Psychiatric Publishing.

Consortium on the Management of Disorders of Sexual Development. (2006). *Clinical guidelines for the management of disorders of sexual development.* Rohnert, CA: Intersex Society of North America.

Constantine, N. A. (2008). Converging evidence leaves policy behind: Sex education in the United States. *Journal of Adolescent Health, 42,* 324–326.

Conway, M., & Rubin, D. (1993). The structure of autobiographical memory. In A. F. Collins, S. E. Gathercole, M. A. Conway, & P. E. Morris (Eds.), *Theories of memory.* Hillsdale, NJ: Erlbaum.

Cook, M. B., & Smallman, H. S. (2008). Human factors of the confirmation bias in intelligence analysis: Decision support from graphical evidence landscapes. *Human Factors, 50,* 745–754.

Cook, R. J., Cusack, S., & Dickens, B. M. (2010). Unethical female stereotyping in reproductive health. *International Journal of Gynecology and Obstetrics.* (in press)

Cooper, M., & others. (2010). Randomized controlled trial of school-based humanistic counseling for emotional distress in young people: Feasibility study and preliminary indications of efficacy. *Child and Adolescent Psychiatry and Mental Health.* (in press)

Cooper, M. L. (1994). Motivations for alcohol use among adolescents: Development and validation of a four-factor model. *Psychological Assessment, 6,* 117–128.

Cooper, M. L. (2010). Toward a person × situation model of sexual risk-taking behaviors: Illuminating the conditional effects of traits across sexual situations and relationship contexts. *Journal of Personality and Social Psychology, 98,* 319–341.

Cooper, M. L., Pioli, M., Levitt, A., Talley, A. E., Micheas, L., & Collins, N. L. (2006). Attachment styles, sex motives, and sexual behavior: Evidence for gender-specific expressions of attachment dynamics. In M. Mikulincer & G. S. Goodman (Eds.),

Dynamics of romantic love: Attachment, care-giving, and sex (pp. 243–274). New York: Guilford.

Cooper, M. L., Russell, M., Skinner, J. B., & Windle, M. (1992). Development and validation of a three-dimensional measure of drinking motives. *Psychological Assessment, 4,* 123–132.

Cooper M. L., Shapiro, C. M., & Powers, A. M. (1998). Motivations for sex and risky sexual behavior among adolescents and young adults: A functional perspective. *Journal of Personality and Social Psychology, 75,* 1528–1558.

Cooper, M. L., Talley, A., Sheldon, M. S., Levitt, A., & Barber, L. (2008). A dyadic perspective on approach and avoidance motives for sex. In A. J. Elliot (Ed.), *Handbook of approach and avoidance motivation.* New York: Psychology Press.

Cooper, R. M., & Zubek, J. P. (1958). Effects of enriched and restricted early environments on the learning ability of bright and dull rats. *Canadian Journal of Psychology, 12,* 159–164.

Cooper-Hakim, A., & Viswesvaran, C. (2005). The construct of work commitment: Testing an integrative framework. *Psychological Bulletin, 131,* 241–259.

Copeland, D. E., Radvansky, G. A., & Goodwin, K. A. (2009). A novel study: Forgetting curves and the reminiscence bump. *Memory, 17,* 323–336.

Cornell, J. L., & Halpern-Felsher, B. L. (2006). Adolescents tell us why teens have oral sex. *Journal of Adolescent Health, 38,* 299–301.

Cornwell, B., Schumm, L. P., & Laumann, E. O. (2008). The social connectedness of older adults. *American Sociological Review, 73,* 185–203.

Cornwell, E. Y., & Waite, L. J. (2009). Social disconnectedness, perceived isolation, and health among older adults. *Journal of Health and Social Behavior, 50,* 31–48.

Corr, P. J. (2008). Reinforcement sensitivity theory (RST): Introduction. In P. J. Corr (Ed.), *The reinforcement sensitivity theory of personality* (pp. 1–43). New York: Cambridge University Press.

Correa, T., Hinsley, A. W., & de Zuniga, H. G. (2010). Who interacts on the web?: The intersection of users' personality and social media use. *Computers in Human Behavior, 26,* 247–253.

Corrigan, P. W. (2007). How clinical diagnosis might exacerbate the stigma of mental illness. *Social Work, 52,* 31–39.

Cortina, M. (2010). The future of psychodynamic psychotherapy. *Psychiatry, 73,* 43–56.

Cosmides, L. (2011). Evolutionary psychology. *Annual Review of Psychology* (vol. 62). Palo Alto, CA: Annual Reviews.

Costa, L. C., Vasconcelos, F. A., & Peres, K. G. (2010). Influence of biological, social, and psychological factors on abnormal eating attitudes among female university students in Brazil. *Journal of Health, Population, and Nutrition, 28,* 173–181.

Costa, P. T., & McCrae, R. R. (1992). *Revised NEO personality inventory.* Odessa, FL: Psychological Assessment Resources.

Costa, P. T., Terraciano, A., McCrae, R. R., Scally, M., & Abecasis, G. (2010). An alternative to the search for single polymorphisms: Toward molecular personality scales for the five-factor model. *Journal of Personality and Social Psychology.* (in press)

Costa, V. D., Lang, P. J., Sabatinelli, D., Versace, F., & Bradley, M. M. (2010). Emotional imagery: Assessing pleasure and arousal in the brain's reward circuitry. *Human Brain Mapping.* (in press)

Costafreda, S. G., Khanna, A., Mourao-Miranda, J., & Fu, C. H. (2009). Neural correlates of sad faces predict clinical remission to cognitive behavioral therapy in depression. *NeuroReport, 20,* 637–641.

Coulson, S., & Wu, Y. C. (2005). Right hemisphere activation of joke-related information: An event-related brain potential study. *Journal of Cognitive Neuroscience, 17,* 494–506.

Courtet, P., & others. (2004). Serotonin transporter gene may be involved in short-term risk of subsequent suicide attempts. *Biological Psychiatry, 55,* 46–51.

Courtois, E. T., & others. (2010). In vitro and in vivo enhanced generation of human A9 dopamine neurons from neural stem cells by Bcl-XL. *Journal of Biological Chemistry.* (in press)

Cowan, R. L., Roberts, D. M., & Joers, J. M. (2008). Neuroimaging in human MDMA (Ecstasy) users. *Annals of the New York Academy of Sciences, 1139,* 291–298.

Cowansage, K. K., LeDoux, J. E., & Monfils, M. H. (2010). Brain-deprived neurotrophic factor: A dynamic gatekeeper of neural plasticity. *Current Molecular Pharmacology, 3,* 12–29.

Cox, R. E., & Bryant, R. A. (2008) Advances in hypnosis research: Methods, designs, and contributions of intrinsic and instrumental hypnosis. In M. R. Nash & A. J. Barnier (Eds.), *The Oxford handbook of hypnosis: Research theory and practice* (pp. 311–336). New York: Oxford University Press.

Coxon, J. P., Goble, D. J., Van Impe, A., De Vos, J., Wenderoth, N., & Swinnen, S. P. (2010). Reduced basal ganglia function when elderly switch between coordinated movement patterns. *Cerebral Cortex.* (in press)

Craddock, N., & Forty, L. (2006). Genetics of affective (mood) disorders. *European Journal of Human Genetics, 14,* 660–668.

Craig, I., & Plomin, R. (2006). Quantitative trait loci for IQ and other complex traits: Single-nucleotide polymorphism genotyping using pooled DNA and microarrays. *Genes, Brain, and Behavior, 5,* 32–37.

Craik, F. I. M., & Lockhart, R. S. (1972). Levels of processing: A framework for memory research. *Journal of Verbal Learning and Verbal Behavior, 11,* 671–684.

Craik, F. I. M., & Tulving, E. (1975). Depth of processing and retention of words in episodic memory. *Journal of Experimental Psychology: General, 104,* 268–294.

Cramer, P. (2008). Longitudinal study of defense mechanisms: Late childhood to late adolescence. *Journal of Personality, 75,* 1–23.

Cramer, P. (2008a). Seven pillars of defense mechanism theory. *Social and Personality Psychology Compass, 2,* 1963–1981.

Cramer, P. (2009). An increase in early adolescent undercontrol is associated with the use of denial. *Journal of Personality Assessment, 91,* 331–339.

Cramer, P., & Jones, C. J. (2007). Defense mechanisms predict differential lifespan change in self-control and self-acceptance. *Journal of Research in Personality, 41,* 841–855.

Crampton, S. M., & Wagner, J. A., III. (1994). Percept-percept inflation in microorganizational research: An investigation of prevalence and effect. *Journal of Applied Psychology, 79,* 67–76.

Crandall, C. S. (2004). Social contagion of binge eating. In R. M. Kowalski & M. R. Leary (Eds.), *The interface of social and clinical psychology: Key readings* (pp. 99–115). New York: Psychology Press.

Cranley, L., Doran, D. M., Tourangeau, A. E., Kushniruk, A., & Nagle, L. (2009). Nurses' uncertainty in decision-making: A literature review. *Worldviews in Evidence-Based Nursing, 6,* 3–15.

Creer, D. J., Romberg, C., Saksida, L. M., van Praag, H., & Bussey, T. J. (2010). Running enhances spatial pattern separation in mice. *Proceedings of the National Academy of Sciences USA, 107,* 2367–2372.

Crescentini, C., Shallice, T., Del Missier, F., & Macaluso, E. (2010). Neural correlates of episodic retrieval: An fMRI study of the part-list cueing effect. *NeuroImage, 50,* 678–692.

Crespo-Garcia, M., Cantero, J. L., Pomyalov, A., Boccaletti, S., & Atienza, M. (2010). Functional neural networks underlying semantic encoding of associative memories. *NeuroImage.* (in press)

Cress, M. E., Buchner, D. M., Prohaska, T., Rimmer, J., Brown, M., Macera, C., DiPietro, L., & Chodzko-Zajko, W. (2005). Best practices for physical activity programs and behavior counseling in older adult populations. *Journal of Aging and Physical Activity, 13,* 61–74.

Cresswell, M. (2008). Szasz and his interlocutors: Reconsidering Thomas Szasz's "Myth of Mental Illness" thesis. *Journal for the Theory of Social Behaviour, 38,* 23–44.

Crick, N. R., & Grotpeter, J. K. (1995). Relational aggression, gender, and social-psychological adjustment. *Child Development, 66,* 710–722.

Crick, N. R., & Rose, A. J. (2000). Toward a gender-balanced approach to the study of social-emotional development: A look at relational aggression. In P. H. Miller & E. Kofsky Scholnick (Eds.), *Toward a feminist developmental psychology* (pp. 153–168). Florence, KY: Taylor & Frances/Routledge.

Crooks, R. L., & Baur, K. (2011). *Our sexuality* (11th ed.). Boston: Cengage.

Crowley, K., Pickle, J., Dale, R., & Fattal, O. (2008). A critical examination of bifrontal electroconvulsive therapy: Clinical efficacy, cognitive side effects, and directions for future research. *Journal of ECT, 24,* 268–271.

Csikszentmihalyi, M. (1990). *Flow: The psychology of optimal experience.* New York: Harper Perennial.

Csikszentmihalyi, M., & Rathunde, K. (1998). The development of the person: An experiential perspective on the ontogenesis of psychological complexity. In W. Damon (Ed.), *Handbook of child psychology* (5th ed., vol. 1). New York: Wiley.

Cuijpers, P. (2001). Mortality and depressive symptoms in inhabitants of residential homes. *International Journal of Geriatric Psychiatry, 16,* 131–138.

Cullen, K. (2010, January 14). The untouchable mean girls. *Boston Globe.* http://www.boston.com/news/local/massachusetts/articles/2010/01/24/the_untouchable_mean_girls/ (accessed May 16, 2010)

Cullen, K., Klimes-Dougan, B., & Kumra, S. (2009). Pediatric depression: Issues and treatment recommendations. *Minnesota Medicine, 92,* 45–48.

Culp, M. C. (2005, December 25). The business case for compassion. *San Bernardino Sun.* http://www.sbsun.com/workwise/ci_3829431 (accessed June 15, 2006)

Culpepper, L. (2010). The social and economic burden of shift-work disorder. *Journal of Family Practice, 59, Suppl. 1,* S3–S11.

Cumming, E., & Henry, W. E. (1961). *Growing older: The process of disengagement.* New York: Basic.

Cunha, C., Monfils, M. H., & LeDoux, J. E. (2010). GABA(C) receptors in the lateral amygdala: A possible novel target for the treatment of fear and anxiety disorders? *Frontiers in Behavioral Neuroscience.* (in press)

Cunningham, R. L., & McGinnis, M. Y. (2007). Factors influencing aggression toward females by male rats exposed to anabolic androgenic steroids during puberty. *Hormones and Behavior, 51,* 135–141.

Curran, K., DuCette, J., Eisenstein, J., & Hyman, I. A. (2001, August). *Statistical analysis of the cross-cultural data: The third year.* Paper presented at the meeting of the American Psychological Association, San Francisco.

Curtiss, S. (1977). *Genie.* New York: Academic.

Cuthbert, B., & Insel, T. (2010). Classification issues in women's mental health: Clinical utility and etiological mechanisms. *Archives of Women's Mental Health, 13,* 57–59.

Cutrona, C. E. (1982). Transition to college: Loneliness and the process of social adjustment. In L. A. Peplau & D. Perlman (Eds.), *Loneliness.* New York: Wiley.

D

Daadi, M. M., & others (2010). Human neural stem cell grafts modify microglial response and enhance axon sprouting in neonatal hypoxic-ischemic brain injury. *Stroke.* (in press)

Dadds, M. R., Holland, D. E., Barrett, P. M., & Spence, S. H. (1999). Early intervention and prevention of anxiety disorders in children:

Results at 2-year follow-up. *Journal of Consulting & Clinical Psychology, 67,* 145–150.

Dahl, R., & Spear, L. P. (Eds.). (2004). Adolescent brain development: Vulnerabilities and opportunities. *Annals of the New York Academy of Sciences, 1021.*

Dale, K. Y., Berg, R., Elden, A., Odegard, A., & Holte, A. (2009). Testing the diagnosis of dissociative identity disorder through measures of dissociation, absorption, hypnotizability, and PTSD: A Norwegian pilot study. *Journal of Trauma and Dissociation, 10,* 102–112.

Dalton, M., Hoyle, D. G., & Watts, M. W. (2011). *Human relations* (4th ed.). Boston: Cengage.

Damm, J., & others. (2010). Influence of age on effectiveness and tolerability of electroconvulsive therapy. *Journal of ECT.* (in press)

Damon, W. (2008). *The path to purpose: Helping our children find their calling in life.* New York: Free Press.

Damsa, C., Kosel, M., & Moussally, J. (2009). Current status of brain imaging in anxiety disorders. *Current Opinion in Psychiatry, 22,* 96–110.

Daniels, H. (2011). Vygotsky and psychology. In U. Goswami (Ed.), *Wiley-Blackwell handbook of childhood cognitive development* (2nd ed.). New York: Wiley Blackwell.

Danner, D. D., Snowdon, D. A., & Friesen, W. V. (2001). Positive emotions in early life and longevity: Findings from the Nun Study. *Journal of Personality and Social Psychology, 80,* 804–813.

Danoff-Burg, S., Mosher, C. E., & Grant, C. A. (2006). Relations of agentic and communal personality traits to health behavior and substance use among college students. *Personality and Individual Differences, 40,* 353–363.

Darley, J. M., & Latané, B. (1968). Bystander intervention in emergencies: Diffusion of responsibility. *Journal of Personality and Social Psychology, 8,* 377–383.

Darvas, M., & Palmiter, R. D. (2010). Restricting dopaminergic signaling to either dorsolateral or medial striatum facilitates cognition. *Journal of Neuroscience, 30,* 1158–1165.

Darwin, C. (1862). *On the various contrivances by which British and foreign orchids are fertilised by insects, and on the good effects of intercrossing.* London: John Murray.

Darwin, C. (1871). *The descent of man and selection in relation to sex.* London: John Murray.

Darwin, C. (1965). *The expression of the emotions in man and animals.* Chicago: University of Chicago Press. (original work published 1872)

Darwin, C. (1979). *On the origin of species.* New York: Avenal Books. (original work published 1859)

da Silva Cais, C. F., Stefanello, S., Fabrício Mauro, M. L., Vaz Scavacini de Freitas, G., & Botega, N. J. (2009). Factors associated with repeated suicide attempts: Preliminary results of the WHO Multisite Intervention Study on Suicidal Behavior (SUPRE-MISS) from Campinas, Brazil. *Crisis: The Journal of Crisis Intervention and Suicide Prevention, 30,* 73–78.

Davidson, J. R. (2009). First-line pharmacotherapy approaches for generalized anxiety disorder. *Journal of Clinical Psychiatry, 70, Suppl. 2,* S25–S31.

Davidson, K. W., & others. (2006). Assessment and treatment of depression in patients with cardiovascular disease: National Heart, Lung, and Blood Institute Working Group Report. *Psychosomatic Medicine, 68,* 645–650.

Davidson, P. S., Cook, S. P., & Glisky, E. L. (2006). Flashbulb memories for September 11th can be preserved in older adults. *Neuropsychology, Development, and Cognition B, 13,* 196–206.

Davidson, R. J. (2000). Affective style, psychopathology, and resilience: Brain mechanisms and plasticity. *American Psychologist, 55,* 196–214.

Davidson, R. J. (2005). Neural substrates of affective style and value. In Y. Christen (Series Ed.) & J.-P. Changeux, A. R. Damasio, W. Singer, & Y. Christen (Vol. Eds.), *Research and perspectives in neurosciences: Neurobiology of human values* (pp. 67–90). Germany: Springer-Verlag.

Davidson, R. J. (2010). Empirical explorations of mindfulness: Conceptual and methodological conundrums. *Emotion.* (in press)

Davidson, R. J. (2010a, April 22). *Change your brain by transforming your mind.* Paper presented at the Wisconsin Symposium on Emotion, University of Wisconsin, Madison.

Davidson, R. J., Kabat-Zinn, J., Schumacher, J., Rosenkranz, M. M., Daniel, S., Saki, F., Urbanowski, F., Harrington, A., Bonus, K., & Sheridan, J. F. (2003). Alterations in brain and immune function produced by mindfulness meditation. *Psychosomatic Medicine, 65* (4), 564–570.

Davidson, R. J., Scherer, K. R., & Goldsmith, H. H. (Eds.). (2002). *Handbook of affective sciences.* New York: Oxford University Press.

Davidson, R. J., Shackman, A., & Pizzagalli, D. (2002). The functional neuroanatomy of emotion and affective style. In R. J. Davidson, K. R. Scherer, & H. H. Goldsmith (Eds.), *Handbook of affective sciences.* New York: Oxford University Press.

Davis, C., Patte, K., Curtis, C., & Reid, C. (2010). Immediate pleasures and future consequences: A neuropsychological study of binge eating and obesity. *Appetite, 54,* 208–213.

Davis, C. M., & Riley, A. L. (2010). Conditioned taste aversion learning: Implications for animal models of drug abuse. *Annals of the New York Academy of Sciences, 1187,* 247–275.

Davis, E., Sawyer, M. G., Lo, S. K., Priest, N., & Wake, M. (2010). Socioeconomic risk factors for mental health problems in 4–5-year old children: Australian population study. *Academic Pediatrics, 10,* 41–47.

Davis, J. I., Senghas, A., & Ochsner, K. N. (2009). How does facial feedback modulate emotional experience? *Journal of Research in Personality, 43,* 822–829.

Davis, M. C., Zautra, A. J., Johnson, L. M., Murray, K. E., & Okvat, H. A. (2007). Psychosocial stress, emotion regulation, and resilience among older adults. In C. M. Aldwin,

C. L. Park, & A. Spiro (Eds.), *Handbook of health and aging*. New York: Guilford.

Davison, K. P., Pennebaker, J. W., & Dickerson, S. S. (2000). Who talks? The social psychology of illness support groups. *American Psychologist, 55,* 205–217.

Davoli, T., Denchi, E. L., & de Lange, T. (2010). Persistent telomere damage induces bypass of mitosis and teraploidy. *Cell, 141,* 81–83.

Dawson, A., & List, T. (2009). Comparison of pain thresholds and pain tolerance levels between Middle Easterners and Swedes and between genders. *Journal of Oral Rehabilitation, 36,* 271–278.

Deal, T. E., & Kennedy, A. A. (1982). *Corporate cultures: The rites and rituals of corporate life.* New York: Penguin.

De Angelis, T. (2002). Binge-eating disorder: What's the best treatment? *Monitor on Psychology, 33.* http://www.apa.org/monitor/mar02/binge.html

Deary, I. J., Johnson, W., & Starr, J. M. (2010). Are processing speed tasks biomarkers of aging? *Psychology and Aging, 25,* 219–228.

Deaux, K. (2001). Social identity. In J. Worell (Ed.), *Encyclopedia of gender and women.* San Diego: Academic.

Deaux, K., & LaFrance, M. (1998). Gender. In D. T. Gilbert, S. T. Fiske, & G. Lindzey (Eds.), *The handbook of social psychology* (vols. 1 and 2, 4th ed., pp. 788–827). New York: McGraw-Hill.

Debiec, J., Diaz-Mataix, L., Bush, D. E., Doyere, V., & LeDoux, J. E. (2010). The amygdala encodes specific sensory features of an aversive reinforcer. *Nature Neuroscience, 13,* 536–537.

Decety, J., & Cacioppo, J. T. (2011). *Handbook of social neuroscience.* New York: Oxford University Press.

Deci, E., Koestner, R., & Ryan, R. (1999). The undermining effect is a reality after all—Extrinsic rewards, task interest, and self-determination: Repy to Eisenberger, Pierce, and Cameron (1999) and Lepper, Henderlong, and Gingras (1999). *Psychological Bulletin, 125,* 692–700.

Deci, E. L., & Ryan, R. M. (2000). The "what" and "why" of goal pursuits: Human needs and the self-determination of behavior. *Psychological Inquiry, 4,* 227–268.

Deci, E. L., & Ryan, R. M. (Eds.). (2002). *Handbook of self-determination research.* Rochester, NY: University of Rochester Press.

Dedert, E. A., & others. (2009). Association of trauma exposure with psychiatric morbidity in military veterans who have served since September 11, 2001. *Journal of Psychiatric Research, 43,* 830–836.

Degenhardt, L., Bruno, R., & Topp, L. (2010). Is ecstasy a drug of dependence? *Drug and Alcohol Dependence, 107,* 1–10.

Degenhardt, L., & others. (2010). Evaluating the drug use "gateway" theory using cross-national data: Consistency and associations of the order of initiation of drug use among participants in the WHO World Mental Health Surveys. *Drug and Alcohol Dependence, 108,* 84–97.

Degnin, F. D. (2009). Difficult patients, overmedication, and groupthink. *Journal of Clinical Ethics, 20,* 64–74.

de Graaf, L. E., Hollon, S. D., & Huibers, J. J. (2010). Predicting outcome in computerized cognitive behavior therapy for depression in primary care: A randomized trial. *Journal of Consulting and Clinical Psychology, 78,* 184–189.

de Graaf, L. E., Huibers, J. J., Cuijpers, P., & Arntz, A. (2010). Minor and major depression in the general population: Does dysfunctional thinking play a role? *Comprehensive Psychiatry, 51,* 266–274.

de Groot, E. R., Verheul, R., & Trijsburg, R. W. (2008). An integrative perspective on psychotherapeutic treatments for borderline personality disorder. *Journal of Personality Disorders, 22,* 332–352.

Dehaene, S., Changeux, J., Naccache, L., Sackur, J., & Sergent, C. (2006). Conscious, preconscious, and subliminal processing: A testable taxonomy. *Trends in Cognitive Sciences, 10,* 204–211.

de Hevia, M. D., & Spelke, E. S. (2010). Number-space mapping in human infants. *Psychological Science.* (in press)

DeLamater, J., & Moorman, S. M. (2007). Sexual behavior in later life. *Journal of Aging and Health, 19,* 921–945.

de Lange, F. P., Jensen, O., & Dehaene, S. (2010). Accumulation of evidence during sequential decision making: The importance of top-down factors. *Journal of Neuroscience, 30,* 731–738.

Del Cul, A., Dehaene, S., Reyes, P., Bravo, E., & Slachevsky, A. (2009). Causal role of prefrontal cortex in the threshold for access to consciousness. *Brain, 132,* 2531–2540.

Del Giudice, M. J. (2010). What might this be? Rediscovering the Rorschach as a tool for personnel selection in organizations. *Journal of Personality Assessment, 92,* 78–89.

Dell, P. F., & Eisenhower, J. W. (1990). Adolescent multiple personality disorder: A preliminary study of eleven cases. *Journal of the American Academy of Child & Adolescent Psychiatry, 29,* 359–366.

Dell, P. F., & O'Neil, J. A. (Eds.). (2009). *Dissociation and the dissociative disorders: DSM-V and beyond.* New York: Routledge/Taylor & Francis.

Del Missier, F., & Terpini, C. (2009). Part-set cueing in option generation. *Memory and Cognition, 37,* 265–276.

Delprato, D. J. (2005). Retroactive interference as a function of degree of interpolated study without overt retrieval practice. *Psychonomic Bulletin and Review, 12,* 345–349.

DeLuga, R. J., & Mason, S. (2000). Relationship of resident assistant conscientiousness, extraversion, and positive affect with rated performance. *Journal of Research in Personality, 34,* 225–235.

DeMarree, K. G., & Petty, R. E. (2007). The elaboration likelihood model of persuasion. In R. F. Baumeister & K. D. Vohs (Eds.), *Encyclopedia of social psychology.* Thousand Oaks, CA: Sage.

Demeure, V., Bonnefon, J. F., & Raufaste, E. (2009). Politeness and conditioned reasoning: Interpersonal cues to the indirect suppression of

deductive inferences. *Journal of Experimental Psychology: Learning, Memory, and Cognition, 35,* 260–266.

Deming, W. E. (1986). *Out of the crisis.* Cambridge, MA: MIT Press.

Denham, S. A., Bassett, H. H., & Wyatt, T. (2007). The socialization of emotional competence. In J. E. Grusec & P. D. Hastings (Eds.), *Handbook of socialization.* New York: Guilford.

Dennis, A. (2005). Osama bin Laden: The sum of all fears. In W. T. Schultz (Ed.), *Handbook of psychobiography* (pp. 311–322). Oxford, U.K.: Oxford University Press.

De Pauw, S. S., & Mervielde, I. (2010). Temperament, personality, and developmental psychopathology: A review on the conceptual dimensions underlying childhood traits. *Child Psychiatry and Human Development, 41,* 313–329.

Depue, R. A., & Collins, P. F. (1999). Neurobiology of the structure of personality: Dopamine, facilitation of incentive motivation, and extraversion. *Behavioural and Brain Sciences, 22,* 491–569.

De Raad, B., Barelds, D. P. H., Levert, E., Ostendorf, F., Mlacic, B., Di Blas, L., Hrebickova, M., Perugini, M., Church, A. T., & Katigbak, M. S. (2010). Only three factors of personality description are fully replicable across languages: A comparison of 14 trait taxonomies. *Journal of Personality and Social Psychology, 98,* 160–173.

De Raedt, R., & Koster, E. H. W. (2010). Understanding vulnerability for depression from a cognitive neuroscience perspective: A reappraisal of attentional factors and a new conceptual framework. *Cognitive, Affective & Behavioral Neuroscience, 10,* 50–70.

Derks, D., Bos, A. F. R., & von Grumbkow, J. (2008). Emoticons in computer-mediated communication: Social motives and social context. *CyberPsychology & Behavior, 11,* 99–101.

de Roon-Cassini, T. A., Mancini, A. D., Rusch, M. D., & Bonanno, G. A. (2010). Psychopathology and resilience following traumatic injury: A latent growth mixture model analysis. *Rehabilitation Psychology, 55,* 1–11.

Desmond, D. M., & MacLachlan, M. (2010). Prevalence and characteristics of phantom limb pain and residual limb pain in the long term after upper limb amputation. *International Journal of Rehabilitation Research.* (in press)

Deutsch, M. (2006). Cooperation and competition. In M. Deutsch, P. T. Coleman, & E. C. Marcus (Eds.), *Handbook of conflict resolution.* San Francisco: Jossey-Bass.

Deutsch, M., Coleman, P. T., & Marcus, E. C. (Eds.). (2006). *Handbook of conflict resolution* (2nd ed.). San Francisco: Jossey-Bass.

Deutsch, S. (2010). Consciousness platform: The greatest mystery of all time. *IEEE Engineering in Medicine and Biology Magazine, 29,* 60–62.

Devlin, S., & Arneill, A. B. (2003). Health care environments and patient outcomes: A review of the literature. *Environment and Behavior, 35,* 665–694.

De Vries, G. J. (2004). Sex differences in adult and developing brains: Compensation, compensation, compensation. *Endocrinology, 145,* 1063–1068.

de Waal, F. B. M., Leimgruber, K., & Greenberg, A. R. (2008). Giving is self-rewarding for monkeys. *PNAS Proceedings of the National Academy of Sciences USA, 105,* 13685–13689.

DeWall, C. N., Twenge, J. M., Gitter, S. A., & Baumeister, R. F. (2009). It's the thought that counts: The role of hostile cognition in shaping aggressive responses to social exclusion. *Journal of Personality and Social Psychology, 96,* 45–59.

Dewar, M., Cowan, N., & Della Sala, S. (2010). Forgetting due to retroactive interference in amnesia findings and implications. In S. D. Sala (Ed.), *Forgetting.* New York: Psychology Press.

Dewar, M., Della Sala, S., Beschin, N., & Cowan, N. (2010a). Profound retroactive interference in anterograde amnesia: What interferes? *Neuropsychology.* (in press)

de Zoysa, P., Newcombe, P. A., & Rajapakse, L. (2008). Consequences of parental corporal punishment on 12-year-old children in the Colombo district. *Ceylon Medical Journal, 53,* 7–9.

de Zwaan, M., Mitchell, J. E., Crosby, R. D., Mussell, M. P., Raymond, N. C., Specker, S. M., & Seim, H. C. (2005). Short-term cognitive behavioral treatment does not improve outcome of a comprehensive very-low-calorie diet program in obese women with binge eating disorder. *Behavior Therapy, 36,* 89–99.

Diamond, A. (2009). The interplay of biology and the environment broadly defined. *Developmental Psychology, 45,* 1–8.

Diamond, A. (2009a). All or none hypothesis: A global-default mode that characterizes the brain and mind. *Developmental Psychology, 45,* 130–138.

Diamond, A., Casey, B. J., & Munakata, Y. (2011). *Developmental cognitive neuroscience.* New York: Oxford University Press.

Diamond, L. M. (2008a). *Sexual fluidity: Understanding women's love and desire.* Cambridge, MA: Harvard University Press.

Diamond, L. M. (2008b). Female bisexuality from adolescence to adulthood: Results from a 10-year longitudinal study. *Developmental Psychology, 44,* 5–14.

Diamond, L. M. (2009). Emotion in relationships. In H. R. Reis & S. Sprecher (Eds.), *Encyclopedia of human relationships.* Thousand Oaks, CA: Sage.

Diamond, L. M., & Savin-Williams, R. C. (2009). Adolescent sexuality. In R. M. Lerner & L. Steinberg (Eds.), *Handbook of adolescent psychology* (3rd ed.). New York: Wiley.

Diamond, L. M., & Savin-Williams, R. C. (2011). Same-sex activity in adolescence: Multiple meanings and implications. In L. Morrow & R. F. Fassinger (Eds.), *Sex in the margins.* Washington, DC: American Psychological Association. (in press)

Diamond, M., & Sigmundson, H. K. (1997). Sex reassignment at birth. *Archives of Pediatric and Adolescent Medicine, 151,* 298–304.

Dichter, G. S., Felder, J. N., & Smoski, M. J. (2010). The effects of brief behavioral activation therapy for depression on cognitive control in affective contexts: An fMRI investigation. *Journal of Affective Disorders.* (in press)

DiClemente, C. C. (2006). Natural change and the troublesome use of substances: A life-course perspective. In W. R. Miller & K. M. Carroll (Eds.), *Rethinking substance abuse: What the science shows, and what we should do about it* (pp. 81–96). New York: Guilford.

Diefenbach, G. J., Disch, W. B., Robinson, J. T., Baez, E., & Coman, E. (2009). Anxious depression among Puerto Rican and African American older adults. *Aging and Mental Health, 13,* 118–126.

Diekelmann, S., Wilhelm, I., & Born, J. (2009). The whats and whens of sleep-dependent memory consolidation. *Sleep Medicine Reviews, 13,* 309–321.

Diekman, A. B., & Eagly, A. H. (2008). Of women, men, and motivation: A role congruity account. In J. Y. Shah & W. L. Gardner (Eds.), *Handbook of motivational science* (pp. 434–447). New York: Guilford.

Dien, J. (2009). A tale of two recognition systems: Implications of the fusiform face area and the visual work face area for lateralized object recognition models. *Neuropsychologia, 47,* 1–16.

Diener, E. (1999). Introduction to the special section on the structure of emotion. *Journal of Personality and Social Psychology, 76,* 803–804.

Diener, E. (2000). Subjective well-being: The science of happiness and a proposal for a national index. *American Psychologist, 55,* 34–43.

Diener, E., & Diener, C. (1996). Most people are happy. *Psychological Science, 7,* 181–185.

Diener, E., Emmons, R. A., Larsen, R. J., & Griffin, S. (1985). The Satisfaction with Life Scale. *Journal of Personality Assessment, 49,* 71–75.

Digman, J. M. (1990). Personality structure: Emergence of the five-factor model. *Annual Review of Psychology* (vol. 41). Palo Alto, CA: Annual Reviews.

Digman, J. M. (2002). Historical antecedents of the five-factor model. In P. T. Costa & T. A. Widiger (Eds.), *Personality disorders and the five-factor model of personality* (2nd ed., pp. 17–22). Washington, DC: American Psychological Association.

Dijksterhuis, A., Bos, M. W., Van der Leij, A., & Van Baaren, R. B. (2009). Predicting soccer matches after unconscious and conscious thought as a function of expertise. *Psychological Science, 20,* 1381–1387.

Dijksterhuis, A., & Nordgren, L. F. (2006). A theory of unconscious thought. *Perspectives on Psychological Science, 1,* 95–109.

Dijksterhuis, A., & Van Knippenberg, A. (1998). The relation between perception and behavior or how to win a game of Trivial Pursuit. *Journal of Personality and Social Psychology, 74,* 865–877.

Dijkstra, P., Gibbons, F., & Buunk, A. P. (2010). Social comparison theory. In *Social psychological foundations of clinical psychology.* New York: Guilford. (in press)

Dimeff, L. A., Koerner, K., & Linehan, M. M. (2007). *Dialectical behavior therapy in clinical practice: Applications across disorders and settings.* New York: Guilford.

Dishion, T. J., & Piehler, T. F. (2009). Deviant by design: Peer contagion in development, interventions, and schools. In K. H. Rubin, W. M. Bukowski, & B. Laursen (Eds.), *Handbook of peer interactions, relationships, and groups.* New York: Guilford.

Distel, M. A., Trull, T. J., Derom, C. A., Thiery, E. W., Grimmer, M. A., Martin, N. G., Willemsen, G., & Boomsma, D. I. (2008). Heritability of borderline personality disorder features is similar across three countries. *Psychological Medicine, 38,* 1219–1229.

Dixon, M. L., Ruppel, J., Pratt, J., & De Rosa, E. (2009). Learning to ignore: Acquisition of sustained attentional suppression. *Psychonomic Bulletin and Review, 16,* 418–423.

Dodge, K. A., Coie, J. D., & Lynam, D. (2006). Aggression and antisocial behavior in youth. In W. Damon & R. Lerner (Eds.), *Handbook of child psychology* (6th ed.). New York: Wiley.

Doerr, C. E., & Baumeister, R. F. (2010). Self-regulatory strength and adjustment: Implications of the limited resource model of self-regulation. In J. E. Maddux & J. P. Tagney (Eds.), *Social psychological foundations of clinical psychology.* New York: Guilford.

Doherty, M. J. (2009). *Theory of mind: How children understand others' thoughts and feelings.* New York: Psychology Press.

Dolan, M., & Fullam, R. (2006). Face affect recognition deficits in personality disordered offenders: Associate with psychopathy. *Psychological Medicine, 36,* 1563–1569.

Dollard, J., Doob, L. W., Miller, N. E., Mowrer, O. H., & Sears, R. R. (1939). *Frustration and aggression.* New Haven, CT: Yale University Press.

Domènech-Llaberia, E., Vinas, F., Pla, E., Jane, M. C., Mitjavila, M., Corbella, T., & Canals, J. (2009). Prevalence of major depression in school children. *European Child and Adolescent Psychiatry, 18* (10), 597–604.

Domhoff, G. W. (2007). Realistic simulation and bizarreness in dream content: Past findings and suggestions for future research. In D. Barrett & P. McNamara (Eds.), *The new science of dreaming: Content, recall, and personality correlates* (vol. 2, pp. 1–27). Westport, CT: Praeger.

Dominquez Coello, S., & others. (2010). Association between glycemic index, glycemic load, and fructose with insulin resistance: The CDC of the Canary Islands study. *European Journal of Nutrition.* (in press)

Domjan, M. (2010). *The principles of learning and behavior* (6th ed.). Boston: Cengage.

Donatelle, R. J. (2011). *Health* (9th ed.). Upper Saddle River, NJ: Pearson.

Donnellan, M. B., Larsen-Rife, D., & Conger, R. D. (2005). Personality, family history, and competence in early adult romantic relationships. *Journal of Personality and Social Psychology, 88,* 562–576.

Donnellan, M. B., Lucas, R. E., & Fleeson, W. (2009). Introduction to personality and assessment at age 40: Reflections on the legacy of the person-situation debate and the future of person-situation integration. *Journal of Research in Personality, 43,* 117–119.

Donnellan, M. B., Trzesniewski, K., & Robins, R. (2009). An emerging epidemic of narcissism or much ado about nothing? *Journal of Research in Personality.*

Donnellan, M. B., Trzesniewski, K., Robins, R. W., Moffitt, T. E., & Caspi, A. (2005). Low self-esteem is related to aggression, anti-social behavior, and delinquency. *Psychological Science, 16,* 328–335.

Donovan, M. A. (2000). Cognitive, affective, and satisfaction variables as predictors of organizational behaviors: A structural equation modeling examination of alternative models. *Dissertation Abstracts International, 60* (9-B), 4943 (UMI No. AAI9944835).

Dougherty, S. (2010). Computing the unconscious. *Psychoanalytic Quarterly, 79,* 171–201.

Dovidio, J. F., Gaertner, S. L., & Saguy, T. (2009). Commonality and the complexity of "we": Social attitudes and social change. *Personality and Social Psychology Review, 13,* 3–20.

Dovidio, J. F., Kawakami, K., & Gaertner, S. L. (2002). Implicit and explicit prejudice and interracial interaction. *Journal of Personality and Social Psychology, 82,* 62–68.

Doyle, W. J., & others. (2010). The interleukin 6-174C/C genotype predicts greater rhinovirus illness. *Journal of Infectious Diseases, 201,* 199–206.

Drake, C., Levine, R., & Laska, E. A. (2007). Identifying prognostic factors that predict recovery in the presence of loss to follow-up. In K. Hopper, G. Harrison, A. Janca, & N. Sartorius (Eds.), *Recovery from schizophrenia: An international perspective: A report from the WHO Collaborative Project, the international study of schizophrenia* (pp. 69–72). New York: Oxford University Press.

Dreisbach, G., & Goschke, T. (2004). How positive affect modulates cognitive control: Reduced perseveration at the cost of increased distractibility. *Journal of Experimental Psychology: Learning, Memory, and Cognition, 30,* 343–353.

Dricot, L., Sorger, B., Schiltz, C., Goebel, R., & Rossion, B. (2008). Evidence for individual face discrimination in non-face selective areas of the visual cortex in acquired prosopagnosia. *Behavioral Neuroscience, 19,* 75–79.

Drigotas, S. M., Safstrom, C. A., & Gentilia, T. (1999). An investment model prediction of dating infidelity. *Journal of Personality and Social Psychology, 77,* 509–524.

Duan, J., Sanders, A. R., & Gejman, P. V. (2010). Genome-wide approaches to schizophrenia. *Brain Research Bulletin.* (in press)

Dubový, P., Klusáková, I., Svíženská, I., & Brázda, V. (2010). Spatio-temporal changes of SDF1 and its CXCR4 receptor in the dorsal root ganglia following unilateral sciatic nerve injury as a model of neuropathic pain. *Histochemistry and Cell Biology, 133,* 323–337.

Dubow, E. F., Huesmann, L. R., & Greenwood, D. (2007). Media and youth socialization: Underlying processes and moderators of effects. In J. E. Grusec & P. D. Hastings (Eds.), *Handbook of socialization* (pp. 404–430). New York: Guilford.

Dudley, M., Goldney, R., & Hadzi-Pavlovic, D. (2010). Are adolescents dying by suicide taking SSRI antidepressants? A review of observational studies. *Australasian Psychiatry, 18,* 242–245.

Duffy, M. K., Ganster, D. C., & Pagon, M. (2002). Social undermining and social support in the workplace. *Academy of Management Journal, 45,* 331–351.

Duncan, A. E., Scherrer, J., Fu, Q., Bucholz, K. K., Heath, A. C., True, W. R., Haber, J. R., Howell, D., & Jacob, T. (2006). Exposure to paternal alcoholism does not predict development of alcohol-use disorders in offspring: Evidence from an offspring-of-twins study. *Journal of Studies on Alcohol, 67,* 649–656.

Duncan, G. E. (2010). The "fit but fat" concept revisited: Population-based estimates using NHANES. *International Journal of Behavioral Nutrition and Physical Activity.* (in press)

Dunlap, E., Golub, A., Johnson, B. D., & Benoit, E. (2009). Normalization of violence: Experiences of childhood abuse by inner-city crack users. *Journal of Ethnicity in Substance Abuse, 8,* 15–34.

Dunn, E. W., Aknin, L. B., & Norton, M. I. (2008). Spending money on others promotes happiness. *Science, 319,* 1687–1688.

Dupoux, E., de Gardelle, V., & Kouider, S. (2008). Subliminal speech perception and auditory streaming. *Cognition, 109,* 267–273.

Dupré, K. E., & Barling, J. (2006). Predicting and preventing supervisory workplace aggression. *Journal of Occupational Health Psychology, 11,* 13–26.

Durand, V. M., & Barlow, D. H. (2010). *Essentials of abnormal psychology* (5th ed.). Boston: Cengage.

Durantini, M. R., Albarracin, D., Mitchell, A. L., Earl, A. N., & Gillette, J. C. (2006). Conceptualizing the influence of social agents of behavior change: A meta-analysis of the effectiveness of HIV-prevention interventionists for different groups. *Psychological Bulletin, 132,* 212–248.

Durrant, J. E. (2008). Physical punishment, culture, and rights: Current issues for professionals. *Developmental and Behavioral Pediatrics, 29,* 55–66.

Dutton, D., & Aron, A. (1974). Some evidence for heightened sexual attraction under conditions of high anxiety. *Journal of Personality and Social Psychology, 30,* 510–517.

Duvarci, S., Nader, K., & LeDoux, J. E. (2008). De novo mRNA synthesis is required for both consolidation and reconsolidation of fear memories in the amygdala. *Learning and Memory, 15,* 747–755.

Dweck, C. S. (2006). *Mindset.* New York: Random House.

Dweck, C. S., & Master, A. (2009). Self-theories and motivation: Students' beliefs about intelligence. In K. R. Wentzel & A. Wigfield (Eds.), *Handbook of motivation at school.* New York: Routledge.

Dysart, J. E., & Lindsay, R. C. L. (2007). The effects of delay on eyewitness identification witness accuracy: Should we be concerned? In R. C. L. Lindsay, D. F. Ross, J. D. Read, & M. P. Toglia (Eds.), *The handbook of eyewitness memory: Vol. II.* Mahwah, NJ: Erlbaum.

E

Eagleman, D. M. (2010). Synaesthesia. *British Medical Journal, 340,* 4616.

Eagly, A. H. (1987). *Sex differences in social behavior: A social-role interpretation.* Hillsdale, NJ: Erlbaum.

Eagly, A. H. (2010a). Gender roles. In J. Levine & M. Hogg (Eds.), *Encyclopedia of group processes and intergroup relations.* Thousand Oaks, CA: Sage. (in press)

Eagly, A. H. (2010b). The his and hers of prosocial behavior: An examination of the social psychology of gender. *American Psychologist.* (in press)

Eagly, A. H., & Crowley, M. (1986). Gender and helping behavior: A meta-analytic review of the social psychological literature. *Psychological Bulletin, 100,* 283–308.

Eagly, A. H., & Diekman, A. B. (2003). The malleability of sex differences in response to changing social roles. In L. G. Aspinwall & U. M. Staudinger (Eds.), *A psychology of human strengths: Fundamental questions and future directions for a positive psychology* (pp. 103–115). Washington, DC: American Psychological Association.

Eagly, A. H., & Fischer, A. (2009). Gender inequities in power in organizations. In B. van Krippenberg & D. Tjosvold (Eds.), *Power and interdependence in organizations.* New York: Cambridge University Press.

Eagly, A. H., & Sczesny, S. (2009). Stereotypes about women, men, and leaders: Have times changed? In M. Barreto, M. K. Ryan, & M. T. Schmitt (Eds.), *The glass ceiling in the 21st century.* Washington, DC: APA Books.

Eagly, A. H., & Wood, W. (2010). Gender roles in a biosocial world. In P. van Lange, A. Kruglanski, & E. T. Higgins (Eds.), *Handbook of theories in social psychology.* Thousand Oaks, CA: Sage. (in press)

Eagly, A. H., Wood, W., & Johannesen-Schmidt, M. C. (2004). Social role theory of sex differences and similarities: Implications for the partner preferences of women and men. In A. H. Eagly, A. Beall, & R. S. Sternberg (Eds.). *The psychology of gender* (2nd ed., pp. 269–295). New York: Guilford.

Eastman, K. K. (1994). In the eyes of the beholder: An attributional approach to ingratiation and organizational citizenship behavior. *Academy of Management Journal, 37,* 1379–1391.

Eaton, D. K., & others. (2008). Youth risk behavior surveillance—United States, 2007. *Morbidity and Mortality Weekly Reports, 57,* 1–131.

Eby, L. T. (2010). Mentoring. In S. Zedeck (Ed.), *APA handbook of industrial and organizational psychology.* Washington, DC: APA. (in press)

Eby, L. T., Maher, C. P., & Butts, M. M. (2010). The intersection of work and family life: The role of affect. *Annual Review of Psychology* (vol. 61). Palo Alto, CA: Annual Reviews.

Edmonds, G. W., Jackson, J. J., Fayard, J. V., & Roberts, B. W. (2007). Is character fate or is there hope to change my personality yet? *Social and Personality Psychology Compass, 2,* 399–413.

Eells, T. D. (2000). Can therapy affect physical health? *Journal of Psychotherapy Practice and Research, 9,* 100–104.

Effros, R. B. (2009). Kleemeir Award Lecture 2008—The canary in the coal mine: Telomeres and human healthspan. *Journals of Gerontology: Biological Sciences and Medical Sciences, 64,* 511–515.

Efklides, A. (2009). The role of metacognitive experiences in the learning process. *Psicothema, 21,* 76–82.

Eghigian, G. (Ed.). (2010). *From madness to mental health: Psychiatric disorder and its treatment in Western civilization.* New Brunswick, NJ: Rutgers University Press.

Ehrhart, M. G., Ehrhart, K. H., Roesch, S. C., Chung-Herrera, B. G., Nadler, K., & Bradshaw, K. (2009). Testing the latent factor structure and construct validity of the Ten-Item Personality Inventory. *Personality and Individual Differences, 47,* 900–905.

Eisenberg, D. P., Sarpal, D., Kohn, P. D., Meyer-Lindenberg, A., Wint, D., Kolachana, B., Apud, J., Weinberger, D. R., & Berman, K. F. (2010). Catechol-o-methyltransferase valine(158)methionine genotype and resting regional cerebral blood flow in medication-free patients with schizophrenia. *Biological Psychiatry, 67,* 287–290.

Eisenberg, M. E., & others. (2008). Support for comprehensive sexuality education: Perspectives from parents of school-age youth. *Journal of Adolescent Health, 42,* 352–359.

Eisenberg, N. (2010). Empathy-related responding: Links with self-regulation, moral judgment, and moral behavior. In M. Mikulincer & P. R. Shaver (Eds.), *Prosocial motives, emotions, and behavior: The better angels of our nature* (pp. 129–148). Washington, DC: American Psychological Association.

Eisenberg, N., Fabes, R. A., & Spinrad, T. L. (2006). Prosocial development. In W. Damon & R. Lerner (Eds.), *Handbook of child psychology* (2nd ed.). New York: Wiley.

Eisenberg, N., Morris, A. S., McDaniel, B., & Spinrad, T. L. (2009). Moral cognitions and prosocial responding. In R. M. Lerner & L. Steinberg (Eds.), *Handbook of adolescent psychology* (3rd ed.). New York: Wiley.

Eisenberg, N., & Murphy, B. (1995). Parenting and children's moral development. In M. H. Bornstein (Ed.), *Children and parenting* (vol. 4). Hillsdale, NJ: Erlbaum.

Eisenberg, N., & Valiente, C. (2002). Parenting and children's prosocial and moral development. In M. H. Bornstein (Ed.), *Handbook of parenting* (2nd ed.). Mahwah, NJ: Erlbaum.

Eisenberger, R., & Aselage, J. (2009). Incremental effects of reward on experienced performance pressure: Positive outcomes for intrinsic interest and creativity. *Journal of Organizational Behavior, 30,* 95–117.

Ekman, P. (1980). *The face of man.* New York: Garland.

Ekman, P. (1996). Lying and deception. In N. L. Stein, C. Brainerd, P. A. Ornstein, & B. Tversky (Eds.), *Memory for everyday emotional events.* Mahwah, NJ: Erlbaum.

Ekman, P. (2003). Emotions inside out: 130 years after Darwin's "The expression of emotions in man and animal." *Annals of the New York Academy of Sciences, 1000,* 1–6.

Ekman, P., Davidson, R. J., & Friesen, W. V. (1990). The Duchenne smile: Emotional expression and brain physiology: II. *Journal of Personality and Social Psychology, 58,* 342–353.

Ekman, P., Davidson, R. J., Ricard, M., & Wallace, B. A. (2005). Buddhist and psychological perspectives on emotions and well-being. *Current Directions in Psychological Science, 14,* 59–63.

Ekman, P., & Friesen, W. V. (1969). The repertoire of nonverbal behavior: Categories, origins, usage, and coding. *Semiotica, 1,* 49–98.

Ekman, P., & Friesen, W. V. (1971). Constants across cultures in the face and emotion. *Journal of Personality and Social Psychology, 17,* 124–129.

Ekman, P., Levenson, R. W., & Friesen, W. V. (1983). Autonomic nervous system activity distinguishes among emotions. *Science, 223,* 1208–1210.

Ekman, P., & O'Sullivan, M. (1991). Facial expressions: Methods, means, and moues. In R. S. Feldman & B. Rime (Eds.), *Fundamentals of nonverbal behavior.* Cambridge, U.K.: Cambridge University Press.

El-Hai, J. (2005). *The lobotomist: A maverick medical genius and his tragic quest to rid the world of mental illness.* Hoboken, NJ: Wiley.

Elias, W. J., & Cosgrove, G. R. (2008). Psychosurgery. *Neurosurgery Focus, 25,* E1.

Elkind, D. (1978). Understanding the young adolescent. *Adolescence, 13,* 127–134.

Elliott, T., Kuang, X., Shadbolt, N. R., & Zauner, K. P. (2009). Adaptation in multisensory neurons: Impact of cross-modal enhancement. *Network, 20,* 1–31.

Ellis, A. (1962). *Reason and emotion in psychotherapy.* New York: Lyle Stuart.

Ellis, A. (1996). A rational-emotive behavior therapist's perspective on Ruth. In G. Corey (Ed.), *Case approach to counseling and psychotherapy.* Pacific Grove, CA: Brooks/Cole.

Ellis, A. (2000). Rational emotive behavior therapy. In A. Kazdin (Ed.), *Encyclopedia of psychology.* Washington, DC, & New York: American Psychological Association and Oxford University Press.

Ellis, A. (2002). Rational emotive behavior therapy. In M. Hersen & W. H. Sledge (Eds.), *Encyclopedia of psychotherapy.* San Diego: Academic.

Ellis, A. (2005). Why I (really) became a therapist. *Journal of Clinical Psychology, 61,* 945–948.

Emmons, R. A. (2005). Striving for the sacred: Personal goals, life meaning, and religion. *Journal of Social Issues, 61,* 731–745.

Emmons, R. A., & Diener, E. (1986). Situation selection as a moderator of response consistency and stability. *Journal of Personality and Social Psychology, 51,* 1013–1019.

Emmons, R. A., & King, L. A. (1988). Conflict among personal strivings: Immediate and long-term implications for psychological and physical well-being. *Journal of Personality and Social Psychology, 48,* 1040–1048.

Emmons, R. A., & McCullough, M. E. (2003). Counting blessings versus burdens: An experimental investigation of gratitude and subjective well-being in daily life. *Journal of Personality and Social Psychology, 84,* 377–389.

Emmons, R. A., & McCullough, M. E. (Eds.). (2004). *The psychology of gratitude.* New York: Oxford University Press.

Emslie, G. J., Croarkin, P., & Mayes, T. L. (2010). Antidepressants. In M. K. Dulcan, (Ed.), *Dulcan's textbook of child and adolescent psychiatry* (pp. 701–723). Arlington, VA: American Psychiatric Publishing.

Endler, N. S. (1988). The origins of electroconvulsive therapy (ECT). *Convulsive Therapy, 4,* 5–23.

Eng, P. M., Fitzmaurice, G., Kubzansky, L. D., Rimm, E. B., & Kawachi, I. (2003). Anger expression and risk of stroke and coronary heart disease among male health professionals. *Psychosomatic Medicine, 65,* 100–110.

Engel, A. K., & Singer, W. (2001). Temporal binding and the neural correlates of sensory awareness. *Trends in Cognitive Science, 5,* 16–25.

Engels, R. C. M. E. (2009). Early pubertal maturation and drug use: Underlying mechanisms. *Addiction, 104,* 67–68.

Englander, E. K. (2006). *Understanding violence* (3rd ed.). Mahwah, NJ: Erlbaum.

Ensembl Human. (2010). *Explore the human genome.* www.ensemblhuman.org (accessed February 5, 2010)

Enstrom, J. E. (1999). Smoking cessation and mortality trends among two United States populations. *Journal of Clinical Epidemiology, 52,* 813–825.

Equal Employment Opportunity Commission (EEOC). (2007). *Sexual harassment charges EEOC & FEPAs combined FY 1997–2006.* Washington, DC: Author. http://eeoc.gov/stats/harass/html

Erath, S. A., Flanaggan, K. S., Bierman, K. L., & Tu, K. M. (2010). Friendships moderate psychosocial maladjustment in socially anxious early adolescents. *Journal of Applied Developmental Psychology, 31,* 15–26.

Erber, R., & Erber, M. (2011). *Intimate relationships* (2nd ed.). Upper Saddle River, NJ: Prentice-Hall.

Erdle, S., Irwing, P., Rushton, J. P., & Park, J. (2010). The general factor of personality and its relation to self-esteem in 628,640 internet respondents. *Personality and Individual Differences, 48,* 343–346.

Erickson, K. I., & Kramer, A. F. (2009). Aerobic exercise effects on cognitive and neural plasticity in older adults. *British Journal of Sports Medicine, 43,* 22–24.

Eriksen, J., Jorgensen, T. N., & Gether, U. (2010). Regulation of the dopamine transporter function by protein-protein interactions: New discoveries and methodological challenges. *Journal of Neurochemistry.* (in press)

Erikson, E. H. (1968). *Identity: Youth and crisis.* New York: Norton.

Erikson, E. H. (1969). *Gandhi's truth.* New York: Norton.

Erol, A. (2010). Are paradoxical cell cycle activities in neurons and glia related to the metabolic theory of Alzheimer disease? *Journal of Alzheimer's Disease, 19,* 129–135.

Espirito-Santo, H., & Pio-Abreu, J. L. (2009). Psychiatric symptoms and dissociation in conversion, somatization, and dissociative disorders. *Australian and New Zealand Journal of Psychiatry, 43,* 270–276.

Estrada, C., Isen, A. M., & Young, M. J. (1997). Positive affect influences creative problem solving and reported source of practice satisfaction in physicians. *Motivation and Emotion, 18,* 285–299.

Etaugh, C. A., & Bridges, J. S. (2010). *Women's lives* (2nd ed.). Upper Saddle River, NJ: Prentice-Hall.

Etnier, J. (2009). Chronic exercise and cognition in older adults. In T. McMorris, P. Tomporowski, & M. Audiffren (Eds.), *Exercise and cognitive function* (pp. 227–247). New York: Wiley-Blackwell.

Evans, C., & Diekman, A. B. (2009). On motivated role selection: Gender beliefs, distant goals, and career interest. *Psychology of Women Quarterly, 33,* 235–249.

Evans, D. E., & Rothbart, M. K. (2009). A two-factor model of temperament. *Personality and Individual Differences, 47,* 565–570.

Exner, J. E., Jr. (2003). *The Rorschach: A comprehensive system* (4th ed.). Hoboken, NJ: Wiley.

Eysenck, H. J. (1967). *The biological basis of personality.* Springfield, IL: Thomas.

Eysenck, M. W., & Keane, M. (2010). *Cognitive psychology.* New York: Psychology Press.

F

Faber, M. A., & Mayer, J. D. (2009). Resonance to archetypes in media: There's some accounting for taste. *Journal of Research in Personality, 43,* 307–322.

Faedda, G. L., Becker, I., Baroni, A., Tondo, L., Aspland, E., & Koukopoulos, A. (2010). The origins of electroconvulsive therapy: Prof. Bini's first report on ECT. *Journal of Affective Disorders, 120,* 12–15.

Fagan, M. K., & Pisoni, D. B. (2010). Hearing experience and receptive vocabulary development in deaf children with cochlear implants. *Journal of Deaf Studies and Deaf Education.* (in press)

Fahey, T. D., Insel, P. M., & Roth, W. T. (2011). *Fit and well* (9th ed.). New York: McGraw-Hill.

Fahlman, S. E. (2003). *Smiley lore.* http://www.cs.cmu.edu/~sef/sefSmiley.htm (accessed April 29, 2009)

Falk, C. F., Heine, S. J., Yuki, M., & Takemura, K. (2009). Why do Westerners self-enhance more than East Asians? *European Journal of Personality, 23,* 183–203.

Family and Youth Services Bureau. (2004). *Fact sheet: Section 510 state abstinence education program.* Bethesda, MD: U.S. Department of Health and Human Services.

Fant, R. V., Buchhalter, A. R., Buchman, A. C., & Heningfield, J. E. (2009). Pharmacotherapy for tobacco dependence. *Handbook of Experimental Pharmacology, 192,* 487–510.

Farin, A., Liu, C. Y., Langmoen, I. A., & Apuzzo, M. L. (2009). The biological restoration of central nervous system architecture and function: Part 2—emergence of the realization of adult neurogenesis. *Neurosurgery, 64,* 581–600.

Farrell, S. W., Fitzgerald, S. J., McAuley, P., & Barlow, C. E. (2010). Cardiorespiratory fitness, adiposity, and all-cause mortality in women. *Medicine and Science in Sports and Exercise.* (in press)

Farris, M. (2009, November 2). *Man donates kidney to complete stranger.* http://www.wwltv.com/home/wwl110209cbstranger-68784452.html (accessed April 10, 2010)

Fatemi, S. H., & Folsom, T. D. (2009). The neurodevelopmental hypothesis of schizophrenia, revisited. *Schizophrenia Bulletin, 35,* 528–548.

Faul, L. A., Jim, H. S., Williams, C., Loftus, L., & Jacobsen, P. B. (2009). Relationship of stress management skill to psychological distress and quality of life in adults with cancer. *Psychooncology, 19* (1), 102–109.

Fava, G. A. (2006). The intellectual crisis in psychiatric research. *Psychotherapy and Psychosomatics, 75,* 202–208.

Fava, G. A., Ruini, C., & Belaise, C. (2007). The concept of recovery in depression. *Psychological Medicine, 37,* 307–317.

Faymonville, M. E., Boly, M., & Laureys, S. (2006). Functional neuroanatomy of the hypnotic state. *Journal of Physiology, Paris, 99,* 463–469.

Fazio, R. H., Chen, J., McDonel, E. C., & Sherman, S. J. (1982). Attitude accessibility, attitude-behavior consistency, and the strength of the object-evaluation association. *Journal of Experimental Social Psychology, 18,* 339–357.

Fazio, R. H., & Olsen, A. (2007). Attitudes. In M. A. Hogg & J. Cooper (Eds.), *The Sage handbook of social psychology* (concise 2nd ed.). Thousand Oaks, CA: Sage.

Fearon, R. P., & others. (2010). The significance of insecure attachment and disorganization in the development of children's externalizing behavior: A meta-analytic study. *Child Development, 81,* 435–456.

Federal Emergency Management Agency (FEMA). (2003, July 10). *Disaster search canine readiness evaluation process.* Washington, DC: Author.

Fehm, H. L., Kern, W., & Peters, A. (2006). The selfish brain: Competition for energy resources. *Progress in Brain Research, 153,* 129–140.

Fei-Fei, L., Iyer, A., Koch, C., & Perona, P. (2007). What do we perceive in a glance at a real-world scene? *Journal of Vision, 7,* 10.

Feldman, D. (2009). Synaptic mechanisms for plasticity in neocortex. *Annual Review of Neuroscience* (vol. 32). Palo Alto, CA: Annual Reviews.

Ferguson, C. J., & Kilburn, J. (2010). Much ado about nothing: The misestimation and overinterpretation of violent video game effects in Eastern and Western nations: Comment on Anderson et al. (2010). *Psychological Bulletin, 136,* 174–178.

Ferguson, C. J., Rueda, S. M., Cruz, A. M., Ferguson, D. E., Fritz, S., & Smith, S. M. (2008). Violent video games and aggression: Causal relationship or byproduct of family violence and intrinsic violence motivation? *Criminal Justice and Behavior, 35,* 311–332.

Ferrari, P. F., Paukner, A., Ruggiero, A., Darcey, L., Unbehagen, S., & Suomi, S. J. (2009). Interindividual differences in neonatal imitation and the development of action chains in rhesus macaques. *Child Development, 80,* 1057–1068.

Ferretti, F., & Coluccia, A. (2009). Socioeconomic factors and suicide rates in European Union countries. *Legal Medicine, 11, Suppl. 1,* S92–S94.

Ferris, G. R., Judge, T. A., Rowland, K. M., & Fitzgibbons, D. E. (1994). Subordinate influence and the performance evaluation process: Test of a model. *Organizational and Human Decision Processes, 58,* 101–135.

Ferro, A. (2009). Transformations in dreaming and characters in the psychoanalytic field. *International Journal of Psychoanalysis, 90,* 209–230.

Feshbach, S., & Weiner, B. (1996). *Personality* (4th ed.). Lexington, MA: Heath.

Festinger, L. (1954). A theory of social comparison processes. *Human Relations, 7,* 117–140.

Festinger, L. (1957). *A theory of cognitive dissonance.* Evanston, IL: Row Peterson.

Festinger, L., & Carlsmith, J. M. (1959). Cognitive consequences of forced compliance. *Journal of Abnormal and Social Psychology, 58,* 203–211.

Field, T. M., Diego, M., & Hernandez-Reif, M. (2010). Preterm infant massage therapy research: A review. *Infant Behavior and Development.* (in press)

Fields, R. (2010). *Drugs in perspective* (7th ed.). New York: McGraw-Hill.

Fiese, B. H., Foley, K. P., & Spagnola, M. (2006). Routine and ritual elements in family mealtimes: Contexts for child well-being and family identity. *New Directions in Child and Adolescent Development, 111,* 67–89.

Fifer, W. P., & Myers, M. M. (2002) Sudden fetal and infant deaths: Shared observations and distinctive features. *Seminar in Perinatology, 26,* 89–96.

Figueroa-Moseley, C., Jean-Pierre, P., Roscoe, J. A., Ryan, J. L., Kohli, S., Palesh, O. G., Ryan, E. P., & Finch, C. E. (2009). The neurobiology of middle-age has arrived. *Neurobiology and Aging, 30,* 515–520.

Finch, E. A., Linde, J. A., Jeffery, R. W., Rothman, A. J., King, C. M., & Levy, R. L. (2005). The effects of outcome expectations and satisfaction on weight loss and maintenance:

Correlational and experimental analyses—a randomized trial. *Health Psychology, 24* (6), 608–616.

Fine, S. A., & Wiley, W. W. (1971). *An introduction to functional job analysis.* Kalamazoo, MI: W. E. Upjohn Institute.

Fink, B., Brewer, G., Fehl, K., & Neave, N. (2007). Instrumentality and lifetime number of sexual partners. *Personality and Individual Differences, 43,* 747–756.

Finkbeiner, M., & Palermo, R. (2009). The role of spatial attention in nonconscious processing: A comparison of face and nonface stimuli. *Psychological Science, 20,* 42–51.

Finzi-Dottan, R., & Zubery, E. (2009). The role of depression and anxiety in impulsive and obsessive-compulsive behaviors among anorexic and bulimic patients. *Eating Disorders, 17,* 162–182.

First, M. B. (2011). The clinical utility of psychiatric diagnoses. *Annual Review of Clinical Psychology* (vol. 7). Palo Alto, CA: Annual Reviews.

Fischer, J., Spotswood, N., & Whitney, D. (2010). The emergence of perceived position in the visual system. *Journal of Cognitive Neuroscience.* (in press)

Fischhoff, B., Bruine de Bruin, W., Parker, A. M., Millstein, S. G., & Halpern-Felsher, B. L. (2010). Adolescents' perceived risk of dying. *Journal of Adolescent Health, 46,* 265–269.

Fishbein, M., & Ajzen, I. (2010). *Predicting and changing behavior.* New York: Psychology Press.

Fisher, A. J., Granger, D. A., & Newman, M. G. (2010). Sympathetic arousal moderates self-reported physiological arousal symptoms at baseline and physiological flexibility in response to a stressor in generalized anxiety disorder. *Biological Psychology, 83,* 191–200.

Fiske, A., Wetherell, J. L., & Gatz, M. (2009). Depression in older adults. *Annual Review of Clinical Psychology, 5,* 363–389.

Fitzgerald, L. F. (2003). Sexual harassment and social justice: Reflections on the distance yet to go. *American Psychologist, 58,* 915–924.

Fivush, R. (2011). The development of autobiographical memory. *Annual Review of Psychology* (vol. 62). Palo Alto, CA: Annual Reviews.

Flegal, K. M., Carroll, M. G., Ogden, C. L., & Curin, L. R. (2010). Prevalence and trends in obesity among U.S. adults, 1999–2008. *Journal of the American Medical Association, 303,* 235–241.

Fleischhaker, S., Schulz, E., Tepper, K., Martin, M., Hennighausen, K., & Remschmidt, H. (2005). Long-term course of adolescent schizophrenia. *Schizophrenia Bulletin, 31,* 769–780.

Fleming, S. M. (2009). Shaping what we see: Pinning down the influence of value on perceptual judgements. *Frontiers in Human Neuroscience, 3,* ArtID 9.

Flom, R., & Bahrick, L. E. (2010). The effects of intersensory redundancy on attention and memory: Infants' long-term memory for orientation in audiovisual events. *Developmental Psychology, 46,* 428–436.

Flor, H., & Diers, M. (2009). Sensorimotor training and cortical reorganization. *NeuroRehabilitation, 25,* 19–27.

Floyd, D. L., Prentice-Dunn, S., & Rogers, R. W. (2000). A meta-analysis of research on protection motivation theory. *Journal of Applied Social Psychology, 30,* 407–429.

Flynn, J. R. (1999). Searching for justice: The discovery of IQ gains over time. *American Psychologist, 54,* 5–20.

Flynn, J. R. (2006). The history of the American mind in the 20th century: A scenario to explain gains over time and a case for the irrelevance of *g*. In P. C. Kyllonen, R. D. Roberts, & L. Stankov (Eds.), *Extending intelligence.* Mahwah, NJ: Erlbaum.

Foa, E. B., & Franklin, M. E. (2011). Obsessive compulsive disorder. *Annual Review of Clinical Psychology* (vol. 7). Palo Alto, CA: Annual Reviews.

Fodor, I., & Epstein, J. (2002). Agoraphobia, panic disorder, and gender. In J. Worell (Ed.), *Encyclopedia of women and gender.* San Diego: Academic.

Foer, J. (2008). The unspeakable odyssey of the motionless boy. *Esquire.* http://www.esquire.com/features/unspeakable-odyssey-motionless-boy-1008

Foley, P., & Kirschbaum, C. (2010). Human hypothalamic-pituitary-adrenal axis responses to acute psychosocial stress in laboratory settings. *Neuroscience and Biobehavioral Reviews.* (in press)

Folkman, S., & Lazarus, R. S. (1980). An analysis of coping in a middle-aged community sample. *Journal of Health and Social Behavior, 21,* 219–239.

Folkman, S., & Moskowitz, J. T. (2004). Coping: Pitfalls and promises. *Annual Review of Psychology* (vol. 54). Palo Alto, CA: Annual Reviews.

Fontaine, R. G., Yang, C., Burks, V. S., Dodge, K. A., Price, J. M., Pettit, G. S., & Bates, J. E. (2009). Loneliness as a partial mediator of the relation between low social preference in childhood and anxious/depressed symptoms in adolescence. *Development and Psychopathology, 21,* 479–491.

Fontana, M. A., & Wohlgemuth, S. D. (2010). The surgical treatment of metabolic disease and morbid obesity. *Gastroenterology Clinics of North America, 39,* 125–133.

Fontanini, A., Grossman, S. E., Figueroa, J. A., & Katz, D. B. (2009). Distinct subtypes of basolateral amygdala taste neurons reflect palatability and reward. *Journal of Neuroscience, 29,* 2486–2495.

Foote, B., Smolin, Y., Kaplan, M., Legatt, M. E., & Lipschitz, D. (2006). Prevalence of dissociative disorders in psychiatric outpatients. *American Journal of Psychiatry, 163,* 566–568.

Forbey, J. D., & Ben-Porath, Y. S. (2007). Computerized adaptive personality testing: A review and illustration with the MMPI-2 computerized adaptive version. *Psychological Assessment, 19,* 14–24.

Forbush, K., Heatherton, T. F., & Keel, P. K. (2007). Relationships between perfectionism and specific disordered eating behaviors. *International Journal of Eating Disorders, 40,* 37–41.

Forgas, J. P., Baumeister, R. F., & Tice, D. M. (2009). The psychology of self-regulation: An introduction. In J. P. Forgas, R. F. Baumeister, & D. M. Tice (Eds.), *Psychology of self-regulation.* New York: Psychology Press.

Forgas, J. P., Dunn, E., & Granland, S. (2008). Are you being served . . . ? An unobtrusive experiment of affective influences on helping in a department store. *European Journal of Social Psychology, 38,* 333–342.

Forman-Hoffman, V. L., & Cunningham, C. L. (2008). Geographical clustering of eating disordered behaviors in U.S. high school students. *International Journal of Eating Disorders, 41,* 209–214.

Forouzan, B. A. (2007). *Data communication networking* (4th ed.). New York: McGraw-Hill.

Forrest, L. (2010). Linking international psychology, professional competence, and leadership: Counseling psychologists as learning partners. *The Counseling Psychologist, 38,* 96–120.

Forsythe, C., Bernard, M. L., & Goldsmith, T. E. (Eds.). (2006). *Cognitive systems.* Mahwah, NJ: Erlbaum.

Foulkes, D. (1993). Cognitive dream theory. In M. A. Carskadon (Ed.), *Encyclopedia of sleep and dreams.* New York: Macmillan.

Foulkes, D. (1999). *Children's dreaming and the development of consciousness.* Cambridge, MA: Harvard University Press.

Fountas, K. N., & Smith, J. R. (2007). Historical evolution of stereotactic amygdalotomy for the management of severe aggression. *Journal of Neurosurgery, 106,* 710–713.

Fox, R., & Millam, J. R. (2010). The use of ratings and direct behavioural observation to measure temperament traits in cockatiels (*nymphicus hollandicus*). *Ethology, 116,* 59–75.

Frank, J. D. (1982). Therapeutic components shared by all psychotherapies. In J. H. Harvey & M. M. Parks (Eds.), *Psychotherapy research and behavior change.* Washington, DC: American Psychological Association.

Frank, J. D., & Frank, J. B. (1993). *Persuasion and healing: A comparative study of psychotherapy.* Baltimore: Johns Hopkins University Press.

Frank, M. C., Vul, E., & Johnson, S. P. (2009). Development of infants' attention to faces during the first year. *Cognition, 110,* 160–170.

Frank, M. G. (2006). The mystery of sleep function: Current perspectives and future directions. *Reviews in the Neurosciences, 17,* 375–392.

Frank, M. G., & Benington J. H. (2006). The role of sleep in memory consolidation and brain plasticity: Dream or reality? *Neuroscientist, 12,* 477–488.

Franke, R. H., & Kaul, J. D. (1978). The Hawthorn experiments: First statistical interpretation. *American Sociological Review, 43,* 623–643.

Frankl, V. E. (1963/1984). *Man's search for meaning* (3rd ed.). New York: First Washington Square Press. (original work published 1946)

Frattaroli, J. (2006). Experimental disclosure and its moderators: A meta-analysis. *Psychological Bulletin, 132,* 823–865.

Fredrick, S., & Loewenstein, G. (1999). Hedonic adaptation. In D. Kahneman, E. Diener, & N. Schwarz (Eds.), *Well-being: The foundations of hedonic psychology* (pp. 302–329). New York: Russell Sage Foundation.

Fredrickson, B. L. (1998). What good are positive emotions? *Review of General Psychology, 2,* 300–319.

Fredrickson, B. L. (2001). The role of positive emotions in positive psychology. *American Psychologist, 56,* 218–226.

Fredrickson, B. L. (2006). Unpacking positive emotions: Investigating the seeds of human flourishing. *Journal of Positive Psychology, 1,* 57–60.

Fredrickson, B. L. (2009). *Positivity.* New York: Crown.

Fredrickson, B. L., & Roberts, T. (1997). Objectification theory: Toward understanding women's lived experiences and mental health risks. *Psychology of Women Quarterly, 21,* 173–206.

Fredrickson, B. L., Roberts, T., Noll, S. M., Quinn, D. M., & Twenge, J. M. (1998). That swimsuit becomes you: Sex differences in self-objectification, restrained eating, and math performance. *Journal of Personality and Social Psychology, 75,* 269–284.

Fredrickson, B. L., Tugade, M. M., Waugh, C. E., & Larkin, G. R. (2003). What good are positive emotions in crisis? A prospective study of resilience and emotions following the terrorist attacks on the United States on September 11th, 2001. *Journal of Personality and Social Psychology, 84,* 365–376.

Freedman, J. L., & Fraser, S. C. (1966). Compliance without pressure: The foot-in-the-door technique. *Journal of Personality and Social Psychology, 4,* 195–202.

Freeland, A., Manchanda, R., Chiu, S., Sharma, V., & Merskey, H. (1993). Four cases of supposed multiple personality disorder: Evidence of unjustified diagnoses. *Canadian Journal of Psychiatry, 38,* 245–247.

Freeman, S., & Herron, J. C. (2007). *Evolutionary analysis* (4th ed.). Upper Saddle River, NJ: Prentice-Hall.

Freestone, D. M., & Church, R. M. (2010). The importance of the reinforcer as a time marker. *Behavioral Processes.* (in press)

French, C. C., Santomauro, J., Hamilton, V., Fox, R., & Thalbourne, M. A. (2008). Psychological aspects of alien contact experience. *Cortex, 44,* 1387–1395.

Freud, S. (1911). *The interpretation of dreams* (3rd ed.). A. A. Brill (Trans). New York: Macmillan. (original work published 1899)

Freud, S. (1917). *A general introduction to psychoanalysis.* New York: Washington Square Press.

Freud, S. (1953). The interpretation of dreams. In J. Strachey (Ed.), *The standard edition of the complete psychological works of Sigmund Freud.* New York: Washington Square Press. (original work published 1900)

Freud, S. (1996). Number 23091. In R. Andrews, M. Seidel, & M. Biggs (Eds.), *Columbia world of quotations.* New York: Columbia University Press. (original work published 1918)

Freyer, T., & others. (2010). Frontostriatal activation in patients with obsessive-compulsive disorder before and after cognitive behavioral therapy. *Psychological Medicine.* (in press)

Fried, S. (2008, October 9). Commentary in "Think fat just hangs around, does nothing." *USA Today,* 6D.

Friedel, E., & others. (2009). 5-HTT genotype effect on prefrontal-amygdala coupling differs between major depression and controls. *Psychopharmacology, 205* (2), 261–271.

Friedman, J. M. (2009). Leptin at 14 y of age: An ongoing story. *American Journal of Clinical Nutrition, 89,* 973S–979S.

Friedman, M., & Rosenman, R. (1974). *Type A behavior and your heart.* New York: Knopf.

Friedman, N. P., Miyake, A., Young, S. E., DeFries, J. C., Corley, R. P., & Hewitt, J. K. (2008). Individual differences in executive functions are almost entirely genetic in origin. *Journal of Experimental Psychology: General, 137* (2), 201–225.

Friedman, R., Myers, P., & Benson, H. (1998). Meditation and the relaxation response. In H. S. Friedman (Ed.), *Encyclopedia of mental health* (vol. 2). San Diego: Academic.

Frijda, N. H. (2007). *The laws of emotion.* Mahwah, NJ: Erlbaum.

Frisch, M. B., & others. (2004). Predictive and treatment validity of life satisfaction and the Quality of Life Inventory. *Assessment, 10,* 1–13.

Frishman, W. H., Mitta, W., Kupersmith, A., & Ky, T. (2006). Nicotine and non-nicotine smoking cessation pharmacotherapies. *Cardiology in Review, 14,* 57–73.

Fritz, C., & Sonnentag, S. (2006). Recovery, well-being, and performance-related outcomes: The role of work overload and vacation experiences. *Journal of Applied Psychology, 91,* 936–945.

Frohlich, P., & Meston, C. M. (2005). Fluoxetine-induced changes in tactile sensation and sexual functioning among clinically depressed women. *Journal of Sex & Marital Therapy, 31* (2), 113–128.

Fromm, E. (1947). *Man for himself.* New York: Holt, Rinehart & Winston.

Frosch, Z. A., Dierker, L. C., Rose, J. S., & Waldinger, R. J. (2009). Smoking trajectories, health, and mortality across the adult lifespan. *Addictive Behaviors, 34* (8), 701–704.

Fry, P. S., & Debats, D. L. (2009). Perfectionism and the five-factor personality traits as predictors of mortality in older adults. *Journal of Health Psychology, 14,* 513–524.

Fry, R. B., & Prentice-Dunn, S. (2006). Effects of a psychosocial intervention on breast self-examination attitudes and behaviors. *Health Education Research, 21,* 287–295.

Fryberg, S. A., & Markus, H. R. (2003). On being American Indian: Current and possible selves. *Self and Identity, 2,* 325–344.

Fujiwara, E., Levine, B., & Anderson, A. K. (2008). Intact implicit and reduced explicit memory for negative self-related information in repressive coping. *Cognitive, Affective, and Behavioral Neuroscience, 8,* 254–263.

Fullam, R. S., McKie, S., & Dolan, M. C. (2009). Psychopathic traits and deception: Functional magnetic resonance imaging study. *British Journal of Psychiatry, 194,* 229–235.

Fulton, S. (2010). Appetite and reward. *Frontiers in Neuroendocrinology, 31,* 85–103.

Fultz, J., Batson, C. D., Fortenbach, V. A., McCarthy, P. M., & Varney, L. L. (1986). Social evaluation and the empathy-altruism hypothesis. *Journal of Personality and Social Psychology, 50,* 761–769.

Funder, D. C. (2009). Persons, behaviors, and situations: An agenda for personality psychology in the postwar era. *Journal of Research in Personality, 43,* 120–126.

Fung, H. H., & Ng, S. K. (2006). Age differences in the sixth personality factor: Age difference in interpersonal relatedness among Canadians and Hong Kong Chinese. *Psychology and Aging, 21,* 810–814.

Fung, M. T., Raine, A., Loeber, R., Lynam, D. R., Steinhauer, S. R., Venables, P. H., & Stouthamer-Loeber, M. (2005). Reduced electrodermal activity in psychopathy-prone adolescents. *Journal of Abnormal Psychology, 114,* 187–196.

G

Gabelle, A., & Dauvilliers, Y. (2010). Editorial: Sleep and dementia. *Journal of Nutrition, Health, and Aging, 14,* 201–202.

Gagnepain, P., Henson, R., Chetelat, G., Desgranges, B., Lebreton, K., & Eustache, F. (2010). Is neocortical–hippocampal connectivity a better predictor of subsequent recollection than local increases in hippocampal activity? New insights on the role of priming. *Journal of Cognitive Neuroscience.* (in press)

Gaillard, R., Dehaene., S., Adam, C., Clémenceau, S., Hasboun, D., Baulac, M., Cohen, L., & Naccache, L. (2009). Converging intracranial markers of conscious access. *PLoS Biology, 7,* e1000061.

Galambos, N. L., Berenbaum, S. A., & McHale, S. M. (2009). Gender development in adolescence. In R. M. Lerner & L. Steinberg (Eds.), *Handbook of adolescent psychology* (3rd ed.). New York: Wiley.

Galan, R. F., Weidert, M., Menzel, R., Herz, A. V., & Galizia, C. G. (2006). Sensory memory for odors is encoded in spontaneous correlated activity between olfactory glomeruli. *Neural Computation, 18,* 10–25.

Gallagher, K. E., & Parrott, D. J. (2010). Influence of heavy episodic drinking on the relation between men's locus of control and aggression toward intimate partners. *Journal of Studies on Alcohol and Drugs, 71,* 299–306.

Gallo, I. S., Keil, A., McCulloch, K. C., Rockstroh, B., & Gollwitzer, P. M. (2009). Strategic automation of emotion regulation. *Journal of Personality and Social Psychology, 96,* 11–31.

Gallo, W. T., Bradley, E. H., Dubin, J. A., Jones, R. N., Falba, T. A., Teng, H. M., & Kasi, S. V. (2006). The persistence of depressive symptoms in older workers who experience involuntary job loss: Results from the health and retirement survey. *Journals of Gerontology B: Psychological Sciences and Social Sciences, 61,* S221–S228. doi:10.1093/scan/nsp005

Ganis, G., Morris, R. R., & Kosslyn, S. M. (2009). Neural processes underlying self- and other-related lies: An individual difference approach using MRI. *Social Neuroscience, 4,* 539–553.

Gao, D., & Vasconcelos, N. (2009). Decision-theoretic saliency: Computational principles, biological plausibility, and implications for neurophysiology. *Neural Computation, 21,* 239–271.

Gao, Y., & Raine, A. (2010). Successful and unsuccessful psychopaths: A neurobiological model. *Behavioral Sciences and Law, 28,* 194–210.

Gao, Y. J., & Ji, R. R. (2010). Chemokines, neuronal-glial interactions, and central processing of neuropathic pain. *Pharmacology & Therapeutics.* (in press)

Garb, H. N., Wood, J. M., Nezworski, M. T., Grove, W. M., & Stejskal, W. J. (2001). Toward a resolution of the Rorschach controversy. *Psychological Assessment, 13,* 433–448.

Garbett, K. A., & others. (2010). Novel animal models for studying complex brain disorders: BAC-driven *mi*RNA-mediated *in vivo* silencing of gene expression. *Molecular Psychiatry.* (in press)

Garcia, B. G., Neely, M. D., & Deutsch, A. Y. (2010). Cortical regulation of striatal medium spiny neuron dendritic remodeling in Parkinsonism: Modulation of glutamate release reverses dopamine depletion-induced dendritic spine loss. *Cerebral Cortex.* (in press)

Garcia, J. (1989). Food for Tolman: Cognition and cathexis in concert. In T. Archer & L. Nilsson (Eds.), *Aversion, avoidance, and anxiety.* Mahwah, NJ: Erlbaum.

Garcia, J., Ervin, F. E., & Koelling, R. A. (1966). Learning with prolonged delay of reinforcement. *Psychonomic Science, 5,* 121–122.

Garcia, J., & Koelling, R. A. (1966). Relation of cue to consequence in avoidance learning. *Psychonomic Science, 4,* 123–124.

Garcia, J., & Koelling, R. A. (2009). Specific hungers and poison avoidance as adaptive specializations of learning. In D. Shanks (Ed.), *Psychology of learning.* Thousand Oaks, CA: Sage.

Garcia, L. F., Aluja, A., Fibla, J., Cuevas, L., & Garcia, O. (2010). Incremental effect for antisocial personality disorder genetic risk combining 5-HTTLPR and 5-HTTVNTR polymorphisms *Psychiatry Research, 177,* 161–166.

Gardner, H. (1983). *Frames of mind.* New York: Basic.

Gardner, H. (1993). *Multiple intelligences.* New York: Basic.

Gardner, H. (2002). The pursuit of excellence through education. In M. Ferrari (Ed.), *Learning from extraordinary minds.* Mahwah, NJ: Erlbaum.

Gardner, W. L., & Martinko, M. J. (1996). Using the Myers-Briggs Type Indicator to study managers: A literature review and research agenda. *Journal of Management, 22,* 45–83.

Garfield, A. S., & Heisler, L. K. (2009). Pharmacological targeting of the serotonergic system for the treatment of obesity. *Journal of Physiology, 587,* 49–60.

Garner, M., Mohler, H., Stein, D. J., Mueggler, T., & Baldwin, D. S. (2009). Research in anxiety disorders: From the bench to the bedside. *European Neuropsychopharmacology, 19,* 381–390.

Garrison, G. D., & Dugan, S. E. (2009). Varenicline: A first-line treatment for smoking cessation. *Clinical Therapeutics, 31,* 463–491.

Garry, M., & Loftus, E. F. (2009). Repressed memory. In D. Clark (Ed.), *Encyclopedia of law and society* (pp. 555–556). Thousand Oaks, CA: Sage.

Garver, D. L. (2006). Evolution of antipsychotic intervention in the schizophrenic psychosis. *Current Drug Targets, 7,* 1205–1215.

Garzon, C., Guerrero, J. M., Aramburu, O., & Guzman, T. (2009). Effect of melatonin administration on sleep, behavioral disorders, and hypnotic drug discontinuation in the elderly: A randomized, double-blind, placebo-controlled study. *Aging: Clinical and Experimental Research, 21,* 38–42.

Gasper, K. (2004). Permission to seek freely? The effect of happy and sad moods on generating old and new ideas. *Creativity Research Journal, 16* (2–3), 215–229.

Gastil, J. W. (2009). *The group in society.* Thousand Oaks, CA: Sage.

Gaunt, R., & Trope, Y. (2007). Attribution and person perception. In M. A. Hogg & J. Cooper (Eds.), *The Sage handbook of social psychology* (concise 2nd ed.). Thousand Oaks, CA: Sage.

Gauthier, I., Behrmann, M., & Tarr, M. J. (2004). Are greebles like faces? Using the neuropsychological exception to test the rule. *Neuropsychologia, 42,* 1961–1970.

Gauthier, I., & Bukach, C. (2007). Should we reject the expertise hypothesis? *Cognition, 103,* 322–330.

Gauthier, I., Skudlarski, P., Gore, J. C., & Anderson, A. W. (2000). Expertise for cars and birds recruits brain areas involved in face recognition. *Nature Neuroscience, 3,* 191–197.

Gauthier, I., Tarr, M. J., & Bub, D. (Eds.). (2010). *Perceptual expertise: Bridging brain and behavior.* New York: Oxford University Press.

Gauvain, M., & Parke, R. D. (2010). Socialization. In M. H. Bornstein (Ed.), *Handbook of cultural developmental science.* New York: Psychology Press.

Gavlak, D. (2009, April 12). Jordan honor killing: Man confesses to brutally stabbing to death pregnant sister. http://www.huffingtonpost.com/2009/04/12/jordan-honor-killing-man-_n_185977.html (accessed May 29, 2009)

Gazzaniga, M. S. (Ed.). (2010). *The cognitive neurosciences* (4th ed.). New York: Cambridge University Press.

Gazzaniga, M. S., Dorn, K. W., & Funk, C. M. (2010). Looking towards the future: Perspectives on examining the architecture and function of the human brain as a complex system. In M. S. Gazzaniga (Ed.), *The cognitive neurosciences* (4th ed.). New York: Cambridge University Press.

Ge, X., Natsuaki, M. N., Neiderhiser, J. M., & Reiss, D. (2009). The longitudinal effects of stressful life events on adolescent depression are buffered by parent-child closeness. *Development and Psychopathology, 21,* 621–635.

Geary, D. C. (2010). *Male, female: The evolution of human sex differences* (2nd ed.). Washington, DC: American Psychological Association.

Gehar, D. R. (2010). *Mastering competencies in family therapy.* Boston: Cengage.

Gelder, B. D., Meeren, H. K., Righart, R., Stock, J. V., van de Riet, W. A., & Tamietto, M. (2006). Beyond the face: Exploring rapid influences of context on face processing. *Progress in Brain Research, 155PB,* 37–48.

Gelernter, J., & Stein, M. B. (2009). Heritability and genetics of anxiety disorders. In M. M. Antony &. M. B. Stein (Eds.), *Oxford handbook of anxiety and related disorders* (pp. 87–96). New York: Oxford University Press.

Geller, E. S. (2002). The challenge of increasing proenvironmental behavior. In R. B. Bechtel & A. Churchman (Eds.), *Handbook of environmental psychology* (pp. 525–540). Hoboken, NJ: Wiley.

Geller, E. S. (2006). Occupational injury prevention and applied behavior analysis. In A. C. Gielen, D. A. Sleet, & R. J. DiClemente (Eds.), *Injury and violence prevention: Behavioral science theories, methods, and applications* (pp. 297–322). San Francisco: Jossey-Bass.

Gelman, S. A. (2009). Learning from others: Children's constructions of concepts. *Annual Review of Psychology* (vol. 60). Palo Alto, CA: Annual Reviews.

Gentile, D. A., & Anderson, C. A. (2006). Violent video games: Effects on youth and public policy implications. In N. Dowd, D. G. Singer, & R. F. Wilson (Eds.), *Handbook of children, culture, and violence* (pp. 225–246). Thousand Oaks, CA: Sage.

Gentile, S. (2010). Antidepressant use in children and adolescents diagnosed with major depressive disorder: What can we learn from published data? *Reviews on Recent Clinical Trials, 5,* 63–75.

George, J. M. (1995). Leader positive mood and group performance: The case of customer service. *Journal of Applied Social Psychology, 25,* 778–795.

George, L. K. (2006). Perceived quality of life. In R. H. Binstock & L. K. George (Eds.), *Handbook of aging and the social sciences* (6th ed.). San Diego: Academic.

George, L. K. (2009). Religiousness and spirituality, later life. In D. Carr (Ed.), *Encyclopedia of the life course and human adjustment.* Boston: Gale Cengage.

Geraerts, E., Lindsay, D. S., Merckelbach, H., Jelicic, M., Raymaekers, L., Arnold, M. M., & Schooler, J. W. (2009). Cognitive mechanisms underlying recovered-memory experiences of childhood sexual abuse. *Psychological Science, 20,* 92–98.

Gershman, S. J., Blei, D. M., & Niv, Y. (2010). Context, learning, and extinction. *Psychological Review, 117,* 197–209.

Gershoff, E. T. (2002). Corporal punishment by parents and associated child behaviors and experiences: A meta-analysis and theoretical review. *Psychological Bulletin, 128,* 539–579.

Gerson, L. S., & Braun, B. (2006). Effect of high cardiorespiratory fitness and high body fat on insulin resistance. *Medicine and Science in Sports and Exercise, 38,* 1709–1715.

Gervai, J. (2009). Environmental and genetic influences on early attachment. *Child and Adolescent Psychiatry and Mental Health, 3,* ArtID 25.

Giang, D. W., and others. (1996). Conditioning of cyclophosphamide-induced leukopenia in humans. *Journal of Neuropsychiatry and Clinical Neuroscience, 8,* 194–201.

Gibbons, C. J., & others. (2010). The clinical effectiveness of cognitive behavior therapy in an outpatient clinic. *Journal of Affective Disorders.* (in press)

Gibbons, R. D., Hedeker, D., & DuToit, S. (2010). Advances in analysis of longitudinal data. *Annual Review of Clinical Psychology* (vol. 6). Palo Alto, CA: Annual Reviews.

Gibbs, J. C. (2010). *Moral development and reality: Beyond the theories of Kohlberg and Hoffman* (2nd ed.). Boston: Allyn & Bacon.

Gibson, E. J. (2001). *Perceiving the affordances.* Mahwah, NJ: Erlbaum.

Gidron, Y., & Nyklicek, I. (2009). Experimentally testing Taylor's stress, coping, and adaptation framework. *Anxiety, Stress, and Coping, 22,* 1477–2205.

Giedd, J. N. (2008). The teen brain: Insights from neuroimaging. *Journal of Adolescent Medicine, 42,* 335–343.

Gifford, R. (2009). Environmental psychology: Manifold visions, unity of purpose. *Journal of Environmental Psychology, 29,* 387–389.

Gigerenzer, G. (2011). Heuristic decision making in individuals and organizations. *Annual Review of Psychology* (vol. 62). Palo Alto, CA: Annual Reviews.

Gijs, L. (2008). Paraphilia and paraphilia-related disorders: An introduction. In D. L. Rowland & L. Incrocci (Eds.), *Handbook of sexual and gender identity disorders* (pp. 491–528). Hoboken, NJ: Wiley.

Gijs, L., & Brewaeys, A. (2007). Surgical treatment of gender dysphoria in adults and adolescents: Recent developments, effectiveness, and challenges. *Annual Review of Sex Research, 18,* 178–224.

Gilbert, A. L., Regier, T., Kay, P., & Ivry, R. B. (2006). Whorf hypothesis is supported in the right visual field but not the left. *Proceedings of the National Academy of Sciences USA, 103* (2), 489–494.

Gilbert, L. A., & Kearney, L. K. (2006). The psychotherapeutic relationship as a positive and powerful resource for girls and women. In J. Worell & C. D. Goodheart (Eds.), *Handbook of girls' and women's psychological health: Gender and well-being across the lifespan.* New York: Oxford University Press.

Gillard, E., Van Dooren, W., Schaeken, W., & Verschaffel, L. (2009). Proportional reasoning as a heuristic-based processs. *Experimental Psychology, 56,* 92–99.

Gilligan, C. (1982). *In a different voice.* Cambridge, MA: Harvard University Press.

Gillihan, S. J., & Farah, M. J. (2005). Is self special? A critical review of evidence from experimental psychology and cognitive neuroscience. *Psychological Bulletin, 131,* 76–97.

Gil-Mohapel, J., Simpson, J. M., Titerness, A. K., & Christie, B. R. (2010). Characterization of the neurogenesis quiet zone in the rodent brain: Effects on age and exercise. *European Journal of Neuroscience, 31,* 797–807.

Giltay, E. J., Zitman, F. G., & Kromhout, D. (2006). Dispositional optimism and the risk of depressive symptoms during 15 years of follow-up: The Zutphen Elderly Study. *Journal of Affective Disorders, 91,* 45–52.

Gino, F., Ayal, S., & Ariely, D. (2009). Contagion and differentiation in unethical behavior: The effect of one bad apple on the barrel. *Psychological Science, 20,* 393–398.

Gittelman, M. (2008). Editor's introduction: Why are the mentally ill dying? *International Journal of Mental Health, 37,* 3–12.

Glaser, R., & Kiecolt-Glaser, J. K. (2005). Stress-induced immune dysfunction: Implications for health. *Nature Reviews: Immunology, 5,* 243–251.

Glaw, X. M., Garrick, T. M., Terwee, P. J., Patching, J. R., Blake, H., & Harper, C. (2009). Brain donation: Who and why? *Cell and Tissue Banking, 10* (3), 241–246.

Glenn, D. (2010, February 5). Divided attention. *Chronicle of Higher Education, 56,* B5–B8.

Go, C. L., Raosales, R. L., Caraos, R. J., & Fernandez, H. H. (2009). The current prevalence and factors associated with tardive dyskinesia among Filipino schizophrenic patients. *Parkinsonism and Related Disorders, 15* (9), 655–659.

Gobet, F., & Clarkson, G. (2004). Chunks in expert memory: Evidence for the magical number four . . . or is it two? *Memory, 12,* 732–747.

Godden, D. R., & Baddeley, A. D. (1975). Context-dependent memory in two natural environments: On land and under water. *British Journal of Psychology, 66,* 325–331.

Goebel, M. U., Trebst, A. E., Steiner, J., Xie, Y. F., Exton, M. S., and others. (2002). Behavioral conditioning of immunosuppression is possible in humans. *Federation of American Societies for Experimental Biology Journal, 16,* 1869–1873.

Goel, N., & others. (2009). Circadian rhythm profiles in women with night eating syndrome. *Journal of Biological Rhythms, 24,* 85–94.

Goethals, G. R., & Demorest, A. P. (1995). The risky shift is a sure bet. In M. E. Ware & D. E. Johnson (Eds.), *Demonstrations and activities in teaching of psychology* (vol. 3). Mahwah, NJ: Erlbaum.

Gogtay, N., & Thompson, P. M. (2010). Mapping gray matter development: Implications for typical development and vulnerability to psychopathology. *Brain and Cognition, 72,* 6–15.

Goldberg, A., & Adriano, J. (2008, June 27). "I'm a girl"—Understanding transgender children: Parents of transgender 6 year old support her choice. ABC News. http://abcnews.go.com/2020/story?id=5261464&page=1 (accessed January 10, 2010)

Goldberg, L. R., & Digman, J. M. (1994). Revealing structure in the data: Principles of exploratory factor analysis. In S. Strack & M. Lorr (Eds.), *Differentiating normal and abnormal personality* (pp. 216–242). New York: Springer.

Goldberg, R. (2010). *Drugs across the spectrum* (6th ed.). Boston: Cengage.

Goldfield, B. A., & Snow, C. E. (2009). Individual differences: Implications for the study of language acquisition. In J. Berko Gleason & N. Ratner (Eds.), *The development of language* (7th ed.). Boston: Allyn & Bacon.

Goldin, P., Ramel, W., & Gross, J. (2009). Mindfulness meditation training and self referential processing in social anxiety disorder: Behavioral and neural effects. *Journal of Cognitive Psychotherapy, 23,* 242–257.

Goldman, S. E., & others. (2008). Sleep problems associated with daytime fatigue in community-dwelling older individuals. *Journals of Gerontology A: Biological Sciences and Medical Sciences, 63,* 1069–1075.

Goldschmidt, L., Richardson, G. A., Willford, J., & Day, N. L. (2008). Prenatal marijuana exposure and intelligence test performance at age 6. *Journal of the American Academy of Child and Adolescent Psychiatry, 47,* 254–263.

Goldsmith, H. H. (2011). Human development: Biological and genetic processes in development. *Annual Review of Psychology* (vol. 62). Palo Alto, CA: Annual Reviews.

Goldstein, E. B. (2010). *Sensation and perception* (8th ed.). Boston: Cengage.

Goldstein, J. M., Seidman, L. J., Horton, N. J., Makris, N., Kennedy, D. N., Caviness, C., Faraone, S. V. & Tsuang, M. T. (2001). Normal sexual dimorphism of the adult human brain assessed by *in vivo* magnetic resonance imaging. *Cerebral Cortex, 11,* 490–497.

Goldstein, R., & Reynolds, C. R. (Eds.). (1999). *Handbook of neurodevelopmental and genetic disorders in children.* New York: Guilford.

Goldston, D. B., Molock, S. D., Whibeck, L. B., Murakami, J. L., Zayas, L. H., & Hall, G. C. (2008). Cultural considerations in adolescent suicide prevention and psychosocial treatment. *American Psychologist, 63,* 14–31.

Goldstrom, I. D., Campbell, J., Rogers, J. A., Lambert, D. B., Blacklow, B., Henderson, M. J., & Manderscheid, R. W. (2006). National estimates for mental health mutual support groups, self-help organizations, and consumer-operated services. *Administration and Policy in Mental Health, 33,* 92–103.

Goleman, D., Kaufman, P., & Ray, M. (1993). *The creative mind.* New York: Plume.

Golombok, S., Perry, B., Burston, A., Murray, C., Mooney-Somers, J., Stevens, M., & Golding, J. (2003). Children with lesbian parents: A community study. *Developmental Psychology, 39,* 20–33.

Golombok, S., & Tasker, F. (1996). Do parents influence the sexual orientation of their children? Findings from a longitudinal study of lesbian families. *Developmental Psychology, 32,* 3–11.

Gonda, X., & others. (2009). Association of the s allele of the 5-HTTLPR with neuroticism-related traits and temperaments in a psychiatrically healthy population. *European Archives of Psychiatry and Clinical Neuroscience, 259,* 106–113.

Gonzales-Backen, M. A., & Umana-Taylor, A. J. (2010). Examining the role of physical appearance in Latino adolescents' ethnic identity. *Journal of Adolescence.* (in press)

Gonzalez-Maeso, J., & Sealfon, S. C. (2009). Psychedelics and schizophrenia. *Trends in Neuroscience, 32,* 225–232.

Gonzalez-Vallejo, C., Lassiter, G. D., Bellezza, F. S., & Lindberg, M. J. (2008). "Save angels perhaps": A critical examination of unconscious thought theory and the deliberation-without-attention effect. *Review of General Psychology, 12,* 282–296.

Goodnow, J. J. (2010). Culture. In M. H. Bornstein (Ed.), *Handbook of cultural developmental science.* New York: Psychology Press.

Goodwin, R. D., & Cowles, R. A. (2008). Household smoking and childhood asthma in the United States: A state-level analysis. *Journal of Asthma, 45,* 607–610.

Gorin, A., Phelan, S., Wing, R. R., & Hill, J. O. (2004). Promoting long-term weight control: Does dieting consistency matter? *International Journal of Obesity Related Metabolic Disorder, 28,* 278–281.

Gormley, B., & Lopez, F. G. (2010). Authoritarian and homophobic attitudes: Gender and adult attachment style differences. *Journal of Homosexuality, 57,* 525–538.

Gosling, S. D. (2008). Personality in nonhuman animals. *Social and Personality Psychology Compass, 2,* 985–1001.

Gosling, S. D. (2008a). *Snoop: What your stuff says about you.* New York: Basic.

Gosling, S. D., & John, O. P. (1999). Personality dimensions in nonhuman animals: A cross-species review. *Current Directions in Psychological Science, 8,* 69–75.

Gosling, S. D., Kwan, V. S. Y., & John, O. (2003). A dog's got personality: A cross-species comparison of personality judgments in dogs and humans. *Journal of Personality and Social Psychology, 85,* 1161–1169.

Gosling, S. D., Rentfrow, P. J., & Swann, W. B. (2003). A very brief measure of the Big-Five personality domains. *Journal of Research in Personality, 37,* 504–528.

Gotthold, J. J. (2009). Peeling the onion: Understanding layers of treatment. *Annals of the New York Academy of Sciences, 1159,* 301–312.

Gottlieb, G. (2007). Probabilistic epigenesis. *Developmental Science, 10,* 1–11.

Gottman, J. M. (1994). *What predicts divorce?* Mahwah, NJ: Erlbaum.

Gottman, J. M. (2006, April 29). Secrets of long term love. *New Scientist, 2549,* 40.

Gottman, J. M., Gottman, J. S., & Declaire, J. (2006). *10 lessons to transform your marriage: America's love lab experts share their strategies for strengthening your relationship.* New York: Random House.

Gottman, J. M., Levenson, R. W., Swanson, C., Swanson, K., Tyson, R., & Yoshimoto, D. (2003). Observing gay, lesbian and heterosexual couples' relationships: Mathematical modeling of conflict interaction. *Journal of Homosexuality, 45,* 65–91.

Gouin, J. P., Hantsoo, L., & Kiecolt-Glaser, J. K. (2008). Immune dysregulation and chronic stress among older adults: A review. *Neuro-immunomodulation, 15,* 251–259.

Gould, E., Reeves, A. J., Graziano, M. S., & Gross, C. G. (1999). Neurogenesis in the neocortex of adult primates. *Science, 286* (1), 548–552.

Gouzoulis-Mayfrank, E., & Daumann, J. (2009). Neurotoxicity of drugs of abuse—the case of methylenedioxyamphetamines (MDMA, ecstasy), and amphetamines. *Dialogues in Clinical Neurscience, 11,* 305–317.

Graber, J. A. (2007). Pubertal and neuroendocrine development and risk for depressive disorders. In N. B. Allen & L. Sheeber (Eds.), *Adolescent emotional development and the emergence of depressive disorders.* New York: Cambridge University Press.

Graber, J. A., Brooks-Gunn, J., & Warren, M. P. (2006). Pubertal effects on adjustment in girls: Moving from demonstrating effects to identifying pathways. *Journal of Youth and Adolescence, 35,* 391–401.

Graber, J. A., & Sontag, L. M. (2009). Internalizing problems during adolescence. In R. M. Lerner & L. Steinberg (Eds.), *Handbook of adolescent psychology* (3rd ed.). New York: Wiley.

Grady, C. L. (2008). Cognitive neuroscience of aging. *Annals of the New York Academy of Sciences, 1124,* 127–144.

Graffin, N. F., Ray, W. J., & Lundy, R. (1995). EEG concomitants of hypnosis and hypnotic susceptibility. *Journal of Abnormal Psychology, 104,* 123–131.

Graham, J. E., Christian, L. M., & Kiecolt-Glaser, J. K. (2006). Stress, age, and immune function: Toward a lifespan approach. *Journal of Behavioral Medicine, 29,* 389–400.

Grandey, A. A., Kern, J. H., & Frone, M. R. (2007). Verbal abuse from outsiders versus insiders: Comparing frequency, impact on emotional exhaustion, and the role of emotional labor. *Journal of Occupational Health Psychology, 12,* 63–79.

Grandin, T. (1995/2006). *Thinking in pictures: My life with autism* (expanded ed.). New York: Random House.

Grant, A. M., & Wrzesniewski, A. (2010). I won't let you down . . . or will I? Core self-evaluations, other orientation, anticipated guilt, and gratitude, and job performance. *Journal of Applied Psychology, 95,* 108–121.

Grant, B. F., Stinson, F. S., Dawson, D. A., Chou, P., Dufour, M. C., Compton, W., Pickering, R. P., & Kaplan, K. (2004). Prevalence and co-occurrence of substance use disorders and independent mood and anxiety disorders: Results from the national epidemiologic survey on alcohol and related conditions. *Archives of General Psychiatry, 61,* 807–816.

Gravetter, F. J. (2009). *Research methods for the behavioral sciences* (3rd ed.). Belmont, CA: Wadsworth.

Gray, J. (2004). *Men are from Mars, Women are from Venus.* New York: HarperCollins.

Gray, J. A. (1987). *The psychology of fear and stress.* Cambridge, U.K.: Cambridge University Press.

Gray, J. A., & McNaughton, N. (2000). *The neuropsychology of anxiety: An enquiry into the functions of the septo-hippocampal system.* Oxford, U.K.: Oxford University Press.

Graziano, A. M., & Raulin, M. L. (2010). *Research methods* (7th ed.). Boston: Allyn & Bacon.

Graziano, W. G., & Habashi, M. M. (2010). Motivational processes underlying both prejudice and helping. *Personality and Social Psychology Review.* (in press)

Grealish, S., Johnsson, M. E., Li, M., Kirik, D., Bjorklund, A., & Thompson, L. H. (2010). The A9 dopamine neuron component in grafts of ventral mesencephalon is an important determinant for recovery of motor function in a rat model of Parkinson's disease. *Brain.* (in press)

Green, J. P., Page, R. A., Handley, G. W., & Rasekhy, R. (2005). The "hidden observer" and ideomotor responding: A real–simulator comparison. *Contemporary Hypnosis, 22,* 123–137.

Green, R. (1987). *The "sissy boy syndrome" and the development of homosexuality.* New Haven, CT: Yale University Press.

Green, R. J., Bettinger, M., & Zacks, E. (1996). Are lesbian couples fused and gay male couples disengaged? Questioning gender straitjackets. In J. Laird & R. J. Green (Eds.), *Lesbian and gays in couples and families: A handbook for therapists* (pp. 185–230). New York: Jossey-Bass.

Greene, R. L. (1999). Applied memory research: How far from bankruptcy? *Contemporary Psychology, 44,* 29–31.

Greenfield, P. M. (2009). Linking social change and developmental change: Shifting pathways of human development. *Developmental Psychology, 43,* 401–418.

Greenfield, R. (2006). *Timothy Leary: A biography.* New York: Harcourt.

Greenwald, A. G., Poehlman, T. A., Uhlmann, E., & Banaji, M. R. (2009). Understanding and using the Implicit Association Test: III. Meta-analysis of predictive validity. *Journal of Personality and Social Psychology, 97,* 17–41.

Greeson, J. M., Lewis, J. G., Achanzar, K., Zimmerman, E., Young K. H., & Suarez, E. C. (2009). Stress-induced changes in the expression of monocytic beta-2-integrins: The impact of arousal of negative affect and adrenergic responses to the Anger Recall interview. *Brain, Behavior, and Immunity, 23,* 251–256.

Gregg, A. P., & Sedikides, C. (2010). Narcissistic fragility: Rethinking its link to explicit and implicit self-esteem. *Self and Identity, 9,* 142–146.

Gregory, R. J. (2011). *Psychological testing* (6th ed.). Upper Saddle River, NJ: Pearson.

Greitemeyer, T. (2009). Effects of songs with prosocial lyrics on prosocial thoughts, affect, and behavior. *Journal of Experimental Social Psychology, 45,* 186–190.

Greitemeyer, T., & Osswald, S. (2010). Effects of prosocial video games on prosocial behavior. *Journal of Personality and Social Psychology, 98,* 211–221.

Grewen, K. M., Davenport, R. E., & Light, K. C. (2010). An investigation of plasma and salivary oxytocin responses in breast- and formula-feeding mothers of infants. *Psychophysiology.* (in press)

Griffin, M. A., & Clarke, S. (2010). Stress and well-being at work. In S. Zedeck (Ed.), *APA handbook of industrial and organizational psychology.* Washington, DC: APA. (in press)

Griffin, R. W., & Lopez, Y. P. (2005). "Bad behavior" in organizations: A review and typology for future research. *Journal of Management, 31,* 988–1005.

Griffin, R. W., & Moorhead, G. (2010). *Organizational behavior* (9th ed.). Boston: Cengage.

Grigorenko, E., & Takanishi, R. (2010). *Immigration, diversity, and education.* New York: Routledge.

Grigorenko, E. L., Jarvin, L., Tan, M., & Sternberg, R. J. (2008). Something new in the garden: Assessing creativity in academic domains. *Psychology Science Quarterly, 50,* 295–307.

Grilo, C. M., Masheb, R. M., & White, M. A. (2010). Significance of overvaluation of shape/weight in binge-eating disorder: Comparative study with overweight and bulimia nervosa. *Obesity, 18,* 499–504.

Grinspoon, L. (1994). *Marihuana reconsidered.* Cambridge, MA: Harvard University Press.

Grippo, A. J., & Johnson, A. K. (2009). Stress, depression, and cardiovascular dysregulation: A review of neurobiological mechanisms and the integration of research from preclinical disease models. *Stress, 12,* 1–21.

Groenewould, J. H., & others. (2010). Rotterdam Amblyopia Screening Effectiveness Study: Detection and causes of amblyopia in a large birth cohort. *Investigative Ophthalmology & Visual Science.* (in press)

Gronlund, N. E. (2006). *Assessment of student achievement* (8th ed.). Boston: Allyn & Bacon.

Grosse, S. D. (2010). Late-treated phenylketonuria and partial reversibility of intellectual impairment. *Child Development, 81,* 200–211.

Grossi, E., Buscema, M. P., Snowdon, D., & Antuono, P. (2007). Neuropathological findings processed by artificial neural networks (ANNs) can perfectly distinguish Alzheimer's patients from controls in the Nun Study. *BMC Neurology, 7,* 15.

Grossman, I., Na, J., Varnum, M. E. W., Park, D. C., Kitayama, S., & Nisbett, R. E. (2010). Reasoning about social conflicts improves into old age. *Proceedings of the National Academy of Science.* (in press)

Grubin, D., & Madsen, L. (2006). Accuracy and utility of post-conviction polygraph testing of sex offenders. *British Journal of Psychiatry, 188,* 479–483.

Grusec, J. E. (2009). Unpublished review of J. W. Santrock's *Child Development* (13th ed.). New York: McGraw-Hill.

Grusec, J. E. (2011). Human development: Development in the family. *Annual Review of Psychology* (vol. 62). Palo Alto, CA: Annual Reviews.

Guérard, K., Tremblay, S., & Saint-Aubin, J. (2009). The processing of spatial information in short-term memory: Insights from eye-tracking the path length effect. *Acta Psychologica.* (in press)

Guerrini, I., Thomson, A. D., & Gurling, H. M. (2009). Molecular genetics of alcohol-related brain damage. *Alcohol and Alcoholism, 44,* 166–170.

Gueta, R., Barlam, D., Shneck, R. Z., & Rousso, I. (2006). Measurement of the mechanical properties of isolated tectorial membrane using atomic force microscopy. *Proceedings of the National Academy of Sciences USA, 103,* 14790–14795.

Gulwadi, B. (2006). Seeking restorative experiences: Elementary school teachers' choices for places that enable coping with stress. *Environment and Behavior, 38,* 503–520.

Gump, B., & Matthews, K. (2000, March). Are vacations good for your health? The 9-year mortality experience after the multiple risk factor intervention trial. *Psychosomatic Medicine, 62,* 608–612.

Gunderson, J. (2008). Borderline personality disorder: An overview. *Social Work in Mental Health, 6,* 5–12.

Gunderson, J. G., Bender, D., Sanislow, C., Yen, S., Rettew, J. B., Dolan-Sewell, R., Dyck, I., Morey, L. C., McGlashan, T. H., Shea, M. T., & Skodol, A. E. (2003). Plausibility and possible determinants of sudden "remissions" in borderline patients. *Psychiatry: Interpersonal and Biological Processes, 66,* 111–119.

Guo, Q., Johnson, C. A., Unger, J. B., Lee, L., Xie, B., Chou, C. P., Palmer, P. H., Sun, P., Gallaher, P., & Pentz, M. (2007). Utility of theory of reasoned action and theory of planned behavior for predicting Chinese adolescent smoking. *Addictive Behaviors, 32,* 1066–1081.

Guo, Y. (2005). Filial therapy for children's behavioral and emotional problems in mainland China. *Journal of Child and Adolescent Psychiatric Nursing, 18,* 171–180.

Gurung, R. A. R. (2010). *Health psychology* (2nd ed.). Boston: Cengage.

Guttmacher Institute. (2010, January). *Facts on American teens' sexual and reproductive health.* Washington, DC: Author.

Guttman, N., & Kalish, H. I. (1956). Discriminability and stimulus generalization. *Journal of Experimental Psychology, 51,* 79–88.

Gwaltney, C. J., Metrik, J., Kahler, C. W., & Shiffman, S. (2009). Self-efficacy and smoking cessation: A meta-analysis. *Psychology of Addictive Behaviors, 23,* 56–66.

Gwernan-Jones, R., & Burden, R. L. (2010). Are they just lazy? Student teachers' attitudes about dyslexia. *Dyslexia: An International Journal of Research and Practice, 16,* 66–86.

Gynther, L. M., Hewitt, J. K., Heath, A. C., & Eaves, L. J. (1999). Phenotypic and genetic factors in motives for smoking. *Behavior Genetics, 29,* 291–302.

H

Haas, B. W., Omura, K., Constable, R. T., & Canli, T. (2007). Emotional conflict and neuroticism: Personality-dependent activation in the amygdala and subgenual anterior cingulate. *Behavioral Neuroscience, 121,* 249–256.

Habbal, O. A., & Al-Jabri, A. A. (2009). Circadian rhythm and the immune system: A review. *International Reviews of Immunology, 28,* 93–108.

Habeck, C., Rakitin, B. C., Moeller, J., Scarmeas, N., Zarahn, E., Brown, T., & Stern, Y. (2004). An event-related fMRI study of the neuro-behavioral impact of sleep deprivation on performance of a delayed-match-to-sample task. *Brain Research, 18,* 306–321.

Hackett, G. I. (2008). Disorders of male sexual desire. In D. L. Rowland & L. Incrocci (Eds.), *Handbook of sexual and gender identity disorders* (pp. 5–29). Hoboken, NJ: Wiley.

Hagadorn, J. A., & Seilacher. A. (2009). Hermit arthropods 500 million years ago? *Geology, 37,* 295–298.

Hagenauer, M. H., Perryman, J. L., Lee, T. M., & Carskadon, M. A. (2009). Adolescent changes in homeostatic and circadian regulation of sleep. *Developmental Neuroscience, 31,* 276–284.

Hagerman, R. J. (2009). Fragile X syndrome and associated disorders in adulthood. *CONTINUUM: Lifelong Learning in Neurology, 15,* 32–49.

Hagg, T. (2009). From neurotransmitters to neurotrophic factors to neurogenesis. *Neuroscientist, 15,* 20–27.

Hagner, M. (2007). Mind reading, brain mirror, neuroimaging: Insight into the brain or the mind? In M. Ash & T. Sturm (Eds.), *Psychology's territories.* Mahwah, NJ: Erlbaum.

Hahn, D. B., Payne, W. A., & Lucas, E. B. (2007). *Focus on health* (8th ed.). New York: McGraw-Hill.

Halberstadt, J. (2010). Dumb but lucky: Fortuitous affect cues and their disruption by analytic thought. *Social and Personality Psychology Compass, 4,* 64–76.

Hald, G. M., Malamuth, N. M., & Yuen, C. (2010). Pornography and attitudes supporting violence against women: Revisiting the relationship in nonexperimental studies. *Aggressive Behavior, 36,* 14–20.

Hales, D. (2011). *An invitation to health* (14th ed.). Boston: Cengage.

Halgunseth, L. C., Ispa, J. M., & Rudy, D. (2006). Parental control in Latino families: An integrated review of the literature. *Child Development, 77,* 1282–1297.

Hall, B. J., & others. (2010). Exploring the association between posttraumatic growth and PTSD: A national study of Jews and Arabs following the 2006 Israeli-Hezbollah war. *Journal of Nervous and Mental Disease, 198,* 180–186.

Hall, D. L., Matz, D. C., & Wood, W. (2010). Why don't we practice what we preach? A meta-analytic review of racism. *Personality and Social Psychology Review, 14,* 126–139.

Hall, J. A., & Matsumoto, D. (2004). Gender differences in judgments of multiple emotions from facial expressions. *Emotion, 14,* 201–206.

Hall, J. A., Park, N., Song, H., & Cody, M. J. (2010). Strategic misrepresentation in online dating: The effects of gender, self-monitoring, and personality traits. *Journal of Social and Personal Relationships, 27,* 117–135.

Hall, R. C. W., & Hall, R. C. W. (2007). A profile of pedophilia: Definition, characteristics of offenders, recidivism, treatment outcomes, and forensic issues. *Mayo Clinic Proceedings, 82,* 457–471.

Hallal, P. C., Victora, C. G., Azevedo, M. R., & Wells, J. C. (2006). Adolescent physical activity and health: A systematic review. *Sports Medicine, 36,* 1019–1030.

Halpern, D. S., Benbow, C. P., Geary, D. C., Gur, R. C., Hyde, J. S., & Gernsbacher, M. A. (2007). The science of sex differences in science and mathematics. *Psychological Science in the Public Interest, 8,* 1–51.

Halpern, J. H. (2003). Hallucinogens: An update. *Current Psychiatry Reports, 5,* 347–354.

Halpern, J. H., & Sewell, R. A. (2005). Hallucinogenic botanicals of America: A growing need for focused drug education and research. *Life Sciences, 78,* 519–526.

Halpern, J. H., Sherwood, A. R., Hudson, J. I., Yurgelun-Todd, D., & Pope, H. G. (2005). Psychological and cognitive effects of long-term peyote use among Native Americans. *Biological Psychiatry, 58,* 624–631.

Hamann, S. (2005). Sex differences in the responses of the human amygdala. *Neuroscientist, 11,* 288–293.

Hamer, M., Chida, Y., & Molloy, G. J. (2009). Psychological distress and cancer mortality. *Journal of Psychosomatic Research, 66,* 255–258.

Hamer, M., Tanaka, G., Okamura, H., Tsuda, A., & Steptoe, A. (2007). The effects of depressive symptoms on cardiovascular and catecholamine responses to the induction of depressive mood. *Biological Psychology, 74,* 20–25.

Hammad, T. A. (2004, September 13). *Results of the analysis of suicidality in pediatric trials of newer antidepressants.* Presentation at the U.S. Food and Drug Administration, Psychopharmacologic Drugs Advisory Committee and the Pediatric Advisory Committee. www.fda.gov/ohrms/dockets/ac/04/slides/2004-4065S1 08 FDA-Hammad files/frame.htm (accessed July 26, 2006)

Hammond, D. C. (2010). Hypnosis in the treatment of anxiety- and stress-related disorders. *Expert Review of Neurotherapeutics, 10,* 263–273.

Hammond, T. A., Laughren, T., & Racoosin, J. (2006). Suicidality in pediatric patients treated with antidepressant drugs. *Archives of General Psychiatry, 63,* 332–339.

Hampton, J. (2008). Abstinence-only programs under fire. *Journal of the American Medical Association, 17,* 2013–2015.

Handel, R. W., Ben-Porath, Y. S., Tellegen, A., & Archer, R. P. (2010). Psychometric functioning of the MMPI-2-RF VRIN-r and TRIN-r scales with varying degrees of randomness, acquiescence, and counter-acquiescence. *Psychological Assessment, 22,* 87–95.

Haney, C., & Zimbardo, P. G. (2009). Persistent dispositionalism in interactionist clothing: Fundamental attribution error in explaining prison abuse. *Personality and Social Psychology Bulletin, 35,* 807–814.

Hankin, B. L., Stone, L., & Wright, P. A. (2010). Corumination, interpersonal stress generation, and internalizing symptoms: Accumulating effects and transactional influences in a multiwave study of adolescents. *Development and Psychopathology, 22,* 217–235.

Hanley, J. R., & Chapman, E. (2008). Partial knowledge in a tip-of-the-tongue state about two- and three-word proper names. *Psychonomic Bulletin and Review, 15,* 156–160.

Hannum, R. D., Rosellini, R. A., & Seligman, M. E. P. (1976). Learned helplessness in the rat: Retention and immunization. *Developmental Psychology, 12,* 449–454.

Hanowski, R. J., Olson, R. L., Hickman, J. S., & Bocanegra, J. (2009, September). *Driver distraction in commercial vehicle operations.* Paper presented at the First International Conference on Driver Distraction and Inattention, Gothenburg, Sweden.

Hansimayr, S., Leipold, P., Pastotter, B., & Baumi, K. H. (2009). Anticipatory signatures of voluntary memory suppression. *Journal of Neuroscience, 29,* 2742–2747.

Haq, I. U., Foote, K. D., Goodman, W. G., Wu, S. S., Sudhyadhom, A., Ricciuti, N., Siddiqui, M. S., Bowers, D., Jacobson, C. E., Ward, H., & Okun, M. S. (2010). Smile and laughter induction and intraoperative predictors of response to deep brain stimulation for obsessive-compulsive disorder. *NeuroImage.* (in press)

Hardy, L., Arthur, C. A., Jones, G., Shariff, A., Munnoch, K., Isaacs, I., & Allsopp, A. J. (2010). The relationship between transformational leadership behaviors, psychological, and training outcomes in elite military recruits. *Leadership Quarterly, 21,* 20–32.

Hare, M., Jones, M., Thomson, C., Kelly, S., & McRae, K. (2009). Activating event knowledge. *Cognition, 11,* 151–167.

Harel, A., Gilaie-Dotan, S., Mlach, R., & Bentin, S. (2010). Top-down engagement modulates the neural expressions of visual expertise. *Cerebral Cortex.* (in press)

Harker, L. A., & Keltner, D. (2001). Expressions of positive emotion in women's college yearbook pictures and their relationship to personality and life outcomes across adulthood. *Journal of Personality and Social Psychology, 80,* 112–124.

Harkness, S., & Super, C. M. (1995). Culture and parenting. In M. H. Bornstein (Ed.), *Children and parenting* (vol. 2). Hillsdale, NJ: Erlbaum.

Harley, R., Sprich, S., Safren, S., Jacobo, M., & Fava, M. (2008). Adaptation of dialectical behavior therapy skills training group for treatment-resistant depression. *Journal of Nervous and Mental Disease, 196,* 136–143.

Harlow, H. F. (1958). The nature of love. *American Psychologist, 13,* 673–685.

Harms, P., Roberts, B. W., & Woods, D. D. (2007). Who shall lead? An integrative personality approach to the study of the antecedents of status in informal social organizations. *Journal of Research in Personality, 41,* 689–699.

Harms, P. D., & Crede, M. (2010). Emotional intelligence and transformational and transactional leadership: A meta-analysis. *Journal of Leadership and Organizational Studies, 17,* 5–17.

Harpaz, Y., Levkovitz, Y., & Lavidor, M. (2009). Lexical ambiguity resolution in Wernicke's area and its right homologue. *Cortex, 45,* 1097–1103.

Harris, C. B., Sutton, J., & Barnier, A. J. (2010). Autobiographical forgetting. In S. D. Sala (Ed.), *Forgetting.* New York: Psychology Press.

Harris, D. M., & Kay, J. (1995). I recognize your face but I can't remember your name: Is it because names are unique? *British Journal of Psychology, 86,* 345–358.

Harris, J. L., Brownell, K. D., & Bargh, J. A. (2010). The food marketing defense model: Integrating psychological research to protect youth and inform public policy. *Social Issues and Policy Review.* (in press)

Harris, J. R. (1998). *The nurture assumption: Why children turn out the way they do.* New York: Free Press.

Harris, J. R. (2009). *The nurture assumption* (rev. and updated edition). New York: Free Press.

Harris, M., & Grunstein, R. R. (2009). Treatments for somnambulism in adults: Assessing the evidence. *Sleep Medicine Reviews, 13,* 295–297.

Harris Interactive. (2006, October 10). *7 in 10 report knowing someone who is gay.* http://www.harrisinteractive.com/news/allnewsbydate.asp?NewsID=1099 (accessed April 2010)

Harrison, A., Jolicoeur, P., & Marois, R. (2010). "What" and "where" in the intraparietal sulcus: An fMRI study of object identity and location in visual short-term memory. *Cerebral Cortex.* (in press)

Harro, J., Merenakk, L., Nordquist, N., Konstabel, K., Comasco, E., & Oreland, L. (2009). Personality and the serotonin transporter gene: Associations in a longitudinal population-based study. *Biological Psychology, 81,* 9–13.

Harshbarger, J. L., Ahlers-Schmidt, C. R., Mayans, L., Mayans, D., & Hawkins, J. H. (2009). Pro-anorexia websites: What a clinician should know. *International Journal of Eating Disorders, 42,* 367–370.

Hart, B., & Risley, T. R. (1995). *Meaningful differences in the everyday experience of young Americans.* Baltimore: Paul H. Brookes.

Hartenbaum, N., & others. (2006). Sleep apnea and commercial motor vehicle operators. *Chest, 130,* 902–905.

Harter, S. (2006). The development of self-esteem. In M. H. Kernis (Ed.), *Self-esteem issues and* answers: *A sourcebook of current perspectives* (pp. 144–150). New York: Psychology Press.

Hartley, S. L., & Maclean, W. E. (2009). Depression in adults with mild intellectual disability: Role of stress, attributions, and coping. *American Journal on Intellectual and Developmental Disabilities, 114,* 147–160.

Hartmann, E. (1993). Nightmares. In M. A. Carskadon (Ed.), *Encyclopedia of sleep and dreams.* New York: Macmillan.

Hartmann, P., & Apaolaza-Ibanez, V. (2010). Beyond savanna: An evolutionary and environmental psychology approach to behavioral effects of nature scenery in green advertising. *Journal of Environmental Psychology, 30,* 119–128.

Harvey, J. L., Anderson, L. E., Baranowski, L. E., & Morath, R. (2007). Job analysis: Gathering job specific information. In D. L. Whetzel & G. R. Wheaton (Eds.), *Applied measurement.* Mahwah, NJ: Erlbaum.

Hasegawa, H., & Unuma, H. (2010). Facial features in perceived intensity of schematic facial expressions. *Perceptual and Motor Skills, 110,* 129–149.

Haselton, M. G. (2006, April 29). How to pick a perfect mate. *New Scientist, 2549,* 36.

Haslam, S. A., & Reicher, S. D. (2006). Debating the psychology of tyranny: Fundamental issues of theory, perspective and science. *British Journal of Social Psychology, 45,* 55–63.

Hassett, J. M., Siebert, E. R., & Wallen, K. (2008). Sex differences in rhesus monkey toy preferences parallel those of children. *Hormones and Behavior, 54,* 359–364.

Hatzinger, M., Brand, S., Perren, S., Stadelmann, S., von Wyl, A., von Klitzing, K., & Holsboer-Trachsler, E. (2010). Sleep actigraphy pattern and behavioral/emotional difficulties in kindergarten children: Association with hypothalamic-pituitary-adrenocortical (HPA) activity. *Journal of Psychiatric Research, 44,* 253–261.

Haviland-Jones, J., Rosario, H. H., Wilson, P., & McGuire, T. R. (2005). An environmental approach to positive emotion: Flowers. *Evolutionary Psychology, 3,* 104–132.

Hawkley, L. C., & Cacioppo, J. T. (2009). Loneliness. In M. R. Leary & R. H. Hoyle (Eds.), *Handbook of individual differences in social behavior* (pp. 227–240). New York: Guilford.

Hawkley, L. C., Preacher, K. J., & Cacioppo, J. T. (2010). Loneliness impairs daytime functioning but not sleep duration. *Health Psychology, 29,* 124–129.

Hawkley, L. C., Thisted, R. A., & Cacioppo, J. T. (2009). Loneliness predicts reduced physical activity: Cross-sectional and longitudinal analyses. *Health Psychology, 28,* 354–363.

Hawkley, L. C., Thisted, R. A., Masi, C. M., & Cacioppo, J. T. (2010). Loneliness predicts increased blood pressure: Five-year cross-lagged analyses in middle-aged and older adults. *Psychology and Aging, 25,* 132–141.

Haworth, C. M., Dale, P. S., & Plomin, R. (2009). The etiology of science performance: Decreasing heritability and increasing importance of shared

environment from 9 to 12 years of age. *Child Development, 80,* 662–673.

Hay, P. P., Bacaltchuk, J., Stefano, S., & Kashyap, P. (2009). Psychological treatments for bulimia nervosa and binging. *Cochrane Database of Systematic Reviews, 4,* CD000562.

Hayflick, L. (1977). The cellular basis for biological aging. In C. E. Finch & L. Hayflick (Eds.), *Handbook of the biology of aging.* New York: Van Nostrand.

Hazell, P. (2009). Depression in children and adolescents. *Clinical Evidence, 15,* 398–414.

Hazler, R. J. (2007). Person-centered therapy. In D. Capuzzi & D. Gross (Eds.), *Counseling and psychotherapy* (4th ed.). Upper Saddle River, NJ: Prentice-Hall.

Hazlett-Stevens, H., & Craske, M. G. (2009). Breathing retraining and diaphragmatic breathing techniques. In W. T. O'Donohue & J. E. Fisher (Eds.), *General principles and empirically supported techniques of cognitive behavior therapy* (pp. 167–172). Hoboken, NJ: Wiley.

Healy, D. (2009). Are selective serotonin reuptake inhibitors a risk factor for adolescent suicide? *Canadian Journal of Psychiatry, 54,* 69–71.

Hearold, S. (1986). A synthesis of 1043 effects of television on social behavior. In G. Comstock (Ed.), *Public communication of behavior* (pp. 65–133). San Diego: Academic.

Hebb, D. O. (1980). *Essay on mind.* Mahwah, NJ: Erlbaum.

Heckman, C. J., & Clay, D. L. (2005). Hardiness, history of abuse, and women's health. *Journal of Health Psychology, 10,* 767–777.

Hedden, T., & Yoon, C. (2006). Individual differences in executive processing predict susceptibility to interference in verbal working memory. *Neuropsychology, 20,* 511–528.

Heflick, N. A., & Goldenberg, J. L. (2009). Objectifying Sarah Palin: Evidence that objectification causes women to be perceived as less competent and less fully human. *Journal of Experimental Social Psychology, 45,* 598–601.

Hegarty, M., Canham, M. S., & Fabrikant, S. I. (2010). Thinking about the weather: How salience and knowledge affect performance in the graphic interference task. *Journal of Experimental Psychology: Learning, Memory, and Cognition, 36,* 37–53.

Hegarty, P. (2009). Toward an LGBT-informed paradigm for children who break gender norms: A comment on Drummond, et al., (2008) and Rieger et al., (2008). *Developmental Psychology, 45,* 895–900.

Heidelbaugh, J. J. (2010). Management of erectile dysfunction. *American Family Physician, 81,* 305–312.

Heider, F. (1958). *The psychology of interpersonal relations.* Hoboken, NJ: Wiley.

Heiman, G. W. (2011). *Basic statistics for the behavioral sciences* (6th ed.). Boston: Cengage.

Heine, S. J. (2005). Constructing good selves in Japan and North America. In R. M. Sorrentino, D. Cohen, J. M. Olson, & M. P. Zanna (Eds.), *Cultural and social behavior: The Ontario symposium* (vol. 10, pp. 95–116). Mahwah, NJ: Erlbaum.

Heine, S. J., & Buchtel, E. E. (2009). Personality: The universal and the culturally specific. *Annual Review of Psychology* (vol. 60). Palo Alto, CA: Annual Reviews.

Heine, S. J., & Hamamura, T. (2007). In search of East Asian self-enhancement. *Personality and Social Psychology Review, 11,* 1–24.

Heine, S. J., Lehman, D. R., Markus, H. R., & Kitayama, S. (1999). Is there a universal need for positive self-regard? *Psychological Review, 106,* 766–794.

Heine, S. J., & Raineri, A. (2009). Self-improving motivations and collectivism: The case of Chileans. *Journal of Cross-Cultural Psychology, 40,* 158–163.

Helgeson, V. S. (1994). Relation of agency and communion to well-being: Evidence and potential explanations. *Psychological Bulletin, 116,* 412–428.

Heller, A. C., Amar, A. P., Liu, C. Y., & Apuzzo, M. L. (2006). Surgery of the mind and mood: A mosaic of issues in time and evolution. *Neurosurgery, 59,* 720–733.

Hellriegel, D., & Slocum, J. W. (2011). *Organizational behavior* (13th ed.). Boston: Cengage.

Helson, R., & Soto, C. J. (2005). Up and down in middle age: Monotonic and nonmonotonic changes in roles, status, and personality. *Journal of Personality and Social Psychology, 89,* 194–204.

Helson, R., Soto, C. J., & Cate, R. A. (2006). From young adulthood through the middle ages. In D. K. Mroczek & T. D. Little (Eds.), *Handbook of personality development.* Mahwah, NJ: Erlbaum.

Hemmer, P., & Steyvers, M. (2009). Integrating episodic memories and prior knowledge at multiple levels of abstraction. *Psychonomic Bulletin and Review, 16,* 80–87.

Henderson, M. (2008, February 18). Welcome to the town that will make you lose weight. *Times Online.* http://www.timesonline.co.uk/tol/news/uk/health/article3386817.ece

Hendrick, C., & Hendrick, S. S. (2006). Styles of romantic love. In R. J. Sternberg & K. Weis (Eds.), *The new psychology of love* (pp. 149–170). New Haven, CT: Yale University Press.

Hendrick, C., & Hendrick, S. S. (2009). Love. In S. Lopez & C. R. Snyder (Eds.), *Oxford handbook of positive psychology* (2nd ed., pp. 447–454). New York: Oxford University Press.

Hendricks, J., & Hatch, L. R. (2006). Lifestyle and aging. In R. H. Binstock & L. K. George (Eds.), *Handbook of aging and the social sciences* (6th ed.). San Diego: Academic.

Henrich, J., Ensminger, J., McElreath, R., Barr, A., Barrett, C., Bolyanatz, A., Cardenas, J. C., Gurven, M., Gwako, E., Henrich, N., Lesorogoi, C., Marlowe, F., Tracer, D., & Ziker, J. (2010). Markets, religion, community size, and the evolution of fairness and punishment. *Science, 327,* 1480–1484.

Hepper, E. G., & Sedikides, C. (2010). Self-enhancing feedback. In R. Sutton, M. Hornsey, & K. Douglas (Eds.), *Feedback: The handbook of praise, criticism, and advice.* Bern, Switzerland: Peter Lang. (in press)

Hepple, R. T. (2009). Why eating less keeps mitochondria working in aged skeletal muscle. *Exercise and Sport Sciences Reviews, 37,* 23–38.

Hepting, U., & Solle, R. (1973). Sex-specific differences in color coding. *Archiv fur Psychologie, 125* (2–3), 184–202.

Herbert, J. (1988). The physiology of aggression. In J. Groebel & R. Hinde (Eds.), *Aggression and war: The biological and social bases.* New York: Cambridge University Press.

Herek, G. M. (1991). Stigma, prejudice, and violence against lesbians and gay men. In J. Gonsiorek & J. Weinrich (Eds.), *Homosexuality: Research implications for public policy* (pp. 60–80). Newbury Park, CA: Sage.

Hering, E. (1878). *Zur Lehre vom Lichtsinne* (illustration, 2nd ed.). Wien: C. Gerold's Sohn.

Herlihy, B., & McCollum, V. (2007). Feminist theory. In D. Capuzzi & D. Gross (Eds.), *Counseling and psychotherapy* (4th ed.). Upper Saddle River, NJ: Prentice-Hall.

Hernandez, P., Siegel, A., & Almeida, R. (2009). The cultural context model: How does it facilitate couples' therapeutic change? *Journal of Marital and Family Therapy, 35,* 97–110.

Hernstein, R. J. (2009). Selection by consequences. In D. Shanks (Ed.), *Psychology of learning.* Thousand Oaks, CA: Sage.

Herry, C., Bach, D. R., Esposito, F., Di Salle, F., Perrig, W. J., Scheffler, K., Luthi, A., & Seifritz, E. (2007). Processing of temporal unpredictability in human and animal amygdala. *Journal of Neuroscience, 27,* 5958–5966.

Hersen, M., & A. M. Gross, A. M. (Eds.). (2008). *Handbook of clinical psychology, vol 2: Children and adolescents.* Hoboken, NJ: Wiley.

Herz, R. S. (1998). Are odors the best cues to memory? A cross-modal comparison of associative memory stimuli. *Annals of the New York Academy of Sciences, 855,* 670–674.

Herz, R. S. (2004). A naturalistic analysis of autobiographical memories triggered by olfactory, visual, and auditory stimuli. *Chemical Senses, 29,* 217–224.

Herz, R. S., & Cupchik, G. C. (1995). The emotional distinctiveness of odor-evoked memories. *Chemical Senses, 20,* 517–528.

Herz, R. S., Schankler, C., & Beland, S. (2004). Olfaction, emotion and associative learning: Effects on motivated behavior. *Motivation and Emotion, 28,* 363–383.

Herzog, H. (2006). Forty-two thousand and one Dalmatians: Fads, social contagion, and dog breed popularity. *Society & Animals, 14,* 383–397.

Hess, E., & Cameron, K. S. (2006). *Developing management skills* (6th ed.). Upper Saddle River, NJ: Prentice-Hall.

Hess, Y. D., & Pickett, C. L. (2010). Social rejection and self- versus other-awareness. *Journal of Experimental Social Psychology, 46,* 453–456.

Hetherington, E. M. (2006). The influence of conflict, marital problem solving, and parenting on children's adjustment in nondivorced, divorced, and remarried families. In A. Clarke-Stewart & J. Dunn (Eds.), *Families count.* New York: Cambridge University Press.

Hetherington, E. M., & Stanley-Hagan, M. (2002). Parenting in divorced and remarried families. In M. Bornstein (Ed.), *Handbook of parenting* (2nd ed.). Mahwah, NJ: Erlbaum.

Hewlin, P. F. (2009). Wearing the cloak: Antecedents and consequences of creating facades of conformity. *Journal of Applied Psychology, 94,* 727–741.

Hibbard, S., Porcerelli, J., Kamoo, R., Schwartz, M., & Abell, S. (2010). Defense and object relational maturity on thematic apperception test scales indicate levels of personality organization. *Journal of Personality Assessment, 92,* 241–253.

Hickok, G. (2010). The role of mirror neurons in speech and language processing. *Brain and Language, 112,* 1–2.

Hicks, J. A, Cicero, D. C., Trent, J., Burton, C. M., & King, L. A. (2010). Positive affect, intuition, and the feeling of meaning. *Journal of Personality and Social Psychology.* (in press)

Higham, P. A., Perfect, T. J., & Bruno, D. (2009). Investigating strength and frequency effects in recognition memory using type-2 signal detection theory. *Experimental Psychology: Learning, Memory, and Cognition, 35,* 57–80.

Hilgard, E. R. (1977). *Divided consciousness: Multiple controls in human thought and action.* New York: Wiley.

Hilgard, E. R. (1992). Dissociation and theories of hypnosis. In E. Fromm & M. R. Nash (Eds.), *Contemporary hypnosis research.* New York: Guilford.

Hill, C. E. (2000). Client-centered therapy. In A. Kazdin (Ed.), *Encyclopedia of psychology.* Washington, DC, & New York: American Psychological Association and Oxford University Press.

Hill, T. D., Burdette, A. M., Ellison, C. G., & Musick, M. A. (2006). Religious attendance and the health behaviors of Texas adults. *Preventive Medicine: An International Journal Devoted to Practice and Theory, 42,* 309–312.

Hillman, C. H., Erickson, K. I., & Kramer. A. F. (2008). Be smart, exercise your heart: Exercise effects on the brain and cognition. *Nature Reviews: Neuroscience, 9,* 58–65.

Hingson, R. W., Heeren, T., & Winter, M. R. (2006). Age at drinking onset and alcohol dependence: Age of onset, duration, and severity. *Archives of Pediatric and Adolescent Medicine, 160,* 739–746.

Hinshaw, S. P. (2007). *The mark of shame: Stigma of mental illness and an agenda for change.* New York: Oxford University Press.

Hirata, A., & Castro-Alamancos, M. A. (2010). Neocortex network activation and deactivation states controlled by the thalamus. *Journal of Neurophysiology.* (in press)

Hirsch, I. (2010). Discussion: On some contributions of the interpersonal tradition to contemporary psychoanalytic praxis. *American Journal of Psychoanalysis, 70,* 86–93.

Hirsch, J. K., Wolford, K., Lalonde, S. M., Brunk, L., & Parker-Morris, A. (2009). Optimistic explanatory style as a moderator between negative life events and suicide ideation. *Crisis, 30,* 48–53.

Hnasko, T. S., & others. (2010). Vesicular glutamate transport promotes dopamine storage and glutamate corelease in vivo. *Neuron, 65,* 643–656.

Ho, R. C., Neo, L. F., Chua, A. N., Cheak, A. A., & Mak, A. (2010). Research on psychoneuroimmunology: Does stress influence immunity and cause coronary artery disease? *Annals of the Academy of Medicine, Singapore, 39,* 191–196.

Hobson, J. A. (1999). Dreams. In R. Conlan (Ed.), *States of mind.* New York: Wiley.

Hobson, J. A. (2000). Dreams: Physiology. In A. Kazdin (Ed.), *Encyclopedia of psychology.* Washington, DC, and New York: American Psychological Association and Oxford University Press.

Hobson, J. A. (2002). *Dreaming.* New York: Oxford University Press.

Hobson, J. A. (2004). Freud returns? Like a bad dream. *Scientific American, 290,* 89.

Hobson, J. A., Pace-Schott, E. F., & Stickgold, R. (2000). Dreaming and the brain. *Behavior and Brain Sciences, 23,* 793–842.

Hodges, T. D., & Clifton, D. O. (2004). Strengths-based development in practice. In A. Linley & S. Joseph (Eds.), *Positive psychology in practice* (pp. 256–268). Hoboken, NJ: Wiley.

Hodgins, D. C. (2005). Weighing the pros and cons of changing change models: A comment on West (2005). *Addiction, 100,* 1042–1043.

Hodgson, T. L., Parris, B. A., Gregory, N. J., & Jarvis, T. (2009). The saccadic Stroop effect: Evidence for involuntary programming of eye movements by linguistic cues. *Vision Research, 49,* 569–574.

Hoek, H. W. (2006). Incidence, prevalence and mortality of anorexia nervosa and other eating disorders. *Current Opinion in Psychiatry, 19,* 389–394.

Hoffman, I. Z. (2006). The myths of free association and the potentials of the analytic relationship. *International Journal of Psychoanalysis, 87,* 43–61.

Hoffman, J. P. (2009). Drug use, adolescent. In D. Carr (Ed.), *Encyclopedia of the life course and human development.* Boston: Cengage.

Hogan, E. H., Hornick, B. A., & Bouchoux, A. (2002). Focus on communications: Communicating the message: Clarifying the controversies about caffeine. *Nutrition Today, 37,* 28–35.

Hogan, R. (2006). *Personality and the fate of organizations.* Mahwah, NJ: Erlbaum.

Hogan, R. (2009). Much ado about nothing. *Journal of Research in Personality, 43,* 249.

Hogg, M. A., & Abrams, D. (2007). Intergroup behavior and social identity. In M. A. Hogg & J. Cooper (Eds.), *The Sage handbook of social psychology* (concise 2nd ed.). Thousand Oaks, CA: Sage.

Hogh, A., Henriksson, M. E., & Burr, H. (2005). A 5-year follow-up study of aggression at work and psychological health. *International Journal of Behavioral Medicine, 12,* 256–265.

Holland, P. C. (1996). The effects of intertrial and feature-target intervals on operant serial feature-positive discrimination learning. *Animal Learning & Behavior, 24,* 411–428.

Hollich, G. J., & Huston, D. M. (2007). Language development: From speech to first words. In A. Slater & M. Lewis (Eds.), *Introduction to infant development* (2nd ed.). New York: Oxford University Press.

Holliday, E. G., & others. (2009). Strong evidence for a novel schizophrenia risk locus on chromosome 1p31.1 in homogeneous pedigrees from Tamil Nadu, India. *American Journal of Psychiatry, 166,* 206–215.

Hollingsworth, S. A., Burgess, P. M., & Whiteford, H. A. (2010). Affective and anxiety disorders: Prevalence, treatment, and antidepressant medication use. *Australian and New Zealand Journal of Psychiatry, 44,* 513–519.

Hollins, M. (2010). The somesthetic senses. *Annual Review of Psychology* (vol. 61). Palo Alto, CA: Annual Reviews.

Holmes, J. (2010). Charles Rycroft's contribution to contemporary psychoanalytic psychotherapy. *American Journal of Psychoanalysis, 70,* 180–192.

Holmes, J. G., Miller, D. T., & Lerner, M. J. (2002). Committing altruism under the cloak of self-interest: The exchange fiction. *Journal of Experimental Social Psychology, 38* (2), 144–151.

Holmes, S. (1993). Food avoidance in patients undergoing cancer chemotherapy. *Support Care Cancer, 1* (6), 326–330.

Holsboer, F., & Ising, M. (2010). Stress hormone regulation: Biological role and translation into therapy. *Annual Review of Psychology* (vol. 61). Palo Alto, CA: Annual Reviews.

Holzman, L. (2009). *Vygotsky at work and play.* Oxford, U.K.: Routledge.

Hong, S. W., & Shevell, S. K. (2009). Color-binding errors during rivalrous suppression of form. *Psychological Science, 20,* 1084–1091.

Honts, C. (1998, June). Commentary. *APA Monitor, 30.*

Hooper, J., & Teresi, D. (1993). *The 3-pound universe.* New York: Tarcher/Putnam.

Hopf, F. W., & others. (2010). Reduced nucleus accumbens SK channel activity enhances alcohol seeking abstinence. *Neuron, 65,* 682–694.

Horgan, J. (2005, February 26). Psychedelic medicine: Mind bending, health giving. *New Scientist, 2488,* 36.

Horn, H., & others. (2010). Gray matter volume differences specific to formal thought disorder in schizophrenia. *Psychiatry Research.* (in press)

Horney, K. (1945). *Our inner conflicts.* New York: Norton.

Horney, K. (1967). *Feminine psychology (collected essays, 1922–1937).* New York: Norton.

Hornickel, J., Skoe, E., & Kraus, N. (2009). Subcortical laterality of speech encoding. *Audiology and Neuro-Otology, 14,* 198–207.

Hornsey, M. J., Dwyer, L., Oei, T. P., & Dingle, G. A. (2009). Group processes and outcomes in group psychotherapy: Is it time to let go of "cohesiveness"? *International Journal of Group Psychotherapy, 59,* 267–278.

Horowitz, J. L., & Garber, J. (2006). The prevention of depressive symptoms in children and adolescents: A meta-analytic review. *Journal of Consulting and Clinical Psychology, 74* (3), 401–415.

Horry, R., Wright, D. B., & Tredoux, C. G. (2010). Recognition and context memory for faces from own and other ethnic groups: A remember-know investigation. *Memory and Cognition, 38,* 134–141.

Horst, J. S., Ellis, A. E., Samuelson, L. K., Trejo, E., Worzalla, S. L., Peltan, J. R., & Oakes, L. M. (2009). Toddlers can adaptively change how they categorize: Same objects, same session, two different categorical distinctions. *Developmental Science, 12,* 96–105.

Hoss, R. A., & Langlois, J. H. (2003). Infants prefer attractive faces. In O. Pascalis & A. Slater (Eds.), *The development of face processing in infancy and early childhood: Current perspectives* (pp. 27–38). Hauppauge, NY: Nova Science.

Hotard, S. R., McFatter, R. M., McWhirter, R. M., & Stegall, M. E. (1989). Interactive effects of extraversion, neuroticism, and social relationships on subjective well-being. *Journal of Personality and Social Psychology, 57,* 321–331.

House, J. S., Landis, K. R., & Umberson, D. (1988). Social relationships and health. *Science, 241,* 540–545.

Houser-Marko, L., & Sheldon, K. M. (2008). Eyes on the prize or nose to the grindstone? The effects of level of goal evaluation on mood and motivation. *Personality and Social Psychology Bulletin, 34,* 1556–1569.

Hovland, C. I., Janis, I. L., & Kelley, H. H. (1953). *Communication and persuasion.* New Haven, CT: Yale University Press.

Howard, K. I., Moras, K., Brill, P. L., Martinovich, Z., & Lutz, W. (1996). Evaluation of psychotherapy: Efficacy, effectiveness, and patient progress. *American Psychologist, 51,* 1059–1064.

Howe, M. J. A., Davidson, J. W., Moore, D. G., & Sloboda, J. A. (1995). Are there early childhood signs of musical ability? *Psychology of Music, 23,* 162–176.

Howell, D. C. (2010). *Fundamental statistics for the behavioral sciences* (7th ed.). Belmont, CA: Wadsworth.

Howes, M. B. (2006). *Human memory.* Thousand Oaks, CA: Sage.

Howes, O. D., & others. (2009). Elevated striatal dopamine function linked to prodromal signs of schizophrenia. *Archives of General Psychiatry, 66,* 13–20.

Hoyer, D., Hannon, J. P., & Martin, G. R. (2002). Molecular, pharmacological, and functional diversity of 5-HT receptors. *Pharmacology, Biochemistry, and Behavior, 71,* 533–554.

Hoyer, W. J., & Roodin, P. A. (2009). *Adult development and aging* (6th ed.). New York: McGraw-Hill.

Hoyle, R. H. (2009). *Handbook of personality and social regulation.* Malden, MA: Blackwell.

Hsieh, L. T., Hung, D. L., Tzeng, O. J., Lee, J. R., & Cheng, S. K. (2009). An event-related potential investigation of the processing of remember/forget cues and item encoding in item-method directed forgetting. *Brain Research, 1250,* 190–201.

Hu, F. B., Willett, W. C., Li, T., Stampfer, M. J., Colditz, G. A., & Manson, J. E. (2004). Adiposity as compared with physical activity in predicting mortality among women. *New England Journal of Medicine, 351,* 2694–2703.

Huang, C. C., & Chang, Y. C. (2009). The long-term effects of febrile seizures on the hippocampal neuronal plasticity—clinical and experimental evidence. *Brain and Development, 31,* 383–387.

Huang, X., Lei, Z., Li, X. P., & El-Mallakh, R. S. (2009). Response of sodium pump to ouabain challenge in human glioblastoma cells in culture. *World Journal of Biological Psychiatry, 10,* 884–892.

Huart, C., Collet, S., & Rombaux, P. (2009). Chemosensory pathways: From periphery to cortex. *B-ENT, 5, Suppl. 13,* S3–S9.

Hubble, M. A., & Miller, S. D. (2004). The client: Psychotherapy's missing link for promoting a positive psychology. In A. Linley & S. Joseph (Eds.), *Positive psychology in practice* (pp. 335–353). Hoboken, NJ: Wiley.

Hubel, D. H., & Wiesel, T. N. (1963). Receptive fields of cells in striate cortex of very young, visually inexperienced kittens. *Journal of Neurophysiology, 26,* 994–1002.

Hudson, A. J. (2009). Consciousness: Physiological dependence on rapid memory access. *Frontiers in Biology, 14,* 2779–2800.

Huff, C. R. (2002). What can we learn from other nations about the problem of wrongful conviction? *Judicature, 86,* 91–97.

Huffcutt, A. L., & Culbertson, S. S. (2010). Interviews. In S. Zedeck (Ed.), *APA handbook of industrial and organizational psychology.* Washington, DC: APA. (in press)

Hughes, I. A., Houk, C., Ahmed, F., Lee, P. A., & LWPES-ESPE Consensus Group. (2006). Consensus statement on management of intersex disorders. *Archives of Disease in Childhood, 91,* 554–563.

Hummer, R. A., Ellison, C. G., Rogers, R. G., Moulton, B. C., & Romero, R. R. (2004). Religious involvement and adult mortality in the United States: Review and perspective. *Southern Medical Journal, 97,* 1223–1230.

Hung, Y., Smith, M. L., Bayle, D. J., Mills, T., Cheyne, D., & Taylor, M. J. (2010). Unattended emotional faces elicit early lateralized amygdala-frontal and fusiform activations. *NeuroImage.* (in press)

Hunsley, J., & Bailey, J. M. (2001). Whither the Rorschach? An analysis of the evidence. *Psychological Assessment, 13,* 472–485.

Hunsley, J., Lee, C. M., & Wood, J. M. (2004). Controversial and questionable assessment techniques. In S. O. Lilienfeld, J. M. Lohr, & S. J. Lynn (Eds.), *Science and pseudoscience in clinical psychology* (pp. 39–76). New York: Guilford.

Hunt, R. R., & Ellis, H. C. (2004). *Fundamentals of cognitive psychology* (7th ed.). New York: McGraw-Hill.

Hurkmans, E. J., & others. (2010). Motivation as a determinant of physical activity in patients with rheumatoid arthritis. *Arthritis Care Research, 62,* 371–377.

Hurleman, R., & others. (2010). Oxytocin enhances amygdala-dependent, socially reinforced learning and empathy in humans. *Journal of Neuroscience, 30*, 4999–5007.

Hurst, J. L. (2009). Female recognition and assessment of males through scent. *Behavioural Brain Research, 200*, 295–303.

Husain, O. (2009). Paul Lerner and the heart of assessment: A tale of three relations. *Journal of Personality Assessment, 91*, 30–34.

Huston, J. P., Schulz, D., & Topic, B. (2009). Toward an animal model of extinction-induced despair: Focus on aging and physiological indices. *Journal of Neural Transmission, 116*, 1029–1036.

Huttenlocher, P. R., & Dabholkar, A. S. (1997). Regional differences in synaptogenesis in human cerebral cortex. *Journal of Comparative Neurology, 37* (2), 167–178.

Hutton, J. L., Baracos, V. E., & Wismer, W. V. (2007). Chemosensory dysfunction is a primary factor in the evolution of declining nutritional status and quality of life in patients with advanced cancer. *Journal of Pain Symptom Management, 33* (2), 156–165.

Hyde, J. S. (2005). The gender similarities hypothesis. *American Psychologist, 60*, 581–592.

Hyde, J. S. (2006). Gender similarities in mathematics and science. *Science, 314*, 599–600.

Hyde, J. S. (2007). New directions in the study of gender similarities and differences. *Current Directions in Psychological Science, 16*, 259–263.

Hyde, J. S., & DeLamater, J. D. (2011). *Understanding human sexuality* (11th ed.). New York: McGraw-Hill.

Hyde, M., Punch, R., & Komesaroff, L. (2010). Coming to a decision about cochlear implantation: Parents making choices for their deaf children. *Journal of Deaf Studies and Deaf Education.* (in press)

Hyman, S. (2001, October 23). *Basic and clinical neuroscience in the post-genomic era.* Paper presented at the centennial symposium on the Celebration of Excellence in Neuroscience, the Rockefeller University, New York City.

Hyman, S. E. (2010). The diagnosis of mental disorders: The problem of reification. *Annual Review of Clinical Psychology* (vol. 6). Palo Alto, CA: Annual Reviews.

Iacono, W. G., & Lykken, D. T. (1997). The validity of the lie detector: Two surveys of scientific opinion. *Journal of Applied Psychology, 82*, 426–433.

Ideguchi, M., Palmer, T. D., Recht, L. D., & Weimann, J. M. (2010). Murine embryonic stem cell–derived pyramidal neurons integrate into the cerebral cortex and appropriate project axons to subcortical targets. *Journal of Neuroscience, 30*, 894–904.

Ikeda, B. E., Collins, C. E., Alvaro, F., Marshall, G., & Garg, M. L. (2006). Well-being and nutrition-related side effects in children undergoing chemotherapy. *Nutrition and Dietetics, 63*, 227–239.

Ikeda, K., Sekiguchi, T., & Hayashi, A. (2010). Concentrated pitch discrimination modulates auditory brainstem responses during contralateral noise exposure. *NeuroReport.* (in press)

Ilies, R., Arvey, R. D., & Bouchard T. J., Jr. (2006). Darwinism, behavioral genetics, and organizational behavior: A review and agenda for future research. *Journal of Organizational Behavior, 27* (2), 121–141.

Imayoshi, I., Sakamoto, M., Ohtsuka, T., & Kageyama, R. (2009). Continuous neurogenesis in the adult brain. *Development, Growth, and Differentiation, 51*, 379–386.

Imeri, L., & Opp, M. R. (2009). How (and why) the immune system makes us sleep. *Nature Reviews: Neuroscience, 10*, 199–210.

Impett, E. A., Peplau, L. A., & Gable, S. L. (2005). Approach and avoidance sexual motives: Implications for personal and interpersonal well-being. *Personal Relationships, 12*, 465–482.

Inaba, A., Thoits, P. A., Ueno, K., Gove, W. R., Evenson, R. J., & Sloan, M. (2005). Depression in the United States and Japan: Gender, marital status, and SES patterns. *Social Science & Medicine, 61*, 2280–2292.

Ingram, R. E. (Ed.). (2009). *The international encyclopedia of depression.* New York: Springer.

Innocence Project. (2009). *Eyewitness misidentification.* http://www.innocenceproject.org/understand/Eyewitness-Misidentification.php (accessed February 18, 2010)

Insel, P. M., & Roth, W. T. (2008). *Core concepts in health* (10th ed.). New York: McGraw-Hill.

Insko, C. A., & Wilson, M. (1977). Interpersonal attraction as a function of social interaction. *Journal of Personality and Social Psychology, 35*, 903–911.

Institute of Medicine. (2006, April). *Sleep disorders and sleep deprivation: An unmet public health problem.* Washington, DC: National Academies.

Irmansyah, I., Dharmono, S., Maramis, A., & Minas, H. (2010). Determinants of psychological morbidity in survivors of the earthquake and tsunami in Aceh and Nias. *International Journal of Mental Health Systems.* (in press)

Ironson, G., Solomon, G., Balbin, E., O'Cleirigh, C., George, A., Schneiderman, N., & Woods, T. (2001, March). *Religious behavior, religious coping, and compassionate view of others is associated with long-term survival with AIDS.* Paper presented at the meeting of the American Psychosomatic Society, Monterey, CA.

Ironson, G., Stuetzle, R., & Fletcher, M. A. (2006). An increase in religiousness/spirituality occurs after HIV diagnosis and predicts slower disease progression over 4 years in people with HIV. *Journal of General Internal Medicine, 21*, S62–S68.

Irwin, M. R., Wang, M., Campomayor, C. O., Coliado-Hidalgo, A., & Cole, S. (2006). Sleep deprivation and activation of morning levels of cellular and genomic markers of inflammation. *Archives of Internal Medicine, 166*, 1756–1762.

Isbell, L. M. (2004). Not all people are lazy or stupid: Evidence of systematic processing in happy moods. *Journal of Experimental Social Psychology, 40*, 341–349.

Isen, A. M. (2004). Some perspectives on positive feelings and emotions: Positive affect facilitates thinking and problem solving. In A. S. R. Manstead, N. Frijda, & A. Fischer (Eds.), *Feelings and emotions: The Amsterdam symposium* (pp. 263–281). New York: Cambridge University Press.

Isen, A. M. (2007a). Positive affect, cognitive flexibility, and self-control. In Y. Shoda, D. Cervone, & G. Downey (Eds.), *Persons in context.* New York: Guilford.

Isen, A. M. (2007b). Positive affect. In R. Baumeister & K. Vohs (Eds.), *Encyclopedia of social psychology.* Thousand Oaks, CA: Sage.

Isen, A. M. (2008). Some ways in which positive affect influences problem solving and decision making. In M. Lewis, J. Haviland-Jones, & L. F. Barrett (Eds.), *Handbook of emotions* (3rd ed.). New York: Guilford.

Isen, A. M., & Means, B. (1983). The influence of positive affect on decision-making strategy. *Social Cognition, 2*, 18–31.

Issa, E. B., & Wang, X. (2008). Sensory responses during sleep in primary and secondary auditory cortex. *Journal of Neuroscience, 28*, 14467–14480.

Istaphanous, G. K., & Loepke, A. W. (2009). General anesthetics and the developing brain. *Current Opinion in Anesthesiology, 22*, 368–373.

Iturbide, M. I., Raffaelli, M., & Carlo, G. (2009). Protective effects of ethnic identity on Mexican American college students' psychological well-being. *Hispanic Journal of Behavioral Sciences, 31*, 536–552.

Ivancevich, J. M., & Konopaske, R. (2011). *Organizational behavior and management* (9th ed.). New York: McGraw-Hill.

Iwassa, H., Masul, Y., Gondo, Y., Inagaki, H., Kawaal, C., & Suzuki, T. (2008). Personality and all-cause mortality among older adults dwelling in a Japanese community: A five-year population-based prospective study. *American Journal of Geriatric Psychiatry, 16*, 399–405.

Iwassa, H., & others. (2009). Personality and participation in mass health checkups among Japanese community-dwelling elderly. *Journal of Psychosomatic Research, 66*, 155–159.

Izard, C. E. (2009). Emotion theory and research: Highlights, unanswered questions, and emerging issues. *Annual Review of Psychology* (vol. 60). Palo Alto, CA: Annual Reviews.

Jablensky, E. (2000). Epidemiology of schizophrenia: The global burden of disease and disability. *European Archives of Psychiatry and Clinical Neuroscience, 250*, 274–285.

Jablensky, E., & others. (1992). Schizophrenia: Manifestations, incidence and course in different cultures: A World Health Organization 10-country study. *Psychological Medicine, Monograph Suppl. 20*, 1–97.

Jack, R. E., Blais, C., Scheepers, C., Schyns, P. G., & Caldara, R. (2009). Cultural confusions show that facial expressions are not universal. *Current Biology, 19*, 1543–1548.

Jackson, G. (2010). Come fly with me: Jet lag and melatonin. *International Journal of Clinical Practice, 64,* 135.

Jackson, L., Langille, L., Lyons, R., Hughes, J., Martin, D., & Winstanley, V. (2009). Does moving from a high-poverty to lower-poverty neighborhood improve mental health? A realist view of "Moving to Opportunity." *Health and Place, 15* (4), 961–970.

Jackson, L. C., & Greene, B. (2000). *Psychotherapy with African-American women.* New York: Guilford.

Jacobsen, P. B., Bovbjerg, D. H., Schwartz, M. D., Andrykowski, M. A., Futterman, A. D., Gilewski, T., Norton, L., & Redd, W. H. (1993). Formation of food aversions in cancer patients receiving repeated infusions of chemotherapy. *Behavior Reseach Therapy, 31* (8), 739–748.

Jaeger, A., Johnson, J. D., Corona, M., & Rugg, M. D. (2009). ERP correlates of the incidental retrieval of emotional information: Effects of study-test delay. *Brain Research, 1269,* 105–113.

Jaeggi, S. M., Buschkuehl, M., Jonides, J., & Perrig, W. J. (2008). Improving fluid intelligence with training on working memory. *Proceedings of the National Academy of Sciences USA, 105* (19), 6829–6833.

Jakupcak, M., Salters, K., Gratz, K. L., & Roemer, L. (2003). Masculinity and emotionality: An investigation of men's primary and secondary emotional responding. *Sex Roles, 49,* 111–120.

James, W. (1950). *Principles of psychology.* New York: Dover. (original work published 1890)

James, W. H. (2005). Biological and psychosocial determinants of male and female human sexual orientation. *Journal of Biosocial Science, 37,* 555–567.

Jameson, D., & Hurvich, L. M. (1989). Essay concerning color constancy. *Annual Review of Psychology* (vol. 40). Palo Alto, CA: Annual Reviews.

Janata, P. (2009). The neural architecture of music-evoked autobiographical memories. *Cerebral Cortex, 19,* 2579–2594.

Jang, K. L., Livesley, W. J., & Vernon, P. A. (1996). Heritability of the big five personality dimensions and their facets: A twin study. *Journal of Personality, 64,* 577–591.

Janicki-Deverts, D., Cohen, S., & Doyle, W. J. (2010). Cynical hostility and stimulated Th1 and Th2 cytokine production. *Brain, Behavior, and Immunity, 24,* 58–63.

Janis, I. (1972). *Victims of groupthink: A psychological study of foreign-policy decisions and fiascos.* Boston: Houghton Mifflin.

Janis, I. L., & Hovland, C. I. (1959). An overview of persuasability research. In C. I. Hovland & I. L. Janis (Eds.), *Personality and persuasability* (pp. 1–26). New Haven, CT: Yale University Press.

Janowsky, D. S., Addario, D., & Risch, S. C. (1987). *Psychopharmacology case studies* (2nd ed.). New York: Guilford.

Jarrett, R. B., Kraft, D., Doyle, J., Foster, B. M., Eaves, G. G., & Silver, P. C. (2001). Preventing recurrent depression using cognitive therapy with and without a continuation phase: A randomized clinical trial. *Archives of General Psychiatry, 58,* 381–388.

Jaurrieta, N., & others. (2008). Individual versus group cognitive behavioral treatment for obsessive-compulsive disorder: Follow-up. *Psychiatry and Clinical Neuroscience, 62,* 697–704.

Jefferson, S. D., & Bramlett, F. (2010). The moderating roles of gender and anti-gay prejudice in explaining stigma by association in male dyads. *Journal of Homosexuality, 57,* 401–414.

Jemmott, J. B., III, Jemmott, L. S., & Fong, G. T. (2010). Efficacy of a theory-based abstinence-only intervention over 24 months: A randomized controlled trial with young adolescents. *Archives of Pediatrics and Adolescent Medicine, 164,* 52–159.

Jennings, L., & Skovholt, T. M. (1999). The cognitive, emotional, and relational characteristics of master therapists. *Journal of Counseling Psychology, 46,* 3–11.

Jensen, L. W., & Wadkins, T. A. (2007). Mental health success stories: Finding paths to recovery. *Issues in Mental Health Nursing, 28,* 325–340.

Jensen, M. P. (2009). The neurophysiology of pain perception and hypnotic analgesia: Implications for clinical practice. *American Journal of Clinical Hypnosis, 51,* 123–148.

Jensen-Campbell, L. A., & Malcolm, K. T. (2007). The importance of conscientiousness in adolescent interpersonal relationships. *Personality and Social Psychology Bulletin, 33,* 368–383.

Jeong, J., Kim, D. J., Kim, S. Y., Chae, J. H., Go, H. J., & Kim, K. S. (2001). Effect of total sleep deprivation on the dimensional complexity of the waking EEG. *Sleep, 15,* 197–202.

Jerrell, J. M. (2010). Neuroendocrine-related adverse events associated with antidepressant treatment in children and adolescents. *CNS Neuroscience & Therapeutics, 16,* 83–90.

Jespersen, A. E., Lalumiere, M. L,, & Seto, M. C. (2009). Sexual abuse history among adult sex offenders and non–sex offenders: Meta-analysis. *Child Abuse and Neglect, 33,* 179–192.

Jiang, Y. H., & others. (2010). Clinical efficacy of acupuncture on the morphine-related side effects in patients undergoing spinal-epidural anesthesia and analgesia. *Chinese Journal of Integrative Medicine, 16,* 71–74.

Jimenez-Sanchez, A. R., & others. (2009). Morphological background detection and enhancement of images with poor lighting. *IEEE Transactions on Image Processing, 18,* 613–623.

Job, R. F. S. (1987). The effect of mood on helping behavior. *Journal of Social Psychology, 127,* 323–328.

Johnson, A. M., Vernon, P. A., Harris, J. A., & Jang, K. L. (2004). Behavior genetic investigation of the relationship between leadership and personality. *Twin Research, 7* (1), 27–32.

Johnson, G. B. (2008). *The living world* (5th ed.). New York: McGraw-Hill.

Johnson, J. S., & Newport, E. L. (1991). Critical period effects on universal properties of language: The status of subjacency in the acquisition of a second language. *Cognition, 39,* 215–258.

Johnson, J. T., Robinson, M., & Mitchell, E. B. (2004). Inferences about the authentic self: When do actions say more than mental states? *Journal of Personality and Social Psychology, 87,* 615–630.

Johnson, P. L., & others. (2010). A key role for orexin in panic anxiety. *Nature Medicine, 16,* 111–115.

Johnson, R. E., & Chang, C. (2006). "I" is to continuance as "we" is to affective: The relevance of the self-concept for organizational commitment. *Journal of Organizational Behavior, 27* (5), 549–570.

Johnson, S. P. (2010a). Perceptual completion in infancy. In S. P. Johnson (Ed.), *Neoconstructionism: The new science of cognitive development.* New York: Oxford University Press. (in press)

Johnson, S. P. (2010b). A constructivist view of object perception in infancy. In L. M. Oakes, C. H. Cashon, M. Cassola, & D. H. Rakison (Eds.), *Early perceptual and cognitive development.* New York: Oxford University Press. (in press)

Johnson-Laird, P. N., Mancini, F., & Gangemi, A. (2006). A hyper-emotion theory of psychological illnesses. *Psychological Review, 113,* 822–841.

Johnston, L. D., O'Malley, P. M., Bachman, J. G., & Schulenberg, J. E. (2008). *Monitoring the Future national survey results on drug use, 1975–2007.* Bethesda, MD: National Institute on Drug Abuse.

Johnston, L. D., O'Malley, P. M., Bachman, J. G., & Schulenberg, J. E. (2009). *Monitoring the Future national results on adolescent drug use: Overview of key findings, 2008.* Bethesda, MD: National Institute on Drug Abuse.

Johnston, L. D., O'Malley, P. M., Bachman, J. G., & Schulenberg, J. E. (2010). *Monitoring the Future national survey results on drug use, 1975–2009.* Bethesda, MD: National Institute on Drug Abuse. (in press)

Johnstone, E., Benowitz, N., Cargill, A., Jacob, R., Hinks, L., Day, I., Murphy, M., & Walton, R. (2006). Determinants of the rate of nicotine metabolism and the effects on smoking behavior. *Clinical Pharmacology and Therapeutics, 80,* 319–330.

Joiner, T. E., Jr. (2005). *Why people die by suicide.* Cambridge, MA: Harvard University Press.

Joiner, T. E., Jr., Hollar, D., & Van Orden, K. (2006). On Buckeyes, Gators, Super Bowl Sunday, and the miracle on ice: "Pulling together" is associated with lower suicide rates. *Journal of Social & Clinical Psychology, 25,* 179–195.

Jones, E. E. (1998). Major developments in five decades of social psychology. In D. T. Gilbert, S. T. Fiske, & G. Lindzey (Eds.), *Handbook of social psychology* (4th ed., vol. 1). New York: McGraw-Hill.

Jones, E. E., & Harris, V. A. (1967). The attribution of attitudes. *Journal of Experimental Social Psychology, 3,* 1–24.

Jones, G. R., & George, J. M. (2007). *Essentials of contemporary management* (2nd ed.). New York: McGraw-Hill.

Joorman, J., Teachman, B. A., & Gotlib, I. H. (2009). Sadder and less accurate? False memory for negative material in depression. *Journal of Abnormal Psychology, 118,* 412–417.

Jordan, C. E., Campbell, R., & Follingstad, D. (2010). Violence and women's mental health: The impact of physical, sexual, and psychological aggression. *Annual Review of Clinical Psychology* (vol. 6). Palo Alto, CA: Annual Reviews.

Joseph, J. (2006). *The missing gene.* New York: Algora.

Joseph, J., Breslin, C., & Skinner, H. (1999). Critical perspectives on the transtheoretical model and stages of change. In J. A. Tucker, D. M. Donovan, & G. A. Marlatt (Eds.), *Changing addictive behavior: Bridging clinical and public health strategies* (pp. 160–190). New York: Guilford.

Joseph, S., & Linley, P. A. (2004). Positive therapy: A positive psychological approach to therapeutic practice. In P. A. Linley & S. Joseph (Eds.), *Positive psychology in practice* (pp. 354–368). Hoboken, NJ: Wiley.

Jost, J. T., Federico, C. M., & Napier, J. L. (2009). Attitude structure. *Annual Review of Psychology* (vol. 60). Palo Alto, CA: Annual Reviews.

Joy, J. E., Watson, S. J., & Benson, J. A. (Eds.). (1999). *Institute of medicine. Marijuana and medicine: Assessing the science base.* Washington, DC: National Academy Press.

Juang, L., & Syed, M. (2010). Family cultural socialization practices and ethnic identity in college-going emerging adults. *Journal of Adolescence.* (in press)

Juckel, G., Uhl, I., Padberg, F., Brune, M., & Winter, C. (2009). Psychosurgery and deep brain stimulation as ultima ratio treatment for refractory depression. *European Archives of Psychiatry and Clinical Neuroscience, 259,* 1–7.

Judge, T. A., Piccolo, R. F., & Kosalka, T. (2009). The bright and dark sides of leader traits: A review and theoretical extension of the leader trait paradigm. *Leadership Quarterly, 20,* 855–875.

Judge, T. A., Thorson, C. J., Bono, J. E., & Patton, G. K. (2001). The job satisfaction–job performance relationship: A qualitative and quantitative review. *Psychological Bulletin, 127,* 376–407.

Julien, E., Senecal, C., & Guay, F. (2009). Longitudinal relations among perceived autonomy support from health care practitioners, motivation, coping strategies and dietary compliance in a sample of adults with type 2 diabetes. *Journal of Health Psychology, 14,* 457–470.

Jung, C. (1917). *Analytic psychology.* New York: Moffat, Yard.

K

Kaasa, S. O., & Loftus, E. F. (2009). False memories. In F. T. L. Leong (Ed.), *Encyclopedia of counseling.* Thousand Oaks, CA: Sage.

Kabat-Zinn, J. (2006). *Coming to our senses: Healing ourselves and the world through mindfulness.* New York: Hyperion.

Kabat-Zinn, J. (2009, March 18). This analog life; Reconnecting with what is important in an always uncertain world. Presentation at the 7th Annual Conference at the Center for Mindful Meditation, Worcester, MA.

Kabat-Zinn, J., Lipworth, L., & Burney, R. (1985). The clinical use of mindfulness meditation for the self-regulation of chronic pain. *Journal of Behavioral Medicine, 8,* 163–190.

Kabat-Zinn, J., Wheeler, E., Light, T., Skillings, A., Scharf, M. J., Cropley, T. G., Hosmer, D., & Bernhard, J. D. (1998). Influence of a mindfulness meditation–based stress reduction intervention on rates of skin clearing in patients with moderate to severe psoriasis undergoing phototherapy (UVB) and photochemotherapy (PUVA). *Psychosomatic Medicine, 60,* 625–632.

Kagan, J. (2010). Emotions and temperament. In M. H. Bornstein (Ed.), *Handbook of cultural developmental science.* New York: Psychology Press.

Kahn, A., & others. (1992) Sleep and cardiorespiratory characteristics of infant victim of sudden death: A prospective case-control study. *Sleep, 15,* 287–292.

Kahneman, D., & Klein, G. (2009). Conditions for intuitive experience: A failure to disagree. *American Psychologist, 64,* 515–526.

Kaiser Family Foundation. (2001). *Inside-OUT: A report on the experiences of lesbians, gays, and bisexuals in America and the public's views on issues and policies related to sexual orientation.* Menlo Park, CA: Henry J. Kaiser Family Foundation.

Kaiser, S., & others. (2010). Maintenance of real objects and their verbal designations in working memory. *Neuroscience Letters, 469,* 65–69.

Kaiyala, K. J., & others. (2010). Identification of body fat mass as a major determinant of metabolic rate in mice. *Diabetes.* (in press)

Kalichman, S. C. (2007). The theory of reasoned action and advances in HIV/AIDS prevention. In I. Ajzen, D. Albarracin, & R. Hornik (Eds.), *Prediction and change of health behavior.* Mahwah, NJ: Erlbaum.

Kamel, R. M. (2010). The onset of human parturition. *Archives of Gynecology and Obstetrics.* (in press)

Kameyama, K., Sohya, K., Ebina, T., Fukuda, A., Yanagawa, Y., & Tsumoto, T. (2010). Difference in binocularity and ocular dominance plasticity between GABAergic and excitatory cortical neurons. *Journal of Neuroscience, 30,* 1551–1559.

Kamin, L. J. (1968). Attention-like processes in classical conditioning. In M. R. Jones (Ed.), *Miami symposium on the prediction of behavior: Aversive stimuli.* Coral Gables, FL: University of Miami Press.

Kamphaus, R. W., & Kroncke, A. P. (2004). "Back to the future" of the Stanford-Binet Intelligence Scales. In M. Hersen (Ed.), *Comprehensive handbook of psychological assessment* (vol. 1). New York: Wiley.

Kanamaru, T., & Aihara, K. (2010). Roles of inhibitory neurons in rewiring-induced synchronization in pulse-coupled neural networks. *Neural Computation.* (in press)

Kandel, E. R., & Schwartz, J. H. (1982). Molecular biology of learning: Modulation of transmitter release. *Science, 218,* 433–443.

Kanov, J. M., Maitlis, S., Worline, M. C., Dutton, J. E., Frost, P. J., & Lilius, J. M. (2006). Compassion in organizational life. In J. V. Gallos (Ed.), *Organization development: A Jossey-Bass reader* (pp. 793–812). San Francisco: Jossey-Bass.

Kantowitz, B. H., Roediger, H. L., & Elmes, D. G. (2009). *Experimental psychology* (9th ed.). Belmont, CA: Wadsworth.

Kanwisher, N. (2006). Neuroscience: What's in a face? *Science, 311,* 617–618.

Kanwisher, N., & Yovel, G. (2010). Cortical specialization for face perception in humans. In J. T. Cacioppo & G. G. Berentson (Eds.), *Handbook of neuroscience for the behavioral sciences.* New York: Wiley. (in press)

Kaplan, H. S. (1974). *The new sex therapy: Active treatment of sexual dysfunctions.* New York: Routledge.

Kapur, S. (2003). Psychosis as a state of aberrant salience: A framework linking biology, phenomenology, and pharmacology. *American Journal of Psychiatry, 160,* 13–23.

Karasik, L. B., Adolph, K. E., Tamis-LeMonda, C. S., & Bornstein, M. H. (2010). WEIRD walking: Cross-cultural differences in motor development. *Behavior and Brain Sciences.* (in press)

Karau, S. J., & Williams, K. D. (1993). Social loafing: A meta-analytic review and theoretical integration. *Journal of Personality and Social Psychology, 65,* 681–706.

Karlsen, P. J., Allen, R. J., Baddeley, A. D., & Hitch, G. J. (2010). Binding across space and time in visual working memory. *Memory and Cognition, 33,* 292–303.

Karnes, F. A., & Stephens, K. R. (2008). *Achieving excellence: Educating the gifted and the talented.* Upper Saddle River, NJ: Prentice-Hall.

Kaskutas, L. A. (2009). Alcoholics Anonymous effectivness: Faith meets science. *Journal of Addictive Diseases, 28,* 145–157.

Kaskutas, L. A., Subbaraman, M. S., Witbordt, J., & Zemore, S. E. (2009). Effectiveness of making Alcoholics Anonymous easier: A group format 12-step facilitation approach. *Journal of Substance Abuse Treatment, 37* (3), 228–239.

Kasliwal, R., Wilton, L. V., & Shakir, S. A. (2009). Safety and drug utilization profile of varenicline as used in general practice in England: Interim results from a prescription-event monitoring study. *Drug Safety, 32,* 499–507.

Kasser, T., & Ryan, R. M. (1993). A dark side of the American dream: Correlates of financial success as a central life aspiration. *Journal of Personality and Social Psychology, 65,* 410–422.

Kasser, T., & Ryan, R. M. (1996). Further examining the American dream: Differential correlates of intrinsic and extrinsic goals. *Personality and Social Psychology Bulletin, 22,* 280–287.

Kasser, T., Ryan, R. M., Couchman, C. E., & Sheldon, K. M. (2004). Materialistic values: Their causes and consequences. In T. Kasser & A. D. Kanner (Eds.), *Psychology and consumer culture: The struggle for a good life in a materialistic world* (pp. 11–28). Washington, DC: American Psychological Association.

Kasser, T., & Sharma, Y. S. (1999). Reproductive freedom, educational equality, and females' preference for resource-acquisition characteristics in mates. *Psychological Science, 10,* 374–377.

Kato, I., & others. (2003). Incomplete arousal processes in infants who were victims of sudden death. *American Journal of Respiratory Critical Care Medicine, 168,* 1298–1303.

Katschnig, H. (2010). Are psychiatrists an endangered species? Observations on internal and external challenges to the profession. *World Psychiatry, 9,* 21–28.

Katz, J. N. (1995). *The invention of heterosexuality.* New York: Dutton.

Katzman, M. A. (2009). Current considerations in the treatment of generalized anxiety disorder. *CNS Drugs, 23,* 103–120.

Kauffman, C., & Silberman, J. (2009). Finding and fostering the positive in relationships: Positive interventions in couples therapy. *Journal of Clinical Psychology, 65,* 520–531.

Kaye, W. (2008). Neurobiology of anorexia and bulimia nervosa. *Physiology & Behavior, 94,* 121–135.

Kazdin, A. E. (2007). Mediators and mechanisms of change in psychotherapy change. *Annual Review of Clinical Psychology* (vol. 3). Palo Alto, CA: Annual Reviews.

Kazdin, A. E., & Benjet, C. (2003). Spanking children: Evidence and issues. *Current Directions in Psychological Science, 12,* 99–103.

Keeley, J., Zayac, R., & Correia, C. (2008). Curvilinear relationships between statistics anxiety and performance among undergraduate students: Evidence for optimal anxiety. *Statistics Education Research Journal, 7,* 4–15.

Keen, R. (2011). Prefatory. *Annual Review of Psychology* (vol. 62). Palo Alto, CA: Annual Reviews.

Keeton, C. P., Kolos, A. C., & Walkup, J. T. (2009). Pediatric generalized anxiety disorder: Epidemiology, diagnosis, and management. *Pediatric Drugs, 11,* 171–183.

Kegeles, L. S., & others. (2010). Increased synaptic dopamine function in associative regions of the striatum in schizophrenia. *Archives of General Psychiatry, 67,* 231–239.

Keillor, J. M., Barrett, A. M., Crucian, G. P., Kortenkamp, S., & Heilman, K. M. (2002). Emotional experience and perception in the absence of facial feedback. *Journal of the International Neuropsychological Society, 8,* 130–135.

Keitner, G. I., Ryan, C. E., & Solomon, D. A. (2009). Family focused therapy shortens recovery time from depression but not mania in adolescents with bipolar disorder. *Evidence Based Mental Health, 12,* 48.

Keller, M. P., & Attie, A. D. (2010). Physiological insights gained from gene expression analysis in obesity and diabetes. *Annual Review of Nutrition* (vol. 30). Palo Alto, CA: Annual Reviews.

Kellerman, A. L., & others. (1993). Gun ownership as a risk factor for homicide in the home. *New England Journal of Medicine, 329,* 1084–1091.

Kelley, H. H. (1973). The processes of causal attribution. *American Psychologist, 28,* 107–128.

Kellner, C. H., Knapp, R. G., Petrides, G., Rummans, T. A., Husain, M. M., Rasmussen, K., Mueller, M., & Kelly, G. F. (2006). *Sexuality today* (8th ed.). New York: McGraw-Hill.

Kelly, J. F., Dow, S. J., Yeterian, J. D., & Kahler, C. W. (2010). Can 12-step group participation strengthen and extend the benefits of adolescent addiction treatment? A prospective analysis. *Drug and Alcohol Dependence.* (in press)

Kelly, J. W., & McNamara, T. P. (2009). Facilitated pointing to remembered objects: Evidence for egocentric retrieval or for spatial priming. *Psychonomic Bulletin and Review, 16,* 295–300.

Kelsch, W., Sim, S., & Lois, C. E. (2010). Watching synaptogenesis in the human brain. *Annual Review of Neuroscience* (vol. 33). Palo Alto, CA: Annual Reviews.

Keltner, D., & Ekman, P. (2000). Emotion: An overview. In A. Kazdin (Ed.), *Encyclopedia of psychology.* Washington, DC, and New York: American Psychological Association and Oxford University Press.

Kemmerer, D., & Gonzalez-Castillo, J. (2010). The two-level theory of verb meaning: An approach to integrating the semantics of action with the mirror neuron system. *Brain and Language, 112,* 54–76.

Kemp, C., & Tenenbaum, J. B. (2009). Structured statistical models of inductive reasoning. *Psychological Review, 116,* 20–58.

Kemppainen, H., Raivio, N., Nurmi, H., & Kiianmaa, K. (2010). GABA and glutamate overflow in the VTA and ventral pallidum of alcohol-preferring AA and alcohol-avoiding ANA rats after ethanol. *Alcohol and Alcoholism, 45,* 111–118.

Kennard, B. D., & others. (2008). Cognitive-behavioral therapy to prevent relapse in pediatric responders to pharmacotherapy for major depressive disorder. *Journal of the American Academy of Child and Adolescent Psychiatry, 47,* 1395–1404.

Kennedy, G. J., Haque, M., & Zarankow, B. (1997). Human sexuality in late life. *International Journal of Mental Health, 26,* 35–46.

Kennedy, J. E., & others. (2010). Posttraumatic stress symptoms in OIF/OEF service members with blast-related and non-blast-related mild TBI. *NeuroRehabilitation, 26,* 223–231.

Kenrick, D. T., Griskevicius, V., Neuberg, S. L., & Schaller, M. (2010). Renovating the pyramid of needs: Contemporary extensions built upon ancient foundations. *Perspectives on Psychological Science, 5,* 292–314.

Kensinger, E. A., & Choi, E. S. (2009). When side matters: Hemispheric processing and the visual specificity of emotional memories. *Journal of Experimental Psychology: Learning, Memory, and Cognition, 35,* 247–253.

Kern, M. L., & Friedman, H. S. (2008). Do conscientious individuals live longer? A quantitative review. *Health Psychology, 27,* 505–512.

Kerns, J. G., Berenbaum, H., Barch, D. M., Banich, M. T., & Stolar, N. (1999). Word production in schizophrenia and its relationship to positive symptoms. *Psychiatry Research, 87,* 29–37.

Kerr, N. L. (2010). Explorations in juror emotion and juror judgment. In B. H. Bornstein & R. L. Wiener (Eds.), *Emotion and the law: Psychological perspectives* (pp. 97–132). New York: Springer.

Kessler, R. C., Chiu, W. T., Demler, O., & Walters, E. E. (2005). Prevalence, severity, and comorbidity of twelve-month DSM-IV disorders in the National Comorbidity Survey Replication (NCS-R). *Archives of General Psychiatry, 62,* 617–627.

Khatapoush, S., & Hallfors, D. (2004). "Sending the wrong message": Did medical marijuana legalization in California change attitudes about and use of marijuana? *Journal of Drug Issues, 34,* 751–770.

Kibler, J. L. (2009). Posttraumatic stress and cardiovascular disease risk. *Journal of Trauma and Dissociation, 10,* 135–150.

Kiecolt-Glaser, J. K. (2009). Psychoneuroimmunology: Psychology's gateway to the biomedical future. *Perspectives on Psychological Science, 4,* 367–369.

Kiecolt-Glaser, J. K. (2010). Stress, food, and inflammation: Psychoneuroimmunology and nutrition at the cutting edge. *Psychosomatic Medicine, 72,* 365–372.

Kiecolt-Glaser, J. K., & others. (2010). Stress, inflammation, and yoga practice. *Psychosomatic Medicine, 72,* 113–121.

Kiess, H. O., & Green, B. A. (2010). *Statistical concepts for the behavioral sciences* (4th ed.). Boston: Allyn & Bacon.

Kihlstrom, J. (2005). Is hypnosis an altered state of consciousness or what?: Comment. *Contemporary Hypnosis, 22,* 34–38.

Kilicarslan, A., Isildak, M., Guven, G. S., Oz, S. G., Tannover, M. D., Duman, A. E., Saracbasi, O., & Sozen, T. (2006). Demographic, socio-economic, and educational aspects of obesity in an adult population. *Journal of the National Medical Association, 98,* 1313–1317.

Killgore, W., & Yurgelun-Todd, D. (2001). Sex differences in amygdala activation during the perception of facial affect. *NeuroReport, 12,* 2543–2547.

Killgore, W. D., Rosso, I. M., Gruber, S. A., & Yurgelun-Todd, D. A. (2009). Amygdala volume and verbal memory performance in schizophrenia and bipolar disorder. *Cognitive and Behavioral Neurology, 22,* 28–37.

Killgore, W. D. S., Killgore, D. B., Day, L. M., Li, C., Kamimori, G. H., & Balkin, T. J. (2007). The effects of 53 hours of sleep deprivation on moral judgment. *SLEEP, 30,* 345–352.

Kim, J. N., & Lee, B. M. (2007). Risk factors, health risks, and risk management for aircraft personnel and frequent flyers. *Journal of Toxicology and Environmental Health B: Critical Reviews, 10,* 223–234.

Kim, J. Y., Oh, D. J., Yoon, T. Y., Choi, J. M., & Choe, B. K. (2007). The impacts of obesity on psychological well-being: A cross-sectional study about depressive mood and quality of life. *Journal of Preventive Medicine and Public Health, 40,* 191–195.

Kim, S. C., Jo, Y. S., Kim, I. H., Kim, H., & Choi, J. S. (2010). Lack of medial prefrontal cortex activation underlies the immediate extinction deficit. *Journal of Neuroscience, 30,* 832–837.

Kimbrough, E., Magyari, T., Langenberg, P., Chesney, M., & Berman, B. (2010). Mindfulness intervention with child abuse survivors. *Journal of Clinical Psychology, 66,* 17–33.

Kindt, M., Soeter, M., & Vervliet, B. (2009). Beyond extinction: Erasing human fear responses and preventing the return of fear. *Nature Neuroscience, 12,* 256–258.

King, B. M. (2005). *Human sexuality today* (5th ed.). Upper Saddle River, NJ: Prentice-Hall.

King, L. A. (2001). The health benefits of writing about life goals. *Personality and Social Psychology Bulletin, 27,* 798–807.

King, L. A. (2002). Gain without pain: Expressive writing and self regulation. In S. J. Lepore & J. Smyth (Eds.), *The writing cure.* Washington, DC: American Psychological Association.

King, L. A. (2003). Measures and meanings: The use of qualitative data in social and personality psychology. In C. Sansone, C. Morf, & A. Panter (Eds.), *Handbook of methods in social psychology* (pp. 173–194). New York: Sage.

King, L. A. (2008). Personal goals and life dreams: Positive psychology and motivation in daily life. In W. Gardner & J. Shah (Eds.), *Handbook of motivation science* (pp. 518–532). New York: Guilford.

King, L. A., Burton, C. M., & Geise, A. (2009). The good (gay) life: The search for signs of maturity in the narratives of gay adults. In P. Hammack & B. J. Kohler (Eds.), *The story of sexual identity: Narrative, social change, and the development of sexual orientation* (pp. 375–396). New York: Oxford University Press.

King, L. A., & Hicks, J. A. (2007). Whatever happened to "what might have been"? Regret, happiness, and maturity. *American Psychologist, 62,* 625–636.

King, L. A., & Hicks, J. A. (2010). Positive affect and meaning in life: The intersection of hedonism and eudaimonia. In P. T. Wong, P. T. Wong, & P. S. Fry (Eds.), *The human quest for meaning* (2nd ed.). New York: Oxford University Press. (in press)

King, L. A., Hicks, J. A., Krull, J., & Del Gaiso, A. K. (2006). Positive affect and the experience of meaning in life. *Journal of Personality and Social Psychology, 90,* 179–196.

King, L. A., & Miner, K. N. (2000). Writing about the perceived benefits of traumatic life events: Implications for physical health. *Personality and Social Psychology Bulletin, 26,* 220–230.

King, L. A., Scollon, C. K., Ramsey, C. M., & Williams, T. (2000). Stories of life transition: Happy endings, subjective well-being, and ego development in parents of children with Down syndrome. *Journal of Research in Personality, 34,* 509–536.

King, L. A., & Smith, S. N. (2005). Happy, mature, and gay: Intimacy, power, and difficult times in coming out stories. *Journal of Research in Personality, 39,* 278–298.

King, P. E., & Roeser, R. W. (2009). Religion and spirituality in adolescent development. In R. W. Lerner & L. Steinberg (Eds.), *Handbook of adolescent psychology* (3rd ed.). New York: Wiley.

Kinney, A. (2005, September 1). Looting or finding? *Salon.com.* http://dir.salon.com/story/news/feature/2005/09/01/photo_controversy/index.html (accessed March 21, 2009)

Kinney, H. (2009). Neuropathology provides new insight in the pathogenesis of the sudden infant death syndrome. *Acta Neuropathologica, 117,* 247–255.

Kinnish, K. K., Strassberg, D. S., & Turner, C. M. (2005). Sex differences in the flexibility of sexual orientation: A multidimensional retrospective assessment. *Archives of Sexual Behavior, 35,* 173–183.

Kinon, B. J., Chen, L., Ascher-Svanum, H., Stauffer, V. L., Kollack-Walker, S., Zhou, W., Kapur, S., Kane, J. M., & Naber, D. (2010). Challenging the assumption that improvement in functional outcomes is delayed relative to improvement in symptoms in the treatment of schizophrenia. *Schizophrenia Research.* (in press)

Kinsey, A. C., Martin, C. E., & Pomeroy, W. B. (1953). *Sexual behavior in the human female.* Philadelphia: Saunders.

Kinsey, A. C., Pomeroy, W. B., & Martin, C. E. (1948). *Sexual behavior in the human male.* Philadelphia: Saunders.

Kirby, D. B. (2008). The impact of abstinence and comprehensive sex and STD/HIV education programs on adolescent sexual behavior. *Sexuality Research & Social Policy, 5,* 18–27.

Kirby, D. B., Laris, B. A., & Rolleri, L. A. (2007). Sex and HIV education programs: Their impact on sexual behavior of young people throughout the world. *Journal of Adolescent Health, 40,* 206–217.

Kirchhoff, B. A., & Buckner, R. L. (2006). Functional-anatomic correlates of individual differences in memory. *Neuron, 51,* 263–274.

Kishioka, A., & others. (2009). A novel form of memory for auditory fear conditioning at a low-intensity unconditioned stimulus. *PLoS One, 4,* e4157.

Kitayama, S. (2011). Psychology and culture: Cross-country or regional comparisons. *Annual Review of Psychology* (vol. 62). Palo Alto, CA: Annual Reviews.

Kitayama, S., & Cohen, D. (Eds.). (2007). *Handbook of cultural psychology.* New York: Guilford.

Kitchener, K. S., King, P. M., & DeLuca, S. (2006). The development of reflective judgment in adulthood. In C. Hoare (Ed.), *Handbook of adult development and learning.* New York: Oxford University Press.

Kjaer, S. L., Wegener, G., Rosenberg, R., Lund, S. P., & Hougaard, K. S. (2010). Prenatal and adult stress interplay—Behavioral implications. *Brain Research, 1320,* 106–113.

Kjelsberg, E. (2005). Conduct disordered adolescents hospitalised 1963–1990. Secular trends in criminal activity. *European Journal of Child and Adolescent Psychiatry, 14,* 191–199.

Klein, B., & others. (2010). A therapist-assisted cognitive behavior therapy internet intervention for posttraumatic stress disorder: Pre-, post-, and 3-month follow-up results from an open trial. *Journal of Anxiety Disorders, 24,* 635–644.

Klein, S. B. (2009). *Learning.* Thousand Oaks, CA: Sage.

Kligman, D. H. (2010). The logic of psychoanalytic interpretation. *Psychoanalytic Quarterly, 79,* 491–522.

Klimstra, T. A., Hale, W. W., Raaijmakers, Q. A., Branje, S. J., & Meeus, W. H. (2009). Maturation of personality in adolescence. *Journal of Personality and Social Psychology, 96,* 898–912.

Klinesmith, J., Kasser, T., & McAndrew, F. T. (2006). Guns, testosterone, and aggression: An experimental test of a mediational hypothesis. *Psychological Science, 17,* 568–571.

Klingenberg, C. P., & others. (2010). Prenatal alcohol exposure alters the pattern of facial asymmetry. *Alcohol.* (in press)

Klosterhalfen, S., Rüttgers, A., Krumrey, E., Otto, B., Stockhorst, U., Riepl, R. L., Probst, T., & Enck, P. (2000). Pavlovian conditioning of taste aversion using a motion sickness paradigm. *Psychosomatic Medicine, 62,* 671–677.

Klucharev, V., Hytonen, K., Rijpkema, M., Smidts, A., & Fernandez, G. (2009). Reinforcement learning signal predicts social conformity. *Neuron, 61,* 140–151.

Klumpp, H., & Amir, N. (2009). Examination of vigilance and disengagement of threat in social anxiety with a probe detection task. *Anxiety, Stress, and Coping, 2,* 1–13.

Klusmann, V., & others. (2010)). Complex mental and physical activity in older women and cognitive performance: A 6-month randomized controlled trial. *Journals of Gerontology A: Biological Sciences and Medical Sciences, 65,* 680–688.

Knapp, H. (2007). *Therapeutic communication.* Thousand Oaks, CA: Sage.

Knapp, S., & VandeCreek, L. (2000). Recovered memories of childhood abuse: Is there an underlying consensus? *Professional Psychology: Research and Practice, 31,* 365–371.

Knight, D. C., Waters, N. S., King, M. K., & Bandettini, P. A. (2010). Learning-related diminution of unconditioned SCR and fMRI signal responses. *NeuroImage, 49,* 843–848.

Knoblauch, S. H. (2009). From self psychology to selves in relationships: A radical process of micro and macro expansion in conceptual experience. *Annals of the New York Academy of Sciences, 1159,* 262–278.

Knowles, E. S., Nolan, J., & Riner, D. D. (2007). Resistance to persuasion. In R. Baumeister & K. Vohs (Eds.), *Encyclopedia of social psychology.* Newbury Park, CA: Sage.

Kobasa, S., Maddi, S., & Kahn, S. (1982). Hardiness and health: A prospective study. *Journal of Personality and Social Psychology, 42,* 168–177.

Kobasa, S. C., Maddi, S. R., Puccetti, M. C., & Zola, M. (1986). Relative effectiveness of hardiness, exercise, and social support as resources against illness. *Journal of Psychosomatic Research, 29,* 525–533.

Kobayashi, S., Pinto de Carvalho, O., & Schultz, W. (2010). Adaptation of reward sensitivity in orbitofrontal neurons. *Journal of Neuroscience, 30,* 534–544.

Koch, C. (2011). Neuroscience of consciousness. *Annual Review of Psychology* (vol. 62). Palo Alto, CA: Annual Reviews.

Kochanek, K. D., Murphy, S. L. Anderson, R. N, & Scott, C. (2004, October 12). Deaths: Final data for 2002. *National Vital Statistics Reports, 53* (5). Washington, DC: U.S. Department of Health and Human Services.

Kochanska, G., Aksan, N., Prisco, T. R., & Adams, E. E. (2008). Mother-child and father-child mutually responsive orientation in the first two years and children's outcomes at preschool age: Mechanisms of influence. *Child Development, 79,* 30–44.

Kodama, S., & others. (2009). Cardiorespiratory fitness as a quantitative predictor of all-cause mortality and cardiovascular events in healthy men and women: A meta-analysis. *Journal of the American Medical Association, 301,* 2024–2035.

Koepp, M. J., Hammers, A., Lawrence, A. D., Asselin, M. C., Grasby, P. M., & Bench, C. J. (2009). Evidence for endogenous opioid release in the amygdale during positive emotion. *NeuroImage, 44,* 252–256.

Koestner, R., Horberg, E. J., Gaudreau, P., Powers, T., Di Dio, P., Bryan, C., Jochum, R., & Salter, N. (2006). Bolstering implementation plans for the long haul: The benefits of simultaneously boosting self-concordance or self-efficacy. *Personality and Social Psychology Bulletin, 32,* 1547–1558.

Kohlberg, L. (1958). *The development on modes of moral thinking and choice in the years 10 to 16.* Unpublished doctoral dissertation, University of Chicago.

Kohlberg, L. (1986). A current statement on some theoretical issues. In S. Modgil & C. Modgil (Eds.), *Lawrence Kohlberg.* Philadelphia: Falmer.

Kohler, C. L., Schoenberger, Y., Tseng, T., & Ross, L. (2008). Correlates of transitions in stage of change for quitting among adolescent smokers. *Addictive Behaviors, 33,* 1615–1618.

Kohler, P. K., Manhart, L. E., & Lafferty, W. E. (2008). Abstinence-only and comprehensive sex education and the initiation of sexual activity and teen pregnancy. *Journal of Adolescent Health, 42,* 344–351.

Köhler, W. (1925). *The mentality of apes.* New York: Harcourt Brace Jovanovich.

Kohrt, B. A., & others. (2009). Culture in psychiatric epidemiology: Using ethnography and multiple mediator models to assess the relationship of caste with depression and anxiety in Nepal. *Annals of Human Biology, 36,* 261–280.

Kohut, H. (1977). *Restoration of the self.* New York: International Universities Press.

Koitabashi, T., Oyaizu, T., & Ouchi, T. (2009). Low bispectral index values following electroconvulsive therapy associated with memory impairment. *Journal of Anesthesiology, 23,* 182–187.

Kok, B. E., Catalino, L. I., & Fredrickson, B. L. (2008). The broadening, building, buffering effects of positive emotion. In S. J. Lopez (Ed.), *Positive psychology: Exploring the best of people* (vol. 3). Westport, CT: Greenwood.

Kok, G., & de Vries, N. K. (2006). Social psychology and health promotion. In P. A. M. Van Lange (Ed.), *Bridging social psychology.* Mahwah, NJ: Erlbaum.

Kong, L. L., Allen, J. J. B., & Glisky, E. L. (2008). Interidentity memory transfer in dissociative identity disorder. *Journal of Abnormal Psychology, 117,* 686–692.

Konrath, S., Bushman, B. J., & Campbell, W. K. (2006). Attenuating the link between threatened egotism and aggression. *Psychological Science, 17,* 995–1001.

Koo, M. S., Kim, E. J., Roh, D., & Kim, C. H. (2010). Role of dopamine in the pathophysiology and treatment of obsessive-compulsive disorder. *Expert Review of Neurotherapeutics, 10,* 275–290.

Koob, G. F. (2006). The neurobiology of addiction: A neuroadaptational view. *Addiction, 101, Suppl. 1,* S23–S30.

Kopell, B. H., Machado, A. G., & Rezai, A. R. (2006). Not your father's lobotomy: Psychiatric surgery revisited. *Clinical Neurosurgery, 52,* 315–330.

Korczak, D. J., & Goldstein, B. I. (2009). Childhood onset major depressive disorder: Course of illness and psychiatric comorbidity in a community sample. *Journal of Pediatrics, 155,* 118–123.

Korzekwa, M. I., Dell, P. F., Links, P. S., Thabane, L., & Webb, S. P. (2008). Estimating the prevalence of borderline personality disorder in psychiatric outpatients using a two-phase procedure. *Comprehensive Psychiatry, 49* (4), 380–386.

Kosslyn, S. M., Thompson, W. L., Kim, I. J., Rauch, S. L., & Alpert, N. M. (1996). Individual differences in cerebral blood flow in Area 17 predict the time to evaluate visualized letters. *Journal of Cognitive Neuroscience, 8,* 78–82.

Koszycki, D., Taljaard, M., Segal, Z., & Bradwein, J. (2010). A randomized trial of sertraline, self-administered cognitive behavior therapy, and their combination for panic disorder. *Psychological Medicine.* (in press)

Kovacs, A. M. (2009). Early bilingualism enhances mechanisms of false-belief reasoning. *Developmental Science, 12,* 48–54.

Kovacs, K., Lajtha, A., & Sershen, H. (2010). Effect of nicotine and cocaine on neurofilaments and receptors in whole brain tissue and synaptoneurosome preparations. *Brain Research Bulletin.* (in press)

Kovalszky, I., & others. (2010). Leptin-based glycopeptide induces weight loss and simultaneously restores fertility in animal models. *Diabetes, Obesity, and Metabolism, 12,* 393–402.

Kozaric-Kovacic, D. (2008). Integrative psychotherapy. *Psychiatria Danubina, 20,* 352–363.

Kozel, F. A., & others. (2009). Functional MRI detection of deception after commiting a mock sabotage crime. *Journal of Forensic Science, 54,* 220–231.

Kraemer, B., Noll, T., Delsignore, A., Milos, G., Schnyder, U., & Hepp, U. (2006). Finger length ratio (2D:4D) and dimensions of sexual orientation. *Neuropsychobiology, 53,* 210–214.

Kramer, A. F., & Morrow, D. (2010). Cognitive training and expertise. In D. Park & N. Schwartz (Eds.), *Cognitive aging: A primer.* New York: Psychology Press. (in press)

Kranz, G. S., Kasper, S., & Lanzenberger, R. (2010). Reward and the serotonergic system. *Neuroscience.* (in press)

Krause, N. (2006). Religion and health in late life. In J. E. Birren & K. W. Schaie (Eds.), *Handbook of the psychology of aging* (6th ed.). San Diego: Academic.

Krebs, T. S., Johansen, P. Ø., Jerome, L., & Halpern, J. H. (2009). Importance of psychiatric confounding in non-randomized studies of heavy ecstasy users. *Psychological Medicine, 39,* 876–878.

Kressel, L. M., & Uleman, J. S. (2010). Personality traits function as causal concepts. *Journal of Experimental Social Psychology, 46,* 213–216.

Kring, A. M., Davison, G. C., Neale, J. M., & Johnson, S. L. (2007). *Abnormal psychology* (10th ed.). New York: Wiley.

Kristof-Brown, A., & Guay, R. P. (2010). Person–environment fit. In S. Zedeck (Ed.), *APA handbook of industrial and organizational psychology.* Washington, DC: APA. (in press)

Kroger, J., Martinussen, M., & Marcia, J. E. (2010). Identity change in adolescence and young adulthood: A meta-analysis. *Journal of Adolescence.* (in press)

Krogstad, U., Hofoss, D., Veenstra, M., & Hjortdahl, P. (2006). Predictors of job satisfaction among doctors, nurses and auxiliaries in Norwegian hospitals: Relevance for micro unit culture. *Human Resources for Health, 4,* 3.

Kroth, R., & others. (2010). Murine features of neurogenesis in the human hippocampus across the lifespan from 0 to 100 years. *PLoS One, 5,* e8809.

Krueger, J. I. (2007). From social projection to social behaviour. *European Review of Social Psychology, 18,* 1–35.

Krueger, K. A., & Dayan, P. (2009). Flexible shaping: How learning in small steps helps. *Cognition, 110,* 380–394.

Krueger, R. F., Markon, K. E., & Bouchard, T. J. (2003). The extended genotype: The heritability of personality accounts for the heritability of recalled family environments in twins reared apart. *Journal of Personality, 71,* 809–833.

Kruger, J., Blanck, H. M., & Gillespie, C. (2006). Dietary and physical activity behaviors among adults successful at weight loss maintenance. *International Journal of Behavioral Nutrition and Physical Activity, 3,* 17.

Ksir, C. J., Hart, C. L., & Ray, O. S. (2008). *Drugs, society, and human behavior* (12th ed.). New York: McGraw-Hill.

Kuan, T. S. (2009). Current studies on myofascial pain syndrome. *Current Pain and Headache Reports, 13,* 365–369.

Kuczynski, B., & others. (2010). White matter integrity and cortical metabolic associations in aging and dementia. *Alzheimer's and Dementia, 6,* 54–62.

Kudo, K., & others. (2010). Differences in CT perfusion maps generated by different commercial software: Quantitative analysis by using identical source data of acute stroke patients. *Radiology, 254,* 200–209.

Kuhl, P. K. (2000). A new view of language acquisition. *Proceedings of the National Academy of Sciences USA, 97,* 11850–11857.

Kuhl, P. K. (2007). Is speech learning "gated" by the social brain? *Developmental Science, 10,* 110–120.

Kuhl, P. K., & Damasio, A. (2009). In E. R. Kandel & others (Eds.), *Principles of neural science* (5th ed.). New York: McGraw-Hill.

Kuhn, D. (2008). Formal operations from a twenty-first-century perspective. *Human Development, 51,* 48–55.

Kuhn, D. (2009). Adolescent thinking. In R. M. Lerner & L. Steinberg (Eds.), *Handbook of adolescent psychology* (3rd ed.). New York: Wiley.

Kuhn, D. (2011). What is scientific thinking and how does it develop? In U. Goswami (Ed.), *Wiley-Blackwell handbook of childhood cognitive development* (2nd ed.). New York: Wiley Blackwell.

Kujanik, S., & Mikulecky, M. (2010). Circadian and ultradian extrasystole rhythms in healthy individuals at elevated versus lowland altitudes. *International Journal of Biometeorology.* (in press)

Kullmann, D. M. (2010). The neurological channelpathies. *Annual Review of Neuroscience* (vol. 33). Palo Alto, CA: Annual Reviews.

Kumar, C. T. S. (2004). Physical illness and schizophrenia. *British Journal of Psychiatry, 184,* 541.

Kuntsche, E., Knibbe, R., Gmel, G., & Engels, R. (2006). Who drinks and why? A review of socio-demographic, personality, and contextual issues behind the drinking motives in young people. *Addictive Behaviors, 31,* 1844–1857.

Kurdek, L. (1992). Relationship quality in gay and lesbian cohabiting couples: A prospective longitudinal test of the contextual and interdependence models. *Journal of Social and Personal Relationships, 9,* 125–142.

Kurdek, L. (2004). Are gay and lesbian cohabiting couples *really* different from heterosexual married couples? *Journal of Marriage and Family, 66,* 880–900.

Kurson, R. (2007). *Crashing through: A true story of risk, adventure, and the man who dared to see.* New York: Random House.

Kurtz, J. (2008). Looking to the future to appreciate the present. *Psychological Science, 19,* 1238–1241.

Kushner, M. G. (2007). The use of cognitive-behavioral therapy in the University of Minnesota's outpatient psychiatry clinic. *Minnesota Medicine, 90,* 31–33.

Kushner, R. F. (2007). Obesity management. *Gastroenterology Clinics of North America, 36,* 191–210.

Kuyper, P. (1972). The cocktail party effect. *Audiology, 11,* 277–282.

L

Labouvie-Vief, G. (1986, August). *Modes of knowing and life-span cognition.* Paper presented at the meeting of the American Psychological Association, Washington, DC.

Labouvie-Vief, G. (2006). Emerging structures of adult thought. In J. J. Arnett & J. L. Tanner (Eds.), *Emerging adults in America* (pp. 60–84). Washington, DC: American Psychological Association.

Lac, A., Alvaro, E. M., Crano, W. D., & Siegel, J. T. (2009). Pathways from parental knowledge and warmth to adolescent marijuana use: An extension to the theory of planned behavior. *Prevention Science, 10,* 22–32.

Lachman, M. E., Rocke, C., Rosnick, C., & Ryff, C. D. (2008). Realism and illusion in Americans' temporal views of their life satisfaction: Age differences in reconstructing the past and anticipating the future. *Psychological Science, 19,* 89–897.

Lader, M., Tylee, A., & Donoghue, J. (2009). Withdrawing benzodiazepines in primary care. *CNS Drugs, 23,* 19–34.

LaFromboise, T. D., Albright, K., & Harris, A. (2010). Patterns of hopelessness among American Indian adolescents: Relationships by levels of acculturation and residence. *Cultural Diversity and Ethnic Minority Psychology, 16,* 68–76.

Lai, C., & Bird, S. (2010). Querying linguistic trees. *Journal of Logic, Language and Information, 19,* 53–73.

Laible, D. J., & Thompson, R. A. (2000). Mother–child discourse, attachment security, shared positive affect, and early conscience development. *Child Development, 71,* 1424–1440.

Laible, D. J., & Thompson, R. A. (2002). Mother–child conflict in the toddler years: Lessons in emotion, morality, and relationships. *Child Development, 73,* 1187–1203.

Laible, D. J., & Thompson, R. A. (2007). Early socialization: A relationship perspective. In J. E. Grusec & P. D. Hastings (Eds.), *Handbook of socialization.* New York: Guilford.

Lam, C. B., & McBride-Chang, C. A. (2007). Resilience in young adulthood: The moderating influences of gender-related personality traits and coping flexibility. *Sex Roles, 56,* 159–172.

Lambert, M. J. (2001). The effectiveness of psychotherapy: What a century of research tells us about the effects of treatment. *Psychotherapeutically speaking--Updates from the Division of Psychotherapy* (29). Washington, DC: American Psychological Association.

Lamberton, L., & Minor-Evans, L. (2010). *Human relations* (4th ed.). New York: McGraw-Hill.

Lambon Ralph, M. A., Sage, K., Jones, R. W., & Mayberry, E. J. (2010). Coherent concepts are computed in the anterior temporal lobes. *Proceedings of the National Academy of Sciences USA.* (in press)

Laming, D. (2010). Serial position curves in free recall. *Psychological Review, 117,* 93–133.

Landau, M. E., & Barner, K. C. (2009). Vestibulocochlear nerve. *Seminars in Neurology, 29,* 66–73.

Landis, C., & Erlick, D. (1950). An analysis of the Porteus Maze Test as affected by psychosurgery. *American Journal of Psychology, 63,* 557–566.

Lane, S. M., & Schooler, J. W. (2004). Skimming the surface: Verbal overshadowing of analogical retrieval. *Psychological Science, 15,* 715–719.

Laney, C., & Loftus, E. F. (2009). Eyewitness memory. In R. N. Kocsis (Ed.), *Applied criminal psychology.* Springfield, IL: Thomas.

Lange, C. G. (1922). *The emotions.* Baltimore: Williams & Wilkins.

Langer, E., Blank, A., & Chanowitz, B. (1978). The mindlessness of ostensibly thoughtful action: The role of "placebic" information in interpersonal interaction. *Journal of Personality and Social Psychology, 36* (6), 635–642.

Langer, E. J. (1997). *The power of mindful learning.* Reading, MA: Addison-Wesley.

Langer, E. J. (2000). Mindful learning. *Current Directions in Psychological Science, 9,* 220–223.

Langer, E. J. (2005). *On becoming an artist.* New York: Ballantine.

Langer, E. J., & Rodin, J. (1976). The effects of choice and enhanced personal responsibility for the aged: A field experiment in an institutional setting. *Journal of Personality and Social Psychology, 34,* 191–198.

Langer, J. J. (1991). *Holocaust testimonies: The ruins of memory.* New Haven, CT: Yale University Press.

Langleben, D. D., & Dattilio, F. M. (2008). Commentary: The future of forensic functional brain imaging. *Journal of the American Academy of Psychiatry and the Law, 36,* 502–504.

Langlois, J. H., Kalakanis, L., Rubenstein, A. J., Larson, A., Hallam, M., & Smoot, M. (2000). Maxims or myths of beauty? A meta-analytic and theoretical review. *Psychological Bulletin, 126,* 390–423.

Langlois, J. H., Roggman, L. A., & Musselman, L. (1994). What is average and what is not average about attractive faces? *Psychological Science, 5,* 214–220.

Langston, W. (2011). *Research methods: Laboratory manual for psychology* (3rd ed.). Boston: Cengage.

Langstrom, N. (2010). The DSM diagnostic criteria for exhibitionism, voyeurism, and frotteurism. *Archives of Sexual Behavior, 39,* 317–324.

Langstrom, N., Rahman, Q., Carlstrom, E., & Lichtenstein, P. (2010). Genetic and environmental effects on same-sex sexual behaviour: A population study of twins in Sweden. *Archives of Sexual Behavior, 39,* 75–80.

Lapierre, L. M., Spector, P. E., & Leck, J. D. (2005). Sexual versus non-sexual workplace aggression and victims' overall job satisfaction: A meta-analysis. *Journal of Occupational Health Psychology, 10,* 155–169.

Larson-Prior, L. J., Zempel, J. M., Nolan, T. S., Prior, F. W., Snyder, A. Z., & Rachlie, M. E. (2009). Cortical network functional connectivity in the descent to sleep. *Proceedings of the National Academy of Sciences USA, 106,* 4489–4494.

La Rue, A. (2010). Healthy brain aging: Role of cognitive reserve, cognitive stimulation, and cognitive exercises. *Clinics in Geriatric Medicine, 26*, 99–111.

Larzerele, R. E., & Kuhn, B. R. (2005). Comparing child outcomes of physical punishment and alternative discipline practices: A meta-analysis. *Clinical Child and Family Psychology Review, 8*, 1–37.

Lashley, K. (1950). In search of the engram. In *Symposium of the Society for Experimental Biology* (vol. 4). New York: Cambridge University Press.

Last, C. G. (2009). *When someone you love is bipolar.* New York: Guilford.

Latané, B. (1981). The psychology of social impact. *American Psychologist, 36*, 343–356.

Latrémolière, A., & Woolf, C. J. (2009). Central sensitization: A generator of pain hypersensitivity by central neural plasticity. *Journal of Pain, 10*, 895–926.

Laumann, E. O., Nicolosi, A., Glasser, D. B., Paik, A., & Gingell, C. (2005). Sexual problems among men and women aged 40–80 yrs: Prevalence and correlates identified in the global study of sexual attitudes and behaviours. *International Journal of Impotence Research, 17*, 39–57.

Laurence, J. (2006). Editorial: Treating HIV with one pill per day. *AIDS Patient Care and STD, 20*, 610–603.

Lawler-Row, K. A., Karremans, J. C., Scott, C., Edlis-Matityahou, M., & Edwards, L. (2008). Forgiveness, physiological reactivity, and health: The role of anger. *International Journal of Psychophysiology, 68*, 51–58.

Lazarus, A. A., Beutler, L. E., & Norcross, J. C. (1992). The future of technical eclecticism. *Psychotherapy, 29*, 11–20.

Lazarus, R. S. (1991). On the primacy of cognition. *American Psychologist, 39*, 124–129.

Lazarus, R. S. (1993). Coping theory and research: Past, present, and future. *Psychosomatic Medicine, 55*, 234–247.

Lazarus, R. S. (2000). Toward better research on stress and coping. *American Psychologist, 55*, 665–673.

Lazarus, R. S. (2003). Does the positive psychology movement have legs? *Psychological Inquiry, 14*, 93–109.

Leaper, C., & Friedman, C. K. (2007). The socialization of gender. In J. E. Grusec & P. D. Hastings (Eds.), *Handbook of socialization.* New York: Guilford.

Leary, M. R. (2008). *Introduction to behavioral research methods* (5th ed.). Boston: Allyn & Bacon.

Leary, M. R., & Hoyle, R. H. (Eds.). (2009a). *Handbook of individual differences in social behavior.* New York: Guilford.

Leary, M. R., & Hoyle, R. H. (Eds.). (2009b). Situations, dispositions, and the study of social behavior. In M. R. Leary & R. H. Hoyle (Eds.), *Handbook of individual differences in social behavior* (pp. 3–11). New York: Guilford.

Leasure, J. L., & Decker, L. (2009). Social isolation prevents exercise-induced proliferation of hippocampal progenitor cells in female rats. *Hippocampus, 19*, 907–912.

Le Bel, R. M., Pineda, J. A., & Sharma, A. (2009). Motor-auditory-visual integration: The role of the human mirror neuron system in communication and communication disorders. *Journal of Communication Disorders, 42*, 299–304.

Lebrun-Julien, F., & others. (2010). ProNGF induces TNF (alpha)-dependent death of retinal ganglion cells through a p75NTR non-cell-autonomous signaling pathway. *Proceedings of the National Academy of Sciences USA.* (in press)

LeDoux, J. E. (1996). *The emotional brain: The mysterious underpinnings of emotional life.* New York: Simon & Schuster.

LeDoux, J. E. (2000). Emotion circuits in the brain. *Annual Review of Neuroscience, 23*, 155–184.

LeDoux, J. E. (2001). *Emotion, memory, and the brain.* http://www.cns.nyu.edu/home/ledoux.html (accessed October 15, 2001)

LeDoux, J. E. (2002). *The synaptic self.* New York: Viking.

LeDoux, J. E. (2008). Amygdala. *Scholarpedia, 3*, 2698.

LeDoux, J. E. (2009). Emotional coloration of consciousness: How feelings come about. In L. W. Weiskrantz & M. Davis (Eds.), *Frontiers of consciousness.* New York: Oxford University Press.

Lee, C. D., Blair, S. N., & Jackson, A. S. (1999). Cardiorespiratory fitness, body composition, and all-cause and cardiovascular disease mortality in men. *American Journal of Clinical Nutrition, 69*, 373–380.

Lee, J. W., & others. (2010). Evaluation of postoperative sharp waveforms through EEG and magnetoencephalography. *Journal of Clinical Neurophysiology, 27*, 7–11.

Lee, J. W. Y. (2010). Neuroleptic-induced catatonia: Clinical presentation, response to benzodiazepines, and relationship to neuroleptic malignant syndrome. *Journal of Clinical Psychopharmacology, 30*, 3–10.

Lee, M.-J., & Fried, S. K. (2009). Integration of hormonal and nutrient signals that regulate leptin synthesis and secretion. *American Journal of Physiology, Endocrinology, and Metabolism.* doi:10.1152/ajpendo.90927.2008

Lee, P. A., Houk, C. P., Ahmed, S. F., & Hughes, I. A. (2006). Consensus statement on management of intersex disorders. *Pediatrics, 118*, e488–e500.

Leedy, P. D., & Ormrod, J. E. (2010). *Practical research* (9th ed.). Upper Saddle River, NJ: Prentice-Hall.

Lefkowitz, J. (2000). The role of interpersonal affective regard in supervisory performance ratings: A literature review and proposed causal model. *Journal of Occupational and Organizational Psychology, 73*, 67–85.

Legaree, T. A., Turner, J., & Lollis, S. (2007). Forgiveness and therapy: A critical review of conceptualizations, practices, and values in the literature. *Journal of Marital and Family Therapy, 33*, 192–213.

le Grange, D., Lock, J., Loeb, K., & Nicholls, D. (2010). Academy for Eating Disorders position paper: The role of the family in eating disorders. *International Journal of Eating Disorders, 43*, 1–5.

Leibel, R. L. (2008). Molecular physiology of weight regulation in mice and humans. *International Journal of Obesity, 32, Suppl. 7*, S98–S108.

Leichtman, M. (2009). Concepts of development and the Rorschach: The contributions of Paul Lerner and John Exner in historical context. *Journal of Personality Assessment, 91*, 24–29.

Leigh, E. G. (2010). The group selection controversy. *Journal of Evolutionary Biology, 23*, 6–19.

Leo, J. L. (2005). Editorial: Methylphenidate-induced neuropathology in the developing rat brain: Implications for humans. *Ethical Human Psychology and Psychiatry, 7*, 107–110.

Leon, I. G. (2010). Understanding and treating infertility: Psychoanalytic considerations. *Journal of the American Academy of Psychoanalysis and Dynamic Psychiatry, 38*, 47–75.

Leonard, B. E., & Myint, A. (2009). The psychoneuroimmunology of stress. *Human Psychopharmacology, 24*, 165–175.

Lepage, J. F., & Theoret, H. (2010). Brain connectivity: Finding a cause. *Current Biology, 20*, R66–R67.

Lepper, M., Greene, D., & Nisbett, R. E. (1973). Undermining children's intrinsic interest with extrinsic rewards. *Journal of Personality and Social Psychology, 28*, 129–137.

Lepore, S. J., & Smyth, J. (Eds.). (2002). *The writing cure.* Washington, DC: American Psychological Association.

Lerner, B. H. (2005). Last-ditch medical therapy—revisiting lobotomy. *New England Journal of Medicine, 353*, 119–121.

Lerner, J. V., Phelps, E., Forman, Y. E., & Bowers, E. (2009). Positive youth development. In R. M. Lerner & L. Steinberg (Eds.), *Handbook of adolescent psychology* (3rd ed.). New York: Wiley.

Lerner, R. D., Boyd, M., & Du, D. (2008). Adolescent development. In I. B. Weiner & C. B. Craighead (Eds.), *Encyclopedia of psychology* (4th ed.). New York: Wiley.

Leslie, A. M., German, T. P., & Polizzi, P. (2005). Belief-desire reasoning as a process of selection. *Cognitive Psychology, 50*, 45–85.

Leslie, J. C., Shaw, D., Gregg, G., McCormick, N., Reynolds, D. S., & Dawson, G. R. (2006). Effects of reinforcement schedule on facilitation of operant extinction by chlordiazepoxide. *Journal of the Experimental Analysis of Behavior, 84*, 327–338.

Leszczynski, J. P. (2009). A state conceptualization: Are individuals' masculine and feminine personality traits situationally influenced? *Personality and Individual Differences, 47*, 157–162.

Leucht, S., Kissling, W., & Davis, J. M. (2009). Second-generation antipsychotics for schizophrenia: Can we resolve the conflict? *Psychological Medicine, 39*, 1591–1602.

Leung, A. K., Maddux, W. W., Galinsky, A. D., & Chiu, C. (2008). Multicultural experience enhances creativity. *American Psychologist, 63*, 169–181.

Lev, A. I. (2007). Transgender communities: Developing identity through connection. In K. J. Bieschke, R. M. Perez, & K. A. DeBord, (Eds.), *Handbook of counseling and psychotherapy with lesbian, gay, bisexual, and transgender clients* (2nd ed., pp. 147–175). Washington, DC: American Psychological Association.

Levenson, M. R., & Aldwin, C. M. (2006). Change in personality processes and health outcomes. In D. K. Mroczek & T. D. Little (Eds.), *Handbook of personality development* (pp. 423–444). Mahwah, NJ: Erlbaum.

Leventhal, H., & Tomarken, A. J. (1986). Emotion: Today's problems. *Annual Review of Psychology* (vol. 37). Palo Alto, CA: Annual Reviews.

Levi, D. (2007). *Group dynamics for teams* (2nd ed.). Thousand Oaks, CA: Sage.

Levin, B. E. (2010). Developmental gene × environment interactions affecting systems regulating homeostasis and obesity. *Frontiers in Neuroscience.* (in press)

Levin, C. (2010). The mind as a complex internal object: Inner estrangement. *Psychoanalytic Quarterly, 79,* 95–27.

Levin, J., & Fox, J. A. (2011). *Elementary statistics for social research* (3rd ed.). Upper Saddle River, NJ: Prentice-Hall.

Levine, D. S. (2000). *Introduction to neural and cognitive modeling* (2nd ed.). Mahwah, NJ: Erlbaum.

Levine, M., Cassidy, C., & Jentzsch I. (2010). The implicit identity effect: Identity primes, group size, and helping. *British Journal of Social Psychology.* (in press)

Levine, R. L. (2002). Endocrine aspects of eating disorders in adolescents. *Adolescent Medicine, 13,* 129–144.

Levine, S. C., Huttenlocher, J., Taylor, A., & Langrock, A. (1999). Early sex differences in spatial skill. *Developmental Psychology, 35,* 940–949.

Levinthal, C. F. (2010). *Drugs, behavior, and modern society* (6th ed.). Upper Saddle River, NJ: Prentice-Hall.

Levitan, E. B., Wolk, A., & Mittleman, M. A. (2009). Consistency with the DASH diet and the incidence of heart failure. *Archives of Internal Medicine, 169,* 851–857.

Levy, B. R., Slade, M. D., & Kasl, S. V. (2002). Increased longevity by positive self-perceptions of aging. *Journal of Personality and Social Psychology, 83,* 261–270.

Lewis, A., Williams, P., Lawrence, O., Wong, R. O., & Brockerhoff, S. E. (2010). Wild-type cone photoreceptors persist despite neighboring mutant cone degeneration. *Journal of Neuroscience, 30,* 382–389.

Lewis, G. D., & others. (2010). Metabolic signatures of exercise in human plasma. *Science Translation Medicine.* (in press)

Lewis, R. W., Yuan, J., & Wang, R. (2008). Male sexual arousal disorder. In D. L. Rowland & L. Incrocci (Eds.), *Handbook of sexual and gender identity disorders* (pp. 32–67). Hoboken, NJ: Wiley.

Li, Y., & Epley, N. (2009). When the best appears to be saved for last: Serial position effects on choice. *Journal of Behavioral Decision Making, 22,* 378–389.

Liang, B., Williams, L. M., & Siegel, J. A. (2006). Relational outcomes of childhood sexual trauma in female survivors: A longitudinal study. *Journal of Interpersonal Violence, 21,* 42–57.

Liao, K., Walker, M. F., Joshi, A. C., Reschke, M., Strupp, M., Wagner, J., & Leigh, R. J. (2010). The linear vestibulo-ocular reflex, locomotion and falls in neurological disorders. *Restorative Neurology and Neuroscience, 28,* 91–103.

Light, S. N., Goldsmith, H. H., Coan, J. A., Frye, C., & Davidson, R. J. (2009). Dynamic variation in pleasure in children predicts non-linear change in lateral frontal activity. *Developmental Psychology, 45,* 525–533.

Lilienfeld, S. O., Wood, J. M., & Garb, H. N. (2000, November). The scientific status of projective techniques. *Psychological Science in the Public Interest, 1* (2).

Lim, J., Bogossian, F., & Ahern, K. (2010). Stress and coping in Australian nurses: A systematic review. *International Nursing Review, 57,* 22–31.

Lin, L. (2009). Breadth-biased versus focused cognitive control in media multitasking behaviors. *Proceedings of the National Academy of Sciences USA, 106,* 15521–15522.

Lin, Y.-C., & Koleske, A. J. (2010). Mechanisms of synapse and dendrite maintenance and their disruption in psychiatric and neurogenerative disorders. *Annual Review of Neuroscience* (vol. 33). Palo Alto, CA: Annual Reviews.

Lindau, S. T., & Gavrilova, N. (2010). Sex, health, and years of sexually active life gained due to good health: Evidence from two U.S. population based cross sectional surveys of aging. *British Medical Journal.* (in press)

Linden, W., Lenz, J. W., & Con, A. H. (2001). Individualized stress management for primary hypertension: A randomized trial. *Archives of Internal Medicine, 161,* 1071–1080.

Lindvall, O., & Kokaia, Z. (2010). Stem cells in neurodegenerative disorders—time for clinical translation? *Journal of Clinical Investigation, 120,* 29–40.

Lindwall, M., Rennemark, M., Halling, A., Berglund, J., & Hassmen, P. (2007). Depression and exercise in elderly men and women: Findings from the Swedish national study on aging and care. *Journal of Aging and Physical Activity, 15,* 41–55.

Ling, G., Bandak, F., Armonda, R., Grant, G., & Ecklund, J. (2009). Explosive blast neurotrauma. *Journal of Neurotrauma, 26,* 815–825.

Lingjaerde, O., Foreland, A. R., & Engvik, H. (2001). Personality structure in patients with winter depression, assessed in a depression-free state according to the five-factor model of personality. *Journal of Affective Disorders, 62,* 165–174.

Linke, S. E., & others. (2009). Depressive symptom dimensions and cardiovascular prognosis among women with suspected myocardial ischemia: A report from the National Heart, Lung, and Blood Institute-sponsored women's Ischemia Syndrome Foundation. *Archives of General Psychiatry, 66,* 499–507.

Linnman, C., Appel, L., Furark, T., Soderlund, A., Gordh, T., Langstrom, B., & Fredrikson, M. (2010). Ventromedial prefrontal neurokinin 1 receptor availability is reduced in chronic pain. *Pain.* (in press)

Lippa, R. (2000). Gender-related traits in gay men, lesbian women and heterosexual men and women: The virtual identity of homosexual-heterosexual diagnosticity and gender diagnosticity. *Journal of Personality, 68,* 899–926.

Lippa, R. (2003). Handedness, sexual orientation, and gender-related personality traits in men and women. *Archives of Sexual Behavior, 32,* 103–114.

Lippa, R. A. (2005). *Gender: Nature and nurture* (2nd ed.). Mahwah, NJ: Erlbaum.

Lippa, R. (2008). The relation between childhood gender nonconformity and adult masculinity-femininity and anxiety in heterosexual and homosexual men and women. *Sex Roles, 59,* 684–693.

Lippke, S., & Plotnikoff, R. C. (2006). Stages of change in physical exercise: A test of stage discrimination and nonlinearity. *American Journal of Health Behavior, 30,* 290–301.

Lippke, S., Ziegelmann, J. P., Schwarzer, R., & Velicer, W. F. (2009). Validity of stage assessment in the adoption and maintenance of physical activity and fruit and vegetable consumption. *Health Psychology, 28,* 183–193.

Lipsey, M. W., & Wilson, D. B. (1993). The efficacy of psychological, educational, and behavioral treatment: Confirmation from meta-analysis. *American Psychologist, 48,* 1181–1209.

Lissek, S., & others. (2010). Overgeneralization of conditioned fear as a pathogenic marker of panic disorder. *American Journal of Psychiatry, 167,* 47–55.

Little, K. Y., Zhang, L., & Cook, E. (2006). Fluoxetine-induced alterations in human platelet serotonin transporter expression: Serotonin transporter polymorphism effects. *Psychiatry and Neuroscience, 31,* 333–339.

Little, T. D., Snyder, C. R., & Wehmeyer, M. (2006). The agentic self: On the nature and origins of personal agency across the life span. In D. K. Mroczek & T. D. Little (Eds.), *Handbook of personality development.* Mahwah, NJ: Erlbaum.

Littlefield, A. K., & Sher, K. J. (2010). Alcohol use disorders in young adulthood. In J. E. Grant (Ed.), *Young adult mental health* (pp. 292–310). New York: Oxford University Press.

Littrell, J. H., & Girvin, H. (2002). Stages of change: A critique. *Behavior Modification, 26,* 223–273.

Liu, C. C., Doong, J. L., Hsu, W. S., Huang, W. S., & Jeng, M. C. (2009). Evidence from the selective attention mechanism and dual-task interference. *Applied Ergonomics, 40,* 341–347.

Liu, P. D., & McBride-Chang, C. (2010). What is morphological awareness? Tapping lexical compounding awareness in Chinese third graders. *Journal of Educational Psychology, 102,* 62–73.

Liu, R., & Huang, X. (1999). A study on time-perceptual cues in visual information. *Acta Psychologic Sinica, 31,* 15–20.

Lo, S. (2008). The nonverbal communication functions of emotions in computer-mediated communication. *CyberPsychology & Behavior, 11,* 595–597.

Lobbestael, J., & Arntz, A. (2010). Emotional, cognitive, and physiological correlates of abuse-related stress in borderline and antisocial personality disorder. *Behavior Research and Therapy, 48,* 116–124.

Loftus, E. F. (1975). Spreading activation within semantic categories. *Journal of Experimental Psychology, 104,* 234–240.

Loftus, E. F. (1993). Psychologists in the eyewitness world. *American Psychologist, 48,* 550–552.

Loftus, E. F. (2009). Crimes of memory: False memories and social justice. In M. A. Gernsbacher, L. Hough, R. Pew, & J. Pomerantz (Eds.), *Psychology in the real world.* New York: Worth.

Loftus, E. F., & Frenda, S. J. (2010). Bad theories can harm victims. *Science, 327,* 1329–1330.

Loftus, E. F., & Ketcham, K. (1991). *Witness for the defense: The accused, the eyewitness, and the expert who puts memory on trial.* New York: St. Martin's Press.

Loftus, E. F., & Pickrell, J. E. (2001, June). *Creating false memories.* Paper presented at the meeting of the American Psychological Society, Toronto.

Longo, D. A., Lent, R. W., & Brown, S. D. (1992). Social cognitive variables in the prediction of client motivation and attribution. *Journal of Counseling Psychology, 39,* 447–452.

Lopes, M., & Santos-Victor, J. (2007). A developmental roadmap for learning by imitation in robots. *IEEE Transactions on Systems, Man, and Cybernetics B, 37,* 308–321.

Lopez-Munoz, F., & Alamo, C. (2009). Mono-aminergic neurotransmission: The history of the discovery of antidepressants from 1950s until today. *Current Pharmaceutical Design, 15,* 1563–1586.

Lorant, V., Croux, C., Weich, S., Deliege, D., Mackenbach, J., & Ansseau, M. (2007). Depression and socioeconomic risk factors: 7-year longitudinal population study. *British Journal of Psychiatry, 190,* 293–298.

Lord, R. G., Diefendorff, J. M., Schmidt, A. M., & Hall, R. J. (2010). Self-regulation at work. *Annual Review of Psychology* (vol. 61). Palo Alto, CA: Annual Reviews.

Lorenz, K. Z. (1965). *Evolution and the modification of behavior.* Chicago: University of Chicago Press.

Loring-Meier, S., & Halpern, D. F. (1999). Sex differences in visual-spatial working memory: Components of cognitive processing. *Psychonomic Bulletin & Review, 6,* 464–471.

Lo Sauro, C., Ravaldi, C., Cabras, P. L., Faravelli, C., & Ricca, V. (2008). Stress, hypothalamic-pituitary-adrenal axis, and eating disorders. *Neuropsychobiology, 57,* 95–115.

Lovinger, D. M. (2010). Neurotransmitter roles in synaptic modulation, plasticity, and learning in the dorsal striatum. *Neuropharmacology.* (in press)

Low, C. A., Stanton, A., & Danoff-Burg, S. (2006). Expressive disclosure and benefit finding among breast cancer patients: Mechanisms for positive health effects. *Health Psychology, 25,* 181–189.

Lu, J., Sherman, D., Devor, M., & Saper, C. B. (2006). A putative flip-flop switch for control of REM sleep. *Nature, 441,* 589–594.

Lubinski, D., Benbow, C. P., Webb, R. M., & Bleske-Rechek, A. (2006). Tracking exceptional human capital over two decades. *Psychological Science, 17,* 194–199.

Lubinski, D., Webb, R. M., Morelock, M. J., & Benbow, C. P. (2001). Top 1 in 10,000: A 10-year follow-up of the profoundly gifted. *Journal of Applied Psychology, 86,* 718–729.

Luborsky, L., Rosenthal, R., Diguer, L., Andrusyna, T. P., Berman, J. S., Levitt, J. T., Seligman, D. A., & Krause, E. D. (2002). The dodo bird verdict is alive and well—mostly. *Clinical Psychology: Science and Practice, 9,* 2–12.

Lucas, R. E. (2007). Extraversion. In R. Baumeister & K. Vohs (Eds.), *The encyclopedia of social psychology.* Thousand Oaks, CA: Sage.

Lucas, R. E. (2008). Personality and subjective well-being. In M. Eid & R. J. Larsen (Eds.), *The science of subjective well-being* (pp. 171–194). New York: Psychology Press.

Lucas, R. E., Clark, A. E., Yannis, G., & Diener, E. (2004). Unemployment alters the setpoint for life satisfaction. *Psychological Science, 15,* 8–13.

Ludlow, K. H., & others. (2009). Acute and chronic ethanol modulate dopamine d2-subtype receptor responses in ventral tegmental area GABA neurons. *Alcoholism: Clinical and Experimental Research, 33,* 804–811.

Luo, X., Galvin, J. J., & Fu, Q. J. (2010). Effects of stimulus duration on amplitude modulation processing with cochlear implants. *Journal of Acoustical Society of America, 127,* EL23.

Luo, Y., & Baillargeon, R. (2005). Can a self-propelled box have a goal? Psychological reasoning in 5-month-old infants. *Psychological Science, 16,* 601–608.

Luria, A. R. (1968/1987). *The mind of a mnemonist.* L. Solotaroff (Trans.). Cambridge, MA: Harvard University Press.

Lutchmaya, S., Baron-Cohen, S., Raggatt, P., Knickmeyer, R., & Manning, J. T. (2004). 2nd to 4th digit ratios, fetal testosterone and estradiol. *Early Human Development, 77,* 23–28.

Luthans, F. (2011). *Organizational behavior* (12th ed.). New York: McGraw-Hill.

Lykken, D. (1999). *Happiness: What studies on twins show us about nature, nurture, and the happiness set-point.* New York: Golden Books.

Lykken, D. T. (1987). The probity of the polygraph. In S. M. Kassin & L. S. Wrightsman (Eds.), *The psychology of evidence and trial procedures.* Newbury Park, CA: Sage.

Lykken, D. T. (1998). *A tremor in the blood: Uses and abuses of the lie detector* (2nd ed.). New York: Plenum Press.

Lykken, D. T. (2001). Lie detection. In W. E. Craighead & C. B. Nemeroff (Eds.), *The Corsini encyclopedia of psychology and behavioral science* (3rd ed.). New York: Wiley.

Lynam, D. R., Caspi, A., Moffitt, T. E., Loeber, R., & Stouthamer-Loeber, M. (2007). Longitudinal evidence that psychopathy scores in early adolescence predict adult psychopathy. *Journal of Abnormal Psychology, 116,* 155–165.

Lynn, S. J. (2007). Hypnosis reconsidered. *American Journal of Clinical Hypnosis, 49,* 195–197.

Lynn, S. J., Boycheva, E., & Barnes, S. (2008). To assess or not assess hypnotic susceptibility? That is the question. *American Journal of Clinical Hypnosis, 51,* 161–165.

Lynn, S. J., Green, J. P., Accardi, M., & Cleere, C. (2010). Hypnosis and smoking cessation: The state of the science. *American Journal of Clinical Hypnosis, 52,* 177–181.

Lyubomirsky, S. (2008). *The how of happiness: A scientific approach to getting the life you want.* New York: Penguin.

Lyubomirsky, S., King, L. A., & Diener, E. (2005). The benefits of frequent positive affect: Does happiness lead to success? *Psychological Bulletin, 131,* 803–855.

M

Maccoby, E. E. (2002). Gender and group processes. *Current Directions in Psychological Science, 11,* 54–58.

Macdonald, J. S. P., & Lavie, N. (2008). Load induced blindness. *Journal of Experimental Psychology: Human Perception and Performance, 34,* 1078–1091.

Machado, G. M., Oliveira, M. M., & Fernandes, L. A. (2009). A physiologically-based model for simulation of color vision deficiency. *IEEE Transactions on Visualization and Computer Graphics, 15,* 1291–1298.

MacKenzie, S. B., Podsakoff, P. M., & Ahearne, M. (1998). Some possible antecedents and consequences of in-role and extra-role sales-person performance. *Journal of Marketing, 62,* 87–98.

MacLeod, M. (2006, April 1). Mindless imitation teaches us how to be human. *New Scientist, 2545,* 42.

MacQueen, C. E., Brynes, A. E., & Frost, G. S. (2002). Treating obesity. A follow-up study. Can the stages of change model be used as a postal screening tool? *Journal of Human Nutrition and Dietetics, 15* (1), 3–7.

Madan, A., Palaniappan, L., Urizar, G., Wang, Y., Formann, S. P., & Gould, J. B. (2006). Sociocultural factors that affect pregnancy outcomes in two dissimilar immigrant groups in the United States. *Journal of Pediatrics, 148,* 341–346.

Maddi, S. (1998). Hardiness. In H. S. Friedman (Ed.), *Encyclopedia of mental health* (vol. 3). San Diego: Academic.

Maddi, S. R. (2008). The courage and strategies of hardiness as helpful in growing despite major, disruptive stresses. *American Psychologist, 63,* 563–564.

Maddi, S. R., Harvey, R. H., Khoshaba, D. M., Lu, J. L., Persico, M., & Brow, M. (2006). The personality construct of hardiness, III: Relationships with repression, innovativeness, authoritarianism, and performance. *Journal of Personality, 74,* 575–597.

Maddux, J. E. (2010). Social cognitive theories and clinical interventions: Basic processes. In J. E. Maddux & J. P. Tagney (Eds.), *Social psychological foundations of clinical psychology.* New York: Guilford.

Maddux, W. W., & Galinsky, A. D. (2007, September). *Cultural borders and mental barriers: Living in and adapting to foreign countries facilitates creativity.* Working Paper No. 2007/51/B. Fountainbleau, France: INSEAD.

Mader, S. S. (2010). *Biology* (10th ed.). New York: McGraw-Hill.

Mader, S. S. (2011). *Inquiry into life* (13th ed.). New York: McGraw-Hill.

Maes, H. H. M., Neal, M. C., & Eaves, L. J. (1997). Genetic and environmental factors in relative body weight and human adiposity. *Behavior Genetics, 27,* 325–351.

Maggio, N., & Segal, M. (2009). Differential corticosteroid modulation of inhibitory synaptic currents in the dorsal and ventral hippocampus. *Journal of Neuroscience, 29,* 2857–2866.

Maguire, E. A., Gadian, G. D., Johnsrude, I. S., Good, C. D., Ashburner, J., Frackowiak, R. S. J., & Frith, C. D. (2000). Navigation-related structural change in the hippocampi of taxi drivers. *Proceedings of the National Academy of Sciences USA, 97,* 4398–4403.

Mahler, D. A., Murray, J. A., Waterman, L. A., Ward, J., Kraemer, W. J., Zhang, X., & Baird, J. C. (2009). Endogenous opioids modify dyspnoea during treadmill exercise in patients with COPD. *European Respiratory Journal, 33,* 771–777.

Mahoney, M. M. (2010). Shift work, jet lag, and female reproduction. *International Journal of Endocrinology.* (in press)

Maier, N. R. F. (1931). Reasoning in humans. *Journal of Comparative Psychology, 12,* 181–194.

Maier, S. F., & Seligman, M. E. P. (2009). Fears, phobias, and preparedness: Toward an evolved module of fear and fear learning. In D. Shanks (Ed.), *Psychology of learning.* Thousand Oaks, CA: Sage.

Major, B., & Sawyer, P. J. (2009). Attributions to discrimination: Antecedents and consequences. In T. D. Nelson (Ed.), *Handbook of prejudice, stereotyping, and discrimination.* New York: Psychology Press.

Makioka, S. (2009). A self-organizing learning account of number-form synaesthesia. *Cognition, 112,* 397–414.

Malamuth, N. M., Addison, T., & Koss, M. (2000). Pornography and sexual aggression: Are there reliable effects and can we understand them? *Annual Review of Sex Research, 11,* 26–91.

Malcolm-Smith, S., Solms, M., Turnbull, O., & Tredoux, C. (2008). Threat in dreams: An adaptation? *Consciousness and cognition, 17,* 1281–1291.

Malhotra, R. K., & Desai, A. K. (2010). Healthy brain aging: what has sleep got to do with it? *Clinics in Geriatric Medicine, 26,* 46–56.

Mandara, J. (2006). The impact of family functioning on African American males' academic achievement: A review and clarification of the empirical literature. *Teachers College Record, 108,* 206–233.

Mander, B. A., & others. (2008). Sleep deprivation alters functioning within the neural network underlying the covert orienting of attention. *Brain Research, 1217,* 148–156.

Mandler, G. (1980). Recognizing: The judgment of previous occurrence. *Psychological Review, 87,* 252–271.

Maner, J. K., Luce, C. L., Neuberg, S. L., Cialdini, R. B., Brown, S., & Sagarin, B. J. (2002). The effects of perspective taking on motivations for helping: Still no evidence for altruism. *Personality and Social Psychology Bulletin, 28,* 1601–1610.

Manganotti, P., & others. (2010). Changes in cerebral activity after decreased upper-limb hypertonus: An EMG-fMRI study. *Magnetic Resonance Imaging.* (in press)

Manini, T. M., & others. (2006). Daily activity energy expenditure and mortality among older adults. *Journal of the American Medical Association, 296,* 216–218.

Mann, D. M., Ponieman, D., Leventahl, H., & Halm, E. A. (2009). Predictors of adherence to diabetes medications: The role of disease and medication beliefs. *Journal of Behavioral Medicine, 32,* 278–284.

Manning, J. T. (2002). *Digit ratio: A pointer to fertility, behavior and health.* New Brunswick, NJ: Rutgers University Press.

Mantonakis, A., Rodero, P., Lesschaeve, I., & Hastie, R. (2009). Order in choice: Effects of serial position on preferences. *Psychological Science, 20,* 1309–1312.

March, J., Silva, S., Petrycki, S., Curry, J., Wells, K., Fairbank, J., Burns, B., Domino, M., McNulty, S., Vitiello, B., & Severe, J. (2004). Fluoxetine, cognitive-behavioral therapy, and their combination for adolescents with depression: Treatment for Adolescents with Depression Study (TADS) randomized controlled trial. *Journal of the American Medical Association, 292,* 807–820.

Marcia, J. E. (1980). Ego identity development. In J. Adelson (Ed.), *Handbook of adolescent psychology.* New York: Wiley.

Marcia, J. E. (2002). Identity and psychosocial development in adulthood. *Identity, 2,* 7–28.

Marcus, G. F. (2001). *The algebraic mind.* Cambridge, MA: MIT Books.

Marder, S. R., Davis, J. M., & Chouinard, G. (1997). The effects of risperidone on the five dimensions of schizophrenia derived by factor analysis: Combined results of the North American trials. *Journal of Clinical Psychiatry, 58,* 538–546.

Margoob, M. A., Zaffar Ali, Z., & Andrade, C. (2010). Efficacy of ECT in chronic, severe, antidepressant- and CBT-refractory PTSD: An open, prospective study. *Brain Stimulation, 3,* 28–35.

Margrett, J. A., Allaire, J. C., Johnson, T. L., Daugherty, K. E., & Weatherbee, S. R. (2010). Everyday problem solving. In J. C. Cavanaugh, C. K. Cavanaugh, J. Berry, & R. West, (Eds.), *Aging in America, vol 1: Psychological aspects.* (pp. 80–101). Santa Barbara, CA: Praeger/ABC-CLIO.

Maril, A., Wagner, A. D., & Schacter, D. L. (2001). On the tip of the tongue: An event-related fMRI study of semantic retrieval failure and cognitive conflict. *Neuron, 31,* 653–660.

Marine, A., Rutosalainen, J., Serra, C., & Verbeek, J. (2006). Preventing occupational stress in healthcare workers. *Cochrane Database System Review, 18* (4), CD002892.

Marini, A., Martelli, S., Gagliardi, C., Fabbro, F., & Borgatti, R. (2010). Narrative language in Williams syndrome and its neuropsychological correlates. *Journal of Neurolinguistics, 23,* 97–111.

Maris, R. W. (1998). Suicide. In H. S. Friedman (Ed.), *Encyclopedia of mental health* (vol. 3). San Diego: Academic.

Markessis, E., & others. (2009). Effect of presentation level on diagnosis of dead regions using the threshold equalizing noise test. *International Journal of Audiology, 48,* 55–62.

Markowitsch, H. J. (2008). Autobiographical memory: A biocultural relais between subject and environment. *European Archives of Psychiatry and Clinical Neuroscience, 258,* Suppl. 5, S98–S103.

Markowitz, J. C., Milrod, B., Bleiberg, K., & Marshall, R. D. (2009). Interpersonal factors in understanding and treating posttraumatic stress disorder. *Journal of Psychiatric Practice, 15,* 133–140.

Markowitz, S., & Cuellar, A. (2007). Antidepressants and youth: Healing or harmful? *Social Science Medicine, 64,* 2138–2151.

Marks, I., & Cavanaugh, K. (2009). Computer-aided psychological treatments. *Annual Review of Clinical Psychology, 5,* 121–141.

Marlatt, M. W., Lucassen, P. J., & van Pragg, H. (2010). Comparison of neurogenic effects of fluoxetine, duloxetine, and running in mice. *Brain Research.* (in press)

Marlow, A. (1999). *How to stop time: Heroin from A to Z.* New York: Basic.

Marom, M., & Berent, I. (2010). Phonological constraints on the assembly of skeletal structure in reading. *Journal of Psycholinguistic Research, 39,* 67–88.

Maron, E., Hettema, J. M., & Shlik, J. (2010). Advances in molecular genetics of panic disorder. *Molecular Psychiatry.* (in press)

Marques, J. K., Wiederanders, M., Day, D. M., Nelson, C., & van Ommeren A. (2005). Effects of a relapse prevention program on sexual recidivism: Final results from California's Sex Offender Treatment Evaluation Project (SOTEP). *Sex Abuse, 17,* 79–107.

Marrazzo, J. M., Coffey, P., & Bingham, A. (2005). Sexual practices, risk perception, and knowledge of bacterial vaginosis among lesbian and bisexual women. *Perspectives on Sexual and Reproductive Health, 37,* 6–12.

Marshall, D. A., Walizer, E. M., & Vernalis, M. N. (2009). Achievement of heart health characteristics through participation in an intensive lifestyle change program (Coronary

Artery Disease Reversal Study). *Journal of Cardiopulmonary Rehabilitation and Prevention, 29,* 84–94.

Marshall, D. S. (1971). Sexual behavior in Mangaia. In D. S. Marshall & R. C. Suggs (Eds.), *Human sexual behavior: Variations in the ethnographic spectrum* (pp. 103–162). New York: Basic.

Marshall, M., & Rathbone, J. (2006). Early intervention for psychosis. *Cochrane Database of Systematic Reviews, 4,* CD004718.

Martin, C. L., & Ruble, D. N. (2010). Patterns of gender development. *Annual Review of Psychology* (vol. 61). Palo Alto, CA: Annual Reviews.

Martin, G. L., & Pear, J. (2007). *Behavior modification* (8th ed.). Upper Saddle River, NJ: Prentice-Hall.

Martin, L. R., Friedman, H. S., & Schwartz, J. E. (2007). Personality and mortality risk across the lifespan: The importance of conscientiousness as biopsychosocial attribute. *Health Psychology, 26,* 428–436.

Martinez, M. E. (2010). *Learning and cognition.* Upper Saddle River, NJ: Merrill.

Martin-Joy, J., & Vaillant, G. E. (2010). Recognizing and promoting resilience. In C. A. Depp & D. V. Jeste (Eds.), *Successful cognitive and emotional aging* (pp. 363–381). Arlington, VA: American Psychiatric Publishing.

Maruyama, Y., Pereira, M., Margolskee, R. F., Chaudhari, N., & Roper, S. D. (2006). Umami responses in mouse taste cells indicate more than one receptor. *Journal of Neuroscience, 26,* 2227–2234.

Marx, R. F., & Didziulis, V. (2009, March 1). A life, interrupted. *New York Times.*

Mascaro, N., & Rosen, D. H. (2006). The role of existential meaning as a buffer against stress. *Journal of Humanistic Psychology, 46,* 168–190.

Maslow, A. H. (1954). *Motivation and personality.* New York: Harper & Row.

Maslow, A. H. (1971). *The farther reaches of human nature.* New York: Viking.

Mason, C. (2009, May 12). Belgian city plans "veggie" days. BBC. http://news.bbc.co.uk/2/hi/europe/8046970.stm

Mason, T. B., & Pack, A. I. (2005). Sleep terrors in childhood. *Journal of Pediatrics, 147,* 388–392.

Massimini, F., & Delle Fave, A. (2000). Individual development in bio-cultural perspective. *American Psychologist, 55,* 24–33.

Masten, A. S. (2006). Developmental psychopathology: Pathways to the future. *International Journal of Behavioral Development, 31,* 46–53.

Masten, A. S. (2007). Resilience in developing systems: Progress and promise as the fourth wave rises. *Development and Psychopathology, 19,* 921–930.

Masten, A. S. (2009). Ordinary magic: Lessons from research on human development. *Education Canada, 19,* 28–32.

Masten, A. S., Obradovic, J., & Burt, K. B. (2006). Resilience in emerging adulthood. In J. J. Arnett & J. L. Tanner (Eds.), *Emerging adults in America.* Washington, DC: American Psychological Association.

Masten, A. S., & Wright, M. O'D. (2009). Resilience over the lifespan: Developmental perspectives on resistance, recovery, and transformation. In J. W. Reich, A. J. Zautra, & J. S. Hall (Eds.), *Handbook of adult resilience.* New York: Guilford.

Masters, W. H., & Johnson, V. E. (1966). *Human sexual response.* Boston: Little, Brown.

Mate, J., & Baques, J. (2009). Visual similarity at encoding and retrieval in an item recognition task. *Quarterly Journal of Experimental Psychology, 18,* 1–8.

Mathew, K. L., Whitford, H. S., Kenny, M. A., & Denson, L. A. (2010). The long-term effects of mindfulness-based cognitive therapy as a relapse prevention treatment for major depressive disorder. *Behavioral and Cognitive Psychotherapy.* (in press)

Matis, G., & Birbilis, T. (2009). The Glasgow Coma Scale—A brief review. Past, present, future. *Acta Neurologica Belgica, 108,* 75–89.

Matlin, M. W. (2001). *Cognition* (5th ed.). Fort Worth, TX: Harcourt Brace.

Matsumoto, D., & others. (2008) Mapping expressive differences around the world: The relationship between emotional display rules and individualism versus collectivism. *Journal of Cross-Cultural Psychology, 39,* 55–74.

Mattes, K., Spezio, M., Kim, H., Todorov, A., Adolphs, R., & Alvarez, R. M. (2010). Predicting election outcomes from positive and negative trait assessments of candidate images. *Political Psychology, 31,* 41–58.

Matthews, K., & Gallo, L. C. (2011). Psychological perspectives on the association of socioeconomic status and physical health. *Annual Review of Psychology* (vol. 62). Palo Alto, CA: Annual Reviews.

Matthews, K. A., Gump, B. B., Harris, K. F., Haney, T. L., & Barefoot, J. C. (2004). Hostile behaviors predict cardiovascular mortality among men enrolled in the multiple risk factor intervention trial. *Circulation, 109,* 66–70.

Matthews, K. A., Schott, L. L., Bromberger, J., Cyranowski, J., Everson-Rose, S. A., & Sowers, M. F. (2007). Associations between depressive symptoms and inflammatory/hemostatic markers in women during the menopausal transition. *Psychosomatic Medicine, 69,* 124–130.

Matthews, R. A., Bulger, C. A., & Barnes-Farrell, J. L. (2010). Work social supports, role stressors, and work–family conflict: The moderating effect of age. *Journal of Vocational Behavior, 76,* 78–90.

Matzel, L. D., & Kolata, S. (2010). Selective attention, working memory, and animal intelligence. *Neuroscience and Biobehavioral Reviews, 34,* 23–30.

Maurer, T. J., Mitchell, D. R. D., & Barbeite, F. G. (2002). Predictors of attitudes toward a 360-degree feedback system and involvement in post-feedback management development activity. *Journal of Occupational and Organizational Psychology, 75,* 87–107.

May, F. B. (2006). *Teaching reading creatively* (7th ed.). Upper Saddle River, NJ: Prentice-Hall.

May, M. (2003). *Vision diary.* http://www.guardian.co.uk/g2/story/0,3604,1029268,00.html (accessed October 11, 2006)

Mayer, J. D., Salovey, P., & Caruso, D. R. (2008). Emotional intelligence: New ability or eclectic traits? *American Psychologist, 63,* 503–517.

Mayer, R. (2000). Problem solving. In M. A. Runco & S. Pritzker (Eds.), *Encyclopedia of psychology.* San Diego: Academic.

Mayer, R. E. (2011). *Applying the science of learning.* Boston: Allyn & Bacon.

Mayo Foundation. (2006). *Electroconvulsive therapy (ECT):* Treating severe depression and mental illness. Rochester, MN: Author. http://www.mayo-clinic.com/health/electroconvulsive-therapy/MH00022

McAdams, D. P. (1989). *Intimacy: The need to be close.* New York: Doubleday.

McAdams, D. P. (2001). The psychology of life stories. *Review of General Psychology, 5,* 100–122.

McAdams, D. P. (2006). *The redemptive self: Stories Americans live by.* New York: Oxford University Press.

McAdams, D. P. (2009). *The person* (5th ed.). New York: Wiley.

McAdams, D. P., Bauer, J. J., Sakaeda, A. R., Anyidoho, N. A., Machado, M. A., Magrino-Failla, K., White, K. W., & Pals, J. L. (2006). Continuity and change in life story: A longitudinal study of autobiographical memories in emerging adulthood. *Journal of Personality, 74,* 1371–1400.

McAdams, D. P., & Bryant, F. B. (1987). Intimacy motivation and subjective mental health in a nationwide sample. *Journal of Personality, 55,* 395–413.

McAdams, D. P., & Olson, B. D. (2010). Personality development: Continuity and change over the lifespan. *Annual Review of Psychology* (vol. 61). Palo Alto, CA: Annual Reviews.

McBurney, D. H., & White, T. L. (2010). *Research methods* (8th ed.). Boston: Cengage.

McCabe, J., Tanner, A., & Heiman, J. R. (2010). The impact of gender expectations on meanings of sex and sexuality: Results from a cognitive interview study. *Sex Roles, 62,* 252–263.

McCarthy, M. M., Auger, A. P., Bale, T. L., De Vries, G. J., Dunn, G. A., Forger, N. G., Murray, E. K., Nugent, B. M., Schwarz, J. M., & Wilson, M. E. (2009). The epigenetics of sex differences in the brain. *Journal of Neuroscience, 29,* 12815–12823.

McCauley, C., & Segal, M. E. (2009). Social psychology of terrorist groups. In J. Victoroff & A. W. Kruglanski (Eds.), *Psychology of terrorism: Classic and contemporary insights* (pp. 331–346). New York: Psychology Press.

McCaulley, M. H. (2000). Myers-Briggs Type Indicator: A bridge between counseling and consulting. *Consulting Psychology Journal: Practice and Research, 52,* 117–132.

McClelland, J. L., & Rumelhart, D. E. (2009). Why there are complementary learning systems in the hippocampus and neocortex: Insights from the successes and failures of connectionist models of learning and memory. In D. Shanks (Ed.), *Psychology of learning.* Thousand Oaks, CA: Sage.

McConnell, A. R., & Brown, C. M. (2010). Dissonance averted: Self-concept organization moderates the effect of hypocrisy on attitude change. *Journal of Experimental Social Psychology, 46,* 361–366.

McCorkle, B. H., Rogers, E. S., Dunn, E. C., Lyass, A., & Wan, Y. M. (2008). Increasing social support for individuals with serious mental illness: Evaluating the compeer model of intentional friendship. *Community Mental Health Journal, 44,* 359–366.

McCrae, R. R., & Costa, P. T. (2006). Cross-cultural perspectives on adult personality trait development. In D. K. Mroczek & T. D. Little (Eds.), *Handbook of personality development.* Mahwah, NJ: Erlbaum.

McCrae, R. R., & Sutin, A. R. (2007). New frontiers for the five factor model: A preview of the literature. *Social and Personality Psychology Compass, 1,* 423–440.

McCrae, R. R., & Sutin, A. R. (2009). Openness to experience. In M. R. Leary & R. H. Hoyle (Eds.), *Handbook of individual differences in social behavior* (pp. 257–273). New York: Guilford.

McCulloch, K. C., Ferguson, M. J., Kawada, C. C. K., & Bargh, J. A. (2008). Taking a closer look: On the operation of nonconscious impression formation. *Journal of Experimental Social Psychology, 44,* 614–623.

McCullough, J. L., & Kelly, K. M. (2006). Prevention and treatment of skin aging. *Annals of the New York Academy of Sciences, 1067,* 323–331.

McCullough, M. E., Bono, G., & Root, L. M. (2007). Rumination, emotion, and forgiveness: Three longitudinal studies. *Journal of Personality and Social Psychology, 92,* 490–505.

McCullough, M. E., Emmons, R. A., & Tsang, J. (2002). The grateful disposition: A conceptual and empirical topography. *Journal of Personality and Social Psychology, 82,* 112–127.

McCullough, M. E., Hoyt, W. T., Larson, D. B., Koenig, H. G., & Thoresen, C. (2000). Religious involvement and mortality: A meta-analytic review. *Health Psychology, 19,* 211–222.

McCullough, M. E., & Willoughby, B. L. (2009). Religion, self-regulation, and self-control: Associations, explanations, and implications. *Psychological Bulletin, 135,* 69–93.

McDaniel, M. A., & Einstein, G. O. (2007). *Prospective memory: An overview and synthesis of an emerging field.* Thousand Oaks, CA: Sage.

McDermott, R. (2009). Medical decision making: Lessons from psychology. *Urologic Oncology, 26,* 665–668.

McDonald, M. A., Hildebrand, J. A., Wiggins, S. M., Johnston, D. W., & Polovina, J. J. (2009). An acoustic survey of beaked whales at Cross Seamount near Hawaii. *Journal of the Acoustical Society of America, 125,* 624–627.

McDonald, S. D., & others. (2010). Preterm birth and low birth weight among in vitro fertilization twins: A systematic review and meta-analyses. *European Journal of Obstetrics, Gynecology, and Reproductive Biology, 148,* 105–113.

McFadden, D. (2008) What do sex, twins, spotted hyenas, ADHD, and sexual orientation have in

common? *Perspectives on Psychological Science, 3,* 309–323.

McFadden, D., Loehlin, J. C., Breedlove, S. M., Lippa, R. A., Manning, J. T., & Rahman, Q. (2005). A reanalysis of five studies on sexual orientation and the relative length of the 2nd and 4th fingers (the 2D:4D ratio). *Archives of Sexual Behavior, 34,* 341–356.

McFadden, D., & Shubel, E. (2002). Relative lengths of fingers and toes in human males and females. *Hormones and Behavior, 42,* 492–500.

McFadden, S. H., & Basting, A. D. (2010). Healthy aging persons and their brains: Promoting resilience through creative engagement. *Clinics in Geriatric Medicine, 26,* 149–161.

McFarlane, A. C. (2010). The long-term costs of traumatic stress: Intertwined physical and psychological consequences. *World Psychiatry, 9,* 3–10.

McGettigan, C., & others. (2010). Neural correlates of sublexical processing in phonological working memory. *Journal of Cognitive Neuroscience.* (in press)

McGhee, K. E., & Travis, J. (2010). Repeatable behavioural type and stable dominance rank in the bluefin killifish. *Animal Behaviour, 79,* 497–507.

McGregor, D. M. (1960). *The human side of enterprise.* New York: McGraw-Hill.

McGugin, R. W., & Gauthier, I. (2010). Perceptual expertise with objects predicts another hallmark of face perception. *Journal of Vision.* (in press)

McGuire, M. T., Wing, R. R, Klem, M. L., Lang, W., & Hill, J. O. (1999). What predicts weight regain in a group of successful weight losers? *Journal of Consulting and Clinical Psychology, 67,* 177–185.

McGuire, W. J. (2003). Doing psychology my way. In R. J. Sternberg (Ed.), *Psychologists defying the crowd: Stories of those who battled the establishment and won* (pp. 119–137). Washington, DC: American Psychological Association.

McGuire, W. J. (2004). The morphing of attitude-change into social-cognition. In G. V. Bodenhausen & A. J. Lambert (Eds.), *Foundations of social cognition.* Mahwah, NJ: Erlbaum.

McGuire, W. J., & Papageorgis, D. (1961). The relative efficacy of various types of prior belief-defense in producing immunity against persuasion. *Public Opinion Quarterly, 26,* 24–34.

McIntosh, W. D., Harlow, T. F., & Martin, L. L. (1995). Linkers and non-linkers: Goal beliefs as a moderator of the effects of everyday hassles on rumination, depression, and physical complaints. *Journal of Applied Social Psychology, 25,* 1231–1244.

McKay, K. M., Imel, Z. E., & Wampold, B. E. (2006). Psychiatrist effects in the psychopharmacological treatment of depression. *Journal of Affective Disorders, 92,* 287–290.

McKone, E., Crookes, K., & Kanwisher, N. (2010). The cognitive and neural development of face recognition in humans. In M. Gazzaniga (Ed.), *The cognitive neurosciences* (4th ed.). New York: Cambridge University Press.

McMahon, D. B., & Olson, C. R. (2009). Linearly additive shape and color signals in monkey inferotemporal cortex. *Journal of Neurophysiology, 101,* 1867–1875.

McMain, S., & Pos, A. E. (2007). Advances in psychotherapy of personality disorders: A research update. *Current Psychiatry Reports, 9,* 46–52.

McManus, M. A., & Ferguson, M. W. (2003). Biodata, personality, and demographic differences of recruits from three sources. *International Journal of Selection and Assessment, 11,* 175–183.

McMillan, J. H. (2008). *Educational research* (5th ed.). Boston: Allyn & Bacon.

McMillan, J. H., & Wergin, J. F. (2010). *Understanding and evaluating educational research* (4th ed.). Upper Saddle River, NJ: Merrill.

McMillan, K. A., Enns, M. W., Asmundson, G. J., & Sareen, J. (2010). The association between income and distress, mental disorders, and suicidal ideation and attempts: Findings from the collaborative psychiatric epidemiology surveys. *Journal of Clinical Psychology.* (in press)

McNamara, P., McLaren, D., & Durso, K. (2007). Representation of the self in REM and NREM dreams. *Dreaming, 17,* 113–126.

McNaughton, N., & Corr, P. J. (2008). The neuropsychology of fear and anxiety: A foundation for reinforcement sensitivity theory. In P. J. Corr (Ed.), *The reinforcement sensitivity theory of personality* (pp. 44–94). New York: Cambridge University Press.

McNeil, D. G. (2009, February 2). A company prospers by saving poor people's lives. *New York Times,* D4.

McNiel, J. M., Lowman, J. C., & Fleeson, W. (2010). The effect of state extraversion on four types of affect. *European Journal of Personality, 24,* 18–35.

McRae, K., Hughes, B., Chopra, S., Gabrieli, J. D. E., Gross, J. J., & Ochsner, K. N. (2010). The neural bases of distraction and reappraisal. *Journal of Cognitive Neuroscience, 22,* 248–262.

McRobbie, H., & others. (2010). A randomized trial of the effects of two novel nicotine replacement therapies on tobacco withdrawal symptoms and user satisfaction. *Addiction.* (in press)

McVay, J. C., & Kane, M. J. (2010). Does mind wandering reflect executive function or executive failure? Comment on Smallwood and Schooler (2006) and Watkins (2008). *Psychological Bulletin, 136,* 188–197.

Meade, C. S., Wang, J., Lin, X., Wu, H., & Poppen, P. J. (2010). Stress and coping in HIV-positive former plasma/blood donors in China: A test of cognitive appraisal theory. *AIDS Behavior, 14,* 328–338.

Medland, S. E., & Loehlin, J. C. (2008). Multivariate genetic analyses of the 2D:4D ratio: Examining the effects of hand and measurement technique in data from 757 twin families. *Twin Research and Human Genetics, 11,* 335–341.

Medley-Rath, S. R. (2007). "Am I still a virgin?": What counts as sex in 20 years of *Seventeen.*

Sexuality & Culture: An Interdisciplinary Quarterly, 11, 24–38.

Medvec, V. H., Madey, S. F., & Gilovich, T. (1995). When less is more: Counterfactual thinking and satisfaction among Olympic medalists. *Journal of Personality and Social Psychology, 69*, 603–610.

Meehl, P. (1962). Schizotonia, schizotypy, schizophrenia. *American Psychologist, 17*, 827–838.

Mehl, M. R., Vazire, S., Ramirez-Esparza, N., Slatcher, R. B., & Pennebaker, J. W. (2007). Are women really more talkative than men? *Science, 317*, 82.

Meissner, W. W. (2009). Religion in the psychoanalytic relationship—some aspects of transference and countertransference. *Journal of the American Academy of Psychoanalysis and Dynamic Psychiatry, 37*, 123–136.

Mejia-Arauz, R., Rogoff, B., & Paradise, R. (2005). Cultural variation in children's observation during a demonstration. *International Journal of Behavioral Development, 29*, 282–291.

Mello, J. A. (2011). *Strategic human resource management* (3rd ed.). Boston: Cengage.

Mellon, S., & others. (2009). Predictors of decision making in families at risk for inherited breast/ovarian cancer. *Health Psychology, 28*, 38–47.

Melton, L. (2005, December 17). How brain power can help you cheat old age. *New Scientist, 2530*, 32.

Meltzoff, A. N. (2011). Social cognition and the origins of imitation, empathy, and theory of mind. In U. Goswami (Ed.), *Wiley-Blackwell handbook of childhood cognitive development* (2nd ed.). New York: Wiley Blackwell.

Mendes, W. B. (2007). Social facilitation. In R. Baumeister & K. Vohs (Eds.), *Encyclopedia of social psychology*. Thousand Oaks, CA: Sage.

Menn, L., & Stoel-Gammon, C. (2009). Phonological development: Learning sounds and sound patterns. In J. Berko Gleason & N. Ratner (Eds.), *The development of language* (7th ed.). Boston: Allyn & Bacon.

Mercer, C. H., Bailey, J. V., Johnson, A. M., Erens, B., Wellings, K., Fenton, K. A., & Copas, A. J. (2007). Women who report having sex with women: British national probability data on prevalence, sexual behaviors, and health outcomes. *American Journal of Public Health, 97*, 1126–1133.

Mercer, V. E. (2009). Stress management intervention. In W. T. O'Donohue & J. E. Fisher (Eds.), *General principles and empirically supported techniques of cognitive behavior therapy* (pp. 631–639). Hoboken, NJ: Wiley.

Merkl, A., Heuser, I., & Bajbouj, M. (2009). Antidepressant electroconvulsive therapy: Mechanism of action, recent advances, and limitations. *Experimental Neurology, 219* (1), 20–26.

Merlino, G., & others. (2010). Daytime sleepiness is associated with dementia and cognitive decline in older Italian adults: A population-based study. *Sleep Medicine*. (in press)

Mesquita, B. (2002). Emotions as dynamic cultural phenomena. In R. J. Davidson, K. R. Scherer, & H. H. Goldsmith (Eds.), *Handbook of affective sciences*. New York: Oxford University Press.

Messenger, J. C. (1971). Sex and repression in an Irish folk community. In D. S. Marshall & R. C. Suggs (Eds.), *Human sexual behavior*. New York: Basic.

Messer, S. B., & Abbass, A. A. (2010). Evidence-based psychodynamic therapy with personality disorders. In J. J. Magnavita (Ed.), *Evidence-based treatment of personality dysfunction: Principles, methods, and processes* (pp. 79–111). Washington, DC: American Psychological Association.

Messner, S. F., Raffalovich, L. E., & Shrock, P. (2002). Reassessing the cross-national relationship between income inequality and homicide rates: Implications of data quality control in the measurement of income distribution. *Journal of Quantitative Criminology, 18*, 377–395.

Meston, C. M., & Buss, D. M. (2009). *Why women have sex: Understanding sexual motivations from adventure to revenge (and everything in between)*. New York: Holt.

Meston, C. M., Seal, B. N., & Hamilton, L. D. (2008). Problems with arousal and orgasm in women. In D. L. Rowland & L. Incrocci (Eds.), *Handbook of sexual and gender identity disorders* (pp. 188–219). Hoboken, NJ: Wiley.

Metcalfe, J., & Mischel, W. (1999). A hot/cool system analysis of delay of gratification: Dynamics of will power. *Psychological Review, 106*, 3–19.

Mettler, F. A. (Ed.). (1952). *Psychosurgical problems*. Oxford: Blakiston.

Meyer, J. P., Becker, T. E., & Vandenberghe, C. (2004). Employee commitment and motivation: A conceptual analysis and integrative model. *Journal of Applied Psychology, 89*, 991–1007.

Meyer, J. P., & Herscovitch, L. (2001). Commitment in the workplace: Toward a general model. *Human Resource Management Review, 11*, 299–326.

Meyer, J. P., Stanley, D. J., Herscovitch, L., & Topolnytsky, L. (2002). Affective, continuance, and normative commitment to the organization: A meta-analysis of antecedents, correlates, and consequences. *Journal of Vocational Behavior, 61*, 20–52.

Meyer, P. J., Meshul, C. K., & Phillips, T. J. (2009). Ethanol- and cocaine-induced locomotion are genetically related to increases in accumbal dopamine. *Genes, Brain, and Behavior, 8*, 346–355.

Meyer-Bahlburg, H. F. L. (1998). Gender assignment in intersexuality. *Journal of Psychology and Human Sexuality, 10*, 1–21.

Meyer-Bahlburg, H. F. L. (2005). Gender identity outcome in female-raised 46, XY persons with penile agenesis, cloacal exstrophy of the bladder, or penile ablation. *Archives of Sexual Behavior, 34*, 423–438.

Meyer-Bahlburg, H. F. L. (2010). From mental disorder to iatrogenic hypogonadism: Dilemmas in conceptualizing gender identity variants as psychiatric conditions. *Archives of Sexual Behavior, 39*, 461–476.

Meyer-Bahlburg, H. F. L, Dolezal, C., Baker, S. W., & New, M. I. (2008). Sexual orientation in women with classical or non-classical congenital adrenal hyperplasia as a function of degree of prenatal androgen excess. *Archives of Sexual Behavior, 37*, 85–99.

Miacic, B., & Goldberg, L. R. (2007). An analysis of a cross-cultural personality inventory: The IPIP big five factors markers in Croatia. *Journal of Personality Assessment, 88*, 168–177.

Michael, R. T., Gagnon, J. H., Laumann, E. O., & Kolata, G. (1994). *Sex in America*. Boston: Little, Brown.

Middeldorp, C. M., de Geus, E. J. C., Beem, A. L., Lakenberg, N., Hottenga, J., Slagboom, P. E., & Boomsma, D. I. (2007). Family based association analyses between the serotonin transporter gene polymorphism (5-HTTLPR) and neuroticism, anxiety and depression. *Behavior Genetics, 37*, 294–301.

Migneault, J. P., Adams, T. B., & Read, J. P. (2005). Application of the transtheoretical model to substance abuse: Historical development and future directions. *Drug and Alcohol Review, 24*, 437–448.

Mihashi, M., & others. (2009). Predictive factors of psychological disorder development during recovery following SARS outbreak. *Health Psychology, 28*, 91–100.

Mikolajczyk, E., Grzywacz, A., & Samochowlec, J. (2010). The association of catechol-O-methyl-transferace genotype with the phenotype of women with eating disorders. *Brain Research, 1307*, 142–148.

Milane, M. S., Suchard, M. A., Wong, M., & Licinio, J. (2006). Modeling of the temporal patterns of fluoxetine prescriptions and suicide rates in the United States. *PloS Medicine, 3*, e190. doi:10.1371/jo.

Milgram, S. (1965). Some conditions of obedience and disobedience to authority. *Human Relations, 18*, 56–76.

Milgram, S. (1974). *Obedience to authority*. New York: Harper & Row.

Miller, A. G. (2004). What can the Milgram obedience experiments tell us about the Holocaust? Generalizing from the social psychology laboratory. In A. G. Miller (Ed.), *The social psychology of good and evil* (pp. 193–239). New York: Guilford.

Miller, C. A., & Golden, N. H. (2010). An introduction to eating disorders: Clinical presentation, epidemiology, and prognosis. *Nutrition in Clinical Practice, 25*, 110–115.

Miller, D. J., Vachon, D. D., & Lynam, D. R. (2009). Neuroticism, negative affect, and negative affect instability: Establishing convergent and discriminant validity using ecological momentary assessment. *Personality and Individual Differences, 47*, 873–877.

Miller, D. T. (1999). The norm of self-interest. *American Psychologist, 54* (12), 1053–1060.

Miller, D. T. (2001). The norm of self-interest. In J. Dienhart, D. Moberg, & R. Duska (Eds.), *The next phase of business ethics: Integrating psychology and ethics* (pp. 193–210). New York: Elsevier Science/JAI Press.

Miller, G., Chen, E., & Cole, S. W. (2009). Health psychology: Developing biologically plausible models linking the social world and physical health. *Annual Review of Psychology* (vol. 60). Palo Alto, CA: Annual Reviews.

Miller, G. A. (1956). The magical number seven, plus or minus two: Some limits on our capacity for information processing. *Psychological Review, 48,* 337–442.

Miller, J. J., Fletcher, K., & Kabat-Zinn, J. (1995). Three-year follow-up and clinical implications of a mindfulness meditation–based stress reduction intervention in the treatment of anxiety disorders. *General Hospital Psychiatry, 17,* 192–200.

Miller, N. E. (1941). The frustration-aggression hypothesis. *Psychological Review, 48,* 337–442.

Miller, N. E. (1985). The value of behavioral research on animals. *American Psychologist, 40,* 432–440.

Miller, P. H. (2011). Piaget's theory: Past, present, and future. In U. Goswami (Ed.), *Wiley-Blackwell handbook of childhood cognitive development* (2nd ed.). New York: Wiley Blackwell.

Miller, R., Perlman, D., & Brehm, S. S. (2009). *Intimate relationships* (5th ed.). New York: McGraw-Hill.

Milling, L. S., Coursen, E. L., Shores, J. S., & Waszkiewicz, J. A. (2010). The predictive utility of hypnotizability: The change in suggestibility produced by hypnosis. *Journal of Consulting and Clinical Psychology, 78,* 126–130.

Miltenberger, R. G. (2008). Behavior modification. In M. Hersen & A. M. Gross (Eds.), *Handbook of clinical psychology, vol. 2: Children and adolescents* (pp. 626–652). Hoboken, NJ: Wiley.

Milton, F., & others. (2010). Remote memory deficits in transient epileptic amnesia. *Brain.* (in press)

Minde, K., & Zelkowitz, P. (2008). Premature babies. In M. M. Haith & J. B. Benson (Eds.), *Encyclopedia of infant and early childhood development.* Oxford, U.K.: Elsevier.

Mindell, J. A., Meltzer, L. J., Carskadon, M. A., & Chervin, R. D. (2009). Developmental aspects of sleep hygiene: Findings from the 2004 National Sleep in America Poll. *Sleep Medicine, 10,* 771–779.

Mineka, S., & Ohman, A. (2002). Phobias and preparedness: The selective, automatic, and encapsulated nature of fear. *Biological Psychiatry, 52,* 927–937.

Miner-Rubino, K., Twenge, J. M., & Fredrickson, B. L. (2002). Trait self-objectification in women: Affective and personality correlates. *Journal of Research in Personality, 36,* 147–172.

Mirilas, P., & others. (2010). Serum beta-endorphin response to stress before and after operation under fentanyl anesthesia in neonates, infants, and preschool children. *European Journal of Pediatric Surgery.* (in press)

Mischel, W. (1968). *Personality and assessment.* New York: Wiley.

Mischel, W. (2004). Toward an integrative science of the person. *Annual Review of Psychology* (vol. 55). Palo Alto, CA: Annual Reviews.

Mischel, W. (2009). From *Personality and Assessment* (1968) to personality science, 2009. *Journal of Research in Personality, 43,* 282–290.

Mischel, W., & Ayduk, O. (2004). Willpower in a cognitive-affective processing system: The dynamics of delay of gratification. In R. F. Baumeister & K. D. Vohs (Eds.), *Handbook of self-regulation: Research, theory, and applications* (pp. 99–129). New York: Guilford.

Mischel, W., Cantor, N., & Feldman, S. (1996). Principles of self-regulation: The nature of will power and self-control. In E. T. Higgins & A. W. Kruglanski (Eds.), *Social psychology: Handbook of basic principles.* New York: Guilford.

Mischel, W., & Moore, B. S. (1980). The role of ideation in voluntary delay for symbolically presented rewards. *Cognitive Therapy and Research, 4,* 211–221.

Mischel, W., & Shoda, Y. (1999). Integrating dispositions and processing dynamics within a unified theory of personality: The cognitive-affective personality system. In L. A. Pervin & O. P. John (Eds.), *Handbook of personality: Theory and research* (2nd ed., pp. 197–218). New York: Guilford.

Mitchell, C. J., & others. (2010). Do reaction times in the Perruchet effect reflect variations in the strength of the associative link? *Journal of Experimental Psychology: Learning, Memory, and Cognition, 36,* 567–572.

Mitchell, D. L., Gallagher, T. V., & Thomas, R. E. (2008). The human factors of implementing shift work in logging operations. *Journal of Agricultural Safety and Health, 14,* 391–404.

Mitchell, H. A., & Weinshenker, D. (2010). Good night and good luck: Norephinephrine in sleep pharmacology. *Biochemical Pharmacology, 79,* 801–809.

Mitchell, K. E., Alliger, G. M., & Morfopoulos, R. (1997). Toward an ADA-appropriate job analysis. *Human Resource Management Review, 7,* 5–26.

Mittag, W., & Schwarzer, R. (1993). Interaction of employment status and self-efficacy on alcohol consumption: A two-wave study on stressful life transitions. *Psychology and Health, 8,* 77–87.

Miyamoto, M. (2009). Pharmacology of ramelteon, a selective MT1/MT2 receptor agonist: A novel therapeutic drug for sleep disorders. *CNS Neuroscience and Therapeutics, 15,* 32–51.

Mizes, J. S., & Miller, K. J. (2000). Eating disorders. In M. Hersen & R. T. Ammerman (Eds.), *Advanced abnormal child psychology* (2nd ed.). Mahwah, NJ: Erlbaum.

Moberly, N. J., & Watkins, E. R. (2009). Negative affect and ruminative self-focus during everyday goal pursuit. *Cognition and Emotion,* 1–15.

Mock, S., & Boerner, K. (2010). Sense making and benefit finding among patients with amyotrophic lateral sclerosis and their primary caregivers. *Journal of Health Psychology, 15,* 115–121.

Moffitt, T. E., Brammer, G. L., Caspi, A., Fawcet, J. P., Raleigh, M., Yuwiler, A., & Silva, P. A. (1998). Whole blood serotonin relates to violence in an epidemiological study. *Biological Psychiatry, 43,* 446–457.

Mojza, E. J., Lorenz, C., Sonnentag, S., & Binnewies, C. (2010). Daily recovery experiences: The role of volunteer work during leisure time. *Journal of Occupational Health Psychology, 15,* 60–74.

Mojzisch, A., & Schulz-Hardt, S. (2010). Knowing others' preferences degrades the quality of group decisions. *Journal of Personality and Social Psychology, 98,* 794–808.

Mokhber, N., & others. (2010). Randomized, single-blind, trial of sertraline and buspirone for treatment of elderly patients with generalized anxiety disorder. *Psychiatry and Clinical Neurosciences, 64,* 128–134.

Molles, M. C. (2010). *Ecology* (5th ed.). New York: McGraw-Hill.

Mondy, R. W. (2010). *Human resource management* (11th Ed.). Upper Saddle River, NJ: Prentice-Hall.

Money, J. (1986). *Lovemaps: Clinical concepts of sexual/erotic health and pathology, paraphilia, and gender transposition in childhood, adolescence, and maturity.* New York: Irvington.

Money, J., Hampson, J. G., & Hampson, J. L. (1955). Hermaphroditism: Recommendations concerning assignment of sex, change of sex, and psychological management. *Bulletin of Johns Hopkins Hospital, 97,* 284–300.

Money, J., Hampson, J. G., & Hampson, J. L. (1957). Imprinting and the establishment of gender role. *Archives of Neurology and Psychiatry, 77,* 333–336.

Money, J., & Tucker P. (1975). *Sexual signatures: On being a man or woman.* Boston: Little, Brown.

Monteleone, G. T., Phan, K. L., Nusbaum, H. C., Fitzgerald, D., Irick, J. S., Fienberg, S. E., & Cacioppo, J. T. (2009). Detection of deception using fMRI: Better than chance, but well below perfection. *Social Neuroscience, 4,* 528–538.

Montgomery, E. (2010). Trauma and resilience in young refugees: A 9-year follow-up study. *Developmental Psychology, 22,* 477–489.

Moore, D. W. (2005, June 16). Three in four Americans believe in paranormal (press release). Washington, DC: Gallup News Service.

Moos, R. H. (1986). Work as a human context. In M. S. Pallack & R. Perloff (Eds.), *Psychology and work.* Washington, DC: American Psychological Association.

Moradi, B., & Huang, Y. (2008). Objectification theory and psychology of women: A decade of advances and future directions. *Psychology of Women Quarterly, 32,* 377–398.

Moreines, J. L., McClintock, S. M., & Holtzheimer, P. E. (2010). Neuropsychologic effects of neuromodulation techniques for treatment-resistant depression: A review. *Brain Stimulation.* (in press)

Morgan, C. D., & Murray, H. A. (1935). A method of investigating fantasies: The Thematic Apperception Test. *Archives of Neurology and Psychiatry, 34,* 289–306.

Morgeson, F. P., Reider, M. H., & Campion, M. A. (2005). Selecting individuals in team settings: The importance of social skills, personality characteristics, and teamwork knowledge. *Personnel Psychology, 58,* 583–611.

Moritsugu, J., Wong, F. Y., & Duffy, K. G. (2010). *Community psychology* (4th ed.). Boston: Allyn & Bacon.

Morrison, F. J., Ponitz, C. C., & McClelland, M. M. (2010). Self-regulation and academic achievement in the transition to school. In S. D. Calkins & M. A. Bell (Eds.), *Child development at the intersection of emotion and cognition*. Washington, DC: American Psychological Association.

Mortimer, J. A., Snowdon, D. A., & Markesbery, W. R. (2009). The effect of APOE-epsilon4 on dementia is mediated by Alzheimer neuropathology. *Alzheimer Disease and Associated Disorders, 23,* 152–157.

Moscovici, S. (1985). Social influence and conformity. In G. Lindzey & E. Aronson (Eds.), *Handbook of social psychology* (3rd ed., vol. 2). New York: Random House.

Moses, T. (2010). Being treated differently: Stigma experiences with family, peers, and school staff among adolescents with mental health disorders. *Social Science Medicine, 70,* 985–993.

Mosher, C. E., & Danoff-Burg, S. (2008). Agentic and communal personality traits: Relations to disordered eating behavior, body shape concern, and depressive symptoms. *Eating Behaviors, 9,* 497–500.

Mosher, W. D., Chandra, A., & Jones, J. (2005). Sexual behavior and selected health measures: Men and women 15–44 years of age, United States, 2002. *Advance data from vital and health statistics, no. 362.* Hyattsville, MD: National Center for Health Statistics.

Moskowitz, D. S. (2010). Quarrelsomeness in daily life. *Journal of Personality. 78,* 39–66.

Moskowitz, M., & Levering, R. (2007). 2007 "100 Best Companies to Work For" in America. http://www.greatplacetowork.com/best/100best2007.php

Moskowitz, M., & Levering, R. (2010). 2010 "100 Best Companies to Work For" in America. http://www.greatplacetowork.com/what_we_do/lists-us-bestusa-2010.htm

Mouilso, E. R., Calhoun, K. S., & Gidycz, C. A. (2010). Effects of participation in a sexual assault risk reduction program on psychological distress following revictimization. *Journal of Interpersonal Violence.* (in press)

Moulton, S. T., & Kosslyn, S. M. (2008). Using neuroimaging to resolve the psi debate. *Journal of Cognitive Neuroscience, 20,* 182–192.

Mroczek, D. K. (2001). Age and emotion in adulthood. *Current Directions in Psychological Science, 10,* 87–90.

Mroczek, D. K., & Kolarz, C. M. (1998). The effect of age on positive and negative affect: A developmental perspective on happiness. *Journal of Personality and Social Psychology, 75,* 1333–1349.

Mroczek, D. K., & Spiro, A. (2005). Change in life satisfaction during adulthood: Findings from the Veterans Affairs Normative Aging Study. *Journal of Personality and Social Psychology, 88,* 189–202.

Mueller, D. L. (2010). Mechanisms maintaining peripheral tolerance. *Nature Immunology, 11,* 21–27.

Mullington, J. M., Haack, M., Toth, M., Serrador, J. M., & Meier-Ewert, H. K. (2009). Cardiovascular, inflammatory, and metabolic consequences of sleep deprivation. *Progress in Cardiovascular Diseases, 51,* 294–302.

Mullis, I. V. S., Marting, M. O., Gonzales, E. J., & Kennedy, A. M. (2003). *PIRLS 2001 International Report: IEA's study of reading literacy achievement in primary schools.* Chestnut Hill, MA: Boston College. timss.bc.edu/pirls2001html (accessed April 15, 2010)

Mumford, M. D., Scott, G., & Hunter, S. T. (2006). Theory—charismatic, ideological, and pragmatic leaders: How do they lead, why do they lead, and who do they lead? In M. D. Mumford (Ed.), *Pathways to outstanding leadership.* Mahwah, NJ: Erlbaum.

Munafo, M. R., Yalcin, B., Willis-Owen, S. A., & Flint, J. (2008). Association of the dopamine D4 receptor (DRD4) gene and approach-related personality traits: Meta-analysis and new data. *Biological Psychiatry, 63,* 197–206.

Munoz-Laboy, M., Hirsch, J. S., & Quispe-Lazaro, A. (2009). Loneliness as a sexual risk for male Mexican migrant workers. *American Journal of Public Health, 99,* 802–810.

Mur, M., Ruff, D. A., Bodurka, J., Bandettini, P. A., & Kriegeskorte, N. (2010). Face-identity change activation outside the face system: "Release from adaptation" may not always indicate neuronal selectivity. *Cerebral Cortex.* (in press)

Murray, E. A. (2007). Visual memory. *Annual Review of Neuroscience* (vol. 29). Palo Alto, CA: Annual Reviews.

Murray, L., Halligan, S. L., Goodyer, I., & Herbert, J. (2010). Disturbances in early parenting of depressed mothers and cortisol secretion in offspring: A preliminary study. *Journal of Affective Disorders, 122,* 218–223.

Murray-Swank, A. B., Lucksted, A., Medoff, D. R., Yang, Y., Wohlheiter, K., & Dixon, L. B. (2006). Religiosity, psychosocial adjustment, and subjective burden of persons who care for those with mental illness. *Psychiatric Services, 57,* 361–365.

Murre, J. M. J. (2010). Connectionist models of forgetting. In S. D. Sala (Ed.), *Forgetting.* New York: Psychology Press.

Mussweiler, T. (2009). Social comparison. In F. Strack & J. Forster (Eds.), *Social cognition: The basis of human interaction.* New York: Psychology Press.

Mykletun, A., Bjerkeset, O., Dewey, M., Prince, M., Overland, S., & Stewart, R. (2007). Anxiety, depression, and cause-specific mortality: The Hunt Study. *Psychosomatic Medicine, 69,* 323–331.

N

Naar-King, S., Wright, K., Parsons, J. T., Frey, M., Templin, T., & Ondersma, S. (2006). Transtheoretical model and condom use in HIV-positive youths. *Health Psychology, 25,* 648–652.

Nagase, Y., & others. (2009). Coping strategies and their correlates with depression in the Japanese general population. *Psychiatry Research, 168,* 57–66.

Nagashima, J., & others. (2010). Three-month exercise and weight loss program improves heart rate recovery in obese persons along with cardiopulmonary function. *Journal of Cardiology.* (in press)

Nakao, M. (2010). Work-related stress and psychosomatic medicine. *Biopsychosocial Medicine.* (in press)

Nakao, T., & others. (2009). Working memory dysfunction in obsessive-compulsive disorder: A neuropsychological and functional MRI study. *Journal of Psychiatric Research, 43,* 784–791.

Nanda, S. (2008). Cross-cultural issues. In D. L. Rowland & L. Incrocci (Eds.), *Handbook of sexual and gender identity disorders* (pp. 457–485). Hoboken, NJ: Wiley.

Narayanan, L., Menon, S., & Spector, P. E. (1999). A cross-cultural comparison of job stressors and reactions among employees holding comparable jobs in two countries. *International Journal of Stress Management, 6,* 197–212.

Nardi, P. M. (2006). *Doing survey research* (2nd ed.). Boston: Allyn & Bacon.

Narvaez, D., & Lapsley, D. (2009). *Moral personality, identity, and character: An interdisciplinary future.* New York: Cambridge University Press.

Nash, M. R., Perez, N., Tasso, A., & Levy, J. J. (2009). Clinical research on the utility of hypnosis in the prevention, diagnosis, and treatment of medical and psychiatric disorders. *International Journal of Clinical and Experimental Hypnosis, 57,* 443–450.

Nasrallah, H. A., & others. (2009). Proceedings and data from the Schizophrenia Summit: A critical appraisal to improve management of schizophrenia. *Journal of Clinical Psychiatry, 70,* Suppl. 1, 4–46.

Nassi, J. J., & Callaway, E. M. (2009). Parallel processing strategies of the primate visual system *Nature Review Neuroscience, 10,* 360–372.

Nath, A. (2010). Human immunodeficiency virus-associated neurocognitive disorder: Pathophysiology in relation to drug addiction. *Annals of the New York Academy of Sciences, 1187,* 122–128.

National Alliance for the Mentally Ill, American Psychiatric Association, National Mental Health Association (NAMI/APA, NMHA). (2005, June 24). *Joint statement in response to Tom Cruise's Today Show interview.* Author.

National Center for Health Statistics. (2002). *Sexual behavior and selected health measures: Men and women 15–44 years of age, United States, 2002.* Atlanta: Centers for Disease Control and Prevention.

National Center for Health Statistics. (2005). *Early release of selected estimates from Jan–Mar 2005 National Health Interview Survey.* Washington, DC: Author.

National Center for Health Statistics. (2005a). *Death statistics.* Atlanta: Centers for Disease Control and Prevention.

National Center for Health Statistics. (2006). *Vital and health statistics.* Atlanta: Centers for Disease Control and Prevention.

National Center for Health Statistics. (2006a). *Health United States, 2006.* Atlanta: Centers for Disease Control and Prevention.

National Center for Health Statistics. (2009). Cigarette smoking among adults and trends in smoking cessation—United States, 2008. Atlanta: Centers for Disease Control and Prevention.

National Center for Health Statistics. (2010). *HIV/AIDS in the United States*. Atlanta: Centers for Disease Control and Prevention.

National Center for Post-Traumatic Stress Disorder (PTSD). (2006). *Facts about PTSD*. www.ncptsd.va.gov (accessed November 25, 2006)

National Heart, Lung, and Blood Institute. (2009). BMI calculator. http://www.nhlbisupport.com/bmi/

National Highway Traffic Safety Administration (NHTSA). (2007, December). *Traffic safety facts: Crash stats*. Washington, DC: NHTSA's Center for Statistics and Analysis.

National Institute on Drug Abuse (NIDA). (2009a). *Research report series—MDMA (Ecstasy) abuse*. Bethesda, M.D: Author.

National Institute on Drug Abuse (NIDA). (2009b). *NIDA infacts: Marijuana*. Bethesda, MD: Author.

National Institute of Mental Health (NIMH). (2008). *The numbers count: Mental disorders in America*. Bethesda, MD: U.S. Department of Health and Human Services. http://www.nimh.nih.gov/health/publications/the-numbers-count-mental-disorders-in-america/index.shtml

National Institute of Mental Health (NIMH). (2009). *Eating disorders*. Bethesda, MD: Author.

National Sleep Foundation. (2007, March 6). *Stressed-out American women have no time for sleep*. Washington, DC: Author.

Naumann, L. P., Vazire, S., Rentfrow, P. J., & Gosling, S. D. (2009). Personality judgments based on physical appearance. *Personality and Social Psychology Bulletin, 35*, 1661–1671.

Neacsiu, A. D., Rizvi, S. L., Vitaliano, P. P., Lynch, T. R., & Linehan, M. M. (2010). The dialectical behavior therapy ways of coping checklist: Developmental and psychometric properties. *Journal of Clinical Psychology, 66*, 563–582.

Needham, A. (2009). Learning in infants' object perception, object-directed action, and tool use. In A. Woodward & A. Needham (Eds.), *Learning and the infant mind*. New York: Oxford University Press.

Needham, A., Barrett, T., & Peterman, K. (2002). A pick-me-up for infants' exploratory skills: Early simulated experiences reaching for objects using "sticky mittens" enhances young infants' object exploration skills. *Infant Behavior and Development, 25*, 279–295.

Nefti, W., Chaumontet, C., Fromentin, G., Tomé, D., & Darcel, N. (2009). A high fat diet attenuates the central response to within-meal satiation signals and modifies the receptor expression of vagal afferents in mice. *American Journal of Physiology: Regulatory, Integrative, and Comparative Physiology, 296*, R1681–R1686.

Neisser, U., Boodoo, G., Bouchard, T. J., Boykin, A. W., Brody, N., Ceci, S. J.,

Halpern, D. F., Loehlin, J. C., Perloff, R., Sternberg, R. J., & Urbina, S. (1996). Intelligence: Knowns & unknowns. *American Psychologist, 51*, 77–101.

Neisser, U., & Harsch, N. (1992). Phantom flashbulbs: False recollections of hearing the news about *Challenger*. In E. Winograd & U. Neisser (Eds.), *Affect and accuracy in recall: Studies of "flashbulb" memories* (pp. 9–31). New York: Cambridge University Press.

Nelson, C. A. (2011). Brain development and behavior. In A. M. Rudolph, C. Rudolph, L. First, G. Lister, & A. A. Gershon (Eds.), *Rudolph's pediatrics* (22nd ed.). New York: McGraw-Hill.

Nelson, D. L., & Quick, J. C. (2011). *ORGB 2* (2nd ed.). Boston: Cengage.

Nelson, K. J., Bowman-Fowler, N., Berkowitz, S. R., & Loftus, E. F. (2009). Eyewitness testimony. In C. Edwards (Ed.), *Encyclopedia of forensic science*. New York: Wiley.

Nelson, T. D. (Ed.). (2009). *Handbook of prejudice, stereotyping, and discrimination*. New York: Psychology Press.

Nenadic, I., Sauer, H., & Gaser, C. (2010). Distinct pattern of brain structural deficits in subsyndromes of schizophrenia delineated by psychopathology. *NeuroImage, 49*, 1153–1160.

Neukrug, E. S., & Fawcett, R. C. (2010). *Essentials of testing and assessment* (2nd ed.). Boston: Cengage.

Neumann, I. D., Veenema, A. H., & Beiderbeck, D. I. (2010). Aggression and anxiety: Social context and neurobiological links. *Frontiers in Behavioral Neuroscience*. (in press)

Nevels, R. M., Dehon, E. E., Alexander, K., & Gontkovsky, S. T. (2010). Psychopharmacology of aggression in children and adolescents with primary neuropsychiatric disorders: A review of current and potentially promising treatment options. *Experimental and Clinical Psychopharmacology, 18*, 184–201.

Neville, H. J. (2006). Different profiles of plasticity within human cognition. In Y. Munakata & M. H. Johnson (Eds.), *Attention and performance*. Oxford, U.K.: Oxford University Press.

Nevsimalova, S. (2009). Narcolepsy in childhood. *Sleep Medicine Reviews, 13*, 169–180.

Newberg, A. B. (2010). The neurobiology of meditation. In D. A. Monti & B. D. Beitman (Eds.), *Integrative psychiatry* (pp. 339–358). New York: Oxford University Press.

Nicholls, J. G., & Paton, J. F. R. (2009). Brainstem: Neural networks vital for life. *Philosophical Transactions of the Royal Society B: Biological Sciences, 364*, 2447–2451.

Nicholson, C. (2008). In the news: Scanning sexuality. *Nature Reviews Neuroscience. 9*, 582.

Nickerson, R. S., & Adams, M. J. (1979). Long-term memory for a common object. *Cognitive Psychology, 11*, 287–307.

Nides, M. (2008). Update on pharmacological options for smoking cessation treatment. *American Journal of Medicine, 121, Suppl. 4*, S20–S31.

Nielsen, K., & Munir, F. (2009). How do transformational leaders influence followers'

affective well-being? Exploring the mediating role of self-efficacy. *Work & Stress, 23*, 31–329.

Nijstad, B. (2009). *Group performance*. New York: Psychology Press.

Nilsson, H., Juslin, P., & Olsson, H. (2008). Exemplars in the mist: The cognitive substrate of the representativeness heuristic. *Scandinavian Journal of Psychology, 49*, 201–212.

Niparko, J. K. (2004). Speech, language, and reading skills after early cochlear implantation. *Journal of the American Medical Association, 291*, 2378–2380.

Nir, Y., & Tononi, G. (2010). Dreaming and the brain: From phenomenology to neurophysiology. *Trends in Cognitive Science, 14*, 88–100.

Nisbett, R. E. (1987). Lay trait theory: Its nature, origins, and utility. In N. E. Grunberg, R. E. Nisbett, J. Rodin, & J. E. Singer (Eds.), *A distinctive approach to psychological research: The influence of Stanley Schachter*. Hillsdale, NJ: Erlbaum.

Nisbett, R. E. (2009). *Intelligence and how to get it: Why schools and cultures count*. New York: Norton.

Nisbett, R. E., & Ross, L. (1980). *Human inference*. Upper Saddle River, NJ: Prentice-Hall.

Nishida, A., Miyaoka, T., Inagaki, T., & Horiguchi, J. (2009). New approaches to antidepressant drug design: Cytokine-regulated pathways. *Current Pharmaceutical Design, 15*, 1683–1687.

Niswender, C. M., & Conn, P. J. (2010). Metabotropic glutamate receptors: Physiology, pharmacology, and disease. *Annual Review of Toxicology and Pharmacology, 50*, 295–322.

Nixon, K., & McClain, J. A. (2010). Adolescence as a critical window for developing an alcohol use disorder: Current findings in neuroscience. *Current Opinion in Psychiatry*. (in press)

Nkomo, S. M., Fottler, M. D., & McAfee, R. B. (2011). *Human resource management applications*. (7th Ed.). Boston: Cengage.

Noe, R. A., Hollenbeck, J. R., Gerhart, B., & Wright, P. M. (2007). *Fundamentals of human resource management* (2nd ed.). New York: McGraw-Hill.

Noel, N. E., Maisto, S. A., Johnson, J. D., & Jackson, L. A. (2009). The effects of alcohol and cue salience on young men's acceptance of sexual aggression. *Addictive Behaviors, 34*, 386–394.

Noftle, E. E., & Fleeson, W. (2010). Age differences in big five behavior averages and variabilities across the adult life span: Moving beyond retrospective, global summary accounts of personality. *Psychology and Aging, 25*, 95–107.

Noftle, E. E., & Robins, R. W. (2007). Personality predictors of academic outcomes: Big five correlates of GPA and SAT scores. *Journal of Personality and Social Psychology, 93*, 116–130.

Nolen-Hoeksema, S. (2011). *Abnormal psychology* (5th ed.). New York: McGraw-Hill. (in press)

Norcross, J. C., Mrykalo, M. S., & Blagys, M. D. (2002). Auld lang syne: Success predictors, change processes, and self-reported outcomes of New Year's resolvers and nonresolvers. *Journal of Clinical Psychology, 58*, 397–405.

Nordenskjold, A., Knorring, L. V., & Engstrom, I. (2010). Rehospitalization rate after continued electroconvulsive therapy: A retrospective chart review of patients with severe depression. *Nordic Journal of Psychiatry.* (in press)

Nordgren, L. F., & Dijksterhuis, A. P. (2009). The devil is in the deliberation: Thinking too much reduces preference consistency. *Journal of Consumer Research, 36,* 39–46.

Nordt, C., Rossler, W., & Lauber, C. (2006). Attitudes of mental health professionals toward people with schizophrenia and major depression. *Schizophrenia Bulletin, 32,* 709–714.

Norman, G. J., Devries, A. C., Cacioppo, J. T., & Bernsten, G. G. (2010). Multilevel analyses of stress. In J. Contrada & A. Baum (Eds.), *Handbook of stress science.* Springer.

Norman, W. T. (1963). Toward an adequate taxonomy of personality attributes. *Journal of Abnormal and Social Psychology, 66,* 574–583.

Norris, J., & others. (2009). Cognitive mediation of alcohol's effects on women's in-the-moment sexual decision making. *Health Psychology, 28,* 20–28.

Noseda, R., & others. (2010). A neural mechanism for exacerbation of headache by light. *Nature Neuroscience, 13,* 239–245.

Nosek, B. A., & Banaji, M. R. (2007). Implicit attitude. In P. Wilken, T. Bayne, & A. Cleeremans (Eds.), *Oxford companion to consciousness.* Oxford, U.K.: Oxford University Press.

Notman, M. T., & Nadelson, C. C. (2002). Women's issues. In M. Hersen & W. H. Sledge (Eds.), *Encyclopedia of psychotherapy.* San Diego: Academic.

Nowak, M. A., Page, K. M., & Sigmund, K. (2000). Fairness versus reason in the ultimatum game. *Science, 289,* 1773–1775.

Nrugham, L., Holen, A., & Sund, A. M. (2010). Associations between attempted suicide, life events, depressive symptoms, and resilience in adolescents and young adults. *Journal of Nervous and Mental Disease, 198,* 131–136.

Nystul, M. S. (1999). *Introduction to counseling.* Boston: Allyn & Bacon.

O

Oakley, D. A., & Halligan, P. W. (2010). Using hypnosis to gain insights into healthy and pathological cognitive functioning. *Consciousness and Cognition.* (in press)

O'Barr, W. M. (2006). Multiculturalism in the marketplace: Targeting Latinas, African American women, and gay consumers. *Advertising and Society Review, 7* (4). http://muse.jhu.edu/journals/advertising_and_society_review/

Obler, L. K. (2009). Development in the adult years. In J. Berko Gleason & N. Ratner (Eds.), *The development of language* (7th ed.). Boston: Allyn & Bacon.

Occupational Safety and Health Administration (OSHA). (2002). *Fact sheet.* http://www.osha.gov/OshDoc/data_General_ Facts/factsheet-workplace-violence.pdf. Washington, DC: Author.

O'Connor, D. B., Conner, M., Jones, F., McMillan, B., & Ferguson, E. (2009). Exploring the benefits of conscientiousness: An investigation of the role of daily stressors and health behaviors. *Annals of Behavioral Medicine, 37,* 184–196.

O'Donnell, M. L., Creamer, M., McFarlane, A. C., Silove, D., & Bryant, R. A. (2010). Should A2 be a diagnostic requirement for posttraumatic stress disorder in DSM-V? *Psychiatry Research, 176,* 257–260.

Ogden, C. L., & Carroll, M. D. (June 2010). *Prevalence of Overweight, Obesity, and Extreme Obesity Among Adults: United States, Trends 1976–1980 Through 2007–2008.* Hyattsville, MD: National Center for Health Statistics.

Ogden, T. H. (2010). On three forms of thinking: Magical thinking, dream thinking, and transformative thinking. *Psychoanalytic Quarterly, 79,* 317–347.

Ogilvie, R. D., & Wilkinson, R. T. (1988). Behavioral versus EEG-based monitoring of all-night sleep/wake patterns. *Sleep, 11* (2), 139–155.

Ogle, L., Sen, A., Pahlke, E., Jocelyn, L., Kostberg, D., Roey, S., & Williams, T. (2003). *International comparisons in fourth grade reading literacy: Finding from the Progress in International Literacy Study (PIRLS) of 2001.* (NCES 2003-073). Washington, DC: U.S. Government Printing Office.

Ohayon, M. M. (2009). Difficulty in resuming or inability to resume sleep and the links to daytime impairment: Definition, prevalence, and comorbidity. *Journal of Psychiatric Research, 43,* 934–940.

Ohman, A. (2010). Post-traumatic fear memories: Analysing a case study of a sexual assault. In L. Backman & L. Nyberg (Eds.), *Memory, aging, and the brain: A Festschrift in honour of Lars-Goran Nilsson* (pp. 211–228). New York: Psychology Press.

Ohman, A., & Mineka, S. (2001). Fears, phobias, and preparedness: Toward an evolved module of fear and fear learning. *Psychological Review, 108,* 483–522.

Ohman, A., & Mineka, S. (2003). The malicious serpent: Snakes as a prototypical stimulus for an evolved module of fear. *Current Directions in Psychological Science, 12,* 5–9.

Ohman, A., & Soares, J. J. P. (1998). Emotional conditioning to masked stimuli: Expectancies for aversive outcomes following nonrecognized fear-relevant stimuli. *Journal of Experimental Psychology, 127,* 69–82.

Olds, J. M. (1958). Self-stimulation experiments and differential reward systems. In H. H. Jasper, L. D. Proctor, R. S. Knighton, W. C. Noshay, & R. T. Costello (Eds.), *Reticular formation of the brain.* Boston: Little, Brown.

Olds, J. M., & Milner, P. M. (1954). Positive reinforcement produced by electrical stimulation of the septal area and other areas of the rat brain. *Journal of Comparative and Physiological Psychology, 47,* 419–427.

Olfson, M., & Marcus, S. C. (2009). National patterns in antidepressant medication treatment. *Archives of General Psychiatry, 66,* 848–856.

Oliver, M. B., & Hyde, J. S. (1993). Gender differences in sexuality: A meta-analysis. *Psychological Bulletin, 114,* 29–51.

Oliver, N. S., Toumazou, C., Cass, A. E., & Johnston, D. G. (2009). Glucose sensors: A review of current and emerging technology. *Diabetic Medicine, 26,* 197–2010.

Olivola, C. Y., & Todorov, A. (2010). Fooled by first impressions? Reexamining the diagnostic value of appearance-based inferences. *Journal of Experimental Social Psychology, 46,* 315–324.

Ollendick, T. H., Raishevich, N., Davis, T. E., Sirbu, C., & Ost, L. G. (2010). Specific phobia in youth: Phenomenology and psychological characteristics. *Behavior Therapy, 41,* 133–141.

Olness, K., & Ader, R. (1992). Conditioning as an adjunct in the pharmacotherapy of lupus erythematosus. *Journal of Developmental and Behavioral Pediatrics, 13,* 124–125.

Olson, M., & Hergenhahn, B. R. (2009). *Introduction to theories of learning* (8th ed.). Upper Saddle River, NJ: Prentice-Hall.

Oltmanns, T. F., & Emery, R. E. (2010). *Abnormal psychology* (6th ed.). Boston: Allyn & Bacon.

Olver, J. S., & others. (2009). Dopamine D1 receptor binding in the striatum of patients with obsessive-compulsive disorder. *Journal of Affective Disorders, 114,* 321–326.

Ones, D. S., & Viswesvaran, C. (1998). Gender, age, and race differences in overt integrity tests: Results across four large-scale job applicant datasets. *Journal of Applied Psychology, 83,* 35–42.

Ones, D. S., & Viswesvaran, C., & Schmidt, F. L. (1993). Comprehensive meta-analysis of integrity test validities: Finding and implications for personnel selection and theories of job performance. *Journal of Applied Psychology, 78,* 679–703.

Ong, A. D., Bergeman, C. S., & Boker, S. M. (2009). Resilience comes of age: Defining features in later adulthood. *Journal of Personality, 77,* 1777–1804.

Online Publishers Association. (2005, October). *Online paid content U.S. market spending report.* New York: Online Publishers Association and Comscore Networks.

Ophir, E., Nass, C., & Wagner, A. D. (2009). Cognitive control in media multitaskers. *Proceedings of the National Academy of Sciences USA, 106,* 15583–15587.

Orduna, V., Garcia, A., & Hong, E. (2010). Choice behavior in spontaneously hypertensive rats: Variable vs. fixed schedules of reinforcement. *Behavioural Processes.* (in press)

O'Regan, D., Wong, K., Bouras, I., Foot, C., & Wigmore, T. (2010). Falling in and out of consciousness: Catatonia in a postoperative patient. *Journal of Research in Social Medicine, 103,* 107–108.

Organ, D. W., Podsakoff, P. M., & Podsakoff, N. P. (2010). Expanding the criterion domain to include organizational citizenship behavior: Implications for employee selection. In S. Zedeck (Ed.), *APA handbook of industrial and organizational psychology.* Washington, DC: APA. (in press)

Organ, D. W., & Ryan, K. (1995). A meta-analytic review of attitudinal and dispositional predictors of organizational citizenship behavior. *Personnel Psychology, 48,* 775–802.

Orlacchio, A., Bernardi, G., Orlacchio, A., & Martino, S. (2010). Stem cells: An overview of the current status of therapies for central and peripheral nervous system diseases. *Current Medicinal Chemistry.* (in press)

Orom, H., & Cervone, D. (2009). Personality dynamics, meaning, and idiosyncrasy: Identifying cross-situational coherence by assessing personality architecture. *Journal of Research in Personality, 43,* 228–240.

O'Shea, P. G., Foti, R. J., Haunenstein, N. M. A., & Bycio, P. (2009). Are the best leaders both transformational and transactional? A pattern-oriented analysis. *Leadership, 5,* 237–259.

Ostir, G. V., Markides, K. S., Black, S. A., & Goodwin, J. S. (2000). Emotional well-being predicts subsequent functional independence and survival. *Journal of the American Geriatrics Society, 48,* 473–478.

Oswald, F. L., & Hough, L. M. (2010). Personality and its assessment in organizations: Theoretical and empirical developments. In S. Zedeck (Ed.), *APA handbook of industrial and organizational psychology.* Washington, DC: APA. (in press)

Otake, K., Shimai, S., Tanaka-Matsumi, J., Otsui, K., & Fredrickson, B. L. (2006). Happy people becoming happier through kindness: A counting kindnesses intervention. *Journal of Happiness Studies, 7,* 361–375.

Otto, J. M., Bach, M., & Kommerell, G. (2010). Advantage of binocularity in the presence of external visual voice. *Graefe's Archive for Clinical and Experimental Ophthalmology.* (in press)

Oyama, H., & others. (2010). A community-based survey and screening for depression in the elderly. *Crisis, 31,* 100–108.

Ozer, D. J., & Benet-Martinez, V. (2006). Personality and the prediction of consequential outcomes. *Annual Review of Psychology* (vol. 57). Palo Alto, CA: Annual Reviews.

P

Packer, D. J. (2008). Identifying systematic disobedience in Milgram's obedience experiments: A meta-analytic review. *Perspectives on Psychological Science, 3,* 301–304.

Packer, D. J. (2009). Avoiding groupthink: Whereas weakly identified members stay silent, strongly identified members dissent about collective matters. *Psychological Science, 20,* 546–548.

Page, J. H., Rexrode, K. M., Hu, F., Albert, C. M., Chae, C. U., & Manson, J. E. (2009). Waist-height ratio as a predictor of coronary heart disease among women. *Epidemiology, 20,* 361–366.

Page, S. (2009, December 29). Americans most admire Obama, Clinton, Palin. *USA Today.* http://www.usatoday.com/news/washington/2009-12-29-admire-gallup-poll_N.htm (accessed February 3, 2010)

Paivio, A. (1971). *Imagery and verbal processes.* New York: Holt, Rinehart & Winston.

Paivio, A. (1986). *Mental representations: A dual coding approach.* New York: Oxford University Press.

Paivio, A. (2007). *Mind and its evolution: A dual coding theoretical approach.* Mahwah, NJ: Erlbaum.

Paller, C. J., Campbell, C. M., Edwards, R. R., & Dobs, A. S. (2009). Sex-based differences in pain perception and treatment. *Pain Medicine, 10,* 289–299.

Palmieri, P. A., & Fitzgerald, L. F. (2005). Confirmatory factor analysis of posttraumatic stress symptoms in sexually harassed women. *Journal of Traumatic Stress, 18,* 657–666.

Palomo, T., Beninger, R. J., Kostrzewa, R. M., & Archer, T. (2008). Focusing on symptoms rather than diagnoses in brain dysfunction: Conscious and nonconscious expression in impulsiveness and decision-making. *Neurotoxicity Research, 14,* 1–20.

Paluck, E. C., McCormack, J. P., Ensom, M. H. H., Levine, M., Soon, J. A., & Fielding, D. W. (2006). Outcomes of bupropion therapy for smoking cessation during routine clinical use. *Annals of Pharmacotherapy, 40,* 185–190.

Pan, B. A., & Uccelli, P. (2009). Semantic development. In J. Berko Gleason & N. Ratner (Eds.), *The development of language* (7th ed.). Boston: Allyn & Bacon.

Pant, S., & Ramaswamy, B. (2009). Association of major stressors with elevated risk of breast cancer incidence or relapse. *Drugs Today, 45,* 115–126.

Pantazopoulos, H., Woo, T. U., Lim, M. P., Lange, N., & Berretta, S. (2010). Extracellular matrix-glial abnormalities in the amygdale and entorhinal cortex of subjects diagnosed with schizophrenia. *Archives of General Psychiatry, 67,* 155–166.

Papousek, I., Nauschnegg, K., Paechter, M., Lackner, H. K., Goswami, N., & Schulter, G. (2010). Trait and state positive affect and cardiovascular recovery from experimental academic stress. *Biological Psychology, 83,* 108–115.

Papousek, I., Schulter, G., & Lang, B. (2009). Effects of emotionally contagious films on changes in hemisphere-specific cognitive performance. *Emotion, 9,* 510–519.

Paris, J. (2010). Effectiveness of different therapeutic approaches in the treatment of borderline personality disorder. *Current Psychiatric Reports, 12,* 56–80.

Park, B. H., Lee, M. S., Hong, J. Y., Bas, S. H., Kim, E. Y., Kim, K. K., & Kim, D. K. (2009). The stages of physical activity and exercise behavior: An integrated approach to the theory of planned behavior. *Asia-Pacific Journal of Mental Health, 21,* 71–83.

Park, C. (2009). Meaning making in cancer survivorship. In P. T. P. Wong (Ed.), *Handbook of meaning* (2nd ed.). Thousand Oaks, CA: Sage.

Park, C. L. (2010). Making sense of the meaning literature: An integrative review of meaning making and its effects on adjustment to stressful life events. *Psychological Bulletin, 136,* 257–301.

Park, C. L., Lechner, S. C., Antoni, M. H., & Stanton, A. L. (Eds.). (2009). *Medical illness and positive life change: Can crisis lead to personal transformation?* Washington, DC: American Psychological Association.

Park, D. C., & Huang, C. M. (2010). Culture wires the brain: A cognitive neuroscience perspective. *Perspectives on Psychological Science.* (in press)

Park, D. C., & Reuter-Lorenz, P. (2009). The adaptive brain: Aging and neurocognitive scaffolding. *Annual Review of Psychology* (vol. 60). Palo Alto, CA: Annual Reviews.

Park, D. H., Eve, D. J., Borlongan, C. V., Klasko, S. K., Cruz, L. E., & Sanberg, P. R. (2009). From the basics to application of cell therapy, a steppingstone to the conquest of neurodegeneration: A meeting report. *Medical Science Monitor, 15,* RA23–31.

Park, M. (2009, April 4). Teen tries to quiet the voices caused by schizophrenia. *CNN.com.* http://www.cnn.com/2009/HEALTH/04/24/schizophrenia.soloist.brain/index.html (accessed April 14, 2009)

Parker, M., Brugeaud, A., & Edge, A. S. (2010). Primary culture and plasmid electroporation of the murine organ of corti. *Journal of Visualized Experiments.* (in press)

Parker, P. S. (2006). *Race, gender, and leadership.* Mahwah, NJ: Erlbaum.

Parks, M. R. (2007). *Personal relationships and personal networks.* Mahwah, NJ: Erlbaum.

Parry, A., & Matthews, P. M. (2002). Functional magnetic resonance imaging: A window into the brain. *Interdisciplinary Science Reviews, 27,* 50–60.

Parsons, H. M. (1974). What happened at Hawthorne? *Science, 183,* 922–932.

Pascalls, O., & Kelly, D. J. (2008). Face processing. In M. M. Haith & J. B. Benson (Eds.), *Encyclopedia of infant and early childhood development.* Oxford, U.K.: Elsevier.

Paschalis, V., & others. (2010). A weekly bout of eccentric exercise is sufficient to induce health-promoting effects. *Medicine and Science in Sports and Exercise.* (in press)

Passie, T., Halpern, J. H., Stichtenoth, D. O., Emrich, H. M., & Hintzen, A. (2008). The pharmacology of lysergic acid diethylamide: A review. *CNS Neuroscience and Therapeutics, 14,* 295–314.

Patalano, A. L., Wengrovitz, S. M., & Sharpes, K. M. (2009). The influence of category coherence on inference about cross-classified entities. *Memory and Cognition, 37,* 21–38.

Patel, A. R., Hui, H., J. T., Pandian, N. G., & Karas, R. H. (2009). Modestly overweight women have vascular endothelial dysfunction. *Clinical Cardiology, 32,* 269–273.

Patel, S. R., Zhu, X., Storfer-Isser, A., Mehra, A., Jenny, N. S., Tracy, R., & Redline, S. (2009). Sleep duration and biomarkers of inflammation. *Sleep, 32,* 200–204.

Patell, E. A., Cooper, H., & Robinson, J. C. (2008). The effects of choice on intrinsic motivation and related outcomes: A meta-analysis of research findings. *Psychological Bulletin, 134,* 270–300.

Paton, C., & others. (2010). Lithium in bipolar and other affective disorders: Prescribing practice in the UK. *Journal of Psychopharmacology.* (in press)

Patten, S. B., Wang, J. L., Williams, J. V., Currie, S., Beck, C. A., Maxwell, C. A., &

el-Guebaly, N. (2006). Descriptive epidemiology of major depression in Canada. *Canadian Journal of Psychology, 51,* 84–90.

Patterson, C. J., & Farr, R. H. (2010). Children of gay and lesbian parents: Reflections on the research-policy interface. In H. R. Schaffer & K. Durkin (Eds.), *Blackwell handbook of developmental psychology in action.* London: Blackwell. (in press)

Patterson, C. J., & Wainright, J. L. (2010). Adolescents with same-sex parents: Findings from the National Longitudinal Study of Adolescent Health. In D. Brodzinsky, A. Pertman, & D. Kunz (Eds.), *Lesbian and gay adoption: A new American reality.* New York: Oxford University Press. (in press)

Pattillo, R. (2010). Are students as good at multitasking as they think? *Nurse Educator, 35,* 24.

Paul-Samojedny, M., & others. (2010). Functional polymorphism in the interleukin-6 and interleukin-10 genes in patients with paranoid schizophrenia—a case control study. *Journal of Molecular Neuroscience.* (in press)

Paunonen, S., Jackson, D., Trzebinski, J., & Forserling, F. (1992). Personality structures across cultures: A multimethod evaluation. *Journal of Personality and Social Psychology, 62,* 447–456.

Paus, T. (2009). Brain development. In R. M. Lerner & L. Steinberg (Ed.), *Handbook of adolescent psychology* (3rd ed.). New York: Wiley.

Paus, T., Toro, R., Leonard, G., Lerner, J. V., Lerner, R. M., Perron, M., Pike, G. B., Richer, L., Steinberg, L., Veillete, S., & Pausova, Z. (2008). Morphological properties of the action-observation cortical network in adolescents with low and high resistance to peer influence. *Social Neuroscience, 3,* 303–316.

Pavlov, I. P. (1927). *Conditioned reflexes.* G. V. Anrep (Trans.). New York: Dover.

Pavot, W., & Diener, E. (2008). The Satisfaction with Life Scale and the emerging construct of life satisfaction. *Journal of Positive Psychology, 3,* 137–152.

Payne, B. K. (2001). Prejudice and perception: The role of automatic and controlled processes in misperceiving a weapon. *Journal of Personality and Social Psychology, 81,* 181–192.

Payne, B. K. (2010). Divided minds, divided morals: How implicit social cognition underpins and undermines our sense of social justice. In B. Gawronski & B. K. Payne (Eds.), *Handbook of implicit social cognition.* New York: Guilford.

Pearce, J. M., & Hall, G. (2009). A model for stimulus generalization in Pavlovian conditioning. In D. Shanks (Ed.), *Psychology of learning.* Thousand Oaks, CA: Sage.

Pearson, C. M., Andersson, L. M., & Porath, C. L. (2005). Workplace incivility. In S. Fox & P. E. Spector (Eds.), *Counterproductive work behavior: Investigations of actors and targets* (pp. 177–200). Washington, DC: American Psychological Association.

Pearson, N. J., Johnson, L. L., & Nahin, R. L. (2006). Insomnia, trouble sleeping, and complementary and alternative medicine: Analysis of the 2002 National Health Interview Survey data. *Archives of Internal Medicine, 166,* 1775–1782.

Peeters, A., & Barendregt, J. J., Willekens, F., Mackenbach, J. P., Al Mamun, A., & Bonneux, L. (2003). Obesity in adulthood and its consequences for life expectancy: A Life-Table analysis. *Annals of Internal Medicine, 138,* 24–32.

Pelleymounter, M. A., & others. (1995). Effects of the obese gene product on body weight regulation in ob/ob mice. *Science, 269,* 540–543.

Penedo, F. J., Molton, I., Dahn, J. R., Shen, B. J., Kinsinger, D., Traeger, L., Siegel, S., Schneiderman, N., & Antoni, M. (2006). A randomized clinical trial of group-based cognitive-behavioral stress management in localized prostate cancer: Development of stress management skills improves quality of life and benefit finding. *Annals of Behavioral Medicine, 31,* 261–270.

Penfield, W. (1947). Some observations in the cerebral cortex of man. *Proceedings of the Royal Society, 134,* 349.

Pennebaker, J. W. (1997a). *Opening up: The healing power of expressing emotions* (rev. ed.). New York: Guilford.

Pennebaker, J. W. (1997b). Writing about emotional experiences as a therapeutic experience. *Psychological Science, 8,* 162–166.

Pennebaker, J. W. (2004). *Writing to heal: A guided journal for recovering from trauma emotional upheaval.* Oakland, CA: New Harbinger Press.

Pennebaker, J. W., & Chung, C. K. (2007). Expressive writing, emotional upheavals, and health. In H. S. Friedman & R. C. Silver (Eds.), *Foundations of health psychology* (pp. 263–284). New York: Oxford University Press.

Pennebaker, J. W., & Graybeal, A. (2001). Patterns of natural language use: Disclosure, personality, and social integration. *Current Directions in Psychological Science, 32,* 90–93.

Pennebaker, J. W., & O'Heeron, R. C. (1984). Confiding in others and illness rate among spouses of suicide and accidental-death victims. *Journal of Abnormal Psychology, 93,* 473–476.

Penner, J., Rupsingh, R., Smith, M., Wells, J. L., Borrie, M. J., & Bartha, R. (2010). Increased glutamate in the hippocampus after galantamine treatment for Alzheimer disease. *Progress in Neuro-Psychopharmacology and Biological Psychiatry, 34,* 104–110.

Peplau, L. A. (2001). Rethinking women's sexual orientation: An interdisciplinary, relationship-focused approach. *Personal Relationships, 8,* 1–19.

Peplau, L. A. (2003). Human sexuality: How do men and women differ? *Current Directions in Psychological Science, 12,* 37–40.

Peplau, L. A., & Fingerhut, A. W. (2007). The close relationships of lesbians and gay men. *Annual Review of Psychology* (vol. 58). Palo Alto, CA: Annual Reviews.

Peplau, L. A., Spalding, L. R., Conley, T. D., & Veniegas, R. C. (1999). The development of sexual orientation in women. *Annual Review of Sex Research, 10,* 70–99.

Perez-Costas, E., Melendez-Ferro, M., & Roberts, R. C. (2010). Basal ganglia pathology in schizophrenia: Dopamine connections and anomalies. *Journal of Neurochemistry.* (in press)

Perkins, D. (1994, September). Creativity by design. *Educational Leadership,* 18–25.

Perlis, R. H., & others. (2009). A genomewide association study of response to lithium for prevention of recurrence in bipolar disorder. *American Journal of Psychiatry, 166,* 718–725.

Perlman, D. M., Salomons, T. V., Davidson, R. J., & Lutz, A. (2010). Differential effects of pain intensity and unpleasantness of two meditation practices. *Emotion, 10,* 65–71.

Perrin, P. B., Heesacker, M., Pendley, C., & Smith, M. B. (2010). Social influence processes and persuasion in psychotherapy and counseling. In J. E. Maddux & J. P. Tagney (Eds.), *Social psychological foundations of clinical psychology.* New York: Guilford.

Pert, C. B. (1999). *Molecules of emotion.* New York: Simon & Schuster.

Pert, C. B., & Snyder, S. H. (1973). Opiate receptor: Demonstration in a nervous tissue. *Science, 179,* 1011.

Pessoa, L. (2009). How do emotion and motivation direct executive control? *Trends in Cognitive Science, 13,* 160–166.

Peters, E., & others. (2010). A randomized controlled trial of cognitive behavior therapy for psychosis in a routine clinical service. *Acta Psychiatrica Scandinavica.* (in press)

Petersen, J. L., & Hyde, J. S. (2010). A meta-analytic review of research on gender differences in sexuality, 1973–2007. *Psychological Bulletin, 136,* 21–38.

Peterson, C., Seligman, M. E. P., & Vaillant, G. E. (1988). Pessimistic explanatory style is a risk factor for physical illness: A thirty-five year longitudinal study. *Journal of Personality and Social Psychology, 55,* 23–27.

Peterson, C. C., Garnett, M., Kelly, A., & Attwood, T. (2009). Everyday social and conversation applications of theory-of-mind understanding by children with autism-spectrum disorders or typical development. *European Child and Adolescent Psychology, 18,* 105–115.

Peterson, N. G., & Jeanneret, P. R. (2007). Job analysis: An overview and description of deductive methods. In D. L. Whetzel & G. R. Wheaton (Eds.), *Applied measurement.* Mahwah, NJ: Erlbaum.

Pettigrew, T. F., & Tropp, L. R. (2006). A meta-analytic test of intergroup contact theory. *Journal of Personality and Social Psychology, 90,* 751–783.

Petty, R. E., & Brinol, P. (2008). Persuasion: From single to multiple to metacognitive processes. *Perspectives on Psychological Science, 3,* 137–147.

Petty, R. E., & Cacioppo, J. T. (1986). The elaboration likelihood of persuasion. In L. Berkowitz (Ed.), *Advances in experimental social psychology* (vol. 19). New York: Academic.

Pew Research Center. (2007, January 9). *A portrait of "Generation Next": How young people view their lives, futures and politics.* Washington, DC: Author.

Pfafflin, F. (2010). Understanding transgendered phenomena. In S. B. Levine, C. B. Risen, & S. E. Althof (Eds.), *Handbook of clinical sexuality for mental health professionals* (2nd ed., pp. 425–447). New York: Routledge/Taylor & Francis.

Phan, M. L., & Vicario, D. S. (2010). Hemispheric differences in processing of vocalizations depend on early experience. *Proceedings of the National Academy of Sciences USA, 107,* 2301–2306.

Phaneuf, L., & McIntyre, L. L. (2007). Effects of individualized video feedback combined with group parent training on inappropriate maternal behavior. *Journal of Applied Behavior Analysis, 40* (4), 737–741.

Phelan, J. E., & Basow, S. A. (2007). College students' attitudes toward mental illness: An examination of the stigma process. *Journal of Applied Social Psychology, 37,* 2877–2902.

Phelan, S., Hill, J. O., Lang, W., Dibello, J. R., & Wing, R. R. (2003). Recovery from relapse among successful weight maintainers. *American Journal of Clinical Nutrition, 78,* 1079–1084.

Phillips, D. A., & Lowenstein, A. (2011). Early care, education, and child development. *Annual Review of Psychology* (vol. 62). Palo Alto, CA: Annual Reviews.

Phillips, K. J., & Mudford, O. C. (2008). Functional analysis skills training for residential caregivers. *Behavioral Interventions, 23* (1), 1–12.

Phillips, T., Ferguson, E., & Rijsdijk, F. (2010). A link between altruism and sexual selection: Genetic influence on altruistic behavior and mate preference towards it. *British Journal of Psychology.* (in press)

Phinney, J. S., Berry, J. W., Berry, D. L., & Vedder, S. P. (2006). Understanding immigrant youth: Conclusions and implications. In J. W. Berry, J. S. Phinney, D. L. Sam, & S. P. Vedder (Eds.), *Immigrant youth in cultural transmission.* Mahwah, NJ: Erlbaum.

Piaget, J. (1952). *The origins of intelligence in children.* New York: Oxford University Press.

Pickering, A. D., & Smillie, L. D. (2008). The behavioral activation system: Challenges and opportunities. In P. J. Corr (Ed.), *The reinforcement sensitivity theory of personality* (pp. 120–154). New York: Cambridge University Press.

Pierrehumbert, B., Torrisi, R., Laufer, D., Halfon, O., Ansermet, F., & Beck Popovic, M. (2010). Oxytocin response to an experimental psychosocial challenge in adults exposed to traumatic experiences during childhood or adolescence. *Neuroscience, 166,* 168–177.

Pierucci, M., Di Matteo, V., Benigno, A., Crescimanno, G., Esposito, E., & Di Giovanni, G. (2009). The unilateral nigral lesion induces dramatic bilateral modification on a rat brain monoamine neurochemistry. *Annals of the New York Academy of Sciences, 1155,* 316–323.

Pillemer, D. B. (1998). *Momentous events: Vivid memories.* Cambridge, MA: Harvard University Press.

Pilnick, A., & Coleman, T. (2010). "Do your best for me": The difficulties of finding a clinically effective endpoint in smoking cessation consultations in primary care. *Health, 14,* 57–74.

Pine, D. S. (2009). A social neuroscience approach to adolescent depression. In M. de Haan & M. R. Gunnar (Eds.), *Handbook of developmental social neuroscience.* New York: Guilford.

Pinel, J. P. J. (2009). *Biopsychology* (7th ed.). Upper Saddle River, NJ: Prentice-Hall.

Pinel, P., & Dehaene, S. (2010). Beyond hemispheric dominance: Brain regions underlying the joint lateralization of language and arithmetic to the left hemisphere. *Journal of Cognitive Neuroscience, 22* (1), 48–66.

Pines, A. M., & Maslach, C. (2002). *Experiencing social psychology* (4th ed.). New York: McGraw-Hill.

Pinker, S. (2007). The mystery of consciousness. *Time, 169,* 58–62.

Piolino, P., Desgranges, B., Clarys, D., Guillery-Girard, B., Taconnat, L., Isingrini, M., & Eustache, F. (2006). Autobiographical memory, autonoetic consciousness, and self-perspective in aging. *Psychology and Aging, 21,* 510–525.

Pirucello, L. M. (2010). Preventing adolescent suicide. *Journal of Psychosocial Nursing and Mental Health Services.* (in press)

Pittenger, D. J. (2005). Cautionary comments regarding the Myers-Briggs Type Indicator. *Consulting Psychology Journal: Practice and Research, 57,* 210–221.

Pitychoutis, P. M., Zisaki, A., Dallas, C., & Papadopoulou-Daifoti, Z. (2010). Pharmacogenic insights into depression and antidepressant response: Does sex matter? *Current Pharmaceutical Design.* (in press)

Plant, E. A., & Peruche, B. M. (2005). The consequences of race for police officers' responses to criminal suspects. *Psychological Science, 16,* 180–183.

Plaza-Zabala, A., Martin-Garcia, E., de Lecea, L., Maldonado, R., & Berrendero, F. (2010). Hypcretins regulate the anxiogenic-like effects of nicotine and induce reinstatement of nicotine-seeking behavior. *Journal of Neuroscience, 30,* 2300–2310.

Plomin, R., DeFries, J. C., McClearn, G. E., & McGuffin, P. (2009). *Biological psychology and neuroscience* (5th ed.). New York: Worth.

Ploog, B. O., & Williams, B. A. (2010). Serial discrimination reversal learning in pigeons as a function of intertrial interval and delay of reinforcement. *Learning & Behavior, 38,* 96–102.

Ployhart, R. E., & MacKenzie, W. I. (2010). Situational judgment tests: A critical review and agenda for the future. In S. Zedeck (Ed.), *APA handbook of industrial and organizational psychology.* Washington, DC: APA. (in press)

Poisnel, G., Dhilly, M., Boisselier, R. L., Barre, L., & Debruyne, D. (2009). Comparison of five benzodiazepine-receptor agonists on buprenorphine-induced mu-opioid receptor regulation. *Journal of Pharmacological Sciences, 110,* 36–46.

Pollack, M. H. (2009). Refractory generalized anxiety disorder. *Journal of Clinical Psychiatry, 70,* Suppl. 2, S32–S38.

Polyn, S. M., Norman, K. A., & Kahana, M. J. (2009). Task context and organization in free recall. *Neuropsychologia, 47,* 2158–2163.

Pomerantz, E. M., Saxon, J. L., & Oishi, S. (2000). The psychological trade-offs of goal investment. *Journal of Personality and Social Psychology, 79,* 617–630.

Pompili, M., & others. (2007). Suicide risk in schizophrenia: Learning from the past to change the future. *Annals of General Psychiatry, 6,* 10.

Pompili, M., & others. (2010). The hypothalamic-pituitary-adrenal axis and serotonin abnormalities: A selective overview for the implications of suicide prevention. *European Archives of Psychiatry and Clinical Neuroscience.* (in press)

Popeo, D. M. (2009). Electroconvulsive therapy for depressive episodes: A brief review. *Geriatrics, 64,* 9–12.

Popova, N. K., Naumenko, V. S., Cybko, A. S., & Bazovkina, D. V. (2010). Receptor-genes cross-talk: Effect of chronic 5-HT1A agonist 8-OH-DPAT treatment on the expression of key genes in brain serotonin system and on behavior. *Neuroscience.* (in press)

Popp, A. (2006, November). *Inequality and segregation as correlates of urban crime rates.* Paper presented at the annual meeting of the American Society of Criminology (ASC), Los Angeles.

Poppenk, J., Moscovitch, M., McIntosh, A. R., Ozcelik, E., & Craik, F. L. (2010). Encoding the future: Successful processing of intentions engages predictive brain networks. *NeuroImage, 49,* 905–913.

Porter, S., & ten Brinke, L. (2008). Reading between the lies: Identifying concealed and falsified emotions in universal facial expressions. *Psychological Science, 19,* 508–514.

Portnuff, C. D. F., & Fligor, B. J. (2006, October). *Output levels of portable music players.* Presented at the American Auditory Society Conference, Cincinnati.

Poryazova, R., Schnepf, B., Werth, E., Khatami, R., Dydak, U., Meier, D., Boesiger, P., & Bassetti, C. L. (2009). Evidence for metabolic hypothalamo-amygdala dysfunction in narcolepsy. *Sleep: Journal of Sleep and Sleep Disorders Research, 32,* 607–613.

Posner J., Russell J., & Peterson, B. S. (2005). The circumplex model of affect: An integrative approach to affective neuroscience, cognitive development, and psychopathology. *Developmental Psychopathology, 17,* 715–734.

Posner, M. I., & Rothbart, M. K. (2010). Brain states and hypnosis research. *Consciousness and Cognition.* (in press)

Postel, M. G., de Haan, H. A., & de Jong, C. A. (2010). Evaluation of an e-therapy program for problem drinkers: A pilot study. *Substance Use and Misuse.* (in press)

Postel, M. G., de Jong, C. A. J., & de Haan, H. A. (2005). Does e-therapy for problem drinking reach hidden populations? *American Journal of Psychiatry, 162,* 2393.

Powell, R. A., Symbaluk, D. G., & Honey, P. L. (2009). *Introduction to learning and behavior* (3rd ed.). Belmont, CA: Cengage.

Prakash, R. S., Snook, T., Motl, R. W., & Kramer, A. F. (2010). Aerobic fitness is associated with gray matter volume and white matter integrity in multiple sclerosis. *Brain Research.* (in press)

Prescott, T. J., & Humphries, M. D. (2007). Who dominates the dark basements of the brain? *Behavioral and Brain Sciences, 30,* 104–105.

Pressman, J. (1998). *Last resort, Psychosurgery and the limits of medicine.* New York: Cambridge University Press.

Preston, T. J., Kourtzi, Z., & Welchman, A. E. (2009). Adaptive estimation of three-dimensional structure in the human brain. *Journal of Neuroscience, 29,* 1688–1699.

Price, D. D., Finniss, D. G., & Benedetti, F. (2008). A comprehensive review of the placebo effect. *Annual Review of Psychology* (vol. 59). Palo Alto: Annual Reviews.

Probstner, D., Thuler, L. C., Ishikawa, N. M., & Alvarenga, R. M. (2010). Phantom limb phenomena in cancer amputees. *Pain Practice.* (in press)

Prochaska, J. O., DiClemente, C. C., & Norcross, J. C. (1992). In search of how people change: Applications to addictive behaviors. *American Psychologist, 47,* 1102–1114.

Prochaska, J. O., & Norcross, J. C. (2010). *Systems of psychotherapy* (7th ed.). Pacific Grove, CA: Brooks/Cole.

Prochaska, J. O., Norcross, J. C., & DiClemente, C. C. (1994). *Changing for good: A revolutionary six-stage program for overcoming bad habits and moving your life positively forward.* New York: Avon Books.

Proctor, R. W., & Vu, K. (2010). Cumulative knowledge and progress in human factors. *Annual Review of Psychology* (vol. 61). Palo Alto, CA: Annual Reviews.

Pronk, T. M., Karremans, J. C., Overbeek, G., Vermulst, A. A., & Wigboldus, D. H. J. (2010). What it takes to forgive: When and why executive functioning facilitates forgiveness. *Journal of Personality and Social Psychology, 98,* 119–131.

Provenzo, E. F. (2002). *Teaching, learning, and schooling in American culture: A critical perspective.* Boston: Allyn & Bacon.

Provine, R. R., Spencer, R. J., & Mandell, D. L. (2007). Emotional expression online: Emoticons punctuate website text messages. *Journal of Language and Social Psychology, 26,* 299–307.

Pujadas, L., & others. (2010). Reelin regulates postnatal neurogenesis and enhances spin hypertrophy and long-term potentiating. *Journal of Neuroscience, 30,* 4636–4649.

Pukrop, R., Sass, H., & Steinmeyer, E. M. (2000). Circumplex models for the similarity relationships between higher-order factors of personality and personality disorders: An empirical analysis. *Contemporary Psychiatry, 41,* 438–445.

Puterman, E., Lin, J., Blackburn, E., O'Donovan, A., Adler, N., & Epel, E. (2010). The power of exercise: Buffering the effect of chronic stress on telomere length. *PLoS One, 5,* e10837.

Q

Qian, Z. (2009). Mate selection. In D. Carr (Ed.), *Encyclopedia of the life course and human development.* Boston: Gale Cengage.

Quan, S. F., Parthasarathy, S., & Budhiraja, R. (2010). Healthy sleep education—a salve for obesity. *Journal of Clinical Sleep Medicine, 6,* 18–19.

Quang, P. N., & Schmidt, B. L. (2010). Endothelin-A receptor antagonism attenuates carcinoma-induced pain through opioids in mice. *Journal of Pain.* (in press)

Quinn, J. G., & McConnell, J. (2006). The interval for interference in conscious visual imagery. *Memory, 14,* 241–252.

Quinn, P. C. (2011). Born to categorize. In U. Goswami (Ed.), *Wiley-Blackwell handbook of childhood cognitive development* (2nd ed.). New York: Wiley Blackwell.

R

Raabe, B., & Beehr, T. A. (2003). Formal mentoring versus supervisor and co-worker relationships: Differences in perceptions and impact. *Journal of Organizational Behavior, 24,* 271–293.

Racagni, G., & Popoli, M. (2010). The pharmacological properties of antidepressants. *International Clinical Psychopharmacology, 25,* 117–131.

Rachlin, H., & Green, L. (2009). The neural basis of drug craving: An incentive-sensitization theory of addiction. In D. Shanks (Ed.), *Psychology of learning.* Thousand Oaks, CA: Sage.

Rachman, S. (2009). Psychological treatment of anxiety: The evolution of behavior therapy and cognitive-behavior therapy. *Annual Review of Clinical Psychology* (vol. 5). Palo Alto, CA: Annual Reviews.

Racsmany, M., Conway, M. A., & Demeter, G. (2010). Consolidation of episodic memory during sleep: Long-term effects of retrieval practice. *Psychological Science, 21,* 80–85.

Radel, R., Sarrazin, P., & Pelletier, L. (2009). Evidence of subliminally primed motivational orientations: The effects of unconscious motivational processes on the performance of a new motor task. *Journal of Sport and Exercise Psychology, 31,* 657–674.

Rafanelli, C., Milaneschi, Y., Roncuzzi, R., & Pancaldi, L. G. (2010). Dysthymia before myocardial infarction as a cardiac risk factor at 2.5-year follow-up. *Psychosomatics, 51,* 8–13.

Raffone, A., & Srinivasan, N. (2010). The exploration of meditation in the neuroscience of attention and consciousness. *Cognitive Processes.* (in press)

Ragins, B. R., Cotton, J. L., & Miller, J. S. (2000). Marginal mentoring: The effects of type of mentor, quality of relationship, and program design on work and career attitudes. *Academy of Management Journal, 43,* 1177–1194.

Rahman, Q. (2005). The neurodevelopment of human sexual orientation. *Neuroscience & Biobehavioral Reviews, 29,* 1057–1066.

Rahman, Q., Clarke, K., & Morera, T. (2009). Hair whorl direction and sexual orientation in human males. *Behavioral Neuroscience, 123,* 252–256.

Rahman, Q., & Wilson, G. D. (2003). Sexual orientation and the 2nd to 4th finger length ratio: Evidence for organising effects of sex hormones or developmental instability? *Psychoneuroendocrinology, 28,* 288–303.

Raine, A. (2008). From genes to brain to antisocial behavior. *Current Directions in Psychological Science, 17,* 323–328.

Raine, A., Venables, P. H., & Williams, M. (1990). Relationships between N1, P300 and CNV recorded at age 15 and criminal behavior at age 24. *Psychophysiology, 27,* 567–575.

Rajkumar, R., & Mahesh, R. (2010). The auspicious role of the 5-HT3 receptor in depression: A probably neuronal target? *Journal of Psychopharmacology.* (in press)

Ram, N., Morelli, S., Lindberg, C., & Carstensen, L. L. (2008). From static to dynamic: The ongoing dialectic about human development. In K. W. Schaie & R. P. Abeles (Eds.), *Social structures and aging individuals.* Mahwah, NJ: Erlbaum.

Ramey, C. T., Ramey, S. L., & Lanzi, R. G. (2006). Children's health and education. In W. Damon & R. Lerner (Eds.), *Handbook of child psychology* (6th ed.). New York: Wiley.

Ramirez-Esparza, N., Gosling, S. D., Benet-Martinez, V., Potter, J. P., & Pennebaker, J. W. (2006). Do bilinguals have two personalities? A special case of cultural frame switching. *Journal of Research in Personality, 40,* 99–120.

Rammstedt, B., Goldberg, L. R., & Borg, I. (2010). The measurement equivalence of Big Five factor markers for persons with different levels of education. *Journal of Research in Personality, 44,* 53–61.

Ramon, J. M., & Bruguera, E. (2009). Real world study to evaluate the effectiveness of varenicline and cognitive-behavioral interventions for smoking cessation. *International Journal of Environmental Research and Public Health, 6,* 1530–1538.

Ramsey, J. L., Langlois, J. H., Hoss, R. A., Rubenstein, A. J., & Griffin, A. M. (2004). Origins of a stereotype: Categorization of facial attractiveness by 6-month-old infants. *Developmental Science, 7* (2), 201–211.

Ramsey, R., & de C. Hamilton, A. F. (2010). Understanding actors and object-goals in the human brain. *NeuroImage, 50,* 1142–1147.

Ramsoy, T. Z., Liptrot, M. G., Skimminge, A., Lund, T. E., Sidaros, K., Christensen, M. S., Baare, W., Paulson, O. B., & Jernigan, T. L. (2009). Regional activation of the human medial temporal lobe during intentional encoding of objects and positions. *NeuroImage, 47,* 1863–1872.

Rao, U., Hammen, C. L., & Poland, R. E. (2009). Risk markers for depression in adolescents: Sleep and HPA measures. *Neuropsychopharmacology, 34,* 1936–1945.

Rapanelli, M., Lew, S. E., Frick, L. R., & Zanutto, B. S. (2010). Plasticity in the rate prefrontal cortex: Linking gene expression and an operant learning with a computational theory. *PLoS One, 5,* e8656.

Rapaport, D. (1967). On the psychoanalytic theory of thinking. In M. M. Gill (Ed.), *The collected papers of David Rapaport*. New York: Basic.

Rapaport, S. (1994, November 28). Interview. *U.S. News and World Report*, 94.

Rapee, R. M., Gaston, J. E., & Abbott, M. J. (2009). Testing the efficacy of theoretically derived improvements in the treatment of social phobia. *Journal of Consulting and Clinical Psychology, 77*, 317–327.

Raposo, A., Han, S., & Dobbins, I. G. (2009). Ventrolateral prefrontal cortex and self-initiated semantic elaboration during memory retrieval. *Neuropsychologia, 47*, 2261–2271.

Rathunde, K., & Csikszentmihalyi, M. (2006). The developing person: An experiential perspective. In W. Damon & R. Lerner (Eds.), *Handbook of child psychology* (6th ed.). New York: Wiley.

Ratner, N. B. (1993). Learning to speak. *Science, 262*, 260.

Rauch, S. L., Shin, L. M., & Phelps, E. A. (2006). Neurocircuitry models of posttraumatic stress disorder and extinction: Human neuro-imaging research—past, present, and future. *Biological Psychiatry, 60*, 376–382.

Raudies, F., & Neumann, H. (2010). A neural model of the temporal dynamics of figure-ground segregation in motion perception. *Neural Networks, 23*, 160–176.

Ravassard, P., & others. (2009). Paradoxical (REM) sleep deprivation causes a large and rapidly reversible decrease in long-term potentiation, synaptic transmission, glutamate receptor protein levels, and ERK/MAPK activation in the dorsal hippocampus. *Sleep, 32*, 227–240.

Raven, P. H., Johnson, G. B., Mason, K. A., Losos, J. B., & Singer, S. S. (2011). *Biology* (9th ed.). New York: McGraw-Hill.

Rawson, N. E., & Yee, K. K. (2006). Transduction and coding. *Advances in Otorhinolaryngology, 63*, 23–43.

Ray, W. J. (2009). *Methods toward a science of behavior and experience* (9th ed.). Belmont, CA: Wadsworth.

Raynor, H. A., Jeffrey, R. W., Phelan, S., Hill, J. O., & Wing, R. R. (2005). Amount of food groups variety consumed in the diet and long term weight loss maintenance. *Obesity Research, 13*, 883–890.

Raz, A., Schwiezer, H. R., Zhu, H., & Bowles, E. N. (2010). Hypnotic dreams as a lens into hypnotic dynamics. *International Journal of Clinical and Experimental Hypnosis, 58*, 69–81.

Rector, N. A., & Beck, A. T. (2001). Cognitive behavioral therapy for schizophrenia: An empirical review. *Journal of Nervous and Mental Disorders, 189*, 278–287.

Recupero, P. R., & Rainey, S. E. (2006). Characteristics of E-therapy, web sites. *Journal of Clinical Psychiatry, 67*, 1435–1440.

Reder, L. M., Park, H., & Kieffaber, P. D. (2009). Memory systems do not divide on consciousness: Reinterpreting memory in terms of activation and binding. *Psychological Bulletin, 135*, 23–49.

Redondo, J. L., Fernandez, J., Garcia, I., & Ortigosa, P. M. (2009). Solving the multiple competitive facilities location and design problem on the plane. *Evolutionary Computation, 17*, 21–53.

Ree, M. J., & Carretta, T. R. (2007). Tests of cognitive ability. In D. L. Whetzel & G. R. Wheaton (Eds.), *Applied measurement*. Mahwah, NJ: Erlbaum.

Reece, B. L., Brandt, R., & Howie, K. T. (2011). *Effective human relations* (11th ed.). Boston: Cengage.

Reed, S. K. (2010). *Thinking visually*. New York: Psychology Press.

Reeve, C. (2000, May 1). Use the body's repair kit. *Time, 155*, 18.

Reeve, C. L., & Charles, J. E. (2008). Survey of opinions on the primacy of *g* and social consequences of ability testing: A comparison of expert and non-expert views. *Intelligence, 36*, 681–688.

Reeves, R. R., & Burke, R. S. (2010). Carisoprodol: Abuse potential and withdrawal syndrome. *Current Drug Abuse Reviews, 3*, 33–38.

Reger, M. A., & Gahm, G. A. (2009). A meta-analysis of the effects of internet- and computer-based cognitive-behavioral treatments for anxiety. *Journal of Clinical Psychology, 65*, 53–75.

Reich, J. (2009). Avoidant personality disorder and its relationship to social phobia. *Current Psychiatry Reports, 11*, 89–93.

Reichel, C. M., & Bevins, R. A. (2010). Competition between novelty and cocaine conditioned reward is sensitive to drug dose and retention interval. *Behavioral Neuroscience, 124*, 141–151.

Reimer, T., & Rieskamp, J. (2007). Fast and frugal heuristics. In R. F. Baumeister & K. D. Vohs (Eds.), *Encyclopedia of social psychology*. Thousand Oaks, CA: Sage.

Reinhardt, I., & others. (2010). Neural correlates of aversive conditioning: Development of a functional imaging paradigm for the investigation of anxiety disorders. *European Archives of Psychiatry and Clinical Neuroscience*. (in press)

Reis, H. T., Sheldon, K. M., Gable, S. L., Roscoe, J., & Ryan, R. M. (2000). Daily well-being: The role of autonomy, competence, and relatedness. *Personality and Social Psychology Bulletin, 26*, 419–435.

Reisner, S. L., Mimiaga, M. J., Skeer, M., & Mayer, K. H. (2009). Beyond anal sex: Sexual practices associated with HIV risk reduction among men who have sex with men in Boston, Massachusetts. *AIDS Patient Care and STDs, 23*, 545–550.

Reivich, K., & Gillham, J. (2003). Learned optimism: The measurement of explanatory style. In S. J. Lopez & C. R. Snyder (Eds.), *Positive psychological assessment: A handbook of models and measures* (pp. 57–74). Washington, DC: American Psychological Association.

Remington, G. (2007). Tardive dyskinesia: Eliminated, forgotten or overshadowed? *Current Opinion in Psychiatry, 20*, 131–137.

Rendell, P. G., & Craik, F. I. M. (2000). Virtual week and actual week: Age-related differences in prospective memory. *Applied Cognitive Psychology, 14*, S43–S62.

Rescorla, R. A. (1966). Predictability and number of pairings in Pavlovian fear conditioning. *Psychonomic Science, 4*, 383–384.

Rescorla, R. A. (1988). Pavlovian conditioning: It's not what you think it is. *American Psychologist, 43*, 151–160.

Rescorla, R. A. (2003). Contemporary study of Pavlovian conditioning. *Spanish Journal of Psychology, 6*, 185–195.

Rescorla, R. A. (2004). Spontaneous recovery varies inversely with the training-extinction interval. *Learning and Behavior, 32*, 401–408.

Rescorla, R. A. (2005). Spontaneous recovery of excitation but not inhibition. *Journal of Experimental Psychology: Animal Behavior Processes, 31*, 277–288.

Rescorla, R. A. (2006a). Stimulus generalization of excitation and inhibition. *Quarterly Journal of Experimental Psychology, 59*, 53–67.

Rescorla, R. A. (2006b). Spontaneous recovery from overexpectation. *Learning and Behavior, 34*, 13–20.

Rescorla, R. A. (2006c). Deepened extinction from compound stimulus presentation. *Journal of Experimental Psychology: Animal Behavior Processes, 32*(2), 135–144.

Rescorla, R. A. (2009). A theory of Pavlovian conditioning: Variations in the effectiveness of reinforcement and nonreinforcement. In D. Shanks (Ed.), *Psychology of learning*. Thousand Oaks, CA: Sage.

Rescorla, R. A., & Wagner, A. R. (2009). A theory of attention: Variations in the associability of stimuli with reinforcement. In D. Shanks (Ed.), *Psychology of learning*. Thousand Oaks, CA: Sage.

Rethorst, C. D., Wipfli, B. M., & Landers, D. M. (2009). The antidepressive effects of exercise: A meta-analysis of randomized trials. *Sports Medicine, 39*, 491–511.

Reuter-Lorenz, P., & Davidson, R. J. (1981). Differential contributions of the two cerebral hemispheres to the perception of happy and sad faces. *Neuropsychologia, 19*, 609–613.

Revelle, W. (2008). The contribution of reinforcement sensitivity theory to personality theory. In P. J. Corr (Ed.), *The reinforcement sensitivity theory of personality* (pp. 508–527). New York: Cambridge University Press.

Reverberi, C., Shallice, T., D'Agostini, S., Skrap, M., & Bonatti, L. L. (2009). Cortical bases of elementary deductive reasoning, inference, memory, and metadeduction. *Neuropsychologia, 47*, 1107–1116.

Revonsuo, A., Kallio, S., & Sikka, P. (2009). What is an altered state of consciousness? *Philosophical Psychology, 22*, 187–204.

Reynolds, C. R., Livingston, R., & Willson, V. (2006). *Measurement and assessment in education*. Boston: Allyn & Bacon.

Rhoades, G. K., Stanley, S. M., & Markham, H. J. (2009). The pre-engagement cohabitation effect: A replication and extension of previous findings. *Journal of Family Psychology, 23*, 107–111.

Rieger, G., Linsenmeier, J. A. W., & Bailey, J. M. (2009). Childhood gender nonconformity remains a robust and neutral correlate of sexual orientation: Reply to Hegary (2009). *Developmental Psychology, 45*, 901–903.

Rieger, G., Linsenmeier, J. A. W., Gygax, L., & Bailey, J. M. (2008). Sexual orientation and childhood gender nonconformity: Evidence from home videos. *Developmental Psychology, 44*, 46–58.

Riezzo, I., Cerretani, D., Fiore, C., Bello, S., Centini, F., D'Errico, S., Fiaschi, A. I., Giorgi, G., Neri, M., Pomara, C., Turillazzi, E., & Fineschi, V. (2010). Enzymatic-nonenzymatic cellular antioxidant defense systems response and immunohistochemical detection of MDMA, VMAT2, HSP70, and apoptosis as biomarkers for MDMA (ecstasy) neurotoxicity. *Journal of Neuroscience Research, 88*, 905–916.

Riketta, M. (2002). Attitudinal organizational commitment and job performance: A meta-analysis. *Journal of Organizational Behavior, 23*, 257–266.

Rilling, J. K., & Sanfey, A. (2011). The neuroscience of decision making. *Annual Review of Psychology* (vol. 62). Palo Alto, CA: Annual Reviews.

Risley, T. R., & Hart, B. (2006). Promoting early language development. In N. F. Watt, C. Ayoub, R. H. Bradley, J. E. Puma, & W. A. LeBoeuf (Eds.), *The crisis in youth mental health: Critical issues and effective programs, vol. 4: Early intervention programs and policies* (pp. 83–88). Westport, CT: Praeger.

Ritchey, M., Labar, K. S., & Cabeza, R. (2010). Level of processing modulates the neural correlates of emotional memory formation. *Journal of Cognitive Neuroscience.* (in press)

Ritskes, R., Ritskes-Hoitinga, M., Stodkilde-Jorgensen, H., Baerentsen, K., & Hartman, T. (2003). MRI scanning during Zen meditation: The picture of enlightenment? *Constructivism in the Human Sciences, 8* (1), 85–90.

Ritter, D., & Elsea, M. (2005). Hot sauce, toy guns, and graffiti: A critical account of current laboratory aggression paradigms. *Aggressive Behavior, 31*, 407–419.

Ro, H. S., & Wampler, R. S. (2009). What's wrong with these people? Clinicians' views of clinical couples. *Journal of Marital and Family Therapy, 35*, 3–17.

Robbins, T. L., & DeNisi, A. S. (1994). A closer look at interpersonal affect as a distinct influence on cognitive processing in performance evaluations. *Journal of Applied Psychology, 79*, 341–353.

Roberts, B. W., Caspi, A., & Moffitt, T. E. (2003). Work experiences and personality development in young adulthood. *Journal of Personality and Social Psychology, 84*, 582–593.

Roberts, B. W., Jackson, J. J., Fayard, J. V., Edmonds, G., & Meints, J. O. (2009). Conscientiousness. In M. Leary & R. Hoyle (Eds.), *Handbook of individual differences in social behavior* (pp. 369–381). New York: Guilford.

Roberts, B. W., Kuncel, N., Shiner, R. N., Caspi, A., & Goldberg, L. (2007). The power of personality: A comparative analysis of the predictive validity of personality traits, SES,

and IQ. *Perspectives on Psychological Science, 2*, 313–345.

Roberts, B. W., & Mroczek, D. (2008). Personality trait change in adulthood. *Current Directions in Psychological Science, 17*, 31–35.

Roberts, B. W., Walton, K. E., & Viechtbauer, W. (2006). Patterns of mean level change in personality traits across the life course: A meta-analysis of longitudinal studies. *Psychological Bulletin, 132*, 1–25.

Roberts, B. W., Wood, D., & Caspi, A. (2008). Personality development. In O. P. John, R. W., Robins, & L. A. Pervin (Eds.), *Handbook of personality: Theory and research* (3rd ed.). New York: Guilford.

Roberts, D. F., Henriksen, L., & Foehr, U. G. (2009). Adolescence, adolescents, and the media. In R. M. Lerner & L. Steinberg (Eds.), *Handbook of adolescent psychology* (3rd ed.). New York: Wiley.

Robinson, A., Shore, B. M., & Enersen, D. L. (2007). Best practices in gifted education: An evidence-based guide. Waco, TX: Prufrock Press.

Robinson, A. J. (2008). McGregor's Theory X-Theory Y model. In J. Gordon (Ed.), *The Pfeiffer book of successful leadership development tools: The most enduring, effective, and valuable training activities for developing leaders* (pp. 63–66). San Francisco: Pfeiffer/Wiley.

Rodgers, J. L. (2007). The shape of things to come: Diagnosing social contagion from adolescent smoking and drinking curves. In T. D. Little, J. A. Bovaird, & N. A. Card (Eds.), *Modeling contextual effects in longitudinal studies* (pp. 343–362). Mahwah, NJ: Erlbaum.

Rodgers, R. J., Holch, P., & Tallett, A. J. (2010). Behavioral satiety sequence (BSS): Separating wheat from chaff in the behavioral pharmacology of appetite. *Pharmacology, Biochemistry, and Behavior.* (in press)

Rodin, J. (1984, December). Interview: A sense of control. *Psychology Today*, 38–45.

Rodriquez, M. L., & Walden, N. J. (2010). Socializing relationships. In D. P. Swanson, M. C. Edwards, & M. B. Spencer (Eds.), *Adolescence: Development in a global era.* San Diego: Academic.

Roediger, H. L., & Marsh, E. J. (2003). Episodic and autobiographical memory. In I. B. Weiner (Ed.), *Handbook of psychology* (vol. 4). New York: Wiley.

Roese, N. J., & Summerville, A. (2005). What we regret most . . . and why. *Personality and Social Psychology Bulletin, 31*, 1273–1285.

Roethlisberger, F. J. (1941). *Management and morale.* Cambridge, MA: Harvard University Press.

Roethlisberger, F. J., & Dickson, W. J. (1939). *Management and the worker.* Cambridge, MA: Harvard University Press.

Rogers, C. R. (1961). *On becoming a person.* Boston: Houghton Mifflin.

Rogers, C. R. (1980). *A way of being.* Boston: Houghton Mifflin.

Rogers, G., & others. (2009). The harmful health effects of recreational Ecstasy: A systematic review of observational evidence. *Health Technology Assessment, 13*, 1–315.

Rojas, A., Khoo, A., Tejedo, J. R., Bedoya, F. J., Soria, B., & Martin, F. (2010). Islet cell development. *Advances in Experimental Medicine and Biology, 654*, 59–75.

Rojas, Y., & Stenberg, S. A. (2010). Early life circumstances and male suicide—a 30-year follow-up of a Stockholm cohort born in 1953. *Social Science Medicine, 70*, 420–427.

Rolland, Y., van Kan, G. A., & Vellas, B. (2010). Healthy brain aging: Role of exercise and physical activity. *Clinics in Geriatric Medicine, 26*, 75–87.

Romero-Canyas, R., Downey, G., Berenson, K., Ayduk, O., & Kang, N. J. (2010). Rejection sensitivity and the rejection-hostility link in romantic relationships. *Journal of Personality, 78*, 119–148.

Ronningstam, E. (2010). Narcissistic personality disorder: A current review. *Current Psychiatry Reports, 12*, 68–75.

Rosa-Alcazar, A. I., Sanchez-Meca, J., Gomez-Conesa, A., & Marin-Martinez, F. (2008). Psychological treatment of obsessive-compulsive disorder: A meta-analysis. *Clinical Psychology Review, 28*, 1310–1325.

Rosack, J. (2007). Impact of FDA warning questioned in suicide rise. *Psychiatric News, 5*, 1.

Rose, A. J. (2002). Co-rumination in the friendships of girls and boys. *Child Development, 73*, 1830–1843.

Rose, A. J., Carlson, W., & Waller, E. M. (2007). Prospective associations of co-rumination with friendship and emotional adjustment: Considering the socioemotional trade-offs of co-rumination. *Developmental Psychology, 43*, 1019–1031.

Rose, A. J., & Smith, R. L. (2009). Sex differences in peer relationships. In K. H. Rubin, W. M. Bukowski, & B. Laursen (Eds.), *Handbook of peer interactions, relationships, and groups.* New York: Guilford.

Rose, M., Haider, H., & Buchel, C. (2010). The emergence of explicit memory during learning. *Cerebral Cortex.* (in press)

Rosell, D. R., & others. (2010). Increased serotonin 2A receptor availability in the orbitofrontal cortex of physically aggressive personality disordered patients. *Biological Psychiatry.* (in press)

Roseman, I. J., & Smith, C. A. (2009). Appraisal theory: Overview, assumptions, varieties, controversies. In K. R. Scherer, A. Schorr, T. Johnstone (Eds.), *Appraisal processes in emotion: Theory, methods, research* (pp. 3–19). Oxford, U.K.: Oxford University Press.

Rosen, K., & Garety, P. (2005). Predicting recovery from schizophrenia: A retrospective comparison of characteristics at onset of people with single and multiple episodes. *Schizophrenia Bulletin, 31*, 735–750.

Rosenberg, M. S., Westling, D. L., & McLeskey, J. (2011). *Special education for today's teachers* (2nd ed.). Upper Saddle River, NJ: Merrill.

Rosenhan, D. L. (1973). On being sane in insane places. *Science, 179*, 250–258.

Rosenthal, R. (1966). *Experimenter effects in behavioral research.* New York: Appleton-Century-Crofts.

Rosenthal, R., & DiMatteo, M. R. (2001). Meta-analysis: Recent developments in quantitative methods for literature reviews. *Annual Review of Psychology* (vol. 52). Palo Alto, CA: Annual Reviews.

Rosenthal, R., & Jacobsen, L. (1968). *Pygmalion in the classroom*. Fort Worth, TX: Harcourt Brace.

Rosenzweig, S., Greenson, J. M., Reibel, D. K., Green, J. S., Jasser, S. A., & Beasley, D. (2010). Mindfulness-based stress reduction for chronic pain conditions: Variations in treatment outcomes and role of home meditation practice. *Journal of Psychosomatic Research, 68*, 29–36.

Rosier, J. P., Stephan, K. E., den Ouden, H. E. M., Friston, K. J., & Joyce, E. M. (2010). Adaptive and aberrant reward prediction signals in the human brain. *NeuroImage, 50*, 657–664.

Rosmarin, D. H., Krumrei, E. J., & Andersson, G. (2009). Religion as a predictor of psychological distress in two religious communities. *Cognitive Behavior Therapy, 38*, 54–64.

Rosnow, R. L., & Rosenthal, R. (2008). *Beginning behavioral research* (6th ed.). Upper Saddle River, NJ: Prentice-Hall.

Ross, K., Handel, P. J., Clark, E. M., & Vander Wal, J. S. (2009a). The relationship between religion and religious coping: Religious coping as a moderator between coping and adjustment. *Journal of Religion and Health*.

Ross, K. M., Milsom, V. A., Debraganza, N., Gibbons, L. M., Murawski, M. E., & Perri, M. G. (2009b). The contributions of weight loss and increased physical fitness to improvements in health-related quality of life. *Eating Behaviors, 10*, 84–88.

Ross, L., Kohler, C. L., Grimley, D. M., & Anderson-Lewis, C. (2007). The theory of reasoned action and intention to seek cancer information. *American Journal of Health Behavior, 31*, 123–134.

Ross, R. S., Brown, T. I., & Stern, C. E. (2009). The retrieval of learned sequences engages the hippocampus: Evidence from fMRI. *Hippocampus, 19*, 790–799.

Rossi, E. L. (2009). The psychosocial genomics of therapeutic hypnosis, psychotherapy, and rehabilitation. *American Journal of Clinical Hypnosis, 51*, 281–298.

Rotella, R. J. (2010). *Case studies in sport psychology*. Sudbury, MA: Jones & Bartlett.

Roten, R. G. (2007). DSM-IV and the taxonomy of roles: How can the taxonomy of roles complement the DSM-IV to create a more holistic diagnostic tool? *The Arts in Psychotherapy, 34*, 53–68.

Rotge, J. Y., & others. (2009). Inverse relationship between thalamic and orbitofrontal volumes in obsessive-compulsive disorder. *Progress in Neuro-Psychopharmacology & Biological Psychiatry, 33*, 682–686.

Rothbart, M. K., & Gartstein, M. A. (2008). Temperament. In M. M. Haith & J. B. Benson (Eds.), *Encyclopedia of infant and early childhood development*. London: Elsevier.

Rouder, J. N., & Morey, R. D. (2009). The nature of psychological thresholds. *Psychological Review, 116*, 655–660.

Roughgarden, J., Oishi, M., & Akcay, E. (2006). Reproductive social behavior: Cooperative games to replace sexual selection. *Science, 311*, 965–968.

Rowland, D. L., & McMahon, C. G. (2008). Premature ejaculation. In D. L. Rowland & L. Incrocci (Eds.), *Handbook of sexual and gender identity disorders* (pp. 68–97). Hoboken, NJ: Wiley.

Roy, M., & others. (2010). Medial frontal cortex activity during memory encoding of pictures and its relation to symptomatic improvement after citalopram treatment in patients with major depression. *Journal of Psychiatry and Neuroscience, 35*, 152–162.

Roy-Byrne, P., & others. (2010). Delivery of evidence-based treatment for multiple anxiety disorders in primary care: A randomized controlled trial. *Journal of the American Medical Association, 303*, 1921–1928.

Rubin, K. H., Cheah, C., & Menzer, M. M. (2010). Peers. In M. H. Bornstein (Ed.), *Handbook of cultural developmental science*. New York: Psychology Press.

Rubin, Z., & Mitchell, C. (1976). Couples research as couples counseling: Some unintended effects of studying close relationships. *American Psychologist, 31*, 17–25.

Ruck, C. (2003). Psychosurgery. *Journal of Neurosurgery, 99*, 1113–1114.

Rudy, D., & Grusec, J. E. (2006). Authoritarian parenting in individualist and collectivist groups: Associations with maternal emotion and cognition and children's self-esteem. *Journal of Family Psychology, 20*, 68–78.

Ruini, C., Belaise, C., Brombin, C., Caffo, E., & Fava, G. A. (2006). Well-being therapy in school settings: A pilot study. *Psychotherapy and Psychosomatics, 75*, 331–336.

Ruini, C., & Fava, G. A. (2004). Clinical applications of well-being therapy. In A. Linley & S. Joseph (Eds.), *Positive psychology in practice* (pp. 371–387). Hoboken, NJ: Wiley.

Ruini, C., & Fava, G. A. (2009). Well-being therapy for generalized anxiety disorder. *Journal of Clinical Psychology, 65*, 510–519.

Ruiz, A., Campanac, E., Scott, R. S., Rusakov, D. A., & Kullman, D. M. (2010). Presynaptic GABA (A) receptors enhance transmission and LTP induction at hippocampal mossy fiber synapses. *Nature Neuroscience, 13*, 431–438.

Rule, N. O., Ambady, N., Adams, R. B., Ozono, H., Nakashima, S., Yoshikawa, S., & Watabe, M. (2010). Polling the face: Prediction and consensus across cultures. *Journal of Personality and Social Psychology, 98*, 1–15.

Rummel, J. (2010). Psychological distance to a prospective memory cue influences the probability of fulfilling a delayed intention. *Memory*. (in press)

Runyon, W. M. (2007). *Psychology and historical interpretation*. New York: Oxford University Press.

Rusbult, C. E., & Agnew, C. R. (2010). Prosocial motivation and behavior in close relationships. In M. Mikulincer & P. R. Shaver (Eds.), *Prosocial motives, emotions, and behavior: The better angels of our nature* (pp. 327–345). Washington, DC: American Psychological Association.

Rusbult, C. E., Finkel, E. J., & Kumashiro, M. (2009). The Michelangelo phenomenon. *Current Directions in Psychological Science, 18*, 305–309.

Rusbult, C. E., Kumashiro, M., Coolsen, M. K., & Kirchner, J. L. (2004). Interdependence, closeness, and relationships. In D. J. Mashek & A. P. Aaron (Eds.), *Handbook of closeness and intimacy* (pp. 137–161). Mahwah, NJ: Erlbaum.

Rush, C. C., Becker, S. J., & Curry, J. F. (2009). Personality factors and styles among college students who binge eat and drink. *Psychology of Addictive Behaviors, 23*, 140–145.

Russell, K. L, & Bray, S. R. (2010). Promoting self-determined motivation for exercise in cardiac rehabilitation: The role of autonomy support. *Rehabilitation Psychology, 55*, 74–80.

Russo, S. J., & others. (2010). The addicted synapse: Mechanisms of synaptic and structural plasticity in nucleus accumbens. *Trends in Neuroscience*. (in press)

Rustin, J. (2009). The interface of self psychology, infant research, and neuroscience in clinical practice. *Annals of the New York Academy of Sciences, 1159*, 204–217.

Rutishauser, U., Ross, I. B., Mamelak, A. N., & Schuman, E. M. (2010). Human memory strength is predicted by theta-frequency phase-locking of single neurons. *Nature*. (in press)

Rutter, M. (2007). Gene-environment interplay and developmental psychopathology. In A. S. Masten (Ed.), *Multilevel dynamics in developmental psychology*. Mahwah, NJ: Erlbaum.

Ryan, M. P. (2008). The antidepressant effects of physical activity: Mediating self-esteem and self-efficacy mechanisms. *Psychology and Health, 23*, 279–307.

Ryan, R. M., & Deci, E. L. (2000). Self-determination theory and the facilitation of intrinsic motivation, social development, and well-being. *American Psychologist, 55*, 68–78.

Ryan, R. M., & Deci, E. L. (2009). Promoting self-determined school engagement, motivation, learning, and well-being. In K. R. Wentzel & A. Wigfield (Eds.), *Handbook of research on schools, schooling, and human development*. New York: Routledge.

Rycroft, C. (2010). Why analysts need their patients' transferences. *American Journal of Psychoanalysis, 70*, 112–118.

Rydell, R. J., & Boucher, K. L. (2010). Capitalizing on multiple social identities to prevent stereotype threat: The moderating role of self-esteem. *Personality and Social Psychology Bulletin, 36*, 239–250.

Ryff, C. D., & Singer, B. (1998). Contours of positive human health. *Psychological Inquiry, 9*, 1–28.

Ryff, C. D., & Singer, B. H. (2009). Understanding healthy aging: Key components and their integration. In V. L. Bengtson, D. Gans, N. Pulney, & M. Silverstein, (Eds.), *Handbook of theories of aging* (2nd ed., pp. 117–144). New York: Springer.

Ryff, C. D., Singer, B. H., & Love, G. D. (2004). Positive health: Connecting well-being with biology. *Philosophical Transactions of the Royal Society of London, 359,* 1383–1394.

Rymer, R. (1993). *Genie.* New York: HarperCollins.

S

Saad, L. (2008, December 26). Obama, Hillary Clinton share "Most Admired" billing. Gallup Press Release. http://www.gallup.com/poll/113572/Obama-Hillary-Clinton-Share-Most-Admired-Billing.aspx (accessed January 19, 2009)

Saarni, C., Campos, J. J., Camras, L. A., & Witherington, D. (2006). Emotional development: Action, communication, and understanding. In W. Damon & R. Lerner (Eds.), *Handbook of child psychology* (6th ed.). New York: Wiley.

Sacco, D. F., & Hugenberg, K. (2009). The look of anger and fear: Facial maturity modulates recognition of fearful and angry expressions. *Emotion, 9,* 39–49.

Sachdev, P. S., & Chen, X. (2009). Neurosurgical treatment of mood disorders: Traditional psychosurgery and the advent of deep brain stimulation. *Current Opinion in Psychiatry, 22,* 25–31.

Sachs, J. (2009). Communication development in infancy. In J. Berko Gleason & N. Ratner (Eds.), *The development of language* (7th ed.). Boston: Allyn & Bacon.

Sack, R. L. (2009). The pathology of jet lag. *Travel Medicine and Infectious Disease, 7,* 102–110.

Sack, R. L. (2010). Clinical practice. Jet lag. *New England Journal of Medicine, 362,* 440–447.

Sacks, O. (2006, June 19). Stereo Sue. *New Yorker,* 64–73.

Sadeghniiat-Haghighi, K., Aminian, O., Pouryaghoub, G., & Yazdi, Z. (2008). Efficacy and hypnotic effects of melatonin in shift-work nurses: Double-blind, placebo-controlled crossover trial. *Journal of Circadian Rhythms, 6,* 10.

Sado, M., Knapp, M., Yamauchi, K., Fujisawa, D., So, M., Nakagawa, A., Kikuchi, T., & Ono, Y. (2009). Cost-effectiveness of combination therapy versus antidepressant therapy for management of depression in Japan. *Australian and New Zealand Journal of Psychiatry, 43,* 539–547.

Safren, S. A., & others. (2009). A randomized controlled trial of cognitive behavioral therapy for adherence and depression (CBT-AD) in HIV-infected individuals. *Health Psychology, 28,* 1–10.

Sahin, E., & DePinho, R. A. (2010). Linking functional decline of telomeres, mitochondria, and stem cells during aging. *Nature, 464,* 520–528.

Saito, H., & others. (2010). Hearing handicap predicts the development of depressive symptoms after 3 years in older community-dwelling Japanese. *Journal of the American Geriatrics Society, 58,* 93–97.

Salas, E., DeRouin, R. E. & Gade, P. A. (2007). The military's contribution to our science and practice: People, places, and findings. In L. L. Koppes (Ed.), *Historical perspectives in industrial and organizational psychology.* Mahwah, NJ: Erlbaum.

Salkind, J. J. (Ed.). (2009). *Encyclopedia of educational psychology.* Thousand Oaks, CA: Sage.

Salminen, N. H., Tiitnen, H., Yrttiaho, S., & May, P. J. (2010). The neural code for interaural time difference in human auditory cortex. *Journal of Acoustical Society of America, 127,* EL60.

Salthouse, T. A. (1994). The nature of the influence of speed on adult age differences in cognition. *Developmental Psychology, 30,* 240–259.

Salthouse, T. A. (2009). When does age-related cognitive decline begin? *Neurobiology of Aging, 30,* 507–514.

Salvia, J., Ysseldyke, J. E., & Bolt, S. (2010). *Assessment* (11th ed.). Boston: Cengage.

Salzman, C. D., & Fusi, S. (2010). Emotion, cognition, and mental state representation in amygdala and cerebral cortex. *Annual Review of Neuroscience* (vol. 33). Palo Alto, CA: Annual Reviews.

Sameroff, A. (2006). Identifying risk and protective factors for healthy child development. In A. Clarke-Stewart & J. Dunn (Eds.), *Families count.* New York: Oxford University Press.

Sampaio, A. S., & others. (2010). Association between polymorphisms in GRIK2 gene and obsessive-compulsive disorder: A family-based study. *CNS Neuroscience and Therapeutics.* (in press)

Sampaio, C., & Brewer, W. F. (2009). The role of unconscious memory errors in judgments of confidence for sentence recognition. *Memory and Cognition, 37,* 158–163.

Sanchez-Burks, J. (2007). Cultural differences. In R. Baumeister & K. Vohs (Eds.), *Encyclopedia of social psychology.* Thousand Oaks, CA: Sage.

Sand, S. (2010, February 7). Small town mayor issues big weight loss challenge. *Digital Journal.* http://www.digitaljournal.com/article/287210

Sandler, I., Wolchik, S., & Schoenfelder, E. (2011). Evidence-based family-focused prevention programs for children. *Annual Review of Psychology* (vol. 62). Palo Alto, CA: Annual Reviews.

Santtila, P., Sandnabba, N. K., Harlaar, N., Varjonen, M., Alanko, K., & von der Pahlen, B. (2008). Potential for homosexual response is prevalent and genetic. *Biological Psychology, 77,* 102–105.

Sapolsky, R. M. (2004). *Why zebras don't get ulcers* (3rd ed.). New York: Henry Holt.

Sapp, S. (2010). What have religion and spirituality to do with religion? Three approaches. *Gerontologist.* (in press)

Sar, V., Akyuz, G., & Dogan, O. (2007). Prevalence of dissociative disorders among women in the general population. *Psychiatry Research, 149,* 169–176.

Sar, V., Koyuncu, A., Ozturk, E., Yargic, L. I., Kundakci, T., Yazici, A., Kuskonmaz, E., & Aksut, D. (2007). Dissociative disorders in the psychiatric emergency ward. *General Hospital Psychiatry, 29,* 45–50.

Sarkar, U., Ali, S., & Whooley, M. A. (2009). Self-efficacy as a marker of cardiac function and predictor of heart failure hospitalization and mortality in patients with stable coronary heart disease: Findings from the Heart and Soul Study. *Health Psychology, 28,* 166–173.

Sarkar, U., Fisher, L., & Schillinger, D. (2006). Is self-efficacy associated with diabetes self-management across race/ethnicity and health literacy? *Diabetes Care, 29,* 323–329.

Sarma, K., & Kola, S. (2010). Firearms, hanging, and drowning suicides in the Republic of Ireland. *Crisis, 31,* 69–75.

Saroglou, V. (2010). Religiousness as a cultural adaptation of basic traits: A five-factor model perspective. *Personality and Social Psychology Review, 14,* 108–125.

Sartor, C. E., Agrawal, A., Lynskey, M. T., Bucholz, K. K., Madden, P. A., & Heath, A. C. (2009). Common genetic influences on the timing of first use for alcohol, cigarettes, and cannabis in young African-American women. *Drug and Alcohol Dependence, 102,* 49–55.

Sato, W., Kochiyama, T., Unono, S., & Yoshikawa, S. (2010). Amygdala integrates emotional expression and gaze direction in response to dynamic facial expressions. *NeuroImage, 50,* 1658–1665.

Saul, S. (2006, March 8). Some sleeping pill users range far beyond bed. *New York Times.*

Saunders, F. W. (1991). *Katherine and Isabel: Mother's light, daughter's journey.* Palo Alto, CA: Consulting Psychologists Press.

Saurer, T. B., Ijames, S. G., Carrigan, K. A., & Lysle, D. T. (2008). Neuroimmune mechanisms of opioid-mediated conditioned immunomodulation. *Brain, Behavior, and Immunity, 22,* 89–97.

Sauter, D. A., Eisner, F., Ekman, P., & Scott, S. K. (2010). Cross-cultural recognition of basic emotions through nonverbal emotional vocalizations. *Proceedings of the National Academy of Sciences USA, 107,* 2408–2412.

Sava, F. A., Yates, B. T., Lupu, V., Szentagotal, A., & David, D. (2009). Cost-effectiveness and cost-utility of cognitive therapy, rational emotive behavioral therapy, and fluoxetine (Prozac) in treating depression: A randomized clinical trial. *Journal of Clinical Psychology, 65,* 36–52.

Savage, J. (2008). The role of exposure to media violence in the etiology of violent behavior: A criminologist weighs in. *American Behavioral Scientist, 51,* 1123–1136.

Savage, J., & Yancey, C. (2008). The effects of media violence exposure on criminal aggression: A meta-analysis. *Criminal Justice and Behavior, 35,* 772–791.

Savic, I., & Lindström, P. (2008). PET and MRI show differences in cerebral asymmetry and functional connectivity between homo- and heterosexual subjects. *Proceedings of the National Academy of Sciences, 105,* 9403–9408.

Savin-Williams, R. (2006). *The new gay teenager.* Cambridge, MA: Harvard University Press.

Savin-Williams, R. C., & Ream, G. L. (2007). Prevalence and stability of sexual orientation components during adolescence and young adulthood. *Archives of Sexual Behavior, 36,* 385–394.

Savitz, J. B., & Ramesar R. S. (2004). Genetic variants implicated in personality: A review of the more promising candidates. *American Journal of Medical Genetics Part B, Neuropsychiatric Genetics, 131B,* 20–32.

Saxe, L. (1998, June). Commentary. *APA Monitor,* 30.

Sayal, K., Heron, J., Golding, J., & Emond, A. (2007). Prenatal alcohol exposure and gender differences in childhood mental health problems: A longitudinal population-based study. *Pediatrics, 119,* e426–e434.

Scarr, S. (1984, May). Interview. *Psychology Today,* 59–63.

Scarr, S. (1992). Keep our eyes on the prize: Family and child care policy in the United States, as it should be. In A. Booth (Ed.), *Child care in the 1990s: Trends and consequences* (pp. 215–222). Hillsdale, NJ: Erlbaum.

Scarr, S. (2000). Toward voluntary parenthood. *Journal of Personality, 68,* 615–623.

Schacter, D. L., & Wagner, A. D. (2011). Learning and memory. In E. R. Kandel, J. R. Schwartz, & T. M. Jessell (Eds.), *Principles of neural science* (5th ed.). New York: McGraw-Hill.

Schachter, S., & Singer, J. E. (1962). Cognitive, social, and physiological determinants of emotional state. *Psychological Review, 69,* 379–399.

Schaie, K. W. (1994). The life course of adult intellectual abilities. *American Psychologist, 49,* 304–313.

Schaie, K. W. (2006). Intelligence. In R. Schultz (Ed.), *Encyclopedia of aging* (4th ed.). New York: Springer.

Schaie, K. W. (2007). Generational differences: The age-cohort period model. In J. E. Birren & K. W. Schaie (Eds.), *Encyclopedia of gerontology.* Oxford, U.K.: Elsevier.

Schaie, K. W. (2009). "When does age-related cognitive decline begin?" Salthouse again reifies the "cross-sectional fallacy." *Neurobiology of Aging, 30,* 528–529.

Schaie, K. W. (2010). Adult intellectual abilities. *Corsini encyclopedia of psychology.* New York: Wiley.

Schaie, K. W. (2011). *Developmental influences on adult intellectual development.* New York: Oxford University Press. (in press)

Schank, R., & Abelson, R. (1977). *Scripts, plans, goals, and understanding.* Mahwah, NJ: Erlbaum.

Scheer, F. A., Hilton, M. F., Mantzoros, C. S., & Shea, S. A. (2009). Adverse metabolic and cardiovascular consequences of circadian misalignment. *Proceedings of the National Academy of Sciences USA, 106,* 4453–4458.

Scheibe, S., & Carstensen, L. L. (2010). Emotional aging: Recent findings and future trends. *Journals of Gerontology B: Psychological Sciences and Social Sciences, 65B,* 135–144.

Scheid, T. L., & Brown, T. N. (Eds.). (2010). *A handbook for the study of mental health: Social contexts, theories, and systems* (2nd ed.). New York: Cambridge University Press.

Schieffelin, B., & Ochs, E. (Eds.). (1986). *Language socialization across cultures.* Cambridge, U.K.: Cambridge University Press.

Schienle, A., Schaefer, A., Stark, R., & Vaiti, D. (2009). Long-term effects of cognitive behavior therapy on brain activation in spider phobia. *Psychiatry Research, 172,* 99–102.

Schiff, W. J. (2011). *Nutrition for healthy living* (2nd ed.). New York: McGraw-Hill.

Schiffman, J., & Walker, E. (1998). Schizophrenia. In H. S. Friedman (Ed.), *Encyclopedia of mental health* (vol. 2). San Diego: Academic.

Schira, M. M., Tyler, C. W., Spehar, B., & Breakspear, M. (2010). Modeling magnification and anisotropy in the primate foveal confluence. *PLoS Computational Biology, 6,* e1000651.

Schkade, D. A., & Kahneman, D. (1998). Does living in California make people happy? A focusing illusion in judgments of life satisfaction. *Psychological Science, 9,* 340–346.

Schlosser, R. G., Nenadic, I., Wagner, G., Zysset, S., Koch, K., & Sauer, H. (2009). Dopaminergic modulation of brain systems subserving decision making under uncertainty: A study with fMRI and methylphenidate challenge. *Synapse, 63,* 429–442.

Schmader, T., Forbes, C. E., Zhang, S., & Berry Mendes, W. (2009). A metacognitive perspective on the cognitive deficits experiences in intellectually threatening environments. *Personality and Social Psychology Bulletin, 35,* 584–596.

Schmeichel, B. J., Harmon-Jones, C., & Harmon-Jones, E. (2010). Exercising self-control increases approach motivation. *Journal of Personality and Social Psychology.* (in press)

Schmidt, N. B., & Keough, M. E. (2010). Treatment of panic. *Annual Review of Clinical Psychology* (vol. 6). Palo Alto, CA: Annual Reviews.

Schmidt, N. B., & Koselka, M. (2000). Gender differences in patients with panic disorder: Evaluating cognitive mediation of phobic avoidance. *Cognitive Therapy and Research, 24,* 533–550.

Schmidtke, J. I., & Heller, W. (2004). Personality, affect, and EEG: Predicting patterns of regional brain activity related to extraversion and neuroticism. *Personality and Individual Differences, 36,* 717–732.

Schmiedek, F., Li, S. C., & Lindenberger, U. (2009). Interference and facilitation in spatial working memory: Age-associated differences in lure effects in the n-back paradigm. *Psychology and Aging, 24,* 203–210.

Schmitt, K. C., & Reith, M. E. (2010). Regulation of the dopamine transporter: Aspects relevant to psychostimulant drugs of abuse. *Annals of the New York Academy of Sciences, 1187,* 316–340.

Schnall, E., & others. (2010). The relationship between religion and cardiovascular outcomes and all-cause mortality in the women's health initiative observational study. *Psychology and Health, 25,* 249–263.

Schnall, S., Roper, J., & Fessler, D. M. (2010). Elevation leads to altruistic behavior. *Psychological Science, 21,* 315–320.

Schneider, D. W., & Logan, G. D. (2009). Selecting a response in task switching: Testing a model of compound cue retrieval. *Journal of Experimental Psychology: Learning, Memory, and Cognition, 35,* 122–136.

Schneider, K. J. (2002). Humanistic psychotherapy. In M. Hersen & W. H. Sledge (Eds.), *Encyclopedia of psychotherapy.* San Diego: Academic.

Schneider, K. J. (2009). Editor's commentary. *Journal of Humanistic Psychology, 49,* 6–8.

Schomerus, G., Matschinger, H., & Angermeyer, M. C. (2009). Attitudes that determine willingness to seek psychiatric help for depression: A representative population survey applying the theory of planned behavior. *Psychological Medicine, 39,* 1855–1865.

Schooler, J. W. (2002). Re-representing consciousness: Dissociations between experience and meta-consciousness. *Trends in Cognitive Sciences, 6,* 339–344.

Schooler, J. W., Ambadar, Z., & Bendiksen, M. (1997). A cognitive corroborative case study approach for investigating discovered memories of sexual abuse. In J. D. Read & D. S. Lindsay (Eds.), *Recollections of trauma: Scientific evidence and clinical practice* (pp. 379–387). New York: Plenum Press.

Schooler, J. W., Ariely, D., & Loewenstein, G. (2003). The explicit pursuit and assessment of happiness can be self-defeating. In I. Brocas & J. Carrillo (Eds.), *The psychology of economic decisions.* Oxford, U.K.: Oxford University Press.

Schooler, J. W., & Eich, E. (2000). Memory for emotional events. In E. Tulving & F. I. M. Craik (Eds.), *The Oxford handbook of memory* (pp. 379–392). New York: Oxford University Press.

Schredl, M. (2009). Dreams in patients with sleep disorders. *Sleep Medicine Reviews, 13,* 215–221.

Schredl, M. (2010). Nightmare frequency and nightmare topics in a representative German sample. *European Archives of Psychiatry and Clinical Neuroscience.* (in press)

Schredl, M., & Erlacher, D. (2008). Relation between waking sport activities, reading, and dream content in sport students and psychology students. *Journal of Psychology, 142,* 267–275.

Schuckit, M. A. (2009). Alcohol-use disorders. *Lancet, 373,* 492–501.

Schulenberg, J. E., & Zarrett, N. R. (2006). Mental health in emerging adulthood: Continuities and discontinuities in course, content, and meaning. In J. J. Arnett & J. Tanner (Eds.), *Advances in emerging adulthood.* Washington, DC: American Psychological Association.

Schultheiss, O. C., & Brunstein, J. C. (2005). An implicit motive perspective on competence.

In A. J. Elliot & C. S. Dweck (Eds.), *Handbook of competence and motivation* (pp. 31–51). New York: Guilford.

Schultz, W. (2006). Behavioral theories and the neurophysiology of reward. *Annual Review of Psychology* (vol. 57). Palo Alto, CA: Annual Reviews.

Schultz, W., Dayan, P., & Montague, P. R. (1997). A neural substrate of prediction and reward. *Science, 275,* 1593–1599.

Schultz, W., Dayan, P., & Montague, P. R. (2009). Context, time, and memory retrieval in the interference paradigms of Pavlovian conditioning. In D. Shanks (Ed.), *Psychology of learning.* Thousand Oaks, CA: Sage.

Schultz, W. T. (Ed.). (2005). *The handbook of psychobiography.* New York: Oxford University Press.

Schulz, R. (2007). Cardiovascular health study. In K. S. Markides (Ed.), *Encyclopedia of health and aging.* Thousand Oaks, CA: Sage.

Schulz-Stubner, S., Krings, T., Meister, I. G., Rex, S., Thron, A., & Rossaint, R. (2004). Clinical hypnosis modulates functional magnetic resonance imaging signal intensities and pain perception in a thermal stimulation paradigm. *Regional Anesthesia and Pain Medicine, 29,* 549–556.

Schumann, A., John, U., Rumpf, H., Hapke, U., & Meyer, C. (2006). Changes in the "stages of change" as outcome measures of a smoking cessation intervention: A randomized controlled trial. *Preventive Medicine: An International Journal Devoted to Practice and Theory, 43,* 101–106.

Schunk, D. H. (2011). *Learning theories* (6th ed.). Boston: Allyn & Bacon. (in press)

Schunk, D. H., Pintrich, P. R., & Meece, J. L. (2008). *Motivation in education* (3rd ed.). Upper Saddle River, NJ: Prentice-Hall.

Schupak, C., & Rosenthal, J. (2009). Excessive daydreaming: A case history and discussion of mind wandering and high fantasy proneness. *Consciousness and Cognition, 18,* 290–292.

Schur, E. A., Heckbert, S. R., & Goldberg, J. H. (2010). The association of restrained eating with weight change over time in a community-based sample of twins. *Obesity.* (in press)

Schütz-Bosbach, S., Tausche, P., & Weiss, C. (2009). Roughness perception during the rubber band illusion. *Brain and Cognition, 70* (1), 136–144.

Schutzwohl, A., Fuchs, A., McKibbin, W. F., & Shackelford, T. K. (2009). How willing are you to accept sexual requests from slightly unattractive to exceptionally attractive imagined requestors? *Human Nature, 20,* 282–293.

Schuz, B., Sniehotta, F. F., Mallach, N., Wiedemann, A. U., & Schwarzer, R. (2009). Predicting transitions from preintentional, intentional, and actional stages of change. *Health Education Research, 24,* 64–75.

Schwabe, L., Bohringer, A., & Wolf, O. T. (2009). Stress disrupts context-dependent memory. *Learning and Memory, 16,* 110–113.

Schwartz, B., Ward, A. H., Monterosso, J., Lyubomirsky, S., White, K., & Lehman, D. (2002). Maximizing versus satisficing: Happiness is a matter of choice. *Journal of Personality and Social Psychology, 83,* 1178–1197.

Schwartz, S. (2010). Life goes on in dreams. *Sleep, 33,* 15–16.

Schwartz, S., & Corcoran, C. (2010). Biological theories of psychiatric disorders: A sociological approach. In T. L. Scheid & T. N. Brown (Eds.), *A handbook for the study of mental health: Social contexts, theories, and systems* (2nd ed., pp. 64–88). New York: Cambridge University Press.

Schweinsburg, A. D., McQueeny, T., Nagle, B. J., Eyler, L. T., & Tapert, S. F. (2010). A preliminary study of functional magnetic resonance imaging response during verbal encoding among adolescent binge drinkers. *Alcohol, 44,* 111–117.

Scott, S. K., Rabito, F. A., Price, P. D., Butler, N. N., Schwartzbaum, J. A., Jackson, B. M., Love, R. L., & Harris, R. E. (2006). Comorbidity among the morbidly obese: A comparative study of 2002 U.S. hospital patient surcharges. *Surgery for Obesity and Related Disorders, 2,* 105–111.

Scott-Phillips, T. C. (2010). Animal communication: Insights from linguistic pragmatics. *Animal Behaviour, 79,* e1–e4.

Scott-Sheldon, L. A. J., & Johnson, B. T. (2006). Eroticizing creates safer sex: A research synthesis. *Journal of Primary Prevention, 27,* 619–640.

Seacat, J. D., & Mickelson, K. D. (2009). Stereotype threat and the exercise/dietary health intentions of overweight women. *Journal of Health Psychology, 14,* 556–567.

Sears, D. O. (2008). The American color line 50 years after *Brown v. Board:* Many "peoples of color" or Black exceptionalism? In G. Adams, M. Biernat, N. R. Branscombe, C. S. Crandall, & L. S. Wrightsman (Eds.), *Commemorating Brown: The social psychology of racism and discrimination.* Washington, DC: American Psychological Association.

Sears, D. O., & Henry, P. J. (2007). Symbolic racism. In R. Baumeister & K. Vohs (Eds.), *Encyclopedia of social psychology.* Newbury Park, CA: Sage.

Sedikides, C. (2007). Self-enhancement and self-protection: Powerful, pancultural, and functional. *Hellenic Journal of Psychology, 4,* 1–13.

Sedikides, C. (2009). On self-protection and self-enhancement regulation: The role of self-improvement and social norms. In J. P. Forgas, R. F. Baumeister, & D. Tice (Eds.), *The psychology of self-regulation.* New York: Psychology Press.

Sedikides, C., Gaertner, L., & Vevea, J. L. (2005). Pancultural self-enhancement reloaded: A meta-analytic reply to Heine (2005). *Journal of Personality and Social Psychology, 89,* 539–551.

Sedikides, C., & Gregg, A. P. (2008). Self-enhancement: Food for thought. *Perspectives on Psychological Science, 3,* 102–116.

Sedikides, C., & Skowronski, J. J. (2009). Social cognition and self-cognition: Two sides of the same evolutionary coin? *European Journal of Social Psychology, 39,* 1245–1249.

Segal, D. L., & Coolidge, F. L. (2004). Objective assessment of personality and psychopathology. In M. Hersen (Ed.), *Comprehensive handbook of psychological assessment* (vol. 2). New York: Wiley.

Segal, S. K., & Cahill, L. (2009). Endogenous noradrenergic activation and memory for emotional material in men and women. *Psychoneuroendocrinology, 34,* 1263–1271.

Segall, L. A., & Amir, S. (2010). Glucocorticoid regulation of clock gene expression in the mammalian limbic forebrain. *Journal of Molecular Neuroscience.* (in press)

Segerstrom, S. C. (2003). Individual differences, immunity, and cancer: Lessons from personality psychology. *Brain, Behavior and Immunity, 17, Suppl. 1,* S92–S97.

Segerstrom, S. C. (2005). Optimism and immunity: Do positive thoughts always lead to positive effects? *Brain, Behavior and Immunity, 19,* 195–200.

Segerstrom, S. C. (2006). *Breaking Murphy's law: How optimists get what they want from life and pessimists can too.* New York: Guilford.

Selby, E. A., Anestis, M. D., Bender, T. W., & Joiner, T. E. (2009). An exploration of the emotional cascade model of borderline personality disorder. *Journal of Abnormal Psychology, 118,* 375–387.

Selby, E. A., & others. (2010). Overcoming the fear of lethal injury: Evaluating suicide in the military through the lens of the interpersonal-psychological theory of suicide. *Clinical Psychology Review, 30,* 298–307.

Seligman, M. E. P. (1970). On the generality of the laws of learning. *Psychological Review, 77,* 406–418.

Seligman, M. E. P. (1990). *Learned optimism.* New York: Knopf.

Seligman, M. E. P. (1994). *What you can change and what you can't.* New York: Knopf.

Seligman, M. E. P. (2000). Positive psychology. In J. E. Gillham (Ed.), *The science of optimism and hope: Research essays in honor of Martin E. P. Seligman* (pp. 415–429). West Conshohocken, PA: Templeton Foundation Press.

Seligman, M. E. P., & Csikszentmihalyi, M. (2000). Positive psychology: An introduction. *American Psychologist, 55,* 5–14.

Seligman, M. E. P., & Maier, S. F. (1967). Failure to escape traumatic shock. *Journal of Experimental Psychology, 74,* 1–9.

Seligman, M. E. P., & Pawelski, J. O. (2003). Positive psychology: FAQs. *Psychological Inquiry, 14,* 159–163.

Seligman, M. E. P., Rosellini, R. A., & Kozak, M. J. (1975). Learned helplessness in the rat: Time course, immunization, and reversibility. *Journal of Comparative and Physiological Psychology, 88,* 542–547.

Sellbom, M., Toomey, J. A., Wygant, D. B., Kucharski, L. T., & Duncan, S. (2010). Utility of the MMPI-2-RF (restructured form) validity scales in detecting malingering in a criminal forensic setting: A known-groups design. *Psychological Assessment, 22,* 22–31.

Sellers, R. M., Copeland-Linder, N., Martin, P. P., & Lewis, R. L. (2006). Racial identity matters: The relationship between racial discrimination and psychological functioning in African American adolescents. *Journal of Research on Adolescence, 16,* 187–216.

Selye, H. (1974). *Stress without distress.* Philadelphia: Saunders.

Selye, H. (1983). The stress concept: Past, present, and future. In C. I. Cooper (Ed.), *Stress research.* New York: Wiley.

Serretti, A., Drago, A., & DeRonchi, D. (2009). Lithium pharmacogenetics. *Current Medicinal Chemistry, 16,* 1917–1948.

"Sertraline versus other antidepressant agents for depression." *Cochrane Database of Systematic Reviews, 4,* CD006117.

Sesardic, N. (2006). *Making sense of heritability.* New York: Cambridge University Press.

Sessa, B. (2007). Is there a case for MDMA-assisted psychotherapy in the UK? *Journal of Psychopharmacology, 21,* 220–224.

Seto, M. C. (2009). Pedophilia. *Annual Review of Clinical Psychology, 5,* 391–407.

Sewell, R. A., Halpern, J. H., & Pope, H. G. (2006). Response of cluster headache to psilocybin and LSD. *Neurology, 66,* 1920–1922.

Seymour, K., Clifford, C. W., Logothetis, N. K., & Bartels, A. (2009). The coding of color, motion, and their conjunction in the human visual cortex. *Current Biology, 19,* 177–183.

Seymour, T. L., Seifert, C. M., Shafto, M. G., & Mosmann, A. L. (2000). Using response time measures to assess "guilty knowledge." *Journal of Applied Psychology, 85,* 30–37.

Shamay-Tsoory, S. G., Harari, H., Aharon-Peretz, J., & Levkovitz, Y. (2010). The role of the orbitofrontal cortex in affective theory of mind deficits in criminal offenders with psychopathic tendencies. *Cortex, 46,* 668–677.

Shanks, D. R. (2010). Learning: From association to cognition. *Annual Review of Psychology* (vol. 61). Palo Alto, CA: Annual Reviews.

Sharp, E. S., Reynolds, C. A., Pedersen, N. L., & Gatz, M. (2010). Cognitive engagement and cognitive aging: Is openness protective? *Psychology and Aging, 25,* 60–73.

Shaver, P., & Mikulincer, M. (2011). Recent advances in the study of close relationships. *Annual Review of Psychology* (vol. 62). Palo Alto, CA: Annual Reviews.

Shaw, D. S., Connell, A., Dishion, T. J., Wilson, M. N., & Gardner, F. (2009). Improvements in maternal depression as a mediator of intervention effects on early childhood problem behavior. *Development and Psychopathology, 21,* 417–439.

Shay, J. W., & Wright, W. E. (2007). Hallmarks of telomere aging research. *Journal of Pathology, 211,* 114–123.

Shea, N., Krug, K., & Tobler, P. N. (2008). Conceptual representations in goal-directed decision making. *Cognitive, Affective, and Behavioral Neuroscience, 8,* 418–428.

Sheese, B. E., Voleker, P., Posner, M. I., & Rothbart, M. K. (2009). Genetic variation influences on early development of reactive emotions and their regulation. *Cognitive Neuropsychiatry, 14,* 4–5.

Sheldon, K. M. (2002). The self-concordance model of healthy goal-striving: When personal goals correctly represent the person. In E. L. Deci & R. M. Ryan (Eds.), *Handbook of self-determination research* (pp. 65–86). Rochester, NY: University of Rochester Press.

Sheldon, K. M., & Elliot, A. J. (1998). Not all personal goals are personal: Comparing autonomous and controlled reasons for goals as predictors of effort and attainment. *Personality and Social Psychology Bulletin, 24,* 546–557.

Sheldon, K. M., Elliot, A. J., Kim, Y., & Kasser, T. (2001). What is satisfying about satisfying events? Testing 10 candidate psychological needs. *Journal of Personality and Social Psychology, 80,* 325–339.

Sheldon, K. M., & Gunz, A. (2009). Psychological needs as basic motives, not just experiential requirements. *Journal of Personality, 77,* 1467–1492.

Sheldon, K. M., Kasser, T., Houser-Marko, L., Jones, T., & Turban, D. (2005). Doing one's duty: Chronological age, felt autonomy, and subjective well-being. *European Journal of Personality, 19,* 97–115.

Sheldon, K. M., & Lyubomirsky, S. (2007). Is it possible to become happier? (And if so, how?). *Social and Personality Psychology Compass, 1,* 129–145.

Shelton, R. C., & Miller, A. H. (2010). Eating ourselves to death and despair: The contribution of adiposity and inflammation to depression. *Progress in Neurobiology.* (in press)

Shelton, R. C., Osuntokun, O., Heinloth, A. N., & Corya, S. A. (2010). Therapeutic options for treatment-resistant depression. *CNS Drugs, 24,* 131–161.

Shen, K., & Scheiffele, P. (2010). Genetics and cell biology of synapse recognition and formation. *Annual Review of Neuroscience* (vol. 33). Palo Alto, CA: Annual Reviews.

Sherif, M., Harvey, O. J., White, B. J., Hood, W. R., & Sherif, C. W. (1961). *Intergroup cooperation and competition: The Robbers Cave experiment.* Norman: University of Oklahoma Press.

Sherman, A. C., Plante, T. G., Simonton, U. L., & Anaissie, E. J. (2009). Prospective study of religious coping among patients undergoing autologous stem cell transplantation. *Journal of Behavioral Science, 32,* 118–128.

Sherman, F. T. (2009). Life-saving treatment for depression in the elderly: Always think of electroconvulsive therapy (ECT). *Geriatrics, 64,* 8, 12.

Sherman, R. A., Nave, C., & Funder, D. C. (2010). Situational similarity and personality predict behavioral consistency. *Journal of Personality and Social Psychology,* (in press)

Shibata, S. B., & others. (2010). Transgenic BDNF induces nerve fiber regrowth into the auditory epithelium in deaf cochleae. *Experimental Neurology.* (in press)

Shields, S. A. (1991). Gender in the psychology of emotion. In K. T. Strongman (Ed.), *International Review of Studies of Emotion* (vol. 1). New York: Wiley.

Shier, D. N., Butler, J. L., & Lewis, R. (2010). *Hole's human anatomy and physiology* (12th ed.). New York: McGraw-Hill.

Shih, M., Bonam, C., Sanchez, D., & Peck, C. (2007). The social construction of race: Biracial identity and vulnerability to stereotypes. *Cultural Diversity & Ethnic Minority Psychology, 13,* 125–133.

Shih, M., Yang, Y.-H., & Koo, M. (2009). A meta-analysis of hypnosis in the treatment of depressive symptoms: A brief communication. *International Journal of Clinical and Experimental Hypnosis, 57,* 431–432.

Shinn, M., & Thaden, E. (2010). *Current directions in community psychology.* Boston: Allyn & Bacon.

Shipp, S., Adams, D. L, Moutoussis, K., & Zeki, S. (2009). Feature binding in the feedback layers of area V2. *Cerebral Cortex, 19,* 2230–2239.

Shiraev, E., & Levy, D. (2010). *Cross-cultural psychology* (4th ed.). Boston: Allyn & Bacon.

Shoda, Y., & Mischel, W. (2006). Applying meta-theory to achieve generalisability and precision in personality science: Comment. *Applied Psychology: An International Review, 55,* 439–452.

Shyn, S. I., & Hamilton, S. P. (2010). The genetics of major depression: Moving beyond the monoamine hypothesis. *Psychiatric Clinics of North America, 33,* 125–140.

Sieber, W. J., Rodin, J., Larson, L., Ortega, S., & Cummings, N. (1992). Modulation of human natural killer cell activity by exposure to uncontrollable stress. *Brain, Behavior, and Immunity, 6,* 141–156.

Siebner, H. R., Hartwigsen, G., Kassuba, T., & Rothwell, J. C. (2009). How does transcranial magnetic stimulation modify neuronal activity in the brain? Implications for studies of cognition. *Cortex, 45,* 1035–1042.

Siegel, J. M. (2005). Clues to the functions of mammalian sleep. *Nature, 437,* 1264–1271.

Siegel, S. (1988). State dependent learning and morphine tolerance. *Behavioral Neuroscience, 102,* 228–232.

Sienaert, P., Vansteelandt, K., Demyttenaere, K., & Peuskens, J. (2010). Randomized comparison of ultra-brief bifrontal and unilateral electroconvulsive therapy for major depression: Cognitive side-effects. *Journal of Affective Disorders, 122,* 60–67.

Sieswerda, S., Arntz, A., Mertens, I., & Vertommen, S. (2007). Hypervigilance in patients with borderline personality disorder: Specificity, automaticity, and predictors. *Behaviour Research and Therapy, 45,* 1011–1024.

Sigel, E. (2008). Eating disorders. *Adolescence Medicine: State of the Art Reviews, 19,* 547–572.

Sigurdsson, T., Doyere, V., Cain, C. K., & LeDoux, J. E. (2007). Long-term potentiation in the amygdale: A cellular mechanism of learning and memory. *Neuropharmacology, 52,* 215–227.

Sikorskii, A., Given, C., Given, B., Jeon, S., & McCorkle, R. (2006). Testing the effects of treatment complications on a cognitive-behavioral intervention for reducing symptom severity. *Journal of Pain and Symptom Management, 32,* 129–139.

Silva de Lima, M., Farrell, M., Lima Reisser, A. A., & Soares, B. (2010). WITHDRAWN: Antidepressants for cocaine dependence.

Cocharine Database of Systematic Reviews, CD002950.

Silvia, P. J., Nusbaum, E. C., Berg, C., Martin, C., & O'Connor, A. (2009). Openness to experience, plasticity, and creativity: Exploring lower-order, high-order, and interactive effects. *Journal of Research in Personality, 43,* 1087–1090.

Sim, T. N., & Ong, L. P. (2005). Parent punishment and child aggression in a Singapore Chinese preschool sample. *Journal of Marriage and the Family, 67,* 85–99.

Simms, L. J. (2007). The big seven model of personality and its relevance to personality pathology. *Journal of Personality, 75,* 65–94.

Simola, S. K., Barling, J., & Turner, N. (2010). Transformational leadership and leader moral orientation: Contrasting an ethic of justice and an ethic of care. *Leadership Quarterly, 21,* 179–188.

Simon, H. A. (1969). *The sciences of the artificial.* Cambridge, MA: MIT Press.

Simons, D. J., & Chabris, C. F. (1999). Gorillas in our midst: Sustained inattentional blindness for dynamic events. *Perception, 28* (9), 1059–1074.

Simpson, J. R. (2008). Functional fMRI lie detection: Too good to be true? *Journal of the American Academy of Psychiatry and Law, 36,* 491–498.

Sims, C. S., Drasgow, F., & Fitzgerald, L. F. (2005). The effects of sexual harassment on turnover in the military: Time-dependent modeling. *Journal of Applied Psychology, 90,* 1141–1152.

Sin, N. L., & Lyubomirsky, S. (2009). Enhancing well-being and alleviating depressive symptoms with positive psychology interventions: A practice-friendly meta-analysis. *Journal of Clinical Psychology, 65,* 467–487.

Singer, J. A., & Conway, M. A. (2008). Should we forget about forgetting? *Memory Studies, 1,* 279–285.

Singh, M., & others. (2010). Brain glutamatergic characteristics of pediatric offspring of parents with bipolar disorder. *Psychiatry Research.* (in press)

Sinn, D. L., Gosling, S. D., & Moltschaniwskyj, N. A. (2008). Development of shy/bold behaviour in squid: Context-specific phenotypes associated with developmental plasticity. *Animal Behaviour, 75,* 433–442.

Sinn, D. L., Moltschaniwskyj, N. A., Wapstra, E., & Dall, S. R. X. (2010). Are behavioral syndromes invariant? Spatiotemporal variation in shy/bold behavior in squid. *Behavioral Ecology and Sociobiology, 64,* 693–702.

Sintov, N. D., & others. (2010). Empirically defined subtypes of alcohol dependence in an Irish family sample. *Drug and Alcohol Dependence, 107,* 230–236.

Sitnikova, T., Goff, D., & Kuperberg, G. R. (2009). Neurocognitive abnormalities during comprehension of real-world goal-directed behaviors in schizophrenia. *Journal of Abnormal Psychology, 118,* 256–277.

Sivacek, J., & Crano, W. D. (1982). Vested interest as a moderator of attitude-behavior

consistency. *Journal of Personality and Social Psychology, 43* (2), 210–221.

Sivanathan, N., Arnold, K. A., Turner, N., & Barling, J. (2004). Leading well: Transformational leadership and well-being. In P. A. Linley & S. Joseph (Eds.), *Positive psychology in practice* (pp. 241–255). Hoboken, NJ: Wiley.

Skinner, B. F. (1938). *The behavior of organisms: An experimental analysis.* New York: Appleton-Century-Crofts.

Skinner, B. F. (1957). *Verbal behavior.* New York: Appleton-Century-Crofts.

Skinner, E. I., & Fernandes, M. A. (2009). Illusory recollection in older adults and younger adults under divided attention. *Psychology and Aging, 24,* 211–216.

Skolin I., Wahlin, Y. B., Broman, D. A., Koivisto Hursti, U., Vikström, L. M., & Hernell, O. (2006). Altered food intake and taste perception in children with cancer after start of chemotherapy: Perspectives of children, parents and nurses. *Supportive Care in Cancer, 14,* 369–378.

Slater, A., Field, T., & Hernandez-Reif, M. (2007). The development of the senses. In A. Slater & M. Lewis (Eds.), *Introduction to infant development* (2nd ed.). New York: Oxford University Press.

Slater, A. M., Riddell, P., Quinn, P. C., Pacalis, O., Lee, K., & Kelly, D. J. (2011). Visual perception. In U. Goswami (Ed.), *Wiley-Blackwell handbook of childhood cognitive development* (2nd ed.). New York: Wiley Blackwell.

Slavin, R. E. (2006). Translating research into widespread practice: The case of success for all. In M. A. Constas & R. J. Sternberg (Eds.), *Translating theory and research into educational practice: Developments in content domains, large-scale reform, and intellectual capacity* (pp. 113–126). Mahwah, NJ: Erlbaum.

Slaymaker, V. J., & Sheehan, T. (2008). The impact of AA on professional treatment. *Recent Developments in Alcoholism, 18,* 59–70.

Slotnick, S. D., & Schacter, D. L. (2006). The nature of memory related activity in early visual areas. *Neuropsychologia, 44,* 2874–2886.

Slutske, W. S. (2005). Alcohol use disorders among US college students and their non-college-attending peers. *Archives of General Psychiatry, 62,* 321–327.

Smetana, J. G., Tasopoulos-Chan, M., Gettman, D. C., Villalobos, M., Campione-Barr, N., & Metzger, A. (2009). Adolescents' and parents' evaluations of helping versus fulfilling personal desires in family situations. *Child Development, 80,* 280–294.

Smieskova, R., & others. (2010). Neuroimaging predictors of transition to psychosis—A systematic review and meta-analysis. *Neuroscience and Biobehavioral Reviews.* (in press)

Smit, F., Willemse, G., Koopmanschap, M., Onrust, S., Cuijpers, P., & Beekman, A. (2006). Cost-effectiveness of preventing depression in primary care patients: Randomized trial. *British Journal of Psychiatry, 188,* 330–336.

Smith, B. (2007). *The psychology of sex and gender.* Belmont, CA: Wadsworth.

Smith, C. A., & Kirby, L. D. (2009). Putting appraisal in context: Toward a relational model of appraisal and emotion. *Cognition and Emotion, 23,* 1352–1372.

Smith, C. P. (Ed.). (1992). *Thematic content analysis for motivation and personality research.* New York: Cambridge University Press.

Smith, D. (2004, February 7). Love that dare not squeak its name. *New York Times.* http://www.nytimes.com/2004/02/07/arts/07GAY.html

Smith, G. P. (1995). Dopamine and food reward. *Progress in Psychobiology and Physiological Psychology, 16,* 83–144.

Smith, H. S. (2010). The role of genomic oxidative-reductive balance as predictor of complex regional pain syndrome development: A novel theory. *Pain Physician, 13,* 79–90.

Smith, M. B. (2001). Humanistic psychology. In W. E. Craighead & C. B. Nemeroff (Eds.), *The Corsini encyclopedia of psychology and behavioral science* (3rd ed.). New York. Wiley.

Smith, P. B., Bond, M. H., & Kagitcibasi, C. (2006). *Understanding social psychology across cultures: Living and working in a changing world.* Thousand Oaks, CA: Sage.

Smith, P. K., & Bargh, J. A. (2008). Nonconscious effects of power on basic approach and avoidance tendencies. *Social Cognition, 26,* 1–24.

Smith, R. A., & Davis, S. F. (2010). *Psychologist as detective* (5th ed.). Boston: Cengage.

Smith, R. L., Rose, R. J., & Schwartz-Mette, R. A. (2010). Relational and overt aggression in childhood and adolescence: Clarifying mean-level gender differences and associations with peer acceptance. *Social Development, 19,* 243–269.

Smith, S. J., Axelton, A. M., & Saucier, D. A. (2009). The effects of contact on sexual prejudice: A meta-analysis. *Sex Roles, 61,* 178–191.

Smith, S. R., Gorske, T. T., Wiggins, C., & Little, J. A. (2010). Personality assessment use by clinical neuropsychologists. *International Journal of Testing, 10,* 6–20.

Smith, T. E., Weston, C. A., & Lieberman, J. A. (2009, April 16). Schizophrenia (maintenance treatment). *Clinical Evidence,* PMID: 19445748.

Smith, T. W., & MacKenzie, J. (2006). Personality and risk of physical illness. *Annual Review of Clinical Psychology* (vol. 2). Palo Alto, CA: Annual Reviews.

Smyth, J. (1998). Written emotional expression: Effect sizes, outcome types, and moderating variables. *Journal of Consulting and Clinical Psychology, 66,* 174–184.

Snarey, J. R. (1993). *How fathers care for the next generation: A four-decade study.* Cambridge, MA: Harvard University Press.

Snell, R. S., & Wong, Y. L. (2007). Differentiating good soldiers from good actors. *Journal of Management Studies.* doi:10.1111/j.1467-6486.2007.00699.x

Snowdon, D. A. (2003). Healthy aging and dementia: Findings from the Nun study. *Annals of Internal Medicine, 139,* 450–454.

Snowdon, D. A. (2007, April). *Aging with grace: findings from the nun study.* Paper presented at the 22nd annual Alzheimer's regional conference, Seattle.

Snyder, C. R., & Lopez, S. J. (Eds.). (2007). *Positive psychology: The scientific and practical explorations of human strengths.* Thousand Oaks, CA: Sage.

Snyder, C. R., & Lopez, S. (2009). *The Oxford handbook of positive psychology* (2nd ed.). New York: Oxford University Press.

Sofuoglu, M. (2010). Cognitive enhancement as a pharmacotherapy target for stimulant addiction. *Addiction, 105,* 38–48.

Sofuoglu, M., Sugarman, D. E., & Carroll, K. M. (2010). Cognitive function as an emerging treatment target for marijuana addiction. *Experimental and Clinical Psychopharmacology, 18,* 109–119.

Sokol, M. S., Carroll, A. K., Heebink, D. M., Hoffman-Riken, K. M., Goudge, C. S., & Ebers, D. D. (2009). Anorexia nervosa in identical triplets. *CNS Spectrums, 14,* 156–162.

Solberg Nes, L., Evans, D. R., & Segerstrom, S. C. (2009). Optimism and college retention: Mediation by motivation, performance, and adjustment. *Journal of Applied Social Psychology, 39,* 1887–1912.

Solberg Nes, L., & Segerstrom, S. C. (2006). Dispositional optimism and coping: A meta-analytic review. *Personality and Social Psychology Review, 10,* 235–251.

Soldan, A., Hilton, H. J., Cooper, L. A., & Stern, Y. (2009). Priming of familiar and unfamiliar visual objects over delays in young and older adults. *Psychology and Aging, 24,* 93–104.

Soloff, P. H., & others. (1994). Self-mutilation and suicidal behavior in borderline personality disorder. *Journal of Personality Disorders, 8,* 257–267.

Soltesz, E. G., & Cohn, L. H. (2007). Minimally invasive valve surgery. *Cardiology Review, 15,* 109–115.

Sommer, M., Hajak, G., Dohnel, K., Schwerdtner, J., Meinhardt, J., & Muller, J. L. (2006). Integration of emotion and cognition in patients with psychopathy. *Progress in Brain Research, 156C,* 457–466.

Sommer, V., & Vasey, P. L. (Eds.). (2006). *Homosexual behaviour in animals: An evolutionary perspective.* New York: Cambridge University Press.

Song, H., & Ming, G.-L. (2010). Application of neurons from stem cells for neurological diseases. *Annual Review of Neuroscience* (vol. 33). Palo Alto, CA: Annual Reviews.

Song, S. (2006, March 27). Mind over medicine. *Time, 167,* 13.

Sonnenfeld, J. A. (1985). Shedding light on the Hawthorne studies. *Journal of Occupational Behavior, 6,* 111–130.

Sorrentino, R., Cohen, D., Olson, J. M., & Zanna, M. P. (2005). *Cultural and social behavior: The Ontario symposium* (vol. 10). Mahwah, NJ: Erlbaum.

Sotres-Bayon, F., Diaz-Mataix, L., Bush, D. E., & LeDoux, J. E. (2009). Dissociable roles for the ventromedial prefrontal cortex and amygdale in fear extinction: NR2B contribution. *Cerebral Cortex, 19,* 472–482.

Sourial-Bassillious, N., Rydelius, P. A., Aperia, A., & Aizman, O. (2009). Glutamate-mediated calcium signaling: A potential target for lithium action. *Neuroscience, 161* (4), 1126–1134.

South, S. C., & Krueger, R. F. (2008). An interactionist on genetic and environmental contributions to personality. *Social and Personality Psychology Compass, 2,* 929–948.

South, S. C., & Krueger, R. F. (2010). Genetic and environmental influences on internalizing psychopathology vary as a function of economic status. *Psychological Medicine.* (in press)

Spanos, N. P. (1996). *Multiple identities and false memories: A sociocognitive perspective.* Washington, DC: American Psychological Association.

Spanos, N. P., & Chaves, J. F. (Eds.). (1989). *Hypnosis: The cognitive-behavior perspective.* Buffalo, NY: Prometheus.

Sparks, J. R., & Areni, C. S. (2008). Style versus substance: Multiple roles of language power in persuasion. *Journal of Applied Social Psychology, 38,* 37–60.

Sparling, P., & Redican, K. (2011). *MP iHealth.* New York: McGraw-Hill.

Spaulding, L. H. (1998). Florida's 1997 chemical castration law: A return to the Dark Ages. *Florida State University Law Review, 117,* 125–135.

Spaulding, S. (2010). Embodied cognition and mindreading. *Mind & Language, 25,* 119–140.

Spearman, C. (1904). "General intelligence" objectively determined and measured. *American Journal of Psychology, 15,* 201–293.

Spector, P. E., & others. (2001). Do national levels of individualism and internal locus of control relate to well-being? An ecological level international study. *Journal of Organizational Behavior, 22,* 815–832.

Spellman, B. A. (2005). Could reality shows become reality experiments? *APS Observer, 18,* 34–35.

Spencer, S. J., Steele, C. M., & Quinn, D. M. (1999). Stereotype threat and women's math performance. *Journal of Experimental Social Psychology, 35,* 4–28.

Speranza, M., Corcos, M., Atger, F., Paterniti, S., & Jeammet, P. (2003). Binge eating behaviours, depression and weight control strategies. *Eating and Weight Disorders, 8,* 201–206.

Sperling, G. (1960). The information available in brief presentations. *Psychological Monographs, 74* (11).

Sperry, R. W. (1968). Hemisphere deconnection and unity in conscious awareness. *American Psychologist, 23,* 723–733.

Sperry, R. W. (1974). Lateral specialization in surgically separated hemispheres. In F. O. Schmitt & F. G. Worden (Eds.), *The neurosciences: Third study program.* Cambridge, MA: MIT Press.

Spiegel, D. (2006). Editorial: Recognizing traumatic dissociation. *American Journal of Psychiatry, 163,* 566–568.

Spiegel, D. (2010). Hypnosis testing. In A. F. Barabasz, K. Olness, R. Boland, & S. Kahn (Eds.), *Medical hypnosis primer: Clinical and research evidence* (pp. 11–18). New York: Routledge/Taylor & Francis.

Spiegler, M. D., & Guevremont, D. C. (2010). *Contemporary behavior therapy* (5th ed.). Boston: Cengage.

Spielberger, C. D. (2004, August). *Type A behavior, anger-hostility, and heart disease.* Paper presented at the 28th International Congress of Psychology, Beijing, China.

Spritz, B. L., Fergusson, A. S., & Bankoff, S. M. (2010). False beliefs and the development of deception. In E. H. Sandberg & B. L. Spritz (Eds.), *A clinician's guide to normal cognitive development in childhood* (pp. 101–120). New York: Routledge/Taylor & Francis.

Spyer, K. M., & Gourine, A. V. (2009). Chemosensory pathways in the brainstem controlling cardiorespiratory activity, *Philosophical Transactions of the Royal Society B: Biological Sciences 364,* 2603–2610.

Squire, L. R. (1990, June). *Memory and brain systems.* Paper presented at the meeting of the American Psychological Society, Dallas.

Squire, L. R. (2004). Memory systems of the brain: A brief history and current perspective. *Neurobiology of Learning and Memory, 82,* 171–177.

Squire, L. R. (2007). Memory systems as a biological concept. In H. L. Roediger, Y. Dudai, & S. Fitzpatrick (Eds.), *Science of memory: Concepts.* New York: Oxford University Press.

Sriram, N., & Greenwald, A. G. (2009). The Brief Implicit Association Test. *Experimental Psychology, 56,* 283–204

Sroufe, L. A., Coffino, B., & Carlson, E. A. (2010). Conceptualizing the role of early experience: Lessons from the Minnesota Longitudinal Study. *Developmental Review, 30,* 36–51.

Staddon, J. E., Chelaru, I. M., & Higa, J. J. (2002). A tune-trace theory of interval-timing dynamics. *Journal of the Experimental Analysis of Behavior, 77,* 105–124.

Stadler, G., Oettingen, G., & Gollwitzer, P. M. (2010). Intervention effects of information and self-regulation on eating fruits and vegetables over two years. *Health Psychology, 29,* 274–283.

Stake, R. E. (2010). *Qualitative research.* New York: Guilford.

Stangor, C. (2009). The study of stereotyping, prejudice, and discrimination within social psychology: A quick history of theory and research. In T. D. Nelson (Ed.), *Handbook of prejudice, stereotyping, and discrimination.* New York: Psychology Press.

Stangor, C. (2011). *Research methods for the behavioral sciences* (4th ed.). Boston: Cengage.

Stanovich, K. E. (2010). *How to think straight about psychology* (9th ed.). Upper Saddle River, NJ: Prentice-Hall.

Stanovich, K. E., & West, R. F. (2000). Individual differences in reasoning: Implications for the rationality debate. *Behavioral and Brain Sciences, 23,* 645–665.

Stanton, A. L., Revenson, T. A., & Tennen, H. (2007). Health psychology: Psychological adjustment to chronic disease. *Annual Review of Psychology* (vol. 58). Palo Alto, CA: Annual Reviews.

Starcevic, V. (2006). Anxiety states: A review of conceptual and treatment issues. *Current Opinions in Psychiatry, 19,* 79–83.

Staresina, B. P., Gray, J. C., & Davachi, L. (2010). Event congruency enhances episodic memory encoding through semantic elaboration and relational binding. *Cerebral Cortex, 19,* 1198–1207.

Stasiewicz, P. R., Brandon, T. H., & Bradizza, C. M. (2007). Effects of extinction context and retrieval cues on renewal of alcohol-cue reactivity among alcohol-dependent outpatients. *Psychology of Addictive Behaviors, 21* (2), 244–248.

Staub, E., & Vollhardt, J. (2008). Altruism born of suffering: The roots of caring and helping after victimization and other trauma. *American Journal of Orthopsychiatry, 78,* 267–280.

Staudinger, U. M., & Gluck, J. (2011). Psychological wisdom research. *Annual Review of Psychology* (vol. 62). Palo Alto, CA: Annual Reviews.

Staudt, M. (2010). Brain plasticity following early life brain injury: Insights from neuuroimaging. *Seminars in Perinatology, 34,* 87–92.

Staw, B. M., & Barsade, S. G. (1993). Affect and managerial performance: A test of the sadder-but-wiser vs. happier-and-smarter hypothesis. *Administrative Science Quarterly, 38,* 304–331.

Staw, B. M., Bell, N. E. & Clausen, J. A. (1986). The dispositional approach to job attitudes: A lifetime longitudinal test. *Administrative Science Quarterly, 31,* 56–77.

Staw, B. M., Sutton, R. I., & Pelled, L. H. (1994). Employee positive emotion and favorable outcomes at the workplace. *Organization Science, 5,* 51–71.

Steblay, N., & Loftus, E. (2009). Eyewitness memory and the legal system. In E. Shafir (Ed.), *The behavioral foundations of policy.* Princeton, NJ: Princeton University Press and the Russell Sage Foundation.

Steel, P., Schmidt, J., & Schultz, J. (2008). Refining the relationship between personality and subjective well-being. *Psychological Bulletin, 134,* 138–161.

Steele, C. M., & Aronson, J. (1995). Stereotype threat and the intellectual test performance of African-Americans. *Journal of Personality and Social Psychology, 69,* 797–811.

Steele, C. M., & Aronson, J. A. (2004). Stereotype threat does not live by Steele and Aronson (1995) alone. *American Psychologist, 59,* 47–48.

Steele, H., & Siever, L. (2010). An attachment perspective on borderline personality disorder: Advances in gene-environment considerations. *Current Psychiatry Reports, 12,* 61–67.

Steeves, J., Dricot, L., Goltz, H. C., Sorger, B., Peters, J., Milner, A. D., Goodale, M. A., Goebel, R., & Rossion, B. (2009). Abnormal face identity coding in the middle fusiform gyrus of two brain-damaged prosopagnosic patients. *Neuropsychologia, 47,* 2584–2592.

Steger, M. F., & Frazier, P. (2005). Meaning in life: One link in the chain from religion to well-being. *Journal of Counseling Psychology, 52,* 574–582.

Stein, R. (2003). *Blinded by the light.* http://www.theage.com.au/articles/2003/09/01/1062403448264.html (accessed October 11, 2006)

Stein, T., Peelen, M. V., Funk, J., & Seidi, K. N. (2010). The fearful-face advantage is modulated by task demands: Evidence from the attentional blink. *Emotion, 10,* 136–140.

Steinberg, L. (2009). Adolescent development and juvenile justice. *Annual Review of Clinical Psychology* (vol. 5). Palo Alto, CA: Annual Reviews.

Steinbrook, R. (1992). The polygraph test: A flawed diagnostic method. *New England Journal of Medicine, 327,* 122–123.

Stenfelt, S. (2006). Middle ear ossicles motion at hearing thresholds with air conduction and bone conduction stimulation. *Journal of the Acoustical Society of America, 119,* 2848–2858.

Stern, Y., Alexander, G. E., Prohovnik, I., & Mayeux, R. (1992). Inverse relationship between education and parietotemporal perfusion deficit in Alzheimer's disease. *Annals of Neurology, 32,* 371–375.

Stern, Y., Scarmeas, N., & Habeck, C. (2004). Imaging cognitive reserve. *International Journal of Psychology, 39,* 18–26.

Sternberg, E. M., & Gold, P. W. (1996). The mind–body interaction in disease. *Mysteries of the mind.* New York: Scientific American.

Sternberg, R. J. (1986). *Intelligence applied.* Fort Worth, TX: Harcourt Brace.

Sternberg, R. J. (Ed.). (2004). *Definitions and conceptions of giftedness.* Thousand Oaks, CA: Corwin.

Sternberg, R. J. (2007a). *G, g's, or Jeez:* Which is the best model for developing abilities, competencies, and expertise? In P. C. Kyllonen, R. D. Roberts, & L. Stankov (Eds.), *Extending intelligence.* Mahwah, NJ: Erlbaum.

Sternberg, R. J. (2007b). Developing successful intelligence in all children: A potential solution to underachievement in ethnic minority children. In M. C. Wang & R. D. Taylor (Eds.), *Closing the achievement gap.* Philadelphia: Laboratory for Student Success at Temple University.

Sternberg, R. J. (2008). The triarchic theory of human intelligence. In N. Salkind (Ed.), *Encyclopedia of educational psychology.* Thousand Oaks, CA: Sage.

Sternberg, R. J. (2009a). *Cognitive psychology* (5th ed.). Belmont, CA: Wadsworth.

Sternberg, R. J. (2009b). Teaching for creativity. In R. A. Beghetto & J. C. Kaufman (Eds.), *Nurturing creativity in the classroom.* New York: Cambridge University Press.

Sternberg, R. J. (2009c). Successful intelligence as a framework for understanding cultural adaption. In S. Ang & L. van Dyne (Eds.), *Handbook on cultural intelligence.* New York: M. E. Sharpe.

Sternberg, R. J. (2009d). The triarchic theory of intelligence. In B. Kerr (Ed.), *Encyclopedia of giftedness, creativity, and talent.* Thousand Oaks, CA: Sage.

Sternberg, R. J. (2009e). Wisdom, intelligence, creativity, synthesized: A model of giftedness. In T. Balchin, B. Hymer, & D. Matthews (Eds.), *International companion to gifted education.* London: RoutledgeFalmer.

Sternberg, R. J. (2009f). Wisdom. In S. J. Lopez (Ed.), *Encyclopedia of positive psychology.* Amsterdam: Springer.

Sternberg, R. J. (2011). Human intelligence. In V. S. Ramachandran (Ed.), *Encyclopedia of human behavior* (2nd ed.). New York: Elsevier.

Sternberg, R. J., & Grigorenko, E. L. (2008). Ability testing across cultures. In L. Suzuki (Ed.), *Handbook of multicultural assessment* (3rd ed., pp. 335–359). New York: Jossey-Bass.

Sternberg, R. J., Grigorenko, E. L., & Kidd, K. K. (2005). Intelligence, race, and genetics. *American Psychologist, 60,* 46–59.

Sternberg, R. J., Roediger, H., & Halpern, D. (Eds.). (2007). *Critical thinking in psychology.* New York: Cambridge University Press.

Sterponi, L. (2010). Learning communicative competence. In D. F. Lancy, J. Bock, & S. Gaskins (Eds.), *The anthropology of learning in childhood* (pp. 235–259). Walnut Creek, CA: AltaMira.

Stevens, M. J., & Gielen, U. P. (Eds.). (2007). *Toward a global psychology: Theory, research, intervention, and pedagogy.* Mahwah, NJ: Erlbaum.

Stewart, J. L., Silton, R. L., Sass, S. M., Fisher, J. E., Edggar, J. C., Heller, W., & Miller, G. A. (2010). Attentional bias to negative emotion as a function of approach and withdrawal anger styles: An ERP investigation. *International Journal of Psychophysiology.* (in press)

Stewart, S. H., & Chambers, L. (2000). Relationships between drinking motives and drinking restraint. *Addictive Behaviors, 25,* 269–274.

Stice, E., Shaw, H., & Marti, C. N. (2006). A meta-analytic review of obesity prevention programs for children and adolescents: The skinny on interventions that work. *Psychological Bulletin, 132,* 667–691.

Stickgold, R. (2001). Watching the sleeping brain watch us: Sensory processing during sleep. *Trends in Neuroscience, 24,* 307–309.

Stirling, J. D. (2002). *Introducing neuropsychology.* East Sussex, U.K.: Psychology Press.

Stokes, M. B., & Payne, B. K. (2010). Mental control and visual illusions: Errors of action and construal in race-based weapon misidentification. In R. B. Adams, N. Ambady, K. Nakayama, & S. Shimojo (Eds.), *The science of social vision.* New York: Oxford University Press.

Stone, J. (2002). Battling doubt by avoiding practice: The effects of stereotype threat on self-handicapping in white athletes. *Personality and Social Psychology Bulletin, 28,* 1667–1678.

Stoner, J. (1961). *A comparison of individual and group decisions, including risk.* Unpublished master's thesis, School of Industrial Management, MIT.

Storbeck, J., & Clore, G. L. (2008). The affective regulation of cognitive priming. *Emotion, 8,* 208–215.

Storch, E. A., & others. (2010). Does cognitive-behavior therapy response among adults with obsessive-compulsive disorder differ as a function of certain comorbidities? *Journal of Anxiety Disorders.* (in press)

Stores, G., Montgomery, P., & Wiggs, L. (2006). The psychosocial problems of children with narcolepsy and those with excessive daytime sleepiness of unknown origin. *Pediatrics, 118,* e1116–e1123.

Strack, F., & Forster, J. (2009). Social cognition: An introduction. In F. Strack & J. Forster (Eds.), *Social cognition: The basis of human interaction.* New York: Psychology Press.

Strahan, E., Spencer, S. J., & Zanna, M. P. (2002). Subliminal priming and persuasion: Striking while the iron is hot. *Journal of Experimental Social Psychology, 38,* 556–568.

Straus, M. A., & Stewart, J. H. (1999). Corporal punishment by American parents: National data on prevalence, chronicity, severity, and duration in relation to child and family characteristics. *Clinical Child and Family Psychology Review, 2,* 55–70.

Straus, M. A., Sugarman, D. B., & Giles-Sims, J. (1997). Spanking by parents and subsequent antisocial behavior of children. *Archives of Pediatric and Adolescent Medicine, 151,* 761–767.

Streff, F. M., & Geller, E. S. (1986). Strategies for motivating safety belt use: The application of applied behavior analysis. *Health Education Research, 1* (1), 47–59.

Strick, M., Dijksterhuis, A., & van Baaren, R. B. (2010). Unconscious-thought effects take place off-line, not on-line. *Psychological Science, 21,* 484–488.

Striegel-Moore, R. H., & Franko, D. L. (2008). Should binge eating disorder be included in the DSM-V? A critical review of the state of the evidence. *Annual Review of Clinical Psychology, 4,* 305–324.

Strike, P. C., Magid, K., Whitehead, D. L., Brydon, L., Bhattacharyya, M. R., & Steptoe, A. (2006). Pathophysiological processes underlying emotional triggering of acute cardiac events. *Proceedings of the National Academy of Sciences USA, 103,* 4322–4327.

Stroop, J. R. (1935). Studies of interference in serial verbal reactions. *Journal of Experimental Psychology, 28,* 643–662.

Strupp, H. H. (1995). The psychotherapist's skills revised. *Clinical Psychology: Science and Practice, 2,* 70–74.

Stulhofer, A., Busko, V., & Landripet, I. (2010). Pornography, sexual socialization, and satisfaction among young men. *Archives of Sexual Behavior, 39,* 168–178.

Sturmer, T., Hasselbach, P., & Amelang, M. (2006). Personality, lifestyle, and risk of cardiovascular disease and cancer: Follow-up of population-based cohort. *British Medical Journal, 332,* 1359.

Sue, D., Sue, D. W., & Sue, S. (2010). *Understanding abnormal behavior* (9th ed.). Boston: Cengage.

Sui, X., Laditka, J. N., Church, T. S., Hardin, J. W., Chase, N., Davis, K., & Blair, S. N. (2009). Prospective study of cardiovascular fitness and depressive symptoms in women and men. *Journal of Psychiatric Research, 43,* 546–552.

Sui, X., LaMonte, M. J., Laditka, J. N., Hardin, J. W., Chase, N., Hooker, S. P., & Blair, S. N. (2007). Cardiorespiratory fitness and adiposity as mortality predictors in older adults. *Journal of the American Medical Association, 298,* 2507–2516.

Suinn, R. M. (1984). *Fundamentals of abnormal psychology.* Chicago: Nelson-Hall.

Sullivan, H. S. (1953). *The interpersonal theory of psychiatry.* New York: Norton.

Sullivan, P. W., Morrato, E. H., Ghushchyan, V., Wyatt, H. R., & Hill, J. O. (2005). Obesity, inactivity, and the prevalence of diabetes and diabetes-related cardiovascular comorbidities in the U.S., 2000–2002. *Diabetes Care, 28,* 1599–1603.

Suls, J., & Swain, A. (1998). Type A–Type B personalities. In H. S. Friedman (Ed.), *Encyclopedia of mental health* (vol. 3). San Diego: Academic.

Suls, J. M., Davidson, K. W., & Kaplan, R. M. (Eds.). (2010). *Handbook of health psychology and behavioral medicine.* New York: Guilford.

Surmeier, D. J., Guzman, J. N., & Sanchez-Padilla, J. (2010). Calcium, cellular aging, and selective neuronal vulnerability in Parkinson's disease. *Cell Calcium.* (in press)

Susman, E. J., & Dorn, L. D. (2009). Puberty: Its role in development. In R. M. Lerner & L. Steinberg (Eds.), *Handbook of adolescent psychology* (3rd ed.). New York: Wiley.

Suzuki, C., Tsukiura, T., Mochiizuki-Kawai, H., Shigemune, Y., & Iijima, T. (2009). Prefrontal and medial temporal contributions to episodic memory-based reasoning. *Neuroscience Research, 63,* 177–183.

Swanson, D. P. (2010). Adolescent psychosocial processes: Identity, stress, and competence. In D. P. Swanson, M. C. Edwards, & M. B. Spencer (Eds.), *Adolescence: Development in a global era.* San Diego: Academic.

Swanson, D. P., Edwards, M. C., & Spencer, M. B. (Eds.). (2010). *Adolescence: Development during a global era.* Burlington, MA: Academic.

Swanson, J. (Ed.). (1999). *Sleep disorders sourcebook.* New York: Omnigraphics.

Swisher, J. D., Gatenby, J. C., Gore, J. C., Wolfe, B. A,, Moon, C. H., Kim, S. G., & Tong, F. (2010). Multiscale pattern analysis of orientation-selective activity in the primary visual cortex. *Journal of Neuroscience, 30,* 325–330.

Szasz, T. S. (1961). *The myth of mental illness: Foundations of a theory of personal conduct.* New York: Hoeber-Harper.

Szczepanski, S. M., Konen, C. S., & Kastner, S. (2010). Mechanisms of spatial attention control in frontal and parietal cortex. *Journal of Neuroscience, 30,* 148–160.

Szulwach, K. E., & others. (2010). Cross talk between microRNA and epigenetic regulation in adult neurogenesis. *Journal of Cell Biology, 189,* 127–141.

T

Taga, K. A., Markey, C. N., & Friedman, H. S. (2006). A longitudinal investigation of associations between boys' pubertal timing and adult behavioral health and well-being. *Journal of Youth and Adolescence, 35,* 380–390.

Tager-Flusberg, H., & Zukowski, A. (2009). Putting words together; Morphology and syntax in the preschool years. In J. Berko Gleason & N. Ratner (Eds.), *The development of language* (7th ed.). Boston: Allyn & Bacon.

Tagliamonte, S. A., & Denis, D. (2008). Linguistic ruin? LOL! Instant messaging and teen language. *American Speech, 83,* 3–34.

Tajfel, H. (1978). The achievement of group differentiation. In H. Tajfel (Ed.), *Differentiation between social groups.* London: Academic.

Takahashi, A., Nagaoka, T., Ishiko, S., Kameyama, D., & Yoshida, A. (2010). Foveal anatomic changes in a progressing stage 1 macular hole documented by spectral-domain optical coherence tomography. *Ophthalmology, 117,* 806–810.

Takahashi, M., Shimizu, H., Saito, S., & Tomoyori, H. (2006). One percent ability and ninety-nine percent perspiration: A study of a Japanese memorist. *Journal of Experimental Psychology: Learning, Memory, and Cognition, 32,* 1195–1200.

Takeuchi, T., & De Valois, K. K. (2009). Visual motion mechanisms under low retinal illuminance revealed by motion-reversal. *Vision Research, 49,* 801–809.

Talarico, J. M. (2009). Freshman flashbulbs: Memories of unique and first-time events in starting college. *Memory, 17,* 256–265.

Tam, L., Bagozzi, R. P., & Spanjol, J. (2010). When planning isn't enough: The self-regulatory effect of implementation intentions on changing snacking habits. *Health Psychology, 29,* 284–292.

Tamada, K., Machida, S., Oikawa, T., Miyamoto, H., Nishimura, T., & Kurosaka, D. (2010). Correlation between photopic negative response of focal electroretinograms and local loss of retinal neurons in glaucoma. *Current Eye Research, 35,* 155–164.

Tamis-LeMonda, C., & McFadden, K. E. (2010). The United States of America. In M. H. Bornstein (Ed.), *Handbook of cultural developmental science.* New York: Psychology Press.

Tamminga, C. A. (2006). The neurobiology of cognition in schizophrenia. *Journal of Clinical Psychology, 67,* e11.

Tamnes, C. K., Ostby, Y., Fjell, A. M., Westlye, L. T., Due-Tønnessen, P., & Walhovd, K. W. (2010). Brain maturation in adolescence and young adulthood: Regional age-related changes in cortical thickness and white matter volume and microstructure. *Cerebral Cortex, 20,* 534–548.

Tannenbaum, S. I. (2006). Applied measurement: Practical issues and challenges. In W. Bennett, C. E. Lance, & D. J. Woehr (Eds.), *Performance measurement.* Mahwah, NJ: Erlbaum.

Tarokh, L., & Carskadon, M. A. (2008). In L. R. Squire (Ed.), *New Encyclopedia of Neuroscience.* London: Elsevier.

Tarr, M. J., & Gauthier, I. (2000). FFA: A flexible fusiform area for subordinate-level visual processing automatized by expertise. *Nature Neuroscience, 3,* 764–769.

Tarter, R. E., Vanyukov, M., Kirisci, L., Reynolds, M., & Clark, D. B. (2006). Predictors of marijuana use in adolescents before and after illicit drug use: Examination of the gateway hypothesis. *American Journal of Psychiatry, 163,* 2134–2140.

Tavris, C., & Wade, C. (1984). *The longest war: Sex differences in perspective* (2nd ed.). Fort Worth, TX: Harcourt Brace.

Tay, C., Ang, S., & Van Dyne, L. (2006). Personality, biographical characteristics, and job interview success: A longitudinal study of the mediating effects of self-efficacy and the moderating effects of internal locus of causality. *Journal of Applied Psychology, 91,* 446–454.

Taylor, F. W. (1911). *Scientific management.* New York: Harper & Row.

Taylor, H. G., & others (2010). Post-concussive symptoms in children with mild traumatic brain injury. *Neuropsychology, 24,* 148–159.

Taylor, S. E. (2011). *Health psychology* (8th ed.). New York: McGraw-Hill.

Taylor, S. E., Brown, J. D., Colvin, C. R., Block, J., & Funder, D. C. (2007). Issue 6: Do positive illusions lead to healthy behavior? In J. A. Nier (Ed.), *Taking sides: Clashing views in social psychology* (2nd ed., pp. 116–137). New York: McGraw-Hill.

Taylor, S. E., Lerner, J. S., Sherman, D. K., Sage, R. M., & McDowell, N. K. (2003a). Are self-enhancing cognitions associated with healthy or unhealthy biological profiles? *Journal of Personality and Social Psychology, 85,* 605–615.

Taylor, S. E., Lerner, J. S., Sherman, D. K., Sage, R. M., & McDowell, N. K. (2003b). Portrait of the self-enhancer: Well adjusted and well liked or maladjusted and friendless? *Journal of Personality and Social Psychology, 84,* 165–176.

Taylor, S. E., Saphire-Bernstein, S., & Seeman, T. E. (2010). Are plasma oxytocin in women and plasma vasopressin in men biomarkers of distressed pair bond relationships? *Psychological Science, 21,* 3–7.

Taylor, S. E., & Sherman, D. K. (2008). Self-enhancement and self-affirmation: The consequences of positive self-thoughts for motivation and health. In W. Gardner & J. Shah (Eds.), *Handbook of motivation science.* New York: Guilford.

Teague, H. F., Rouch, P. A., Woodard, J. S., Hatch, D. R., Zdanski, C. J., Buss, E., & Buchman, C. A. (2010). Cochlear implantation in children with auditory neuropathy spectrum disorder. *Ear and Hearing.* (in press)

Teesson, M., & Vogl, L. (2006). Major depressive disorder is common among Native Americans, women, the middle aged, the poor, the widowed, separated, or divorced people. *Evidence-Based Mental Health, 9,* 59.

Tellegen, A., Ben-Porath, Y. S., & Sellbom, M. (2009). Construct validity of the MMPI-2 restructured clinical (RC) scales: Reply to Rouse, Green, Butcher, Nichols, and Williams. *Journal of Personality Assessment, 91,* 211–221.

Tenenbaum, J. B., Griffiths, T. L., & Kemp, C. (2006). Theory-based Bayesian models of inductive learning and reasoning. *Trends in Cognitive Science, 10,* 309–318.

Teodorescu, M., & others. (2006). Correlates of daytime sleepiness in patients with asthma. *Sleep Medicine, 7,* 607–613.

Tepper, B. J., Duffy, M. K., Hoobler, J., & Ensley, M. D. (2004). Moderators of the relationships between coworkers' organizational citizenship behavior and fellow employees' attitudes. *Journal of Applied Psychology, 89,* 455–465.

Terman, L. (1925). *Genetic studies of genius. Vol. 1: Mental and physical traits of a thousand gifted children.* Stanford, CA: Stanford University Press.

Terr, L. C. (1988). What happens to early memories of trauma? *Journal of the American Academy of Child and Adolescent Psychiatry, 27,* 96–104.

Terry, S. (2009). *Learning and memory* (4th ed.). Upper Saddle River, NJ: Prentice-Hall.

Tharoor, H., Dinesh, N., Chauhan, A., Mathew, A., & Sharma, P. S. V. N. (2007). Dissociative amnesia related to pregnancy. *German Journal of Psychiatry, 10,* 119–121.

Thaxton, L., Emshoff, J. G., & Guessous, O. (2005). Prostate cancer support groups: A literature review. *Journal of Psychosocial Oncology, 23* (1), 25–40.

Theeuwes, J., Belopolsky, A., & Olivers, C. N. (2009). Interactions between working memory, attention, and eye movements. *Acta Psychologica, 132,* 106–114.

Thigpen, C. H., & Cleckley, H. M. (1957). *Three faces of Eve.* New York: McGraw-Hill.

Thomas, M., Sing, H., Belenky, G., Holcomb, H., Mayberg, H., Dannals, R., Wagner, H., Thorne, D., Popp, K., Rowland, L., Welsh, A., Balwinksi, S., & Redmond, D. (2001). Neural basis of alertness and cognitive performance impairments during sleepiness: I. Effects of 24 hours of sleep deprivation on waking human regional brain activity. *Journal of Sleep Research, 9,* 335–352.

Thomas, M., Tyers, P., Lazic, S. E., Barker, R. A., Beazley, L., & Ziman, M. (2009). Graft outcomes influences by co-expression of Pax7 in graft and host tissue. *Journal of Anatomy, 214,* 396–405.

Thomas, M. S. C., & Johnson, M. H. (2008). New advances in understanding sensitive periods in brain development. *Current Directions in Psychological Science, 17,* 1–5.

Thompson, L., & others. (2005). Dispositional forgiveness of self, others, and situations. *Journal of Personality, 73,* 313–359.

Thompson, P. M., Giedd, J. N., MacDonald, D., Evans, A. C., & Toga, A. W. (2000). Growth patterns in the developing brain by using continuum sensor maps. *Nature, 404,* 190–193.

Thompson, R. A. (2009). Unpublished review of J. W. Santrock's *Life-Span Development* (13th ed.). New York: McGraw-Hill.

Thompson, R. A. (2009b). Early foundations: Conscience and the development of moral character. In D. Narvaez & D. Lapsley (Eds.), *Moral self, identity, and character.* New York: Cambridge University Press.

Thompson, R. A. (2010). Feeling and understanding through the prism of relationships. In S. D. Calkins & M. A. Bell (Eds.), *Child development at the intersection of emotion and cognition* (pp. 79–95). Washington, DC: American Psychological Association.

Thompson, R. A., & Newton, E. (2009). Infant-caregiver communicaton. In H. T. Reis & S. Sprecher (Eds.), *Encyclopedia of human relationships.* Thousand Oaks, CA: Sage.

Thompson, S. C. (2001). The role of personal control in adaptive functioning. In C. R. Snyder & S. J. Lopez (Eds.), *Handbook of positive psychology.* New York: Oxford University Press.

Thompson-Brenner, H., Boisseau, C. L., & Satir, D. A. (2010). Adolescent eating disorders: Treatment and response in a naturalistic study. *Journal of Clinical Psychology, 66,* 277 301.

Thomsen, D. K. (2009). There is more to life stories than memory. *Memory, 17,* 1–13.

Thomsen, M., Hall, F. S., Uhl, G. R., & Caine, S. B. (2009). Dramatically decreased cocaine self-administration in dopamine but not serotonin transporter knock-out mice. *Journal of Neuroscience, 29,* 1087–1092.

Thoresen, C. J., Kaplan, S. A., Barsky, A. P., Warren, C. R., & de Chermont, K. (2003). The affective underpinnings of job perceptions and attitudes: A meta-analytic review and integration. *Psychological Bulletin, 129,* 914–945.

Thorndike, E. L. (1898). *Animal intelligence: An experimental study of the associative processes in animals* (Psychological Review, monograph supplements, no. 8). New York: Macmillan.

Thornicroft, G., Brohan, E., Rose, D., Sartorius, N., Lees, M., & the INDIGO Study Group. (2009). Global pattern of experienced and anticipated discrimination against people with schizophrenia: A cross-sectional survey. *Lancet, 373,* 408–415.

Thunedborg, K., Black, C. H., & Bech, P. (1995). Beyond the Hamilton depression scores in long-term treatment of manic-melancholic patients: Prediction of recurrence of depression by quality of life measurements. *Psychotherapy and Psychosomatics, 64,* 131–140.

Tikhomirov, A. A., & Spangler, W. D. (2010). Neo-charismatic leadership and the fate of mergers and acquisitions: An institutional model of CEO leadership. *Journal of Leadership and Organizational Studies, 17,* 44–60.

Timimi, S. (2004). A critique of the international consensus statement on ADHD. *Clinical Child and Family Psychology Review, 7* (1), 59–63.

Tinbergen, N. (1969). *The study of instinct.* New York: Oxford University Press.

Todorov, A., Mandisodza, A. N., Goren, A., & Hall, C. C. (2005). Inferences of competence from faces predict election outcomes. *Science, 308* (5728), 1623–1626.

Todd, R. M., Evans, J. W., Morris, D., Lewis, M. D., & Taylor, M. J. (2010). The changing face of emotion: Age-related patterns of amygdala activation to salient faces. *Social Cognitive and Affective Neuroscience.* (in press)

Tolman, E. C. (1932). *Purposive behavior in animals and man.* New York: Appleton-Century-Crofts.

Tolman, E. C., & Honzik, C. H. (1930). Degrees of hunger, reward and non-reward, and maze performance in rats. *University of California Publications in Psychology, 4,* 21–256.

Tong, E. K., Strouse, R., Hall, J., Kovac, M., & Schroeder, S. A. (2010). National survey of U.S. health professionals' smoking prevalence, cessation practices, and beliefs. *Nicotine and Tobacco Research.* (in press)

Tong, F., Nakayama, K., Moscovitch, M., Weinrib, O., & Kanwisher, N. (2000). Response properties of the human fusiform face area. *Cognitive Neuropsychology, 17,* 257–279.

Tononi, G., & Cirelli, C. (2011). Sleep and synaptic plasticity. *Annual Review of Psychology* (vol. 62). Palo Alto, CA: Annual Reviews.

Topolinski, S., & Strack, F. (2008). Where there's a will—there's no intuition: The unintentional basis of semantic coherence judgments. *Journal of Memory and Language, 58,* 1032–1048.

Topolinski, S., & Strack, F. (2010). Scanning the "fringe of consciousness": What is felt and what is not felt in intuition about semantic coherence. *Consciousness and Cognition.* (in press)

Torchinsky, A., & Toder, V. (2010). Mechanisms of the embryo's response to embryopathic stressors: A focus on p53. *Journal of Reproductive Immunology.* (in press)

Torriero, S., & others. (2010). Changes in cerebello–motor connectivity during procedural learning by actual execution and observation. *Journal of Cognitive Neuroscience.* (in press)

Tourian, K. A., Jiang, Q., & Ninan, P. T. (2010). Analysis of the effect of desvenlafaxine on anxiety symptoms associated with major depressive disorder: Pooled data from 9 short-term, double-blind, placebo controlled trials. *CNS Spectrums, 15,* 187–93.

Travis, F., & Shear, J. (2010). Focused attention, open monitoring, and automatic self-transcending: Categories to organize meditations from Vedic, Buddhist, and Chinese traditions. *Consciousness and Cognition.* (in press)

Trawaiter, S., & Shapiro, J. R. (2010). Racial bias and stereotyping: Interpersonal processes. In B. Gawronski & B. K. Payne (Eds.), *Handbook of implicit cognition.* New York: Guilford.

Treasure, J., Claudino, A. M., & Zucker, N. (2010). Eating disorders. *Lancet, 375,* 583–593.

Tremblay, T., Monetta, L., & Joanette, Y. (2009). Complexity and hemispheric abilities: Evidence for a differential impact on semantics and phonology. *Brain and Language, 108,* 67–72.

Triandis, H. C. (2000). Cross-cultural psychology: History of the field. In A. Kazdin (Ed.), *Encyclopedia of psychology.* Washington, DC, & New York: American Psychological Association and Oxford University Press.

Triandis, H. C. (2007). Culture and psychology: A history of the study of their relationship. In S. Kitayama & D. Cohen (Eds.), *Handbook of cultural psychology* (pp. 59–76). New York: Guilford.

Trickett, E. J. (2009). Multilevel community-based culturally situated interventions and community impact: An ecological perspective. *American Journal of Community Psychology, 43,* 257–266.

Trinkler, I., King, J. A., Doeller, C. F., Rugg, M. D., & Burgess, N. (2009). Neural bases of autobiographical support for episodic recollection of faces. *Hippocampus, 19,* 718–730.

Triplett, N. (1898). The dynamogenic factors in pacemaking and competition. *American Journal of Psychology, 9,* 507–533.

Tropp, L. R., & Wright, S. C. (2003). Evaluations and perceptions of self, ingroup, and outgroup: Comparisons between Mexican-American and European-American children. *Self and Identity, 2,* 203–221.

Trudel, E., & Bourque, C. W. (2010). Central clock excites vasopressin neurons by waking osmosensory afferents during late sleep. *Nature Neuroscience.* (in press)

Trull, T. J., & Widiger, T. A. (2003). Personality disorders. In I. B. Weiner (Ed.), *Handbook of Psychology* (vol. 8). New York: Wiley.

Truxillo, D. M., & Bauer, T. N. (2010). Applicant reactions to organizations and selection systems. In S. Zedeck (Ed.), *APA handbook of industrial and organizational psychology.* Washington, DC: APA. (in press)

Tryon, R. C. (1940). Genetic differences in maze-learning ability in rats. In *39th Yearbook, National Society for the Study of Education.* Chicago: University of Chicago Press.

Trzesniewski, K. H., & Donnellan, M. B. (2009). Reevaluating the evidence for increasingly positive self-views among high school students: More evidence for consistency across generations (1976–2006). *Psychological Science, 20,* 920–922.

Trzesniewski, K. H., & Donnellan, M. B. (2010). Rethinking "Generation Me": A study of cohort effects from 1976–2006. *Perspectives on Psychological Science, 5,* 58–75.

Trzesniewski, K. H., Donnellan, M. B., Moffitt, T. E., Robins, R. W., Poulton, R., & Caspi, A. (2006). Low self-esteem during adolescence predicts poor health, criminal behavior, and limited economic prospects during adulthood. *Developmental Psychology, 42,* 381–390.

Trzesniewski, K. H., Donnellan, M. B., & Robins, R. W. (2008). Do today's young people really think they are so extraordinary? An examination of secular trends in narcissism and self-enhancement. *Psychological Science, 19,* 181–188.

Tsai, W., Chen, C., & Chiu, S. (2005). Exploring boundaries of the effects of applicant impression management tactics in job interviews. *Journal of Management, 31,* 108–125.

Tsenkova, V. K., Dienberg Love, G., Singer, B. H., & Ryff, C. D. (2008). Coping and positive affect predict longitudinal change in glycosylated hemoglobin. *Health Psychology, 27, Suppl. 2,* S163–S171.

Tsushima, Y., Sasaki, Y., & Watanabe, T. (2006). Greater disruption due to failure of inhibitory control on an ambiguous distractor. *Science, 314,* 1786–1788.

Tugade, M. M., Fredrickson, B. L., & Feldman Barrett, L. (2004). Psychological resilience and positive emotional granularity: Examining the benefits of positive emotions on coping and health. *Journal of Personality, 72,* 1161–1190.

Tulving, E. (1972). Episodic and semantic memory. In E. Tulving & W. Donaldson (Eds.), *Origins of memory.* San Diego: Academic.

Tulving, E. (1983). *Elements of episodic memory.* New York: Oxford University Press.

Tulving, E. (1989). Remembering and knowing the past. *American Scientist, 77,* 361–367.

Tulving, E. (2000). Concepts of memory. In E. Tulving & F. I. M. Craik (Eds.), *The Oxford handbook of memory.* New York: Oxford University Press.

Tural, U., & Onder, E. (2010). Clinical and pharmacologic risk factors for neuroleptic malignant syndrome and their association with death. *Psychiatry and Clinical Neurosciences, 64,* 79–87.

Turkheimer, E., Haley, A., Waldron, M., D'Onofrio, B., & Gottesman, I. I. (2003). Socioeconomic status modifies heritability of IQ in young children. *Psychological Science, 14,* 623–628.

Turrigiano, G. (2010). Synaptic homeostasis. *Annual Review of Neuroscience* (vol. 33). Palo Alto, CA: Annual Reviews.

Tversky, A., & Kahneman, J. (1974). Judgment under uncertainty: Heuristics and biases. *Science, 185,* 1124–1131.

Twenge, J. M. (2006). *Generation Me: Why today's young Americans are more confident, assertive, entitled—and more miserable than ever before.* New York: Free Press.

Twenge, J. M. (2008). Social exclusion, motivation, and self-defeating behavior: Why breakups lead to drunkenness and ice cream. In J. Y Shah & W. L. Gardner (Eds.), *Handbook of motivation science* (pp. 508–517). New York: Guilford.

Twenge, J. M., & Campbell, S. M. (2010). Generation Me and the changing world of work. In A. P. Linley, S. Harrington, & N. Garcea (Eds.), *Oxford handbook of positive psychology and work* (pp. 25–35). New York: Oxford University Press.

Twenge, J. M., & Campbell, W. K. (2008). Increases in positive self-views among high school students: Birth cohort changes in anticipated performance, self-satisfaction, self-liking, and self-competence. *Psychological Science, 19,* 1082–1086.

Twenge, J. M., & Campbell, W. K. (2009). *The narcissism epidemic: Living in the age of enlightenment.* New York: Free Press

Twenge, J. M., & Foster, J. D. (2008). Mapping the scale of the narcissism epidemic: Increases in narcissism 2002–2007 within ethnic groups. *Journal of Research in Personality, 42,* 1619–1622.

Tye, K. M., & Janak, P. H. (2007). Amygdala neurons differentially encode motivation and reinforcement. *Journal of Neuroscience, 27,* 3937–3945.

U

Uchida, H., & Mamo, D. C. (2009). Dosing of antipsychotics across the life-spectrum. *Progress in Neuro-Psychopharmacology and Biological Psychiatry, 33* (6), 917–920.

Uguz, F., Akman, C., Kaya, N., & Cilli, A. S. (2007). Postpartum-onset obsessive-compulsive disorder: Incidence, clinical features, and related factors. *Journal of Clinical Psychiatry, 68,* 132–138.

Ullman, A. D. (1952). Review of "Antabuse" in the treatment of alcoholism. *Psychological Bulletin, 49,* 557–558.

Ulrich, R. S. (1991). Stress recovery during exposure to natural and urban environments. *Journal of Environmental Psychology, 11,* 201–230.

Umana-Taylor, A. J., & Guimond, A. B. (2010). A longitudinal examination of parenting behaviors and perceived discrimination predicting Latino adolescents' ethnic identity. *Developmental Psychology, 46,* 636–650.

Underhill, K., Montgomery, P., & Operario, D. (2007). Sexual abstinence programs to prevent HIV infection in high-income countries. *British Medical Journal, 335,* 248.

United Nations Office on Drugs and Crime (UNODC). (2008). *World drug report.* Vienna: United Nations.

United Nations World Youth Report. (2005). *World youth report 2005: Young people today and in 2015.* Geneva, Switzerland: United Nations.

Unkelbach, C. (2007). Reversing the truth effect: Learning the interpretation of processing fluency in judgments of truth. *Journal of Experimental Psychology: Learning, Memory, and Cognition, 33,* 219–230.

Urban, E. (2008). The "self" in analytical psychology: The function of the "central archetype" within Fordham's model. *Journal of Analytical Psychology, 53,* 329–350.

Urcelay, G. P., Wheeler, D. S., & Miller, R. R. (2009). Spacing extinction trials alleviates renewal and spontaneous recovery. *Learning and Behavior, 37,* 60–73.

Urdan, T. (2010). Classroom goal structures, motivation, and learning. In J. L. Meece & J. S. Eccles (Eds.), *Handbook of schools, schooling, and human development.* New York: Routledge.

Urry, H. L. (2010). Seeing, thinking, and feeling: Emotion regulating effects of gaze-directed cognitive reappraisal. *Emotion, 10,* 125–135.

Urry, H. L., Nitschke, J. B., Dolski, I., Jackson, D. C., Dalton, K. M., Mueller, C. J., Rosenkranz, M. A., Ryff, C. D., Singer, B. H., & Davidson, R. J. (2004). Making a life worth living: Neural correlates of well-being. *Psychological Science, 15,* 367–372.

USA Today. (2008, April 4). *Jackpot winner to boss: I'm outta here!* http://www.usatoday.com/news/nation/2008-04-04-jackpot-winner_N.htm (accessed April 10, 2010)

U.S. Bureau of Labor Statistics. (2006, October 27). *Survey of workplace violence prevention, 2005.* http://www.bls.gov/iif/oshwc/osnr0026.pdf. Washington, DC: Author. (accessed June 13, 2007)

U.S. Census Bureau. (2008). *People.* Washington, DC: U.S. Department of Labor.

U.S. Department of Justice. (2007). *Homicide trends in the U.S.* http://www.ojp.usdoj.gov/bjs/homicide/tables/totalstab.htm (accessed May 29, 2009)

U.S. Department of Labor. (2010–2011). *Occupational outlook handbook.* Washington, DC: Bureau of Labor Statistics.

U.S. Department of Labor. (2010). *O*NET database.* http://www.bls.gov/oco/

U.S. Food and Drug Administration. (2004, October 15). *FDA launches a multi-pronged strategy to strengthen safeguards for children treated with antidepressant medications.* News release. Washington, DC: Author.

U.S. Food and Drug Administration. (2009). *Office of Device Evaluation annual report, fiscal year 2008.* Washington, DC: Center for Devices and Radiological Health.

U.S. General Accounting Office. (1996, September). *Cycle of sexual abuse: Research inconclusive about whether child victims become adult abusers.* Report to the Chairman, Subcommittee on the Judiciary, House of Representatives.

Ussher, J., Kirsten, L., Butow, P., & Sandoval, M. (2006). What do cancer support groups provide which other supportive relationships do not? The experience of peer support groups for people with cancer. *Social Science & Medicine, 62,* 2565–2576.

Uusi-Oukari, M., & Korpi, E. R. (2010). Regulation of GABAA receptor subunit expression by pharmacological agents. *Pharmacological Reviews.* (in press)

V

Vacek, J. E. (2009). Using a conceptual approach with a concept map of psychosis as an exemplar to promote critical thinking. *Journal of Nursing Education, 48,* 49–53.

Vaes, J., Heflick, N. A., & Goldenberg, J. L. (2010). "We are people": Ingroup humanization as an existential defense. *Journal of Personality and Social Psychology, 98,* 750–760.

Vaillant, G. (2003). A 60-year follow-up of alcoholic men. *Addiction, 98,* 1043–1051.

Vakily, M., Lee, R. D., Wu, J., Gunawardhana, L., & Mulford, D. (2009). Drug interaction studies with dexiansoprazole modified release (TAK-390MR), a proton pump inhibitor with a dual delayed-release formulation. *Clinical Drug Investigation, 29,* 35–50.

Vallido, T., Jackson, D., & O'Brien, L. (2009). Mad, sad, and hormonal: The gendered nature of adolescent sleep disturbance. *Journal of Child Health Care, 13,* 7–18.

van Apeldoorn, F. J., & others. (2010). A randomized trial of cognitive-behavioral therapy or selective serotonin reuptake inhibitor or both combined for panic disorder with or without agoraphobia: treatment results through 1-year follow-up. *Journal of Clinical Psychology, 71,* 574–586.

van Atteveldt, N. M, Blau, V. C, Blomert, L., & Goebel, R. (2010). fMR-adaptation indicates selectivity to audiovisual content congruency in distributed clusters in human superior temporal cortex. *BMC Neuroscience, 11,* 11.

van Bokhoven, I., van Goozen, S. H. M., van Engeland, H., Schaal, B., Arseneault, L., Seguin, J. R., Assaad, J., Nagin, D. S., Vitaro, F., & Tremblay, R. E. (2006). Salivary testosterone and aggression, delinquency, and social dominance in a population-based longitudinal study of adolescent males. *Hormones and Behavior, 50,* 118–125.

Vandello, J. A., & Cohen, D. (2008). Culture, gender, and men's intimate partner violence. *Social and Personality Psychology Compass, 2,* 652–667.

Vandello, J. A., Cohen, D., Grandon, R., & Franiuk, R. (2009). Stand by your man: Indirect prescriptions for honorable violence and feminine loyalty in Canada, Chile, and the United States. *Journal of Cross-Cultural Psychology, 40,* 81–104.

van der Geest, V., Blokland, A., & Bijleveld, C. (2009). Delinquent development in a sample of high-risk youth: Shape, content, and predictors of delinquent trajectories from age 12 to 32. *Journal of Research in Crime and Delinquency, 46,* 111–143.

Van der Werf, J., Jensen, O., Fries, P., & Medendorp, W. P. (2010). Neuronal synchronization in human posterior parietal cortex during reach planning. *Journal of Neuroscience, 30,* 1402–1412.

Van Dick, R., Becker, T. E., & Meyer, J. P. (2006). Commitment and identification: Forms, foci, and future. *Journal of Organizational Behavior, 27,* 545–548.

van Driel, M. A., & Brunner, H. G. (2006). Bioinformatics methods for identifying candidate disease genes. *Human Genomics. 2,* 429–432.

van Ettinger-Veenstra, H. M., & others. (2010). Right-hemispheric brain activation correlates to language performance. *NeuroImage, 49,* 3481–3488.

van IJzendoorn, M. H., & Sagi-Schwartz, A. (2008). Cross-cultural patterns of attachment: Universal and contextual dimensions. In J. Cassidy & P. R. Shaver (Eds.), *Handbook of attachment.* New York: Guilford.

van Ingen, D. J., & Novicki, D. J. (2009). An effectiveness study of group therapy for anxiety disorders. *International Journal of Group Psychotherapy, 59,* 243–251.

Van Katwyk, P. T., Fox, S., Spector, P. E., & Kelloway, E. K. (2000). Using the job-related affective well-being scale (JAWS) to investigate affective responses to work stressors. *Journal of Occupational Health Psychology, 52,* 219–230.

Van Lange, P. A. M., Rusbult, C. E., Drigotas, S. M., & Arriaga, X. B. (1997). Willingness to sacrifice in close relationships. *Journal of Personality and Social Psychology, 72,* 1373–1395.

van Lankveld, J. (2008). Problems with sexual interest and desire in women. In D. L. Rowland & L. Incrocci (Eds.), *Handbook of sexual and gender identity disorders* (pp. 154–185). Hoboken, NJ: Wiley.

Van Orden, K. A., Whitte, T. K., Gordon, K. H., Bender, T. W., & Joiner, T. E. (2008). Suicidal desire and the capability of suicide: Tests of the interpersonal-psychological theory of suicidal behavior among adults. *Journal of Consulting and Clinical Psychology, 76,* 72–83.

Van Orden, K. A., & others. (2010). The interpersonal theory of suicide. *Psychological Review, 117,* 575–600.

van Os, J., & Kapur, S. (2009). Schizophrenia. *Lancet, 374,* 635–645.

van Remmen, H., & Jones, D. P. (2009). Current thoughts on the role of mitochondria and free radicals in the biology of aging. *Journals of Gerontology A: Biological Sciences and Medical Sciences, 64,* 171–174.

Van Riper, M. (2007). Families of children with Down syndrome: Responding to "a change in plans" with resilience. *Journal of Pediatric Nursing, 22,* 116–128.

van Son, G. E., van Hoeken, D., van Furth, E. F., Donker, G. A., & Hoek, H. W. (2010). Course and outcome of eating disorders in a primary care–based cohort. *International Journal of Eating Disorders, 43,* 130–138.

Van Voorhees, B. W., & others. (2009). Randomized clinical trial of an Internet-based depression prevention program for adolescents (Project CATCH-IT) in primary care: 12-week outcomes. *Journal of Developmental and Behavioral Pediatrics, 30,* 23–37.

Vassilopoulos, S. P., & Watkins, E. R. (2009). Adaptive and maladaptive self-focus: A pilot extension study with individuals high and low in fear of negative evaluation. *Behavior Therapy, 40,* 181–189.

Vaughn, S., Bos, C. S., & Schumm, J. S. (2003). *Teaching exceptional, diverse, and at-risk students in the general education classroom* (3rd ed.). Boston: Allyn & Bacon.

Vazire, S. (2010). Who knows what about a person? The self-other knowledge asymmetry (SOKA) model. *Journal of Personality and Social Psychology, 98,* 281–300.

Vazsonyi, A. T., & Huang, L. (2010). Where self-control comes from: On the development of self-control and its relationship to deviance over time. *Developmental Psychology, 46,* 245–257.

Vega, G. L., Barlow, C. E., & Grundy, S. M. (2010). Prevalence of the metabolic syndrome as influenced by the measure of obesity employed. *American Journal of Cardiology, 105,* 1306–1302.

Vega, V., & Malamuth, N. M. (2007). Predicting sexual aggression: The role of pornography in the context of general and specific risk factors. *Aggressive Behavior, 33,* 104–117.

Vermetten, E., Schmahl, C., Lindner, S., Loewenstein, R. J., & Bremner, J. D. (2006). Hippocampal and amygdalar volumes in dissociative identity disorder. *American Journal of Psychiatry, 163,* 630–636.

Verquer, M. L., Beehr, T. A., & Wagner, S. H. (2003). A meta-analysis of relations between person–organization fit and work attitudes. *Journal of Vocational Behavior, 63,* 473–489.

Verschuere, B., Crombez, G., De Clercq, A., & Koster, E. H. W. (2005). Psychopathic traits and autonomic responding to concealed information in a prison sample. *Psychophysiology, 42,* 239–245.

Vervaet, M., van Heeringen, C., & Audenaert, K. (2004). Personality-related characteristics in restricting versus binging and purging eating disordered patients. *Comprehensive Psychiatry, 45,* 37–43.

Veselka, L., Schermer, J. A., Petrides, K. V., & Verson, P. A. (2009). Evidence for a heritable general factor of personality in two studies. *Twin Research and Human Genetics, 12,* 254–260.

Vetter, S., & others. (2010). Impact of resilience enhancing programs on youth surviving the Belsan school siege. *Child and Adolescent Psychiatry and Mental Health.* (in press)

Vickerman, K. A., & Margolin, G. (2009). Rape treatment outcome research: Empirical findings and state of the literature. *Clinical Psychology Review, 29* (5), 431–448.

Victor, A. M., & Bernstein, G. A. (2009). Anxiety disorders and posttraumatic stress disorder update. *Psychiatric Clinics of North America, 32,* 57–69.

Videtic, A., Zupanic, T., Pregelj, P., Balazic, J., Tomori, M., & Komel, R. (2009). Suicide, stress, and serotonin receptor 1A promotor polymorphism -1019>G in Slovenian suicide victims. *European Archives of Psychiatry and Clinical Neuroscience, 259,* 234–238.

Vidoni, E. D., Acerraa, N. E., Dao, E., Meehan, S. K., & Boyd, L. A. (2010). Role of the primary somatosensory cortex in motor learning: An rTMS study. *Neurobiology of Learning and Memory.* (in press)

Vimal, R. L., & others. (2009). Activation of the suprachiasmatic nuclei and primary visual cortex depends upon time of day. *European Journal of Neuroscience, 29,* 399–410.

Vinberg, M., Mellerup, E., Andersen, P. K., Bennike, B., & Kessing, L. V. (2010). Variations in 5-HTTLPR: Relation to familiar risk of affective disorder, life events, neuroticism, and cortisol. *Progress in Neuro-Psychopharmacology & Biological Psychiatry, 34,* 86–91.

Vinchur, A. J., & Koppes, L. L. (2010). A historical survey of research and practice in industrial and organizational psychology. In S. Zedeck (Ed.), *APA handbook of industrial and organizational psychology.* Washington, DC: APA. (in press)

Vismara, L. A., & Rogers, S. J. (2010). Behavioral treatments in autism spectrum disorder: What do we know? *Annual Review of Clinical Psychology, 6,* 447–468.

Vogt, T. M., Mullooly, J. P., Ernst, D., Pople, C. R., & Hollis, J. F. (1992). Social networks as predictors of ischemic heart disease, cancer, stroke, and hypertension. *Journal of Clinical Epidemiology, 45,* 659–666.

Volskuijl, O. F., & Evers, A. (2008). Job analysis and competency modeling. In S. Cartwright & C. L. Cooper (Eds.), *The Oxford handbook of personnel psychology* (pp. 138–162). New York: Oxford University Press.

von Békésy, G. (1960). Vibratory patterns of the basilar membrane. In E. G. Wever (Ed.), *Experiments in hearing.* New York: McGraw-Hill.

von Helmholtz, H. (1852). On the theory of compound colors. *Philosophical Magazine, 4,* 519–534.

Voshaar, R. C., & others. (2006). Predictors of long-term benzodiazepine abstinence in participants of a randomized controlled benzodiazepine withdrawal program. *Canadian Journal of Psychiatry, 51,* 445–452.

Voss, J. L., & Paller, K. A. (2009). An electro-physiological signature of unconscious recognition memory. *Nature Neuroscience, 13,* 349–355.

Voyvodic, J. T., Petrella, J. R., & Friedman, A. H. (2009). fMRI activation mapping as a percentage of local excitation: Consistent presurgical motor maps without threshold adjustment. *Journal of Magnetic Resonance Imaging, 29,* 751–759.

Vuillermot, S., Weber, L., Feldon, J., & Meyer, U. (2010). A longitudinal examination of the neurodevelopmental impact of prenatal immune activation in mice reveals primary defects in dopaminergic development relevant to schizophrenia. *Journal of Neuroscience, 30,* 1270–1287.

Vukovic, J., & others. (2009). Lack of fibulin-3 alters regenerative tissue responses in the primary olfactory pathway. *Matrix Biology, 28,* 406–415.

Vygotsky, L. S. (1962). *Thought and language.* Cambridge, MA: MIT Press.

W

Waddell, E. L., & Jacobs-Lawson, J. M. (2010). Predicting positive well-being in older men and women. *International Journal of Aging and Human Development, 70,* 181–197.

Wagner, A. D., Schacter, D. L., Rotte, M., Koutstaal, B., Maril, A., Dale, A. M., Rosen, B. R., & Buckner, R. L. (1998). Building memories: Remembering and forgetting of verbal experiences as predicted by brain activity. *Science, 281,* 1185–1187.

Wai, J., Lubinski, D., & Benbow, C. P. (2005). Creativity and occupational accomplishments among intellectually precocious youths: An age 13 to age 33 longitudinal study. *Journal of Educational Psychology, 97,* 484–492.

Wainwright, J. L., & Patterson, C. J. (2008). Peer relations among adolescents with female same-sex parents. *Developmental Psychology, 44,* 117–126.

Wald, A., Langenberg, A. G., & Krantz, E. (2005). The relationship between condom use and herpes simplex virus acquisition. *Annals of Internal Medicine, 143,* 707–713.

Walker, D. D., Roffman, R. A., Stephens, R. S., Wakana, K., & Berghuis, J. (2006). Motivational enhancement therapy for adolescent marijuana users: A preliminary randomized controlled trial. *Journal of Consulting and Clinical Psychology, 74,* 628–632.

Walker, D. R., & Milton, G. A. (1966). Memory transfer vs. sensitization in cannibal planarians. *Psychonomic Science, 5,* 293–294.

Walker, H. (2008). *Breaking free: My life with dissociative disorder.* New York: Simon & Schuster.

Walker, L. E. A. (2009). *The battered woman syndrome* (3rd ed.). New York: Springer.

Walker, L. J., & Frimer, J. A. (2011). The science of moral development. In M. K. Underwood & L. H. Rosen (Eds.), *Social development.* New York: Guilford. (in press)

Waller, E. A., Bendel, R. E., & Kaplan, J. (2008). Sleep disorders and the eye. *Mayo Clinic Proceedings, 83,* 1251–1261.

Wallerstein, R. S. (1989). The psychotherapy research project of the Menninger Foundation: An overview. *Journal of Consulting and Clinical Psychology, 57,* 195–205.

Walter, K. H., Horsey, K. J., Palmieri, P. A., & Hobfoll, S. E. (2010). The role of protective self-cognitions in the relationship between childhood trauma and later resource loss. *Journal of Traumatic Stress, 23,* 264–273.

Wampold, B. E. (2001). *The great psychotherapy debate: Models, methods, and findings.* Mahwah, NJ: Erlbaum.

Wampold, B. E., & Brown, G. S. (2005). Estimating variability in outcomes attributable to therapists: A naturalistic study of outcomes of managed care. *Journal of Consulting and Clinical Psychology, 73,* 914–923.

Wamsley, E. J., Perry, K., Djonlagic, I., Reaven, L. B., & Stickgold, R. (2010). Cognitive replay of visuomotor learning at sleep onset: Temporal dynamics and relationship to task performance. *Sleep, 33,* 59–88.

Wanat, M. J., Sparta, D. R., Hopf, F. W., Bowers, M. S., Melis, M., & Bonci, A. (2009). Strain specific synaptic modifications on ventral tegmental area dopamine neurons after ethanol exposure. *Biological Psychiatry, 65,* 646–653.

Wang, L., Li, C. C., Wang, G. W., & Cai, J. X. (2009). The effects of centrally administered fluorocitrate via inhibiting glial cells on working memory in rats. *Science in China. Series C, Life Sciences, 52,* 701–719.

Wang, S.-H., & Morris, R. G. M. (2010). Hippocampal-neocortical interactions in memory formation, consolidation, and reconsolidation. *Annual Review of Psychology* (vol. 61). Palo Alto, CA: Annual Reviews.

Wangberg, S. C., Gammon, D., & Spitznogle, K. (2007). In the eyes of the beholder: Exploring psychologists' attitudes towards the use of e-therapy in Norway. *CyberPsychology and Behavior, 10,* 418–423.

Ward, J. (2010). *The student's guide to cognitive neuroscience* (2nd ed.). New York: Psychology Press.

Ward, J., Jonas, C., Dienes, Z., & Seth, A. (2010). Grapheme-colour synaesthesia improves detection of embedded shapes, but without pre-attentive "pop-out" of synaesthetic color. *Proceedings: Biological Sciences.* (in press)

Ward, T. B. (2007). Creative cognition as a window on creativity. *Methods, 42,* 28–37.

Wardlaw, G. M., & Smith, A. M. (2011). *Contemporary nutrition* (8th ed.). New York: McGraw-Hill.

Warnecke, R. B., Morera, O., Turner, L., Mermelstein, R., Johnson, T. P., Parsons, J., Crittenden, K., Freels, S., & Flay, B. (2001). Changes in self-efficacy and readiness for smoking cessation among women with high school or less education. *Journal of Health and Social Behavior, 42,* 97–109.

Warren, G., Schertler, E., & Bull, P. (2009). Detecting deception from emotional and unemotional cues. *Journal of Nonverbal Behavior, 33,* 59–69.

Warren, J. I., Stein, J. A., & Grella, C. E. (2007). Role of social support and self-efficacy in treatment outcomes among clients with co-occurring disorders. *Drug and Alcohol Dependence, 89,* 267–274.

Wasserman, D., Wasserman, J., & Sokolowski, M. (2010). Genetics of HPA-axis, depression, and suicidality. *European Psychiatry.* (in press)

Watanabe, H., & Mizunami, M. (2007). Pavlov's cockroach: Classical conditioning of salivation in an insect. *PloS One, 6,* e529.

Watson, A., El-Deredy, W., Bentley, D. E., Vogt, B. A., & Jones, A. K. (2006). Categories of placebo response in the absence of site-specific stimulation of analgesia. *Pain, 126,* 115–122.

Watson, D. (2001). Positive affectivity: The disposition to experience pleasurable emotional states. In C. R. Snyder & S. J. Lopez (Eds.), *Handbook of positive psychology.* New York: Oxford University Press.

Watson, D. (2009). Differentiation of mood and anxiety disorders. *Annual Review of Clinical Psychology* (vol. 5). Palo Alto, CA: Annual Reviews.

Watson, D., & Clark, L. A. (1997). Extraversion and its positive emotional core. In R. Hogan, J. A. Johnson, & S. R., Briggs (Eds.), *Handbook of personality psychology* (pp. 767–793). San Diego: Academic.

Watson, D., & Naragon, K. (2009). Positive affectivity: The disposition to experience positive emotional states. In S. J. Lopez & C. R. Snyder (Eds.), *Oxford handbook of positive psychology* (2nd ed., pp. 207–215). New York: Oxford University Press.

Watson, J. B., & Rayner, R. (1920). Conditioned emotional reactions. *Journal of Experimental Psychology, 3,* 1–14.

Waugaman, R. M. (2005). Substance abuse and borderline personality disorder. *American Journal of Psychiatry, 162,* 1759.

Wayment, H. A., & O'Mara, E. M. (2008). The collective and compassionate consequences of downward social comparisons. In H. A. Wayment & J. J. Bauer (Eds.), *Transcending self-interest: Psychological explorations of the quiet ego* (pp. 159–169). Washington, DC: American Psychological Association.

Weaver, K., Garcia, S. M., Schwarz, N., & Miller, D. T. (2007). Inferring the popularity of an opinion from its familiarity: A repetitive voice can sound like a chorus. *Journal of Personality and Social Psychology, 92,* 821–833.

Webb, W. B. (2000). Sleep. In A. Kazdin (Ed.), *Encyclopedia of psychology.* Washington, DC, & New York: American Psychological Association and Oxford University Press.

Weber, S., Habel, U., Amunts, K., & Schneider, F. (2008). Structural brain abnormalities in psychopaths—A review. *Behavioral Sciences and the Law, 26,* 7–28.

Webster, J. M., Smith, R. H., Rhodes, A., & Whatley, M. A. (1999). The effect of a favor on public and private compliance: How internalized is the norm of reciprocity? *Basic and Applied Social Psychology, 21,* 251–260.

Wechsler, H., Lee, J. E., Kuo, M., & Lee, H. (2000). College binge drinking in the 1990s—A continuing health problem: Results of the Harvard University School of Public Health 1999 College Alcohol Study. *Journal of American College Health, 48,* 199–210.

Wechsler, H., Lee, J. E., Kuo, M., Seibring, M., Nelson, T. F., & Lee, H. (2002). Trends in college binge drinking during a period of increased prevention efforts: Findings from 4 Harvard School of Public Health college alcohol study surveys: 1993–2001. *Journal of American College Health, 50,* 203–217.

Wecker, L., & others. (2010). *Brody's human pharmacology* (5th ed.). London: Elsevier.

Weerda, R., Muehlhan, M., Wolf, O. T., & Thiel, C. M. (2010). Effects of acute psychosocial stress on working memory related brain activity in men. *Human Brain Mapping.* (in press)

Wegener, D. T., Clark, J. K., & Petty, R. E. (2006). Not all stereotyping is created equal: Differential consequences of thoughtful versus non-thoughtful stereotyping. *Journal of Personality and Social Psychology, 90,* 42–59.

Weiner, B. (2006). Social motivation, justice, and the moral emotions: An attributional approach. Mahwah, NJ: Erlbaum.

Weiner, I. B. (2004). Rorschach assessment: Current status. In M. Hersen (Ed.), *Comprehensive handbook of psychological assessment* (vol. 2). New York: Wiley.

Weinstein, T. A. R., Capitanio, J. P., & Gosling, S. D. (2008). Personality in animals. In O. P. John, R. W. Robins, & L. A. Pervin (Eds.), *Handbook of personality theory and research* (3rd ed., pp. 328–350). New York: Guilford.

Weir, W. (1984, October 15). Another look at subliminal "facts." *Advertising Age,* 46.

Weis, C. O., & others. (2010). Relationships of cardiac, pulmonary, and muscle reserves and frailty to exercise capacity in older women. *Journals of Gerontology A: Biological Sciences and Medical Sciences, 65A,* 287–294.

Weismiller, D. G. (2009). Menopause. *Primary Care, 36,* 199–226.

Weiss, B., & Feldman, R. S. (2006). Looking good and lying to do it: Deception as an impression management strategy in job interviews. *Journal of Applied Social Psychology, 36,* 1070–1086.

Weissman, M., & Olfson, M. (1995). Depression in women: Implications for health care research. *Science, 269,* 99–801.

Weissman, M. M. (2009). Teenaged, depressed, and treatment resistant: What predicts self-harm? *American Journal of Psychiatry, 166*, 385–387.

Wellen, M. (2010). Differentiation between demoralization, grief, and anhedonic depression. *Current Psychiatry Reports, 12*, 229–233.

Wellman, H. M., & Woolley, J. D. (1990). From simple desires to ordinary beliefs: The early development of everyday psychology. *Cognition, 35*, 245–275.

Wenzel, M. (2009). Social identity and justice: Implications for intergroup relations. In S. Otten, K. Sassenberg, & T. Kessler (Eds.), *Intergroup relations*. New York: Psychology Press.

Werner, J. M., & Bolino, M. C. (1997). Explaining U.S. courts of appeals decisions involving performance appraisal: Accuracy, fairness, and validation. *Personnel Psychology, 50*, 1–24.

Werner, K., & Gross, J. J. (2010). Emotion regulation and psychopathology: A conceptual framework. In A. M. Kring & D. M. Sloan (Eds.), *Emotion regulation and psychopathology: A transdiagnostic approach to etiology and treatment* (pp. 13–37). New York: Guilford.

Wesson, M. J., & Gogus, C. I. (2005). Shaking hands with a computer: An examination of two methods of organizational newcomer orientation. *Journal of Applied Psychology, 90*, 1018–1026.

West, R. (2005). Time for a change: Putting the transtheoretical (stages of change) model to rest. *Addiction, 100*, 1036–1039.

Westen, D., Gabbard, G. O., & Soto, C. J. (2008). Psychoanalytic approaches to personality. In O. P. John, R. W. Robins, & L. A. Pervin (Eds.) *Handbook of personality theory and research* (3rd ed., pp. 61–113). New York: Guilford.

Weyers, P., Muhlberger, A., Kund, A., Hess, U., & Pauli, P. (2009). Modulation of facial reactions to avatar emotional faces by nonconscious competition priming. *Psychophysiology, 46*, 328–335.

Wheeler, D. S., & Miller, R. R. (2008). Determinants of cue interactions. *Behavioral Processes, 78*, 191–203.

Whiffen, V. E., & Demidenko, N. (2006). Mood disturbances across the lifespan. In J. Worell & C. D. Goodheart (Eds.), *Handbook of girls' and women's health: Gender and well-being across the lifespan*. New York: Oxford University Press.

Whitaker, R. (2002). Mad in America: Bad science, bad medicine, and the mistreatment of the mentally ill. Cambridge, MA: Perseus.

White, J. W., & Frabutt, J. M. (2006). Violence against girls and women: An integrative developmental perspective. In J. Worell & C. D. Goodheart (Eds.), *Handbook of girls' and women's psychological health: Gender and well-being across the lifespan* (pp. 85–93). New York: Oxford University Press.

White, R. C., & Aimola Davies, A. (2008). Attention set for numbers: Expectation and perceptual load in inattentional blindness. *Journal of Experimental Psychology: Human Perception and Performance, 34*, 1092–1107.

White, R. W. (1992). Exploring personality the long way: The study of lives. In R. A. Zucker, A. I. Rabin, J. Aronoff, & S. J. Frank (Eds.), *Personality structure in the life course: Essays on personology in the Murray tradition* (pp. 3–21). New York: Springer.

Whorf, B. L. (1956). *Language, thought, and creativity.* New York: Wiley.

Widiger, T. A. (2009). Neuroticism. In M. R. Leary & R. H. Hoyle (Eds.), *Handbook of individual differences in social behavior* (pp. 129–146). New York: Guilford.

Wiebe, R. P. (2004). Delinquent behavior and the Five Factor model: Hiding in the adaptive landscape? *Individual Differences Research, 2*, 38–62.

Wiedeman, R. (2008, March 25). Digital man. *Boston Globe.* http://www.boston.com/news/education/higher/articles/2008/03/25/digital_man/

Wiegand, B., & others. (2010). Efficacy of a comprehensive program for reducing stress in women: A prospective, randomized trial. *Current Medical Research and Opinion, 26*, 991–1002.

Wiegand, D. M., & Geller, E. S. (2004). Connecting positive psychology and organizational behavior management: Achievement motivation and the power of positive reinforcement. *Journal of Organizational Behavior Management, 24*, 3–24.

Wiersma, D., Nienhuis, F. J., Slooff, C. J., & Giel, R. (1998). Natural course of schizophrenic disorders: A 15-year follow up of a Dutch incidence cohort. *Schizophrenia Bulletin, 24*, 75–85.

Wiese, H., & Schweinberger, S. R. (2010). Accessing semantic person knowledge: Temporal dynamics of nonstrategic categorical and associative priming. *Journal of Cognitive Neurosceince.* (in press)

Wigfield, A., Eccles, J. S., Schiefele, U., Roeser, R. W., & Davis-Kean, P. (2006). Development of achievement motivation. In W. Damon & R. Lerner (Eds.), *Handbook of child psychology* (6th ed.). New York: Wiley.

Wijesiri, L. (2005, October 21). Meditation's effect on the brain. *Ceylon Daily News.* http://www.maithri.com/links/articles/meditation_effect_brain.htm (accessed April 23, 2010)

Wijnen, V. J., & van Boxtel, G. J. (2010). The continuing problem of diagnosing unresponsive patients: Searching for neuropsychological correlates of consciousness. *Clinical Neurophysiology.* (in press)

Wildman, J. L., Bedwell, W. L., Salas, E., & Smith-Jentsch, K. A. (2010). Performance measurement at work: A multilevel perspective. In S. Zedeck (Ed.), *APA handbook of industrial and organizational psychology*. Washington, DC: APA. (in press)

Wilfley, D. E., Friedman, M. A., Dounchis, J. Z., Stein, R. I., Welch, R. R., & Ball, S. A. (2000). Comorbid psychopathology in binge eating disorder: Relation to eating disorder severity at baseline and following treatment. *Journal of Consulting and Clinical Psychology, 68*, 641–649.

Wilkowski, B. M., & Robinson, M. D. (2010). Associative and spontaneous appraisal processes

independently contribute to anger elicitation in daily life. *Emotion, 10*, 181–189.

Willcox, D. C., Willcox, B. J., He, Q., Wang, N. C., & Suzuki, M. (2008). They really are that old: A validation study of centenarian prevalence in Okinawa. *Journals of Gerontology A: Biological Sciences and Medical Sciences, 63*, 338–349.

Willenbockel, V., & others. (2010). Does face inversion change spatial frequency tuning? *Journal of Experimental Psychology: Human Perception and Performance, 36*, 122–135.

Willert, M. V., Thulstrup, A. M., & Hertz, J. (2009). Changes in stress and coping from a randomized controlled trial of a three-month stress management intervention. *Scandinavian Journal of Work and Environmental Health, 35*, 145–152.

Williams, K. D. (2007). Ostracism. *Annual Review of Psychology* (vol. 58). Palo Alto, CA: Annual Reviews.

Williams, L. M. (1995). Recovered memories of abuse in women with documented child sexual victimization histories. *Journal of Traumatic Stress, 19*, 257–267.

Williams, L. M. (2003). Understanding child abuse and violence against women: A life-course perspective. *Journal of Interpersonal Violence, 18*, 441–451.

Williams, L. M. (2004). Researcher-advocate collaborations to end violence against women. *Journal of Interpersonal Violence, 19*, 1350–1357.

Williams, R. B. (2001). Hostility (and other psychosocial risk factors): Effects on health and the potential for successful behavioral approaches to prevention and treatment. In A. Baum, T. A. Revenson, & J. E. Singer (Eds.), *Handbook of health psychology*. Mahwah, NJ: Erlbaum.

Williams, R. B. (2002). Hostility, neuroendocrine changes, and health outcomes. In H. G. Koenig & H. J. Cohen (Eds.), *The link between religion and health*. New York: Oxford University Press.

Williams, S. K., & Davidson, K. W. (2009). Psychological distress and cardiovascular disease with emphasis on acute coronary syndromes. *Journal of the American College of Cardiology, 53*, 1339.

Willis, J., & Todorov, A. (2006). First impressions: Making up your mind after a 100-ms exposure to a face. *Psychological Science, 17*, 592–598.

Willis, S. L., & Schaie, K. W. (2005). Cognitive trajectories in midlife and cognitive functioning in old age. In S. L. Willis & M. Martin (Eds.), *Middle adulthood*. Thousand Oaks, CA: Sage.

Wilsey, B., Marcotte, T., Tsodikov, A., Millman, J., Bentley, H., Gouaux, B., & Fishman, S. (2008). A randomized, placebo-controlled, crossover trial of cannabis cigarettes in neuropathic pain. *Journal of Pain, 9*, 506–521.

Wilson, A., & Godin, J. J. (2010). Boldness and intermittent locomotion in the bluegill sunfish, *Lepomis macrochirus. Behavioral Ecology, 21*, 57–62.

Wilson, G. T., Grilo, C. M., & Vitousek, K. M. (2007). Psychological treatment of eating disorders. *American Psychologist, 62*, 199–216.

Wilson, J. F. (2007). Posttraumatic stress disorder needs to be recognized in primary care. *Annals of Internal Medicine, 146,* 617–620.

Wilson, R. S., Mendes de Leon, D. F., Bienias, J. L., Evans, D. A., & Bennett, D. A. (2004). Personality and mortality in old age. *Journals of Gerontology: Psychological Sciences and Social Sciences, 59B,* 110–116.

Wilt, J., & Revelle, W. (2009) Extraversion. In M. Leary & R. Hoyle (Eds.), *Handbook of individual differences in social behavior* (pp. 27–45). New York: Guilford.

Wiltermuth, S. S., & Heath, C. (2009). Synchrony and cooperation. *Psychological Science, 20,* 1–5.

Winecoff, A., Labar, K. S., Madden, D. J., Cabeza, R., & Huettel, S. A. (2010). Cognitive and neural contributors to emotion regulation in aging. *Social Cognitive and Affective Neuroscience.* (in press)

Winer, R. L., Hughes, J. P., Feng, O., O'Reilly, S., Kiviat, N. B., Holmes, K. K., & Koutsky, L. A. (2006). Condom use and the risk of genital human papilloma virus infection in young women. *New England Journal of Medicine, 354,* 2645–2654.

Wingo, A. P., Fani, N., Bradley, B., & Ressler, K. J. (2010). Psychological resilience and neurocognitive performance in a traumatized community sample. *Depression and Anxiety.* (in press)

Winner, E. (1996). *Gifted children: Myths and realities.* New York: Basic.

Winner, E. (2000). The origins and ends of giftedness. *American Psychologist, 55,* 159–169.

Winner, E. (2006). Development in the arts. In W. Damon & R. Lerner (Eds.), *Handbook of child psychology* (6th ed.). New York: Wiley.

Winter, D. G. (2005). Measuring the motives of political actors at a distance. In J. M. Post (Ed.), *The psychological assessment of political leaders: With profiles of Saddam Hussein and Bill Clinton* (pp. 153–177). Ann Arbor: University of Michigan Press.

Wirtz, P. H., Redwine, L. S., Ehlert, U., & von Kanel, R. (2009). Independent association between lower level of social support and higher coagulation activity before and after acute psychosocial stress. *Psychosomatic Medicine, 71,* 30–37.

Wirtz, P. H., Siegrist, J., Schuhmacher, A., Hoefels, S., Maier, W., & Zobel, A. W. (2010). Higher overcommitment to work is associated with higher plasma cortisol but not ACTH responses in the combined dexamethasone/CRH test in apparently healthy men and women. *Psychoneuroendocrinology, 35,* 536–543.

Wiseman, R., & Watt, C. (2006). Belief in psychic ability and the misattribution hypothesis: A qualitative review. *British Journal of Psychology, 97,* 323–338.

Witelson, S. F., Kigar, D. L., & Harvey, T. (1999). The exceptional brain of Albert Einstein. *Lancet, 353,* 2149–2153.

Witelson, S. F., Kigar, D. L., Scamvougeras, A., Kideckel, D. M., Buck, B., Stanchev, P. L., Bronskill, M., & Black, S. (2008). Corpus callosum anatomy in right-handed homosexual and heterosexual men. *Archives of Sexual Behavior, 37,* 857–863.

Woike, B. A. (2001). Working with free response data: Let's not give up hope. *Psychological Inquiry, 12,* 157–159.

Woike, B. A. (2008). The state of the story in personality psychology. *Social and Personality Psychology Compass, 2,* 434–443.

Woike, B. A., & Matic, D. (2004). Cognitive complexity in response to traumatic experiences. *Journal of Personality, 72,* 633–657.

Woike, B. A., Mcleod, S., & Goggin, M. (2003). Implicit and explicit motives influence accessibility to different autobiographical knowledge. *Personality and Social Psychology Bulletin, 29,* 1046–1055.

Wojtczak, M., & Oxenham, A. J. (2009). Pitfalls in behavioral estimates of basilar-membrane compression in humans. *Journal of the Acoustical Society of America, 125,* 270–281.

Wolf, A. (2000). Emotional expression online: Gender differences in emoticon use. *CyberPsychology & Behavior, 3,* 827–833.

Wolf, R., Matzke, K., Paelchen, K., Dobrokolny, H., Goverts, B., & Schwegler, H. (2010). Reduction of prepulse inhibition (PPI) after neonatal excitotoxic lesion of the ventral thalamus in pubertal and adult rats. *Pharmacopsychiatry.* (in press)

Wolitzky, K. B., & Telch, M. J. (2009). Augmenting in vivo exposure with fear antagonistic actions: A preliminary test. *Behavior Therapy, 40,* 57–71.

Wolkove, N., Elkholy, O., Baltzan, M., & Palayew, M. (2007). Sleep and aging: 1. Sleep disorders commonly found in older people. *Canadian Medical Association Journal, 176,* 1299–1304.

Wolkowitz, O. M., Epel, E. S., Reus, V. I., & Mellon, S. H. (2010). Depression gets old fast: Do stress and depression accelerate cell aging? *Depression and Anxiety, 27,* 327–338.

Wolpe, J. (1963). Behavior therapy in complex neurotic states. *British Journal of Psychiatry, 110,* 28–34.

Wong, A. C., Jobard, G., James, K. H., James, T. W., & Gauthier, I. (2009). Expertise with characters in alphabetic and non-alphabetic writing systems engage overlapping occipito-temporal areas. *Cognitive Neuropsychology, 26* (1), 111–127.

Wong, Y. J., Kim, S. H., & Tran, K. K. (2010). Asian Americans' adherence to Asian values, attributions about depression, and coping strategies. *Cultural Diversity and Ethnic Minority Psychology, 16* (1), 1–8.

Wood, A. H., & Eagly, A. H. (2010). Gender. In S. Fiske, D. Gilbert, & G. Lindzey (Eds.), *Handbook of social psychology.* New York: Oxford University Press.

Wood, D., Harms, P., & Vazire, S. (2010). Perceiver effects as projective tests: What your perceptions of others say about you. *Journal of Personality and Social Psychology, 99* (1), 174–190.

Wood, R. L., & Liossi, C. (2006). Neuropsychological and neurobehavioral correlates of aggression following traumatic brain injury. *Journal of Neuropsychiatry & Clinical Neurosciences, 18,* 333–341.

Woolf, N. J., & Butcher, L. L. (2010). Cholinergic systems media action from movement to higher consciousness. *Behavioural Brain Research.* (in press)

World Health Organization (WHO). (2009). *Suicide rates per 100,000 by country.* http://www.who.int/mental_health/prevention/suicide_rates/en/index.html (accessed April 20, 2010

World Health Organization (WHO). (2010). *Health through safe drinking water and basic sanitation.* http://www.who.int/water_sanitation_health/mdg1/en/index.html (accessed May 6, 2010)

Worthington, R. L., Navarro, R. L., Savoy, H. B., & Hampton, D. (2008). Development, reliability, and validity of the Measure of Sexual Identity Exploration and Commitment (MoSIEC). *Developmental Psychology, 44,* 22–33.

Wortman, C. B., & Boerner, K. (2007). Reactions to death of a loved one: Beyond the myths of coping with loss. In H. S. Friedman & R. C. Silver (Eds.), *Foundations of health psychology.* New York: Oxford University Press.

Wright, R. G. (2008). Sex offender post-incarceration sanctions: Are there any limits? *Criminal and Civil Confinement, 34,* 17–50.

Wright, T. A., & Cropanzano, R. (2000). Psychological well-being and job satisfaction as predictors of job performance. *Journal of Occupational Health Psychology, 5,* 84–94.

Wright, T. A., & Staw, B. M. (1999). Affect and favorable work outcomes: Two longitudinal tests of the happy–productive worker thesis. *Journal of Organizational Behavior, 20,* 1–23.

Wrzesniewski, A. (2003). Finding positive meaning in work. In K. S. Cameron, J. E. Dutton, & R. E. Quinn (Eds.), *Positive organizational scholarship: Foundations of a new discipline* (pp. 296–308). San Francisco: Berrett-Koehler.

Wrzesniewski, A., Dutton, J. E., & Debebe, G. (2003). Interpersonal sense-making and the meaning of work. In R. M. Kramer, M. Roderick, & B. M. Staw (Eds.), *Research in organizational behavior: An annual series of analytical essays and critical reviews* (vol. 25, pp. 93–135). Oxford: Elsevier.

Wrzesniewski, A., McCauley, C. I., Rozin, P., & Schwartz, B. (1997). Jobs, careers, and callings: People's relations to their work. *Journal of Research in Personality, 31,* 21–33.

Wykes, T., Brammer, M., Mellers, J., Bray, P., Reeder, C., Williams, C., & Corner, J. (2002). Effects on the brain of a psychological treatment: Cognitive remediation therapy: Functional magnetic resonance imaging in schizophrenia. *British Journal of Psychiatry, 181,* 144–152.

X

Xu, H., Kotak, V. C., & Sanes, D. H. (2010). Normal hearing is required for the emergence of long-lasting inhibitory potentiation in the cortex. *Journal of Neuroscience, 30,* 331–341.

Y

Yalom, I. D., & Leszcz, M. (2006). *Theory and practice of group psychotherapy* (5th ed.). New York: Basic.

Yamada, M., & Decety, J. (2009). Unconscious affective processing and empathy: An investigation of subliminal priming on the detection of painful facial expressions. *Pain, 143,* 71–75.

Yamanishi, T., & others. (2009). Changes after behavior therapy among responsive and non-responsive patients with obsessive-compulsive disorder. *Psychiatry Research, 172,* 242–250.

Yamazaki, Y., Yokochi, H., Tanaka, M., Okanoya, K., & Iriki, A. (2010). Potential role of monkey inferior parietal neurons coding action semantic equivalences as precursors of parts of speech. *Social Neuroscience, 5,* 105–117.

Yamin, S., & Vaddadi, K. (2010). Are we using excessive neuroleptics? An argument for systematic neuroleptic dose reduction in stable patients with schizophrenia with specific reference to clozapine. *International Review of Psychiatry, 22,* 138–147.

Yang, H., & others. (2010). Residual sleep disturbance and risk of relapse during the continuation/maintenance phase treatment of major depressive disorder with the selective serontonin reuptake inhibitor fluoxetine. *Annals of General Psychiatry, 9,* 10.

Yang, Y. (2008). Social inequalities in happiness in the United States, 1972–2004: An age-period-cohort analysis. *American Sociological Review, 73,* 204–226.

Yang, Y., Glenn, A. L., & Raine, A. (2008). Brain abnormalities in antisocial individuals: Implications for the law. *Behavioral Sciences & the Law, 26,* 65–83.

Yang, Y., & Raine, A. (2009). Prefrontal structural and functional brain imaging findings in antisocial, violent, and psychopathic individuals: A meta-analysis. *Psychiatry Research, 174,* 81–88.

Yang, Y., Raine, A., Lencz, T., Bihrle, S., LaCasse, L., & Colletti, P. (2005). Volume reduction in prefrontal gray matter in unsuccessful criminal psychopaths. *Biological Psychiatry, 57,* 1103–1108.

Ye, C. Q., Poo, M. M., Dan, Y., & Zhang, X. H. (2010). Synaptic mechanisms of direction selectivity in primary auditory cortex. *Journal of Neuroscience, 30,* 1861–1868.

Yen, C. F., Chen, C. C., Lee, Y, Tang, T. C., Ko, C. H., & Yen, J. Y. (2009). Association between quality of life and self-stigma, insight, and adverse effects of medication in patients with depressive disorders. *Depression and Anxiety, 26* (11), 1033–1039.

Yeshurun, Y., & Sobel, N. (2010). An odor is not worth a thousand words: From multidimensional odors to unidimensional objects. *Annual Review of Psychology* (vol. 61). Palo Alto, CA: Annual Reviews.

Yi, Y., Driesen, N., & Leung, H. (2009). Behavioral and neural correlates of memory selection and interference resolution during a digit working memory task. *Cognitive, Affective & Behavioral Neuroscience, 9,* 249–259.

Yip, T., Kiang, L., & Fuligni, A. J. (2008). Multiple social identities and reactivity to daily stress among ethnically diverse young adults. *Journal of Research in Personality, 42,* 1160–1172.

Yordanova, J., Kolev, V., & Verleger, R. (2009). Awareness of knowledge or awareness of processing? Implications for sleep-related memory consolidation. *Frontiers in Human Neuroscience, 3,* ARTID 40.

Young, L. J. (2009). Being human: Love: Neuroscience reveals all. *Nature, 457,* 148.

Young, S. G., & Claypool, H. M. (2010). Mere exposure has differential effects on attention allocation to threatening and neutral stimuli. *Journal of Experimental Social Psychology, 46,* 424–427.

Young, T. (1802). On the theory of light and colors. *Philosophical Transactions of the Royal Society of London, 92,* 12–48.

Ystad, M., Eichele, T., Lundervold, A. J., & Lundervold, A. (2010). Subcortical functional connectivity and verbal episodic memory in healthy elderly—a resting state fMRI study. *NeuroImage.* (in press)

Yuan, J., Luo, Y., Yan, J. H., Meng, X., Yu, F., & Li, H. (2009). Neural correlates of the female's susceptibility to negative emotions: An insight into gender-related prevalence of affective disturbances. *Human Brain Mapping, 30,* 3676–3686.

Yuan, Y., Zhang, Z., Bai, F., You, J., Yu, H., Shi, Y., & Liu, W. (2010). Genetic variation in apolipoprotein E alters regional gray matter volumes in remitted late-onset depression. *Journal of Affective Disorders, 121,* 273–277.

Z

Zajonc, R. B. (1965). Social facilitation. *Science, 149,* 269–274.

Zajonc, R. B. (1968). Attitudinal effects of mere exposure. *Journal of Personality and Social Psychology, 9,* 1–27.

Zajonc, R. B. (1984). On the primacy of affect. *American Psychologist, 39,* 117–123.

Zajonc, R. B. (2001). Mere exposure: A gateway to the subliminal. *Current Directions in Psychological Science, 10,* 224–228.

Zedeck, S. (Ed.). (2010). *APA handbook of industrial and organizational psychology.* Washington, DC: APA. (in press)

Zeidan, F., Gordon, N. S., Merchant, J., & Goolkasian, P. (2010). The effects of brief mindfulness meditation training on experimentally induced pain. *Journal of Pain, 11,* 199–209.

Zhang, L.-F., & Sternberg, R. J. (2009). Learning in a cross-cultural perspective. In T. Husén & T. N. Postlethwaite (Eds.), *International encyclopedia of education* (3rd ed.), *Learning and cognition.* Oxford, U.K.: Elsevier.

Zhang, Y., & others. (2010). Serotonin (5-HT) receptor 5A sequence variants affect human plasma triglyceride levels. *Physiological Genomics.* (in press)

Zhang, Z., Ilies, R., & Arvey, R. D. (2009). Beyond genetic explanations for leadership: The moderating role of the social environment. *Organizational Behavior and Human Decision Processes, 110,* 118–128.

Zhao, H., Seibert, S. E., & Lumpkin, G. T. (2010). The relationship of personality to entrepreneurial intentions and performance: A meta-analytic review. *Journal of Management, 36,* 381–404.

Zhao, F., Manchiaiah, V. K., French, D., & Price, S. M. (2010). Music exposure and hearing disorders: An overview. *International Journal of Audiology, 49,* 54–64.

Zhou, X., Tang, W., Greenwood, T. A., Guo, S., He, L., Geyer, M. A., & Kelsoe, J. R. (2009a). Transcription factor SP4 is a susceptibility gene for bipolar disorder. *PLoS ONE, 4,* e5196.

Zhou, Z., Zhen, J., Karpowich, N. K., Law, C. J., Rith, M. E., & Wang, D. N. (2009). Antidepressant specificity of serotonin transporter suggested by three LeuT-SSRI structures. *Nature Structure and Molecular Biology, 16,* 652– 657.

Zhu, B., & others. (2010). Individual differences in false memory from misinformation: Personality characteristics and their interactions with cognitive abilities. *Personality and Individual Differences, 48,* 889–894.

Zhu, D. C., Zacks, R. T., & Slade, J. M. (2010). Brain activation during interference resolution in young and older adults: An fMRI study. *NeuroImage, 50,* 810–817.

Zietsch, B. P., Morley, K. I., Shekar, S. N., Verweij, K. J. H., Keller, M. C., Macgregor, S., Wright, M. J., & Zilney, L. A. (2011). *Drugs.* Upper Saddle River, NJ: Prentice-Hall.

Zimbardo, P. (2007). *The Lucifer effect: Understanding how good people turn evil.* New York: Random House.

Zimmer-Gembeck, M. J., Hunter, T. A., Waters, A. M., & Pronk, R. (2009). Depression as a longitudinal outcome and antecedent of preadolescents' peer relationships and peer-relevant cognitions. *Development and Psychopathology, 21,* 555–557.

Ziol-Guest, K. M. (2009). Child custody and support. In D. Carr (Ed.), *Encyclopedia of the life course and human development.* Boston: Cengage.

Zou, L., & others. (2010). Proliferation, migration, and neuronal differentiation of the endogenous neural progenitors in hippocampus after fimbria fornix transaction. *International Journal of Neuroscience, 120,* 192–200.

Zou, Y., Misri, S., Shay, J. W., Pandita, T. K., & Wright, W. E. (2009). Altered states of telomere deprotection and the two-stage mechanism of replicative aging. *Molecular and Cellular Biology, 29* (9), 2390–2397.

Zucker, K. J. (1999). Intersexuality and gender identity differentiation. *Annual Review of Sex Research, 10,* 1–69.

Zurron, M., Pouso, M., Lindin, M., Galdo, S., & Diaz, F. (2009). Event-related potentials with the Stroop color-word task: Timing of semantic conflict. *International Journal of Psychophysiology, 72,* 246–252.

Zwanzger, P., & others. (2009). Effects of the GABA-reuptake inhibitor tiagabine on panic and anxiety in patients with panic disorder. *Pharmacopsychiatry, 42,* 266–269.

Text and Line Art Credits

Chapter 2

Figure 2.1: From Laura King, *Experience Psychology*, 1e. Copyright © 2010 The McGraw-Hill Companies, Inc. Reproduced with permission of The McGraw-Hill Companies.

Figure 2.3: From Laura King, *Experience Psychology*, 1e. Copyright © 2010 The McGraw-Hill Companies, Inc. Reproduced with permission of The McGraw-Hill Companies.

p. 31: "Satisfaction with Life Scale." Ed Diener, Robert A. Emmons, Randy J. Larson, Sharon Griffin, U. Illinois at Urbana-Champaign, *J. of Personality Assessment*, 1985, 49, 1, p. 72.

Chapter 3

Figure 3.1: From Laura King, *Experience Psychology*, 1e. Copyright © 2010 The McGraw-Hill Companies, Inc. Reproduced with permission of The McGraw-Hill Companies.

Figure 3.3: From R. Lewis, *Life*, 3rd ed. Copyright © 1998 McGraw-Hill Companies, Inc. Reproduced with permission of The McGraw-Hill Companies.

Figure 3.4: From R. Lewis, *Life*, 3rd ed. Copyright © 1998 McGraw-Hill Companies, Inc. Reproduced with permission of The McGraw-Hill Companies.

Figure 3.6: From *Mapping the Mind* by Rita Carter, 1998. Reprinted by permission of Moonrunner Design, Ltd.

Figure 3.11: From *Brain, Mind, and Behavior* by Floyd Bloom, Charles A. Nelson, Arlyne Lazerson. Copyright 1985, 1988, 2001 by Educational Broadcasting Corporation. Used with permission of Worth Publishers.

Figure 3.16: From *Brain, Mind, and Behavior* by Floyd Bloom, Charles A. Nelson, Arlyne Lazerson. Copyright 1985, 1988, 2001 by Educational Broadcasting Corporation. Used with permission of Worth Publishers.

Figure 3.17: From Laura King, *Experience Psychology*, 1e. Copyright © 2010 The McGraw-Hill Companies, Inc. Reproduced with permission of The McGraw-Hill Companies.

Figure 3.18: From Laura King, *Experience Psychology*, 1e. Copyright © 2010 The McGraw-Hill Companies, Inc. Reproduced with permission of The McGraw-Hill Companies.

Figure 3.19: From Laura King, *Experience Psychology*, 1e. Copyright © 2010 The McGraw-Hill Companies, Inc. Reproduced with permission of The McGraw-Hill Companies.

Chapter 4

Figure 4.1: From Laura King, *Experience Psychology*, 1e. Copyright © 2010 The McGraw-Hill Companies, Inc. Reproduced with permission of The McGraw-Hill Companies.

Figure 4.2: From Laura King, *Experience Psychology*, 1e. Copyright © 2010 The McGraw-Hill Companies, Inc. Reproduced with permission of The McGraw-Hill Companies.

Figure 4.16: Reproduced from *Ishihara's Tests for Colour Deficiency* published by Kanehara Trading Inc., located at Tokyo in Japan. But tests for color deficiency cannot be conducted with this material. For accurate testing, the original plates should be used. Used with permission.

Figure 4.17: From Atkinson/Hilgard/Smith/Hoeksema/Frederickson, *Atkinson and Hilgard's Introduction to Psychology*, 14E. © 2003 Wadsworth, a part of Cengage Learning. Reproduced by permission. www.cengage.com/permissions.

Figure 4.24: From James J. Gibson, *The Perception of the Visual World*. © 1950 Wadsworth, a part of Cengage Learning, Inc. Reproduced by permission. www.cengage.com/permissions.

Figure 4.26: From *Brain, Mind and Behavior* by Floyd Bloom, Charles A. Nelson, Arlyne Lazerson. Copyright 1985, 1988, 2001 by Educational Broadcasting Corporation. Used with permission of Worth Publishers.

Chapter 5

Figure 5.6: From H. P. Roffwarg, J. N. Muzio, and W. C. Dement, "Ontogenetic Development of Human Dream-Sleep-Cycle," *Science* 152, 604–609. Copyright 1966 American Association for the Advancement of Science.

p. 150, Psychological Inquiry: From *Brain, Mind, and Behavior*, by Floyd Bloom, Charles A. Nelson, Arlyne Lazerson. Copyright 1985, 1988, 2001 by Educational Broadcasting Corporation. Used with permission of Worth Publishers.

p. 155, Psychological Inquiry: From Laura King, *Experience Psychology*, 1e. Copyright © 2010 The McGraw-Hill Companies, Inc. Reproduced with permission of The McGraw-Hill Companies.

Figure 5.9: (line art) From Laura King, *Experience Psychology*, 1e. Copyright © 2010 The McGraw-Hill Companies, Inc. Reproduced with permission of The McGraw-Hill Companies.

Figure 5.10: (line art) From Laura King, *Experience Psychology*, 1e. Copyright © 2010 The McGraw-Hill Companies, Inc. Reproduced with permission of The McGraw-Hill Companies.

Figure 5.11: From Laura King, *Experience Psychology*, 1e. Copyright © 2010 The McGraw-Hill Companies, Inc. Reproduced with permission of The McGraw-Hill Companies

Chapter 6

Figure 6.3: From Laura King, *Experience Psychology*, 1e. Copyright © 2010 The McGraw-Hill Companies, Inc. Reproduced with permission of The McGraw-Hill Companies.

Chapter 7

Figure 7.4: From Laura King, *Experience Psychology*, 1e. Copyright © 2010 The McGraw-Hill Companies, Inc. Reproduced with permission of The McGraw-Hill Companies.

Figure 7.9: From John Santrock, *Life-Span Development*, 11th Ed. Copyright © 2008 The McGraw-Hill Companies, Inc. Reproduced with permission of The McGraw-Hill Companies.

p. 224, Psychological Inquiry: Copyright © 1974 From *Human Memory: Theory and Data*, by B. Murdock, Jr. Reproduced by permission of Lawrence Erlbaum Associates, Inc. a division of Taylor & Francis Group.

Figure 7.15: © Exploratorium, www.exploratorium.edu. Used with permission.

Chapter 8

Figure 8.1: (line art) From Laura King, *Experience Psychology*, 1e. Copyright © 2010 The McGraw-Hill Companies, Inc. Reproduced with permission of The McGraw-Hill Companies.

Figure 8.5: From Laura King, *Experience Psychology*, 1e. Copyright © 2010 The McGraw-Hill Companies, Inc. Reproduced with permission of The McGraw-Hill Companies.

p. 256, Psychological Inquiry: From John Santrock, *Children*, 7th Ed. Copyright © 2003 The McGraw-Hill Companies, Inc. Reproduced with permission of The McGraw-Hill Companies.

Figure 8.9: From "The Increase in IQ Scores from 1932–1997," by Ulric Neisser. Used with permission.

Figure 8.11: From John Santrock, *Educational Psychology*. Copyright © 2001 The McGraw-Hill Companies, Inc. Reprinted with permission of The McGraw-Hill Companies, Inc.

Chapter 9

Figure 9.2: From Laura King, *Experience Psychology*, 1e. Copyright © 2010 The McGraw-Hill Companies, Inc. Reproduced with permission of The McGraw-Hill Companies.

Figure 9.5: From John Santrock, *A Topical Approach to Life-Span Development*, 2002. Copyright © The McGraw-Hill Companies, Inc. Reprinted by permission of the McGraw-Hill Companies, Inc.

Figure 9.8: (line art) From John Santrock, *Life-Span Development*, 9e. Copyright © The McGraw-Hill Companies, Inc. Reproduced with permission of The McGraw-Hill Companies.

Figure 9.12: From John Santrock, *Life-Span Development*, 11th Ed. Copyright © 2008 The McGraw-Hill Companies, Inc. Reproduced with permission of The McGraw-Hill Companies.

p. 302, Psychological Inquiry: From John Santrock, *Life-Span Development*, 8th Ed. Copyright © 2002 The McGraw-Hill Companies, Inc. Reproduced with permission of The McGraw-Hill Companies.

Figure 9.15: From John Santrock, *Life-Span Development*, 8th Ed. Copyright © 2002 The McGraw-Hill Companies, Inc. Reproduced with permission of The McGraw-Hill Companies.

Chapter 10

Figure 10.4: From Laura King, *Experience Psychology*, 1e. Copyright © 2010 The McGraw-Hill Companies, Inc. Reproduced with permission of The McGraw-Hill Companies.

Figure 10.6: From Laura King, *Experience Psychology*, 1e. Copyright © 2010 The McGraw-Hill Companies, Inc. Reproduced with permission of The McGraw-Hill Companies.

p. 339, Psychological Inquiry: From Laura King, *Experience Psychology*, 1e. Copyright © 2010 The McGraw-Hill Companies, Inc. Reproduced with permission of The McGraw-Hill Companies.

Chapter 11

Figure 11.3: From J. M. Tanner et al., in *Archives of Diseases in Childhood* 41, 1966. Reproduced with permission from BMJ Publishing Group, Ltd.

Figure 11.4: From Santrock, *Child Development*, 10e, Fig 13.3. Copyright © 2008 The McGraw-Hill Companies. Reprinted by permission.

p. 361, Psychological Inquiry: From Clark, R. D. & Hatfield, E. (1989). "Gender Differences in Receptivity to Sexual Offers." *Journal of Psychology & Human Sexuality*, 2(1), 39–55. doi:10.1300/J056v02n01_04. Reprinted by permission of Taylor & Francis Ltd. http://www.tandf.co.uk/journals.

p. 370, **Psychological Inquiry:** From *Sex In America* by Robert T. Michael, John H. Gagnon, Edward O. Laumann, and Gina Kolata. Copyright © 1994 by Robert T. Michael, John H. Gagnon, Edward O. Laumann, and Gina Kolata. By permission of Little Brown & Company and Brockman, Inc.

Figure 11.7: From Laura King, *Experience Psychology,* 1e. Copyright © 2010 The McGraw-Hill Companies, Inc. Reproduced with permission of The McGraw-Hill Companies.

Chapter 13

Figure 13.5: (text) This figure was published in "Types of Identity" by K. Deaux in *Encyclopedia of Women and Gender: Sex Similarities and Differences and the Impact of Society and Gender,* 2-volume set, edited by Judith Worell. Copyright 2001, Elsevier USA. Reprinted by permission.

Figure 13.6: "Attitudes toward the Out-Group Following Competitive and Cooperative Activities." From M. Sherif, O. J. Harvey, B. J. White, W. E. Hood, C. W. Sherif, "The Robber's Cave Experiment: Intergroup Conflict and Cooperation" © 1988 by Muzafer Sherif and reprinted by permission of Wesleyan University Press. www.wesleyan.edu/wespress.

Chapter 15

Figure 15.5: From *Annual Review of Neuroscience, Online,* Vol. 20, by Annual Review. Copyright 1997 by Annual Reviews, Inc. Reproduced with permission of Annual Reviews, Inc. in the format Textbook via Copyright Clearance Center. www.annualreviews.org.

p. 501, Psychological Inquiry: From Weissman and Olfson, *Science,* 269, p. 779, Fig 1. Copyright © 1995 American Association for the Advancement of Science. Reprinted with permission from AAAS.

Figure 15.8: From Laura King, *Experience Psychology,* 1e. Copyright © 2010 The McGraw-Hill Companies, Inc. Reproduced with permission of The McGraw-Hill Companies.

p. 510, Psychological Inquiry: © Irving I. Gottesman, 2004. Used by permission.

Figure 15.11: (text) From Laura King, *Experience Psychology,* 1e. Copyright © 2010 The McGraw-Hill Companies, Inc. Reproduced with permission of The McGraw-Hill Companies.

Figure 15.12: From Laura King, *Experience Psychology,* 1e. Copyright © 2010 The McGraw-Hill Companies, Inc. Reproduced with permission of The McGraw-Hill Companies.

Chapter 16

Figure 16.4: From Laura King, *Experience Psychology,* 1e. Copyright © 2010 The McGraw-Hill Companies, Inc. Reproduced with permission of The McGraw-Hill Companies.

p. 534, Psychological Inquiry: From Laura King, *Experience Psychology,* 1e. Copyright © 2010 The McGraw-Hill Companies, Inc. Reproduced with permission of The McGraw-Hill Companies.

p. 536: From A. T. Beck, A. J. Rush, B. F. Shaw, G. Emery, *Cognitive Therapy of Depression.* 1979, pp. 145–146 Reprinted with permission of The Guilford Press.

p. 546, Psychological Inquiry: Reprinted with permission of Michael J. Lambert, professor of Psychology, Brigham Young University.

Figure 16.5: Adapted from A. Freeman and M. A. Reinecke, "Cognitive Therapy" in A. S. Gurman, ed., *Essential Psychotherapies.* Adapted with permission of The Guilford Press.

Figure 16.6: Copyright © 1999, American Psychological Association.

Figure 16.7: From Laura King, *Experience Psychology,* 1e. Copyright © 2010 The McGraw-Hill Companies, Inc. Reproduced with permission of The McGraw-Hill Companies.

Figure 16.8: From "A Survival Analysis of Clinically Significant Change in Outpatient Psychotherapy" by Anderson & Lambert from *Journal of Clinical Psychology,* 57, 875–888. Copyright © 2010 Wiley Periodicals, Inc., A Wiley Company.

Chapter 17

Figure 17.1: From Laura King, *Experience Psychology,* 1e. Copyright © 2010 The McGraw-Hill Companies, Inc. Reproduced with permission of The McGraw-Hill Companies.

Figure 17.2: Figure, "Hans Selye's General Adaptation Syndrome" from *The Stress of Life,* 2nd ed., by Hans Selye, p. 476, 1976. New York: McGraw-Hill. Reprinted by permission of The McGraw-Hill Companies, Inc.

Figure 17.3: Copyright © 1998, American Psychological Association.

p. 562, Psychological Inquiry: From Laura King, *Experience Psychology,* 1e. Copyright © 2010 The McGraw-Hill Companies, Inc. Reproduced with permission of The McGraw-Hill Companies.

p. 570, Psychological Inquiry: From John Santrock, *Life-Span Development,* 11th Ed. Copyright © 2008 The McGraw-Hill Companies, Inc. Reproduced with permission of The McGraw-Hill Companies.

Figure 17.5: This article was published in *Journal of Psychosomatic Research,* Vol. 29, S. C. Kobasa, S. R. Maddi, M. C. Puccette, and M. A. Zola, pp. 525–533. Copyright © 1985, Elsevier Used with permission.

Figure 17.7: From Laura King, *Experience Psychology,* 1e. Copyright © 2010 The McGraw-Hill Companies, Inc. Reproduced with permission of The McGraw-Hill Companies.

Figure 17.10: From John Santrock, *Life-Span Development,* 11th Ed. Copyright © 2008 The McGraw-Hill Companies, Inc. Reproduced with permission of The McGraw-Hill Companies.

Figure 17.11: From Laura King, *Experience Psychology,* 1e. Copyright © 2010 The McGraw-Hill Companies, Inc. Reproduced with permission of The McGraw-Hill Companies.

Photo Credits

Frontmatter

p. i © Image Source/Getty Images; p. ii: © Image Source/Getty Images; p. vi: Courtesy of Laura King; p. vii: © PhotoAlto/PunchStock; p. xxi: © Stockbyte/Getty Images; p. xxii: © Jae Rew/Photonica/Getty Images; p. xxvi: © Burke/Triolo/Brand X Pictures/Jupiterimages; p. xxvi: © The McGraw-Hill Companies, Inc./Ken Karp photographer; p. xxvii: © PhotoAlto/PunchStock; p. xxix: © RubberBall Productions; p. xxxi: © Fly Fernandez/Corbis.

Chapter 1

Opener: © Michael Blann/Digital Vision/Getty; p. 4: © PhotoAlto/PunchStock; p. 5 (inset): © GlowImages/Alamy; p. 5: © Brand X Pictures/PunchStock; p. 8: AP Photo/Carolyn Kaster; p. 9 (both): © Bettmann/Corbis; p. 10: © Michele Burgess/Corbis; p. 11: AP Photo; p. 12: © Time & Life Pictures/Getty; p. 13: © Kevin Dodge/Corbis; p. 15: Courtesy of Richard Davidson, University of Wisconsin, Madison. Photo by Jeff Miller.; p. 16: Courtesy of Carol S. Dweck, Stanford University; p. 17 (top left): © Atlantide Phototravel/Corbis; p. 17 (top middle): © Chip Somodevilla/Getty; p. 17 (top right): © Peter Foley/Reuters/Corbis; p. 17 (bottom left): © Dennis MacDonald/PhotoEdit; p. 17 (bottom right): © David McNew/Getty; p. 19: Courtesy of the Suicide Prevention Center; p. 20: © artpartner-images.com/Alamy; p. 21: © Ryan McVay/Getty.

Chapter 2

Opener: © Dimitri Vervitsiotis/Photographer's Choice RF/Getty; p. 26 (top): © PhotoAlto/PunchStock; p. 26 (middle): © Creatas/PunchStock; p. 26 (bottom): © George Doyle & Ciaran Griffin/Stockbyte/Getty; p. 27 (left): © Stockdisc/PunchStock; p. 27 (right): © Masterfile/Royalty Free; p. 28: © Peter Ciresa Cires/Index Stock/Photolibrary; p. 30 (top): © The McGraw-Hill Companies, Inc./John Flournoy, photographer; p. 30 (bottom): © Photographers Choice RF/SuperStock; p. 31: © Bettmann/Corbis; p. 33 (yawn): © Doug Menuez/Getty Images; p. 33 (tired student): © BananaStock/JupiterImages; p. 33 (library): © Veer; p. 33 (friends): © Stockbyte/PunchStock; p. 33 (cone): © Photodisc/PunchStock; p. 34: © Tony Savino/Corbis; p. 36: AP Photo/Richard Vogel; p. 38: © Stockbyte/Getty; p. 39: Image courtesy of The Advertising Archives; p. 40: © Visions of America, LLC/Alamy; p. 41 (left): © Peter Arnold/Photolibrary; p. 41 (right): © Elsa/Staff/Getty; p. 42 (left): © Michael Nichols/National Geographic/Getty; p. 42 (right): Courtesy of Barbara Fredrickson, University of North Carolina; p. 44: AP Photo/Ted S. Warren; p. 45: © RF@PPS/Alamy; p. 47: © Josef Lindau/Corbis; p. 49: © age fotostock/SuperStock; p. 50: © CBS/Photofest; p. 52: © Stockbyte/PunchStock; p. 53 (top): Courtesy of James W. Pennebaker, University of Texas. Photo by Marsha Miller; p. 53 (bottom): © Brand X Pictures.

Chapter 3

Opener: © Hybrid Medical/Photo Researchers; p. 58 (top): © PhotoAlto/PunchStock; p. 58 (bottom left): © Amana Productions, Inc./Getty; p. 58 (bottom right): © Digital Vision/Getty; p. 59: Press Association via AP Images; p. 60: © RubberBall Productions; p. 63: AP Photo/Kevin Ferguson; p. 3T-1: © Chad Baker/Thomas Northcut/Stone/Getty Images; p. 66: Cen-ters for Disease Control; p. 69: © Jonathan Nourok/PhotoEdit; p. 70: © Blend Images/Alamy; p. 71: © Peter Arnold, Inc./Alamy; p. 72: © Lennart Nilsson/Albert Bonniers Forlag AB; p. 76 (top): © John Whiley, California Institute of Technology, estate of James Olds; p. 76 (bottom): © A. Glauberman/Photo Researchers, Inc.; p. 77: From: Damasio H., Grabowski T., Frank R., Galaburda A. M., Damasio A. R.: The return of Phineas Gage: Clues about the brain from the skull of a famous patient. Science, 264:1102–1105, 1994. Departments of Neurology and Image Analysis Facility, University of Iowa; p. 78: Courtesy of Michael J. Tarr, Ph.D.; p. 84: © Yann Arthus-Bertrand/Corbis; p. 85: © PhotoAlto/PunchStock; p. 86: © Lennart Nilsson/Albert Bonniers Forlag AB; p. 87: © Riccardo Cassiani-Ingoni/Photo Researchers; p. 88: © Rick Rickman; p. 89: © Punchstock/BananaStock; p. 90: © Enrico Ferorelli; p. 91: © Joe Murphy/NBAE via Getty.

Chapter 4

Opener: © Brand New Images/Stone/Getty; p. 98: © PhotoAlto/PunchStock; p. 99: © Ariel Skelley/Riser/Getty; p. 100 (owl): © Ron Austing; Frank Lane Picture Agency/Corbis; p. 100 (rabbit): © Image Source/PunchStock; p. 100 (eye): © Barbara Penoyar/Getty Images; p. 100 (ear): © The McGraw-Hill Companies, Inc./Eric Wise, photographer; p. 100 (foot): The McGraw-Hill Companies, Inc./Jill Braaten, photographer; p. 100 (smelling): © ZenShui/Sigrid Olsson/Getty; p. 100 (eating): © istockphoto.com/Zorani; p. 101: © Stockbyte/PunchStock; p. 102 (top): © Photodisc; p. 102 (bottom): © Stockdisc; p. 108: © Jose Luis Pelaez, Inc./Blend Images/Corbis; p. 111: Courtesy of X-Rite, Inc.; p. 112: © Frank S. Werblin; p. 113: © Editorial Image, LLC/Alamy; p. 114: © RubberBall Productions/Getty; p. 115: © Silver Screen Collection/Hulton Archives/Getty; p. 118: © Erich Lessing/Art Resource, NY; p. 119: © Steve Allen/Getty; p. 124: © Mary Kate Denny/PhotoEdit; p. 4T-1: © Jae Rew/Photonica/Getty Images; p. 129: © Chip Simons; p. 131: © Dominic Rouse/The Image Bank/Getty; p. 131 (inset): © Lennart Nilsson/Albert Bonniers Forlag AB.

Chapter 5

Opener: © hana/Datacraft/Getty; p. 138 (top): © PhotoAlto/PunchStock; p. 138 (bottom): © Comstock/Alamy; p. 142: © Newscom; p. 144: © Philip Lee Harvey/Getty; p. 145 (top): © Frank Greenaway/Getty; p. 145 (bottom): © Royalty Free/Corbis; p. 146: © Will and Deni McIntyre/Photo Researchers, Inc.; p. 147: © J. Allan Hobson & Hoffman La Roche, Inc.; p. 149: © RubberBall/Alamy; p. 150: © Steve Cole/Getty; p. 153: © Thinkstock/PunchStock; p. 155: © PhotoAlto/PictureQuest; p. 156: © Ingram Publishing/Alamy; p. 157 (top): © George Doyle/Stockbyte/Getty; p. 157 (bottom): © Royalty-Free/Corbis; p. 158: © Ingram Publishing/SuperStock; p. 160 (top): © Image Source/Getty; p. 164: AP Photo/Reed Saxon; p. 166: © Stanford News Service; p. 167: © Erin Koran/McGraw-Hill; p. 168: © Jules Frazier/Getty.

NAME INDEX

Page numbers followed by "*f*" refer to figures.

Henson, R., 223
Hepp, U., 365
Hepper, E. G., 423
Hepple, R. T., 305
Hepting, U., 264
Herbert, J., 433, 564
Herek, G. M., 355
Hergenhahn, B. R., 174
Hering, E., 115
Herlihy, B., 545
Hernandez, P., 543
Hernandez-Reif, M., 284, 286
Hernell, O., 181
Hernstein, R. J., 184
Heron, J., 284
Herry, C., 75
Herscovitch, L., 474
Hersen, M., 16
Hertz, J., 568
Herz, A. V., 222
Herz, R. S., 222
Herzog, H., 442
Hess, E., 476
Hess, U., 141
Hess, Y. D., 325
Hetherington, E. M., 281, 282
Hettema, J. M., 494
Heuser, I., 527
Hewitt, J. K., 257, 560
Hewlin, P. F., 438
Heywood, C. A., 116
Hibbard, S., 391, 409, 411
Hickman, J. S., 106
Hickok, G., 61
Hicks, B. M., 407
Hicks, J. A., 36, 237, 248, 272,
    310, 311, 395
Higham, P. A., 104
Hilgard, E. R., 166, 166f
Hill, C. E., 393, 532
Hill, J. O., 558, 572, 573
Hill, L. E., 569
Hill, T. D., 562
Hillman, C. H., 308, 311
Hilton, H. J., 219
Hines, M., 352
Hingson, R. W., 158
Hinks, L., 574
Hinshaw, S. P., 515
Hinsley, A. W., 395
Hintzen, A., 164
Hippocrates, 403
Hirata, A., 75, 127
Hirsch, I., 389
Hirsch, J. K., 500
Hirsch, J. S., 451
Hitch, G. J., 214
Hitler, A., 398f
Hjortdahl, P., 472
Hnasko, T. S., 155
Ho, M., 379
Ho, R. C., 564
Hobbs, S., 458
Hobfoll, S. E., 497
Hobson, J. A., 147, 153, 154
Hodges, T. D., 471
Hodgins, D. C., 559
Hodgkins, D. C., 516
Hodgson, T. L., 105
Hoefels, S., 482
Hoek, H. W., 321, 322
Hoffman, I. Z., 531
Hoffman, J. P., 156
Hoffman-Riken, K. M., 322
Hofoss, D., 472
Hogan, D., 464

Hogan, E. H., 159
Hogan, R., 395, 402
Hogg, M. A., 444
Hogh, A., 480
Hohl, E., 529
Holch, P., 320
Holcomb, H., 145
Holen, A., 503
Holland, A. K., 83
Holland, D. E., 538
Holland, P. C., 191
Hollar, D., 504
Hollenbeck, J. R., 466
Holliday, E. G., 509
Hollingsworth, S. A., 524
Hollins, M., 126
Hollis, J. F., 451
Hollon, S. D., 499
Holmes, J., 531
Holmes, J. G., 430
Holmes, K. K., 379
Holmes, S., 181
Holmstrom, A., 543
Holsboer, F., 17, 61, 555
Holsboer-Trachsler, E., 564
Holte, A., 506
Holtzheimer, P. E., 527
Holyoak, K. J., 12, 15
Holzman, L., 292
Honey, P. L., 179, 180
Hong, E., 189
Hong, J. Y., 555
Hong, S. W., 114
Honkonen, T., 482
Honts, C., 330
Honzik, C. H., 196
Hoobler, J., 469
Hood, M., 323
Hood, W. R., 448
Hooker, S. P., 570
Hooper, J., 154
Hopf, F. W., 156
Hoption, C., 475, 476
Horberg, E. J., 559
Horgan, J., 164
Horiguchi, J., 523
Horn, H., 509
Horney, K., 388, 389, 389f
Hornick, B. A., 159
Hornickel, J., 267
Hornsey, M. J., 541
Horowitz, J. L., 502
Horry, R., 230
Horsey, K. J., 497
Horst, J. S., 263
Horton, N. J., 349
Hosmer, D., 168
Hoss, R. A., 420
Hotard, S. R., 415
Hottenga, J., 405
Hougaard, K. S., 564
Hough, L. M., 464
Houk, C., 350
Houk, C. P., 350
Houlihan, D., 430
House, J. S., 451
Houser-Marko, L., 325, 327
Hovland, C. I., 428
Howard, K. I., 546
Howe, M. J. A., 259
Howell, D., 158
Howell, D. C., 44
Howes, M. B., 209
Howes, O. D., 510
Howie, K. T., 458

Hoyer, D., 67
Hoyer, W. J., 308
Hoyle, D. G., 458
Hoyle, R. H., 398
Hoyt, W. T., 562
Hrebickova, M., 397
Hsieh, L. T., 231
Hu, F., 304
Hu, F. B., 573
Huang, C. C., 86
Huang, C. M., 282
Huang, L., 297
Huang, X., 62, 358
Huang, Y., 424
Huart, C., 130
Hubble, M. A., 546, 547
Hubel, D. H., 113, 114
Hudson, A. J., 243
Hudson, J. I., 164
Huesmann, L. R., 435, 436
Huettel, S. A., 333
Huff, C. R., 230
Huffcutt, A. L., 464, 465
Hugdahl, K., 215
Hugenberg, K., 335
Hughes, B., 271
Hughes, I. A., 350
Hughes, J., 544
Hughes, J. P., 379
Hughes, M. E., 451
Huibers, J. J., 499
Hummer, R. A., 562
Humphries, M. D., 73
Hung, D. L., 231
Hung, Y., 78
Hunsley, J., 410, 411
Hunt, R. R., 210
Hunter, S. T., 476
Hunter, T. A., 502
Hurkmans, E. J., 559
Hurleman, R., 333, 527
Hurst, J. L., 130
Hurvich, L. M., 115
Husain, M. M., 527
Husain, O., 409
Hussong, A., 156
Huston, D. M., 268
Huston, J. P., 187
Huttenlocher, J., 358
Huttenlocher, P. R., 286
Hutton, J. L., 181
Hyde, J. S., 348, 353, 357, 358, 359,
    360, 361, 367, 373
Hyde, M., 124
Hyman, I. A., 192
Hyman, S., 59, 493
Hytonen, K., 439

I

Iacono, W. G., 330, 407
Ialongo, N., 502
Ideguchi, M., 87
Ihori, N., 436
Iijima, T., 223
Ijames, S. G., 181
Ikeda, B. E., 181
Ikeda, K., 102
Ilies, R., 477
Imayoshi, I., 306
Imel, Z. E., 547
Imeri, L., 149
Impett, E. A., 380
Inaba, A., 500
Inagaki, H., 413

Inagaki, T., 523
INDIGO Study Group, 515
Ingram, R. E., 498
Innocence Project, 230
Insel, P. M., 481, 483,
    568, 572
Insel, T., 490
Insko, C. A., 449
Institute of Medicine, 145
Irick, J. S., 331
Iriki, A., 61
Irmansyah, I., 497
Ironson, G., 562–563
Irwin, M. R., 149
Irwing, P., 397
Isaacs, I., 476
Isbell, L. M., 252
Isen, A. M., 252
Ishikawa, N. M., 101
Ishiko, S., 111
Isildak, M., 481
Ising, M., 17, 61, 555
Isingrini, M., 226, 306
Isometsa, E., 482
Ispa, J. M., 296
Issa, E. B., 141
Istaphanous, G. K., 522
Iturbide, M. I., 302, 303
Iverson, P., 270
Ivry, R. B., 264
Iwassa, H., 413
Iyer, A., 107
Izard, C. E., 16, 338

J

Jablensky, E., 511
Jack, R. E., 337
Jackson, A. S., 573
Jackson, B. M., 152
Jackson, D., 148, 397
Jackson, D. C., 84, 333
Jackson, G., 144
Jackson, J., 84
Jackson, J. J., 407, 412
Jackson, L., 544
Jackson, L. A., 156
Jackson, L. C., 545
Jacob, R., 574
Jacob, T., 158
Jacobo, M., 539
Jacobs, R. H., 499
Jacobsen, L., 421
Jacobsen, P. B., 181, 566
Jacobs-Lawson, J. M., 562
Jacobson, C. E., 527
Jacobson, K. C., 432
Jaeger, A., 232
Jaeggi, S. M., 262
Jakupcak, M., 338
Jalinous, R., 71
James, W., 9, 9f, 138, 331
James, W. H., 365
Jameson, D., 115
Janak, P. H., 499
Janata, P., 220
Jancke, L., 71, 101
Jane, M. C., 502
Jang, K. L., 406, 477
Janicki-Deverts, D., 565
Janis, I., 443
Janis, I. L., 428
Janowsky, D. S., 510
Jarrett, R. B., 538
Jarvin, L., 12, 259

Sagan, C., 164
Sagarin, B. J., 429
Sage, K., 77
Sage, R. M., 423
Sagi-Schwartz, A., 294
Saguy, T., 444
Sahin, E., 305, 570
Saito, H., 132
Saito, S., 207
Sakaeda, A. R., 227, 236
Sakamoto, A., 436
Sakamoto, M., 306
Saki, F., 84, 168
Saksida, L. M., 86
Salas, E., 457, 468
Saleem, M., 436
Salminen, N. H., 126
Salomons, T. V., 168
Salovey, P., 261
Salter, N., 559
Salters, K., 338
Salthouse, T. A., 308
Salvia, J., 254
Salzman, C. D., 11, 76, 83
Sameroff, A., 258
Samochowiec, J., 322
Sampaio, A. S., 496
Sampaio, C., 141
Sampson, S., 527
Samuelson, L. K., 263
Sanberg, P. R., 67
Sanchez, D., 425
Sanchez, J. L., 472
Sanchez-Burks, J., 444
Sanchez-Meca, J., 534
Sanchez-Padilla, J., 67
Sand, S., 553
Sandberg, L. S., 530
Sanders, A. R., 509
Sanderson, C. A., 238
Sandler, I., 14, 281
Sandnabba, N. K., 361
Sandoval, M., 543
Sanes, D. H., 98
Sanfey, A., 15
Sanislow, C., 514
Santomauro, J., 109
Santos-Victor, J., 243
Santtila, P., 361
Saper, C. B., 154
Saphire-Bernstein, S., 68
Sapolsky, R. M., 92, 202
Sapp, S., 562
Sar, V., 505, 506, 507
Saracbasi, O., 481
Sarkar, U., 401, 413
Sarma, K., 504
Saroglou, V., 397
Sarpal, D., 510
Sarrazin, P., 103
Sartor, C. E., 90
Sartorius, N., 515
Sasaki, Y., 103
Sass, H., 397
Sass, S. M., 106
Satir, D. A., 323
Sato, W., 335
Saucier, D. A., 367
Sauer, H., 186, 490
Sauer, J., 428
Saul, S., 151
Saunders, F. W., 410
Saurer, T. B., 181
Sauter, D. A., 336, 337
Sava, F. A., 535, 537, 538
Savage, J., 433, 435, 436

Savage, P. D., 569
Savic, I., 365
Savin-Williams, R., 300, 360, 363, 367
Savoy, H. B., 367
Sawalani, G. M., 359
Sawyer, M. G., 489
Sawyer, P. J., 447
Saxe, L., 330
Saxon, J. L., 342
Sayal, K., 284
Scally, M., 406
Scamvougeras, A., 365
Scardamalia, M., 246
Scarmeas, N., 145, 237
Scarr, S., 25, 281
Schaal, B., 360, 433
Schachter, S., 333
Schacter, D. L., 208, 210, 218, 222, 233, 234
Schaefer, A., 495
Schaefer, H. S., 84
Schaie, K. W., 279, 282, 307, 308
Schaller, M., 324, 430
Schank, R., 220
Schankler, C., 222
Scharf, M. J., 168
Scharrer, E., 435
Scheepers, C., 337
Scheffler, K., 75
Scheibe, S., 282
Scheid, T. L., 490
Scheier, M. F., 326, 414, 567
Scheiffele, P., 66
Scherer, K. R., 329
Schermer, J. A., 406
Scherrer, J., 158
Schertler, E., 330
Schiefele, U., 326
Schieffelin, B., 266
Schienle, A., 495
Schiff, W. J., 483, 572
Schillinger, D., 401
Schira, M. M., 113
Schkade, D. A., 341
Schlaepfer, T. E., 527
Schlaug, G., 71
Schleicher, A., 71
Schlosser, R. G., 186
Schmader, T., 425
Schmahl, C., 505
Schmeichel, B. J., 405
Schmidt, A. M., 456
Schmidt, B. L., 128
Schmidt, F. L., 464
Schmidt, J., 415
Schmidt, N. B., 495, 538
Schmidtke, J. I., 404
Schmiedek, F., 232
Schmitt, K. C., 155
Schnall, E., 562
Schnall, S., 430
Schneider, D. W., 232
Schneider, F., 512
Schneider, K. J., 393, 532
Schneiderman, N., 547, 562–563
Schnepf, B., 151
Schnyder, U., 365
Schoen, L. S., 201
Schoenberger, Y., 558
Schoenfelder, E., 14, 281
Schomerus, G., 426
Schooler, J. W., 227, 228, 229, 341
Schott, L. L., 305
Schoueri, P., 530
Schraw, G. J., 235
Schredl, M., 147, 151, 153

Schroeder, S. A., 574
Schuckit, M. A., 158
Schuhmacher, A., 482
Schulenberg, J. E., 154, 155, 157, 159, 162, 163, 304
Schulter, G., 83, 339
Schultheiss, O. C., 411
Schultz, J., 415
Schultz, W., 76, 186, 196, 218, 565
Schultz, W. T., 399
Schultz-Hardt, S., 442
Schulz, D., 187
Schulz, E., 511
Schulz-Stubner, S., 167
Schumacher, J., 84, 168
Schuman, E. M., 221
Schumann, A., 558
Schumm, J. S., 260
Schumm, L. P., 310
Schunk, D. H., 194, 195, 196, 245, 326, 327, 401
Schur, E. A., 322
Schutzwohl, A., 360
Schuz, B., 559
Schwabe, L., 226
Schwartz, B., 252, 475
Schwartz, J. E., 413
Schwartz, J. H., 221
Schwartz, J. M., 502
Schwartz, M., 391, 409, 411
Schwartz, M. D., 181
Schwartz, S., 153, 489
Schwartzbaum, J. A., 152
Schwartz-Mette, R. A., 359
Schwarz, J. M., 349
Schwarz, N., 422, 435
Schwarzer, R., 413, 559
Schwegler, H., 69
Schweinberger, S. R., 219
Schweinsburg, A. D., 71
Schweizer, S., 499, 566
Schwerdtner, J., 180, 534
Schwiezer, H. R., 166
Schyns, P. G., 337
Scollon, C. K., 399
Scott, C., 7, 504
Scott, G., 476
Scott, R. S., 221
Scott, S. K., 152, 336, 337
Scott-Phillips, T. C., 263
Scott-Sheldon, L. A. J., 379
Sczesny, S., 355
Seacat, J. D., 425
Seal, B. N., 377
Sealfon, S. C., 163
Sears, D. O., 446
Sears, R. R., 433
Sedikides, C., 423
Seeman, T. E., 68
Segal, D. L., 408
Segal, M., 61
Segal, M. E., 438
Segal, S. K., 349
Segal, Z., 540
Segall, L. A., 143
Segerstrom, S. C., 340, 414, 567
Seguin, J. R., 360, 433
Seibert, S. E., 395, 397
Seibt, J., 145
Seidi, K. N., 335
Seidman, L. J., 349
Seifert, C. M., 330
Seifritz, E., 75
Seilacher, A., 72
Seim, H. C., 323
Sekiguchi, T., 102

Selby, E. A., 504, 513
Seligman, D. A., 545, 546
Seligman, M. E. P., 8, 180, 187, 199, 202, 245, 313, 413, 414, 414f, 500, 527
Selin, C. E., 502
Sellers, R. M., 303, 445
Selye, H., 563, 564
Sen, A., 358
Senecal, C., 559
Senghas, A., 336
Sergent, C., 138
Serra, C., 415
Serrador, J. M., 145
Serretti, A., 168, 322, 524
Sershen, H., 159
Sesardic, N., 257
Sessa, B., 164
Seth, A., 101
Seto, M. C., 361, 376, 377
Severe, J., 525
Sewell, R. A., 164
Seymour, K., 114
Seymour, T. L., 330
Sforza, L., 90, 91
Sgobio, C., 222
Shackelford, T. K., 360
Shackman, A., 333
Shadbolt, N. R., 107
Shafto, M. G., 330
Shakir, S. A., 575
Shallice, T., 225, 248
Shamay-Tsoory, S. G., 513
Shanks, D. R., 12, 15
Shapiro, C. M., 379
Shapiro, J. R., 446
Shapiro, S. J., 547
Shariff, A., 476
Sharma, A., 61
Sharma, P. S. V. N., 506
Sharma, V., 505
Sharma, Y. S., 356
Sharp, E. S., 395
Sharpes, K. M., 244
Shattuck, D. W., 257
Shaver, P., 16
Shaw, B. F., 536
Shaw, D., 188
Shaw, D. S., 502
Shaw, H., 559
Shay, J. W., 305
Shea, M. T., 514
Shea, N., 244
Shear, J., 169
Sheehan, T., 543
Sheese, B. E., 292
Shekar, S. N., 363
Sheldon, K. M., 12, 28, 325, 326, 327, 340, 341
Sheldon, M. S., 560
Shelton, J., 38
Shelton, R. C., 320, 499, 528
Shen, B. J., 547
Shen, K., 66
Sher, K. J., 157
Sheridan, J. F., 84, 168
Sherif, C. W., 448
Sherif, M., 448
Sherman, D., 154
Sherman, D. K., 423
Sherman, F. T., 527
Sherman, R. A., 402
Sherman, S. J., 426
Sherwood, A. R., 164
Shetty, A. K., 87
Shevell, S. K., 114

Watabe, M., 420
Watanabe, H., 177
Watanabe, T., 103
Waterman, L. A., 67
Waters, A. M., 502
Waters, E., 293
Waters, N. S., 186
Watkins, E. R., 252, 533
Watson, A., 128
Watson, D., 93, 338, 340, 415
Watson, J. B., 12, 179, 180, 182
Watson, S. J., 164
Watt, C., 109
Watts, M. W., 458
Waugaman, R. M., 513
Waugh, C. E., 340
Wayman, C., 68
Wayment, H. A., 425
Weatherbee, S. R., 15
Weaver, K., 422
Webb, R. M., 259
Webb, S. P., 513
Webb, W. B., 148
Weber, L., 509
Weber, S., 512
Weber, T., 476
Weber, T. J., 16, 477
Webster, J., 464
Wechsler, H., 157
Wecker, L., 68
Wee, S., 103
Weerda, R., 71
Wegener, D. T., 420
Wegener, G., 564
Wehmeyer, M., 413
Weich, S., 500
Weidert, M., 222
Weihenmayer, E., 315
Weimann, J. M., 87
Weinberg, M. S., 363
Weinberger, D. R., 510
Weiner, B., 411, 422
Weiner, I. B., 411
Weinrib, O., 78
Weinshenker, D., 149
Weinstein, T. A. R., 397
Weir, W., 103
Weis, C. O., 305
Weisberg, R. B., 516
Weismiller, D. G., 305
Weiss, A., 415
Weiss, B., 465
Weissman, M., 501
Weissman, M. M., 525
Welchman, A. E., 107, 117
Wellen, M., 499
Wellings, K., 371
Wellman, H. M., 142
Wells, J. C., 569
Wells, J. L., 66
Wells, K., 525
Welsh, A., 145
Wendel, S., 395
Wenderoth, N., 75
Wengrovitz, S. M., 244
Wenzel, M., 444
Wergin, J. F., 30
Werkle-Bergner, M., 223
Werner, J. M., 469
Werner, K., 329
Wernicke, C., 80
Werth, E., 151
Wesson, M. J., 460, 466, 469
West, M. J., 268
West, R., 559
West, R. F., 248

Westen, D., 384
Westling, D. L., 492
Westlye, L. T., 286
Weston, C. A., 526
Wetherell, J. L., 499, 565
Weyers, P., 141
Wheeler, D., 428
Wheeler, D. S., 178
Wheeler, E., 168
Wheelwright, S., 352
Whibeck, L. B., 504
Whiffen, V. E., 500
Whitaker, R., 528
White, B. J., 448
White, F., 569, 569f
White, J. W., 359
White, K., 252
White, K. W., 227
White, M., 516
White, M. A., 323
White, R. C., 106
White, R. W., 400
White, T. L., 26
Whiteford, H. A., 524
Whitehead, D. L., 565
Whitchead, J., 251
Whitelaw, S., 558
Whitfield, S. L., 404
Whitford, H. S., 499
Whitman, C., 432
Whitney, D., 112
Whitte, T. K., 504
Whooley, M. A., 413
Whorf, B. L., 264, 265
Widiger, T. A., 395, 514
Widmaier, E. P., 61, 85, 432
Wiebe, R. P., 397
Wiedeman, R., 207
Wiedemann, A. U., 559
Wiederanders, M., 376
Wiegand, B., 145
Wiegand, D. M., 478
Wiersma, D., 511
Wiese, H., 219
Wiesel, T. N., 113, 114
Wigboldus, D. H. J., 8
Wigfield, A., 326
Wiggins, C., 409
Wiggs, L., 151
Wigmore, T., 138
Wijesiri, L., 167
Wijnen, V. J., 138
Wilcox, T., 352
Wild, J., 496
Wildman, J. L., 468
Wiley, W. W., 460
Wilhelm, I., 145, 147
Wilkinson, R. T., 141
Wilkowski, B. M., 334
Willcox, B. J., 305
Willcox, D. C., 305
Willekens, F., 573
Willemse, G., 548
Willemsen, G., 513
Willenbockel, V., 98
Willert, M. V., 568
Willett, W. C., 573
Willford, J., 162
Williams, B. A., 15
Williams, C., 540, 566
Williams, J. V., 481
Williams, K. D., 325, 442
Williams, L. M., 228
Williams, M., 512
Williams, P., 111, 569
Williams, R. B., 405, 415

Williams, S. K., 565
Williams, T., 358, 399
Willis, J., 421
Willis, S. L., 308
Willis-Owen, S. A., 405
Willoughby, B. L., 562
Willson, V., 256
Wilsey, B., 164
Wilson, A., 397
Wilson, B., 5
Wilson, D. B., 545
Wilson, G. D., 365
Wilson, G. T., 323, 540
Wilson, J. F., 460
Wilson, M., 449
Wilson, M. E., 349
Wilson, M. N., 502
Wilson, P., 133
Wilson, R. S., 413
Wilt, J., 415
Wiltermuth, S. S., 437
Wilton, L. V., 575
Windle, M., 560
Windmann, S., 252
Winecoff, A., 333
Winer, R. L., 379
Wing, R. R., 558, 572
Wingo, A. P., 502
Winner, E., 259, 260
Winstanley, V., 544
Wint, D., 510
Winter, C., 528
Winter, D. G., 399
Winter, M. R., 158
Wipfli, B. M., 569
Wirtz, D., 252
Wirtz, P. H., 85, 482
Wiseman, R., 109
Wismer, W. V., 181
Witbordt, J., 543
Witcomb, D., 569
Witelson, S. F., 78, 365
Witherington, D., 430
Witkowska, H. E., 145
Wittlinger, R. P., 217
Wohlgemuth, S. D., 149
Wohlheiter, K., 563
Woike, B. A., 411
Wojtczak, M., 123
Wolchik, S., 14, 281
Wolf, A., 338
Wolf, O. T., 71, 226
Wolf, R., 69
Wolfe, B. A., 76, 98
Wolford, K., 500
Wolitzky, K. B., 533
Wolk, A., 572
Wolkove, N., 149
Wolkowitz, O. M., 305–306
Wolpe, J., 533
Wong, F. Y., 19, 544
Wong, K., 138
Wong, M., 525
Wong, R. O., 111, 569
Wong, Y. J., 500
Woo, T. U., 62
Wood, A. H., 13, 16, 355, 356
Wood, D., 397, 407
Wood, J. M., 410, 411
Wood, R. L., 433
Wood, W., 355, 356, 445
Woodard, J. S., 123
Woods, D. D., 477
Woods, K. F., 482
Woods, R., 352
Woods, T., 562–563

Woolf, C. J., 127
Woolf, N. J., 66
Woolley, J. D., 142
World Health Organization (WHO), 241, 504
Worline, M. C., 478
Worthington, R. L., 367
Wortman, C. B., 451
Worzalla, S. L., 263
Wright, D. B., 230
Wright, K., 558
Wright, M. J., 257, 363
Wright, M. O'D., 502
Wright, P. A., 502
Wright, P. M., 466
Wright, R. G., 376
Wright, S. C., 20
Wright, T. A., 473
Wright, W. E., 305
Wrzesniewski, A., 467, 475
Wu, D., 291
Wu, H., 271
Wu, J., 522
Wu, K. D., 495
Wu, S. S., 527
Wu, Y. C., 83
Wundt, W., 9, 9f
Wyatt, H. R., 573
Wyatt, T., 436
Wykes, T., 540

X

Xie, B., 555
Xie, Y. F., 181
Xu, H., 98

Y

Yalcin, B., 405
Yalom, I. D., 541
Yamada, M., 141
Yamanishi, T., 533
Yamauchi, K., 538
Yamazaki, Y., 61
Yamin, S., 524
Yan, J. H., 400
Yan, S., 291
Yanagawa, Y., 113
Yancey, C., 433, 435, 436
Yancura, L. A., 311
Yang, C., 502
Yang, H., 149
Yang, Y., 279, 433, 512, 513, 563
Yang, Y.-H., 167
Yannis, G., 469
Yates, B. T., 535, 537, 538
Yazdi, Z., 144
Ye, C. Q., 100
Yee, K. K., 130
Yen, C. F., 515
Yen, J. Y., 515
Yen, S., 514
Yeshurun, Y., 15
Yeterian, J. D., 543
Yi, Y., 232
Yildirim, H., 496
Yim, E., 527
Yip, T., 302
Yokochi, H., 61
Yoon, C., 232
Yoon, D. P., 562
Yoon, T. Y., 516
Yordanova, J., 146
Yoshida, A., 111

SUBJECT INDEX

Note: Page references in bold refer to definitions. Page references followed by "*f*" refer to figures.

infant attachment, **293**–294, 293*f*
infants and babies
  attachment in, 293–294, 293*f*
  brain in, 286–287, 286*f*, 287*f*
  inhibition in, 292
  motor and perceptual skills in, 284–286, 285*f*
  preference for attractive faces by, 420
  preterm infants, 284
  reflexes in, 284, 285*f*
  sudden infant death syndrome, 152
  temperament in, 292
inferential statistics, **47**
infinite generativity, **262**
informational social influence, **438**
information processing, 12–13
informed consent, 48, 50
in-groups/out-groups, 445
inhibition, in infants, 292
inner ear, 122*f*, **123**, 123*f*
Innocence Project, 230
inoculation, 429
insight learning, **197**–198, 197*f*
insight therapies, 533
insomnia, 150
instinct, **316**
instinctive drift, **198**, 198*f*
institutional review board (IRB), 48, 50
instrumental conditioning. *See* operant conditioning
instrumentality, 348
insulin, hunger and, 319
integrative therapy, **539**–540
integrity tests, **464**
integrity *vs.* despair, 295*f*, 309
intellectual disability, **260**–261
intelligence, **253**
  crystallized and fluid, 307
  cultural bias in tests, 255–257, 256*f*
  g (general ability), 253
  genetic and environmental influences on, 257–259, 258*f*
  giftedness, 259–260
  intellectual disability, 260–261
  intelligence quotient, 254
  IQ tests, 254–255
  theories of multiple intelligences, 261–262
intelligence quotient (IQ), 254–**255**
interference theory, **232**, 233*f*
intergroup relations, 444–448, 445*f*, 448*f*
internal locus of control, 401
internal validity, **38**
Internet
  cybertherapy, 529
  job ads on, 464*f*
  O*NET, 461
  online support groups, 543
interpretation, **530**–531
intersex conditions, 350
interval schedules, 189, 190*f*
interviewer illusion, 465
interviews, 30, 464–466
intimacy motive, 399
intimacy *vs.* isolation, 295*f*, 308
intrinsic motivation, **326**–327
introspection, 9
intuitive processing, 248
Inuit people, 31
inventions, 241
investment model, **450**–451
in vitro fertilization, 87
ion channels, 63–64, 64*f*
I/O psychology. *See* industrial and organizational psychology
IQ (intelligence quotient), 254–**255**

IRB (institutional review board), 48, 50
iris, 111, 112*f*
Islets of Langerhans, 85

J

James-Lange theory, **331**, 332*f*
"Japanese" management style, 470, 472*f*, 479*f*
jigsaw classroom, 448
Jim twins, 90
job analysis, **460**–463, 461*f*, 462*f*
job crafting, **475**
jobs. *See* employment
job stress, **482**
journal keeping, 34, 53–54
justice perspective, 299
just noticeable difference, 102–103

K

Katrina, Hurricane, 446
kinesthetic senses, **131**–132
The Kinsey Reports, 369–370
KSAOs (or KSAs), **460**–462, 461*f*
Ku Klux Klan, 441, 441*f*

L

labia, 347
language, **262**
  basic properties of, 262–263
  biological influences on, 266–267
  brain and, 266–267
  Broca's area and, 80, 80*f*
  environmental influences on, 267–268, 268*f*
  gender differences in, 265
  learning second languages, 270, 270*f*
  left hemisphere and, 81
  over the life span, 268–270, 269*f*, 270*f*
  people-first, 492
  role in cognition, 263–266
  sign, 124
  somniloquy, 151
  Wernicke's area and, 80, 80*f*
latency period, 388
latent content, **154**, 531
latent learning, **196**–197
lateral hypothalamus, 319–320
lateralization, 306, 306*f*
law of effect, 183–**184**, 184*f*
leadership, 475–477
learned helplessness, **187**, 202
learning, **174**. *See also* classical conditioning; operant conditioning
  animal models of stress, 201–202
  breaking habits, 180
  cultural influences, 199–200
  expectancy learning and information, 196
  fears, 179–180
  insight, 197–198, 197*f*
  instinctive drift, 198, 198*f*
  latent, 196–197
  mindset and, 200–201
  observational, 175, 194–195, 195*f*, 400–401
  overlearning, 467
  placebo effect, 180
  preparedness, 199
  remembering learned material, 217, 217*f*
  second languages, 270, 270*f*

study of, 15
  taste aversion, 181–182, 199
  types of, 174–175, 174*f*
left-brained, 83
leisure, **482**
lens, 111, 112*f*
leptin, 319–320, 319*f*
lesbian women. *See* sexual orientation
levels of processing, **209**, 210*f*
lexical approach, 394
lie detectors, 330, 330*f*
life changes. *See* health psychology
life span. *See also* aging; longevity
  development and, 311–312
  language development over, 268–270, 269*f*, 270*f*
  life-span experiences, 282
  sleep over, 148–149, 148*f*
life story approach, 399–400
Lifestraw, 241
life themes, 280–281, 311–312
light, 110, 110*f*
limbic system, **74**–75
linear perspective, 118, 118*f*
linguistic relativity hypothesis, 264
lithium, **524**
lobotomies, 528
locked-in syndrome, 137
loneliness, 451–452
longevity
  conscientiousness and, 412–413
  happiness and, 34, 35
  obesity and fitness and, 573
  personal control and, 413
  physical activity and, 569–570, 570*f*
  quitting smoking and, 574*f*
  religion and, 562, 562*f*
longitudinal design, **34**–36
longitudinal studies, 279
long-term memory, **216**
  components of, 216, 216*f*
  explicit memory, 216–218, 216*f*, 217*f*
  implicit memory, 216*f*, 218–219
  location of stored memories, 221–223, 223*f*
  organization of, 219–221
  smell and, 222
long-term potentiation, 221–222
lottery winners, 455
loudness, 121, 121*f*
love, 449–450
LSD (lysergic acid diethylamide), 162–163, 164

M

MA (mental age), **255**
Maasai people, 31–32
magnetic resonance imaging (MRI), 70–71, 71*f*
Maier string problem, 246*f*
maintenance stage, 556*f*, 558
major depressive disorder (MDD), **498**, 514*f*. *See also* depression/depressive disorders
major histocompatibility complex (MHC), 130–131
majority influence, 444
management approaches, 470–471, 472*f*
mandala, 389
mania, 500–501, 503*f*
manifest content, **514**, 531
Man's Search for Meaning (Frankl), 311
MAO inhibitors, 523
marijuana, 162
marriage, 308–309, 368

Maslow's hierarchy of needs, **324**, 324*f*
massage, infant, 284*f*
masturbation, 361–362
maturation, 278
MBTI (Myers-Briggs Type Indicator), 409, 410
MDD (major depressive disorder), **498**, 514*f*. *See also* depression/depressive disorders
MDMA (Ecstasy), 162, 164
mean, **45**
measures of central tendency, 44–45
measures of dispersion, 45–46
mechanoreception, 100, 100*f*
media
  altruism and, 431–432
  classical conditioning in, 182
  disordered eating and, 322
  on psychological research results, 51–52
  violence in, 435–436
median, **45**
medical marijuana, 164
medical model, **489**
meditation, 84, 167–169
medulla, 72, 73*f*
memory, **208, 209**
  aging and, 307–308
  Atkinson-Shiffrin theory of, 212, 212*f*
  brain structures and, 222–223, 223*f*
  encoding, 208–212
  false memories, 229
  forgetting. *See* forgetting
  health and wellness and, 236–238
  hippocampus and, 75
  levels of processing, 209, 210*f*
  long-term. *See* long-term memory
  neural networks and, 69, 69*f*
  preserving brain function, 237
  processing steps, 208*f*
  prospective, 233–234
  retrieval of. *See* retrieval of memories
  sensory, 212–213, 212*f*
  short-term, 212*f*, 213–215
  sleep and, 145
  smell and, 222
  study tips, 234–236
  temporal lobes and, 77
  working, 214–215
  world champions of, 211*f*
memory loss. *See* forgetting
memory span, 213
men and boys. *See also* gender differences
  brain in, 349
  maturation rate in, 300
  sexual harassment and, 479–480, 480*f*
menopause, 305
mental age (MA), **255**
mental health professionals, 529, 529*f*, 543
mental processes, **4**
mentoring, **467**
mere exposure effect, **449**
meta-analysis, **29**, 53–54
metacognition, 138
meth, 161
MHC (major histocompatibility complex), 130–131
midbrain, **73**
middle ear, **122**, 122*f*
Milgram obedience experiments, 439–440, 440*f*, 441
mindfulness, **251**
mindfulness meditation, 84, 167–168
mindset, 200–201

social constructions, 507
social contagion, 441–442
social desirability, 408
social exchange theory, 450
social facilitation, 442
social identity, 444–445, 445f
social identity theory, 445
social influence, 437–444, 438f, 440f, 441f. See also social behavior
social loafing, 442
social phobia, 495
social psychology, 419–452, 420
    brain and, 439
    close relationships, 449–451
    intergroup relations, 444–448, 445f, 448f
    social behavior, 429–436
    social cognition, 420–429, 422f, 427f
    social influence, 437–444, 438f, 440f, 441f
    study of, 16, 17f
    wellness and, 451–452
social role theory, 355–356, 357f
social sharing, 561
social support, 558, 561, 562–563
social ties, health and, 451–452
sociocultural approach, 13
    to depression, 500
    of Horney, 389
    to psychological disorders, 489
    in therapy, 541–545
socioeconomic status (SES), 435, 500
socioemotional development
    in adolescents, 301–303
    in adults, 308–310
    Erikson's theory of, 294–296, 294f–295f
    infant attachment, 293–294, 293f
    parenting styles and, 296–297
    temperament, 292
socioemotional selectivity theory, 310
sodium ion channels, 63–64, 64f
somatic nervous system, 60f, 61
somatosensory cortex, 77f, 79–80, 79f
somnambulism, 151
somniloquy, 151
sound, 121, 121f. See also auditory system
sound shadow, 126, 126f
spanking children, 192
speech, 80, 80f, 151, 508
Sperling sensory memory experiment, 213, 213f
split-brain research, 80–83, 80f, 81f, 82f
splitting, 513
spontaneous recovery, in classical conditioning, 178–179, 179f
sport psychology, 19
SRY gene, 348
SSRIs (selective serotonin reuptake inhibitors), 523, 523f
stages of change model, 556–559, 556f
standard deviation, 46
standardization, in intelligence tests, 254
Stanford-Binet test, 255, 256f
statistics, 43, 45–47
stem cells, 87
stereotypes, 420
    gender influences in emotion, 338
    racial prejudice and, 447
    self-fulfilling prophecies and, 421
stereotype threat, 424–425
stick problem, 197
stigma, psychological disorders and, 514–516, 515f
stimulants, 159–162, 160f, 161f

stimulus generalization, 188, 188f
stirrup, 122, 122f
STIs (sexually transmitted infections), 284, 378–379. See also HIV/AIDS
storage, memory, 212–213, 212f
strange situation, 293–294
stream of consciousness, 138
strengths-based management, 471, 472f
stress, 92
    acute vs. chronic, 92–93
    aging and, 305–306
    animal models of, 201–202
    cancer and, 565–566, 566f
    cardiovascular disease and, 565
    cognitive appraisal and, 271
    cognitive reappraisal and, 271–272
    coping with, 566–568, 568f
    helping and, 561
    hormones, 61, 564
    immune system and, 563, 564–565, 565f, 568, 568f
    leisure and, 482
    nervous system in, 61
    schizophrenia and, 511
    stages of, 563–564, 563f
    stress management programs, 568–569
    telomere shortening and, 570
    at work, 482
stress management programs, 568–569
stressors, 92
stress response, 61, 68, 92
striatum, 73
Stroop effect, 105–106, 105f
structuralism, 8, 9
structured interviews, 465
Study of Mathematically Precocious Youth (SMPY), 259
study tips, 234–236
subconscious awareness, 139f, 140–141
subgoals, 245
subjective well-being, 415–416
sublimation, 386f, 387, 388f
subliminal perception, 103–104
substance abuse. See psychoactive drugs
substantia nigra, 73, 73f
sudden infant death syndrome (SIDS), 152
suicide, 503–505, 504f, 525
suicide prevention, 504f
superego, 385–386
"superparenting," 281
Super Size Me (film), 557
support groups, 543–544, 558
suprachiasmatic nucleus (SCN), 143, 143f
surveys, 30, 40f
sustained attention, 209
SWLS (Satisfaction with Life Scale), 27–28, 31–32
sympathetic nervous system, 61, 329–330, 329f
synaesthesia, 101
synapses, 65
    in infant brains, 286–287, 286f, 287f
    structure of, 64–66, 65f
synaptic gap, 65–66, 65f
syntax, 263
system 1/system 2, 248–249
systematic desensitization, 533, 533f

T

tardive dyskinesia, 524
taste
    categories of, 129
    chemoreception in, 100f

threshold for, 102f
    tongue papillae, 128–129
taste aversion learning, 181–182, 199
TAT (Thematic Apperception Test), 398, 411, 411f
tectorial membrane, 123, 123f
telomerase, 305
telomeres, 305, 570
temperament, 292
temporal lobes, 77, 77f
temptation, 328
"tend and befriend," 68
teratogens, 283–284
terminal buttons, 65–66, 65f
test anxiety, 533f
testes, 85, 85f, 346
testosterone, 300, 365, 433
tetracyclics, 523
texture gradient, 118, 118f
thalamus, 73f, 75, 127
THC, 162
Thematic Apperception Test (TAT), 398, 411, 411f
theory, 26, 27
theory of mind, 142
theory of mind mechanism (TOMM), 142
theory of planned behavior, 555–556
theory of reasoned action, 555–556
Theory X managers, 470, 472
Theory Y managers, 470–471, 472f
therapeutic alliance, 547
therapies, 521–548
    for alcoholism, 158
    behavior therapies, 533–535, 533f, 534f
    brain changes from, 540
    client participation in, 547
    cognitive-remediation therapy, 540
    cognitive therapies, 535–539, 537f, 538f, 539f
    community mental health, 544
    comparison of, 539f
    drug therapy, 522–526, 526f
    effectiveness of, 545–546, 546f
    electroconvulsive therapy, 526–527
    ethnicity and, 544–545
    family and couples therapy, 541–543
    gender and, 545
    group therapy, 541
    humanistic therapies, 532
    hypnosis in, 167
    integrative therapy, 539–540
    prevention and, 548
    psychodynamic therapies, 530–532
    psychosurgery, 528
    self-help support groups, 543–544
    therapeutic alliance, 547
    well-being therapy, 547–548
thermoreceptors, 127, 127f
theta waves, 146, 147f
thinking, 243–244
    artificial intelligence, 242–243
    biases and heuristics, 249–251, 259f
    concepts, 244, 244f
    convergent vs. divergent, 253
    creative, 252–253
    critical, 5, 51–52, 251
    decision making, 104–105, 248
    emotions and, 252
    health and wellness and, 270–272
    intuitive processing in, 248–249
    problem solving, 244–247, 246f, 247f, 252
    reasoning, 247–248, 247f
    role of language in, 263–266

third variable problem, 33
Thorndike's puzzle box, 183–184, 184f
thought disorder, 508
"three faces of Eve," 506–507, 507f
360-degree feedback, 468, 468f
thresholds
    absolute, 101–102, 102f, 104
    difference, 102–103
    subliminal perception, 103–104
timbre, 121, 121f
time and motion studies, 457
time-out, 191
tip-of-the-tongue (TOT) phenomenon, 233
TMS (transcranial magnetic stimulation), 71–72
tobacco use
    health effects of, 159–161, 160f
    nicotine, 159, 574
    reinforcement of, 193
    smoking cessation, 413, 414, 572–575, 574f
tolerance, to psychoactive drugs, 154, 159
TOMM (theory of mind mechanism), 142
top-down processing, 98–99
TOT (tip-of-the-tongue) phenomenon, 233
touch, 100f, 102f, 126–127
training, 466–467, 529–530, 529f
trait perspectives, 393–398, 395f, 396f, 412f
tranquilizers, 158, 522–523
transactional leaders, 476–477
transcendence, 558
transcranial magnetic stimulation (TMS), 71–72
transference, 531
transformational leaders, 476–477
transgender individuals, 351–352
transvestic fetishes, 375, 376f
traumatic memories, 228
treatment. See therapies
triarchic theory of intelligence, 261
trichromatic theory, 114–116, 115, 116f
tricyclics, 523
TV violence, 435
twin studies
    on bipolar disorder, 501
    fraternal vs. identical twins in, 90–91
    Jim twins, 90
    on leadership, 477
    on obesity, 320
    on personality, 406
    on physical aggression, 432
    on schizophrenia, 509, 510f
    on sexual orientation, 364
2D:4D ratio, 365
two-factor theory of emotion, 333–334, 334f
Type A/Type B behavior patterns, 414–415

U

umami, 129
unconditional positive regard, 392, 393, 532
unconditioned response (UCR), 176–178, 177f
unconditioned stimulus (UCS), 176–178, 177f
unconscious thought, 141, 384

V

vacations, 482–483
valence, 338, 339*f*
validity, 37, **254**
varenicline, 574–575
variable-interval schedules, 189, 190*f*
variable-ratio schedules, 189, 190*f*
variables, **26, 27,** 33, 36–37
ventral tegmental area (VTA), 155, 155*f*, 156
ventromedial hypothalamus, 319–320
vestibular sense, **131**–132, 131*f*
vicarious punishment, 195
vicarious reinforcement, 195
video games, 431–432, 436
vigilance, 209
violence. *See also* aggression
  alcohol use and, 156
  domestic, 187, 202
  media, 435–436
  in pornography, 435–436
  workplace, 480–481
virginity, 369
virtual lesions, 71
virtue, organizational, 479
vision, 109–120
  binding, 114
  blind spot in, 112, 113*f*
  color perception, 111, 112*f*, 114–116, 115*f*, 116*f*
  depth perception, 117–118, 118*f*
  eye structure and, 111–112, 112*f*
  illusions, 120*f*
  light and, 110, 110*f*
  motion perception, 119
  nutrition and, 132
  occipital lobes and, 76–77
  parallel processing in, 114
  perceptual constancy, 119–120
  photoreception in, 100*f*
  shape perception, 116–117, 117*f*
  threshold for, 102*f*
  visual processing in the brain, 112–114, 114*f*
visual cortex, 113–114, 114*f*
visuospatial working memory, 215, 215*f*
volley principle, **125**
voyeurism, 375, 376*f*
VTA (ventral tegmental area), 155, 155*f*, 156

W

waigawa system, **471**
wavelength, 110, 110*f*, 111*f*
WBT (well-being therapy), **547**–548
Weber's law, **102**–103
weight. *See* obesity
weight loss
  community support for, 553
  exercise and, 571–572, 571*f*, 572*f*
  motivation in, 559
  stages of change model in, 556*f*
  success of strategies for, 572*f*
well-being therapy (WBT), **547**–548
wellness
  cognitive appraisal and, 270–272
  human development and, 310–312
  meditation and, 167–168
  memory and, 236–238
  motivation, emotion, and, 340–342
  personality and, 412–415, 414*f*
  religion and, 562–563, 562*f*
  sensation and perception and, 132–133
  sexual behavior and, 378–380
  social psychology and, 451–452
  therapies and, 547–548
  writing about traumas and, 53–54
Wernicke's area, 80, 80*f*
Williams syndrome, 266
windigo, 490*f*
wisdom, **308**
women and girls. *See also* gender differences
  brain in, 349
  Freud on, 385, 387–388, 389
  maturation age in, 300
  menopause in, 305
  psychology of, 16
  self-objectification in, 424
  sexual harassment of, 479–480, 480*f*
  in violent pornography, 435–436
"word salad," 508
working memory, **214**–215
workplace. *See* employment
workplace aggression, 480–481
workplace incivility, 479
work samples, 466
work settings, 14*f*
writing, healing power of, 53–54

X

X rays, 70

Y

Yerkes-Dodson law, **317**–318

Z

Zyban, 574